KT-195-249

COLLINS
ENGLISH
SPELLING
DICTIONARY

HarperCollins*Publishers*

First published 1993
© HarperCollins Publishers 1993
ISBN 0 00 433634-8

All Rights Reserved

A catalogue record for this book is
available from the British Library

Computer typeset by Barbers Ltd.,
Wrotham, England

Printed and bound in Great Britain by
HarperCollins Manufacturing
PO Box, Glasgow G4 ONB

Entered words that we have reason to believe con-
stitute trademarks have been designated as such.
However, neither the presence nor absence of
such designation should be regarded as affecting
the legal status of any trademark.

EDITORIAL STAFF

MANAGING EDITOR
Marian Makins

SENIOR EDITOR
Diana Adams

EDITORS
Tom Shearer
Elspeth Summers   Danielle McGinley
Andrew Holmes   Sheila Ferguson

EDITORIAL ASSISTANCE
Donna Jordan
Anne Young   Cathy Forde
Alice Grandison   Lorna Knight
Elizabeth Scott

COMPUTING STAFF
Ray Carrick   Colette Clenaghan
Tim Lane (*Collins Cobuild*)

Introduction

English is often regarded as a particularly difficult language to spell. Our modern language is a blend of words from many different origins: the Germanic dialects of the Anglo-Saxons, the Scandinavian dialects of the Vikings, the French of the Normans, words derived from Greek, Latin, and the Romance languages, to mention only the main sources. This variety while providing richness in our vocabulary results in what appear arbitrary spelling conventions. The *qu* in *queen*, for instance, was introduced by Norman scribes after the Conquest, replacing the simpler Anglo-Saxon *cw* (*cwen*). The *k* in words like *knight* and *know* is a survival of the Anglo-Saxon pronunciation of those words.

For many centuries this feature of English was not a problem, because consistency of spelling was not regarded as a matter of any importance. Milton's contemporaries were not concerned that he spelt music with the ending *ck*, nor Shakespeare's that he spelt his own name in more than one way. By the nineteenth century, however, spelling conventions had become established, retaining a number of inconsistencies especially between letters and the sounds they represent in different words. Nowadays, the most frequent purpose of using a dictionary is simply to check spelling.

The **Collins English Spelling Dictionary** is a list of words that shows the spelling, not only of the main word form but of all the inflected forms associated with it. It is often these which may present difficulty; do you double the *l* in travel when adding *ed?* or drop the *e* of *glide* when adding *ing?* The dictionary shows all the possible inflections, clearly set out as a simple list at the entry for the main word.

The dictionary also provides a full guide to hyphenation. Every word for which one or more acceptable hyphenation breaks exist has these shown by a small plus sign, printed in red to make it easily distinguishable. The hyphenation system is based on pronunciation and is acceptable in all written and printed contexts.

All material in the dictionary is derived from a machine-readable electronic dictionary of spelling and hyphenation, which was itself created from the authoritative **Collins English Dictionary**. It is thus a comprehensive and up-to-date listing, and includes thousands of geographical and other proper names. The word listing is of British English, but US forms are also given, with labels.

Further information about the electronic dictionary may be obtained from *Collins Electronic Reference*, details of which will be found on the last page of this dictionary.

USING THIS BOOK

The *Collins English Spelling Dictionary* shows the spelling of many thousands of English words and proper names, together with the points at which it is acceptable to hyphenate them.

All inflected forms, that is, plurals of nouns, different tenses of verbs, and comparatives and superlatives of adjectives, are shown in the text. They are placed on a separate line, immediately following the word they are derived from, and slightly set in from the margin.

The plus signs in a word indicate the points, if any, at which it can be hyphenated at the end of a line. A hyphen indicates a point at which it must be hyphenated in all circumstances.

ORDER OF INFLECTIONS

Inflections are shown in the following order:

plural
3rd person singular
present participle
past tense
past participle (not shown if same as past tense)
comparative
superlative

A few words have all these forms, for example

brown
  browns
  browns
  brown+ing
  browned
  brown+er
  brown+est

However, it is more common for a word to be used only as a verb, only as an adjective, etc., for example

back+track
  back+tracks
  back+track+ing
  back+tracked

big
  big+ger
  big+gest

In other cases a word can be a noun and a verb, or a noun and an adjective, for example

gain
  gains
  gains
  gain+ing
  gained

cold
  colds
  cold+er
  cold+est

VARIANT FORMS

Where a word has an acceptable variant form or spelling, the variants follow each other on separate lines, linked by the word *or.*

gold+fish
  gold+fish *or*
  gold+fishes

hic+cup
  hic+cups
  hic+cups
  hic+cup+ing *or*
  hic+cup+ping
  hic+cuped *or*
  hic+cupped

REGIONAL, HISTORICAL, AND LINGUISTIC LABELS

Occasionally, the Dictionary labels a variant to show that it is restricted to one part of the world, is now old-fashioned, or is only used in a certain context.

The most common of these labels is *U.S.*, to show that this form is the one used in the United States.

Where a label applies to all the inflections of a word, it comes immediately after the main word and is not set in from the margin:

col+or
U.S.
  col+ors
  col+ors
  col+or+ing
  col+ored

Where a label applies only to one particular inflection, it comes after that inflected form and is set in from the margin:

mar+vel
  mar+vels
  mar+vels
  mar+vel+ling *or*
  mar+vel+ing
  U.S.
  mar+velled *or*
  mar+veled
  U.S.

Other labels used in this way include *Obsolete, Not standard* (used when a form is widely encountered but generally considered to be incorrect), *Poetic, Austral., N.Z., Scots, Canada,* and *Archaic.*

SIMILAR WORDS

Where two or more words with different meanings have the same spelling, but are hyphenated differently or have different inflections, they are shown separately, with a brief note to distinguish one from the other.

re+fuse
reject
  re+fuses
  re+fus+ing
  re+fused

ref+use
rubbish

Personal names are not usually hyphenated:

Es+sex
place name

Essex
surname

MULTIWORD TERMS

This book follows the spelling conventions of the **Collins English Dictionary.**

In general, multiword terms such as *greenhouse effect* or *word processor* are not included because the words which form the compound are included in the dictionary in their own right.

The exception is where a multiword term is almost identical to a solid or hyphenated word. In these instances both are shown and labelled to make the distinction in their meaning or use clear, for example

May+day
distress signal

May Day
holiday

kick-off
  kick-offs

kick off
verb

The inflected forms of a multiword verb such as kick off are not shown at the multiword form, but can be found at the entry for the main word.

ABBREVIATIONS USED IN THE DICTIONARY

adj.	adjective
adv.	adverb
interj.	interjection
Austral.	Australian
N.Z.	New Zealand
U.S.	United States
masc.	masculine
fem.	feminine
Naut.	Nautical
Pathol.	Pathology
Physiol.	Physiology

A

a
a's
A
A's *or*
As
Aachen
Aal+borg
Aale+sund
Aalto
Aarau
aard+vark
aard+varks
Aar+gau
Aar+hus
Aaron
aba
abas
aba+ca
aba+cas
aback
aba+cus
aba+cuses
Abad+don
abaft
Aba+kan
aba+lo+ne
aba+lo+nes
aban+don
aban+dons
aban+don+ing
aban+doned
aban+doned
aban+don+ment
abase
abases
abas+ing
abased
abase+ment
abash
abashes
abash+ing
abashed
abate
abates
abat+ing

abat+ed
abate+ment
abate+ments
aba+tis
aba+tis *or*
aba+tises
ab+at+tis
ab+at+tis *or*
ab+at+tises
ab+at+toir
ab+at+toirs
Abba
ab+ba+cy
ab+ba+cies
Abbado
ab+ba+tial
Abbe
abbé
abbés
ab+bess
ab+besses
Abbe+vill+ian
ab+bey
ab+beys
ab+bot
ab+bots
ab+bot+cy
ab+bot+cies
ab+bot+ship
ab+bot+ships
ab+bre+vi+ate
ab+bre+vi+ates
ab+bre+viat+ing
ab+bre+viat+ed
ab+bre+via+tion
ab+bre+via+
tions
ABC
ABCs
Abdias
ab+di+cate
ab+di+cates
ab+di+cat+ing
ab+di+cat+ed
ab+di+ca+tion

ab+di+ca+tions
ab+di+ca+tor
ab+di+ca+tors
ab+do+men
ab+do+mens
ab+domi+nal
ab+duct
ab+ducts
ab+duct+ing
ab+duct+ed
ab+duc+tion
ab+duc+tions
ab+duc+tor
ab+duc+tors
abeam
abed
Abednego
Abel
Abelard
Ab+eo+ku+ta
Ab+er+dare
Ab+er+deen
place name
Aberdeen
surname
Ab+er+deen+
shire
Ab+er+do+nian
Ab+er+do+
nians
Aber+fan
ab+er+rance
ab+er+rancy
ab+er+ran+cies
ab+er+rant
ab+er+ra+tion
ab+er+ra+tions
Ab+er+yst+wyth
abet
abets
abet+ting
abet+ted
abet+ment
abet+ments
abey+ance

ab+hor
ab+hors
ab+hor+ring
ab+horred
ab+hor+rence
ab+hor+rences
ab+hor+rent
ab+hor+rer
ab+hor+rers
abide
abides
abid+ing
abode *or*
abid+ed
abid+er
abid+ers
abid+ing
A+bid+jan
Abi+gail
abil+ity
abil+ities
Ab+ing+don
ab ini+tio
abio+gen+esis
ab+ject
ab+jec+tion
ab+ject+ly
ab+ject+ness
ab+ju+ra+tion
ab+jure
ab+jures
ab+jur+ing
ab+jured
ab+jur+er
ab+jur+ers
Ab+kha+zia
ab+late
ab+lates
ab+lat+ing
ab+lat+ed
ab+la+tion
ab+la+tions
ab+la+tive
ab+la+tives
ab+laut

ablaze
able
 abler
 ablest
able-bodied
abloom
ab+lu+tion
 ab+lu+tions
ab+lu+tion+ary
ab+ne+gate
 ab+ne+gates
ab+ne+gat+ing
ab+ne+gat+ed
ab+ne+ga+tion
ab+ne+ga+tor
 ab+ne+ga+tors
ab+nor+mal
ab+nor+mal+ity
 ab+nor+mal+
  ities
ab+nor+mal+ly
Abo
 Abos
Abo
aboard
abode
 abodes
abol+ish
 abol+ishes
 abol+ish+ing
 abol+ished
abol+ish+able
abol+ish+er
 abol+ish+ers
abol+ish+ment
abo+li+tion
abo+li+tion+ary
abo+li+tion+ism
abo+li+tion+ist
 abo+li+tion+ists
abo+ma+sum
 abo+ma+sa
A-bomb
 A-bombs
abomi+nable
abomi+nably
abomi+nate
 abomi+nates
 abomi+nat+ing
 abomi+nat+ed
abom+ina+tion
 abom+ina+tions
abomi+na+tor
 abomi+na+tors
abon+dance

abon+dances
abo+rigi+nal
Abo+rigi+nal
 Abo+rigi+nals
Abo+rigi+nal+ity
abo+rigi+nal+ly
abo+rigi+ne
 abo+rigi+nes
Abo+rigi+ne
 Abo+rigi+nes
abort
 aborts
 aborts
 abort+ing
 abort+ed
abor+ti+fa+cient
 abor+ti+fa+
  cients
abor+tion
 abor+tions
 abor+tion+ist
 abor+tion+ists
abor+tive
abou+lia
abound
 abounds
 abound+ing
 abound+ed
about
about-face
 about-faces
 about-faces
 about-facing
 about-faced
about face
 interj.
about-turn
 about-turns
 about-turns
 about-turning
 about-turned
about turn
 interj.
above
ab+ra+ca+dab+ra
abrade
 abrades
 abrad+ing
 abrad+ed
 abrad+er
 abrad+ers
Abraham
abran+chial
abran+chi+ate
abra+sion

abra+sions
abra+sive
 abra+sives
ab+re+ac+tion
 ab+re+ac+tions
abreast
abridg+able
abridge
 abridges
 abridg+ing
 abridged
abridgea+ble
abridge+ment
 abridge+ments
abridg+er
 abridg+ers
abridg+ment
 abridg+ments
abroad
ab+ro+gate
 ab+ro+gates
 ab+ro+gat+ing
 ab+ro+gat+ed
ab+ro+ga+tion
ab+ro+ga+tor
 ab+ro+ga+tors
ab+rupt
ab+rupt+ly
ab+rupt+ness
Abruz+zi
Absalom
ab+scess
 ab+scesses
 ab+scesses
 ab+scess+ing
 ab+scessed
ab+scis+sa
 ab+scis+sas *or*
 ab+scis+sae
ab+scis+sion
ab+scond
 ab+sconds
 ab+scond+ing
 ab+scond+ed
 ab+scond+er
 ab+scond+ers
ab+seil
 ab+seils
 ab+seils
 ab+seil+ing
 ab+seiled
ab+sence
 ab+sences
ab+sent

ab+sents
 ab+sent+ing
 ab+sent+ed
ab+sen+tee
 ab+sen+tees
ab+sen+tee+ism
ab+sent+er
 ab+sent+ers
absent-minded
absent-minded+
 ly
absent-minded+
 ness
ab+sinth
ab+sinthe
ab+so+lute
 ab+so+lutes
Ab+so+lute
ab+so+lute+ly
ab+so+lu+tion
 ab+so+lu+tions
ab+so+lut+ism
ab+so+lut+ist
 ab+so+lut+ists
ab+solve
 ab+solves
 ab+solv+ing
 ab+solved
ab+solv+er
 ab+solv+ers
ab+sorb
 ab+sorbs
 ab+sorb+ing
 ab+sorbed
ab+sorb+abil+ity
ab+sorb+able
 ab+sorbed
ab+sor+ben+cy
ab+sor+bent
 ab+sor+bents
ab+sorb+ing
ab+sorb+ing+ly
ab+sorp+tance
ab+sorp+tion
ab+sorp+tive
ab+stain
 ab+stains
ab+stain+ing
ab+stained
ab+stain+er
 ab+stain+ers
ab+ste+mi+ous
ab+ste+mi+ous+
 ly

ab+ste+mi+ous+
    ness
ab+sten+tion
ab+sten+tions
ab+sti+nence
ab+sti+nent
ab+stract
ab+stracts
ab+stracts
ab+stract+ing
ab+stract+ed
ab+stract+ed+ly
ab+strac+tion
ab+strac+tions
ab+strac+tive
ab+struse
ab+struse+ly
ab+struse+ness
ab+surd
ab+surd+ity
ab+surd+ities
ab+surd+ly
ab+surd+ness
Abu Dha+bi
Abu+ja
abu+lia
abun+dance
abun+dant
abun+dant+ly
Abu Qîr
abuse
abuses
abuses
abus+ing
abused
abus+er
abus+ers
Abu Sim+bel
abu+sive
abu+sive+ly
abu+sive+ness
abut
abuts
abut+ting
abut+ted
abut+ment
abut+ments
abut+tal
abut+tals
abut+ter
abut+ters
abuzz
Aby+dos
abysm

abysms
abys+mal
abys+mal+ly
abyss
abysses
a+bys+sal
Ab+ys+sinia
Ab+ys+sin+ian
Ab+ys+sin+ians
aca+cia
aca+cias
aca+deme
aca+demes
aca+dem+ic
aca+dem+ics
aca+dem+ical+ly
acad+emi+cian
acad+emi+cians
acad+emy
acad+emies
Aca+dia
Aca+dian
Aca+dians
Aca+die
acan+thus
acan+thuses
    or
acan+thi
a cap+pel+la
Acapul+co
Acapul+co de Juá+
    rez
aca+ria+sis
aca+rid
aca+rids
acari+dan
acari+dans
acar+pous
ACAS
Acas
Ac+cad
Ac+ca+dian
Ac+ca+dians
ac+cede
ac+cedes
ac+ced+ing
ac+ced+ed
ac+ced+ence
ac+cel+er+an+do
ac+cel+er+ant
ac+cel+er+ants
ac+cel+er+ate
ac+cel+er+ates
ac+cel+er+at+
    ing

ac+cel+er+at+
    ed
ac+cel+era+tion
ac+cel+era+
    tions
ac+cel+era+tive
ac+cel+era+tor
ac+cel+era+tors
ac+cel+er+om+
    eter
ac+cel+er+om+
    eters
ac+cent
ac+cents
ac+cents
ac+cent+ing
ac+cent+ed
ac+cen+tor
ac+cen+tors
ac+cen+tual
ac+cen+tu+al+ly
ac+cen+tu+ate
ac+cen+tu+ates
ac+cen+tu+at+
    ing
ac+cen+tu+at+
    ed
ac+cen+tua+tion
ac+cept
ac+cepts
ac+cept+ing
ac+cept+ed
ac+cept+abil+ity
ac+cept+able
ac+cept+able+
    ness
ac+cept+ably
ac+cept+ance
ac+cept+ances
ac+cep+ta+tion
ac+cept+ed
ac+cept+er
ac+cept+ers
ac+cep+tor
ac+cep+tors
ac+cess
ac+cesses
ac+cess+ing
ac+cessed
ac+ces+sibil+ity
ac+ces+sible
ac+ces+sion
ac+ces+sions
ac+ces+sion+al
ac+ces+so+rial

ac+ces+so+ri+ly
ac+ces+so+ry
ac+ces+so+ries
ac+ciac+ca+tu+
    ra
ac+ciac+ca+tu+
    ras or
ac+ciac+ca+tu+
    re
ac+ci+dence
ac+ci+dent
ac+ci+dents
ac+ci+den+tal
ac+ci+den+tals
ac+ci+den+tal+ly
ac+cident-prone
ac+ci+die
ac+cipi+ter
ac+cipi+ters
ac+cipi+trine
acclaim
ac+claims
ac+claims
ac+claim+ing
ac+claimed
ac+claim+er
ac+claim+ers
ac+cla+ma+tion
ac+cla+ma+
    tions
ac+clama+tory
ac+cli+ma+tis+
    able
ac+cli+ma+ti+sa+
    tion
ac+cli+ma+tise
ac+cli+ma+tises
ac+cli+ma+tis+
    ing
ac+cli+ma+tised
ac+cli+ma+tiz+
    able
ac+cli+ma+ti+za+
    tion
ac+cli+ma+tize
ac+cli+ma+tizes
ac+cli+ma+tiz+
    ing
ac+cli+ma+tized
ac+cliv+itous
ac+cliv+ity
ac+cliv+ities
ac+co+lade
ac+co+lades

ac+com+mo+date
ac+com+mo+dates
ac+com+mo+dat+ing
ac+com+mo+dat+ed
ac+com+mo+dat+ing
ac+com+mo+da+tion
ac+com+mo+da+tions
ac+com+pa+ni+ment
ac+com+pa+ni+ments
ac+com+pa+nist
ac+com+pa+nists
ac+com+pa+ny
ac+com+pa+nies
ac+com+pa+ny+ing
ac+com+pa+nied
ac+com+plice
ac+com+plices
ac+com+plish
ac+com+plishes
ac+com+plish+ing
ac+com+plished
ac+com+plished
ac+com+plish+ment
ac+com+plish+ments
ac+cord
ac+cords
ac+cord+ing
ac+cord+ed
ac+cord+ance
ac+cord+ing
ac+cord+ing+ly
ac+cor+di+on
ac+cor+di+ons
ac+cor+di+on+ist
ac+cor+di+on+ists
ac+cost
ac+costs
ac+cost+ing

ac+cost+ed
ac+cost+able
ac+couche+ment
ac+couche+ments
ac+count
ac+counts
ac+counts
ac+count+ing
ac+count+ed
ac+count+abil+ity
ac+count+able
ac+count+ably
ac+count+an+cy
ac+count+ant
ac+count+ants
ac+count+ing
ac+cou+ter
U.S.
ac+cou+ters
ac+cou+ter+ing
ac+cou+tered
ac+cou+ter+ment
U.S.
ac+cou+ter+ments
ac+cou+tre
ac+cou+tres
ac+cou+tring
ac+cou+tred
ac+cou+tre+ment
ac+cou+tre+ments
Ac+cra
ac+cred+it
ac+cred+its
ac+cred+it+ing
ac+cred+it+ed
ac+credi+ta+tion
ac+crete
ac+cretes
ac+cret+ing
ac+cret+ed
ac+cre+tion
ac+cre+tions
ac+cre+tive
ac+cru+al
ac+crue
ac+crues
ac+cru+ing
ac+crued
ac+cul+tur+ate

ac+cul+tur+ates
ac+cul+tur+at+ing
ac+cul+tur+at+ed
ac+cul+tura+tion
ac+cu+mu+lable
ac+cu+mu+late
ac+cu+mu+lates
ac+cu+mu+lat+ing
ac+cu+mu+lat+ed
ac+cu+mu+la+tion
ac+cu+mu+la+tions
ac+cu+mu+la+tive
ac+cu+mu+la+tor
ac+cu+mu+la+tors
ac+cu+ra+cy
ac+cu+ra+cies
ac+cu+rate
ac+cu+rate+ly
ac+curs+ed
ac+curs+ed+ly
ac+curs+ed+ness
ac+curst
ac+cu+sa+tion
ac+cu+sa+tions
ac+cu+sa+ti+val
ac+cu+sa+tive
ac+cu+sa+tives
ac+cu+sa+tive+ly
ac+cu+sa+to+rial
ac+cu+sa+tory
ac+cuse
ac+cuses
ac+cus+ing
ac+cused
ac+cused
ac+cus+er
ac+cus+ers
ac+cus+ing
ac+cus+ing+ly
ac+cus+tom
ac+cus+toms
ac+cus+tom+ing
ac+cus+tomed
ac+cus+tomed
AC/DC
ace

aces
acedia
acepha+lous
acer
acers
ac+er+bate
ac+er+bates
ac+er+bat+ing
ac+er+bat+ed
acer+bic
acer+bity
acer+bities
ac+etabu+lum
ac+etabu+la
ac+etal
ac+etals
ac+et+al+de+hyde
ac+et+ani+lide
ac+etate
ac+etates
acetic
aceti+fi+ca+tion
aceti+fy
aceti+fies
aceti+fy+ing
aceti+fied
ac+etone
ac+etose
ac+etous
ac+etyl
ac+etyl+cho+line
acety+lene
ac+etyl+sali+cyl+ic
Achaea
Achae+an
Achae+ans
Achaia
Achaian
Achaians
Acha+tes
Acha+teses
ache
aches
aches
ach+ing
ached
Achebe
Achelous
achene
achenes
Ach+er+on
Acheson
Acheu+lean

Acheu+lian
achiev+able
achieve
　achieves
achiev+ing
achieved
achieve+ment
　achieve+ments
achiev+er
　achiev+ers
a+chil+lea
　a+chil+leas
Ach+il+lean
Achilles
ach+ing
Achitophel
ach+ro+mat
　ach+ro+mats
ach+ro+ma+tic
achro+ma+ti+cal+
　ly
achro+ma+tic+ity
achro+ma+tism
acid
　acids
acid-fast
Acid-House
adj.
Acid House
　noun
acid+ic
acidi+fi+able
acidi+fi+ca+tion
acidi+fy
　acidi+fies
　acidi+fy+ing
　acidi+fied
acid+ity
　acid+ities
ac+id+ly
ac+id+ness
aci+do+sis
　aci+do+ses
aci+dot+ic
acidu+late
　acidu+lates
acidu+lat+ing
acidu+lat+ed
acidu+la+tion
acidu+lent
acidu+lous
aci+nus
　aci+ni
Acis
ack-ack

ac+knowl+edge
ack+nowl+
　edges
ack+nowl+edg+
　ing
ack+nowl+
　edged
ack+nowl+edge+
　able
ac+knowl+edge+
　ment
ac+knowl+edge+
　ments
ac+knowl+edg+
　ment
ac+knowl+edg+
　ments
acme
acmes
acne
aco+lyte
aco+lytes
Acon+ca+gua
aco+nite
aco+nites
aco+nit+ic
Açô+res
acorn
　acorns
acous+tic
acous+ti+cal
acous+ti+cal+ly
acous+tics
ac+quaint
　ac+quaints
ac+quaint+ing
ac+quaint+ed
ac+quaint+ance
ac+quaint+
　ances
ac+quaint+ance+
　ship
ac+quaint+ance+
　ships
ac+quaint+ed
ac+qui+esce
ac+qui+esces
ac+qui+esc+ing
ac+qui+esced
ac+qui+es+cence
ac+qui+es+cent
ac+quir+able
ac+quire
ac+quires
ac+quir+ing

ac+quired
ac+quire+ment
ac+quire+ments
ac+qui+si+tion
ac+qui+si+tions
ac+quisi+tive
ac+quisi+tive+ly
ac+quisi+tive+
　ness
ac+quit
ac+quits
ac+quit+ting
ac+quit+ted
ac+quit+tal
ac+quit+tals
ac+quit+tance
ac+quit+tances
ac+quit+ter
ac+quit+ters
acre
acres
Acre
acre+age
　acre+ages
ac+rid
ac+ri+dine
acrid+ity
ac+rid+ly
ac+ri+fla+vine
Ac+ri+lan
Trademark
ac+ri+mo+ni+ous
ac+ri+mo+ny
　ac+ri+mo+nies
ac+ro+bat
　ac+ro+bats
ac+ro+bat+ic
ac+ro+bati+cal+
　ly
ac+ro+bat+ics
ac+ro+gen
ac+ro+gens
acrog+enous
ac+ro+mega+lic
ac+ro+mega+ly
ac+ro+nym
ac+ro+nyms
ac+ro+pho+bia
ac+ro+pho+bic
acropo+lis
　acropo+lises
Acropo+lis
across
across-the-board
acros+tic

acros+tics
acryl+ic
act
acts
act+ing
act+ed
act+abil+ity
act+able
Actaeon
ac+tin
act+ing
ac+tinia
　ac+tiniae or
　ac+tinias
ac+tin+ic
ac+tini+cal+ly
ac+tin+ism
ac+tin+ium
ac+tino+bi+ol+
　ogy
ac+tin+oid
ac+ti+nom+eter
ac+ti+nom+
　eters
ac+ti+no+my+cin
ac+ti+no+my+
　cins
ac+ti+no+zo+an
ac+ti+no+zo+
　ans
ac+tion
ac+tions
ac+tions
ac+tion+ing
ac+tioned
ac+tion+able
ac+tion+ably
Ac+tium
ac+ti+vate
ac+ti+vates
ac+ti+vat+ing
ac+ti+vat+ed
ac+ti+va+tion
ac+ti+va+tions
ac+ti+va+tor
ac+ti+va+tors
ac+tive
ac+tives
ac+tive+ly
ac+tive+ness
ac+tiv+ism
ac+tiv+ist
ac+tiv+ists
ac+tiv+ity

ac+tiv+ities
ac+ton
ac+tons
ac+tor
ac+tors
ac+tress
ac+tresses
ac+tual
ac+tu+al+i+sa+
tion
ac+tu+al+ise
ac+tu+al+ises
ac+tu+al+is+ing
ac+tu+al+ised
ac+tu+al+ity
ac+tu+al+ities
ac+tu+aliza+tion
ac+tu+al+ize
ac+tu+al+izes
ac+tu+al+iz+ing
ac+tu+al+ized
ac+tu+al+ly
ac+tuals
ac+tu+ari+al
ac+tu+ary
ac+tu+aries
ac+tu+ate
ac+tu+ates
ac+tu+at+ing
ac+tu+at+ed
ac+tua+tion
ac+tua+tions
ac+tua+tor
ac+tua+tors
acu+ity
acu+leate
acu+leus
acu+leuses
acu+men
acu+min+ate
acu+min+ates
acu+min+at+ing
acu+min+at+ed
acu+mi+na+tion
acu+mi+na+
tions
acu+mi+nous
acu+pres+sure
acu+punc+ture
acu+punc+tur+ist
acu+punc+tur+
ists
acute
acutes
acute+ly

acute+ness
ad+age
ad+ages
ada+gio
ada+gios
Adam
ada+mant
ada+mants
ada+man+tine
Ad+ams
mountain
Adams
surname
Ada+na
a+dapt
a+dapts
a+dapt+ing
a+dapt+ed
adapt+abil+ity
adapt+able
ad+ap+ta+tion
ad+ap+ta+tions
adapt+er
adapt+ers
adap+tive
adap+tor
adap+tors
add
adds
add+ing
add+ed
Addams
ad+dax
ad+daxes
ad+dend
ad+dends
ad+den+dum
ad+den+da
ad+der
ad+ders
snake
add+er
add+ers
person, machine
adder's-tongue
adder's-tongues
ad+dict
ad+dicts
ad+dicts
ad+dict+ing
ad+dict+ed
ad+dic+tion
ad+dic+tions
ad+dic+tive
Addington

Ad+dis Aba+ba
Addison
ad+di+tion
ad+di+tions
ad+di+tion+al
ad+di+tive
ad+di+tives
ad+dle
ad+dles
ad+dling
ad+dled
add-on
add-ons
ad+dress
ad+dresses
ad+dresses
ad+dress+ing
ad+dressed *or*
ad+drest
Obsolete, Poetic
ad+dressee
ad+dressees
ad+dress+er
ad+dress+ers
ad+dres+sor
ad+dres+sors
ad+duce
ad+duces
ad+duc+ing
ad+duced
ad+du+cent
ad+duc+ible
ad+duct
ad+ducts
ad+ducts
ad+duct+ing
ad+duct+ed
ad+duc+tion
ad+duc+tor
ad+duc+tors
Ad+elaide
Aden
Adenauer
ad+enine
ad+enines
ad+enoid+al
ad+enoids
ad+eno+ma
ad+eno+mas
or
ad+eno+ma+ta
ad+eno+pa+thy
adeno+sine
adept
adepts

adept+ness
ad+equa+cy
ad+equate
ad+equate+ly
à deux
ad+here
ad+heres
ad+her+ing
ad+hered
ad+her+ence
ad+her+ences
ad+her+ent
ad+her+ents
ad+he+sion
ad+he+sions
ad+he+sive
ad+he+sives
ad+he+sive+ly
ad+he+sive+ness
ad hoc
ad ho+mi+nem
adia+ba+tic
adia+ba+tics
Adie
adieu
ad in+fi+ni+tum
ad in+ter+im
adi+po+cere
adi+pose
Adi+ron+dacks
adit
adits
ad+ja+cen+cy
ad+ja+cent
ad+ja+cent+ly
ad+jec+ti+val
ad+jec+tive
ad+jec+tives
ad+join
ad+joins
ad+join+ing
ad+joined
ad+join+ing
ad+journ
ad+journs
ad+journ+ing
ad+journed
ad+journ+ment
ad+journ+ments
ad+judge
ad+judges
ad+judg+ing
ad+judged
ad+ju+di+cate
ad+ju+di+cates

ad+ju+di+cat+
  ing
ad+ju+di+cat+
  ed
ad+ju+di+ca+tion
ad+ju+di+ca+
  tions
ad+ju+di+ca+tor
ad+ju+di+ca+
  tors
ad+junct
ad+juncts
ad+junc+tive
ad+junct+ly
ad+ju+ra+tion
ad+ju+ra+tions
ad+jura+tory
ad+jure
ad+jures
ad+jur+ing
ad+jured
ad+jur+er
ad+jur+ers
ad+ju+ror
ad+ju+rors
ad+just
ad+justs
ad+just+ing
ad+just+ed
ad+just+able
ad+just+er
ad+just+ers
ad+just+ment
ad+just+ments
ad+ju+tan+cy
ad+ju+tan+cies
ad+ju+tant
ad+ju+tants
ad+ju+tant gen+
  er+al
ad+ju+tants gen+
  er+al
ad+ju+vant
ad+ju+vants
Adler
Ad+ler+ian
ad-lib
ad-libs
ad-libs
ad-libbing
ad-libbed
ad libi+tum
ad+man
ad+men
ad+mass

ad+meas+ure
ad+meas+ures
ad+meas+ur+
  ing
ad+meas+ured
Admetus
ad+min
ad+mins
ad+min+is+ter
ad+min+is+ters
ad+min+is+ter+
  ing
ad+min+is+
  tered
ad+min+is+trate
ad+min+is+
  trates
ad+min+is+trat+
  ing
ad+min+is+trat+
  ed
ad+min+is+tra+
  tion
ad+min+is+tra+
  tions
ad+min+is+tra+
  tive
ad+min+is+tra+
  tive+ly
ad+min+is+tra+
  tor
ad+min+is+tra+
  tors
ad+mi+rable
ad+mi+rably
ad+mi+ral
ad+mi+rals
ad+mi+ral+ship
ad+mi+ral+ships
Ad+mi+ral+ties
ad+mi+ral+ty
ad+mi+ral+ties
ad+mi+ra+tion
ad+mi+ra+tions
ad+mire
ad+mires
ad+mir+ing
ad+mired
ad+mir+er
ad+mir+ers
ad+mir+ing
ad+mir+ing+ly
ad+mis+sibil+ity
ad+mis+sible
ad+mis+sion

ad+mis+sions
ad+mis+sive
ad+mit
ad+mits
ad+mit+ting
ad+mit+ted
ad+mit+tance
ad+mit+ted+ly
ad+mix
ad+mixes
ad+mix+ing
ad+mixed
ad+mix+ture
ad+mix+tures
ad+mon+ish
ad+mon+ishes
ad+mon+ish+ing
ad+mon+ished
ad+moni+tion
ad+moni+tions
ad+moni+tory
ad nau+seam
ado
ado+be
ado+bes
ado+les+cence
ado+les+cent
ado+les+cents
Adonai
Adonis
adopt
adopts
adopt+ing
adopt+ed
adopt+ed
adop+tion
adop+tions
adop+tive
ador+able
ador+ably
ado+ra+tion
ado+ra+tions
adore
adores
ador+ing
adored
ador+er
ador+ers
ador+ing
ador+ing+ly
adorn
adorns
adorn+ing
adorned
adorn+ment

adorn+ments
Ado+wa
Adrastus
ad rem
ad+ren+al
ad+ren+als
adrena+line
Adri+ano+ple
Adria+nopo+lis
Adri+at+ic
adrift
adroit
adroit+ly
adroit+ness
ad+sorb
ad+sorbs
ad+sorb+ing
ad+sorbed
ad+sorb+able
ad+sorb+ate
ad+sorb+ates
ad+sor+bent
ad+sorp+tion
Adua
adu+late
adu+lates
adu+lat+ing
adu+lat+ed
adu+la+tion
adu+la+tor
adu+la+tors
adu+la+tory
adult
adults
adul+ter+ant
adul+ter+ants
adul+ter+ate
adul+ter+ates
adul+ter+at+ing
adul+ter+at+ed
adul+tera+tion
adul+tera+tions
adul+tera+tor
adul+tera+tors
adul+ter+er
adul+ter+ers
adul+ter+ess
adul+ter+esses
adul+ter+ous
adul+ter+ous+ly
adul+tery
adul+teries
adult+hood
adult+hoods
ad+um+brate

ad+um+brates
ad+um+brat+ing
ad+um+brat+ed
ad+um+bra+tion
ad+um+bra+
tions
ad+um+bra+tive
Adu+wa
ad va+lo+rem
ad+vance
ad+vances
ad+vances
ad+vanc+ing
ad+vanced
ad+vanced
ad+vance+ment
ad+vance+
ments
ad+vanc+er
ad+vanc+ers
ad+vances
ad+van+tage
ad+van+tages
ad+van+tages
ad+van+tag+ing
ad+van+taged
ad+van+ta+
geous
ad+van+ta+
geous+ly
ad+vec+tion
ad+vec+tions
ad+vent
ad+vents
Ad+vent
Ad+vent+ist
Ad+vent+ists
ad+ven+ti+tious
ad+ven+ti+tious+
ly
ad+ven+ture
ad+ven+tures
ad+ven+tures
ad+ven+tur+ing
ad+ven+tured
ad+ven+tur+er
ad+ven+tur+ers
ad+ven+ture+
some
ad+ven+tur+ess
ad+ven+tur+
esses
ad+ven+tur+ism
ad+ven+tur+ist
ad+ven+tu+rists

ad+ven+tur+ous
ad+verb
ad+verbs
ad+ver+bial
ad+ver+sar+ial
ad+ver+sary
ad+ver+saries
ad+ver+sa+tive
ad+ver+sa+tives
ad+verse
ad+verse+ly
ad+verse+ness
ad+ver+sity
ad+ver+sities
ad+vert
ad+verts
ad+verts
ad+vert+ing
ad+vert+ed
ad+ver+tise
ad+ver+tises
ad+ver+tis+ing
ad+ver+tised
ad+ver+tise+
ment
ad+ver+tise+
ments
ad+ver+tis+er
ad+ver+tis+ers
ad+ver+tis+ing
ad+vice
ad+vices
ad+vis+abil+ity
ad+vis+able
ad+vis+able+
ness
ad+vis+ably
ad+vise
ad+vises
ad+vis+ing
ad+vised
ad+vised
ad+vis+ed+ly
ad+vis+er
ad+vis+ers
ad+vi+sor
ad+vi+sors
ad+vi+so+ry
ad+vo+caat
ad+vo+caats
ad+vo+ca+cy
ad+vo+ca+cies
ad+vo+cate
ad+vo+cates
ad+vo+cates

ad+vo+cat+ing
ad+vo+cat+ed
ad+vow+son
ad+vow+sons
adz
U.S.
adzes
adze
adzes
Adzha+ria
aedes
aedeses
aedile
aediles
Aeëtes
Aegean
Aegeus
Aegi+na
Aegir
aegis
Aegisthus
Aegos+pota+mi
aegro+tat
aegro+tats
Aeneas
Aene+id
Aeo+lia
aeo+lian
Aeo+lis
aeo+lo+trop+ic
Aeolus
aeon
aeons
aer+ate
aer+ates
aer+at+ing
aer+at+ed
aera+tion
aera+tor
aera+tors
aer+ial
aer+ials
aeri+al+ist
aeri+al+ists
aerie
aeries
aeri+form
aero
aero+bat+ics
aer+obe
aer+obes
aero+bic
aero+bics
aero+bium
aero+bia

aero+drome
aero+dromes
aero+dy+nam+ic
aero+dy+nami+
cal+ly
aero+dy+nam+
ics
aero+em+bo+
lism
aero+foil
aero+foils
aero+gram
aero+grams
aero+gramme
aero+grammes
aero+lite
aero+lites
aero+logi+cal
aer+olo+gist
aer+olo+gists
aer+ol+ogy
aero+mechani+
cal
aero+mechan+ics
aero+nau+ti+cal
aero+naut+ics
aero+pause
aero+plane
aero+planes
aero+sol
aero+sols
aero+space
aero+stat
aero+stats
aero+stat+ic
aero+stat+ics
aeru+gin+ous
aeru+go
aery
aeries
Aes+chy+lean
Aeschylus
Aes+cu+la+pian
Aesculapius
Aesir
Aesop
Aesop+ian
aes+the+sia
aes+thete
aes+thetes
aes+thet+ic
aes+theti+cal
aes+theti+cal+ly
aes+theti+cism
aes+thet+ics

aes+ti+val
aes+ti+vate
aes+ti+vates
aes+ti+vat+ing
aes+ti+vat+ed
aes+ti+va+tion
aether
aethers
aetio+logi+cal
aetio+logi+cal+ly
aeti+olo+gist
aeti+olo+gists
aeti+ol+ogy
aeti+ol+ogies
Aet+na
Aeto+lia
afar
Afars and the Is+
  sas
afeard
afeared
af+fa+bil+ity
af+fable
af+fair
  af+fairs
af+fairs
af+fect
  af+fects
af+fects
af+fect+ing
af+fect+ed
af+fec+ta+tion
  af+fec+ta+tions
af+fect+ed
af+fect+ed+ly
af+fect+ing
af+fect+ing+ly
af+fec+tion
  af+fec+tions
af+fec+tion+al
af+fec+tion+ate
af+fec+tion+ate+
  ly
af+fec+tive
af+fec+tiv+ity
af+fer+ent
af+fiance
  af+fiances
af+fianc+ing
af+fianced
af+fi+da+vit
  af+fi+da+vits
af+fili+ate
  af+fili+ates
af+fili+ates

af+fili+at+ing
af+fili+at+ed
af+filia+tion
af+filia+tions
af+fine
af+fini+tive
af+fin+ity
af+fin+ities
af+firm
af+firms
af+firm+ing
af+firmed
af+firm+ant
af+firm+ants
af+fir+ma+tion
  af+fir+ma+tions
af+firma+tive
af+firma+tives
af+firma+tive+ly
af+firm+er
af+firm+ers
af+fix
af+fixes
af+fixes
af+fix+ing
af+fixed
af+fix+ture
af+fix+tures
af+fla+tus
af+flict
af+flicts
af+flict+ing
af+flict+ed
af+flic+tion
af+flic+tions
af+flic+tive
af+flu+ence
af+flu+ent
af+flu+ents
af+flux
af+fluxes
af+ford
af+fords
af+ford+ing
af+ford+ed
af+forda+bil+ity
af+ford+able
af+for+est
af+for+ests
af+for+est+ing
af+for+est+ed
af+for+esta+tion
af+for+esta+
  tions
af+fran+chise

af+fran+chises
af+fran+chis+ing
af+fran+chised
af+fran+chise+
  ment
af+fran+chise+
  ments
af+fray
af+frays
af+fri+cate
  af+fri+cates
af+fright
af+frights
af+frights
af+fright+ing
af+fright+ed
af+front
af+fronts
af+fronts
af+front+ing
af+front+ed
af+ghan
af+ghans
Af+ghan
Af+ghans
Af+ghani
Af+ghanis
Af+ghani+stan
afi+cio+na+do
  afi+cio+na+dos
afield
afire
aflame
af+la+tox+in
  af+la+tox+ins
afloat
aflut+ter
afoot
afore
afore+men+
  tioned
afore+said
afore+thought
a for+tio+ri
afraid
af+reet
  af+reets
afresh
Af+ri+ca
Af+ri+can
  Af+ri+cans
Af+ri+can+der
Af+ri+can+ders
Af+ri+kaans
Af+ri+kan+er

Af+ri+kan+ers
af+rit
af+rits
Afro
Afros
af+ror+mo+sia
aft
af+ter
after+birth
  after+births
after+burn+er
  after+burn+ers
after+care
after+damp
after+effect
  after+effects
after+glow
after+image
  after+images
after+life
  after+lives
after+math
after+most
after+noon
  after+noons
after+noons
after+pains
af+ters
after+shave
aftershaves
after+taste
  after+tastes
after+thought
  after+thoughts
after+ward
after+wards
aga
  agas
Agade
Aga+dir
again
against
Aga Khan
Agamemnon
agam+ic
aga+mo+gen+
  esis
aga+pan+thus
  aga+pan+thuses
agape
Agape
  Agapes
agar
agar-agar
aga+ric

aga+rics
Agar+ta+la
ag+ate
 ag+ates
aga+ve
 aga+ves
age
 ages
 ages
 age+ing *or*
 ag+ing
 aged
 aged
Agee
age+ing
age+ism
age+ist
age+less
age-long
agen+cy
 agen+cies
agen+da
 agen+das
agen+dum
 agen+dums *or*
 agen+da
agent
 agents
agent-general
 agents-general
agen+tial
Agent Or+ange
agent pro+vo+ca+
 teur
 agents pro+vo+
 ca+teurs
age-old
ag+era+tum
ag+era+tums
ag+glom+er+ate
ag+glom+er+
 ates
ag+glom+er+
 ates
ag+glom+er+at+
 ing
ag+glom+er+at+
 ed
ag+glom+era+
 tion
ag+glom+era+
 tions
ag+glom+era+
 tive
ag+glu+ti+nable

ag+glu+ti+nant
ag+glu+ti+nate
ag+glu+ti+nates
ag+glu+ti+nat+
 ing
ag+glu+ti+nat+
 ed
ag+glu+ti+na+
 tion
ag+glu+ti+na+
 tions
ag+gran+dise
ag+gran+dises
ag+gran+dis+
 ing
ag+gran+dised
ag+gran+dise+
 ment
ag+gran+di+ser
ag+gran+di+
 sers
ag+gran+dize
ag+gran+dizes
ag+gran+diz+ing
ag+gran+dized
ag+gran+dize+
 ment
ag+gran+di+zer
ag+gran+di+
 zers
ag+gra+vate
ag+gra+vates
ag+gra+vat+ing
ag+gra+vat+ed
ag+gra+va+tion
ag+gra+va+
 tions
ag+gre+gate
ag+gre+gates
ag+gre+gates
ag+gre+gat+ing
ag+gre+gat+ed
ag+gre+ga+tion
ag+gre+ga+
 tions
ag+gre+ga+tive
ag+gress
ag+gresses
ag+gress+ing
ag+gressed
ag+gres+sion
ag+gres+sions
ag+gres+sive
ag+gres+sive+ly

ag+gres+sive+
 ness
ag+gres+sor
 ag+gres+sors
ag+grieve
 ag+grieves
ag+griev+ing
ag+grieved
ag+grieved
ag+griev+ed+ly
ag+gro
agha
 aghas
aghast
ag+ile
ag+ile+ly
agil+ity
agin
Ag+in+court
ag+ing
agio
 agios
ag+ism
ag+ist
agi+tate
 agi+tates
agi+tat+ing
agi+tat+ed
agi+tat+ed
agi+tat+ed+ly
agi+ta+tion
agi+ta+tions
agi+ta+to
agi+ta+tor
 agi+ta+tors
agit+prop
Aglaia
agleam
aglee
ag+let
 ag+lets
ag+ley
aglit+ter
agloo
 agloos
aglow
aglu
 aglus
ag+nail
 ag+nails
ag+nate
 ag+nates
Agnes
Agnesi
Agnew

Agni
ag+nos+tic
ag+nos+tics
ag+nos+ti+cism
Ag+nus Dei
 Ag+nus Deis
ago
agog
agon+ic
ago+nise
 ago+nises
ago+nis+ing
ago+nised
ago+nis+ing+ly
ago+nize
 ago+nizes
ago+niz+ing
ago+nized
ago+niz+ing+ly
ago+ny
 ago+nies
ago+ra
 ago+rae *or*
 ago+ras
 Greek
  marketplace
ago+ra
 ago+rot
 Israeli coin
ago+ra+pho+bia
ago+ra+pho+bic
ago+ra+pho+
 bics
agou+ti
agou+tis *or*
 agou+ties
Agra
Agram
agrar+ian
 agrar+ians
agrari+an+ism
agree
 agrees
agree+ing
agreed
agree+able
agree+able+ness
agree+ably
agreed
agree+ment
 agree+ments
ag+ri+busi+ness
Agricola
ag+ri+cul+tur+al

ag+ri+cul+tur+al+ist
ag+ri+cul+tur+al+ists
ag+ri+cul+ture
ag+ri+cul+tur+ist
ag+ri+cul+tur+ists
Agri+gen+to
ag+ri+mo+ny
ag+ri+mo+nies
Agrippa
Agrippina
ag+ro+bi+ol+ogy
ag+ro+for+est+ry
ag+ro+nom+ic
ag+ro+nom+ics
agrono+mist
agrono+mists
agrono+my
ag+ro+stem+ma
ag+ro+stem+mas
aground
Aguas+ca+lien+tes
ague
aguish
ah
aha
Ahab
Ahasuerus
ahead
ahem
ahim+sa
Ahithophel
Ah+mada+bad
Ah+mad+na+gar
Ah+meda+bad
Ah+med+na+gar
ahoy
Ahriman
Ahura Mazda
Ah+vaz
Ah+ve+nan+maa
Ah+waz
ai
ais
aid
aids
aids
aid+ing
aid+ed
Aid
Aidan

aid-de-camp
aids-de-camp
aide
aides
aide-de-camp
aides-de-camp
aide-mémoire
aides-mémoire
aid+er
aid+ers
Aidin
Aids
AIDS
aig+let
aig+lets
aigret
aigrets
aigrette
aigrettes
aiguille
aiguilles
aiguil+lette
aiguil+lettes
aikido
ail
ails
ail+ing
ailed
ailan+thus
ailan+thuses
ailer+on
ailer+ons
ail+ing
ail+ment
ail+ments
aim
aims
aims
aim+ing
aimed
aim+less
aim+less+ly
aim+less+ness
Ain
ain't
Ain+tree
Ainu
Ainus or
Ainu
air
airs
airs
air+ing
aired
Aïr

air+borne
air+brick
air+bricks
air+brush
air+brushes
air+brushes
air+brush+ing
air+brushed
air-condition
air-conditions
air-condition+ing
air-conditioned
air-cool
air-cools
air-cooling
air-cooled
air+craft
air+craft
air+craft+man
air+craft+men
air+craft+wom+an
air+craft+wom+en
Air+drie
air+drop
air+drops
air+drops
air+drop+ping
air+dropped
Aire
Aire+dale
Aire+dales
air+field
air+fields
air+foil
air+foils
air+frame
air+frames
air+head
air+heads
airi+ly
airi+ness
air+ing
air+ings
air+less
air+less+ness
air+lift
air+lifts
air+lifts
air+lift+ing
air+lift+ed
air+line
air+lines
air+lin+er

air+lin+ers
air+lock
air+locks
air-mail
verb, adj.
air-mails
air-mailing
air-mailed
air mail
noun
air+man
air+men
air+plane
U.S.
air+planes
air+play
air+plays
air+port
air+ports
airs
air+screw
air+screws
air+ship
air+ships
air+show
air+shows
air+sick
air+side
air+sides
air+space
air+spaces
air+speed
air+speeds
air+strip
air+strips
air+tight
air-to-air
air+waves
air+way
air+ways
air+worthy
airy
airi+er
airi+est
Aisha
aisle
aisles
aisled
Aisne
aitch
aitches
aitch+bone
aitch+bones
Aitken
Aix

Aix-en-Provence
Aix-la-Chapelle
Aix-les-Bains
Aï+yi+na
Ajac+cio
ajar
Ajax
Aj+mer
Aka+ba
Akbar
akene
akenes
Akhaïa
Akhenaten
Akhenaton
Akhmatova
Akihito
akim+bo
akin
Ak+kad
Ak+ka+dian
Ak+ka+dians
Ak+ker+man
Ak+mo+linsk
Ak+tyu+binsk
Aku+re
ak+va+vit
ak+va+vits
ala
alae
à la
Ala+bama
Ala+bam+ian
ala+bas+ter
ala+bas+trine
à la carte
alack
alacka+day
alac+rity
Ala Dagh
Ala+gez
Ala+go+as
Ala+göz
Alai
Alain-Fournier
Ala+mein
Ala+mo
ala+mode
à la mode
Alan+brooke
Åland
alar
Alar
Alar+cón
Alaric

alarm
alarms
alarms
alarm+ing
alarmed
alarm+ing
alarm+ist
alarm+ists
alar+um
alar+ums
alas
Alas+ka
Alas+kan
Alas+kans
alate
alb
albs
Alba
al+ba+core
al+ba+cores
Alba Lon+ga
Alban
Al+ba+nia
Al+ba+nian
Al+ba+nians
Al+ba+ny
al+ba+tross
al+ba+trosses
al+be+do
al+be+dos
Albee
al+be+it
Alberich
Albers
al+bert
al+berts
Albert
Al+ber+ta
Al+ber+tan
Al+ber+tans
Alberti
Albertus Magnus
al+bes+cence
al+bes+cent
Albi
Al+bi+gen+ses
Al+bi+gen+sian
Al+bi+gen+si+an+
  ism
al+bi+nism
al+bi+nisms
al+bi+no
al+bi+nos
Albinoni
al+bi+not+ic

Albinus
Al+bi+on
al+bite
al+bum
al+bums
al+bu+men
al+bu+mens
al+bu+min
al+bu+mins
al+bu+mi+nous
al+bu+mi+nu+ria
al+bu+mose
al+bu+moses
Al+bu+quer+que
place name
Albuquerque
surname
al+bur+num
Al+bu+ry
al+cade
al+cades
Alcaeus
Al+ca+ic
Al+ca+ics
al+cal+des
Al+ca+traz
al+ca+zar
al+ca+zars
Al+ca+zar de San
  Juan
Alcestis
al+che+mic
al+chemi+cal
al+che+mise
al+che+mises
al+che+mis+ing
al+che+mised
al+che+mist
al+che+mists
al+che+mize
al+che+mizes
al+che+miz+ing
al+che+mized
al+che+my
al+che+mies
al+che+rin+ga
Al+ci+bia+dean
Alcibiades
Alcides
Alcinoüs
Alcock
al+co+hol
al+co+hols
al+co+hol+ic

al+co+hol+ics
al+co+holi+sa+
  tion
al+co+hol+ise
al+co+hol+ises
al+co+hol+is+
  ing
al+co+hol+ised
al+co+hol+ism
al+co+holi+za+
  tion
al+co+hol+ize
al+co+hol+izes
al+co+hol+iz+
  ing
al+co+hol+ized
Al+co+ran
Al+co+ran+ic
Alcott
al+cove
al+coves
Alcuin
Al+dab+ra
Al+dan
Alde+burgh
al+de+hyde
al+de+hydes
al+de+hy+dic
al den+te
al+der
al+ders
al+der+man
al+der+men
al+der+man+ic
Al+der+mas+ton
Al+der+ney
Al+der+shot
Aldington
Aldiss
Aldridge-
  Brownhills
al+drin
Aldrin
ale
ales
alea+to+ric
alea+to+ry
alec
alecs
aleck
alecks
Alecto
alee
ale+house
ale+houses

Aleichem
Aleksan+dro+pol
Aleksan+drovsk
Alembert
alem+bic
 alem+bics
Alençon
Alep
aleph
 alephs
aleph-null
 aleph-nulls
aleph-zero
 aleph-zeros
Alep+po
alert
 alerts
 alerts
 alert+ing
 alert+ed
 alert+ly
 alert+ness
Ales+san+dria
aleu+ron
aleu+rone
Al+eut
 Al+euts
Aleu+tian
 Aleu+tians
A lev+el
 A lev+els
ale+wife
 ale+wives
Alexander
Alexandra
Al+ex+an+dret+
 ta
Al+ex+an+dria
Al+ex+an+drian
 Al+ex+an+
 drians
Al+ex+an+drine
 Al+ex+an+
 drines
al+ex+an+drite
Alexan+droú+po+
 lis
alexia
Alexis
 Mikhailovich
al+fal+fa
 al+fal+fas
Alfonso
al+fres+co
Alfvén

alga
al+gal
Al+garve
al+ge+bra
 al+ge+bras
al+ge+bra+ic
al+ge+brai+cal
al+ge+bra+ist
 al+ge+bra+ists
Al+ge+ci+ras
Alger
Al+ge+ria
Al+ge+rian
Al+ge+rians
Al+gé+rie
Al+gé+rine
 Al+gé+rines
al+gid
al+gid+ity
Al+giers
al+gi+nate
 al+gi+nates
al+goid
Al+gol
al+go+lag+nia
Al+gon+kian
Al+gon+kians
 or
Al+gon+kian
Al+gon+kin
Al+gon+kins
 or
Al+gon+kin
Al+gon+quian
Al+gon+quians
 or
Al+gon+quian
Al+gon+quin
Al+gon+quins
 or
Al+gon+quin
al+go+rism
 al+go+risms
al+go+rithm
 al+go+rithms
al+go+rith+mic
Algren
Al+ham+bra
Al+ham+bresque
Al Hijra
Al Hijras
Al Hijrah
Al Hijrahs
Al Hof+uf
Al Huf+uf

Ali
ali+as
 ali+ases
 ali+as+ing
ali+bi
 ali+bis
 ali+bis
 ali+bi+ing
 ali+bied
Ali+can+te
Al+ice
Alice-in-Wonder+
 land
ali+cy+clic
ali+dad
 ali+dads
 ali+dade
 ali+dades
al+ien
 al+iens
al+ien+abil+ity
al+ien+able
al+ien+ate
 al+ien+ates
 al+ien+at+ing
 al+ien+at+ed
al+iena+tion
 al+iena+tions
al+iena+tor
 al+iena+tors
al+ienee
 al+ienees
al+ien+ist
 al+ien+ists
al+ien+or
 al+ien+ors
ali+form
Ali+garh
alight
 alights
 alight+ing
 alight+ed or
 alit
align
 aligns
 align+ing
 aligned
 align+ment
 align+ments
alike
ali+ment
 ali+ments
ali+men+ta+ry
ali+men+ta+tion
ali+mo+ny

ali+mo+nies
A-line
Ali Pasha
ali+phat+ic
ali+quant
ali+quot
alit
alit+er+ate
 alit+er+ates
alive
aliza+rin
Al-Jezair
al+ka+li
al+ka+lis or
 al+ka+lies
al+ka+line
al+ka+lin+ity
al+ka+lis+able
al+ka+lise
 al+ka+lises
al+ka+lis+ing
al+ka+lised
al+ka+liz+able
al+ka+lize
 al+ka+lizes
al+ka+liz+ing
al+ka+lized
al+ka+loid
 al+ka+loids
al+kane
 al+kanes
al+ka+net
 al+ka+nets
al+kene
 al+kenes
Alkmaar
Al+ko+ran
Al+ko+ran+ic
al+kyl
 al+kyls
al+kyne
 al+kynes
all
alla bre+ve
 alla bre+ves
Allah
Al+laha+bad
al+lan+to+ic
al+lan+to+is
 al+lan+toi+des
al+lay
 al+lays
 al+lay+ing
 al+layed
All Blacks

Allcock
all-dayer
all-dayers
al+le+ga+tion
al+le+ga+tions
al+lege
al+leges
al+leg+ing
al+leged
al+leged
al+leg+ed+ly
Al+le+ghe+nies
Al+le+ghe+ny
al+le+giance
al+le+giances
al+le+gor+ic
al+le+gori+cal
al+le+gori+sa+
   tion
al+le+gori+sa+
   tions
al+le+go+rise
al+le+go+rises
al+le+go+ris+ing
al+le+go+rised
al+le+go+rist
al+le+go+rists
al+le+gori+za+
   tion
al+le+gori+za+
   tions
al+le+go+rize
al+le+go+rizes
al+le+go+riz+ing
al+le+go+rized
al+le+go+ry
al+le+go+ries
al+le+gret+to
al+le+gret+tos
Allegri
al+le+gro
al+le+gros
al+lele
al+leles
al+le+lo+morph
al+le+lo+morphs
al+le+luia
al+le+mande
al+le+mandes
Al+len
place name
Allen
surname
Allenby
Allende

al+ler+gen
al+ler+gens
al+ler+gen+ic
al+ler+gic
al+ler+gist
al+ler+gists
al+ler+gy
al+ler+gies
al+le+vi+ate
al+le+vi+ates
al+le+vi+at+ing
al+le+vi+at+ed
al+le+via+tion
al+le+via+tions
al+le+via+tor
al+le+via+tors
al+ley
al+leys
alley+way
alley+ways
All+hal+lows
al+lia+ceous
al+li+ance
al+li+ances
al+lied
Al+lied
Al+lier
Al+lies
al+li+ga+tor
al+li+ga+tors
all-important
all-in
Allingham
al+lit+er+ate
al+lit+er+ates
al+lit+er+at+ing
al+lit+er+at+ed
al+lit+era+tion
al+lit+era+tions
al+lit+era+tive
al+lium
al+liums
all-nighter
all-nighters
Al+loa
al+lo+cat+able
al+lo+cate
al+lo+cates
al+lo+cat+ing
al+lo+cat+ed
al+lo+ca+tion
al+lo+ca+tions
al+lo+cu+tion
al+lo+cu+tions
al+lo+mer+ic

al+lom+er+ism
al+lom+er+ous
al+lo+morph
al+lo+morphs
al+lo+mor+phic
al+lo+path
al+lo+paths
al+lo+pa+thic
al+lopa+thist
al+lopa+thists
al+lopa+thy
al+lo+phone
al+lo+phones
al+lo+phon+ic
al+lot
al+lots
al+lot+ting
al+lot+ted
al+lot+ment
al+lot+ments
al+lo+trope
al+lo+tropes
al+lo+trop+ic
al+lot+ro+pism
al+lot+ro+pisms
al+lo+tro+py
al+lo+tro+pies
all-out
all-over
al+low
al+lows
al+low+ing
al+lowed
al+low+able
al+low+ably
al+low+ance
al+low+ances
al+low+ances
al+low+anc+ing
al+low+anced
Al+lo+way
al+low+ed+ly
al+loy
al+loys
al+loys
al+loy+ing
al+loyed
all-right
all-round
all-rounder
all-rounders
all+spice
all+spices
all-star
all-time

al+lude
al+ludes
al+lud+ing
al+lud+ed
al+lure
al+lures
al+lures
al+lur+ing
al+lured
al+lure+ment
al+lure+ments
al+lur+ing
al+lu+sion
al+lu+sions
al+lu+sive
al+lu+sive+ness
al+lu+vial
al+lu+vials
al+lu+vion
al+lu+vions
al+lu+vium
al+lu+viums
ally
al+lies
al+lies
al+ly+ing
al+lied
Alma-Ata
al+ma+can+tar
al+ma+can+tars
Al+ma+da
Al Ma+di+nah
alma ma+ter
alma ma+ters
al+ma+nac
al+ma+nacs
al+ma+nack
al+ma+nacks
al+man+dine
al+man+dines
Al Man+su+rah
Al Marj
Alma-Tadema
al+mighty
Al+mighty
al+mond
al+monds
almond-eyed
al+mon+er
al+mon+ers
al+most
alms
alms+house
alms+houses
al+mu+can+tar

al+mu+can+tars
aloe
aloes
aloes
aloe vera
aloft
alone
along
along+shore
along+side
aloof
aloof+ly
aloof+ness
alo+pecia
aloud
Aloysius
alp
alps
al+paca
al+pacas
alpen+horn
alpen+horns
alpen+stock
alpen+stocks
Alpes-de-Haute-
Pro+vence
Alpes Ma+ri+
times
al+pha
al+phas
al+pha+bet
al+pha+bets
al+pha+bet+ic
al+pha+beti+cal
al+pha+beti+cal+
ly
al+pha+beti+sa+
tion
al+pha+bet+ise
al+pha+bet+ises
al+pha+bet+is+
ing
al+pha+bet+ised
al+pha+beti+za+
tion
al+pha+bet+ize
al+pha+bet+izes
al+pha+bet+iz+
ing
al+pha+bet+ized
alpha-fetoprotein
al+pha+mer+ic
al+pha+nu+mer+
ic
Alpheus

alp+horn
alp+horns
al+pine
al+pines
Al+pine
al+pin+ist
al+pin+ists
Alps
al+ready
al+right
Not standard
Al+sace
Alsace-Lorraine
Al+sa+tia
Al+sa+tian
Al+sa+tians
also
also-ran
also-rans
al+stroe+meria
al+stroe+merias
alt
Al+tai
Al+ta+ic
Al+ta+mi+ra
al+tar
al+tars
altar+piece
altar+pieces
alt+azi+muth
alt+azi+muths
Alt+dorf
al+ter
al+ters
al+ter+ing
al+tered
al+ter+able
al+tera+tion
al+tera+tions
al+tera+tive
al+tera+tives
al+ter+cate
al+ter+cates
al+ter+cat+ing
al+ter+cat+ed
al+ter+ca+tion
al+ter+ca+tions
al+ter+nate
al+ter+nates
al+ter+nat+ing
al+ter+nat+ed
al+ter+nate+ly
al+ter+na+tion
al+ter+na+tions
al+ter+na+tive

al+ter+na+tives
al+ter+na+tive+ly
al+ter+na+tor
al+ter+na+tors
al+thaea
al+thaeas
al+thea
al+theas
alt+horn
alt+horns
al+though
al+time+ter
al+time+ters
Al+ti+pla+no
al+ti+tude
al+ti+tudes
alto
altos
alto+cu+mu+lus
alto+cu+mu+li
al+to+geth+er
alto+ist
alto+ists
al+to+stra+tus
al+to+stra+ti
al+tri+cial
al+tri+cials
Al+trin+cham
al+tru+ism
al+tru+ist
al+tru+ists
al+tru+is+tic
al+tru+is+ti+cal+
ly
alum
alums
alu+mi+na
alu+mi+nise
alu+mi+nises
alu+mi+nis+ing
alu+mi+nised
alu+min+ium
alu+mi+nize
alu+mi+nizes
alu+mi+niz+ing
alu+mi+nized
alu+mi+nous
alu+mi+num
alum+na
alum+nae
alum+nus
alum+ni
Alva
Alvarez
al+veo+lar

al+veo+lars
al+veo+late
al+veo+la+tion
al+veo+la+tions
al+veo+lus
al+veo+li
al+way
al+ways
Alwyn
alys+sum
alys+sums
Alzheimer's
Alzheimer's
am
ama+da+vat
ama+da+vats
ama+dou
amah
amahs
amain
Amal+fi
amalgam
amalgams
amal+gam+ate
amal+gam+ates
amal+gam+at+
ing
amal+ga+mat+
ed
amal+gama+tion
amal+gama+
tions
amanu+en+sis
amanu+en+
sises
Amanullah Khan
Ama+pá
ama+ranth
ama+ranths
ama+ret+to
ama+ret+tos
ama+ryl+lis
ama+ryl+lises
amass
amasses
amass+ing
amassed
amass+er
amass+ers
ama+teur
ama+teurs
ama+teur+ish
ama+teur+ish+ly
ama+teur+ism
Amati

Amatis
ama+tive
ama+to+rial
ama+tory
amau+ro+sis
amau+ro+ses
amau+rot+ic
amaze
amazes
amaz+ing
amazed
amaze+ment
amaz+ing
Ama+zon
Ama+zons
Ama+zo+nas
Ama+zo+nian
Am+ba+la
am+bas+sa+dor
am+bas+sa+
  dors
am+bas+sa+dor+
  ial
am+bas+sa+dor+
  ships
am+bas+sa+
  dress
am+ber
am+bers
am+ber+gris
amber+jack
amber+jacks
am+bi+ance
am+bi+dex+ter+
  ity
am+bi+dex+trous
am+bi+dex+trous+
  ness
am+bi+ence
am+bi+ent
am+bi+gu+ity
am+bi+gu+ities
am+bigu+ous
am+bigu+ous+ly
am+bigu+ous+
  ness
ambi+sex+ual
am+bit
am+bits
am+bi+tion
am+bi+tions
am+bi+tious
am+bi+tious+
  ness
am+biva+lence

am+biva+len+cy
am+biva+lent
am+ble
am+bles
am+bles
am+bling
am+bled
Ambler
Am+ble+side
am+blyo+pia
am+blyop+ic
am+boi+na
Am+boi+na
Am+boise
Ambon
ambo+sex+ual
am+boy+na
Ambrose
am+bro+sia
am+bro+sias
am+bro+sial
am+bro+sian
Am+bro+sian
am+bry
am+bries
am+bu+lance
am+bu+lances
am+bu+lant
am+bu+late
am+bu+lates
am+bu+lat+ing
am+bu+lat+ed
am+bu+la+tion
am+bu+la+tions
am+bu+la+tory
am+bu+la+
  tories
am+bus+cade
am+bus+cades
am+bus+cades
am+bus+cad+
  ing
am+bus+cad+
  ed
am+bush
am+bushes
am+bushes
am+bush+ing
am+bushed
ame+ba
  U.S.
ame+bae *or*
ame+bas
ame+bic
  U.S.

ameer
ameers
ame+lio+rate
ame+lio+rates
ame+lio+rat+ing
ame+lio+rat+ed
ame+lio+ra+tion
ame+lio+ra+
  tions
ame+lio+ra+tive
ame+lio+ra+tor
ame+lio+ra+tors
amen
amens
Amen
ame+nabil+ity
ame+nable
ame+nable+ness
ame+nably
amend
amends
amend+ing
amend+ed
amend+able
amend+er
amend+ers
amend+ment
amend+ments
amends
amen+ity
amen+ities
amen+or+rhea
  U.S.
amen+or+rhoea
Amen-Ra
am+ent
am+ents
am+en+ta+ceous
amen+tia
amen+tum
amerce
amerces
amerc+ing
amerced
amerce+ment
amerce+ments
Ameri+ca
Ameri+cas
Ameri+can
Ameri+cans
Ameri+ca+na
Ameri+cani+sa+
  tion
Ameri+cani+sa+
  tions

Ameri+can+ise
Ameri+can+ises
Ameri+can+is+
  ing
Ameri+can+ised
Ameri+can+ism
Ameri+can+
  isms
Ameri+cani+za+
  tion
Ameri+cani+za+
  tions
Ameri+can+ize
Ameri+can+izes
Ameri+can+iz+
  ing
Ameri+can+ized
am+eri+cium
Am+er+in+dian
Am+er+in+dians
Am+er+in+dic
am+ethyst
am+ethysts
am+ethys+tine
Am+ha+ra
Am+har+ic
Amherst
ami+abil+ity
ami+able
ami+able+ness
ami+ably
ami+an+thus
ami+an+thuses
ami+cabil+ity
ami+cable
ami+cable+ness
ami+cably
am+ice
am+ices
ami+cus cu+riae
ami+ci cu+riae
amid
am+ide
am+ides
amid+ships
amidst
Ami+ens
ami+go
ami+gos
Amin
amine
amines
ami+no
amir
amirs

amir+ate
amir+ates
Amis
Amish
amiss
ami+to+sis
ami+tot+ic
am+ity
am+ities
Am+man
am+meter
am+meters
ammo
Ammon
am+mo+nia
am+mo+nias
am+mo+ni+ac
am+mo+nia+cal
am+mo+ni+ate
am+mo+ni+ates
am+mo+ni+at+ing
am+mo+ni+at+ed
am+mo+nia+tion
am+mo+nia+tions
am+moni+fi+ca+tion
am+moni+fi+ca+tions
am+moni+fy
am+moni+fies
am+moni+fy+ing
am+moni+fied
am+mo+nite
am+mo+nites
am+mo+nium
am+mu+ni+tion
am+ne+sia
am+ne+si+ac
am+ne+si+acs
am+ne+sic
am+ne+sics
am+nes+ty
am+nes+ties
am+nes+ties
am+nes+ty+ing
am+nes+tied
am+nio+cen+tesis
am+nio+cen+teses
am+ni+on

am+ni+ons *or*
am+nia
am+ni+ot+ic
amoe+ba
amoe+bae *or*
amoe+bas
amoe+bic
amok
among
amongst
amon+til+la+do
amon+til+la+dos
amor+al
amo+ral+ity
amo+rist
amo+rists
amo+ro+so
amo+rous
amo+rous+ly
amo+rous+ness
amor+phism
amor+phisms
amor+phous
amor+phous+ness
amor+ti+sa+tion
amor+ti+sa+tions
amor+tise
amor+tises
amor+tis+ing
amor+tised
amor+ti+za+tion
amor+ti+za+tions
amor+tize
amor+tizes
amor+tiz+ing
amor+tized
Amos
amount
amounts
amounts
amount+ing
amount+ed
amour
amours
amour-propre
Amoy
amp
amps
am+pe+lop+sis
am+per+age
am+per+ages
am+pere

am+peres
Ampère
ampere-turn
ampere-turns
am+per+sand
am+per+sands
am+pheta+mine
am+pheta+mines
am+phib+ian
am+phib+ians
am+phibi+ous
am+phibi+ous+ness
am+phi+bole
am+phi+boles
am+phi+bol+ogy
am+phi+bol+ogies
am+phibo+ly
am+phibo+lies
am+phi+mic+tic
am+phi+mix+is
am+phi+mixes
am+phi+ox+us
am+phi+oxi *or*
am+phi+oxes
am+phi+pod
am+phi+pods
am+phip+ro+style
am+phip+ro+styles
am+phis+bae+na
am+phis+bae+nae *or*
am+phis+bae+nas
am+phi+thea+ter *U.S.*
am+phi+thea+ters
am+phi+thea+tre
am+phi+thea+tres
Amphitrite
am+pho+ra
am+pho+rae *or*
am+pho+ras
am+pho+ter+ic
am+pi+cil+lin
am+ple
am+ple+ness

am+pli+fi+ca+tion
am+pli+fi+ca+tions
am+pli+fi+er
am+pli+fi+ers
am+pli+fy
am+pli+fies
am+pli+fy+ing
am+pli+fied
am+pli+tude
am+pli+tudes
am+ply
am+poule
am+poules
am+pule *U.S.*
am+pules
am+pul+la
am+pul+lae
am+pu+tate
am+pu+tates
am+pu+tat+ing
am+pu+tat+ed
am+pu+ta+tion
am+pu+ta+tions
am+pu+tee
am+pu+tees
Am+rit+sar
Am+ster+dam
amuck
Amu Dar+ya
amu+let
amu+lets
Amundsen
Amur
amuse
amuses
amus+ing
amused
amuse+ment
amuse+ments
amus+ing
amus+ing+ly
amyg+da+lin
amyl
amy+la+ceous
am+yl+ase
am+yl+ases
amy+loid
amy+loids
amy+lop+sin
amy+lum
Amy+tal
Trademark

an
An
an'
ana
adv.
ana
Ana+bap+tism
Ana+bap+tist
Ana+bap+tists
ana+bas
ana+bases
anaba+sis
anaba+ses
ana+bat+ic
ana+bio+sis
ana+bio+ses
ana+bi+ot+ic
ana+bol+ic
anabo+lism
anabo+lisms
anach+ro+nism
anach+ro+nisms
anach+ro+nis+tic
anach+ro+nis+ti+
cal+ly
ana+co+lu+thon
ana+co+lu+tha
ana+con+da
ana+con+das
Anacreon
Anac+reon+tic
Anac+reon+tics
ana+cru+sis
ana+cru+ses
anad+ro+mous
Ana+dyr
anaemia
anaemic
an+aer+obe
an+aer+obes
an+aero+bic
an+aero+bium
an+aero+bia
an+aes+the+sia
an+aes+thet+ic
an+aes+thet+ics
an+aes+thet+ics
anaes+the+ti+sa+
tion
anaes+the+ti+sa+
tions
anaes+the+tise
anaes+the+
tises

anaes+the+tis+
ing
anaes+the+
tised
anaes+the+tist
anaes+the+tists
anaes+the+ti+za+
tion
anaes+the+ti+za+
tions
anaes+the+tize
anaes+the+tizes
anaes+the+tiz+
ing
anaes+the+tized
ana+glyph
ana+glyphs
ana+glyph+ic
Ana+glyp+ta
Trademark
ana+gram
ana+grams
ana+gram+mat+
ic
ana+gram+mati+
cal
ana+gram+ma+
tise
ana+gram+ma+
tises
ana+gram+ma+
tis+ing
ana+gram+ma+
tised
ana+gram+ma+
tize
ana+gram+ma+
tizes
ana+gram+ma+
tiz+ing
ana+gram+ma+
tized
anal
ana+lec+ta
ana+lects
ana+lep+tic
ana+lep+tics
an+al+gesia
an+alge+sic
an+alge+sics
an+al+gia
anal+ly
ana+log
ana+logs
ana+logi+cal

analo+gise
analo+gises
analo+gis+ing
analo+gised
analo+gize
analo+gizes
analo+giz+ing
analo+gized
analo+gous
ana+logue
ana+logues
anal+ogy
anal+ogies
analy+sand
analy+sands
ana+lyse
ana+lyses
ana+lys+ing
ana+lysed
ana+lys+er
ana+lys+ers
analy+sis
analy+ses
ana+lyst
ana+lysts
ana+lyt+ic
ana+lyti+cal
ana+lyti+cal+ly
Anam+bra
an+an+drous
Ananias
ana+paest
ana+paests
ana+paes+tic
ana+pest
ana+pests
ana+pes+tic
anapho+ra
anapho+ras
an+aph+ro+dis+
iac
an+aph+ro+dis+
iacs
ana+phy+lax+is
ana+plas+mo+sis
an+ap+tyx+is
an+ap+tyxes
Ana+pur+na
an+ar+chic
an+ar+chism
an+ar+chist
an+ar+chists
an+ar+chy
an+ar+chies
Anastasia

an+as+tig+mat
an+as+tig+mats
an+as+tig+mat+
ic
anas+to+mose
anas+to+moses
anas+to+mos+
ing
anas+to+mosed
anas+to+mo+sis
anas+to+mo+
ses
anas+tro+phe
anas+tro+phes
anath+ema
anath+emas
anath+ema+tise
anath+ema+
tises
anath+ema+tis+
ing
anath+ema+
tised
anath+ema+tize
anath+ema+
tizes
anath+ema+tiz+
ing
anath+ema+
tized
Ana+to+lia
Ana+to+lian
Ana+to+lians
ana+tomi+cal
anato+mise
anato+mises
anato+mis+ing
anato+mised
anato+mist
anato+mists
anato+mize
anato+mizes
anato+miz+ing
anato+mized
anato+my
anato+mies
anat+to
anat+tos
Anaxagoras
Anaximander
an+ces+tor
an+ces+tors
an+ces+tral
an+ces+tress
an+ces+try

an+ces+tries
Anchises
an+chor
an+chors
an+chors
an+chor+ing
an+chored
an+chor+age
an+chor+ages
An+chor+age
an+cho+ress
an+cho+rite
an+cho+rites
anchor+man
anchor+men
anchor+woman
anchor+women
an+cho+vy
an+cho+vies
or
an+cho+vy
an+chu+sa
an+chu+sas
an+chy+lose
an+chy+loses
an+chy+los+ing
an+chy+losed
an+chy+lose
an+chy+loses
an+chy+los+ing
an+chy+losed
an+chy+lo+sis
an+chy+lot+ic
an+cien ré+gime
an+ciens ré+
    gimes
an+cient
an+cients
an+cient+ly
an+cient+ness
an+cil+lary
an+cil+laries
An+co+hu+ma
an+con
an+cones
An+co+na
an+cone
an+cones
an+cy+los+to+
    mia+sis
An+cy+ra
and
An+da+lu+sia
an+dan+te
an+dan+tes

an+dan+ti+no
an+dan+ti+nos
AND cir+cuit
AND cir+cuits
An+dean
Andersen
An+der+son
place name
Anderson
surname
An+des
and+iron
and+irons
An+dong
and/or
An+dor+ra
An+dor+ra la Ve+
    lla
An+dor+ran
An+dorre la
    Vieille
Andrássy
Andrea del Sarto
Andrew
Andrewes
Andrews
Andric
Androcles
Androclus
an+droe+cium
an+droe+cia
an+dro+gen
an+dro+gens
an+dro+gen+ic
an+dro+gyne
an+dro+gynes
an+drogy+nous
an+drogy+ny
an+droid
an+droids
Andromache
An+drom+eda
constellation
Andromeda
Greek myth
An+drop+ov
place name
Andropov
surname
An+dros
an+dros+ter+one
Andvari
ane
an+ec+dot+age
an+ec+do+tal

an+ec+do+tal+ist
an+ec+do+tal+
    ists
an+ec+dote
an+ec+dotes
an+ec+dot+ic
an+ec+do+tist
an+ec+to+tists
an+echo+ic
Aneirin
anemia
U.S.
anemic
U.S.
anemo+graph
anemo+graphs
an+emom+eter
an+emom+eters
an+emo+met+ric
an+emom+etry
anemo+ne
anemo+nes
an+emophi+lous
an+emophi+ly
anent
an+es+the+sia
U.S.
an+es+thesi+olo+
    gist
an+es+thesi+olo+
    gists
an+es+the+si+ol+
    ogy
U.S.
an+es+thet+ic
U.S.
an+es+thet+ics
anes+the+tist
U.S.
anes+the+tists
anes+the+ti+za+
    tion
U.S.
anes+the+ti+za+
    tions
anes+the+tize
U.S.
anes+the+tizes
anes+the+tizing
anes+the+tized
Aneto
aneu+rism
aneu+risms
aneu+rysm
aneu+rysms

anew
Anfinsen
An+ga+ra
an+ga+ry
an+gel
an+gels
angel+fish
angel+fish *or*
angel+fishes
an+gel+ic
an+gel+ica
an+gel+icas
an+geli+cal
an+geli+cal+ly
Angelico
Angell
Angelou
An+ge+lus
An+ge+luses
an+ger
an+gers
an+gers
an+ger+ing
an+gered
An+ge+vin
An+ge+vins
an+gi+na
an+gio+ma
an+gio+mas *or*
an+gio+ma+ta
an+gio+plas+ty
an+gio+sperm
an+gio+sperms
Ang+kor
an+gle
an+gles
an+gles
an+gling
an+gled
An+gle
An+gles
an+gler
an+glers
An+gle+sey
An+glia
An+glian
An+gli+can
An+gli+cans
An+gli+can+ism
an+gli+cise
an+gli+cises
an+gli+cis+ing
an+gli+cised
An+gli+cism
An+gli+cisms

an+gli+cize
an+gli+cizes
an+gli+ciz+ing
an+gli+cized
an+gling
An+glo
An+glos
Anglo-American
Anglo-
Americans
Anglo-Catholic
Anglo-Catholics
Anglo-
Catholicism
Anglo-French
Anglo-Indian
Anglo-Indians
An+glo+ma+nia
An+glo+ma+ni+
ac
An+glo+ma+ni+
acs
Anglo-Norman
Anglo-Normans
An+glo+phil
An+glo+phils
An+glo+phile
An+glo+philes
An+glo+phobe
An+glo+phobes
An+glo+phone
An+glo+phones
Anglo-Saxon
Anglo-Saxons
An+go+la
An+go+lan
An+go+lans
an+go+ra
An+go+ra
An+go+ras
An+go+stu+ra
an+gri+ly
an+gry
an+gri+er
an+gri+est
angst
ang+strom
ang+stroms
An+guil+la
an+guine
an+guish
an+guishes
an+guish+ing
an+guished
an+guished

an+gu+lar
an+gu+lar+ity
an+gu+lar+ities
An+gus
Angus Og
An+halt
an+he+dral
An+hui
An+hwei
an+hy+dride
an+hy+drides
an+hy+drous
Ani+ak+chak
anil
anils
ani+line
ani+ma
ani+mad+ver+
sion
ani+mad+ver+
sions
ani+mad+vert
ani+mad+verts
ani+mad+vert+
ing
ani+mad+vert+
ed
ani+mal
ani+mals
ani+mal+cu+lar
ani+mal+cule
ani+mal+cules
ani+mali+sa+tion
ani+mal+ise
ani+mal+ises
ani+mal+is+ing
ani+mal+ised
ani+mal+ism
ani+mal+isms
ani+mal+ity
ani+mali+za+tion
ani+mal+ize
ani+mal+izes
ani+mal+iz+ing
ani+mal+ized
ani+mate
ani+mates
ani+mat+ing
ani+mat+ed
ani+mat+ed+ly
ani+ma+tion
ani+ma+tions
ani+ma+to
ani+mé
ani+més

ani+mism
ani+mis+tic
ani+mos+ity
ani+mos+ities
ani+mus
an+ion
an+ions
ani+on+ic
an+ise
ani+seed
ani+sette
an+iso+trop+ic
an+iso+tropi+cal+
ly
an+isot+ro+py
An+jou
An+ka+ra
ankh
ankhs
An+king
an+kle
an+kles
ankle+bone
ankle+bones
an+klet
an+klets
an+ky+lose
an+ky+loses
an+ky+los+ing
an+ky+losed
an+ky+lo+sis
an+ky+los+to+
mia+sis
an+ky+los+to+
mia+ses
an+ky+lot+ic
anna
annas
An+na+ba
an+nal+ist
an+nal+ists
an+nal+is+tic
An+napo+lis
An+na+pur+na
Ann Ar+bor
an+nates
an+nat+to
an+nat+tos
Anne
an+neal
an+neals
an+neals
an+neal+ing
an+nealed
an+neal+er

an+neal+ers
Anne+cy
an+nelid
an+nelids
an+neli+dan
an+neli+dans
an+nex
an+nexes
an+nexes
an+nex+ing
an+nexed
an+nex+able
an+nexa+tion
an+nexa+tions
an+nexe
an+nexes
Annigoni
an+ni+hi+late
an+ni+hi+lates
an+ni+hi+lat+ing
an+ni+hi+lat+ed
an+ni+hi+la+tion
an+ni+hi+la+
tions
an+ni+hi+la+tor
an+ni+hi+la+
tors
an+ni+ver+sa+ry
an+ni+ver+sa+
ries
anno Domi+ni
an+no+tate
an+no+tates
an+no+tat+ing
an+no+tat+ed
an+no+ta+tion
an+no+ta+tions
an+no+ta+tive
an+no+ta+tor
an+no+ta+tors
an+nounce
an+nounces
an+nounc+ing
an+nounced
an+nounce+ment
an+nounce+
ments
an+nounc+er
an+nounc+ers
an+noy
an+noys
an+noy+ing
an+noyed
an+noy+ance
an+noy+ances

an+noy+er
an+noy+ers
an+noy+ing
an+noy+ing+ly
an+nual
an+nuals
an+nual+ise
an+nual+ises
an+nual+is+ing
an+nual+ised
an+nual+ize
an+nual+izes
an+nual+iz+ing
an+nual+ized
an+nual+ly
an+nui+tant
an+nui+tants
an+nu+ity
an+nu+ities
an+nul
an+nuls
an+nul+ling
an+nulled
an+nu+lar
an+nu+late
an+nu+la+tion
an+nu+la+tions
an+nu+let
an+nu+lets
an+nul+lable
an+nul+ment
an+nul+ments
an+nu+lus
an+nu+li or
an+nu+luses
an+nun+ci+ate
an+nun+ci+ates
an+nun+ci+at+ing
an+nun+ci+at+ed
An+nun+cia+tion
an+nun+cia+tor
an+nun+cia+tors
an+nus mi+ra+bi+lis
anni mi+ra+bi+les
anoa
anoas
an+od+al
an+ode
an+odes
an+od+ic

ano+dise
ano+dises
ano+dis+ing
ano+dised
ano+dize
ano+dizes
ano+diz+ing
ano+dized
ano+dyne
ano+dynes
anoint
anoints
anoint+ing
anoint+ed
anoint+er
anoint+ers
anoint+ment
anoint+ments
anoma+lis+tic
anoma+lous
anoma+lous+ness
anoma+ly
anoma+lies
anom+ic
an+omie
an+omy
anon
ano+nym
ano+nyms
ano+nym+ity
anony+mous
anophe+les
anophe+les
ano+rak
ano+raks
ano+rec+tic
ano+rec+tics
ano+rexia
ano+rexia ner+vo+sa
ano+rex+ic
ano+rex+ics
an+os+mat+ic
an+os+mia
an+os+mic
an+oth+er
Anouilh
an+oxia
an+ox+ic
An+qing
An+schluss
Anselm
an+ser+ine
Ansermet

an+swer
an+swers
an+swers
an+swer+ing
an+swered
an+swer+able
ant
ants
ant+acid
ant+acids
Antaeus
an+tago+ni+sa+tion
an+tago+ni+sa+tions
an+tago+nise
an+tago+nises
an+tago+nis+ing
an+tago+nised
an+tago+nism
an+tago+nisms
an+tago+nist
an+tago+nists
an+tago+nis+tic
an+tago+nis+ti+cal+ly
an+tago+ni+za+tion
an+tago+ni+za+tions
an+tago+nize
an+tago+nizes
an+tago+niz+ing
an+tago+nized
An+ta+ki+ya
An+ta+kya
ant+al+ka+li
ant+al+ka+lis or
ant+al+ka+lies
An+ta+na+na+ri+vo
Ant+arc+tic
Ant+arc+ti+ca
ante
an+tes
an+tes
an+te+ing
an+ted or
an+teed
ant+eater
ant+eaters
ante+bel+lum
ante+cede

ante+cedes
ante+ced+ing
ante+ced+ed
ante+ced+ence
ante+ced+ent
ante+ced+ents
ante+cham+ber
ante+cham+bers
ante+date
ante+dates
ante+dates
ante+dat+ing
ante+dat+ed
ante+di+lu+vian
ante+di+lu+vians
ante+lope
ante+lopes or
ante+lope
ante+me+rid+ian
ante me+ridi+em
ante+na+tal
an+ten+na
an+ten+nae
insect organ
an+ten+nas
aerial
an+ten+nal
an+ten+nary
ante+pen+dium
ante+pen+dia
ante+penult
ante+penults
ante+penul+ti+mate
ante+penul+ti+mates
ante+ri+or
ante+room
ante+rooms
ant+he+li+on
ant+he+lia
an+thel+min+thic
an+them
an+thems
an+ther
an+thers
an+ther+id+ium
an+ther+idia
an+tholo+gise
an+tholo+gises
an+tholo+gis+ing
an+tholo+gised

an+tholo+gist
an+tholo+gists
an+tholo+gize
an+tholo+gizes
an+tholo+giz+
ing
an+tholo+gized
an+thol+ogy
an+thol+ogies
Anthony
an+tho+zo+an
an+tho+zo+ans
an+thra+cene
an+thra+cite
an+thra+cit+ic
an+thra+co+sis
an+thrax
an+thra+ces
an+thro+po+cen+
tric
an+thro+po+gen+
esis
an+thro+po+
geny
an+thro+poid
an+thro+poids
an+thro+po+logi+
cal
an+thro+polo+
gist
an+thro+polo+
gists
an+thro+pol+ogy
an+thro+po+met+
ric
an+thro+po+met+
ri+cal
an+thro+pom+
etry
an+thro+po+
morph
an+thro+po+
morphs
an+thro+po+mor+
phic
an+thro+po+
morphi+cal+ly
an+thro+po+mor+
phism
an+thro+po+mor+
phous
an+thro+popha+
gi
anti
antis

anti-abortion
anti-abrasion
anti-ageing
anti-aircraft
anti-alien
anti-American
anti-apartheid
an+ti+ar
an+ti+ars
anti-aristocratic
anti+bac+te+rial
anti+bal+lis+tic
An+tibes
anti+bib+li+cal
anti+bio+sis
anti+bi+ot+ic
anti+bi+ot+ics
anti+body
anti+bodies
anti-Bolshe+vik
anti-Bolshe+viks
anti-Bolshe+vism
anti-Bolshe+vist
anti-Bolshe+
vists
anti-British
an+tic
an+tics
anti+capi+tal+ist
anti+capi+tal+
ists
anti+capi+tal+is+
tic
anti+cath+ode
anti+cath+odes
anti-Catho+lic
anti-Catho+lics
anti-Catholi+cism
anti+cen+sor+
ship
anti+cen+sor+
ships
Anti+christ
Anti+christs
anti+church
an+tici+pant
an+tici+pants
an+tici+pate
an+tici+pates
an+tici+pat+ing
an+tici+pat+ed
an+tici+pa+tion
an+tici+pa+tions
an+tici+pa+tive
an+tici+pa+tor

an+tici+pa+tors
an+tici+pa+tory
anti+clas+si+cal
anti+cleri+cal
anti+cleri+cals
anti+cleri+cal+
ism
anti+cli+mac+tic
anti+cli+max
anti+cli+maxes
anti+cli+nal
anti+cline
anti+clines
anti+clock+wise
anti+co+agu+lant
anti+co+agu+
lants
anti+co+agu+lat+
ing
anti-Com+mu+
nist
anti-Com+mu+
nists
an+ti+con+scrip+
tion
anti+con+sti+tu+
tion+al
anti+con+vul+
sant
anti+con+vul+
sants
anti+cor+ro+sive
An+ti+cos+ti
anti+cy+clone
anti+cy+clones
anti+cy+clon+ic
anti-Darwin+ian
anti-Darwin+ians
anti+daz+zle
anti+demo+crat+
ic
anti+de+pres+
sant
anti+de+pres+
sants
anti+diu+ret+ic
anti+diu+ret+ics
anti+dot+al
anti+dote
anti+dotes
anti-ecclesi+as+ti+
cal
anti-ecclesi+as+ti+
cal+ly
anti+emet+ic

anti+emet+ics
anti-episco+pal
anti-episco+pals
anti-erosion
anti-
Establishment
anti-evolu+tion
anti-evolu+tion+
ist
anti-evolu+tion+
ists
anti+fac+tion
anti+fas+cist
anti+fas+cists
anti+freeze
anti-Freudian
anti-Freudians
anti+fun+da+men+
tal+ist
anti+fun+da+
men+tal+ists
anti+gen
anti+gens
Antigone
An+ti+gua
An+ti+guan
An+ti+guans
anti+he+ro
anti+he+roes
anti+his+ta+mine
anti+his+ta+
mines
anti+hu+man+
ism
anti+hu+man+ist
anti+hu+man+
ists
anti-imperi+al+
ism
anti-imperi+al+ist
anti-imperi+al+
ists
anti-inflamma+
tory
anti-inflationary
anti+knock
anti+knocks
anti+la+bour
Anti-Leba+non
anti+li+tur+gi+cal
An+til+les
anti+lock
anti+log
anti+logs
anti+loga+rithm

anti+loga+
rithms
anti+loga+rith+
mic
an+til+ogy
an+til+ogies
anti+ma+cas+sar
anti+ma+cas+
sars
anti+mag+net+ic
anti+ma+lar+ial
anti+ma+lar+ials
anti+masque
anti+masques
anti+ma+teri+al+
is+tic
anti+mat+ter
anti+me+tabo+
lite
anti+me+tabo+
lites
anti+mi+cro+bial
anti+mili+ta+rism
anti+mili+ta+rist
anti+mili+ta+
rists
anti+mili+ta+ris+
tic
anti+mis+sile
anti+mis+siles
anti+mod+ern+ist
anti+mod+ern+
ists
anti+mo+nar+
chic+al
anti+mo+nar+
chist
anti+mo+nar+
chists
anti+mo+nial
anti+mo+ny
anti+muon
anti+muons
anti+nar+cot+ic
anti+nar+cot+
ics
anti+na+tion+al+
ist
anti+na+tion+al+
ists
anti+na+tion+al+
is+tic
anti-Nazi
anti-Nazis
anti+noise

anti+no+mian
anti+no+mians
anti+no+mian+
ism
anti+nom+ic
an+tino+my
an+tino+mies
anti+nov+el
anti+nov+els
anti+nu+clear
An+ti+och
anti+paci+fist
anti+paci+fists
anti+par+ti+cle
anti+par+ti+cles
anti+pas+to
anti+pas+tos
anti+pa+thet+ic
anti+pa+thet+ical
anti+patho+gen
anti+patho+
gens
anti+patho+gen+
ic
an+tipa+thy
an+tipa+thies
anti+per+son+nel
anti+per+spi+rant
anti+per+spi+
rants
anti+phlo+gis+tic
anti+phlo+gis+
tics
anti+phon
anti+phons
an+tipho+nal
an+tipho+nary
an+tipho+naries
an+tipho+ny
an+tipho+nies
an+tipo+dal
anti+pode
anti+podes
an+tipo+dean
an+tipo+des
anti+po+liti+cal
anti+pol+lu+tion
anti+pol+lu+
tions
anti+pope
anti+popes
anti+pro+hi+bi+
tion
anti+pro+hi+bi+
tions

anti+pro+hi+bi+
tion+ist
anti+pro+hi+bi+
tion+ists
anti-Protes+tant
anti-Protes+
tants
anti+pu+ri+tan
anti+pu+ri+tans
anti+py+ret+ic
anti+py+ret+ics
anti+quar+ian
anti+quar+ians
anti+quari+an+
ism
anti+quark
anti+quarks
anti+quary
anti+quaries
anti+quate
anti+quates
anti+quat+ing
anti+quat+ed
anti+quat+ed
an+tique
an+tiques
an+tiques
an+tiqu+ing
an+tiqued
an+tiq+uity
an+tiq+uities
anti+rac+ism
anti+rac+ist
anti+rac+ists
anti+ra+tion+al
anti+ra+tion+al+
ism
anti+reli+gious
anti+repub+li+
can
anti+repub+li+
cans
anti+revo+lu+tion+
ary
anti+revo+lu+
tion+aries
anti+riot
anti-roll
an+tir+rhi+num
anti+rust
An+ti+sa+na
anti+sci+en+tif+
ic
anti+scor+bu+tic

anti+scor+bu+
tics
anti-Semite
anti-Semites
anti-Semitic
anti-Semitism
anti+sep+sis
anti+sep+tic
anti+sep+tics
anti+sep+ti+cal+
ly
anti+serum
anti+serums *or*
anti+sera
anti+shock
anti+skid
anti+so+cial
anti-Soviet
anti-Soviets
anti+spas+mod+
ic
anti+spas+mod+
ics
anti+spir+it+ual
anti+stat+ic
an+tis+tro+phe
an+tis+tro+phes
anti+strophi+cal+
ly
anti+sub+ma+
rine
anti+tank
anti+tar+nish+ing
anti+ter+ror+ist
anti+theft
anti+the+ism
anti+the+ist
anti+the+ists
an+tith+esis
an+tith+eses
anti+theti+cal
anti+tox+ic
anti+tox+in
anti+tox+ins
anti+trades
anti+trini+tar+ian
anti+trini+tar+
ians
anti+trust
anti+tus+sive
anti+tus+sives
anti+type
anti+types
anti+typi+cal
anti+ven+ene

anti+ven+enes
anti+ven+in
anti+ven+ins
anti+vivi+sec+
  tion
anti+vivi+sec+
  tion+ist
anti+vivi+sec+
  tion+ists
anti+war
anti-Zion+ism
anti-Zion+ist
anti-Zion+ists
ant+ler
ant+lers
ant+li+on
ant+li+ons
Antoinette
Antonello da
  Messina
Antonescu
An+to+nine
Antoninus
Antonioni
an+to+no+ma+
  sia
an+to+no+ma+
  sias
Antony
an+to+nym
an+to+nyms
an+tony+mous
an+tral
An+trim
an+trum
an+tra
An+tung
Ant+werp
Ant+werp+en
Anu
Anubis
Anu+ra+dha+pu+
  ra
anu+resis
anus
anuses
An+vers
an+vil
an+vils
anxi+ety
anxi+eties
anx+ious
anx+ious+ly
anx+ious+ness
any

An+yang
any+body
any+bodies
any+how
any+more
any+one
any+place
any+thing
any+way
any+where
any+wise
ANZAAS
An+zac
An+zacs
An+zio
ANZUS
A-one
Aoran+gi
aorist
aor+ta
aor+tas or
aor+tae
aor+tal
aor+tic
Aosta
aou+dad
aou+dads
Aouita
apace
apache
apaches
Apache
Apaches or
  Apache
apa+nage
apa+nages
apart
apart+heid
apart+ment
apart+ments
apa+thet+ic
apa+theti+cal+ly
apa+thy
apa+tite
ape
apes
apes
ap+ing
aped
Apel+doorn
ape+like
Apelles
ape+man
ape+men
Ap+en+nines

aper+çu
aper+çus
aperi+ent
aperi+ents
aperi+od+ic
aperio+dic+ity
apé+ri+tif
apé+ri+tifs
ap+er+ture
ap+er+tures
apet+al+ous
apex
apexes or
api+ces
APEX
Apex+ian
Apex+ians
aphaer+esis
apha+sia
ap+he+li+on
ap+he+lia
apher+esis
aph+esis
aphet+ic
aphid
aphids
aphis
aphi+des
apho+nia
apho+ny
apho+rism
apho+risms
apho+rist
apho+rists
apho+ris+tic
aph+ro+disi+ac
aph+ro+disi+acs
Aphrodite
aphyl+lous
apian
apia+rist
apia+rists
api+ary
api+aries
api+cal
api+cal+ly
api+ces
api+cul+tur+al
api+cul+ture
api+cul+tur+ist
api+cul+tur+ists
apiece
Apis
ap+ish
ap+ish+ly

ap+ish+ness
ap+la+nat+ic
aplen+ty
aplomb
ap+nea
ap+noea
Apo
Apos
apoca+lypse
apoca+lypses
Apoca+lypse
apoca+lyp+tic
apo+car+pous
apo+chro+mat
apo+chro+mats
apoco+pe
apo+crine
Apoc+ry+pha
apoc+ry+phal
apo+dal
apodo+sis
apodo+ses
apo+dous
apo+gean
apo+gee
apo+gees
apo+liti+cal
Apollinaire
Apollo
god
Apol+lo
spacecraft
Apol+los
Apollyon
apolo+get+ic
apolo+geti+cal+ly
apolo+get+ics
apo+lo+gia
apo+lo+gias
apolo+gise
apolo+gises
apolo+gis+ing
apolo+gised
apolo+gist
apolo+gists
apolo+gize
apolo+gizes
apolo+giz+ing
apolo+gized
apo+logue
apo+logues
apol+ogy
apol+ogies
apo+phthegm
apo+phthegms

apo+plec+tic
apo+plec+ti+cal+
  ly
apo+plexy
aport
apos+ta+sy
apos+ta+sies
apos+tate
apos+tates
apo+stati+cal
apos+ta+tise
apos+ta+tises
apos+ta+tis+ing
apos+ta+tised
apos+ta+tize
apos+ta+tizes
apos+ta+tiz+ing
apos+ta+tized
a pos+terio+ri
apos+tle
apos+tles
apos+to+late
apos+to+lates
ap+os+tol+ic
ap+os+toli+cal
apos+tro+phe
apos+tro+phes
apos+tro+phise
apos+tro+
  phises
apos+tro+phis+
  ing
apos+tro+
  phised
apos+tro+phize
apos+tro+phizes
apos+tro+phiz+
  ing
apos+tro+
  phized
apoth+ecary
apoth+ecaries
apo+thegm
apo+thegms
apo+them
apo+thems
apoth+eo+sis
apoth+eo+ses
apoth+eo+sise
apoth+eo+sises
apoth+eo+sis+
  ing
apoth+eo+sised
apoth+eo+size
apoth+eo+sizes

apoth+eo+siz+
  ing
apoth+eo+sized
ap+pal
ap+pals
ap+pal+ling
ap+palled
Ap+pa+la+chia
Ap+pa+la+chian
Ap+pa+la+chians
ap+pall
U.S.
ap+palls
ap+pall+ing
ap+palled
ap+pal+ling
ap+pal+ling+ly
Ap+pa+loo+sa
Ap+pa+loo+sas
ap+pa+nage
ap+pa+nages
ap+pa+rat+chik
ap+pa+rat+chiks
ap+pa+rat+us
ap+pa+rat+us
  or
ap+pa+rat+uses
ap+par+el
ap+par+els
ap+par+els
ap+par+el+ling
  or
ap+par+el+ing
U.S.
ap+par+elled
  or
ap+par+eled
U.S.
ap+par+ent
ap+par+ent+ly
ap+pa+ri+tion
ap+pa+ri+tions
ap+pas+sio+na+
  to
ap+peal
ap+peals
ap+peals
ap+peal+ing
ap+pealed
ap+peal+able
ap+peal+er
ap+peal+ers
ap+peal+ing
ap+peal+ing+ly
ap+pear

ap+pears
ap+pear+ing
ap+peared
ap+pear+ance
ap+pear+ances
ap+pease
ap+peases
ap+peas+ing
ap+peased
ap+pease+ment
ap+pease+
  ments
ap+peas+er
ap+peas+ers
Appel
ap+pel+lant
ap+pel+lants
ap+pel+late
ap+pel+la+tion
ap+pel+la+tions
ap+pel+la+tive
ap+pel+la+tives
ap+pend
ap+pends
ap+pend+ing
ap+pend+ed
ap+pend+age
ap+pend+ages
ap+pen+dant
ap+pen+dants
ap+pen+dec+to+
  my
ap+pen+dec+to+
  mies
ap+pen+di+cec+
  to+my
ap+pen+di+cec+
  to+mies
ap+pen+di+ci+tis
ap+pen+dix
ap+pen+dixes
  or
ap+pen+di+ces
Ap+pen+zell
ap+per+ceive
ap+per+ceives
ap+per+ceiv+ing
ap+per+ceived
ap+per+cep+tion
ap+per+cep+
  tions
ap+per+cep+tive
ap+per+tain
ap+per+tains
ap+per+tain+ing

ap+per+tained
ap+pe+tence
ap+pe+tences
ap+pe+ten+cy
ap+pe+ten+cies
ap+pe+tis+er
ap+pe+tis+ers
ap+pe+tis+ing
ap+pe+tite
ap+pe+tites
ap+peti+tive
ap+pe+tiz+er
ap+pe+tiz+ers
ap+pe+tiz+ing
ap+plaud
ap+plauds
ap+plaud+ing
ap+plaud+ed
ap+plause
ap+ple
ap+ples
apple-pie
Appleton
ap+pli+ance
ap+pli+ances
ap+plic+abil+ity
ap+pli+cable
ap+pli+cably
ap+pli+cant
ap+pli+cants
ap+pli+ca+tion
ap+pli+ca+tions
ap+pli+ca+tor
ap+pli+ca+tors
ap+pli+ca+tory
ap+pli+er
ap+pli+ers
ap+pli+qué
ap+pli+qués
ap+pli+qués
ap+pli+qué+ing
ap+pli+quéd
ap+ply
ap+plies
ap+ply+ing
ap+plied
ap+pog+gia+tu+
  ra
ap+pog+gia+tu+
  ras or
ap+pog+gia+tu+
  re
ap+point
ap+points
ap+point+ing

ap+point+ed
ap+poin+tee
ap+poin+tees
ap+point+er
ap+point+ers
ap+poin+tive
ap+point+ment
ap+point+ments
ap+por+tion
ap+por+tions
ap+por+tion+ing
ap+por+tioned
ap+por+tion+able
ap+por+tion+ment
ap+por+tion+ments
ap+pos+able
ap+pose
ap+poses
ap+pos+ing
ap+posed
ap+po+site
ap+po+site+ly
ap+po+site+ness
ap+po+si+tion
ap+po+si+tions
ap+po+si+tion+al
ap+posi+tive
ap+posi+tive+ly
ap+prais+able
ap+prais+al
ap+prais+als
ap+praise
ap+praises
ap+prais+ing
ap+praised
ap+praise+ment
ap+praise+ments
ap+prais+er
ap+prais+ers
ap+pre+ci+able
ap+pre+ci+ably
ap+pre+ci+ate
ap+pre+ci+ates
ap+pre+ci+at+ing
ap+pre+ci+at+ed
ap+pre+cia+tion
ap+pre+cia+tions
ap+pre+cia+tive

ap+pre+cia+tive+ly
ap+pre+cia+tive+ness
ap+pre+cia+tor
ap+pre+cia+tors
ap+pre+cia+tory
ap+pre+hend
ap+pre+hends
ap+pre+hend+ing
ap+pre+hend+ed
ap+pre+hen+sibil+ity
ap+pre+hen+sible
ap+pre+hen+sion
ap+pre+hen+sions
ap+pre+hen+sive
ap+pre+hen+sive+ly
ap+pre+hen+sive+ness
ap+pren+tice
ap+pren+tices
ap+pren+tices
ap+pren+tic+ing
ap+pren+ticed
ap+pren+tice+ship
ap+pren+tice+ships
ap+prise
ap+prises
ap+pris+ing
ap+prised
ap+pro
ap+proach
ap+proaches
ap+proaches
ap+proach+ing
ap+proached
ap+proach+abil+ity
ap+proach+able
ap+pro+ba+tion
ap+pro+ba+tive
ap+pro+ba+tory
ap+pro+pri+ate
ap+pro+pri+ates
ap+pro+pri+at+ing

ap+pro+pri+at+ed
ap+pro+pri+ate+ly
ap+pro+pri+ate+ness
ap+pro+pria+tion
ap+pro+pria+tions
ap+pro+pria+tor
ap+pro+pria+tors
ap+prov+al
ap+prov+als
ap+prove
ap+proves
ap+prov+ing
ap+proved
ap+proxi+mate
ap+proxi+mates
ap+proxi+mat+ing
ap+proxi+mat+ed
ap+proxi+mate+ly
ap+proxi+ma+tion
ap+proxi+ma+tions
ap+pur+te+nance
ap+pur+te+nances
apraxia
après-ski
apri+cot
apri+cots
April
Aprils
a prio+ri
apri+or+ity
apron
aprons
aprons
apron+ing
aproned
ap+ro+pos
apse
apses
ap+si+dal
ap+sis
ap+si+des
apt
apt+er
apt+est

ap+ter+ism
ap+ter+ous
ap+ter+yx
ap+ter+yxes
ap+ti+tude
ap+ti+tudes
apt+ly
apt+ness
Apuleius
Apu+lia
Aqa+ba
aqua
aquae *or*
aquas
aqua+cul+ture
aquaero+bics
aqua for+tis
aqua+lung
aqua+lungs
aqua+marine
aqua+marines
aqua+naut
aqua+nauts
aqua+plane
aqua+planes
aqua+planes
aqua+plan+ing
aqua+planed
aqua re+gia
aqua+rist
aqua+rists
aquar+ium
aquar+iums *or*
aquaria
Aquar+ius
aquat+ic
aquat+ics
aqua+tint
aqua+tints
aqua+tints
aqua+tint+ing
aqua+tint+ed
aqua+vit
aqua vi+tae
aque+duct
aque+ducts
aque+ous
aqui+cul+tur+al
aqui+cul+ture
aqui+cul+tur+ist
aqui+cul+tur+ists
aqui+fer
aqui+fers
Aqui+la

constellation
Aqui+la
city
aqui+legia
aqui+line
Aquinas
Aquino
Aqui+taine
Arab
 Arabs
ara+besque
 ara+besques
Ara+bia
Ara+bian
 Ara+bians
Ara+bic
ara+bi+ca
ara+bis
Ar+ab+ist
 Ar+ab+ists
ar+able
Ara+by
Ara+ca+jú
Arachne
arach+nid
 arach+nids
arach+ni+dan
 arach+ni+dans
arach+noid
 arach+noids
Arafat
Ara+gats
Ara+gon
place name
Aragon
surname
Ara+go+nese
Ara+guaia
Ara+guaya
arak
Ara+kan Yoma
Araks
Aral
Ar+al+dite
Trademark
Aram
Ara+maean
 Ara+maeans
Ara+ma+ic
Ara+mean
 Ara+means
Aran
Ara+rat
Aras
Arau+ca+nia

Arau+ca+nian
Arau+ca+nians
arau+ca+ria
arau+ca+rias
Arax+es
ar+ba+lest
ar+ba+lests
ar+ba+list
ar+ba+lists
Ar+be+la
Arber
Ar+bil
ar+bi+ter
ar+bi+ters
ar+bit+ra+ment
ar+bit+ra+ments
ar+bi+trari+ly
ar+bi+trari+ness
ar+bi+trary
ar+bi+trate
ar+bi+trates
ar+bi+trat+ing
ar+bi+trat+ed
ar+bi+tra+tion
ar+bi+tra+tions
ar+bi+tra+tor
ar+bi+tra+tors
ar+bi+tress
Arblay
ar+bor
ar+bors
ar+bora+ceous
ar+bor+eal
ar+bo+res+cence
ar+bo+res+cent
ar+bo+retum
ar+bo+reta *or*
ar+bo+retums
ar+bori+cul+ture
ar+bori+cul+tur+
 ist
ar+bori+cul+tur+
 ists
ar+bor vi+tae
ar+bour
ar+bours
Ar+broath
Arbus
Arbuthnot
ar+bu+tus
ar+bu+tuses
arc
arcs
arcs
arc+ing *or*

arck+ing
arced *or*
arcked
ar+cade
ar+cades
Ar+ca+dia
Ar+ca+dian
Ar+ca+dians
Ar+ca+di+an+
 ism
Ar+ca+dy
ar+cane
ar+ca+num
ar+ca+na
Arc de Triomphe
arch
arches
arches
arch+ing
arched
Ar+chaean
ar+chaeo+logi+
 cal
ar+chae+olo+gist
ar+chae+ol+ogy
ar+chae+op+ter+
 yx
ar+cha+ic
ar+chai+cal+ly
ar+cha+ism
 ar+cha+isms
ar+cha+ist
 ar+cha+ists
ar+cha+is+tic
arch+angel
arch+angels
Arch+an+gel
arch+angelic
arch+bishop
 arch+bishops
arch+bishop+ric
arch+bishop+
 rics
arch+deacon
 arch+deacons
arch+deacon+ry
arch+deacon+
 ries
arch+dioc+esan
arch+dio+cese
arch+dio+ceses
arch+ducal
arch+duchess
 arch+duchesses
arch+duchy

arch+duchies
arch+duke
arch+dukes
Ar+chean
U.S.
ar+che+go+nium
ar+che+go+nia
arch+en+emy
arch+en+emies
ar+cheo+logi+cal
ar+che+olo+gist
ar+che+olo+
 gists
ar+che+ol+ogy
arch+er
arch+ers
Arch+er
constellation
Archer
surname
archer+fish
 archer+fish *or*
 archer+fishes
ar+chery
ar+che+typ+al
ar+che+type
 ar+che+types
arch+fiend
 arch+fiends
archi+di+aco+nal
archi+di+aco+
 nate
archi+di+aco+
 nates
archi+epis+co+
 pal
archi+epis+co+
 pate
archi+epis+co+
 pates
ar+chil
ar+chils
archi+man+drite
archi+man+
 drites
Archi+medean
Archimedes
mathematician
Archi+medes
moon's plain
archi+pelag+ic
archi+pela+go
archi+pela+gos
 or
archi+pela+goes

archi+tect
archi+tects
archi+tec+ton+ic
archi+tec+ton+
ics
archi+tec+tur+al
archi+tec+ture
archi+tec+tures
archi+trave
archi+traves
ar+chiv+al
ar+chive
ar+chives
archi+vist
archi+vists
arch+ly
arch+ness
ar+chon
ar+chons
ar+chon+ship
ar+chon+ships
arch+priest
arch+priests
arch+way
arch+ways
arc+tic
arc+tics
Arc+tic
Arc+tu+rus
ar+cu+ate
Ar+dèche
Ar+den
place name
Arden
surname
ar+den+cy
Ar+dennes
ar+dent
ar+dent+ly
ar+dor
U.S.
ar+dour
ar+du+ous
ar+du+ous+ly
ar+du+ous+ness
are
verb
are
ares
area
areas
ar+eal
area+way
area+ways
arena

arenas
ar+ena+ceous
Arendt
aren´t
areo+la
areo+lae *or*
areo+las
areo+lar
areo+late
areole
areoles
Ar+eopa+gite
Ar+eopa+gites
Ar+eopa+gus
Arequi+pa
Ares
arête
arêtes
Arethusa
Arez+zo
ar+gal
ar+gals
ar+ga+li
ar+ga+lis
ar+gent
Ar+gen+teuil
ar+gen+tif+er+
ous
Ar+gen+ti+na
ar+gen+tine
ar+gen+tines
Ar+gen+tine
Ar+gen+tines
Ar+gen+tin+ian
Ar+gen+tin+ians
argie-bargie
argie-bargies
ar+gil+la+ceous
Ar+give
Ar+gives
Argo
ar+gol
Ar+go+lis
ar+gon
Ar+go+naut
Ar+go+nauts
Ar+go+naut+ic
Ar+gonne
Ar+gos
ar+go+sy
ar+go+sies
ar+got
ar+gots
Ar+go+vie
ar+gu+able

ar+gu+ably
ar+gue
ar+gues
ar+gu+ing
ar+gued
ar+gu+er
ar+gu+ers
ar+gu+fy
ar+gu+fies
ar+gu+fy+ing
ar+gu+fied
ar+gu+ment
ar+gu+ments
ar+gu+men+ta+
tion
ar+gu+men+ta+
tions
ar+gu+men+ta+
tive
Argus
Arguses
Argus-eyed
argy-bargy
argy-bargies
Ar+gyll+shire
aria
arias
Ariadne
Arian
Arians
Ari+an+ism
Arias
Ari+ca
arid
arid+ity
ar+id+ness
Ariège
Aries
aright
aril
arils
ar+il+late
Ari+ma+thaea
Ari+ma+thea
Arimi+num
ario+so
ario+sos *or*
ario+si
Ariosto
arise
arises
aris+ing
arose
aris+en
ar+is+toc+ra+cy

ar+is+toc+ra+
cies
aris+to+crat
aris+to+crats
aris+to+crat+ic
aris+to+crati+cal+
ly
Aristophanes
Ar+is+to+telian
Ar+is+to+telians
Aristotle
philosopher
Ar+is+tot+le
moon´s crater
arith+me+tic
arith+meti+cal+ly
arith+meti+cian
arith+meti+cians
Arius
Ari+zo+na
Arjuna
ark
arks
Ark
Ar+kan+sas
Ar+khan+gelsk
Arkwright
Arles
Ar+ling+ton
Ar+lon
arm
arms
arms
arm+ing
armed
ar+ma+da
ar+ma+das
ar+ma+dil+lo
ar+ma+dil+los
Ar+ma+ged+don
Ar+magh
Ar+ma+lite
Trademark
Ar+ma+lites
ar+ma+ment
ar+ma+ments
Armani
ar+ma+ture
ar+ma+tures
arm+chair
arm+chairs
armed
Ar+me+nia
Ar+me+nian
Ar+me+nians

Ar+men+tières
arm+ful
arm+fuls
arm+hole
arm+holes
Ar+mi+dale
Ar+mini+an
Ar+mini+an+ism
ar+mi+stice
ar+mi+stices
arm+let
arm+lets
ar+moire
ar+moires
ar+mor
U.S.
ar+mors
ar+mors
ar+mor+ing
ar+mored
ar+mored
U.S.
ar+mor+er
U.S.
ar+mor+ers
ar+mo+ri+al
ar+mory
U.S.
ar+mories
ar+mour
ar+mours
ar+mours
ar+mour+ing
ar+moured
ar+moured
ar+mour+er
ar+mour+ers
ar+moury
ar+mouries
arm+pit
arm+pits
arm+rest
arm+rests
Armstrong
army
armies
Arnaud
Arne
Arn+hem
ar+ni+ca
ar+ni+cas
Arnim
Arno
Ar+nold
place name

Arnold
surname
aroha
ar+oid
aro+ma
aro+mas
aroma+thera+pist
aroma+thera+
  pists
aroma+thera+py
aro+mat+ic
aro+mat+ics
aro+mati+cal+ly
aro+ma+tic+ity
aro+ma+ti+sa+
  tion
aro+ma+tise
aro+ma+tises
aro+ma+tis+ing
aro+ma+tised
aro+ma+ti+za+
  tion
aro+ma+tize
aro+ma+tizes
aro+ma+tiz+ing
aro+ma+tized
arose
around
arous+al
arous+als
arouse
arouses
arous+ing
aroused
arous+er
arous+ers
Arp
ar+peg+gio
ar+peg+gios
ar+que+bus
ar+que+buses
ar+rack
ar+raign
ar+raigns
ar+raign+ing
ar+raigned
ar+raign+er
ar+raign+ers
ar+raign+ment
ar+raign+ments
Ar+ran
ar+range
ar+ranges
ar+rang+ing
ar+ranged

ar+range+able
ar+range+ment
ar+range+ments
ar+rang+er
ar+rang+ers
ar+rant
ar+rant+ly
ar+ras
ar+rases
Ar+ras
Arrau
ar+ray
ar+rays
ar+rays
ar+ray+ing
ar+rayed
ar+ray+al
ar+ray+als
ar+rear+age
ar+rears
ar+rest
ar+rests
ar+rests
ar+rest+ing
ar+rest+ed
ar+rest+ing
ar+rest+ing+ly
Ar+re+tine
Ar+re+tium
ar+rhyth+mia
arrière-pensée
Ar Ri+mal
ar+ris
  ar+ris *or*
ar+rises
ar+ri+val
ar+ri+vals
ar+rive
ar+rives
ar+riv+ing
ar+rived
ar+ri+veder+ci
ar+ri+viste
ar+ri+vistes
ar+ro+gance
ar+ro+gant
ar+ro+gant+ly
ar+ro+gate
ar+ro+gates
ar+ro+gat+ing
ar+ro+gat+ed
ar+ro+ga+tion
ar+ro+ga+tions
ar+roga+tive

ar+ron+disse+
  ment
ar+ron+disse+
  ments
ar+row
ar+rows
arrow+head
arrow+heads
arrow+root
ar+royo
ar+royos
arse
arses
arse+hole
arse+holes
ar+senal
ar+senals
ar+senate
ar+senates
ar+senic
ar+seni+cal
ar+seni+cals
ar+seni+ous
ar+sen+ous
ar+son
ar+son+ist
ar+son+ists
art
arts
Artaud
Art Deco
ar+te+fact
ar+te+facts
ar+tel
ar+tels
Artemis
ar+te+rial
ar+te+ri+ali+sa+
  tion
ar+te+ri+al+ise
ar+te+ri+al+ises
ar+te+ri+al+is+
  ing
ar+te+ri+al+ised
ar+te+ri+ali+za+
  tion
ar+te+ri+al+ize
ar+te+ri+al+izes
ar+te+ri+al+iz+
  ing
ar+te+ri+al+ized
ar+te+ri+al+ly
ar+te+ri+ole
ar+te+ri+oles

ar+te+rio+sclero+
  sis
ar+te+rio+sclero+
  ses
ar+te+rio+sclerot+
  ic
ar+tery
  ar+teries
ar+te+sian
Ar+tex
  Trademark
art+ful
art+ful+ly
art+ful+ness
ar+thral+gia
ar+thral+gic
ar+thrit+ic
  ar+thrit+ics
ar+thri+tis
arthro+pod
  arthro+pods
Arthur
Ar+thu+rian
ar+tic
  ar+tics
ar+ti+choke
  ar+ti+chokes
ar+ti+cle
  ar+ti+cles
  ar+ti+cles
  ar+ti+cling
  ar+ti+cled
ar+ticu+lar
ar+ticu+late
  ar+ticu+lates
  ar+ticu+lat+ing
  ar+ticu+lat+ed
ar+ticu+late+ly
ar+ticu+late+
  ness
ar+ticu+la+tion
  ar+ticu+la+tions
ar+ticu+la+tor
  ar+ticu+la+tors
ar+ti+fact
  ar+ti+facts
ar+ti+fice
  ar+ti+fices
ar+tifi+cer
  ar+tifi+cers
ar+ti+fi+cial
ar+ti+fi+ci+al+ity
ar+ti+fi+cial+ly
ar+til+lery
arti+ness

ar+tio+dac+tyl
  ar+tio+dac+tyls
ar+tio+dac+ty+
  lous
ar+ti+san
  ar+ti+sans
ar+ti+san+al
art+ist
  art+ists
ar+tiste
  ar+tistes
ar+tis+tic
ar+tis+ti+cal+ly
art+ist+ry
art+less
art+less+ly
Art Nou+veau
arty
arti+er
arti+est
Aru+ba
arum
Aru+na+chal Pra+
  desh
Ar+un+del
arvo
Aryan
  Aryans
as
asa+feti+da
asa+foeti+da
As+ben
as+bes+tos
as+bes+to+sis
Ascanius
as+ca+rid
  as+ca+rids
as+cend
  as+cends
  as+cend+ing
  as+cend+ed
  as+cend+ance
  as+cend+ancy
  as+cend+ant
  as+cend+ants
  as+cend+ence
  as+cend+ency
  as+cend+ent
  as+cend+ents
  as+cend+er
  as+cend+ers
as+cen+sion
  as+cen+sions
As+cen+sion
as+cen+sion+al

as+cent
  as+cents
as+cer+tain
  as+cer+tains
  as+cer+tain+ing
  as+cer+tained
as+cer+tain+able
as+cer+tain+
  ment
as+cet+ic
  as+cet+ics
as+ceti+cal+ly
Asch
Aschaf+fen+burg
Ascham
as+cid+ian
  as+cid+ians
as+cid+ium
  as+cidia
Asclepius
as+co+my+cete
  as+co+my+
  cetes
as+co+my+
  cetous
ascor+bic
As+cot
as+crib+able
as+cribe
  as+cribes
  as+crib+ing
  as+cribed
as+crip+tion
  as+crip+tions
as+dic
ASEAN
asep+sis
asep+tic
asexu+al
asexu+al+ity
asexu+al+ly
As+gard
As+garth
ash
  ashes
ASH
ashamed
asham+ed+ly
Ashan+ti
  Ashan+ti *or*
  Ashan+tis
Ashcroft
Ash+dod
Ashdown
Ashe

ash+en
Asher
Ashes
Ash+ford
Ash+ke+na+zi
  Ash+ke+na+zim
Ashkenazy
Ash+kha+bad
ash+lar
  ash+lars
ash+ler
  ash+lers
Ashley
ashore
ash+ram
  ash+rams
Ashton
Ashton-under-
  Lyne
Ashtoreth
ash+tray
  ash+trays
Ashur
ashy
  ashi+er
  ashi+est
Asi
Asia
Asian
  Asians
Asi+at+ic
  Asi+at+ics
aside
  asides
A-side
  A-sides
Asimov
asi+nine
asi+nine+ly
asi+nin+ity
Asir
ask
  asks
  ask+ing
  asked
Ask
askance
askant
ask+er
  ask+ers
askew
Askey
Ask+ja
aslant
asleep

ASLEF
As+ma+ra
As+nières
Aso
aso+cial
asp
 asps
as+para+gus
as+par+tame
as+pect
 as+pects
as+pen
 as+pens
as+per+ity
 as+per+ities
as+perse
 as+perses
as+pers+ing
as+persed
as+pers+er
 as+pers+ers
as+per+sion
 as+per+sions
as+per+sive
as+phalt
 as+phalts
 as+phalts
as+phalt+ing
as+phalt+ed
as+phal+tic
as+pho+del
 as+pho+dels
as+phyxia
as+phyx+ial
as+phyxi+ant
as+phyxi+ate
 as+phyxi+ates
as+phyxi+at+ing
as+phyxi+at+ed
as+phyxia+tion
as+phyxia+tions
as+phyxia+tor
as+phyxia+tors
as+pic
 as+pics
as+pi+dis+tra
 as+pi+dis+tras
as+pir+ant
 as+pir+ants
as+pi+rate
 as+pi+rates
as+pi+rat+ing
as+pi+rat+ed
as+pi+ra+tion
 as+pi+ra+tions

as+pi+ra+tor
 as+pi+ra+tors
as+pira+tory
as+pire
 as+pires
as+pir+ing
as+pired
as+pi+rin
 Trademark
as+pi+rin or
 as+pi+rins
as+pir+ing
asquint
Asquith
ass
 asses
Assad
as+sa+gai
 as+sa+gais
as+sai
as+sail
 as+sails
as+sail+ing
as+sailed
as+sail+able
as+sail+ant
 as+sail+ants
as+sail+er
 as+sail+ers
As+sam
As+sa+mese
As+sa+mese
as+sas+sin
 as+sas+sins
as+sas+si+nate
 as+sas+si+
  nates
as+sas+si+nat+
  ing
as+sas+si+nat+
  ed
as+sas+si+na+
  tion
as+sas+si+na+
  tions
as+sault
 as+saults
 as+saults
as+sault+ing
as+sault+ed
as+saul+tive
as+say
 as+says
 as+says
as+say+ing

as+sayed
as+say+er
 as+say+ers
as+se+gai
 as+se+gais
as+sem+blage
 as+sem+blages
as+sem+ble
 as+sem+bles
as+sem+bling
as+sem+bled
as+sem+blé
as+sem+bler
 as+sem+blers
as+sem+bly
 as+sem+blies
As+sem+bly
 As+sem+blies
As+sen
as+sent
 as+sents
 as+sents
as+sent+ing
as+sent+ed
as+sert
 as+serts
as+sert+ing
as+sert+ed
as+sert+er
 as+sert+ers
as+ser+tion
 as+ser+tions
as+ser+tive
as+ser+tive+ly
as+ser+tive+ness
as+ser+tor
 as+ser+tors
as+sess
 as+sesses
as+sess+ing
as+sessed
as+sess+able
as+sess+ment
 as+sess+ments
as+ses+sor
 as+ses+sors
as+ses+so+rial
as+set
 as+sets
asset-stripper
asset-strippers
asset-stripping
as+sev+er+ate
 as+sev+er+ates

as+sev+er+at+
 ing
as+sev+er+at+
 ed
as+sev+era+tion
as+sev+era+
 tions
Asshur
as+sibi+late
 as+sibi+lates
as+sibi+lat+ing
as+sibi+lat+ed
as+sibi+la+tion
 as+sibi+la+tions
as+si+du+ity
 as+si+du+ities
as+sidu+ous
as+sidu+ous+
 ness
as+sign
 as+signs
 as+signs
as+sign+ing
as+signed
as+sign+able
as+sig+na+tion
 as+sig+na+tions
as+signee
 as+signees
as+sign+er
 as+sign+ers
as+sign+ment
 as+sign+ments
as+sign+or
 as+sign+ors
as+simi+lable
as+simi+late
 as+simi+lates
as+simi+lat+ing
as+simi+lat+ed
as+simi+la+tion
 as+simi+la+
  tions
as+simi+la+tive
as+simi+la+tor
 as+simi+la+tors
as+simi+la+tory
As+sini+boine
As+sini+boine
 or
As+sini+boines
As+si+si
as+sist
 as+sists
 as+sists

as+sist+ing
as+sist+ed
as+sis+tance
as+sis+tant
as+sis+tants
as+sist+er
as+sist+ers
as+size
as+sizes
as+so+ci+able
as+so+ci+ate
as+so+ci+ates
as+so+ci+ates
as+so+ci+at+ing
as+so+ci+at+ed
as+so+ci+ate+
ship
as+so+ci+ate+
ships
as+so+cia+tion
as+so+cia+tions
as+so+cia+tive
as+so+cia+tor
as+so+cia+tors
as+so+nance
as+so+nant
as+so+nants
as+sort
as+sorts
as+sort+ing
as+sort+ed
as+sorta+tive
as+sort+ed
as+sort+ment
as+sort+ments
As+souan
as+suage
as+suages
as+suag+ing
as+suaged
as+suage+ment
as+suage+
ments
as+suag+er
as+suag+ers
As+suan
as+sum+able
as+sume
as+sumes
as+sum+ing
as+sumed
as+sumed
as+sum+er
as+sum+ers
as+sum+ing

as+sump+tion
as+sump+tions
As+sump+tion
as+sump+tive
Assur
as+sur+able
as+sur+ance
as+sur+ances
as+sure
as+sures
as+sur+ing
as+sured
as+sured
as+sur+ed+ly
as+sur+er
as+sur+ers
As+syria
As+syr+ian
As+syr+ians
Astaire
Astarte
astat+ic
astati+cal+ly
as+ta+tine
Astbury
as+ter
as+ters
as+ter+isk
as+ter+isks
as+ter+isks
as+ter+isk+ing
as+ter+isked
as+ter+ism
as+ter+isms
astern
as+ter+oid
as+ter+oids
as+teroi+dal
as+the+nia
as+then+ic
as+then+ics
asth+ma
asth+mat+ic
asth+mat+ics
asth+mati+cal+ly
Asti
as+tig+mat+ic
as+tig+mati+cal+
ly
astig+ma+tism
astig+mia
astil+be
astil+bes
astir
As+to+lat

Aston
aston+ish
aston+ishes
aston+ish+ing
aston+ished
aston+ish+ing
aston+ish+ment
aston+ish+
ments
Astor
astound
astounds
astound+ing
astound+ed
astound+ing
astrad+dle
as+tra+gal
as+tra+gals
astraga+lus
astraga+li
as+tra+khan
as+tra+khans
As+tra+khan
as+tral
astray
astride
as+trin+gen+cy
as+trin+gent
as+trin+gents
as+trin+gent+ly
as+tro+bi+ol+
ogy
as+tro+chem+is+
try
as+tro+dome
as+tro+domes
as+tro+labe
as+tro+labes
as+trolo+ger
as+trolo+gers
as+tro+logi+cal
as+trolo+gist
as+trolo+gists
as+trol+ogy
as+tro+naut
as+tro+nauts
as+tro+nau+ti+
cal
as+tro+nau+tics
as+trono+mer
as+trono+mers
as+tro+nom+ic
as+tro+nomi+cal
as+tro+nomi+cal+
ly

as+trono+my
as+tro+physi+
cist
as+tro+physi+
cists
as+tro+phys+ics
As+tu+ri+as
place name
Asturias
surname
as+tute
as+tute+ly
as+tute+ness
Asun+ción
asun+der
Asur
As+wan
asy+lum
asy+lums
asym+met+ric
asym+met+ri+cal
asym+met+ri+cal+
ly
asym+me+try
asymp+to+mat+
ic
as+ymp+tote
as+ymp+totes
as+ymp+tot+ic
as+ymp+toti+cal
asys+to+le
asys+tol+ic
at
at
currency unit
at
Atabalipa
Ata+ca+ma
Atahualpa
Atalanta
ata+rac+tic
ata+rac+tics
ata+raxia
ata+rax+ic
ata+rax+ics
ata+raxy
Atatürk
ata+vism
ata+visms
ata+vis+tic
ataxia
atax+ic
ataxy
At+ba+ra
ate

Ate	At+lan+tis	at+ra+bili+ar	at+taint+ing
at+el+ier	at+las	at+ra+bil+ious	at+taint+ed
at+el+iers	*book of maps*	at+ra+bil+ious+	at+tar
a tem+po	at+lases	ness	at+tempt
Aten	at+las	atra+zine	at+tempts
Atget	*column*	Atreus	at+tempts
Atha+bas+ca	at+lan+tes	atrial	at+tempt+ing
Atha+bas+can	Atlas	atrium	at+tempt+ed
Atha+bas+cans	At+las Moun+	atria	at+tempt+able
Atha+bas+ka	tains	atro+cious	Attenborough
Atha+bas+kan	Atli	atro+cious+ness	at+tend
Atha+bas+kans	at+man	atroc+ity	at+tends
Atha+na+sian	at+moly+sis	atroc+ities	at+tend+ing
Athanasius	at+moly+ses	atroph+ic	at+tend+ed
Atha+pas+can	at+mos+phere	at+ro+phy	at+tend+ance
Atha+pas+cans	at+mos+pheres	at+ro+phies	at+tend+ances
Atha+pas+kan	at+mos+pher+ic	at+ro+phies	at+tend+ant
Atha+pas+kans	at+mos+pheri+	at+ro+phy+ing	at+tend+ants
athe+ism	cal+ly	at+ro+phied	at+ten+tion
athe+ist	at+mos+pher+ics	at+ro+pine	at+ten+tions
athe+ists	at+oll	Atropos	at+ten+tive
athe+is+tic	at+olls	at+tach	at+ten+tive+ly
Athelstan	atom	at+taches	at+ten+tive+ness
athe+mat+ic	atoms	at+tach+ing	at+tenu+ate
Athena	atom+ic	at+tached	at+tenu+ates
ath+enaeum	ato+mic+ity	at+tach+able	at+tenu+at+ing
ath+enaeums	at+om+ise	at+ta+ché	at+tenu+at+ed
Athene	at+om+ises	at+ta+chés	at+tenua+tion
ath+eneum	at+om+is+ing	at+tached	at+tenua+tions
ath+eneums	at+om+ised	at+tach+er	at+test
Athe+nian	at+om+is+er	at+tach+ers	at+tests
Athe+nians	at+om+is+ers	at+tach+ment	at+test+ing
Ath+ens	at+om+ize	at+tach+ments	at+test+ed
ath+ero+scle+ro+	at+om+izes	at+tack	at+test+able
sis	at+om+iz+ing	at+tacks	at+test+ant
ath+ero+scle+rot+	at+om+ized	at+tacks	at+test+ants
ic	at+om+iz+er	at+tack+ing	at+tes+ta+tion
athirst	at+om+iz+ers	at+tacked	at+tes+ta+tions
ath+lete	ato+my	at+tack+er	at+test+ed
ath+letes	ato+mies	at+tack+ers	at+test+er
ath+let+ic	Aton	at+tain	at+test+ers
ath+leti+cal+ly	aton+al	at+tains	at+tes+tor
ath+leti+cism	ato+nal+ity	at+tain+ing	at+tes+tors
ath+let+ics	atone	at+tained	at+tic
at-home	atones	at+tain+abil+ity	at+tics
at-homes	aton+ing	at+tain+able	At+tic
Ath+os	atoned	at+tain+able+	At+ti+ca
athwart	atone+ment	ness	At+ti+cism
Atkinson	atone+ments	at+tain+der	At+ti+cisms
At+lan+ta	aton+er	at+tain+ders	Attila
At+lan+tean	aton+ers	at+tain+ment	at+tire
At+lan+tic	aton+ic	at+tain+ments	at+tires
At+lan+ti+cism	aton+ics	at+taint	at+tir+ing
At+lan+ti+cist	atop	at+taints	at+tired
At+lan+ti+cists	ATP	at+taints	at+ti+tude

at+ti+tudes
at+ti+tu+di+nal
at+ti+tu+di+nise
at+ti+tu+di+
 nises
at+ti+tu+di+nis+
 ing
at+ti+tu+di+
 nised
at+ti+tu+di+nize
at+ti+tu+di+
 nizes
at+ti+tu+di+niz+
 ing
at+ti+tu+di+
 nized
Attlee
at+tor+ney
at+tor+neys
at+torney-at-law
at+torneys-at-
 law
at+tor+ney gen+
 er+al
at+tor+neys gen+
 er+al or
at+tor+ney gen+
 er+als
at+tor+ney+ship
at+tor+ney+
 ships
at+tract
at+tracts
at+tract+ing
at+tract+ed
at+tract+able
at+trac+tion
at+trac+tions
at+trac+tive
at+trac+tive+ly
at+trac+tor
at+trac+tors
at+trib+ut+able
at+trib+ute
at+trib+utes
at+trib+utes
at+trib+ut+ing
at+trib+ut+ed
at+tribu+tion
at+tribu+tions
at+tribu+tive
at+tri+tion
Attu
at+tune
at+tunes

at+tun+ing
at+tuned
Atwood
atypi+cal
atypi+cal+ly
aubade
aubades
Aube
auber+gine
auber+gines
aubre+tia
aubre+tias
Aubrey
aubrie+ta
aubrie+tas
aubrie+tia
aubrie+tias
auburn
Aubus+son
Auck+land
au cou+rant
auc+tion
auc+tions
auc+tions
auc+tion+ing
auc+tioned
auc+tion+eer
auc+tion+eers
auc+tion+eers
auc+tion+eer+
 ing
auc+tion+eered
auc+to+rial
auda+cious
auda+cious+ness
audac+ity
audac+ities
Aude
Auden
audibil+ity
audible
audible+ness
audibly
audi+ence
audi+ences
audio
audi+olo+gist
audi+olo+gists
audi+ol+ogy
audi+om+eter
audi+om+eters
audi+om+etrist
audi+om+etrists
audi+om+etry
audio+phile

audio+philes
audio+typing
audio+typist
audio+typists
audio+visual
audio+visual+ly
audit
audits
audits
audit+ing
audit+ed
audi+tion
audi+tions
audi+tions
audi+tion+ing
audi+tioned
audi+tor
audi+tors
audi+to+ri+al
audi+to+rium
audi+to+riums
 or
audi+to+ria
audi+tory
Audubon
Auerbach
au fait
au fond
auf Wie+der+seh+
 en
Augean
augend
augends
auger
augers
aught
aug+ment
aug+ments
aug+ment+ing
aug+ment+ed
aug+ment+able
aug+men+ta+tion
aug+men+ta+
 tions
aug+menta+tive
aug+ment+ed
aug+ment+er
aug+ment+ers
au gra+tin
Augs+burg
augur
augurs
augurs
augur+ing
augured

augur+al
augu+ry
augu+ries
august
August
Augusts
Au+gus+ta
Augus+tan
Augus+tans
Augustine
Augus+tin+ian
Augus+tin+ians
august+ness
Augustus
auk
auks
au lait
auld
auld+er
auld+est
auld lang syne
Auld Reekie
Aulis
aum+bry
aum+bries
au na+tu+rel
aunt
aunts
auntie
aunties
Auntie
Aunt Sal+ly
Aunt Sal+lies
aunty
aunties
au pair
au pairs
aura
auras or
aurae
aural
aural+ly
aure+ate
Aurelian
Aurelius
aureo+la
aureo+las
aure+ole
aure+oles
au re+voir
auric
Auric
auri+cle
auri+cles
auri+cled

auricu+la
auricu+lae *or*
auricu+las
auricu+lar
aurif+er+ous
Aurig+na+cian
Auriol
aurochs
aurochs
auro+ra
auro+ras *or*
auro+rae
Aurora
goddess
Auro+ra
place name
auro+ra aus+tra+
lis
auro+ra bo+real+
is
auro+ral
aur+ous
Ausch+witz
aus+cul+tate
aus+cul+tates
aus+cul+tat+ing
aus+cul+tat+ed
aus+cul+ta+tion
aus+cul+ta+
tions
aus+cul+ta+tory
aus+pice
aus+pices
aus+pi+cious
aus+pi+cious+ly
aus+pi+cious+
ness
Aus+sie
Aus+sies
Austen
aus+tere
aus+tere+ly
aus+ter+ity
aus+ter+ities
Aus+ter+litz
Aus+tin
place name
Austin
surname
aus+tral
adj.
aus+trales
aus+tral
Aus+tral+asia
Aus+tral+asian

Aus+tralia
Aus+tral+ian
Aus+tral+ians
Aus+tral+ia+na
Aus+tra+loid
Aus+tra+loids
aus+tra+lo+pithe+
cine
aus+tra+lo+
pithe+cines
Aus+tral+orp
Aus+tral+orps
Aus+tra+sia
Aus+tria
Aus+trian
Aus+trians
Aus+tro+nesia
Aus+tro+nesian
autar+chic
autar+chi+cal
autar+chy
autar+chies
autar+kic
autar+kist
autar+kists
autar+ky
autar+kies
authen+tic
authen+ti+cal+ly
authen+ti+cate
authen+ti+cates
authen+ti+cat+
ing
authen+ti+cat+
ed
authen+ti+ca+
tion
authen+ti+ca+
tions
au+then+ti+ca+
tor
au+then+ti+ca+
tors
au+then+tic+ity
author
authors
authors
author+ing
authored
autho+rial
authori+sa+tion
authori+sa+tions
author+ise
author+ises
author+is+ing

author+ised
authori+tar+ian
authori+tar+ians
authori+ta+tive
authori+ta+tive+
ly
authori+ta+tive+
ness
author+ity
author+ities
authori+za+tion
authori+za+tions
author+ize
author+izes
author+iz+ing
author+ized
author+ship
author+ships
autism
autis+tic
auto
autos
auto+bahn
auto+bahns
auto+bi+og+ra+
pher
auto+bi+og+ra+
phers
auto+bio+graphi+
cal
auto+bi+og+ra+
phy
auto+bi+og+ra+
phies
auto+cepha+lous
autoch+thon
autoch+thons
or
autoch+tho+nes
autoch+tho+nous
auto+clave
auto+claves
autoc+ra+cy
autoc+ra+cies
auto+crat
auto+crats
auto+crat+ic
auto+crati+cal+ly
auto+cross
Auto+cue
Trademark
Auto+cues
auto-da-fé
autos-da-fé
auto+erot+ic

auto+eroti+cism
auto+ero+tism
autoga+mous
autoga+my
autog+enous
autog+enous+ly
auto+gi+ro
auto+gi+ros
auto+graph
auto+graphs
auto+graphs
auto+graph+ing
auto+graphed
auto+graph+ic
auto+graphi+cal+
ly
auto+gy+ro
auto+gy+ros
auto+hyp+no+sis
auto+im+mune
auto+im+mun+ity
auto+intoxi+ca+
tion
autolo+gous
Autoly+cus
moon's crater
Autolycus
name
autoly+sis
auto+lyt+ic
auto+mat
auto+mats
auto+mate
auto+mates
auto+mat+ing
auto+mat+ed
auto+mat+ic
auto+mat+ics
auto+mati+cal+ly
auto+ma+tion
automa+ti+sa+
tion
automa+ti+sa+
tions
automa+tise
automa+tises
automa+tis+ing
automa+tised
automa+tism
automa+tist
automa+tists
automa+ti+za+
tion
automa+tize
automa+tizes

automa+tiz+ing	availed	aver+sion	avouch+ment
automa+tized	avail+abil+ity	aver+sions	avow
automa+ton	avail+abil+ities	avert	avows
automa+tons	avail+able	averts	avow+ing
or	avail+able+ness	avert+ing	avowed
automa+ta	avail+ably	avert+ed	avow+al
auto+mo+bile	ava+lanche	avert+able	avow+als
auto+mo+biles	ava+lanches	avert+ible	avowed
auto+mo+bilia	ava+lanches	Aves+ta	avow+ed+ly
auto+mo+bil+ist	ava+lanch+ing	Aves+tan	avow+er
auto+mo+bil+ ists	ava+lanched	Avey+ron	avow+ers
auto+mo+tive	Ava+lon	avian	avun+cu+lar
auto+nom+ic	avant-garde	aviary	AWACS
auto+nomi+cal+ ly	avan+tu+rine	aviaries	Awacs
	ava+rice	avia+tion	await
auto+nom+ics	ava+ri+cious	avia+tor	awaits
autono+mous	avast	avia+tors	await+ing
autono+mous+ly	ava+tar	avia+tress	await+ed
autono+my	ava+tars	avia+trix	awake
autono+mies	avaunt	Avicenna	awakes
auto+pi+lot	ave	avid	awak+ing
auto+pi+lots	Ave	avid+ity	awoke *or*
autop+sy	Aves	av+id+ly	awaked
autop+sies	Ave+bury	Avie+more	awok+en *or*
auto+route	Avei+ro	avi+fau+na	awaked
auto+routes	Ave Ma+ria	avi+fau+nal	awak+en
auto+stra+da	avenge	Avi+gnon	awak+ens
auto+stra+das	avenges	Ávi+la	awak+en+ing
auto+sug+ges+ tion	aveng+ing	avi+on+ic	*or*
	avenged	avi+on+ics	awak+ened
auto+tom+ic	aveng+er	avita+mino+sis	award
autoto+my	aveng+ers	avita+mino+ses	awards
autoto+mies	av+ens	Av+lo+na	awards
auto+troph	av+ens	avo+ca+do	award+ing
auto+trophs	Av+en+tine	avo+ca+dos	award+ed
auto+troph+ic	aven+tu+rine	avo+ca+tion	award+er
autumn	av+enue	avo+ca+tions	award+ers
autumns	av+enues	avo+cet	aware
autum+nal	aver	avo+cets	aware+ness
Auvergne	avers	Avogadro	awash
auxa+nom+eter	aver+ring	avoid	away
auxa+nom+ eters	averred	avoids	aways
	av+er+age	avoid+ing	awe
Aux Cayes	av+er+ages	avoid+ed	awes
Auxerre	av+er+ages	avoid+able	aw+ing
aux+ilia+ry	av+er+ag+ing	avoid+ably	awed
aux+ilia+ries	av+er+aged	avoid+ance	aweigh
aux+in	av+er+age+ly	avoid+er	awe-inspiring
Av	aver+ment	avoid+ers	awe+some
ava+da+vat	aver+ments	av+oir+du+pois	awe+some+ly
ava+da+vats	Aver+no	Avon	awe+some+ness
avail	Averroës	avouch	awe-stricken
avails	averse	avouches	awe-struck
avail+ing	averse+ly	avouch+ing	aw+ful
	averse+ness	avouched	aw+ful+ly

aw+ful+ness
awhile
awk+ward
awk+ward+ly
awk+ward+ness
awl
 awls
awn
 awns
awned
awn+ing
 awn+ings
awoke
AWOL
awry
ax
U.S.
 axes
axes
ax+ing
axed
axe
 axes
 axes
 ax+ing
 axed
axel
 axels
axe+man
 axe+men

axes
ax+ial
axi+al+ity
axi+al+ly
axil
 axils
ax+il+la
 ax+il+lae
 ax+il+lar
 ax+il+lary
 ax+il+laries
axi+om
 axi+oms
axio+mat+ic
axio+mati+cal+ly
axis
 geometry
 axes
 axis
 deer
 axises
Axis
axle
 axles
axle+tree
axle+trees
Ax+min+ster
 Ax+min+sters
axo+lotl
 axo+lotls

axon
 axons
ay
 ays
Aya+cu+cho
ayah
 ayahs
aya+tol+lah
 aya+tol+lahs
Ayckbourn
Ay+cliffe
Ay+din
aye
 ayes
aye-aye
 aye-ayes
Ayer
Ayers
Ayesha
Ayles+bury
Aylward
Ay+ma+ra
 Ay+ma+ras *or*
 Ay+ma+ra
Ayr
Ayr+shire
Ayub Khan
Ayut+tha+ya
azalea
 azaleas

Aza+nia
Aza+nian
 Aza+nians
Az+bine
azeo+trope
 azeo+tropes
azeo+trop+ic
Azer+bai+jan
Azer+bai+ja+ni
azer+ty
az+ide
 az+ides
Azikiwe
Azil+ian
azi+muth
 azi+muths
azi+muth+al
az+ine
 az+ines
azo
azo+ic
Azores
Azorín
Azov
Az+tec
 Az+tecs
az+ure
 az+ures
az+ur+ite
azy+gous

B

b
 bs
B
 Bs *or*
 B's
Ba
baa
 baas
 baas
 baa+ing
 baaed
Baal
Baal+bek
Baal Shem Tob
Baal Shem Tov
baas
baas+kap
baas+skap
Bab
baba
 babas
Babar
Babbage
bab+bitt
 bab+bitts
 bab+bitt+ing
 bab+bitt+ed
Babbitt
 Babbitts
Bab+bitt+ry
bab+ble
 bab+bles
 bab+bles
 bab+bling
 bab+bled
bab+bler
 bab+blers
babe
 babes
Ba+bel
 Ba+bels
Babel
surname
Bab el Man+deb
Baber

Babeuf
Babington
babi+ru+sa
 babi+ru+sas
Bab+ism
ba+boon
 ba+boons
babu
 babus
Babur
ba+bush+ka
 ba+bush+kas
baby
 babies
 babies
 baby+ing
 babied
baby-boomer
 baby-boomers
ba+by+hood
ba+by+ish
Baby+lon
Baby+lo+nia
Baby+lo+nian
 Baby+lo+nians
baby-sit
 baby-sits
 baby-sitting
 baby-sat
baby-sitter
 baby-sitters
baby-sitting
bac+ca+lau+re+
 ate
bac+ca+lau+re+
 ates
bac+ca+rat
bac+cate
Bac+chae
bac+cha+nal
 bac+cha+nals
bac+cha+na+lia
bac+cha+na+lian
bac+chant
 bac+chants *or*

bac+chan+tes
bac+chan+te
 bac+chan+tes
Bac+chic
Bacchus
bac+cy
 bac+cies
bach
bach
Austral., N.Z.
 baches
bach+ing
 bached
Bach
bach+elor
 bach+elors
bach+elor+hood
bachelor's-
 buttons
ba+cil+lar
ba+cil+lary
ba+cil+li+form
ba+cil+lus
 ba+cil+li
back
 backs
 backs
 back+ing
 backed
back+bencher
 back+benchers
back+bite
 back+bites
 back+bit+ing
 back+bit
 back+bit+ten *or*
 back+bit
back+biter
 back+biters
back+board
 back+boards
back+bone
 back+bones
back+breaking
back+burn

back+burns
 back+burns
 back+burn+ing
 back+burned
back+chat
back+cloth
 back+cloths
back+comb
 back+combs
 back+comb+ing
 back+combed
back+date
 back+dates
 back+dat+ing
 back+dat+ed
back+down
 back+downs
back down
verb
back+drop
 back+drops
backed
back+er
 back+ers
back+field
 back+fields
back+fill
 back+fills
 back+fill+ing
 back+filled
back+fire
 back+fires
 back+fires
 back+fir+ing
 back+fired
back+gam+mon
 back+gam+
 mons
back+ground
 back+grounds
back+hand
 back+hands
 back+hand+ed
 back+hand+er
 back+hand+ers

back+ing	*noun, adj.*	*excellent*	bag+ging
back+ings	back up	bad+der	bagged
back+lash	*verb*	bad+dest	ba+gasse
back+lashes	back+veld	bad	baga+telle
back+log	back+veld+er	*a past tense of*	baga+telles
back+logs	back+veld+ers	*bid*	Bag+dad
back+most	back+ward	Ba+da+joz	Bagehot
back+pack	back+warda+tion	Ba+da+lo+na	ba+gel
back+packs	back+ward+ness	bad+dish	ba+gels
back+packs	back+wards	bade	bag+ful
back+pack+ing	back+wash	Ba+den	bag+fuls
back+packed	back+washes	Baden-Baden	bag+gage
back-pedal	back+water	Baden-Powell	bag+gages
back-pedals	back+waters	Baden-Württem+	bag+gi+ly
back-pedalling	back wa+ter	berg	bag+gi+ness
or	*verb*	Bader	bag+gy
back-pedaling	back+woods	badge	bag+gi+er
U.S.	back+woods+	badges	bag+gi+est
back-pedalled	man	badg+er	Bagh+dad
or	back+woods+	badg+ers	Bagley
back-pedaled	men	badg+ers	bag+man
U.S.	bac+la+va	badg+er+ing	bag+men
Backs	bac+la+vas	badg+ered	bagnio
back-seat	Ba+co+lod	badi+nage	bagnios
adj.	ba+con	bad+lands	Bagnold
back+sheesh	ba+cons	Bad Lands	bag+pipes
back+side	Bacon	*area of the U.S.*	bags
back+sides	Ba+co+nian	bad+ly	ba+guet
back+slide	Ba+co+nians	bad+min+ton	ba+guets
back+slides	bac+te+ria	bad+min+tons	ba+guette
back+slid+ing	bac+te+rial	Bad+min+ton	ba+guettes
back+slid	bac+te+ri+al+ly	bad-mouth	Ba+guio
back+slid *or*	bac+te+ri+cid+al	bad-mouths	bah
back+slid+den	bac+te+ri+cide	bad-mouthing	Ba+ha'i
back+slid+er	bac+te+ri+cides	bad-mouthed	Ba+ha'is
back+slid+ers	bac+te+rio+logi+	bad+ness	Ba+ha'ism
back+space	cal	bad-tempered	Ba+ha'ist
back+spaces	bac+te+ri+olo+	Bae+de+ker	Ba+ha'ists
back+spac+ing	gist	Bae+de+kers	Ba+ha'ite
back+spaced	bac+te+ri+olo+	Baez	Ba+ha'ites
back+spin	gists	Baf+fin	Ba+ha+ma
back+stage	bac+te+ri+ol+ogy	baf+fle	Ba+ha+mas
back+stairs	bac+te+rio+	baf+fles	Ba+ha+mian
back+stay	phage	baf+fles	Ba+ha+mians
back+stays	bac+te+rio+	baf+fling	Ba+ha+wal+pur
back+street	phages	baf+fled	Ba+hia
back+streets	bac+te+rium	baf+fle+ment	Ba+hía Blan+ca
back+stroke	bac+te+ria	baf+fler	Bah+rain
back+strokes	Bac+tria	baf+flers	Bah+rai+ni
back-to-back	Bac+trian	baf+fling	Bah+rai+nis
back+track	Bac+trians	baf+fling+ly	Bah+rein
back+tracks	bad	BAFTA	Bah+rei+ni
back+track+ing	worse	bag	Bah+rei+nis
back+tracked	worst	bags	bail
back+up	bad	bags	bails

bails
bail+ing
bailed
bail+er
bail+ers
bai+ley
bai+leys
Bailey
bailie
bailies
bail+iff
bail+iffs
baili+wick
baili+wicks
Bainbridge
bain-marie
bains-marie
Bai+ram
Bai+rams
Baird
bairn
bairns
bait
baits
baits
bait+ing
bait+ed
baize
bake
bakes
bakes
bak+ing
baked
Ba+ke+lite
Trademark
bak+er
bak+ers
Baker
bak+ery
bak+eries
Bakewell
Bakh+ta+ran
bak+la+va
bak+la+vas
bak+sheesh
Bakst
Baku
Bakunin
Bala
Balaam
Bala+cla+va
Balakirev
Bala+kla+va
bala+lai+ka
bala+lai+kas

bal+ance
bal+ances
bal+ances
bal+anc+ing
bal+anced
Bal+ance
bal+ance+able
bal+anc+er
bal+anc+ers
Balanchine
bala+ta
bala+tas
Ba+la+ton
Balboa
surname
Bal+boa
place name
Balcon
bal+co+nied
bal+co+ny
bal+co+nies
bald
bald+er
bald+est
bal+da+chin
bal+da+chins
bal+da+quin
bal+da+quins
Balder
bal+der+dash
bald+faced
bald+ing
bald+ish
bald+ly
bald+ness
bal+dric
bal+drics
Baldwin
bale
bales
bales
bal+ing
baled
Bale
Bales
Bâle
ba+leen
bale+ful
bale+ful+ly
bale+ful+ness
Balenciaga
bal+er
bal+ers
Balfour
Bali

Ba+lik+pa+pan
Ba+li+nese
Ba+li+nese
Baliol
balk
balks
balks
balk+ing
balked
Bal+kan
Balkh
Bal+khash
balky
balki+er
balki+est
ball
balls
balls
ball+ing
balled
Ball
bal+lad
bal+lads
bal+lade
bal+lades
bal+lad+eer
bal+lad+eers
Ballance
Bal+la+rat
Ballard
bal+last
bal+lasts
bal+lasts
bal+last+ing
bal+last+ed
ball+break+er
ball+break+ers
bal+le+ri+na
bal+le+ri+nas
Ballesteros
bal+let
bal+lets
bal+let+ic
bal+leto+mane
bal+leto+manes
bal+leto+ma+nia
Balliol
bal+lis+ta
bal+lis+tae
bal+lis+tic
bal+lis+ti+cal+ly
bal+lis+tics
bal+locks
bal+loon
bal+loons

bal+loons
bal+loon+ing
bal+looned
bal+loon+ist
bal+loon+ists
balloon-like
bal+lot
bal+lots
bal+lots
bal+lot+ing
bal+lot+ed
bal+lo+ti+ni
ball+park
ball+parks
ball+point
ball+points
ball+room
ball+rooms
balls
balls-up
balls-ups
bal+ly
bal+ly+hoo
bal+ly+hoos
bal+ly+hoos
bal+ly+hoo+ing
bal+ly+hooed
bal+ly+rag
bal+ly+rags
bal+ly+rag+ging
bal+ly+ragged
balm
balms
Balmain
balmi+ly
balmi+ness
Bal+mor+al
Bal+mor+als
balmy
balmi+er
balmi+est
bal+neo+logi+cal
bal+ne+olo+gist
bal+ne+olo+
  gists
bal+ne+ol+ogy
ba+lo+ney
BALPA
bal+sa
bal+sas
bal+sam
bal+sams
bal+sam+ic
balsa+wood
Bal+tha+zar

wine bottle	band+ing	ban+di+est	bank+er
Bal+tha+zars	band+ed	bandy-legged	bank+ers
Balthazar	Banda	bane	Bankhead
personal name	*surname*	banes	bank+ing
Balthus	Ban+da	bane+berry	bank+ings
Bal+tic	*sea*	bane+berries	bank+note
Bal+tics	band+age	bane+ful	bank+notes
Bal+ti+more	band+ages	Banff	bank+roll
place name	band+ages	Banff+shire	bank+rolls
Baltimore	band+ag+ing	bang	bank+rolls
surname	band+aged	bangs	bank+roll+ing
Ba+lu+chi+stan	ban+dana	bangs	bank+rolled
bal+us+ter	ban+danas	bang+ing	bank+rupt
bal+us+ters	ban+dan+na	banged	bank+rupts
bal+us+trade	ban+dan+nas	Ban+ga+lore	bank+rupts
bal+us+trades	Bandaranaike	bang+er	bank+rupt+ing
Balzac	Ban+dar Seri Be+	bang+ers	bank+rupt+ed
Bama+ko	ga+wan	Bang+ka	bank+rupt+cy
Bam+berg	band+box	Bang+kok	bank+rupt+cies
bam+bi+no	band+boxes	Bang+la	Banks
bam+bi+nos *or*	ban+deau	Bang+la+desh	bank+sia
bam+bi+ni	ban+deaux	Bang+la+deshi	bank+sias
bam+boo	ban+de+rol	Bang+la+deshis	ban+ner
bam+boos	ban+de+rols	ban+gle	ban+ners
bam+boo+zle	ban+de+role	ban+gles	ban+nered
bam+boo+zles	ban+de+roles	Ban+gor	Bannister
bam+boo+zling	ban+di+coot	bang+tail	ban+nis+ters
bam+boo+zled	ban+di+coots	bang+tails	ban+nock
bam+boo+zle+	band+ing	Ban+gui	ban+nocks
ment	ban+dit	Bang+weu+lu	Ban+nock+burn
bam+boo+zler	ban+dits *or*	ban+ian	banns
bam+boo+zlers	ban+dit+ti	ban+ians	ban+quet
ban	ban+dit+ry	ban+ish	ban+quets
bans	Band+jar+ma+sin	ban+ishes	ban+quets
bans	Band+jer+ma+sin	ban+ish+ing	ban+quet+ing
ban+ning	band+master	ban+ished	ban+quet+ed
banned	band+masters	ban+ish+ment	ban+quet+er
ban	ban+do+leer	ban+ish+ments	ban+quet+ers
Romanian money	ban+do+leers	ban+is+ters	ban+quette
bani	ban+do+lier	Ban+ja Luka	ban+quettes
Ba+na+ba	ban+do+liers	Ban+jar+ma+sin	bans
Ba+na+ban	bands+man	ban+jo	ban+shee
Ba+na+bans	bands+men	ban+jos *or*	ban+shees
ba+nal	band+stand	ban+joes	Ban+stead
ba+nal+ity	band+stands	ban+jo+ist	ban+tam
ba+nal+ities	Ban+dung	ban+jo+ists	ban+tams
ba+nal+ly	band+wagon	Ban+jul	bantam+weight
ba+na+na	band+wagons	bank	bantam+weights
ba+na+nas	band+width	banks	ban+ter
Ba+na+ras	band+widths	banks	ban+ters
Ban+at	ban+dy	bank+ing	ban+ters
Ban+bury	ban+dies	banked	ban+ter+ing
band	ban+dy+ing	Ban+ka	ban+tered
bands	ban+died	bank+book	ban+ter+er
bands	ban+di+er	bank+books	ban+ter+ers

Banting	bar+ba+ri+sa+	bar+bi+tu+rates	barg+ing
Bantock	tion	Bar+bu+da	barged
Ban+tu	bar+ba+ri+sa+	bar+bule	barge+board
Ban+tu or	tions	bar+bules	barge+boards
Ban+tus	bar+ba+rise	Barbusse	bar+gee
Ban+tu+stan	bar+ba+rises	Barca	bar+gees
Ban+tu+stans	bar+ba+ris+ing	Bar+ca	barge+pole
ban+yan	bar+ba+rised	bar+ca+role	barge+poles
ban+yans	bar+ba+rism	bar+ca+roles	Bari
ban+zai	bar+ba+risms	bar+ca+rolle	Baring
bao+bab	bar+bar+ity	bar+ca+rolles	bar+ite
bao+babs	bar+bar+ities	Bar+ce	U.S.
Bao+ding	bar+ba+ri+za+	Bar+ce+lo+na	bar+ites
Bao+tou	tion	Bar+ci+no	bari+tone
bap	bar+ba+rize	Barclay de Tolly	bari+tones
baps	bar+ba+rizes	bard	bar+ium
bap+tise	bar+ba+riz+ing	bards	bark
bap+tises	bar+ba+rized	bards	barks
bap+tis+ing	Barbarossa	bard+ing	barks
bap+tised	bar+ba+rous	bard+ed	bark+ing
bap+tism	bar+ba+rous+ly	Bard	barked
bap+tisms	bar+ba+rous+	Bardeen	bar+ken+tine
bap+tis+mal	ness	bard+ic	U.S., Canada
bap+tis+mal+ly	Bar+ba+ry	bar+die	bar+ken+tines
Bap+tist	Bar+ba+ries	bar+dies	bark+er
Bap+tists	bar+bate	Bardot	bark+ers
bap+tist+ery	bar+becue	bare	Barker
bap+tist+eries	bar+becues	bares	bark+ing
bap+tist+ry	bar+becues	bar+ing	Bar+let+ta
bap+tist+ries	bar+becu+ing	bared	bar+ley
bap+tize	bar+becued	bar+er	bar+leys
bap+tizes	barbed	bar+est	barley+corn
bap+tiz+ing	bar+bel	bare+back	barley+corns
bap+tized	bar+bels	bare+backed	barm
bar	bar+bell	bare+faced	barms
bars	bar+bells	bare+fac+ed+ly	bar+maid
bars	bar+ber	bare+fac+ed+	bar+maids
bar+ring	bar+bers	ness	bar+man
barred	bar+bers	bare+foot	bar+men
Bar	bar+ber+ing	bare+footed	Bar+mecide
Bars	bar+bered	bare+headed	Bar Mitz+vah
Barabbas	bar+ber+ry	Ba+reil+ly	Bar Mitz+vahs
bara+thea	bar+ber+ries	bare+ly	bar+my
barb	barber+shop	Barenboim	bar+mi+er
barbs	U.S.	bare+ness	bar+mi+est
barbs	barber+shops	bar+gain	barn
barb+ing	bar+bi+can	bar+gains	barns
barbed	bar+bi+cans	bar+gains	Barnabas
Bar+ba+dian	Bar+bi+can	bar+gain+ing	bar+na+cle
Bar+ba+dians	bar+bi+cel	bar+gained	bar+na+cles
Bar+ba+dos	bar+bi+cels	bar+gain+er	bar+na+cled
bar+bar+ian	Barbirolli	bar+gain+ers	Barnard
bar+bar+ians	bar+bi+tal	barge	Barnardo
bar+bar+ic	bar+bi+tone	barges	Bar+na+ul
bar+bari+cal+ly	bar+bi+tu+rate	barges	Bar+net

bar+ney
 bar+neys
 bar+neys
 bar+ney+ing
 bar+neyed
Barns+ley
Barn+sta+ple
barn+storm
 barn+storms
 barn+storm+ing
 barn+stormed
 barn+storm+ing
Barnum
barn+yard
 barn+yards
baro+cep+tor
 baro+cep+tors
Ba+ro+da
baro+gram
 baro+grams
baro+graph
 baro+graphs
baro+graphic
Baroja
ba+rom+eter
 ba+rom+eters
baro+met+ric
baro+met+ri+cal
ba+rom+etry
bar+on
 bar+ons
bar+on+age
 bar+on+ages
bar+on+ess
 bar+on+esses
bar+on+et
 bar+on+ets
bar+on+et+age
 bar+on+et+ages
bar+on+et+cy
 bar+on+et+cies
ba+ro+nial
baro+ny
 baro+nies
ba+roque
 ba+roques
baro+re+cep+tor
 baro+re+cep+
 tors
baro+scope
 baro+scopes
baro+scop+ic
ba+rouche
 ba+rouches
Barozzi

bar+per+son
 bar+per+sons
bar+quan+tine
 bar+quan+tines
barque
 barques
bar+quen+tine
 bar+quen+tines
Bar+qui+si+me+
 to
Bar+ra
bar+rack
 bar+racks
 bar+rack+ing
 bar+racked
 bar+racks
bar+ra+cou+ta
 bar+ra+cou+tas
bar+ra+cu+da
 bar+ra+cu+da
 or
 bar+ra+cu+das
bar+rage
 bar+rages
bar+ra+mun+di
 bar+ra+mun+dis
 or
 bar+ra+mun+di
 or
 bar+ra+mun+
 dies
Bar+ran+qui+lla
bar+ra+tor
 bar+ra+tors
bar+ra+trous
bar+ra+try
 bar+ra+tries
Barrault
barre
 barres
bar+ré
 bar+rés
bar+rel
 bar+rels
 bar+rels
bar+rel+ling or
 bar+rel+ing
 U.S.
bar+relled or
 bar+reled
 U.S.
barrel-chested
bar+rel+ful
 bar+rel+fuls
barrel-roll

verb
bar+rel roll
 bar+rel rolls
bar+ren
bar+ren+ness
bar+retrous
bar+retry
 bar+retries
bar+ri+cade
 bar+ri+cades
 bar+ri+cades
 bar+ri+cad+ing
 bar+ri+cad+ed
Barrie
bar+ri+er
 bar+ri+ers
barrier-nurse
 barrier-nurses
 barrier-nursing
 barrier-nursed
bar+ring
bar+ris+ter
 bar+ris+ters
bar+rister-at-law
 bar+risters-at-
 law
bar+row
 bar+rows
Bar+row
bar+row+ful
 bar+row+fuls
Barrow-in-
 Furness
Bar+ry
place name
Barry
surname
Barrymore
Bart
bar+tender
 bar+tenders
bar+ter
 bar+ters
 bar+ters
 bar+ter+ing
 bar+tered
Barth
Barthes
Barth+ian
 Barth+ians
Bartholdi
Bartholomew
bar+ti+zan
 bar+ti+zans
 bar+ti+zaned

Bartók
Bartolommeo
Barton
Baruch
bary+on
 bary+ons
bary+on+ic
Baryshnikov
ba+ry+ta
 ba+ry+tes
ba+sal
bas+alt
 bas+alts
ba+sal+tic
bas+cule
 bas+cules
base
 bases
 bases
bas+ing
 based
bas+er
bas+est
base+ball
 base+balls
base+born
Ba+sel
base+less
 base+less+ness
base+line
 base+lines
base+ment
 base+ments
base+ness
ba+sen+ji
 ba+sen+jis
ba+ses
plural of basis
bases
plural of base
bash
 bashes
 bashes
bash+ing
 bashed
bash+ful
bash+ful+ly
bash+ful+ness
Bash+kir
 Bash+kir or
 Bash+kirs
Basho
ba+sic
 ba+sics
BASIC

ba+si+cal+ly
ba+sic+ity
ba+sic+ities
ba+sidio+my+
cete
ba+sidio+my+
cetes
ba+sidio+my+cet+
ous
Basie
bas+il
bas+ils
Basil
Ba+si+lan
basi+lar
basi+lary
Ba+sil+don
ba+sil+ic
ba+sili+ca
ba+sili+cas
ba+sili+can
Ba+si+li+ca+ta
basi+lisk
basi+lisks
ba+sin
ba+sins
ba+sin+ful
ba+sin+fuls
Ba+sing+stoke
ba+sis
ba+ses
bask
basks
bask+ing
basked
bas+ket
bas+kets
basket+ball
basket+balls
bas+ket+ful
bas+ket+fuls
bas+ket+ry
basket+work
Basle
ba+so+phil
ba+so+phils
ba+so+phile
ba+so+philes
ba+so+phil+ic
Basotho-
Qwaqwa
basque
basques
Basque
Basques

Bas+ra
Bas+rah
bas-relief
bas-reliefs
Bas-Rhin
bass
basses
Bas+sein
Basse-Norman+
die
Bas+sen+thwaite
Basses-Alpes
Basses-Pyrénées
bas+set
bas+sets
Basse+terre
St Kitts
Basse-Terre
Guadeloupe
bas+si+net
bas+si+nets
bass+ist
bass+ists
bas+so
bas+sos *or*
bas+si
bas+soon
bas+soons
bas+soon+ist
bas+soon+ists
bas+so ri+lievo
bas+so ri+lievos
bast
bas+tard
bas+tards
bas+tard+ise
bas+tard+ises
bas+tard+is+ing
bas+tard+ised
bas+tard+ize
bas+tard+izes
bas+tard+iz+ing
bas+tard+ized
bas+tardy
baste
bastes
bast+ing
bast+ed
Bas+tia
Bas+tille
bas+ti+na+do
bas+ti+na+does
bas+ti+na+does
bas+ti+na+do+
ing

bas+ti+na+doed
bast+ing
bas+ti+on
bas+ti+ons
Ba+stogne
Ba+su+to+land
bat
bats
bats
bat+ting
bat+ted
Ba+taan
Ba+tan+gas
Ba+ta+via
Ba+ta+vi+an
Ba+ta+vi+ans
batch
batches
batches
batch+ing
batched
bate
bates
bates
bat+ing
bat+ed
ba+teau
ba+teaux
Bates
bath
baths
baths
bath+ing
bathed
Bath
bathe
bathes
bathes
bath+ing
bathed
bath+er
bath+ers
bath+ers
ba+thet+ic
bath+house
bath+houses
batho+lite
batho+lites
batho+lith
batho+liths
batho+lith+ic
batho+lit+ic
ba+thom+eter
ba+thom+eters
batho+met+ric

ba+thom+etry
ba+thos
bath+robe
bath+robes
bath+room
bath+rooms
Bathsheba
bath+tub
bath+tubs
Bath+urst
bathy+scape
bathy+scapes
bathy+scaph
bathy+scaphs
bathy+scaphe
bathy+scaphes
bathy+sphere
bathy+spheres
ba+tik
Batista
ba+tiste
Bat+ley
bat+man
bat+men
ba+ton
ba+tons
Bat+on Rouge
ba+tra+chi+an
ba+tra+chi+ans
bats
bats+man
bats+men
bat+tal+ion
bat+tal+ions
bat+ten
bat+tens
bat+tens
bat+ten+ing
bat+tened
Batten
bat+ter
bat+ters
bat+ters
bat+ter+ing
bat+tered
bat+ter+er
bat+ter+ers
bat+ter+ing
bat+ter+ings
Bat+ter+sea
bat+tery
bat+teries
bat+ting
bat+tle
bat+tles

bat+tles
bat+tling
bat+tled
Bat+tle
battle-axe
battle-axes
bat+tle+dore
bat+tle+dores
bat+tle+dress
bat+tle+dresses
battle+field
battle+fields
battle+ground
battle+grounds
bat+tle+ment
bat+tle+ments
bat+tle+ment+ed
bat+tler
bat+tlers
bat+tle roy+al
bat+tles roy+al
battle+ship
battle+ships
bat+ty
bat+ti+er
bat+ti+est
Ba+tum
Ba+tu+mi
bat+woman
bat+women
bau+ble
bau+bles
Bau+chi
baud
bauds
Baudelaire
Bau+haus
bau+hinia
bau+hinias
baulk
baulks
baulks
baulk+ing
baulked
baulky
baulki+er
baulki+est
Bau+tzen
baux+ite
Ba+varia
Ba+var+ian
Ba+var+ians
bawd
bawds
bawdi+ly

bawdi+ness
bawd+ry
bawdy
bawdi+er
bawdi+est
bawdy+house
bawdy+houses
bawl
bawls
bawls
bawl+ing
bawled
bawl+er
bawl+ers
bawl+ing
bawl+ings
Bax
Baxter
bay
bays
bays
bay+ing
bayed
Ba+ya+món
bay+berry
bay+berries
Bay+ern
Ba+yeux
Baylis
bayo+net
bayo+nets
bayo+nets
bayo+net+ing
  or
bayo+net+ting
bayo+net+ed
  or
bayo+net+ted
Ba+yonne
bayou
bayous
Bay+reuth
ba+zaar
ba+zaars
ba+zar
ba+zars
ba+zoo+ka
ba+zoo+kas
bdel+lium
bdel+liums
be
am
are
is
be+ing

was
were
been
beach
beaches
beaches
beach+ing
beached
beach+comber
beach+combers
beach+head
beach+heads
Beachy Head
bea+con
bea+cons
Bea+cons+field
  town
Beaconsfield
  surname
bead
beads
beads
bead+ing
bead+ed
bead+ed
beadi+ness
bead+ing
bead+ings
bea+dle
bea+dles
bea+dle+ship
bea+dle+ships
beads+man
beads+men
bead+work
beady
beadi+er
beadi+est
bea+gle
bea+gles
bea+gles
bea+gling
bea+gled
Beaglehole
beak
beaks
beaked
beak+er
beak+ers
beaky
Beale
beam
beams
beams
beam+ing

beamed
beam-ends
beam+ing
bean
beans
bean+bag
bean+bags
bean+feast
bean+feasts
beano
beanos
bean+pole
bean+poles
bean+stalk
bean+stalks
bear
  in most senses
bears
bear+ing
bore
borne
bear
  give birth to
bears
bear+ing
bore
born
bear
  lower the price of
  shares etc.
bears
bear+ing
beared
bear
bears *or*
bear
Bear
bear+able
bear-baiting
beard
beards
beards
beard+ing
beard+ed
beard+ed
beard+less
Beardsley
bear+er
bear+ers
bear+ing
bear+ings
bear+ish
bear+ish+ness
bear+skin
bear+skins

beast	beau+jo+lais	Bechua+na	bed+chambers
beasts	beau+jo+lais	Bechua+nas *or*	bed+clothes
beast+ings	Beau+lieu	Bechua+na	bed+dable
beast+li+ness	Beaumarchais	Bechua+na+land	bed+ding
beast+li+nesses	Beau+mar+is	beck	bed+dings
beast+ly	beau monde	becks	Bede
beast+li+er	Beau+mont	Beckenbauer	be+deck
beast+li+est	*place name*	Becker	be+decks
beat	Beaumont	Becket	be+deck+ing
beats	*surname*	Beckett	be+decked
beats	Beaune	Beckford	bedes+man
beat+ing	Beaunes	Beckmann	bedes+men
beat	beaut	beck+on	be+dev+il
beat+en	beauts	beck+ons	be+dev+ils
beat+able	beau+te+ous	beck+ons	be+dev+il+ling
beat+box	beau+te+ous+	beck+on+ing	*or*
beat+boxes	ness	beck+oned	be+dev+il+ing
beat+en	beau+ti+cian	beck+on+er	*U.S.*
beat+er	beau+ti+cians	beck+on+ers	be+dev+illed
beat+ers	beau+ti+fi+ca+	beck+on+ing	*or*
bea+tif+ic	tion	be+cloud	be+dev+iled
bea+tifi+cal+ly	beau+ti+fi+er	be+clouds	*U.S.*
be+ati+fi+ca+tion	beau+ti+fi+ers	be+cloud+ing	be+dev+il+ment
be+ati+fi+ca+	beau+ti+ful	be+cloud+ed	be+dev+il+
tions	beau+ti+ful+ly	be+come	ments
be+ati+fy	beau+ti+fy	be+comes	be+dew
be+ati+fies	beau+ti+fies	be+com+ing	be+dews
be+ati+fy+ing	beau+ti+fy+ing	be+came	be+dew+ing
be+ati+fied	beau+ti+fied	be+come	be+dewed
beat+ing	beau+ty	be+com+ing	bed+fellow
beat+ings	beau+ties	be+com+ing+ly	bed+fellows
be+ati+tude	Beau+vais	be+com+ing+	Bed+ford
be+ati+tudes	Beauvoir	ness	*place name*
Be+ati+tude	beaux	bec+que+rel	Bedford
Be+ati+tudes	beaux-arts	bec+que+rels	*surname*
Beat+les	bea+ver	Becquerel	Bed+ford+shire
beat+nik	bea+vers	bed	be+dight
beat+niks	bea+vers	beds	be+dights
Beaton	bea+ver+ing	beds	be+dight+ing
Beatrix	bea+vered	bed+ding	be+dight *or*
Beatty	Beaverbrook	bed+ded	be+dight+ed
beat-up	Beb+ing+ton	be+daub	be+dim
adj.	be+bop	be+daubs	be+dims
beat up	be+bop+per	be+daub+ing	be+dim+ming
verb	be+bop+pers	be+daubed	be+dimmed
beau	be+calmed	be+daz+zle	Bedivere
beaus *or*	be+came	be+daz+zles	be+di+zen
beaux	be+cause	be+daz+zling	be+di+zens
Beaufort	Be+char	be+daz+zled	be+di+zen+ing
surname	bêche-de-mer	be+daz+zle+ment	be+di+zened
Beau+fort	bêches-de-mer	be+daz+zle+	be+di+zen+ment
scale, Sea	*or*	ments	be+di+zen+
beau geste	bêche-de-mer	bed+bug	ments
beaux gestes	Bechet	bed+bugs	bed+lam
Beauharnais	Bechstein	bed+chamber	bed+lams

Bedou+in
 Bedou+ins *or*
 Bedou+in
bed+pan
 bed+pans
be+drag+gle
 be+drag+gles
 be+drag+gling
 be+drag+gled
be+drag+gled
bed+rid+den
bed+rock
 bed+rocks
bed+roll
 bed+rolls
bed+room
 bed+rooms
bed+side
 bed+sides
bed+sitter
 bed+sitters
bed+sore
 bed+sores
bed+spread
 bed+spreads
bed+stead
 bed+steads
bed+straw
 bed+straws
bed+time
 bed+times
Bedu+in
 Bedu+ins *or*
 Bedu+in
bed-wetting
 bed-wettings
Bed+worth
bee
 bees
Beeb
bee+bread
beech
 beeches
Beecham
beech+en
beech+nut
 beech+nuts
beechy
bee-eater
 bee-eaters
beef
 beeves
 cattle
 beefs
 complaints

beefs
beef+ing
beefed
beef+bur+ger
 beef+bur+gers
beef+cake
beef+eater
 beef+eaters
beefi+ness
beef+steak
 beef+steaks
beefy
beefi+er
beefi+est
bee+hive
 bee+hives
bee+keeper
 bee+keepers
bee+keeping
bee+line
 bee+lines
Beelzebub
been
beep
 beeps
 beeps
beep+ing
beeped
beep+er
 beep+ers
beer
 beers
Beerbohm
beeri+ly
beeri+ness
Beer+she+ba
beery
 beeri+er
 beeri+est
beest+ings
bees+wax
bees+wing
 bees+wings
beet
 beets
Beethoven
bee+tle
 bee+tles
 bee+tles
 bee+tling
 bee+tled
beetle-browed
bee+tling
Beeton
beet+root

beet+roots
beeves
be+fall
 be+falls
 be+fall+ing
 be+fell
 be+fall+en
be+fit
 be+fits
 be+fit+ting
 be+fit+ted
be+fit+ting
be+fit+ting+ly
be+fog
 be+fogs
 be+fog+ging
 be+fogged
be+fore
before+hand
be+foul
 be+fouls
 be+foul+ing
 be+fouled
be+friend
 be+friends
 be+friend+ing
 be+friend+ed
be+fud+dle
 be+fud+dles
 be+fud+dling
 be+fud+dled
be+fud+dle+ment
beg
 begs
 beg+ging
 begged
be+gan
be+get
 be+gets
 be+get+ting
 be+got *or*
 be+gat
 be+got+ten *or*
 be+got
be+get+ter
 be+get+ters
beg+gar
 beg+gars
 beg+gars
 beg+gar+ing
 beg+gared
beg+gar+dom
beg+gar+li+ness
beg+gar+ly

beggar-my-
 neighbour
beg+gary
be+gin
 be+gins
 be+gin+ning
 be+gan
 be+gun
Begin
be+gin+ner
 be+gin+ners
 be+gin+ning
 be+gin+nings
be+gird
 be+girds
 be+gird+ing
 be+gird+ed *or*
 be+girt
be+gone
be+gonia
 be+gonias
be+gor+ra
be+got
 be+got+ten
be+grime
 be+grimes
 be+grim+ing
 be+grimed
be+grudge
 be+grudges
 be+grudg+ing
 be+grudged
be+grudg+ing+ly
be+guile
 be+guiles
 be+guil+ing
 be+guiled
be+guile+ment
 be+guile+ments
be+guil+er
 be+guil+ers
 be+guil+ing
 be+guil+ing+ly
be+guine
 be+guines
be+gum
 be+gums
be+gun
be+half
Behan
be+have
 be+haves
 be+hav+ing
 be+haved
be+hav+ior

U.S.
be+hav+iors
be+hav+ior+al
U.S.
be+hav+ior+ism
U.S.
be+hav+ior+
isms
be+hav+ior+ist
U.S.
be+hav+ior+ists
be+hav+ior+is+
tic
U.S.
be+hav+iour
be+hav+iours
be+hav+iour+al
be+hav+iour+ism
be+hav+iour+
isms
be+hav+iour+ist
be+hav+iour+
ists
be+hav+iour+is+
tic
be+head
be+heads
be+head+ing
be+head+ed
be+held
be+he+moth
be+he+moths
be+hest
be+hests
be+hind
be+hinds
behind+hand
Be+his+tun
Behn
be+hold
be+holds
be+hold+ing
be+held
be+hold+en
be+hold+er
be+hold+ers
be+hoof
be+hooves
be+hove
be+hoves
be+hov+ing
be+hoved
Behring
Beiderbecke
beige

beiges
bei+gel
bei+gels
Bei+jing
be+ing
be+ings
Bei+ra
Bei+rut
be+jab+bers
be+ja+bers
be+jew+el
be+jew+els
be+jew+el+ling
or
be+jew+el+ing
U.S.
be+jew+elled
or
be+jew+eled
U.S.
Be+kaa
bel
bels
Bel
be+la+bor
U.S.
be+la+bors
be+la+bor+ing
be+la+bored
be+la+bour
be+la+bours
be+la+bour+ing
be+la+boured
be+lat+ed
be+lat+ed+ly
be+lat+ed+ness
Be+lau
be+lay
be+lays
be+lays
be+lay+ing
be+layed
bel can+to
belch
belches
belches
belch+ing
belched
bel+dam
bel+dams
bel+dame
bel+dames
be+lea+guer
be+lea+guers

be+lea+guer+
ing
be+lea+guered
Be+lém
bel+em+nite
bel+em+nites
Bel+fast
Bel+fort
bel+fry
bel+fries
Bel+gaum
Bel+gian
Bel+gians
Bel+gium
Belgorod-
Dnestrov+ski
Bel+grade
Bel+gra+via
Belial
be+lie
be+lies
be+ly+ing
be+lied
be+lief
be+liefs
be+liev+able
be+lieve
be+lieves
be+liev+ing
be+lieved
be+liev+er
be+liev+ers
be+like
Belisarius
be+lit+tle
be+lit+tles
be+lit+tling
be+lit+tled
be+lit+tle+ment
be+lit+tle+
ments
be+lit+tler
be+lit+tlers
Be+li+tung
Be+lize
bell
bells
bells
bell+ing
belled
Bell
bel+la+don+na
bel+la+don+nas
Bellamy
Bellay

bell+bird
bell+birds
bell-bottomed
bell-bottoms
bell+boy
bell+boys
belle
belles
Bellerophon
belles-lettres
bel+let+rist
bel+let+rists
bell+flower
bell+flowers
bell+founder
bell+founders
bell glass
bell+hop
U.S.
bell+hops
bel+li+cose
bel+li+cos+ity
bel+lig+er+ence
bel+lig+er+en+cy
bel+lig+er+ent
bel+lig+er+ents
Bellini
Bel+lin+zo+na
bell+man
bell+men
Belloc
bel+low
bel+lows
bel+lows
bel+low+ing
bel+lowed
Bellow
bel+lows
bel+lows
bell-ringer
bell-ringers
bell-ringing
bell+wether
bell+wethers
bel+ly
bel+lies
bel+lies
bel+ly+ing
bel+lied
belly+ache
belly+aches
belly+aches
belly+ach+ing
belly+ached
belly+acher

belly+achers
belly+band
belly+bands
belly+button
belly+buttons
belly-dance
belly-dances
belly-dancing
belly-danced
bel+ly dance
bel+ly dances
bel+ly danc+er
bel+ly danc+ers
belly-flop
belly-flops
belly-flopping
belly-flopped
bel+ly flop
bel+ly flops
bel+ly+ful
bel+ly+fuls
Bel+mo+pan
Belo Ho+ri+zon+
  te
be+long
be+longs
be+long+ing
be+longed
be+long+ing
be+long+ings
Be+lo+rus+sian
Be+lo+rus+sians
Be+lo+stock
Be+los+tok
be+lov+ed
be+lov+eds
Be+lo+vo
be+low
Bel Pa+ese
Bel+sen
Belshazzar
belt
belts
belts
belt+ing
belt+ed
Bel+tane
Bel+tanes
belt+er
belt+ers
belt+ing
belt+ings
be+lu+ga
be+lu+gas
bel+vedere

bel+vederes
Bembo
be+mire
be+mires
be+mir+ing
be+mired
be+moan
be+moans
be+moan+ing
be+moaned
be+muse
be+muses
be+mus+ing
be+mused
be+mused
ben
bens
Be+na+res
Ben Bella
Benbow
bench
benches
benches
bench+ing
benched
bench+er
bench+ers
bench+mark
bench+marks
  noun, adj.
bench mark
bench marks
bend
bends
bends
bend+ing
bent
Ben+del
bend+er
bend+ers
Ben+di+go
bends
bendy
bendi+er
bendi+est
be+neath
ben+edi+ci+te
ben+edi+ci+tes
Benedict
Ben+edic+tine
Ben+edic+tines
ben+edic+tion
ben+edic+tions
ben+edic+tory
Ben+edic+tus

ben+efac+tion
ben+efac+tions
ben+efac+tor
ben+efac+tors
ben+efac+tress
ben+efac+tresses
ben+efice
ben+efices
be+nefi+cence
be+nefi+cences
be+nefi+cent
ben+efi+cial
bene+fi+ciary
bene+fi+ciaries
ben+efit
ben+efits
ben+efits
ben+efit+ing
  or
ben+efit+ting
ben+efit+ed *or*
ben+efit+ted
Bene+lux
Be+ne+ven+to
be+nevo+lence
be+nevo+lences
be+nevo+lent
Ben+fleet
Ben+gal
Ben+ga+li
Ben+ga+lis
Ben+ga+si
Beng+bu
Ben+gha+zi
Ben+guela
Ben-Gurion
Beni
be+night+ed
be+night+ed+
  ness
be+nign
be+nig+nan+cy
be+nig+nan+
  cies
be+nig+nant
be+nig+nity
be+nig+nities
be+nign+ly
Beni Ha+san
Be+nin
Be+ni+nese
Be+ni+nese
beni+son
beni+sons
Benjamin

Benjamins
Benn
Bennett
Ben Ne+vis
Ben+ning+ton
Benny
Be+no+ni
bent
bents
Bentham
Ben+tham+ism
Ben+tham+ite
Ben+tham+ites
ben+thic
ben+thos
Bentinck
Bentley
ben+ton+ite
bent+wood
Be+nue
be+numb
be+numbs
be+numb+ing
be+numbed
Ben+xi
Benz
Ben+ze+drine
  Trademark
ben+zene
ben+zin
ben+zine
ben+zo+ate
ben+zo+ates
ben+zo+caine
benzo+di+az+
  epine
benzo+di+az+
  epines
ben+zo+ic
ben+zo+in
ben+zo+ins
ben+zol
ben+zole
Beo+grad
Be+qaa
be+queath
be+queaths
be+queath+ing
be+queathed
be+quest
be+quests
Be+rar
be+rate
be+rates
be+rat+ing

be+rat+ed
Ber+ber
Ber+bers
Ber+bera
ber+ber+is
ber+ceuse
ber+ceuses
Berch+tes+ga+
den
be+reave
be+reaves
be+reav+ing
be+reaved
be+reave+ment
be+reave+
ments
be+reft
be+ret
be+rets
Be+re+zi+na
Be+rez+ni+ki
berg
bergs
Berg
Ber+ga+mo
ber+ga+mot
ber+ga+mots
Ber+gen
Bergerac
Berg+ie
Berg+ies
Bergius
Bergman
berg+schrund
berg+schrunds
Bergson
Berg+son+ian
Berg+son+ism
Beria
beri+beri
Bering
Beriosova
berk
berks
Berkeley
ber+kelium
Berk+shire
ber+ley
ber+leys
ber+ley+ing
ber+leyed
ber+lin
ber+lins
Ber+lin
place name

Berlin
surname
Ber+lin+er
Ber+lin+ers
Berlioz
berm
berms
berme
bermes
Ber+mejo
Ber+mu+da
Ber+mu+dan
Ber+mu+dans
Ber+mu+dian
Ber+mu+dians
Bern
Bernadotte
Bernard
Berne
Bernhardt
Ber+ni+na
Bernini
Bernouilli
Bernoulli
Bernstein
ber+ret+ta
ber+ret+tas
ber+ry
ber+ries
ber+ries
ber+ry+ing
ber+ried
Berry
ber+serk
ber+serks
ber+serk+er
ber+serk+ers
berth
berths
berths
berth+ing
berthed
ber+tha
ber+thas
Bertolucci
Ber+wick
place name
Berwick
surname
Ber+wick+shire
Berwick-upon-
Tweed
ber+yl
ber+yls
ber+yl+ine

be+ryl+lium
Berzelius
Be+san+çon
Besant
be+seech
be+seeches
be+seech+ing
be+sought *or*
be+seeched
be+seem
be+seems
be+seem+ing
be+seemed
be+set
be+sets
be+set+ting
be+set
be+set+ting
be+side
be+sides
be+siege
be+sieges
be+sieg+ing
be+sieged
be+sieg+er
be+sieg+ers
be+smear
be+smears
be+smear+ing
be+smeared
be+smirch
be+smirches
be+smirch+ing
be+smirched
be+som
be+soms
be+sot+ted
be+sought
be+span+gle
be+span+gles
be+span+gling
be+span+gled
be+spat+ter
be+spat+ters
be+spat+ter+ing
be+spat+tered
be+speak
be+speaks
be+speak+ing
be+spoke
be+spo+ken *or*
be+spoke
be+spec+ta+cled
be+spoke
be+sprin+kle

be+sprin+kles
be+sprin+kling
be+sprin+kled
Bes+sa+ra+bia
Bessel
best
bests
bests
best+ing
best+ed
Best
be+stead
be+steads
be+stead+ing
be+stead+ed
be+stead+ed
or
be+stead
bes+tial
bes+ti+al+ise
bes+ti+al+ises
bes+ti+al+is+ing
bes+ti+al+ised
bes+ti+al+ity
bes+ti+al+ities
bes+ti+al+ize
bes+ti+al+izes
bes+ti+al+iz+ing
bes+ti+al+ized
bes+ti+ary
bes+ti+aries
be+stir
be+stirs
be+stir+ring
be+stirred
be+stow
be+stows
be+stow+ing
be+stowed
be+stow+al
be+strew
be+strews
be+strew+ing
be+strewed
be+strewn *or*
be+strewed
be+stride
be+strides
be+strid+ing
be+strode *or*
be+strid
Archaic
be+strid+den
or
be+strid

Archaic
best+sell+er
best+sell+ers
best-selling
bet
  bets
  bets
  bet+ting
  bet *or*
  bet+ted
beta
  betas
beta-blocker
  beta-blockers
be+ta+caro+tene
be+take
  be+takes
  be+tak+ing
  be+took
  be+tak+en
be+ta+tron
be+ta+trons
be+tel
bête noire
  bêtes noires
beth
  beths
Betha+ny
Bethe
Beth+el
Be+thes+da
  Be+thes+das
be+think
  be+thinks
  be+think+ing
  be+thought
Beth+le+hem
Beth+sai+da
be+tide
  be+tides
  be+tid+ing
  be+tid+ed
  be+times
Betjeman
be+to+ken
  be+to+kens
  be+to+ken+ing
  be+to+kened
beto+ny
  beto+nies
be+tray
  be+trays
  be+tray+ing
  be+trayed
be+tray+al

be+tray+als
be+tray+er
be+tray+ers
be+troth
  be+troths
  be+troth+ing
  be+trothed
  be+troth+al
  be+troth+als
  be+trothed
  be+trothed
bet+ter
  bet+ters
  bet+ters
  bet+ter+ing
  bet+tered
bet+ter+ment
bet+ter+ments
be+tween
be+tween+times
be+tween+whiles
be+twixt
Betws-y-Coed
Beu+lah
Beu+then
Bevan
Bevan+ite
  Bevan+ites
beva+tron
  beva+trons
bev+el
  bev+els
  bev+els
  bev+el+ling *or*
  bev+el+ing
  U.S.
  bev+elled *or*
  bev+eled
  U.S.
bev+er+age
  bev+er+ages
Beveridge
Bev+er+ley
Bev+er+ly Hills
Bevin
bev+vy
  bev+vies
bevy
  bevies
be+wail
  be+wails
  be+wail+ing
  be+wailed
  be+wail+er
  be+wail+ers

be+ware
be+wares
be+war+ing
be+wared
Bewick
be+wil+der
  be+wil+ders
be+wil+der+ing
be+wil+dered
be+wil+der+ing
be+wil+der+ing+
  ly
be+wil+der+ment
be+witch
  be+witches
  be+witch+ing
  be+witched
  be+witch+ing
be+wray
  be+wrays
  be+wray+ing
  be+wrayed
Bex+hill
Bex+ley
bey
  beys
be+yond
Bey+routh
Beza
bez+el
  bez+els
Bé+ziers
be+zique
  be+ziques
Bez+wa+da
Bha+gal+pur
bha+ji
  bha+jis
bhang
bhan+gra
bhar+al
  bhar+als
Bha+rat
Bhat+pa+ra
Bhav+na+gar
bhin+di
  bhin+dis
Bho+pal
Bhu+ba+nes+war
Bhu+tan
Bhu+tan+ese
  Bhu+tan+ese
Bhutto
bi
Bi+afra

Bi+afran
Bi+afrans
Biak
bi+an+nual
bi+an+nu+al+ly
Biar+ritz
bias
  biases
  biases *or*
  biasses
  bias+ing *or*
  bias+sing
  biased *or*
  biassed
  bi+ased
  bi+assed
bi+ath+lon
  bi+ath+lons
bi+ax+ial
bib
  bibs
  bibs
bib+bing
bibbed
bib+cock
  bib+cocks
bi+belot
  bi+belots
Bi+ble
  Bi+bles
Bible-basher
  Bible-bashers
Bible-thumper
  Bible-thumpers
Bible-thumping
  Bible-thumpings
bib+li+cal
Bib+li+cist
  Bib+li+cists
bib+li+og+ra+
  pher
bib+li+og+ra+
  phers
bib+lio+graph+ic
bib+lio+graphi+
  cal
bib+li+og+ra+phy
bib+li+og+ra+
  phies
bib+lio+man+cy
bib+lio+ma+nia
bib+lio+ma+ni+ac
bib+lio+ma+ni+
  acs
bib+lio+phil

bib+lio+phils
bib+lio+phile
bib+lio+philes
bib+li+ophi+lism
bib+lio+pole
bib+lio+poles
bib+li+opo+list
bib+li+opo+lists
bib+li+opo+ly
Bib+list
Bib+lists
bibu+lous
bibu+lous+ly
bibu+lous+ness
bi+cam+er+al
bi+cam+er+al+
ism
bi+carb
bi+car+bo+nate
bi+car+bo+
nates
bice
bices
bi+cen+tenary
bi+cen+tenaries
bi+cen+ten+nial
U.S.
bi+cen+ten+
nials
bi+cepha+lous
bi+ceps
bi+ceps
bi+chlo+ride
bi+chlo+rides
bi+chro+mate
bi+chro+mates
bick+er
bick+ers
bick+ers
bick+er+ing
bick+ered
bick+er+er
bick+er+ers
bi+col+or
U.S.
bi+col+ored
U.S.
bi+col+our
bi+col+oured
bi+con+cave
bi+con+di+tion+
al
bi+con+di+tion+
als
bi+con+vex

bi+cus+pid
bi+cus+pids
bi+cus+pi+date
bi+cus+pi+dates
bi+cy+cle
bi+cy+cles
bi+cy+cles
bi+cy+cling
bi+cy+cled
bi+cy+cler
bi+cy+clers
bi+cy+clist
bi+cy+clists
bid
bids
bids
bid+ding
bad *or*
bade *or*
bid
bid+den *or*
bid
Bida
bid+dable
bid+dable+ness
bid+dable+
nesses
bid+der
bid+ders
bid+ding
bid+dy
bid+dies
biddy-biddy
biddy-biddies
bide
bides
bid+ing
bid+ed *or*
bode
bid+ed
bi+den+tate
bi+det
bi+dets
Biel
Bie+lefeld
Biel+er+see
Bien Hoa
Bienne
bi+en+nial
bi+en+nials
bi+en+ni+al+ly
bier
biers
Bierce
biest+ings

biff
biffs
biffs
biff+ing
biffed
bi+fid
bi+fid+ity
bi+fid+ly
bi+fo+cal
bi+fo+cals
bi+fur+cate
bi+fur+cates
bi+fur+cat+ing
bi+fur+cat+ed
bi+fur+ca+tion
bi+fur+ca+tions
big
big+ger
big+gest
biga+mist
biga+mists
biga+mous
biga+my
biga+mies
big+head
big+heads
big+headed
big+headed+ness
big+horn
big+horns *or*
big+horn
bight
bights
big+mouth
big+mouths
big-mouthed
big+ness
big+no+nia
big+no+nias
big-note
big-notes
big-noting
big-noted
big+ot
big+ots
big+ot+ed
big+ot+ry
big+ot+ries
big time
big-timer
big-timers
big+wig
big+wigs
Bi+har
Biisk

Bi+ja+pur
bi+jou
bi+joux
bi+ju+gate
bi+ju+gous
Bi+ka+ner
bike
bikes
bikes
bik+ing
biked
bik+er
bik+ers
bikie
bikies
bi+ki+ni
bi+ki+nis
Bi+ki+ni
Biko
bi+la+bial
bi+la+bials
bi+la+bi+ate
bi+lat+er+al
Bil+bao
bil+berry
bil+berries
bil+boes
Bild+ungs+ro+
man
Bild+ungs+ro+
mans
bile
bilge
bilges
bilges
bilg+ing
bilged
bil+har+zia
bil+har+zias
bil+har+zia+sis
bil+har+zio+sis
bili+ary
bi+lin+gual
bi+lin+guals
bi+lin+gual+ism
bili+ous
bil+ious+ness
bilk
bilks
bilks
bilk+ing
bilked
bilk+er
bilk+ers
bill

bills
bills
bill+ing
billed
bil+la+bong
bil+la+bongs
bill+board
bill+boards
bil+let
bil+lets
bil+lets
bil+let+ing
bil+let+ed
billet-doux
billets-doux
bill+hook
bill+hooks
bil+liard
bil+liards
bill+ing
bill+ings
bil+lings+gate
Bil+lings+gate
bil+lion
bil+lions *or*
bil+lion
bil+lion+aire
bil+lion+aires
bil+lionth
bil+lionths
Bil+li+ton
bil+low
bil+lows
bil+lows
bil+low+ing
bil+lowed
bil+lowi+ness
bil+low+ing
bil+lowy
bill+poster
bill+posters
bill+posting
bill+sticker
bill+stickers
bill+sticking
bil+ly
bil+lies
bil+ly+can
bil+ly+cans
bi+lo+bate
bi+lobed
bil+tong
bima+nous
bi+manu+al
bim+bo

bim+bos *or*
bim+boes
bi+me+tal+lic
bi+met+al+lism
bi+met+al+list
bi+met+al+lists
bi+month+ly
bi+month+lies
bi+morph
bi+morphs
bin
bins
bins
bin+ning
binned
bi+na+ry
bi+na+ries
bi+nate
bi+nate+ly
bin+aural
bind
binds
binds
bind+ing
bound
bind+er
bind+ers
bind+ery
bind+eries
bindi-eye
bindi-eyes
bind+ing
bind+ings
bind+weed
bind+weeds
bine
bines
binge
binges
binges
bing+ing *or*
binge+ing
binged
Bing+en
bin+go
bin+gos
bin+man
bin+men
bin+na+cle
bin+na+cles
bin+ocu+lar
bin+ocu+lars
bi+no+mial
bi+no+mials
bi+no+mi+al+ly

bint
bints
bin+tu+rong
bin+tu+rongs
Binyon
bio
bio+as+say
bio+as+says
bio+as+says
bio+as+say+ing
bio+as+sayed
bio+as+tro+nau+
tics
Bío-Bío
bio+ceno+sis
bio+chemi+cal
bio+chem+ist
bio+chem+ists
bio+chem+is+try
bio+cid+al
bio+cide
bio+cides
bio+coeno+sis
bio+deg+ra+da+
bil+ity
bio+deg+ra+da+
bil+ities
bio+degrad+able
bio+en+gi+neer
bio+en+gi+
neers
bio+en+gi+neer+
ing
bio+eth+ics
bio+feed+back
bio+gen+esis
bio+genet+ic
bio+geneti+cal
bi+og+raph+er
bi+og+raph+ers
bio+graphi+cal
bi+og+ra+phy
bi+og+ra+phies
Bio+ko
bio+logi+cal
bio+logi+cals
bi+olo+gist
bi+olo+gists
bi+ol+ogy
bi+ol+ogies
bio+lu+mi+nes+
cence
bio+lu+mi+nes+
cent
bio+mass

bio+masses
bio+math+emat+
ics
bio+medi+cal
bio+medi+cine
bio+met+ric
bio+met+rics
bi+om+etry
bi+on+ic
bi+on+ics
bio+nomic
bio+nom+ics
bi+ono+mist
bi+ono+mists
bio+physi+cal
bio+physi+cal+ly
bio+physi+cist
bio+physi+cists
bio+phys+ics
bio+pic
bio+pics
bi+op+sy
bi+op+sies
bio+rhythm
bio+rhythms
bio+scope
bio+scopes
bi+os+co+py
bi+os+co+pies
bio+sphere
bio+syn+the+sis
bio+syn+thet+ic
bio+syn+theti+
cal+ly
bio+tech+nol+
ogy
bio+tech+nol+
ogies
bi+ot+ic
bio+tin
bi+par+ti+san
bi+par+ti+san+
ship
bi+par+tite
bi+par+tite+ly
bi+par+ti+tion
bi+par+ti+tions
bi+ped
bi+peds
bi+ped+al
bi+pin+nate
bi+pin+nate+ly
bi+plane
bi+planes
bi+po+lar

bi+prism
bi+prisms
bi+quad+rat+ic
bi+quad+rat+ics
bi+ra+cial
bi+ra+cial+ism
birch
birches
birches
birch+ing
birched
birch+en
bird
birds
bird+bath
bird+baths
bird-brained
bird+cage
bird+cages
bird-foot
bird-foots
birdie
birdies
bird+lime
bird+limes
bird+limes
bird+lim+ing
bird+limed
bird-nesting
bird+seed
bird's-eye
bird's-foot
bird's-foots
bird+shot
birds'-nesting
bird-watcher
bird-watchers
bird-watching
bi+refrin+gence
bi+refrin+gent
bi+reme
bi+remes
bi+ret+ta
bi+ret+tas
Birgitta
bi+ria+ni
bi+ria+nis
Birkbeck
Bir+ken+head
place name
Birkenhead
surname
birl
birls
birls

birl+ing
birled
Bir+ming+ham
Biro
Trademark
Biros
Bi+ro+bi+dzhan
birth
births
births
birth+ing
birthed
birth+day
birth+days
birth+mark
birth+marks
birth+place
birth+places
birth+right
birth+rights
birth+stone
birth+stones
Birtwistle
birya+ni
birya+nis
Bi+sa+yas
Bis+cay
bis+cuit
bis+cuits
bise
bises
bi+sect
bi+sects
bi+sect+ing
bi+sect+ed
bi+sec+tion
bi+sec+tions
bi+sec+tor
bi+sec+tors
bi+sex+ual
bi+sex+uals
bi+sexu+al+ity
bish+op
bish+ops
Bish+op Auck+
land
bish+op+ric
bish+op+rics
Bi+si+tun
Bisk
Bis+kra
Bis+ley
Bis+marck
place name
Bismarck

surname
bis+muth
bi+son
bi+son
bisque
bisques
Bis+sau
bi+sta+ble
bi+sta+bles
bis+ter
U.S.
bis+ters
bis+tort
bis+torts
bis+tou+ry
bis+tou+ries
bis+tre
bis+tres
bis+tro
bis+tros
bi+sul+phate
bi+sul+phates
bi+sul+phide
bi+sul+phides
Bi+su+tun
bit
bits
bits
bit+ting
bit+ted
bitch
bitches
bitches
bitch+ing
bitched
bitchi+ness
bitchy
bitchi+er
bitchi+est
bite
bites
bites
bit+ing
bit
bit+ten
bit+er
bit+ers
Bi+thynia
bit+ing
bit+ing+ly
Bi+to+la
Bi+tolj
bitt
bitts
bitts

bitt+ing
bitt+ed
bit+ten
bit+ter
bit+ters
bit+ter+er
bit+ter+est
bit+ter+ly
bit+tern
bit+terns
bit+ter+ness
bit+ters
bitter+sweet
bitter+sweets
bit+ti+ness
bit+ty
bit+ti+er
bit+ti+est
bi+tu+men
bi+tu+mens
bi+tu+mi+nise
bi+tu+mi+nises
bi+tu+mi+nis+
ing
bi+tu+mi+nised
bi+tu+mi+nize
bi+tu+mi+nizes
bi+tu+mi+niz+
ing
bi+tu+mi+nized
bi+tu+mi+nous
bi+va+len+cy
bi+va+len+cies
bi+va+lent
bi+valve
bi+valves
bivou+ac
bivou+acs
bivou+acs
bivou+ack+ing
bivou+acked
bi+week+ly
bi+week+lies
bi+year+ly
Biysk
biz
bi+zarre
bi+zarre+ness
Bi+zer+ta
Bi+zer+te
Bizet
Björ+ne+borg
blab
blabs
blabs

blab+bing
blabbed
blab+ber
blab+bers
blab+bers
blab+ber+ing
blab+bered
black
 blacks
 blacks
 black+ing
 blacked
 black+er
 black+est
Black
 Blacks
blacka+moor
 blacka+moors
black-and-blue
black-and-white
 black-and-
  whites
black+ball
 black+balls
 black+balls
 black+ball+ing
 black+balled
Blackbeard
black+berry
 black+berries
 black+berries
 black+berry+ing
 black+berried
black+bird
 black+birds
 black+birds
 black+bird+ing
 black+bird+ed
black+board
 black+boards
black+boy
 black+boys
black+buck
 black+bucks
Black+burn
black+butt
 black+butts
black+cap
 black+caps
black+cock
 black+cocks
black+cur+rant
 black+cur+rants
black+damp
 black+damps

black+en
 black+ens
 black+en+ing
 black+ened
Blackett
black+face
 black+faces
black+fish
 black+fish or
 black+fishes
black+fly
 black+flies
black+guard
 black+guards
 black+guards
 black+guard+ing
 black+guard+ed
 black+guard+ism
 black+guard+ly
black+head
 black+heads
Black+heath
black+ing
 black+ings
black+jack
 black+jacks
 black+jacks
 black+jack+ing
 black+jacked
black+leg
 black+legs
 black+legs
 black+leg+ging
 black+legged
black+list
 black+lists
 black+lists
 black+list+ing
 black+list+ed
black+mail
 black+mails
 black+mails
 black+mail+ing
 black+mailed
 black+mail+er
 black+mail+ers
black-market
 black-markets
 black-marketing
 black-marketed
black mar+ket
 noun
Blackmore
black+ness
black+out

black+outs
black out
 verb
Black+pool
Black+shirt
 Black+shirts
black+smith
 black+smiths
black+snake
 black+snakes
black+thorn
 black+thorns
black+top
 black+tops
Black+wood
 *bridge-playing
 term*
Blackwood
blad+der
 blad+ders
bladder+wort
 bladder+worts
bladder+wrack
 bladder+wracks
blad+dery
blade
 blades
blad+ed
blae+berry
 blae+berries
blag
 blags
 blags
blag+ging
 blagged
blag+ger
 blag+gers
Bla+go+vesh+
 chensk
blah
 blahs
blain
 blains
Blake
blam+able
blam+ably
blame
 blames
 blam+ing
 blamed
blame+able
blame+ably
blame+ful
blame+ful+ly
blame+ful+ness

blame+less
blame+less+ness
blame+worthi+
 ness
blame+worthy
Blanc
blanch
 blanches
 blanch+ing
 blanched
blanc+mange
 blanc+manges
Blanco
bland
 bland+er
 bland+est
blan+dish
 blan+dishes
 blan+dish+ing
 blan+dished
 blan+dish+ments
bland+ly
bland+ness
blank
 blanks
 blanks
 blank+ing
 blanked
 blank+er
 blank+est
blan+ket
 blan+kets
blank+ety
blank+ness
Blantyre-Limbe
blare
 blares
 blares
 blar+ing
 blared
blar+ney
 blar+neys
 blar+neys
 blar+ney+ing
 blar+neyed
bla+sé
blas+pheme
 blas+phemes
 blas+phem+ing
 blas+phemed
 blas+phem+er
 blas+phem+ers
blas+phe+mous
blas+phe+my
 blas+phe+mies

blast
blasts
blasts
blast+ing
blast+ed
blast+ed
blast+er
blast+ers
blast+off
blast+offs
blast off
verb
blas+to+sphere
blas+to+spheres
blas+tu+la
blas+tu+las *or*
blas+tu+lae
blas+tu+lar
blat
blats
bla+tan+cy
bla+tant
blath+er
blath+ers
blath+ers
blath+er+ing
blath+ered
blather+skite
blather+skites
Blavatsky
Blay+don
blaze
blazes
blazes
blaz+ing
blazed
blaz+er
blaz+ers
blazes
bla+zon
bla+zons
bla+zons
bla+zon+ing
bla+zoned
bla+zon+er
bla+zon+ers
bla+zon+ry
bla+zon+ries
bleach
bleaches
bleaches
bleach+ing
bleached
bleach+er
bleach+ers

bleak
bleak+er
bleak+est
bleak+ness
blear
blears
blear+ing
bleared
blear+er
blear+est
blear-eyed
bleari+ness
bleary
bleari+er
bleari+est
bleary-eyed
bleat
bleats
bleats
bleat+ing
bleat+ed
bleat+er
bleat+ers
bleat+ing
bleat+ings
bleb
blebs
bleed
bleeds
bleed+ing
bled
bleed+er
bleed+ers
bleed+ing
bleep
bleeps
bleeps
bleep+ing
bleeped
bleep+er
bleep+ers
blem+ish
blem+ishes
blem+ishes
blem+ish+ing
blem+ished
blench
blenches
blench+ing
blenched
blend
blends
blends
blend+ing
blend+ed

blende
blendes
blend+er
blend+ers
Blen+heim
Blen+heims
blen+ny
blen+nies
blent
blepha+ri+tis
Blériot
bles+bok
bles+boks *or*
bles+bok
bles+buck
bles+bucks *or*
bles+buck
bless
blesses
bless+ing
blessed *or*
blest
bless+ed
bless+ed+ly
bless+ed+ness
bless+ing
bless+ings
blest
bleth+er
bleth+ers
bleth+ers
bleth+er+ing
bleth+ered
blew
Bli+da
Bligh
blight
blights
blights
blight+ing
blight+ed
blight+er
blight+ers
Blighty
Blighties
bli+mey
blimp
blimps
blind
blinds
blinds
blind+ing
blind+ed
blind+er
blind+est

blind+er
blind+ers
blin+ders
blind+fold
blind+folds
blind+folds
blind+fold+ing
blind+fold+ed
blind+ly
blind+ness
blind+sight
blind+worm
blind+worms
blink
blinks
blinks
blink+ing
blinked
blink+er
blink+ers
blink+ers
blink+er+ing
blink+ered
blink+ered
blink+ers
blink+ing
blip
blips
blips
blip+ping
blipped
bliss
blisses
Bliss
bliss+ful
bliss+ful+ly
bliss+ful+ness
blis+ter
blis+ters
blis+ters
blis+ter+ing
blis+tered
blis+tered
blithe
blithe+ly
blithe+ness
blith+er+ing
blithe+some
blitz
blitzes
blitzes
blitz+ing
blitzed
Blitz
Blitzes

blitz+krieg
blitz+kriegs
Blixen
bliz+zard
bliz+zards
bloat
bloats
bloat+ing
bloat+ed
bloat+ed
bloat+er
bloat+ers
blob
blobs
bloc
blocs
Bloch
block
blocks
blocks
block+ing
blocked
block+ade
block+ades
block+ades
block+ad+ing
block+ad+ed
block+ad+er
block+ad+ers
block+age
block+ages
block+board
block+boards
block+bust+er
block+bust+ers
block+er
block+ers
block+head
block+heads
block+headed
block+house
block+houses
block+ish
block+ish+ly
Bloem+fon+tein
Blois
bloke
blokes
bloke+ish
bloke+ish+ness
blok+ish
blok+ish+ness
blond
masc.
blonds

blond+er
blond+est
blonde
blondes
blond+er
blond+est
blonde+ness
Blondin
blond+ness
blood
bloods
bloods
blood+ing
blood+ed
blood-and-
thunder
blood+curdling
blood+curdling+ly
blood+ed
blood+hound
blood+hounds
bloodi+ly
bloodi+ness
blood+less
blood+less+ly
blood+less+ness
blood-letting
blood-lettings
blood+line
blood+lines
blood+shed
blood+shot
blood+stain
blood+stains
blood+stained
blood+stock
blood+stone
blood+stones
blood+stream
blood+streams
blood+sucker
blood+suckers
blood+thirsti+ly
blood+thirsti+
ness
blood+thirsty
blood+thirsti+er
blood+thirsti+
est
blood+wood
blood+woods
bloody
blood+ies
bloody+ing
blood+ied

bloodi+er
bloodi+est
bloody-minded
bloom
blooms
blooms
bloom+ing
bloomed
bloom+er
bloom+ers
bloom+ers
Bloomfield
bloom+ing
Bloom+ing+ton
Blooms+bury
blos+som
blos+soms
blos+soms
blos+som+ing
blos+somed
blos+somy
blot
blots
blots
blot+ting
blot+ted
blotch
blotches
blotches
blotch+ing
blotched
blotchy
blotchi+er
blotchi+est
blot+ter
blot+ters
blot+ting
blot+to
blouse
blouses
blouses
blous+ing
bloused
blou+son
blou+sons
blow
blows
blows
blow+ing
blew
blown *or*
blowed
damned
blow-by-blow
blow-dry

blow-dries
blow-dries
blow-drying
blow-dried
blow+er
blow+ers
blow+fish
blow+fish *or*
blow+fishes
blow+fly
blow+flies
blow+gun
blow+guns
blow+hard
blow+hards
blow+hole
blow+holes
blow-in
Austral.
blow-ins
blow+lamp
blow+lamps
blown
blow+out
blow+outs
blow out
verb
blow+pipe
blow+pipes
blowsy
blowsi+er
blowsi+est
blow+torch
blow+torches
blow-up
blow-ups
blow up
verb
blowy
blowi+er
blowi+est
blowzy
blowzi+er
blowzi+est
blub
blubs
blub+bing
blubbed
blub+ber
blub+bers
blub+bers
blub+ber+ing
blub+bered
blub+ber+er
blub+ber+ers

blub +bery
Blücher
bludge
 bludges
 bludges
 bludg +ing
 bludged
bludg +eon
 bludg +eons
 bludg +eons
 bludg +eon +ing
 bludg +eoned
bludg +er
 bludg +ers
blue
 blues
 blu +er
 blu +est
Blue
Blue +beard
 Blue +beards
blue +bell
 blue +bells
blue +berry
 blue +berries
blue +bird
 blue +birds
blue-blooded
blue +book
 blue +books
blue +bottle
 blue +bottles
blue-collar
blue-eyed
blue +fish
 blue +fish or
 blue +fishes
blue +grass
 blue +grasses
blue-green
blue +ish
blue +jacket
 blue +jackets
blue +ness
blue-pencil
 blue-pencils
 blue-pencil +ling
 or
 blue-pencil +ing
 U.S.
 blue-pencilled
 or
 blue-penciled
 U.S.
blue pen +cil

blue pen +cils
blue +print
 blue +prints
 blue +prints
 blue +print +ing
 blue +print +ed
blue-ribbon
 adj.
blue rib +bon
 noun
 blues
blue-sky
blue +stocking
 blue +stockings
blue +stone
 blue +stones
blue +tit
 blue +tits
blu +ey
 blu +eys
bluff
 bluffs
 bluffs
 bluff +ing
 bluffed
 bluff +er
 bluff +est
bluff +er
 bluff +ers
bluff +ly
 bluff +ness
blu +ing
 blu +ings
blu +ish
Blum
Blunden
blun +der
 blun +ders
 blun +ders
 blun +der +ing
 blun +dered
blun +der +buss
 blun +der +
 busses
 blun +der +er
 blun +der +ers
 blun +der +ing
 blun +der +ings
blunge
 blunges
 blung +ing
 blunged
 blung +er
 blung +ers
blunt

blunts
blunt +ing
blunt +ed
blunt +er
blunt +est
Blunt
blunt +ly
blunt +ness
 blunt +nesses
blur
 blurs
 blurs
 blur +ring
 blurred
blurb
 blurbs
blurred
blur +ry
 blur +ri +er
 blur +ri +est
blurt
 blurts
 blurt +ing
 blurt +ed
blush
 blushes
 blushes
 blush +ing
 blushed
 blush +er
 blush +ers
blus +ter
 blus +ters
 blus +ters
 blus +ter +ing
 blus +tered
 blus +ter +er
 blus +ter +ers
 blus +tery
Blyth
Blyton
B-movie
 B-movies
bo
boa
 boas
Boadicea
boar
 boars
board
 boards
 boards
 board +ing
 board +ed
board +er

board +ers
board +ing
board +ings
board +room
 board +rooms
board +walk
 board +walks
boart
boast
 boasts
 boasts
 boast +ing
 boast +ed
boast +er
 boast +ers
boast +ful
 boast +ful +ly
 boast +ful +ness
 boast +ing
 boast +ings
boat
 boats
 boats
 boat +ing
 boat +ed
boat +er
 boat +ers
boat +hook
 boat +hooks
boat +house
 boat +houses
boat +ie
 boat +ies
 boat +ing
 boat +ings
boat +load
 boat +loads
boat +man
 boat +men
boat +swain
 boat +swains
Boa Vis +ta
Boaz
bob
 bobs
 bobs
 bob +bing
 bobbed
 bob
 shilling
 bob
bob +be +jaan
bob +be +jaans
bob +bin
 bob +bins

bob+ble
  bob+bles
bob+by
  bob+bies
bobby-dazzler
  bobby-dazzlers
bob+cat
  bob+cats
Bobo-Dioulas+so
bobo+link
  bobo+links
bo+bo+tie
  bo+bo+ties
Bo+bru+isk
Bo+bru+ysk
bob+sled
  bob+sleds
  bob+sleds
  bob+sled+ding
  bob+sled+ded
bob+sleigh
  bob+sleighs
  bob+sleighs
  bob+sleigh+ing
  bob+sleighed
bob+stay
  bob+stays
bobsy-die
bob+tail
  bob+tails
  bob+tails
  bob+tail+ing
  bob+tailed
bob+tailed
Boccaccio
Boccherini
Boche
Boches
Bo+chum
bock+edy
bod
  bods
bode
  bodes
  bod+ing
  bod+ed
bo+dega
  bo+degas
bode+ment
  bode+ments
Bo+den+see
bodge
  bodges
  bodg+ing
  bodged

bodgie
  bodgies
Bodh Gaya
Bodhidharma
Bo+dhi+satt+va
bod+ice
  bod+ices
bodi+less
bodi+ly
bod+kin
  bod+kins
Bod+min
body
  bodies
  bodies
  body+ing
  bod+ied
body+check
  body+checks
  body+checks
  body+check+ing
  body+checked
body+guard
  body+guards
body-line
body+suit
  body+suits
body-swerve
  body-swerves
  body-swerving
  body-swerved
body swerve
  body swerves
body+work
Boeo+tia
Boeo+tian
Boeo+tians
Boer
  Boers
boer+bul
  boer+buls
boere+mu+siek
boer+perd
  boer+perde
Boethius
bof+fin
  bof+fins
bof+fo
Bo+fors
bog
  bogs
bo+gan
  bo+gans
Bogarde
Bogart

bog+bean
  bog+beans
bo+gey
  bo+geys
bogey+man
  bogey+men
bog+gi+ness
bog+gle
  bog+gles
  bog+gling
  bog+gled
bog+gy
  bog+gi+er
  bog+gi+est
bo+gie
  bo+gies
bo+gle
  bo+gles
Bog+nor Re+gis
bo+gong
  bo+gongs
Bo+gor
Bo+go+tá
bog+trotter
  bog+trotters
bo+gus
bo+gus+ly
bo+gus+ness
bogy
  bogies
boh
Bo+hai
bo+hea
Bo+he+mia
Bo+he+mian
  Bo+he+mians
Bo+he+mi+an+ism
Böhm
Böh+men
Bo+hol
Bohr
boil
  boils
  boils
  boil+ing
  boiled
Boileau
boil+er
  boil+ers
boiler+maker
  boiler+makers
boiler+plate
  boiler+plates

Bois de Bou+logne
Boi+se
Bois-le-Duc
bois+ter+ous
bois+ter+ous+ly
bois+ter+ous+ness
Boito
Bo+kha+ra
bola
  bolas
Bo+lan
bo+las
  bo+lases
bold
  bold+er
  bold+est
bold+face
adj.
bold face
noun
bold+ly
bold+ness
Boldrewood
bole
  boles
bo+lero
  bo+leros
Boleyn
Bolingbroke
Bolivar
Bo+livia
Bo+liv+ian
  Bo+liv+ians
bo+li+via+no
  bo+li+via+nos
boll
  bolls
bol+lard
  bol+lards
bol+lock+ing
  bol+lock+ings
bol+locks
Bo+lo+gna
place name
Bologna
surname
Bo+lo+gnese
bo+lom+eter
  bo+lom+eters
bo+lo+met+ric
bo+lo+ney
  bo+lo+neys
Bol+she+vik

Bol+she+viks
or
Bol+she+vi+ki
Bol+she+vism
Bol+she+vist
Bol+she+vists
bol+shie
bol+shies
bol+shi+er
bol+shi+est
bol+shy
bol+shies
bol+shi+er
bol+shi+est
bol+ster
bol+sters
bol+sters
bol+ster+ing
bol+stered
bolt
bolts
bolts
bolt+ing
bolt+ed
Bolt
bolt+er
bolt+ers
Bol+ton
bolt+rope
bolt+ropes
Boltzmann
bo+lus
bo+luses
Bol+za+no
Bo+ma
bomb
bombs
bombs
bomb+ing
bombed
bom+bard
bom+bards
bom+bards
bom+bard+ing
bom+bard+ed
bom+bar+dier
bom+bar+diers
bom+bard+ment
bom+bard+
   ments
bom+ba+sine
bom+bast
bom+basts
bom+bas+tic

bom+bas+ti+cal+
   ly
Bom+bay
bom+ba+zine
bomb+er
bomb+ers
bom+bora
bom+boras
bomb+shell
bomb+shells
bomb+sight
bomb+sights
Bomu
Bon
Bons
Bona
bona fide
bona fi+des
Bon+aire
bo+nan+za
bo+nan+zas
Bonaparte
Bonapartes
Bonaventura
Bonaventure
bon+bon
bon+bons
bonce
bonces
bond
bonds
bonds
bond+ing
bond+ed
Bond
bond+age
bond+ages
bond+ed
bond+holder
bond+holders
Bondi
bond+ing
bond+ings
bond+maid
bond+maids
bond+servant
bond+servants
bonds+man
bonds+men
bone
bones
bones
bon+ing
boned
Bône

bone-dry
bone+head
bone+heads
bone+headed
bone+less
bon+er
bon+ers
bone+set+ter
bone+set+ters
bone+shaker
bone+shakers
bon+fire
bon+fires
bong
bongs
bongs
bong+ing
bonged
bon+go
antelope
bon+go *or*
bon+gos
bon+go
drum
bon+gos *or*
bon+goes
Bonhoeffer
bon+ho+mie
Boniface
Bonington
bo+ni+to
bo+ni+tos
bonk
bonks
bonk+ing
bonked
bonk+ers
bonk+ing
bonk+ings
bon mot
bons mots
Bonn
Bonnard
bon+net
bon+nets
bon+ny
bon+ni+er
bon+ni+est
Bon+ny
Bo+no+nia
bon+sai
bon+sai
bon+te+bok
bon+te+boks
or

bon+te+bok
bo+nus
bo+nuses
bon vi+vant
bons vi+vants
bon vi+veur
bons vi+veurs
bon vo+yage
bony
boni+er
boni+est
Bonynge
bonze
bonzes
bon+zer
boo
boos
boo+ing
booed
boob
boobs
boobs
boob+ing
boobed
boo+bi+al+la
boo+bi+al+las
boo-boo
boo-boos
boo+by
boo+bies
booby-trap
booby-traps
booby-trapping
booby-trapped
boo+by trap
noun
boo+dle
boo+dles
boo+gie
boo+gies
boo+gie+ing
boo+gied
boogie-woogie
boogie-woogies
boo+hai
boo+hais
boo+hoo
boo+hoos
boo+hoos
boo+hoo+ing
boo+hooed
book
books
books
book+ing

booked
book+binder
book+binders
book+bindery
book+binderies
book+bind+ing
book+case
book+cases
bookie
bookies
book+ing
book+ings
book+ish
book+ish+ness
book-keeper
book-keepers
book-keeping
book-learning
book+let
book+lets
book+maker
book+makers
book+making
book+mark
book+marks
book+marker
book+markers
book+plate
book+plates
book+stall
book+stalls
book+worm
book+worms
Boole
boom
booms
booms
boom+ing
boomed
boom+er
boom+ers
boom+er+ang
boom+er+angs
boom+er+angs
boom+er+ang+
  ing
boom+er+anged
boom+slang
boom+slangs
boon
boons
boon+docks
boong
boongs
boon+gary

boon+garies
boor
boors
boor+ish
boor+ish+ly
boor+ish+ness
boost
boosts
boosts
boost+ing
boost+ed
boost+er
boost+ers
boot
boots
boots
boot+ing
boot+ed
boot+black
boot+blacks
bootee
bootees
Boö+tes
booth
booths
Booth
boot+jack
boot+jacks
Boo+tle
boot+leg
boot+legs
boot+legs
boot+leg+ging
boot+legged
boot+leg+ger
boot+leg+gers
boot+less
boot+lick+er
boot+lick+ers
boot+strap
boot+straps
boot+straps
boot+strap+ping
boot+strapped
boo+ty
boo+ties
booze
boozes
boozes
booz+ing
boozed
booz+er
booz+ers
booze-up
booze-ups

boozy
boozi+er
boozi+est
bop
bops
bops
bop+ping
bopped
bo-peep
bo-peeps
Bo+phu+that+
  swa+na
bop+per
bop+pers
bora
boras
Bora Bora
bo+ra+cic
bor+age
bor+ages
bo+rate
bo+rates
bo+rates
bo+rat+ing
bo+rat+ed
bo+rax
bo+raxes or
bo+ra+ces
bo+ra+zon
bor+bo+ryg+mus
bor+bo+ryg+mi
Bor+deaux
Bor+deaux
bor+der
bor+ders
bor+ders
bor+der+ing
bor+dered
Bor+der
Bor+ders
bor+der+er
bor+der+ers
border+land
border+lands
border+line
border+lines
bore
bores
bores
bor+ing
bored
bo+real
Bo+real
Boreas
bored

bore+dom
boree
borees
bor+er
bor+ers
Borg
Bor+ger+hout
Borges
Borgia
Borgias
bo+ric
bor+ing
bor+lot+ti
Bormann
born
Born
born-again
borne
Bor+ne+an
Bor+ne+ans
Bor+neo
Born+holm
Bor+no
Borodin
Bo+ro+di+no
bo+ron
bo+ro+nia
bo+ro+nias
bor+ough
bor+oughs
Borromini
bor+row
bor+rows
bor+row+ing
bor+rowed
Borrow
bor+row+er
bor+row+ers
Bors
borsch
borscht
borsh
borshch
bor+stal
bor+stals
bort
bortz
bor+zoi
bor+zois
bos+cage
Bosch
bosch+bok
bosch+boks or
bosch+bok
Bose

bosh
  boshes
bosk
  bosks
bos+kage
bosky
  boski+er
  boski+est
bo's'n
  bo's'ns
Bos+nia
Bos+nian
bos+om
  bos+oms
  bos+oms
  bos+om+ing
  bos+omed
bos+omy
bos+on
  bos+ons
Bos+pho+rus
Bos+po+rus
boss
  bosses
  bosses
  boss+ing
  bossed
bos+sa nova
  bos+sa novas
bos+set
  bos+sets
bossi+ly
bossi+ness
bossy
  bossi+er
  bossi+est
Bos+ton
bo+sun
  bo+suns
Boswell
Bos+wel+lian
Bos+worth
bot
  bots
  bots
  bot+ting
  bot+ted
bo+tan+ic
bo+tan+ics
bo+tani+cal
bo+tani+cals
bo+tani+cal+ly
bota+nise
  bota+nises
  bota+nis+ing

bota+nised
bota+nist
  bota+nists
bota+nize
  bota+nizes
  bota+niz+ing
  bota+nized
bota+ny
  bota+nies
Bota+ny
botch
  botches
  botches
  botch+ing
  botched
  botch+er
  botch+ers
botchy
  botchi+er
  botchi+est
bot+fly
  bot+flies
both
Botha
Botham
  both+er
  both+ers
  both+ers
  both+er+ing
  both+ered
  both+era+tion
  both+er+some
Both+nia
Bothwell
bothy
  bothies
bo tree
  bo trees
Bot+swa+na
bott
  botts
Botticelli
bot+tle
  bot+tles
  bot+tles
  bot+tling
  bot+tled
bottle+brush
  bottle+brushes
bot+tled
bottle-feed
  bottle-feeds
  bottle-feeding
  bottle-fed
bottle+ful

bottle+fuls
bottle-jack
  bottle-jacks
bottle+neck
  bottle+necks
bottle+nose
bot+tler
  bot+tlers
bot+tom
  bot+toms
  bot+toms
  bot+tom+ing
  bot+tomed
  bot+tom+ing
  bot+tom+less
  bot+tom+ry
  bot+tom+ries
bottom-up
Bot+trop
botu+lin
  botu+lins
botu+lism
Boua+ké
Boucher
Bouches-du-
  Rhône
bou+clé
  bou+clés
Boudicca
Boudin
bou+doir
  bou+doirs
bouf+fant
Bou+gain+ville
  place name
Bougainville
  surname
bou+gain+vil+lea
  bou+gain+vil+
  leas
bough
  boughs
bought
bou+gie
  bou+gies
bouil+la+baisse
  bouil+la+baisses
bouil+lon
  bouil+lons
Boulanger
boul+der
  boul+ders
boule
  boules
  boules

boule+vard
  boule+vards
Boulez
boulle
  boulles
Bou+logne
Boulogne-Billan+
  court
boult
  boults
  boult+ing
  boult+ed
Boult
  boult+er
  boult+ers
Boulton
Boumédienne
bounce
  bounces
  bounces
  bounc+ing
  bounced
  bounc+er
  bounc+ers
  bounc+ing
bouncy
  bounci+er
  bounci+est
bound
  bounds
  bounds
  bound+ing
  bound+ed
bounda+ry
  bounda+ries
bound+en
bound+er
  bound+ers
bound+less
  bound+less+ly
bounds
boun+te+ous
  boun+te+ous+ly
  boun+te+ous+
  ness
boun+ti+ful
  boun+ti+ful+ly
boun+ty
  boun+ties
bou+quet
  bou+quets
bou+quet gar+ni
  bou+quets gar+
  nis
bour+bon

bour+bons
Bourbon
bour+don
bour+dons
bour+geois
bour+geois
bour+geoise
bour+geoises
bour+geoi+sie
bour+geoi+sies
bour+geon
bour+geons
bour+geons
bour+geon+ing
bour+geoned
Bourges
Bour+gogne
Bourguiba
bourn
bourns
bourne
bournes
Bourne+mouth
bour+rée
bour+rées
Bourse
Bourses
bou+stro+
  phedon
bout
bouts
bou+tique
bou+tiques
bou+ton+ni+ere
bou+ton+ni+
  eres
bou+zouki
bou+zoukis
bo+vine
Bov+ril
Trademark
bov+ver
bow
bows
bows
bow+ing
bowed
bowd+leri+sa+
  tion
bowd+leri+sa+
  tions
bowd+ler+ise
bowd+ler+ises
bowd+ler+is+
  ing

bowd+ler+ised
bowd+ler+ism
bowd+leri+za+
  tion
bowd+leri+za+
  tions
bowd+ler+ize
bowd+ler+izes
bowd+ler+iz+ing
bowd+ler+ized
bow+el
bow+els
Bowen
bow+er
bow+ers
bower+bird
bower+birds
Bow+ery
bow+fin
bow+fins
bow+head
bow+heads
bowie
Bowie
bowl
bowls
bowls
bowl+ing
bowled
bow-legged
bow+ler
bow+lers
Bowles
bowl+ful
bowl+fuls
bow+line
bow+lines
bowl+ing
bowls
bow+man
bow+men
bow+ser
bow+sers
bow+shot
bow+shots
bow+sprit
bow+sprits
bow+string
bow+strings
bow-wow
bow-wows
bow-wows
bow-wowing
bow-wowed
bow+yangs

box
boxes
boxes
box+ing
boxed
box+er
box+ers
Box+er
Box+ers
box+ers
box+ful
box+fuls
box+ing
box+like
box+room
box+rooms
box+wood
box+woods
boxy
boxi+er
boxi+est
boy
boys
Boyce
boy+cott
boy+cotts
boy+cotts
boy+cott+ing
boy+cott+ed
Boycott
Boyd
Boyer
boy+friend
boy+friends
boy+hood
boy+hoods
boy+ish
Boyle
Boyne
boyo
boyos
boysen+berry
boysen+berries
Boz
Boz+caa+da
Bo+zen
bra
bras
braai
braais
braai+vleis
braai+vleises
Bra+bant
Brabham
brace

braces
braces
brac+ing
braced
brace+let
brace+lets
brace+lets
brac+er
brac+ers
braces
bra+chial
bra+chi+ate
bra+chi+ates
bra+chi+at+ing
bra+chi+at+ed
bra+chia+tion
bra+chia+tions
bra+chio+pod
bra+chio+pods
bra+chio+saur+
  us
bra+chio+saur+
  uses
bra+chium
bra+chia
brachy+cephal+ic
brachy+cepha+ly
brac+ing
brac+ings
brack+en
brack+ens
brack+et
brack+ets
brack+ets
brack+et+ing
brack+et+ed
brack+ish
brack+ish+ness
Brack+nell
bract
bracts
bract+eal
brac+te+ate
brac+te+ole
brac+te+oles
bract+let
bract+lets
brad
brads
brad+awl
brad+awls
Bradbury
Brad+ford
Bradley
Bradman

Bradshaw
 Bradshaws
brady+car+dia
brae
 braes
Brae+mar
brag
 brags
 brags
 brag+ging
 bragged
Bra+ga
Brage
Bragg
brag+ga+do+cio
 brag+ga+do+
  cios
brag+gart
 brag+garts
brag+ger
 brag+gers
Bragi
Brahe
Brah+ma
 Brah+mas
Brah+man
 Brah+mans
Brah+man+ic
Brah+mani+cal
Brah+man+ism
Brah+man+ist
 Brah+man+ists
Brah+ma+pu+tra
Brah+min
 Brah+min or
Brah+mins
Brah+min+ism
Brah+min+ist
 Brah+min+ists
Brahms
braid
 braids
 braids
 braid+ing
 braid+ed
braid+er
 braid+ers
braid+ing
 braid+ings
Braille
 Brailles
 Brailles
 Braill+ing
 Brailled
brain

brains
brains
brain+ing
brained
brain+child
brain+children
brain+dead
brain death
Braine
braini+ness
brain+less
brain+pan
 brain+pans
brain+stem
 brain+stems
brain+storm
 brain+storms
brain+storming
 brain+stormings
brain-teaser
 brain-teasers
brain-twister
 brain-twisters
brain+wash
 brain+washes
brain+wash+ing
brain+washed
brain+wash+ing
 brain+wash+
  ings
brainy
braini+er
braini+est
braise
 braises
brais+ing
braised
brake
 brakes
 brakes
 brak+ing
 braked
brake-fade
 brake-fades
brake+less
brakes+man
 brakes+men
Brak+pan
Bramante
bram+ble
 bram+bles
 bram+bles
 bram+bling
 bram+bled
bram+bling

bram+blings
bram+bly
bram+bli+er
bram+bli+est
bran
Branagh
branch
 branches
 branches
 branch+ing
 branched
bran+chia
 bran+chiae
bran+chial
bran+chi+ate
branch+like
Brancusi
brand
 brands
 brands
 brand+ing
 brand+ed
Bran+den+burg
brand+er
 brand+ers
bran+dish
 bran+dishes
 bran+dishes
 bran+dish+ing
 bran+dished
bran+dish+er
 bran+dish+ers
brand+ling
 brand+lings
brand-new
Brando
Brandt
bran+dy
 bran+dies
Branson
brant
 brants or
 brant
Brant+ford
Braque
brash
 brash+er
 brash+est
 brash+ly
 brash+ness
brashy
 brashi+er
 brashi+est
bra+si+er
 bra+si+ers

Bra+sil
Bra+sília
Bra+şov
brass
 brasses
bras+sard
 bras+sards
bras+sart
 bras+sarts
bras+se+rie
 bras+se+ries
bras+si+ca
 bras+si+cas
brassie
 brassies
bras+siere
 bras+sieres
brassi+ly
brassi+ness
Brassó
brassy
 brassies
brassi+er
 brassi+est
brat
 brats
Bra+ti+sla+va
brat+pack
 brat+packs
brat+pack+er
 brat+pack+ers
Brattain
brat+tice
 brat+tices
Braun
Braun+schweig
bra+va+do
 bra+va+does
  or
 bra+va+dos
brave
 braves
 braves
 brav+ing
 braved
brav+er
 brav+est
brave+ly
brave+ness
brav+ery
bra+vo
 shout of
  appreciation
bra+vos
bra+vo

65

breeding

hired killer
bra+voes *or*
bra+vos
bra+vu+ra
braw
braw+er
braw+est
brawl
brawls
brawls
brawl+ing
brawled
brawl+er
brawl+ers
brawn
brawni+ness
brawny
brawni+er
brawni+est
bray
brays
brays
bray+ing
brayed
braze
brazes
braz+ing
brazed
bra+zen
bra+zens
bra+zen+ing
bra+zened
bra+zen+ly
bra+zen+ness
braz+er
braz+ers
bra+zi+er
bra+zi+ers
bra+zi+ery
bra+zi+eries
bra+zil
bra+zils
Bra+zil
Bra+zil+ian
Bra+zil+ians
Braz+za+ville
breach
breaches
breaches
breach+ing
breached
bread
breads
breads
bread+ing

bread+ed
bread-and-butter
adj.
bread and but+ter
noun
bread+basket
bread+baskets
bread+board
bread+boards
bread+fruit
bread+fruits *or*
bread+fruit
bread+line
bread+lines
breadth
breadths
breadth+ways
breadth+wise
bread+winner
bread+winners
break
breaks
breaks
break+ing
broke
bro+ken
break+able
break+ables
break+age
break+ages
break+away
break+aways
break away
verb
break-dance
break-dances
break-dancing
break-danced
break dance
noun
break danc+er
break danc+ers
break danc+ing
break+down
noun, adj.
break+downs
break down
verb
break+er
break+ers
break+even
noun, adj.
break even
verb
break+fast

break+fasts
break+fasts
break+fast+ing
break+fast+ed
break-in
break-ins
break in
verb
break+neck
break-out
break-outs
break out
verb
break+through
break+throughs
break through
verb
break-up
noun, adj.
break-ups
break up
verb
break+water
break+waters
bream
bream
bream
breams
bream+ing
breamed
breast
breasts
breasts
breast+ing
breast+ed
breast+bone
breast+bones
breast-feed
breast-feeds
breast-feeding
breast-fed
breast+pin
breast+pins
breast+plate
breast+plates
breast+stroke
breast+strokes
breast+work
breast+works
breath
breaths
breatha+lyse
breatha+lyses
breatha+lys+ing
breatha+lysed

Breatha+lys+er
Trademark
Breatha+lys+ers
breathe
breathes
breath+ing
breathed
breath+er
breath+ers
breathi+ly
breathi+ness
breath+ing
breath+ings
breath+less
breath+less+ly
breath+less+ness
breath+taking
breath+taking+ly
breathy
breathi+er
breathi+est
brec+cia
brec+cias
brec+ci+at+ed
Brecht
Brechtian
Brechtians
Breck+nock
Breck+nock+
shire
Brec+on
Brec+on+shire
bred
Bre+da
breech
breeches
breeches
breech+ing
breeched
breech+block
breech+blocks
breeches
breech+ing
breech+ings
breech-loader
breech-loaders
breech-loading
breed
breeds
breeds
breed+ing
bred
breed+er
breed+ers
breed+ing

breeze
breezes
breezes
breez+ing
breezed
breeze+way
breeze+ways
breezi+ly
breezi+ness
breezy
breezi+er
breezi+est
Bre+genz
Breiz
Bre+men
Brem+er+ha+ven
brems+strah+
  lung
Bren
Brendel
Brennan
brent
brents
Brent
Brenton
Brent+wood
Bre+scia
Bres+lau
Brest
Brest Li+tovsk
Bre+tagne
breth+ren
Bret+on
(person) from
  Brittany
Bret+ons
Breton
surname
Breuer
Breughel
breve
breves
bre+vet
bre+vets
bre+vets
bre+vet+ting
  or
bre+vet+ing
bre+vet+ted *or*
bre+vet+ed
brev+et+cy
brev+et+cies
brevia+ry
brevia+ries
brev+ity

brev+ities
brew
brews
brews
brew+ing
brewed
brew+er
brew+ers
brew+ery
brew+eries
brew+ing
brew+ings
Brezhnev
Brian
Brian Boru
Briand
bri+ar
bri+ars
Bri+ar+ean
Briareus
briar+root
briar+wood
bri+ary
bribe
bribes
bribes
brib+ing
bribed
brib+ery
brib+er+ies
bric-a-brac
brick
bricks
bricks
brick+ing
bricked
brick+bat
brickie
brickies
brick+layer
brick+layers
brick+laying
brick+work
brick+works
bricky
bricki+er
bricki+est
brick+yard
brick+yards
brid+al
bride
brides
Bride
bride+groom
bride+grooms

brides+maid
brides+maids
bridge
bridges
bridges
bridg+ing
bridged
Bridge
bridge+able
bridge+head
bridge+heads
Bridge+port
Bridget
Bridge+town
bridge+work
bridge+works
bridg+ing
Bridg+wa+ter
Bridie
bri+dle
bri+dles
bri+dles
bri+dling
bri+dled
Brie
brief
briefs
briefs
brief+ing
briefed
brief+er
brief+est
brief+case
brief+cases
brief+ing
brief+ings
brief+less
brief+ly
brief+ness
briefs
bri+er
bri+ers
brier+root
brier+wood
bri+ery
brig
brigs
bri+gade
bri+gades
bri+gades
bri+gad+ing
bri+gad+ed
briga+dier
briga+diers
briga+low

briga+lows
brig+and
brig+ands
brig+and+age
brig+and+ages
brig+and+ry
brig+and+ries
brig+an+tine
brig+an+tines
Briggs
Brig+house
place name
Brighouse
surname
bright
bright+er
bright+est
Bright
bright+en
bright+ens
bright+en+ing
bright+en+ed
bright+ly
bright+ness
Bright+on
bright+work
Brigid
brill
brills *or*
brill
bril+liance
bril+lian+cy
bril+liant
bril+liants
bril+lian+tine
bril+liant+ly
brim
brims
brims
brim+ming
brimmed
brim+ful
brim+full
brim+less
brim+stone
brim+stones
Brin+di+si
brin+dle
brin+dles
brin+dled
Brindley
brine
brines
brines
brin+ing

brined
bring
brings
bring+ing
brought
bring+er
bring+ers
brini+ness
brin+ish
brin+jal
brin+jals
brink
brinks
brink+man+ship
briny
brini+er
brini+est
brio
bri+oche
bri+oches
brio+ny
brio+nies
bri+quet
bri+quets
bri+quette
bri+quettes
Bris+bane
brisk
brisks
brisk+ing
brisked
brisk+er
brisk+est
bris+ket
bris+kets
brisk+ly
brisk+ness
bris+ling
bris+lings
bris+tle
bris+tles
bris+tles
bris+tling
bris+tled
bris+tly
bris+tli+er
bris+tli+est
Bris+tol
bris+tols
Brit
Brits
Brit+ain
Bri+tan+nia
Bri+tan+nias
Bri+tan+nic

britches
Briti+cism
Briti+cisms
Brit+ish
Brit+ish+er
Brit+ish+ers
Brit+ish+ism
Brit+ish+isms
Brit+ish+ness
Brit+on
Brit+ons
Brit+ta+ny
Britten
brit+tle
brit+tles
brit+tler
brit+tlest
brit+tle+ness
brit+tle+nesses
brittle-star
brittle-stars
Bri+xia
Brno
broach
broaches
broaches
broach+ing
broached
broad
broads
broad+er
broad+est
B-road
B-roads
broad+cast
broad+casts
broad+casts
broad+cast+ing
broad+cast or
broad+cast+ed
broad+cast+er
broad+cast+ers
broad+cast+ing
Broad-Church
adj.
Broad Church
noun
broad+cloth
broad+cloths
broad+en
broad+ens
broad+en+ing
broad+ened
broad-gauge
adj.

broad gauge
noun
broad-leaved
broad+loom
broad+looms
broad+ly
broad-minded
broad-minded+ly
broad-minded+
ness
Broads
broad+sheet
broad+sheets
broad+side
broad+sides
broad-spectrum
broad+sword
broad+swords
broad+tail
broad+tails
Broad+way
Brob+ding+na+gian
Broca
bro+cade
bro+cades
bro+cades
bro+cad+ing
bro+cad+ed
broc+co+li
broch
brochs
bro+chette
bro+chettes
bro+chure
bro+chures
brock
brocks
Brock+en
brock+et
brock+ets
bro+de+rie an+
glaise
Broeder+bond
Broglie
brogue
brogues
broil
broils
broils
broil+ing
broiled
broil+er
broil+ers
broke
bro+ken

broken-down
broken+hearted
broken+hearted+
ly
Bro+ken Hill
broken-in
bro+ken+ly
bro+ker
bro+kers
bro+ker+age
bro+ker+ages
brol+ga
brol+gas
brol+ly
brol+lies
Brom+berg
bro+meli+ad
bro+meli+ads
bro+mide
bro+mides
bro+mine
Brom+ley
Broms+grove
bron+chi
bron+chial
bron+chi+al+ly
bron+chi+ec+ta+
sis
bron+chio+lar
bron+chi+ole
bron+chi+oles
bron+chit+ic
bron+chi+tis
bron+cho
bron+chos
bron+cho+di+la+
tor
bron+cho+di+la+
tors
bron+cho+pneu+
mo+nia
bron+cho+pneu+
mo+nias
bron+cho+scope
bron+cho+
scopes
bron+chus
bron+chi
bron+co
bron+cos
Brontë
Brontës
bron+to+saur
bron+to+saurs
bron+to+sau+rus

bron +to +sau +
ruses
Bronx
bronze
bronzes
bronzes
bronz +ing
bronzed
bronz +ing
bronzy
brooch
brooches
brood
broods
broods
brood +ing
brood +ed
brood +er
brood +ers
broodi +ness
brood +ing
brood +ings
broody
broodi +er
broodi +est
brook
brooks
brooks
brook +ing
brooked
Brooke
brook +let
brook +lets
brook +lime
brook +limes
Brook +lyn
Brookner
Brooks
broom
brooms
brooms
broom +ing
broomed
Broome
broom +rape
broom +stick
broom +sticks
brose
broth
broths
broth +el
broth +els
broth +er
broth +ers or
breth +ren

Archaic
brother +hood
brother +hoods
brother-in-law
brothers-in-law
broth +er +li +ness
broth +er +ly
brough +am
brough +ams
brought
brou +ha +ha
brou +ha +has
brow
brows
brow +beat
brow +beats
brow +beat +ing
brow +beat
brow +beat +en
brown
browns
browns
brown +ing
browned
brown +er
brown +est
Brown
Browne
browned-off
Brown +ian
brownie
brownies
Brownie
Brownies
brown +ing
Browning
surname
Browning
gun
Brownings
brown +ish
brown +ness
brown +stone
brown +stones
browny
browse
browses
browses
brows +ing
browsed
brows +er
brows +ers
Broz
Brubeck
Bruce

bru +cel +lo +sis
Bruch
Bruckner
Brudenell
Bruegel
Brueghel
Bruges
Brug +ge
bru +in
bru +ins
bruise
bruises
bruises
bruis +ing
bruised
bruis +er
bruis +ers
bruit
bruits
bruits
bruit +ing
bruit +ed
brum +by
brum +bies
brume
brumes
Brum +ma +gem
Brummell
brunch
brunches
Brun +dis +ium
Bru +nei
Brunel
Brunelleschi
bru +nette
bru +nettes
Brunhild
Brünn
Brünnhilde
Bruno
Bruns +wick
brunt
brunts
Bru +sa
brush
brushes
brushes
brush +ing
brushed
brushed
brush +er
brush +ers
brush +mark
brush +marks
brush +off

brush +offs
brush off
verb
brush-up
brush-ups
brush up
verb
brush +wood
brush +work
brushy
brushi +er
brushi +est
brusque
brusque +ly
brusque +ness
Brus +sel
Brus +sels
Brus +sels sprout
Brus +sels
sprouts
brut
bru +tal
bru +tali +sa +tion
bru +tali +sa +
tions
bru +tal +ise
bru +tal +ises
bru +tal +is +ing
bru +tal +ised
bru +tal +ism
bru +tal +ity
bru +tal +ities
bru +tali +za +tion
bru +tali +za +
tions
bru +tal +ize
bru +tal +izes
bru +tal +iz +ing
bru +tal +ized
bru +tal +ly
brute
brutes
brut +ish
brut +ish +ly
brut +ish +ness
Brutus
Brux +elles
Bry +ansk
Brynhild
bryo +logi +cal
bry +olo +gist
bry +olo +gists
bry +ol +ogy
bryo +ny
bryo +nies

bryo+phyte
bryo+phytes
bryo+phyt+ic
bryo+zoan
bryo+zoans
Bry+thon+ic
Brześć nad Bu+
giem
B-side
B-sides
bub+ble
bub+bles
bub+bles
bub+bling
bub+bled
bub+bly
bub+bli+er
bub+bli+est
Buber
bubo
buboes
bu+bon+ic
Bu+ca+ra+man+
ga
buc+cal
buc+ca+neer
buc+ca+neers
buc+ca+neers
buc+ca+neer+
ing
buc+ca+neered
buc+ci+na+tor
buc+ci+na+tors
Buchan
Buchanan
Bu+cha+rest
Buch+en+wald
Büchner
buck
bucks
bucks
buck+ing
bucked
Buck
buck+bean
buck+beans
buck+board
buck+boards
buck+er
buck+ers
buck+et
buck+ets
buck+ets
buck+et+ing
buck+et+ed

buck+et+ful
buck+et+fuls
buck+et+fuls
buck+eye
buck+eyes
buck+horn
buck+horns
Buck+ing+ham
in place names
Buckingham
surname
Buck+ing+ham+
shire
buck+jump+er
buck+jump+ers
Buckland
buck+le
buck+les
buck+les
buck+ling
buck+led
buck+ler
buck+lers
Buck+ley's
chance
bucko
buckoes
buck+ram
buck+rams
buck+shee
buck+skin
buck+skins
buck+thorn
buck+thorns
buck+tooth
buck+teeth
buck+wheat
bu+col+ic
bu+col+ics
bu+coli+cal
bu+coli+cal+ly
Bu+co+vi+na
Bu+cu+reşti
bud
buds
buds
bud+ding
bud+ded
Bu+da+pest
Buddha
Bud+dha Gaya
Buddh Gaya
Bud+dhism
Bud+dhist
Bud+dhists
bud+dleia

bud+dleias
bud+dy
bud+dies
bud+dies
bud+dy+ing
bud+died
budge
budges
budges
budg+ing
budged
budg+eri+gar
budg+eri+gars
budg+et
budg+ets
budg+ets
budg+et+ing
budg+et+ed
Budg+et
Budg+ets
budg+et+ary
budgie
budgies
Bue+na+ven+tu+
ra
Bue+na Vis+ta
Bueno
Bue+nos Aires
buff
buffs
buffs
buff+ing
buffed
buf+fa+lo
buf+fa+loes *or*
buf+fa+los
Buf+fa+lo
buff+er
buff+ers
buff+ers
buff+er+ing
buff+ered
buf+fet
buf+fets
buf+fets
buf+fet+ing
buf+fet+ed
Buffet
buf+fet+ing
buf+fet+ings
buffle+head
buffle+heads
buf+fo
buf+fi *or*
buf+fos

buf+foon
buf+foons
buf+foon+ery
bug
bugs
bugs
bug+ging
bugged
Bug
buga+boo
buga+boos
Bu+gan+da
Bugatti
bug+bear
bug+bears
bug+ger
bug+gers
bug+gers
bug+ger+ing
bug+gered
bug+gery
bug+gy
bug+gies
bug+gi+er
bug+gi+est
bu+gle
bu+gles
bu+gles
bu+gling
bu+gled
bu+gler
bu+glers
bu+gloss
bu+gong
bu+gongs
buhl
buhls
build
builds
builds
build+ing
built
build+er
build+ers
build+ing
build+ings
build-up
build-ups
build up
verb
built
built-in
built-ins
built-up
Bui+ten+zorg

Bu+jum+bu+ra
Bu+ka+vu
Bu+kha+ra
Bu+ko+vi+na
Bu+la+wa+yo
bulb
 bulbs
bul+bil
 bul+bils
bulb+ous
bul+bul
 bul+buls
Bulgakov
Bulganin
Bul+garia
Bul+gar+ian
 Bul+gar+ians
bulge
 bulges
 bulges
bulg+ing
 bulged
bulg+ing
bul+gur
bulgy
bu+limia
bulk
 bulks
 bulks
 bulk+ing
 bulked
bulk+head
 bulk+heads
bulki+ly
bulki+ness
bulky
 bulki+er
 bulki+est
bull
 bulls
 bulls
 bull+ing
 bulled
Bull
Bul+la+ma+kanka
bull+dog
 bull+dogs
bull+doze
 bull+dozes
 bull+doz+ing
 bull+dozed
bull+doz+er
 bull+doz+ers
bul+let
 bul+lets

bul+letin
bul+letins
bul+letins
bul+letin+ing
bul+letined
bullet+proof
bullet+proofs
bullet+proof+ing
bullet+proofed
bullet+wood
bull+fight
bull+fights
bull+fighter
bull+fighters
bull+fighting
bull+finch
bull+finches
bull+frog
bull+frogs
bull+head
bull+heads
bull-headed
bull-headed+ly
bull-headed+ness
bull+horn
bull+horns
bul+lion
bull+ish
bull+ish+ness
bull-necked
bull+ock
bull+ocks
bull+ocks
bull+ock+ing
bull+ocked
bull+ocky
bull+ockies
bull+ring
bull+rings
bull+roarer
bull+roarers
bull's-eye
bull's-eyes
bull+shit
bull+shits
bull+shits
bull+shit+ting
bull+shit+ted
 or
bull+shit
bul+ly
bul+lies
bul+lies
bul+ly+ing
bul+lied

bully-off
bully-offs
bully+rag
bully+rags
bully+rag+ging
bully+ragged
Bülow
bul+rush
bul+rushes
bul+wark
bul+warks
bul+warks
bul+wark+ing
bul+warked
Bulwer-Lytton
bum
bums
bums
bum+ming
bummed
bum+bailiff
bum+bailiffs
bum+ble
bum+bles
bum+bling
bum+bled
bumble+bee
bumble+bees
bum+bler
bum+blers
bum+bling
bum+blings
bumf
bum+ma+lo
bum+ma+lo
bum+mer
bum+mers
bump
bumps
bumps
bump+ing
bumped
bump+er
bump+ers
bumph
bumpi+ly
bumpi+ness
bump+kin
bump+kins
bump+tious
bump+tious+ly
bump+tious+
 ness
bumpy
bumpi+er

bumpi+est
bun
buns
bunch
bunches
bunches
bunch+ing
bunched
bunchy
bunchi+er
bunchi+est
bun+combe
Bun+da+berg
Bun+del+khand
bun+dle
bun+dles
bun+dles
bun+dling
bun+dled
bun+dler
bun+dlers
bung
bungs
bungs
bung+ing
bunged
bun+ga+low
bun+ga+lows
bung+hole
bung+holes
bun+gle
bun+gles
bun+gles
bun+gling
bun+gled
bun+gler
bun+glers
bun+gling
bun+ion
bun+ions
bunk
bunks
bunks
bunk+ing
bunked
bun+ker
bun+kers
bun+kers
bun+ker+ing
bun+kered
bunk+house
bunk+houses
bun+kum
bun+net
bun+nets

bun+ny
  bun+nies
Bunsen
surname
Bun+sen burn+er
  Bun+sen burn+
    ers
bunt+ing
bunt+line
  bunt+lines
Buñuel
bunya
  bunyas
bunya-bunya
  bunya-bunyas
Bunyan
bun+yip
  bun+yips
Buonaparte
Buonarroti
buoy
  buoys
  buoys
  buoy+ing
  buoyed
buoy+an+cy
  buoy+an+cies
buoy+ant
bu+pi+va+caine
bur
  burs
  burs
  bur+ring
  burred
Bu+rai+da
Bu+ray+dah
Burbage
bur+ble
  bur+bles
  bur+bles
  bur+bling
  bur+bled
bur+bler
  bur+blers
bur+bot
  bur+bots *or*
  bur+bot
Burckhardt
bur+den
  bur+dens
  bur+dens
  bur+den+ing
  bur+dened
bur+den+some
bur+dock

bur+docks
bu+reau
  bu+reaus *or*
  bu+reaux
bu+reau+cra+cy
  bu+reau+cra+
    cies
bu+reau+crat
  bu+reau+crats
bu+reau+crat+ic
bu+reau+crati+
  cal+ly
bu+reau+crati+sa+
  tion
bu+reau+cra+tise
  bu+reau+cra+
    tises
bu+reau+cra+tis+
  ing
bu+reau+cra+
  tised
bu+reau+crati+za+
  tion
bu+reau+cra+tize
bu+reau+cra+
  tizes
bu+reau+cra+tiz+
  ing
bu+reau+cra+
  tized
bu+ret
  U.S.
bu+rets
bu+rette
  bu+rettes
burg
  burgs
burg+age
Bur+gas
Bur+gen+land
bur+geon
  bur+geons
  bur+geons
  bur+geon+ing
  bur+geoned
burg+er
  burg+ers
bur+gess
  bur+gesses
Burgess
burgh
  burghs
burgh+al
burgh+er
  burgh+ers

Burghley
  surname
Burgh+ley
  place name
bur+glar
  bur+glars
bur+glari+ous
bur+gla+ry
  bur+gla+ries
bur+gle
  bur+gles
  bur+gling
  bur+gled
bur+go+mas+ter
  bur+go+mas+
    ters
Burgos
Burgoyne
Bur+gun+dian
  Bur+gun+dians
Bur+gun+dy
  Bur+gun+dies
bur+hel
  bur+hels
bur+ial
  bur+ials
bu+rin
  bu+rins
burk
  burks
Burke
Burkina-Faso
burl
  burls
  burls
burl+ing
  burled
bur+lap
  bur+laps
Burleigh
burl+er
  burl+ers
bur+lesk
  U.S.
  bur+lesks
bur+lesque
  bur+lesques
  bur+lesques
  bur+lesqu+ing
  bur+lesqued
bur+les+quer
  bur+les+quers
bur+ley
  bur+leys
  bur+leys

bur+ley+ing
bur+leyed
bur+li+ness
Bur+ling+ton
bur+ly
  bur+li+er
  bur+li+est
Bur+ma
Bur+man
Bur+mese
  Bur+mese
burn
  burns
  burns
  burn+ing
  burnt *or*
  burned
Burne-Jones
burn+er
  burn+ers
bur+net
  bur+nets
Burnet
Burnett
Burney
burn+ing
bur+nish
  bur+nishes
  bur+nishes
  bur+nish+ing
  bur+nished
burn+ish+er
  burn+ish+ers
Burn+ley
bur+noose
  U.S.
  bur+nooses
bur+nous
  bur+nouses
bur+nouse
  bur+nouses
burn+out
  burn+outs
burn out
  verb
Burns
burnt
burp
  burps
  burps
burp+ing
burped
burr
  burrs
  burrs

burr+ing
burred
Burren
bur+ri+to
bur+ri+tos
bur+ro
bur+ros
Burroughs
bur+row
bur+rows
bur+rows
bur+row+ing
bur+rowed
bur+row+er
bur+row+ers
bur+ry
bur+ri+er
bur+ri+est
bur+sa
bur+sae *or*
bur+sas
Bur+sa
bur+sal
bur+sar
bur+sars
bur+sar+ial
bur+sar+ship
bur+sar+ships
bur+sa+ry
bur+sa+ries
bur+si+tis
burst
bursts
bursts
burst+ing
burst
bur+then
bur+thens
bur+then+some
bur+ton
bur+tons
Burton
Burton-upon-
Trent
Bu+run+di
bury
buries
bury+ing
bur+ied
Bury
Bur+yat
Bur+yats
Bury St Ed+
munds
bus

buses *or*
bus+ses
buses *or*
bus+ses
bus+ing *or*
bus+sing
bused *or*
bussed
bus+bar
bus+bars
bus+by
bus+bies
Busby
bush
bushes
bushes
bush+ing
bushed
Bush
bush+baby
bush+babies
bush+buck
bush+bucks *or*
bush+buck
bushed
Bu+shehr
bush+el
bush+els
bush+fire
bush+fires
bush+fly
bush+flies
Bu+shi+do
bushie
bushies
bushi+ly
bushi+ness
bush+ing
Bu+shire
bush-line
bush-lines
bush+man
bush+men
Bush+man
Bush+man *or*
Bush+men
bush+master
bush+masters
bush+ranger
bush+rangers
Bush+veld
bush+whack
bush+whacks
bush+whack+
ing

bush+whacked
bush+whacker
bush+whackers
bushy
bushi+er
bushi+est
bushy
bushies
busi+ly
busi+ness
busi+nesses
business+like
business+man
business+men
business+woman
business+
women
busk
busks
busk+ing
busked
busk+er
busk+ers
bus+kin
bus+kins
Bus+ra
Bus+rah
buss
busses
busses
buss+ing
bussed
Buss
bust
busts
bust+ing
bust+ed *or*
bust
bus+tard
bus+tards
bust+ier
bust+iers
bus+tle
bus+tles
bus+tles
bus+tling
bus+tling
bus+tled
bust-up
bust-ups
busy
busies
busy+ing
bus+ied
busi+er

busi+est
busy+body
busy+bodies
busy+ness
but
buts
bu+ta+di+ene
bu+tane
bu+ta+nol
bu+ta+none
butch
butches
butch+er
butch+est
butch+er
butch+ers
butch+ers
butch+er+ing
butch+ered
butcher+bird
butcher+birds
butcher's-broom
butch+ery
butch+eries
Bute
Butenandt
Bute+shire
Buthelezi
but+ler
but+lers
Butler
but+lery
but+leries
butt
butts
butts
butt+ing
butt+ed
butte
buttes
butt+er
person or thing
that butts
butt+ers
but+ter
spread made
from cream
but+ters
but+ters
but+ter+ing
but+tered
but+ter+bur
but+ter+burs
butter+cup
butter+cups

butter+fat
Butterfield
butter+fingered
butter+fingers
butter+fingers
butter+fish *or*
butter+fishes
butter+flies
butter+fly
butter+flies
but+teri+ness
but+teri+nesses
But+ter+mere
butter+milk
butter+nut
butter+nuts
butter+scotch
butter+scotches
butter+wort
butter+worts
Butterworth
but+tery
but+teries
but+tock
but+tocks
but+ton
but+tons
but+tons
but+ton+ing
but+toned
but+ton+er
but+ton+ers
button+hole
button+holes
button+holes
button+hol+ing
button+holed

button+hook
button+hooks
but+ton+less
but+tress
but+tresses
but+tresses
but+tress+ing
but+tressed
but+ty
but+ties
Bu+tung
bu+tyl
bux+om
bux+om+ness
Buxtehude
Bux+ton
buy
buys
buys
buy+ing
bought
buy-back
buy-backs
buy+er
buy+ers
buy-in
buy-ins
buy in
verb
buy-out
buy-outs
buy out
verb
buzz
buzzes
buzzes
buzz+ing
buzzed

buz+zard
buz+zards
buzz+er
buzz+ers
bwa+na
by
byes
by-and-by
noun
by and by
adv.
Byd+goszcz
bye
byes
bye-bye
bye-byes
bye-byes
bye-election
bye-elections
bye-law
bye-laws
by-election
by-elections
Byelgorod-
Dnestrov+ski
Bye+lo+rus+sian
Bye+lo+rus+
sians
Bye+lo+stok
Bye+lo+vo
by+gone
by+gones
by+law
by+laws
by-line
by-lines
Byng
BYO

BYOs
by+pass
by+passes
by+passes
by+pass+ing
by+passed *or*
by+past
by+path
by+paths
by-play
by-plays
by-product
by-products
Byrd
byre
byres
by+road
by+roads
Byron
By+ron+ic
By+roni+cal+ly
By+ron+ism
bys+si+no+sis
by+stander
by+standers
byte
bytes
By+tom
by+way
by+ways
by+word
by+words
Byz+an+tine
Byz+an+tines
Byz+an+tin+ism
By+zan+tium

C

c
c's
C
C's *or*
Cs
Caa+ba
cab
  cabs
ca+bal
  ca+bals
  ca+bals
  ca+bal+ling
  ca+balled
  ca+ba+la
  ca+ba+las
Caballé
ca+bal+le+ro
  ca+bal+le+ros
ca+ba+na
  ca+ba+nas
caba+ret
  caba+rets
cab+bage
  cab+bages
  cab+ba+la
  cab+ba+las
cab+ba+lism
cab+ba+list
  cab+ba+lists
  cab+ba+lis+tic
cab+bie
  cab+bies
cab+by
  cab+bies
ca+ber
  ca+bers
Cab+er+net Sau+
  vi+gnon
  Cab+er+net Sau+
  vi+gnons
cab+in
  cab+ins
  cab+ins
  cab+in+ing
  cab+ined

Ca+bin+da
cabi+net
  cabi+nets
cabinet-maker
  cabinet-makers
cabinet-making
cabinet+work
ca+ble
  ca+bles
  ca+ble+gram
  ca+ble+grams
cabo+chon
  cabo+chons
ca+boo+dle
ca+boose
  ca+booses
Cabot
cabo+tage
Cabral
cab+ri+ole
  cab+ri+oles
cab+rio+let
  cab+rio+lets
ca+cao
  ca+caos
cacha+lot
  cacha+lots
cache
  caches
  caches
  cach+ing
  cached
cache+pot
  cache+pots
ca+chet
  ca+chets
ca+chexia
ca+chexy
cach+in+nate
  cach+in+nates
  cach+in+nat+ing
  cach+in+nat+ed
cach+in+na+tion
  cach+in+na+
  tions

cach+in+na+tory
ca+chou
  ca+chous
ca+cique
  ca+ciques
cack-handed
cack+le
  cack+les
  cack+les
  cack+ling
  cack+led
caco+dyl
caco+ethes
caco+graph+ic
ca+cog+ra+phy
ca+copho+nous
ca+copho+ny
  ca+copho+nies
cac+ta+ceous
cac+tus
  cac+tuses *or*
  cac+ti
ca+cu+mi+nal
  ca+cu+mi+nals
cad
  cads
ca+dav+er
  ca+dav+ers
  ca+dav+er+ic
  ca+dav+er+ous
  ca+dav+er+ous+
  ness
Cadbury
CAD+CAM
cad+die
  cad+dies
  cad+dies
  cad+dy+ing
  cad+died
cad+dis
cad+dish
cad+dy
  cad+dies
  cad+dies
  cad+dy+ing

cad+died
Cade
ca+dence
  ca+dences
ca+den+cy
  ca+den+cies
ca+den+za
  ca+den+zas
ca+det
  ca+dets
  ca+det+ship
  ca+det+ships
cadge
  cadges
  cadges
  cadg+ing
  cadged
cadg+er
  cadg+ers
cadi
  ca+dis
Cá+diz
Cad+mean
cad+mium
Cadmus
ca+dre
  ca+dres
ca+du+ceus
  ca+du+cei
ca+du+cous
Cadwalader
cae+cal
cae+cil+ian
  cae+cil+ians
cae+cum
  cae+ca
Cædmon
Cae+lian
Caen
Cae+no+zo+ic
Caer+nar+fon
Caer+nar+von
Caer+nar+von+
  shire
Caer+phil+ly

Caesar
  Caesars
Cae+sar+augus+
  ta
Caesa+rea
Cae+sar+ean
Cae+sar+ian
cae+si+ous
cae+sium
cae+su+ra
  cae+su+ras or
  cae+su+rae
cae+su+ral
Caetano
café
  cafés
café au lait
caf+eteria
  caf+eterias
caff
  caffs
caf+fein
caf+feine
caf+tan
  caf+tans
cage
  cages
  cages
  cag+ing
  caged
Cage
cag+ey
  cagi+er
  cagi+est
  cagi+ness
Ca+glia+ri
Cagliari
Cagney
ca+goule
  ca+goules
cagy
  cagi+er
  cagi+est
ca+hoots
Caiaphas
cai+man
  cai+mans
Cain
Caine
Cai+no+zo+ic
caïque
  caïques
Cai+rene
cairn
  cairns

cairn+gorm
cairn+gorms
Cai+ro
cais+son
cais+sons
Caith+ness
cai+tiff
cai+tiffs
Caius
ca+jole
ca+joles
ca+jol+ing
ca+joled
ca+jole+ment
ca+jole+ments
ca+jol+er
ca+jol+ers
ca+jol+ery
ca+jol+eries
cake
cakes
cakes
cak+ing
caked
cake+walk
cake+walks
Cala+bar
cala+bash
cala+bashes
cala+boose
cala+booses
cala+bre+se
Ca+lab+ria
Ca+lab+ri+an
Ca+lab+ri+ans
Cal+ais
cala+man+der
cala+mine
cala+mint
cala+mints
ca+lami+tous
ca+lam+ity
ca+lam+ities
Calamity Jane
cala+mus
cala+mi
cal+an+dria
cal+an+drias
ca+lash
ca+lashes
cal+ca+neum
cal+ca+nei
cal+ca+neus
cal+ca+nei
cal+car+eous

cal+ceo+lar+ia
cal+ceo+lar+ias
cal+ces
cal+cif+er+ol
cal+cif+er+ous
cal+ci+fi+ca+tion
cal+ci+fi+ca+
  tions
cal+ci+fy
cal+ci+fies
cal+ci+fy+ing
cal+ci+fied
cal+ci+na+tion
cal+ci+na+tions
cal+cine
cal+cines
cal+cin+ing
cal+cined
cal+cite
cal+cium
calc+spar
cal+cu+labil+ity
cal+cu+lable
cal+cu+lably
cal+cu+late
cal+cu+lates
cal+cu+lat+ing
cal+cu+lat+ed
cal+cu+lat+ed
cal+cu+lat+ing
cal+cu+lat+ing+ly
cal+cu+la+tion
cal+cu+la+tions
cal+cu+la+tive
cal+cu+la+tor
cal+cu+la+tors
cal+cu+lous
cal+cu+lus
cal+cu+luses
  or
cal+cu+li
Cal+cut+ta
Calder
cal+de+ra
cal+de+ras
cal+dron
cal+drons
Caldwell
ca+lèche
ca+lèches
Cal+edo+nia
Cal+edo+nian
Cal+edo+nians
cal+efa+cient
cal+efa+cients

cal+en+dar
cal+en+dars
cal+en+dars
cal+en+dar+ing
cal+en+dared
cal+en+der
cal+en+ders
cal+en+ders
cal+en+der+ing
cal+en+dered
ca+len+dric
ca+len+dri+cal
cal+ends
ca+len+du+la
ca+len+du+las
calf
calves
calf+skin
calf+skins
Cal+ga+ry
Cal+gon
  Trademark
cali+ber
  U.S.
cali+bers
cali+bered
  U.S.
cali+brate
cali+brates
cali+brat+ing
cali+brat+ed
cali+bra+tion
cali+bra+tor
cali+bra+tors
cali+bre
cali+bres
cali+bred
cali+ces
cali+co
cali+coes or
cali+cos
ca+lif
ca+lifs
Cali+for+nia
Cali+for+nian
Cali+for+nians
cali+for+nium
Caligula
cali+pash
cali+pee
cali+per
  U.S.
cali+pers
cali+pers
cali+per+ing

cali+pered
ca+liph
ca+liphs
ca+li+phate
ca+li+phates
cal+is+then+ic
cal+is+then+ics
ca+lix
cali+ces
calk
calks
calks
calk+ing
calked
cal+kin
cal+kins
cal+kins
cal+kin+ning
cal+kinned
call
calls
calls
call+ing
called
cal+la
cal+las
Callaghan
Cal+lane+tics
Trademark
Callas
call+boy
call+boys
call+er
call+ers
Callicrates
cal+lig+ra+pher
cal+lig+ra+phers
cal+li+graph+ic
cal+lig+ra+phist
cal+lig+ra+
 phists
cal+lig+ra+phy
Callimachus
call+ing
call+ings
cal+lio+pe
cal+lio+pes
Cal+lio+pe
cal+li+pash
cal+li+per
cal+li+pers
cal+li+pers
cal+li+per+ing
cal+li+pered
cal+liste+mon

cal+liste+mons
cal+lis+then+ic
cal+lis+then+ics
Callisto
Cal+lis+to
cal+lose
cal+los+ity
cal+los+ities
cal+lous
cal+louses
cal+lous+ing
cal+loused
cal+lous+ly
cal+lous+ness
cal+low
cal+low+ness
call-up
call-ups
call up
verb
cal+lus
cal+luses
calm
calms
calms
calm+ing
calmed
calm+er
calm+est
cal+ma+tive
calm+ly
calm+ness
calo+mel
Cal+or
Trademark
calo+rie
calo+ries
Calo+rie
Calo+ries
calo+rif+ic
calo+rifi+cal+ly
calo+rim+eter
calo+rim+eters
calo+ri+met+ric
calo+rim+etry
cal+or+ize
cal+or+izes
cal+or+iz+ing
cal+or+ized
calo+ry
calo+ries
Cal+pe
calque
calques

calu+met
calu+mets
ca+lum+ni+ate
ca+lum+ni+ates
ca+lum+ni+at+
 ing
ca+lum+ni+at+
 ed
ca+lum+niation
ca+lum+ni+ator
ca+lum+ni+
 ators
ca+lum+nia+tory
ca+lum+ni+ous
cal+um+ny
cal+um+nies
Cal+va+dos
Cal+va+ry
calve
calves
calv+ing
calved
Calvert
calves
Calvin
Cal+vin+ism
Cal+vin+ist
Cal+vin+ists
Cal+vin+is+tic
Cal+vin+is+tic+al
Calvino
calx
calxes *or*
cal+ces
caly+ces
ca+lyp+so
ca+lyp+sos
Calypso
ca+lyx
ca+lyxes *or*
caly+ces
cal+zone
cam
cams
Cam
Ca+ma+güey
ca+ma+ra+derie
Ca+margue
cama+ril+la
cama+ril+las
Cam+bay
cam+ber
cam+bers
cam+bers
cam+ber+ing

cam+bered
cam+bial
cam+bium
cam+biums *or*
 cam+bia
Cam+bo+dia
Cam+bo+dian
Cam+bo+dians
Camborne-
 Redruth
Cam+brai
Cam+bria
Cam+brian
Cam+brians
cam+bric
Cam+bridge
Cam+bridge+
 shire
Cambyses
cam+cord+er
cam+cord+ers
Cam+den
Camden
came
cam+el
cam+els
cam+el+eer
cam+el+eers
ca+mel+lia
ca+mel+lias
ca+melo+pard
ca+melo+pards
Cam+elot
Cam+em+bert
cameo
cameos
cam+era
cam+eras *or*
cam+erae
camera+man
camera+men
cam+era ob+scu+
 ra
cam+era ob+scu+
 ras
Cameron
Cam+eroon
Cam+eroons
Came+roun
cami+knick+ers
cami+sole
cami+soles
camo+mile
camo+miles
camou+flage

camou+flages
camou+flag+ing
camou+flaged
camp
camps
camps
camp+ing
camped
Cam+pa+gna
cam+paign
cam+paigns
cam+paigns
cam+paign+ing
cam+paigned
cam+paign+er
cam+paign+ers
Campanella
Cam+pa+nia
cam+pa+ni+le
cam+pa+ni+les
cam+pa+nolo+
ger
cam+pa+nolo+
gers
cam+pa+no+logi+
cal
cam+pa+nolo+
gist
cam+pa+nolo+
gists
cam+pa+nol+ogy
cam+panu+la
cam+panu+las
Campbell
Campbell-
Bannerman
camp-drafting
camp-draftings
Cam+peche
camp+er
camp+ers
Campese
cam+phor
cam+pho+rate
cam+pho+rates
cam+pho+rat+
ing
cam+pho+rat+
ed
cam+phor+ic
Campin
camp+ing
camp+ings
cam+pi+on
cam+pi+ons

Campion
Cam+po+bel+lo
Cam+po+for+mi+
do
Cam+po For+mio
Cam+po Gran+de
cam+pus
cam+puses
campy
cam+pylo+bac+
ter
Cam Ranh
cam+shaft
cam+shafts
Ca+mu+lo+du+
num
Camus
can
cans
cans
can+ning
canned
Cana
Ca+naan
Ca+naan+ite
Ca+naan+ites
Cana+da
Ca+na+dian
Ca+na+dians
Ca+na+di+an+
ism
ca+naille
cana+kin
cana+kins
ca+nal
ca+nals
ca+nals
ca+nal+ling or
ca+nal+ing
U.S.
ca+nalled or
ca+naled
U.S.
Canaletto
cana+licu+lar
cana+licu+late
cana+licu+lus
cana+licu+li
cana+li+sa+tion
cana+lise
cana+lises
cana+lis+ing
cana+lised
cana+li+za+tion
cana+lize

cana+lizes
cana+liz+ing
cana+lized
cana+pé
cana+pés
Ca+na+ra
ca+nard
ca+nards
Ca+naries
ca+nary
ca+naries
ca+nas+ta
can+as+ter
Ca+nav+er+al
Can+ber+ra
can+can
can+cans
can+cel
can+cels
can+cel+ling or
can+cel+ing
U.S.
can+celled or
can+celed
U.S.
can+cel+er
U.S.
can+cel+ers
can+cel+late
can+cel+lat+ed
can+cel+la+tion
can+cel+la+
tions
can+cel+ler
can+cel+lers
can+cer
can+cers
Can+cer
can+cero+phobia
can+cer+ous
can+croid
can+croids
can+de+la
can+de+las
Candela
can+de+la+bra
can+de+la+bras
can+de+la+brum
can+de+la+bra
or
can+de+la+
brums
can+des+cence
can+des+cent
Can+dia

can+did
can+dida
can+didas
can+di+da+cy
can+di+da+cies
can+di+date
can+di+dates
can+di+da+ture
can+di+da+
tures
can+did+ly
can+did+ness
can+died
can+dle
can+dles
can+dles
can+dling
can+dled
candle+berry
candle+berries
candle+holder
candle+holders
candle+light
Candle+mas
candle+nut
candle+nuts
candle+power
can+dler
can+dlers
candle+stick
candle+sticks
candle+wick
candle+wicks
Candolle
can+dor
U.S.
can+dour
can+dy
can+dies
can+dies
can+dy+ing
can+died
candy+floss
candy-striped
candy+tuft
candy+tufts
cane
canes
canes
can+ing
caned
Ca+nea
cane+brake
cane+brakes
can+er

can+ers
Canetti
can+ful
can+fuls
cang
cangs
cangue
cangues
cani+kin
cani+kins
ca+nine
ca+nines
can+ing
can+ings
Ca+nis
can+is+ter
can+is+ters
can+ker
can+kers
can+kers
can+ker+ing
can+kered
can+ker+ous
canker+worm
canker+worms
can+na
can+nas
can+na+bis
Can+nae
canned
can+nel
can+nel+lo+ni
can+ne+lo+ni
can+ner
can+ners
can+nery
can+neries
Cannes
can+ni+bal
can+ni+bals
can+ni+bali+sa+
tion
can+ni+bal+ise
can+ni+bal+ises
can+ni+bal+is+
ing
can+ni+bal+ised
can+ni+bal+ism
can+ni+bali+za+
tion
can+ni+bal+ize
can+ni+bal+izes
can+ni+bal+iz+
ing
can+ni+bal+ized

can+ni+kin
can+ni+kins
can+ni+ly
can+ni+ness
can+ning
can+nings
Canning
Can+nock
can+non
can+nons or
can+non
can+nons
can+non+ing
can+noned
can+non+ade
can+non+ades
can+non+ades
can+non+ad+ing
can+non+ad+ed
cannon+ball
cannon+balls
cannon+balls
cannon+ball+ing
cannon+balled
can+non+eer
can+non+eers
can+not
can+nu+la
can+nu+las or
can+nu+lae
can+ny
can+ni+er
can+ni+est
ca+noe
ca+noes
ca+noes
ca+noe+ing
ca+noed
ca+noe+ist
ca+noe+ists
can+on
can+ons
ca+ñon
ca+ñons
ca+non+ic
ca+noni+cal
ca+noni+cal+ly
ca+noni+cals
can+on+ic+ity
can+on+ic+ities
can+oni+sa+tion
can+oni+sa+
tions
can+on+ise
can+on+ises

can+on+is+ing
can+on+ised
can+on+ist
can+on+ists
can+oni+za+tion
can+oni+za+
tions
can+on+ize
can+on+izes
can+on+iz+ing
can+on+ized
can+on+ry
can+on+ries
ca+noo+dle
ca+noo+dles
ca+noo+dling
ca+noo+dled
Ca+no+pic
Ca+no+pus
cano+py
cano+pies
cano+pies
cano+py+ing
cano+pied
canst
cant
cants
cants
cant+ing
cant+ed
can't
can+ta+bi+le
can+ta+bi+les
Can+ta+brig+ian
Can+ta+brig+
ians
Can+tal
can+ta+loup
can+ta+loups
can+ta+loupe
can+ta+loupes
can+tan+ker+ous
can+tan+ker+ous+
ly
can+tan+ker+ous+
ness
can+ta+ta
can+ta+tas
can+teen
can+teens
Canteloube
can+ter
can+ters
can+ters
can+ter+ing

can+tered
Can+ter+bury
can+thari+des
can+thus
can+thi
can+ti+cle
can+ti+cles
can+ti+lena
can+ti+lever
can+ti+levers
can+til+late
can+til+lates
can+til+lat+ing
can+til+lat+ed
can+til+la+tion
can+til+la+tions
cant+ing+ly
can+tle
can+tles
can+to
can+tos
can+to fer+mo
can+ton
can+tons
can+tons
can+ton+ing
can+toned
Can+ton
can+ton+al
Can+ton+ese
Can+ton+ese
can+ton+ment
can+ton+ments
can+tor
can+tors
can+to+ri+al
can+tor+is
can+tus fir+mus
Ca+nuck
Ca+nucks
canu+la
canu+las or
canu+lae
Canute
can+vas
can+vases
canvas+back
canvas+backs
or
canvas+back
can+vass
can+vasses
can+vasses
can+vass+ing
can+vassed

can+vass+er
can+vass+ers
can+yon
can+yons
can+zo+net
can+zo+nets
can+zo+net+ta
can+zo+net+tas
caou+tchouc
cap
caps
caps
cap+ping
capped
Capa
ca+pa+bil+ity
ca+pa+bil+ities
Capablanca
ca+pable
ca+pable+ness
ca+pably
ca+pa+cious
ca+pa+cious+ly
ca+pa+cious+
ness
ca+paci+tance
ca+paci+tive
ca+paci+tor
ca+paci+tors
ca+pac+ity
ca+pac+ities
cap-a-pie
ca+pari+son
ca+pari+sons
ca+pari+sons
ca+pari+son+ing
ca+pari+soned
cape
capes
Cape
cap+elin
cap+elins
ca+pell+meis+ter
ca+pell+meis+
ters
ca+per
ca+pers
ca+pers
ca+per+ing
ca+pered
cap+er+cail+lie
cap+er+cail+lies
cap+er+cail+zie
cap+er+cail+zies
Ca+per+na+um

ca+pers
Capet
Ca+petian
Ca+petians
Cap-Haitien
ca+pi+as
ca+pi+ases
cap+il+lar+ity
ca+pil+lary
ca+pil+laries
capi+tal
capi+tals
capi+tali+sa+tion
capi+tali+sa+
tions
capi+tal+ise
capi+tal+ises
capi+tal+is+ing
capi+tal+ised
capi+tal+ism
capi+tal+ist
capi+tal+ists
capi+tal+ist+ic
capi+tali+za+tion
capi+tali+za+
tions
capi+tal+ize
capi+tal+izes
capi+tal+iz+ing
capi+tal+ized
capi+tal+ly
capi+ta+tion
capi+ta+tions
Capi+tol
Capi+to+line
ca+pitu+late
ca+pitu+lates
ca+pitu+lat+ing
ca+pitu+lat+ed
ca+pitu+la+tion
ca+pitu+la+tions
ca+pitu+la+tor
ca+pitu+la+tors
ca+pitu+la+tory
ca+pitu+lum
ca+pitu+la
cap+lin
cap+lins
capo
capos
ca+pon
ca+pons
Capone
ca+pon+ise
ca+pon+ises

ca+pon+is+ing
ca+pon+ised
ca+pon+ize
ca+pon+izes
ca+pon+iz+ing
ca+pon+ized
Capo+ret+to
capo tas+to
capo tas+tos
ca+pote
ca+potes
Capote
Capp
Cap+pa+do+cia
Cap+pa+do+cian
Cap+pa+do+
cians
cap+puc+ci+no
cap+puc+ci+nos
Capra
Ca+pri
ca+pric+cio
ca+pric+cios
or
ca+pric+ci
ca+pric+cio+so
ca+price
ca+prices
ca+pri+cious
ca+pri+cious+ly
Cap+ri+corn
Cap+ri+corns
Cap+ri+cor+nia
Cap+ri+cor+nus
cap+rine
cap+ri+ole
cap+ri+oles
cap+ri+oles
cap+ri+ol+ing
cap+ri+oled
cap+si+cum
cap+si+cums
cap+sid
cap+sids
cap+siz+al
cap+siz+als
cap+size
cap+sizes
cap+siz+ing
cap+sized
cap+stan
cap+stans
cap+stone
cap+stones
cap+su+late

cap+sule
cap+sules
cap+sul+ise
cap+sul+ises
cap+sul+is+ing
cap+sul+ised
cap+sul+ize
cap+sul+izes
cap+sul+iz+ing
cap+sul+ized
cap+tain
cap+tains
cap+tains
cap+tain+ing
cap+tained
cap+tain+cy
cap+tain+cies
cap+tain+ship
cap+tain+ships
cap+tion
cap+tions
cap+tions
cap+tion+ing
cap+tioned
cap+tious
cap+tious+ly
cap+tious+ness
cap+ti+vate
cap+ti+vates
cap+ti+vat+ing
cap+ti+vat+ed
cap+ti+va+tion
cap+ti+va+tions
cap+tive
cap+tives
cap+tiv+ity
cap+tiv+ities
cap+tor
cap+tors
cap+ture
cap+tures
cap+tures
cap+tur+ing
cap+tured
cap+tur+er
cap+tur+ers
Capua
Capuana
capu+chin
capu+chins
Capu+chin
Capu+chins
capy+ba+ra
capy+ba+ras
Ca+que+tá

car
cars
cara+bi+neer
cara+bi+neers
cara+bi+ner
cara+bi+ners
cara+bi+nier
cara+bi+niers
cara+cal
cara+cals
Caracalla
ca+ra+ca+ra
ca+ra+ca+ras
Ca+ra+cas
cara+col
cara+cols
cara+cols
cara+col+ing
cara+coled
cara+cole
cara+coles
cara+coles
cara+col+ing
cara+coled
Caractacus
cara+cul
Caradoc
ca+rafe
ca+rafes
cara+geen
ca+ram+bo+la
ca+ram+bo+las
cara+mel
cara+mels
cara+mel+ise
cara+mel+ises
cara+mel+is+ing
cara+mel+ised
cara+mel+ize
cara+mel+izes
cara+mel+iz+ing
cara+mel+ized
cara+pace
car+at
car+ats
Caratacus
Caravaggio
cara+van
cara+vans
cara+vans
cara+van+ning
cara+vanned
cara+van+sa+ry
cara+van+sa+
  ries

cara+van+se+rai
cara+van+se+
  rais
cara+vel
cara+vels
cara+way
cara+ways
car+bide
car+bine
car+bines
car+bi+neer
car+bi+neers
car+bo+cy+clic
car+bo+hy+drate
car+bo+hy+
  drates
car+bon
car+bons
carbon-14
car+bo+na+
  ceous
car+bo+nade
car+bo+nades
car+bo+na+do
car+bo+na+dos
  or
car+bo+na+
  does
car+bon+ate
car+bon+ates
car+bon+ates
car+bon+at+ing
car+bon+at+ed
car+bon+ette
car+bon+ettes
car+bon+ic
carbonic-acid
  adj.
car+bon+if+er+
  ous
Car+bon+if+er+
  ous
car+boni+sa+tion
car+boni+sa+
  tions
car+bon+ise
car+bon+ises
car+bon+is+ing
car+bon+ised
car+boni+za+tion
car+boni+za+
  tions
car+bon+ize
car+bon+izes
car+bon+iz+ing

car+bon+ized
Car+bo+run+dum
  Trademark
Car+bo+run+
  dums
car+boy
car+boys
car+bun+cle
car+bun+cles
car+bun+cu+lar
car+bu+ra+tion
car+bu+ra+tions
car+bu+ret
car+bu+rets
car+bu+ret+ting
car+bu+ret+ted
car+bu+retor
  U.S.
car+bu+retors
car+bu+ret+ter
car+bu+ret+ters
car+bu+ret+tor
car+bu+ret+tors
car+ca+jou
car+ca+jous
car+case
car+cases
car+cass
car+casses
Car+cas+sonne
car+cino+gen
car+cino+gens
car+cino+gene+
  sis
car+cino+gen+ic
car+ci+no+ma
car+ci+no+mas
  or
car+ci+no+ma+
  ta
card
cards
cards
card+ing
card+ed
car+da+mom
car+da+moms
car+da+mum
car+da+mums
card+board
card-carrying
car+di+ac
car+di+acs
cardie
cardies

Car+diff
car+di+gan
car+di+gans
Car+di+gan
Car+di+gan+shire
Cardin
car+di+nal
car+di+nals
car+di+nal+ate
car+di+nal+ates
car+di+nal+ly
car+di+nal+ship
car+di+nal+
  ships
card-index
card-indexes
card-indexing
card-indexed
card in+dex
  noun
card+ing
card+ings
car+dio+cen+te+
  sis
car+dio+gram
car+dio+grams
car+dio+graph
car+dio+graphs
car+di+og+ra+
  pher
car+di+og+ra+
  phers
car+di+og+ra+
  phy
car+di+olo+gist
car+di+olo+
  gists
car+di+ol+ogy
car+dio+ple+gia
car+dio+ple+
  gias
car+dio+vas+cu+
  lar
car+doon
car+doons
cards
card+sharp
card+sharps
card+sharper
card+sharpers
Cardus
cardy
cardies
care
cares

cares	cari+ca+tur+ing	car+na+tions	carou+sel
car+ing	cari+ca+tured	car+nau+ba	carou+sels
cared	cari+ca+tur+ist	car+nau+bas	ca+rous+er
ca+reen	cari+ca+tur+ists	Carné	ca+rous+ers
ca+reens	cari+es	Carnegie	carp
ca+reen+ing	cari+es	car+nel+ian	carp *or*
ca+reened	ca+ril+lon	car+nel+ians	carps
ca+reen+age	ca+ril+lons	car+net	carps
ca+reen+ages	ca+ri+na	car+nets	carp+ing
ca+reer	ca+ri+nae *or*	Car+nio+la	carped
ca+reers	ca+ri+nas	car+ni+val	Carpaccio
ca+reers	cari+nate	car+ni+vals	car+pal
ca+reer+ing	cari+nat+ed	car+ni+vore	car+pals
ca+reered	car+ing	car+ni+vores	Car+pa+thians
ca+reer+ist	Ca+rin+thia	car+nivo+rous	Carpatho-Ukraine
ca+reer+ists	cario+ca	car+nivo+rous+	car+pe diem
care+free	cario+cas	ness	car+pel
care+free+ness	cario+gen+ic	Carnot	car+pels
care+ful	cari+ole	Caro	car+pel+lary
care+ful+ly	cari+oles	car+ob	Car+pen+ta+ria
care+ful+ness	cari+ose	car+obs	car+pen+ter
care+less	cari+ous	car+ol	car+pen+ters
care+less+ly	carl	car+ols	car+pen+ters
care+less+ness	carls	car+ols	car+pen+ter+ing
Carême	carle	car+ol+ling *or*	car+pen+tered
car+er	carles	car+ol+ing	Carpenter
car+ers	Car+lisle	*U.S.*	Carpentier
ca+ress	Carlos	car+olled *or*	car+pen+try
ca+resses	Carlota	car+oled	carp+er
ca+resses	Car+lov+ingian	*U.S.*	carp+ers
ca+ress+ing	Car+lov+ingians	Caro+lean	car+pet
ca+ressed	Car+low	Caro+li+na	car+pets
car+et	Carls+bad	Caro+li+nas	car+pets
car+ets	Carlyle	Caro+line	car+pet+ing
care+taker	car+ma+gnole	Caro+lin+gian	car+peted
care+takers	car+ma+gnoles	Caro+lin+gians	carpet+bag
Carew	Car+mar+then	Caro+lin+ian	carpet+bags
care+worn	Car+mar+then+	Caro+lin+ians	carpet+bag+ger
Carey	shire	car+om	carpet+bag+
car+go	Car+mel	car+oms	gers
car+goes *or*	Car+mel+ite	ca+rot+enoid	car+pet+ing
car+gos	Car+mel+ites	ca+rot+enoids	carpet-sweeper
U.S.	Carmichael	ca+rot+id	carpet-sweepers
Car+ib	car+mina+tive	ca+rot+ids	carp+ing
Car+ibs *or*	car+mina+tives	caro+tin	car+port
Car+ib	car+mine	caro+tins	car+ports
Car+ib+bean	Car+nac	ca+roti+noid	car+pus
Car+ib+bees	car+nage	ca+roti+noids	car+pi
Cari+boo	car+nal	ca+rous+al	Carracci
cari+bou	car+nal+ity	ca+rous+als	car+rack
cari+bous *or*	car+nal+ities	ca+rouse	car+racks
cari+bou	car+nal+ly	ca+rouses	car+ra+geen
cari+ca+ture	Carnap	ca+rouses	car+ra+gheen
cari+ca+tures	Car+nar+von	ca+rous+ing	Car+ra+ra
cari+ca+tures	car+na+tion	ca+roused	car+rel

car+rels
Carrel
car+rell
car+rells
Carreras
car+riage
car+riages
carriage+way
carriage+ways
Car+rick+fer+gus
car+ri+er
car+ri+ers
Carrington
car+ri+ole
car+ri+oles
car+ri+on
Carroll
car+rot
car+rots
car+roty
car+rou+sel
car+rou+sels
car+ry
car+ries
car+ry+ing
car+ried
carry+all
carry+alls
carry+cot
carry+cots
carry-forward
carry-forwards
car+ry for+ward
verb
carrying-on
carryings-on
carry-on
carry-ons
car+ry on
verb
carry-out
carry-outs
car+ry out
verb
carry-over
carry-overs
car+ry over
verb
carse
carses
car+sick
car+sick+ness
Carson
surname
Car+son

place name
Car+stensz
cart
carts
carts
cart+ing
cart+ed
cart+age
Car+ta+gena
carte blanche
cartes blanches
car+tel
car+tels
cart+er
cart+ers
Carter
Carteret
Car+tesian
Car+tesi+an+ism
Car+thage
Car+tha+gin+ian
Car+tha+gin+ians
cart+horse
cart+horses
Car+thu+sian
Car+thu+sians
Cartier
Cartier-Bresson
car+ti+lage
car+ti+lagi+nous
Cartland
cart+load
cart+loads
car+to+gram
car+to+grams
car+tog+ra+pher
car+tog+ra+phers
car+to+graph+ic
car+to+graphi+cal
car+tog+ra+phy
car+ton
car+tons
car+toon
car+toons
car+toon+ist
car+toon+ists
car+touch
car+touches
car+touche
car+touches
car+tridge
car+tridges

cart+wheel
cart+wheels
Cartwright
car+un+cle
car+un+cles
ca+run+cu+lar
ca+run+cu+lous
Caruso
carve
carves
carv+ing
carved
car+vel
car+vels
carvel-built
carv+en
carv+er
carv+ers
car+very
car+veries
carve-up
carve-ups
carve up
verb
carv+ing
carv+ings
Cary
cary+at+id
cary+at+ids *or*
cary+ati+des
Casa+blan+ca
Casals
Casanova
Casanovas
cas+bah
cas+bahs
cas+cade
cas+cades
cas+cades
cas+cad+ing
cas+cad+ed
cas+ca+ra
cas+ca+ras
cas+ca+ra sa+gra+da
cas+ca+ra sa+gra+das
case
cases
cases
cas+ing
cased
case+book
case+books
case-harden

case-hardens
case-harden+ing
case-hardened
ca+sein
case+mate
case+mates
case+ment
case+ments
Casement
ca+seous
ca+sern
ca+serns
ca+serne
ca+sernes
Ca+ser+ta
case+work
case+worker
case+workers
case+worm
case+worms
cash
cash
Cash
cash+able
cash-and-carry
cash-and-carries
cash-book
cash-books
cash+ew
cash+ews
cash+ier
cash+iers
cash+iers
cash+ier+ing
cash+iered
cash+mere
Cash+mere
cash-point
cash-points
cas+ing
cas+ings
ca+si+no
ca+si+nos
cask
casks
cas+ket
cas+kets
Caspar
casque
casques
casqued
Cassandra
Cassandras
Cassatt
cas+sa+va

cas+sa+vas
Cas+sel
cas+se+role
cas+se+roles
cas+se+roles
cas+se+rol+ing
cas+se+roled
cas+sette
cas+settes
cas+sia
cas+sias
Cassini
cas+si+no
Cassiodorus
Cassiopeia
Cassirer
cas+sis
cas+sit+er+ite
Cassius Longinus
Cassivelaunus
cas+sock
cas+socks
Casson
cas+so+wary
cas+so+waries
cast
casts
casts
cast+ing
cast
Cas+ta+lia
Cas+ta+lian
cas+ta+nets
cast+away
cast+aways
cast away
verb
caste
castes
Cas+tel+lam+ma+
re di Sta+bia
cas+tel+lan
cas+tel+lans
cas+tel+lat+ed
cas+tel+la+tion
cas+tel+la+tions
cast+er
cast+ers
cas+ti+gate
cas+ti+gates
cas+ti+gat+ing
cas+ti+gat+ed
cas+ti+ga+tion
cas+ti+ga+tions
cas+ti+ga+tor

cas+ti+ga+tors
Castiglione
Cas+tile
Cas+til+ian
Cas+til+ians
Cas+ti+lla
Cas+ti+lla la Vie+
ja
cast+ing
cast+ings
cast-iron
cas+tle
cas+tles
cas+tles
cas+tling
cas+tled
Cas+tle+bar
Castlereagh
Castner
cast-off
cas+tor
cas+tors
Cas+tor
castor-oil
cas+trate
cas+trates
cas+trat+ing
cas+trat+ed
cas+tra+tion
cas+tra+tions
cas+tra+to
cas+tra+ti or
cas+tra+tos
Cas+tries
Castro
cas+ual
cas+uals
casu+ali+sa+tion
casu+ali+sa+
tions
casu+ali+za+tion
casu+ali+za+
tions
casu+al+ly
casu+al+ness
casu+al+ty
casu+al+ties
casua+ri+na
casua+ri+nas
casu+ist
casu+ists
casu+is+tic
casu+is+ti+cal
casu+ist+ry
casu+ist+ries

cat
cats
cats
cat+ting
cat+ted
cata+bol+ic
ca+tabo+lism
ca+tabo+lisms
cata+chre+sis
cata+chres+tic
cata+clysm
cata+clysms
cata+clys+mal
cata+clys+mic
cata+clys+mi+cal+
ly
cata+comb
cata+combs
ca+tad+ro+mous
cata+falque
cata+falques
Cata+lan
Cata+lans
cata+lep+sy
cata+lep+tic
cata+log
U.S.
cata+logs
cata+logs
cata+log+ing
cata+loged
cata+logue
cata+logues
cata+logues
cata+logu+ing
cata+logued
cata+logu+er
cata+logu+ers
Cata+lo+nia
ca+tal+pa
ca+tal+pas
cata+lyse
cata+lyses
cata+lys+ing
cata+lysed
ca+taly+sis
ca+taly+ses
cata+lyst
cata+lysts
cata+lyt+ic
cata+lyze
cata+lyzes
cata+lyz+ing
cata+lyzed
cata+ma+ran

cata+ma+rans
cata+mite
cata+mites
cata+mount
cata+mounts
cata+moun+tain
cata+moun+
tains
cat+an+an+che
cat+an+an+ches
Ca+ta+nia
cata+plec+tic
cata+plexy
cata+pult
cata+pults
cata+pults
cata+pult+ing
cata+pult+ed
cata+ract
cata+racts
ca+tarrh
ca+tarrh+al
cat+arrh+ine
cat+arrh+ines
ca+tas+tro+phe
ca+tas+tro+
phes
cata+stroph+ic
cata+strophi+cal+
ly
ca+tas+tro+
phism
cata+to+nia
cata+ton+ic
cat+bird
cat+birds
cat+boat
cat+boats
cat+call
cat+calls
cat+calls
cat+call+ing
cat+called
catch
catches
catch+ing
caught
catch-22
catch-22s
catch+able
catch-as-catch-
can
catch+fly
catch+flies
catch+ing

catch+ment
catch+ments
catch+penny
catch+weight
catch+word
catch+words
catchy
catchi+er
catchi+est
cat+echet+ic
cate+cheti+cal
cat+echeti+cal+ly
cat+echise
cat+echises
cat+echis+ing
cat+echised
cate+chis+er
cate+chis+ers
cat+echism
cat+echis+mal
cat+echist
cat+echists
cat+echize
cat+echizes
cat+echiz+ing
cat+echized
cate+chiz+er
cate+chiz+ers
cat+echu
cat+echu+men
cat+echu+mens
cat+ego+rial
cat+egor+ic
cat+egori+cal
cat+egori+cal+ly
cat+ego+ri+sa+tion
cat+ego+ri+sa+tions
cat+ego+rise
cat+ego+rises
cat+ego+ris+ing
cat+ego+rised
cat+ego+ri+za+tion
cat+ego+ri+za+tions
cat+ego+rize
cat+ego+rizes
cat+ego+riz+ing
cat+ego+rized
cat+ego+ry
cat+ego+ries
ca+tena
ca+tenae

ca+ten+ac+cio
ca+tena+ry
ca+tena+ries
cat+enate
cat+enates
cat+enat+ing
cat+enat+ed
cat+ena+tion
cat+ena+tions
ca+ter
ca+ters
ca+ter+ing
ca+tered
cater-cornered
ca+ter+er
ca+ter+ers
ca+ter+ing
ca+ter+ings
cat+er+pil+lar
cat+er+pil+lars
cat+er+waul
cat+er+wauls
cat+er+wauls
cat+er+waul+ing
cat+er+wauled
cates
Catesby
cat+fish
cat+fish or
cat+fishes
cat+gut
Cath+ar
Cath+ars or
Cath+ari
Cath+ar+ism
Cath+ar+ist
Cath+ar+ists
ca+thar+sis
ca+thar+ses
ca+thar+tic
ca+thar+tics
ca+thar+ti+cal+ly
Ca+thay
cat+head
cat+heads
ca+thedral
ca+thedrals
Cather
Catherine
Catherine de' Medici
Catherine of Bra+gan+za
cath+eter

cath+eters
cath+eter+ise
cath+eter+ises
cath+eter+is+ing
cath+eter+ised
cath+eter+ize
cath+eter+izes
cath+eter+iz+ing
cath+eter+ized
ca+thex+is
ca+thexes
ca+thod+al
cath+ode
cath+odes
ca+thod+ic
catho+lic
Catho+lic
Catho+lics
ca+tholi+cal+ly
ca+tholi+cise
ca+tholi+cises
ca+tholi+cis+ing
ca+tholi+cised
Ca+tholi+cism
catho+lic+ity
ca+tholi+cize
ca+tholi+cizes
ca+tholi+ciz+ing
ca+tholi+cized
ca+thol+ic+ly
Cati+li+nar+ian
Catiline
cati+on
cati+ons
cati+on+ic
cat+kin
cat+kins
cat+like
cat+mint
cat+nap
cat+naps
cat+naps
cat+nap+ping
cat+napped
cat+nip
Cato
cat-o'-nine-tails
cat-o'-nine-tails
Cats+eye
Trademark
Cats+eyes
cat's-eye
cat's-eyes

Cats+kills
cat's-paw
cat's-paws
cat+sup
Cat+te+gat
cat+tery
cat+teries
cat+ti+ly
cat+ti+ness
cat+tish
cat+tish+ly
cat+tish+ness
cat+tle
cattle-cake
cattle-cakes
cattle-grid
cattle-grids
cattle+man
cattle+men
cattle-stop
cattle-stops
cat+ty
cat+ti+er
cat+ti+est
catty-cornered
Ca+tul+lan
Catullus
cat+walk
cat+walks
Cau+ca
Cau+ca+sia
Cau+ca+sian
Cau+ca+sians
Cau+ca+soid
Cau+ca+sus
cau+cus
cau+cuses
cau+cuses
cau+cus+ing
cau+cused
cau+dal
cau+dal+ly
cau+date
cau+dat+ed
cau+da+tion
cau+da+tions
cau+dil+lo
cau+dil+los
cau+dle
caught
caul
cauls
caul+dron
caul+drons
cau+li+flow+er

cau +li +flow +ers
caulk
  caulks
  caulk +ing
  caulked
caus +al
cau +sal +ity
  cau +sal +ities
caus +al +ly
cau +sa +tion
  cau +sa +tions
cau +sa +tion +al
causa +tive
  causa +tives
causa +tive +ly
cause
  causes
  causes
  caus +ing
  caused
cause cé +lè +bre
  causes cé +lè +
  bres
cause +less
cau +serie
  cau +series
cause +way
  cause +ways
caus +tic
  caus +tics
caus +ti +cal +ly
caus +tic +ity
  caus +tic +ities
cau +teri +sa +tion
  cau +teri +sa +
  tions
cau +ter +ise
  cau +ter +ises
  cau +ter +is +ing
  cau +ter +ised
cau +teri +za +tion
  cau +teri +za +
  tions
cau +ter +ize
  cau +ter +izes
  cau +ter +iz +ing
  cau +ter +ized
cau +tery
  cau +teries
cau +tion
  cau +tions
  cau +tions
  cau +tion +ing
  cau +tioned
cau +tion +ary

cau +tious
cau +tious +ly
cau +tious +ness
Cavaco Silva
Cavafy
cav +al +cade
  cav +al +cades
Cavalcanti
cava +lier
  cava +liers
Cava +lier
  Cava +liers
cava +lier +ly
Cavallini
cav +al +ry
  cav +al +ries
cav +al +ry +man
  cav +al +ry +men
Cav +an
cava +ti +na
  cava +ti +ne
cave
  caves
  caves
  cav +ing
  caved
ca +veat
  ca +veats
ca +veat emp +tor
cave-in
  cave-ins
cave in
  verb
ca +vel
  ca +vels
Cavell
cave +man
  cave +men
cav +en +dish
Cavendish
cav +er
  cav +ers
cav +ern
  cav +erns
  cav +erns
  cav +ern +ing
  cav +erned
cav +ern +ous
cavi +ar
  cavi +ars
cavi +are
  cavi +ares
cav +il
  cav +ils
  cav +ils

cav +il +ling *or*
cav +il +ing
U.S.
cav +illed *or*
cav +iled
U.S.
cav +il +ler
  cav +il +lers
cav +ing
cav +ity
  cav +ities
ca +vort
  ca +vorts
  ca +vort +ing
  ca +vort +ed
  ca +vort +er
  ca +vort +ers
Cavour
cavy
  cavies
caw
  caws
  caws
  caw +ing
  cawed
Cawley
Cawn +pore
Cawn +pur
Cax +ton
  Cax +tons
Caxton
cay
  cays
cay +enne
Cay +enne
Cayes
Cayley
cay +man
  cay +mans
ca +zique
  ca +ziques
CD-video
  CD-videos
Cea +rá
cease
  ceases
  ceases
  ceas +ing
  ceased
cease-fire
  cease-fires
cease +less
cease +less +ly
Ceaușescu
Cebú

ce +cal
Čechy
Cecil
Ce +cilia
ce +cum
  ce +ca
ce +dar
  ce +dars
cede
  cedes
  ced +ing
  ced +ed
ced +er
  ced +ers
ce +dil +la
  ce +dil +las
Cee +fax
  Trademark
ceil
  ceils
  ceil +ing
  ceiled
cei +lidh
  cei +lidhs
ceil +ing
  ceil +ings
Cela
cela +don
Celan
cel +an +dine
  cel +an +dines
ce +leb
  ce +lebs
Cel +ebes
cel +ebrant
  cel +ebrants
cel +ebrate
  cel +ebrates
  cel +ebrat +ing
  cel +ebrat +ed
  cel +ebrat +ed
cel +ebra +tion
  cel +ebra +tions
cel +ebra +tor
  cel +ebra +tors
cel +ebra +tory
ce +leb +rity
  ce +leb +rities
ce +leri +ac
ce +ler +ity
cel +ery
ce +les +ta
  ce +les +tas
ce +leste
  ce +lestes

ce+les+tial
ce+les+ti+al+ly
ce+li+ac
U.S.
celi+ba+cy
celi+bate
 celi+bates
Céline
cell
 cells
cel+lar
 cel+lars
 cel+lars
 cel+lar+ing
 cel+lared
cel+lar+age
cel+lar+er
cel+lar+ers
cel+lar+et
cel+lar+ets
Cellini
cel+list
 cel+lists
Cell+net
Trademark
 Cell+nets
cel+lo
 cel+los
Cel+lo+phane
Trademark
cell+phone
 cell+phones
cel+lu+lar
cel+lule
 cel+lules
cel+lu+lite
cel+lu+li+tis
cel+lu+loid
 cel+lu+loids
cel+lu+lose
ce+lom
U.S.
 ce+loms
ce+lom+ic
Celsius
celt
 celts
Celt
 Celts
Celt+ic
Celti+cism
cem+ba+lo
 cem+ba+li *or*
 cem+ba+los
ce+ment

ce+ments
ce+ments
ce+ment+ing
ce+ment+ed
ce+men+tum
cem+etery
 cem+eteries
Ce+nis
ce+no+bite
 ce+no+bites
ceno+taph
 ceno+taphs
Ceno+taph
Ce+no+zo+ic
cen+ser
 cen+sers
cen+sor
 cen+sors
 cen+sors
 cen+sor+ing
 cen+sored
cen+so+rial
cen+so+ri+ous
cen+so+ri+ous+
 ly
cen+sor+ship
 cen+sor+ships
cen+sur+able
cen+sure
 cen+sures
 cen+sures
 cen+sur+ing
 cen+sured
cen+sus
 cen+suses
cent
 cents
cen+tare
 cen+tares
cen+taur
 cen+taurs
cen+tau+rea
 cen+tau+reas
cen+tau+ry
 cen+tau+ries
cen+ta+vo
 cen+ta+vos
cen+te+nar+ian
 cen+te+nar+ians
cen+te+nary
 cen+te+naries
cen+ten+nial
 cen+ten+nials
cen+ter
U.S.

cen+ters
cen+ters
cen+ter+ing
cen+tered
center+fold
U.S.
 center+folds
cen+ter+ing
U.S.
 cen+ter+ings
cen+tesi+mal
 cen+tesi+mals
cen+tesi+mal+ly
cen+tesi+mo
 cen+tesi+mos
cen+ti+are
 cen+ti+ares
cen+ti+grade
cen+ti+gram
 cen+ti+grams
cen+ti+gramme
cen+ti+
 grammes
cen+ti+li+ter
U.S.
 cen+ti+li+ters
cen+ti+li+tre
 cen+ti+li+tres
cen+time
 cen+times
cen+ti+me+ter
U.S.
 cen+ti+me+ters
cen+ti+me+tre
 cen+ti+me+tres
cen+timetre-
 gram-second
cén+ti+mo
 cén+ti+mos
cen+ti+pede
 cen+ti+pedes
cen+to
 cen+tos
CENTO
cen+tral
Cen+tra+lia
cen+trali+sa+tion
cen+trali+sa+
 tions
cen+tral+ise
 cen+tral+ises
cen+tral+is+ing
cen+tral+ised
cen+tral+ism
cen+tral+ist

cen+tral+ists
cen+tral+ity
cen+tral+ities
cen+trali+za+tion
cen+trali+za+
 tions
cen+tral+ize
 cen+tral+izes
cen+tral+iz+ing
cen+tral+ized
cen+tral+ly
cen+tre
cen+tres
cen+tres
cen+tring
cen+tred
Cen+tre
centre+board
centre+boards
centre+fold
centre+folds
centre+piece
centre+pieces
cen+tric
cen+tri+cal
cen+tric+ity
cen+trifu+gal
cen+trifu+gal+ly
cen+trifu+ga+tion
cen+trifu+ga+
 tions
cen+tri+fuge
 cen+tri+fuges
 cen+tri+fuges
 cen+tri+fug+ing
 cen+tri+fuged
cen+tring
cen+trings
cen+trip+etal
cen+trip+etal+ly
cen+trism
 cen+trisms
cen+trist
 cen+trists
cen+tro+some
 cen+tro+somes
cen+tu+pli+cate
cen+tu+pli+
 cates
cen+tu+pli+
 cates
cen+tu+pli+cat+
 ing
cen+tu+pli+cat+
 ed

cen +tu +ri +on
cen +tu +ri +ons
cen +tu +ry
cen +tu +ries
cep
ceps
ce +phal +ic
Cepha +lo +nia
cepha +lo +pod
cepha +lo +pods
cepha +lopo +dan
cepha +lo +tho +
rax
cepha +lo +tho +
raxes or
cepha +lo +tho +
races
Ce +pheid
Ce +pheus
Cepheus
Ce +ram
ce +ram +ic
ce +ram +ics
ce +ram +ics
cera +mist
cera +mists
Cer +berean
Cerberus
cere
ceres
ce +real
ce +reals
cer +ebel +lar
cer +ebel +lum
cer +ebel +lums
or
cer +ebel +la
cere +bral
cer +ebral +ly
cer +ebrate
cer +ebrates
cer +ebrat +ing
cer +ebrat +ed
cer +ebra +tion
cer +ebra +tions
cer +ebric
cer +ebro +spi +nal
cer +ebro +vas +cu +
lar
cer +ebrum
cer +ebrums or
cer +ebra
cere +cloth
cere +cloths
cere +ment

cere +ments
cer +emo +nial
cer +emo +nials
cer +emo +ni +al +
ism
cer +emo +ni +al +
ist
cer +emo +ni +al +
ists
cer +emo +ni +al +
ly
cer +emo +ni +ous
cer +emo +ni +ous +
ly
cer +emo +ny
cer +emo +nies
Cerenkov
Ceres
ce +rise
ce +rium
CERN
Cernuda
ce +rog +ra +phy
ce +ro +plas +tic
Cer +ro de Pas +co
cert
certs
cer +tain
cer +tain +ly
cer +tain +ty
cer +tain +ties
cer +tes
cer +ti +fi +able
cer +tifi +cate
cer +tifi +cates
cer +tifi +cates
cer +tifi +cat +ing
cer +tifi +cat +ed
cer +ti +fi +ca +tion
cer +ti +fi +ca +
tions
cer +tifi +ca +tory
cer +ti +fied
cer +ti +fy
cer +ti +fies
cer +ti +fy +ing
cer +ti +fied
cer +tio +ra +ri
cer +tio +ra +ris
cer +ti +tude
cer +ti +tudes
ce +ru +lean
ce +ru +men
ce +ru +mi +nous
Cervantes

cer +ve +lat
cer +ve +lats
cer +vi +cal
Cer +vin
cer +vine
cer +vix
cer +vixes or
cer +vi +ces
Ce +sar +ean
U.S.
Ce +sar +ian
U.S.
ce +si +ous
U.S.
ce +sium
U.S.
ce +sium
U.S.
Čes +ko +slo +ven +
sko
cess
cesses
ces +sa +tion
ces +sa +tions
ces +sion
ces +sions
ces +sion +ary
ces +sion +aries
cess +pool
cess +pools
ces +toid
ce +su +ra
ce +su +ras or
ce +su +rae
ce +ta +cean
ce +ta +ceans
ce +tane
Cetewayo
Ce +ti +nje
ce +tri +mide
Cetshwayo
Ceu +ta
Cé +vennes
Cey +lon
Cey +lo +nese
Cézanne
Chab +rier
Chabrol
cha-cha
cha-chas
cha-chas
cha-cha +ing
cha-chaed
cha-cha-cha

cha-cha-chas
cha-cha-chas
cha-cha-chaing
cha-cha-chaed
Cha +co
cha +conne
cha +connes
Chad
Chadwick
chafe
chafes
chafes
chaf +ing
chafed
chaf +er
chaf +ers
chaff
chaffs
chaff +ing
chaffed
chaff +er
chaff +ers
chaf +fer
chaf +fers
chaf +fer +ing
chaf +fered
chaf +fer +er
chaf +fer +ers
chaf +finch
chaf +finches
chaffy
Chagall
cha +grin
cha +grins
cha +grins
cha +grin +ing
cha +grined
chain
chains
chains
chain +ing
chained
Chain
chain-react
chain-reacts
chain-reacting
chain-reacted
chain-smoke
chain-smokes
chain-smoking
chain-smoked
chain-stitch
chain-stitches
chain-stitching
chain-stitched

chair
chairs
chairs
chair+ing
chaired
chair+man
chair+men
chair+person
chair+persons
chaise
chaises
chaise longue
chaise longues
or
chaises longues
Chaka
chak+ra
chak+ras
cha+la+za
cha+la+zas or
cha+la+zae
chal+cedon+ic
chal+cedo+ny
chal+cedo+nies
Chal+cidi+ce
Chal+cis
chal+co+lith+ic
chal+co+py+rite
Chal+daea
Chal+dea
chal+dron
chal+drons
cha+let
cha+lets
Chaliapin
chal+ice
chal+ices
chalk
chalks
chalki+ness
chalk+like
chalk+pit
chalk+pits
chalky
chalki+er
chalki+est
chal+lenge
chal+lenges
chal+lenges
chal+leng+ing
chal+lenged
chal+lenge+able
chal+leng+er
chal+leng+ers
chal+leng+ing

chal+lie
chal+lis
Cha+lon
Châ+lons
Châlons-sur-
  Marne
Chalon-sur-Saône
cha+lyb+eate
cham+ber
cham+bers
cham+ber+lain
cham+ber+lains
Chamberlain
chamber+maid
chamber+maids
cham+bers
Cham+bé+ry
cham+bray
cha+me+le+on
cha+me+le+ons
cha+meleon+ic
cham+fer
cham+fers
cham+fers
cham+fer+ing
cham+fered
cham+ois
cham+ois
chamo+mile
chamo+miles
Cha+mo+nix
champ
champs
champs
champ+ing
champed
cham+pagne
cham+pagnes
Champagne-
  Ardenne
Champaigne
cham+pers
cham+per+ty
cham+per+ties
Champigny-sur-
  Marne
cham+pi+on
cham+pi+ons
cham+pi+ons
cham+pi+on+ing
cham+pi+oned
cham+pi+on+
  ship
cham+pi+on+
  ships

Cham+plain
Champlain
champ+le+vé
Champollion
Champs Ely+sées
chance
chances
chances
chanc+ing
chanced
chance+ful
chan+cel
chan+cels
chan+cel+lery
chan+cel+leries
chan+cel+lor
chan+cel+lors
chan+cel+lor+
  ship
chan+cel+lor+
  ships
chan+cel+lo+ry
chan+cel+lo+
  ries
chance-medley
chance-medleys
chan+cer
chan+cers
chan+cery
chan+ceries
chancey
chanci+er
chanci+est
chan+cre
chan+cres
chan+croid
chan+croids
chan+crous
chancy
chanci+er
chanci+est
chan+de+lier
chan+de+liers
Chan+der+na+
  gore
Chan+di+garh
chan+dler
chan+dlers
Chandler
chan+dlery
chan+dleries
Chandragupta
Chandrasekhar
Chanel
Chang

Chang+an
Chang+chia+k'ou
Chang+chia+kow
Ch'ang-chou
Chang+chow
Chang+chun
Ch'ang Ch'un
Chang+de
change
changes
changes
chang+ing
changed
change+abil+ity
change+able
change+ably
change+ful
change+less
change+ling
change+lings
change+over
change+overs
change over
verb
chang+er
chang+ers
change-ringing
change-ringings
Chang+sha
Ch'ang-sha
Ch'ang-te
Chang+teh
chan+nel
chan+nels
chan+nels
chan+nel+ling
or
chan+nel+ing
U.S.
chan+nelled or
chan+neled
U.S.
Chan+nel
chan+son de
  geste
chan+sons de
  geste
chant
chants
chants
chant+ing
chant+ed
chant+er
chant+ers
chan+te+relle

chan +te +relles
chan +teuse
chan +teuses
chan +ti +cleer
chan +ti +cleers
Chan +til +ly
chan +try
chan +tries
chan +ty
chan +ties
Cha +nu +kah
Cha +nu +kahs
Chao +an
Chao +chow
chao +lo +gy
cha +os
cha +ot +ic
cha +oti +cal +ly
chap
chaps
chaps
chap +ping
chapped
chapa +ra +jos
chapa +rejos
chap +ar +ral
chap +ar +rals
cha +pa +ti
cha +pa +ti or
cha +pa +tis or
cha +pa +ties
cha +pat +ti
cha +pat +ti or
cha +pat +tis or
cha +pat +ties
chap +book
chap +books
chap +el
chap +els
chap +er +on
chap +er +ons
chap +er +ons
chap +er +on +ing
chap +er +oned
chap +er +on +age
chap +er +one
chap +er +ones
chap +er +ones
chap +er +on +ing
chap +er +oned
chap +fallen
chap +lain
chap +lains
chap +lain +cy
chap +lain +cies

chap +let
chap +lets
chap +let +ed
Chaplin
Chap +lin +esque
chap +man
chap +men
Chapman
Chappell
chap +pie
chap +pies
chaps
chap +ter
chap +ters
chap +ter +house
chap +ter +houses
char
char or
chars
chars
char +ring
charred
chara +banc
chara +bancs
char +ac +ter
char +ac +ters
char +ac +ter +ful
char +ac +teri +sa +tion
char +ac +teri +sa +tions
char +ac +ter +ise
char +ac +ter +ises
char +ac +ter +is +ing
char +ac +ter +ised
char +ac +ter +is +tic
char +ac +ter +is +tics
char +ac +ter +is +ti +cal +ly
char +ac +teri +za +tion
char +ac +teri +za +tions
char +ac +ter +ize
char +ac +ter +izes
char +ac +ter +iz +ing

char +ac +ter +ized
char +ac +ter +less
cha +rade
cha +rades
cha +rades
char +coal
char +coals
char +coals
char +coal +ing
char +coaled
Charcot
chard
chards
Chardin
Char +don +nay
Char +don +nays
Chardonnet
Cha +rente
Charente-Maritime
charge
charges
charges
charg +ing
charged
charge +able
charge-cap
charge-caps
charge-capping
charge-capped
charge-capping
charge-cappings
char +gé d'af +faires
char +gés d'af +faires
charg +er
charg +ers
chari +ly
chari +ness
Char +ing
chari +ot
chari +ots
chari +ot +eer
chari +ot +eers
char +ism
char +isms
cha +ris +ma
cha +ris +mas
char +is +mat +ic
chari +table
chari +table +ness
chari +tably
char +ity

char +ities
chari +vari
chari +varis
char +lady
char +ladies
char +la +tan
char +la +tans
char +la +tan +ism
char +la +tan +ry
Charlemagne
charles +ton
charles +tons
Charles +ton
Charleville-Mézières
char +lie
char +lies
char +lock
char +locks
char +lotte
char +lottes
Char +lotte
Char +lot +ten +burg
char +lotte russe
char +lottes russe
Char +lotte +town
Charlton
charm
charms
charms
charm +ing
charmed
charm +er
charm +ers
charm +ing
charm +ing +ly
char +nel
char +nels
Charnley
Charon
Charpentier
charr
charr or
charrs
chart
charts
charts
chart +ing
chart +ed
char +ter
char +ters
char +ter +er
char +ter +ers

Charteris
Chart+ism
Chart+ist
  Chart+ists
chart+less
Char+tres
char+treuse
char+woman
  char+women
chary
  chari+er
  chari+est
Cha+ryb+dis
chase
  chases
  chases
  chas+ing
  chased
  chas+er
  chas+ers
chasm
  chasms
chas+mal
chas+mic
chas+seur
  chas+seurs
Chas+sid
Chas+sid+ic
chas+sis
  chas+sis
chaste
  chaste+ly
chas+ten
  chas+tens
  chas+ten+ing
  chas+tened
  chas+ten+er
  chas+ten+ers
chaste+ness
chas+tise
  chas+tises
  chas+tis+ing
  chas+tised
chas+tise+ment
  chas+tise+
    ments
chas+tis+er
  chas+tis+ers
chas+tity
chasu+ble
  chasu+bles
chat
  chats
  chats
  chat+ting

chat+ted
cha+teau
  cha+teaux or
  cha+teaus
châ+teau
  châ+teaux or
  châ+teaus
Chateaubriand
Châ+teau+roux
Château-Thierry
chat+elain
  chat+elains
chat+elaine
  chat+elaines
Chat+ham
chat+line
  chat+lines
Chat+ta+noo+ga
chat+tel
  chat+tels
chat+ter
  chat+ters
  chat+ters
  chat+ter+ing
  chat+tered
chatter+box
  chatter+boxes
chat+ter+er
  chat+ter+ers
chat+ti+ly
chat+ti+ness
chat+ty
  chat+ti+er
  chat+ti+est
Chaucer
chauf+feur
  chauf+feurs
chauf+feurs
  chauf+feur+ing
  chauf+feured
chauf+feuse
chaunt
  chaunts
chaunt+er
  chaunt+ers
chau+vin+ism
  chau+vin+isms
chau+vin+ist
  chau+vin+ists
  chau+vin+is+tic
  chau+vin+is+ti+
    cal+ly
cheap
  cheap+er
  cheap+est

cheap+en
  cheap+ens
  cheap+en+ing
  cheap+ened
  cheap+en+er
  cheap+en+ers
  cheap-jack
  cheap-jacks
cheap+ly
cheap+ness
cheapo
cheap+skate
  cheap+skates
cheat
  cheats
  cheats
  cheat+ing
  cheat+ed
  cheat+er
  cheat+ers
Che+bo+ksa+ry
Checheno-Ingush
check
  checks
  checks
  check+ing
  checked
check
  U.S.
  checks
check+able
check+book
  U.S.
  check+books
  checked
  check+er
  U.S.
  check+ers
  check+ers
  check+er+ing
  check+ered
checker+board
  checker+boards
check+ered
  U.S.
  check+ers
check-in
  check-ins
check in
  verb
check+mate
  check+mates
  check+mates
  check+mat+ing
  check+mat+ed

check+out
  check+outs
check out
  verb
check+point
  check+points
check+up
  check+ups
check up
  verb
Ched+dar
  Ched+dars
cheek
  cheeks
  cheeks
  cheek+ing
  cheeked
cheek+bone
  cheek+bones
cheeki+ly
cheeki+ness
cheeky
  cheeki+er
  cheeki+est
cheep
  cheeps
  cheeps
  cheep+ing
  cheeped
  cheep+er
  cheep+ers
cheer
  cheers
  cheers
  cheer+ing
  cheered
cheer+ful
  cheer+ful+ly
  cheer+ful+ness
cheeri+ly
cheeri+ness
cheerio
  cheerios
cheer+leader
  cheer+leaders
cheer+less
  cheer+less+ly
  cheer+less+ness
  cheers
cheery
  cheeri+er
  cheeri+est
cheese
  cheeses
cheese+burg+er

cheese+burg+
ers
cheese+cake
cheese+cakes
cheese+cloth
cheese+paring
cheese+parings
cheesi+ness
cheesy
cheesi+er
cheesi+est
chee+tah
chee+tahs
Cheever
chef
chefs
Che+foo
Che Guevara
Cheiron
Che+ju
Chekhov
Che+khov+ian
Che+kiang
Chekov
Che+kov+ian
che+la
che+lae
che+la
che+las
che+late
che+lates
che+lates
che+lat+ing
che+lat+ed
che+la+tion
che+la+tions
che+lic+era
che+lic+erae
Chelms+ford
che+loid
che+loids
che+loi+dal
che+lo+nian
che+lo+nians
Chel+sea
Chel+ten+ham
Chel+ya+binsk
Che+lyus+kin
chemi+cal
chemi+cals
chemi+cal+ly
chemi+lu+mi+nes+
cence
chemi+lu+mi+nes+
cent

che+min de fer
che+mise
che+mises
chem+ist
chem+ists
chem+is+try
chem+is+tries
Chem+nitz
chemo+cep+tor
chemo+cep+
tors
chemo+recep+
tor
chemo+recep+
tors
chemo+syn+
thesis
chemo+thera+py
Che+mul+po
chem+ur+gic
chem+ur+gi+cal
chem+ur+gy
Che+nab
Cheng-chiang
Cheng-chou
Cheng+chow
Cheng+de
Cheng+du
Ch'eng-te
Cheng+teh
Cheng+tu
Ch'eng-tu
Chénier
che+nille
che+nilles
cheong+sam
cheong+sams
Cheops
Chep+stow
cheque
cheques
cheque+book
cheque+books
cheq+uer
cheq+uers
cheq+uers
cheq+uer+ing
cheq+uered
cheq+uers
Cheq+uers
Cher
Cher+bourg
Cherenkov
Che+ri+bon

cher+ish
cher+ishes
cher+ish+ing
cher+ished
Chernenko
Cher+no+byl
Cher+nov+tsy
cher+no+zem
Chero+kee
Chero+kees *or*
Chero+kee
che+root
che+roots
cher+ry
cher+ries
chert
Chert+sey
cherty
cher+ub
cher+ubs *or*
cheru+bim
che+ru+bic
che+ru+bi+cal
che+ru+bi+cal+ly
Cherubini
cher+vil
cher+vils
Cherwell
Chesh+ire
place name
Cheshire
surname
chess
chesses
chess+board
chess+boards
chess+man
chess+men
chest
chests
chest+ed
Ches+ter
ches+ter+field
ches+ter+fields
Ches+ter+field
place name
Chesterfield
surname
Chesterton
chesti+ness
chest+nut
chest+nuts
chesty
chesti+er
chesti+est

che+tah
che+tahs
cheva+lier
cheva+liers
Chevalier
Che+vi+ot
Che+vi+ots
chèvre
chèvres
chev+ron
chev+rons
chev+ro+tain
chev+ro+tains
chevy
chevies
chevies
chevy+ing
chev+ied
chew
chews
chews
chew+ing
chewed
chew+able
chew+er
chew+ers
chew+ing
chewy
chewi+er
chewi+est
Chey+enne
Chey+enne *or*
Chey+ennes
chez
chi
ch'i
chi+ack
chi+acks
chi+ack+ing
chi+acked
Chiang Ch'ing
Chiang Kai-shek
chi+an+ti
Chia+pas
chia+ro+scu+ro
chia+ro+scu+
ros
chi+as+ma
chi+as+mas *or*
chi+as+ma+ta
chi+as+mus
chi+as+mi
chi+as+tic
Chi+ba
chic

Chi+ca+go
chi+cane
chi+canes
chi+canes
chi+can+ing
chi+caned
chi+can+er
chi+can+ers
chi+can+ery
chi+can+eries
chi+ca+no
chi+ca+nos
Chi+chen Itzá
Chich+es+ter
place name
Chichester
surname
chi+chi
chi+chis
Chi+chi+haerh
Ch'i-chi'i-haerh
chick
chicks
chicka+dee
chicka+dees
chick+en
chick+ens
chicken-hearted
chicken-livered
chicken+pox
chick+pea
chick+peas
chick+weed
chick+weeds
Chi+cla+yo
chic+le
chic+ly
chico+ry
chico+ries
chide
chides
chid+ing
chid+ed *or*
chid *or*
chid+den
chid+er
chid+ers
chid+ing+ly
chief
chiefs
chief+ly
chief+tain
chief+tains
chief+tain+cy
chief+tain+ship

chief+tain+ships
chiff+chaff
chiff+chaffs
chif+fon
chif+fo+nier
chif+fo+niers
chif+fon+nier
chif+fon+niers
chig+etai
chig+etais
chig+ger
chig+gers
chi+gnon
chi+gnons
chigoe
chigoes
Chig+well
Chih+li
Chi+hua+hua
Chi+hua+huas
chil+blain
chil+blains
chil+blained
child
chil+dren
child-abuse
child-bearing
child+bed
child+birth
child+care
Childers
child+hood
child+hoods
child+ish
child+ish+ly
child+ish+ness
child+less
child+less+ness
child+like
chil+dren
chile
chiles
Chile
Chil+ean
Chil+eans
chili+ad
chili+ads
chill
chills
chills
chill+ing
chilled
chill+er
chill+ers
chil+li

chil+lies
chil+li con car+ne
chil+li+ness
chill+ing+ly
chill+ness
chil+ly
chil+li+er
chil+li+est
Chil+pan+cin+go
Chil+tern
Chi+lung
Chi-lung
chi+maera
chi+maeras
chimb
chimbs
Chim+bo+ra+zo
Chim+bo+te
chime
chimes
chimes
chim+ing
chimed
chim+er
chim+ers
chi+mera
chi+meras
chi+mer+ic
chi+meri+cal
chi+meri+cal+ly
Chim+kent
chim+ney
chim+neys
chimney+pot
chimney+pots
chimp
chimps
chim+pan+zee
chim+pan+zees
chin
chins
chins
chin+ning
chinned
chi+na
chi+nas
Chi+na
China+graph
Trademark
China+graphs
China+man
China+men
Chi+nan
Chi-nan
China+town

China+towns
china+ware
chin+che+rin+
chee
chin+che+rin+
chees
chin+chil+la
chin+chil+las
chin-chin
Chin-Chou
Chin+chow
Chin+dit
Chin+dits
Chin+dwin
chine
chines
chines
chin+ing
chined
Chi+nese
Chi+nese
Ching+hai
Ch'ing-hai
Ching+tao
Ch'ing-tao
Ch'ing-yüan
Chin-Hsien
chink
chinks
chinks
chink+ing
chinked
Chin+kiang
chi+noi+serie
chi+nook
chi+nooks
Chi+nook
Chi+nook *or*
Chi+nooks
chi+nos
chintz
chintzy
chintzi+er
chintzi+est
chin+wag
chin+wags
Chios
chip
chips
chips
chip+ping
chipped
chip-based
chip+board
chip+munk

chip+munks
chipo+la+ta
chipo+la+tas
Chippendale
chip+per
chip+py
chip+pies
Chirac
chiral
chiral+ity
Chirico
chi+rog+ra+pher
chi+rog+ra+
phers
chi+ro+graph+ic
chi+ro+graphi+
cal
chi+rog+ra+phy
chi+ro+man+cer
chi+ro+man+
cers
chi+ro+man+cy
Chiron
chi+ropo+dist
chi+ropo+dists
chi+ropo+dy
chi+ro+prac+tic
chi+ro+prac+tor
chi+ro+prac+
tors
chirp
chirps
chirps
chirp+ing
chirped
chirp+er
chirp+ers
chirpi+ly
chirpi+ness
chirpy
chirpi+er
chirpi+est
chirr
chirrs
chirrs
chirr+ing
chirred
chir+rup
chir+rups
chir+rups
chir+rup+ping
chir+rupped
chir+rup+er
chir+rup+ers
chir+rupy

chis+el
chis+els
chis+els
chis+el+ling *or*
chis+el+ing
U.S.
chis+elled *or*
chis+eled
U.S.
chis+el+ler
chis+el+lers
Chi+shi+ma
Chi+si+maio
chi-square
chit
chits
Chi+ta
chi+tal
chi+tals
chit+chat
chit+chats
chit+chats
chit+chat+ting
chit+chat+ted
chi+tin
chi+tin+ous
chit+lings
chi+ton
chi+tons
Chit+ta+gong
chit+ter+lings
chit+ty
chit+ties
chiv
chivs
chivs
chiv+ving
chivvved
chiv+al+ric
chiv+al+rous
chiv+al+rous+ly
chiv+al+rous+
ness
chiv+al+ry
chiv+al+ries
chiva+ree
U.S.
chiva+rees
chive
chives
chiv+vy
chiv+vies
chiv+vies
chiv+vy+ing
chiv+vied

chivvy
chiv+ies
chiv+ies
chivvy+ing
chiv+ied
Chka+lov
chla+myd+ia
chla+myd+ias
chlo+ral
chlo+ram+pheni+
col
chlo+rate
chlo+rates
chlor+dan
chlor+dane
chlor+hexi+dine
chlo+ric
chlo+ride
chlo+rides
chlo+rin
chlo+rin+ate
chlo+rin+ates
chlo+rin+at+ing
chlo+rin+at+ed
chlo+rina+tion
chlo+rina+tions
chlo+rina+tor
chlo+rina+tors
chlo+rine
chlo+rite
chlo+rites
chlo+rit+ic
chloro+fluoro+car+
bon
chloro+fluoro+
car+bons
chlo+ro+form
Chlo+ro+my+ce+
tin
Trademark
chlo+ro+phyl
U.S.
chlo+ro+phyll
chlo+ro+phyl+
loid
chlo+ro+phyl+
lous
chlo+ro+plast
chlo+ro+plasts
chlo+ro+sis
chlo+rot+ic
chlo+rous
chlor+proma+
zine

chlor+tet+ra+cy+
cline
chock
chocks
chocks
chock+ing
chocked
chock-a-block
chock+er
chock-full
chocko
chockos
choco
chocos
choco+late
choco+lates
chocolate-box
adj.
choco+laty
Choc+taw
Choc+taws *or*
Choc+taw
choice
choices
choic+er
choic+est
choice+ly
choice+ness
choir
choirs
choir+boy
choir+boys
Choi+seul
choke
chokes
chokes
chok+ing
choked
choked
choke-full
chok+er
chok+ers
chok+ey
chok+eys
cho+ko
cho+kos
choky
chokies
chol+an+gio+
graphy
chol+an+gio+
graphies
chol+er
chol+era
chol+er+ic

chol +eri +cal +ly
cho +les +ter +in
cho +les +ter +ol
cho +line
Cho +lu +la
chomp
chomps
chomps
chomp +ing
chomped
Chomsky
Chom +sky +an
Chom +sky +ans
chon +drite
chon +drites
Chong +qinq
chook
chooks
chook +ie
chook +ies
choose
chooses
choos +ing
chose
cho +sen
choos +er
choos +ers
choosy
choosi +er
choosi +est
chop
chops
chops
chop +ping
chopped
chop +fallen
chop +house
chop +houses
Chopin
chop +logic
chop +per
chop +pers
chop +pi +ly
chop +pi +ness
chop +py
chop +pi +er
chop +pi +est
chops
chop +sticks
chop suey
cho +ral
cho +rals
cho +rale
cho +rales
cho +ral +ly

chord
chords
chords
chord +ing
chord +ed
chord +al
chor +date
chor +dates
chore
chores
cho +rea
cho +reas
cho +reg +ra +pher
cho +reg +ra +
   phers
cho +regraph +ic
cho +regraphi +cal +
   ly
cho +reg +ra +phy
cho +reg +ra +
   phies
cho +reo +graph
cho +reo +graphs
cho +reo +graph +
   ing
cho +reo +
   graphed
cho +reog +ra +
   pher
cho +reog +ra +
   phers
cho +reo +graph +
   ic
cho +reo +graphi +
   cal +ly
cho +reog +ra +
   phy
cho +reog +ra +
   phies
cho +ric
cho +ri +oid
cho +ri +oids
cho +ri +on
cho +ri +ons
cho +ri +on +ic
chor +is +ter
chor +is +ters
Chor +ley
cho +roid
cho +roids
chor +tle
chor +tles
chor +tles
chor +tling
chor +tled

chor +tler
chor +tlers
cho +rus
cho +ruses
cho +ruses
cho +rus +ing
cho +rused
Chor +zów
chose
cho +sen
Cho +sen
Cho +sŏn
Cho +ta Nag +pur
Chou En-lai
chough
choughs
chow
chows
chow-chow
chow-chows
chow +der
chow +ders
chow mein
Chrétien de
   Troyes
chrism
chris +mal
chris +om
chris +oms
Christ
Chris +ta +del +
   phian
Chris +ta +del +
   phians
Christ +church
chris +ten
chris +tens
chris +ten +ing
chris +tened
Chris +ten +dom
chris +ten +ing
chris +ten +ings
Chris +tian
Chris +tians
Christian
Chris +tia +nia
Chris +tiani +sa +
   tion
Chris +tiani +sa +
   tions
Chris +tian +ise
Chris +tian +ises
Chris +tian +is +
   ing
Chris +tian +ised

Chris +tian +is +er
Chris +tian +is +
   ers
Chris +ti +an +ity
Chris +tiani +za +
   tion
Chris +tiani +za +
   tions
Chris +tian +ize
Chris +tian +izes
Chris +tian +iz +
   ing
Chris +tian +ized
Chris +tian +iz +er
Chris +tian +iz +
   ers
chris +tian +ly
Chris +tian +sand
Christie
surname
Chris +tie
Skiing
Chris +ties
Christina
Christine de Pisan
Christ +like
Christ +likeness
Christ +ly
Christ +mas
Christ +mases
Christ +massy
Christmas +tide
Christmas +tides
Christoff
Christopher
Chris +ty
Chris +ties
chro +ma
chro +mas
chro +mate
chro +mates
chro +mat +ic
chro +mati +cal +ly
chro +mati +cism
chro +ma +tic +ity
chro +ma +tic +
   ities
chro +mat +ics
chro +ma +tin
chro +ma +tins
chro +ma +tog +ra +
   phy
chrome
chromes
chrom +ing

chromed
chro+mel
chro+mic
chro+mite
chro+mium
chro+mo
chro+mos
chro+mo+litho+
  graph
chro+mo+litho+
  graphs
chro+mo+li+thog+
  ra+pher
chro+mo+li+
  thog+ra+phers
chro+mo+litho+
  graph+ic
chro+mo+li+thog+
  ra+phy
chro+mo+so+mal
chro+mo+some
chro+mo+
  somes
chro+mo+sphere
chro+mo+
  spheres
chro+mo+spher+
  ic
chro+mous
chron+ic
chroni+cal+ly
chro+nic+ity
chroni+cle
chroni+cles
chroni+cles
chroni+cling
chroni+cled
chroni+cler
chroni+clers
chrono+graph
chrono+graphs
chrono+graph+ic
chrono+log+ic
chrono+logi+cal
chrono+logi+cal+
  ly
chro+nolo+gist
chro+nolo+gists
chro+nol+ogy
chro+nol+ogies
chro+nom+eter
chro+nom+eters
chrono+met+ric
chrono+met+ri+
  cal

chrono+met+ri+
  cal+ly
chro+nom+etry
chro+non
chro+nons
chrysa+lid
chrysa+lids
chrysa+lis
chrysa+lises or
chry+sali+des
chry+san+
  themum
chry+san+
  themums
chrys+el+ephan+
  tine
chryso+ber+yl
chryso+ber+yls
chryso+lite
chryso+lites
chryso+prase
chryso+prases
Chrysostom
chtho+nian
chtho+nic
chub
chub or
chubs
chub+bi+ness
chub+by
chub+bi+er
chub+bi+est
Chu Chiang
chuck
chucks
chucks
chuck+ing
chucked
chuck-in
  Austral.
chuck-ins
chuck in
  verb
chuck+le
chuck+les
chuck+les
chuck+ling
chuck+led
chuckle+head
chuckle+heads
chud+dy
chuff
chuffs
chuffs
chuff+ing

chuffed
chug
chugs
chugs
chug+ging
chugged
chu+kar
chu+kars
Chu Kiang
chuk+ka
chuk+kas
chuk+ker
chuk+kers
chum
chums
chums
chum+ming
chummed
chum+mi+ly
chum+mi+ness
chum+my
chum+mi+er
chum+mi+est
chump
chumps
chumps
chump+ing
chumped
chun+der
chun+ders
chun+der+ing
chun+dered
Ch'ung-ch'ing
Chung+king
chunk
chunks
chunki+ness
chunky
chunki+er
chunki+est
Chun+nel
chun+ter
chun+ters
chun+ter+ing
chun+tered
Chu+qui+sa+ca
Chur
church
churches
churches
church+ing
churched
church+goer
church+goers
church+going

church+goings
Churchill
church+li+ness
church+ly
church+man
church+men
church+warden
church+wardens
church+woman
church+women
church+yard
church+yards
chu+rin+ga
chu+rin+ga or
chu+rin+gas
churl
churls
churl+ish
churn
churns
churns
churn+ing
churned
churn+er
churn+ers
churr
churrs
churrs
churr+ing
churred
chute
chutes
chut+ist
chut+ists
chut+ney
chut+neys
chutz+pah
chutz+pahs
chy+ack
chy+acks
chy+ack+ing
chy+acked
chy+la+ceous
chyle
chy+lous
chyme
chy+mous
chypre
Ciano
Cibber
ci+bo+rium
ci+bo+ria
ci+ca+da
ci+ca+das or
ci+ca+dae

ci+ca+la
ci+ca+las *or*
ci+ca+le
cica+tri+cial
cica+tri+sa+tion
cica+tri+sa+
  tions
cica+trise
cica+trises
cica+tris+ing
cica+trised
cica+trix
cica+tri+ces
cica+tri+za+tion
cica+tri+za+
  tions
cica+trize
cica+trizes
cica+triz+ing
cica+trized
cic+ely
cic+elies
Cicero
cic+ero+ne
cic+ero+nes *or*
cic+ero+ni
ci+der
ci+ders
cig
cigs
ci+gar
ci+gars
ciga+ret
ciga+rets
ciga+rette
ciga+rettes
ciga+ril+lo
ciga+ril+los
cig+gy
cig+gies
cili+ary
cili+ate
cili+at+ed
cil+ium
cil+ia
Cimarosa
cinch
cinches
cinches
cinch+ing
cinched
cin+cho+na
cin+cho+nas
cin+chon+ic
Cin+cin+nati

Cincinnatus
cinc+ture
cinc+tures
cin+der
cin+ders
Cinderella
Cinderellas
cin+dery
cine
cin+easte
cin+eastes
cin+ema
cin+emas
cin+emat+ic
cin+emati+cal+ly
cin+emato+graph
cin+emato+
  graphs
cin+emato+
  graphs
cin+emato+
  graph+ing
cin+emato+
  graphed
cin+ema+tog+ra+
  pher
cin+ema+tog+ra+
  phers
cin+emato+graph+
  ic
cin+emato+
  graphi+cal+ly
cin+ema+tog+ra+
  phy
ci+né+ma vé+ri+
  té
cin+eraria
cin+erarias
cin+erar+ium
cin+eraria
cin+erary
cin+era+tion
cin+era+tions
cin+era+tor
cin+era+tors
cin+na+bar
cin+na+bars
cin+na+mon
cin+na+mons
cinque
cinques
Cinque
cin+quecen+to
cinque+foil
cinque+foils

Cin+tra
ci+pher
ci+phers
ci+phers
ci+pher+ing
ci+phered
cir+ca
cir+ca+dian
Cir+cas+sia
Circe
Cir+cean
cir+cle
cir+cles
cir+cles
cir+cling
cir+cled
cir+cler
cir+clers
cir+clet
cir+clets
cir+cuit
cir+cuits
cir+cuits
cir+cuit+ing
cir+cuit+ed
cir+cuit+al
cir+cui+tous
cir+cui+tous+ly
cir+cui+tous+
  ness
cir+cuit+ry
cir+cuit+ries
cir+cu+ity
cir+cu+ities
cir+cu+lar
cir+cu+lars
cir+cu+lari+sa+
  tion
cir+cu+lari+sa+
  tions
cir+cu+lar+ise
cir+cu+lar+ises
cir+cu+lar+is+
  ing
cir+cu+lar+ised
cir+cu+lar+ity
cir+cu+lari+za+
  tion
cir+cu+lari+za+
  tions
cir+cu+lar+ize
cir+cu+lar+izes
cir+cu+lar+iz+
  ing
cir+cu+lar+ized

cir+cu+lar+ly
cir+cu+late
cir+cu+lates
cir+cu+lat+ing
cir+cu+lat+ed
cir+cu+la+tion
cir+cu+la+tions
cir+cu+la+tive
cir+cu+la+tor
cir+cu+la+tors
cir+cu+la+tory
cir+cum+am+bi+
  ence
cir+cum+am+bi+
  en+cy
cir+cum+am+bi+
  ent
cir+cum+am+bu+
  late
cir+cum+am+bu+
  lates
cir+cum+am+bu+
  lat+ing
cir+cum+am+bu+
  lat+ed
cir+cum+am+bu+
  la+tion
cir+cum+am+bu+
  la+tions
cir+cum+cise
cir+cum+cises
cir+cum+cis+ing
cir+cum+cised
cir+cum+ci+sion
cir+cum+ci+
  sions
cir+cum+fer+
  ence
cir+cum+fer+
  ences
cir+cum+fer+en+
  tial
cir+cum+fer+en+
  tial+ly
cir+cum+flex
cir+cum+flexes
cir+cum+flex+ion
cir+cum+flex+
  ions
cir+cum+fuse
cir+cum+fuses
cir+cum+fus+ing
cir+cum+fused
cir+cum+fu+sion

cir+cum+fu+
sions
cir+cum+lo+cu+
tion
cir+cum+lo+cu+
tions
cir+cum+locu+
tory
cir+cum+navi+
gate
cir+cum+navi+
gates
cir+cum+navi+
gat+ing
cir+cum+navi+
gat+ed
cir+cum+navi+ga+
tion
cir+cum+navi+
ga+tions
cir+cum+navi+ga+
tor
cir+cum+navi+
ga+tors
cir+cum+scrib+
able
cir+cum+scribe
cir+cum+scribes
cir+cum+scrib+
ing
cir+cum+scribed
cir+cum+scrib+er
cir+cum+scrib+
ers
cir+cum+scrip+
tion
cir+cum+scrip+
tions
cir+cum+spect
cir+cum+spec+
tion
cir+cum+spect+
ly
cir+cum+stance
cir+cum+
stances
cir+cum+
stances
cir+cum+stanc+
ing
cir+cum+
stanced
cir+cum+stan+
tial

cir+cum+stan+ti+
al+ity
cir+cum+stan+ti+
al+ities
cir+cum+stan+
tial+ly
cir+cum+stan+ti+
ate
cir+cum+stan+ti+
ates
cir+cum+stan+ti+
at+ing
cir+cum+stan+ti+
at+ed
cir+cum+stan+tia+
tion
cir+cum+stan+
tia+tions
cir+cum+val+late
cir+cum+val+
lates
cir+cum+val+lat+
ing
cir+cum+val+lat+
ed
cir+cum+val+la+
tion
cir+cum+val+la+
tions
cir+cum+vent
cir+cum+vents
cir+cum+vent+
ing
cir+cum+vent+
ed
cir+cum+ven+
tion
cir+cum+ven+
tions
cir+cus
cir+cuses
ciré
cirés
Cir+enai+ca
Ci+ren+ces+ter
cirque
cirques
cir+rho+sis
cir+rhot+ic
cir+ri+ped
cir+ri+peds
cir+ri+pede
cir+ri+pedes
cir+ro+cu+mu+
lus

cir+ro+cu+mu+li
cir+ro+stra+tus
cir+ro+stra+ti
cir+rus
cir+ri
cis+al+pine
Cis+cau+ca+sia
cis+co
cis+coes or
cis+cos
Cis+kei
cis+lu+nar
cis+mon+tane
cis+pa+dane
cis+pla+tin
cis+sing
cis+sy
cis+sies
cist
cists
Cis+ter+cian
Cis+ter+cians
cis+tern
cis+terns
cis+ter+na
cis+ter+nae
cis+tus
cis+tuses
cit+able
cita+del
cita+dels
ci+ta+tion
ci+ta+tions
ci+ta+tory
cite
cites
cit+ing
cit+ed
cite+able
citha+ra
citha+ras
cith+er
cith+ers
cith+ern
cith+erns
citi+fied
citi+zen
citi+zens
citi+zen+ry
citi+zen+ries
citi+zen+ship
citi+zen+ships
Ci+tlal+té+petl
cit+rate
cit+rates

cit+ric
cit+rine
cit+rines
cit+ron
cit+rons
cit+ron+el+la
cit+rous
cit+rus
cit+ruses
Cit+tà del Va+ti+
ca+no
cit+tern
cit+terns
city
cities
city+fied
city+scape
city+scapes
city-state
city-states
Ciu+dad
civ+et
civ+ets
civ+ic
civi+cal+ly
civ+ics
civies
civ+il
ci+vil+ian
ci+vil+ians
civi+lis+able
civi+li+sa+tion
civi+li+sa+tions
civi+lise
civi+lises
civi+lis+ing
civi+lised
ci+vil+ity
ci+vil+ities
civi+liz+able
civi+li+za+tion
civi+li+za+tions
civi+lize
civi+lizes
civi+liz+ing
civi+lized
civi+lized
civ+il+ly
civ+vy
civ+vies or
civ+vies
cla+chan
cla+chans
clack

clacks
clacks
clack+ing
clacked
clack+er
clack+ers
Clack+man+nan+
 shire
Clac+ton
Clacton-on-Sea
clad
 clads
 clad+ding
 clad
clad+ding
clade
 clades
cla+dism
 cla+disms
cla+dist
 cla+dists
cla+dis+tics
claim
 claims
 claims
 claim+ing
 claimed
claim+able
claim+ant
 claim+ants
claim+er
 claim+ers
Clair
clair+voy+ance
clair+voy+ant
 clair+voy+ants
clair+voy+ant+ly
clam
 clams
 clams
 clam+ming
 clammed
clam
 clams
 clam+ming
 clammed
cla+mant
clam+ber
 clam+bers
 clam+bers
 clam+ber+ing
 clam+bered
clam+ber+er
 clam+ber+ers
clam+mi+ly

clam+mi+ness
clam+my
 clam+mi+er
 clam+mi+est
clam+or
U.S.
 clam+ors
 clam+ors
 clam+or+ing
 clam+ored
clam+or+ous
clam+or+ous+ly
clam+or+ous+
 ness
clam+our
 clam+ours
 clam+ours
 clam+our+ing
 clam+oured
clamp
 clamps
 clamps
 clamp+ing
 clamped
clamp+down
 clamp+downs
clamp down
verb
clan
 clans
clan+des+tine
clan+des+tine+ly
clang
 clangs
 clangs
 clang+ing
 clanged
clang+er
 clang+ers
clang+or
U.S.
 clang+ors
 clang+ors
 clang+or+ing
 clang+ored
clang+or+ous
clang+or+ous+ly
clang+our
 clang+ours
 clang+ours
 clang+our+ing
 clang+oured
clank
 clanks
 clanks

clank+ing
 clanked
clank+ing+ly
clan+nish
clan+nish+ly
clan+nish+ness
clans+man
 clans+men
clans+woman
 clans+women
clap
 claps
 claps
 clap+ping
 clapped
clap+board
 clap+boards
 clap+boards
 clap+board+ing
 clap+board+ed
clap+per
 clap+pers
clapper+board
 clapper+boards
Clapton
clap+trap
claque
 claques
Clare
Clar+en+don
Clarendon
clar+et
 clar+ets
clari+fi+ca+tion
 clari+fi+ca+tions
clari+fi+er
 clari+fi+ers
clari+fy
 clari+fies
 clari+fy+ing
 clari+fied
clari+net
 clari+nets
clari+net+ist
 clari+net+ists
clari+net+tist
 clari+net+tists
clari+on
 clari+ons
 clari+ons
 clari+on+ing
 clari+oned
clar+ity
Clark
Clarke

clarkia
 clarkias
Clarkson
clary
 claries
clash
 clashes
 clashes
 clash+ing
 clashed
clash+er
 clash+ers
clasp
 clasps
 clasps
 clasp+ing
 clasped
clasp+er
 clasp+ers
class
 classes
 classes
 class+ing
 classed
class-conscious
class-conscious+
 ness
clas+sic
 clas+sics
clas+si+cal
clas+si+cal+ism
clas+si+cal+
 isms
clas+si+cal+ity
clas+si+cal+ly
clas+si+cal+ness
clas+si+cise
 clas+si+cises
 clas+si+cis+ing
 clas+si+cised
clas+si+cism
 clas+si+cisms
clas+si+cist
 clas+si+cists
clas+si+cize
 clas+si+cizes
 clas+si+ciz+ing
 clas+si+cized
clas+sics
clas+si+fi+able
clas+si+fi+ca+
 tion
 clas+si+fi+ca+
 tions

clas+si+fi+ca+
 tory
clas+si+fied
clas+si+fi+er
 clas+si+fi+ers
clas+si+fy
 clas+si+fies
 clas+si+fy+ing
 clas+si+fied
classi+ness
class+less
class+less+ness
class+mate
 class+mates
class+room
 class+rooms
classy
 classi+er
 classi+est
clat+ter
 clat+ters
 clat+ters
 clat+ter+ing
 clat+tered
clat+ter+er
 clat+ter+ers
clat+ter+ing+ly
Claudius
claus+al
clause
 clauses
Clausewitz
Clausius
claus+tro+phobe
 claus+tro+
  phobes
claus+tro+pho+
 bia
claus+tro+pho+
 bic
cla+vate
cla+vate+ly
clave
 claves
clavi+chord
 clavi+chords
clavi+cle
 clavi+cles
cla+vicu+lar
cla+vier
 cla+viers
clavi+form
claw
 claws
 claws

claw+ing
 clawed
claw+back
 claw+backs
 claw back
 verb
claw+er
 claw+ers
clay
 clays
 clay+ey
 clay+ish
 clay+like
 clay+more
 clay+mores
clean
 cleans
 cleans
 clean+ing
 cleaned
 clean+er
 clean+est
 clean+able
 clean-cut
 clean+er
 clean+ers
 clean+li+ly
 clean+li+ness
 clean+ly
 clean+li+er
 clean+li+est
 clean+ness
cleanse
 cleanses
 cleans+ing
 cleansed
 cleans+er
 cleans+ers
clean-shaven
 clean+up
 clean+ups
 clean up
 verb
clear
 clears
 clears
 clear+ing
 cleared
 clear+er
 clear+est
 clear+ance
 clear+ances
clear-cut
 clear+er
 clear+ers

clear+ing
 clear+ings
clear+ly
clear+ness
clear+storied
clear+story
 clear+stories
clear+way
 clear+ways
cleat
 cleats
 cleats
 cleat+ing
 cleat+ed
cleav+able
cleav+age
 cleav+ages
cleave
 cleaves
 cleav+ing
 cleaved *or*
 cleft *or*
 clove *or*
 clo+ven
cleav+er
 cleav+ers
 cleav+ers
Cleese
Clee+thorpes
clef
 clefs
cleft
 clefts
 clefts
 cleft+ing
 cleft+ed
cleg
 clegs
Cle+land
clema+tis
Clemenceau
clem+en+cy
 clem+en+cies
Clemens
clem+ent
clem+en+tine
 clem+en+tines
clench
 clenches
 clenches
 clench+ing
 clenched
Cleon
Cleopatra
clep+sy+dra

clep+sy+dras
 or
clep+sy+drae
clep+to+ma+nia
clere+storied
clere+story
 clere+stories
cler+gy
 cler+gies
clergy+man
 clergy+men
cler+ic
 cler+ics
cleri+cal
 cleri+cal+ism
 cleri+cal+ist
 cleri+cal+ists
 cleri+cal+ly
 cleri+cals
cleri+hew
 cleri+hews
clerk
 clerks
clerk+ess
clerk+ish
clerk+ship
 clerk+ships
Clermont-Ferrand
Cleve+land
 place name
Cleveland
 surname
clev+er
 clev+er+er
 clev+er+est
 clev+er+ly
 clev+er+ness
clev+is
 clev+ises
clew
 clews
 clews
 clew+ing
 clewed
cli+an+thus
 cli+an+thuses
cli+ché
 cli+chés
 cli+chéd
 cli+ché'd
click
 clicks
 clicks
 click+ing
 clicked

click+er
click+ers
cli+ent
cli+ents
cli+en+tage
cli+en+tal
cli+en+tele
cliff
cliffs
cliff+hanger
cliff+hangers
cliff+hanging
cliffy
cli+mac+ter+ic
cli+mac+ter+ics
cli+mac+teri+cal
cli+mac+tic
cli+mac+ti+cal
cli+mac+ti+cal+ly
cli+mate
cli+mates
cli+mat+ic
cli+mati+cal
cli+mati+cal+ly
cli+ma+to+log+ic
cli+ma+to+logi+
cal
cli+ma+tolo+gist
cli+ma+tolo+
gists
cli+ma+tol+ogy
cli+max
cli+maxes
cli+maxes
cli+max+ing
cli+maxed
climb
climbs
climbs
climb+ing
climbed
climb+able
climb-down
climb-downs
climb down
verb
climb+er
climb+ers
clime
climes
clin+al
clinch
clinches
clinches
clinch+ing

clinched
clinch+er
clinch+ers
clincher-built
cline
clines
cling
clings
cling+ing
clung
cling+film
clingi+ness
cling+ing
cling+ing+ly
cling+ing+ness
cling+stone
cling+stones
clingy
clin+ic
clin+ics
clini+cal
clini+cal+ly
cli+ni+cian
cli+ni+cians
clink
clinks
clinks
clink+ing
clinked
clink+er
clink+ers
clink+ers
clink+er+ing
clink+ered
clinker-built
cli+nom+eter
cli+nom+eters
cli+no+met+ric
cli+no+met+ri+
cal
cli+nom+etry
Clio
clip
clips
clips
clip+ping
clipped
clip+board
clip+boards
clipped
clip+per
clip+pers
clip+pers
clip+pie
clip+pies

clip+ping
clip+pings
clips
clique
cliques
cli+quey
cli+quish
cli+quish+ly
cli+quish+ness
cli+quy
clito+ral
cli+tori+dec+
tomy
cli+tori+dec+
tomies
clito+ris
clito+rises
cloa+ca
cloa+cae
cloa+cal
cloak
cloaks
cloaks
cloak+ing
cloaked
cloak-and-dagger
cloak+room
cloak+rooms
clob+ber
clob+bers
clob+ber+ing
clob+bered
cloche
cloches
clock
clocks
clocks
clock+ing
clocked
clock-watcher
clock-watchers
clock+wise
clock+work
clock+works
clod
clods
clod+dish
clod+dish+ly
clod+dy
clod+di+er
clod+di+est
clod+hop+per
clod+hop+pers
clod+pate
clod+pates

clog
clogs
clogs
clog+ging
clogged
clog+gy
cloi+son+né
cloi+son+nés
clois+ter
clois+ters
clois+ters
clois+ter+ing
clois+tered
clois+tered
clois+tral
clomb
clomp
clomps
clone
clones
clones
clon+ing
cloned
clon+ic
clo+nic+ity
clonk
clonks
clonks
clonk+ing
clonked
Clon+mel
clo+nus
clo+nuses
clop
clops
clop+ping
clopped
close
clos+er
clos+est
close
closes
closes
clos+ing
closed
closed
closed-circuit
adj.
closed cir+cuit
noun
close-down
close-downs
close down
verb
close-fisted

close-fisted+ness
close-hauled
close+ly
close+ness
clos+er
 clos+ers
clos+et
 clos+ets
 clos+ets
 clos+et+ing
 clos+et+ed
close-up
 close-ups
close up
 verb
clo+sure
 clo+sures
 clo+sures
 clo+sur+ing
 clo+sured
clot
 clots
 clots
 clot+ting
 clot+ted
cloth
 cloths
clothe
 clothes
 cloth+ing
 clothed *or*
 clad
clothes
clothes+horse
 clothes+horses
clothes+line
 clothes+lines
clothes-press
 clothes-presses
clo+thi+er
 clo+thi+ers
cloth+ing
Clotho
clot+ted
clot+ting
clo+ture
 clo+tures
 clo+tures
 clo+tur+ing
 clo+tured
cloud
 clouds
 clouds
 cloud+ing
 cloud+ed

cloud+burst
 cloud+bursts
cloud-cuckoo-
 land
cloudi+ly
cloudi+ness
cloud+less
 cloud+less+ly
 cloud+less+ness
cloudy
 cloudi+er
 cloudi+est
clough
 cloughs
Clough
clout
 clouts
clove
 cloves
Clo+vel+ly
clo+ven
cloven-footed
cloven-hoofed
clo+ver
 clo+vers
clover+leaf
 clover+leaves
clown
 clowns
 clowns
 clown+ing
 clowned
clown+ery
clown+ish
 clown+ish+ly
 clown+ish+ness
cloy
 cloys
cloy+ing
 cloyed
cloy+ing+ly
cloze
club
 clubs
 clubs
 club+bing
 clubbed
club+ber
 club+bers
 club+bing
 club+bings
club-footed
club+house
 club+houses
club+man

club+men
club+woman
 club+women
cluck
 clucks
 clucks
 cluck+ing
 clucked
clucky
clue
 clues
 clues
 clu+ing
 clued
clued-up
clue+less
clump
 clumps
 clumps
 clump+ing
 clumped
clumpy
clum+si+ly
clum+si+ness
clum+sy
 clum+si+er
 clum+si+est
clung
Clu+ni+ac
clunk
 clunks
 clunks
 clunk+ing
 clunked
Clu+ny
clus+ter
 clus+ters
 clus+ters
 clus+ter+ing
 clus+tered
 clus+tered
 clus+tery
clutch
 clutches
 clutches
 clutch+ing
 clutched
Clu+tha
clut+ter
 clut+ters
 clut+ters
 clut+ter+ing
 clut+tered
Clw+yd
Clyde

Clyde+bank
Clydes+dale
 Clydes+dales
clyp+eal
clyp+eate
clyp+eus
clypei
Clytaemnestra
Clytemnestra
Cnos+sus
Cnut
coach
 coaches
 coaches
 coach+ing
 coached
coach-builder
 coach-builders
coach-built
coach+er
 coach+ers
coach+man
 coach+men
coach+work
 coach+works
co+ad+ju+tor
 co+ad+ju+tors
co+agu+lant
 co+agu+lants
co+agu+late
 co+agu+lates
 co+agu+lat+ing
 co+agu+lat+ed
 co+agu+la+tion
 co+agu+la+tions
 co+agu+la+tive
 co+agu+la+tor
 co+agu+la+tors
Coa+hui+la
coal
 coals
 coals
 coal+ing
 coaled
coal+er
 coal+ers
coa+lesce
 coa+lesces
 coa+lesc+ing
 coa+lesced
 coa+les+cence
 coa+les+cences
 coa+les+cent
coal+face
 coal+faces

coal+field
coal+fields
coal+fish
coal+fish *or*
coal+fishes
coa+li+tion
coa+li+tions
coa+li+tion+ist
coa+li+tion+ists
coal-tar
coaly
coam+ing
coam+ings
coarse
coars+er
coars+est
coarse+ly
coars+en
coars+ens
coars+en+ing
coars+ened
coarse+ness
coast
coasts
coasts
coast+ing
coast+ed
coast+al
coast+er
coast+ers
Coast+er
Coast+ers
coast+guard
coast+guards
coast+guards+
  man
coast+guards+
  men
coast+line
coast+lines
coat
coats
coats
coat+ing
coat+ed
Coates
coa+ti
coa+tis
coati-mondi
coati-mondis
coati-mundi
coati-mundis
coat+ing
coat+ings
coat-of-mail

coat-tail
coat-tails
co+author
co+authors
co+authors
co+author+ing
co+authored
coax
coaxes
coax+ing
coaxed
coax
coaxes
co+ax+al
coax+er
coax+ers
co+ax+ial
coax+ing+ly
cob
cobs
co+balt
cob+ber
cob+bers
Cobbett
cob+ble
cob+bles
cob+bles
cob+bling
cob+bled
cob+bler
cob+blers
cob+blers
cobble+stone
cobble+stones
Cobden
co+bel+lig+er+
  ent
co+bel+lig+er+
  ents
Cobham
Co+blenz
cob+nut
cob+nuts
COBOL
Co+bol
co+bra
co+bras
Co+burg
cob+web
cob+webs
cob+webbed
cob+web+by
cob+webs
coca
cocas

Coca-Cola
Trademark
  Coca-Colas
co+cain
co+caine
coc+cal
coc+coid
coc+cus
coc+ci
coc+cyg+eal
coc+cyx
coc+cyges
Co+chin
cochi+neal
cochi+neals
coch+lea
coch+leae
coch+lear
coch+leate
coch+leat+ed
cock
cocks
cocks
cock+ing
cocked
cocka+bul+ly
cocka+bul+lies
cock+ade
cock+ades
cock+ad+ed
cock-a-doodle-
  doo
cock-a-hoop
cock-a-leekie
cocka+lo+rum
cocka+lo+rums
cocka+too
cocka+toos
cocka+trice
cocka+trices
cock+boat
cock+boats
cock+chafer
cock+chafers
cock+crow
cock+crows
Cocker
cock+er+el
cock+er+els
Cockerell
cock+er span+iel
cock+er span+
  iels
cock+eyed
cock+fight

cock+fights
cock+fighting
cock+horse
cock+horses
cockie+leekie
cocki+ly
cocki+ness
cock+le
cock+les
cock+les
cock+ling
cock+led
cockle+boat
cockle+boats
cockle+shell
cockle+shells
cock+ney
cock+neys
cock+ney+ish
cock+ney+ism
cock+ney+isms
cock+pit
cock+pits
cock+roach
cock+roaches
cocks+comb
cocks+combs
cock+shy
cock+shies
cock+sure
cock+sure+ness
cock+swain
cock+swains
cock+tail
cock+tails
cock+up
cock+ups
cock up
verb
cocky
cocki+er
cocki+est
cocky
cockies
cocky+leeky
coco
cocos
co+coa
cocoa+nut
cocoa+nuts
coco+nut
coco+nuts
co+coon
co+coons
co+coons

co+coon+ing
co+cooned
co+co+pan
co+co+pans
Co+cos
co+cotte
co+cottes
Cocteau
cod
 cod *or*
 cods
 cods
 cod+ding
 cod+ded
coda
 codas
cod-act
 cod-acts
 cod-acting
 cod-acted
cod+dle
 cod+dles
 cod+dling
 cod+dled
 cod+dler
 cod+dlers
code
 codes
 codes
 cod+ing
 cod+ed
co+deine
cod+er
 cod+ers
co+dex
 co+di+ces
cod+fish
 cod+fish *or*
 cod+fishes
codg+er
 codg+ers
codi+cil
 codi+cils
codi+cil+la+ry
codi+fi+ca+tion
 codi+fi+ca+tions
codi+fi+er
 codi+fi+ers
codi+fy
 codi+fies
 codi+fy+ing
 codi+fied
cod+lin
 cod+lins
cod+ling

cod+lings
cod-liver
codo+lo+gy
cod+piece
cod+pieces
cods+wallop
Cody
Coe
co-ed
 co-eds
co+edu+ca+tion
co+edu+ca+tion+
 al
co+edu+ca+tion+
 al+ly
co+ef+fi+cient
 co+ef+fi+cients
coe+la+canth
coe+la+canths
coe+len+ter+ate
 coe+len+ter+
 ates
coe+li+ac
coe+lom
 coe+loms
 coe+lom+ic
coe+no+bite
 coe+no+bites
 coe+no+bit+ic
 coe+no+biti+cal
co+en+zyme
 co+en+zymes
co+equal
 co+equals
 co+equali+ty
co+erce
 co+erces
 co+erc+ing
 co+erced
 co+erc+er
 co+erc+ers
 co+er+ci+ble
 co+er+cion
 co+er+cions
 co+er+cive
 co+er+cive+ly
Coeur
co+eval
 co+evals
 co+eval+ity
 co+eval+ly
co+ex+ecu+tor
 co+ex+ecu+tors
co+ex+ist
 co+ex+ists

co+ex+ist+ing
co+ex+ist+ed
co+ex+ist+ence
co+ex+ist+
 ences
co+ex+ist+ent
co+ex+tend
co+ex+tends
co+ex+tend+ing
co+ex+tend+ed
co+ex+ten+sion
co+ex+ten+
 sions
co+ex+ten+sive
cof+fee
 cof+fees
coffee+pot
coffee+pots
coffee-table
 adj.
cof+fee ta+ble
 noun
cof+fer
 cof+fers
coffer+dam
 coffer+dams
cof+fin
 cof+fins
cof+fle
 cof+fles
cog
 cogs
 cogs
 cog+ging
 cogged
co+gen+cy
co+gent
co+gent+ly
cogi+tate
 cogi+tates
 cogi+tat+ing
 cogi+tat+ed
cogi+ta+tion
 cogi+ta+tions
 cogi+ta+tive
 cogi+ta+tor
 cogi+ta+tors
Cog+nac
 Cog+nacs
cog+nate
 cog+nates
 cog+nate+ly
 cog+nate+ness
cog+na+tion
 cog+na+tions

cog+ni+sable
cog+ni+sance
cog+ni+sant
cog+ni+tion
 cog+ni+tions
cog+ni+tion+al
cog+ni+tive
cog+ni+zable
cog+ni+zance
cog+ni+zant
cog+no+men
 cog+no+mens
 or
cog+nomi+na
cog+nomi+nal
co+gno+scen+te
 co+gno+scen+ti
co+gno+scen+ti
cog+wheel
 cog+wheels
co+hab+it
 co+hab+its
 co+hab+it+ing
 co+hab+it+ed
 co+hab+it+ant
 co+hab+it+ants
 co+habi+ta+tion
 co+habi+ta+
 tions
co+hab+it+er
 co+hab+it+ers
co+heir
 co+heirs
 co+heir+ess
Cohen
co+here
 co+heres
 co+her+ing
 co+hered
co+her+ence
co+her+en+cy
co+her+ent
co+her+ent+ly
co+he+sion
co+he+sive
coho
 coho *or*
 cohos
co+hort
 co+horts
COHSE
coif
 coifs
 coifs
coif+fing

coiffed
coif+feur
coif+feurs
coif+feuse
coif+feuses
coif+fure
coif+fures
coif+fures
coif+fur+ing
coif+fured
coign
coigns
coil
  coils
  coils
  coil+ing
  coiled
Coim+bra
coin
  coins
  coins
  coin+ing
  coined
coin+age
  coin+ages
co+in+cide
  co+in+cides
  co+in+cid+ing
  co+in+cid+ed
  co+in+ci+dence
  co+in+ci+
    dences
  co+in+ci+dent
  co+in+ci+dent+al
  co+in+ci+dent+al+
    ly
coin-op
  coin-ops
Coin+treau
  Trademark
  Coin+treaus
coir
Coire
coi+tal
coi+tion
coi+tus
coke
  cokes
  cok+ing
  coked
Coke
  Cokes
col
  cols
  cola

colas
col+an+der
  col+an+ders
Colbert
Col+ches+ter
col+chi+cine
col+chi+cum
  col+chi+cums
Col+chis
cold
  cold+er
  cold+est
  cold-blooded
  cold-blooded+ly
  cold-blooded+
    ness
  cold-hearted
  cold-hearted+ly
  cold-hearted+
    ness
  cold+ish
  Col+ditz
  cold+ly
  cold+ness
  cold-rolled
  cold-shoulder
    cold-shoulders
    cold-shouldering
    cold-shouldered
  cold shoul+der
    noun
  Cold+stream
cole
  coles
Cole
Coleman
cole+op+ter
  cole+op+ters
col+eop+ter+an
  col+eop+ter+
    ans
col+eop+ter+on
  col+eop+ter+
    ons
Coleridge
Coleridge-Taylor
cole+slaw
co+les+ti+pol
Colet
cole+tit
  cole+tits
Colette
co+leus
  co+le+uses
cole+wort

cole+worts
col+ey
  col+eys
col+ic
col+icky
coli+form
Coligni
Coligny
Co+li+ma
coli+seum
  coli+seums
co+li+tis
col+labo+rate
  col+labo+rates
  col+labo+rat+
    ing
  col+labo+rat+ed
  col+labo+ra+tion
  col+labo+ra+
    tions
col+labo+ra+tive
col+labo+ra+tor
  col+labo+ra+
    tors
col+lage
  col+lages
col+la+gen
col+lag+ist
  col+lag+ists
col+lapsa+ble
col+lap+sar
  col+lap+sars
col+lapse
  col+lapses
  col+lapses
  col+laps+ing
  col+lapsed
col+laps+ibil+ity
col+laps+ible
col+lar
  col+lars
  col+lars
  col+lar+ing
  col+lared
collar+bone
  collar+bones
col+lard
  col+lards
col+late
  col+lates
  col+lat+ing
  col+lat+ed
col+lat+er+al
  col+lat+er+als
  col+lat+er+al+ly

col+la+tion
  col+la+tions
col+la+tor
  col+la+tors
col+league
  col+leagues
col+lect
  col+lects
  col+lects
  col+lect+ing
  col+lect+ed
col+lect+able
  col+lect+ables
col+lect+ed
col+lect+ed+ly
col+lect+ed+ness
col+lect+ible
  col+lect+ibles
col+lec+tion
  col+lec+tions
col+lec+tive
  col+lec+tives
col+lec+tive+ly
col+lec+tivi+
  sation
col+lec+tivi+sa+
  tions
col+lec+ti+vise
  col+lec+ti+vises
  col+lec+ti+vis+
    ing
  col+lec+ti+vised
col+lec+tiv+ism
col+lec+tiv+ist
  col+lec+tiv+ists
col+lec+tiv+is+tic
col+lec+tiv+ity
col+lec+tivi+za+
  tion
col+lec+tivi+za+
  tions
col+lec+ti+vize
  col+lec+ti+vizes
  col+lec+ti+viz+
    ing
  col+lec+ti+vized
col+lec+tor
  col+lec+tors
col+leen
  col+leens
col+lege
  col+leges
col+le+gial
col+legian

col+legians
col+legi+ate
col le+gno
Colles
col+let
col+lets
col+lide
col+lides
col+lid+ing
col+lid+ed
col+lid+er
col+lid+ers
col+lie
col+lies
col+li+er
col+li+ers
col+liery
col+lieries
col+li+mate
col+li+mates
col+li+mat+ing
col+li+mat+ed
col+li+ma+tion
col+li+ma+tions
col+li+ma+tor
col+li+ma+tors
col+lin+ear
col+lin+ear+ity
collins
collinses
Collins
col+li+sion
col+li+sions
col+lo+cate
col+lo+cates
col+lo+cat+ing
col+lo+cat+ed
col+lo+ca+tion
col+lo+ca+tions
col+lo+cu+tor
col+lo+cu+tors
col+lo+di+on
col+lo+dium
col+logue
col+logues
col+lo+guing
col+logued
col+loid
col+loids
col+loi+dal
col+lop
col+lops
col+lo+quial
col+lo+qui+al+ism

col+lo+qui+al+isms
col+lo+qui+al+ly
col+lo+qui+al+ness
col+lo+quist
col+lo+quists
col+lo+quium
col+lo+quiums or
col+lo+quia
col+lo+quy
col+lo+quies
col+lo+type
col+lo+types
col+lude
col+ludes
col+lud+ing
col+lud+ed
col+lud+er
col+lud+ers
col+lu+sion
col+lu+sions
col+lu+sive
col+ly+wob+bles
Col+mar
colo+bus
colo+buses
co+loga+rithm
co+loga+rithms
co+logne
co+lognes
Co+logne
Colomb-Béchar
Co+lombes
Co+lom+bia
Co+lom+bian
Co+lom+bians
Co+lom+bo
co+lon
co+lons or
co+la
co+lón
co+lóns or
co+ló+nes
Co+lón
colo+nel
colo+nels
colo+nel+cy
colo+nel+cies
colo+nel+ship
colo+nel+ships
co+lo+nial
co+lo+nials
co+lo+ni+al+ism

co+lo+ni+al+ist
co+lo+ni+al+ists
co+lo+ni+al+ly
co+lon+ic
Colo+nies
colo+ni+sa+tion
colo+ni+sa+tions
colo+nise
colo+nises
colo+nis+ing
colo+nised
colo+nis+er
colo+nis+ers
colo+nist
colo+nists
colo+ni+za+tion
colo+ni+za+tions
colo+nize
colo+nizes
colo+niz+ing
colo+nized
colo+niz+er
colo+niz+ers
col+on+nade
col+on+nades
col+on+nad+ed
Col+on+say
colo+ny
colo+nies
colo+phon
colo+phons
co+lopho+ny
col+or
U.S.
col+ors
col+ors
col+or+ing
col+ored
Colo+ra+do
col+or+ant
col+or+ants
col+ora+tion
col+ora+tions
colo+ra+tu+ra
colo+ra+tu+ras
col+or+if+ic
col+or+im+eter
col+or+im+eters
col+ori+met+ric
col+orim+etry
col+ori+za+tion
U.S.
col+ori+za+tions

col+or+ize
U.S.
col+or+izes
col+or+iz+ing
col+or+ized
co+los+sal
co+los+sal+ly
col+os+seum
col+os+seums
Col+os+seum
co+los+sus
co+los+si or
co+los+suses
co+los+to+my
co+los+to+mies
co+los+trum
co+loto+my
co+loto+mies
col+our
col+ours
col+our+able
colour-blind
col+oured
Col+oured
Col+oureds or
Col+oured
colour+fast
colour+fastness
col+our+ful
col+our+ful+ly
col+our+ing
col+our+ings
col+ouri+sa+tion
col+ouri+sa+tions
col+our+ise
col+our+ises
col+our+is+ing
col+our+ised
col+our+ist
col+our+ists
col+ouri+za+tion
col+ouri+za+tions
col+our+ize
col+our+izes
col+our+iz+ing
col+our+ized
col+our+less
col+our+less+ly
col+ours
colour+way
colour+ways
colpo+scope
colpo+scopes

colt
  colts
col+ter
  col+ters
colt+ish
colt+ish+ness
Coltrane
colts+foot
  colts+foots
colu+brine
Colum
Co+lum+ba
Columba
Co+lum+bia
col+um+bine
  col+um+bines
Columbine
Co+lum+bus
Columbus
col+umn
  col+umns
co+lum+nar
col+umned
col+umn+ist
  col+umn+ists
co+lure
  co+lures
Col+wyn
col+za
coma
  unconsciousness
comas
coma
  Astronomy,
  botany
comae
Comaneci
co+mate
co+ma+tose
comb
  combs
  combs
  comb+ing
combed
com+bat
  com+bats
  com+bats
com+bat+ing
com+bat+ed
com+bat+ant
  com+bat+ants
com+bat+ive
com+bat+ive+
  ness
combe

combes
comb+er
  comb+ers
com+bin+abili+ty
com+bin+able
com+bi+na+tion
  com+bi+na+
  tions
com+bi+na+tion+
  al
com+bi+na+tions
com+bi+na+tive
com+bi+na+tory
com+bine
  com+bines
  com+bines
  com+bin+ing
  com+bined
comb+ings
com+bin+ing
com+bo
  com+bos
comb-out
  comb-outs
comb out
  verb
com+bus+tibil+
  ity
com+bus+tible
  com+bus+tibles
com+bus+tible+
  ness
com+bus+tion
  com+bus+tions
com+bus+tive
  com+bus+tives
com+bus+tor
  com+bus+tors
come
  comes
  com+ing
  came
  come
come+back
  come+backs
come back
  verb
Com+econ
co+median
  co+medians
co+medic
co+medi+enne
  co+medi+ennes
com+edo
  com+edos *or*

com+edo+nes
come+down
  come+downs
come down
  verb
com+edy
  com+edies
come-hither
come+li+ness
come+ly
  come+li+er
  come+li+est
come-on
  come-ons
come on
  verb
come+over
  noun
come over
  verb
com+er
  com+ers
co+mes+tible
  co+mes+tibles
com+et
  com+ets
com+etary
co+met+ic
come+up+pance
  come+up+
  pances
com+fit
  com+fits
com+fort
  com+forts
  com+forts
com+fort+ing
com+fort+ed
com+fort+able
com+fort+ably
com+fort+er
  com+fort+ers
Com+fort+er
com+fort+ing
com+fort+less
com+frey
  com+freys
com+fy
  com+fi+er
  com+fi+est
com+ic
  com+ics
comi+cal
comi+cal+ly
com+ing

com+ings
Com+in+tern
com+ity
  com+ities
com+ma
  com+mas
com+mand
  com+mands
  com+mands
com+mand+ing
com+mand+ed
com+man+dant
  com+man+
  dants
com+man+deer
  com+man+
  deers
com+man+deer+
  ing
com+man+
  deered
com+mand+er
  com+mand+ers
com+mand+er+
  ship
com+mand+er+
  ships
com+mand+ing
com+mand+ing+
  ly
com+mand+ment
  com+mand+
  ments
com+man+do
  com+man+dos
  or
  com+man+does
com+media
  dell'ar+te
comme il faut
com+memo+rate
  com+memo+
  rates
com+memo+rat+
  ing
com+memo+rat+
  ed
com+memo+ra+
  tion
com+memo+ra+
  tions
com+memo+ra+
  tive
com+memo+ra+
  tor

com+memo+ra+
tors
com+mence
com+mences
com+menc+ing
com+menced
com+mence+
ment
com+mence+
ments
com+mend
com+mends
com+mend+ing
com+mend+ed
com+mend+able
com+mend+ably
com+men+da+
tion
com+men+da+
tions
com+menda+
tory
com+men+sal
com+men+sals
com+men+sal+
ism
com+men+sal+
ity
com+men+su+
rabil+ity
com+men+su+
rable
com+men+su+
rably
com+men+su+
rate
com+men+su+
rate+ly
com+ment
com+ments
com+ments
com+ment+ing
com+ment+ed
com+men+tary
com+men+
taries
com+men+tate
com+men+tates
com+men+tat+
ing
com+men+tat+
ed
com+men+ta+tor
com+men+ta+
tors

com+ment+er
com+ment+ers
com+merce
com+mer+cial
com+mer+cials
com+mer+ciali+
sa+tion
com+mer+ciali+
sa+tions
com+mer+cial+
ise
com+mer+cial+
ises
com+mer+cial+
is+ing
com+mer+cial+
ised
com+mer+cial+
ism
com+mer+ci+al+
ity
com+mer+ci+al+
ities
com+mer+ciali+
za+tion
com+mer+ciali+
za+tions
com+mer+cial+
ize
com+mer+cial+
izes
com+mer+cial+
iz+ing
com+mer+cial+
ized
com+mer+cial+ly
com+mie
com+mies
com+mi+na+tion
com+mi+na+
tions
com+mina+tory
com+min+gle
com+min+gles
com+min+gling
com+min+gled
com+mi+nute
com+mi+nutes
com+mi+nut+
ing
com+mi+nut+ed
com+mi+nu+tion
com+mi+nu+
tions
com+mis

com+mis
com+mis+er+ate
com+mis+er+
ates
com+mis+er+at+
ing
com+mis+er+at+
ed
com+mis+era+
tion
com+mis+era+
tions
com+mis+era+
tor
com+mis+era+
tors
com+mis+sar
com+mis+sars
com+mis+sar+ial
com+mis+sari+at
com+mis+sari+
ats
com+mis+sary
com+mis+saries
com+mis+sion
com+mis+sions
com+mis+sions
com+mis+sion+
ing
com+mis+
sioned
com+mis+sion+
aire
com+mis+sion+
aires
com+mis+sioned
com+mis+sion+
er
com+mis+sion+
ers
com+mis+sion+
er+ship
com+mis+sion+
er+ships
com+mit
com+mits
com+mit+ting
com+mit+ted
com+mit+ment
com+mit+ments
com+mit+table
com+mit+tal
com+mit+tals
com+mit+tee
com+mit+tees

committee+man
committee+men
committee+
woman
committee+
women
com+mit+ter
com+mit+ters
com+mode
com+modes
com+mo+di+ous
com+mo+di+ous+
ness
com+mod+ity
com+mod+ities
com+modo
com+mo+dore
com+mo+dores
Commodus
com+mon
com+mons
com+mon+er
com+mon+est
com+mon+age
com+mon+al+ity
com+mon+al+
ities
com+mon+al+ty
com+mon+al+
ties
com+mon+er
com+mon+ers
com+mon+ly
com+mon+ness
common+place
common+places
common+
placeness
com+mons
Com+mons
common-sense
common-sensical
common+weal
common+wealth
Common+wealth
com+mo+tion
com+mo+tions
com+mu+nal
com+mu+nali+sa+
tion
com+mu+nali+
sa+tions
com+mu+nal+ise
com+mu+nal+
ises

com+mu+nal+is+ing
com+mu+nal+ised
com+mu+nal+ism
com+mu+nal+ist
com+mu+nal+ists
com+mu+nal+is+tic
com+mu+nal+ity
com+mu+nali+za+tion
com+mu+nali+za+tions
com+mu+nal+ize
com+mu+nal+izes
com+mu+nal+iz+ing
com+mu+nal+ized
com+mu+nal+ly
com+mune
com+munes
com+munes
com+mun+ing
com+muned
Com+mune
com+mu+ni+cabil+ity
com+mu+ni+cable
com+mu+ni+cably
com+mu+ni+cant
com+mu+ni+cants
com+mu+ni+cate
com+mu+ni+cates
com+mu+ni+cat+ing
com+mu+ni+cat+ed
com+mu+ni+ca+tion
com+mu+ni+ca+tions
com+mu+ni+ca+tions
com+mu+ni+ca+tive

com+mu+ni+ca+tor
com+mu+ni+ca+tors
com+mu+ni+ca+tory
com+mun+ion
com+mun+ions
Com+mun+ion
Com+mun+ions
com+mu+ni+qué
com+mu+ni+qués
com+mu+ni+sa+tion
com+mu+ni+sa+tions
com+mu+nise
com+mu+nises
com+mu+nis+ing
com+mu+nised
com+mun+ism
com+mun+ist
com+mun+ists
com+mu+nis+tic
com+mu+nity
com+mu+nities
com+mu+ni+za+tion
com+mu+ni+za+tions
com+mu+nize
com+mu+nizes
com+mu+niz+ing
com+mu+nized
com+mut+abil+ity
com+mut+able
com+mu+tate
com+mu+tates
com+mu+tat+ing
com+mu+tat+ed
com+mu+ta+tion
com+mu+ta+tions
com+mu+ta+tive
com+mu+ta+tor
com+mu+ta+tors
com+mute
com+mutes
com+mut+ing

com+mut+ed
com+mut+er
com+mut+ers
com+my
com+mies
Como
co+modo
Como+ros
co+mose
comp
comps
comps
comp+ing
comped
com+pact
com+pacts
com+pacts
com+pact+ing
com+pact+ed
com+pact+ly
com+pact+ness
com+pages
com+pan+ion
com+pan+ions
com+pan+ions
com+pan+ion+ing
com+pan+ioned
com+pan+ion+able
com+pan+ion+able+ness
com+pan+ion+ably
com+pan+ion+ate
com+pan+ion+ship
com+pan+ion+way
com+pan+ion+ways
com+pa+ny
com+pa+nies
com+pa+nies
com+pa+ny+ing
com+pa+nied
com+pa+rabil+ity
com+pa+rable
com+pa+rable+ness
com+para+tive
com+para+tives
com+para+tive+ly

com+para+tive+ness
com+pare
com+pares
com+par+ing
com+pared
com+pari+son
com+pari+sons
com+part+ment
com+part+ments
com+part+men+tal
com+part+men+tali+sa+tion
com+part+men+tali+sa+tions
com+part+men+tal+ise
com+part+men+tal+ises
com+part+men+tal+is+ing
com+part+men+tal+ised
com+part+men+tali+za+tion
com+part+men+tali+za+tions
com+part+men+tal+ize
com+part+men+tal+izes
com+part+men+tal+iz+ing
com+part+men+tal+ized
com+part+men+tal+ly
com+pass
com+passes
com+passes
com+pass+ing
com+passed
com+pass+able
com+pas+sion
com+pas+sion+ate
com+pas+sion+ate+ly
com+pat+ibil+ity
com+pat+ible
com+pat+ibly
com+pat+ri+ot
com+pat+ri+ots

com+pat+ri+ot+ic
com+peer
 com+peers
com+pel
 com+pels
 com+pel+ling
 com+pelled
com+pel+lable
com+pel+ling
com+pen+di+ous
com+pen+di+ous+ly
com+pen+di+ous+ness
com+pen+dium
 com+pen+diums
 or
com+pen+dia
com+pen+sate
 com+pen+sates
 com+pen+sat+ing
 com+pen+sat+ed
com+pen+sa+tion
 com+pen+sa+tions
com+pen+sa+tion+al
com+pen+sa+tive
com+pen+sa+tory
com+pere
 com+peres
 com+peres
 com+per+ing
 com+pered
com+pete
 com+petes
 com+pet+ing
 com+pet+ed
com+pe+tence
com+pe+ten+cy
 com+pe+ten+cies
com+pe+tent
com+pe+tent+ly
com+pe+ti+tion
 com+pe+ti+tions
com+peti+tive

com+peti+tive+ness
com+peti+tor
 com+peti+tors
Com+piègne
com+pi+la+tion
 com+pi+la+tions
com+pile
 com+piles
 com+pil+ing
 com+piled
com+pil+er
 com+pil+ers
com+pla+cence
 com+pla+cences
com+pla+cen+cy
 com+pla+cen+cies
com+pla+cent
com+pla+cent+ly
com+plain
 com+plains
 com+plain+ing
 com+plained
com+plain+ant
 com+plain+ants
com+plain+er
 com+plain+ers
com+plain+ing+ly
com+plaint
 com+plaints
com+plai+sance
 com+plai+sances
com+plai+sant
com+ple+ment
 com+ple+ments
 com+ple+ments
 com+ple+ment+ing
 com+ple+ment+ed
com+ple+men+ta+ri+ly
com+ple+men+ta+ri+ness
com+ple+men+tary
com+ple+men+ta+tion
com+ple+men+ta+tions
com+plete
 com+pletes

com+plet+ing
com+plet+ed
com+plete+ly
com+plete+ness
com+ple+tion
 com+ple+tions
com+plex
 com+plexes
com+plex+ion
 com+plex+ions
com+plex+ion+al
com+plex+ioned
com+plex+ity
 com+plex+ities
com+plex+ness
com+pli+ance
 com+pli+ances
com+pli+an+cy
 com+pli+an+cies
com+pli+ant
com+pli+ant+ly
com+pli+cate
 com+pli+cates
 com+pli+cat+ing
 com+pli+cat+ed
 com+pli+cat+ed+ly
com+pli+ca+tion
 com+pli+ca+tions
com+plic+ity
 com+plic+ities
com+pli+ment
 com+pli+ments
 com+pli+ments
 com+pli+ment+ing
 com+pli+ment+ed
com+pli+men+ta+ri+ly
com+pli+men+tary
com+plin
com+pline
com+ply
 com+plies
 com+ply+ing
 com+plied
com+po
 com+pos
com+po+nent
 com+po+nents

com+po+nen+tial
com+port
 com+ports
 com+port+ing
 com+port+ed
 com+port+ment
com+pose
 com+poses
 com+pos+ing
 com+posed
com+posed
 com+pos+ed+ly
 com+pos+er
 com+pos+ers
com+po+site
 com+po+sites
 com+po+sites
 com+po+sit+ing
 com+po+sit+ed
com+pos+ite+ly
com+pos+ite+ness
com+po+si+tion
com+po+si+tions
com+posi+tor
 com+posi+tors
com+pos men+tis
com+post
 com+posts
 com+posts
 com+post+ing
 com+post+ed
Com+po+ste+la
com+po+sure
com+pote
 com+potes
com+pound
 com+pounds
 com+pounds
 com+pound+ing
 com+pound+ed
com+pound+able
com+pre+hend
 com+pre+hends
 com+pre+hend+ing
 com+pre+hend+ed
com+pre+hen+sibil+ity
com+pre+hen+sible

com+pre+hen+
sibly
com+pre+hen+
sion
com+pre+hen+
sions
com+pre+hen+
sive
com+pre+hen+
sives
com+pre+hen+
sive+ly
com+pre+hen+
sive+ness
com+press
com+presses
com+presses
com+press+ing
com+pressed
com+pressed
com+press+ibil+
ity
com+press+ible
com+pres+sion
com+pres+sions
com+pres+sive
com+pres+sor
com+pres+sors
com+pris+able
com+prise
com+prises
com+pris+ing
com+prised
com+pro+mise
com+pro+mises
com+pro+mises
com+pro+mis+
ing
com+pro+mised
com+pro+mis+er
com+pro+mis+
ers
com+pro+mis+
ing+ly
compte ren+du
comptes ren+
dus
Compton
Compton-Burnett
comp+trol+ler
comp+trol+lers
com+pul+sion
com+pul+sions
com+pul+sive
com+pul+sive+ly

com+pul+so+ri+
ly
com+pul+so+ri+
ness
com+pul+so+ry
com+punc+tion
com+punc+tious
com+punc+tious+
ly
com+put+abil+ity
com+put+able
com+pu+ta+tion
com+pu+ta+
tions
com+pu+ta+tion+
al
com+pute
com+putes
com+put+ing
com+put+ed
com+put+ed
com+put+er
com+put+ers
computer-aided
com+put+er+ate
com+put+eri+sa+
tion
com+put+eri+sa+
tions
com+put+er+ise
com+put+er+
ises
com+put+er+is+
ing
com+put+er+
ised
com+put+eri+za+
tion
com+put+eri+za+
tions
com+put+er+ize
com+put+er+
izes
com+put+er+iz+
ing
com+put+er+
ized
com+put+er+ized
com+rade
com+rades
com+rade+ly
com+rade+ship
com+sat
com+sats
Comte

Comt+ian
Comt+ians
Comt+ism
Comt+ist
Comt+ists
Comus
con
cons
cons
con+ning
conned
Co+na+kry
con amo+re
Conan Doyle
con+cat+enate
con+cat+enates
con+cat+enat+
ing
con+cat+enat+
ed
con+cat+ena+
tion
con+cat+ena+
tions
con+cave
con+caves
con+cav+ing
con+caved
con+cave+ly
con+cave+ness
con+cav+ity
con+cav+ities
concavo-concave
concavo-convex
con+ceal
con+ceals
con+ceal+ing
con+cealed
con+ceal+er
con+ceal+ers
con+ceal+ment
con+ceal+ments
con+cede
con+cedes
con+ced+ing
con+ced+ed
con+ced+er
con+ced+ers
con+ceit
con+ceits
con+ceits
con+ceit+ing
con+ceit+ed
con+ceit+ed
con+ceit+ed+ly

con+ceit+ed+
ness
con+ceiv+abil+ity
con+ceiv+able
con+ceiv+ably
con+ceive
con+ceives
con+ceiv+ing
con+ceived
con+cel+ebrate
con+cel+ebrates
con+cel+ebrat+
ing
con+cel+ebrat+
ed
con+cel+ebra+
tion
con+cel+ebra+
tions
con+cen+trate
con+cen+trates
con+cen+trates
con+cen+trat+
ing
con+cen+trat+
ed
con+cen+tra+tion
con+cen+tra+
tions
con+cen+tra+tive
con+cen+tra+tor
con+cen+tra+
tors
con+cen+tre
con+cen+tres
con+cen+tring
con+cen+tred
con+cen+tric
con+cen+tri+cal+
ly
Con+cep+ción
con+cept
con+cepts
con+cep+tion
con+cep+tions
con+cep+tion+al
con+cep+tive
con+cep+tual
con+cep+tu+ali+
sa+tion
con+cep+tu+ali+
sa+tion
con+cep+tu+al+
ise

con+cep+tu+al+
ises
con+cep+tu+al+
is+ing
con+cep+tu+al+
ised
con+cep+tu+ali+
za+tion
con+cep+tu+ali+
za+tions
con+cep+tu+al+
ize
con+cep+tu+al+
izes
con+cep+tu+al+
iz+ing
con+cep+tu+al+
ized
con+cep+tu+al+
ly
con+cern
con+cerns
con+cerns
con+cern+ing
con+cerned
con+cerned
con+cern+ed+ly
con+cern+ing
con+cern+ment
con+cern+
ments
con+cert
con+certs
con+certs
con+cert+ing
con+cert+ed
con+cer+tan+te
con+cer+tan+ti
con+cert+ed
Con+cert+
gebouw
con+cer+ti+na
con+cer+ti+nas
con+cer+ti+nas
con+cer+ti+na+
ing
con+cer+ti+
naed
con+cer+ti+nist
con+cer+ti+
nists
con+cer+ti+no
con+cer+ti+ni
concert+master

concert+
masters
con+cer+to
con+cer+tos
or
con+cer+ti
con+cer+to gros+
so
con+cer+ti gros+
si or
con+cer+to gros+
sos
con+ces+sible
con+ces+sion
con+ces+sions
con+ces+sion+
aire
con+ces+sion+
aires
con+ces+sion+
ary
con+ces+sion+
aries
con+ces+sion+er
con+ces+sion+
ers
con+ces+sive
conch
conchs or
conches
con+chie
con+chies
Conchobar
con+cholo+gist
con+cholo+gists
con+chol+ogy
con+chy
con+chies
con+ci+erge
con+ci+erges
con+cili+able
con+cili+ar
con+cili+ate
con+cili+ates
con+cili+at+ing
con+cili+at+ed
con+cili+ation
con+cili+ations
con+cilia+tive
con+cili+ator
con+cili+ators
con+cilia+to+ri+
ly
con+cilia+tory
con+cise

con+cise+ly
con+cise+ness
con+ci+sion
con+ci+sions
con+clave
con+claves
con+clude
con+cludes
con+clud+ing
con+clud+ed
con+clu+sion
con+clu+sions
con+clu+sive
con+clu+sive+ly
con+coct
con+cocts
con+coct+ing
con+coct+ed
con+coct+er
con+coct+ers
con+coc+tion
con+coc+tions
con+coc+tor
con+coc+tors
con+comi+tance
con+comi+
tances
con+comi+tant
con+comi+tants
con+cord
con+cords
Con+cord
con+cord+ance
con+cord+ances
con+cord+ant
con+cord+ant+ly
con+cor+dat
con+cor+dats
con+course
con+courses
con+crete
con+cretes
con+cretes
con+cret+ing
con+cret+ed
con+crete+ly
con+crete+ness
con+cre+tion
con+cre+tions
con+cre+tion+ary
con+cre+tise
con+cre+tises
con+cre+tis+ing
con+cre+tised
con+cre+tize

con+cre+tizes
con+cre+tiz+ing
con+cre+tized
con+cu+bi+nage
con+cu+bi+nary
con+cu+bine
con+cu+bines
con+cu+pis+
cence
con+cu+pis+cent
con+cur
con+curs
con+cur+ring
con+curred
con+cur+rence
con+cur+rent
con+cur+rent+ly
con+cuss
con+cusses
con+cuss+ing
con+cussed
con+cus+sion
con+cus+sions
Condé
con+demn
con+demns
con+demn+ing
con+demned
con+demn+able
con+dem+na+
tion
con+dem+na+
tions
con+dem+na+
tory
con+den+sable
con+den+sate
con+den+sates
con+den+sa+tion
con+den+sa+
tions
con+den+sa+tion+
al
con+dense
con+denses
con+dens+ing
con+densed
con+densed
con+den+ser
con+den+sers
con+den+sible
con+de+scend
con+de+scends
con+de+scend+
ing

con+de+scend+ed
con+de+scend+ing
con+de+scend+ing+ly
con+de+scen+sion
con+de+scen+sions
con+dign
con+dign+ly
con+di+ment
con+di+ments
con+di+tion
con+di+tions
con+di+tion+al
con+di+tion+als
con+di+tion+al+ity
con+di+tion+al+ly
con+di+tioned
con+di+tion+er
con+di+tion+ers
con+di+tion+ing
con+do
con+dos
con+dole
con+doles
con+dol+ing
con+doled
con+do+lence
con+do+lences
con+dom
con+doms
con+do+min+ium
con+do+min+iums
con+do+na+tion
con+done
con+dones
con+don+ing
con+doned
con+don+er
con+don+ers
con+dor
con+dors
con+dot+tiere
con+dot+tieri
con+duce
con+duces
con+duc+ing
con+duced
con+du+cive

con+duct
con+ducts
con+ducts
con+duct+ing
con+duct+ed
con+duct+ance
con+duct+ibil+ity
con+duct+ible
con+duct+ing
con+duc+tion
con+duc+tions
con+duc+tion+al
con+duc+tive
con+duc+tiv+ity
con+duc+tiv+ities
con+duc+tor
con+duc+tors
con+duc+tor+ship
con+duc+tor+ships
con+duc+tress
con+duc+tresses
con+duit
con+duits
con+dy+lar
con+dyle
con+dyles
cone
cones
cones
con+ing
coned
co+ney
co+neys
Co+ney
con+fab
con+fabs
con+fabs
con+fab+bing
con+fabbed
con+fabu+late
con+fabu+lates
con+fabu+lat+ing
con+fabu+lat+ed
con+fabu+la+tion
con+fabu+la+tions
con+fect
con+fects
con+fect+ing

con+fect+ed
con+fec+tion
con+fec+tions
con+fec+tion+er
con+fec+tion+ers
con+fec+tion+ery
con+fec+tion+eries
con+fed+era+cy
con+fed+era+cies
Con+fed+era+cy
con+fed+er+ate
con+fed+er+ates
con+fed+er+ates
con+fed+er+at+ing
con+fed+er+at+ed
Con+fed+er+ate
Con+fed+er+ates
con+fed+era+tion
con+fed+era+tions
Con+fed+era+tion
con+fed+era+tion+ist
con+fed+era+tion+ists
con+fer
con+fers
con+fer+ring
con+ferred
con+feree
con+ferees
con+fer+ence
con+fer+ences
con+fer+enc+ing
con+fer+en+tial
con+fer+ment
con+fer+ments
con+fer+rable
con+fer+ral
con+fer+rals
con+fer+ree
con+fer+rees
con+fess
con+fesses
con+fess+ing
con+fessed

con+fess+ed+ly
con+fes+sion
con+fes+sions
con+fes+sion+al
con+fes+sion+als
con+fes+sion+ary
con+fes+sor
con+fes+sors
con+fet+ti
con+fi+dant
con+fi+dants
con+fi+dante
con+fi+dantes
con+fide
con+fides
con+fid+ing
con+fid+ed
con+fi+dence
con+fi+dences
con+fi+dent
con+fi+den+tial
con+fi+den+ti+al+ity
con+fi+den+tial+ly
con+fi+dent+ly
con+fid+er
con+fid+ers
con+fid+ing
con+fid+ing+ly
con+fid+ing+ness
con+figu+ra+tion
con+figu+ra+tions
con+figu+ra+tion+al
con+figu+ra+tive
con+fine
con+fines
con+fines
con+fin+ing
con+fined
con+fined
con+fine+ment
con+fine+ments
con+fin+er
con+fin+ers
con+firm
con+firms
con+firm+ing
con+firmed
con+fir+ma+tion

con+fir+ma+
tions
con+firma+tive
con+firma+tory
con+firmed
con+fis+cate
con+fis+cates
con+fis+cat+ing
con+fis+cat+ed
con+fis+ca+tion
con+fis+ca+
tions
con+fis+ca+tor
con+fis+ca+tors
con+fis+ca+tory
Con+fit+eor
con+fla+gra+tion
con+fla+gra+
tions
con+flate
con+flates
con+flat+ing
con+flat+ed
con+fla+tion
con+fla+tions
con+flict
con+flicts
con+flicts
con+flict+ing
con+flict+ed
con+flict+ing
con+flict+ing+ly
con+flic+tion
con+flic+tions
con+flu+ence
con+flu+ences
con+flu+ent
con+flux
con+fluxes
con+form
con+forms
con+form+ing
con+formed
con+form+abil+
ity
con+form+able
con+form+ably
con+for+mal
con+form+ance
con+form+
ances
con+for+ma+tion
con+for+ma+
tions
con+form+er

con+form+ers
con+form+ist
con+form+ists
con+form+ity
con+form+ities
con+found
con+founds
con+found+ing
con+found+ed
con+found+ed
con+found+ed+ly
con+found+er
con+found+ers
con+fra+ter+nity
con+fra+ter+
nities
con+frère
con+frères
con+front
con+fronts
con+front+ing
con+front+ed
con+fron+ta+tion
con+fron+ta+
tions
con+fron+ta+tion+
al
Con+fu+cian
Con+fu+cians
Con+fu+cian+ism
Con+fu+cian+ist
Con+fu+cian+
ists
Confucius
con+fus+able
con+fuse
con+fuses
con+fus+ing
con+fused
con+fus+ed+ly
con+fus+ing
con+fus+ing+ly
con+fu+sion
con+fu+sions
con+fut+able
con+fu+ta+tion
con+fu+ta+tions
con+fute
con+futes
con+fut+ing
con+fut+ed
con+ga
con+gas
con+gas
con+ga+ing

con+gaed
con+gé
con+gés
con+geal
con+geals
con+geal+ing
con+gealed
con+geal+able
con+geal+ment
con+geal+ments
con+ge+la+tion
con+ge+la+
tions
con+ge+ner
con+ge+ners
con+gen+ial
con+ge+ni+al+ity
con+geni+tal
con+geni+tal+ly
con+ger
con+gers
con+ge+ries
con+gest
con+gests
con+gest+ing
con+gest+ed
con+ges+tion
con+glom+er+ate
con+glom+er+
ates
con+glom+er+
ates
con+glom+er+at+
ing
con+glom+er+at+
ed
con+glom+era+
tion
con+glom+era+
tions
Con+go
Con+go+lese
Con+go+lese
con+grats
con+gratu+late
con+gratu+lates
con+gratu+lat+
ing
con+gratu+lat+
ed
con+gratu+la+
tion
con+gratu+la+
tions

con+gratu+la+
tions
con+gratu+la+
tive
con+gratu+la+
tory
con+gre+gate
con+gre+gates
con+gre+gat+
ing
con+gre+gat+ed
con+gre+ga+tion
con+gre+ga+
tions
con+gre+ga+tion+
al+ism
Con+gre+ga+tion+
al+ist
Con+gre+ga+tion+
al+ist
Con+gre+ga+
tion+al+ists
con+gress
con+gresses
Con+gress
con+gres+sion+
al
Con+gres+sion+
al
con+gres+sion+
al+ist
con+gres+sion+
al+ists
Congress+man
Congress+men
Congress+
woman
Congress+
women
Congreve
con+gru+ence
con+gru+ences
con+gru+en+cy
con+gru+en+
cies
con+gru+ent
con+gru+ity
con+gru+ities
con+gru+ous
con+ic
con+ics
coni+cal
coni+cal+ly
con+ics
co+nid+ium

co+nidia
co+ni+fer
co+ni+fers
co+nif+er+ous
Con+is+ton
con+jec+tur+able
con+jec+tur+al
con+jec+tur+al+ly
con+jec+ture
con+jec+tures
con+jec+tures
con+jec+tur+ing
con+jec+tured
con+join
con+joins
con+join+ing
con+joined
con+join+er
con+join+ers
con+joint
con+joint+ly
con+ju+gal
con+ju+gal+ity
con+ju+gal+ly
con+ju+gate
con+ju+gates
con+ju+gat+ing
con+ju+gat+ed
con+ju+ga+tion
con+ju+ga+tions
con+ju+ga+tion+al
con+ju+ga+tive
con+ju+ga+tor
con+ju+ga+tors
con+junct
con+juncts
con+junc+tion
con+junc+tions
con+junc+tion+al
con+junc+ti+va
con+junc+ti+vas
or
con+junc+ti+vae
con+junc+ti+val
con+junc+tive
con+junc+tives
con+junc+ti+vi+tis
con+junc+ture
con+junc+tures
con+jura+tion
con+jura+tions

con+jure
con+jures
con+jur+ing
con+jured
con+jur+er
con+jur+ers
con+jur+ing
con+jur+ings
con+jur+or
con+jur+ors
conk
conks
conks
conk+ing
conked
conk+er
conk+ers
conk+ers
con moto
conn
conns
conns
conn+ing
conned
Con+nacht
con+nate
Con+naught
con+nect
con+nects
con+nect+ing
con+nect+ed
con+nect+able
con+nect+er
con+nect+ers
con+nect+ible
Con+necti+cut
con+nect+ing
con+nec+tion
con+nec+tions
con+nec+tion+al
con+nec+tive
con+nec+tives
con+nect+or
con+nect+ors
Con+ne+ma+ra
Connery
con+nex+ion
con+nex+ions
con+nex+ion+al
con+ning
con+niv+ance
con+niv+ances
con+nive
con+nives
con+niv+ing

con+nived
con+niv+er
con+niv+ers
con+nois+seur
con+nois+seurs
con+nois+seur+ship
Connolly
Connors
con+no+ta+tion
con+no+ta+tions
con+no+ta+tive
con+note
con+notes
con+not+ing
con+not+ed
con+nu+bial
con+nu+bi+al+ity
co+noid
co+noids
co+noi+dal+ly
cono+scen+te
cono+scen+ti
cono+scen+ti
con+quer
con+quers
con+quer+ing
con+quered
con+quer+able
con+quer+ing
con+quer+or
con+quer+ors
Con+quer+or
con+quest
con+quests
con+quis+ta+dor
con+quis+ta+dors or
con+quis+ta+do+res
Conrad
con+san+guine
con+san+guin+eous
con+san+guin+ity
con+science
con+sciences
conscience-smitten
conscience-stricken
con+sci+en+tious

con+sci+en+tious+ly
con+sci+en+tious+ness
con+scious
con+scious+ly
con+scious+ness
con+script
con+scripts
con+scripts
con+script+ing
con+script+ed
con+scrip+tion
con+scrip+tions
con+se+crate
con+se+crates
con+se+crat+ing
con+se+crat+ed
con+se+cra+tion
con+se+cra+tions
Con+se+cra+tion
con+se+cra+tor
con+se+cra+tors
con+se+cra+tory
con+secu+tive
con+secu+tive+ly
con+secu+tive+ness
con+sen+sual
con+sen+su+al+ly
con+sen+sus
con+sent
con+sents
con+sent+ing
con+sent+ed
con+sent+ing
con+se+quence
con+se+quences
con+se+quent
con+se+quen+tial
con+se+quen+ti+al+ity
con+se+quen+tial+ly
con+se+quent+ly
con+serv+an+cy
con+serv+an+cies
con+ser+va+tion

con+ser+va+tion+
al
con+ser+va+tion+
ist
con+ser+va+
tion+ists
con+serva+tism
con+serva+tive
con+serva+tives
Con+serva+tive
Con+serva+
tives
con+serva+tive+
ness
con+serva+toire
con+serva+
toires
con+ser+va+tor
con+ser+va+
tors
con+serva+to+
rium
con+serva+to+
riums
con+serva+tory
con+serva+
tories
con+serve
con+serves
con+serves
con+serv+ing
con+served
con+sid+er
con+sid+ers
con+sid+er+ing
con+sid+ered
con+sid+er+able
con+sid+er+ably
con+sid+er+ate
con+sid+er+ate+
ly
con+sid+era+tion
con+sid+era+
tions
con+sid+ered
con+sid+er+ing
con+sign
con+signs
con+sign+ing
con+signed
con+sign+able
con+signee
con+signees
con+sign+er
con+sign+ers

con+sign+ment
con+sign+ments
con+sign+or
con+sign+ors
con+sist
con+sists
con+sist+ing
con+sist+ed
con+sist+ence
con+sist+ences
con+sist+en+cy
con+sist+en+
cies
con+sist+ent
con+sist+ent+ly
con+sis+to+rial
con+sis+tory
con+sis+tories
con+sol+able
con+sol+a+tion
con+so+la+tions
con+sola+tory
con+sole
con+soles
con+soles
con+sol+ing
con+soled
con+sol+er
con+sol+ers
con+soli+date
con+soli+dates
con+soli+dat+
ing
con+soli+dat+
ed
con+soli+dat+ed
con+soli+da+tion
con+soli+da+tor
con+soli+da+
tors
con+sol+ing+ly
con+sols
con+som+mé
con+so+nance
con+so+nances
con+so+nant
con+so+nants
con+so+nan+tal
con+so+nant+ly
con+sort
con+sorts
con+sorts
con+sort+ing
con+sort+ed
con+sor+tium

con+sor+tia
con+spec+tus
con+spec+tuses
con+spicu+ous
con+spicu+ous+
ly
con+spicu+ous+
ness
con+spira+cy
con+spira+cies
con+spira+tor
con+spira+tors
con+spira+to+rial
con+spire
con+spires
con+spir+ing
con+spired
con spi+ri+to
con+sta+ble
con+sta+bles
Constable
con+sta+ble+
ship
con+stabu+lary
con+stabu+
laries
Con+stance
con+stan+cy
con+stant
con+stants
Con+stan+ta
Con+stan+tia
Con+stan+tine
Constantine
Con+stan+ti+no+
ple
con+stant+ly
con+stel+late
con+stel+lates
con+stel+lat+ing
con+stel+lat+ed
con+stel+la+tion
con+stel+la+
tions
con+stel+la+tory
con+ster+nate
con+ster+nates
con+ster+nat+
ing
con+ster+nat+
ed
con+ster+na+tion
con+sti+pate
con+sti+pates
con+sti+pat+ing

con+sti+pat+ed
con+sti+pat+ed
con+sti+pa+tion
con+stitu+en+cy
con+stitu+en+
cies
con+stitu+ent
con+stitu+ents
con+stitu+ent+ly
con+sti+tute
con+sti+tutes
con+sti+tut+ing
con+sti+tut+ed
con+sti+tu+tion
con+sti+tu+
tions
con+sti+tu+tion+
al
con+sti+tu+tion+
al+ism
con+sti+tu+tion+
al+ist
con+sti+tu+tion+
al+ists
con+sti+tu+tion+
al+ity
con+sti+tu+tion+
al+ly
con+sti+tu+tive
con+sti+tu+tive+
ly
con+sti+tu+tor
con+sti+tu+tors
con+strain
con+strains
con+strain+ing
con+strained
con+strain+er
con+strain+ers
con+straint
con+straints
con+strict
con+stricts
con+strict+ing
con+strict+ed
con+stric+tion
con+stric+tions
con+stric+tive
con+stric+tor
con+stric+tors
con+stru+able
con+struct
con+structs
con+structs

con+struct+ing
con+struct+ed
con+struct+er
con+struct+ers
con+struc+tion
con+struc+tions
con+struc+tion+
al
con+struc+tion+
al+ly
con+struc+tive
con+struc+tive+
ly
con+struc+tiv+
ism
con+struc+tiv+ist
con+struc+tiv+
ists
con+struc+tor
con+struc+tors
con+strue
con+strues
con+stru+ing
con+strued
con+sub+stan+
tial
con+sub+stan+ti+
al+ity
con+sub+stan+
tia+tion
con+suetude
con+suetudes
con+sul
con+suls
con+su+lar
con+su+late
con+su+lates
con+sul gen+er+
al
con+suls gen+er+
al
con+sul+ship
con+sul+ships
con+sult
con+sults
con+sult+ing
con+sult+ed
con+sul+tan+cy
con+sul+tan+
cies
con+sult+ant
con+sult+ants
con+sul+ta+tion
con+sul+ta+
tions

con+sul+ta+tive
con+sult+ing
con+sum+able
con+sume
con+sumes
con+sum+ing
con+sumed
con+sum+ed+ly
con+sum+er
con+sum+ers
con+sum+er+ism
con+sum+er+ist
con+sum+er+
ists
con+sum+ing
con+sum+mate
con+sum+mates
con+sum+mat+
ing
con+sum+mat+
ed
con+sum+mate+
ly
con+sum+ma+
tion
con+sum+ma+
tions
con+sump+tion
con+sump+tive
con+sump+tives
con+sump+tive+
ly
con+sump+tive+
ness
con+tact
con+tacts
con+tacts
con+tact+ing
con+tact+ed
con+tac+tual
con+ta+gion
con+ta+gions
con+ta+gious
con+tain
con+tains
con+tain+ing
con+tained
con+tain+able
con+tain+er
con+tain+ers
con+tain+eri+sa+
tion
con+tain+er+ise
con+tain+er+
ises

con+tain+er+is+
ing
con+tain+er+
ised
con+tain+eri+za+
tion
con+tain+er+ize
con+tain+er+
izes
con+tain+er+iz+
ing
con+tain+er+
ized
con+tain+ment
con+tami+nable
con+tami+nant
con+tami+nants
con+tami+nate
con+tami+nates
con+tami+nat+
ing
con+tami+nat+
ed
con+tami+na+
tion
con+tami+na+
tions
con+tami+na+tor
con+tami+na+
tors
con+tan+go
con+tan+gos
conte
contes
con+té
con+tés
con+temn
con+temns
con+temn+ing
con+temned
con+temn+er
con+temn+ers
con+tem+plate
con+tem+plates
con+tem+plat+
ing
con+tem+plat+
ed
con+tem+pla+
tion
con+tem+pla+
tive
con+tem+pla+
tives
con+tem+pla+tor

con+tem+pla+
tors
con+tem+po+ra+
neity
con+tem+po+ra+
neous
con+tem+po+ra+
neous+ness
con+tem+po+rari+
ly
con+tem+po+rari+
ness
con+tem+po+
rary
con+tem+po+
raries
con+tem+po+rise
con+tem+po+
rises
con+tem+po+ris+
ing
con+tem+po+
rised
con+tem+po+rize
con+tem+po+
rizes
con+tem+po+riz+
ing
con+tem+po+
rized
con+tempt
con+tempts
con+tempt+ibil+
ity
con+tempt+ible
con+tempt+ible+
ness
con+tempt+ibly
con+temp+tu+
ous
con+temp+tu+
ous+ly
con+tend
con+tends
con+tend+ing
con+tend+ed
con+tend+er
con+tend+ers
con+tent
con+tents
con+tents
con+tent+ing
con+tent+ed
con+tent+ed+ly

con+tent+ed+
ness
con+ten+tion
con+ten+tions
con+ten+tious
con+ten+tious+
ness
con+tent+ment
con+ter+mi+nous
con+test
con+tests
con+tests
con+test+ing
con+test+ed
con+test+able
con+test+ant
con+test+ants
con+test+er
con+test+ers
con+text
con+texts
con+tex+tual
con+tigu+ous
con+tigu+ous+ly
con+ti+nence
con+ti+nent
con+ti+nents
Con+ti+nent
Con+ti+nents
con+ti+nen+tal
Con+ti+nen+tal
Con+ti+nen+tals
con+ti+nen+tal+
ly
con+tin+gence
con+tin+gences
con+tin+gen+cy
con+tin+gen+
cies
con+tin+gent
con+tin+gents
con+tin+ual
con+tinu+al+ly
con+tinu+ance
con+tinu+ant
con+tinu+ants
con+tinu+ation
con+tinu+ations
con+tinue
con+tinues
con+tinu+ing
con+tinued
con+ti+nu+ity
con+ti+nu+ities
con+tinuo

con+tinuos
con+tinu+ous
con+tinu+ous+ly
con+tin+uum
con+tinua or
con+tin+uums
con+tort
con+torts
con+tort+ing
con+tort+ed
con+tor+tion
con+tor+tions
con+tor+tion+ist
con+tor+tion+
ists
con+tor+tive
con+tour
con+tours
con+tours
con+tour+ing
con+toured
contra+band
contra+band+ist
contra+band+
ists
contra+bass
contra+basses
contra+bas+soon
contra+bas+
soons
contra+cep+tion
contra+cep+tive
contra+cep+
tives
con+tract
con+tracts
con+tracts
con+tract+ing
con+tract+ed
con+tract+ible
con+trac+tile
con+trac+tion
con+trac+tions
con+trac+tive
con+trac+tor
con+trac+tors
con+trac+tual
contra+dance
contra+dances
contra+dict
contra+dicts
contra+dict+ing
contra+dict+ed
contra+dic+tion

contra+dic+
tions
con+tra+dic+tor
con+tra+dic+
tors
contra+dic+to+ri+
ly
contra+dic+to+ri+
ness
contra+dic+tory
contra+dis+tinc+
tion
contra+dis+tinc+
tions
contra+dis+tinc+
tive
contra+flow
contra+flows
con+trail
con+trails
con+tral+to
con+tral+tos
or
con+tral+ti
contra+po+si+
tion
contra+po+si+
tions
con+trap+tion
con+trap+tions
contra+pun+tal
contra+pun+tal+
ist
contra+pun+tal+
ists
contra+pun+tal+
ly
contra+pun+tist
contra+pun+
tists
contra+ri+ety
contra+ri+eties
con+tra+ri+ly
con+tra+ri+ness
con+tra+ri+wise
con+tra+ry
con+tra+ries
con+trast
con+trasts
con+trasts
con+trast+ing
con+trast+ed
con+trast+ing
con+tras+tive
contra+vene

contra+venes
contra+ven+ing
contra+vened
contra+ven+er
contra+ven+ers
contra+ven+tion
contra+ven+
tions
con+tre+danse
con+tre+danses
con+tre+temps
con+tre+temps
con+trib+ute
con+trib+utes
con+trib+ut+ing
con+trib+ut+ed
con+tri+bu+tion
con+tri+bu+
tions
con+tribu+tive
con+tribu+tor
con+tribu+tors
con+tribu+tory
con+tribu+tories
con+trite
con+trite+ly
con+trite+ness
con+tri+tion
con+triv+ance
con+triv+ances
con+trive
con+trives
con+triv+ing
con+trived
con+trived
con+triv+er
con+triv+ers
con+trol
con+trols
con+trols
con+trol+ling
con+trolled
con+trol+labil+ity
con+trol+lable
con+trol+lably
con+trol+ler
con+trol+lers
con+trol+ler+ship
con+trol+ler+
ships
con+trol+ling
con+tro+ver+sial
con+tro+ver+sial+
ism

con+tro+ver+sial+ist
con+tro+ver+sial+ists
con+tro+ver+sy
con+tro+ver+sies
con+tro+vert
con+tro+verts
con+tro+vert+ing
con+tro+vert+ed
con+tro+vert+ible
con+tu+ma+cious
con+tu+ma+cious+ly
con+tu+ma+cy
con+tu+ma+cies
con+tu+meli+ous
con+tu+meli+ous+ly
con+tu+mely
con+tu+melies
con+tuse
con+tuses
con+tus+ing
con+tused
con+tu+sion
con+tu+sions
co+nun+drum
co+nun+drums
con+ur+ba+tion
con+ur+ba+tions
con+va+lesce
con+va+lesces
con+va+lesc+ing
con+va+lesced
con+va+les+cence
con+va+les+cent
con+va+les+cents
con+vec+tion
con+vec+tion+al
con+vec+tive
con+vec+tor
con+vec+tors
con+vene
con+venes
con+ven+ing

con+vened
con+ven+er
con+ven+ers
con+veni+ence
con+veni+ences
con+veni+ent
con+veni+ent+ly
con+ven+or
con+ven+ors
con+vent
con+vents
con+ven+ti+cle
con+ven+ti+cles
con+ven+tion
con+ven+tions
con+ven+tion+al
con+ven+tion+ali+sa+tion
con+ven+tion+ali+sa+tions
con+ven+tion+al+ise
con+ven+tion+al+ises
con+ven+tion+al+is+ing
con+ven+tion+al+ised
con+ven+tion+al+ism
con+ven+tion+al+isms
con+ven+tion+al+ity
con+ven+tion+al+ities
con+ven+tion+ali+za+tion
con+ven+tion+ali+za+tions
con+ven+tion+al+ize
con+ven+tion+al+izes
con+ven+tion+al+iz+ing
con+ven+tion+al+ized
con+ven+tion+al+ly
con+ven+tual
con+ven+tuals
con+ven+tu+al+ly
con+verge

con+verges
con+verg+ing
con+verged
con+ver+gence
con+ver+gences
con+ver+gen+cy
con+ver+gent
con+vers+able
con+ver+sance
con+ver+san+cy
con+ver+sant
con+ver+sant+ly
con+ver+sa+tion
con+ver+sa+tions
con+ver+sa+tion+al
con+ver+sa+tion+al+ist
con+ver+sa+tion+al+ists
con+ver+sa+tion+al+ly
con+verse
con+verses
con+verses
con+vers+ing
con+versed
con+verse+ly
con+vers+er
con+vers+ers
con+ver+sion
con+ver+sions
con+vert
con+verts
con+verts
con+vert+ing
con+vert+ed
con+vert+er
con+vert+ers
con+vert+ibil+ity
con+vert+ible
con+vert+ibles
con+vert+ibly
con+ver+tor
con+ver+tors
con+vex
con+vex+ity
con+vex+ities
con+vex+ly
convexo-concave
convexo-convex
con+vey
con+veys
con+vey+ing

con+veyed
con+vey+able
con+vey+ance
con+vey+ances
con+vey+anc+er
con+vey+anc+ers
con+vey+anc+ing
con+vey+er
con+vey+ers
con+vey+or
con+vey+ors
con+vict
con+victs
con+victs
con+vict+ing
con+vict+ed
con+vic+tion
con+vic+tions
con+vic+tion+al
con+vic+tive
con+vince
con+vinces
con+vinc+ing
con+vinced
con+vinc+er
con+vinc+ers
con+vinc+ible
con+vinc+ing
con+vinc+ing+ly
con+viv+ial
con+vivi+al+ity
con+vo+ca+tion
con+vo+ca+tions
con+vo+ca+tion+al
con+voke
con+vokes
con+vok+ing
con+voked
con+vok+er
con+vok+ers
con+vo+lute
con+vo+lutes
con+vo+lut+ing
con+vo+lut+ed
con+vo+lut+ed+ly
con+vo+lu+tion
con+vo+lu+tions
con+vo+lu+tion+al

con+vo+lu+tion+
  ary
con+volve
  con+volves
  con+volv+ing
  con+volved
con+vol+vu+lus
con+vol+vu+
  luses *or*
  con+vol+vu+li
con+voy
  con+voys
  con+voys
  con+voy+ing
  con+voyed
con+vulse
  con+vulses
  con+vuls+ing
  con+vulsed
con+vul+sion
  con+vul+sions
con+vul+sive
con+vul+sive+ly
Con+way
Con+wy
cony
  conies
Conybeare
coo
  coos
  coos
  coo+ing
  cooed
Cooch Be+har
cooee
  cooees
  cooees
  cooee+ing
  cooeed
coo+ey
  coo+eys
  coo+eys
  coo+ey+ing
  coo+eyed
coo+ing+ly
cook
  cooks
  cooks
  cook+ing
  cooked
Cook
cook+able
cook+book
  cook+books
cook-chill

cook+er
  cook+ers
cook+ery
  cook+eries
  U.S., Canada
cook-general
  cooks-general
cookie
  cookies
cook+ing
Cookson
cook-up
  noun
cook up
  verb
cooky
  cookies
cool
  cools
  cool+ing
  cooled
  cool+er
  cool+est
coo+la+bah
  coo+la+bahs
cool+ant
  cool+ants
cool+er
  cool+ers
Coolidge
coolie
  coolies
cooling-off
cool+ly
cool+ness
cooly
  coolies
Coomaraswamy
coomb
  coombs
coombe
  coombes
coon
  coons
coon+skin
  coon+skins
coop
  cage or basket
  coops
  coops
  coop+ing
  cooped
coop
  cooperative
  coops

co-op
  co-ops
coop+er
  coop+ers
  coop+ers
  coop+er+ing
  coop+ered
Cooper
coop+er+age
  coop+er+ages
co+oper+ate
  co+oper+ates
  co+oper+at+ing
  co+oper+at+ed
co-operate
  co-operates
  co-operat+ing
  co-operat+ed
co+opera+tion
  co+opera+tions
co-operation
  co-operations
co+opera+tion+
  ist
co+opera+tion+
  ists
co-operation+ist
co-operation+
  ists
co+opera+tive
  co+opera+tives
co-operative
  co-operatives
co+opera+tor
  co+opera+tors
co-operator
  co-operators
coop+ery
  coop+eries
co+opt
  co+opts
  co+opt+ing
  co+opt+ed
co-opt
  co-opts
  co-opting
  co-opted
co+opta+tion
  co+opta+tions
co-optation
  co-optations
co+option
  co+options
co-option
  co-options

co+or+di+nate
  co+or+di+nates
  co+or+di+nates
  co+or+di+nat+
    ing
  co+or+di+nat+
    ed
co-ordinate
  co-ordinates
  co-ordinates
  co-ordinat+ing
  co-ordinat+ed
co+or+di+nates
co+or+di+nat+
  ing
co+or+di+na+
  tion
co-ordina+tion
co+or+di+na+tive
co-ordina+tive
co+or+di+na+tor
  co+or+di+na+
    tors
co-ordina+tor
  co-ordina+tors
coot
  coots
cootie
  cooties
cop
  cops
  cops
  cop+ping
  copped
co+pal
co+part+ner
  co+part+ners
co+part+ner+ship
  co+part+ner+
    ships
cope
  copes
  copes
  cop+ing
  coped
co+peck
  co+pecks
Co+pen+ha+gen
co+pepod
  co+pepods
co+per
  co+pers
Co+per+ni+can
Copernicus
Co+per+ni+cus

cope+stone
cope+stones
copi+er
copi+ers
co+pi+lot
co+pi+lots
cop+ing
co+pi+ous
co+pi+ous+ly
co+pi+ous+ness
co+pla+nar
co+pla+nar+ity
Copland
co+poly+mer
co+poly+mers
cop-out
cop-outs
cop out
verb
cop+per
cop+pers
cop+pers
cop+per+ing
cop+pered
cop+per+as
copper-bottomed
copper-fasten
copper-fastens
copper-fasten+
 ing
copper-fastened
copper+head
copper+heads
copper+plate
copper+plates
copper+smith
copper+smiths
cop+pice
cop+pices
cop+pices
cop+pic+ing
cop+piced
cop+piced
Coppola
cop+ra
cop+ras
cop+rol+ogy
cop+ropha+gous
copse
copses
Copt
Copts
Cop+tic
copu+la
copu+las *or*

copu+lae
copu+lar
copu+late
copu+lates
copu+lat+ing
copu+lat+ed
copu+la+tion
copu+la+tions
copu+la+tive
copu+la+tory
copy
copies
copies
copy+ing
copied
copy+book
copy+books
copy+cat
copy+cats
copy+hold
copy+holds
copy+ist
copy+ists
copy+reader
copy+readers
copy+right
copy+rights
copy+rights
copy+right+ing
copy+right+ed
copy+writer
copy+writers
copy+writing
co+quet
co+quets
co+quet+ting
co+quet+ted
co+quet+ry
co+quet+ries
co+quette
co+quettes
co+quet+tish
co+quet+tish+
 ness
cora+cle
cora+cles
cora+coid
cora+coids
cor+al
cor+als
Cor+al
coral+root
coral+roots
cor an+glais
cors an+glais

Co+ran+tijn
cor+bel
cor+bels
cor+bels
cor+bel+ling *or*
cor+bel+ing
U.S.
cor+belled *or*
cor+beled
U.S.
cor+bie
cor+bies
corbie-step
corbie-steps
Corbusier
Cor+co+va+do
Cor+cy+ra
cord
cords
cords
cord+ing
cord+ed
cord+age
cor+date
Corday
cord+ed
cor+dial
cor+dials
cor+di+al+ity
cor+di+al+ities
cor+di+al+ly
cor+dil+lera
Cor+dil+leras
cord+ite
cord+ites
cord+less
cord-like
Cór+do+ba
Córdoba
cor+don
cor+dons
cor+dons
cor+don+ing
cor+doned
cor+don bleu
cor+don sa+ni+
 taire
Cor+do+va
Córdova
cor+do+van
cords
cor+du+roy
cor+du+roys
cord+wainer
cord+wainers

cord+wood
core
cores
cores
cor+ing
cored
co+reli+gion+ist
co+reli+gion+
 ists
Corelli
co+reop+sis
co-respond+ent
co-respond+
 ents
corf
corves
Cor+fu
cor+gi
cor+gis
co+ri+an+der
Co+rini+um
Cor+inth
Co+rin+thian
Co+rin+thians
Coriolanus
Coriolis
co+rium
co+ria
cork
corks
corks
cork+ing
corked
Cork
cork+age
corked
cork+er
cork+ers
cork+like
cork+screw
cork+screws
cork+screws
cork+screw+ing
cork+screwed
corm
corms
cor+mo+rant
cor+mo+rants
corn
corns
corns
corn+ing
corned
corn+cob
corn+cobs

corn+cockle
corn+cockles
corn+crake
corn+crakes
cor+nea
cor+neas *or*
cor+neae
cor+neal
corned
Corneille
cor+nel
cor+nels
cor+nel+ian
cor+nel+ians
cor+ner
cor+ners
cor+ners
cor+ner+ing
cor+nered
corner+back
corner+backs
corner+stone
corner+stones
corner+ways
corner+wise
cor+net
cor+nets
cor+net+ist
cor+net+ists
cor+net+tist
cor+net+tists
corn+field
corn+fields
corn+flakes
corn+flour
corn+flower
corn+flowers
Cornforth
cor+nice
cor+nices
cor+niche
cor+niches
Cor+nish
Cornish+man
Cornish+men
Cor+no
corn+starch
cor+nu+co+pia
cor+nu+co+pias
cor+nu+co+pian
Corn+wall
Cornwallis
corny
corni+er
corni+est

co+rol+la
cor+ol+lary
cor+ol+laries
Coro+man+del
co+ro+na
co+ro+nas *or*
co+ro+nae
co+ro+nach
co+ro+nachs
coro+nary
coro+naries
coro+na+tion
coro+na+tions
coro+ner
coro+ners
coro+ner+ship
coro+ner+ships
coro+net
coro+nets
Corot
co-routine
co-routines
cor+po+ral
cor+po+rals
cor+po+ra+le
cor+po+ra+les
cor+po+ral+ity
cor+po+ral+ly
cor+po+rate
cor+po+ra+tion
cor+po+ra+tions
cor+po+rat+ism
cor+po+ra+tive
cor+po+real
cor+po+real+ity
cor+po+real+ly
cor+po+reity
corps
corps
corps dip+lo+ma+
tique
corpse
corpses
cor+pu+lence
cor+pu+lent
cor pul+mon+ale
cor+pus
cor+po+ra
Cor+pus Chris+ti
Cor+pus Chris+
tis
cor+pus+cle
cor+pus+cles
cor+pus+cu+lar
cor+pus+cule

cor+pus+cules
cor+pus de+lic+ti
cor+pus ju+ris
cor+pus lu+teum
cor+po+ra lu+
tea
cor+ral
cor+rals
cor+rals
cor+ral+ling
cor+ralled
cor+ra+sion
cor+ra+sions
cor+rea
cor+reas
cor+rect
cor+rects
cor+rect+ing
cor+rect+ed
cor+rec+tion
cor+rec+tions
cor+rec+tion+al
cor+rec+tive
cor+rec+tives
cor+rect+ly
cor+rect+ness
Correggio
Cor+regi+dor
cor+re+late
cor+re+lates
cor+re+lates
cor+re+lat+ing
cor+re+lat+ed
cor+re+la+tion
cor+re+la+tions
cor+re+la+tion+al
cor+rela+tive
cor+rela+tives
cor+rela+tive+ly
cor+rela+tiv+ity
cor+re+spond
cor+re+sponds
cor+re+spond+
ing
cor+re+spond+
ed
cor+re+spond+
ence
cor+re+spond+
ences
cor+re+spond+
ent
cor+re+spond+
ents

cor+re+spond+
ing+ly
cor+ri+da
cor+ri+das
cor+ri+dor
cor+ri+dors
cor+rie
cor+ries
cor+ri+gen+dum
cor+ri+gen+da
cor+ri+gible
cor+robo+rate
cor+robo+rates
cor+robo+rat+
ing
cor+robo+rat+
ed
cor+robo+ra+tion
cor+robo+ra+
tions
cor+robo+ra+tive
cor+robo+ra+tor
cor+robo+ra+
tors
cor+robo+ra+to+
ry
cor+robo+ree
cor+robo+rees
cor+rode
cor+rodes
cor+rod+ing
cor+rod+ible
cor+ro+sion
cor+ro+sive
cor+ro+sives
cor+ro+sive+ly
cor+ro+sive+
ness
cor+ru+gate
cor+ru+gates
cor+ru+gat+ing
cor+ru+gat+ed
cor+ru+gat+ed
cor+ru+ga+tion
cor+ru+ga+tions
cor+rupt
cor+rupts
cor+rupt+ing
cor+rupt+ed
cor+rupt+er
cor+rupt+ers
cor+rup+tible
cor+rup+tibly
cor+rup+tion

cor+rup+tions
cor+rupt+ly
cor+rupt+ness
cor+rup+tor
cor+rup+tors
cor+sage
cor+sages
cor+sair
cor+sairs
corse
corses
Corse
corse+let
corse+lets
cor+set
cor+sets
cor+sets
cor+set+ing
cor+set+ed
cor+setière
cor+setières
cor+set+ry
Cor+si+ca
Cor+si+can
Cor+si+cans
cors+let
cors+lets
cor+tege
cor+teges
cor+tège
cor+tèges
Cor+tes
Cortés
cor+tex
cor+ti+ces
Cortez
cor+ti+cal
cor+ti+cate
cor+ti+cat+ed
cor+ti+sone
Cor+to+na
Cortot
co+run+dum
Co+run+na
co+rus+cate
co+rus+cates
co+rus+cat+ing
co+rus+cat+ed
cor+us+ca+tion
cor+us+ca+
tions
cor+vée
cor+vées
cor+vette
cor+vettes

cor+vine
Corvo
Corybant
Corybants or
Corybantes
Cory+ban+tic
cor+ymb
cor+ymbs
co+ry+za
cos
Cos
Cosa Nos+tra
co+secant
co+secants
co+set
co+sets
Cosgrave
cosh
coshes
coshes
cosh+ing
coshed
co+sig+na+tory
co+sig+na+
tories
co+si+ly
co+sine
co+sines
co+si+ness
cos+met+ic
cos+met+ics
cos+meti+cal+ly
cos+mic
cos+mi+cal+ly
cos+mo+gon+ic
cos+mo+goni+
cal
cos+mogo+nist
cos+mogo+
nists
cos+mogo+ny
cos+mogo+nies
cos+mog+ra+
pher
cos+mog+ra+
phers
cos+mo+graph+
ic
cos+mo+graphi+
cal
cos+mog+ra+phy
cos+mo+log+ic
cos+mo+logi+cal
cos+molo+gist
cos+molo+gists

cos+mol+ogy
cos+mo+naut
cos+mo+nauts
cos+mo+poli+tan
cos+mo+poli+
tans
cos+mo+poli+tan+
ism
cos+mopo+lite
cos+mopo+lites
cos+mopo+lit+
ism
cos+mos
cos+mos or
cos+moses
Cosmos
Cosmoses
Cos+sack
Cos+sacks
cos+set
cos+sets
cos+sets
cos+set+ing
cos+set+ed
cost
costs
costs
cost+ing
cost or
cost+ed
estimate
cos+ta
cos+tae
Cos+ta Bra+va
cos+tal
Cos+ta Rica
Cos+ta Ri+can
Cos+ta Ri+cans
cost-benefit
cost-effective
cost-
effectiveness
cos+ter
cos+ters
cos+ter+mon+
ger
cos+ter+mon+
gers
cos+tive
cos+tive+ness
cost+li+ness
cost+ly
cost+li+er
cost+li+est
cost-plus

cos+tume
cos+tumes
cos+tumes
cos+tum+ing
cos+tumed
cos+tum+er
cos+tum+ers
cos+tumi+er
cos+tumi+ers
cosy
cosies
cosi+er
cosi+est
cot
cots
co+tan+gent
co+tan+gents
cote
cotes
Côte d'Azur
Côte d'Ivoire
Côte-d'Or
co+terie
co+teries
co+ter+mi+nous
Côtes-du-Nord
coth
coths
co+til+lion
co+til+lions
co+til+lon
co+til+lons
co+tin+ga
co+tin+gas
co+to+neas+ter
co+to+neas+
ters
Coto+paxi
Cots+wolds
cot+ta
cot+tas
cot+tage
cot+tages
cot+tag+er
cot+tag+ers
cot+tag+ing
cot+tar
cot+tars
cot+ter
cot+ters
Cot+tian
cot+ton
cot+tons
Cotton
cotton-picking

cotton+seed
cotton+seeds
or
cotton+seed
cot+tony
coty+ledon
coty+ledons
coty+ledo+nal
coty+ledo+nous
cou+cal
 cou+cals
couch
 couches
 couches
 couch+ing
 couched
cou+chant
cou+chette
cou+chettes
Coué
Coué+ism
cou+gar
 cou+gars
cough
 coughs
 coughs
 cough+ing
 coughed
cough+er
 cough+ers
could
couldn't
couldst
cou+lee
 cou+lees
cou+lomb
 cou+lombs
Coulomb
coul+ter
 coul+ters
cou+ma+rin
coun+cil
 coun+cils
 coun+cil+lor
 coun+cil+lors
council+man
 council+men
coun+ci+lor
U.S.
 coun+ci+lors
coun+sel
 coun+sels
 coun+sels
 coun+sel+ling
 or

coun+sel+ing
U.S.
coun+selled *or*
coun+seled
U.S.
coun+sel+ing
U.S.
coun+sel+ling
coun+sel+lor
 coun+sel+lors
coun+se+lor
U.S.
 coun+se+lors
counselor-at-law
counselors-at-
 law
count
 counts
 counts
count+ing
count+ed
count+able
count+down
 count+downs
count down
verb
coun+te+nance
coun+te+nances
coun+te+nances
coun+te+nanc+
 ing
coun+te+nanced
coun+ter
 coun+ters
 coun+ters
 coun+ter+ing
 coun+tered
counter+act
 counter+acts
 counter+act+ing
 counter+act+ed
counter+ac+tion
counter+ac+
 tions
counter+ac+tive
counter+at+tack
counter+at+
 tacks
counter+at+
 tacks
counter+at+tack+
 ing
counter+at+
 tacked

counter+bal+
 ance
counter+bal+
 ances
counter+bal+
 ances
counter+bal+anc+
 ing
counter+bal+
 anced
counter+blast
 counter+blasts
counter+check
 counter+checks
 counter+checks
 counter+check+
 ing
 counter+
 checked
counter+claim
 counter+claims
 counter+claims
 counter+claim+
 ing
 counter+claimed
counter+claim+
 ant
counter+claim+
 ants
counter+
 clockwise
counter+culture
 counter+cultures
counter+es+pio+
 nage
counter+feit
 counter+feits
 counter+feits
 counter+feit+ing
 counter+feit+ed
 counter+feit+er
 counter+feit+ers
counter+foil
 counter+foils
counter+in+sur+
 gen+cy
counter+in+tel+li+
 gence
counter+ir+ri+
 tant
 counter+ir+ri+
 tants
counter+ir+ri+ta+
 tion

counter+ir+ri+ta+
 tions
counter+mand
 counter+mands
 counter+mands
 counter+mand+
 ing
 counter+mand+
 ed
counter+march
 counter+
 marches
 counter+
 marches
 counter+march+
 ing
 counter+
 marched
counter+meas+
 ure
counter+meas+
 ures
counter+move
 counter+moves
 counter+moves
 counter+mov+
 ing
 counter+moved
counter+move+
 ment
 counter+move+
 ments
counter+of+fen+
 sive
 counter+of+fen+
 sives
counter+of+fer
 counter+of+fers
counter+pane
 counter+panes
counter+part
 counter+parts
counter+plot
 counter+plots
 counter+plots
 counter+plot+
 ting
 counter+plot+
 ted
counter+point
 counter+points
 counter+points
 counter+point+
 ing

counter+point+
ed
counter+poise
counter+poises
counter+poises
counter+pois+
ing
counter+poised
counter+pro+duc+
tive
counter+pro+pos+
al
counter+pro+
pos+als
Counter-Reforma+
tion
counter-revolu+
tion
counter-revolu+
tions
counter-revo+lu+
tion+ary
counter-revo+lu+
tion+aries
counter-revolu+
tion+ist
counter-revolu+
tion+ists
counter+shaft
counter+shafts
counter+sign
counter+signs
counter+signs
counter+sign+
ing
counter+signed
counter+sig+na+
ture
counter+sig+na+
tures
counter+sink
counter+sinks
counter+sinks
counter+sink+
ing
counter+sank
counter+sunk
counter+ten+or
counter+ten+ors
counter+vail
counter+vails
counter+vail+ing
counter+vailed
counter+vail+ing
counter+weigh

counter+weighs
counter+weigh+
ing
counter+
weighed
counter+weight
counter+
weights
coun+tess
coun+tesses
count+ing
count+less
coun+tri+fied
coun+try
coun+tries
coun+try+fied
country+man
country+men
country+side
country+woman
country+women
coun+ty
coun+ties
coup
coups
coup de grâce
coups de grâce
coup d'état
coups d'état
coupe
coupes
cou+pé
cou+pés
Couperin
cou+ple
cou+ples
cou+ples
cou+pling
cou+pled
cou+pler
cou+plers
cou+plet
cou+plets
cou+pling
cou+plings
cou+pon
cou+pons
cour+age
cou+ra+geous
cou+ra+geous+ly
cou+ra+geous+
ness
cou+rante
cou+rantes
Cour+an+tyne

cour+ba+ril
cour+ba+rils
Courbet
cou+reur de bois
cou+reurs de
bois
cour+gette
cour+gettes
cou+ri+er
cou+ri+ers
Cournand
Courrèges
course
courses
courses
cours+ing
coursed
cours+er
cours+ers
course+work
cours+ing
court
courts
courts
court+ing
court+ed
Court
court-bouillon
Cour+telle
Trademark
cour+teous
cour+teous+ly
cour+teous+ness
cour+tesan
cour+tesans
cour+tesy
cour+tesies
cour+tezan
cour+tezans
court+house
court+houses
cour+ti+er
cour+ti+ers
court+li+ness
court+ly
court+li+er
court+li+est
court-martial
court-martials
court-martial+
ing
court-martialed
court mar+tial
court mar+tials
or

courts mar+tial
court+room
court+rooms
court+ship
court+ships
court+yard
court+yards
cous+cous
cous+in
cous+ins
cous+in+hood
cous+in+ly
cous+in+ship
Cousteau
cou+ture
cou+tu+ri+er
cou+tu+ri+ers
cou+tu+ri+ère
cou+vade
co+va+lence
U.S.
co+va+lences
co+va+len+cy
co+va+len+cies
co+va+lent
co+va+lent+ly
cove
coves
cov+en
cov+ens
cov+enant
cov+enants
cov+enants
cov+enant+ing
cov+enant+ed
cov+enan+tal
cov+enant+er
cov+enant+ers
Cov+enant+er
Cov+enant+ers
cov+enan+tor
cov+enan+tors
Cov+ent Gar+den
Cov+en+try
cov+er
cov+ers
cov+ers
cov+er+ing
cov+ered
cov+er+able
cov+er+age
Coverdale
cov+ered
cov+er+er
cov+er+ers

cov+er+ing
cov+er+ings
cov+er+let
cov+er+lets
cov+ert
cov+erts
cov+ert+ly
cov+er+ture
cover-up
cover-ups
cov+er up
verb
cov+et
cov+ets
cov+et+ing
cov+et+ed
cov+et+able
cov+et+ous
cov+et+ous+ly
cov+et+ous+
ness
cov+ey
cov+eys
cow
cows
cows
cow+ing
cowed
cow+ard
cow+ards
cow+ard+ice
cow+ard+li+ness
cow+ard+ly
cow+bell
cow+bells
cow+berry
cow+berries
cow+bird
cow+birds
cow+boy
cow+boys
cow+catcher
cow+catchers
Cowdrey
cow+er
cow+ers
cow+er+ing
cow+ered
Cowes
cow+girl
cow+girls
cow+herd
cow+herds
cow+hide
cow+hides

cowl
cowls
cowls
cowl+ing
cowled
cow+lick
cow+licks
cowl+ing
cowl+ings
cow+man
cow+men
co-worker
co-workers
cow+pat
cow+pats
cow+pea
cow+peas
Cowper
cow+poke
cow+pokes
cow+pox
cow+puncher
cow+punchers
cow+rie
cow+ries
cow+ry
cow+ries
cow+slip
cow+slips
cox
coxes
coxes
cox+ing
coxed
coxa
coxae
cox+al
cox+al+gia
cox+al+gic
cox+comb
cox+combs
cox+comb+ry
cox+comb+ries
cox+less
cox+swain
cox+swains
coy
coy+ly
coy+ness
coy+ote
coy+otes *or*
coy+ote
coy+pu
coy+pus *or*
coy+pu

coz
co+zen
co+zens
co+zen+ing
co+zened
coz+en+age
co+zi+ly
co+zi+ness
cozy
U.S.
cozies
cozi+er
cozi+est
crab
crabs
crabs
crab+bing
crabbed
Crabbe
crab+bed
crab+bed+ly
crab+bed+ness
crab+bi+er
crab+bi+est
crab+wise
crack
cracks
cracks
crack+ing
cracked
crack+brained
crack+down
crack+downs
crack down
verb
cracked
crack+er
crack+ers
cracker+jack
cracker+jacks
crack+ers
crack+head
crack+heads
crack+ing
crack+jaw
crack+jaws
crack+le
crack+les
crack+les
crack+ling
crack+led
crack+ling
crack+lings
crack+pot

crack+pots
crack+up
crack+ups
crack up
verb
Cra+cow
cra+dle
cra+dles
cra+dles
cra+dling
cra+dled
cradle+song
cradle+songs
craft
crafts
crafts
craft+ing
craft+ed
crafti+ly
crafti+ness
crafts+man
crafts+men
crafts+man+ship
crafty
crafti+er
crafti+est
crag
crags
crag+ged
crag+gi+ness
crag+gy
crag+gi+er
crag+gi+est
Craig
Craigie
crake
crakes
cram
crams
cram+ming
crammed
Cram
cram+bo
cram+mer
cram+mers
cramp
cramps
cramps
cramp+ing
cramped
cramped
cram+pon
cram+pons
cran
crans

Cranach
cran+berry
 cran+berries
crane
 cranes
 cranes
 cran+ing
 craned
Crane
cranes+bill
 cranes+bills
cra+nial
cra+ni+al+ly
cra+ni+ate
cra+nio+logi+cal
cra+nio+logi+cal+
 ly
cra+ni+olo+gist
 cra+ni+olo+gists
cra+ni+ol+ogy
cra+nio+met+ric
cra+nio+met+ri+
 cal
cra+nio+met+ri+
 cal+ly
cra+ni+om+etrist
 cra+ni+om+
 etrists
cra+ni+om+etry
cra+ni+oto+my
 cra+ni+oto+
 mies
cra+nium
 cra+niums or
 cra+nia
crank
 cranks
 cranks
 crank+ing
 cranked
crank+case
 crank+cases
cranki+ly
cranki+ness
Cranko
crank+pin
 crank+pins
crank+shaft
 crank+shafts
cranky
 cranki+er
 cranki+est
Cranmer
cran+nied
cran+nog

cran+nogs
cran+ny
 cran+nies
Cran+well
crap
 craps
 craps
 crap+ping
 crapped
crape
 crapes
 craps
crap+shooter
 crap+shooters
crapu+lence
crapu+lent
crapu+lous
crash
 crashes
 crashes
 crash+ing
 crashed
Crashaw
crash-dive
 crash-dives
 crash-diving
 crash-dived or
 crash-dove
 U.S.
crash dive
 crash dives
crash+ing
crash-land
 crash-lands
 crash-landing
 crash-landed
 crash-landing
 crash-landings
crass
cras+si+tude
crass+ly
crass+ness
Crassus
crate
 crates
 crates
 crat+ing
 crat+ed
cra+ter
 cra+ters
 cra+ters
 cra+ter+ing
 cra+tered
crater-like
cra+ter+ous

cra+vat
 cra+vats
crave
 craves
 crav+ing
 craved
cra+ven
 cra+vens
 cra+ven+ly
 cra+ven+ness
crav+er
 crav+ers
crav+ing
 crav+ings
craw
 craws
craw+fish
 craw+fish or
 craw+fishes
Crawford
crawl
 crawls
 crawls
 crawl+ing
 crawled
crawl+er
 crawl+ers
Craw+ley
crawl+ing
 crawl+ing+ly
crawly
 crawli+er
 crawli+est
Craxi
cray+fish
 cray+fish or
 cray+fishes
cray+on
 cray+ons
 cray+ons
 cray+on+ing
 cray+oned
cray+on+ist
 cray+on+ists
craze
 crazes
 crazes
 craz+ing
 crazed
cra+zi+ly
cra+zi+ness
cra+zy
 cra+zi+er
 cra+zi+est
Crazy Horse

creak
 creaks
 creaks
 creak+ing
 creaked
creaki+ly
creaki+ness
creak+ing+ly
creaky
 creaki+er
 creaki+est
cream
 creams
 creams
 cream+ing
 creamed
cream+er
 cream+ers
cream+ery
 cream+eries
creami+ness
cream+like
creamy
 creami+er
 creami+est
crease
 creases
 creases
 creas+ing
 creased
creas+er
 creas+ers
creasy
cre+ate
 cre+ates
 cre+at+ing
 cre+at+ed
crea+tine
crea+tion
 crea+tions
Crea+tion
crea+tive
crea+tive+ly
crea+tive+ness
crea+tiv+ity
crea+tor
 crea+tors
Crea+tor
crea+tor+ship
crea+tur+al
crea+ture
 crea+tures
crea+ture+ly
crèche
 crèches

Cré+cy
cred+al
cre+dence
 cre+dences
cre+den+tial
 cre+den+tials
cre+den+za
 cre+den+zas
cred+ibil+ity
cred+ible
cred+ible+ness
cred+ibly
cred+it
 cred+its
 cred+its
 cred+it+ing
 cred+it+ed
cred+it+abil+ity
cred+it+able
cred+it+able+
 ness
cred+it+ably
credi+tor
 credi+tors
cred+its
credit+worthi+
 ness
credit+worthy
cre+do
 cre+dos
Cre+do
 Cre+dos
cre+du+lity
credu+lous
credu+lous+ly
credu+lous+ness
Cree
 Cree or
 Crees
creed
 creeds
creed+al
creek
 creeks
Creek
 Creek or
 Creeks
creel
 creels
creep
 creeps
 creeps
 creep+ing
 crept
creep+er

creep+ers
creepi+ly
creepi+ness
creeps
creepy
 creepi+er
 creepi+est
creepy-crawly
creepy-crawlies
cre+mate
 cre+mates
 cre+mat+ing
 cre+mat+ed
 cre+ma+tion
 cre+ma+tions
 cre+ma+tor
 cre+ma+tors
crema+to+rium
 crema+to+riums
  or
 crema+to+ria
crema+tory
 crema+tories
crème
 crèmes
crème de la
crème
crème de menthe
crème fraîche
Cre+mo+na
cre+nate
 cre+nat+ed
 cre+nate+ly
 cre+na+tion
 cre+na+tions
cren+el
 cren+els
 cren+el+ate
 U.S.
 cren+el+ates
 cren+el+at+ing
 cren+el+at+ed
 U.S.
 cren+ela+tion
 U.S.
 cren+ela+tions
 cren+el+late
 cren+el+lates
 cren+el+lat+ing
 cren+el+lat+ed
 cren+el+lat+ed
 cren+el+la+tion
 cren+el+la+tions
cre+nelle

cre+nelles
cre+ole
 cre+oles
Cre+ole
 Cre+oles
Creon
creo+sol
creo+sote
 creo+sotes
 creo+sot+ing
 creo+sot+ed
 creo+sot+ic
crepe
crepe de Chine
creper+ie
 creper+ies
crêpe su+zette
crêpes su+
 zettes
crep+ey
crepi+tant
crepi+tate
 crepi+tates
 crepi+tat+ing
 crepi+tat+ed
 crepi+ta+tion
 crepi+ta+tions
crepi+tus
crept
cre+pus+cu+lar
crepy
cre+scen+do
 cre+scen+dos
  or
 cre+scen+di
 cre+scen+does
 cre+scen+do+
 ing
 cre+scen+doed
cres+cent
 cres+cents
cre+sol
cress
 cresses
cres+set
 cres+sets
Cressid
Cressida
Cres+sy
crest
 crests
 crests
crest+ing
crest+ed
crest+ed

crest+fallen
crest+fallen+ly
crest+less
cre+ta+ceous
Cre+ta+ceous
Cre+tan
 Cre+tans
Crete
cret+in
 cret+ins
cret+in+ism
cret+in+ous
cre+tonne
Creutzfeldt-Jakob
cre+vasse
 cre+vasses
cre+vasses
cre+vass+ing
cre+vassed
crev+ice
crev+ices
crew
crews
crews
crew+ing
crewed
Crewe
crew+el
 crew+el+ist
 crew+el+ists
crewel+work
crew-neck
crew-necked
crib
 cribs
 cribs
crib+bing
cribbed
crib+bage
crib+ber
 crib+bers
crib-biting
crib+work
 crib+works
crick
 cricks
 cricks
crick+ing
cricked
crick+et
 crick+ets
 crick+ets
 crick+et+ing
 crick+et+ed
crick+et+er

crick+et+ers
cri+coid
cri+coids
cri de coeur
cris de coeur
cri+er
cri+ers
crime
crimes
Cri+mea
Cri+mean
Cri+means
crimi+nal
crimi+nals
crimi+nali+sa+
tion
crimi+nali+sa+
tions
crimi+nal+ise
crimi+nal+ises
crimi+nal+is+ing
crimi+nal+ised
crimi+nal+ity
crimi+nal+ities
crimi+nali+za+
tion
crimi+nali+za+
tions
crimi+nal+ize
crimi+nal+izes
crimi+nal+iz+ing
crimi+nal+ized
crimi+nal+ly
crimi+no+log+ic
crimi+no+logi+cal
crimi+no+logi+cal+
ly
crimi+nolo+gist
crimi+nolo+gists
crimi+nol+ogy
crimp
crimps
crimps
crimp+ing
crimped
crimp+er
crimp+ers
Crimp+lene
Trademark
crimpy
crim+son
crim+sons
crim+son+ing
crim+soned
crim+son+ness

cringe
cringes
cringes
cring+ing
cringed
cring+er
cring+ers
crin+gle
crin+gles
crin+kle
crin+kles
crin+kles
crin+kling
crin+kled
crin+kly
crin+klies
cri+noid
cri+noids
cri+noi+dal
crino+line
crino+lines
Crippen
crip+ple
crip+ples
crip+ples
crip+pling
crip+pled
crip+pler
crip+plers
Cripps
Criseyde
cri+sis
cri+ses
crisp
crisps
crisps
crisp+ing
crisped
crisp+er
crisp+est
crisp+bread
crisp+breads
crisp+er
crisp+ers
Crispin
crispi+ness
Crispinian
crisp+ly
crisp+ness
crispy
crispi+er
crispi+est
criss+cross
criss+crosses
criss+cross+ing

criss+crossed
cri+teri+on
cri+teria *or*
cri+teri+ons
crit+ic
crit+ics
criti+cal
criti+cal+ity
criti+cal+ly
criti+cal+ness
criti+cis+able
criti+cise
criti+cises
criti+cis+ing
criti+cised
criti+cis+er
criti+cis+ers
criti+cism
criti+cisms
criti+ciz+able
criti+cize
criti+cizes
criti+ciz+ing
criti+cized
criti+ciz+er
criti+ciz+ers
cri+tique
cri+tiques
croak
croaks
croaks
croak+ing
croaked
croak+er
croak+ers
croaki+ness
croaky
Cro+at
Cro+ats
Croa+tia
Croa+tian
Croa+tians
Croce
cro+chet
cro+chets
cro+chet+ing
cro+cheted
cro+chet+er
cro+chet+ers
crock
crocks
crock+ery
crock+et
crock+ets
Crockett

croco+dile
croco+diles
croco+dil+ian
croco+dil+ians
cro+cus
cro+cuses
Croesus
croft
crofts
croft+er
croft+ers
croft+ing
crois+sant
crois+sants
Croix de Guerre
Cro-Magnon
Crom+er
Cromer
crom+lech
crom+lechs
Crompton
Cromwell
Crom+wel+lian
Crom+wel+lians
crone
crones
Cronin
cronk
Cronos
Cronus
cro+ny
cro+nies
crook
crooks
crooks
crook+ing
crooked
crook+ed
crook+ed+ly
crook+ed+ness
Crookes
croon
croons
croons
croon+ing
crooned
croon+er
croon+ers
crop
crops
crops
crop+ping
cropped
crop-dusting
crop-eared

crop+per
crop+pers
cro+quet
cro+quette
cro+quettes
Cros+by
place name
Crosby
surname
cro+sier
cro+siers
cross
crosses
crosses
cross+ing
crossed
Cross
cross+bar
cross+bars
cross+beam
cross+beams
cross-bench
cross-benches
cross-bencher
cross-benchers
cross+bill
cross+bills
cross+bones
cross+bow
cross+bows
cross+bowman
cross+bowmen
cross+bred
cross+breds
cross+breed
cross+breeds
cross+breeds
cross+breed+
ing
cross+bred
cross+check
cross+checks
cross+checks
cross+check+
ing
cross+checked
cross-country
cross-countries
cross+current
cross+currents
cross-curricu+lar
cross+cut
cross+cuts
cross+cuts
cross+cut+ting

cross+cut
crosse
cross-examina+
tion
cross-examina+
tions
cross-examine
cross-examines
cross-examin+
ing
cross-examined
cross-eye
cross-eyes
cross-eyed
cross-fertilize
cross-fertilizes
cross-fertiliz+ing
cross-fertilized
cross+fire
cross-grained
cross+hatch
cross+hatches
cross+hatch+ing
cross+hatched
cross+ing
cross+ings
cross-legged
cross+ly
Crossman
cross-match
cross+ness
cross+over
cross+overs
cross+patch
cross+patches
cross+piece
cross+pieces
cross-ply
cross-pollinate
cross-pollinates
cross-pollinat+
ing
cross-pollinat+
ed
cross-pollina+tion
cross-pollina+
tions
cross-purpose
cross-purposes
cross-question
cross-questions
cross-questions
cross-question+
ing

cross-
questioned
cross-refer
cross-refers
cross-refer+ring
cross-referred
cross-reference
cross-references
cross-references
cross-referenc+
ing
cross-
referenced
cross+road
cross+roads
cross+roads
cross+ruff
cross+ruffs
cross+ruffs
cross+ruff+ing
cross+ruffed
cross-section+al
cross-stitch
cross-stitches
cross-stitches
cross-stitching
cross-stitched
cross+talk
cross+tree
cross+trees
cross+way
cross+ways
cross+ways
cross+wise
crotch
crotches
crotched
crotch+et
crotch+ets
crotch+eti+ness
crotch+ety
cro+ton
cro+tons
crouch
crouches
crouch+ing
crouched
croup
croups
crou+pi+er
crou+pi+ers
croup+ous
croupy
crou+ton
crou+tons

crow
crows
crows
crow+ing
crowed *or*
crew
crow+bar
crow+bars
crowd
crowds
crowds
crowd+ing
crowd+ed
crowd+ed
crowd+ed+ness
crow+foot
plant
crow+foots
crow+foot
Nautical
crow+feet
crow+ing+ly
crown
crowns
crowns
crown+ing
crowned
Crown
Crowns
crown+ing
crown+ings
crow's-foot
crow's-feet
crow's-nest
crow's-nests
Croy+don
cro+zier
cro+ziers
cru+ces
cru+cial
cru+cial+ly
cru+ci+ble
cru+ci+bles
cru+ci+fi+er
cru+ci+fi+ers
cru+ci+fix
cru+ci+fixes
cru+ci+fix+ion
cru+ci+fix+ions
Cru+ci+fix+ion
cru+ci+form
cru+ci+form+ly
cru+ci+fy
cru+ci+fies
cru+ci+fy+ing

cru+ci+fied
crud
  cruds
crud+dy
  crud+di+er
  crud+di+est
crude
  crud+er
  crud+est
crude+ly
Cruden
crude+ness
crud+ity
cru+el
  cru+el+ler
  cru+el+lest
cru+el+ly
cru+el+ness
cru+el+ty
  cru+el+ties
cruelty-free
cru+et
  cru+ets
Cruft
Cruikshank
cruise
  cruises
  cruises
  cruis+ing
  cruised
cruis+er
  cruis+ers
cruiser+weight
  cruiser+weights
crumb
  crumbs
  crumbs
  crumb+ing
  crumbed
crum+ble
  crum+bles
  crum+bles
  crum+bling
  crum+bled
crum+bli+ness
crum+bly
  crum+bli+er
  crum+bli+est
crumby
  crumbi+er
  crumbi+est
crum+my
  crum+mi+er
  crum+mi+est
crum+pet

crum+pets
crum+ple
  crum+ples
  crum+ples
  crum+pling
  crum+pled
crum+ply
crunch
  crunches
  crunches
  crunch+ing
  crunched
crunchi+ly
crunchi+ness
crunchy
  crunchi+er
  crunchi+est
crup+per
  crup+pers
cru+sade
  cru+sades
  cru+sades
  cru+sad+ing
  cru+sad+ed
  cru+sad+er
  cru+sad+ers
cruse
  cruses
crush
  crushes
  crushes
  crush+ing
  crushed
crush+able
crush+er
  crush+ers
Crusoe
crust
  crusts
  crusts
  crust+ing
  crust+ed
crus+ta+cean
  crus+ta+ceans
  crus+ta+ceous
crus+tal
crusti+ly
crusti+ness
crusty
  crusti+er
  crusti+est
crutch
  crutches
  crutches
  crutch+ing

crutched
crutch+ings
crux
  cruxes *or*
  cru+ces
Cruyff
cru+za+do
  cru+za+does
   or
  cru+za+dos
cru+zei+ro
  cru+zei+ros
cry
  cries
  cries
  cry+ing
  cried
cry+baby
  cry+babies
cry+ing
cryo+bi+olo+gist
  cryo+bi+olo+gists
cryo+bi+ol+ogy
cryo+gen
cryo+gen+ic
cryo+gen+ics
cryo+lite
cry+on+ics
cryo+pre+cipi+tate
  cryo+pre+cipi+tates
cryo+stat
  cryo+stats
cryo+sur+gery
crypt
  crypts
crypt+analy+sis
crypt+ana+lyst
  crypt+ana+lysts
crypt+ana+lyt+ic
cryp+tic
cryp+ti+cal+ly
cryp+to+crys+tal+line
cryp+to+gam
  cryp+to+gams
cryp+to+gam+ic
cryp+toga+mous
cryp+to+graph
  cryp+to+graphs
cryp+to+gra+pher

cryp+tog+ra+phers
cryp+to+graph+ic
cryp+to+graphi+cal
cryp+to+graphi+cal+ly
cryp+tog+ra+phist
  cryp+tog+ra+phists
cryp+tog+ra+phy
crys+tal
  crys+tals
crys+tal+line
crys+tal+lis+able
crys+tal+li+sa+tion
  crys+tal+li+sa+tions
crys+tal+lise
  crys+tal+lises
  crys+tal+lis+ing
  crys+tal+lised
crys+tal+liz+able
crys+tal+li+za+tion
  crys+tal+li+za+tions
crys+tal+lize
  crys+tal+lizes
  crys+tal+liz+ing
  crys+tal+lized
crys+tal+log+ra+pher
  crys+tal+log+ra+phers
crys+tal+lo+graph+ic
crys+tal+log+ra+phy
crys+tal+loid
  crys+tal+loids
Crys+tal Pal+ace
C-spanner
  C-spanners
cteno+phore
  cteno+phores
cub
  cubs
  cubs
cub+bing
  cubbed
Cub

Cubs
Cuba
Cu+ban
 Cu+bans
cub+bish
cubby+hole
 cubby+holes
cube
 cubes
 cubes
 cub+ing
 cubed
cube
 cubes
cu+beb
 cu+bebs
cub+er
 cub+ers
cu+bic
cu+bi+cal
cu+bi+cle
 cu+bi+cles
cu+bi+form
cub+ism
cub+ist
 cub+ists
cu+bis+tic
cu+bit
 cu+bits
cu+boid
 cu+boids
Cuchulain
Cuchulainn
Cuchullain
cuck+ing
cuck+old
 cuck+olds
 cuck+olds
 cuck+old+ing
 cuck+old+ed
 cuck+old+ry
cuckoo
 cuckoos
 cuckoos
 cuckoo+ing
 cuckooed
cuckoo+pint
 cuckoo+pints
cu+cum+ber
 cu+cum+bers
cu+cur+bit
 cu+cur+bits
cu+cur+bi+ta+
 ceous
cud

cud+dle
 cud+dles
 cud+dles
 cud+dling
 cud+dled
cud+dle+some
cud+dly
cud+dy
 cud+dies
cudg+el
 cudg+els
 cudg+els
 cudg+el+ling
 or
 cudg+el+ing
 U.S.
 cudg+elled or
 cudg+eled
 U.S.
cudg+erie
 cudg+eries
Cudlipp
cud+weed
 cud+weeds
cue
 cues
 cues
 cue+ing
 cued
Cuer+na+va+ca
 cues+ta
 cues+tas
cuff
 cuffs
 cuffs
 cuff+ing
 cuffed
Cuia+bá
cui bono
cui+rass
 cui+rasses
 cui+rasses
 cui+rass+ing
 cui+rassed
cui+ras+sier
 cui+ras+siers
Cuisenaire
 Trademark
cuish
 cuishes
cui+sine
cuisse
 cuisses
Culbertson
cul-de-sac

culs-de-sac or
 cul-de-sacs
Cu+lebra
cu+lex
 cu+li+ces
Cul+ham
Cu+lia+cán
culi+nari+ly
 culi+nary
cull
 culls
 culls
 cull+ing
 culled
cul+len+der
 cul+len+ders
cull+er
 cull+ers
Cul+lod+en
culm
 culms
cul+mi+nant
cul+mi+nate
 cul+mi+nates
 cul+mi+nat+ing
 cul+mi+nat+ed
cul+mi+na+tion
 cul+mi+na+tions
cu+lottes
cul+pabil+ity
cul+pable
cul+pably
Culpeper
cul+prit
 cul+prits
cult
 cults
cul+tic
cult+ism
cult+ist
 cult+ists
cul+ti+vabil+ity
cul+ti+vable
cul+ti+var
 cul+ti+vars
cul+ti+vat+able
cul+ti+vate
 cul+ti+vates
 cul+ti+vat+ing
 cul+ti+vat+ed
cul+ti+va+tion
 cul+ti+va+tions
cul+ti+va+tor
 cul+ti+va+tors

cul+tur+al
cul+ture
 cul+tures
 cul+tures
 cul+tur+ing
 cul+tured
cul+tured
cul+tur+ist
 cul+tur+ists
cul+tus
 cul+tuses or
 cul+ti
cul+ver+in
 cul+ver+ins
cul+vert
 cul+verts
cum
Cu+mae
Cu+maean
cu+ma+rin
cum+ber
 cum+bers
 cum+ber+ing
 cum+bered
Cum+ber+land
Cumberland
cum+ber+some
cum+ber+some+
 ness
Cum+bria
Cum+brian
 Cum+brians
cum+brous
cum+brous+ness
cum+in
cum+mer+bund
 cum+mer+
 bunds
cum+min
Cummings
cum+quat
 cum+quats
cu+mu+late
 cu+mu+lates
 cu+mu+lat+ing
 cu+mu+lat+ed
cu+mu+la+tion
 cu+mu+la+tions
cu+mu+la+tive
cu+mu+la+tive+ly
cu+mu+la+tive+
 ness
cu+mu+lo+nim+
 bus

cu+mu+lo+nim+
  bi *or*
cu+mu+lo+nim+
  buses
cu+mu+lous
cu+mu+lus
cu+mu+li
Cu+naxa
cu+neal
cu+neate
cu+neate+ly
cu+nei+form
cun+jevoi
  cun+jevois
cun+ni+linc+tus
cun+ni+lin+gus
cun+ning
Cunningham
Cunninghame
cun+ning+ly
cun+ning+ness
Cunobelinus
cunt
  cunts
cup
  cups
  cups
cup+ping
cupped
cup+bearer
  cup+bearers
cup+board
  cup+boards
cup+cake
  cup+cakes
cu+pel
  cu+pels
  cu+pels
cu+pel+ling *or*
cu+pel+ing
  U.S.
  cu+pelled *or*
  cu+peled
  U.S.
cu+pel+la+tion
Cupid
cu+pid+ity
cu+po+la
  cu+po+las
cu+po+lat+ed
cup+pa
  cup+pas
cup+per
  cup+pers
cup+ping

cu+pre+ous
cu+pres+sus
  cu+pres+suses
cu+pric
cu+prif+er+ous
cu+pro+nick+el
cu+prous
cu+pule
  cu+pules
cur
  curs
cur+abil+ity
cur+able
cur+able+ness
Cu+ra+cao
cu+ra+cy
  cu+ra+cies
cu+ra+re
cu+ra+res
cu+ra+ri
cu+ra+ris
cu+ras+sow
  cu+ras+sows
cu+rate
cu+rates
cu+ra+tive
  cu+ra+tives
cura+tive+ly
cura+tive+ness
cu+ra+tor
  cu+ra+tors
cu+ra+to+rial
cu+ra+tor+ship
  cu+ra+tor+ships
curb
  curbs
  curbs
curb+ing
curbed
cur+cu+ma
cur+cu+mas
curd
  curds
  curds
curd+ing
curd+ed
cur+dle
cur+dles
cur+dling
cur+dled
curdy
cure
  cures
  cures
cur+ing

cured
cu+ré
  cu+rés
cure-all
  cure-alls
cure+less
cur+er
cur+ers
cu+ret
  cu+rets
  cu+rets
cu+ret+ting
cu+ret+ted
cu+ret+tage
cu+rette
cu+rettes
cu+rettes
cu+ret+ting
cu+ret+ted
cu+rette+ment
cur+few
  cur+fews
cu+ria
cu+riae
cu+rial
cu+rie
  cu+ries
Curie
cu+rio
  cu+rios
cu+ri+os+ity
  cu+ri+os+ities
cu+ri+ous
cu+ri+ous+ly
cu+ri+ous+ness
Cu+ri+ti+ba
cu+rium
curl
  curls
  curls
curl+ing
curled
curl+er
  curl+ers
cur+lew
  cur+lews
cur+li+cue
  cur+li+cues
curli+ness
curl+ing
curly
curli+er
curli+est
cur+mudg+eon
  cur+mudg+eons

cur+mudg+eon+
  ly
Curnow
cur+rach
  cur+rachs
cur+ra+jong
  cur+ra+jongs
cur+rant
  cur+rants
cur+ra+wong
  cur+ra+wongs
cur+ren+cy
  cur+ren+cies
cur+rent
  cur+rents
current-cost
cur+rent+ly
cur+rent+ness
cur+ri+cle
  cur+ri+cles
cur+ricu+lar
cur+ricu+lum
  cur+ricu+la *or*
cur+ricu+lums
cur+ricu+lum vi+
  tae
  cur+ricu+la vi+
  tae
cur+rish
cur+rish+ly
cur+rish+ness
cur+ry
  cur+ries
  cur+ries
cur+ry+ing
  cur+riea
curry+comb
  curry+combs
curse
  curses
  curses
curs+ing
cursed *or*
curst
curs+ed
curs+ed+ly
curs+ed+ness
curs+er
  curs+ers
cur+sive
  cur+sives
cur+sive+ly
cur+sor
  cur+sors
cur+so+rial

cur+so+ri+ly
cur+so+ri+ness
cur+sory
curst
curt
cur+tail
  cur+tails
  cur+tail+ing
  cur+tailed
cur+tail+er
  cur+tail+ers
cur+tail+ment
cur+tain
  cur+tains
  cur+tains
  cur+tain+ing
  cur+tained
curtain-raiser
  curtain-raisers
cur+tains
Curtin
curt+ly
curt+ness
curt+sey
  curt+seys
  curt+seys
  curt+sey+ing
  curt+seyed
curt+sy
  curt+sies
  curt+sies
  curt+sy+ing
  curt+sied
cur+va+ceous
cur+va+ture
  cur+va+tures
curve
  curves
  curves
  curv+ing
  curved
curv+ed+ness
cur+vet
  cur+vets
  cur+vets
  cur+vet+ting
    or
  cur+vet+ing
  cur+vet+ted *or*
  cur+vet+ed
cur+vi+lin+eal
cur+vi+lin+ear
curvy
  curvi+er
  curvi+est

Curzon
Cusack
Cusanus
Cus+co
cus+cus
  cus+cuses
cu+sec
  cu+secs
cush+at
  cush+ats
Cushing
cush+ion
  cush+ions
  cush+ions
  cush+ion+ing
  cush+ioned
cush+iony
Cush+it+ic
cushy
  cushi+er
  cushi+est
CUSO
cusp
  cusps
cus+pate
cus+pid
  cus+pids
cus+pi+dal
cus+pi+date
  cus+pi+dat+ed
cus+pi+dor
  cus+pi+dors
cuss
  cusses
  cusses
  cuss+ing
  cussed
cuss+ed
cuss+ed+ly
cuss+ed+ness
cus+tard
  cus+tards
Custer
cus+to+dial
cus+to+dian
  cus+to+dians
cus+to+di+an+
  ship
cus+to+dy
  cus+to+dies
cus+tom
  cus+toms
cus+tom+ari+ly
cus+tom+ari+
  ness

cus+tom+ary
  cus+tom+aries
custom-built
cus+tom+er
  cus+tom+ers
cus+tom+ise
  cus+tom+ises
  cus+tom+is+ing
  cus+tom+ised
cus+tom+ize
  cus+tom+izes
  cus+tom+iz+ing
  cus+tom+ized
custom-made
cus+toms
cut
  cuts
  cuts
  cut+ting
  cut
cu+ta+neous
cut+away
  cut+aways
cut+back
  cut+backs
cut back
verb
Cutch
cute
  cut+er
  cut+est
cute+ly
cute+ness
Cuthbert
cu+ti+cle
  cu+ti+cles
cu+ticu+lar
cu+tin
cut-in
noun
cut in
verb
cu+tis
  cu+tes *or*
  cu+tises
cut+lass
  cut+lasses
cut+ler
  cut+lers
cut+lery
cut+let
  cut+lets
cut+off
  cut+offs
cut off

verb
cut+out
  cut+outs
cut out
verb
cut-price
cut+purse
  cut+purses
cut-rate
cut+ter
  cut+ters
cut+throat
  cut+throats
cut+ting
  cut+tings
  cut+ting+ly
cut+tle
  cut+tles
cuttle+bone
  cuttle+bones
cuttle+fish
  cuttle+fish *or*
  cuttle+fishes
cut-up
cut-ups
cut up
verb
cut+water
  cut+waters
cut+worm
  cut+worms
cu+veé
  cu+veés
Cux+ha+ven
Cu+ya+bá
Cuyp
Cuz+co
cwm
cwms
cyan
cya+nate
  cya+nates
cy+an+ic
cya+nid
  cya+nids
cya+ni+da+tion
cya+nide
  cya+nides
cya+nite
cya+nit+ic
cya+no+bac+te+
ria
cya+no+bac+te+
rium

cya+no+bac+te+
  ria
cya+no+co+bala+
  min
cy+ano+gen
cya+no+sis
cya+not+ic
Cybele
cy+ber+nate
  cy+ber+nates
  cy+ber+nat+ing
  cy+ber+nat+ed
cy+ber+na+tion
cy+ber+net+ic
cy+ber+neti+cist
  cy+ber+neti+
    cists
cy+ber+net+ics
cy+ber+pho+bia
cy+ber+pho+bic
cy+ber+punk
  cy+ber+punks
cy+cad
  cy+cads
cyca+da+ceous
Cyc+la+des
Cy+clad+ic
cy+cla+mate
  cy+cla+mates
cyc+la+men
  cyc+la+mens
cy+cle
  cy+cles
  cy+cles
  cy+cling
  cy+cled
cy+cler
  cy+clers
cy+clic
cy+cli+cal
cy+cli+cal+ly
cy+cling
cy+clist
  cy+clists
cy+clo+gi+ro
  cy+clo+gi+ros
cy+clo+hexa+
  none
cy+cloid
  cy+cloids
cy+cloi+dal
cy+clom+eter
  cy+clom+eters
cy+clone

cy+clones
cy+clon+ic
cy+clo+pae+dia
  cy+clo+pae+
    dias
Cy+clo+pean
cy+clo+pedia
  cy+clo+pedias
cy+clo+pen+ta+
    di+ene
cy+clo+phos+
    pha+mide
cy+clo+pro+pane
Cy+clops
Cy+clo+pes or
  Cy+clopses
cy+clo+rama
  cy+clo+ramas
  cy+clo+ram+ic
cy+clo+sporin-A
cy+clos+to+mate
cy+clo+stoma+
    tous
cy+clo+stome
  cy+clo+stomes
cy+clo+style
  cy+clo+styles
  cy+clo+styles
  cy+clo+styl+ing
  cy+clo+styled
  cy+clo+styled
cy+clo+thy+mia
cy+clo+thy+mic
cy+clo+tron
  cy+clo+trons
cy+der
  cy+ders
cyg+net
  cyg+nets
cyl+in+der
  cyl+in+ders
cylinder-like
cy+lin+dric
cy+lin+dri+cal
cy+lin+dri+cal+ity
cy+lin+dri+cal+ly
cym+bal
  cym+bals
  cym+bal+ist
  cym+bal+ists
Cymbeline
cyme
  cymes
cy+mif+er+ous

cy+mose
Cym+ric
Cym+ru
Cym+ry
Cynewulf
cyn+ic
cyn+ics
Cyn+ic
  Cyn+ics
cyni+cal
cyni+cal+ly
cyni+cal+ness
cyni+cism
  cyni+cisms
Cyni+cism
cy+no+sure
  cy+no+sures
Cynthia
Cynwulf
cy+pher
  cy+phers
  cy+phers
cy+pher+ing
cy+phered
cy+press
  cy+presses
Cyp+rian
  Cyp+rians
Cyprian
cy+pri+nid
  cy+pri+nids
cy+pri+noid
  cy+pri+noids
Cyp+ri+ot
  Cyp+ri+ots
Cyp+ri+ote
  Cyp+ri+otes
cyp+ri+pedium
  cyp+ri+pediums
Cy+prus
Cyrano de
  Bergerac
Cyr+ena+ic
  Cyr+ena+ics
Cyr+enai+ca
Cy+re+ne
Cyril
Cy+ril+lic
Cyrus
cyst
  cysts
cys+tec+to+my
cys+tec+to+
  mies

cyst+ic
cys+ti+cer+cus
  cys+ti+cer+ci
cys+ti+tis
cys+toid
  cys+toids
cys+to+scope
  cys+to+scopes
cys+to+scop+ic
cys+tos+co+py
cys+tos+co+
  pies
Cyth+era
Cytherea
Cyth+er+ean
cy+to+genet+ic
cy+to+genet+ics
cy+to+kin+in
  cy+to+kin+ins
cy+to+logi+cal
cy+to+logi+cal+
  ly
cy+tolo+gist
cy+tolo+gists
cy+tol+ogy
cy+tol+ogies
cy+to+meg+alo+
  vi+rus
cy+to+plasm
cy+to+plas+mic
cy+to+sine
cy+to+tox+ic
cy+to+toxi+ci+ty
cy+to+tox+in
  cy+to+tox+ins
Cyzi+cus
czar
  czars
czar+das
czar+dom
  czar+doms
Czech
  Czechs
Czecho+slo+vak
Czecho+slo+va+
  kia
Czecho+slo+va+
  kian
Czecho+slo+va+
  kians
Czer+no+witz
Czerny
Cz+e+sto+cho+wa

D

d
d's
D
D's *or*
Ds
dab
 dabs
 dabs
 dab+bing
 dabbed
dab+ber
 dab+bers
 dab+ble
 dab+bles
 dab+bling
 dab+bled
dab+bler
 dab+blers
 dab+chick
 dab+chicks
da capo
Dac+ca
dace
 dace *or*
 daces
da+cha
 da+chas
Da+chau
dachs+hund
 dachs+hunds
Da+cia
Da+cian
da+coit
 da+coits
Da+cron
 Trademark
dac+tyl
 dac+tyls
dac+tyl+ic
 dac+tyl+ics
dac+tyli+cal+ly
dad
 dads
Dada
Da+da+ism

Da+da+ist
 Da+da+ists
Da+da+is+tic
dad+dy
 dad+dies
daddy-longlegs
dado
 da+does *or*
 da+dos
 da+dos
 da+do+ing
 da+doed
Dae+da+lean
Dae+da+lian
Dae+dal+ic
Daedalus
dae+mon
 dae+mons
dae+mon+ic
daff
 daffs
daf+fo+dil
 daf+fo+dils
daffy
 daffi+er
 daffi+est
daft
 daft+er
 daft+est
 daft+ness
dag
 dags
 dags
 dag+ging
 dagged
Da Gama
Da+gan
Dag+en+ham
Da+ge+stan
dag+ga
dag+ger
 dag+gers
dag+gy
 dag+gi+er
 dag+gi+est

Da+ghe+stan
dag+lock
 dag+locks
dago
da+gos *or*
 da+goes
Da+gon
Daguerre
da+guerreo+type
 da+guerreo+
 types
da+guerreo+typy
Dahl
dahl+ia
 dahl+ias
Dah+na
Da+ho+mey
Dáil Éi+reann
dai+ly
 dai+lies
Daimler
dai+mon
 dai+mons
dai+mon+ic
dain+ti+ly
dain+ty
 dain+ties
 dain+ti+er
 dain+ti+est
dai+qui+ri
 dai+qui+ris
dairy
 dairies
dairy+ing
dairy+man
dairy+men
dais
 daises
dai+sied
dai+sy
 dai+sies
daisy+cutter
 daisy+cutters
daisy+wheel
 daisy+wheels

Da+kar
Da+ko+ta
Da+ko+tan
 Da+ko+tans
dal
 dals
Daladier
Dalai Lama
 Dalai Lamas
dale
 dales
Da+lek
 Da+leks
d'Alembert
Dales
dales+man
 dales+men
Dalglish
Dalhousie
Dali
Dallapiccola
Dal+las
dal+li+ance
 dal+li+ances
dal+ly
 dal+lies
dal+ly+ing
 dal+lied
Dal+ma+tia
Dal+ma+tian
 Dal+ma+tians
dal+mat+ic
 dal+mat+ics
dal seg+no
dal+ton
 dal+tons
Dalton
dal+ton+ism
dam
 dams
 dams
 dam+ming
 dammed
dam+age
 dam+ages

dam+ages	damp	dan+dle	daphnes
dam+ag+ing	damps	dan+dles	Daphne
dam+aged	damp+ing	dan+dling	daph+nia
dam+ages	damped	dan+dled	daph+nias
dam+ag+ing	damp+er	dan+dler	Daphnis
Da+man	damp+est	dan+dlers	Da Ponte
dama+scene	damp+course	dan+druff	dap+per
dama+scenes	damp+courses	dan+dy	dap+per+ly
dama+scenes	damp+en	dan+dies	dap+per+ness
dama+scen+ing	damp+ens	dan+di+er	dap+ple
dama+scened	damp+en+ing	dan+di+est	dap+ples
Dama+scene	damp+ened	dandy-brush	dap+ples
Dama+scenes	damp+en+er	dandy-brushes	dap+pling
Da+mas+cus	damp+en+ers	dan+dy+ish	dap+pled
dam+ask	damp+er	Dane	dapple-grey
dam+asks	damp+ers	Danes	dapple-greys
dam+asks	damp+ness	Dane+geld	Dap+sang
dam+ask+ing	damp-proof	Dane+gelt	dar+bies
dam+asked	damp-proofs	Dane+law	Darcy
dame	damp-proofing	dan+ger	Dar+da+nelles
dames	damp-proofed	dan+gers	dare
Dame	dam+sel	dan+ger+less	dares
Dames	dam+sels	dan+ger+ous	dares
Damien	damsel+fly	dan+ger+ous+ly	dar+ing
damn	damsel+flies	dan+gle	dared
damns	dam+son	dan+gles	dare+devil
damns	dam+sons	dan+gling	dare+devils
damn+ing	dan	dan+gled	dare+devil+ry
damned	dans	dan+gler	dare+devil+try
dam+nabil+ity	Dan	dan+glers	dar+er
dam+nabil+ities	Dans	Daniel	dar+ers
dam+nable	Dana	Dan+ish	Dar es Sa+laam
dam+nable+ness	Danaë	dank	Dar+fur
dam+na+tion	Danaid	dank+er	Dari+en
dam+na+tions	Danaidean	dank+est	dar+ing
dam+na+tory	Danaides	dank+ly	Dario
damned	Da Nang	dank+ness	Dar+jee+ling
damned+est	Dana+üs	Dankworth	dark
dam+ni+fi+ca+	dance	Dan+mark	dark+er
tion	dances	D'Annunzio	dark+est
dam+ni+fi+ca+	dances	danse ma+cabre	dark+en
tions	danc+ing	dan+seur	dark+ens
dam+ni+fy	danced	dan+seurs	dark+en+ing
dam+ni+fies	dance+able	Dante	dark+ened
dam+ni+fy+ing	danc+er	Dan+tean	dark+en+er
dam+ni+fied	danc+ers	Dan+tesque	dark+en+ers
Damo+clean	danc+ing	Danton	dark+ish
Damocles	dan+de+lion	Dan+ube	dark+ling
Damo+dar	dan+de+lions	Danu+bian	dark+ly
damoi+selle	dan+der	Dan+zig	dark+ness
damoi+selles	dan+ders	dap	dark+room
damo+sel	dan+di+fy	daps	dark+rooms
damo+sels	dan+di+fies	dap+ping	dark+some
damo+zel	dan+di+fy+ing	dapped	Darlan
damo+zels	dan+di+fied	daphne	dar+ling

dar+lings
Darling
Dar+ling+ton
Darm+stadt
darn
darns
darns
darn+ing
darned
darn
dar+nel
dar+nels
darn+er
darn+ers
Darnley
dart
darts
darts
dart+ing
dart+ed
dart+board
dart+boards
dart+er
dart+ers
Dart+ford
dart+ing
Dart+moor
Dart+mouth
darts
Dar+win
place name
Darwin
surname
Dar+win+ian
Dar+win+ians
Dar+win+ism
Dar+win+ist
Dar+win+ists
dash
dashes
dashes
dash+ing
dashed
dash+board
dash+boards
dash+er
dash+ers
da+shi+ki
da+shi+kis
dash+ing
Dasht-e-Kavir
Dasht-e-Lut
Dasht-i-Kavir
Dasht-i-Lut
Das+seh+ra

Das+seh+ras
das+sie
das+sies
das+tard+li+ness
das+tard+ly
dasy+ure
dasy+ures
data
data+base
data+bases
dat+able
dat+able
da+tcha
da+tchas
date
dates
dates
dat+ing
dat+ed
date+able
dat+ed
date+less
date+line
date+lines
da+ting
da+ti+val
da+tive
da+tives
da+tive+ly
da+tum
da+ta
da+tu+ra
da+tu+ras
daub
daubs
daubs
daub+ing
daubed
daub+er
daub+ers
Daubigny
Daudet
Dau+ga+va
Dau+gav+pils
daugh+ter
daugh+ters
daugh+ter+hood
daughter-in-law
daughters-in-law
daugh+ter+less
daugh+ter+ly
Daumier
daunt
daunts
daunt+ing
daunt+ed

daunt+ing
daunt+ing+ly
daunt+less
daunt+less+ly
daunt+less+ness
dau+phin
dau+phins
dau+phine
dau+phines
dau+phin+ess
dau+phin+esses
dav+en+port
dav+en+ports
Da+vent+ry
David
Davies
da Vinci
Davis
Davisson
dav+it
dav+its
Da+vos
Davy
daw
daws
daw+dle
daw+dles
daw+dling
daw+dled
daw+dler
daw+dlers
Dawes
Dawkins
dawn
dawns
dawns
dawn+ing
dawned
dawn+like
day
days
Day+ak
Day+aks *or*
Day+ak
Dayan
day+book
day+books
day+boy
day+boys
day+break
day+care
day+centre
day+centres
day+dream
day+dreams

day+dreams
day+dream+ing
day+dreamed
day+dream+er
day+dream+ers
day+dreamy
Day-Glo
Trademark
Day-Lewis
day+light
day+lights
day+long
days
day+time
day+times
day-to-day
day-tripper
day-trippers
Da Yunhe
daze
dazes
dazes
daz+ing
dazed
daz+zle
daz+zles
daz+zles
daz+zling
daz+zled
D-day
DDT
dea+con
dea+cons
dea+con+ess
dea+con+esses
dea+con+ship
dea+con+ships
de+ac+tiv+ate
de+ac+tiv+ates
de+ac+tiv+at+
  ing
de+ac+tiv+at+
  ed
de+ac+ti+va+tor
de+ac+ti+va+
  tors
dead
dead-and-alive
dead+beat
dead+beats
dead beat
adj.
dead+en
dead+ens
dead+en+ing

dead+ened
dead+eye
dead+eyes
dead+fall
dead+falls
dead+head
dead+heads
dead+heads
dead+head+ing
dead+head+ed
dead+light
dead+lights
dead+line
dead+lines
dead+lock
dead+locks
dead+locks
dead+lock+ing
dead+locked
dead+ly
dead+li+er
dead+li+est
dead+ness
dead-nettle
dead-nettles
dead+pan
dead+wood
deaf
deaf+er
deaf+est
deaf-and-dumb
deaf+en
deaf+ens
deaf+en+ing
deaf+ened
deaf+en+ing+ly
deaf-mute
deaf-mutes
deaf+ness
Deakin
deal
deals
deals
deal+ing
dealt
Deal
deal+er
deal+ers
deal+ings
dean
deans
Dean
dean+ery
dean+eries
dear

dears
dear+er
dear+est
dearie
dearies
dear+ly
dear+ness
dearth
dearths
deary
dearies
death
deaths
death+bed
death+beds
death+blow
death+blows
death+less
death+less+ness
death+ly
death's-head
death+trap
death+traps
death+watch
Deau+ville
deb
debs
de+ba+cle
de+ba+cles
de+bag
de+bags
de+bag+ging
de+bagged
de+bar
de+bars
de+bar+ring
de+barred
de+bark
de+barks
de+bark+ing
de+barked
de+bar+ka+tion
de+bar+ka+tions
de+bar+ment
de+bar+ments
de+base
de+bases
de+bas+ing
de+based
de+base+ment
de+base+ments
de+bas+er
de+bas+ers
de+bat+able

de+bate
de+bates
de+bates
de+bat+ing
de+bat+ed
de+bat+er
de+bat+ers
de+bauch
de+bauches
de+bauches
de+bauch+ing
de+bauched
debau+chee
debau+chees
de+bauch+er
de+bauch+ers
de+bauch+ery
de+bauch+eries
de+ben+ture
de+ben+tures
de+ben+tured
de+bili+tate
de+bili+tates
de+bili+tat+ing
de+bili+tat+ed
de+bili+ta+tion
de+bili+ta+tions
de+bili+ta+tive
de+bil+ity
de+bil+ities
deb+it
deb+its
deb+its
deb+it+ing
deb+it+ed
debo+nair
debo+nair+ly
debo+nair+ness
deb+on+naire
Deborah
de+bouch
de+bouches
de+bouch+ing
de+bouched
de+bouch+ment
de+bouch+
ments
Debrett
de+brief
de+briefs
de+brief+ing
de+briefed
de+bris
dé+bris
de Broglie

debt
debts
debt+or
debt+ors
de+bud
de+buds
de+bud+ding
de+bud+ded
de+bug
de+bugs
de+bug+ging
de+bugged
de+bunk
de+bunks
de+bunk+ing
de+bunked
de+bunk+er
de+bunk+ers
de+bus
de+buses *or*
de+busses
de+bus+ing *or*
de+bus+sing
de+bused *or*
de+bussed
Debussy
de+but
de+buts
debu+tante
debu+tantes
Debye
de+ca+dal
dec+ade
dec+ades
deca+dence
deca+dences
deca+den+cy
deca+den+cies
deca+dent
deca+dents
de+caf+fein+ate
de+caf+fein+
ates
de+caf+fein+at+
ing
de+caf+fein+at+
ed
deca+gon
deca+gons
de+cago+nal
deca+he+dral
deca+he+dron
deca+he+drons
de+cal
de+cals

de+cal+ling *or*
de+cal+ing
U.S.
de+called *or*
de+caled
U S.
de+cal+ci+fi+er
de+cal+ci+fi+ers
de+cal+ci+fy
de+cal+ci+fies
de+cal+ci+fy+
  ing
de+cal+ci+fied
de+cal+co+ma+
  nia
deca+li+ter
U.S.
deca+li+ters
deca+li+tre
deca+li+tres
Deca+logue
deca+me+ter
U.S.
deca+me+ters
deca+me+tre
deca+me+tres
de+camp
de+camps
de+camp+ing
de+camped
de+camp+ment
de+camp+
  ments
de+ca+nal
de+ca+ni
de+cant
de+cants
de+cant+ing
de+cant+ed
de+cant+er
de+cant+ers
de+capi+tate
de+capi+tates
de+capi+tat+ing
de+capi+tat+ed
de+capi+ta+tion
de+capi+ta+
  tions
de+capi+ta+tor
de+capi+ta+tors
deca+pod
deca+pods
de+capo+dal
de+capo+dan
de+car+bon+ate

de+car+bon+
  ates
de+car+bon+at+
  ing
de+car+bon+at+
  ed
de+car+bona+
  tion
de+car+bona+tor
de+car+bona+
  tors
de+car+boni+sa+
  tion
de+car+bon+ise
de+car+bon+
  ises
de+car+bon+is+
  ing
de+car+bon+
  ised
de+car+bon+is+
  er
de+car+bon+is+
  ers
de+car+boni+za+
  tion
de+car+bon+ize
de+car+bon+
  izes
de+car+bon+iz+
  ing
de+car+bon+
  ized
de+car+bon+iz+
  er
de+car+bon+iz+
  ers
de+car+boxy+
  lase
de+car+bu+rise
de+car+bu+
  rises
de+car+bu+ris+
  ing
de+car+bu+
  rised
de+car+bu+rize
de+car+bu+rizes
de+car+bu+riz+
  ing
de+car+bu+
  rized
deca+style
deca+styles
deca+syl+lab+ic

deca+syl+la+ble
deca+syl+la+
  bles
de+cath+lete
de+cath+letes
de+cath+lon
de+cath+lons
de+cay
de+cays
de+cay+ing
de+cayed
de+cay+able
Dec+can
de+cease
de+ceases
de+ceas+ing
de+ceased
de+ceased
de+ceit
de+ceits
de+ceit+ful
de+ceiv+able
de+ceive
de+ceives
de+ceiv+ing
de+ceived
de+ceiv+er
de+ceiv+ers
de+cel+er+ate
de+cel+er+ates
de+cel+er+at+
  ing
de+cel+er+at+
  ed
de+cel+era+tion
de+cel+era+
  tions
de+cel+era+tor
de+cel+era+tors
De+cem+ber
De+cem+bers
de+cen+cies
de+cen+cy
de+cen+cies
de+cen+nial
de+cen+nials
de+cen+ni+al+ly
de+cent
de+cent+ly
de+cen+trali+sa+
  tion
de+cen+tral+ise
de+cen+tral+
  ises

de+cen+tral+is+
  ing
de+cen+tral+
  ised
de+cen+tral+ist
de+cen+tral+
  ists
de+cen+trali+za+
  tion
de+cen+tral+ize
de+cen+tral+
  izes
de+cen+tral+iz+
  ing
de+cen+tral+
  ized
de+cep+tion
de+cep+tions
de+cep+tive
de+cep+tive+ly
de+cep+tive+
  ness
deci+bel
deci+bels
de+cid+able
de+cide
de+cides
de+cid+ing
de+cid+ed
de+cid+ed+ly
de+cid+er
de+cid+ers
de+cidu+ous
de+cidu+ous+
  ness
deci+li+ter
U.S.
deci+li+ters
deci+li+tre
deci+li+tres
de+cil+lion
de+cil+lions
de+cil+lionth
deci+mal
deci+mals
deci+mali+sa+
  tion
deci+mal+ise
deci+mal+ises
deci+mal+is+ing
deci+mal+ised
deci+mali+za+
  tion
deci+mal+ize

deci+mal+izes
deci+mal+iz+ing
deci+mal+ized
deci+mal+ly
deci+mate
deci+mates
deci+mat+ing
deci+mat+ed
deci+ma+tion
deci+ma+tor
deci+ma+tors
deci+meter
U.S.
deci+meters
deci+metre
deci+metres
de+ci+pher
de+ci+phers
de+ci+pher+ing
de+ci+phered
de+ci+pher+able
de+ci+pher+ment
de+ci+sion
de+ci+sions
de+ci+sive
de+ci+sive+ly
de+ci+sive+ness
deck
 decks
 decks
 deck+ing
 decked
deck-access
deck+el
 deck+els
deck+er
Decker
deck+le
 deck+les
de+claim
 de+claims
 de+claim+ing
 de+claimed
 de+claim+er
 de+claim+ers
dec+la+ma+tion
 dec+la+ma+
  tions
de+clama+tory
de+clar+able
dec+la+ra+tion
 dec+la+ra+tions
de+clara+tive
de+clara+tive+ly
de+clara+to+ri+ly

de+clara+tory
de+clare
 de+clares
 de+clar+ing
 de+clared
 de+clar+er
 de+clar+ers
de+clas+si+fi+ca+
  tion
 de+clas+si+fi+
  ca+tions
de+clas+si+fy
 de+clas+si+fies
 de+clas+si+fy+
  ing
 de+clas+si+fied
de+clen+sion
 de+clen+sions
 de+clen+sion+al
de+clin+able
dec+li+na+tion
 dec+li+na+tions
 dec+li+na+tion+al
de+cline
 de+clines
 de+clines
 de+clin+ing
 de+clined
 de+clin+er
 de+clin+ers
de+clivi+tous
de+cliv+ity
 de+cliv+ities
de+clutch
 de+clutches
 de+clutch+ing
 de+clutched
de+coct
 de+cocts
 de+coct+ing
 de+coct+ed
 de+coc+tion
 de+coc+tions
de+code
 de+codes
 de+cod+ing
 de+cod+ed
 de+cod+er
 de+cod+ers
de+coke
 de+cokes
 de+cok+ing
 de+coked
dé+colle+tage
dé+colle+té

de+colo+nisa+
  tion
 de+colo+nisa+
  tions
de+colo+nise
 de+colo+nises
 de+colo+nis+ing
 de+colo+nised
 de+colo+niza+
  tion
 de+colo+niza+
  tions
de+colo+nize
 de+colò+nizes
 de+colo+niz+ing
 de+colo+nized
de+col+ori+sa+
  tion
 de+col+ori+sa+
  tions
de+col+or+ise
 de+col+or+ises
 de+col+or+is+
  ing
 de+col+or+ised
de+col+ori+za+
  tion
 de+col+ori+za+
  tions
de+col+or+ize
 de+col+or+izes
 de+col+or+iz+
  ing
 de+col+or+ized
de+col+our
 de+col+ours
 de+col+our+ing
 de+col+oured
de+com+mis+
  sion
 de+com+mis+
  sions
 de+com+mis+
  sion+ing
 de+com+mis+
  sioned
de+com+pose
 de+com+poses
 de+com+pos+
  ing
 de+com+posed
 de+com+pos+er
 de+com+pos+
  ers

de+com+po+si+
  tion
de+com+press
 de+com+
  presses
 de+com+press+
  ing
 de+com+
  pressed
 de+com+pres+
  sion
 de+com+pres+
  sions
de+con+gest+ant
 de+con+gest+
  ants
de+con+secrate
 de+con+
  secrates
 de+con+secrat+
  ing
 de+con+secrat+
  ed
 de+con+secra+
  tion
 de+con+secra+
  tions
de+con+struct
 de+con+structs
 de+con+struct+
  ing
 de+con+struct+
  ed
 de+con+struc+
  tion
 de+con+struc+
  tions
de+con+tami+
  nate
 de+con+tami+
  nates
 de+con+tami+
  nat+ing
 de+con+tami+
  nat+ed
 de+con+tami+na+
  tion
 de+con+tami+
  na+tions
de+con+trol
 de+con+trols
 de+con+trol+
  ling
 de+con+trolled
de+cor

de+cors
dé+cor
dé+cors
deco+rate
deco+rates
deco+rat+ing
deco+rat+ed
deco+ra+tion
deco+ra+tions
deco+ra+tive
deco+ra+tor
deco+ra+tors
deco+rous
deco+rous+ly
deco+rous+ness
de+co+rum
de+cou+page
de+coy
de+coys
de+coys
de+coy+ing
de+coyed
de+crease
de+creases
de+creases
de+creas+ing
de+creased
de+creas+ing+ly
de+cree
de+crees
de+crees
de+cree+ing
de+creed
dec+re+ment
dec+re+ments
de+crep+it
de+crepi+tude
de+cres+cence
de+cres+cences
de+cre+scen+do
de+cre+scen+
dos
de+cres+cent
de+cre+tal
de+cre+tals
de+crimi+nal+ise
de+crimi+nal+
ises
de+crimi+nal+is+
ing
de+crimi+nal+
ised
de+crimi+nal+ize
de+crimi+nal+
izes

de+crimi+nal+iz+
ing
de+crimi+nal+
ized
de+cry
de+cries
de+cry+ing
de+cried
de+cum+ben+cy
de+cum+ben+
cies
de+cum+bent
dedi+cate
dedi+cates
dedi+cat+ing
dedi+cat+ed
dedi+cat+ed
dedi+ca+tion
dedi+ca+tions
dedi+ca+tion+al
dedi+ca+tive
dedi+ca+tor
dedi+ca+tors
dedi+ca+tory
de+duce
de+duces
de+duc+ing
de+duced
de+duc+ible
de+duct
de+ducts
de+duct+ing
de+duct+ed
de+duct+ible
de+duct+ibles
de+duc+tion
de+duc+tions
de+duc+tive
Dee
deed
deeds
deeds
deed+ing
deed+ed
dee+jay
dee+jays
deem
deems
deem+ing
deemed
de-emphasise
de-emphasises
de-emphasis+
ing
de-emphasised

de-emphasize
de-emphasizes
de-emphasiz+
ing
de-emphasized
deem+ster
deem+sters
de-energisation
de-energise
de-energises
de-energis+ing
de-energised
de-energization
de-energize
de-energizes
de-energiz+ing
de-energized
deep
deeps
deep+er
deep+est
deep+en
deep+ens
deep+en+ing
deep+ened
deep+en+er
deep+en+ers
deep+freeze
deep+freezes
deep-freeze
deep-freezes
deep-freezing
deep-froze or
deep-freezed
deep-frozen or
deep-freezed
deep-fry
deep-fries
deep-frying
deep-fried
deep-laid
deep+ly
deep+ness
deep-rooted
deep-sea
deep-seated
deep-set
deer
deer or
deers
deer+skin
deer+skins
deer+stalker
deer+stalkers
deer+stalking

de-escalate
de-escalates
de-escalat+ing
de-escalat+ed
de-escala+tion
de-escala+tions
def
de+face
de+faces
de+fac+ing
de+faced
de+face+able
de+face+ment
de+face+ments
de+fac+er
de+fac+ers
de fac+to
de fac+tos
de+fal+cate
de+fal+cates
de+fal+cat+ing
de+fal+cat+ed
de+fal+ca+tor
de+fal+ca+tors
defa+ma+tion
defa+ma+tions
de+fama+tory
de+fame
de+fames
de+fam+ing
de+famed
de+fault
de+faults
de+faults
de+fault+ing
de+fault+ed
de+fault+er
de+fault+ers
de+feat
de+feats
de+feats
de+feat+ing
de+feat+ed
de+feat+ism
de+feat+ist
de+feat+ists
def+ecate
def+ecates
def+ecat+ing
def+ecat+ed
def+eca+tion
def+eca+tions
def+eca+tor
def+eca+tors
de+fect

de+fects
de+fects
de+fect+ing
de+fect+ed
de+fec+tion
de+fec+tions
de+fec+tive
de+fec+tive+
  ness
de+fec+tor
de+fec+tors
de+fence
de+fences
de+fence+less
de+fend
de+fends
de+fend+ing
de+fend+ed
de+fend+ant
de+fend+ants
de+fend+er
de+fend+ers
de+fen+es+tra+
  tion
de+fen+es+tra+
  tions
de+fense
U.S.
de+fenses
de+fense+less
U.S.
de+fen+sibil+ity
de+fen+sible
de+fen+sible+
  ness
de+fen+sive
de+fen+sive+ly
de+fer
de+fers
de+fer+ring
de+ferred
def+er+ence
def+er+ent
def+er+en+tial
def+er+en+tial+ly
de+fer+ral
de+fer+rals
de+fer+rer
de+fer+rers
de+fi+ance
de+fi+ances
de+fi+ant
de+fib+ril+la+tion
de+fib+ril+la+
  tions

de+fib+ril+la+tor
de+fib+ril+la+
  tors
de+fi+cien+cy
de+fi+cien+cies
de+fi+cient
de+fi+cient+ly
defi+cit
defi+cits
de+fi+er
de+fi+ers
de+file
de+files
de+files
de+fil+ing
de+filed
de+file+ment
de+file+ments
de+fin+able
de+fine
de+fines
de+fin+ing
de+fined
de+fin+er
de+fin+ers
defi+nite
defi+nite+ly
defi+nite+ness
defi+ni+tion
defi+ni+tions
de+fini+tive
de+fini+tives
de+fini+tive+ly
de+flate
de+flates
de+flat+ing
de+flat+ed
de+fla+tion
de+fla+tions
de+fla+tion+ary
de+fla+tion+ist
de+fla+tion+ists
de+fla+tor
de+fla+tors
de+flect
de+flects
de+flect+ing
de+flect+ed
de+flec+tion
de+flec+tions
de+flec+tive
de+flec+tor
de+flec+tors
de+flex+ion
de+flex+ions

de+floc+cu+lant
de+floc+cu+
  lants
de+floc+cu+late
de+floc+cu+
  lates
de+floc+cu+lat+
  ing
de+floc+cu+lat+
  ed
de+floc+cu+la+
  tion
de+floc+cu+la+
  tions
de+flo+ra+tion
de+flo+ra+tions
de+flow+er
de+flow+ers
de+flow+er+ing
de+flow+ered
Defoe
de+fo+li+ant
de+fo+li+ants
de+fo+li+ate
de+fo+li+ates
de+fo+li+at+ing
de+fo+li+at+ed
de+fo+lia+tion
de+fo+lia+tions
de+for+est
de+for+ests
de+for+est+ing
de+for+est+ed
de+for+esta+tion
de+form
de+forms
de+form+ing
de+formed
de+form+able
de+for+ma+tion
de+for+ma+
  tions
de+formed
de+form+ity
de+form+ities
de+fraud
de+frauds
de+fraud+ing
de+fraud+ed
de+fraud+er
de+fraud+ers
de+fray
de+frays
de+fray+ing
de+frayed

de+fray+able
de+fray+al
de+fray+als
de+fray+ment
de+fray+ments
de+frock
de+frocks
de+frock+ing
de+frocked
de+frost
de+frosts
de+frost+ing
de+frost+ed
de+frost+er
de+frost+ers
deft
deft+er
deft+est
deft+ly
deft+ness
de+funct
de+funct+ness
de+fuse
de+fuses
de+fus+ing
de+fused
de+fuze
U.S.
de+fuzes
de+fuz+ing
de+fuzed
defy
de+fies
de+fy+ing
de+fied
Degas
De Gasperi
de Gaulle
de+gauss
de+gausses
de+gauss+ing
de+gaussed
de+gen+era+cy
de+gen+era+
  cies
de+gen+er+ate
de+gen+er+ates
de+gen+er+ates
de+gen+er+at+
  ing
de+gen+er+at+
  ed
de+gen+er+ate+
  ly

de+gen+er+ate+
ness
de+gen+era+tion
de+gen+era+
tions
de+gen+era+tive
de+gra+dable
deg+ra+da+tion
deg+ra+da+
tions
de+grade
de+grades
de+grad+ing
de+grad+ed
de+grad+er
de+grad+ers
de+grad+ing
de+grad+ing+ly
de+gree
de+grees
De Havilland
de+hisce
de+hisces
de+his+cing
de+hisced
de+his+cent
de+horn
de+horns
de+horn+ing
de+horned
de+hu+mani+sa+
tion
de+hu+man+ise
de+hu+man+
ises
de+hu+man+is+
ing
de+hu+man+
ised
de+hu+mani+za+
tion
de+hu+man+ize
de+hu+man+
izes
de+hu+man+iz+
ing
de+hu+man+
ized
de+hu+midi+fi+
ca+tion
de+hu+midi+fi+er
de+hu+midi+fi+
ers
de+hu+midi+fy
de+hu+midi+fies

de+hu+midi+fy+
ing
de+hu+midi+fied
de+hy+drate
de+hy+drates
de+hy+drat+ing
de+hy+drat+ed
de+hy+dra+tion
de+hy+dra+tor
de+hy+dra+tors
de+hydro+gen+
ate
de+hydro+gen+
ates
de+hydro+gen+
at+ing
de+hydro+gen+
at+ed
de+hydro+gena+
tion
de+hydro+geni+
sa+tion
de+hydro+gen+
ise
de+hydro+gen+
ises
de+hydro+gen+
is+ing
de+hydro+gen+
ised
de+hydro+geni+
za+tion
de+hydro+gen+
ize
de+hydro+gen+
izes
de+hydro+gen+
iz+ing
de+hydro+gen+
ized
de-ice
de-ices
de-icing
de-iced
de-icer
de-icers
deic+tic
dei+fi+ca+tion
dei+fi+ca+tions
dei+fi+er
dei+fi+ers
dei+fy
dei+fies
dei+fy+ing
dei+fied

Deighton
deign
deigns
deign+ing
deigned
de+in+di+vidu+
ation
de+ioni+sa+tion
de-ionise
de-ionises
de-ionising
de-ionised
de+ioni+za+tion
de-ionize
de-ionizes
de-ionizing
de-ionized
Deirdre
de+ism
de+ist
de+ists
de+ist+ic
de+is+ti+cal
de+is+ti+cal+ly
de+ity
de+ities
De+ity
déjà vu
de+ject
de+jects
de+ject+ing
de+ject+ed
de+ject+ed+ly
de+jec+tion
de jure
Dekker
dek+ko
dek+kos
de Klerk
del
Delacroix
Dela+goa Bay
de la Mare
Delaroche
Delaunay
Dela+ware
people
Dela+wares *or*
Dela+ware
Dela+ware
place name,
grape
Dela+wares
Dela+war+ean

De La Warr
de+lay
de+lays
de+lays
de+lay+ing
de+layed
de+lay+er
de+lay+ers
de+lay+er+ing
de+lay+er+ings
dele
deles
de+les
de+leing
de+led
de+lec+tabil+ity
de+lec+table
de+lec+table+
ness
de+lec+ta+tion
del+egable
del+egate
del+egates
del+egates
del+egat+ing
del+egat+ed
del+ega+tion
del+ega+tions
de+lete
de+letes
de+let+ing
de+let+ed
del+eteri+ous
del+eteri+ous+
ness
de+letion
de+letions
Delft
Del+hi
deli
delis
de+lib+er+ate
de+lib+er+ates
de+lib+er+at+
ing
de+lib+er+at+ed
de+lib+er+ate+ly
de+lib+er+ate+
ness
de+lib+era+tion
de+lib+era+
tions
de+lib+era+tive
de+lib+era+tive+
ly

de+lib+era+tive+
 ness
de+lib+era+tor
de+lib+era+tors
Delibes
deli+ca+cy
 deli+ca+cies
deli+cate
deli+cate+ly
deli+cate+ness
deli+ca+tes+sen
 deli+ca+tes+
 sens
de+li+cious
de+li+cious+ly
de+li+cious+ness
de+light
 de+lights
 de+lights
 de+light+ing
 de+light+ed
de+light+ed+ly
de+light+ful
de+light+ful+ly
de+light+ful+ness
Delilah
de+lim+it
 de+lim+its
 de+lim+it+ing
 de+lim+it+ed
de+limi+tate
 de+limi+tates
 de+limi+tat+ing
 de+limi+tat+ed
de+limi+ta+tion
 de+limi+ta+tions
de+limi+ta+tive
de+lin+eate
 de+lin+eates
 de+lin+eat+ing
 de+lin+eat+ed
de+lin+ea+tion
 de+lin+ea+tions
de+lin+ea+tive
de+lin+quen+cy
 de+lin+quen+
 cies
de+lin+quent
 de+lin+quents
deli+quesce
 deli+quesces
 deli+quesc+ing
 deli+quesced
deli+ques+cence

deli+ques+
 cences
deli+ques+cent
de+liri+ous
de+liri+ous+ly
de+lir+ium
 de+lir+iums *or*
 de+liria
de+lir+ium tre+
 mens
Delius
de+liv+er
 de+liv+ers
 de+liv+er+ing
 de+liv+ered
de+liv+er+able
de+liv+er+ance
de+liv+er+er
 de+liv+er+ers
de+liv+ery
 de+liv+eries
dell
dells
Deller
Del Mar
Delors
De+los
de los Angeles
de+louse
 de+louses
 de+lous+ing
 de+loused
Del+phi
Del+phian
Del+phic
del+phin+ium
 del+phin+iums
del Sarto
del+ta
 del+tas
 del+ta+ic
del+tic
del+ti+olo+gist
 del+ti+olo+gists
del+ti+ol+ogy
del+toid
 del+toids
de+lud+able
de+lude
 de+ludes
 de+lud+ing
 de+lud+ed
de+lud+er
 de+lud+ers
del+uge

del+uges
del+uges
del+ug+ing
del+uged
de+lu+sion
 de+lu+sions
de+lu+sion+al
de+lu+sive
de+lu+so+ry
de luxe
delve
delves
delv+ing
delved
delv+er
delv+ers
de+mag+neti+sa+
 tion
de+mag+net+ise
 de+mag+net+
 ises
 de+mag+net+is+
 ing
 de+mag+net+
 ised
de+mag+net+is+
 er
 de+mag+net+is+
 ers
de+mag+neti+za+
 tion
de+mag+net+ize
 de+mag+net+
 izes
 de+mag+net+iz+
 ing
 de+mag+net+
 ized
de+mag+net+iz+
 er
 de+mag+net+iz+
 ers
dema+gog
 U.S.
 dema+gogs
dema+gog+ic
dema+gogue
 dema+gogues
dema+gogu+ery
dema+gogy
 dema+gogies
de+mand
 de+mands
 de+mands
 de+mand+ing

de+mand+ed
de+mand+able
de+mand+er
de+mand+ers
de+mand+ing
de+mar+cate
 de+mar+cates
 de+mar+cat+ing
 de+mar+cat+ed
de+mar+ca+tion
 de+mar+ca+
 tions
de+mar+ca+tor
de+mar+ca+tors
dé+marche
dé+marches
de+mar+ka+tion
 de+mar+ka+
 tions
de+ma+teri+ali+
 sa+tion
de+ma+teri+al+
 ise
 de+ma+teri+al+
 ises
 de+ma+teri+al+
 is+ing
 de+ma+teri+al+
 ised
de+ma+teri+ali+
 za+tion
de+ma+teri+al+
 ize
 de+ma+teri+al+
 izes
 de+ma+teri+al+
 iz+ing
 de+ma+teri+al+
 ized
deme
demes
de+mean
 de+means
 de+mean+ing
 de+meaned
de+mean+or
 U.S.
 de+mean+ors
de+mean+our
 de+mean+ours
de+ment
 de+ments
 de+ment+ing
 de+ment+ed
de+ment+ed

de+ment+ed+ly
de+ment+ed+
ness
de+men+tia
dem+erara
dem+eraras
Dem+erara
de+mer+it
de+mer+its
de+meri+to+ri+
ous
de+mer+sal
de+mesne
de+mesnes
demi+god
demi+gods
demi+god+dess
demi+god+
desses
demi+john
demi+johns
de+mili+ta+ri+sa+
tion
de+mili+ta+rise
de+mili+ta+rises
de+mili+ta+ris+
ing
de+mili+ta+rised
de+mili+ta+ri+za+
tion
de+mili+ta+rize
de+mili+ta+rizes
de+mili+ta+riz+
ing
de+mili+ta+rized
De Mille
demi+mon+daine
demi+mon+
daines
demi+monde
de+mis+able
de+mise
de+mises
de+mis+ing
de+mised
demi+semi+qua+
ver
demi+semi+qua+
vers
de+mist
de+mists
de+mist+ing
de+mist+ed
de+mist+er
de+mist+ers

demi+tasse
demi+tasses
demi+urge
demi+urges
demi+ur+gic
demi+ur+gi+cal
demo
demos
de+mob
de+mobs
de+mob+bing
de+mobbed
de+mo+bi+li+sa+
tion
de+mo+bi+li+sa+
tions
de+mo+bi+lise
de+mo+bi+lises
de+mo+bi+lis+
ing
de+mo+bi+lised
de+mo+bi+li+za+
tion
de+mo+bi+li+za+
tions
de+mo+bi+lize
de+mo+bi+lizes
de+mo+bi+liz+
ing
de+mo+bi+lized
de+moc+ra+cy
de+moc+ra+
cies
demo+crat
demo+crats
Demo+crat
Demo+crats
demo+crat+ic
Demo+crat+ic
demo+crati+cal+
ly
de+moc+ra+ti+sa+
tion
de+moc+ra+tise
de+moc+ra+
tises
de+moc+ra+tis+
ing
de+moc+ra+
tised
de+moc+ra+ti+za+
tion
de+moc+ra+tize
de+moc+ra+
tizes

de+moc+ra+tiz+
ing
de+moc+ra+
tized
Democritus
dé+mo+dé
de+modu+late
de+modu+lates
de+modu+lat+
ing
de+modu+lat+
ed
de+modu+la+tion
de+modu+la+
tions
de+modu+la+tor
de+modu+la+
tors
de+mog+ra+pher
de+mog+ra+
phers
de+mo+graph+ic
de+mog+ra+phy
de+mog+ra+
phies
demoi+selle
demoi+selles
de Molina
de+mol+ish
de+mol+ishes
de+mol+ish+ing
de+mol+ished
de+mol+ish+er
de+mol+ish+ers
demo+li+tion
demo+li+tions
demo+li+tion+ist
demo+li+tion+
ists
de+mon
de+mons
de+mon+eti+sa+
tion
de+mon+etise
de+mon+etises
de+mon+etis+
ing
de+mon+etised
de+mon+eti+za+
tion
de+mon+etize
de+mon+etizes
de+mon+etiz+
ing
de+mon+etized

de+mo+ni+ac
de+mo+ni+acs
de+mo+nia+cal
de+mo+nia+cal+
ly
de+mon+ic
de+mon+ism
de+mon+ist
de+mon+ists
de+mon+ola+try
de+mon+ola+
tries
de+mon+olo+gist
de+mon+olo+
gists
de+mon+ol+ogy
de+mon+ol+
ogies
de+mon+strabil+
ity
de+mon+strable
de+mon+strably
dem+on+strate
dem+on+strates
dem+on+strat+
ing
dem+on+strat+
ed
dem+on+stra+
tion
dem+on+stra+
tions
de+mon+stra+
tion+al
de+mon+stra+
tion+ist
de+mon+stra+
tion+ists
de+mon+stra+
tive
de+mon+stra+
tives
de+mon+stra+
tive+ly
de+mon+stra+
tive+ness
de+mon+stra+tor
de+mon+stra+
tors
de+mor+ali+sa+
tion
de+mor+al+ise
de+mor+al+ises
de+mor+al+is+
ing

de+mor+al+ised
de+mor+ali+za+
tion
de+mor+al+ize
de+mor+al+izes
de+mor+al+iz+
ing
de+mor+al+ized
Demosthenes
de+mote
de+motes
de+mot+ing
de+mot+ed
de+mot+ic
de+mo+tion
de+mo+tions
de+mot+ist
de+mot+ists
Dempsey
demp+ster
demp+sters
de+mul+cent
de+mul+cents
de+mur
de+murs
de+murs
de+mur+ring
de+murred
de+mure
de+mure+ly
de+mure+ness
de+mur+rable
de+mur+rage
de+mur+rages
de+mur+rer
de+mur+rers
demy
demies
de+mys+ti+fi+ca+
tion
de+mys+ti+fy
de+mys+ti+fies
de+mys+ti+fy+
ing
de+mys+ti+fied
de+my+tholo+
gise
de+my+tholo+
gises
de+my+tholo+
gis+ing
de+my+tholo+
gised
de+my+tholo+
gize

de+my+tholo+
gizes
de+my+tholo+
giz+ing
de+my+tholo+
gized
den
dens
dens
den+ning
denned
de+nar+ius
de+narii
de+nary
de+na+tion+ali+
sa+tion
de+na+tion+al+
ise
de+na+tion+al+
ises
de+na+tion+al+
is+ing
de+na+tion+al+
ised
de+na+tion+ali+
za+tion
de+na+tion+al+
ize
de+na+tion+al+
izes
de+na+tion+al+
iz+ing
de+na+tion+al+
ized
de+natu+rali+sa+
tion
de+natu+ral+ise
de+natu+ral+
ises
de+natu+ral+is+
ing
de+natu+ral+
ised
de+natu+rali+za+
tion
de+natu+ral+ize
de+natu+ral+
izes
de+natu+ral+iz+
ing
de+natu+ral+
ized
de+na+tur+ant
de+na+tur+ants
de+na+tura+tion

de+na+tura+
tions
de+na+ture
de+na+tures
de+na+tur+ing
de+na+tured
de+na+tur+ise
de+na+tur+ises
de+na+tur+is+
ing
de+na+tur+ised
de+na+tur+ize
de+na+tur+izes
de+na+tur+iz+
ing
de+na+tur+ized
Den+bigh+shire
Den Bosch
Dench
den+drite
den+drites
den+drit+ic
den+dro+chro+
nol+ogy
den+dro+log+ic
den+dro+logi+cal
den+drolo+gist
den+drolo+gists
den+drol+ogy
dene
denes
de+ner+vate
de+ner+vates
de+ner+vat+ing
de+ner+vat+ed
de+ner+va+tion
de+ner+va+
tions
Deneuve
den+gue
Deng Xiaoping
Den Haag
de+ni+able
de+ni+ably
de+ni+al
de+ni+als
den+ier
measure of
fineness
de+ni+er
person who
denies
de+ni+ers
deni+grate

deni+grates
deni+grat+ing
deni+grat+ed
deni+gra+tion
deni+gra+tions
deni+gra+tor
deni+gra+tors
den+im
den+ims
De Niro
Denis
deni+zen
deni+zens
Den+mark
Denning
Dennis
de+nomi+nate
de+nomi+nates
de+nomi+nat+
ing
de+nomi+nat+
ed
de+nomi+na+tion
de+nomi+na+
tions
de+nomi+na+tion+
al
de+nomi+na+tive
de+nomi+na+tor
de+nomi+na+
tors
de+no+ta+tion
de+no+ta+tions
de+no+ta+tive
de+note
de+notes
de+not+ing
de+not+ed
de+noue+ment
de+noue+ments
dé+noue+ment
dé+noue+ments
de+nounce
de+nounces
de+nounc+ing
de+nounced
de+nounce+ment
de+nounce+
ments
de+nounc+er
de+nounc+ers
de novo
dense
dens+er
dens+est

dense+ly
dense+ness
den+sim+eter
 den+sim+eters
den+si+met+ric
den+sim+etry
den+sity
 den+sities
dent
 dents
 dents
 dent+ing
 dent+ed
den+tal
den+tate
den+tate+ly
den+ticu+late
den+ti+frice
 den+ti+frices
den+til
 den+tils
den+tin
den+tin+al
den+tine
den+tist
 den+tists
den+tis+try
den+ti+tion
 den+ti+tions
den+ture
 den+tures
de+nu+cleari+sa+
 tion
de+nu+clear+ise
 de+nu+clear+
 ises
 de+nu+clear+is+
 ing
 de+nu+clear+
 ised
de+nu+cleari+za+
 tion
de+nu+clear+ize
 de+nu+clear+
 izes
 de+nu+clear+iz+
 ing
 de+nu+clear+
 ized
denu+date
 denu+dates
 denu+dat+ing
 denu+dat+ed
denu+da+tion
 denu+da+tions

de+nude
de+nudes
de+nud+ing
de+nud+ed
de+nu+mer+able
de+nu+mer+ably
de+nun+ci+ate
de+nun+ci+ates
de+nun+ci+at+
 ing
de+nun+ci+at+
 ed
de+nun+cia+tion
de+nun+cia+
 tions
de+nun+cia+tor
de+nun+cia+
 tors
de+nun+cia+tory
Den+ver
deny
de+nies
de+ny+ing
de+nied
deo+dar
deo+dars
de+odor+ant
de+odor+ants
de+odori+sa+tion
de+odor+ise
de+odor+ises
de+odor+is+ing
de+odor+ised
de+odor+is+er
de+odor+is+ers
de+odori+za+tion
de+odor+ize
de+odor+izes
de+odor+iz+ing
de+odor+ized
de+odor+iz+er
de+odor+iz+ers
de+on+tic
de+on+tol+ogy
de+oxi+di+sa+
 tion
de+oxi+di+sa+
 tions
de+oxi+dise
de+oxi+dises
de+oxi+dis+ing
de+oxi+dised
de+oxi+dis+er
de+oxi+dis+ers

de+oxi+di+za+
 tion
de+oxi+di+za+
 tions
de+oxi+dize
de+oxi+dizes
de+oxi+diz+ing
de+oxi+dized
de+oxi+diz+er
de+oxi+diz+ers
de+oxy+gen+ate
de+oxy+gen+
 ates
de+oxy+gen+at+
 ing
de+oxy+gen+at+
 ed
de+oxy+gena+
 tion
de+oxy+gen+ise
de+oxy+gen+
 ises
de+oxy+gen+is+
 ing
de+oxy+gen+
 ised
de+oxy+gen+ize
de+oxy+gen+
 izes
de+oxy+gen+iz+
 ing
de+oxy+gen+
 ized
de+oxy+ri+bo+
 nu+cle+ase
Depardieu
de+part
de+parts
de+part+ing
de+part+ed
de+part+ment
de+part+ments
de+part+men+tal
de+part+men+tali+
 sa+tion
de+part+ment+al+
 ise
de+part+ment+
 al+ises
de+part+ment+
 al+is+ing
de+part+ment+
 al+ised

de+part+men+tali+
 za+tion
de+part+ment+al+
 ize
de+part+ment+
 al+izes
de+part+ment+
 al+iz+ing
de+part+ment+
 al+ized
de+par+ture
de+par+tures
de+pend
de+pends
de+pend+ing
de+pend+ed
de+pend+abil+ity
de+pend+able
de+pend+able+
 ness
de+pend+ably
de+pend+ance
 U.S.
de+pend+an+cy
 U.S.
de+pend+an+
 cies
de+pend+ant
de+pend+ants
de+pend+ence
de+pend+en+cy
de+pend+en+
 cies
de+pend+ent
de+pend+ents
de+pend+ent+ly
de+per+son+ali+
 sa+tion
de+per+son+al+
 ise
de+per+son+al+
 ises
de+per+son+al+
 is+ing
de+per+son+al+
 ised
de+per+son+ali+
 za+tion
de+per+son+al+
 ize
de+per+son+al+
 izes
de+per+son+al+
 iz+ing

de+per+son+al+
ized
de+pict
de+picts
de+pict+ing
de+pict+ed
de+pict+er
de+pict+ers
de+pic+tion
de+pic+tions
de+pic+tive
de+pic+tor
de+pic+tors
depi+late
depi+lates
depi+lat+ing
depi+lat+ed
depi+la+tion
depi+la+tions
depi+la+tor
depi+la+tors
de+pila+tory
de+pila+tories
de+plane
de+planes
de+plan+ing
de+planed
de+plete
de+pletes
de+plet+ing
de+plet+ed
de+ple+tion
de+ple+tions
de+plor+able
de+plor+ably
de+plore
de+plores
de+plor+ing
de+plored
de+plor+ing+ly
de+ploy
de+ploys
de+ploy+ing
de+ployed
de+ploy+ment
de+ploy+ments
de+po+lari+sa+
tion
de+po+lar+ise
de+po+lar+ises
de+po+lar+is+
ing
de+po+lar+ised
de+po+lari+za+
tion

de+po+lar+ize
de+po+lar+izes
de+po+lar+iz+
ing
de+po+lar+ized
de+po+nent
de+po+nents
de+popu+late
de+popu+lates
de+popu+lat+
ing
de+popu+lat+ed
de+popu+la+tion
de+popu+la+
tions
de+port
de+ports
de+port+ing
de+port+ed
de+port+able
de+por+ta+tion
de+por+ta+tions
de+por+tee
de+por+tees
de+port+ment
de+pose
de+poses
de+pos+ing
de+posed
de+pos+it
de+pos+its
de+pos+its
de+pos+it+ing
de+pos+it+ed
de+posi+tary
de+posi+taries
depo+si+tion
depo+si+tions
de+posi+tor
de+posi+tors
de+posi+tory
de+posi+tories
de+pot
de+pots
dep+ra+va+tion
dep+ra+va+
tions
de+prave
de+praves
de+prav+ing
de+praved
de+praved
de+prav+ity
de+prav+ities
dep+re+cate

dep+re+cates
dep+re+cat+ing
dep+re+cat+ed
dep+re+cat+ing+
ly
dep+re+ca+tion
dep+re+ca+
tions
dep+re+ca+tive
dep+re+ca+tor
dep+re+ca+tors
dep+re+ca+tory
de+pre+ci+ate
de+pre+ci+ates
de+pre+ci+at+
ing
de+pre+ci+at+
ed
de+pre+ci+at+ing+
ly
de+pre+cia+tion
de+pre+cia+tive
de+pre+cia+tory
dep+re+da+tion
dep+re+da+
tions
de+press
de+presses
de+press+ing
de+pressed
de+pres+sant
de+pres+sants
de+pressed
de+press+ing
de+press+ing+ly
de+pres+sion
de+pres+sions
de+pres+sive
de+pres+sive+ly
de+pres+sor
de+pres+sors
de+pres+sur+isa+
tion
de+pres+sur+ise
de+pres+sur+
ises
de+pres+sur+is+
ing
de+pres+sur+
ised
de+pres+sur+iza+
tion
de+pres+sur+ize
de+pres+sur+
izes

de+pres+sur+iz+
ing
de+pres+sur+
ized
de+priv+al
de+priv+als
dep+ri+va+tion
dep+ri+va+tions
de+prive
de+prives
de+priv+ing
de+prived
de+prived
depth
depths
depu+ra+tion
depu+ra+tions
depu+ta+tion
depu+ta+tions
de+pute
de+putes
de+putes
de+put+ing
de+put+ed
depu+tise
depu+tises
depu+tis+ing
depu+tised
depu+tize
depu+tizes
depu+tiz+ing
depu+tized
depu+ty
depu+ties
De Quincey
de+rac+in+ate
de+rac+in+ates
de+rac+in+at+
ing
de+rac+in+at+
ed
de+raci+na+tion
de+raci+na+
tions
de+rail
de+rails
de+rail+ing
de+railed
de+rail+ment
de+rail+ments
Derain
de+range
de+ranges
de+rang+ing
de+ranged

de +range +ment
de +range +
  ments
der +by
  der +bies
Der +by
place name,
  horse race
Derby
surname
Der +by +shire
de +rec +og +nise
de +rec +og +
  nises
de +rec +og +nis +
  ing
de +rec +og +
  nised
de +rec +og +ni +
  tion
de +rec +og +nize
de +rec +og +
  nizes
de +rec +og +niz +
  ing
de +rec +og +
  nized
de +regu +late
de +regu +lates
de +regu +lat +ing
de +regu +lat +ed
de +regu +la +tion
de +regu +la +
  tions
der +elict
  der +elicts
der +elic +tion
  der +elic +tions
de +re +strict
  de +re +stricts
  de +re +strict +ing
  de +re +strict +ed
  de +re +stric +tion
  de +re +stric +
  tions
de +ride
  de +rides
  de +rid +ing
  de +rid +ed
  de +rid +er
  de +rid +ers
  de +rid +ing +ly
de ri +gueur
der +in +ger
  der +in +gers

de +ris +ible
de +ri +sion
de +ri +sive
de +ri +sive +ly
de +ri +sive +ness
de +ri +sory
de +riv +able
deri +va +tion
  deri +va +tions
  deri +va +tion +al
de +riva +tive
  de +riva +tives
  de +riva +tive +ly
de +rive
  de +rives
  de +riv +ing
  de +rived
  de +riv +er
  de +riv +ers
derm
  derms
der +ma
  der +mas
der +mal
der +ma +ti +tis
der +ma +to +logi +
  cal
der +ma +tolo +
  gist
  der +ma +tolo +
  gists
der +ma +tol +ogy
der +mic
der +mis
der +nier cri
dero +gate
  dero +gates
  dero +gat +ing
  dero +gat +ed
dero +gation
de +roga +tive
de +roga +to +ri +ly
de +roga +tory
der +rick
  der +ricks
Derrida
der +rière
  der +rières
derring-do
der +rin +ger
  der +rin +gers
der +ris
  der +rises
Der +ry
derv

der +vish
  der +vishes
Der +went
Derwent +water
Desai
de +sali +na +tion
de +sali +ni +sa +
  tion
de +sali +ni +za +
  tion
de +scale
  de +scales
  de +scal +ing
  de +scaled
des +cant
  des +cants
des +cant +er
  des +cant +ers
Descartes
de +scend
  de +scends
  de +scend +ing
  de +scend +ed
des +cend +able
de +scend +able
Law
de +scend +ant
  de +scend +ants
  de +scend +ent
  de +scend +er
  de +scend +ers
de +scend +ible
de +scent
  de +scents
de +school
  de +schools
  de +school +ing
  de +schooled
de +scrib +able
de +scribe
  de +scribes
  de +scrib +ing
  de +scribed
  de +scrib +er
  de +scrib +ers
de +scrip +tion
  de +scrip +tions
de +scrip +tive
  de +scrip +tive +ly
  de +scrip +tive +
  ness
de +scry
  de +scries
  de +scry +ing
  de +scried

des +ecrate
  des +ecrates
  des +ecrat +ing
  des +ecrat +ed
  des +ecrat +er
  des +ecrat +ers
des +ecra +tion
des +ecra +tor
  des +ecra +tors
de +seg +re +gate
  de +seg +re +
  gates
  de +seg +re +gat +
  ing
  de +seg +re +gat +
  ed
de +seg +re +ga +
  tion
de +se +lect
  de +se +lects
  de +se +lect +ing
  de +se +lect +ed
de +se +lec +tion
  de +se +lec +tions
de +sen +si +ti +sa +
  tion
de +sen +si +tise
  de +sen +si +tises
  de +sen +si +tis +
  ing
  de +sen +si +tised
  de +sen +si +tis +er
  de +sen +si +tis +
  ers
de +sen +si +ti +za +
  tion
de +sen +si +tize
  de +sen +si +tizes
  de +sen +si +tiz +
  ing
  de +sen +si +tized
  de +sen +si +tiz +er
  de +sen +si +tiz +
  ers
de +sert
abandon,
punishment
  de +serts
  de +serts
  de +sert +ing
  de +sert +ed
des +ert
dry area
  des +erts
de +sert +er

de+sert+ers
des+er+ti+fi+ca+
tion
de+ser+tion
de+ser+tions
de+serve
de+serves
de+serv+ing
de+served
de+served
de+serv+ed+ly
de+serv+ed+
ness
de+serv+ing
de+serv+ing+ly
de+serv+ing+
ness
des+ha+bille
des+ha+billes
de Sica
des+ic+cant
des+ic+cants
des+ic+cate
des+ic+cates
des+ic+cat+ing
des+ic+cat+ed
des+ic+ca+ted
des+ic+ca+tion
de+sid+er+ate
de+sid+er+ates
de+sid+er+at+
ing
de+sid+er+at+
ed
de+sid+era+tion
de+sid+era+
tions
de+sid+era+tum
de+sid+era+ta
de+sign
de+signs
de+signs
de+sign+ing
de+signed
de+sign+able
des+ig+nate
des+ig+nates
des+ig+nat+ing
des+ig+nat+ed
des+ig+na+tion
des+ig+na+tions
des+ig+na+tor
des+ig+na+tors
de+sign+ed+ly
de+sign+er

de+sign+ers
de+sign+ing
de+sir+abil+ity
de+sir+able
de+sirable+ness
de+sir+ably
de+sire
de+sires
de+sires
de+sir+ing
de+sired
de+sir+er
de+sir+ers
de+sir+ous
de+sist
de+sists
de+sist+ing
de+sist+ed
desk
desks
desk-bound
de+skill
de+skills
de+skill+ing
de+skilled
desk+top
desk+tops
des+man
des+mans
Des Moines
Desmoulins
deso+late
deso+lates
deso+lat+ing
deso+lat+ed
deso+late+ly
deso+late+ness
deso+lat+er
deso+lat+ers
deso+la+tion
deso+la+tor
deso+la+tors
De Soto
des+pair
des+pairs
des+pair+ing
des+paired
des+pair+ing
des+pair+ing+ly
des+patch
des+patches
des+patches
des+patch+ing
des+patched
des+patch+er

des+patch+ers
Despenser
des+pe+ra+do
des+pe+ra+
does or
des+pe+ra+dos
des+per+ate
des+per+ate+ly
des+per+ate+
ness
des+pera+tion
des+pic+able
des+pi+cably
des+pise
des+pises
des+pis+ing
des+pised
de+spis+er
de+spis+ers
de+spite
de+spites
de+spoil
de+spoils
de+spoil+ing
de+spoiled
de+spoil+er
de+spoil+ers
de+spoil+ment
de+spo+lia+tion
de+spond
de+sponds
de+spond+ing
de+spond+ed
de+spond+ence
de+spond+en+cy
de+spond+ent
de+spond+ent+ly
de+spond+ing+ly
des+pot
des+pots
des+pot+ic
des+poti+cal
des+poti+cal+ly
des+pot+ism
des Prés
des res
Des+sau
des+sert
des+serts
dessert+spoon
dessert+spoons
des+ti+na+tion
des+ti+na+tions
des+tine
des+tines

des+tin+ing
des+tined
des+tined
des+ti+ny
des+ti+nies
des+ti+tute
des+ti+tu+tion
des+tri+er
des+tri+ers
de+stroy
de+stroys
de+stroy+ing
de+stroyed
de+stroy+er
de+stroy+ers
de+struct
de+structs
de+struct+ing
de+struct+ed
de+struct+ible
de+struc+tion
de+struc+tive
de+struc+tive+ly
de+struc+tive+
ness
de+struc+tor
de+struc+tors
desue+tude
de+sul+phur+ise
de+sul+phur+
ises
de+sul+phur+is+
ing
de+sul+phur+
ised
de+sul+phur+ize
de+sul+phur+
izes
de+sul+phur+iz+
ing
de+sul+phur+
ized
des+ul+to+ri+ly
des+ul+to+ri+
ness
des+ul+tory
de+tach
de+taches
de+tach+ing
de+tached
de+tach+abil+ity
de+tach+abil+
ities
de+tach+able
de+tached

de+tach+ment
de+tach+ments
de+tail
de+tails
de+tails
de+tail+ing
de+tailed
de+tailed
de+tain
de+tains
de+tain+ing
de+tained
de+tain+able
de+tainee
de+tainees
de+tain+ment
de+tect
de+tects
de+tect+ing
de+tect+ed
de+tect+able
de+tect+ible
de+tec+tion
de+tec+tive
de+tec+tives
de+tec+tor
de+tec+tors
de+tent
de+tents
dé+tente
dé+tentes
de+ten+tion
de+ten+tions
de+ter
de+ters
de+ter+ring
de+terred
de+terge
de+terges
de+terg+ing
de+terged
de+ter+gent
de+ter+gents
de+terio+rate
de+terio+rates
de+terio+rat+ing
de+terio+rat+ed
de+terio+ra+tion
de+terio+ra+tive
de+ter+ment
de+ter+ments
de+ter+mi+nable
de+ter+mi+nant
de+ter+mi+
  nants

de+ter+mi+nate
de+ter+mi+nate+
  ness
de+ter+mi+na+
  tion
de+ter+mi+na+
  tive
de+ter+mi+na+
  tives
de+ter+mi+na+
  tive+ly
de+ter+mi+na+
  tive+ness
de+ter+mine
de+ter+mines
de+ter+min+ing
de+ter+mined
de+ter+mined
de+ter+mined+ly
de+ter+min+er
de+ter+min+ers
de+ter+min+ism
de+ter+min+ist
de+ter+min+ists
de+ter+min+is+
  tic
de+ter+rence
de+ter+rences
de+ter+rent
de+ter+rents
de+test
de+tests
de+test+ing
de+test+ed
de+test+abil+ity
de+test+able
de+test+able+
  ness
de+test+ably
de+tes+ta+tion
de+test+er
de+test+ers
de+throne
de+thrones
de+thron+ing
de+throned
de+throne+ment
de+thron+er
de+thron+ers
deto+nate
deto+nates
deto+nat+ing
deto+nat+ed
deto+na+tion
deto+na+tions

deto+na+tor
deto+na+tors
de+tour
de+tours
de+tours
de+tour+ing
de+toured
de+toxi+fi+ca+
  tion
de+toxi+fy
de+toxi+fies
de+toxi+fy+ing
de+toxi+fied
de+tract
de+tracts
de+tract+ing
de+tract+ed
de+trac+tion
de+trac+tions
de+trac+tive
de+trac+tor
de+trac+tors
de+train
de+trains
de+train+ing
de+trained
de+train+ment
de+train+ments
det+ri+ment
det+ri+men+tal
de+tri+tal
de+tri+tus
De+troit
de trop
de+tu+mes+
  cence
de+tu+mes+
  cences
deuce
deuces
deu+ced
Deus
deus ex machi+na
deu+ter+ide
deu+ter+ides
deu+ter+ium
deu+ter+on
deu+ter+ons
Deutsch
Deut+sche Mark
Deut+sche
  Marks
Deutsch+land
Deutsch+mark
Deutsch+marks

deut+zia
deut+zias
Deux-Sèvres
de Valera
de+valu+ate
de+valu+ates
de+valu+at+ing
de+valu+at+ed
de+valua+tion
de+valua+tions
de+value
de+values
de+valu+ing
de+valued
De+va+na+ga+ri
dev+as+tate
dev+as+tates
dev+as+tat+ing
dev+as+tat+ed
dev+as+ta+tion
dev+as+ta+
  tions
dev+as+ta+tor
dev+as+ta+tors
de+vel+op
de+vel+ops
de+vel+op+ing
de+vel+oped
de+vel+op+able
de+vel+op+er
de+vel+op+ers
de+vel+op+ment
de+vel+op+
  ments
de+vel+op+men+
  tal
Devereux
Devi
de+vi+ance
de+vi+ances
de+vi+an+cy
de+vi+an+cies
de+vi+ant
de+vi+ants
de+vi+ate
de+vi+ates
de+vi+ates
de+vi+at+ing
de+vi+at+ed
de+via+tion
de+via+tions
de+via+tor
de+via+tors
de+via+tory
de+vice

de+vices
dev+il
dev+ils
dev+ils
dev+il+ling *or*
dev+il+ing
U.S.
dev+illed *or*
dev+iled
U.S.
devil+fish
devil+fish *or*
devil+fishes
dev+il+ish
dev+il+ish+ly
dev+il+ish+ness
devil-may-care
dev+il+ment
dev+il+ments
dev+il+ry
dev+il+ries
dev+il+try
dev+il+tries
Devine
de+vi+ous
de+vi+ous+ly
de+vi+ous+ness
de+vise
de+vises
de+vises
de+vis+ing
de+vised
de+vis+er
de+vis+ers
de+vi+tali+sa+
tion
de+vi+tal+ise
de+vi+tal+ises
de+vi+tal+is+ing
de+vi+tal+ised
de+vi+tali+za+
tion
de+vi+tal+ize
de+vi+tal+izes
de+vi+tal+iz+ing
de+vi+tal+ized
Devizes
de+void
de+voirs
de+vo+lu+tion
de+vo+lu+tions
de+vo+lu+tion+
ary
de+vo+lu+tion+
ist

de+vo+lu+tion+
ists
de+volve
de+volves
de+volv+ing
de+volved
de+volve+ment
de+volve+
ments
Dev+on
De+vo+nian
Dev+on+shire
de+vote
de+votes
de+vot+ing
de+vot+ed
de+vot+ed+ly
de+vot+ed+ness
devo+tee
devo+tees
de+vo+tion
de+vo+tions
de+vo+tion+al
de+vour
de+vours
de+vour+ing
de+voured
de+vour+er
de+vour+ers
de+vour+ing
de+vout
de+vout+ly
de+vout+ness
De Vries
dew
dews
dew+ing
dewed
Dewar
dew+berry
dew+berries
dew+claw
dew+claws
dew+clawed
dew+drop
dew+drops
Dewey
dewi+ly
dewi+ness
dew+lap
dew+laps
dewy
dewi+er
dewi+est

dex+ter
dex+ter+ity
dex+ter+ities
dex+ter+ous
dex+ter+ous+ly
dex+ter+ous+
ness
dex+tral
dex+tral+ity
dex+tral+ly
dex+tran
dex+trans
dex+trin
dex+trins
dex+trine
dex+trines
dex+tro
dextro+glu+cose
dextro+ro+ta+ry
dextro+ro+ta+
tion
dextro+ro+ta+
tions
dextro+ro+ta+
tory
dex+tror+sal
dex+trorse
dex+trorse+ly
dex+trose
dex+trous
dex+trous+ly
dex+trous+ness
Dha+ka
dhal
dhals
dhar+ma
Dhí+los
dho+bi
dho+bis
dholl
dholls
dhoo+ti
dhoo+tis
dhoo+tie
dhoo+ties
dho+ti
dho+tis
dhow
dhows
dhu+ti
dhu+tis
dia+be+tes
dia+bet+ic
dia+bet+ics
dia+ble+rie

dia+bol+ic
dia+boli+cal
dia+boli+cal+ly
dia+boli+cal+
ness
diabo+lism
di+abo+list
di+abo+lists
di+abo+lo
di+abo+los
dia+chron+ic
di+acid
dia+cid+ic
di+aco+nal
di+aco+nate
di+aco+nates
dia+crit+ic
dia+crit+ics
dia+criti+cal
dia+dem
dia+dems
di+aer+esis
di+aer+eses
Diaghilev
di+ag+nos+able
di+ag+nose
di+ag+noses
di+ag+nos+ing
di+ag+nosed
di+ag+no+sis
di+ag+no+ses
di+ag+nos+tic
di+ago+nal
di+ago+nals
di+ago+nal+ly
dia+gram
dia+grams
dia+grams
dia+gram+ming
or
dia+gram+ing
U.S.
dia+grammed
or
dia+gramed
U.S.
dia+gram+mat+ic
dial
dials
dials
dial+ling *or*
dial+ing
U.S.
dialled *or*
dialed

U.S.
dia+lect
  dia+lects
  dia+lec+tal
  dia+lec+tic
    dia+lec+tics
  dia+lec+ti+cal
  dia+lec+ti+cal+ly
  dia+lec+ti+cian
    dia+lec+ti+cians
  dia+lec+tics
dial+ler
  dial+lers
dia+log
U.S.
  dia+logs
dia+logue
  dia+logues
  dia+ly+sa+tion
  dia+lyse
  dia+lyses
  dia+lys+ing
  dia+lysed
  dia+lys+er
  dia+lys+ers
di+aly+sis
  di+aly+ses
dia+lyt+ic
dia+lyz+er
U.S.
  dia+lyz+ers
dia+mag+net+ic
dia+mag+net+
  ism
dia+man+té
dia+man+tine
di+am+eter
  di+am+eters
  di+am+etral
dia+met+ric
  dia+met+ri+cal
  dia+met+ri+cal+
  ly
dia+mond
  dia+monds
diamond+back
  diamond+backs
dia+mor+phine
di+an+thus
  di+an+thuses
dia+pa+son
  dia+pa+sons
dia+pause
  dia+pauses
dia+per

dia+pers
dia+pers
dia+per+ing
dia+pered
di+apha+nous
di+apha+nous+ly
dia+pho+resis
dia+pho+ret+ic
  dia+pho+ret+ics
dia+phragm
  dia+phragms
dia+phrag+mat+
  ic
dia+posi+tive
  dia+posi+tives
dia+rist
  dia+rists
di+ar+rhea
U.S.
di+ar+rheal
U.S.
di+ar+rhoea
di+ar+rhoeal
di+ar+rhoe+ic
dia+ry
  dia+ries
Dias
Di+as+po+ra
dia+stal+sis
  dia+stal+ses
  dia+stal+tic
dia+stase
dia+stases
dia+sta+sic
di+as+to+le
di+as+tol+ic
dia+stroph+ic
di+as+tro+phism
dia+ther+man+cy
  dia+ther+man+
  cies
dia+ther+man+
  ous
dia+ther+mia
dia+ther+my
dia+tom
  dia+toms
dia+to+ma+
  ceous
dia+tom+ic
di+ato+mite
  di+ato+mites
dia+ton+ic
dia+tribe
  dia+tribes

Diaz
di+az+epam
di+azo
  di+azos *or*
  di+azoes
dia+zo+nium
di+ba+sic
di+ba+sic+ity
dib+ber
  dib+bers
dib+ble
  dib+bles
  dib+bles
  dib+bling
  dib+bled
dibs
dice
  dices
  dic+ing
  diced
dic+er
  dic+ers
dicey
  dici+er
  dici+est
di+chlo+ride
di+chloro+di+
  phenyl+tri+
  chloro+ethane
di+chloro+
  methane
di+choto+mous
di+choto+my
  di+choto+mies
di+chro+ic
di+chro+ism
di+chro+mate
  di+chro+mates
  di+chro+mat+ic
  di+chro+mati+
  cism
di+chro+ma+tism
di+chro+mic
dick
  dicks
dick+ens
Dickens
Dick+en+sian
dick+er
  dick+ers
  dick+ers
  dick+er+ing
  dick+ered
dick+ey
  dick+eys

dick+ey
dicki+er
dicki+est
dick+head
  dick+heads
Dickinson
dicky
  dickies
dicky
  dicki+er
  dicki+est
di+cli+nism
di+cli+nous
di+coty+ledon
  di+coty+ledons
di+coty+ledon+
  ous
dic+ta
Dic+ta+phone
Trademark
Dic+ta+phones
dic+tate
  dic+tates
  dic+tates
  dic+tat+ing
  dic+tat+ed
dic+ta+tion
  dic+ta+tions
dic+ta+tor
  dic+ta+tors
  dic+ta+tor+ial
  dic+ta+to+ri+al+
  ly
dic+ta+tor+ship
  dic+ta+tor+
  ships
dic+tion
  dic+tions
  dic+tion+ary
  dic+tion+aries
dic+tum
  dic+tums *or*
  dic+ta
di+dac+tic
di+dac+ti+cal+ly
di+dac+ti+cism
di+dac+tics
did+dle
  did+dles
  did+dling
  did+dled
did+dler
  did+dlers
Diderot
did+geri+doo

did+geri+doos
didn't
dido
  didos *or*
  didoes
Dido
didst
di+dym+ium
die
  dies
  dies
  dy+ing
  died
die-cast
  die-casts
  die-casting
  die-cast
die-casting
Diefenbaker
die-hard
  die-hards
diel+drin
di+elec+tric
  di+elec+trics
  di+elec+tri+cal+ly
Dien Bien Phu
diene
  dienes
Di+eppe
di+er+esis
  di+er+eses
  di+eret+ic
die+sel
  die+sels
Diesel
Dies Irae
di+esis
  di+eses
die+stock
  die+stocks
diet
  diets
  diets
  diet+ing
  diet+ed
di+etary
  di+etaries
di+et+er
  di+et+ers
di+etet+ic
di+eteti+cal
di+eteti+cal+ly
di+etet+ics
di+eti+cian
  di+eti+cians

di+eti+tian
  di+eti+tians
Dietrich
dif+fer
  dif+fers
  dif+fer+ing
  dif+fered
dif+fer+ence
  dif+fer+ences
dif+fer+ent
  dif+fer+en+tia
  dif+fer+en+tiae
  dif+fer+en+tial
  dif+fer+en+tials
  dif+fer+en+tial+ly
  dif+fer+en+ti+ate
  dif+fer+en+ti+
    ates
  dif+fer+en+ti+at+
    ing
  dif+fer+en+ti+at+
    ed
  dif+fer+en+tia+
    tion
  dif+fer+en+tia+
    tions
  dif+fer+en+tia+
    tor
  dif+fer+en+tia+
    tors
dif+fer+ent+ly
dif+fer+ent+ness
dif+fi+cult
  dif+fi+cult+ly
  dif+fi+cul+ty
  dif+fi+cul+ties
dif+fi+dence
dif+fi+dent
  dif+fi+dent+ly
dif+fract
  dif+fracts
  dif+fract+ing
  dif+fract+ed
dif+frac+tion
  dif+frac+tions
dif+frac+tive
  dif+frac+tive+ly
  dif+frac+tive+
    ness
dif+fuse
  dif+fuses
  dif+fus+ing
  dif+fused
  dif+fuse+ly
  dif+fuse+ness

dif+fus+er
  dif+fus+ers
dif+fus+ible
dif+fu+sion
  dif+fu+sions
dif+fu+sive
  dif+fu+sive+ly
  dif+fu+sive+ness
dif+fu+sor
  dif+fu+sors
dig
  digs
  digs
  dig+ging
  dug
di+gest
  di+gests
  di+gests
  di+gest+ing
  di+gest+ed
Di+gest
di+gest+ant
  di+gest+ants
di+ges+tant
  di+ges+tants
di+gest+ibil+ity
di+gest+ible
di+ges+tion
  di+ges+tion+al
di+ges+tive
  di+ges+tives
  di+ges+tive+ly
dig+ger
  dig+gers
  dig+gings
dight
  dights
  dight+ing
  dight *or*
  dight+ed
dig+it
  dig+its
digi+tal
  digi+tals
  digi+tal+in
  digi+tal+is
  digi+tal+ise
  digi+tal+ises
  digi+tal+is+ing
  digi+tal+ised
  digi+tal+ize
  digi+tal+izes
  digi+tal+iz+ing
  digi+tal+ized
  digi+tal+ly

digi+tate
  digi+tat+ed
  digi+tate+ly
  digi+ta+tion
  digi+ti+grade
  digi+ti+grades
  dig+iti+sa+tion
  dig+it+ise
  dig+it+ises
  dig+it+is+ing
  dig+it+ised
  digi+tis+er
  digi+tis+ers
  dig+iti+za+tion
  dig+it+ize
  dig+it+izes
  dig+it+iz+ing
  dig+it+ized
  digi+tiz+er
  digi+tiz+ers
dig+ni+fied
  dig+ni+fied+ly
  dig+ni+fied+ness
dig+ni+fy
  dig+ni+fies
  dig+ni+fy+ing
  dig+ni+fied
dig+ni+tary
  dig+ni+taries
dig+nity
  dig+nities
di+gox+in
  di+gox+ins
di+graph
  di+graphs
  di+graph+ic
di+gress
  di+gresses
  di+gress+ing
  di+gressed
  di+gress+er
  di+gress+ers
di+gres+sion
  di+gres+sions
  di+gres+sive
  di+gres+sive+ly
  di+gres+sive+
    ness
di+he+dral
  di+he+drals
di+he+dron
  di+he+drons
Di+jon
dik-dik
  dik-diks

dike
  dikes
  dikes
  dik+ing
  diked
dik+tat
  dik+tats
di+lapi+date
  di+lapi+dates
  di+lapi+dat+ing
  di+lapi+dat+ed
  di+lapi+da+ted
  di+lapi+da+tion
di+lat+abil+ity
di+lat+able
di+la+ta+tion
  di+la+ta+tions
di+late
  di+lates
  di+lat+ing
  di+lat+ed
di+la+tion
  di+la+tions
di+la+tive
dila+to+ri+ly
dila+to+ri+ness
di+la+tory
dil+do
  dil+dos
dil+doe
  dil+does
di+lem+ma
  di+lem+mas
dil+em+mat+ic
dil+et+tante
  dil+et+tan+tes
  or
  dil+et+tan+ti
dil+et+tan+teish
dil+et+tan+teism
dil+et+tan+tish
dil+et+tan+tism
dili+gence
  dili+gences
dili+gent
dili+gent+ly
dill
  dills
dil+ly
  dil+lies
dilly-dally
  dilly-dallies
  dilly-dally+ing
  dilly-dallied
di+lute

di+lutes
di+lut+ing
di+lut+ed
di+lut+er
di+lut+ers
di+lu+tion
di+lu+tions
di+lu+vial
di+lu+vian
dim
  dims
  dim+ming
  dimmed
  dim+mer
  dim+mest
Dimbleby
dime
  dimes
di+men+hy+dri+
  nate
di+men+sion
  di+men+sions
  di+men+sions
  di+men+sion+
    ing
  di+men+sioned
  di+men+sion+al
  di+men+sion+
    less
di+mer
  di+mers
di+mer+isa+tion
di+mer+ise
  di+mer+ises
  di+mer+is+ing
  di+mer+ised
di+mer+iza+tion
di+mer+ize
  di+mer+izes
  di+mer+iz+ing
  di+mer+ized
dim+eter
  dim+eters
di+methyl+for+
  ma+mide
di+methyl+sulph+
  ox+ide
di+min+ish
  di+min+ishes
  di+min+ish+ing
  di+min+ished
  di+min+ish+able
  di+min+ished
di+minu+en+do
  di+minu+en+dos

dimi+nu+tion
dimi+nu+tions
di+minu+tive
  di+minu+tives
  di+minu+tive+ly
  di+minu+tive+
    ness
dim+is+sory
Di+mi+tro+vo
dim+ity
  dim+ities
dim+ly
dim+mer
  dim+mers
dim+ness
di+mor+phic
di+mor+phism
  di+mor+phisms
di+mor+phous
dim+ple
  dim+ples
  dim+ples
  dim+pling
  dim+pled
dim+ply
dim sum
dim+wit
  dim+wits
dim-witted
dim-witted+ness
din
  dins
  din+ning
  dinned
DIN
di+nar
  di+nars
d'Indy
dine
  dines
  din+ing
  dined
din+er
  din+ers
Dinesen
di+nette
  di+nettes
ding
  dings
  dings
  ding+ing
  dinged
ding+bat
  U.S.
  ding+bats

ding+bats
  Austral.
ding-dong
  ding-dongs
ding+es
din+ghy
  din+ghies
din+gi+ly
din+gi+ness
din+gle
  din+gles
din+go
  din+goes
din+gy
  din+gi+er
  din+gi+est
dinkie
  dinkies
din+kum
dinky
  dinki+er
  dinki+est
dinky-di
din+ner
  din+ners
dinner-dance
  dinner-dances
di+no+saur
  di+no+saurs
  di+no+saur+ian
dint
  dints
  dints
  dint+ing
  dint+ed
di+oc+esan
  di+oc+esans
dio+cese
  dio+ceses
Diocletian
di+ode
  di+odes
di+oecious
Diogenes
Diomed
Diomede
  king
Dio+mede
  islands
Diomedes
Dio+ny+sian
Dionysius
Dionysos
Dionysus
Diophantus

di+op+ter
U.S.
di+op+ters
di+op+tral
di+op+tre
di+op+tres
di+op+trics
Dior
dio+ra+ma
dio+ra+mas
dio+ram+ic
di+ox+ide
di+ox+ides
di+ox+in
di+ox+ins
dip
dips
dips
dip+ping
dipped
diph+theria
diph+therial
diph+ther+ic
diph+thong
diph+thongs
diph+thon+gal
diph+thongi+sa+
tion
diph+thong+ise
diph+thong+ises
diph+thong+is+
ing
diph+thong+
ised
diph+thongi+za+
tion
diph+thong+ize
diph+thong+izes
diph+thong+iz+
ing
diph+thong+ized
dip+lo+do+cus
dip+lo+do+
cuses
dip+loid
dip+loids
dip+loi+dic
di+plo+ma
di+plo+mas
di+plo+ma+cy
di+plo+ma+cies
dip+lo+mat
dip+lo+mats
dip+lo+mat+ic

dip+lo+mati+cal+
ly
di+plo+ma+tist
di+plo+ma+tists
di+po+lar
di+pole
di+poles
dip+per
dip+pers
dip+py
dip+pi+er
dip+pi+est
dip+so+ma+nia
dip+so+ma+ni+
ac
dip+so+ma+ni+
acs
dip+stick
dip+sticks
dip+ter+an
dip+ter+ans
dip+ter+on
dip+ter+ons
dip+ter+ous
dip+tych
dip+tychs
Dirac
dire
di+rect
di+rects
di+rect+ing
di+rect+ed
di+rec+tion
di+rec+tions
di+rec+tion+al
di+rec+tion+al+
ity
di+rec+tive
di+rec+tives
di+rect+ly
di+rect+ness
di+rec+tor
di+rec+tors
di+rec+to+rate
di+rec+to+rates
di+rector-general
di+rectors-
general
di+rec+to+rial
di+rec+tor+ship
di+rec+tor+
ships
di+rec+tory
di+rec+tories
Di+rec+tory

di+rec+tress
di+rec+tresses
dire+ful
dire+ly
dire+ness
dirge
dirges
dirge+ful
dir+ham
dir+hams
diri+gibil+ity
di+rig+ible
di+rig+ibles
di+rig+isme
di+ri+giste
dirk
dirks
dirks
dirk+ing
dirked
dirndl
dirndls
dirt
dirt-cheap
dirti+ly
dirti+ness
dirty
dirties
dirty+ing
dirt+ied
dirti+er
dirti+est
Dis
dis+abil+ity
dis+abil+ities
dis+able
dis+ables
dis+abling
dis+abled
dis+abled
dis+able+ment
dis+able+ments
dis+abuse
dis+abuses
dis+abus+ing
dis+abused
dis+ad+vant+age
dis+ad+vant+
ages
dis+ad+vant+
ages
dis+ad+vant+ag+
ing
dis+ad+vant+
aged

dis+ad+van+
taged
dis+ad+van+ta+
geous
dis+ad+van+ta+
geous+ly
dis+ad+van+ta+
geous+ness
dis+af+fect
dis+af+fects
dis+af+fect+ing
dis+af+fect+ed
dis+af+fect+ed+
ly
dis+af+fec+tion
dis+af+fili+ate
dis+af+fili+ates
dis+af+fili+at+
ing
dis+af+fili+at+
ed
dis+af+fili+ation
dis+af+for+est
dis+af+for+ests
dis+af+for+est+
ing
dis+af+for+est+
ed
dis+af+for+es+ta+
tion
dis+agree
dis+agrees
dis+agree+ing
dis+agreed
dis+agree+able
dis+agree+able+
ness
dis+agree+ably
dis+agree+ment
dis+agree+
ments
dis+al+low
dis+al+lows
dis+al+low+ing
dis+al+lowed
dis+al+low+able
dis+al+low+ance
dis+al+low+
ances
dis+ap+pear
dis+ap+pears
dis+ap+pear+
ing
dis+ap+peared

dis+ap+pear+
ance
dis+ap+pear+
ances
dis+ap+pli+ca+
tion
dis+ap+pli+ca+
tions
dis+ap+point
dis+ap+points
dis+ap+point+
ing
dis+ap+point+
ed
dis+ap+point+ed
dis+ap+point+ing
dis+ap+point+ing+
ly
dis+ap+point+
ment
dis+ap+point+
ments
dis+ap+pro+ba+
tion
dis+ap+pro+ba+
tions
dis+ap+prov+al
dis+ap+prove
dis+ap+proves
dis+ap+prov+
ing
dis+ap+proved
dis+ap+prov+ing
dis+ap+prov+ing+
ly
dis+arm
dis+arms
dis+arm+ing
dis+armed
dis+arma+ment
dis+arma+
ments
dis+arm+er
dis+arm+ers
dis+arm+ing
dis+arm+ing+ly
dis+ar+range
dis+ar+ranges
dis+ar+rang+ing
dis+ar+ranged
dis+ar+range+
ment
dis+ar+range+
ments
dis+ar+ray

dis+ar+rays
dis+ar+ray+ing
dis+ar+rayed
dis+as+sem+ble
dis+as+sem+
bles
dis+as+sem+
bling
dis+as+sem+
bled
dis+as+sem+bler
dis+as+sem+
blers
dis+as+so+ci+ate
dis+as+so+ci+
ates
dis+as+so+ci+at+
ing
dis+as+so+ci+at+
ed
dis+as+so+cia+
tion
dis+as+so+cia+
tions
dis+as+ter
dis+as+ters
dis+as+trous
dis+avow
dis+avows
dis+avow+ing
dis+avowed
dis+avow+al
dis+avow+als
dis+avow+ed+ly
dis+band
dis+bands
dis+band+ing
dis+band+ed
dis+band+ment
dis+bar
dis+bars
dis+bar+ring
dis+barred
dis+bar+ment
dis+bar+ments
dis+be+lief
dis+be+liefs
dis+be+lieve
dis+be+lieves
dis+be+liev+ing
dis+be+lieved
dis+be+liev+er
dis+be+liev+ers
dis+be+liev+ing
dis+bud

dis+buds
dis+bud+ding
dis+bud+ded
dis+bur+den
dis+bur+dens
dis+bur+den+
ing
dis+bur+dened
dis+burs+able
dis+burse
dis+burses
dis+burs+ing
dis+bursed
dis+burse+ment
dis+burse+
ments
dis+burs+er
dis+burs+ers
disc
discs
dis+cal
dis+card
dis+cards
dis+cards
dis+card+ing
dis+card+ed
dis+cern
dis+cerns
dis+cern+ing
dis+cerned
dis+cern+ible
dis+cern+ibly
dis+cern+ing
dis+cern+ment
dis+cern+ments
dis+charge
dis+charges
dis+charges
dis+charg+ing
dis+charged
dis+charge+able
dis+charg+er
dis+charg+ers
dis+ci+ple
dis+ci+ples
dis+ci+ple+ship
dis+ci+ple+
ships
dis+ci+plin+able
dis+ci+pli+nal
dis+ci+pli+nar+
ian
dis+ci+pli+nar+
ians
dis+ci+pli+nary

dis+ci+pline
dis+ci+plines
dis+ci+plines
dis+ci+plin+ing
dis+ci+plined
dis+ci+plin+er
dis+ci+plin+ers
dis+cipu+lar
dis+claim
dis+claims
dis+claim+ing
dis+claimed
dis+claim+er
dis+claim+ers
dis+close
dis+closes
dis+clos+ing
dis+closed
dis+clos+er
dis+clos+ers
dis+clo+sure
dis+clo+sures
dis+co
dis+cos
dis+cobo+lus
dis+cobo+li
dis+cog+ra+phy
dis+cog+ra+
phies
dis+coid
dis+coids
dis+col+or
_U.S._
dis+col+ors
dis+col+or+ing
dis+col+ored
dis+col+ora+tion
_U.S._
dis+col+our
dis+col+ours
dis+col+our+ing
dis+col+oured
dis+col+oura+
tion
dis+com+bobu+
late
dis+com+bobu+
lates
dis+com+bobu+
lat+ing
dis+com+bobu+
lat+ed
dis+com+fit
dis+com+fits
dis+com+fit+ing

dis+com+fit+ed
dis+com+fi+ture
dis+com+fort
dis+com+forts
dis+com+forts
dis+com+fort+
 ing
dis+com+fort+
 ed
dis+com+mode
dis+com+
 modes
dis+com+mod+
 ing
dis+com+mod+
 ed
dis+com+mo+di+
 ous
dis+com+pose
dis+com+poses
dis+com+pos+
 ing
dis+com+posed
dis+com+po+
 sure
dis+com+po+
 sures
dis+con+cert
dis+con+certs
dis+con+cert+
 ing
dis+con+cert+
 ed
dis+con+cert+ed
dis+con+cert+ing
dis+con+cer+tion
dis+con+cer+
 tions
dis+con+form+ity
dis+con+form+
 ities
dis+con+nect
dis+con+nects
dis+con+nect+
 ing
dis+con+nect+
 ed
dis+con+nect+ed
dis+con+nec+
 tion
dis+con+nec+
 tions
dis+con+so+late
dis+con+so+late+
 ly

dis+con+so+late+
 ness
dis+con+so+la+
 tion
dis+con+so+la+
 tions
dis+con+tent
dis+con+tents
dis+con+tents
dis+con+tent+
 ing
dis+con+tent+
 ed
dis+con+tent+ed
dis+con+tent+ed+
 ness
dis+con+tent+
 ment
dis+con+tinu+
 ance
dis+con+tinu+
 ances
dis+con+tinua+
 tion
dis+con+tinue
dis+con+tinues
dis+con+tinu+
 ing
dis+con+tinued
dis+con+ti+nu+
 ity
dis+con+ti+nu+
 ities
dis+con+tinu+
 ous
dis+con+tinu+
 ous+ly
dis+con+tinu+
 ous+ness
dis+cord
dis+cords
dis+cords
dis+cord+ing
dis+cord+ed
dis+cord+ance
dis+cord+ances
dis+cord+ant
dis+cor+dant+ly
dis+co+theque
dis+co+theques
dis+count
dis+counts
dis+counts
dis+count+ing
dis+count+ed

dis+count+able
dis+coun+
 tenance
dis+coun+
 tenances
dis+coun+
 tenanc+ing
dis+coun+
 tenanced
dis+count+er
dis+count+ers
dis+cour+age
dis+cour+ages
dis+cour+ag+
 ing
dis+cour+aged
dis+cour+age+
 ment
dis+cour+age+
 ments
dis+cour+ag+ing+
 ly
dis+course
dis+courses
dis+courses
dis+cours+ing
dis+coursed
dis+cour+teous
dis+cour+teous+
 ly
dis+cour+teous+
 ness
dis+cour+tesy
dis+cour+tesies
dis+cov+er
dis+cov+ers
dis+cov+er+ing
dis+cov+ered
dis+cov+er+able
dis+cov+er+er
dis+cov+er+ers
dis+cov+ery
dis+cov+eries
dis+cred+it
dis+cred+its
dis+cred+its
dis+cred+it+ing
dis+cred+it+ed
dis+cred+it+able
dis+creet
dis+creet+ly
dis+creet+ness
dis+crep+an+cy
dis+crep+an+
 cies

dis+crep+ant
dis+crete
dis+crete+ly
dis+crete+ness
dis+cre+tion
dis+cre+tions
dis+cre+tion+al
dis+cre+tion+ary
dis+crimi+nate
dis+crimi+nates
dis+crimi+nat+
 ing
dis+crimi+nat+
 ed
dis+crimi+nate+ly
dis+crimi+nat+
 ing
dis+crimi+na+
 tion
dis+crimi+na+
 tions
dis+crimi+na+tive
dis+crimi+na+
 tory
dis+cur+sive
dis+cur+sive+ly
dis+cur+sive+
 ness
dis+cus
dis+cuses *or*
 dis+ci
dis+cuss
dis+cusses
dis+cuss+ing
dis+cussed
dis+cuss+able
dis+cus+sant
dis+cuss+er
dis+cuss+ers
dis+cuss+ible
dis+cus+sion
dis+cus+sions
dis+dain
dis+dains
dis+dain+ing
dis+dained
dis+dain+ful
dis+ease
dis+eases
dis+eased
dis+econo+my
dis+econo+mies
dis+em+bark
dis+em+barks

dis+em+bark+
ing
dis+em+barked
dis+em+bar+ka+
tion
dis+em+bar+ka+
tions
dis+em+bar+rass
dis+em+bar+
rasses
dis+em+bar+
rass+ing
dis+em+bar+
rassed
dis+em+bod+ied
dis+em+bodi+
ment
dis+em+body
dis+em+bodies
dis+em+body+
ing
dis+em+bod+
ied
dis+em+bogue
dis+em+bogues
dis+em+bogu+
ing
dis+em+bogued
dis+em+bow+el
dis+em+bow+
els
dis+em+bow+el+
ling or
dis+em+bow+el+
ing
U.S.
dis+em+bow+
elled or
dis+em+bow+
eled
U.S.
dis+em+bow+el+
ment
dis+em+bow+el+
ments
dis+en+chant
dis+en+chants
dis+en+chant+
ing
dis+en+chant+
ed
dis+en+chant+
ing+ly
dis+en+chant+
ment

dis+en+chant+
ments
dis+en+cum+ber
dis+en+cum+
bers
dis+en+cum+
ber+ing
dis+en+cum+
bered
dis+en+cum+ber+
ment
dis+en+cum+
ber+ments
dis+en+fran+
chise
dis+en+fran+
chises
dis+en+fran+
chis+ing
dis+en+fran+
chised
dis+en+fran+
chise+ment
dis+en+fran+
chise+ments
dis+en+gage
dis+en+gages
dis+en+gag+ing
dis+en+gaged
dis+en+gaged
dis+en+gage+
ment
dis+en+gage+
ments
dis+en+tan+gle
dis+en+tan+gles
dis+en+tan+
gling
dis+en+tan+
gled
dis+en+tan+gle+
ment
dis+en+tan+gle+
ments
dis+equi+lib+rium
dis+es+tab+lish
dis+es+tab+
lishes
dis+es+tab+lish+
ing
dis+es+tab+
lished
dis+es+tab+lish+
ment
dis+es+teem

dis+es+teems
dis+es+teems
dis+es+teem+
ing
dis+es+teemed
dis+fa+vor
U.S
dis+fa+vors
dis+fa+vors
dis+fa+vor+ing
dis+fa+vored
dis+fa+vour
dis+fa+vours
dis+fa+vours
dis+fa+vour+ing
dis+fa+voured
dis+fig+ure
dis+fig+ures
dis+fig+ur+ing
dis+fig+ured
dis+fig+ure+ment
dis+fig+ure+
ments
dis+for+est
dis+for+ests
dis+for+est+ing
dis+for+est+ed
dis+for+es+ta+
tion
dis+fran+chise
dis+fran+chises
dis+fran+chis+
ing
dis+fran+chised
dis+fran+chise+
ment
dis+fran+chise+
ments
dis+gorge
dis+gorges
dis+gorg+ing
dis+gorged
dis+gorge+ment
dis+gorge+
ments
dis+grace
dis+graces
dis+graces
dis+grac+ing
dis+graced
dis+grace+ful
dis+grace+ful+ly
dis+grun+tle
dis+grun+tles
dis+grun+tling

dis+grun+tled
dis+grun+tle+
ment
dis+guise
dis+guises
dis+guises
dis+guis+ing
dis+guised
dis+guised
dis+gust
dis+gusts
dis+gust+ing
dis+gust+ed
dis+gust+ed+ly
dis+gust+ed+
ness
dish
dishes
dishes
dish+ing
dished
dis+ha+bille
dis+har+mo+ni+
ous
dis+har+mo+ny
dis+har+mo+
nies
dish+cloth
dish+cloths
dis+heart+en
dis+heart+ens
dis+heart+en+
ing
dis+heart+en+ed
dis+heart+en+ing+
ly
dis+heart+en+
ment
dished
di+shev+el
di+shev+els
di+shev+el+ling
or
di+shev+el+ing
U.S.
di+shev+elled
or
di+shev+eled
U.S.
di+shev+elled
di+shev+el+ment
dish+like
dis+hon+est
dis+hon+est+ly
dis+hon+es+ty

dis+hon+es+ties
dis+hon+or
U.S.
  dis+hon+ors
  dis+hon+ors
  dis+hon+or+ing
  dis+hon+ored
dis+hon+or+able
U.S.
dis+hon+or+able+
  ness
U.S.
dis+hon+or+ably
U.S.
dis+hon+our
  dis+hon+ours
  dis+hon+ours
  dis+hon+our+
    ing
  dis+hon+oured
dis+hon+our+
  able
dis+hon+our+
  able+ness
dis+hon+our+
  ably
dish+towel
dish+towels
dish+washer
dish+washers
dish+water
dishy
  dishi+er
  dishi+est
dis+il+lu+sion
  dis+il+lu+sions
  dis+il+lu+sions
  dis+il+lu+sion+
    ing
  dis+il+lu+sioned
dis+il+lu+sion+
  ment
dis+in+cen+tive
  dis+in+cen+
    tives
dis+in+cli+na+
  tion
  dis+in+cli+na+
    tions
dis+in+cline
  dis+in+clines
  dis+in+clin+ing
  dis+in+clined
dis+in+fect
  dis+in+fects

dis+in+fect+ing
dis+in+fect+ed
dis+in+fect+ant
  dis+in+fect+
    ants
dis+in+fec+tion
  dis+in+fec+tions
dis+in+fest
  dis+in+fests
  dis+in+fest+ing
  dis+in+fest+ed
dis+in+fes+ta+
  tion
  dis+in+fes+ta+
    tions
dis+in+fla+tion
dis+in+for+ma+
  tion
dis+in+genu+ous
  dis+in+genu+ous+
    ly
  dis+in+genu+ous+
    ness
dis+in+her+it
  dis+in+her+its
  dis+in+her+it+
    ing
  dis+in+her+it+
    ed
dis+in+heri+tance
  dis+in+heri+
    tances
dis+in+te+grate
  dis+in+te+
    grates
  dis+in+te+grat+
    ing
  dis+in+te+grat+
    ed
dis+in+te+gra+
  tion
  dis+in+te+gra+
    tions
dis+in+te+gra+
  tor
  dis+in+te+gra+
    tors
dis+in+ter
  dis+in+ters
  dis+in+ter+ring
  dis+in+terred
dis+in+ter+est
dis+in+ter+est+
  ed

dis+in+ter+est+
  ed+ly
dis+in+ter+est+
  ed+ness
dis+in+ter+me+
  dia+tion
dis+in+ter+ment
dis+in+ter+
  ments
dis+in+vest
  dis+in+vests
  dis+in+vest+ing
  dis+in+vest+ed
dis+in+vest+
  ment
dis+join
  dis+joins
  dis+join+ing
  dis+joined
dis+join+able
dis+joint
  dis+joints
  dis+joint+ing
  dis+joint+ed
dis+joint+ed
dis+joint+ed+ly
dis+junct
  dis+juncts
dis+junc+tion
  dis+junc+tions
dis+junc+tive
  dis+junc+tives
  dis+junc+tive+ly
dis+junc+ture
disk
U.S.
  disks
disk+ette
  disk+ettes
dis+lik+able
dis+like
  dis+likes
  dis+likes
  dis+lik+ing
  dis+liked
dis+like+able
dis+lo+cate
  dis+lo+cates
  dis+lo+cat+ing
  dis+lo+cat+ed
dis+lo+ca+tion
  dis+lo+ca+tions
dis+lodge
  dis+lodges
  dis+lodg+ing

dis+lodged
dis+lodge+ment
dis+lodge+
  ments
dis+lodg+ment
  dis+lodg+ments
dis+loy+al
  dis+loy+al+ly
  dis+loy+al+ty
  dis+loy+al+ties
dis+mal
  dis+mal+ly
  dis+mal+ness
dis+man+tle
  dis+man+tles
  dis+man+tling
  dis+man+tled
dis+man+tle+
  ment
  dis+man+tle+
    ments
dis+mast
  dis+masts
  dis+mast+ing
  dis+mast+ed
dis+may
  dis+mays
  dis+may+ing
  dis+mayed
  dis+may+ing
dis+mem+ber
  dis+mem+bers
  dis+mem+ber+
    ing
  dis+mem+bered
dis+mem+ber+
  ment
  dis+mem+ber+
    ments
dis+miss
  dis+misses
  dis+miss+ing
  dis+missed
dis+mis+sal
  dis+mis+sals
dis+miss+ible
dis+miss+ive
dis+mount
  dis+mounts
  dis+mounts
  dis+mount+ing
  dis+mount+ed
Disney
Disney+esque
dis+obedi+ence

dis+obedi+
  ences
dis+obedi+ent
dis+obedi+ent+ly
dis+obey
dis+obeys
dis+obey+ing
dis+obeyed
dis+obey+er
dis+obey+ers
dis+oblige
dis+obliges
dis+oblig+ing
dis+obliged
dis+oblig+ing
dis+or+der
dis+or+ders
dis+or+ders
dis+or+der+ing
dis+or+dered
dis+or+der+li+
  ness
dis+or+der+ly
dis+or+gani+sa+
  tion
dis+or+gan+ise
dis+or+gan+ises
dis+or+gan+is+
  ing
dis+or+gan+
  ised
dis+or+gani+za+
  tion
dis+or+gan+ize
dis+or+gan+izes
dis+or+gan+iz+
  ing
dis+or+gan+ized
dis+ori+ent
dis+ori+ents
dis+ori+ent+ing
dis+ori+ent+ed
dis+ori+en+tate
dis+ori+en+
  tates
dis+ori+en+tat+
  ing
dis+ori+en+tat+
  ed
dis+ori+en+ta+
  tion
dis+own
dis+owns
dis+own+ing
dis+owned

dis+own+er
dis+own+ers
dis+par+age
dis+par+ages
dis+par+ag+ing
dis+par+aged
dis+par+age+
  ment
dis+par+ag+ing
dis+par+ate
dis+par+ates
dis+par+ate+ly
dis+par+ate+
  ness
dis+par+ity
dis+par+ities
dis+pas+sion+ate
dis+pas+sion+ate+
  ly
dis+patch
dis+patches
dis+patches
dis+patch+ing
dis+patched
dis+patch+er
dis+patch+ers
dis+pel
dis+pels
dis+pel+ling
dis+pelled
dis+pel+ler
dis+pel+lers
dis+pen+sabil+ity
dis+pen+sable
dis+pen+sa+ry
dis+pen+sa+ries
dis+pen+sa+tion
dis+pen+sa+
  tions
dis+pen+sa+tion+
  al
dis+pen+sa+tory
dis+pen+sa+
  tories
dis+pense
dis+penses
dis+pens+ing
dis+pensed
dis+pens+er
dis+pens+ers
dis+per+sal
dis+per+sals
dis+per+sant
dis+per+sants
dis+perse

dis+perses
dis+pers+ing
dis+persed
dis+pers+er
dis+pers+ers
dis+per+sion
dis+per+sions
dis+pir+it
dis+pir+its
dis+pir+it+ing
dis+pir+it+ed
dis+pir+it+ed
dis+pir+it+ed+
  ness
dis+pir+it+ing
dis+place
dis+places
dis+plac+ing
dis+placed
dis+place+ment
dis+place+
  ments
dis+play
dis+plays
dis+plays
dis+play+ing
dis+played
dis+play+er
dis+play+ers
dis+please
dis+pleases
dis+pleas+ing
dis+pleased
dis+pleas+ing
dis+pleas+ing+ly
dis+pleas+ure
dis+port
dis+ports
dis+ports
dis+port+ing
dis+port+ed
dis+pos+able
dis+pos+ables
dis+pos+able+
  ness
dis+pos+al
dis+pos+als
dis+pose
dis+poses
dis+pos+ing
dis+posed
dis+posed
dis+pos+er
dis+pos+ers
dis+po+si+tion

dis+po+si+tions
dis+pos+sess
dis+pos+sesses
dis+pos+sess+
  ing
dis+pos+sessed
dis+pos+ses+
  sion
dis+pos+ses+sor
dis+pos+ses+
  sors
dis+praise
dis+praises
dis+prais+ing
dis+praised
dis+prais+er
dis+prais+ers
dis+proof
dis+pro+por+tion
dis+pro+por+
  tions
dis+pro+por+
  tions
dis+pro+por+
  tion+ing
dis+pro+por+
  tioned
dis+pro+por+tion+
  ate
dis+pro+por+tion+
  ate+ly
dis+pro+por+tion+
  ate+ness
dis+prov+able
dis+prov+al
dis+prove
dis+proves
dis+prov+ing
dis+proved
dis+put+abil+ity
dis+put+able
dis+put+able+
  ness
dis+put+ably
dis+pu+tant
dis+pu+tants
dis+pu+ta+tion
dis+pu+ta+tions
dis+pu+ta+tious
dis+pu+ta+tious+
  ness
dis+pu+ta+tive
dis+pu+ta+tive+
  ness
dis+pute

dis+putes
dis+putes
dis+put+ing
dis+put+ed
dis+put+er
dis+put+ers
dis+quali+fi+ca+
tion
dis+quali+fi+ca+
tions
dis+quali+fy
dis+quali+fies
dis+quali+fy+ing
dis+quali+fied
dis+qui+et
dis+qui+ets
dis+qui+et+ing
dis+qui+et+ed
dis+qui+et+ing
dis+qui+etude
dis+qui+si+tion
dis+qui+si+tions
dis+qui+si+tion+
al
Disraeli
dis+re+gard
dis+re+gards
dis+re+gard+ing
dis+re+gard+ed
dis+re+gard+ful
dis+re+mem+ber
dis+re+mem+
bers
dis+re+mem+
ber+ing
dis+re+mem+
bered
dis+re+pair
dis+repu+table
dis+repu+tably
dis+re+pute
dis+re+spect
dis+re+spect+ful
dis+robe
dis+robes
dis+rob+ing
dis+robed
dis+robe+ment
dis+robe+ments
dis+rupt
dis+rupts
dis+rupt+ing
dis+rupt+ed
dis+rupt+er
dis+rupt+ers

dis+rup+tion
dis+rup+tions
dis+rup+tive
dis+rup+tor
dis+rup+tors
dis+sat+is+fac+
tion
dis+sat+is+fac+
tory
dis+sat+is+fy
dis+sat+is+fies
dis+sat+is+fy+
ing
dis+sat+is+fied
dis+sect
dis+sects
dis+sect+ing
dis+sect+ed
dis+sect+ed
dis+sec+tion
dis+sec+tions
dis+sec+tor
dis+sec+tors
dis+sel+boom
dis+sel+booms
dis+sem+blance
dis+sem+ble
dis+sem+bles
dis+sem+bling
dis+sem+bled
dis+sem+bler
dis+sem+blers
dis+semi+nate
dis+semi+nates
dis+semi+nat+
ing
dis+semi+nat+
ed
dis+semi+na+tion
dis+semi+na+
tions
dis+semi+na+tor
dis+sem+i+na+
tors
dis+sen+sion
dis+sen+sions
dis+sent
dis+sents
dis+sent+ing
dis+sent+ed
dis+sent+er
dis+sent+ers
Dis+sent+er
Dis+sent+ers
dis+sen+tience

dis+sen+tien+cy
dis+sen+tient
dis+sen+tients
dis+sent+ing
dis+ser+ta+tion
dis+ser+ta+
tions
dis+ser+ta+tion+
al
dis+serve
dis+serves
dis+serv+ing
dis+served
dis+ser+vice
dis+ser+vices
dis+sev+er
dis+sev+ers
dis+sev+er+ing
dis+sev+ered
dis+sev+er+ance
dis+sev+er+ment
dis+si+dence
dis+si+dent
dis+si+dents
dis+si+dent+ly
dis+simi+lar
dis+simi+lar+ity
dis+simi+lar+
ities
dis+simi+lar+ly
dis+simi+late
dis+simi+lates
dis+simi+lat+ing
dis+simi+lat+ed
dis+simi+la+tion
dis+simi+la+
tions
dis+si+mili+tude
dis+si+mili+
tudes
dis+simu+late
dis+simu+lates
dis+simu+lat+
ing
dis+simu+lat+ed
dis+simu+la+tion
dis+simu+la+
tions
dis+simu+la+tor
dis+simu+la+
tors
dis+si+pate
dis+si+pates
dis+si+pat+ing
dis+si+pat+ed

dis+si+pat+ed
dis+si+pat+er
dis+si+pat+ers
dis+si+pa+tion
dis+si+pa+tions
dis+si+pa+tive
dis+si+pa+tor
dis+si+pa+tors
dis+so+ci+ate
dis+so+ci+ates
dis+so+ci+at+
ing
dis+so+ci+at+
ed
dis+so+cia+tion
dis+so+cia+
tions
dis+so+cia+tive
dis+sol+ubil+ity
dis+sol+uble
dis+so+lute
dis+so+lute+ly
dis+so+lute+ness
dis+so+lu+tion
dis+so+lu+tions
dis+solv+able
dis+solve
dis+solves
dis+solves
dis+solv+ing
dis+solved
dis+so+nance
dis+so+nan+cy
dis+so+nant
dis+suade
dis+suades
dis+suad+ing
dis+suad+ed
dis+suad+er
dis+suad+ers
dis+sua+sion
dis+sua+sions
dis+sua+sive
dis+syl+lab+ic
dis+syl+la+ble
dis+syl+la+bles
dis+sym+met+ric
dis+sym+met+ri+
cal
dis+sym+me+try
dis+sym+me+
tries
dis+taff
dis+taffs
dis+tal

dis+tal+ly
dis+tance
 dis+tances
 dis+tances
 dis+tanc+ing
 dis+tanced
dis+tant
dis+tant+ly
dis+tant+ness
dis+taste
dis+taste+ful
dis+taste+ful+
 ness
dis+tem+per
 dis+tem+pers
 dis+tem+pers
 dis+tem+per+
 ing
 dis+tem+pered
dis+tend
 dis+tends
 dis+tend+ing
 dis+tend+ed
dis+ten+sible
dis+ten+tion
 dis+ten+tions
dis+tich
 dis+tichs
dis+til
 dis+tils
 dis+til+ling
 dis+tilled
dis+till
U.S.
 dis+tills
 dis+till+ing
 dis+tilled
dis+til+late
 dis+til+lates
 dis+til+la+tion
 dis+til+la+tions
 dis+til+la+tory
dis+till+er
 dis+till+ers
 dis+till+ery
 dis+till+eries
dis+tinct
dis+tinc+tion
 dis+tinc+tions
dis+tinc+tive
dis+tinc+tive+ly
dis+tinc+tive+
 ness
dis+tinct+ly
dis+tinct+ness

dis+tin+gué
dis+tin+guish
 dis+tin+guishes
 dis+tin+guish+
 ing
 dis+tin+guished
dis+tin+guish+
 able
 dis+tin+guished
 dis+tin+guish+ing
dis+tort
 dis+torts
 dis+tort+ing
 dis+tort+ed
dis+tort+ed
dis+tor+tion
 dis+tor+tions
 dis+tor+tion+al
dis+tract
 dis+tracts
 dis+tract+ing
 dis+tract+ed
dis+tract+ed
 dis+tract+ed+ly
dis+trac+tion
 dis+trac+tions
dis+train
 dis+trains
 dis+train+ing
 dis+trained
 dis+train+er
 dis+train+ers
 dis+train+ment
 dis+train+ments
 dis+trai+nor
 dis+trai+nors
dis+traint
 dis+traints
dis+trait
dis+traught
dis+tress
 dis+tresses
 dis+tresses
 dis+tress+ing
 dis+tressed
 dis+tressed
 dis+tress+ful
 dis+tress+ing
 dis+tress+ing+ly
dis+trib+ut+able
dis+trib+ute
 dis+trib+utes
 dis+trib+ut+ing
 dis+trib+ut+ed
dis+tri+bu+tion

dis+tri+bu+tions
dis+tri+bu+tion+
 al
dis+tribu+tive
 dis+tribu+tives
 dis+tribu+tive+ly
 dis+tribu+tive+
 ness
dis+tribu+tor
 dis+tribu+tors
dis+trict
 dis+tricts
dis+trust
 dis+trusts
 dis+trust+ing
 dis+trust+ed
 dis+trust+er
 dis+trust+ers
 dis+trust+ful
dis+turb
 dis+turbs
 dis+turb+ing
 dis+turbed
dis+turb+ance
 dis+turb+ances
 dis+turbed
dis+turb+er
 dis+turb+ers
 dis+turb+ing
 dis+turb+ing+ly
di+sul+phide
di+sul+phides
dis+un+ion
 dis+un+ions
dis+unite
 dis+unites
 dis+unit+ing
 dis+unit+ed
dis+unity
 dis+unities
dis+use
 dis+uses
di+syl+lab+ic
di+syl+la+ble
di+syl+la+bles
ditch
 ditches
 ditches
 ditch+ing
 ditched
ditch+er
 ditch+ers
ditch+water
dith+er
 dith+ers

dith+er+ing
dith+ered
dith+er+er
dith+er+ers
dith+ery
dithy+ramb
dithy+rambs
dithy+ram+bic
dit+ta+ny
dit+ta+nies
dit+to
dit+tos
dit+tos
dit+to+ing
dit+toed
dit+ty
dit+ties
di+uresis
di+uret+ic
di+uret+ics
di+ur+nal
di+ur+nal+ly
diva
divas *or*
dive
di+va+gate
di+va+gates
di+va+gat+ing
di+va+gat+ed
di+va+ga+tion
di+va+ga+tions
di+va+len+cy
di+va+len+cies
di+va+lent
di+van
di+vans
dive
dives
dives
div+ing
dived *or*
dove
U.S.
dive-bomb
dive-bombs
dive-bombing
dive-bombed
div+er
div+ers
di+verge
di+verges
di+verg+ing
di+verged
di+ver+gence
di+ver+gences

di+ver+gen+cy
di+ver+gen+cies
di+ver+gent
di+ver+gent+ly
di+vers
di+verse
di+verse+ly
di+ver+si+fi+ca+
  tion
di+ver+si+fi+ca+
  tions
di+ver+si+fy
di+ver+si+fies
di+ver+si+fy+
  ing
di+ver+si+fied
di+ver+sion
di+ver+sions
di+ver+sion+al
di+ver+sion+ary
di+ver+sity
di+ver+sities
di+vert
di+verts
di+vert+ing
di+vert+ed
di+ver+ticu+li+tis
di+ver+ticu+lum
di+ver+ticu+la
di+ver+ti+men+
  to
di+ver+ti+men+
  ti
di+vert+ing
di+vert+ing+ly
di+ver+tisse+
  ment
di+ver+tisse+
  ments
Dives
di+vest
di+vests
di+vest+ing
di+vest+ed
di+vesti+ture
di+vesti+tures
di+vest+ment
di+vest+ments
di+ves+ture
di+ves+tures
di+vide
di+vides
di+vides
di+vid+ing
di+vid+ed

di+vid+ed
divi+dend
divi+dends
di+vid+er
di+vid+ers
di+vid+ers
divi+na+tion
divi+na+tions
di+vina+tory
di+vine
di+vines
di+vin+ing
di+vined
di+vine+ly
di+vin+er
di+vin+ers
di+vin+ity
di+vin+ities
di+vis+ibil+ity
di+vis+ibil+ities
di+vi+sible
di+vis+ible+ness
di+vis+ibly
di+vi+sion
di+vi+sions
di+vi+sion+al
di+vi+sion+al+ly
di+vi+sion+ary
di+vi+sive
di+vi+sive+ly
di+vi+sive+ness
di+vi+sor
di+vi+sors
di+vorce
di+vorces
di+vorces
di+vorc+ing
di+vorced
di+vor+cé
di+vor+cés
di+vorce+able
di+vor+cée
di+vor+cées
div+ot
div+ots
di+vulge
di+vulges
di+vulg+ing
di+vulged
di+vulge+ment
di+vulge+ments
di+vul+gence
di+vul+gences
di+vulg+er
di+vulg+ers

div+vy
div+vies
div+vies
div+vy+ing
div+vied
dixie
dixies
Dixie
Dixie+land
diz+zi+ly
diz+zi+ness
diz+zy
diz+zies
diz+zy+ing
diz+zied
diz+zi+er
diz+zi+est
Djai+lo+lo
Dja+ja
Dja+ja+pu+ra
Dja+kar+ta
Djam+bi
Dji+bou+ti
djin+ni
djinn
djin+ny
djinn
dl
dm
D-mark
D-marks
D-Mark
D-Marks
DNA
DNAs
DNAase
DNAases
DNase
DNases
Dnepr
Dne+pro+
  petrovsk
Dnestr
Dnie+per
Dnie+ster
D-notice
D-notices
do
dos *or*
do's
does
do+ing
did
done
do+able

dob+bin
dob+bins
Dobell
Do+ber+man pin+
  scher
Do+ber+man pin+
  schers
doc
docs
doc+ile
doc+ile+ly
do+cil+ity
dock
docks
docks
dock+ing
docked
dock+age
dock+ages
dock+er
dock+ers
dock+et
dock+ets
dock+ets
dock+et+ing
dock+et+ed
dock+land
dock+lands
dock+yard
dock+yards
Doc Martens
Trademark
doc+tor
doc+tors
doc+tors
doc+tor+ing
doc+tored
doc+tor+al
doc+tor+ate
doc+tor+ates
doc+to+rial
doc+tri+naire
doc+tri+naires
doc+tri+nair+ism
doc+tri+nal
doc+tri+nal+ly
doc+trine
doc+trines
docu+dra+ma
docu+dra+mas
docu+ment
docu+ments
docu+ments
docu+ment+ing
docu+ment+ed

docu+men+ta+ri+
ly
docu+men+tary
  docu+men+
  taries
docu+men+ta+
tion
  docu+men+ta+
  tions
dod+der
  dod+ders
  dod+ders
  dod+der+ing
  dod+dered
dod+der+er
  dod+der+ers
dod+dery
dod+dle
  dod+dles
do+deca+gon
  do+deca+gons
do+deca+he+dral
do+deca+he+
dron
  do+deca+he+
  drons
Do+deca+nese
do+deca+phon+
ic
dodge
  dodges
  dodges
  dodg+ing
  dodged
Dodg+em
Trademark
  Dodg+ems
dodg+er
  dodg+ers
dodgy
  dodgi+er
  dodgi+est
dodo
  dodos *or*
  dodoes
Do+do+ma
doe
  does *or*
  doe
Doenitz
doer
  doers
doe+skin
  doe+skins
doff

doffs
  doff+ing
  doffed
  doff+er
  doff+ers
dog
  dogs
  dogs
  dog+ging
  dogged
dog+berry
  dog+berries
dog+cart
  dog+carts
dog-catcher
  dog-catchers
doge
  doges
dog-ear
  dog-ears
  dog-ears
  dog-earing
  dog-eared
dog-eared
dog-end
  dog-ends
do+gey
  do+geys
dog+fight
  dog+fights
dog+fish
  dog+fish *or*
  dog+fishes
dog+ged
  dog+ged+ly
  dog+ged+ness
dog+ger+el
dog+gie
  dog+gies
doggie-paddle
  doggie-paddles
  doggie-paddling
  doggie-paddled
dog+gie pad+dle
noun
dog+gish
dog+go
  dog+gone
  dog+goned
dog+gy
  dog+gies
doggy-paddle
  doggy-paddles
  doggy-paddling
  doggy-paddled

dog+gy pad+dle
noun
dog+house
  dog+houses
do+gie
  do+gies
dog+leg
  dog+legs
  dog+legs
  dog+leg+ging
  dog+legged
  dog+leg+ged
dog+ma
  dog+mas *or*
  dog+ma+ta
dog+man
  dog+men
dog+mat+ic
dog+mati+cal
  dog+mati+cal+ly
  dog+mat+ics
dog+ma+tise
  dog+ma+tises
  dog+ma+tis+ing
  dog+ma+tised
dog+ma+tism
dog+ma+tist
  dog+ma+tists
dog+ma+tize
  dog+ma+tizes
  dog+ma+tiz+ing
  dog+ma+tized
do-gooder
  do-gooders
do-gooding
dog+rel
Dogs
dogs+body
  dogs+bodies
  dogs+bodies
  dogs+body+ing
  dogs+bodied
dog+sled
  dog+sleds
Dog Star
dog-tired
dog+tooth
  dog+teeth
dog-tooth
dog+trot
dog+watch
  dog+watches
dog+wood
dogy
  dogies

doh
  dohs
Doha
Dohnányi
doi+ly
  doi+lies
do+ing
  do+ings
do-it-yourself
dol
Dol+by
Trademark
dol+ce
dol+ce vita
dol+drums
dole
  doles
dol+ing
  doled
dole+ful
  dole+ful+ly
  dole+ful+ness
dol+er+ite
  dol+er+ites
Dolgellau
doli+cho+cephal+
ic
doli+cho+cepha+
lous
Dolin
doll
  dolls
  dolls
  doll+ing
  dolled
dol+lar
  dol+lars
dollar+bird
  dollar+birds
Dollfuss
dol+lop
  dol+lops
  dol+lops
  dol+lop+ing
  dol+loped
dol+ly
  dol+lies
  dol+lies
  dol+ly+ing
  dol+lied
dol+ma
  dol+mas *or*
  dol+ma+des
dol+man
dol+men

dol+mens
Dolmetsch
do+lo+mite
do+lo+mites
Do+lo+mites
dolo+mit+ic
dol+or
U.S.
do+lo+ro+so
dol+or+ous
dol+or+ous+ly
dol+os
dol+os+se
dol+our
dol+phin
dol+phins
dol+phin+ar+ium
dol+phin+ar+
  iums
dolt
dolts
dolt+ish
dolt+ish+ness
dom
do+main
do+mains
dome
domes
domes
dom+ing
domed
dome+like
domes+day
do+mes+tic
do+mes+tics
do+mes+ti+cable
do+mes+ti+cal+
  ly
do+mes+ti+cate
do+mes+ti+
  cates
do+mes+ti+cat+
  ing
do+mes+ti+cat+
  ed
do+mes+ti+ca+
  tion
do+mes+ti+ca+
  tions
do+mes+ti+city
do+mes+ti+
  cities
do+mes+ti+cize
do+mes+ti+
  cizes

do+mes+ti+ciz+
  ing
do+mes+ti+
  cized
domi+cal
domi+cil
domi+cils
domi+cils
domi+cil+ing
domi+ciled
domi+cile
domi+ciles
domi+ciles
domi+cil+ing
domi+ciled
domi+cili+ary
domi+cili+ate
domi+cili+ates
domi+cili+at+ing
domi+cili+at+ed
domi+nance
domi+nant
domi+nants
domi+nant+ly
domi+nate
domi+nates
domi+nat+ing
domi+nat+ed
domi+nat+ing
domi+na+tion
domi+na+trix
domi+na+tri+
  ces
do+mi+nee
do+mi+nees
domi+neer
domi+neers
domi+neer+ing
domi+neered
domi+neer+ing
Domingo
Dominic
Domi+ni+ca
do+mini+cal
Do+mini+can
Do+mini+cans
domi+nie
domi+nies
do+min+ion
do+min+ions
domi+no
game piece
domi+noes
domi+no
cloak

domi+noes *or*
domi+nos
Domino
domi+noes
Do+mi+nus
Domitian
don
dons
dons
don+ning
donned
Don
title
Dons
Don
river
Donar
do+nate
do+nates
do+nat+ing
do+nat+ed
Donatello
do+na+tion
do+na+tions
dona+tive
dona+tives
do+na+tor
do+na+tors
Donatus
Do+nau
Don+bas
Don+bass
Don+cas+ter
do+nee
do+nees
Don+egal
do+ner ke+bab
do+ner ke+babs
Do+nets
Do+netsk
dong
dongs
dongs
dong+ing
donged
don+ga
don+gas
Don+go+la
Dong+ting
Dönitz
Donizetti
don+jon
don+jons
Don Juan
Don Juans

don+key
don+keys
donkey-work
Donleavy
Don+na
Don+nas
Donne
don+nish
don+nish+ness
donny+brook
donny+brooks
do+nor
do+nors
Don Quixote
Don Quixotes
don't
doo+dad
U.S.
doo+dads
doo+dah
doo+dahs
doo+dle
doo+dles
doo+dles
doo+dling
doo+dled
doodle+bug
doodle+bugs
doo+dler
doo+dlers
Doolittle
doom
dooms
doom+ing
doomed
dooms+day
doona
Trademark
doonas
door
doors
do-or-die
door+jamb
door+jambs
door+keeper
door+keepers
door+man
door+men
door+mat
door+mats
Doorn
door+nail
door+nails
Doornik
door+post

door+posts
door+sill
door+sills
door+step
door+steps
door+steps
door+step+ping
door+stepped
door+stop
door+stops
door+way
door+ways
doo-wop
dope
dopes
dopes
dop+ing
doped
dopey
dopi+er
dopi+est
dop+pel+gäng+er
dop+pel+gäng+
ers
dopy
dopi+er
dopi+est
dorado
dorados
Doráti
Dorcas
Dor+ches+ter
Dor+dogne
Dor+drecht
Doré
Dor+ic
Dor+ics
Do+ris
place name
Doris
nymph
dorm
dorms
dor+man+cy
dor+mant
dor+mer
dor+mers
dor+mie
dor+mi+tory
dor+mi+tories
Dor+mo+bile
Trademark
Dor+mo+biles
dor+mouse
dor+mice

dor+my
dorp
dorps
Dorpat
dor+sal
dor+sal+ly
Dor+set
Dort
Dort+mund
dory
dories
dos+age
dos+ages
dose
doses
doses
dos+ing
dosed
dosh
do+sim+eter
do+sim+eters
do+si+met+ric
Dos Passos
doss
dosses
doss+ing
dossed
dos+ser
dos+sers
doss+house
doss+houses
dos+si+er
dos+si+ers
Dostoevski
Dostoevsky
Dostoyevski
dot
dots
dots
dot+ting
dot+ted
dot+age
dot+ages
do+tard
do+tards
do+tard+ly
dote
dotes
dot+ing
dot+ed
dot+er
dot+ers
dot+ter
dot+ters
dot+ter+el

dot+ter+els
dot+ti+ly
dot+ti+ness
dot+tle
dot+tles
dot+trel
dot+trels
dot+ty
dot+ti+er
dot+ti+est
Douai
Doua+la
dou+ble
dou+bles
dou+bles
dou+bling
dou+bled
double-bank
double-banks
double-banking
double-banked
double-barrelled
double-bass
adj.
dou+ble bass
noun
double-blind
double-breasted
double-check
double-checks
double-checking
double-checked
dou+ble check
dou+ble checks
double-chinned
double-cross
double-crosses
double-crosses
double-crossing
double-crossed
double-crosser
double-crossers
double-dealer
double-dealers
double-dealing
double-dealings
double-decker
double-deckers
double-declutch
double-
declutches
double-
declutching
double-
declutched

double-edged
double-faced
double-header
double-headers
double-jointed
double-park
double-parks
double-parking
double-parked
double-quick
dou+bler
dou+blers
double-reed
dou+bles
double-space
double-spaces
double-spacing
double-spaced
double-stop
double-stops
double-stopping
double-stopped
dou+blet
dou+blets
dou+ble time
noun
dou+bloon
dou+bloons
dou+bly
Doubs
doubt
doubts
doubts
doubt+ing
doubt+ed
doubt+able
doubt+er
doubt+ers
doubt+ful
doubt+ful+ly
doubt+ful+ness
doubt+ing+ly
doubt+less
doubt+less+ness
douche
douches
douches
douch+ing
douched
dough
doughs
dough+boy
dough+boys
dough+nut
dough+nuts

dough+nuts
dough+nut+ting
dough+nut+ted
dough+ti+ly
dough+ti+ness
dough+ty
dough+ti+er
dough+ti+est
doughy
doughi+er
doughi+est
Doug+las
place name
Douglas
surname
Dou+kho+bor
Dou+kho+bors
Doun+reay
dour
dour+ly
dour+ness
dou+rou+cou+li
dou+rou+cou+
lis
douse
douses
douses
dous+ing
doused
dove
doves
Dove
dove+cot
dove+cots
dove+cote
dove+cotes
dove+like
Do+ver
dove+tail
dove+tails
dowa+ger
dowa+gers
dow+di+ly
dow+di+ness
Dowding
dow+dy
dow+dies
dow+di+er
dow+di+est
dow+dy+ish
dow+el
dow+els
Dowell
dow+er
dow+ers

dow+ers
dow+er+ing
dow+ered
Dowland
down
downs
downs
down+ing
downed
Down
surname, district
Down
sheep
Downs
down-and-out
down-and-outs
down+beat
down+beats
down+cast
down+casts
down+er
down+ers
down+fall
down+falls
down+grade
down+grades
down+grades
down+grad+ing
down+grad+ed
down+hearted
down+hearted+ly
down+hill
down+hills
down+hole
down+home
downi+ness
down+load
down+loads
down+load+ing
down+load+ed
down-market
Down+pat+rick
down+pipe
down+pipes
down+pour
down+pours
down+range
down+right
down+right+ly
down+right+ness
downs
Downs
down+side
down+sides
down+spout

down+spouts
down+stage
down+stairs
down+stream
down+swing
down+swings
down+time
down+times
down-to-earth
down+town
down+trod+den
down+turn
down+turns
down+ward
down+ward+ly
down+wards
down+wind
downy
downi+er
downi+est
dow+ry
dow+ries
dowse
dowses
dows+ing
dowsed
dows+er
dows+ers
doxo+logi+cal
dox+ol+ogy
dox+ol+ogies
doxy
doxies
doy+en
masculine
doy+ens
doy+enne
feminine
doy+ennes
doy+ley
doy+leys
D'Oyly Carte
doze
dozes
dozes
doz+ing
dozed
doz+en
doz+ens
doz+enth
doz+er
doz+ers
dozi+ly
dozi+ness
dozy

dozi+er
dozi+est
drab·
drab+ber
drab+best
drab
drabs
drabs
drab+bing
drabbed
drab+ly
drab+ness
drac
drachm
drachms
drach+ma
drach+mas *or*
drach+mae
drack
Dra+co
constellation
Draco
statesman
Dra+co+nian
Dra+co+ni+an+
ism
Dra+coni+cal+ly
draff
draffs
draft
drafts
drafts
draft+ing
draft+ed
draftee
draftees
draft+er
draft+ers
drafti+ly
U.S.
drafti+ness
U.S.
drafts+man
U.S.
drafts+men
drafts+man+ship
U.S.
drafty
U.S.
drafti+er
drafti+est
drag
drags
drags
drag+ging

dragged
dra+gée
dra+gées
drag+gle
drag+gles
drag+gling
drag+gled
drag-hunt
drag-hunts
drag-hunting
drag-hunted
drag hunt
drag hunts
drag+net
drag+nets
dra+go+man
dra+go+mans
  or
dra+go+men
drag+on
drag+ons
drag+on+et
drag+on+ets
dragon+fly
dragon+flies
drag+on+nade
drag+on+nades
drag+on+nades
drag+on+nad+
  ing
drag+on+nad+
  ed
dra+goon
dra+goons
dra+goons
dra+goon+ing
dra+gooned
drag+ster
drag+sters
drain
drains
drains
drain+ing
drained
drain+age
drain+ages
drain+er
drain+ers
drain+pipe
drain+pipes
drain+pipes
drake
drakes
Drake
Dra+kens+berg

Dra+lon
Trademark
dram
drams
DRAM
D-RAM
dra+ma
dra+mas
dra+mat+ic
dra+mati+cal+ly
dra+mat+ics
drama+ti+sa+tion
drama+ti+sa+
  tions
drama+tise
drama+tises
drama+tis+ing
drama+tised
dra+ma+tis per+
  so+nae
drama+tist
drama+tists
drama+ti+za+tion
drama+ti+za+
  tions
drama+tize
drama+tizes
drama+tiz+ing
drama+tized
drama+turg
drama+turgs
drama+turge
drama+turges
drama+tur+gic
drama+tur+gi+cal
drama+tur+gist
drama+tur+gists
drama+tur+gy
drape
drapes
drapes
drap+ing
draped
drap+er
drap+ers
dra+per+ied
dra+peries
dra+pery
dra+peries
drapes
dras+tic
dras+ti+cal+ly
drat
draught
draughts

draught+board
draught+boards
draughti+ly
draughti+ness
draughts
draughts+man
draughts+men
draughts+man+
  ship
draughty
draughti+er
draughti+est
Dra+vid+ian
Dra+vid+ians
draw
draws
draw+ing
drew
drawn
draw+back
draw+backs
draw back
  verb
draw+bridge
draw+bridges
drawee
drawees
draw+er
draw+ers
drawers
draw+ing
draw+ings
draw+knife
draw+knives
drawl
drawls
drawls
drawl+ing
drawled
drawl+ing
drawn
draw+shave
draw+shaves
draw+string
draw+strings
dray
drays
Drayton
dread
dreads
dreads
dread+ing
dread+ed
dread+ful
dread+fully

dread+locks
dread+nought
dread+noughts
dream
dreams
dreams
dream+ing
dreamt *or*
dreamed
dream+boat
dream+boats
dream+er
dream+ers
dreami+ly
dreami+ness
dreamy
dreami+er
dreami+est
dreari+ly
dreari+ness
dreary
dreari+er
dreari+est
dredge
dredges
dredges
dredg+ing
dredged
dredg+er
dredg+ers
dree
drees
dree+ing
dreed
dregs
dreich
dreigh
drench
drenches
drenches
drench+ing
drenched
drench+ing
drench+ings
Dren+the
Dres+den
dress
dresses
dresses
dress+ing
dressed
dres+sage
dress+er
dress+ers
dressi+ness

dress+ing
  dress+ings
dressing-down
  dressing-downs
dress+maker
  dress+makers
dress+making
dressy
  dressi+er
  dressi+est
drey
  dreys
Dreyfus
drib+ble
  drib+bles
  drib+bles
  drib+bling
  drib+bled
  drib+bler
  drib+blers
  drib+blet
  drib+blets
  drib+bly
drib+let
  drib+lets
dri+er
  dri+ers
drift
  drifts
  drifts
  drift+ing
  drift+ed
drift+age
drift+er
  drift+ers
drift+wood
drill
  drills
  drills
  drill+ing
  drilled
drill+er
  drill+ers
drill+master
  drill+masters
dri+ly
drink
  drinks
  drinks
  drink+ing
  drank
  drunk
drink+able
drink-driving
drink+er

drink+ers
Drinkwater
drip
  drips
  drips
  drip+ping
  dripped
drip-dry
  drip-dries
  drip-drying
  drip-dried
drip-feed
  drip-feeds
  drip-feeding
  drip-fed
drip feed
  drip feeds
drip+ping
  drip+pings
drip+py
drip+pi+er
  drip+pi+est
driv+able
drive
  drives
  drives
  driv+ing
  drove
  driv+en
drive+able
drive-in
driv+el
  driv+els
  driv+el+ling or
  driv+el+ing
  U.S.
  driv+elled or
  driv+eled
  U.S.
  driv+el+ler
  driv+el+lers
  driv+er
  driv+ers
  driv+er+less
drive+way
  drive+ways
driz+zle
  driz+zles
  driz+zles
  driz+zling
  driz+zled
driz+zly
  driz+zli+er
  driz+zli+est
Drobny

Drog+heda
drogue
  drogues
droll
droll+ery
  droll+eries
droll+ness
drol+ly
Drôme
drom+edary
  drom+edaries
drone
  drones
  drones
  dron+ing
  droned
dron+go
  dron+gos
  dron+ing
drool
  drools
  drool+ing
  drooled
droop
  droops
  droops
  droop+ing
  drooped
  droop+ing
droopy
drop
  drops
  drops
  drop+ping
  dropped
drop-forge
  drop-forges
  drop-forging
  drop-forged
drop forge
  drop forges
drop-kick
  drop-kicks
  drop-kicking
  drop-kicked
drop kick
  drop kicks
drop+let
  drop+lets
drop-off
  drop-offs
drop off
  verb
drop+out
  drop+outs

drop out
  verb
drop+per
  drop+pers
drop+pings
drops
drop+si+cal
drop+sy
drosh+ky
  drosh+kies
dros+ky
  dros+kies
dro+sophi+la
  dro+sophi+las
  or
  dro+sophi+lae
dross
drossi+ness
drossy
drought
  droughts
droughty
drove
  droves
  droves
drov+ing
  droved
drov+er
  drov+ers
drown
  drowns
  drown+ing
  drowned
drowse
  drowses
  drows+ing
  drowsed
drowsi+ly
drowsi+ness
drowsy
  drowsi+er
  drowsi+est
drub
  drubs
  drubs
  drub+bing
  drubbed
drudge
  drudges
  drudges
  drudg+ing
  drudged
drudg+er
  drudg+ers
drudg+ery

drudg+eries
drudg+ing+ly
drug
  drugs
  drugs
drug+ging
  drugged
drug+get
drug+gie
  drug+gies
drug+gist
  drug+gists
drug+store
  drug+stores
dru+id
  dru+ids
dru+id+ess
  dru+id+esses
dru+id+ic
dru+idi+cal
dru+id+ism
drum
  drums
  drums
drum+ming
  drummed
drum+beat
  drum+beats
drum+head
  drum+heads
drum+lin
  drum+lins
drum+mer
  drum+mers
drum+stick
  drum+sticks
drunk
  drunks
drunk+er
drunk+est
drunk+ard
  drunk+ards
drunk+en
drunk+en+ly
drunk+en+ness
dru+pa+ceous
drupe
  drupes
dru+pel
  dru+pels
drupe+let
  drupe+lets
Druse
  Druse
Druze

Druze
dry
  drys *or*
  dries
  dries
dry+ing
  dried
dri+er *or*
dry+er
dri+est *or*
dry+est
dry+ad
  dry+ads *or*
  dry+ades
dry-clean
  dry-cleans
  dry-cleaning
  dry-cleaned
  dry-cleaner
  dry-cleaners
  dry-cleaning
Dryden
dry-dock
  dry-docks
  dry-docking
  dry-docked
dry dock
  dry docks
dry+er
  dry+ers
dry+ing
dry+ly
dry+ness
dry+salter
  dry+salters
Drysdale
  surname
  Drys+dale
  sheep
  Drys+dales
dry-stone
dual
  duals
Du+ala
Du+ala *or*
Du+alas
dual+ism
dual+ist
  dual+ists
  dual+is+tic
dual+ity
  dual+ities
dual+ly
dub
  dubs

dubs
dub+bing
  dubbed
Du+bai
dub+bin
dub+bing
du+bi+ety
  du+bi+eties
du+bi+ous
du+bi+ous+ly
du+bi+ous+ness
Dub+lin
Dub+lin+er
  Dub+lin+ers
Du+brov+nik
Dubuffet
du+cal
duc+at
  duc+ats
Duccio di
  Buoninsegna
duce
  duces
Duchamp
duch+ess
  duch+esses
duchy
  duchies
duck
  ducks
  ducks
duck+ing
  ducked
duck+board
  duck+boards
duck+er
  duck+ers
duckie
  duckies
duck+ling
  duck+lings
duck+weed
ducky
  duckies
ducki+er
  ducki+est
duct
  ducts
duc+tile
duc+til+ity
duct+less
dud
  duds
dude
  dudes

dudg+eon
  anger
dudg+eon
  dagger
  dudg+eons
dud+ish
dud+ish+ly
Dud+ley
  place name
Dudley
  surname
due
  dues
duel
  duels
  duels
duel+ling *or*
duel+ing
  U.S.
duelled *or*
dueled
  U.S.
duel+ler
  duel+lers
duel+list
  duel+lists
du+en+na
  du+en+nas
dues
duet
  duets
duet+tist
  duet+tists
duff
  duffs
  duffs
duff+ing
  duffed
duff+er
duff+est
duf+fel
duf+fer
  duf+fers
duf+fle
Dufy
dug
  dugs
du+gong
  du+gongs
dug+out
  dug+outs
dui+ker
  dui+kers *or*
  dui+ker
Duis+burg

Dukas
duke
 dukes
duke+dom
 duke+doms
dukes
Du+kho+bor
 Du+kho+bors
dul+cet
dul+ci+mer
 dul+ci+mers
dull
 dulls
 dull+ing
 dulled
 dull+er
 dull+est
dull+ard
 dull+ards
dull+ish
dull+ness
dul+ly
dul+ness
dulse
 dulses
Dul+wich
duly
du+ma
 du+mas
Dumas
Du Maurier
dumb
 dumb+er
 dumb+est
Dum+bar+ton
dumb+bell
 dumb+bells
dumb+found
 dumb+founds
 dumb+found+
  ing
 dumb+found+ed
dumb+ly
dumb+ness
dumb+struck
dumb+waiter
 dumb+waiters
dum+dum
 dum+dums
dum+found
 dum+founds
 dum+found+ing
 dum+found+ed
Dum+fries
Dum+fries+shire

dum+my
 dum+mies
Du Mont
dump
 dumps
 dumps
 dump+ing
 dumped
 dump+er
 dump+ers
dumpi+ly
 dumpi+ness
dump+ling
 dump+lings
 dumps
dumpy
 dumpi+er
 dumpi+est
dun
 duns
 duns
 dun+ning
 dunned
 dun+ner
 dun+nest
Duna
Dü+na+burg
Du+naj
Dunant
Dun+bar
 place name
Dunbar
 surname
Dun+bar+ton+
 shire
Duncan
dunce
 dunces
Dun+dalk
Dun+dee
 place name
Dundee
 family name
dunder+head
 dunder+heads
 dunder+headed
dune
 dunes
Dun+edin
Dun+ferm+line
dung
 dungs
 dung+ing
 dunged
Dun+gan+non

dun+ga+ree
 dun+ga+rees
Dun+ge+ness
dun+geon
 dun+geons
dung+hill
 dung+hills
dunk
 dunks
 dunk+ing
 dunked
dunk+er
 dunk+ers
Dun+kerque
Dun+kirk
Dún Laoghaire
Dun+leary
dun+lin
 dun+lins
Dunlop
dun+nage
dun+no
dun+nock
 dun+nocks
dun+ny
 dun+nies
Dun+si+nane
Duns Scotus
Dun+sta+ble
 place name
Dunstable
 surname
Dunstan
duo
 duos *or*
 dui
duo+deci+mal
 duo+deci+mals
 duo+deci+mal+ly
duo+deci+mo
 duo+deci+mos
duo+de+nal
duo+denum
 duo+de+na *or*
 duo+de+nums
duo+log
 U.S.
 duo+logs
 duo+logue
 duo+logues
duo+po+lis+tic
duo+po+ly
 duo+po+lies
dup
dup+able

dupe
 dupes
 dupes
 dup+ing
 duped
dup+er
 dup+ers
dup+ery
du+ple
du+plex
 du+plexes
du+plex+ity
du+pli+cable
du+pli+cate
 du+pli+cates
 du+pli+cates
 du+pli+cat+ing
 du+pli+cat+ed
du+pli+ca+tion
 du+pli+ca+tions
du+pli+ca+tor
 du+pli+ca+tors
du+plic+ity
 du+plic+ities
Dupré
du Pré
Du+que de Ca+xi+
 as
du+rabil+ity
du+rable
 du+rables
du+rably
du+ral
Du+ralu+min
 Trademark
dura ma+ter
du+ra+men
Duran
du+rance
 du+rances
Du+ran+go
Durante
Duras
du+ra+tion
 du+ra+tions
du+ra+tion+al
du+ra+tive
 du+ra+tives
Dur+ban
dur+bar
 dur+bars
Dürer
du+ress
Dur+ga Pu+ja
 Dur+ga Pu+jas

Dur+ham
dur+ing
Durkheim
dur+mast
dur+masts
dur+ra
Durrell
Dürrenmatt
dur+ry
dur+ries
durst
du+rum
Duse
Du+shan+be
dusk
dusks
dusks
dusk+ing
dusked
duski+ly
duski+ness
dusky
duski+er
duski+est
Düs+sel+dorf
dust
dusts
dusts
dust+ing
dust+ed
dust+bin
dust+bins
dust+cart
dust+carts
dust+er
dust+ers
dusti+ly
dusti+ness
dusting-powder
dusting-
powders
dust+less
dust+man
dust+men
dust+pan
dust+pans
dust+sheet
dust+sheets
dust-up

dust-ups
dusty
dusti+er
dusti+est
Dutch
Dutch+man
Dutch+men
du+teous
du+teous+ly
du+ti+abil+ity
du+ti+able
du+ti+ful
duty
duties
duty-bound
duty-free
du+um+vir
du+um+virs or
du+um+vi+ri
du+um+vi+rate
du+um+vi+rates
Duvalier
du+vet
du+vets
dux
duxes
duy+ker
duy+kers or
duy+ker
Dvi+na
Dvinsk
dwaal
dwale
dwarf
dwarfs or
dwarves
dwarfs
dwarf+ing
dwarfed
dwarf+ish
dwell
dwells
dwell+ing
dwelt or
dwelled
dwell+er
dwell+ers
dwell+ing
dwell+ings

dwin+dle
dwin+dles
dwin+dling
dwin+dled
dy+able
dyad
dyads
dy+ad+ic
Dyak
Dyaks or
Dyak
dye
dyes
dyes
dye+ing
dyed
dye+able
dyed-in-the-wool
dye+ing
dyer
dyers
dye+stuff
dye+stuffs
Dyf+ed
dyke
dykes
dykes
dyk+ing
dyked
Dylan
dy+nam+ic
dy+nami+cal+ly
dy+nam+ics
dy+na+mism
dy+na+mist
dy+na+mists
dy+na+mis+tic
dy+na+mite
dy+na+mites
dy+na+mit+ing
dy+na+mit+ed
dy+na+mit+er
dy+na+mit+ers
dy+na+mo
dy+na+mos
dy+na+mo+elec+
tric
dy+na+mo+elec+
tri+cal

dy+na+mom+
eter
dy+na+mom+
eters
dy+na+mo+tor
dy+na+mo+tors
dyn+ast
dyn+asts
dy+nas+tic
dyn+as+ty
dyn+as+ties
dyne
dynes
dys+en+ter+ic
dys+en+tery
dys+func+tion
dys+func+tions
dys+func+tion+al
dys+graphia
dys+lec+tic
dys+lexia
dys+men+or+
rhea
U.S.
dys+men+or+
rhoea
dys+pep+sia
dys+pep+tic
dys+pep+tics
dys+pha+sia
dys+pha+sic
dys+pho+ria
dysp+nea
U.S.
dysp+neal
U.S.
dysp+noea
dysp+noeal
dysp+noe+ic
dys+pro+sium
dys+thy+mia
dys+thy+mic
dys+troph+ic
dys+tro+phy
dzo
dzos or
dzo
Dzun+ga+ria

E

e
e's
E
Es *or*
E's
each
Eadred
eager
eager+ly
eager+ness
eagle
eagles
eagle-eyed
eagle-hawk
eagle-hawks
eaglet
eaglets
Eakins
eal+dor+man
eal+dor+men
Ealing
ear
ears
ear+ache
ear+aches
ear+drum
ear+drums
eared
ear+ful
Earhart
earl
earls
earl+dom
earl+doms
ear+less
ear+li+ness
ear+ly
ear+li+er
ear+li+est
early-music
adj.
ear+ly mu+sic
noun
ear+mark
ear+marks

ear+marks
ear+mark+ing
ear+marked
ear+muff
ear+muffs
earn
earns
earn+ing
earned
earn+er
earn+ers
ear+nest
ear+nests
ear+nest+ly
ear+nest+ness
earn+ings
EAROM
EAROMs
ear+phone
ear+phones
ear-piercing
adj.
ear pierc+ing
noun
ear+plug
ear+plugs
ear+ring
ear+rings
ear+shot
ear-splitting
earth
earths
earths
earth+ing
earthed
earth+bound
earth+en
earthen+ware
earthi+ly
earthi+ness
earth+li+ness
earth+ling
earth+lings
earth+ly
earth+li+er

earth+li+est
earth+man
earth+men
earth+nut
earth+nuts
earth+quake
earth+quakes
earth+ward
earth+wards
earth+work
earth+works
earth+worm
earth+worms
earthy
earthi+er
earthi+est
ear+wax
ear+wig
ear+wigs
ear+wig+ging
ear+wig+gings
ease
eases
eas+ing
eased
ease+ful
easel
easels
ease+ment
ease+ments
easi+ly
easi+ness
east
East
east+bound
East+bourne
East+er
East+ers
east+er+ly
east+er+lies
east+ern
East+ern+er
East+ern+ers
East+er+tide
East+er+tides

east+ing
east+ings
East Kil+bride
East+leigh
Eastman
east-northeast
east-southeast
east+ward
east+ward+ly
east+wards
Eastwood
easy
easi+er
easi+est
easy-care
easy-going
eat
eats
eat+ing
ate
eat+en
eat+able
eat+ables
eat+er
eat+ers
eat+ing
eau de Co+logne
eau de nil
eau de vie
eaves
eaves+drop
eaves+drops
eaves+drop+
   ping
eaves+dropped
eaves+drop+per
eaves+drop+
   pers
ebb
ebbs
ebb+ing
ebbed
Ebbinghaus
Ebbw Vale

EBCDIC
Ebert
ebon
eb+on+ise
eb+on+ises
eb+on+is+ing
eb+on+ised
eb+on+ite
eb+on+ize
eb+on+izes
eb+on+iz+ing
eb+on+ized
eb+ony
eb+onies
Ebora+cum
Ebro
ebul+lience
ebul+lien+cy
ebul+lient
ebul+li+om+eter
ebul+li+om+
  eters
ebul+li+tion
ebul+li+tions
Ec+bata+na
ec+cen+tric
ec+cen+trics
ec+cen+tri+cal+
  ly
ec+cen+tri+city
ec+cen+tri+
  cities
Ec+cles
place name
Eccles
surname
ec+cle+si+as+tic
ec+cle+si+as+
  tics
ec+cle+si+as+ti+
  cal
ec+cle+si+as+ti+
  cal+ly
ec+cle+si+as+ti+
  cism
ec+cle+sio+logi+
  cal
ec+cle+si+ol+ogy
ec+crine
ec+crin+ol+ogy
ec+dem+ic
ec+dy+sis
ec+dy+ses
Ecevit
eche+lon

eche+lons
echid+na
echid+nas *or*
echid+nae
echi+no+derm
echi+no+derms
echi+nus
echi+ni
echo
echoes
echoes
echo+ing
echoed
Echo
Echoes
echo+car+di+og+
  ra+phy
echo+car+di+og+
  ra+phies
echo+gra+phy
echo+gra+phies
echo+ic
echo+ing
echo+la+lia
echo+less
echo-like
echo+location
echo+locations
echo+virus
echo+viruses
Eck
Eckert
éclair
éclairs
ec+lamp+sia
éclat
ec+lec+tic
ec+lec+ti+cal+ly
ec+lec+ti+cism
ec+lec+ti+cisms
eclipse
eclipses
eclipses
eclips+ing
eclipsed
eclips+er
eclips+ers
eclip+tic
eclip+ti+cal+ly
ec+logue
ec+logues
eclo+sion
Eco
eco+logi+cal
eco+logi+cal+ly

ecolo+gist
ecolo+gists
ecol+ogy
econo+met+ric
econo+met+ri+
  cal
econo+me+tri+
  cian
econo+me+tri+
  cians
econo+met+rics
econo+met+rist
econo+met+
  rists
eco+nom+ic
eco+nomi+cal
eco+nomi+cal+ly
eco+nom+ics
econo+mi+sa+
  tion
econo+mise
econo+mises
econo+mis+ing
econo+mised
econo+mist
econo+mists
econo+mi+za+
  tion
econo+mize
econo+mizes
econo+miz+ing
econo+mized
econo+my
econo+mies
eco+sphere
écoss+aise
eco+sys+tem
eco+sys+tems
ecru
ec+sta+sy
ec+sta+sies
ec+stat+ic
ec+stat+ics
ec+stati+cal+ly
ec+to+blast
ec+to+blasts
ec+to+blas+tic
ec+to+derm
ec+to+derms
ec+to+der+mal
ec+to+der+mic
ec+to+morph
ec+to+morphs
ec+to+mor+phic
ec+to+morphy

ec+to+plasm
ec+to+plas+mic
ECU
ECUs
Ecua+dor
Ecua+do+ran
Ecua+do+rans
Ecua+do+rian
Ecua+do+rians
ecu+men+ic
ecu+meni+cal
ecu+meni+cal+
  ism
ecu+meni+cal+ly
ecu+meni+cism
ec+ze+ma
ec+zema+tous
Edam
Edberg
Edda
Ed+da+ic
Eddery
Eddington
eddy
eddies
eddies
ed+dy+ing
ed+died
Eddy
Ede
Edelman
edel+weiss
ede+ma
U.S.
ede+ma+ta
Eden
Eden+ic
eden+tate
eden+tates
Edes+sa
Edgar
edge
edges
edges
edg+ing
edged
Edge+hill
edg+er
edg+ers
edge+ways
edge+wise
Edgeworth
edgi+ly
edgi+ness
edg+ing

edg+ings
edgy
  edgi+er
  edgi+est
edh
  edhs
Édhes+sa
ed+ibil+ity
ed+ible
  ed+ibles
edict
  edicts
edi+fi+ca+tion
edi+fice
  edi+fices
edi+fi+er
  edi+fi+ers
edi+fy
  edi+fies
  edi+fy+ing
  edi+fied
  edi+fy+ing
Ed+in+burgh
place name
Edinburgh
name
Edison
edit
  edits
  edit+ing
  edit+ed
edi+tion
  edi+tions
edi+tor
  edi+tors
edi+to+rial
  edi+to+rials
edi+to+ri+ali+sa+
  tion
edi+to+ri+al+ise
  edi+to+ri+al+
  ises
  edi+to+ri+al+is+
  ing
  edi+to+ri+al+
  ised
  edi+to+ri+al+is+
  er
  edi+to+ri+al+is+
  ers
edi+to+ri+al+ize
  edi+to+ri+al+
  izes
  edi+to+ri+al+iz+
  ing

edi+to+ri+al+
  ized
edi+to+ri+al+iz+
  er
edi+to+ri+al+iz+
  ers
edi+to+ri+al+ly
edi+tor+ship
  edi+tor+ships
Ed+mon+ton
Edmund
edu+cabil+ity
edu+cable
edu+cat+abil+ity
edu+cat+able
edu+cate
  edu+cates
  edu+cat+ing
  edu+cat+ed
  edu+cat+ed
edu+ca+tion
  edu+ca+tions
  edu+ca+tion+al
  edu+ca+tion+al+
  ist
  edu+ca+tion+al+
  ists
  edu+ca+tion+ist
  edu+ca+tion+
  ists
edu+ca+tive
edu+ca+tor
  edu+ca+tors
educe
  educes
  educ+ing
  educed
educ+ible
educ+tive
Ed+ward
lake
Edward
name
Ed+ward+ian
Ed+ward+ian+
  ism
Edwin
eel
  eels
  eel+grass
  eel+grasses
  eel-like
  eel+pout
  eel+pouts
  eel+worm

  eel+worms
eely
e'en
  e'ens
e'er
eerie
  eeri+er
  eeri+est
  eeri+ly
  eeri+ness
eff
  effs
  eff+ing
  effed
ef+face
  ef+faces
  ef+fac+ing
  ef+faced
  ef+face+able
  ef+face+ment
  ef+face+ments
  ef+fac+er
  ef+fac+ers
ef+fect
  ef+fects
  ef+fect+ing
  ef+fect+ed
  ef+fect+er
  ef+fect+ers
  ef+fect+ible
ef+fec+tive
  ef+fec+tive+ly
  ef+fec+tive+ness
ef+fec+tual
  ef+fec+tu+al+ity
  ef+fec+tu+al+ly
  ef+fec+tu+al+
  ness
ef+fec+tu+ate
  ef+fec+tu+ates
  ef+fec+tu+at+
  ing
  ef+fec+tu+at+
  ed
ef+fec+tu+ation
ef+femi+na+cy
ef+femi+nate
  ef+femi+nate+
  ness
ef+fen+di
  ef+fen+dis
ef+fer+ence
ef+fer+ent
ef+fer+vesce

ef+fer+vesces
  ef+fer+ves+cing
  ef+fer+vesced
  ef+fer+ves+
  cence
  ef+fer+ves+cent
  ef+fer+ves+cing+
  ly
ef+fete
  ef+fete+ness
ef+fi+ca+cious
  ef+fi+ca+cious+
  ness
ef+fi+ca+cy
ef+fi+cien+cy
  ef+fi+cien+cies
  ef+fi+cient
ef+fi+gy
  ef+fi+gies
eff+ing
eff+ings
ef+fleur+age
ef+flo+resce
  ef+flo+resces
  ef+flo+res+cing
  ef+flo+resced
  ef+flo+res+cence
  ef+flo+res+
  cences
  ef+flo+res+cent
ef+flu+ence
  ef+flu+ences
ef+flu+ent
  ef+flu+ents
ef+flu+vial
ef+flu+vium
  ef+flu+via *or*
  ef+flu+viums
ef+flux
ef+fort
  ef+forts
  ef+fort+ful
  ef+fort+less
ef+fron+tery
  ef+fron+teries
ef+ful+gence
ef+ful+gent
  ef+ful+gent+ly
ef+fuse
  ef+fuses
  ef+fus+ing
  ef+fused
ef+fu+sion
  ef+fu+sions
ef+fu+sive

ef+fu+sive+ly
ef+fu+sive+ness
eft
 efts
EFTA
EFTPOS
egad
egali+tar+ian
 egali+tar+ians
egali+tari+an+ism
 egali+tari+an+
  isms
Egbert
Eger
egg
 eggs
 egg+ing
 egged
eg+gar
 eg+gars
egg+beater
 egg+beaters
eg+ger
 eg+gers
egg+head
 egg+heads
egg+nog
 egg+nogs
egg+plant
 egg+plants
egg+shell
 egg+shells
Eg+ham
eg+lan+tine
 eg+lan+tines
Eg+mont
place name
Egmont
surname
ego
 egos
ego+cen+tric
 ego+cen+trics
ego+cen+tric+ity
ego+cen+trism
ego+ism
ego+ist
 ego+ists
ego+ma+nia
ego+ma+ni+ac
ego+ma+ni+acs
ego+ma+nia+cal
ego+tism
ego+tist
 ego+tists

ego-trip
 ego-trips
 ego-tripping
 ego-tripped
egre+gious
egre+gious+ness
egress
 egresses
egres+sion
egret
 egrets
Egypt
 Egyp+tian
 Egyp+tians
Egyp+tolo+gist
 Egyp+tolo+gists
Egyp+tol+ogy
eh
Ehrenburg
Ehrlich
Eichmann
eider
 eiders
 eider+down
 eider+downs
eidet+ic
eideti+cal+ly
Eid-ul-Adha
 Eid-ul-Adhas
Eid-ul-Fitr
 Eid-ul-Fitrs
Eifel
Eiffel
Eigen
Eiger
eight
 eights
 eight+een
 eight+eens
 eight+eenth
 eight+eenths
eight+fold
eighth
 eighths
eighti+eth
 eighti+eths
eighty
 eighties
Eilat
Eind+ho+ven
Einstein
Ein+stein+ian
ein+stein+ium
Einthoven
Eire

Eisen+ach
Eisenhower
Eisen+stadt
Eisenstein
eistedd+fod
 eistedd+fods
 or
 eistedd+fodau
either
ejacu+late
 ejacu+lates
 ejacu+lat+ing
 ejacu+lat+ed
ejacu+la+tion
 ejacu+la+tions
ejacu+la+tive
ejacu+la+tor
 ejacu+la+tors
ejacu+la+tory
eject
 ejects
 eject+ing
 eject+ed
ejec+tion
 ejec+tions
ejec+tive
ejec+tor
 ejec+tors
eke
 ekes
 ek+ing
 eked
Ekman
El Aaiún
elabo+rate
 elabo+rates
 elabo+rat+ing
 elabo+rat+ed
elabo+rate+ness
elabo+ra+tion
 elabo+ra+tions
elabo+ra+tive
elabo+ra+tor
 elabo+ra+tors
El Ala+mein
Elam
élan
eland
 elands
elapse
 elapses
 elaps+ing
 elapsed
elas+mo+branch

elas+mo+
 branchs
elas+tic
 elas+tics
elas+ti+cal+ly
elas+ti+cate
 elas+ti+cates
 elas+ti+cat+ing
 elas+ti+cat+ed
elas+ti+ca+tion
elas+ti+cise
 elas+ti+cises
 elas+ti+cis+ing
 elas+ti+cised
elas+tici+ty
elas+ti+cize
 elas+ti+cizes
 elas+ti+ciz+ing
 elas+ti+cized
elas+to+mer
 elas+to+mers
elas+to+mer+ic
Elas+to+plast
Trademark
 Elas+to+plasts
elate
 elates
 elat+ing
 elat+ed
elat+ed+ly
elat+ed+ness
ela+tion
Elba
Elbe
El+bert
El+bląg
el+bow
 el+bows
 el+bows
 el+bow+ing
 el+bowed
elbow+room
El+brus
El Capi+tan
El+che
el+der
 el+ders
elder+berry
 elder+berries
el+der+li+ness
el+der+ly
el+der+ship
el+der+ships
eld+est

El Do+ra+do
el+drich
el+dritch
elect
 elects
 elect+ing
 elect+ed
elect+able
elec+tion
 elec+tions
 elec+tion+eer
 elec+tion+eers
 elec+tion+eers
 elec+tion+eer+
  ing
 elec+tion+eered
elec+tive
 elec+tives
 elec+tive+ness
 elec+tiv+ity
elec+tor
 elec+tors
 elec+tor+al
 elec+tor+ate
 elec+tor+ates
 elec+tor+ship
Electra
elec+tret
 elec+trets
elec+tric
 elec+trics
 elec+tri+cal
 elec+tri+cal+ly
electric-discharge
 elec+tri+cian
 elec+tri+cians
 elec+tric+ity
 elec+tri+fi+able
 elec+tri+fi+ca+
  tion
 elec+tri+fi+ca+
  tions
 elec+tri+fi+er
 elec+tri+fi+ers
 elec+tri+fy
 elec+tri+fies
 elec+tri+fy+ing
 elec+tri+fied
elec+tro
 elec+tros
 elec+tro+acous+
  tic
elec+tro+car+dio+
 graph

elec+tro+car+
 dio+graphs
elec+tro+car+dio+
 graph+ic
elec+tro+car+di+
 og+ra+phy
elec+tro+chemi+
 cal
elec+tro+chem+
 ist
 elec+tro+chem+
  ists
 elec+tro+chem+
  is+try
elec+tro+con+vul+
 sive
elec+tro+cute
 elec+tro+cutes
 elec+tro+cut+
  ing
 elec+tro+cut+ed
 elec+tro+cu+tion
 elec+tro+cu+
  tions
elec+trode
 elec+trodes
elec+tro+de+pos+
 it
 elec+tro+de+
  pos+its
 elec+tro+de+
  pos+its
 elec+tro+de+
  pos+it+ing
 elec+tro+de+
  pos+it+ed
elec+tro+depo+si+
 tion
elec+tro+dy+nam+
 ics
elec+tro+en+
 cepha+lo+graph
 elec+tro+en+
  cepha+lo+
  graphs
 elec+tro+en+
  cepha+lo+graph+
  ic
 elec+tro+en+
  cepha+log+ra+
  phy
elec+tro+lyse
 elec+tro+lyses
 elec+tro+lys+ing
 elec+tro+lysed

elec+tro+lys+er
 elec+tro+lys+
  ers
elec+troly+sis
 elec+troly+ses
elec+tro+lyte
 elec+tro+lytes
 elec+tro+lyt+ic
 elec+tro+lyt+ics
 elec+tro+lyti+cal+
  ly
elec+tro+lyze
 U.S.
 elec+tro+lyzes
 elec+tro+lyz+ing
 elec+tro+lyzed
 elec+tro+lyz+er
  U.S.
 elec+tro+lyz+ers
elec+tro+mag+
 net
 elec+tro+mag+
  nets
 elec+tro+mag+
  net+ic
 elec+tro+mag+
  neti+cal+ly
 elec+tro+mag+
  net+ics
 elec+tro+mag+ne+
  tism
elec+trom+eter
 elec+trom+eters
 elec+trom+met+ric
 elec+trom+met+ri+
  cal
 elec+trom+etry
elec+tro+mo+tive
elec+tro+my+og+
 ra+phy
elec+tron
 elec+trons
elec+tro+nega+
 tive
 elec+tron+ic
 elec+troni+cal+ly
 elec+tron+ics
elec+tron+volt
 elec+tron+volts
elec+tro+pho+
 resis
elec+tro+pho+ret+
 ic
elec+tropho+rus

elec+tropho+
 ruses or
elec+tropho+ri
elec+tro+plate
 elec+tro+plates
 elec+tro+plat+
  ing
 elec+tro+plat+
  ed
 elec+tro+plat+er
 elec+tro+plat+
  ers
elec+tro+po+si+
 tive
elec+tro+rheo+
 logi+cal
elec+tro+rhe+ol+
 ogy
elec+tro+scope
 elec+tro+scopes
 elec+tro+scop+ic
elec+tro+stat+ic
 elec+tro+stat+ics
elec+tro+thera+
 peu+tic
 elec+tro+thera+
  peu+ti+cal
 elec+tro+thera+
  peu+tics
 elec+tro+thera+
  pist
 elec+tro+thera+
  pists
 elec+tro+thera+
  py
elec+tro+type
 elec+tro+types
 elec+tro+types
 elec+tro+typ+
  ing
 elec+tro+typed
 elec+tro+typ+er
 elec+tro+typ+
  ers
elec+tro+va+len+
 cy
 elec+tro+va+len+
  cies
elec+tro+weak
elec+trum
elec+tu+ary
 elec+tu+aries
el+eemosy+nary
el+egance
 el+egances

el+egan+cy
el+egan+cies
el+egant
el+egi+ac
el+egi+acs
el+egia+cal+ly
el+egise
el+egises
el+egis+ing
el+egised
el+egist
el+egists
el+egize
el+egizes
el+egiz+ing
el+egized
el+egy
el+egies
el+ement
el+ements
el+ement+al
el+emen+tal+ism
el+emen+ta+ri+
  ness
el+emen+ta+ry
elen+chus
elen+chi
elenc+tic
el+ephant
  el+ephants or
  el+ephant
el+ephan+tia+sis
el+ephan+tine
Eleu+sin+ian
Eleu+sis
el+evate
  el+evates
el+evat+ing
el+evat+ed
el+evat+ed
el+eva+tion
  el+eva+tions
el+eva+tion+al
el+eva+tor
  el+eva+tors
el+eva+tory
elev+en
  elev+ens
eleven-plus
elev+en+ses
elev+enth
  elev+enths
eleventh-hour
adj.
elev+enth hour

noun
elf
  elves
El Fai+yûm
El Fer+rol
elf+in
elf+ish
elf+lock
  elf+locks
Elgar
El+gin
place name
Elgin
surname
El Gîza
El+gon
El Greco
Eli
Elia
Elias
elic+it
  elic+its
elic+it+ing
elic+it+ed
elic+it+able
elici+ta+tion
  elici+ta+tions
elici+tor
  elici+tors
elide
  elides
elid+ing
elid+ed
elid+ible
eli+gibil+ity
eli+gible
eli+gibly
Elijah
elimi+nable
elimi+nate
  elimi+nates
elimi+nat+ing
elimi+nat+ed
elimi+na+tion
  elimi+na+tions
elimi+na+tive
elimi+na+tor
  elimi+na+tors
Eliot
Elis
ELISA
Elisabeth
Élisa+beth+ville
Eli+sa+vet+grad
Eli+sa+vet+pol

Elisha
eli+sion
  eli+sions
elite
  elites
élite
  élites
elit+ism
elit+ist
Eliza+beth
place name
Elizabeth
name
Eliza+bethan
  Eliza+bethans
elk
  elks or
  elk
ell
  ells
Ellington
el+lipse
  el+lipses
el+lip+sis
  el+lip+ses
el+lip+soid
  el+lip+soids
el+lip+soi+dal
el+lip+ti+cal
el+lip+ti+cal+
  ness
Ellis
elm
  elms
El Man+sû+ra
El Min+ya
El Mis+ti
El Obeid
elo+cu+tion
elo+cu+tion+ary
elo+cu+tion+ist
  elo+cu+tion+ists
Elo+him
Elo+hist
  Elo+hists
elon+gate
  elon+gates
elon+gat+ing
elon+gat+ed
elon+ga+tion
  elon+ga+tions
elope
  elopes

elop+ing
eloped
elope+ment
  elope+ments
elop+er
  elop+ers
elo+quence
elo+quent
El Paso
El Sal+va+dor
El+san
Trademark
else
else+where
El+si+nore
Elton
elu+ant
  elu+ants
elu+ate
  elu+ates
elu+ci+date
  elu+ci+dates
elu+ci+dat+ing
elu+ci+dat+ed
elu+ci+da+tion
  elu+ci+da+tions
elu+ci+da+tive
elu+ci+da+tor
  elu+ci+da+tors
elu+ci+da+tory
elude
  eludes
elud+ing
elud+ed
elud+er
  elud+ers
elu+ent
  elu+ents
elu+sion
  elu+sions
elu+sive
elu+sive+ness
elute
  elutes
elut+ing
elut+ed
elu+tion
elu+tri+ate
  elu+tri+ates
elu+tri+at+ing
elu+tri+at+ed
elu+tria+tion
el+ver
  el+vers
elves

elv+ish
Ely
Ély+sée
Ely+sium
ely+tron
ely+tra
ely+trum
ely+tra
em
ems
ema+ci+ate
ema+ci+ates
ema+ci+at+ing
ema+ci+at+ed
ema+ci+at+ed
ema+cia+tion
E-mail
ema+nate
ema+nates
ema+nat+ing
ema+nat+ed
ema+na+tion
ema+na+tions
ema+na+tion+al
ema+na+tive
ema+na+tor
ema+na+tors
ema+na+tory
eman+ci+pate
eman+ci+pates
eman+ci+pat+ing
eman+ci+pat+ed
eman+ci+pat+ed
eman+ci+pa+tion
eman+ci+pa+tor
eman+ci+pa+tors
eman+ci+pa+tory
emas+cu+late
emas+cu+lates
emas+cu+lat+ing
emas+cu+lat+ed
emas+cu+la+tion
emas+cu+la+tor
emas+cu+la+tors
emas+cu+la+tory
em+balm
em+balms
em+balm+ing
em+balmed
em+balm+er

em+balm+ers
em+balm+ment
em+bank
em+banks
em+bank+ing
em+banked
em+bank+ment
em+bank+ments
em+bar+go
em+bar+goes
em+bar+goes
em+bar+go+ing
em+bar+goed
em+bark
em+barks
em+bark+ing
em+barked
em+bar+ka+tion
em+bar+ka+tions
em+bar+rass
em+bar+rasses
em+bar+rass+ing
em+bar+rassed
em+bar+rassed
em+bar+rass+ing
em+bar+rass+ment
em+bar+rass+ments
em+bas+sy
em+bas+sies
em+bat+tle
em+bat+tles
em+bat+tling
em+bat+tled
em+bay
em+bays
em+bay+ing
em+bayed
em+bed
em+beds
em+bed+ding
em+bed+ded
em+bed+ment
em+bed+ments
em+bel+lish
em+bel+lishes
em+bel+lish+ing
em+bel+lished
em+bel+lish+er
em+bel+lish+ers

em+bel+lish+
ment
em+bel+lish+
ments
em+ber
em+bers
em+bez+zle
em+bez+zles
em+bez+zling
em+bez+zled
em+bez+zle+
ment
em+bez+zle+
ments
em+bez+zler
em+bez+zlers
em+bit+ter
em+bit+ters
em+bit+ter+ing
em+bit+tered
em+bit+tered
em+bit+ter+ment
em+bla+zon
em+bla+zons
em+bla+zon+ing
em+bla+zoned
em+bla+zon+
ment
em+bla+zon+
ments
em+blem
em+blems
em+blem+at+ic
em+blem+ati+cal
em+blem+ati+cal+
ly
em+bodi+ment
em+bodi+ments
em+body
em+bod+ies
em+body+ing
em+bod+ied
em+bold+en
em+bold+ens
em+bold+en+
ing
em+bold+ened
em+bol+ic
em+bo+lism
em+bo+lisms
em+bo+lus
em+bo+li
em+bon+point
em+bos+om
em+bos+oms

em+bos+om+
ing
em+bos+omed
em+boss
em+bosses
em+boss+ing
em+bossed
em+boss+er
em+boss+ers
em+boss+ment
em+boss+
ments
em+bou+chure
em+bou+chures
em+bow+er
em+bow+ers
em+bow+er+ing
em+bow+ered
em+brace
em+braces
em+braces
em+brac+ing
em+braced
em+brace+able
em+brace+ment
em+brac+er
em+brac+ers
em+bra+sure
em+bra+sures
em+bra+sured
em+bro+cate
em+bro+cates
em+bro+cat+ing
em+bro+cat+ed
em+bro+ca+tion
em+bro+ca+
tions
em+broi+der
em+broi+ders
em+broi+der+
ing
em+broi+dered
em+broi+der+er
em+broi+der+
ers
em+broi+dery
em+broi+deries
em+broil
em+broils
em+broil+ing
em+broiled
em+broil+er
em+broil+ers
em+bryo

em+bryos
em+bryo+log+ic
em+bryo+logi+cal
em+bry+olo+gist
em+bry+olo+gists
em+bry+ol+ogy
em+bryo+nal
em+bry+on+ic
em+bry+oni+cal+ly
em+cee
 em+cees
 em+cees
 em+cee+ing
 em+ceed
Em+den
emend
 emends
 emend+ing
 emend+ed
emend+able
emen+da+tion
 emen+da+tions
emen+da+tor
 emen+da+tors
 emen+da+tory
em+er+ald
 em+er+alds
emerge
 emerges
 emerg+ing
 emerged
emer+gence
emer+gen+cy
 emer+gen+cies
emer+gent
emeri+tus
emer+sion
Emerson
em+ery
emet+ic
 emet+ics
emi+grant
 emi+grants
emi+grate
 emi+grates
 emi+grat+ing
 emi+grat+ed
emi+gra+tion
emi+gra+tory
émi+gré
 émi+grés
Emilia-Romagna

emi+nence
 emi+nences
Emi+nence
 Emi+nences
émi+nence grise
 émi+nences grises
emi+nen+cy
 emi+nen+cies
Emi+nen+cy
 Emi+nen+cies
emi+nent
emir
 emirs
emir+ate
 emir+ates
em+is+sary
 em+is+saries
emis+sion
 emis+sions
emis+sive
emis+siv+ity
emit
 emits
 emit+ting
 emit+ted
emit+ter
 emit+ters
Emmanuel
Em+men
Em+men+tal
Em+men+thal
Em+men+thal+er
Emmet
Emmy
 Emmys or
 Emmies
emol+lience
emol+lient
 emol+lients
emolu+ment
 emolu+ments
emote
 emotes
 emot+ing
 emot+ed
emot+er
 emot+ers
emo+tion
 emo+tions
emo+tion+al
emo+tion+al+ise
 ises

emo+tion+al+is+ing
emo+tion+al+ised
emo+tion+al+ism
emo+tion+al+ist
 ists
emo+tion+al+is+tic
emo+tion+al+ity
emo+tion+al+ize
 izes
emo+tion+al+iz+ing
emo+tion+al+ized
emo+tive
emo+tive+ness
emo+tiv+ity
em+pan+el
 em+pan+els
em+pan+el+ling
 or
 em+pan+el+ing
 U.S.
 em+pan+elled
 or
 em+pan+eled
 U.S.
 em+pan+el+ment
em+pa+thet+ic
em+path+ic
em+pa+thise
 em+pa+thises
 em+pa+this+ing
 em+pa+thised
em+pa+thize
 em+pa+thizes
 em+pa+thiz+ing
 em+pa+thized
em+pa+thy
Empedocles
em+per+or
 em+per+ors
em+pha+sis
em+pha+ses
em+pha+sise
 em+pha+sises
 em+pha+sis+ing
 em+pha+sised
em+pha+size
 em+pha+sizes
 em+pha+siz+ing

em+pha+sized
em+phat+ic
em+phati+cal+ly
em+phy+sema
em+pire
 em+pires
empire-builder
 empire-builders
empire-building
em+pir+ic
 em+pir+ics
em+piri+cal
em+piri+cal+ness
em+piri+cism
em+piri+cist
 em+piri+cists
em+place
 em+places
em+plac+ing
em+placed
em+place+ment
 em+place+ments
em+plane
 em+planes
em+plan+ing
em+planed
em+ploy
 em+ploys
em+ploys
em+ploy+ing
em+ployed
em+ploy+abil+ity
em+ploy+able
em+ploye
 U.S.
 em+ployes
em+ployee
 em+ployees
em+ploy+er
 em+ploy+ers
em+ploy+ment
 em+ploy+ments
em+po+rium
 em+po+riums
 or
 em+po+ria
em+pow+er
 em+pow+ers
 em+pow+er+ing
 em+pow+ered
em+pow+er+ment
em+press
 em+presses

Empson
emp+ti+able
emp+ti+er
emp+ti+ers
emp+ti+ly
emp+ti+ness
emp+ty
emp+ties
emp+ties
emp+ty+ing
emp+tied
emp+ti+er
emp+ti+est
empty-handed
empty-headed
empty-nester
empty-nesters
em+py+ema
em+py+ema+ta
  or
em+py+emas
em+py+emic
em+py+real
em+py+rean
em+py+reu+ma
em+py+reu+ma+
  ta
Ems
emu
emus
emu+late
emu+lates
emu+lat+ing
emu+lat+ed
emu+la+tion
emu+la+tions
emu+la+tive
emu+la+tor
emu+la+tors
emu+lous
emu+lous+ness
emul+sible
emul+si+fi+able
emul+si+fi+ca+
  tion
emul+si+fi+er
emul+si+fi+ers
emul+si+fy
emul+si+fies
emul+si+fy+ing
emul+si+fied
emul+sion
emul+sions
emul+sive
emu-wren

emu-wrens
en
ens
en+able
en+ables
en+abling
en+abled
en+able+ment
en+able+ments
en+abler
en+ablers
en+act
en+acts
en+act+ing
en+act+ed
en+act+able
en+ac+tion
en+ac+tions
en+ac+tive
en+act+ment
en+act+ments
en+ac+tor
en+ac+tors
en+ac+tory
enam+el
enam+els
enam+els
enam+el+ling
  or
enam+el+ing
  U.S.
enam+elled *or*
enam+eled
  U.S.
enam+el+er
  U.S.
enam+el+ers
enam+el+ler
enam+el+lers
enam+el+list
enam+el+lists
en+am+or
  U.S.
en+am+ors
en+am+or+ing
en+am+ored
  U.S.
en+am+our
en+am+ours
en+am+our+ing
en+am+oured
en+am+oured
en bloc
en brosse

en+camp
en+camps
en+camp+ing
en+camped
en+camp+ment
en+camp+
  ments
en+cap+su+late
en+cap+su+
  lates
en+cap+su+lat+
  ing
en+cap+su+lat+
  ed
en+cap+su+la+
  tion
en+cap+su+la+
  tions
en+case
en+cases
en+cas+ing
en+cased
en+case+ment
en+cash
en+cashes
en+cash+ing
en+cashed
en+cash+able
en+cash+ment
en+cash+ments
en+caus+tic
en+caus+tics
en+ceinte
Enceladus
en+cephal+ic
en+cepha+lin
en+cepha+lit+ic
en+cepha+li+tis
en+cepha+lo+
  gram
en+cepha+lo+
  grams
en+cepha+lon
en+cepha+la
en+cepha+lopa+
  thy
en+cepha+lopa+
  thies
en+cepha+lous
en+chain
en+chains
en+chain+ing
en+chained
en+chain+ment
en+chain+ments

en+chant
en+chants
en+chant+ing
en+chant+ed
en+chant+ed
en+chant+er
en+chant+ers
en+chant+ing
en+chant+ing+ly
en+chant+ment
en+chant+
  ments
en+chant+ress
en+chant+
  resses
en+chase
en+chases
en+chas+ing
en+chased
en+chas+er
en+chas+ers
en+chi+la+da
en+chi+la+das
en+ci+pher
en+ci+phers
en+ci+pher+ing
en+ci+phered
en+ci+pher+er
en+ci+pher+ers
en+ci+pher+ment
en+cir+cle
en+cir+cles
en+cir+cling
en+cir+cled
en+cir+cle+ment
en+clave
en+claves
en+clit+ic
en+clit+ics
en+clos+able
en+close
en+closes
en+clos+ing
en+closed
en+clos+er
en+clos+ers
en+clo+sure
en+clo+sures
en+code
en+codes
en+cod+ing
en+cod+ed
en+code+ment
en+cod+er
en+cod+ers

en+co+mi+ast
en+co+mi+asts
en+co+mi+as+tic
en+co+mium
en+co+miums
or
en+co+mia
en+com+pass
en+com+passes
en+com+pass+
ing
en+com+passed
en+com+pass+
ment
en+core
en+cores
en+cores
en+cor+ing
en+cored
en+coun+ter
en+coun+ters
en+coun+ters
en+coun+ter+
ing
en+coun+tered
en+cour+age
en+cour+ages
en+cour+ag+ing
en+cour+aged
en+cour+age+
ment
en+cour+age+
ments
en+cour+ag+er
en+cour+ag+ers
en+cour+ag+ing
en+cour+ag+ing+
ly
en+croach
en+croaches
en+croach+ing
en+croached
en+croach+er
en+croach+ers
en+croach+ment
en+croach+
ments
en+crust
en+crusts
en+crust+ing
en+crust+ed
en+crus+ta+tion
en+crus+ta+
tions
en+cum+ber

en+cum+bers
en+cum+ber+
ing
en+cum+bered
en+cum+brance
en+cum+
brances
en+cyc+li+cal
en+cyc+li+cals
en+cy+clo+pae+
dia
en+cy+clo+pae+
dias
en+cy+clo+pae+
dic
en+cy+clo+pae+
dism
en+cy+clo+pae+
dist
en+cy+clo+pae+
dists
en+cy+clo+pedia
en+cy+clo+
pedias
en+cy+clo+pedic
en+cy+clo+
pedism
en+cy+clo+
pedist
en+cy+clo+
pedists
en+cyst
en+cysts
en+cyst+ing
en+cyst+ed
en+cys+ta+tion
en+cyst+ment
end
ends
ends
end+ing
end+ed
en+da+meba
U.S.
en+da+mebae
or
en+da+mebas
en+da+moeba
en+da+moebae
or
en+da+moebas
en+dan+ger
en+dan+gers
en+dan+ger+ing
en+dan+gered

en+dan+ger+
ment
en+dan+ger+
ments
en+dear
en+dears
en+dear+ing
en+deared
en+dear+ing+ly
en+dear+ment
en+dear+ments
en+deav+or
U.S.
en+deav+ors
en+deav+ors
en+deav+or+ing
en+deav+ored
en+deav+or+er
U.S.
en+deav+or+ers
en+deav+our
en+deav+ours
en+deav+ours
en+deav+our+
ing
en+deav+oured
en+deav+our+er
en+deav+our+
ers
en+demi+al
en+dem+ic
en+demi+cal+ly
en+de+mic+ity
en+de+mism
end+er
end+ers
en+der+mic
end+game
end+games
end+ing
end+ings
en+dive
en+dives
end+less
end+less+ness
end+most
endo+blast
endo+blasts
endo+blas+tic
endo+car+dit+ic
endo+car+di+tis
endo+carp
endo+carps
endo+car+pal
endo+car+pic

endo+crin+al
endo+crine
endo+cri+nolo+
gist
endo+cri+nolo+
gists
endo+cri+nol+
ogy
endo+derm
endo+derms
endo+der+mal
endo+der+mic
endo+gam+ic
endo+doga+mous
endo+doga+my
endo+doga+mies
endo+dog+enous
endo+dog+eny
endo+metrial
endo+metritis
endo+metrium
endo+metria
endo+morph
endo+morphs
endo+mor+phic
endo+mor+phism
endo+mor+phy
endo+phyte
endo+phytes
endo+phyt+ic
endo+plasm
endo+plas+mic
en+dor+phin
en+dor+phins
en+dors+able
en+dorse
en+dorses
en+dors+ing
en+dorsed
en+dor+see
en+dor+sees
en+dorse+ment
en+dorse+
ments
en+dors+er
en+dors+ers
en+dor+sor
en+dor+sors
endo+scope
endo+scopes
endo+scop+ic
endo+skel+etal
endo+skel+eton
endo+skel+
etons

endo+sperm
endo+sper+mic
endo+ther+mal
endo+ther+mic
endo+ther+mi+
cal+ly
endo+ther+mism
en+dow
en+dows
en+dow+ing
en+dowed
en+dow+ment
en+dow+ments
end+paper
end+papers
en+due
en+dues
en+du+ing
en+dued
en+dur+able
en+dur+ance
en+dure
en+dures
en+dur+ing
en+dured
en+dur+ing
en+dur+ing+ly
en+dur+ing+ness
end-user
adj.
end user
end users
end+ways
end+wise
U.S.
Endymion
en+ema
en+emas *or*
en+ema+ta
en+emy
en+emies
en+er+get+ic
en+er+geti+cal+
ly
en+er+gise
en+er+gises
en+er+gis+ing
en+er+gised
en+er+gis+er
en+er+gis+ers
en+er+gize
en+er+gizes
en+er+giz+ing
en+er+gized
en+er+giz+er

en+er+giz+ers
en+er+gy
en+er+gies
en+er+vate
en+er+vates
en+er+vat+ing
en+er+vat+ed
en+er+vat+ing
en+er+va+tion
en fa+mille
en+fant ter+ri+ble
en+fants ter+ri+
bles
en+fee+ble
en+fee+bles
en+fee+bling
en+fee+bled
en+fee+ble+ment
en+fee+ble+
ments
en+fee+bler
en+fee+blers
en fête
En+field
en+fi+lade
en+fi+lades
en+fi+lades
en+fi+lad+ing
en+fi+lad+ed
en+fold
en+folds
en+fold+ing
en+fold+ed
en+fold+er
en+fold+ers
en+fold+ment
en+force
en+forces
en+forc+ing
en+forced
en+force+abil+ity
en+force+able
en+forc+ed+ly
en+force+ment
en+forc+er
en+forc+ers
en+fran+chise
en+fran+chises
en+fran+chis+
ing
en+fran+chised
en+fran+chise+
ment
en+fran+chise+
ments

en+fran+chis+er
en+fran+chis+
ers
en+gage
en+gages
en+gag+ing
en+gaged
en+ga+gé
en+gaged
en+ga+gée
en+gage+ment
en+gage+ments
en+gag+er
en+gag+ers
en+gag+ing
en garde
Engels
en+gen+der
en+gen+ders
en+gen+der+ing
en+gen+dered
en+gine
en+gines
en+gi+neer
en+gi+neers
en+gi+neers
en+gi+neer+ing
en+gi+neer+ing
Eng+land
Eng+lish
English+man
English+men
Eng+lish+ness
English+woman
English+women
en+gorge
en+gorges
en+gorg+ing
en+gorged
en+gorge+ment
en+graft
en+grafts
en+graft+ing
en+graft+ed
en+grain
en+grains
en+grain+ing
en+grained
en+grave
en+graves
en+grav+ing
en+graved
en+grav+er
en+grav+ers

en+gross
en+grosses
en+gross+ing
en+grossed
en+grossed
en+gross+ing
en+gross+ment
en+gross+
ments
en+gulf
en+gulfs
en+gulf+ing
en+gulfed
en+gulf+ment
en+gulf+ments
en+hance
en+hances
en+hanc+ing
en+hanced
en+hance+ment
en+hance+
ments
en+hanc+er
en+hanc+ers
en+har+mon+ic
en+har+moni+cal+
ly
enig+ma
enig+mas
en+ig+mat+ic
en+ig+mati+cal
en+ig+mati+cal+
ly
Eni+we+tok
en+jambed
en+jambe+ment
en+jambe+
ments
en+jamb+ment
en+jamb+ments
en+join
en+joins
en+join+ing
en+joined
en+join+er
en+join+ers
en+join+ment
en+join+ments
en+joy
en+joys
en+joy+ing
en+joyed
en+joy+able
en+joy+able+
ness

en+joy+ably
en+joy+er
en+joy+ers
en+joy+ment
en+joy+ments
en+kepha+lin
en+kin+dle
en+kin+dles
en+kin+dling
en+kin+dled
en+lace
en+laces
en+lac+ing
en+laced
en+lace+ment
en+lace+ments
en+large
en+larges
en+larg+ing
en+larged
en+large+able
en+large+ment
en+large+ments
en+larg+er
en+larg+ers
en+light+en
en+light+ens
en+light+en+ing
en+light+ened
en+light+en+ing
en+light+en+
ment
En+light+en+
ment
en+list
en+lists
en+list+ing
en+list+ed
en+list+er
en+list+ers
en+list+ment
en+list+ments
en+liv+en
en+liv+ens
en+liv+en+ing
en+liv+ened
en+liv+en+ing
en+liv+en+ment
en masse
en+mesh
en+meshes
en+mesh+ing
en+meshed
en+mesh+ment

en+mesh+
ments
en+mity
en+mities
En+nis
En+nis+kil+len
en+no+ble
en+no+bles
en+no+bling
en+no+bled
en+no+ble+ment
en+no+bler
en+no+blers
en+no+bling
en+nui
Enoch
enol+ogy
U.S.
enor+mity
enor+mities
enor+mous
enor+mous+ly
enor+mous+ness
Enos
eno+sis
enough
en pas+sant
en+print
en+prints
en+quire
en+quires
en+quir+ing
en+quired
en+quir+er
en+quir+ers
en+quiry
en+quiries
en+rage
en+rages
en+rag+ing
en+raged
en rap+port
en+rap+ture
en+rap+tures
en+rap+tur+ing
en+rap+tured
en+rich
en+riches
en+rich+ing
en+riched
en+riched
en+rich+ment
en+rich+ments
Enright
en+rol

en+rols
en+rol+ling
en+rolled
en+roll
U.S.
en+rolls
en+roll+ing
en+rolled
en+rol+lee
en+rol+lees
en+rol+ler
en+rol+lers
en+roll+ment
U.S.
en+roll+ments
en+rol+ment
en+rol+ments
en route
En+schede
en+sconce
en+sconces
en+sconc+ing
en+sconced
en+sem+ble
en+sem+bles
en+shrine
en+shrines
en+shrin+ing
en+shrined
en+shrine+ment
en+shroud
en+shrouds
en+shroud+ing
en+shroud+ed
en+sign
en+signs
en+sign+cy
en+sign+cies
en+sign+ship
en+sign+ships
en+si+lage
en+sile
en+siles
en+sil+ing
en+siled
en+slave
en+slaves
en+slav+ing
en+slaved
en+slave+ment
en+slave+ments
en+slav+er
en+slav+ers
en+snare
en+snares

en+snar+ing
en+snared
en+snare+ment
en+snare+
ments
en+snar+er
en+snar+ers
en+sue
en+sues
en+su+ing
en+sued
en+su+ing
en suite
en+sure
en+sures
en+sur+ing
en+sured
en+sur+er
en+sur+ers
en+tab+la+ture
en+tab+la+tures
en+ta+ble+ment
en+ta+ble+
ments
en+tail
en+tails
en+tails
en+tail+ing
en+tailed
en+tail+er
en+tail+ers
en+tail+ment
en+tail+ments
en+ta+meba
U.S.
en+ta+mebae
or
en+ta+mebas
en+ta+moeba
en+ta+moebae
or
en+ta+moebas
en+tan+gle
en+tan+gles
en+tan+gling
en+tan+gled
en+tan+gle+ment
en+tan+gle+
ments
en+tan+gler
en+tan+glers
en+ta+sis
en+ta+ses
En+teb+be
en+tel+lus

en+tel+luses
en+tente
en+tentes
en+tente cor+
diale
en+ter
en+ters
en+ter+ing
en+tered
en+ter+able
en+ter+al
ent+er+er
ent+er+ers
en+ter+ic
en+teri+tis
en+tero+bi+as+is
en+ter+prise
en+ter+prises
en+ter+pris+er
en+ter+pris+ers
en+ter+pris+ing
en+ter+pris+ing+
ly
en+ter+tain
en+ter+tains
en+ter+tain+ing
en+ter+tained
en+ter+tain+er
en+ter+tain+ers
en+ter+tain+ing
en+ter+tain+
ment
en+ter+tain+
ments
en+thral
en+thrals
en+thral+ling
en+thralled
en+thrall
U.S.
en+thralls
en+thrall+ing
en+thralled
en+thral+ler
en+thral+lers
en+thral+ling
en+thrall+ment
U.S.
en+thrall+ments
en+thral+ment
en+thral+ments
en+throne
en+thrones
en+thron+ing
en+throned

en+throne+ment
en+thuse
en+thuses
en+thus+ing
en+thused
en+thu+si+asm
en+thu+si+asms
en+thu+si+ast
en+thu+si+asts
en+thu+si+as+tic
en+thu+si+as+ti+
cal+ly
en+tice
en+tices
en+tic+ing
en+ticed
en+tice+ment
en+tice+ments
en+tic+er
en+tic+ers
en+tic+ing
en+tic+ing+ly
en+tire
en+tire+ly
en+tire+ness
en+tirety
en+tireties
en+ti+tle
en+ti+tles
en+ti+tling
en+ti+tled
en+ti+tle+ment
en+ti+tle+ments
en+tity
en+tities
ento+derm
ento+derms
ento+der+mal
ento+der+mic
en+tomb
en+tombs
en+tomb+ing
en+tombed
en+tomb+ment
en+tomb+ments
ento+mo+logi+
cal
ento+molo+gist
ento+molo+
gists
ento+mol+ogy
ento+phyt+ic
en+tou+rage
en+tou+rages
en+tr'acte

en+tr'actes
en+trails
en+train
en+trains
en+train+ing
en+trained
en+train+ment
en+train+ments
en+trance
en+trances
en+trances
en+tranc+ing
en+tranced
en+trance+ment
en+trance+
ments
en+tranc+ing
en+trant
en+trants
en+trap
en+traps
en+trap+ping
en+trapped
en+trap+ment
en+trap+ments
en+trap+per
en+trap+pers
en+treat
en+treats
en+treat+ing
en+treat+ed
en+treat+ment
en+treat+ments
en+treaty
en+treaties
en+tre+chat
en+tre+chats
en+tre+côte
en+tre+côtes
en+trée
en+trées
en+tre+mets
en+tre+mets
en+trench
en+trenches
en+trench+ing
en+trenched
en+trenched
en+trench+ment
en+trench+
ments
en+tre+pôt
en+tre+pôts
en+tre+pre+neur

en+tre+pre+
neurs
en+tre+pre+neur+
ial
en+tre+pre+neur+
ship
en+tre+pre+
neur+ships
en+tro+py
en+tro+pies
en+trust
en+trusts
en+trust+ing
en+trust+ed
en+trust+ment
en+trust+ments
en+try
en+tries
en+try+ism
en+try+ist
en+try+ists
en+twine
en+twines
en+twin+ing
en+twined
en+twine+ment
en+twine+
ments
Enu+gu
enu+mer+able
enu+mer+ate
enu+mer+ates
enu+mer+at+ing
enu+mer+at+ed
enu+mera+tion
enu+mera+tions
enu+mera+tive
enu+mera+tor
enu+mera+tors
enun+ci+able
enun+ci+ate
enun+ci+ates
enun+ci+at+ing
enun+ci+at+ed
enun+cia+tion
enun+cia+tions
enun+cia+tive
enun+cia+tor
enun+cia+tors
enun+cia+tory
enu+resis
enu+ret+ic
en+vel+op
en+vel+ops
en+vel+op+ing

en+vel+oped
en+velope
en+velopes
en+vel+op+ment
en+vel+op+
  ments
en+ven+om
en+ven+oms
en+ven+om+ing
en+ven+omed
en+vi+able
en+vi+able+ness
en+vi+er
en+vi+ers
en+vi+ous
en+vi+ous+ly
en+vi+ous+ness
en+vi+ron
en+vi+rons
en+vi+ron+ing
en+vi+roned
en+vi+ron+ment
en+vi+ron+
  ments
en+vi+ron+men+
  tal
en+vi+ron+men+
  tal+ist
en+vi+ron+men+
  tal+ists
en+vi+rons
en+vis+age
en+vis+ages
en+vis+ag+ing
en+vis+aged
en+vis+age+
  ment
en+vis+age+
  ments
en+vi+sion
en+vi+sions
en+vi+sion+ing
en+vi+sioned
en+voi
en+vois
en+voy
en+voys
en+voy+ship
en+voy+ships
envy
envies
envies
envy+ing
envied
en+vy+ing+ly

en+wrap
en+wraps
en+wrap+ping
en+wrapped
en+wreath
en+wreaths
en+wreath+ing
en+wreathed
en+zo+ot+ic
enzo+oti+cal+ly
en+zy+mat+ic
en+zyme
en+zymes
en+zy+mic
Eocene
eohip+pus
eohip+puses
Eolith+ic
eon
U.S.
eons
Eos
eosin
eosine
epact
epacts
Epaminondas
ep+arch
ep+archs
ep+ar+chy
ep+ar+chies
ep+aulet
U.S.
ep+aulets
ep+aulette
ep+aulettes
épée
épées
épée+ist
épée+ists
epei+ro+gen+
  esis
epei+ro+genet+ic
epei+ro+gen+ic
ep+ei+rog+eny
epergne
epergnes
ep+ex+egesis
ep+ex+egeses
ep+ex+eget+ic
ep+ex+egeti+cal
epha
ephas
ephah
ephahs

ephed+rin
ephed+rine
ephem+era
ephem+eras *or*
ephem+erae
ephem+er+al
ephem+er+als
ephem+er+al+ity
ephem+er+al+
  ness
ephem+er+id
ephem+er+ids
ephem+er+is
eph+emer+ides
ephem+er+on
ephem+era *or*
ephem+er+ons
ephem+er+op+
  ter+an
ephem+er+op+
  ter+ans
Eph+esus
ephod
ephods
eph+or
eph+ors *or*
eph+ori
eph+or+al
eph+or+ate
eph+or+ates
Ephraim
Ephra+im+ite
Ephra+im+ites
epic
epics
epi+ca+lyx
epi+ca+lyxes
  or
epi+ca+ly+ces
epi+can+thic
epi+can+thus
epi+can+thi
epi+car+di+ac
epi+car+dial
epi+car+dium
epi+car+dia
epi+carp
epi+carps
epi+cene
epi+cen+ism
epi+cen+ter
U.S.
epi+cen+ters
epi+cen+tral
epi+cen+tre

epi+cen+tres
Epictetus
epi+cure
epi+cures
epi+cu+rean
epi+cu+reans
epi+cu+rean+ism
epi+cu+rean+
  isms
epi+cur+ism
epi+cur+isms
Epicurus
epi+cy+cle
epi+cy+cles
epi+cy+clic
epi+cy+cli+cal
epi+cy+cloid
epi+cy+cloids
epi+cy+cloid+al
Epi+daur+us
epi+dem+ic
epi+dem+ics
epi+demi+cal+ly
epi+demio+logi+
  cal
epi+demi+olo+
  gist
epi+demi+olo+
  gists
epi+demi+ol+ogy
epi+der+mal
epi+der+mic
epi+der+mis
epi+der+moid
epi+dia+scope
epi+dia+scopes
epi+di+dy+mis
epi+di+dymi+
  des
epi+dur+al
epi+dur+als
epi+gam+ic
epi+geal
epi+gean
epi+geous
epi+glot+tal
epi+glot+tic
epi+glot+tis
epi+glot+tises
  or
epi+glot+ti+des
Epigo+ni
epi+gram
epi+grams
epi+gram+mat+ic

epi+gram+mati+cal+ly
epi+gram+ma+tise
epi+gram+ma+tises
epi+gram+ma+tis+ing
epi+gram+ma+tised
epi+gram+ma+tism
epi+gram+ma+tisms
epi+gram+ma+tist
epi+gram+ma+tists
epi+gram+ma+tize
epi+gram+ma+tizes
epi+gram+ma+tiz+ing
epi+gram+ma+tized
epi+graph
epi+graphs
epig+ra+pher
epig+ra+phers
epi+graph+ic
epi+graphi+cal
epig+ra+phist
epig+ra+phists
epig+ra+phy
epi+la+tor
epi+la+tors
epi+lep+sy
epi+lep+tic
epi+lep+tics
epi+lep+ti+cal+ly
epilo+gist
epilo+gists
epi+logue
epi+logues
epi+phan+ic
epipha+ny
epipha+nies
epi+phenom+enal
epi+phenom+enon
epi+phenom+ena
epi+phyt+al
epi+phyte

epi+phytes
epi+phyt+ic
Epi+rus
epis+co+pa+cy
epis+co+pa+cies
epis+co+pal
epis+co+pa+lian
epis+co+pa+lians
epis+co+pa+lian+ism
epis+co+pate
epis+co+pates
epi+si+oto+my
epi+si+oto+mies
epi+sode
epi+sodes
epi+sod+ic
epi+sodi+cal
epi+sodi+cal+ly
epi+stax+is
epis+temo+logi+cal
epis+temolo+gist
epis+temolo+gists
epis+temol+ogy
epis+tle
epis+tles
Epis+tle
Epis+tles
epis+to+lary
epis+to+la+tory
epi+style
epi+styles
epi+taph
epi+taphs
epi+taph+ic
epi+taph+ist
epi+taph+ists
epi+tax+ial
epi+taxy
epi+tha+lam+ic
epi+tha+la+mi+on
epi+tha+la+mia
epi+tha+la+mium
epi+tha+la+mia
epi+thelial
epi+thelium
epi+theli+ums
or
epi+thelia
epi+thet

epi+thets
epi+thet+ic
epi+theti+cal
epito+me
epito+mes
epi+tom+ic
epi+tomi+cal
epito+mi+sa+tion
epito+mise
epito+mises
epito+mis+ing
epito+mised
epito+mist
epito+mists
epito+mi+za+tion
epito+mize
epito+mizes
epito+miz+ing
epito+mized
epi+zo+ot+ic
epi+zo+ot+ics
epoch
epochs
ep+och+al
ep+ode
ep+odes
epo+nym
epo+nyms
epony+mous
epony+mous+ly
epony+my
epoxy
epoxies
Ep+ping
ep+si+lon
ep+si+lons
Ep+som
Epstein
eq+uabil+ity
eq+uable
eq+uable+ness
equal
equals
equals
equal+ling or
equal+ing
U.S.
equalled or
equaled
U.S.
equali+sa+tion
equali+sa+tions
equal+ise
equal+ises
equal+is+ing

equal+ised
equali+tar+ian
equali+tar+ians
equali+tari+an+ism
equali+tari+an+isms
equali+ty
equali+ties
equali+za+tion
equali+za+tions
equal+ize
equal+izes
equal+iz+ing
equal+ized
equal+ly
equa+nim+ity
equani+mous
equat+abil+ity
equat+able
equate
equates
equat+ing
equat+ed
equa+tion
equa+tions
equa+tion+al
equa+tion+al+ly
equa+tor
equa+tors
equa+to+rial
eq+uer+ry
eq+uer+ries
eques+trian
eques+trians
eques+tri+an+ism
equi+an+gu+lar
equi+dis+tance
equi+dis+tant
equi+dis+tant+ly
equi+lat+eral
equi+lat+erals
equili+brant
equili+brants
equili+brate
equili+brates
equili+brat+ing
equili+brat+ed
equi+li+bra+tion
equili+brist
equili+brists
equili+bris+tic
equi+lib+rium

equi+lib+riums	equivo+ca+tor	Ere+tria	ero+genei+ty
or	equivo+ca+tors	erf	ero+gen+ic
equi+lib+ria	equivo+ca+tory	er+ven	erog+enous
equine	er	Erf	Eros
equi+noc+tial	era	Er+furt	ero+sion
equi+noc+tials	eras	erg	ero+sions
equi+nox	eradi+cable	energy unit	ero+sion+al
equi+noxes	eradi+cate	ergs	ero+sive
equip	eradi+cates	erg	erot+ic
equips	eradi+cat+ing	sand dune	eroti+ca
equip+ping	eradi+cat+ed	ergs or	eroti+cal+ly
equipped	eradi+ca+tion	areg	eroti+cism
equi+page	eradi+ca+tions	ergo	ero+tism
equi+pages	eradi+ca+tive	er+go+nom+ic	ero+to+gen+ic
equip+ment	eras+able	er+go+nom+ics	err
equi+poise	erase	er+gono+mist	errs
equi+poises	erases	er+gono+mists	err+ing
equi+pol+lence	eras+ing	er+gos+terol	erred
equi+pol+len+cy	erased	er+got	er+ran+cy
equi+pol+lent	eras+er	er+got+ism	er+ran+cies
equip+per	eras+ers	Erhard	er+rand
equip+pers	Erasmus	eri+ca	er+rands
equi+setum	eras+ure	eri+ca+ceous	er+rant
equi+setums	eras+ures	Ericson	er+rant+ry
or	Erato	Ericsson	er+rant+ries
equi+seta	Er+bil	Erie	er+rat+ic
equi+table	er+bium	Eries or	er+rat+ics
equi+table+ness	ere	Erie	er+rati+cal+ly
equi+ta+tion	Er+ebus	erig+er+on	er+ra+tum
equi+ta+tions	volcano	erig+er+ons	er+ra+ta
equi+ty	Erebus	Erin	er+ro+neous
equi+ties	name	Erin+ys	er+ro+neous+
Equi+ty	Erech+thei+on	Eris	ness
equiva+lence	Erech+theum	Eri+trea	er+ror
equi+va+lence	Erechtheus	Eri+trean	er+rors
chemistry	erect	Eri+treans	error-free
equiva+len+cy	erects	erk	er+satz
equi+va+len+cy	erect+ing	erks	Erse
chemistry	erect+ed	Er+lan+gen	erst
equi+va+lent	erect+able	Erlanger	erst+while
chemistry	erect+er	er+mine	Erté
equiva+lent	erect+ers	er+mines or	eruct
equiva+lents	erec+tile	er+mine	eructs
equiva+lent+ly	erec+til+ity	ern	eruct+ing
equivo+cal	erec+tion	erns	eruct+ed
equivo+cal+ity	erec+tions	erne	eruc+tate
equivo+cal+ness	erect+ness	ernes	eruc+tates
equivo+cate	erec+tor	Erne	eruc+tat+ing
equivo+cates	erec+tors	Er+nie	eruc+tat+ed
equivo+cat+ing	er+emite	Ernst	eruc+ta+tion
equivo+cat+ed	er+emites	erode	eruc+ta+tions
equivo+cat+ing+	er+emit+ic	erodes	eru+dite
ly	er+emit+ism	erod+ing	eru+dite+ness
equivo+ca+tion	erep+sin	erod+ed	eru+di+tion
equivo+ca+tions	er+ethism	erod+ible	erupt

erupts
erupt+ing
erupt+ed
erup+tion
erup+tions
erup+tive
Ery+man+thus
ery+sip+elas
eryth+ro+cyte
eryth+ro+cytes
eryth+ro+cyt+ic
eryth+ro+my+cin
eryth+ro+poi+
esis
eryth+ro+poi+et+
ic
Erz+ge+bir+ge
Er+zu+rum
Esau
Es+bjerg
es+ca+drille
es+ca+drilles
es+ca+lade
es+ca+lades
es+ca+lades
es+ca+lad+ing
es+ca+lad+ed
es+ca+late
es+ca+lates
es+ca+lat+ing
es+ca+lat+ed
es+ca+la+tion
es+ca+la+tions
es+ca+la+tor
es+ca+la+tors
es+cal+lop
es+cal+lops
es+ca+lope
es+ca+lopes
es+cap+able
es+ca+pade
es+ca+pades
es+cape
es+capes
es+capes
es+cap+ing
es+caped
es+capee
es+capees
es+cap+er
es+cap+ers
es+cap+ism
es+cap+ist
es+cap+ists
es+ca+polo+gist

es+ca+polo+
gists
es+ca+pol+ogy
es+car+got
es+car+gots
es+carp+ment
es+carp+ments
Es+caut
es+cha+to+logi+
cal
es+cha+tolo+gist
es+cha+tolo+
gists
es+cha+tol+ogy
es+cheat
es+cheats
es+cheat+able
es+cheat+age
Esche+rich+ia
es+chew
es+chews
es+chew+ing
es+chewed
es+chew+al
es+chew+er
es+chew+ers
esch+schol+tzia
esch+schol+
tzias
esch+schol+zia
esch+schol+zias
Escoffier
Es+co+rial
es+cort
es+corts
es+corts
es+cort+ing
es+cort+ed
es+cri+toire
es+cri+toires
es+crow
es+crows
es+cu+do
es+cu+dos
es+cu+lent
Es+cu+rial
es+cutch+eon
es+cutch+eons
es+cutch+eoned
Es+dra+elon
Esher
es+kar
es+kars
es+ker
es+kers

Eskils+tu+na
Es+ki+mo
Es+ki+mos or
Es+ki+mo
Es+ki+şehir
Esky
Trademark
Eskies
esopha+gus
U.S.
esopha+guses
or
esopha+gi
eso+ter+ic
eso+teri+cal+ly
eso+teri+cism
eso+teri+cisms
es+pa+drille
es+pa+drilles
es+pal+ier
es+pal+iers
es+pal+iers
es+pal+ier+ing
es+pal+iered
es+par+to
es+par+tos
es+pe+cial
es+pe+cial+ly
Es+pe+ran+tist
Es+pe+ran+tists
Es+pe+ran+to
es+pial
es+pials
es+pi+er
es+pi+ers
es+pio+nage
Es+pí+ri+to San+
to
Es+pí+ri+tu San+
to
es+pla+nade
es+pla+nades
Es+poo
es+pous+al
es+pous+als
es+pouse
es+pouses
es+pous+ing
es+poused
es+pous+er
es+pous+ers
es+pres+si+vo
es+pres+so
es+pres+sos
es+prit

es+prit de corps
espy
espies
espy+ing
espied
Es+qui+line
Es+qui+mau
Es+qui+maus
or
Es+qui+mau
es+quire
es+quires
Es+sa+oui+ra
es+say
es+says
es+says
es+say+ing
es+sayed
es+say+ist
es+say+ists
Es+sen
es+sence
es+sences
Es+sene
Es+senes
Es+se+nian
Es+sen+ic
es+sen+tial
es+sen+tials
es+sen+tial+ism
es+sen+tial+ist
es+sen+tial+ists
es+sen+tial+ity
es+sen+tial+ly
es+sen+tial+ness
Es+sequi+bo
Es+sex
place name
Essex
surname
Ess+ling+en
Es+sonne
est
es+tab+lish
es+tab+lishes
es+tab+lish+ing
es+tab+lished
es+tab+lish+er
es+tab+lish+ers
es+tab+lish+
ment
es+tab+lish+
ments
es+tate
es+tates

Este
es+teem
 es+teems
 es+teem+ing
 es+teemed
es+ter
 es+ters
Esterházy
Esther
es+thesia
U.S.
es+thete
U.S.
 es+thetes
Es+tho+nia
es+ti+mable
es+ti+mable+
 ness
es+ti+mably
es+ti+mate
 es+ti+mates
 es+ti+mates
 es+ti+mat+ing
 es+ti+mat+ed
es+ti+ma+tion
 es+ti+ma+tions
es+ti+ma+tive
es+ti+ma+tor
 es+ti+ma+tors
es+ti+val
U.S.
es+ti+vate
U.S.
 es+ti+vates
 es+ti+vat+ing
 es+ti+vat+ed
Es+to+nia
Es+to+nian
 Es+to+nians
es+top
 es+tops
 es+top+ping
 es+topped
es+top+page
es+top+pel
Esto+ril
es+to+vers
es+tra+di+ol
U.S.
es+trange
 es+tranges
 es+trang+ing
 es+tranged
 es+tranged
 es+trange+ment

es+trange+
 ments
Es+tre+ma+du+
 ra
es+tro+gen
U.S.
es+trus
U.S.
es+tu+ar+ial
es+tua+rine
es+tu+ary
 es+tu+aries
eta
Greek letter
eta
outcast
 eta *or*
 etas
eta+lon
 eta+lons
et+cet+era
et cet+era
et+cet+eras
etch
 etches
etch+ing
etched
etch+er
 etch+ers
etch+ing
 etch+ings
Eteocles
eter+nal
eter+nali+sa+tion
eter+nal+ise
 eter+nal+ises
 eter+nal+is+ing
 eter+nal+ised
eter+nal+ity
eter+nali+za+tion
eter+nal+ize
 eter+nal+izes
 eter+nal+iz+ing
 eter+nal+ized
eter+nal+ly
eter+nal+ness
eter+ni+sa+tion
eter+nise
 eter+nises
 eter+nis+ing
 eter+nised
eter+nity
 eter+nities
eter+ni+za+tion
eter+nize

eter+nizes
eter+niz+ing
eter+nized
ete+sian
eth
eths
etha+nal
ethane
ethane+di+ol
etha+nol
Ethelbert
Ethelwulf
eth+ene
ether
ethe+real
ethe+reali+sa+
 tion
ethe+real+ise
 ethe+real+ises
 ethe+real+is+ing
 ethe+real+ised
ethe+real+ity
ethe+reali+za+
 tion
ethe+real+ize
 ethe+real+izes
 ethe+real+iz+ing
 ethe+real+ized
ethe+real+ness
ether+ic
etheri+sa+tion
etheri+sa+tions
ether+is+er
 ether+is+ers
etheri+za+tion
etheri+za+tions
ether+iz+er
 ether+iz+ers
Ether+net
Trademark
eth+ic
 eth+ics
ethi+cal
ethi+cali+ty
ethi+cal+ly
ethi+cal+ness
ethi+cist
 ethi+cists
eth+ics
eth+nic
Ethio+pia
Ethio+pian
 Ethio+pians
Ethio+pic
eth+nic
 eth+nics

eth+ni+cal
eth+ni+cal+ly
eth+nic+ity
eth+no+cen+tric
eth+no+cen+tri+
 cal+ly
eth+no+cen+tric+
 ity
eth+no+cen+
 trism
eth+nog+ra+pher
eth+nog+ra+
 phers
eth+no+graph+ic
eth+no+graphi+
 cal
eth+nog+ra+phy
eth+no+log+ic
eth+no+logi+cal
eth+nolo+gist
 eth+nolo+gists
eth+nol+ogy
eth+no+mu+si+
 col+ogy
etho+logi+cal
etholo+gist
 etholo+gists
ethol+ogy
ethos
eth+oxy+ethane
ethyl
eth+yl+ene
eth+yl+enic
ethyl+ic
ethyne
etio+late
 etio+lates
 etio+lat+ing
 etio+lat+ed
etio+la+tion
eti+ol+ogy
eti+quette
 eti+quettes
Etna
Eton
Eto+nian
 Eto+nians
Etru+ria
Etru+rian
 Etru+rians
Etrus+can
 Etrus+cans
étude
 études
ety+mo+logi+cal

ety+molo+gise
ety+molo+gises
ety+molo+gis+
  ing
ety+molo+gised
ety+molo+gist
ety+molo+gists
ety+molo+gize
ety+molo+gizes
ety+molo+giz+
  ing
ety+molo+gized
ety+mol+ogy
ety+mol+ogies
ety+mon
ety+mons *or*
ety+ma
Etzel
Euboea
Euboean
euca+lypt
euca+lypts
euca+lyp+tus
euca+lyp+tuses
  or
euca+lyp+ti
eu+cary+ote
eu+cary+otes
Eucha+rist
  Eucha+rists
Eucha+ris+tic
Eucha+ris+ti+cal
euchre
  euchres
  euchring
  euchred
Euclid
Euclid+ean
Euclid+ian
eu+cry+phia
eu+cry+phias
eudi+om+eter
eudi+om+eters
Eugène
eugen+ic
eugeni+cal+ly
eugeni+cist
  eugeni+cists
eugen+ics
Eugénie
eu+kary+ote
eu+kary+otes
eu+kary+ot+ic
Euler
Euler-Chelpin

eulo+gise
eulo+gises
eulo+gis+ing
eulo+gised
eulo+gis+er
eulo+gis+ers
eulo+gist
eulo+gists
eulo+gis+tic
eulo+gis+ti+cal
eulo+gium
eulo+giums *or*
eulo+gia
eulo+gize
eulo+gizes
eulo+giz+ing
eulo+gized
eulo+giz+er
eulo+giz+ers
eulogy
  eulogies
Eumeni+des
eunuch
  eunuchs
euony+mus
  euony+muses
eupep+sia
eupep+sy
eupep+tic
euphemise
  euphemises
  euphemis+ing
  euphemised
euphemis+er
euphemis+ers
euphemism
  euphemisms
euphemis+tic
euphemis+ti+cal+
  ly
euphemize
  euphemizes
  euphemiz+ing
  euphemized
euphemiz+er
euphemiz+ers
euphon+ic
euphoni+cal+ly
eupho+ni+ous
eupho+ni+ous+ly
eu+pho+ni+ous+
  ness
eupho+nise
  eupho+nises
  eupho+nis+ing

eupho+nised
eupho+nium
  eupho+niums
eupho+nize
  eupho+nizes
  eupho+niz+ing
  eupho+nized
eupho+ny
  eupho+nies
euphor+bia
  euphor+bias
eupho+ria
eupho+ri+ant
eupho+ri+ants
euphor+ic
eupho+tic
euphra+sy
  euphra+sies
Euphra+tes
Euphrosyne
euphuism
  euphuisms
euphu+ist
  euphu+ists
euphu+is+tic
euphu+is+ti+cal
Eura+sia
Eura+sian
  Eura+sians
Eure
Eure-et-Loir
eureka
eurhyth+mic
eurhyth+mi+cal
eurhyth+mics
eurhyth+my
Euripides
euro+bond
  euro+bonds
euro+cheque
  euro+cheques
Euro+com+mun+
  ism
Euro+com+mun+
  ist
Euro+com+mun+
  ists
euro+crat
  euro+crats
euro+cur+ren+cy
euro+cur+ren+
  cies
euro+dol+lar
  euro+dol+lars
euro+mar+ket

euro+mar+kets
Europa
  Greek myth
Eu+ro+pa
  satellite
Europe
Euro+pean
  Euro+peans
Euro+peani+sa+
  tion
Euro+pean+ise
Euro+pean+ises
Euro+pean+is+
  ing
Euro+pean+ised
Euro+peani+za+
  tion
Euro+pean+ize
Euro+pean+izes
Euro+pean+iz+
  ing
Euro+pean+ized
euro+pium
Euro+poort
Euro+tun+nel
Eurus
Euryale
Eurydice
Eurystheus
euryth+mic
  U.S.
euryth+mi+cal
  U.S.
euryth+mics
  U.S.
euryth+my
  U.S.
Eusebio
Eusebius
Eusta+chian
eustat+ic
eutec+tic
  eutec+tics
Euterpe
Euter+pean
eutha+na+sia
euthen+ics
euthen+ist
  euthen+ists
eutroph+ic
eutrophy
evacu+ate
  evacu+ates
evacu+at+ing
evacu+at+ed

evacu+ation
evacu+ations
evacu+ative
evacu+ator
evacu+ators
evac+uee
evac+uees
evad+able
evade
evades
evad+ing
evad+ed
evad+er
evad+ers
evalu+ate
evalu+ates
evalu+at+ing
evalu+at+ed
evalu+ation
evalu+ations
evalu+ative
evalu+ator
evalu+ators
eva+nesce
eva+nesces
eva+nesc+ing
eva+nesced
eva+nes+cence
eva+nes+cent
evan+gel
evan+gels
evan+geli+cal
evan+geli+cals
evan+geli+cal+ism
evan+geli+cal+ly
evan+geli+sa+tion
evan+gelise
evan+gelises
evan+gelis+ing
evan+gelised
evan+gelis+er
evan+gelis+ers
evan+gelism
evan+gelist
evan+gelists
evan+gelis+tic
evan+geli+za+tion
evan+gelize
evan+gelizes
evan+geliz+ing
evan+gelized
evan+geliz+er

evan+geliz+ers
Evans
Ev+ans+ton
Ev+ans+ville
evapo+rable
evapo+rate
evapo+rates
evapo+rat+ing
evapo+rat+ed
evapo+ra+tion
evapo+ra+tions
evapo+ra+tive
evapo+ra+tor
evapo+ra+tors
eva+sion
eva+sions
eva+sive
eva+sive+ly
eva+sive+ness
eve
eves
Eve
Evelyn
even
evens
even+er
even+ers
even-handed
even-handed+ly
even-handed+ness
eve+ning
eve+nings
even+ly
even+ness
evens
even+song
even+songs
event
events
even-tempered
event+ful
event+ful+ly
event+ful+ness
even+tide
event+ing
even+tual
even+tu+al+ity
even+tu+al+ities
even+tu+al+ly
even+tu+ate
even+tu+ates
even+tu+at+ing
even+tu+at+ed
even+tua+tion

even+tua+tions
ever
Ev+er+est
Ever+glades
ever+green
ever+greens
ever+lasting
ever+lasting+ly
ever+more
evert
everts
evert+ing
evert+ed
Evert
every
every+body
every+day
Every+man
every+one
every+thing
every+where
Eve+sham
evict
evicts
evict+ing
evict+ed
evic+tion
evic+tions
evic+tor
evic+tors
evi+dence
evi+dences
evi+denc+ing
evi+denced
evi+dent
evi+den+tial
evi+den+tial+ly
evi+dent+ly
evil
evils
evil+doer
evil+doers
evil+doing
evil+doings
evil-eyed
evil+ly
evil-minded
evil-minded+ly
evil-minded+ness
evil+ness
evince
evinces
evinc+ing
evinced
evin+cible

evis+cer+ate
evis+cer+ates
evis+cer+at+ing
evis+cer+at+ed
evis+cera+tion
evis+cera+tions
evis+cera+tor
evis+cera+tors
evo+cable
evo+ca+tion
evo+ca+tions
evoca+tive
evoke
evokes
evok+ing
evoked
evok+er
evok+ers
evo+lute
evo+lutes
evo+lu+tion
evo+lu+tions
evo+lu+tion+al
evo+lu+tion+ary
evo+lu+tion+ism
evo+lu+tion+ist
evo+lu+tion+ists
evo+lu+tion+is+tic
evolv+able
evolve
evolves
evolv+ing
evolved
evolve+ment
evony+mus
evony+muses
Évo+ra
Évreux
Év+ros
Év+voia
ev+zone
ev+zones
ewe
ewes
ewer
ewers
ex
exes
ex+ac+er+bate
ex+ac+er+bates
ex+ac+er+bat+ing
ex+ac+er+bat+ed

ex+ac+er+ba+
  tion
ex+act
  ex+acts
  ex+act+ing
  ex+act+ed
  ex+act+able
  ex+act+er
  ex+act+ers
  ex+act+ing
  ex+act+ing+ness
  ex+ac+tion
  ex+ac+tions
  ex+acti+tude
  ex+act+ly
  ex+act+ness
  ex+ac+tor
  ex+ac+tors
exa+cum
  exa+cums
ex+ag+ger+ate
  ex+ag+ger+ates
  ex+ag+ger+at+
    ing
  ex+ag+ger+at+
    ed
  ex+ag+gera+tion
  ex+ag+gera+
    tions
  ex+ag+gera+tor
  ex+ag+gera+
    tors
ex+alt
  ex+alts
  ex+alt+ing
  ex+alt+ed
  ex+al+ta+tion
  ex+al+ta+tions
  ex+alt+er
  ex+alt+ers
exam
  exams
ex+am+in+able
ex+ami+na+tion
  ex+ami+na+
    tions
ex+ami+na+tion+
  al
ex+am+ine
  ex+am+ines
  ex+am+in+ing
  ex+am+ined
  ex+ami+nee
  ex+ami+nees
  ex+am+in+er

ex+am+in+ers
ex+am+in+ing
ex+am+ple
  ex+am+ples
ex+an+thema
ex+an+thema+
  ta *or*
ex+an+themas
ex+as+per+ate
  ex+as+per+ates
  ex+as+per+at+
    ing
  ex+as+per+at+
    ed
  ex+as+per+at+ed+
    ly
  ex+as+per+at+
    ing+ly
  ex+as+pera+tion
ex ca+thedra
ex+ca+vate
  ex+ca+vates
  ex+ca+vat+ing
  ex+ca+vat+ed
  ex+ca+va+tion
  ex+ca+va+tions
  ex+ca+va+tor
  ex+ca+va+tors
ex+ceed
  ex+ceeds
  ex+ceed+ing
  ex+ceed+ed
  ex+ceed+able
  ex+ceed+er
  ex+ceed+ers
  ex+ceed+ing+ly
ex+cel
  ex+cels
  ex+cel+ling
  ex+celled
  ex+cel+lence
  ex+cel+lences
  Ex+cel+lence
  Ex+cel+lences
  Ex+cel+len+cy
  Ex+cel+len+cies
  ex+cel+lent
  ex+cel+lent+ly
  ex+cel+si+or
ex+cept
  ex+cept+ing
  ex+cep+tion
  ex+cep+tions
  ex+cep+tion+
    able

ex+cep+tion+
  able+ness
ex+cep+tion+
  ably
ex+cep+tion+al
ex+cerpt
  ex+cerpts
  ex+cerpt+ible
  ex+cerp+tion
  ex+cerp+tions
  ex+cerp+tor
  ex+cerp+tors
ex+cess
  ex+cesses
  ex+ces+sive
  ex+ces+sive+ly
  ex+ces+sive+
    ness
ex+change
  ex+changes
  ex+changes
  ex+chang+ing
  ex+changed
  ex+change+abil+
    ity
  ex+change+able
  ex+change+ably
  ex+chang+er
  ex+chang+ers
ex+cheq+uer
  ex+cheq+uers
ex+cis+able
ex+cise
  ex+cises
  ex+cis+ing
  ex+cised
  ex+cise+man
  ex+cise+men
ex+ci+sion
  ex+ci+sions
ex+cit+abil+ity
ex+cit+able
ex+cit+able+ness
ex+cit+ant
  ex+cit+ants
ex+ci+ta+tion
  ex+ci+ta+tions
  ex+cita+tive
  ex+cita+tory
ex+cite
  ex+cites
  ex+cit+ing
  ex+cit+ed
  ex+cit+ed+ness
  ex+cite+ment

ex+cite+ments
ex+cit+er
ex+cit+ers
ex+cit+ing+ly
ex+ci+tor
ex+ci+tors
ex+claim
  ex+claims
  ex+claim+ing
  ex+claimed
  ex+claim+er
  ex+claim+ers
  ex+cla+ma+tion
  ex+cla+ma+
    tions
  ex+cla+ma+tion+
    al
  ex+clama+tory
ex+clave
  ex+claves
ex+clo+sure
  ex+clo+sures
ex+clud+able
ex+clude
  ex+cludes
  ex+clud+ing
  ex+clud+ed
  ex+clud+er
  ex+clud+ers
  ex+clud+ible
  ex+clu+sion
  ex+clu+sions
  ex+clu+sion+ary
  ex+clu+sive
  ex+clu+sives
  ex+clu+sive+ly
  ex+clu+sive+
    ness
  ex+clu+sivi+ty
ex+com+muni+
  cate
ex+com+muni+
  cates
ex+com+muni+
  cates
ex+com+muni+
  cat+ing
ex+com+muni+
  cat+ed
ex+com+mu+ni+
  ca+tion
ex+com+mu+ni+
  ca+tions
ex+com+mu+ni+
  ca+tor

ex+com+mu+ni+
 ca+tors
ex+co+ri+ate
 ex+co+ri+ates
 ex+co+ri+at+ing
 ex+co+ri+at+ed
ex+co+ria+tion
 ex+co+ria+tions
ex+cre+ment
ex+cre+men+tal
ex+cre+men+ti+
 tious
ex+cres+cence
 ex+cres+cences
ex+cres+cent
ex+cres+cen+tial
ex+cre+ta
ex+cre+tal
ex+crete
 ex+cretes
 ex+cret+ing
 ex+cret+ed
 ex+cret+er
 ex+cret+ers
ex+cre+tion
ex+cre+tive
ex+cre+tory
ex+cru+ci+at+ing
ex+cul+pate
 ex+cul+pates
 ex+cul+pat+ing
 ex+cul+pat+ed
ex+cul+pa+tion
 ex+cul+pa+tions
ex+cul+pa+tory
ex+cur+sion
 ex+cur+sions
ex+cur+sion+ist
 ex+cur+sion+
 ists
ex+cur+sive
ex+cur+sive+ly
ex+cur+sive+
 ness
ex+cus+able
ex+cus+able+
 ness
ex+cus+ably
ex+cuse
 ex+cuses
 ex+cuses
 ex+cus+ing
 ex+cused
excuse-me
 excuse-mes

ex-directory
ex divi+dend
ex+eat
 ex+eats
ex+ecrable
ex+ecrable+ness
ex+ecrably
ex+ecrate
 ex+ecrates
 ex+ecrat+ing
 ex+ecrat+ed
ex+ecra+tion
 ex+ecra+tions
ex+ecra+tive
ex+ecra+tory
ex+ecut+able
ex+ecu+tant
 ex+ecu+tants
ex+ecute
 ex+ecutes
 ex+ecut+ing
 ex+ecut+ed
 ex+ecut+er
 ex+ecut+ers
ex+ecu+tion
 ex+ecu+tions
ex+ecu+tion+er
 ex+ecu+tion+
 ers
ex+ecu+tive
 ex+ecu+tives
ex+ecu+tor
 ex+ecu+tors
ex+ecu+tor+ship
 ex+ecu+tor+
 ships
ex+ecu+tory
ex+ecu+trix
 ex+ecu+tri+ces
 or
 ex+ecu+trixes
ex+egesis
 ex+egeses
ex+egete
 ex+egetes
ex+eget+ic
ex+egetist
 ex+egetists
ex+em+plar
 ex+em+plars
ex+em+pla+ri+ly
ex+em+pla+ri+
 ness
ex+em+pla+ry

ex+em+pli+fi+
 able
ex+em+pli+fi+ca+
 tion
ex+em+pli+fi+ca+
 tions
ex+em+pli+fi+ca+
 tive
ex+em+pli+fi+er
ex+em+pli+fi+
 ers
ex+em+pli+fy
 ex+em+pli+fies
ex+em+pli+fy+
 ing
ex+em+pli+fied
ex+empt
 ex+empts
 ex+empts
 ex+empt+ing
 ex+empt+ed
ex+emp+tion
 ex+emp+tions
ex+equies
ex+er+cis+able
ex+er+cise
 ex+er+cises
 ex+er+cises
 ex+er+cis+ing
 ex+er+cised
ex+er+cis+er
 ex+er+cis+ers
ex+ert
 ex+erts
ex+ert+ing
ex+ert+ed
ex+er+tion
 ex+er+tions
ex+er+tive
Ex+eter
ex+eunt
exe+unt om+nes
ex+fo+li+ate
 ex+fo+li+ates
 ex+fo+li+at+ing
 ex+fo+li+at+ed
ex+fo+lia+tion
ex+fo+lia+tive
ex gra+tia
ex+hal+able
ex+ha+la+tion
 ex+ha+la+tions
ex+hale
 ex+hales
 ex+hal+ing

ex+haled
ex+haust
 ex+hausts
 ex+hausts
 ex+haust+ing
 ex+haust+ed
ex+haust+ible
 ex+haust+ing
ex+haus+tion
ex+haus+tive
ex+haust+ive+ly
ex+haust+ive+
 ness
ex+hib+it
 ex+hib+its
 ex+hib+its
 ex+hib+it+ing
 ex+hib+it+ed
ex+hi+bi+tion
 ex+hi+bi+tions
ex+hi+bi+tion+er
 ex+hi+bi+tion+
 ers
ex+hi+bi+tion+
 ism
ex+hi+bi+tion+ist
 ex+hi+bi+tion+
 ists
ex+hi+bi+tion+is+
 tic
ex+hibi+tive
ex+hibi+tor
 ex+hibi+tors
ex+hibi+tory
ex+hila+rate
 ex+hila+rates
 ex+hila+rat+ing
 ex+hila+rat+ed
ex+hila+rat+ing
ex+hila+ra+tion
ex+hila+ra+tive
ex+hort
 ex+horts
 ex+hort+ing
 ex+hort+ed
ex+hor+ta+tion
 ex+hor+ta+tions
ex+hor+ta+tive
ex+hor+ta+tory
ex+hort+er
 ex+hort+ers
ex+hu+ma+tion
 ex+hu+ma+
 tions
ex+hume

ex+humes
ex+hum+ing
ex+humed
ex+hum+er
ex+hum+ers
ex hy+poth+esi
exi+gence
exi+gences
exi+gen+cy
exi+gen+cies
exi+gent
exi+gu+ity
ex+igu+ous
ex+igu+ous+ness
ex+ile
ex+iles
ex+iles
ex+il+ing
ex+iled
ex+il+ian
ex+il+ic
ex+ist
ex+ists
ex+ist+ing
ex+ist+ed
ex+ist+ence
ex+ist+ences
ex+ist+ent
ex+is+ten+tial
ex+is+ten+tial+
ism
ex+is+ten+tial+
ist
ex+is+ten+tial+
ists
exit
exits
exits
exit+ing
exit+ed
exi+tance
ex-libris
ex-libris
ex li+bris
adj.
Ex+moor
Ex+mouth
ex new
exo+bi+olo+gist
exo+bi+olo+
gists
exo+bi+ol+ogy
exo+carp
exo+carps
exo+crine

exo+crines
exo+derm
exo+derms
exo+dus
exo+duses
Exo+dus
ex of+fi+cio
exo+gam+ic
ex+oga+mous
ex+oga+my
ex+og+enous
exon
exons
ex+on+er+ate
ex+on+er+ates
ex+on+er+at+
ing
ex+on+er+at+ed
ex+on+era+tion
ex+on+era+
tions
ex+on+era+tive
ex+on+era+tor
ex+on+era+tors
ex+oph+thal+mia
ex+oph+thal+mic
ex+oph+thal+
mos
ex+oph+thal+
mus
ex+or+bi+tance
ex+or+bi+tant
ex+or+bi+tant+ly
ex+or+cise
ex+or+cises
ex+or+cis+ing
ex+or+cised
ex+or+cis+er
ex+or+cis+ers
ex+or+cism
ex+or+cisms
ex+or+cist
ex+or+cists
ex+or+cize
ex+or+cizes
ex+or+ciz+ing
ex+or+cized
ex+or+ciz+er
ex+or+ciz+ers
ex+or+dial
ex+or+dium
ex+or+diums
or
exo+skel+etal

exo+skel+eton
exo+skel+etons
exo+sphere
exo+ther+mal
exo+ther+mal+ly
exo+ther+mic
ex+ot+ic
ex+ot+ics
ex+oti+ca
ex+oti+cal+ly
ex+oti+cism
ex+oti+cisms
ex+ot+ic+ness
ex+pand
ex+pands
ex+pand+ing
ex+pand+ed
ex+pand+able
ex+pand+ed
ex+pand+er
ex+pand+ers
ex+panse
ex+panses
ex+pan+sibil+ity
ex+pan+sible
ex+pan+sion
ex+pan+sions
ex+pan+sion+ary
ex+pan+sion+ism
ex+pan+sion+ist
ex+pan+sion+
ists
ex+pan+sion+is+
tic
ex+pan+sive
ex+pan+sive+
ness
ex+pan+siv+ity
ex par+te
ex+pat
ex+pats
ex+pa+ti+ate
ex+pa+ti+ates
ex+pa+ti+at+ing
ex+pa+ti+at+ed
ex+pa+tia+tion
ex+pa+tia+tions
ex+pa+tia+tor
ex+pa+tia+tors
ex+pat+ri+ate
ex+pat+ri+ates
ex+pat+ri+ates
ex+pat+ri+at+
ing
ex+pat+ri+at+ed

ex+pat+ria+tion
ex+pect
ex+pects
ex+pect+ing
ex+pect+ed
ex+pect+able
ex+pec+tance
ex+pec+tances
ex+pec+tan+cy
ex+pec+tan+
cies
ex+pec+tant
ex+pec+tants
ex+pect+ant+ly
ex+pec+ta+tion
ex+pec+ta+
tions
ex+pec+to+rant
ex+pec+to+
rants
ex+pec+to+rate
ex+pec+to+
rates
ex+pec+to+rat+
ing
ex+pec+to+rat+
ed
ex+pec+to+ra+
tion
ex+pec+to+ra+
tions
ex+pec+to+ra+
tor
ex+pec+to+ra+
tors
ex+pedi+ence
ex+pedi+ences
ex+pedi+en+cy
ex+pedi+en+
cies
ex+pedi+ent
ex+pedi+ents
ex+pedite
ex+pedites
ex+pedit+ing
ex+pedit+ed
ex+pedit+er
ex+pedit+ers
ex+pedi+tion
ex+pedi+tions
ex+pedi+tion+ary
ex+pedi+tious
ex+pedi+tious+ly
ex+pedi+tious+
ness

ex+pedi+tor
ex+pedi+tors
ex+pel
ex+pels
ex+pel+ling
ex+pelled
ex+pel+lable
ex+pel+lant
ex+pel+lants
ex+pel+lent
ex+pel+lents
ex+pel+ler
ex+pel+lers
ex+pend
ex+pends
ex+pend+ing
ex+pend+ed
ex+pend+abil+ity
ex+pend+able
ex+pend+ables
ex+pend+er
ex+pend+ers
ex+pendi+ture
ex+pendi+tures
ex+pense
ex+penses
expense-account
adj.
ex+pense ac+
count
ex+pense ac+
counts
ex+pen+sive
ex+pen+sive+
ness
ex+peri+ence
ex+peri+ences
ex+peri+ences
ex+peri+enc+ing
ex+peri+enced
ex+peri+ence+
able
ex+peri+en+tial
ex+peri+ment
ex+peri+ments
ex+peri+ments
ex+peri+ment+
ing
ex+peri+ment+
ed
ex+peri+men+tal
ex+peri+men+tal+
ism
ex+peri+men+ta+
tion

ex+peri+men+ta+
tions
ex+peri+ment+er
ex+peri+ment+
ers
ex+pert
ex+perts
ex+per+tise
ex+pert+ly
ex+pert+ness
ex+pi+able
ex+pi+ate
ex+pi+ates
ex+pi+at+ing
ex+pi+at+ed
ex+pia+tion
ex+pia+tions
ex+pia+tor
ex+pia+tors
ex+pia+tory
ex+pi+ra+tion
ex+pi+ra+tions
ex+pire
ex+pires
ex+pir+ing
ex+pired
ex+pir+er
ex+pir+ers
ex+pi+ry
ex+pi+ries
ex+plain
ex+plains
ex+plain+ing
ex+plained
ex+plain+able
ex+plain+er
ex+plain+ers
ex+pla+na+tion
ex+pla+na+tions
ex+plana+tive
ex+plana+tory
ex+pletive
ex+pletives
ex+pli+cable
ex+pli+cate
ex+pli+cates
ex+pli+cat+ing
ex+pli+cat+ed
ex+pli+ca+tion
ex+pli+ca+tions
ex+plic+it
ex+plic+it+ly
ex+plic+it+ness
ex+plode
ex+plodes

ex+plod+ing
ex+plod+ed
ex+plod+er
ex+plod+ers
ex+ploit
ex+ploits
ex+ploits
ex+ploit+ing
ex+ploit+ed
ex+ploit+able
ex+ploi+ta+tion
ex+ploi+ta+
tions
ex+ploita+tive
ex+ploit+ive
ex+plo+ra+tion
ex+plo+ra+tions
ex+plora+tive
ex+plora+tory
ex+plore
ex+plores
ex+plor+ing
ex+plored
ex+plor+er
ex+plor+ers
ex+plo+sion
ex+plo+sions
ex+plo+sive
ex+plo+sives
ex+plo+sive+
ness
expo
expos
ex+po+nent
ex+po+nents
ex+po+nen+tial
ex+po+nen+tials
ex+port
ex+ports
ex+ports
ex+port+ing
ex+port+ed
ex+port+abil+ity
ex+port+able
ex+por+ta+tion
ex+por+ta+tions
ex+port+er
ex+port+ers
ex+pos+able
ex+pos+al
ex+pos+als
ex+pose
ex+poses
ex+pos+ing
ex+posed

ex+po+sé
ex+po+sés
ex+posed
ex+pos+er
ex+pos+ers
ex+po+si+tion
ex+po+si+tions
ex+po+si+tion+al
ex+posi+tive
ex+posi+tor
ex+posi+tors
ex+posi+tory
ex post fac+to
ex+pos+tu+late
ex+pos+tu+
lates
ex+pos+tu+lat+
ing
ex+pos+tu+lat+
ed
ex+pos+tu+la+
tion
ex+pos+tu+la+
tions
ex+pos+tu+la+
tor
ex+pos+tu+la+
tors
ex+po+sure
ex+po+sures
ex+pound
ex+pounds
ex+pound+ing
ex+pound+ed
ex+pound+er
ex+pound+ers
ex+press
ex+presses
ex+presses
ex+press+ing
ex+pressed
ex+press+er
ex+press+ers
ex+press+ible
ex+pres+sion
ex+pres+sions
ex+pres+sion+al
ex+pres+sion+
ism
ex+pres+sion+ist
ex+pres+sion+
ists
ex+pres+sion+is+
tic

ex+pres+sion+ less
ex+pres+sive
ex+pres+sive+ ness
ex+press+ly
ex+presso
ex+pressos
ex+press+way
ex+press+ways
ex+pro+pri+ate
ex+pro+pri+ates
ex+pro+pri+at+ ing
ex+pro+pri+at+ ed
ex+pro+pria+tion
ex+pro+pria+ tions
ex+pro+pria+tor
ex+pro+pria+ tors
ex+pul+sion
ex+pul+sions
ex+pul+sive
ex+punc+tion
ex+punc+tions
ex+punge
ex+punges
ex+pung+ing
ex+pung+ed
ex+pung+er
ex+pung+ers
ex+pur+gate
ex+pur+gates
ex+pur+gat+ing
ex+pur+gat+ed
ex+pur+ga+tion
ex+pur+ga+ tions
ex+pur+ga+tor
ex+pur+ga+tors
ex+quis+ite
ex+quis+ites
ex+quis+ite+ly
ex+quis+ite+ness
ex-service+man
ex-service+men
ex-service+ woman
ex-service+ women
ex+tant
ex+tem+po+ra+ neous

ex+tem+po+ra+ neous+ly
ex+tem+po+ra+ neous+ness
ex+tem+po+rari+ ly
ex+tem+po+rari+ ness
ex+tem+po+rary
ex+tem+po+re
ex+tem+po+ri+ sa+tion
ex+tem+po+rise
ex+tem+po+ rises
ex+tem+po+ris+ ing
ex+tem+po+ rised
ex+tem+po+ris+ er
ex+tem+po+ris+ ers
ex+tem+po+ri+za+ tion
ex+tem+po+rize
ex+tem+po+ rizes
ex+tem+po+riz+ ing
ex+tem+po+ rized
ex+tem+po+riz+ er
ex+tem+po+riz+ ers
ex+tend
ex+tends
ex+tend+ing
ex+tend+ed
ex+tend+abil+ity
ex+tend+able
ex+tended-play
ex+tend+er
ex+tend+ers
ex+tend+ibil+ity
ex+tend+ible
ex+ten+sibil+ity
ex+ten+sible
ex+ten+sible+ ness
ex+ten+sile
ex+ten+sion
ex+ten+sions
ex+ten+sion+al

ex+ten+sion+al+ ism
ex+ten+sion+al+ ity
ex+ten+sive
ex+ten+sive+ ness
ex+ten+sor
ex+ten+sors
ex+tent
ex+tents
ex+tenu+ate
ex+tenu+ates
ex+tenu+at+ing
ex+tenu+at+ed
ex+tenu+at+ing
ex+tenu+ation
ex+tenu+ations
ex+tenu+ator
ex+tenu+ators
ex+te+ri+or
ex+te+ri+ors
ex+te+ri+ori+sa+ tion
ex+te+ri+ori+sa+ tions
ex+te+ri+or+ise
ex+te+ri+or+ ises
ex+te+ri+or+is+ ing
ex+te+ri+or+ ised
ex+te+ri+ori+za+ tion
ex+te+ri+ori+za+ tions
ex+te+ri+or+ize
ex+te+ri+or+ izes
ex+te+ri+or+iz+ ing
ex+te+ri+or+ ized
ex+ter+mi+nable
ex+ter+mi+nate
ex+ter+mi+ nates
ex+ter+mi+nat+ ing
ex+ter+mi+nat+ ed
ex+ter+mi+na+ tion

ex+ter+mi+na+ tions
ex+ter+nal
ex+ter+nals
ex+ter+nali+sa+ tion
ex+ter+nal+ise
ex+ter+nal+ises
ex+ter+nal+is+ ing
ex+ter+nal+ised
ex+ter+nal+ity
ex+ter+nal+ities
ex+ter+nali+za+ tion
ex+ter+nal+ize
ex+ter+nal+izes
ex+ter+nal+iz+ ing
ex+ter+nal+ized
ex+ter+nal+ly
ex+ter+ri+to+rial
ex+tinct
ex+tinc+tion
ex+tinc+tions
ex+tin+guish
ex+tin+guishes
ex+tin+guish+ ing
ex+tin+guished
ex+tin+guish+ able
ex+tin+guish+er
ex+tin+guish+ ers
ex+tin+guish+ ment
ex+tir+pate
ex+tir+pates
ex+tir+pat+ing
ex+tir+pat+ed
ex+tir+pa+tion
ex+tir+pa+tions
ex+tir+pa+tor
ex+tir+pa+tors
ex+tol
ex+tols
ex+tol+ling
ex+tolled
ex+toll
U.S.
ex+tolls
ex+toll+ing
ex+tolled
ex+tol+ler

ex+tol+lers
ex+tort
ex+torts
ex+tort+ing
ex+tort+ed
ex+tort+er
ex+tort+ers
ex+tor+tion
ex+tor+tions
ex+tor+tion+ate
ex+tor+tion+ate+ly
ex+tor+tion+er
ex+tor+tion+ers
ex+tor+tion+ist
ex+tor+tion+ists
ex+tor+tive
ex+tra
ex+tras
ex+tract
ex+tracts
ex+tracts
ex+tract+ing
ex+tract+ed
ex+tract+abil+ity
ex+tract+able
ex+trac+tion
ex+trac+tions
ex+trac+tive
ex+trac+tor
ex+trac+tors
extra+cur+ricu+lar
extra+dit+able
extra+dite
extra+dites
extra+dit+ing
extra+dit+ed
extra+di+tion
extra+di+tions
extra+dos
extra+dos *or*
extra+doses
extra+du+ral
extra+ga+lac+tic
extra+mari+tal
extra+mu+ral
extra+neous
extraor+di+nari+ly
extraor+di+nari+ness

extraor+di+nary
ex+trapo+late
ex+trapo+lates
ex+trapo+lat+ing
ex+trapo+lat+ed
ex+trapo+la+tion
ex+trapo+la+tions
ex+trapo+la+tive
ex+trapo+la+tor
ex+trapo+la+tors
ex+trapo+la+tory
extra+sen+so+ry
extra+ter+ri+to+rial
ex+trava+gance
ex+trava+gances
ex+trava+gant
ex+trava+gan+za
ex+trava+gan+zas
extra+vehicu+lar
extra+ver+sion
extra+ver+sive
extra+vert
extra+verts
ex+treme
ex+tremes
ex+treme+ly
ex+treme+ness
ex+trem+ism
ex+trem+ist
ex+trem+ists
ex+trem+ity
ex+trem+ities
ex+tri+cable
ex+tri+cate
ex+tri+cates
ex+tri+cat+ing
ex+tri+cat+ed
ex+tri+ca+tion
ex+trin+sic
ex+trin+si+cal+ly
extro+ver+sion
extro+ver+sive
extro+vert
extro+verts

extro+vert+ed
ex+trude
ex+trudes
ex+trud+ing
ex+trud+ed
ex+tru+sion
ex+tru+sions
ex+tru+sive
exu+ber+ance
exu+ber+ances
exu+ber+ant
exu+ber+ate
exu+ber+ates
exu+ber+at+ing
exu+ber+at+ed
exu+da+tion
exu+da+tions
ex+ude
ex+udes
ex+ud+ing
ex+ud+ed
ex+ult
ex+ults
ex+ult+ing
ex+ult+ed
ex+ult+ant
ex+ult+ant+ly
ex+ul+ta+tion
ex+ul+ta+tions
ex+ult+ing+ly
ex+ur+ban
ex+ur+bia
exu+vi+ate
exu+vi+ates
exu+vi+at+ing
exu+vi+at+ed
exu+via+tion
Eyam
eyas
eyases
eye
eyes
eyes
ey+ing
eyed
eye+ball
eye+balls
eye+bank
eye+banks
eye+bath
eye+baths
eye+black

eye+bright
eye+brights
eye+brow
eye+brows
eye-catching
eye+cup
eye+cups
eyed
eye+ful
eye+fuls
eye+glass
eye+glasses
eye+glasses
eye+hole
eye+holes
eye+lash
eye+lashes
eye+less
eye+let
eye+lets
eye+lev+el
eye+lid
eye+lids
eye+like
eye+liner
eye+liners
eye-opener
eye-openers
eye+piece
eye+pieces
eye+shot
eye+sight
eye+sore
eye+sores
eye+spot
eye+spots
eye+strain
Eye+tie
Eye+ties
eye+tooth
eye+teeth
eye+wash
eye+witness
eye+witnesses
ey+rie
ey+ries
ey+rir
aurar
Eysenck
Ezekiel

F

f
  f's
f/
f:
F
  Fs *or*
  F's
fa
Fabergé
Fa+bian
Fa+bi+an+ism
Fabius Maximus
fa+ble
  fa+bles
  fa+bles
  fa+bling
  fa+bled
fa+bler
  fa+blers
fab+liau
  fab+liaux
Fab+lon
Trademark
Fabre
fab+ric
  fab+rics
fab+ri+cate
  fab+ri+cates
  fab+ri+cat+ing
  fab+ri+cat+ed
fab+ri+ca+tion
  fab+ri+ca+tions
fab+ri+ca+tor
  fab+ri+ca+tors
Fabry
fabu+list
  fabu+lists
fabu+lous
  fabu+lous+ly
  fabu+lous+ness
fa+cade
  fa+cades
fa+çade
  fa+çades
face

faces
faces
fac+ing
faced
face+less
face+less+ness
face-lift
face-lifts
face-off
face-offs
face off
verb
fac+er
  fac+ers
face-saver
  face-savers
face-saving
fac+et
  fac+ets
  fac+ets
  fac+et+ing *or*
  fac+et+ting
  fac+et+ed *or*
  fac+et+ted
fa+cetiae
fa+cetious
  fa+cetious+ly
  fa+cetious+ness
face-to-face
adj.
face to face
adv.
fa+cia
  fa+ciae
fa+cial
  fa+cials
fa+cies
  fa+cies
fac+ile
  fac+ile+ly
  fac+ile+ness
fa+cili+tate
  fa+cili+tates
  fa+cili+tat+ing
  fa+cili+tat+ed

fa+cili+ta+tion
fa+cili+ta+tive
fa+cil+ity
  fa+cil+ities
fac+ing
  fac+ings
fac+simi+le
  fac+simi+les
  fac+simi+les
  fac+simi+le+ing
  fac+simi+led
fact
  facts
fac+tion
  fac+tions
fac+tion+al
fac+tious
  fac+tious+ly
fac+ti+tious
  fac+ti+tious+ly
  fac+ti+tious+
  ness
fac+ti+tive
fac+toid
  fac+toids
fac+tor
  fac+tors
  fac+tors
  fac+tor+ing
  fac+tored
fac+tor+able
fac+torial
fac+to+ri+al+ly
fac+tori+sa+tion
  fac+tori+sa+
  tions
fac+tor+ise
  fac+tor+ises
  fac+tor+is+ing
  fac+tor+ised
fac+tori+za+tion
  fac+tori+za+
  tions
fac+tor+ize
  fac+tor+izes

  fac+tor+iz+ing
  fac+tor+ized
fac+tor+ship
fac+to+ry
  fac+to+ries
fac+to+tum
  fac+to+tums
fact+sheet
  fact+sheets
fac+tual
fac+tu+al+ity
fac+tu+al+ly
fac+tu+al+ness
facu+la
  facu+lae
facu+lar
fac+ul+ta+tive
  fac+ul+ta+tive+ly
fac+ul+ty
  fac+ul+ties
fad
  fads
Fadden
fad+dish
fad+dy
  fad+di+er
  fad+di+est
fade
  fades
  fad+ing
  fad+ed
  fad+ed+ness
fade-in
  fade-ins
fade in
verb
fade+less
fade-out
  fade-outs
fade out
verb
fad+er
  fad+ers
fae+cal
  fae+ces

Fa+en+za
fae+rie
 fae+ries
Fae+roes
Faero+ese
 Faero+ese
fae+ry
 fae+ries
Fae+su+lae
faff
 faffs
 faff+ing
 faffed
Fafnir
fag
 fags
 fags
 fag+ging
 fagged
fag+got
 fag+gots
 fag+gots
 fag+got+ing
 fag+got+ed
 fag+got+ing
fag+ot
U.S.
 fag+ots
 fag+ots
 fag+ot+ing
 fag+ot+ed
 fag+ot+ing
U.S.
fah
Fahd ibn Abdul
 Aziz
Fahr+en+heit
Fai+al
faï+ence
fail
 fails
 fails
 fail+ing
 failed
 fail+ing
 fail+ings
 fail-safe
 fail+ure
 fail+ures
fain
faint
 faints
 faint+ing
 faint+ed
 faint+er

faint+est
faint+ish
faint+ly
faint+ness
fair
 fairs
 fairs
 fair+ing
 faired
 fair+er
 fair+est
Fair+banks
 Fairbanks
 place name
Fairfax
 surname
fair+ground
 fair+grounds
fair+ing
 fair+ings
fair+ish
fair+ly
fair-minded
fair-minded+ness
fair+ness
fair-spoken
fair-spoken+ness
fair+way
 fair+ways
fair-weather
fairy
 fairies
fairy+floss
fairy+land
fairy-like
fairy-tale
 adj.
fairy tale
 noun
Faisal
 Fai+sal+abad
 Faisal Ibn Abdul
 Aziz
 fait ac+com+pli
 faits ac+com+
 plis
faith
 faiths
 faith+ful
 faith+ful+ly
 faith+ful+ness
 faith+less
 faith+less+ness
Fai+yûm
fake

fakes
fakes
fak+ing
faked
fak+er
fak+ers
fak+ery
fa+kir
 fa+kirs
Fa+lange
Fa+lan+gist
 Fa+lan+gists
fal+cate
fal+chion
 fal+chions
fal+ci+form
fal+con
 fal+cons
fal+con+er
 fal+con+ers
 fal+con+et
 fal+con+ets
 fal+con+ry
fal+deral
 fal+derals
Faldo
fald+stool
 fald+stools
Fa+lerii
Fal+kirk
Falkner
fall
 falls
 falls
 fall+ing
 fell
 fall+en
Falla
fal+la+cious
fal+la+cious+ly
fal+la+cy
 fal+la+cies
fall-back
 noun
fall back
 verb
fall+en
fal+libil+ity
fal+lible
fall-off
 noun
fall off
 verb
Fal+lo+pian
fall+out

noun
fall out
verb
fal+low
 fal+lows
 fal+low+ing
 fal+lowed
 fal+low+ness
Fal+mouth
false
 fal+ser
 fal+sest
false+hood
 false+hoods
false+ly
false+ness
fal+set+to
 fal+set+tos
fal+sies
fal+si+fi+able
fal+si+fi+ca+tion
 fal+si+fi+ca+
 tions
fal+si+fy
fal+si+fies
fal+si+fy+ing
fal+si+fied
fal+sity
 fal+sities
Fal+staff+ian
Fal+ster
fal+ter
 fal+ters
 fal+ter+ing
 fal+tered
 fal+ter+er
 fal+ter+ers
 fal+ter+ing+ly
Fa+lun
Fa+ma+gu+sta
fame
 fames
fam+ing
famed
fa+mil+ial
fa+mil+iar
fa+mil+iari+sa+
 tion
fa+mil+iar+ise
 fa+mil+iar+ises
 fa+mil+iar+is+
 ing
 fa+mil+iar+ised
fa+mili+ar+ity
fa+mili+ar+ities

fa+mil+iari+za+
tion
fa+mil+iar+ize
fa+mil+iar+izes
fa+mil+iar+iz+
ing
fa+mil+iar+ized
fa+mili+ar+ly
fa+mili+ar+ness
fa+mille
fami+ly
fami+lies
fam+ine
fam+ines
fam+ish
fam+ishes
fam+ish+ing
fam+ished
fam+ished
fa+mous
fa+mous+ly
fa+mous+ness
fan
fans
fans
fan+ning
fanned
Fana+ga+lo
Fana+ka+lo
fa+nat+ic
fa+nat+ics
fa+nati+cal
fa+nati+cal+ly
fa+nati+cism
fan+cied
fan+ci+er
fan+ci+ers
fan+ci+ful
fan+ci+ful+ly
fan+ci+ful+ness
fan+ci+ly
fan+ci+ness
fan+cy
fan+cies
fan+cies
fan+cy+ing
fan+cied
fan+ci+er
fan+ci+est
fancy-free
fancy+work
fan+dan+gle
fan+dan+gles
fan+dan+go
fan+dan+gos

fane
fanes
fan+fare
fan+fares
fang
fangs
fanged
Fangio
fang+less
fan+jet
fan+jets
fan+light
fan+lights
fan+like
fan+ner
fan+ners
fan+ny
fan+nies
fan+tail
fan+tails
fan-tailed
fan-tan
fan+ta+sia
fan+ta+sias
fan+ta+sise
fan+ta+sises
fan+ta+sis+ing
fan+ta+sised
fan+ta+size
fan+ta+sizes
fan+ta+siz+ing
fan+ta+sized
fan+tas+tic
fan+tas+ti+cal
fan+tas+ti+cal+
ity
fan+tas+ti+cal+ly
fan+tas+ti+cal+
ness
fan+ta+sy
fan+ta+sies
fan+ta+sies
fan+ta+sy+ing
fan+ta+sied
Fantin-Latour
fan+zine
fan+zines
far
far+ther or
fur+ther
far+thest or
fur+thest
far+ad
far+ads
fara+day

fara+days
Faraday
surname
fa+rad+ic
far+an+dole
far+an+doles
far+away
farce
farces
far+ci+cal
far+ci+cal+ity
far+ci+cal+ly
far+del
far+dels
fare
fares
fares
far+ing
fared
far+er
far+ers
fare+well
fare+wells
far-fetched
far-flung
Fargo
fa+ri+na
fari+na+ceous
farm
farms
farms
farm+ing
farmed
farm+able
farm+er
farm+ers
Farmer
farm+house
farm+houses
farm+ing
farm+stead
farm+steads
farm+yard
farm+yards
Farn+bor+ough
Farnese
far+ness
faro
Faroes
Faro+ese
Faro+ese
far-off
fa+rouche
far-out
Farquhar

far+ragi+nous
far+ra+go
far+ra+gos or
far+ra+goes
far-reaching
Farrell
far+ri+er
far+ri+ers
far+ri+ery
far+ri+eries
far+row
far+rows
far+rows
far+row+ing
far+rowed
far-seeing
Farsi
far-sighted
far-sighted+ly
far-sighted+ness
fart
farts
farts
fart+ing
fart+ed
far+ther
farther+most
far+thing
far+things
far+thin+gale
far+thin+gales
fas+ces
fas+cia
fas+ciae
fas+cial
fas+ci+ate
fas+ci+at+ed
fas+ci+cle
fas+ci+cles
fas+ci+cled
fas+cicu+lar
fas+cicu+late
fas+cicu+la+tion
fas+ci+cule
fas+ci+cules
fas+ci+cu+lus
fas+ci+cu+li
fas+ci+nate
fas+ci+nates
fas+ci+nat+ing
fas+ci+nat+ed
fas+ci+nat+ing
fas+ci+na+tion
fas+ci+na+tor
fas+ci+na+tors

fash+ion
  fash+ions
  fash+ions
  fash+ion+ing
  fash+ioned
fash+ion+able
fash+ion+able+
  ness
fash+ion+ably
fash+ion+er
  fash+ion+ers
Fassbinder
fast
  fasts
  fasts
  fast+ing
  fast+ed
  fast+er
  fast+est
fast+back
  fast+backs
fas+ten
  fas+tens
  fas+ten+ing
  fas+tened
fas+ten+er
  fas+ten+ers
fas+ten+ing
  fas+ten+ings
fast+er
  fast+ers
fast-food
adj.
fast food
noun
fast-forward
  fast-forwards
  fast-forward+ing
  fast-forward+ed
fas+tidi+ous
fas+tidi+ous+ly
fas+tidi+ous+
  ness
fas+tigi+ate
fas+tigi+at+ed
fast+ness
fat
  fats
  fats
  fat+ting
  fat+ted
  fat+ter
  fat+test
fa+tal
fa+tal+ism

fa+tal+ist
  fa+tal+ists
  fa+tal+is+tic
fa+tal+ity
  fa+tal+ities
fa+tal+ly
fate
  fates
  fat+ing
  fat+ed
fate+ful
fate+ful+ly
fate+ful+ness
Fates
fat+head
  fat+heads
  fat+headed
fa+ther
  fa+thers
  fa+thers
  fa+ther+ing
  fa+thered
father+hood
father-in-law
fathers-in-law
father+land
  father+lands
fa+ther+less
father-like
fa+ther+li+ness
fa+ther+ly
fath+om
  fath+oms
  fath+oms
  fath+om+ing
  fath+omed
fath+om+able
Fa+thom+eter
  Trademark
Fa+thom+eters
fath+om+less
fath+om+less+
  ness
fa+tig+able
fa+tigue
  fa+tigues
  fa+tigu+ing
  fa+tigued
Fatima
  name
Fáti+ma
  place name
fat+less
fat+ly

fat+ness
Fat+shan
fats+hed+era
  fats+hed+eras
fat+sia
  fat+sias
fat+so
  fat+sos *or*
  fat+soes
fat-soluble
fat+ten
  fat+tens
  fat+ten+ing
  fat+tened
fat+ten+ing
fat+ti+ly
fat+ti+ness
fat+tish
fat+ty
  fat+ties
  fat+ti+er
  fat+ti+est
fa+tui+tous
fa+tu+ity
  fa+tu+ities
fatu+ous
fatu+ous+ly
fatu+ous+ness
fat+wa
  fat+was
  fat+wah
  fat+wahs
fau+cal
fau+ces
  fau+ces
fau+cet
  fau+cets
fau+cial
Faulkner
fault
  faults
  faults
  fault+ing
  fault+ed
fault-finder
  fault-finders
fault-finding
faulti+ly
faulti+ness
fault+less
fault+less+ly
fault+less+ness
faulty
  faulti+er
  faulti+est

faun
  fauns
fau+na
  fau+nas *or*
  fau+nae
fau+nal
faun+like
Faunus
Fauré
Faust
Faust+ian
Faustus
Fauve
  Fauves
Fauv+ism
Fauv+ist
  Fauv+ists
faux pas
  faux pas
fa+vor
  U.S.
  fa+vors
  fa+vors
  fa+vor+ing
  fa+vored
fa+vor+able
  U.S.
fa+vor+er
  U.S.
  fa+vor+ers
fa+vor+ite
  U.S.
  fa+vor+ites
fa+vor+it+ism
  U.S.
fa+vour
  fa+vours
  fa+vours
  fa+vour+ing
  fa+voured
fa+vour+able
fa+vour+er
  fa+vour+ers
fa+vour+ite
  fa+vour+ites
fa+vour+it+ism
Fawcett
Fawkes
fawn
  fawns
  fawns
  fawn+ing
  fawned
fawn+er
  fawn+ers

fawn+like
fax
 faxes
 faxes
 fax+ing
 faxed
fay
 fays
Fay+al
Fa+yum
faze
 fazes
 faz+ing
 fazed
fe+al+ty
 fe+al+ties
fear
 fears
 fears
 fear+ing
 feared
fear+ful
fear+ful+ly
fear+ful+ness
fear+less
fear+less+ly
fear+less+ness
fear+some
fear+some+ly
fea+sibil+ity
fea+sible
fea+sibly
feast
 feasts
 feasts
 feast+ing
 feast+ed
feast+er
 feast+ers
feat
 feats
feath+er
 feath+ers
 feath+ers
 feath+er+ing
 feath+ered
feather+bed
 feather+beds
 feather+bedding
 feather+bedded
feath+er bed
 feath+er beds
feather+bedding
feather+brain
 feather+brains

feather+brained
feather+edge
 feather+edges
feather+head
 feather+heads
 feather+headed
feath+er+ing
 feath+er+ings
feather-like
feather+stitch
 feather+stitches
 feather+stitch+
  ing
 feather+stitched
feather+weight
 feather+weights
feath+ery
fea+ture
 fea+tures
 fea+tures
 fea+tur+ing
 fea+tured
fea+ture+less
fe+brifu+gal
feb+ri+fuge
 feb+ri+fuges
fe+brile
fe+bril+ity
 fe+bril+ities
Feb+ru+ary
 Feb+ru+aries
fe+cal
fe+ces
Fechner
feck+less
feck+less+ly
feck+less+ness
fecu+lence
fecu+lent
fe+cund
fe+cun+date
 fe+cun+dates
 fe+cun+dat+ing
 fe+cun+dat+ed
 fe+cun+da+tion
fe+cun+dity
fed
 feds
fe+da+yee
fe+da+yeen
fed+er+al
fed+er+ali+sa+
 tion
fed+er+al+ise
fed+er+al+ises

fed+er+al+is+
 ing
fed+er+al+ised
fed+er+al+ism
fed+er+al+ist
fed+er+al+ists
fed+er+ali+za+
 tion
fed+er+al+ize
 fed+er+al+izes
fed+er+al+iz+ing
fed+er+al+ized
fed+er+al+ly
fed+er+ate
 fed+er+ates
 fed+er+at+ing
 fed+er+at+ed
fed+era+tion
 fed+era+tions
fed+era+tive
fe+do+ra
 fe+do+ras
fee
 fees
 fees
fee+ing
feed
fee+ble
 fee+bler
 fee+blest
feeble-minded
fee+ble+ness
fee+bly
feed
 feeds
 feeds
 feed+ing
 fed
feed+able
feed+back
 noun
feed back
 verb
feed+er
 feed+ers
feel
 feels
 feel+ing
 felt
feel+er
 feel+ers
feel-good
feel+ing
 feel+ings
feel+ing+ly

feet
feign
 feigns
 feign+ing
 feigned
feign+ing+ly
Feininger
feint
 feints
 feints
feint+ing
feint+ed
Feisal
feld+spar
 feld+spars
feld+spath+ic
fe+lici+tate
 fe+lici+tates
 fe+lici+tat+ing
 fe+lici+tat+ed
fe+lici+ta+tion
 fe+lici+ta+tions
fe+lici+ta+tor
 fe+lici+ta+tors
fe+lici+tous
fe+lici+tous+ly
fe+lic+ity
 fe+lic+ities
fe+line
fe+line+ly
fe+lin+ity
Felix+stowe
fell
 fells
 fells
 fell+ing
 felled
fel+lah
 fel+lahs or
 fel+la+hin or
 fel+la+heen
fell+er
 fell+ers
Fel+ling
Fellini
fel+loe
 fel+loes
fel+low
 fel+lows
Fel+low
 Fel+lows
fel+low+ship
fel+ly
 fel+lies

fel+on
 fel+ons
fe+lo+ni+ous
fe+lo+ni+ous+ly
fe+lo+ni+ous+
 ness
felo+ny
 felo+nies
fel+spar
 fel+spars
fel+spath+ic
felt
 felts
 felts
 felt+ing
 felt+ed
fe+luc+ca
 fe+luc+cas
fe+male
 fe+males
 fe+male+ness
femi+nine
femi+nine+ly
femi+nine+ness
femi+nin+ity
femi+ni+sa+tion
femi+nise
 femi+nises
 femi+nis+ing
 femi+nised
femi+nism
femi+nist
 femi+nists
femi+ni+za+tion
femi+nize
 femi+nizes
 femi+niz+ing
 femi+nized
femme fa+tale
 femmes fa+tales
femo+ral
fe+mur
 fe+murs *or*
 femo+ra
fen
 marshland
 fens
fen
 currency
 fen
fence
 fences
 fences
 fenc+ing
 fenced

fence+less
fenc+er
 fenc+ers
fen+cible
 fen+cibles
fenc+ing
fend
 fends
 fends
 fend+ing
 fend+ed
fend+er
 fend+ers
Fénelon
fe+nes+tra
 fe+nes+trae
 fe+nes+trate
 fe+nes+trat+ed
fen+es+tra+tion
 fen+es+tra+
 tions
Fe+nian
 Fe+nians
Fe+ni+an+ism
fen+nec
 fen+necs
fen+nel
fen+ny
Fenrir
Fenris
Fenriswolf
Fens
Fenton
fenu+greek
feod
 feods
feoff
 feoffs
 feoffs
 feoff+ing
 feoffed
feoffee
 feoffees
feoff+er
 feoff+ers
feoff+ment
 feoff+ments
feof+for
 feof+fors
fe+ral
fer-de-lance
 fer-de-lances
Ferdinand
fer+etory
 fer+etories

Fer+ga+na
Fer+gha+na
Fergus
fe+ria
 fe+rias *or*
 fe+riae
fe+rial
Ferlinghetti
Fer+man+agh
Fermat
fer+ma+ta
 fer+ma+tas *or*
 fer+ma+te
fer+ment
 fer+ments
 fer+ments
 fer+ment+ing
 fer+ment+ed
fer+ment+able
fer+men+ta+tion
 fer+men+ta+
 tions
fer+menta+tive
fer+mi
 fer+mis
Fermi
 surname
fer+mi+on
 fer+mi+ons
 fer+mium
Fermor
fern
 ferns
Fernandel
Fer+nan+do de
 No+ro+nha
Fer+nan+do Po
fern+bird
 fern+birds
ferny
fe+ro+cious
fe+roc+ity
Fer+ra+ra
Ferrari
fer+rate
 fer+rates
fer+ret
 fer+rets
 fer+rets
 fer+ret+ing
 fer+ret+ed
 fer+ret+er
 fer+ret+ers
fer+rety
fer+ri+age

fer+ric
Ferrier
fer+ri+mag+net+
 ic
fer+ri+mag+net+
 ism
Ferris
fer+rite
 fer+rites
fer+ro+cene
fer+ro+con+crete
Fer+rol
fer+ro+mag+net+
 ic
fer+ro+mag+net+
 ism
fer+ro+man+ga+
 nese
fer+rous
fer+ru+gi+nous
fer+rule
 fer+rules
fer+ry
 fer+ries
 fer+ries
 fer+ry+ing
 fer+ried
fer+tile
fer+tile+ly
fer+tile+ness
fer+ti+li+sa+tion
 fer+ti+li+sa+
 tions
fer+ti+lise
 fer+ti+lises
 fer+ti+lis+ing
 fer+ti+lised
 fer+ti+lis+er
 fer+ti+lis+ers
fer+til+ity
fer+ti+li+za+tion
 fer+ti+li+za+
 tions
fer+ti+lize
 fer+ti+lizes
 fer+ti+liz+ing
 fer+ti+lized
 fer+ti+liz+er
 fer+ti+liz+ers
feru+la
 feru+las *or*
 feru+lae
fer+ule
 fer+ules
 fer+ules

fer+ul+ing
fer+uled
fer+ven+cy
fer+ven+cies
fer+vent
fer+vent+ly
fer+vid
fer+vid+ly
fer+vor
U.S.
fer+vors
fer+vour
fer+vours
Fès
fes+cue
fes+cues
fess
fesses
fesse
fesses
fes+tal
fes+tal+ly
fes+ter
fes+ters
fes+ters
fes+ter+ing
fes+tered
fes+ti+val
fes+ti+vals
fes+tive
fes+tive+ly
fes+tiv+ity
fes+tiv+ities
fes+toon
fes+toons
fes+toons
fes+toon+ing
fes+tooned
feta
fe+tal
fetch
fetches
fetches
fetch+ing
fetched
fetch+er
fetch+ers
fetch+ing
fete
fetes
fetes
fet+ing
fet+ed
fête
fêtes

fêtes
fêt+ing
fêt+ed
fet+id
fet+id+ly
fet+id+ness
fet+ish
fet+ishes
fet+ish+ism
fet+ish+ist
fet+ish+ists
fet+ish+is+tic
fet+lock
fet+locks
fe+tor
fe+tors
fet+ter
fet+ters
fet+ters
fet+ter+ing
fet+tered
fet+tle
fet+tles
fet+tles
fet+tling
fet+tled
fet+tler
fet+tlers
fe+tus
fe+tuses
feu
feus
Feuchtwanger
feud
feuds
feuds
feud+ing
feud+ed
feu+dal
feu+dali+sa+tion
feu+dal+ise
feu+dal+ises
feu+dal+is+ing
feu+dal+ised
feu+dal+ism
feu+dal+ist
feu+dal+ists
feu+dal+is+tic
feu+dal+ity
feu+dal+ities
feu+dali+za+tion
feu+dal+ize
feu+dal+izes
feu+dal+iz+ing
feu+dal+ized

feu+da+tory
feu+da+tories
feud+ist
feud+ists
Feuerbach
feuil+le+ton
feuil+le+tons
fe+ver
fe+vers
fe+vers
fe+ver+ing
fe+vered
fe+vered
fe+ver+few
fe+ver+fews
fe+ver+ish
fe+ver+ish+ly
fe+ver+ous
fe+ver+ous+ly
few
few+ness
fey
Feydeau
fey+ness
Feynman
fez
fez+zes
Fez
Fez+zan
Ffes+tin+iog
fia+cre
fia+cres
fi+an+cé
fi+an+cés
fi+an+cée
fi+an+cées
Fi+an+na
fi+as+co
fi+as+cos *or*
fi+as+coes
fiat
fiats
fib
fibs
fib+bing
fibbed
fib+ber
fib+bers
fi+ber
U.S.
fi+bers
fiber+board
U.S.
fi+bered

U.S.
fiber+glass
U.S.
fiber+scope
U.S.
fiber+scopes
Fibonacci
fi+bre
fi+bres
fibre+board
fi+bred
fibre+glass
fibre+scope
fibre+scopes
fi+bril
fi+brils
fi+bril+la
fi+bril+lae
fi+bril+lar
fi+bril+la+tion
fi+bril+la+tions
fi+bril+lose
fi+brin
fi+brino+gen
fi+bro
fi+bro+ce+ment
fi+broid
fi+broids
fi+bro+in
fi+bro+ma
fi+bro+ma+ta
or
fi+bro+mas
fi+bro+sis
fi+bro+si+tis
fi+brous
fi+brous+ly
fibu+la
fibu+lae *or*
fibu+las
fichе
fiches
fichu
fichus
fick+le
fick+le+ness
fic+tile
fic+tion
fic+tions
fic+tion+al
fic+tion+ali+sa+
tion
fic+tion+ali+sa+
tions

fic+tion+al+ise
fic+tion+al+ises
fic+tion+al+is+
  ing
fic+tion+al+ised
fic+tion+ali+za+
  tion
fic+tion+ali+za+
  tions
fic+tion+al+ize
fic+tion+al+izes
fic+tion+al+iz+
  ing
fic+tion+al+ized
fic+tion+al+ly
fic+ti+tious
fic+ti+tious+ly
fic+ti+tious+ness
fic+tive
fid
fids
fid+dle
fid+dles
fid+dles
fid+dling
fid+dled
fiddle-faddle
fiddle-faddles
fiddle-faddles
fiddle-faddling
fiddle-faddled
fiddle-faddler
fiddle-faddlers
fid+dler
fid+dlers
fiddle+stick
fiddle+sticks
fid+dling
fid+dly
fid+dli+er
fid+dli+est
Fi+dei De+fen+
  sor
fi+del+ity
fi+del+ities
fidg+et
fidg+ets
fidg+ets
fidg+et+ing
fidg+et+ed
fidg+ety
fi+du+cial
fi+du+ci+ary
fi+du+ci+aries
fie

fief
fiefs
fief+dom
fief+doms
field
fields
fields
field+ing
field+ed
field+er
field+ers
field+fare
field+fares
Fielding
field+mouse
field+mice
Fields
fields+man
fields+men
field+work
fortification
field+works
field work
research
fiend
fiends
fiend+ish
fierce
fierc+er
fierc+est
fierce+ly
fierce+ness
fiery
fieri+er
fieri+est
Fie+so+le
place name
Fiesole
surname
fi+es+ta
fi+es+tas
FIFA
fife
fifes
fifes
fif+ing
fifed
Fife
fif+er
fif+ers
FIFO
fif+teen
fif+teens
fif+teenth
fif+teenths

fifth
fifths
fifth+ly
fif+ti+eth
fif+ti+eths
fif+ty
fif+ties
fifty-fifty
fig
figs
fight
fights
fights
fight+ing
fought
fight+er
fight+ers
fighter-bomber
fighter-bombers
fight-or-flight
fig+ment
fig+ments
figu+rant
figu+rants
figu+rante
figu+rantes
fig+ura+tion
fig+ura+tions
fig+ura+tive
fig+ura+tive+ly
fig+ura+tive+
  ness
fig+ure
fig+ures
fig+ures
fig+ur+ing
fig+ured
fig+ured
figure+head
figure+heads
fig+ur+er
fig+ur+ers
figu+rine
figu+rines
fig+wort
fig+worts
Fiji
Fijis
Fi+jian
Fi+jians
fila+gree
fila+grees
fila+ment
fila+ments
fila+men+tary

fila+men+tous
fi+laria
fi+lariae
fi+lar+ial
fila+ria+sis
fil+bert
fil+berts
filch
filches
filch+ing
filched
filch+er
filch+ers
file
files
files
fil+ing
filed
file+fish
file+fish *or*
file+fishes
fil+er
fil+ers
fi+let
fi+lets
fil+ial
fil+ial+ly
fili+beg
fili+begs
fili+bus+ter
fili+bus+ters
fili+bus+ters
fili+bus+ter+ing
fili+bus+tered
fili+bus+ter+er
fili+bus+ter+ers
fili+gree
fili+grees
fil+ings
Fili+pi+no
Fili+pi+nos
fill
fills
fill+ing
filled
fill+er
fill+ers
fil+let
fil+lets
fil+lets
fil+let+ing
fil+let+ed
fill-in
fill-ins
fill in

verb
fill+ing
  fill+ings
fil+lip
  fil+lips
  fil+lips
  fil+lip ing
  fil+liped
Fillmore
fill-up
  fill-ups
fill up
verb
fil+ly
  fil+lies
film
  films
  films
  film+ing
  filmed
film+ic
filmi+ly
filmi+ness
fil+mog+ra+phy
  fil+mog+ra+
  phies
film+set
  film+sets
  film+set+ting
  film+set
film set
  film sets
  film+setter
  film+setters
film+setting
filmy
  filmi+er
  filmi+est
Filo+fax
Trademark
  Filo+faxes
fil+ter
  fil+ters
  fil+ters
  fil+ter+ing
  fil+tered
fil+ter+able
filter-tipped
filth
filthi+ly
filthi+ness
filthy
  filthi+er
  filthi+est
fil+trable

fil+trate
fil+trates
fil+trates
fil+trat+ing
fil+trat+ed
fil+tra+tion
fil+tra+tions
fin
fins
fins
fin+ning
finned
fin+able
fin+able+ness
fi+na+gle
fi+na+gles
fi+na+gling
fi+na+gled
fi+na+gler
fi+na+glers
fi+nal
fi+nals
fi+na+le
fi+na+les
fi+na+li+sa+tion
fi+nal+ise
fi+nal+ises
fi+nal+is+ing
fi+nal+ised
fi+nal+ist
fi+nal+ists
fi+nal+ity
fi+nal+ities
fi+na+li+za+tion
fi+nal+ize
fi+nal+izes
fi+nal+iz+ing
fi+nal+ized
fi+nal+ly
fi+nals
fi+nance
fi+nances
fi+nances
fi+nanc+ing
fi+nanced
fi+nan+cial
fi+nan+cial+ly
fi+nan+ci+er
fi+nan+ci+ers
fin+back
  fin+backs
finch
  finches
Finch+ley
find

finds
finds
find+ing
found
find+er
  find+ers
fin de siè+cle
noun
find+ing
  find+ings
fine
  fines
  fines
  fin+ing
  fined
fin+er
fin+est
fine
music
fine+able
fine+able+ness
fine-draw
  fine-draws
  fine-drawing
  fine-drew
  fine-drawn
fine-drawn
fine-grained
fine+ly
fine+ness
fin+ery
  fin+eries
fines herbes
fine+spun
fi+nesse
  fi+nesses
  fi+ness+ing
  fi+nessed
fine-tune
  fine-tunes
  fine-tuning
  fine-tuned
fin+ger
  fin+gers
  fin+gers
  fin+ger+ing
  fin+gered
finger+board
  finger+boards
fin+gered
fin+ger+ing
fin+ger+less
fin+ger+ling
  fin+ger+lings
finger+mark

finger+marks
finger+nail
  finger+nails
finger+print
  finger+prints
  finger+prints
  finger+print+ing
  finger+print+ed
finger+stall
  finger+stalls
finger+tip
  finger+tips
fi+nial
fi+nials
fin+ick+ing
fin+icky
fin+is
fin+ish
  fin+ishes
  fin+ishes
  fin+ish+ing
  fin+ished
  fin+ished
  fin+ish+er
  fin+ish+ers
Fin+is+tère
Fin+is+terre
fi+nite
fi+nite+ly
fi+nite+ness
fink
  finks
Fin+land
Fin+lan+di+sa+
tion
Fin+lan+di+za+
tion
Finlay
fin+less
Finn
  Finns
fin+nan
finned
Finney
Finn+ic
Finn+ish
Finn+mark
Finno-Ugrian
Finno-Ugric
fin+ny
  fin+ni+er
  fin+ni+est
fino
  finos
Finsen

Fin+ster+aar+
  horn
fiord
fiords
fip+ple
fip+ples
fir
  firs
Firbank
Firdausi
Firdusi
fire
  fires
  fires
  fir+ing
  fired
fire+arm
  fire+arms
fire+back
  fire+backs
fire+ball
  fire+balls
fire+boat
  fire+boats
fire+bomb
  fire+bombs
fire+box
  fire+boxes
fire+brand
  fire+brands
fire+break
  fire+breaks
fire+brick
  fire+bricks
fire+bug
  fire+bugs
fire+cracker
  fire+crackers
fire+crest
  fire+crests
fire+damp
fire+dog
  fire+dogs
fire-eater
  fire-eaters
fire-extinguish+er
  fire-extinguish+
  ers
fire+fight+er
  fire+fight+ers
fire+fly
  fire+flies
fire+guard
  fire+guards
fire+lock

fire+locks
fire+man
  fire+men
Fi+ren+ze
fire+place
  fire+places
fire+plug
  fire+plugs
fire+proof
  fire+proofs
  fire+proof+ing
  fire+proofed
fir+er
  fir+ers
fire+side
  fire+sides
fire+storm
  fire+storms
fire+trap
  fire+traps
fire+water
fire+weed
fire+work
  fire+works
  fire+works
fir+ing
  fir+ings
fir+kin
  fir+kins
firm
  firms
  firms
  firm+ing
  firmed
  firm+er
  firm+est
fir+ma+ment
  firm+ly
  firm+ness
  firm+ware
first
  firsts
first-born
  first-borns
first-class
  adj., adv.
  first class
  noun, adj.
first-foot
  first-foots
  first-foots
  first-footing
  first-footed
  first-footing
first-hand

first+ling
  first+lings
first+ly
first-past-the-
  post
first-rate
first-strike
firth
  firths
fis+cal
  fis+cals
  fis+cal+ly
Fischer
Fischer-Dieskau
fish
  fish or
  fishes
  fishes
  fish+ing
  fished
fish+er
  fish+ers
Fisher
fisher+man
  fisher+men
fish+ery
  fish+eries
Fishes
fish+finger
  fish+fingers
Fish+guard
fish-hook
  fish-hooks
fishi+ly
fish+ing
fish+like
fish+monger
  fish+mongers
fish+net
  fish+nets
fish+plate
  fish+plates
fish+tail
  noun
  fish+tails
fish+wife
  fish+wives
fishy
  fishi+er
  fishi+est
fis+sile
fis+sion
  fis+sions
  fis+sion+able
fis+sipa+rous

fis+sipa+rous+ly
fis+sure
  fis+sures
  fis+sures
  fis+sur+ing
  fis+sured
fist
  fists
  fists
  fist+ing
  fist+ed
fist+ful
  fist+fuls
fisti+cuffs
fis+tu+la
  fis+tu+las or
  fis+tu+lae
  fis+tu+lar
  fis+tu+lous
fit
  fits
  fits
  fit+ting
  fit+ted or
  fit
  U.S.
  fit+ter
  fit+test
fitch
  fitches
fit+ful
  fit+ful+ly
fit+ly
fit+ment
  fit+ments
fit+ness
fit+ted
fit+ter
  fit+ters
fit+ting
  fit+tings
  fit+ting+ly
Fittipaldi
Fitzgerald
Fitz+ro+via
Fitzsimmons
Fiu+me
five
  fives
five-a-side
five-eighth
  five-eighths
five-finger
  five-fingers
five+fold

five+pin
five+pins
fiv+er
 fiv+ers
fives
fix
 fixes
 fixes
fix+ing
 fixed
fix+able
fix+ate
 fix+ates
 fix+at+ing
 fix+at+ed
fixa+tion
 fixa+tions
fixa+tive
 fixa+tives
 fixed
fix+ed+ly
fix+ed+ness
fix+er
 fix+ers
fix+ing
 fix+ings
fix+ity
 fix+ities
fix+ture
 fix+tures
fiz+gig
 fiz+gigs
fizz
 fizzes
 fizzes
fizz+ing
 fizzed
fizzi+ness
fiz+zle
 fiz+zles
 fiz+zling
 fiz+zled
fizzy
fjord
 fjords
flab
flab+ber+gast
 flab+ber+gasts
 flab+ber+gast+
  ing
 flab+ber+gast+
  ed
flab+bi+ness
flab+by
 flab+bi+er

flab+bi+est
flac+cid
flac+cid+ity
fla+con
 fla+cons
flag
 flags
 flags
flag+ging
 flagged
flag+el+lant
 flag+el+lants
fla+gel+lar
flag+el+late
 flag+el+lates
flag+el+lat+ing
flag+el+lat+ed
flag+el+lat+ed
flag+el+la+tion
 flag+el+la+tions
flag+el+la+tor
 flag+el+la+tors
fla+gel+lum
fla+gel+la or
 fla+gel+lums
flageo+let
 flageo+lets
flag+ger
 flag+gers
flag+on
 flag+ons
flag+pole
 flag+poles
fla+gran+cy
fla+grant
fla+gran+te de+
 lic+to
fla+grant+ly
flag+ship
 flag+ships
Flagstad
flag+staff
 flag+staffs or
 flag+staves
flag+stone
 flag+stones
flag-waver
 flag-wavers
flag-waving
Flaherty
flail
 flails
 flails
flail+ing
 flailed

flair
 flairs
flak
flake
 flakes
 flakes
flak+ing
 flaked
flakey
flaki+er
 flaki+est
flaki+ly
flaki+ness
flaky
flaki+er
 flaki+est
flam+bé
 flam+bés
 flam+bée+ing
 flam+béed
flam+beau
 flam+beaux or
 flam+beaus
flam+boy+ance
flam+boy+an+cy
flam+boy+ant
flam+boy+ant+ly
flame
 flames
 flames
flam+ing
 flamed
flame+like
fla+men
 fla+mens or
 fla+mi+nes
fla+men+co
 fla+men+cos
flame+out
 flame+outs
flame-thrower
 flame-throwers
flam+ing
fla+min+go
 fla+min+gos or
 fla+min+goes
Flamininus
Flaminius
flam+mabil+ity
flam+mable
Flamsteed
flamy
flan
 flans
Flan+ders

flange
 flanges
 flanges
flang+ing
 flanged
flanged
flange+less
flank
 flanks
 flanks
flank+ing
 flanked
flank+er
 flank+ers
flan+nel
 flan+nels
 flan+nels
flan+nel+ling
 or
 flan+nel+ing
 U.S.
flan+nelled or
 flan+neled
 U.S.
flan+nel+ette
flan+nel+ly
flap
 flaps
 flaps
flap+ping
 flapped
flap+doodle
flap+jack
 flap+jacks
flap+per
 flap+pers
flare
 flares
 flares
flar+ing
 flared
 flares
flare-up
 flare-ups
flash
 flashes
 flashes
flash+ing
 flashed
flash+back
 flash+backs
flash back
 verb
flash+board
 flash+boards

flash+bulb
flash+bulbs
flash+cube
flash+cubes
flash+er
flash+ers
flashi+ly
flashi+ness
flash+ing
flash+light
flash+lights
flashy
flashi+er
flashi+est
flask
flasks
flat
flats
flats
flat+ting
flat+ted
flat+ter
flat+test
flat+boat
flat+boats
flat+ette
flat+ettes
flat+fish
flat+fish or
flat+fishes
flat+foot
flat+foots or
flat+feet
flat-footed
flat-footed+ly
flat-footed+ness
flat+head
flat+head or
flat+heads
flat+iron
flat+irons
flat+let
flat+lets
flat+ly
flat+mate
flat+mates
flat+ness
flat-racing
adj.
flat rac+ing
noun
flat+ten
flat+tens
flat+ten+ing
flat+tened

flat+ten+er
flat+ten+ers
flat+ter
flat+ters
flat+ter+ing
flat+tered
flat+ter+able
flat+ter+er
flat+ter+ers
flat+tery
flat+teries
flat+tie
flat+ties
flat+ties
flat+tish
flat+top
flat+tops
flatu+lence
flatu+len+cy
flatu+lent
flatu+lent+ly
fla+tus
fla+tuses
flat+worm
flat+worms
Flaubert
flaunt
flaunts
flaunt+ing
flaunt+ed
flau+tist
flau+tists
fla+ves+cent
fla+vin
fla+vine
fla+vone
fla+vo+pro+tein
fla+vo+pro+
   teins
fla+vor
U.S.
fla+vors
fla+vors
fla+vor+ing
fla+vored
fla+vor+ful
U.S.
fla+vor+ing
U.S.
fla+vor+ings
fla+vor+less
U.S.
fla+vour
fla+vours
fla+vours

fla+vour+ing
fla+voured
fla+vour+ful
fla+vour+ing
fla+vour+ings
fla+vour+less
flaw
flaws
flaws
flaw+ing
flawed
flaw+less
flax
flax+en
Flaxman
flax+seed
flax+seeds
flay
flays
flay+ing
flayed
flay+er
flay+ers
flea
fleas
flea+bane
flea+banes
flea+bite
flea+bites
flea-bitten
flea+pit
flea+pits
flea+wort
flea+worts
flèche
flèches
fleck
flecks
flecks
fleck+ing
flecked
fleck+er
Flecker
flec+tion
flec+tions
fled
fledge
fledges
fledg+ing
fledged
fledge+ling
fledge+lings
fledg+ling
fledg+lings
flee

flees
flee+ing
fled
flee
Scots
flees
flee+ing or
flow+ing
flew or
flaw
fleece
fleeces
fleeces
fleec+ing
fleeced
fleece-oh
fleece-ohs
fleecie
fleecies
fleeci+ly
fleecy
fleeci+er
fleeci+est
fle+er
fle+ers
fleer
fleers
fleers
fleer+ing
fleered
fleet
fleets
fleets
fleet+ing
fleet+ed
Fleet
fleet+ing
fleet+ing+ly
fleet+ly
fleet+ness
Fleet+wood
Flémalle
Flem+ing
Flemish speaker
Flem+ings
Fleming
surname
Flem+ish
flench
flenches
flench+ing
flenched
Flens+burg
flense
flenses

flens+ing
flensed
flesh
 fleshes
flesh+ing
fleshed
fleshi+ness
flesh+ings
flesh+li+ness
flesh+ly
 flesh+li+er
 flesh+li·est
flesh+pots
fleshy
 fleshi+er
 fleshi+est
fletch
 fletches
fletch+ing
fletched
fletch+er
 fletch+ers
Fletcher
fleur-de-lis
 fleurs-de-lis
fleur-de-lys
 fleurs-de-lys
fleu+ret
 fleu+rets
fleu+rette
 fleu+rettes
Fleury
flew
flews
flex
 flexes
 flexes
 flex+ing
 flexed
flexi+bil+ity
flex+ible
flex+ibly
flex+ile
flex+ion
flex+ion+al
flexi+time
flex+or
 flex+ors
flex+time
flexu+ous
flexu+ous+ly
flex+ure
 flex+ures
flex-wing
 flex-wings

flib+ber+ti+gib+
 bet
flib+ber+ti+gib+
 bets
flick
 flicks
 flicks
flick+ing
flicked
flick+er
 flick+ers
 flick+ers
flick+er+ing
flick+ered
fli+er
 fli+ers
flight
 flights
 flights
flight+ing
flight+ed
flighti+ness
flight+less
flighty
 flighti+er
 flighti+est
flim+flam
 flim+flams
 flim+flams
flim+flam+ming
flim+flammed
flim+flam+mer
 flim+flam+mers
flim+si+ness
flim+sy
 flim+si+er
 flim+si+est
flinch
 flinches
flinch+ing
flinched
flinch+ing+ly
flin+ders
fling
 flings
 flings
fling+ing
 flung
fling+er
 fling+ers
flint
 flints
Flint
flinti+ly
flinti+ness

flint+lock
 flint+locks
Flint+shire
flinty
 flinti+er
 flinti+est
flip
 flips
 flips
flip+ping
 flipped
flip-flop
 flip-flops
 flip-flops
flip-flopping
 flip-flopped
flip+pan+cy
flip+pant
flip+pant+ly
flip+per
 flip+pers
flirt
 flirts
 flirts
flirt+ing
flirt+ed
flir+ta+tion
 flir+ta+tions
flir+ta+tious
flir+ta+tious+ly
flirt+er
 flirt+ers
flit
 flits
 flits
flit+ting
flit+ted
flitch
 flitches
flit+ter
 flit+ters
 flit+ters
flit+ter+ing
 flit+tered
flitter+mouse
 flitter+mice
float
 floats
 floats
float+ing
float+ed
float+abil+ity
float+able
float+age
floata+tion

floata+tions
floa+tel
 floa+tels
float+er
 float+ers
float+ing
float+ing+ly
floats
floaty
floati+er
floati+est
floc+cu+late
 floc+cu+lates
floc+cu+lat+ing
floc+cu+lat+ed
floc+cu+la+tion
floc+cu+lence
floc+cu+lent
floc+cu+lus
floc+cu+li
flock
 flocks
 flocks
flock+ing
flocked
flocky
Flod+den
floe
 floes
flog
 flogs
flog+ging
flogged
flog+ger
 flog+gers
flong
 flongs
flood
 floods
 floods
flood+ing
flood+ed
flood+gate
 flood+gates
flood+ing
flood+light
 flood+lights
 flood+lights
flood+light+ing
flood+lit
floor
 floors
 floors
floor+ing
floored

floor+board
floor+boards
floor+ing
floo+sie
floo+sies
floo+zie
floo+zies
floo+zy
floo+zies
flop
flops
flops
flop+ping
flopped
flop+pi+ly
flop+pi+ness
flop+py
flop+pies
flop+pi+er
flop+pi+est
flo+ra
flo+ras *or*
flo+rae
Flora
flo+ral
flo+ral+ly
flo+reated
Flor+ence
Flor+en+tine
Flor+en+tines
Flo+res
flo+res+cence
flo+ret
flo+rets
Florey
Flo+ria+nópo+lis
flo+ri+at+ed
flo+ri+bun+da
flo+ri+bun+das
flo+ri+cul+tur+al
flo+ri+cul+ture
flo+ri+cul+tur+ist
flo+ri+cul+tur+
  ists
flor+id
Flori+da
Flo+rid+ian
flo+rid+ity
flor+id+ly
flo+rif+er+ous
flor+in
flor+ins
flo+rist
flo+rists
flo+ris+tic

flo+ris+ti+cal+ly
flo+ru+it
floss
flossy
flossi+er
flossi+est
flo+tage
flo+ta+tion
flo+ta+tions
flo+tel
flo+tels
flo+til+la
flo+til+las
flot+sam
flounce
flounces
flounces
flounc+ing
flounced
floun+der
floun+der *or*
floun+ders
floun+ders
floun+der+ing
floun+dered
flour
flours
flours
flour+ing
floured
flour+ish
flour+ishes
flour+ishes
flour+ish+ing
flour+ished
flour+ish+er
flour+ish+ers
floury
flout
flouts
flout+ing
flout+ed
flout+ing+ly
flow
flows
flows
flow+ing
flowed
flow+er
flow+ers
flow+ers
flow+er+ing
flow+ered
flow+ered
flow+er+et

flow+er+ets
flow+eri+ness
flow+er+ing
flow+er+less
flower-like
flower+pot
flower+pots
flow+ery
flown
flow-on
flow-ons
flu
fluc+tu+ant
fluc+tu+ate
fluc+tu+ates
fluc+tu+at+ing
fluc+tu+at+ed
fluc+tua+tion
fluc+tua+tions
flue
flues
flu+en+cy
flu+ent
flu+ent+ly
fluff
fluffs
fluffs
fluff+ing
fluffed
fluffi+ly
fluffi+ness
fluffy
fluffi+er
fluffi+est
flu+gel+horn
flu+gel+horns
flu+id
flu+ids
flu+id+al
flu+id+ic
flu+id+ics
flu+idi+sa+tion
flu+id+ise
flu+id+ises
flu+id+is+ing
flu+id+ised
flu+id+ity
flu+idi+za+tion
flu+id+ize
flu+id+izes
flu+id+iz+ing
flu+id+ized
flu+id+ness
fluke
flukes

flukes
fluk+ing
fluked
fluk+ey
fluki+er
fluki+est
fluki+ness
fluky
fluki+er
fluki+est
flume
flumes
flumes
flum+ing
flumed
flum+mery
flum+meries
flum+mox
flum+moxes
flum+mox+ing
flum+moxed
flung
flunk
flunks
flunk+ing
flunked
flunk+ey
flunk+eys
flunky
flunkies
flu+or
fluo+resce
fluo+resces
fluo+resc+ing
fluo+resced
fluo+res+cence
fluo+res+cent
fluori+date
fluori+dates
fluori+dat+ing
fluori+dat+ed
fluori+da+tion
fluori+da+tions
fluo+ride
fluo+rides
fluo+rim+eter
fluo+rim+eters
fluori+nate
fluori+nates
fluori+nat+ing
fluori+nat+ed
fluori+na+tion
fluori+na+tions
fluo+rine
fluo+rite

fluo+ro+car+bon	fly	Fo	foe+tal
fluo+ro+car+	flies	foal	foet+id
bons	flies	foals	foet+id+ly
fluo+rom+eter	fly+ing	foals	foet+id+ness
fluo+rom+eters	flew	foal+ing	foe+tor
fluoro+scope	flown	foaled	foe+tors
fluoro+scopes	fly+able	foam	foe+tus
fluor+os+co+py	fly+away	foams	foe+tuses
fluo+ro+sis	fly+blow	foams	fog
flu+or+spar	fly+blows	foam+ing	fogs
flur+ry	fly+blowing	foamed	fogs
flur+ries	fly+blew	foam+less	fog+ging
flur+ries	fly+blown	foamy	fogged
flur+ry+ing	fly+blown	foami+er	fog+bound
flur+ried	fly+book	foami+est	fog+bow
flush	fly+books	fob	fo+gey
flushes	fly+by	fobs	fo+geys
flushes	fly+bys	fobs	fo+gey+ish
flush+ing	fly-by-night	fob+bing	Fog+gia
flushed	fly-by-nights	fobbed	fog+gi+ness
flush+er	fly+catcher	fo+cal	fog+gy
flush+ers	fly+catchers	fo+cali+sa+tion	fog+gi+er
Flush+ing	fly+er	fo+cal+ise	fog+gi+est
flush+ness	fly+ers	fo+cal+ises	fog+horn
flus+ter	fly-fish	fo+cal+is+ing	fog+horns
flus+ters	fly-fishes	fo+cal+ised	fogy
flus+ters	fly-fishing	fo+cali+za+tion	fogies
flus+ter+ing	fly-fished	fo+cal+ize	fo+gy+ish
flus+tered	fly-fishing	fo+cal+izes	föhn
flute	fly+ing	fo+cal+iz+ing	foi+ble
flutes	fly+leaf	fo+cal+ized	foi+bles
flutes	fly+leaves	Foch	foie gras
flut+ing	fly+less	fo´c´s´le	foil
flut+ed	Flynn	fo´c´s´les	foils
flute+like	fly+over	fo´c´sle	foils
flut+ing	fly+overs	fo´c´sles	foil+ing
flut+ings	fly+paper	fo+cus	foiled
flut+ist	fly+papers	fo+cuses *or*	foil+able
flut+ists	fly-past	fo+ci	foist
flut+ter	fly-pasts	fo+cuses	foists
flut+ters	fly+posting	fo+cus+ing *or*	foist+ing
flut+ters	fly+screen	fo+cus+sing	foist+ed
flut+ter+ing	fly+screens	fo+cused *or*	Fokine
flut+tered	fly+speck	fo+cussed	Fokker
flut+ter+er	fly+specks	fo+cus+er	*surname*
flut+ter+ers	fly+specks	fo+cus+ers	Fok+ker
flut+tery	fly+speck+ing	fod+der	*aircraft*
fluty	fly+specked	fod+ders	Fok+kers
flu+vial	fly-tipping	fod+der+ing	fola+cin
flux	fly+trap	fod+dered	fold
fluxes	fly+traps	foe	folds
flux+ing	fly+weight	foes	folds
fluxed	fly+weights	foehn	fold+ing
flux+ion	fly+wheel	foe+man	fold+ed
flux+ions	fly+wheels	foe+men	fold+able

fold+away
fold+er
  fold+ers
fol+derol
  fol+derols
fo+ley
  fo+leys
fo+lia+ceous
fo+li+age
fo+li+ar
fo+li+ate
  fo+li+ates
  fo+li+at+ing
  fo+li+at+ed
fo+lia+tion
  fo+lia+tions
fo+lic
fo+lio
  fo+lios
folk
  folk *or*
  folks
Folke+stone
folkie
  folkies
folk+ish
folk+lore
folk+lor+ic
folk+lor+ist
  folk+lor+ists
folk-rock
folk+sy
  folk+si+er
  folk+si+est
folky
  folkies
fol+li+cle
  fol+li+cles
fol+licu+lar
fol+licu+lat+ed
fol+low
  fol+lows
  fol+low+ing
  fol+lowed
fol+low+er
  fol+low+ers
fol+low+ing
  fol+low+ings
follow-on
  follow-ons
follow-through
  follows-through
fol+low through
  verb
follow-up

follow-ups
fol+low up
  verb
fol+ly
  fol+lies
fo+ment
  fo+ments
  fo+ment+ing
  fo+ment+ed
fo+men+ta+tion
  fo+men+ta+
    tions
fo+ment+er
  fo+ment+ers
fond
fond+er
fond+est
Fonda
fon+dant
  fon+dants
fon+dle
  fon+dles
  fon+dling
  fon+dled
fon+dler
  fon+dlers
fond+ly
fond+ness
fon+due
  fon+dues
Fon+seca
font
  fonts
Fon+taine+bleau
fon+ta+nel
  fon+ta+nels
  fon+ta+nelle
  fon+ta+nelles
Fonteyn
Foo+chow
food
  foods
foodie
  foodies
food+stuff
  food+stuffs
foody
  foodies
fool
  fools
  fools
fool+ing
  fooled
fool+ery
  fool+eries

fool+har+di+ly
fool+har+di+ness
fool+hardy
  fool+hardi+er
  fool+hardi+est
fool+ish
fool+ish+ly
fool+ish+ness
fool+proof
fools+cap
  fools+caps
fool's-parsley
foot
  feet
  foots
foot+ing
foot+ed
Foot
foot+age
  foot+ages
foot+ball
  foot+balls
foot+ball+er
  foot+ball+ers
foot+board
  foot+boards
foot+bridge
  foot+bridges
foot+er
  foot+ers
foot+fall
  foot+falls
foot+hill
  foot+hills
foot+hold
  foot+holds
foot+ing
  foot+ings
foot+le
  foot+les
  foot+ling
  foot+led
foot+less
foot+lights
foot+ling
foot+loose
foot+man
  foot+men
foot+note
  foot+notes
  foot+notes
  foot+not+ing
  foot+not+ed
foot+pad
  foot+pads

foot+path
  foot+paths
foot+plate
  foot+plates
foot-pound-
  second
foot-pound-
  seconds
foot+print
  foot+prints
foot+rest
  foot+rests
foot+sie
Foot+sie
foot+sore
foot+soreness
foot+step
  foot+steps
foot+stool
  foot+stools
foot+wear
foot+work
fop
  fops
fop+pery
  fop+peries
fop+pish
for
for+age
  for+ages
  for+ages
  for+ag+ing
  for+aged
for+ag+er
  for+ag+ers
fo+ra+men
fo+rami+na *or*
fo+ra+mens
fora+mini+fer
  fora+mini+fers
for+ay
  for+ays
  for+ays
  for+ay+ing
  for+ayed
for+bad
for+bade
for+bear
  for+bears
  for+bears
  for+bear+ing
for+bore
for+borne
for+bear+ance
Forbes

for+bid
for+bids
for+bid+ding
for+bade or
for+bad
for+bid+den or
for+bid
for+bid+den
for+bid+der
for+bid+ders
for+bid+ding
for+bore
for+borne
force
forces
forces
forc+ing
forced
force+able
forced
force de frappe
force-feed
force-feeds
force-feeding
force-fed
force+ful
force+ful+ly
force+ful+ness
force+less
force+meat
for+ceps
for+ceps or
for+ci+pes
forc+er
forc+ers
Forces
for+cible
for+cibly
ford
fords
fords
ford+ing
ford+ed
Ford
ford+able
fore
fore-and-after
fore-and-afters
fore+arm
fore+arms
fore+arms
fore+arm+ing
fore+armed
fore+bear
fore+bears

fore+bode
fore+bodes
fore+bod+ing
fore+bod+ed
fore+bod+ing
fore+bod+ings
fore+brain
fore+brains
fore+cast
fore+casts
fore+casts
fore+cast+ing
fore+cast or
fore+cast+ed
fore+cast+er
fore+cast+ers
fore+cas+tle
fore+cas+tles
fore+clos+able
fore+close
fore+closes
fore+clos+ing
fore+closed
fore+clo+sure
fore+clo+sures
fore+court
fore+courts
fore+doom
fore+dooms
fore+doom+ing
fore+doomed
fore+father
fore+fathers
fore+father+ly
fore+fend
fore+fends
fore+fend+ing
fore+fend+ed
fore+finger
fore+fingers
fore+foot
fore+feet
fore+front
fore+gather
fore+gathers
fore+gather+ing
fore+gathered
fore+go
fore+goes
fore+go+ing
fore+went
fore+gone
fore+going
fore+gone
fore+gone+ness

fore+ground
fore+hand
fore+hands
fore+head
fore+heads
for+eign
for+eign+er
for+eign+ers
for+eign+ness
fore+know
fore+knows
fore+know+ing
fore+knew
fore+known
fore+know+able
fore+knowl+edge
fore+land
fore+lands
fore+leg
fore+legs
fore+limb
fore+limbs
fore+lock
fore+locks
fore+man
fore+men
Foreman
fore+mast
fore+masts
fore+most
fore+name
fore+names
fore+named
fore+noon
fore+noons
fo+ren+sic
fo+ren+si+cal+ly
fore+or+dain
fore+or+dains
fore+or+dain+
ing
fore+or+dained
fore+or+di+na+
tion
fore+or+di+na+
tions
fore+paw
fore+paws
fore+play
fore+quar+ter
fore+quar+ters
fore+quar+ters
fore+run
fore+runs
fore+run+ning

fore+ran
fore+run
fore+run+ner
fore+run+ners
fore+sail
fore+sails
fore+see
fore+sees
fore+see+ing
fore+saw
fore+seen
fore+see+able
fore+seer
fore+seers
fore+shad+ow
fore+shad+ows
fore+shad+ow+
ing
fore+shad+
owed
fore+shank
fore+shanks
fore+sheet
fore+sheets
fore+shock
fore+shocks
fore+shore
fore+shores
fore+short+en
fore+short+ens
fore+short+en+
ing
fore+short+ened
fore+show
fore+shows
fore+show+ing
fore+showed
fore+shown
fore+sight
fore+sighted
fore+sighted+ly
fore+sighted+
ness
fore+skin
fore+skins
for+est
for+ests
for+ests
for+est+ing
for+est+ed
fore+stall
fore+stalls
fore+stall+ing
fore+stalled
fore+stall+er

fore+stall+ers	for+fei+tures	fork+ing	for+mic
fore+stal+ment	for+fend	forked	For+mi+ca
fore+esta+tion	for+fends	forked	*Trademark*
fore+stay	for+fend+ing	fork+ed+ly	for+mi+dable
fore+stays	for+fend+ed	fork-lift	for+mi+dably
for+est+ed	for+gath+er	for+lorn	form+less
for+est+er	for+gath+ers	for+lorn+ness	form+less+ly
for+est+ers	for+gath+er+ing	form	For+mo+sa
Forester	for+gath+ered	forms	for+mu+la
for+est+ry	for+gave	forms	for+mu+las *or*
for+est+ries	forge	form+ing	for+mu+lae
fore+taste	forges	formed	for+mu+laic
fore+tell	forges	for+mal	for+mu+lar+ise
fore+tells	forg+ing	for+mal+de+hyde	for+mu+lar+ises
fore+tell+ing	forged	for+ma+lin	for+mu+lar+is+
fore+told	forg+er	for+mali+sa+tion	ing
fore+thought	forg+ers	for+mali+sa+	for+mu+lar+ised
fore+thoughts	for+gery	tions	for+mu+lar+ize
fore+to+ken	for+geries	for+mal+ise	for+mu+lar+izes
fore+to+kens	for+get	for+mal+ises	for+mu+lar+iz+
fore+to+kens	for+gets	for+mal+is+ing	ing
fore+to+ken+ing	for+get+ting	for+mal+ised	for+mu+lar+ized
fore+to+kened	for+got	for+mal+ism	for+mu+lary
fore+top	for+got+ten *or*	for+mal+ist	for+mu+laries
fore+tops	for+got	for+mal+ists	for+mu+late
fore-topgal+lant	*Archaic*	for+mal+ity	for+mu+lates
fore-topmast	for+get+ful	for+mal+ities	for+mu+lat+ing
fore-topmasts	for+get+ful+ly	for+mali+za+tion	for+mu+lat+ed
fore-topsail	forget-me-not	for+mali+za+	for+mu+la+tion
fore-topsails	forget-me-nots	tions	for+mu+la+tions
for+ever	for+get+table	for+mal+ize	form+work
noun, adv.	for+get+ter	for+mal+izes	form+works
for ever	for+get+ters	for+mal+iz+ing	for+ni+cate
adv.	for+giv+able	for+mal+ized	for+ni+cates
for+ever+more	for+give	for+mal+ly	for+ni+cat+ing
fore+warn	for+gives	for+mal+ness	for+ni+cat+ed
fore+warns	for+giv+ing	Forman	for+ni+ca+tion
fore+warn+ing	for+gave	for+mant	for+ni+ca+tions
fore+warned	for+giv+en	for+mants	for+ni+ca+tor
fore+warn+er	for+give+ness	for+mat	for+ni+ca+tors
fore+went	for+giv+er	for+mats	Forrest
fore+wing	for+giv+ers	for+mats	for+sake
fore+wings	for+giv+ing	for+mat+ting	for+sakes
fore+word	for+go	for+mat+ted	for+sak+ing
fore+words	for+goes	for+ma+tion	for+sook
for+fait+ing	for+go+ing	for+ma+tions	for+sak+en
For+far	for+went	forma+tive	for+sak+en+ly
for+feit	for+gone	forma+tive+ly	for+sak+en+ness
for+feits	for+got	forma+tive+ness	for+sak+er
for+feits	for+got+ten	Formby	for+sak+ers
for+feit+ing	for+int	forme	for+sook
for+feit+ed	for+ints	formes	for+sooth
for+feit+er	fork	for+mer	Forster
for+feit+ers	forks	for+mers	for+swear
for+fei+ture	forks	for+mer+ly	

for+swears
for+swear+ing
for+swore
for+sworn
for+swear+er
for+swear+ers
for+sworn
for+sworn+ness
Forsyth
for+sythia
for+sythias
fort
forts
For+ta+leza
Fort-de-France
forte
fortes
forte-piano
forte-pianos
forth
Forth
Forths
forth+com+ing
forth+right
forth+right+ly
forth+right+ness
forth+with
for+ti+eth
for+ti+eths
for+ti+fi+able
for+ti+fi+ca+tion
for+ti+fi+ca+
tions
for+ti+fi+er
for+ti+fi+ers
for+ti+fy
for+ti+fies
for+ti+fy+ing
for+ti+fied
for+tis+si+mo
for+ti+tude
fort+night
fort+nights
fort+night+ly
fort+night+lies
For+tran
for+tress
for+tresses
for+tresses
for+tress+ing
for+tressed
for+tui+tous
for+tui+tous+ly
for+tu+ity
for+tu+ities

Fortuna
for+tu+nate
for+tu+nate+ly
for+tune
for+tunes
for+tunes
for+tun+ing
for+tuned
fortune-hunter
fortune-hunters
fortune-teller
fortune-tellers
fortune-telling
for+ty
for+ties
forty-five
forty-fives
Forty-Five
forty-niner
forty-niners
fo+rum
fo+rums or
fo+ra
Fo+rum
for+ward
for+wards
for+ward+ing
for+ward+ed
for+ward+er
for+ward+ers
for+ward+ly
for+ward+ness
for+wards
for+went
for+za
Fo+shan
foss
fosses
fos+sa
trench
fos+sae
fos+sa
animal
fos+sas
fosse
fosses
fos+sick
fos+sicks
fos+sick+ing
fos+sicked
fos+sick+er
fos+sick+ers
fos+sil
fos+sils
fos+sil+if+er+ous

fos+sili+sa+tion
fos+sili+sa+
tions
fos+sil+ise
fos+sil+ises
fos+sil+is+ing
fos+sil+ised
fos+sili+za+tion
fos+sili+za+
tions
fos+sil+ize
fos+sil+izes
fos+sil+iz+ing
fos+sil+ized
fos+so+rial
fos+ter
fos+ters
fos+ter+ing
fos+tered
Foster
fos+ter+age
fos+ter+er
fos+ter+ers
Foth+er+ing+hay
Foucault
Foucquet
fought
foul
fouls
fouls
foul+ing
fouled
foul+er
foul+est
fou+lard
fou+lards
Foulds
Fou-liang
foul+ly
foul+ness
Foul+ness
foul-up
foul-ups
foul up
verb
found
founds
found+ing
found+ed
foun+da+tion
foun+da+tions
foun+da+tion+al
found+er
found+ers
found+ers

found+er+ing
found+ered
found+ling
found+lings
found+ry
found+ries
fount
founts
foun+tain
foun+tains
foun+tained
fountain+head
fountain+heads
Fouqué
Fouquet
Fouquier-Tinville
four
fours
four-ball
four-balls
four+fold
Fourier
four-in-hand
four-in-hands
Fournier
four-o'clock
four-o'clocks
four-poster
four-posters
four+score
four+some
four+somes
four+square
four-stroke
four+teen
four+teens
four+teenth
fourth
fourths
fourth-dimension+
al
fourth+ly
fo+vea
fo+veae
Fowey
fowl
fowls
fowls
fowl+ing
fowled
fowl+er
fowl+ers
Fowler
Fowles
Fow+liang

fowl+ing	frac+tion+ised	frame-up	frank+fur+ters
fox	frac+tion+ize	frame-ups	Frank+fur+ter
foxes *or*	frac+tion+izes	frame+work	frank+in+cense
fox	frac+tion+iz+ing	frame+works	Frank+ish
foxes	frac+tion+ized	franc	frank+lin
fox+ing	frac+tious	francs	frank+lins
foxed	frac+tious+ly	France	Franklin
Fox	frac+tious+ness	Francesca	frank+ly
Fox *or*	frac+tur+al	Franche-Comté	frank+ness
Foxes	frac+ture	fran+chise	fran+tic
Fox	frac+tures	fran+chises	fran+ti+cal+ly
Foxe	frac+tures	fran+chises	fran+tic+ly
fox+fire	frac+tur+ing	fran+chis+ing	frap+pé
fox+glove	frac+tured	fran+chised	frap+pés
fox+gloves	frae+num	fran+chise+ment	Fra+ser
fox+hole	frae+na	fran+chise+	*place name*
fox+holes	frag+ile	ments	Fraser
fox+hound	frag+ile+ly	Francis	*surname*
fox+hounds	fra+gil+ity	Fran+cis+can	fra+ter
fox-hunter	frag+ment	Fran+cis+cans	fra+ters
fox-hunters	frag+ments	fran+cium	fra+ter+nal
fox-hunting	frag+ments	Franck	fra+ter+nal+ism
foxi+ly	frag+ment+ing	Franco	frat+er+ni+sa+
foxi+ness	frag+ment+ed	fran+co+lin	tion
fox+like	frag+men+tal	fran+co+lins	frat+er+nise
fox+tail	frag+men+tary	Fran+co+nia	frat+er+nises
fox+tails	frag+men+ta+	Fran+co+phone	frat+er+nis+ing
fox+trot	tion	Fran+co+	frat+er+nised
fox+trots	frag+men+ta+	phones	frat+er+nis+er
fox+trots	tions	fran+gibil+ity	frat+er+nis+ers
fox+trot+ting	Fragonard	fran+gible	fra+ter+nity
fox+trot+ted	fra+grance	fran+gible+ness	fra+ter+nities
foxy	fra+grances	fran+gi+pane	frat+er+ni+za+
foxi+er	fra+gran+cy	fran+gi+panes	tion
foxi+est	fra+gran+cies	fran+gi+pani	frat+er+nize
foy+er	fra+grant	fran+gi+panis	frat+er+nizes
foy+ers	fra+grant+ly	*or*	frat+er+niz+ing
Fra	frail	fran+gi+pani	frat+er+nized
Fras	frails	Frang+lais	frat+er+niz+er
fra+cas	frail+er	frank	frat+er+niz+ers
fra+cas	frail+est	franks	frat+ri+cid+al
frac+tal	frail+ty	franks	frat+ri+cide
frac+tals	frail+ties	frank+ing	frat+ri+cides
frac+tion	fram+be+sia	franked	Frau
frac+tions	*U.S.*	frank+er	Frau+en *or*
frac+tion+al	fram+boe+sia	frank+est	Fraus
frac+tion+ate	frame	Frank	fraud
frac+tion+ates	frames	Franks	frauds
frac+tion+at+ing	frames	frank+able	fraudu+lence
frac+tion+at+ed	fram+ing	Frankenstein	fraudu+lent
frac+tiona+tion	framed	Frank+en+stein+	fraudu+lent+ly
frac+tiona+tions	Frame	ian	Frau+en+feld
frac+tion+ise	frame+less	Frank+fort	fraught
frac+tion+ises	fram+er	Frank+furt	Fräu+lein
frac+tion+is+ing	fram+ers	frank+fur+ter	Fräu+lein *or*

Fräu+leins
English
Fraunhofer
fraxi+nel+la
fray
frays
frays
fray+ing
frayed
Fray Ben+tos
Frazer
Frazier
fra+zil
fraz+zle
fraz+zles
fraz+zling
fraz+zled
freak
freaks
freaks
freak+ing
freaked
freak+ish
freaky
freaki+er
freaki+est
freck+le
freck+les
freck+les
freck+ling
freck+led
freck+ly
Fre+de+ri+cia
Fred+er+ic+ton
Fred+er+iks+berg
Fred+rik+stad
free
frees
free+ing
freed
fre+er
fre+est
free+base
free+bases
free+bas+ing
free+based
free+bie
free+bies
free+board
free+boot
free+boots
free+boot+ing
free+boot+ed
free+booter

free+booters
free+born
freed+man
freed+men
free+dom
free+doms
free-for-all
free-for-alls
free-form
free+hand
adj.
free hand
noun
free-handed
free-handed+ly
free+hold
free+holds
free+holder
free+holders
free+lance
free+lances
free+lances
free+lanc+ing
free+lanced
free+lancer
free+lancers
free-liver
free-livers
free-living
free+loader
free+loaders
free+man
free+men
free-market
adj.
free mar+ket
free mar+kets
free+martin
free+martins
Free+mason
Free+masons
free+masonry
Free+masonry
free-range
free-select
Trademark
free-selects
free-select+ing
free-select+ed
free-selec+tion
free-selec+tions
free-selec+tor
free-selec+tors
free+sia
free+sias

free-spoken
free-spoken+ly
free+standing
free+stone
free+stones
free+style
free+thinker
free+thinkers
Free+town
free+way
free+ways
free+wheel
free+wheels
free+wheels
free+wheel+ing
free+wheeled
free-will
adj.
free will
noun
freez+able
freeze
freezes
freez+ing
froze
fro+zen
freeze-dry
freeze-dries
freeze-drying
freeze-dried
freeze-frame
freez+er
freez+ers
Frege
Frei+burg
Frei+burg im Breis+
gau
freight
freights
freight+ing
freight+ed
freight+age
freight+er
freight+ers
freight+liner
Trademark
freight+liners
Fre+man+tle
French
French-Canadian
adj.
French Ca+na+
dian
noun
Frenchi+fy

Frenchi+fies
Frenchi+fy+ing
Frenchi+fied
French+man
French+men
French+ness
French-polish
French-polishes
French-polish+
ing
French-polished
French pol+ish
noun
French+woman
French+women
fre+net+ic
fre+neti+cal+ly
fre+num
fre+na
fren+zied
fren+zy
fren+zies
fren+zies
fren+zy+ing
fren+zied
Fre+on
Trademark
fre+quen+cy
fre+quen+cies
fre+quent
fre+quents
fre+quent+ing
fre+quent+ed
fre+quen+ta+tion
fre+quen+ta+tive
fre+quen+ta+
tives
fre+quent+er
fre+quent+ers
fre+quent+ly
fres+co
fres+coes *or*
fres+cos
Frescobaldi
fresh
fresh+er
fresh+est
fresh+en
fresh+ens
fresh+en+ing
fresh+ened
fresh+er
fresh+ers
fresh+et
fresh+ets

fresh+ly
fresh+man
 fresh+men
fresh+ness
fresh+water
fres+nel
 fres+nels
Fresnel
Fres+no
fret
frets
frets
 fret+ting
 fret+ted
fret+ful
fret+ful+ly
fret+ful+ness
fret+less
fret+work
Freud
Freud+ian
Freudi+an+ism
Frey
Freya
Freyja
Freyr
Freytag
fri+abil+ity
fri+able
fri+able+ness
fri+ar
 fri+ars
fri+ary
 fri+aries
Fri+bourg
fric+an+deau
fric+an+deaus
 or
fric+an+deaux
fric+as+see
fric+as+sees
fric+as+sees
fric+as+see+ing
fric+as+seed
frica+tive
frica+tives
fric+tion
fric+tions
fric+tion+al
fric+tion+less
Fri+day
 Fri+days
fridge
 fridges
fried

Friedan
Friedman
Friedman+ite
Friedman+ites
Friedrich
friend
friends
friends
friend+ing
friend+ed
Friend
Friends
friend+less
friend+li+ly
friend+li+ness
friend+ly
friend+lies
friend+li+er
friend+li+est
friend+ship
friend+ships
fri+er
 fri+ers
Friese-Greene
Frie+sian
 Frie+sians
Fries+land
frieze
friezes
frig+ate
 frig+ates
Frigg
Frigga
fright
frights
frights
fright+ing
fright+ed
fright+en
fright+ens
fright+en+ing
fright+ened
fright+en+er
fright+en+ers
fright+en+ing+ly
fright+ful
fright+ful+ly
fright+ful+ness
frig+id
frig+gid+ity
frig+id+ly
frig+id+ness
fri+jol
 fri+joles
frill

frills
frills
frill+ing
frilled
frilli+ness
frilly
fringe
fringes
fringes
fring+ing
fringed
fringe+less
Frink
frip+pery
frip+peries
Fris+bee
 Trademark
Fris+bees
Frisch
Frisch+es Haff
Fri+sian
frisk
frisks
frisks
frisk+ing
frisked
frisk+er
frisk+ers
friski+ly
frisky
friski+er
friski+est
fris+son
 fris+sons
frit
frits
frit+ting
frit+ted
frith
friths
fri+til+lary
fri+til+laries
frit+ter
frit+ters
frit+ters
frit+ter+ing
frit+tered
Friu+li
fri+vol+ity
 fri+vol+ities
frivo+lous
frivo+lous+ly
frivo+lous+ness
frizz
 frizzes

frizzes
frizz+ing
frizzed
friz+zi+ness
friz+zle
friz+zles
friz+zles
friz+zling
friz+zled
friz+zli+ness
friz+zly
friz+zli+er
friz+zli+est
friz+zy
friz+zi+er
friz+zi+est
fro
Fröbel
Frobisher
frock
frocks
frocks
frock+ing
frocked
Fröding
Froebel
frog
frogs
Frog
Frogs
frogged
frog+ging
frog+gy
Frog+gy
Frog+gies
frog+hopper
frog+hoppers
frog+man
frog+men
frog+march
frog+marches
frog+march+ing
frog+marched
frog+mouth
frog+mouths
frog+spawn
frog+spawns
Froissart
frol+ic
frol+ics
frol+ics
frol+ick+ing
frol+icked
frol+ick+er
frol+ick+ers

frol+ic+some
frol+ic+some+ly
from
fro+mage frais
Frome
Fromm
frond
 fronds
front
 fronts
 fronts
front+ing
front+ed
front+age
 front+ages
front+al
 front+als
fron+tal+ly
front-end
adj.
fron+tier
 fron+tiers
 fron+tiers+man
 fron+tiers+men
fron+tiers+
 woman
fron+tiers+
 women
fron+tis+piece
 fron+tis+pieces
front+less
front+let
 front+lets
front-page
adj.
front+runner
 front+runners
front+running
frost
 frosts
 frosts
frost+ing
frost+ed
Frost
frost+bite
 frost+bites
frost+bitten
frost+ed
frosti+ly
frosti+ness
frost+ing
 frost+ings
frosty
 frosti+er
 frosti+est

froth
froths
froths
froth+ing
frothed
frothi+ly
frothy
frothi+er
frothi+est
Froude
frou+frou
fro+ward
fro+ward+ly
fro+ward+ness
frown
frowns
frowns
frown+ing
frowned
frown+er
frown+ers
frown+ing+ly
frowsi+ness
frowst
frowsts
frows+ti+ness
frows+ty
frows+ti+er
frows+ti+est
frowsy
frowsi+er
frowsi+est
frowzi+ness
frowzy
frowzi+er
frowzi+est
froze
fro+zen
fro+zen+ly
fruc+tif+er+ous
fruc+ti+fi+ca+tion
fruc+ti+fi+er
fruc+ti+fi+ers
fruc+ti+fy
fruc+ti+fies
fruc+ti+fy+ing
fruc+ti+fied
fruc+tose
fru+gal
fru+gal+ity
fru+gal+ly
fru+giv+or+ous
fruit
fruits
fruits

fruit+ing
fruit+ed
fruit+cake
fruit+cakes
fruit+er+er
fruit+er+ers
fruit+ful
fruit+ful+ly
fruit+ful+ness
fruiti+ness
frui+tion
fruit+less
fruit+less+ly
fruit+less+ness
fruit+like
fruity
fruiti+er
fruiti+est
fru+men+ty
frump
frumps
frump+ish
frumpy
Frun+ze
frus+trate
frus+trates
frus+trat+ing
frus+trat+ed
frus+trat+ed
frus+tra+tion
frus+tra+tions
frus+tum
frus+tums or
frus+ta
fry
fries
fries
fry+ing
fried
Fry
fry+er
fry+ers
f-stop
f-stops
Fuad I
Fu-chou
Fu-chou
Fuchs
fuch+sia
fuch+sias
fuch+sin
fuch+sine
fuck
fucks
fucks

fuck+ing
fucked
fu+cus
fu+ci or
fu+cuses
fud+dle
fud+dles
fud+dles
fud+dling
fud+dled
fuddy-duddy
fuddy-duddies
fudge
fudges
fudges
fudg+ing
fudged
fuel
fuels
fuels
fuel+ling or
fuel+ing
U.S.
fuelled or
fueled
U.S.
Fuentes
fug
fugs
fu+gac+ity
fu+gal
Fugard
fug+gy
fug+gi+er
fug+gi+est
fu+gi+tive
fu+gi+tives
fu+gi+tive+ly
fugle+man
fugle+men
fugue
fugues
Füh+rer
Füh+rers
Fuji
Fujian
Fuji-san
Fuji+ya+ma
Fu+kien
Fu+kuo+ka
ful+crum
ful+crums or
ful+cra
ful+fil
ful+fils

ful+fil+ling
ful+filled
ful+fill
U.S.
ful+fills
ful+fil+ling
ful+filled
ful+fill+ment
U.S.
ful+fil+ment
ful+gent
ful+gu+rate
ful+gu+rates
ful+gu+rat+ing
ful+gu+rat+ed
ful+gu+rite
ful+gu+rites
Ful+ham
fu+ligi+nous
full
fulls
full+ing
fulled
full+er
full+est
full+back
full+backs
full-blooded
full-blooded+ness
full-blown
full-bodied
full-dress
adj.
full dress
noun
full+er
full+ers
Fuller
full-fledged
full-frontal
adj.
full-length
full+ness
full-scale
full-time
adj.
full time
noun, adv.
full-timer
full-timers
ful+ly
ful+mar
ful+mars
ful+mi+nant
ful+mi+nate

ful+mi+nates
ful+mi+nates
ful+mi+nat+ing
ful+mi+nat+ed
ful+mi+na+tion
ful+mi+na+tions
ful+mi+na+tory
ful+ness
U.S.
ful+some
ful+some+ly
ful+some+ness
Fulton
ful+vous
fu+ma+role
fu+ma+roles
fum+ble
fum+bles
fum+bles
fum+bling
fum+bled
fum+bler
fum+blers
fum+bling+ly
fume
fumes
fumes
fum+ing
fumed
fume+less
fu+mi+gant
fu+mi+gants
fu+mi+gate
fu+mi+gates
fu+mi+gat+ing
fu+mi+gat+ed
fu+mi+ga+tion
fu+mi+ga+tions
fu+mi+ga+tor
fu+mi+ga+tors
fum+ing+ly
fu+mi+tory
fu+mi+tories
fumy
fun
fu+nam+bu+lism
fu+nam+bu+list
fu+nam+bu+lists
Fun+chal
func+tion
func+tions
func+tions
func+tion+ing
func+tioned

func+tion+al
func+tion+al+ism
func+tion+al+ist
func+tion+al+
ists
func+tion+al+ly
func+tion+ary
func+tion+aries
fund
funds
funds
fund+ing
fund+ed
fun+da+ment
fun+da+ments
fun+da+men+tal
fun+da+men+tal+
ism
fun+da+men+tal+
ist
fun+da+men+tal+
ists
fun+da+men+tal+
ity
fun+da+men+tal+
ly
funds
fun+dus
fun+di
Fun+dy
fu+nebrial
Fu+nen
Fü+nen
fu+ner+al
fu+ner+als
fu+ner+ary
fu+nereal
fu+nereal+ly
fun+fair
fun+fairs
fun+gal
fun+gibil+ity
fun+gible
fun+gibles
fun+gi+cid+al
fun+gi+cid+al+ly
fun+gi+cide
fun+gi+cides
fun+goid
fun+gous
fun+gus
fun+gi *or*
fun+guses
fu+nicu+lar
fu+nicu+lars

funk
funks
funks
funk+ing
funked
Funk
funky
funki+er
funki+est
fun+nel
fun+nels
fun+nels
fun+nel+ling *or*
fun+nel+ing
U.S.
fun+nelled *or*
fun+neled
U.S.
funnel-like
funnel-web
funnel-webs
fun+ny
fun+nies
fun+ni+er
fun+ni+est
fur
furs
furs
fur+ring
furred
fur+below
fur+belows
fur+belows
fur+below+ing
fur+belowed
fur+bish
fur+bishes
fur+bish+ing
fur+bished
fur+bish+er
fur+bish+ers
fur+cate
fur+cates
fur+cat+ing
fur+cat+ed
fur+ca+tion
fur+ca+tions
fur+fu+ra+ceous
Furies
fu+rio+so
fu+rio+sos
fu+ri+ous
fu+ri+ous+ly
fu+ri+ous+ness
furl

furls
furls
furl+ing
furled
furl+able
fur+less
fur+long
fur+longs
fur+lough
fur+loughs
fur+loughs
fur+lough+ing
fur+loughed
fur+men+ty
fur+nace
fur+naces
Fur+ness
fur+nish
fur+nishes
fur+nish+ing
fur+nished
fur+nish+er
fur+nish+ers
fur+nish+ings
fur+ni+ture
Furnivall
fu+ror
U.S.
fu+rors
fu+ro+re
fu+ro+res
fur+phy
fur+phies
Furphy
furred
fur+ri+er
fur+ri+ers
fur+ri+ery
fur+ri+eries
fur+ri+ly
fur+ri+ness
fur+ring
fur+rings
fur+row
fur+rows
fur+rows
fur+row+ing

fur+rowed
fur+row+er
fur+row+ers
fur+row+less
fur+rowy
fur+ry
fur+ri+er
fur+ri+est
fur+ther
fur+thers
fur+ther+ing
fur+thered
fur+ther+ance
fur+ther+ances
further+more
further+most
fur+thest
fur+tive
fur+tive+ly
fur+tive+ness
Furtwängler
fu+run+cle
fu+run+cles
fu+run+cu+lar
fu+run+cu+lo+sis
fury
furies
Fury
furze
furzy
fus+cous
fuse
fuses
fuses
fus+ing
fused
fu+see
fu+sees
fu+sel
fu+selage
fu+selages
fuse+less
Fu+shih
Fu-shih
Fu+shun
fu+sibil+ity
fu+sible

fu+sibly
fu+si+form
fu+sil
fu+sils
fu+si+lier
fu+si+liers
fu+sil+lade
fu+sil+lades
fu+sil+lades
fu+sil+lad+ing
fu+sil+lad+ed
fu+sion
fu+sions
fuss
fusses
fusses
fuss+ing
fussed
fuss+er
fuss+ers
fussi+ly
fussi+ness
fuss+pot
fuss+pots
fussy
fussi+er
fussi+est
fus+ta+nel+la
fus+ta+nel+las
fus+tian
fus+tic
fus+tics
fus+ti+ly
fus+ti+ness
fus+ty
fus+ti+er
fus+ti+est
fu+thark
fu+tharks
fu+thorc
fu+thorcs
fu+thork
fu+thorks
fu+tile
fu+tile+ly
fu+til+ity
fu+til+ities

fu+ton
fu+tons
fut+tock
fut+tocks
fu+ture
fu+tures
fu+ture+less
fu+tures
fu+tur+ism
fu+tur+ist
fu+tur+ists
fu+tur+is+tic
fu+tur+is+ti+cal+ly
fu+tur+ity
fu+tur+ities
fu+tur+olo+gist
fu+tur+olo+gists
fu+tur+ol+ogy
fuze
fuzes
fuzes
fuz+ing
fuzed
fu+zee
fu+zees
Fu+zhou
fuzz
fuzzes
fuzzes
fuzz+ing
fuzzed
fuzzi+ly
fuzzi+ness
fuzzy
fuzzi+er
fuzzi+est
fuzzy-wuzzy
fuzzy-wuzzies
or
fuzzy-wuzzy
f-word
f-words
Fylde
fyl+fot
fyl+fots
Fyn

G

g
g's
G
Gs or
G's
gab
gabs
gabs
gab+bing
gabbed
gab+ar+dine
gab+ar+dines
gab+ber
gab+bers
gab+ble
gab+bles
gab+bles
gab+bling
gab+bled
gab+bler
gab+blers
gab+bro
gab+bros
gab+by
gab+bi+er
gab+bi+est
gab+er+dine
gab+er+dines
Gab+ero+nes
Ga+bes
gab+fest
gab+fests
ga+bi+on
ga+bi+ons
ga+ble
ga+bles
Gable
ga+bled
Gabo
Ga+bon
Gabo+nese
Gabo+nese
ga+boon
ga+boons
Gabor

Gabo+ro+ne
Gabriel
Gabrieli
Gabrielli
gaby
gabies
gad
gads
gads
gad+ding
gad+ded
Gad
gad+about
gad+abouts
Gada+rene
Gaddafi
gad+der
gad+ders
gad+fly
gad+flies
gadg+et
gadg+ets
gadg+et+ry
ga+doid
ga+doids
gado+lin+ium
ga+droon
ga+droons
gad+wall
gad+walls or
gad+wall
gad+zooks
Gaea
Gael
Gaels
Gael+dom
Gael+ic
Gael+tacht
Gael+tachts
gaff
gaffs
gaffs
gaff+ing
gaffed
gaffe

gaffes
gaf+fer
gaf+fers
gag
gags
gags
gag+ging
gagged
gaga
Gagarin
gage
gages
gages
gag+ing
gaged
Gage
gag+gle
gag+gles
gag+gles
gag+gling
gag+gled
Gaia
gai+ety
gai+eties
gail+lar+dia
gail+lar+dias
gai+ly
gain
gains
gains
gain+ing
gained
gain+er
gain+ers
gain+ful
gain+ful+ly
gain+ful+ness
gain+say
gain+says
gain+say+ing
gain+said
gain+say+er
gain+say+ers
Gainsborough
'gainst

gainst
Gaiseric
gait
gaits
gaits
gait+ing
gait+ed
gait+er
gait+ers
Gaitskell
Gaius
gal
gals
gala
galas
ga+lac+tic
ga+la+go
ga+la+gos
ga+lah
ga+lahs
Galahad
ga+lan+gal
ga+lan+gals
gal+an+tine
gal+an+tines
Ga+lá+pa+gos
Gala+shiels
Ga+la+ta
Galatea
Ga+laţi
Ga+la+tia
Ga+la+tian
Ga+la+tians
gal+axy
gal+axies
Gal+axy
gal+ba+num
Galbraith
Gal+braith+ian
gale
gales
ga+lea
ga+leae
ga+leate
ga+leat+ed

Galen
ga+lena
Ga+len+ic
ga+lenite
Ga+li+cia
Ga+li+cias
Ga+li+cian
Ga+li+cians
Gali+lean
Gali+leans
Gali+lee
Galileo
gal+in+gale
gal+in+gales
gali+ot
gali+ots
gali+pot
gali+pots
gall
galls
galls
gall+ing
galled
gal+lant
gal+lants
gal+lants
gal+lant+ing
gal+lant+ed
gal+lant+ly
gal+lant+ry
gal+lant+ries
gall-apple
gall-apples
Gal+le
gal+leass
gal+leasses
gal+leon
gal+leons
gal+ler+ied
gal+lery
gal+leries
gal+ley
gal+leys
gall+fly
gall+flies
Gal+lia
gal+liard
gal+liards
Gal+lic
Gal+li+cise
Gal+li+cises
Gal+li+cis+ing
Gal+li+cised
Gal+li+cism
Gal+li+cisms

Gal+li+cize
Gal+li+cizes
Gal+li+ciz+ing
Gal+li+cized
gal+li+gas+kins
gal+li+mau+fry
gal+li+mau+fries
gal+li+na+cean
gal+li+na+ceans
gal+li+na+ceous
Ga+lli+nas
gall+ing
gall+ing+ly
gal+li+nule
gal+li+nules
gal+li+ot
gal+li+ots
Gal+lipo+li
gal+li+pot
gal+li+pots
gal+lium
gal+li+vant
gal+li+vants
gal+li+vant+ing
gal+li+vant+ed
Gäl+li+va+re
gal+li+wasp
gal+li+wasps
gall+nut
gall+nuts
gal+lon
gal+lons
gal+lon+age
gal+lon+ages
gal+loon
gal+loons
gal+loot
gal+loots
gal+lop
gal+lops
gal+lops
gal+lop+ing
gal+loped
gal+lop+er
gal+lop+ers
Gal+lo+way
Gal+lo+ways
gal+lows
gal+lowses *or*
gal+lows
gall+sick+ness
gall+stone
gall+stones
Gallup
Gal+lup Poll

Gal+lup Polls
ga+loot
ga+loots
gal+op
gal+ops
ga+lore
ga+loshes
Galsworthy
Galton
ga+lumph
ga+lumphs
ga+lumph+ing
ga+lumphed
Galvani
gal+van+ic
gal+vani+cal+ly
gal+va+ni+sa+
tion
gal+va+nise
gal+va+nises
gal+va+nis+ing
gal+va+nised
gal+va+nism
gal+va+ni+za+
tion
gal+va+nize
gal+va+nizes
gal+va+niz+ing
gal+va+nized
gal+va+nom+eter
gal+va+nom+
eters
gal+va+no+met+
ric
gal+va+nom+etry
Gal+way
place name
Galway
surname
Gal+we+gian
Gal+we+gians
gam
gams
Gama
Gambetta
Gam+bia
Gam+bian
Gam+bians
gam+bier
gam+bir
gam+bit
gam+bits
gam+ble
gam+bles
gam+bles

gam+bling
gam+bled
gam+bler
gam+blers
gam+bling
gam+boge
gam+boges
gam+bol
gam+bols
gam+bols
gam+bol+ling
or
gam+bol+ing
U.S.
gam+bolled *or*
gam+boled
U.S.
gam+brel
gam+brels
game
games
games
gam+ing
gamed
gam+er
gam+est
game+cock
game+cocks
game+keeper
game+keepers
gam+elan
gam+elans
game+ly
game+ness
games+man+ship
game+some
game+some+
ness
game+ster
game+sters
gam+etan+gium
gam+etan+gia
gam+ete
gam+etes
ga+met+ic
ga+meto+phyte
ga+meto+
phytes
gam+eto+phyt+ic
gam+ey
gami+er
gami+est
gami+ly
gam+in
gam+ins

gam+ine
　gam+ines
gami+ness
gam+ing
gam+ma
　gam+mas
gamma-ray
gam+mer
　gam+mers
gam+mon
　gam+mons
gam+mons
gam+mon+ing
gam+moned
gam+my
　gam+mi+er
　gam+mi+est
gamo+pet+al+
　ous
gamp
gamps
gam+ut
　gam+uts
gamy
gami+er
gami+est
Gance
gan+der
　gan+ders
Gandhi
Gan+dhian
　Gand+hians
Gan+dzha
Ganesa
gang
　gangs
gangs
gang+ing
ganged
gang
　Scots
gangs
gang+ing
gaed
gane
Gan+ga
gang+bang
　gang+bangs
gang+er
　gang+ers
Gan+ges
Gan+get+ic
gang+land
gan+gli+ar
gan+gli+at+ed

gan+gling
gan+gli+on
　gan+gli+ons *or*
　gan+glia
gan+gli+on+ic
gan+gly
gang+plank
　gang+planks
gan+grene
　gan+grenes
gan+gren+ing
gan+grened
gan+gre+nous
gang+ster
　gang+sters
Gang+tok
gangue
gang+way
　gang+ways
gan+is+ter
gan+net
　gan+nets
gan+nis+ter
gan+oid
　gan+oids
Gan+su
gan+try
　gan+tries
Ganymede
　person in Greek
　myth
Gany+mede
　moon of Jupiter
gaol
　gaols
gaols
gaol+ing
gaoled
gaol+er
　gaol+ers
Gao+xiong
gap
　gaps
gaps
gap+ping
gapped
gape
　gapes
gapes
gap+ing
gaped
gap+er
　gap+ers
gapes
gap+ing

gap+py
gap+pi+er
gap+pi+est
gar
　gars *or*
　gar
gar+age
　gar+ages
gar+ages
gar+ag+ing
gar+aged
garb
　garbs
garbs
garb+ing
garbed
gar+bage
gar+ble
　gar+bles
gar+bles
gar+bling
gar+bled
gar+bler
　gar+blers
Garbo
gar+board
　gar+boards
García
gar+çon
　gar+çons
Gard
gar+da
　gar+daí
Gar+da
gar+den
　gar+dens
gar+dens
gar+den+ing
gar+dened
gar+den+er
　gar+den+ers
gar+denia
　gar+denias
gar+den+ing
garde+robe
　garde+robes
Gardiner
Gardner
Garfield
gar+fish
　gar+fishes *or*
　gar+fish
gar+ga+ney
　gar+ga+neys
gar+gan+tuan

gar+gle
gar+gles
gar+gles
gar+gling
gar+gled
gar+goyle
　gar+goyles
gar+ial
　gar+ials
gari+bal+di
　gari+bal+dis
Garibaldi
gar+ish
gar+ish+ly
gar+ish+ness
gar+land
　gar+lands
gar+lands
gar+land+ing
gar+land+ed
Garland
gar+lic
gar+licky
gar+ment
　gar+ments
gar+ments
gar+ment+ing
gar+ment+ed
gar+ner
　gar+ners
gar+ners
gar+ner+ing
gar+nered
Garner
gar+net
　gar+nets
gar+nish
　gar+nishes
gar+nishes
gar+nish+ing
gar+nished
gar+nishee
　gar+nishees
gar+nishees
gar+nishee+ing
gar+nisheed
gar+nish+er
　gar+nish+ers
gar+nish+ment
　gar+nish+ments
gar+ni+ture
　gar+ni+tures
Ga+ronne
ga+rotte
　ga+rottes

ga+rottes
ga+rot+ting
ga+rot+ted
ga+rot+ter
ga+rot+ters
gar+pike
gar+pikes
gar+ret
gar+rets
Garrick
gar+ri+son
gar+ri+sons
gar+ri+sons
gar+ri+son+ing
gar+ri+soned
gar+ron
gar+rons
gar+rotte
gar+rottes
gar+rottes
gar+rot+ting
gar+rot+ted
gar+rott+er
gar+rott+ers
gar+ru+lity
gar+ru+lous
gar+ru+lous+ly
gar+ru+lous+
  ness
garry+owen
garry+owens
gar+ter
gar+ters
gar+ters
gar+ter+ing
gar+tered
Gar+ter
garth
garths
Gary
gas
gases or
gas+ses
gases or
gas+ses
gas+sing
gassed
gas+bag
gas+bags
Gas+cogne
Gascoigne
Gas+con
Gas+cons
gas+con+ade
gas+con+ades

gas+con+ades
gas+con+ad+ing
gas+con+ad+ed
Gas+co+ny
gas-cooled
gas-discharge
gas+eous
gas+eous+ness
gash
gashes
gashes
gash+ing
gashed
gas+holder
gas+holders
gasi+fi+ca+tion
gasi+fy
gasi+fies
gasi+fy+ing
gasi+fied
Gaskell
gas+ket
gas+kets
gas+light
gas+lights
gas+man
gas+men
gaso+lene
gaso+line
gas+om+eter
gas+om+eters
gasp
gasps
gasps
gasp+ing
gasped
Gaspar
Gas+pé
gasp+er
gasp+ers
Gasser
gas+si+ness
gas+sy
gas+si+er
gas+si+est
gas+tero+pod
gas+tero+pods
gas+tric
gas+tri+tis
gas+tro+col+ic
gas+tro+en+teri+
  tis
gas+tro+in+tes+
  ti+nal
gas+tro+nome

gas+tro+nomes
gas+trono+mer
gas+trono+mers
gas+tro+nom+ic
gas+tro+nomi+
  cal
gas+tro+nomi+
  cal+ly
gas+trono+mist
gas+trono+
  mists
gas+trono+my
gas+tro+pod
gas+tro+pods
gas+tropo+dan
gas+tro+scope
gas+tro+scopes
gas+tru+la
gas+tru+las or
gas+tru+lae
gas+works
gas+works
gat
gate
gates
gates
gat+ing
gat+ed
ga+teau
ga+teaux
gâ+teau
gâ+teaux
gate-crash
gate-crashes
gate-crashing
gate-crashed
gate-crasher
gate-crashers
gate+fold
gate+folds
gate+house
gate+houses
gate+keeper
gate+keepers
gate-leg
gate-legged
gate+post
gate+posts
Gates
Gates+head
gate+way
gate+ways
Gath
gath+er
gath+ers

gath+ers
gath+er+ing
gath+ered
gath+er+er
gath+er+ers
gath+er+ing
gath+er+ings
Gatling
Ga+tún
gauche
gauche+ly
gauche+ness
gau+cherie
gau+cheries
gau+cho
gau+chos
gaud
gauds
Gaudí
Gaudier-Brzeska
gaudi+ly
gaudi+ness
gaudy
gaudies
gaudi+er
gaudi+est
gauge
gauges
gauges
gaug+ing
gauged
gauge+able
Gauguin
Gau+ha+ti
Gaul
Gauls
Gau+lei+ter
Gau+lei+ters
Gaul+ish
gaunt
gaunt+let
gaunt+lets
gaunt+ly
gaunt+ness
gaup
gaups
gaup+ing
gauped
gaur
gaurs
gauss
gauss
Gauss
Gauss+ian
Gautier

gauze
  gauzes
gauzi+ly
gauzi+ness
gauzy
  gauzi+er
  gauzi+est
Gavaskar
gave
gav+el
  gav+els
ga+vial
  ga+vials
Gäv+le
ga+vot
  ga+vots
ga+votte
  ga+vottes
gawk
  gawks
  gawks
gawk+ing
gawked
gawki+ly
gawki+ness
gawk+ish
gawky
  gawki+er
  gawki+est
gawp
  gawps
gawp+ing
gawped
gay
  gays
gay+er
gay+est
Gay
Gaya
Gay-Lussac
gay+ness
Gaza
ga+zania
  ga+zanias
Gaz+an+ku+lu
gaze
  gazes
  gazes
gaz+ing
gazed
ga+zebo
  ga+zebos or
  ga+zeboes
ga+zelle
  ga+zelles or

ga+zelle
gaz+er
  gaz+ers
ga+zette
  ga+zettes
  ga+zettes
ga+zet+ting
ga+zet+ted
gaz+et+teer
  gaz+et+teers
Ga+zi+an+tep
gaz+pa+cho
  gaz+pa+chos
ga+zump
  ga+zumps
  ga+zumps
ga+zump+ing
ga+zumped
ga+zump+er
  ga+zump+ers
ga+zund+er
  ga+zund+ers
  ga+zund+ers
ga+zund+er+ing
ga+zund+ered
ga+zund+er+er
  ga+zund+er+ers
Gdańsk
Gdy+nia
Ge
gean
  geans
gear
  gears
  gears
gear+ing
geared
gear+box
  gear+boxes
gear+ing
  gear+ings
gear+shift
  gear+shifts
gear+wheel
  gear+wheels
Geber
gecko
  geckos or
  geckoes
gee
  gees
gee+ing
geed
gee+bung
  gee+bungs

geek
  geeks
geel+bek
  geel+beks
Gee+long
geese
gee+zer
  gee+zers
Ge+hen+na
  Ge+hen+nas
Geiger
Geiger-Müller
gei+sha
  gei+shas or
  gei+sha
Geissler
gel
  gels
gels
gel+ling
gelled
gela+tin
  gela+tins
gela+tine
  gela+tines
ge+lati+ni+sa+
  tion
ge+lati+nise
  ge+lati+nises
ge+lati+nis+ing
ge+lati+nised
ge+lati+ni+za+
  tion
ge+lati+nize
  ge+lati+nizes
ge+lati+niz+ing
ge+lati+nized
ge+lati+nous
ge+lati+nous+ly
ge+lati+nous+
  ness
ge+la+tion
  ge+la+tions
geld
  gelds
geld+ing
geld+ed or
gelt
Gel+der+land
geld+ing
  geld+ings
Geldof
Gelée
Ge+li+bo+lu
gel+id

ge+lid+ity
gel+ig+nite
Gel+li+gaer
Gell-Mann
gel+ly
Gel+sen+kir+
  chen
gelt
gem
  gems
gems
gem+ming
gemmed
Ge+ma+ra
gemi+nate
  gemi+nates
gemi+nat+ing
gemi+nat+ed
gemi+nat+ed
gemi+nate+ly
gemi+na+tion
  gemi+na+tions
Gemi+ni
  Gemi+nis
gem+like
gem+ma
gem+mae
gem+mate
  gem+mates
gem+mat+ing
gem+mat+ed
gem+ma+tion
  gem+ma+tions
gem+mife+rous
gem+mipa+rous
gem+mo+logi+
  cal
gem+molo+gist
gem+molo+
  gists
gem+mol+ogy
gem+mule
  gem+mules
gem+my
gemo+logi+cal
gem+olo+gist
  gem+olo+gists
gem+ol+ogy
gems+bok
  gems+boks or
  gems+bok
gems+buck
  gems+bucks
  or
  gems+buck

gem+stone
  gem+stones
gen
gen+darme
  gen+darmes
gen+dar+me+rie
  gen+dar+me+
    ries
gen+dar+me+ry
  gen+dar+me+
    ries
gen+der
  gen+ders
gender-bender
  gender-benders
gene
  genes
ge+nea+logi+cal
ge+nea+logi+cal+
  ly
ge+nealo+gist
  ge+nealo+gists
ge+neal+ogy
  ge+neal+ogies
gen+ecol+ogy
  gen+ecol+ogies
gen+era
gen+er+able
gen+er+al
  gen+er+als
gen+er+ali+sa+
  tion
  gen+er+ali+sa+
    tions
gen+er+al+ise
  gen+er+al+ises
  gen+er+al+is+
    ing
  gen+er+al+ised
  gen+er+al+is+si+
    mo
  gen+er+al+is+si+
    mos
gen+er+al+ity
  gen+er+al+ities
gen+er+ali+za+
  tion
  gen+er+ali+za+
    tions
gen+er+al+ize
  gen+er+al+izes
  gen+er+al+iz+
    ing
  gen+er+al+ized
gen+er+al+ly

general-purpose
gen+er+ate
  gen+er+ates
  gen+er+at+ing
  gen+er+at+ed
gen+era+tion
  gen+era+tions
gen+era+tive
gen+era+tor
  gen+era+tors
gen+era+trix
  gen+era+tri+ces
ge+ner+ic
ge+neri+cal+ly
gen+er+os+ity
  gen+er+os+ities
gen+er+ous
gen+er+ous+ly
gen+er+ous+
  ness
gen+esis
  gen+eses
Gen+esis
gen+et
  gen+ets
Genet
ge+net+ic
ge+neti+cal
ge+neti+cal+ly
ge+neti+cist
  ge+neti+cists
ge+net+ics
ge+nette
  ge+nettes
Ge+neva
Ge+nevan
  Ge+nevans
Ge+nève
Gen+evese
  Gen+evese
Geneviève
Genf
Genf+er+see
Genghis Khan
gen+ial
  amiable
ge+nial
  of the chin
ge+ni+al+ity
gen+ial+ly
gen+ic
ge+nie
  ge+nies
geni+tal
geni+ta+lia

geni+tals
geni+ti+val
geni+tive
  geni+tives
genito+uri+nary
ge+ni+us
  ge+ni+uses *or*
  ge+nii
ge+ni+zah
  ge+ni+zahs *or*
  ge+ni+zoth
Genk
genoa
  genoas
Genoa
geno+cid+al
geno+cide
  geno+cides
Geno+ese
  Geno+ese
ge+nome
  ge+nomes
geno+type
  geno+types
geno+typ+ic
Ge+no+va
Geno+vese
  Geno+vese
gen+re
  gen+res
gens
  gen+tes
Genseric
gent
  gents
gen+teel
  gen+teel+er
  gen+teel+est
  gen+teel+ly
  gen+teel+ness
gen+tian
  gen+tians
Gen+tile
  non-Jew(ish)
  Gen+tiles
Gentile
  surname
gen+til+ity
  gen+til+ities
gen+tle
  gen+tles
gen+tling
gen+tled
gen+tler

gen+tlest
gentle+folk
gentle+folks
gentle+man
  gentle+men
gentleman-farmer
  gentlemen-
    farmers
gentle+man+li+
  ness
gentle+man+ly
gen+tle+ness
gentle+woman
  gentle+women
gen+tly
gen+tri+fi+ca+
  tion
gen+tri+fi+er
  gen+tri+fi+ers
gen+try
  gen+tries
gents
genu+flect
  genu+flects
  genu+flect+ing
  genu+flect+ed
genu+flec+tion
  genu+flec+tions
genu+flec+tor
  genu+flec+tors
genu+ine
genu+ine+ly
genu+ine+ness
gen up
  gens up
  gen+ning up
  genned up
ge+nus
  ge+nuses *or*
  gen+era
geo
geo+cen+tric
geo+cen+tri+cal+
  ly
geo+chrono+logi+
  cal
geo+chro+nol+
  ogy
geo+chro+nol+
  ogies
ge+ode
  ge+odes
geo+des+ic
geo+des+ics
ge+od+esist

ge+od+esists
geod+esy
geo+det+ic
geo+deti+cal+ly
ge+od+ic
ge+og+ra+pher
ge+og+ra+phers
geo+graph+ic
geo+graphi+cal
geo+graphi+cal+ly
ge+og+ra+phy
ge+og+ra+phies
ge+oid
ge+oids
geo+log+ic
geo+logi+cal
geo+logi+cal+ly
ge+olo+gist
ge+ol+ogy
ge+ol+ogies
geo+mag+net+ic
geo+mag+ne+tism
geo+met+ric
geo+met+ri+cal
geo+met+ri+cal+ly
ge+om+etri+cian
ge+om+etri+cians
ge+om+etrid
ge+om+etrids
ge+om+etry
ge+om+etries
geo+mor+pho+log+ic
geo+mor+pho+logi+cal
geo+mor+pholo+gy
geo+physi+cal
geo+physi+cist
geo+physi+cists
geo+phys+ics
geo+po+liti+cal
geo+poli+tics
Geor+die
Geor+dies
George
Georges
George+town
Guyana
George Town
Malaysia

geor+gette
Geor+gia
Geor+gian
Geor+gians
geo+stat+ics
geo+sta+tion+ary
geo+stroph+ic
geo+syn+chro+nous
geo+syn+cline
geo+syn+clines
geo+tex+tile
geo+tex+tiles
geo+ther+mal
geo+ther+mic
geo+trop+ic
ge+ot+ro+pism
ge+ot+ro+pisms
Gera
ge+ra+nium
ge+ra+niums
Gérard
ger+bera
ger+beras
ger+bil
ger+bils
ger+bille
ger+billes
ger+fal+con
ger+fal+cons
geri+at+ric
geri+at+rics
geria+tri+cian
geria+tri+cians
geri+at+rics
Géricault
Ger+la+chov+ka
germ
germs
ger+man
ger+mans
Ger+man
Ger+mans
ger+man+der
ger+man+ders
ger+mane
ger+mane+ly
ger+mane+ness
Ger+man+ic
Germanicus
ger+ma+nium
Ger+ma+ny
Ger+ma+nies
or
Ger+ma+nys

ger+mi+cid+al
ger+mi+cide
ger+mi+cides
ger+mi+nal
ger+mi+nal+ly
ger+mi+nate
ger+mi+nates
ger+mi+nat+ing
ger+mi+nat+ed
ger+mi+na+tion
ger+mi+na+tive
ger+mi+na+tor
ger+mi+na+tors
Ger+mis+ton
Ge+ro+na
Geronimo
ger+on+to+logi+cal
ger+on+tolo+gist
ger+on+tolo+gists
ger+on+tol+ogy
ger+ry+man+der
ger+ry+man+ders
ger+ry+man+ders
ger+ry+man+der+ing
ger+ry+man+dered
Gers
Gershwin
ger+und
ger+unds
Ge+run+da
ge+run+dial
ger+un+di+val
ge+run+dive
ge+run+dives
Geryon
ges+so
ges+sos
gest
gests
Ge+stalt
Ge+stalts *or*
Ge+stal+ten
Ge+sta+po
ges+tate
ges+tates
ges+tat+ing
ges+tat+ed
ges+ta+tion
ges+ta+tions

geste
gestes
ges+ticu+late
ges+ticu+lates
ges+ticu+lat+ing
ges+ticu+lat+ed
ges+ticu+la+tion
ges+ticu+la+tions
ges+ticu+la+tive
ges+ticu+la+tor
ges+ticu+la+tors
ges+ticu+la+tory
ges+tur+al
ges+ture
ges+tures
ges+tures
ges+tur+ing
ges+tured
get
gets
gets
get+ting
got
got *or*
got+ten
U.S.
get+able
get+away
get+aways
get away
verb
Geth+sema+ne
get+table
get+ter
get+ters
get-togeth+er
get-togeth+ers
Getty
Get+tys+burg
get-up
get-ups
get up
verb
get-up-and-go
Getz
geum
geums
gew+gaw
gew+gaws
gey+ser
gey+sers
Ge+zi+ra
G-force

G-forces	ghost+ed	gib+bose	gift+wrap+ping
Gha+na	ghost+like	gib+bos+ity	gift+wrapped
Gha+na+ian	ghost+ly	gib+bos+ities	Gifu
Gha+na+ians	ghost+li+er	gib+bous	gig
Gha+nian	ghost+li+est	gib+bous+ly	gigs
Gha+nians	ghost+write	gib+bous+ness	gigs
gha+rial	ghost+writes	Gibbs	gig+ging
gha+rials	ghost+writ+ing	gibe	gigged
ghar+ri	ghost+wrote	gibes	gi+ga+flop
ghar+ries	ghost+writ+ten	gibes	gi+ga+flops
ghar+ry	ghost+writ+er	gib+ing	gi+gan+tesque
ghar+ries	ghost+writ+ers	gibed	gi+gan+tic
ghast+li+ness	ghoul	gib+er	gi+gan+ti+cal+ly
ghast+ly	ghouls	gib+ers	gi+gan+tism
ghast+li+er	ghoul+ish	gib+lets	gig+gle
ghast+li+est	ghoul+ish+ly	Gi+bral+tar	gig+gles
ghat	ghoul+ish+ness	Gi+bral+tar+ian	gig+gles
ghats	ghyll	Gi+bral+tar+ians	gig+gling
Ghats	ghylls	Gibran	gig+gled
gha+zi	GI	Gib+son	gig+gler
gha+zis	GIs *or*	Gib+sons	gig+glers
Ghaz+zah	GI's	gid+day	gig+gling
ghee	Giacometti	gid+di+ly	gig+glings
Ghent	Giambologna	gid+di+ness	gig+gly
gher+kin	gi+ant	gid+dy	gig+gli+er
gher+kins	gi+ants	gid+dies	gig+gli+est
ghet+to	gi+ant+ess	gid+dy+ing	Gigli
ghet+tos *or*	gi+ant+esses	gid+died	gigo+lo
ghet+toes	gi+ant+ism	gid+di+er	gigo+los
ghet+to+blaster	gia+our	gid+di+est	gi+got
ghet+to+	gia+ours	Gide	gi+gots
blasters	gib	Gideon	gigue
ghet+toi+sa+tion	gibs	gidgee	gigues
ghet+toi+sa+	gibs	gidgees	Gi+jón
tions	gib+bing	gidjee	Gila
ghet+to+ise	gibbed	gidjees	gil+bert
ghet+to+ises	Gib	gie	gil+berts
ghet+to+is+ing	gib+ber	*Scots*	Gilbert
ghet+to+ised	gib+bers	gies	Gil+bert Is+lands
ghet+toi+za+tion	gib+bers	gie+ing	gild
ghet+toi+za+	gib+ber+ing	gied	gilds
tions	gib+bered	gien	gilds
ghet+to+ize	Gibberd	Gielgud	gild+ing
ghet+to+izes	gib+ber+el+lin	Gies+sen	gild+ed *or*
ghet+to+iz+ing	gib+ber+el+lins	gift	gilt
ghet+to+ized	gib+ber+ish	gifts	gild+er
Ghiberti	gib+bet	gifts	*person who gilds*
ghil+lie	gib+bets	gift+ing	gild+ers
ghil+lies	gib+bets	gift+ed	gil+der
Ghirlandaio	gib+bet+ing	GIFT	*currency*
Ghirlandajo	gib+bet+ed	gift+ed	gil+ders *or*
ghost	gib+bon	gift+ed+ly	gil+der
ghosts	gib+bons	gift+ed+ness	gild+ing
ghosts	Gibbon	gift+wrap	gilds+man
ghost+ing	Gibbons	gift+wraps	gilds+men

Gil+ead
place name
Gilead
Biblical character
Giles
gi+let
　gi+lets
gill
　gills
Gill
gilled
Gillespie
gil+lie
　gil+lies
gil+li+flower
　gil+li+flowers
Gil+ling+ham
Gillray
gills
gil+ly
　gil+lies
gil+ly+flower
　gil+ly+flowers
Gi+lo+lo
gilt
　gilts
gilt-edged
gim+bals
gim+crack
　gim+cracks
gim+crack+ery
gim+let
　gim+lets
　gim+lets
　gim+let+ing
　gim+let+ed
gim+mick
　gim+micks
gim+mick+ry
gim+micky
gimp
　gimps
gin
　gins
　gins
　gin+ning
　ginned
gin
begin
　gins
　gin+ning
　gan
　gun
gin+ger
　gin+gers

ginger+bread
gin+ger+ly
gin+gery
ging+ham
gin+gi+li
gin+gi+va
　gin+gi+vae
　gin+gi+val
　gin+gi+vi+tis
ging+ko
　ging+koes
gin+gly+mus
　gin+gly+mi
gink
　ginks
gink+go
　gink+goes
gi+nor+mous
Ginsberg
gin+seng
　gin+sengs
Ginzburg
Gio+con+da
Giorgione
Giotto
Giovanni
gip
　gips
gip+ping
gipped
Gipps+land
Gip+sy
　Gip+sies
Gip+sy+ish
gi+raffe
　gi+raffes *or*
　gi+raffe
Giraldus
　Cambrensis
gir+an+dole
　gir+an+doles
gira+sol
　gira+sols
gira+sole
　gira+soles
Giraud
Giraudoux
gird
　girds
　girds
gird+ing
gird+ed *or*
girt
gird+er
　gird+ers

gir+dle
　gir+dles
　gir+dles
gir+dling
gir+dled
Gir+gen+ti
girl
　girls
girl+friend
　girl+friends
girl+hood
girlie
　girlies
girl+ish
giro
　giros
Gi+ronde
girt
　girts
girt+ing
girt+ed
girth
　girths
　girths
girth+ing
girthed
Gis+borne
Giscard d'Estaing
Gish
gis+mo
　gis+mos
Gissing
gist
　gists
git
　gits
gîte
　gîtes
git+tern
　git+terns
Giulini
Giulio Romano
giu+sto
giv+able
give
　gives
giv+ing
　gave
giv+en
give+able
give-and-take
give+away
adj., noun
　give+aways
give away

verb
giv+en
giv+er
　giv+ers
Gîza
giz+mo
　giz+mos
giz+zard
gla+bel+la
gla+bel+lae
gla+bel+lar
gla+brous
gla+cé
　gla+cés
gla+cé+ing
gla+céed
gla+cial
gla+ci+al+ly
gla+ci+ate
　gla+ci+ates
gla+ci+at+ing
gla+ci+at+ed
gla+cia+tion
glaci+er
　glaci+ers
glacio+logi+cal
glaci+olo+gist
　glaci+olo+gists
glaci+ol+ogy
glac+is
　glac+ises *or*
　glac+is
glad
　glads
　glads
glad+ding
glad+ded
glad+der
glad+dest
Glad+beck
glad+den
　glad+dens
glad+den+ing
glad+dened
glad+den+er
　glad+den+ers
glade
　glades
gladia+tor
　gladia+tors
gladia+to+rial
gladio+lus
　gladio+luses *or*
　gladio+lus *or*

gladio+li
glad+ly
glad+ness
glad+some
glad+some+ly
glad+some+ness
Glad+stone
carriage or bag
 Glad+stones
Gladstone
surname
Glago+lit+ic
glair
 glairs
 glairs
 glair+ing
 glaired
 glair+eous
 glairy
glam
glam+or
U.S.
Gla+mor+gan
Gla+mor+gan+
 shire
glam+ori+sa+tion
glam+or+ise
 glam+or+ises
 glam+or+is+ing
 glam+or+ised
glam+ori+za+tion
 glam+or+ize
 glam+or+izes
 glam+or+iz+ing
 glam+or+ized
glam+or+ous
glam+or+ous+ly
glam+our
glam+our+ize
U.S.
 glam+our+izes
 glam+our+iz+ing
 glam+our+ized
glance
 glances
 glances
 glanc+ing
 glanced
glanc+ing+ly
gland
 glands
glan+ders
glan+du+lar
glan+du+lar+ly
glan+dule

glan+dules
glan+du+lous
glan+du+lous+ly
glans
 glan+des
glare
 glares
 glares
 glar+ing
 glared
 glar+ing
glar+ing+ly
glar+ing+ness
Gla+ris
Gla+rus
Glaser
glas+nost
glass
 glasses
 glasses
 glass+ing
 glassed
Glass
glass-blower
 glass-blowers
glass-blowing
 glasses
glass+ful
 glass+fuls
glassi+ly
glass+ine
glassi+ness
glass+less
glass+like
glass+ware
glass+wort
 glass+worts
glassy
 glassi+er
 glassi+est
Glas+ton+bury
Glas+we+gian
 Glas+we+gians
Glau+ber
Glauce
glau+co+ma
glau+co+ma+
 tous
glau+cous
glaze
 glazes
 glazes
 glaz+ing
 glazed

glazed
glaz+er
 glaz+ers
gla+zi+er
 gla+zi+ers
 gla+zi+ery
 gla+zi+eries
glaz+ing
Glazunov
gleam
 gleams
 gleams
gleam+ing
 gleamed
gleam+ing
gleam+ing+ly
gleamy
 gleami+er
 gleami+est
glean
 gleans
 glean+ing
 gleaned
glean+er
 glean+ers
 glean+ings
glebe
 glebes
glee
 glees
glee+ful
glee+ful+ly
glee+ful+ness
glee+man
 glee+men
Glei+witz
glen
 glens
Glen+coe
Glendower
glen+gar+ry
 glen+gar+ries
Glenn
Glen+roth+es
Gle+vum
glia
 glias
glib
 glib+ber
 glib+best
glib+ly
glib+ness
glide
 glides
 glides

glid+ing
glid+ed
glid+er
 glid+ers
glid+ing+ly
glim+mer
 glim+mers
 glim+mers
glim+mer+ing
 glim+mered
glim+mer+ing+ly
glimpse
 glimpses
 glimpses
glimps+ing
 glimpsed
glimps+er
 glimps+ers
Glinka
glint
 glints
 glints
glint+ing
glint+ed
glio+ma
 glio+mas *or*
 glio+ma+ta
glis+sade
 glis+sades
 glis+sades
 glis+sad+ing
 glis+sad+ed
glis+san+do
 glis+san+dos
 or
 glis+san+di
glis+ten
 glis+tens
 glis+tens
glis+ten+ing
 glis+tened
glis+ter
 glis+ters
glis+ter+ing
 glis+tered
glitch
 glitches
glit+ter
 glit+ters
 glit+ters
glit+ter+ing
 glit+tered
glit+te+ra+ti
glit+ter+ing+ly
glit+tery

glitzy
 glitzi+er
 glitzi+est
Gli+wi+ce
gloam+ing
gloat
 gloats
 gloats
 gloat+ing
 gloat+ed
gloat+er
 gloat+ers
glob
 globs
glob+al
glob+ali+sa+tion
glob+ali+za+tion
glob+al+ly
globe
 globes
 globes
glob+ing
 globed
globe+fish
 globe+fishes
 or
 globe+fish
globe+flower
 globe+flowers
globe+like
globe+trotter
 globe+trotters
globe+trotting
 globe+trottings
glo+big+eri+na
 glo+big+eri+nas
 or
 glo+big+eri+nae
glo+boid
 glo+boids
glo+bose
glo+bose+ly
glo+bous
globu+lar
glob+ule
 glob+ules
globu+lin
 globu+lins
globu+lous
glock+en+spiel
 glock+en+spiels
glom+er+ate
glom+era+tion
 glom+era+tions
glom+er+ule

glom+er+ules
Glom+ma
gloom
 glooms
 glooms
gloom+ing
 gloomed
gloomi+ly
gloomi+ness
gloomy
 gloomi+er
 gloomi+est
glo+ria
 glo+rias
Glo+ria
 Glo+rias
glo+ri+fi+ca+tion
glo+ri+fi+ca+
 tions
glo+ri+fy
 glo+ri+fies
glo+ri+fy+ing
 glo+ri+fied
glo+ri+ole
 glo+ri+oles
glo+ri+ous
glo+ri+ous+ly
glo+ri+ous+ness
glo+ry
 glo+ries
 glo+ries
glo+ry+ing
 glo+ried
gloss
 glosses
 glosses
gloss+ing
 glossed
glos+sar+ial
glos+sa+rist
 glos+sa+rists
glos+sa+ry
 glos+sa+ries
gloss+eme
 gloss+emes
glossi+ly
glossi+ness
glos+sit+ic
glos+si+tis
glos+so+la+lia
glossy
 glossies
glossi+er
glossi+est
glot+tal

glot+tis
 glot+tises or
 glot+ti+des
Glouces+ter
 place name
Gloucester
 surname
Glouces+ter+
 shire
glove
 gloves
 gloves
glov+ing
 gloved
glov+er
 glov+ers
glow
 glows
 glows
glow+ing
 glowed
glow+er
 glow+ers
 glow+ers
glow+er+ing
 glow+ered
glow+ing
glow-worm
 glow-worms
glox+inia
 glox+inias
gloze
 glozes
gloz+ing
 glozed
Gluck
glu+cose
glu+co+side
 glu+co+sides
glu+co+sid+ic
glue
 glues
 glues
glu+ing or
 glue+ing
 glued
glue+like
glu+er
 glu+ers
glue-sniffer
 glue-sniffers
glue-sniffing
gluey
 glui+er

glui+est
gluh+wein
 gluh+weins
glum
 glum+mer
 glum+mest
glu+ma+ceous
glume
 glumes
glum+ly
glum+ness
glu+on
 glu+ons
glut
 gluts
 gluts
glut+ting
 glut+ted
glu+teal
glu+ten
glu+tenous
glu+teus
glu+tei
glu+ti+nous
glu+ti+nous+ly
glut+ton
 glut+tons
glut+ton+ous
glut+ton+ous+ly
glut+tony
glyc+er+in
glyc+er+ine
glyc+er+ol
gly+cine
gly+co+gen
 gly+co+gens
gly+co+gen+esis
gly+co+gen+ic
gly+col
 gly+cols
gly+col+ic
gly+coly+sis
gly+co+side
 gly+co+sides
gly+co+sid+ic
gly+co+su+ria
Glynde+bourne
glyph
 glyphs
glyph+ic
glyp+tic
glyp+to+dont
 glyp+to+donts
G-man
 G-men

gnarl
gnarls
gnarls
gnarl+ing
gnarled
gnarl
gnarls
gnarl+ing
gnarled
gnarled
gnarly
gnash
gnashes
gnashes
gnash+ing
gnashed
gnat
gnats
gnath+ic
gnaw
gnaws
gnaw+ing
gnawed
gnawed *or*
gnawn
gnaw+ing
gnaw+ings
gneiss
gneiss+ic
gneiss+oid
gneiss+ose
gnoc+chi
gnome
gnomes
gno+mic
gno+mi+cal+ly
gnom+ish
gno+mon
gno+mons
gno+mon+ic
gno+sis
gno+ses
gnos+tic
Gnos+tic
Gnos+tics
Gnos+ti+cism
gno+to+bi+ot+ic
gnu
gnus *or*
gnu
go
goes
going
went
gone

Goa
goad
goads
goads
goad+ing
goad+ed
go-ahead
noun, adj.
goal
goals
goal+ball
goal+balls
goalie
goalies
goal+keeper
goal+keepers
goal+less
go+an+na
go+an+nas
goat
goats
Goat
goatee
goatees
goat+herd
goat+herds
goat+ish
goats+beard
goats+beards
goat's-beard
goat's-beards
goat+skin
goat+skins
goat+sucker
goat+suckers
gob
gobs
gobs
gob+bing
gobbed
gob+bet
gob+bets
Gobbi
gob+ble
gob+bles
gob+bles
gob+bling
gob+bled
gob+ble+de+
gook
gob+ble+dy+
gook
gob+bler
gob+blers
Go+belin

Go+belins
go-between
go-betweens
Gobi
Go+bian
Gobind Singh
gob+let
gob+lets
gob+lin
gob+lins
gobo
gobos *or*
goboes
gob+shite
gob+shites
gob+smacked
goby
gobies *or*
goby
go-by
noun
go by
verb
go-cart
go-carts
god
gods
God
Godard
Go+da+va+ri
god+child
god+children
Goddard
god+daughter
god+daughters
god+dess
god+desses
Gödel
Goderich
Go+des+berg
go+detia
go+detias
god+father
god+fathers
God-fearing
god+forsaken
God+head
god+hood
Godiva
god+less
god+less+ly
god+less+ness
god+like
god+li+ness
god+ly

god+li+er
god+li+est
god+mother
god+mothers
Godolphin
go+down
go+downs
warehouse
go down
verb
god+parent
god+parents
go+droon
go+droons
god+send
god+sends
god+slot
god+son
god+sons
God+speed
god+squad
god+squads
Godt+haab
Godunov
Godwin
God+win Aus+
ten
god+wit
god+wits
Goebbels
goer
goers
Goering
Goethe
go+fer
go+fers
gof+fer
gof+fers
gof+fers
gof+fer+ing
gof+fered
go-getter
go-getters
go-getting
gog+ga
gog+gas
gog+gle
gog+gles
gog+gles
gog+gling
gog+gled
goggle-box
goggle+boxes
goggle-eyed
Gogh

Gogol
Gog+ra
Goiâ+nia
Goi+ás
Goi+del+ic
go+ing
  go+ings
going-over
  goings-over
goings-on
goi+ter
U.S.
  goi+ters
  goi+tered
U.S.
goi+tre
  goi+tres
  goi+tred
  goi+trous
go-kart
  go-karts
Golan
Gol+con+da
gold
  golds
Gold
gold+crest
  gold+crests
gold-digger
  gold-diggers
gold+en
golden+eye
  golden+eyes
    or
golden+eye
gold+en+ly
gold+en+ness
golden+rod
  golden+rods
gold+finch
  gold+finches
gold+fish
  gold+fishes *or*
  gold+fish
Golding
Goldoni
gold-plate
  gold-plates
  gold-plating
  gold-plated
gold plate
noun
Goldschmidt
gold+smith
  gold+smiths

Goldsmith
golf
  golfs
  golf+ing
  golfed
golf+er
  golf+ers
Golgi
Gol+go+tha
Goliath
  Goliaths
gol+li+wog
  gol+li+wogs
gol+lop
  gol+lops
  gol+lop+ing
  gol+loped
gol+ly
  gol+lies
go+loshes
Go+mel
Go+mor+rah
  Go+mor+rahs
Go+mor+rean
Go+mor+rha
  Go+mor+rhas
Go+mor+rhean
Gomulka
gon+ad
  gon+ads
gon+ad+al
go+na+dial
gon+ado+tro+
  phin
  gon+ado+tro+
  phins
gon+ado+trop+ic
gon+ado+tro+pin
  gon+ado+tro+
  pins
Go+na+ïves
Goncharov
Goncourt
Gon+dar
gon+do+la
  gon+do+las
  gon+do+lier
  gon+do+liers
Gond+wa+na+
  land
gone
gon+er
  gon+ers
gon+fa+lon
  gon+fa+lons

gong
  gongs
  gongs
  gong+ing
  gonged
Gon+go+la
go+ni+om+eter
  go+ni+om+eters
go+nio+met+ric
go+ni+ome+try
gono+coc+cus
  gono+coc+ci
gon+or+rhea
  gon+or+rheal
gon+or+rhoea
  gon+or+rhoeal
Gonzales
goo
  goos
Gooch
good
  goods
  bet+ter
  best
good+bye
  good+byes
good-for-nothing
  good-for-
  nothings
good-humoured
good-humoured+
  ly
goodies
good+ish
good+li+ness
good-looking
good+ly
  good+li+er
  good+li+est
good+man
  good+men
Goodman
good-natured
good-natured+ly
good+ness
good-o
good-oh
goods
good-sized
good-tempered
good+wife
  good+wives
good+will
  good+wills
Good+wood

goody
  goodies
Goodyear
goody-goody
  goody-goodies
goo+ey
gooi+er
gooi+est
goof
  goofs
  goofs
  goof+ing
  goofed
goofi+ly
goofi+ness
goofy
goofi+er
goofi+est
goog
  googs
goog+ly
  goog+lies
goo+ily
Goolagong
Goole
gool+ie
  gool+ies
gooly
  gool+ies
goon
  goons
goo+ney
goop
  goops
goopy
goopi+er
goopi+est
goorie
  goories
goory
  goories
goos+an+der
  goos+an+ders
goose
bird
  geese
goose
prod in the behind
  gooses
  gooses
  goos+ing
  goosed
goose+berry
  goose+berries
goose+foot

goose+foots
goose+gog
goose+gogs
goose+grass
goose+neck
goose+necks
goose-step
goose-steps
goose-stepping
goose-stepped
goose step
noun
Goossens
go+pak
go+paks
go+pher
go+phers
Go+rakh+pur
go+ral
go+rals
Gorbachev
Gorbachov
Gor+bals
Gor+dian
Gordimer
Gordon
personal name
Gor+don
place name
gore
gores
gores
gor+ing
gored
gored
gorge
gorges
gorges
gorg+ing
gorged
gor+geous
gor+geous+ly
gor+geous+ness
gor+get
gor+gets
Gor+gio
Gor+gios
Gor+gon
Gor+gons
gor+go+nian
gor+go+nians
Gor+gon+zo+la
Go+ri+ca
go+ril+la
go+ril+las

gori+ly
gori+ness
Göring
Gor+ki
place name
Gorki
surname
Gor+ky
place name
Gorky
surname
Gör+litz
Gor+lov+ka
gor+mand
gor+mands
gor+mand+ise
gor+mand+ises
gor+mand+is+
  ing
gor+mand+ised
gor+mand+is+er
gor+mand+is+
  ers
gor+mand+ize
gor+mand+izes
gor+mand+iz+
  ing
gor+mand+ized
gor+man+dize
gor+mand+iz+er
gor+mand+iz+
  ers
gorm+less
gorse
gorses
gorsy
Gorton
gory
gori+er
gori+est
gosh
gos+hawk
gos+hawks
Go+shen
gos+ling
gos+lings
go-slow
noun, adj.
go-slows
gos+pel
gos+pels
Gos+pel
Gos+pels
gos+port
gos+sa+mer

gos+sa+mers
gos+sa+mery
Gosse
gos+sip
gos+sips
gos+sips
gos+sip+ing
gos+siped
gos+sip+er
gos+sip+ers
gossip+monger
gossip+mongers
gos+sipy
gossy+pol
got
Göta
Gö+teborg
Goth
Goths
Go+tha
Goth+en+burg
Goth+ic
Goth+ics
Gothi+cal+ly
Goth+land
Got+land
got+ten
Göt+ter+däm+
  mer+ung
Gottfried von
  Strass+burg
Göt+tin+gen
Gott+land
gouache
gouaches
Gou+da
gouge
gouges
gouges
goug+ing
gouged
goug+er
goug+ers
gou+jon
gou+jons
gou+lash
gou+lashes
Gould
Gounod
gou+ra+mi
gou+ra+mis *or*
gou+ra+mi
gourd
gourds
gour+mand

gour+mands
gour+mand+ism
gour+mand+
  isms
gour+met
gout
gouts
goût
goûts
gouti+ly
gouti+ness
gout+weed
gouty
gouti+er
gouti+est
gov+ern
gov+erns
gov+ern+ing
gov+erned
gov+ern+able
gov+ern+ance
gov+er+ness
gov+er+nesses
gov+ern+ment
gov+ern+ments
gov+ern+men+tal
gov+ern+men+tal+
  ly
gov+er+nor
gov+er+nors
gov+er+nor gen+
  er+al
gov+er+nor gen+
  er+als *or*
gov+er+nors
  gen+er+al
governor-general+
  ship
governor-
  general+ships
gov+er+nor+ship
gov+er+nor+
  ships
Govind Singh
Gow+er
place name
Gower
surname
gowk
gowks
gown
gowns
gowns
gown+ing
gowned

Gowon
goy
goys *or*
goy+im
Goya
goy+ish
Graaf+ian
grab
grabs
grabs
grab+bing
grabbed
grab+ber
grab+bers
Gracchus
Gracchi
grace
graces
graces
grac+ing
graced
Grace
Graces
grace-and-favour
grace+ful
grace+ful+ly
grace+ful+ness
grace+less
grace+less+ly
grace+less+ness
Graces
gra+cious
gra+cious+ly
gra+cious+ness
grack+le
grack+les
gra+date
gra+dates
gra+dat+ing
gra+dat+ed
gra+da+tion
gra+da+tions
gra+da+tion+al
grade
grades
grades
grad+ing
grad+ed
grade+ly
grade+li+er
grade+li+est
grad+er
grad+ers
gra+di+ent
gra+di+ents

gra+din
gra+dins
gra+dine
gra+dines
grad+ual
grad+uals
gradu+al+ism
gradu+al+ist
gradu+al+ists
gradu+al+is+tic
gradu+al+ly
gradu+al+ness
gradu+and
gradu+ands
gradu+ate
gradu+ates
gradu+ates
gradu+at+ing
gradu+at+ed
gradua+tion
gradua+tions
gradua+tor
gradua+tors
Graeae
Grae+cism
Grae+cisms
Graeco-Roman
Graf
Graf+en
graf+fi+ti
graf+fi+to
graf+fi+ti
graft
grafts
grafts
graft+ing
graft+ed
graft+er
graft+ers
graft+ing
graft+ings
Graham
surname
Gra+ham
in place names
Grahame
Graiae
Gra+ian
Grail
grain
grains
grains
grain+ing
grained
Grainger

graini+ness
grain+ing
grainy
graini+er
graini+est
gral+la+to+rial
gram
grams
gra+mina+ceous
gra+min+eous
grami+nivo+rous
gram+mar
gram+mars
gram+mar+ian
gram+mar+ians
gram+mati+cal
gram+mati+cal+
ly
gram+mati+cal+
ness
gramme
grammes
Grammy
Grammies *or*
Grammys
gramo+phone
gramo+phones
Gram+pian
gram+pus
gram+puses
Gra+na+da
grana+dil+la
grana+dil+las
Granados
grana+ry
grana+ries
Gran Ca+na+ria
Gran Cha+co
grand
grands
grand+er
grand+est
grand
*thousand pounds
or dollars*
grand
gran+dam
gran+dams
gran+dame
gran+dames
grand+aunt
grand+aunts
grand+child
grand+children
grand+dad

grand+dads
grand+daddy
grand+daddies
grand+daughter
grand+
daughters
gran+dee
gran+dees
Grande-Terre
gran+deur
gran+deurs
grand+father
grand+fathers
grand+father+ly
Grand Gui+gnol
Grand Gui+gnols
gran+dilo+
quence
gran+dilo+quent
gran+dilo+quent+
ly
gran+di+ose
gran+di+ose+ly
gran+di+os+ity
grand+ly
grand+ma
grand+mas
grand mal
grand+mama
grand+mamas
grand+mamma
grand+mammas
grand+master
*chess, hip-hop,
etc.*
grand+masters
Grand Mas+ter
*Freemasonry,
martial arts, etc.*
Grand Mas+ters
grand+mother
grand+mothers
grand+mother+ly
grand+nephew
grand+nephews
grand+ness
grand+niece
grand+nieces
grand+pa
grand+pas
grand+papa
grand+papas
grand+parent
grand+parents
Grand Prix

Grand Prixes *or*
Grand Prix *or*
Grands Prix
grand+sire
grand+sires
grand+son
grand+sons
grand+stand
grand+stands
grand+uncle
grand+uncles
grange
granges
Grange+mouth
Gra+ni+cus
gran+ite
gran+ites
granite+ware
gra+nit+ic
grani+vore
grani+vores
gra+nivo+rous
gran+nie
gran+nies
gran+ny
gran+nies
grant
grants
grants
grant+ing
grant+ed
Grant
Gran+ta
grant+able
grantee
grantees
grant+er
grant+ers
Granth
Gran+tham
grant-in-aid
grants-in-aid
grant-maintained
gran tur+is+mo
gran tur+is+mos
granu+lar
granu+lar+ity
granu+late
granu+lates
granu+lat+ing
granu+lat+ed
granu+lat+er
granu+lat+ers
granu+la+tion
granu+la+tions

granu+la+tive
granu+la+tor
granu+la+tors
gran+ule
gran+ules
granu+lo+cyte
granu+lo+cytes
Granville
Granville-Barker
grape
grapes
grape+fruit
grape+fruits *or*
grape+fruit
grape+shot
grape+vine
grape+vines
grap+ey
grapi+er
grapi+est
graph
graphs
graphs
gra+phing
graphed
graph+eme
graph+emes
gra+phemi+cal+ly
graph+ic
graph+ica+cy
graphi+cal
graphi+cal+ly
graph+ic+ness
graph+ics
graph+ite
gra+phit+ic
grapho+logi+cal
graph+olo+gist
graph+olo+gists
graph+ol+ogy
grap+nel
grap+nels
grap+pa
grap+pas
Grappelli
Grappelly
grap+ple
grap+ples
grap+ples
grap+pling
grap+pled
grap+pler
grap+plers
grap+to+lite
grap+to+lites

grapy
grapi+er
grapi+est
Gras+mere
grasps
grasps
grasp+ing
grasped
grasp+able
grasp+er
grasp+ers
grasp+ing
grasp+ing+ly
grasp+ing+ness
grass
grasses
grasses
grass+ing
grassed
Grass
grass+hopper
grass+hoppers
grassi+ness
grass+land
grass+lands
grass+like
grassy
grassi+er
grassi+est
grate
grates
grates
grat+ing
grat+ed
grate+ful
grate+ful+ly
grate+ful+ness
grat+er
grat+ers
Gratian
grati+cule
grati+cules
grati+fi+ca+tion
grati+fi+ca+
tions
grati+fi+er
grati+fi+ers
grati+fy
grati+fies
grati+fy+ing
grati+fied
grati+fy+ing
grati+fy+ing+ly
grat+ing

grat+ings
grat+ing+ly
gra+tis
grati+tude
gra+tui+tous
gra+tui+tous+ly
gra+tui+tous+
ness
gra+tu+ity
gra+tu+ities
gratu+la+tory
Grau+bün+den
grav
gravs
grav+ad+lax
gra+va+men
gra+vami+na
grave
graves
grav+er
grav+est
grave
graves
grav+ing
graved
graved *or*
grav+en
gra+ve
music term
grav+el
grav+els
grav+els
grav+el+ling *or*
grav+el+ing
U.S.
grav+elled *or*
grav+eled
U.S.
gravel-blind
grav+el+ly
grave+ly
grav+en
grave+ness
grav+er
grav+ers
Graves
Graves+end
grave+stone
grave+stones
grave+yard
grave+yards
grav+id
gra+vim+eter
gra+vim+eters
gravi+met+ric

gra+vim+etry
grav+ing
gravi+tate
 gravi+tates
gravi+tat+ing
gravi+tat+ed
gravi+tat+er
 gravi+tat+ers
gravi+ta+tion
 gravi+ta+tions
gravi+ta+tion+al
gravi+ta+tion+al+
 ly
gravi+ta+tive
gravi+ton
 gravi+tons
grav+ity
 grav+ities
grav+lax
gra+vure
 gra+vures
gra+vy
 gra+vies
gray
U.S.
 grays
 grays
gray+ing
grayed
gray+er
gray+est
gray
measure of
 radiation
 grays
Gray
gray+beard
U.S.
 gray+beards
gray+ish
U.S.
gray+lag
U.S.
 gray+lags
gray+ling
 gray+lings *or*
 gray+ling
gray+ly
U.S.
gray+ness
U.S.
Graz
graze
 grazes
 grazes

graz+ing
grazed
gra+zi+er
 gra+zi+ers
graz+ing
graz+ings
grease
greases
greases
greas+ing
greased
grease+paint
greas+er
 greas+ers
greasi+ly
greasi+ness
greasy
greasi+er
greasi+est
great
greats
great+er
great+est
great-aunt
 great-aunts
great+coat
 great+coats
great-hearted
great-hearted+
 ness
great+ly
great-nephew
 great-nephews
great+ness
great-niece
 great-nieces
Greats
great-uncle
 great-uncles
greave
 greaves
grebe
 grebes
Gre+cian
 Gre+cians
Gre+cism
 Gre+cisms
Greco
Greco-Roman
Greece
greed
 greeds
greedi+ly
greedi+ness
greedy

greedi+er
greedi+est
gree+gree
 gree+grees
Greek
 Greeks
Greek+ness
green
 greens
 greens
green+ing
greened
green+er
green+est
Green
Greenaway
green+back
 green+backs
Greene
green+ery
 green+eries
green-eyed
green+field
green+finch
 green+finches
green+fly
 green+flies
green+gage
 green+gages
green+grocer
 green+grocers
green+grocery
 green+groceries
Green+ham
green+heart
 green+hearts
green+horn
 green+horns
green+house
 green+houses
green+ie
 green+ies
green+ish
Green+land
Green+land+er
 Green+land+ers
green+ly
green+mail
green+ness
Green+ock
Greenough
Green+peace
green+room
 green+rooms
green+sand

Greens+boro
green+shank
 green+shanks
green+sickness
green+stone
 green+stones
green+sward
green-wellie
Green+wich
green+wood
 green+woods
greeny
Greer
greet
welcome
greets
greet+ing
greet+ed
greet
cry, weep
greets
greets
greeting
greet+ed *or*
 grat
Scots
greet+ed *or*
 grut+ten
Scots
greet+er
 greet+ers
greet+ing
 greet+ings
gre+gari+ous
gre+gari+ous+ly
gre+gari+ous+
 ness
Gre+go+rian
Gregory
gre+mi+al
 gre+mi+als
grem+lin
 grem+lins
Gre+na+da
gre+nade
 gre+nades
Gre+na+dian
 Gre+na+dians
grena+dier
 grena+diers
grena+dine
Grena+dines
Grendel
Grenfell
Gre+no+ble

Grenville	griev+ous	Grims+by	gris+tles
Gresham	griev+ous+ly	grimy	gris+tli+ness
gres+so+rial	griev+ous+ness	grimi+er	gris+tly
gres+so+ri+ous	grif+fin	grimi+est	gris+tli+er
Gret+na	grif+fins	grin	gris+tli+est
Greville	Griffith	grins	grit
grew	Griffith-Joyner	grins	grits
grey	Griffiths	grin+ning	grit+ting
greys	grif+fon	grinned	grit+ted
greys	grif+fons	grind	Grit
grey+ing	Gri+gio+ni	grinds	Grits
greyed	gri+gri	grinds	grits
grey+er	gri+gris	grind+ing	grit+stone
grey+est	grill	ground	grit+ter
Grey	grills	Grin+del+wald	grit+ters
grey+beard	grills	grind+er	grit+ti+ly
grey+beards	grill+ing	grind+ers	grit+ti+ness
grey+hen	grilled	grind+ing+ly	grit+ty
grey+hens	gril+lage	grind+stone	grit+ti+er
grey+hound	gril+lages	grind+stones	grit+ti+est
grey+hounds	grille	grin+go	griz+zle
grey+ish	grilles	grin+gos	griz+zles
grey+lag	grilled	grin+ning	griz+zles
grey+lags	grill+er	grip	griz+zling
grey+ly	grill+ers	grips	griz+zled
grey+ness	grill+room	grips	griz+zler
grey+wacke	grill+rooms	grip+ping	griz+zlers
grey+wackes	grilse	gripped	griz+zly
grid	grilses *or*	gripe	griz+zlies
grids	grilse	gripes	griz+zli+er
grid+dle	grim	gripes	griz+zli+est
grid+dles	grim+mer	grip+ing	groan
grid+dles	grim+mest	griped	groans
grid+dling	gri+mace	grip+er	groans
grid+dled	gri+maces	grip+ers	groan+ing
griddle+cake	gri+maces	grippe	groaned
griddle+cakes	gri+mac+ing	grip+per	groan+er
grid+iron	gri+maced	grip+pers	groan+ers
grid+irons	gri+mac+er	Gri+qua+land	groan+ing
grid+lock	gri+mac+ers	Gris	groan+ings
grid+locks	Gri+mal+di	gri+saille	groan+ing+ly
grief	*crater*	gri+sailles	groat
griefs	Grimaldi	griseo+ful+vin	groats
Grieg	*clown*	gri+sette	groats
Grierson	gri+mal+kin	gri+settes	gro+cer
griev+ance	gri+mal+kins	gris-gris	gro+cers
griev+ances	grime	gris-gris	gro+ceries
grieve	grimes	Gri+shun	gro+cery
grieves	grimes	gris+li+ness	gro+ceries
griev+ing	grim+ing	gris+ly	Grod+no
grieved	grimed	gris+li+er	grog
griev+er	grimi+ness	gris+li+est	grog+gi+ly
griev+ers	grim+ly	Gri+sons	grog+gi+ness
griev+ing	Grimm	grist	grog+gy
griev+ings	grim+ness	gris+tle	

grog+gi+er	gross+ness	ground+nuts	grows
grog+gi+est	Gross+war+dein	ground+sel	grow+ing
grog+ram	Grosz	ground+sels	grew
grog+rams	grot	ground+sheet	grown
groin	*rubbish, dirt*	ground+sheets	grow+able
groins	grot	ground+sill	grow+er
groins	*grotto*	ground+sills	grow+ers
groin+ing	grots	grounds+man	growl
groined	Grote	grounds+men	growls
grom+met	gro+tesque	ground+speed	growls
grom+mets	gro+tesques	ground+speeds	growl+ing
Gromyko	gro+tesque+ly	ground+work	growled
Gro+ning+en	gro+tesque+ness	ground+works	growl+er
groom	gro+tes+querie	group	growl+ers
grooms	gro+tes+queries	groups	grown
grooms	gro+tes+query	groups	grown-up
groom+ing	gro+tes+queries	group+ing	grown-ups
groomed	Gro+tian	grouped	growth
grooms+man	Grotius	group+er	growths
grooms+men	grot+to	group+ers *or*	groyne
groove	grot+tos *or*	group+er	groynes
grooves	grot+toes	groupie	Groz+ny
grooves	grot+ty	groupies	grub
groov+ing	grot+ti+er	grouse	grubs
grooved	grot+ti+est	*bird*	grubs
groovy	grouch	grouses *or*	grub+bing
groovi+er	grouches	grouse	grubbed
groovi+est	grouches	grouse	grub+ber
grope	grouch+ing	grouses	grub+bers
gropes	grouched	grouses	grub+bi+ly
gropes	grouchi+ly	grous+ing	grub+bi+ness
grop+ing	grouchi+ness	groused	grub+by
groped	grouchy	grous+er	grub+bi+er
grop+er	grouchi+er	grous+ers	grub+bi+est
grop+ers *or*	grouchi+est	grout	grub+stake
grop+er	ground	grouts	grub+stakes
grop+ing+ly	grounds	grouts	grub+stakes
Gropius	grounds	grout+ing	grub+stak+ing
Gros	ground+ing	grout+ed	grub+staked
gros+beak	ground+ed	grout+er	grub+stak+er
gros+beaks	ground+age	grout+ers	grub+stak+ers
gro+schen	ground+ages	grove	grudge
gro+schen	ground+bait	groves	grudges
gros+grain	ground+baits	grov+el	grudges
gros+grains	ground+hog	grov+els	grudg+ing
gros point	ground+hogs	grov+el+ling *or*	grudged
gross	ground+ing	grov+el+ing	grudg+ing
grosses	ground+ings	*U.S.*	grudg+ing+ly
grosses	ground+less	grov+el+led *or*	gru+el
gross+ing	ground+less+ly	grov+el+ed	gru+els
grossed	ground+less+	*U.S.*	gru+el+ing
gross+er	ness	grov+el+ler	*U.S.*
gross+est	ground+ling	grov+el+lers	gru+el+ings
Grosseteste	ground+lings	Groves	gru+el+ling
gross+ly	ground+nut	grow	gru+el+lings

grue+some
grue+some+ly
grue+some+ness
gruff
gruff+er
gruff+est
gruff+ly
gruff+ness
grum+ble
grum+bles
grum+bles
grum+bling
grum+bled
grum+bler
grum+blers
grum+bling
grum+bling+ly
grum+bly
grum+met
grum+mets
grump
grumps
grumps
grump+ing
grumped
grumpi+ly
grumpi+ness
grump+ish
grump+ish+ly
grump+ish+ness
grumpy
grumpi+er
grumpi+est
Grun+dy
Grun+dies
Grun+dy+ism
Grun+dy+isms
Grun+dy+ist
Grun+dy+ists
Grun+dy+ite
Grun+dy+ites
Grünewald
grun+ion
grun+ions
grunt
grunts
grunts
grunt+ing
grunt+ed
grunt+er
grunt+ers
Gru+yère
Gru+yères
gryph+on
gryph+ons

grys+bok
grys+boks
G-string
G-strings
G-suit
G-suits
Gua+da+la+ja+ra
Gua+dal+ca+nal
Gua+dal+qui+vir
Gua+da+lupe Hi+
 dal+go
Gua+de+loupe
Gua+dia+na
guaia+cum
guaia+cums
Guam
Gua+ma+nian
Gua+ma+nians
Gua+na+ba+ra
gua+na+co
gua+na+cos
Gua+na+jua+to
Guang+dong
Guang+zhou
gua+nine
gua+no
Guan+tá+na+mo
Gua+po+ré
Gua+ra+ni
Gua+ra+nis or
Gua+ra+ni
guar+an+tee
guar+an+tees
guar+an+tees
guar+an+tee+
 ing
guar+an+teed
guar+an+tor
guar+an+tors
guar+an+ty
guar+an+ties
guar+an+ties
guar+an+ty+ing
guar+an+tied
guard
guards
guards
guard+ing
guard+ed
Guar+da+fui
guard+ed
guard+ed+ly
guard+ed+ness
guard+er
guard+ers

guard+house
guard+houses
Guardi
guard+ian
guard+ians
guardi+an+ship
guardi+an+ships
guard+room
guard+rooms
Guards
guards+man
guards+men
Guarneri
Guarneris
Guarnerius
Guarneriuses
Guarnieri
Guarnieris
Gua+te+ma+la
Gua+te+ma+lan
Gua+te+ma+
 lans
gua+va
gua+vas
Gua+ya+quil
gua+yu+le
gua+yu+les
gub+bins
gub+binses or
gub+bins
gu+ber+na+to+
 rial
gud+dle
gud+dles
gud+dles
gud+dling
gud+dled
gudg+eon
gudg+eons
gudg+eons
gudg+eon+ing
gudg+eoned
Gud+run
Guel+der+land
guelder-rose
guelder-roses
Guel+ders
Guelph
Guenevere
gue+non
gue+nons
guer+don
guer+dons
guer+dons
guer+don+ing

guer+doned
gue+ril+la
gue+ril+las
Guer+ni+ca
Guern+sey
Guern+seys
Guer+rero
guer+ril+la
guer+ril+las
guess
guesses
guesses
guess+ing
guessed
guess+er
guess+ers
guess+ti+mate
guess+ti+mates
guess+ti+mates
guess+ti+mat+
 ing
guess+ti+mat+
 ed
guess+work
guess+works
guest
guests
guests
guest+ing
guest+ed
guest+house
guest+houses
gues+ti+mate
gues+ti+mates
gues+ti+mates
gues+ti+mat+
 ing
gues+ti+mat+ed
Guevara
guff
guffs
guf+faw
guf+faws
guf+faws
guf+faw+ing
guf+fawed
Guggenheim
Gui+ana
Gui+an+an
Gui+an+ans
Guia+nese
guid+able
guid+ance
guide
guides

guides
guid+ing
guid+ed
Guide
Guides
guide+book
guide+books
guid+ed
guide+line
guide+lines
guide+post
guide+posts
guid+er
guid+ers
Guid+er
Guid+ers
Guido d'Arezzo
gui+don
gui+dons
Gui+enne
guild
guilds
guil+der
guil+ders *or*
guil+der
Guild+ford
guild+hall
guild+halls
guilds+man
guilds+men
guile
guiles
guile+ful
guile+ful+ly
guile+ful+ness
guile+less
guile+less+ly
guile+less+ness
Gui+lin
Guillaume de
  Lorris
guil+lemot
guil+lemots
guil+loche
guil+loches
guil+lo+tine
guil+lo+tines
guil+lo+tines
guil+lo+tin+ing
guil+lo+tined
guil+lo+tin+er
guil+lo+tin+ers
guilt
guilts
guilti+ly

guilti+ness
guilt+less
guilt+less+ly
guilt+less+ness
guilty
guilti+er
guilti+est
guinea
guineas
Guinea
Guinea-Bissau
Guin+ean
Guin+eans
Guinever
Guinevere
Guinness
gui+pure
gui+pures
guise
guises
guis+er
guis+ers
gui+tar
gui+tars
gui+tar+ist
gui+tar+ists
Guitry
Gui+yang
Gui+zhou
Guizot
Gu+ja+rat
Gu+je+rat
Guj+ran+wa+la
Gu+lag
Gulbenkian
gulch
gulches
Gü+lek Bo+gaz
gules
gulf
gulfs
gulfs
Gulf
gulf+weed
gulf+weeds
gull
gulls
gulls
gull+ing
gulled
gul+let
gul+lets
gul+ley

gul+leys
gul+leys
gul+ley+ing
gul+leyed
gul+li+bil+ity
gul+lible
gul+li+bly
gul+ly
gul+lies
gul+lies
gul+ly+ing
gul+lied
gulp
gulps
gulps
gulp+ing
gulped
gulp+er
gulp+ers
gulp+ing+ly
gulpy
gum
gums
gums
gum+ming
gummed
gum+bo
gum+bos
gum+boil
gum+boils
gum+boots
gum+drop
gum+drops
gum+mi+ness
gum+my
gum+mies
gum+mi+er
gum+mi+est
gump+tion
gum+tree
gum+trees
gun
guns
guns
gun+ning
gunned
gun+boat
gun+boats
gun+cotton
gun+fight
gun+fights
gun+fighter
gun+fighters
gun+fire
gunge

gunges
gung+ing
gunged
gun+gy
gun+gi+er
gun+gi+est
gunk
gun+lock
gun+locks
gun+man
gun+men
gun+metal
Gunn
Gunnar
gun+nel
gun+nels
gun+ner
gun+ners
gun+nery
gun+ny
gun+nies
gun+play
gun+point
gun+powder
gun+powders
gun+runner
gun+runners
gun+running
gun+shot
gun+shots
gun+slinger
gun+slingers
gun+smith
gun+smiths
gun+stock
gun+stocks
Gunter
Günter
forename
Gunther
Gun+tur
gun+wale
gun+wales
gun+yah
gun+yahs
gup+py
gup+pies
Gurdjieff
gurd+wa+ra
gurd+wa+ras
gur+gle
gur+gles
gur+gles
gur+gling
gur+gled

Gur+kha
Gur+khas *or*
Gur+kha
gur+nard
gur+nards *or*
gur+nard
gur+net
gur+nets *or*
gur+net
guru
gurus
gush
gushes
gushes
gush+ing
gushed
gush+er
gush+ers
gushi+ly
gushi+ness
gush+ing
gush+ing+ly
gushy
gushi+er
gushi+est
gus+set
gus+sets
gus+sets
gus+set+ing
gus+set+ed
gus+set+ed
gust
gusts
gusts
gust+ing
gust+ed
gus+ta+tion
gus+ta+tions
gus+ta+tory
Gustavus
gusti+ly
gusti+ness
gus+to
gusty
gusti+er
gusti+est
gut
guts
guts
gut+ting
gut+ted
GUT
GUTs
Gutenberg
Gü+ters+loh

Guthrie
Guth+run
gut+less
gutsy
gutsi+er
gutsi+est
gutta-percha
gutta-perchas
gut+tate
gut+ted
gut+ter
gut+ters
gut+ters
gut+ter+ing
gut+tered
gut+ter+ing
gutter+snipe
gutter+snipes
gut+tur+al
gut+tur+als
gut+tur+al+ly
guy
guys
guys
guy+ing
guyed
Guy+ana
Guy+an+an
Guy+an+ans
Guya+nese
Guya+nese
Guy+enne
Guzmán Blanco
guz+zle
guz+zles
guz+zling
guz+zled
guz+zler
guz+zlers
Gwa+li+or
Gwe+lo
Gwent
Gwe+ru
Gwyn
Gwyn+edd
gybe
gybes
gybes
gyb+ing
gybed
gym
gyms
gym+kha+na
gym+kha+nas
gym+na+sium

gym+na+siums
or
gym+na+sia
gym+nast
gym+nasts
gym+nas+tic
gym+nas+ti+cal+ly
gym+nas+tics
gym+no+sperm
gym+no+sperms
gym+no+sper+mous
gym+pie
gym+pies
gym+slip
gym+slips
gy+nae+ceum
gy+nae+cea
gy+nae+co+log+ic
gy+nae+co+logi+cal
gy+nae+colo+gist
gy+nae+colo+gists
gy+nae+col+ogy
gy+nan+dro+morph
gy+nan+dro+morphs
gy+nan+drous
gy+ne+cium
gy+ne+cia
gy+ne+co+logi+cal *U.S.*
gy+ne+colo+gist *U.S.*
gy+ne+colo+gists
gy+ne+col+ogy *U.S.*
gy+noe+cium
gy+noe+cia
gy+no+phore
gy+no+phores
Györ
gyp
gyps
gyp+ping
gypped
gyp

severe pain
gyp
college servant
gyps
gyp+se+ous
gyp+sophi+la
gyp+sophi+las
gyp+sum
Gyp+sy
Gyp+sies
Gyp+sy+ish
gy+rate
gy+rates
gy+rat+ing
gy+rat+ed
gy+ra+tion
gy+ra+tions
gy+ra+tor
gy+ra+tors
gy+ra+tory
gyre
gyres
gyres
gyr+ing
gyred
gyr+fal+con
gyr+fal+cons
gyro
gyros
gy+ro+com+pass
gy+ro+com+passes
gy+ro+dyne
gy+ro+dynes
gy+ro+mag+net+ic
gy+ro+scope
gy+ro+scopes
gy+ro+scop+ic
gy+ro+scopi+cal+ly
gy+ro+sta+bi+lis+er
gy+ro+sta+bi+lis+ers
gy+ro+sta+bi+liz+er
gy+ro+sta+bi+liz+ers
gyve
gyves
gyves
gyv+ing
gyved

H

h
h's
H
H's *or*
Hs
haar
haars
Haar+lem
Habakkuk
Ha+ba+na
ha+ba+nera
ha+ba+neras
ha+beas cor+pus
hab+er+dash+er
hab+er+dash+ers
hab+er+dash+ery
hab+er+dash+eries
hab+er+geon
hab+er+geons
ha+bili+ment
ha+bili+ments
ha+bili+tate
ha+bili+tates
ha+bili+tat+ing
ha+bili+tat+ed
ha+bili+ta+tion
ha+bili+ta+tions
hab+it
hab+its
hab+its
hab+it+ing
hab+it+ed
hab+it+abil+ity
hab+it+able
hab+it+able+ness
hab+it+ably
hab+it+ant
hab+it+ants
habi+tat
habi+tats
habi+ta+tion
habi+ta+tions
habit-forming

ha+bitu+al
ha+bitu+al+ly
ha+bitu+al+ness
ha+bitu+ate
ha+bitu+ates
ha+bitu+at+ing
ha+bitu+at+ed
ha+bitua+tion
ha+bitua+tions
habi+tude
habi+tudes
ha+bitué
ha+bitués
Habsburg
ha+chure
haci+en+da
haci+en+das
hack
hacks
hacks
hack+ing
hacked
hacka+more
hacka+mores
hack+berry
hack+berries
hack+er
hack+ers
hack+ery
hack+le
hack+les
hack+les
hack+ling
hack+led
hack+ney
hack+neys
hack+neys
hack+ney+ing
hack+neyed
Hack+ney
hack+neyed
hack+saw
hack+saws
hack+work
had

had+dock
had+docks *or*
had+dock
hade
hades
hades
had+ing
had+ed
ha+de+dah
ha+de+dahs
Ha+des
Ha+dhra+maut
hadj
hadjes
hadji
hadjis
hadn't
Ha+dra+maut
Hadrian
had+ron
had+rons
had+ron+ic
hadst
haec+ce+ity
haec+ce+ities
haem
hae+mal
haema+tem+esis
hae+mat+ic
haema+tin
haema+tite
haema+tit+ic
haema+to+crit
haema+to+crits
haema+to+log+ic
haema+to+logi+cal
haema+tol+ogy
haema+toly+sis
haema+toly+ses
haema+to+ma
haema+to+mas
or
haema+to+ma+ta

haema+tu+ria
haemo+cya+nin
haemo+cy+tom+eter
haemo+cy+tom+eters
haemo+di+aly+sis
haemo+di+aly+ses
haemo+glo+bin
hae+moly+sis
hae+moly+ses
haemo+lyt+ic
haemo+philia
haemo+phili+ac
haemo+phili+acs
haemo+phil+ic
haem+op+ty+sis
haem+op+ty+ses
haem+or+rhage
haem+or+rhages
haem+or+rhages
haem+or+rhag+ing
haem+or+rhaged
haem+or+rhoi+dal
haem+or+rhoids
haemo+sta+sis
haemo+stat
haemo+stats
haemo+stat+ic
hae+re+mai
Ha-erh-pin
ha+fiz
ha+fizes
haf+nium
haft
hafts

hafts
haft+ing
haft+ed
hag
hags
Hagen *person*
Ha+gen *city*
hag+fish
hag+fish *or*
hag+fishes
hag+gad+ic
Haggai
hag+gard
hag+gards
Haggard
hag+gard+ly
hag+gard+ness
hag+gis
hag+gises
hag+gish
hag+gle
hag+gles
hag+gling
hag+gled
hag+gler
hag+glers
Hagi+og+ra+pha
hagi+og+ra+pher
hagi+og+ra+phers
hagio+graph+ic
hagio+graphi+cal
hagi+og+ra+phist
hagi+og+ra+phists
hagi+og+ra+phy
hagi+og+ra+phies
hagi+ola+try
hagio+logi+cal
hagi+olo+gist
hagi+olo+gists
hagi+ol+ogy
hagi+ol+ogies
hag-ridden
Hague
hah
ha-ha
ha-has
Hahn
Hahnemann
hah+nium
haick

haicks
Hai+fa
Haig
haik
haiks
hai+ku
hai+ku
hail
hails
hails
hail+ing
hailed
Haile Selassie
hail-fellow-well-met
hail+stone
hail+stones
hail+storm
hail+storms
Hailwood
Hai+nan Tao
Hai+nault
Hai+naut
Hai+phong
hair
hairs
hair+brained
hair+cloth
hair+cut
hair+cuts
hair+do
hair+dos
hair+dresser
hair+dressers
hair+dressing
hair+grip
hair+grips
hairi+ness
hair+less
hair+like
hair+line
hair+lines
hair+net
hair+nets
hair+piece
hair+pieces
hair+pin
hair+pins
hair-raising
hair's-breadth
hair+splitter
hair+splitters
hair+splitting
hair+spring
hair+springs

hair+streak
hair+streaks
hair+style
hair+styles
hair+stylist
hair+stylists
hairy
hairi+er
hairi+est
Hai+ti
Hai+tian
Haitink
haji
hajis
hajj
hajjes
haj+ji
haj+jis
haka
hakas
hake
hake *or*
hakes
ha+kea
ha+keas
ha+keem
ha+keems
ha+kim
ha+kims
Hakluyt
Ha+ko+da+te
Ha+la+cha
Ha+la+cha
hal+al
hal+als
hal+al+ling
hal+alled
ha+la+tion
ha+la+vah
ha+la+vahs
hal+berd
hal+berds
hal+ber+dier
hal+ber+diers
Hal+ber+stadt
hal+bert
hal+berts
hal+cy+on
hal+cy+ons
Hal+cyo+ne
Haldane
hale
hales
hal+ing
haled

Hale
Ha+lea+ka+la
hale+ness
ha+ler *Czech money*
ha+lers *or*
ha+leru
Hales+ow+en
Haley
half
halves
half-afraid
half-alive
half-and-half
half-anglicised
half-anglicized
half-ashamed
half-asleep
half-awake
half+back
half+backs
half-baked
half-barrel
half-barrels
half+beak
half+beaks
half-begging
half-binding
half-blind
half-blood
half-bloods
half-blooded
half-board
half-boards
half-boot
half-boots
half-bottle
half-bottles
half-breed
half-breeds
half-brother
half-brothers
half-butt
half-butts
half-caste
half-castes
half-century
half-centuries
half-circle
half-circles
half-civilised
half-civilized
half-civilly
half-clad
half-closed

half-clothed
half-cock
half-cocked
half-complet+ed
half-concealed
half-conscious
half-conscious+ly
half-consumed
half-convinced
half-convincing
half-convincing+
ly
half-cooked
half-covered
half-crazy
half-crown
half-crowns
half-day
half-days
half-dazed
half-dazedly
half-deaf
half-deafened
half-demented
half-deserted
half-developed
half-digested
half-done
half-dozen
half-dozens
half-dressed
half-dried
half-drowned
half-drunk
half-eaten
half-educat+ed
half-empty
half-English
half-expectant
half-expectant+ly
half-filled
half-finished
half-forgotten
half-formed
half-frozen
half-full
half-grown
half-hardy
half-heard
half-hearted
half-heartedly
half-hitch
half-hitches
half-hoping
half-hour

half-hours
half-hourly
half-human
half-hunter
half-hunters
half-inclined
half-informed
half-instinctive
half-instinctive+ly
half-intoxi+cat+
ed
half-joking
half-jokingly
half-knowledge
half-learned
half-lie
half-lies
half-life
half-light
half-lights
half-mad
half-mast
half-mile
half-miles
half-minute
half-minutes
half-monthly
half-moon
half-moons
half-naked
half-nelson
half-nelsons
half-note
half-notes
half-open
half-pagan
half-pay
half+penny
half+pennies
or
half+pence
half+penny+
worth
half+penny+
worths
half-petrified
half-pie
half-plate
half-plates
half-playful
half-playfully
half-pleased
half-protesting
half-proved
half-proven

half-questioning
half-questioning+
ly
half-raw
half-reluctant
half-reluctant+ly
half-remembered
half-repentant
half-right
half-rotted
half-rotten
half-ruined
half-savage
half-savagely
half-second
half-seconds
half-section
half-sections
half-seen
half-sensed
half-serious
half-serious+ly
half-shut
half-sister
half-sisters
half-size
half-sizes
half-smile
half-smiles
half-sole
half-soles
half-starved
half-stated
half-submerged
half-timber
half-timbered
half-timbering
half-time
half-times
half-title
half-titles
half+tone
half+tones
half-track
half-tracks
half-trained
half-true
half-truth
half-truths
half-understood
half-used
half-verified
half+way
half-wild
half-wildly

half+wit
half+wits
half+witted
half-wrong
half-year
half-years
half-yearly
hali+but
hali+buts or
hali+but
Ha+liç
Hali+car+nas+
sian
Hali+car+nas+sus
hal+id
hal+ids
hal+ide
hal+ides
Hali+fax
place name
Halifax
surname
hal+ite
hali+to+sis
hall
halls
hall+al
hall+als
hall+al+ling
hall+alled
Hal+le
Hallé
hal+le+lu+iah
hal+le+lu+iahs
hal+le+lu+jah
hal+le+lu+jahs
Haller
Hallett
Halley
hal+liard
hal+liards
hall+mark
hall+marks
hall+marks
hall+mark+ing
hall+marked
hal+lo
hal+los
hal+los
hal+lo+ing
hal+loed
hal+loa
hal+loas
hal+loas
hal+loa+ing

hal+loaed
hal+loo
hal+loos
hal+loos
hal+loo+ing
hal+looed
hal+low
hal+lows
hal+low+ing
hal+lowed
Hal+low+e'en
Hal+low+een
hal+low+er
hal+low+ers
Hall+statt
hal+lu+ci+nate
hal+lu+ci+nates
hal+lu+ci+nat+ing
hal+lu+ci+nat+ed
hal+lu+ci+na+tion
hal+lu+ci+na+tions
hal+lu+ci+na+tor
hal+lu+ci+na+tors
hal+lu+ci+na+tory
hal+lu+cino+gen
hal+lu+cino+gens
hal+lu+ci+no+gen+ic
hal+lux
hal+luxes
hall+way
hall+ways
halm
halms
hal+ma
Hal+ma+he+ra
Halm+stad
halo
haloes *or*
halos
haloes *or*
halos
halo+ing
haloed
halo+gen
halo+gens
halo+gen+ate
halo+gen+ates

halo+gen+at+ing
halo+gen+at+ed
halo+gena+tion
halo+gena+tions
ha+log+enous
hal+oid
hal+oids
hal+on
hal+ons
Hals
Häl+sing+borg
halt
halts
halts
halt+ing
halt+ed
hal+ter
hal+ters
hal+ters
hal+ter+ing
hal+tered
hal+tere
hal+te+res
halt+ing
halt+ing+ly
hal+va
hal+vas
hal+vah
hal+vahs
halve
halves
halv+ing
halved
hal+yard
hal+yards
ham
hams
hams
ham+ming
hammed
Hama
hama+dry+ad
hama+dry+ads
hama+dry+as
hama+dry+ases
Ha+ma+ma+tsu
ham+ba
Ham+burg
ham+burg+er
ham+burg+ers
hame
hames
Ha+meln
ham-fisted

ham-handed
Ham+heung
Ham+hung
Hamilcar Barca
Ham+il+ton
place name
Hamilton
surname
Ham+it+ic
ham+let
ham+lets
Hamm
Hammarskjöld
ham+mer
ham+mers
ham+mers
ham+mer+ing
ham+mered
Ham+mer+fest
hammer+head
hammer+heads
hammer+headed
hammer-like
hammer+lock
hammer+locks
Ham+mer+smith
Hammerstein
hammer+toe
hammer+toes
Hammett
ham+mock
ham+mocks
Ham+mond
place name
Hammond
surname
Hammurabi
Hammurapi
ham+my
ham+mi+er
ham+mi+est
Hampden
ham+per
ham+pers
ham+pers
ham+per+ing
ham+pered
Hamp+shire
Hamp+stead
Hamp+ton
place name
Hampton
surname
ham+ster
ham+sters

ham+string
ham+strings
ham+strings
ham+string+ing
ham+strung
Hamsun
hamu+lus
hamu+li
Ha+nau
hand
hands
hands
hand+ing
hand+ed
hand+bag
hand+bags
hand+ball
hand+balls
hand+balls
hand+ball+ing
hand+balled
hand+barrow
hand+barrows
hand+bill
hand+bills
hand+book
hand+books
hand+brake
hand+brakes
hand+breadth
hand+cart
hand+carts
hand+craft
hand+crafts
hand+crafts
hand+craft+ing
hand+craft+ed
hand+cuff
hand+cuffs
hand+cuffs
hand+cuff+ing
hand+cuffed
Handel
hand+ful
hand+fuls
hand+gun
hand+guns
handi+cap
handi+caps
handi+caps
handi+cap+ping
handi+capped
handi+cap+per
handi+cap+pers

handi+craft
handi+crafts
handi+ly
handi+ness
handi+work
hand+ker+chief
hand+ker+chiefs
han+dle
han+dles
han+dles
han+dling
han+dled
handle+bars
han+dler
han+dlers
hand+less
han+dling
han+dlings
hand+made
hand+maid
hand+maids
hand+maiden
hand+maidens
hand-me-down
hand-me-downs
hand-off
hand-offs
hand off
verb
hand-out
hand-outs
hand out
verb
hand+over
hand+overs
hand over
verb
hand-pick
hand-picks
hand-picking
hand-picked
hand+rail
hand+rails
hand+saw
hand+saws
hand's-breadth
hand+sel
hand+sels
hand+sels
hand+sel+ling
or
hand+sel+ing
U.S.
hand+selled *or*

hand+seled
U.S.
hand+set
hand+sets
hand+shake
hand+shakes
hands-off
hand+some
hand+som+er
hand+som+est
hand+some+ly
hand+some+ness
hands-on
hand+spring
hand+springs
hand+stand
hand+stands
hand-to-hand
hand-to-mouth
hand+work
hand+worked
hand+writing
hand+written
handy
handi+er
handi+est
handy+man
handy+men
hang
hangs
hang+ing
hung *or*
hanged
executed
hang+ar
hang+ars
Hang+chow
hang+dog
hang+er
hang+ers
hanger-on
hangers-on
hang-glider
hang-gliders
hang-gliding
han+gi
han+gis
hang+ing
hang+ings
hang+man
hang+men
hang+nail
hang+nails
hang-out
hang-outs

hang out
verb
hang+over
hang+overs
Han+guk
hang-up
hang-ups
hang up
verb
Hang+zhou
hank
hanks
hank+er
hank+ers
hank+er+ing
hank+ered
hank+er+ing
hank+er+ings
hankie
hankies
Han-k'ou
Han+kow
hanky
hankies
hanky-panky
Hanley
Hannah
Hannibal
Han+no+ver
Ha+noi
Hano+ver
Hano+verian
Hano+verians
Han+sard
Hanse
Hanses
Han+seat+ic
han+sel
han+sels
han+sels
han+sel+ling *or*
han+sel+ing
U.S.
han+selled *or*
han+seled
U.S.
han+som
han+soms
Ha+nuk+kah
Hanu+man
Hanu+mans
Han+yang
Han-yang
hap
haps

haps
hap+ping
happed
ha'penny
ha'pennies
hap+haz+ard
hap+haz+ard+ly
hap+haz+ard+
ness
hap+less
hap+less+ly
hap+less+ness
hap+log+ra+phy
hap+log+ra+
phies
hap+loid
hap+loids
hap+lol+ogy
hap+ly
ha'+p'orth
ha'+p'orths
hap+pen
hap+pens
hap+pen+ing
hap+pened
hap+pen+ing
hap+pen+ings
hap+pi+ly
hap+pi+ness
hap+py
hap+pi+er
hap+pi+est
happy-go-lucky
Hapsburg
hap+tic
ha+pu+ka
ha+pu+kas
ha+pu+ku
ha+pu+kus
hara-kiri
ha+rangue
ha+rangues
ha+rangues
ha+rangu+ing
ha+rangued
ha+rangu+er
ha+rangu+ers
Ha+ra+re
har+ass
har+asses
har+ass+ing
har+ass+ed
har+ass+ment
har+ass+ments
Har+bin

har+bin+ger
har+bin+gers
har+bin+gers
har+bin+ger+ing
har+bin+gered
har+bor
U.S.
har+bors
har+bors
har+bor+ing
har+bored
har+bor+age
har+bor+ages
har+bour
har+bours
har+bours
har+bour+ing
har+boured
har+bour+age
har+bour+ages
hard
hard+er
hard+est
hard+back
hard+backs
hard-bitten
hard+board
hard-boiled
hard+core
Hardecanute
hard+en
hard+ens
hard+en+ing
hard+ened
Hardenberg
hard+en+er
hard+en+ers
hard-hat
adj.
hard hat
noun
hard-headed
hard+hearted
hard+hearted+
  ness
Hardicanute
Hardie
har+di+hood
har+di+ly
har+di+ness
Harding
hard+liner
hard+liners
hard+ly
hard+ness

hard-nosed
hard+pan
hard-pressed
hard+rock
hard+rocks
hard-shell
hard-shelled
hard+ship
hard+ships
hard+tack
hard+tacks
hard+top
hard+tops
hard+ware
hard-wired
hard+wood
hard+woods
har+dy
har+di+er
har+di+est
Hardy
hare
hares *or*
hare
hares
har+ing
hared
hare+bell
hare+bells
hare+brained
har+eem
har+eems
Hare Krish+na
Hare Krish+nas
hare+like
hare+lip
hare+lips
hare+lipped
har+em
har+ems
hare's-foot
Har+fleur
Har+gei+sa
Hargreaves
hari+cot
hari+cots
Ha+ri+jan
Ha+ri+jans
hari-kari
Ha+rin+gey
hark
harks
hark+ing
harked
hark+en

hark+ens
hark+en+ing
hark+ened
hark+en+er
hark+en+ers
harl
harls
Har+lech
Har+lem
har+lequin
har+lequins
har+lequin+ade
har+lequin+ades
Harley
Har+ley Street
har+lot
har+lots
har+lot+ry
Har+low
place name
Harlow
surname
harm
harms
harm+ing
harmed
har+mat+tan
harm+ful
harm+ful+ly
harm+less
harm+less+ly
har+mon+ic
har+mon+ics
har+moni+ca
har+moni+cas
har+moni+cal+ly
har+mo+ni+ous
har+mo+ni+sa+
  tion
har+mo+ni+sa+
  tions
har+mo+nise
har+mo+nises
har+mo+nis+ing
har+mo+nised
har+mo+nist
har+mo+nists
har+mo+nium
har+mo+niums
har+mo+ni+za+
  tion
har+mo+ni+za+
  tions
har+mo+nize
har+mo+nizes

har+mo+niz+ing
har+mo+nized
har+mo+ny
har+mo+nies
Harmsworth
har+ness
har+nesses
har+nesses
har+ness+ing
har+nessed
har+ness+er
har+ness+ers
Harold
harp
harps
harps
harp+ing
harped
harp+er
harp+ers
harp+ist
harp+ists
har+poon
har+poons
har+poons
har+poon+ing
har+pooned
har+poon+er
har+poon+ers
harp+si+chord
harp+si+chords
harp+si+chord+
ist
harp+si+chord+
  ists
har+py
har+pies
Har+py
Har+pies
har+que+bus
har+que+buses
Har+rer
har+ri+dan
har+ri+dans
har+ri+er
har+ri+ers
Harriman
Har+ris
place name
Harris
surname
Har+ris+burg
Harrison
Har+ro+gate
Har+ro+vian

Har+ro+vians
har+row
har+rows
har+rows
har+row+ing
har+rowed
Har+row
har+row+er
har+row+ers
har+rumph
har+rumphs
har+rumph+ing
har+rumphed
har+ry
har+ries
har+ry+ing
har+ried
harsh
harsh+er
harsh+est
harsh+ly
harsh+ness
hars+let
hars+lets
hart
harts *or*
hart
har+tal
hart+beest
hart+beests
har+te+beest
har+te+beests
Hart+ford
Harthacanute
Hartington
Har+tle+pool
Hartley
Hartnell
harts+horn
hart's-tongue
harum-scarum
harum-scarums
ha+rus+pex
ha+rus+pi+ces
ha+rus+pi+cy
ha+rus+pi+cies
har+vest
har+vests
har+vests
har+vest+ing
har+vest+ed
har+vest+er
har+vest+ers
har+vest+ing
har+vest+ings

harvest+man
harvest+men
Harvey
Har+well
Har+wich
Har+ya+na
Harz
has
has-been
has-beens
Hasdrubal
hash
hashes
hashes
hash+ing
hashed
hash+eesh
Hash+emite
hash+ish
has+let
has+lets
hasn't
hasp
hasps
hasps
hasp+ing
hasped
Has+selt
Has+sid
Has+si+dim
has+sle
has+sles
has+sles
has+sling
has+sled
has+sock
has+socks
hast
has+tate
haste
hastes
hastes
hast+ing
hast+ed
has+ten
has+tens
has+ten+ing
has+tened
has+ten+er
has+ten+ers
hasti+ly
hasti+ness
Hast+ings
place name
Hastings

surname
has+ty
has+ti+er
has+ti+est
hat
hats
hats
hat+ting
hat+ted
hat+able
hat+band
hat+bands
hat+box
hat+boxes
hatch
hatches
hatches
hatch+ing
hatched
hatch+back
hatch+backs
hatch+ery
hatch+eries
hatch+et
hatch+ets
hatch+ment
hatch+ments
hatch+way
hatch+ways
hate
hates
hates
hat+ing
hat+ed
hate+able
hate+ful
hate+ful+ly
hate+ful+ness
Hat+field
hath
Hathaway
Hathor
Ha+thor+ic
hat+less
ha+tred
ha+treds
Hatshepset
Hatshepsut
hat+ter
hat+ters
Hat+ter+as
Hattersley
hau+berk
hau+berks
Haughey

haugh+ti+ly
haugh+ti+ness
haugh+ty
haugh+ti+er
haugh+ti+est
haul
hauls
hauls
haul+ing
hauled
haul+age
haul+ages
haul+er
haul+ers
haul+ier
haul+iers
haulm
haulms
haunch
haunches
haunt
haunts
haunts
haunt+ing
haunt+ed
haunt+ing+ly
Hauptmann
Hau+ra+ki
Hau+sa
Hau+sas *or*
Hau+sa
haus+frau
haus+frau+en
or
haus+fraus
Haussmann
haut+boy
haut+boys
haute cou+ture
haute cui+sine
haute école
Haute-Garonne
Haute-Loire
Haute-Marne
Haute-Norman+
die
Hautes-Alpes
Haute-Saône
Haute-Savoie
Hautes-Pyrénées
hau+teur
Haute-Vienne
haut monde
Haut-Rhin
Hauts-de-Seine

Ha+vana
Hav+ant
have
  haves
  has
  hav+ing
  had
Ha+vel
river
Havel
surname
have+lock
  have+locks
ha+ven
  ha+vens
  ha+vens
  ha+ven+ing
  ha+vened
have-not
  have-nots
haven't
ha+ver
  ha+vers
  ha+vers
  ha+ver+ing
  ha+vered
Ha+ver+ing
hav+er+sack
  hav+er+sacks
hav+er+sine
  hav+er+sines
hav+il+dar
  hav+il+dars
hav+oc
Ha+vre
haw
  haws
  haws
  haw+ing
  hawed
Ha+waii
Ha+wai+ki
haw+finch
  haw+finches
haw-haw
  haw-haws
Haw-Haw
Haw+ick
hawk
  hawks
  hawks
  hawk+ing
  hawked
hawk+er
  hawk+ers

hawk-eyed
Hawking
Hawkins
hawk+ish
hawk+like
hawks+bill
  hawks+bills
Hawksmoor
hawk+weed
  hawk+weeds
Ha+worth
place name
Haworth
surname
hawse
  hawses
hawse+hole
  hawse+holes
hawse+pipe
  hawse+pipes
haws+er
  haws+ers
haw+thorn
  haw+thorns
hay
  hays
  hays
  hay+ing
  hayed
hay+box
  hay+boxes
hay+cock
  hay+cocks
Haydn
Hayek
hay+maker
  hay+makers
  hay+making
hay+mow
  hay+mows
hay+rick
  hay+ricks
hay+seed
  hay+seeds
hay+stack
  hay+stacks
hay+wire
haz+ard
  haz+ards
  haz+ards
  haz+ard+ing
  haz+ard+ed
haz+ard+ous
  haz+ard+ous+ly

haz+ard+ous+
  ness
haze
  hazes
  hazes
  haz+ing
  hazed
ha+zel
  ha+zels
hazel+hen
  hazel+hens
hazel+nut
  hazel+nuts
ha+zi+ly
ha+zi+ness
Hazlitt
hazy
hazi+er
hazi+est
H-bomb
  H-bombs
he
  hes
head
  heads
  heads
  head+ing
  head+ed
head+ache
  head+aches
head+achy
head+band
  head+bands
head+bang
  head+bangs
  head+bang+ing
  head+banged
head-banger
  head-bangers
head+board
  head+boards
head-butt
  head-butts
head-butting
  head-butted
head+dress
  head+dresses
head+ed
head+er
  head+ers
head+first
head+gear
head-hunter
  head-hunters
head-hunting

headi+ly
headi+ness
head+ing
  head+ings
head+lamp
  head+lamps
head+land
  head+lands
head+less
head+light
  head+lights
head+line
  head+lines
head+long
head+man
  head+men
head+master
  head+masters
head+mistress
  head+
    mistresses
head+most
head-on
head+phones
head+piece
  head+pieces
head+pin
  head+pins
head+quarters
head+race
  head+races
head+rest
  head+rests
head+room
head+scarf
  head+scarves
head+set
  head+sets
head+ship
head+shrinker
  head+shrinkers
heads+man
  heads+men
head+stall
  head+stalls
head+stock
  head+stocks
head+stone
  head+stones
head+stream
  head+streams
head+strong
head+waters
head+way
head+wind

head+winds	heart+breakers	hea+then+ism	He+brai+cal
head+word	heart+breaking	hea+then+ize	He+brai+cal+ly
head+words	heart+burn	hea+then+izes	He+bra+ise
head+work	heart+en	hea+then+iz+ing	He+bra+ises
heady	heart+ens	hea+then+ized	He+bra+is+ing
headi+er	heart+en+ing	heath+er	He+bra+ised
headi+est	heart+ened	heath+ers	He+bra+ism
heal	heart+felt	heath+ery	He+bra+isms
heals	hearth	heath+like	He+bra+ist
heal+ing	hearths	heathy	He+bra+ists
healed	hearth+stone	heat-seeking	He+bra+ize
heal+er	hearth+stones	heat+stroke	He+bra+izes
heal+ers	hearti+ly	heat-treat	He+bra+iz+ing
Healey	hearti+ness	heat-treats	He+bra+ized
heal+ing	heart+land	heat-treating	He+brew
heal+ings	heart+lands	heat-treated	He+brews
health	heart+less	heave	Heb+ri+dean
health+ful	heart+less+ly	heaves	Heb+ri+deans
healthi+ly	heart+less+ness	heav+ing	Heb+ri+des
healthi+ness	heart-rending	heaved or	He+brid+ian
healthy	heart-rending+ly	hove	He+brid+ians
healthi+er	heart-searching	heave-ho	Heb+ron
healthi+est	hearts+ease	heav+en	Heca+te
heap	heart's-ease	heav+ens	heca+tomb
heaps	heart+sick	heav+en+li+ness	heca+tombs
heaps	heart+sickness	heav+en+ly	heck
heap+ing	heart+strings	heav+en+ward	heck+el+phone
heaped	heart-throb	heav+en+wards	heck+el+phones
hear	heart-throbs	heav+er	heck+le
hears	heart-to-heart	heav+ers	heck+les
hear+ing	heart-to-hearts	heaves	heck+ling
heard	heart-warming	heavi+ly	heck+led
hear+er	heart+wood	heavi+ness	heck+ler
hear+ers	hearty	Heaviside	heck+lers
hear+ing	hearties	heavy	hec+tare
hear+ings	hearti+er	heavies	hec+tares
heark+en	hearti+est	heavi+er	hec+tic
heark+ens	heat	heavi+est	hec+tics
heark+en+ing	heats	heavy-duty	hec+ti+cal+ly
heark+ened	heats	heavy-handed	hec+to+gram
hear+say	heat+ing	heavy-handed+ly	hec+to+grams
hearse	heat+ed	heavy-hearted	hec+to+gramme
hearses	heat+ed+ly	heavy-water	hec+to+
Hearst	heat+er	heavy+weight	grammes
heart	heat+ers	heavy+weights	hec+to+graph
hearts	heath	Hebbel	hec+to+graphs
hearts	heaths	heb+doma+dal	hec+tor
heart+ing	hea+then	Hebe	hec+tors
heart+ed	hea+thens or	He+bei	hec+tors
heart+ache	hea+then	heb+etate	hec+tor+ing
heart+aches	hea+then+dom	heb+etates	hec+tored
heart+beat	hea+then+ise	heb+etat+ing	Hector
heart+beats	hea+then+ises	heb+etat+ed	Hecuba
heart+break	hea+then+is+ing	heb+eta+tion	he'd
heart+breaker	hea+then+ised	He+bra+ic	hed+dle

hed+dles
hed+era
hedge
  hedges
  hedges
  hedg+ing
  hedged
hedge+hog
  hedge+hogs
hedge+hop
  hedge+hops
  hedge+hop+
   ping
  hedge+hopped
hedg+er
  hedg+ers
hedge+row
  hedge+rows
hedg+ing
  hedg+ings
He+djaz
he+don+ics
he+don+ism
he+don+ist
  he+don+ists
he+don+is+tic
heebie-jeebies
heed
  heeds
  heed+ing
  heed+ed
heed+ful
heed+ful+ly
heed+ful+ness
heed+less
heed+less+ly
heed+less+ness
hee+haw
heel
  heels
  heels
  heel+ing
  heeled
heel+ball
heel+er
  heel+ers
heel+less
heel+tap
  heel+taps
He+fei
heft
  hefts
  hefts
  heft+ing
  heft+ed

hefti+ly
hefty
  hefti+er
  hefti+est
Hegel
He+gelian
He+geli+an+ism
heg+emon+ic
he+gemo+ny
  he+gemo+nies
Hegi+ra
  Hegi+ras
Heidegger
Hei+del+berg
heif+er
  heif+ers
Heifetz
heigh-ho
height
  heights
height+en
  height+ens
  height+en+ing
  height+ened
Heil+bronn
Hei+long+jiang
Hei+long Jiang
Hei+lung+kiang
Heine
Heinkel
hei+nous
  hei+nous+ly
heir
  heirs
heir+dom
heir+ess
  heir+esses
heir+loom
  heir+looms
heir+ship
  heir+ships
heist
  heists
  heists
  heist+ing
  heist+ed
Heitler
He+jaz
Heji+ra
  Heji+ras
Heka+te
Hek+la
held
Helen
Hel+ena

place name
Helena
  saint
he+leni+um
  he+leni+ums
Hel+go+land
he+lia+cal
he+li+an+the+
  mum
  he+li+an+the+
  mums
he+li+an+thus
  he+li+an+thuses
heli+cal
heli+ces
heli+chry+sum
  heli+chry+sums
heli+coid
  heli+coids
heli+con
  heli+cons
Heli+con
heli+cop+ter
  heli+cop+ters
Heli+go+land
helio+cen+tric
helio+cen+tri+cal+
  ly
Heliogabalus
helio+graph
  helio+graphs
he+li+og+ra+phy
he+li+om+eter
  he+li+om+eters
he+li+om+etry
He+li+opo+lis
Helios
helio+stat
  helio+stats
helio+stat+ic
helio+trope
  helio+tropes
helio+trop+ic
he+li+ot+ro+pism
heli+port
  heli+ports
he+lium
he+lix
  heli+ces *or*
  he+lixes
hell
  hells
he'll
Hel+lad+ic
Hel+las

hell+bent
hell+cat
  hell+cats
Helle
hel+le+bore
  hel+le+bores
Hellen
Hel+lene
  Hel+lenes
Hel+le+nian
  Hel+le+nians
Hel+len+ic
Hel+leni+sa+tion
  Hel+leni+sa+
  tions
Hel+len+ise
  Hel+len+ises
  Hel+len+is+ing
  Hel+len+ised
Hel+len+ism
  Hel+len+isms
Hel+len+ist
  Hel+len+ists
Hel+len+is+tic
Hel+len+is+ti+cal
  Hel+len+is+ti+cal+
  ly
Hel+leni+za+tion
  Hel+leni+za+
  tions
Hel+len+ize
  Hel+len+izes
  Hel+len+iz+ing
  Hel+len+ized
Heller
Hel+les
Hel+les+pont
hell+fire
hel+lion
  hell+lions
hell+ish
Hellman
hel+lo
  hel+los
helm
  helms
  helms
  helm+ing
  helmed
hel+met
  hel+mets
  hel+met+ed
Helmholtz
hel+minth
  hel+minths

hel+min+thia+sis
hel+min+thic
hel+min+thoid
helms+man
 helms+men
Héloïse
hel+ot+ism
hel+ot+ry
help
 helps
 helps
 help+ing
 helped
help+er
 help+ers
help+ful
help+ful+ly
help+ful+ness
help+ing
 help+ings
help+less
help+less+ly
help+less+ness
help+line
 help+lines
Helpmann
help+mate
 help+mates
help+meet
 help+meets
Hel+sing+borg
Hel+sing+ør
Hel+sin+ki
helter-skelter
 helter-skelters
helve
 helves
Hel+vel+lyn
Hel+ve+tia
Hel+ve+tian
 Hel+ve+tians
Helvétius
hem
 hems
 hems
 hem+ming
 hemmed
he+mal
he-man
 he-men
hema+tem+esis
U.S.
he+mat+ic
U.S.
hema+tin

U.S.
hema+tite
hema+tit+ic
hema+to+crit
U.S.
 hema+to+crits
hema+tol+ogy
U.S.
 hema+toly+sis
U.S.
 hema+toly+ses
hema+to+ma
U.S.
 hema+to+mas
 or
 hema+to+ma+ta
hema+tu+ria
U.S.
heme
U.S.
Hem+el Hemp+
 stead
hem+era+lo+pia
hem+ero+cal+lis
 hem+ero+cal+
 lises
hemi+demi+semi+
 quaver
hemi+demi+
 semi+quavers
Hemingway
hemi+plegia
hemi+ple+gic
hemi+pode
 hemi+podes
he+mip+ter+an
 he+mip+ter+ans
he+mip+ter+ous
hemi+sphere
 hemi+spheres
hemi+spher+ic
hemi+spheri+cal
hemi+stich
 hemi+stichs
hem+line
 hem+lines
hem+lock
 hem+locks
hem+mer
 hem+mers
hemo+cya+nin
U.S.
hemo+cy+tom+
 eter
U.S.

hemo+cy+tom+
 eters
hemo+di+aly+sis
U.S.
 hemo+di+aly+
 ses
hemo+glo+bin
U.S.
he+moly+sis
U.S.
 he+moly+ses
hemo+philia
U.S.
hemo+phili+ac
U.S.
 hemo+phili+acs
hemo+phil+ic
U.S.
hem+op+ty+sis
U.S.
 hem+op+ty+ses
hem+or+rhage
U.S.
 hem+or+rhages
 hem+or+rhages
hem+or+rhag+
 ing
 hem+or+rhaged
hem+or+rhoi+dal
U.S.
 hem+or+rhoids
U.S.
hemo+sta+sis
U.S.
hemo+stat
U.S.
 hemo+stats
hemo+stat+ic
U.S.
hemp
 hemps
hemp+en
hemp+like
hem+stitch
 hem+stitches
 hem+stitches
 hem+stitch+ing
 hem+stitched
hen
 hens
He+nan
hen+bane
hence
hence+forth
hence+forward

hence+forwards
hench+man
 hench+men
hen+deca+gon
hen+deca+gons
hen+de+cago+
 nal
hen+deca+syl+la+
 ble
 hen+deca+syl+
 la+bles
Henderson
hen+dia+dys
Hendrix
Hendry
hen+equen
 hen+equens
hen+equin
 hen+equins
henge
 henges
Hengist
Heng+yang
hen+house
 hen+houses
Henie
heni+quen
 heni+quens
Henley-on-
 Thames
hen+na
hen+nas
hen+nas
hen+na+ing
hen+naed
heno+theism
heno+theis+tic
hen+peck
 hen+pecks
 hen+peck+ing
 hen+pecked
hen+ry
hen+ry or
hen+ries or
hen+rys
Henryson
Henslowe
hep
hep+per
hep+pest
hepa+rin
he+pat+ic
he+pat+ics
he+pati+ca
he+pati+cas

hepa+ti+tis
Hepburn
Hephaestus
Hephaistos
Hepplewhite
hep+tad
  hep+tads
hep+ta+gon
  hep+ta+gons
hep+tago+nal
hep+ta+he+dral
hep+ta+he+dron
  hep+ta+he+
    drons *or*
  hep+ta+he+dra
hep+tam+eter
  hep+tam+eters
hepta+met+ri+cal
hep+tane
hep+tarch
  hep+tarchs
hep+tar+chic
hep+tar+chy
  hep+tar+chies
hep+tath+lete
  hep+tath+letes
hep+tath+lon
  hep+tath+lons
hep+tava+lent
Hepworth
her
Hera
Hera+clea
Hera+clean
Heracleides
Heracles
Heraclitus
Heraclius
He+ra+klei+on
Herakles
He+ra+kli+on
her+ald
  her+alds
  her+alds
  her+ald+ing
  her+ald+ed
he+ral+dic
he+ral+di+cal+ly
her+ald+ist
  her+ald+ists
her+ald+ry
  her+ald+ries
He+rat
Hé+rault
herb

herbs
her+ba+ceous
herb+age
herb+al
  herb+als
herb+al+ist
  herb+al+ists
her+bar+ium
her+bar+iums
    or
  her+baria
Herbert
herbi+cide
  herbi+cides
her+bi+vore
  her+bi+vores
her+bivo+rous
herb+like
herby
herbi+er
herbi+est
Her+ce+go+vi+
  na
Her+cu+la+neum
her+cu+lean
Hercules
  classical hero
Her+cu+les
  constellation
herd
  herds
  herds
  herd+ing
  herd+ed
herds+man
herds+men
here
here+about
here+abouts
here+after
here+at
here+by
he+redi+tabil+ity
he+redi+table
her+edita+ment
he+redi+tari+ly
he+redi+tari+
  ness
he+redi+tary
he+red+ity
  he+red+ities
Her+eford
Her+eford+shire
here+in
here+in+after

here+into
here+of
here+on
he+resi+arch
  he+resi+archs
her+esy
  her+esies
her+etic
  her+etics
he+reti+cal
he+reti+cal+ly
here+to
here+to+fore
here+under
here+upon
Hereward
here+with
heri+ot
  heri+ots
He+ri+sau
her+it+abil+ity
her+it+able
her+it+ably
her+it+age
  her+it+ages
herl
  herls
Hermann
Her+mann+stadt
her+maph+ro+
  dite
  her+maph+ro+
    dites
her+maph+ro+dit+
  ic
her+maph+ro+
  diti+cal
her+maph+ro+dit+
  ism
Hermaphroditus
her+meneu+tic
her+meneu+ti+
  cal
her+meneu+ti+
  cal+ly
her+meneu+tics
Hermes
  messenger of the
  gods
Her+mes
  asteroid
her+met+ic
her+meti+cal
her+meti+cal+ly
her+mit

her+mits
her+mit+age
  her+mit+ages
her+mit+ic
her+miti+cal
Her+mo+si+llo
Her+mou+po+lis
Her+ne
her+nia
  her+nias *or*
  her+niae
her+nial
her+ni+at+ed
hero
  heroes
Herod
Herod Antipas
Herodias
Herodotus
he+ro+ic
he+roi+cal
he+roi+cal+ly
he+ro+ics
hero+in
hero+ine
  hero+ines
hero+ism
her+on
  her+ons
her+on+ry
  her+on+ries
Herophilus
hero-worship
hero-worships
hero-worship+
  ping *or*
hero-worship+
  ing
  U.S.
hero-
  worshipped
    or
  hero-worshiped
  U.S.
hero wor+ship
  noun
hero-worship+per
hero-worship+
  pers
her+pes
her+pes sim+plex
her+pes zos+ter
her+pet+ic
  her+pet+ics

her+pe+to+log+
 ic
her+pe+to+logi+
 cal
Herr
 Her+ren
Her+ren+volk
Herrick
her+ring
 her+rings or
 her+ring
herring+bone
 herring+bones
 herring+boning
 herring+boned
Herriot
hers
Herschel
her+self
Herst+mon+ceux
Hert+ford
Hert+ford+shire
Her+to+gen+
 bosch
hertz
 hertz
Hertz
Hertz+ian
Hertzog
Herzegovina
Herzl
Herzog
he's
Heseltine
Hesiod
Hesi+od+ic
Hesione
hesi+tan+cy
hesi+tant
hesi+tant+ly
hesi+tate
 hesi+tates
 hesi+tat+ing
 hesi+tat+ed
hesi+tat+ing+ly
hesi+ta+tion
 hesi+ta+tions
Hes+peria
Hes+pe+rian
Hes+per+id+ean
Hesperides
Hes+per+id+ian
hes+per+id+ium
Hes+per+us

Hess
Hesse
Hesse-Nassau
hes+sian
Hes+sian
 Hes+sians
hest
 hests
Hestia
het
he+tae+ra
he+tae+rae
he+tae+rism
he+tae+risms
he+tai+ra
he+tai+rai
he+tai+rism
he+tai+risms
hetero+clite
hetero+clites
hetero+clit+ic
hetero+cy+clic
hetero+dox
hetero+doxy
hetero+dyne
hetero+dynes
hetero+dyn+ing
hetero+dyned
het+er+oecious
het+er+oecism
hetero+gam+ete
hetero+gam+
 etes
heteroga+mous
het+er+oga+my
hetero+geneity
hetero+geneous
hetero+geneous+
 ness
het+er+ogo+
 nous
heter+ogo+ny
het+er+olo+gous
het+er+ol+ogy
het+er+om+er+
 ous
hetero+mor+phic
hetero+mor+
 phism
hetero+mor+
 phous
het+er+ono+
 mous
het+er+ono+my
hetero+nym

hetero+nyms
hetero+phyl+lous
hetero+phyl+ly
het+er+op+ter+
 an
het+er+op+ter+
 ous
hetero+sex+ism
hetero+sex+ist
 hetero+sex+ists
hetero+sex+ual
 hetero+sex+uals
hetero+sexu+al+
 ity
hetero+tax+is
hetero+taxy
hetero+troph
 hetero+trophs
hetero+troph+ic
hetero+zy+gote
 hetero+zy+
 gotes
hetero+zy+gous
het+man
 het+mans
heu+chera
heu+ris+tic
 heu+ris+tics
heu+ris+ti+cal+ly
Hevesy
hew
 hews
hew+ing
hewed
 hewed or
 hewn
hew+er
 hew+ers
Hewish
hex
 hexes
 hexes
hex+ing
hexed
hexa+chloro+
 phene
hexa+chord
 hexa+chords
hex+ad
 hex+ads
hexa+decane
hexa+deci+mal
hexa+gon
 hexa+gons
hex+ago+nal

hexa+gram
 hexa+grams
hexa+he+dral
hexa+he+dron
 hexa+he+drons
 or
 hexa+he+dra
hex+am+eter
 hex+am+eters
hexa+met+ric
hexa+met+ri+cal
hex+ane
hexa+pla
hexa+plar
hexa+pod
 hexa+pods
hexa+va+lent
hex+ose
hey
hey+day
 hey+days
Heyer
Heyerdahl
Hey+sham
Hey+wood
 place name
Heywood
 surname
Hezekiah
hi
Hia+leah
hia+tus
 hia+tuses or
 hia+tus
Hiawatha
hi+ba+chi
 hi+ba+chis
hi+ba+ku+sha
 hi+ba+ku+sha
 or
 hi+ba+ku+shas
hi+ber+nal
hi+ber+nate
 hi+ber+nates
 hi+ber+nat+ing
 hi+ber+nat+ed
hi+ber+na+tion
 hi+ber+na+tions
hi+ber+na+tor
 hi+ber+na+tors
Hi+ber+nia
Hi+ber+nian
 Hi+ber+nians
Hi+ber+ni+cism

Hi+ber+ni+
  cisms
hi+bis+cus
hi+bis+cuses
hic+cup
hic+cups
hic+cups
hic+cup+ing *or*
hic+cup+ping
hic+cuped *or*
hic+cupped
hic ja+cet
hick
hicks
hicko+ry
hicko+ries
hid
hi+dal+go
  hi+dal+gos
Hi+dal+go
hid+den
hide
conceal
  hides
  hides
  hid+ing
  hid
  hid+den *or*
  hid
hide
skin, thrash
  hides
  hides
  hid+ing
  hid+ed
hide-and-go-seek
hide-and-seek
hide+away
  hide+aways
hide+bound
hid+eous
hid+eous+ly
hid+eous+ness
hide-out
  hide-outs
hid+er
  hid+ers
hidey-hole
  hidey-holes
hid+ing
  hid+ings
hi+dro+sis
hi+drot+ic
hidy-hole
  hidy-holes

hie
hies
hie+ing *or*
hy+ing
hied
hi+er+arch
  hi+er+archs
hi+er+ar+chal
hi+er+ar+chic
hi+er+ar+chi+cal
hi+er+arch+ism
hi+er+ar+chy
hi+er+ar+chies
hi+er+at+ic
hi+er+ati+cal+ly
hi+ero+glyph
hi+ero+glyph+ic
hi+ero+glyph+
  ics
hi+ero+glyphi+cal
hi+ero+glyphi+cal+
  ly
Hi+ero+nym+ian
Hi+ero+nym+ic
Hieronymus
hi+ero+phant
  hi+ero+phants
hi+ero+phant+ic
hi-fi
  hi-fis
Higgins
higgledy-piggle+
  dy
high
  highs
high+er
high+est
high+ball
  high+balls
high+born
high+boy
  high+boys
high+brow
  high+brows
high+browed
high+chair
  high+chairs
High-Churchman
  High-Churchmen
high-class
high-coloured
high+er
  high+ers
higher-up
high+fa+lu+tin

high+fa+lu+ting
high-five
high-flier
  high-fliers
high-flown
high-flyer
  high-flyers
high-flying
high-handed
high-handed+
  ness
high-hat
  high-hats
  high-hats
  high-hatting
  high-hatted
high+jack
  high+jacks
  high+jacks
  high+jack+ing
  high+jacked
high+jack+er
  high+jack+ers
high-key
high+land
  high+lands
High+land
  High+lands
high+lander
  high+landers
High+lander
  High+landers
high-level
high+light
  high+lights
  high+lights
  high+light+ing
  high+light+ed
high+ly
high-minded
high-minded+
  ness
High+ness
  High+nesses
high-octane
high-pitched
high-powered
high-pressure
high-rise
  high-rises
high-risk
high+road
  high+roads
Highsmith
high-sounding

high-spirit+ed
high-spirit+ed+
  ness
high-strung
high+tail
  high+tails
  high+tail+ing
  high+tailed
high-tech
  adj.
high tech
  noun
high-tension
high-toned
high-up
high+veld
high-water
high+way
  high+ways
highway+man
highway+men
hi+jack
  hi+jacks
  hi+jacks
  hi+jack+ing
  hi+jacked
hi+jack+er
  hi+jack+ers
Hi+jaz
hike
  hikes
  hikes
  hik+ing
  hiked
hik+er
  hik+ers
hi+lari+ous
hi+lari+ous+ly
hi+lari+ous+ness
hi+lar+ity
Hilary
Hilbert
Hildebrand
Hilde+bran+dian
  Hilde+bran+
    dians
Hilde+brand+ine
Hildegard
Hil+des+heim
hill
  hills
  hills
  hill+ing
  hilled
Hillary

hill+bil+ly
 hill+bil+lies
Hiller
Hilliard
Hil+ling+don
hill+ock
 hill+ocks
hill+ocked
hill+ocky
hilly
 hilli+er
 hilli+est
hilt
 hilts
hi+lum
 hi+la
Hil+ver+sum
him
Hi+ma+chal Pra+
 desh
Hima+la+yan
Hima+la+yas
hi+mati+on
 hi+matia
Hi+meji
Himmler
him+self
Hi+na+ya+na
Hinck+ley
hind
 hind+er
 hind+most or
 hinder+most
hind
female deer
 hinds or
 hind
Hindemith
Hin+den+burg
place name
Hindenburg
surname
hin+der
 hin+ders
 hin+der+ing
 hin+dered
hind+er
adj.
hinder+most
Hin+di
 Hin+dis
hind+most
Hin+doo
 Hin+doos
Hin+doo+ism

hind+quarter
 hind+quarters
hin+drance
 hin+drances
hind+sight
 hind+sights
Hin+du
 Hin+dus
Hin+du+ism
Hin+du Kush
Hin+du+stan
Hin+du+sta+ni
hinge
 hinges
 hinges
 hing+ing
 hinged
hin+ny
 hin+nies
hint
 hints
 hints
 hint+ing
 hint+ed
hinter+land
 hinter+lands
hip
 hips
hip+per
hip+pest
hip+bone
 hip+bones
hip-hop
hip+less
Hipparchus
person's name
Hip+par+chus
moon's crater
hip+pe+as+trum
hipped
hip+pie
 hip+pies
hip+po
 hip+pos
hippo+campus
 hippo+campi
hip+po+cras
Hippocrates
Hip+po+crat+ic
Hip+po+crati+cal
Hip+po+crene
Hip+po+crenian
hippo+drome
 hippo+dromes
hip+po+griff

hip+po+griffs
hip+po+gryph
 hip+po+gryphs
Hippolyta
Hip+poly+tan
Hippolyte
Hippolytus
Hippomenes
hippo+pota+mus
 hippo+pota+
 muses *or*
 hippo+pota+mi
Hip+po Re+gius
hip+py
 hip+pies
hip+pi+er
hip+pi+est
hip+ster
 hip+sters
hir+able
Hiram
hir+cine
hire
 hires
 hires
 hir+ing
 hired
hire+able
hire+ling
 hire+lings
hire-purchase
hir+er
 hir+ers
Hirohito
Hiroshige
Hi+ro+shi+ma
hir+sute
hir+sute+ness
his
His+pania
His+pan+ic
 His+pan+ics
His+pani+cism
 His+pani+cisms
His+panio+la
his+pid
hiss
 hisses
 hisses
hiss+ing
 hissed
hist
his+ta+mine
his+ta+min+ic
his+to+gen+esis

his+to+genet+ic
his+to+gen+ic
his+to+gram
 his+to+grams
his+to+log+ic
his+to+logi+cal
his+tol+ogy
his+toly+sis
his+to+lyt+ic
his+to+rian
 his+to+rians
his+tor+ic
his+tori+cal
his+tori+cal+ly
his+tori+cism
his+tori+cist
 his+tori+cists
his+to+ric+ity
his+to+ri+og+ra+
 pher
his+to+ri+og+ra+
 phers
his+to+ri+og+ra+
 phy
his+to+ry
 his+to+ries
his+tri+on+ic
his+tri+on+ics
his+tri+oni+cal+ly
hit
 hits
 hits
hit+ting
hit
Hi+ta+chi
hit-and-run
hitch
 hitches
 hitches
hitch+ing
 hitched
Hitchcock
hitch+er
 hitch+ers
hitch+hike
 hitch+hikes
hitch+hik+ing
 hitch+hiked
hitch+hiker
 hitch+hikers
hi-tech
adj.
hi tech
noun
hith+er

hither+most
hither+to
Hitler
 Hitlers
Hit+ler+ism
hit+ter
 hit+ters
Hit+tite
 Hit+tites
hive
 hives
 hives
 hiv+ing
 hived
hiya
h'm
hoar
hoard
 hoards
 hoards
 hoard+ing
 hoard+ed
 hoard+er
 hoard+ers
 hoard+ing
 hoard+ings
hoar+frost
hoar+hound
 hoar+hounds
hoari+ness
hoarse
 hoars+er
 hoars+est
 hoarse+ly
 hoars+en
 hoars+ens
 hoars+en+ing
 hoars+ened
 hoarse+ness
hoary
 hoari+er
 hoari+est
ho+at+zin
 ho+at+zins
hoax
 hoaxes
 hoaxes
 hoax+ing
 hoaxed
 hoax+er
 hoax+ers
hob
 hobs
Ho+bart
Hobbema

Hobbes
hob+bit
 hob+bits
hob+ble
 hob+bles
 hob+bles
 hob+bling
 hob+bled
hobble+dehoy
 hobble+dehoys
hob+bler
 hob+blers
Hobbs
hob+by
 hob+bies
hobby+horse
 hobby+horses
hob+by+ist
 hob+by+ists
hob+goblin
 hob+goblins
hob+nail
 hob+nails
 hob+nailed
hob+nob
 hob+nobs
 hob+nob+bing
 hob+nobbed
hobo
 hoboes or
 hobos
hobo+ism
Ho+bo+ken
Hobson
Hochhuth
Ho Chi Minh
hock
 hocks
 hocks
 hock+ing
 hocked
hock+ey
 hock+eys
Hockney
ho+cus
 ho+cuses
 ho+cus+ing or
 ho+cus+sing
 ho+cused or
 ho+cussed
hocus-pocus
 hocus-pocuses
 hocus-pocusing
   or

hocus-
   pocussing
 hocus-pocused
   or
 hocus-pocussed
hod
 hods
hodge+podge
 hodge+podges
Hodgkin
hodo+graph
 hodo+graphs
ho+dom+eter
 ho+dom+eters
 ho+dom+etry
hoe
 hoes
 hoes
 hoe+ing
 hoed
hoe+down
 hoe+downs
hoer
 hoers
Ho+fei
Hoffman
Ho+fuf
hog
 hogs
 hogs
 hog+ging
 hogged
ho+gan
 ho+gans
Hogarth
Ho+garth+ian
hog+back
 hog+backs
hog+fish
 hog+fish or
 hog+fishes
Hogg
hog+ger
 hog+gers
hog+gish
hog+like
Hog+ma+nay
 Hog+ma+nays
hogs+head
 hogs+heads
hog+tie
 hog+ties
 hog+ty+ing
 hog+tied
hog+wash

hog+weed
hog+weeds
Hohenstaufen
Hohenzollern
Hoh+hot
hoick
 hoicks
 hoick+ing
 hoicked
hoi+den
 hoi+dens
 hoi+den+ish
hoi pol+loi
hoist
 hoists
 hoists
 hoist+ing
 hoist+ed
 hoist+er
 hoist+ers
hoity-toity
ho+key co+key
Hok+kai+do
hok+ku
 hok+ku
ho+ko+nui
ho+kum
Hokusai
Hol+arc+tic
Holbein
hold
 holds
 holds
 hold+ing
 held
hold+able
hold+all
 hold+alls
hold+er
 hold+ers
Hölderlin
hold+fast
 hold+fasts
 hold+ing
 hold+ings
hold+over
hold over
 verb
hold-up
 hold-ups
hole
 holes
 holes
 hol+ing
 holed

hole-and-corner
holey
Hol+guín
Holi
holi+day
 holi+days
 holi+days
 holi+day+ing
 holi+dayed
Holiday
holiday-maker
 holiday-makers
ho+li+ly
ho+li+ness
Ho+li+ness
 Ho+li+nesses
Holingshed
Holinshed
ho+lism
ho+lis+tic
hol+la
 hol+las
 hol+las
 hol+la+ing
 hol+laed
hol+land
Hol+land
place name
Holland
surname
hol+lan+daise
Hol+lan+dia
Hol+lands
hol+ler
 hol+lers
 hol+lers
 hol+ler+ing
 hol+lered
hol+lo
 hol+los
 hol+los
 hol+lo+ing
 hol+loed
hol+low
 hol+lows
 hol+lows
 hol+low+ing
 hol+lowed
hollow-eyed
hol+low+ly
hol+low+ness
hol+ly
 hol+lies
Holly
hol+ly+hock

hol+ly+hocks
Hol+ly+wood
holm
holms
Holmes
hol+mium
holo+caust
holo+causts
Holo+cene
Holofernes
holo+gram
 holo+grams
holo+graph
 holo+graphs
holo+graph+ic
holo+graphi+cal+ly
ho+log+ra+phy
holo+he+dral
holo+phyt+ic
holo+thu+rian
 holo+thu+rians
hols
Holst
Hol+stein
hol+ster
 hol+sters
holt
holts
holy
holies
holi+er
holi+est
Holy+head
Holyoake
ho+ly+stone
ho+ly+stones
ho+ly+stones
ho+ly+ston+ing
ho+ly+stoned
hom+age
hom+ages
hom+burg
hom+burgs
home
homes
homes
hom+ing
homed
Home
home+boy
home+boys
home-brew
home-brews
home-brewed

home+coming
home+comings
home+girl
home+girls
home+land
home+lands
home+less
home+less+ness
home+li+ness
home+ly
home+li+er
home+li+est
home-made
homeo+path
homeo+paths
homeo+path+ic
homeopa+thist
homeopa+thists
homeopa+thy
homeo+sta+sis
hom+er
hom+ers
Homer
Ho+mer+ic
home+sick
home+sick+ness
home+spun
home+stead
home+steads
home+stead+er
home+stead+
 ers
home+ward
home+work
homey
homi+er
homi+est
homey+ness
homi+ci+dal
homi+cide
homi+cides
homi+let+ic
homi+let+ics
homi+list
homi+lists
homi+ly
homi+lies
homi+ness
hom+ing
homi+nid
homi+nids
homi+noid
homi+noids
homi+ny
homo

homos
Homo
homo+cy+clic
homoeo+path
homoeo+paths
homoeo+path+ic
homoeopa+thist
homoeopa+
 thists
homoeopa+thy
homoeo+sta+sis
ho+moga+mous
ho+moga+my
homo+genei+ty
homo+geneous
homo+geneous+
 ness
ho+mog+eni+sa+
 tion
ho+mog+eni+sa+
 tions
ho+mog+enise
ho+mog+enises
ho+mog+enis+
 ing
ho+mog+enised
ho+mog+enis+er
ho+mog+enis+
 ers
ho+mog+eni+za+
 tion
ho+mog+eni+za+
 tions
ho+mog+enize
ho+mog+enizes
ho+mog+eniz+
 ing
ho+mog+enized
ho+mog+eniz+er
ho+mog+eniz+
 ers
ho+mog+enous
ho+mog+eny
homo+graph
homo+graphs
homo+graph+ic
ho+moio+ther+
 mic
ho+moio+ther+
 my
homo+log
homo+logs
homo+log+ic
homo+logi+cal
homo+logi+cal+ly

ho+molo+gise
ho+molo+gises
ho+molo+gis+
  ing
ho+molo+gised
ho+molo+gize
ho+molo+gizes
ho+molo+giz+
  ing
ho+molo+gized
ho+molo+gous
homo+logue
homo+logues
ho+mol+ogy
ho+mol+ogies
homo+mor+phic
homo+mor+
  phism
homo+mor+
  phous
homo+mor+phy
homo+nym
homo+nyms
homo+nym+ic
ho+mony+mous
homo+phobe
homo+phobes
homo+pho+bia
homo+phone
homo+phones
homo+phon+ic
ho+mop+ter+an
ho+mop+ter+ous
Homo sa+pi+ens
homo+sex+ual
homo+sex+uals
homo+sex+ual+
  ity
homo+ther+mal
homo+ther+my
homo+zy+gote
homo+zy+gotes
homo+zy+got+ic
homo+zy+gous
ho+mun+cu+lar
ho+mun+cu+lus
ho+mun+cu+li
homy
  homi+er
  homi+est
Ho+nan
hon+cho
hon+chos
Hon+du+ran
  Hon+du+rans

Hon+du+ras
hone
  hones
  hones
  hon+ing
  honed
Honecker
Honegger
hon+est
hon+est+ly
hon+es+ty
hon+es+ties
hon+ey
hon+eys
hon+eys
hon+ey+ing
hon+eyed *or*
hon+ied
honey+bee
honey+bees
honey+comb
honey+combs
honey+combs
honey+combing
honey+combed
honey+dew
honey+dews
honey-eater
honey-eaters
honey-like
honey+moon
honey+moons
honey+moons
honey+mooning
honey+mooned
honey+moon+er
honey+moon+
  ers
honey+suckle
honey+suckles
Hong Kong
Ho+nia+ra
honk
  honks
  honks
  honk+ing
  honked
honky
  honkies
honky-tonk
honky-tonks
Hono+lu+lu
hon+or
  U.S.
  hon+ors

hon+ors
hon+or+ing
hon+ored
hon+or+able
Hon+or+able
hon+or+ably
hono+rar+ium
hono+rar+iums
  or
  hono+raria
hon+or+ary
hon+or+if+ic
hon+or+ifi+cal+ly
hon+our
  hon+ours
  hon+ours
  hon+our+ing
  hon+oured
Hon+our
  Hon+ours
hon+our+able
Hon+our+able
hon+our+ably
Hon+shu
hooch
hood
  hoods
  hoods
  hood+ing
  hood+ed
hood+like
hood+lum
hood+lums
hoodman-blind
hoo+doo
  hoo+doos
  hoo+doos
  hoo+doo+ing
  hoo+dooed
hood+wink
  hood+winks
  hood+wink+ing
  hood+winked
hoo+ey
hoof
  hooves *or*
  hoofs
  hoofs
  hoof+ing
  hoofed
Hoogh+ly
hoo-ha
hook
  hooks
  hooks

hook+ing
hooked
hooka
hookas
hook+ah
hook+ahs
Hooke
hook+er
hook+ers
hookey
hook+like
hook-up
hook-ups
hook up
  verb
hook+worm
hook+worms
hooky
hoo+li+gan
hoo+li+gans
hoo+li+gan+ism
hoop
  hoops
  hoops
  hoop+ing
  hooped
hoop+la
hoop+las
hoo+poe
hoo+poes
hoo+rah
hoo+rahs
hoo+rah+ing
hoo+rahed
hoo+ray
hoo+rays
hoo+ray+ing
hoo+rayed
Hooray Henry
  Hooray Henries
  or
  Hooray Henrys
hoose+gow
hoose+gows
hoos+gow
hoos+gows
hoot
  hoots
  hoots
  hoot+ing
  hoot+ed
hootch
hoot+en+an+ny
hoot+en+an+
  nies

hoot+er
  hoot+ers
hoot+nan+ny
  hoot+nan+nies
hoo+ver
  hoo+vers
  hoo+ver+ing
  hoo+vered
Hoo+ver
Trademark
  Hoo+vers
Hoover
surname
hooves
hop
  hops
  hops
  hop+ping
  hopped
hope
  hopes
  hopes
  hop+ing
  hoped
hope+ful
  hope+fuls
hope+ful+ly
hope+ful+ness
Ho+peh
Ho+pei
hope+less
hope+less+ly
Hopi
  Hopis *or*
  Hopi
Hopkins
hop+lite
  hop+lites
hop+per
  hop+pers
hop+ping
hop+sack
hop+scotch
Horace
ho+ra+ry
Ho+ra+tian
horde
  hordes
hore+hound
  hore+hounds
ho+ri+zon
  ho+ri+zons
hori+zon+tal
  hori+zon+tals
hori+zon+tal+ity

hori+zon+tal+ly
hor+mo+nal
hor+mone
  hor+mones
Hor+muz
horn
  horns
  horns
  horn+ing
  horned
horn+beam
  horn+beams
horn+bill
  horn+bills
horn+blende
horn+book
  horn+books
horned
hor+net
  hor+nets
horni+ness
horn+less
horn+pipe
  horn+pipes
horns+wog+gle
  horns+wog+
    gles
  horns+wog+
    gling
  horns+wog+
    gled
horny
  horni+er
  horni+est
horo+loge
  horo+loges
ho+rolo+ger
  ho+rolo+gers
horo+log+ic
horo+logi+cal
ho+rolo+gist
  ho+rolo+gists
ho+rol+ogy
horo+scope
  horo+scopes
horo+scop+ic
ho+ros+co+py
  ho+ros+co+pies
Horowitz
hor+ren+dous
hor+ren+dous+ly
hor+ri+ble
hor+ri+ble+ness
hor+ri+bly
hor+rid

hor+rid+ly
hor+rid+ness
hor+rif+ic
hor+rifi+cal+ly
hor+ri+fi+ca+tion
hor+ri+fy
  hor+ri+fies
  hor+ri+fy+ing
  hor+ri+fied
hor+ri+fy+ing+ly
hor+ripi+la+tion
hor+ror
  hor+rors
Horsa
hors de com+bat
hors d'oeu+vre
  hors d'oeu+vre
    or
  hors d'oeu+vres
horse
  horses
  horses
  hors+ing
  horsed
horse+back
horse+box
  horse+boxes
horse+flesh
horse+fly
  horse+flies
horse+hair
horse+hide
  horse+hides
horse+leech
  horse+leeches
horse+like
horse+man
  horse+men
horse+man+ship
Hor+sens
horse+play
horse+power
horse+radish
horse+shoe
  horse+shoes
horse+tail
  horse+tails
horse+whip
  horse+whips
  horse+whips
horse+whip+
  ping
horse+whipped
horse+whip+per

horse+whip+
  pers
horse+woman
horsey
horsi+er
horsi+est
horsi+ly
horsi+ness
horst
  horsts
horsy
  horsi+er
  horsi+est
hor+ta+tion
  hor+ta+tions
hor+ta+tive
hor+ta+tive+ly
hor+ta+to+ri+ly
hor+ta+tory
Hortense
hor+ti+cul+tur+al
hor+ti+cul+ture
hor+ti+cul+tur+
  ist
  hor+ti+cul+tur+
    ists
Horus
ho+san+na
hose
  hoses
  hoses
  hos+ing
  hosed
hose
stockings
  hose *or*
  hos+en
Hosea
ho+sier
  ho+siers
ho+siery
hos+pice
  hos+pices
hos+pi+table
hos+pi+table+
  ness
hos+pi+tably
hos+pi+tal
  hos+pi+tals
hos+pi+tal+er
U.S.
  hos+pi+tal+ers
Hos+pi+tal+er
U.S.
  Hos+pi+tal+ers

Hos+pi+ta+let	hot+ter	houghs	house+men
hos+pi+tali+sa+ tion	hot+test	hough+ing	house-proud
hos+pi+tali+sa+ tions	hot-air	houghed	house+room
	Ho+tan	Houghton-le- Spring	house+top
hos+pi+tal+ise	hot+bed		house+tops
hos+pi+tal+ises	hot-beds	hou+mous	house-train
hos+pi+tal+is+ ing	hot-blooded	hound	house-trains
	hotch+potch	hounds	house-training
hos+pi+tal+ised	hotch+potches	hounds	house-trained
hos+pi+tal+ity	hot-dog	hound+ing	house-warming
hos+pi+tal+ities	hot-dogs	hound+ed	house-warmings
hos+pi+tali+za+ tion	hot-dogging	hound+er	house+wife
	hot-dogged	hound+ers	house+wives
hos+pi+tali+za+ tions	hot dog	hound's-tongue	house+wife+ly
	noun	Houns+low	house+wif+ery
hos+pi+tal+ize	ho+tel	Houphouet- Boigny	house+work
hos+pi+tal+izes	ho+tels		housey-housey
hos+pi+tal+iz+ ing	ho+tel+ier	hour	hous+ing
	ho+tel+iers	hours	hous+ings
hos+pi+tal+ized	hot+foot	hour+glass	Housman
hos+pi+tal+ler	hot-gospeller	hour+glasses	Hou+ston
hos+pi+tal+lers	hot-gospellers	hou+ri	hove
Hos+pi+tal+ler	hot+head	hou+ris	hov+el
Hos+pi+tal+lers	hot+heads	hour+ly	hov+els
host	hot-headed	house	hov+er
hosts	hot-headed+ness	houses	hov+ers
hosts	hot+house	houses	hov+er+ing
host+ing	hot+houses	hous+ing	hov+ered
host+ed	Ho+tien	housed	hover+craft
hos+ta	Ho-t'ien	house+boat	hover+crafts
hos+tas	hot+ly	house+boats	hov+er+er
hos+tage	hot+ness	house+bound	hov+er+ers
hos+tages	hot+plate	house+break+er	hover+port
hos+tel	hot+plates	house+break+ ers	hover+ports
hos+tels	hot+pot		hover+train
hos+tel+er	hot+pots	house+break+ing	hover+trains
U.S.	hot-press	house+coat	how
hos+tel+ers	hot-presses	house+coats	hows
hos+tel+ing	hot-presses	house-craft	Howard
U.S.	hot-pressing	house+fly	how+be+it
hos+tel+ler	hot-pressed	house+flies	how+dah
hos+tel+lers	hot+spur	house+hold	how+dahs
hos+tel+ling	hot+spurs	house+holds	how-do-you-do
hos+tel+ry	Hotspur	house+holder	how-do-you-dos
hos+tel+ries	Hot+ten+tot	house+holders	how+dy
host+ess	Hot+ten+tot *or*	house+holder+ ship	Howe
host+esses	Hot+ten+tots		how+ever
hos+tile	hot+tish	house+keeper	how+itz+er
hos+tile+ly	hot-wire	house+keepers	how+itz+ers
hos+til+ity	hot-wires	house+keeping	howl
hos+til+ities	hot-wiring	house+leek	howls
host+ler	hot-wired	house+leeks	howls
host+lers	Houdini	house+maid	howl+ing
hot	hough	house+maids	howled
	houghs	house+man	howl+er

howl+ers
How+rah
how+so+ever
Hoxha
hoy
 hoys
hoya
 hoyas
hoy+den
 hoy+dens
hoy+den+ish
Hoy+lake
Hoyle
Hsia Kuei
Hsia-men
Hsian
Hsiang
Hsin-hai-lien
Hsi+ning
Hsin+king
Hsüan T'ung
Hsü-chou
Hua Guo Feng
Huai+nan
Huam+bo
Huang Hai
Huang Ho
Huang Hua
Huas+cán
Huáscar
Huas+ca+rán
hub
 hubs
Hubble
hubble-bubble
 hubble-bubbles
hub+bub
hub+bubs
hub+by
 hub+bies
hub+cap
 hub+caps
Hu+bei
Hub+li
hu+bris
hu+bris+tic
hucka+back
huckle+berry
 huckle+berries
huck+ster
 huck+sters
huck+sters
huck+ster+ing
huck+stered
Hud+ders+field

hud+dle
hud+dles
hud+dles
hud+dling
hud+dled
hud+dler
hud+dlers
Huddleston
Hudson
 surname
Hud+son
 place name
hue
 hues
Hué
hued
Huel+va
Hues+ca
huff
huffs
huff+ing
huffed
huffi+ly
huff+ish
huff+ish+ly
huffy
huffi+er
huffi+est
hug
hugs
hugs
hug+ging
hugged
huge
hug+er
hug+est
huge+ly
huge+ness
hug+gable
hug+ger+mug+
 ger
hug+ger+mug+
 gers
hug+ger+mug+
 ger+ing
hug+ger+mug+
 gered
Hugo
Hu+guenot
 Hu+guenots
huh
Hu+he+hot
Hu-ho-hao-t'e
huhu

huhus
hui
huies
huia
huias
hula
Hula-Hoop
 Trademark
 Hula-Hoops
hula-hula
hulk
hulks
hull
hulls
hulls
hull+ing
hulled
hul+la+bal+loo
hul+la+bal+loos
hul+la+ba+loo
hul+la+ba+loos
hul+lo
hul+los
hum
hums
hums
hum+ming
hummed
hu+man
hu+mans
hu+mane
hu+mane+ly
hu+mane+ness
hu+mani+sa+tion
hu+mani+sa+
 tions
hu+man+ise
hu+man+ises
hu+man+is+ing
hu+man+ised
hu+man+ism
hu+man+ist
hu+man+ists
hu+man+ist+ic
hu+mani+tar+ian
hu+mani+tar+
 ians
hu+mani+tari+an+
 ism
hu+man+ity
hu+man+ities
hu+mani+za+tion
hu+mani+za+
 tions
hu+man+ize

hu+man+izes
hu+man+iz+ing
hu+man+ized
human+kind
hu+man+ly
hu+man+ness
hu+man+oid
hu+man+oids
Hum+ber
Humber+side
hum+ble
hum+bles
hum+bling
hum+bled
hum+bler
hum+blest
hum+ble+bee
hum+ble+bees
hum+ble+ness
hum+bly
Humboldt
hum+bug
hum+bugs
hum+bugs
hum+bug+ging
hum+bugged
hum+bug+ger
hum+bug+gers
hum+bug+gery
hum+ding+er
hum+ding+ers
hum+drum
hum+drums
Hume
hu+mec+tant
hu+mec+tants
hu+mer+al
hu+mer+us
hu+meri
hu+mid
hu+midi+fi+ca+
 tion
hu+midi+fi+ca+
 tions
hu+midi+fi+er
hu+midi+fi+ers
hu+midi+fy
hu+midi+fies
hu+midi+fy+ing
hu+midi+fied
hu+mid+ity
hu+mid+ly
hu+mid+ness
hu+mi+dor
hu+mi+dors

hu+mi+fi+ca+tion
hu+mi+fi+ca+
  tions
hu+mi+fy
hu+mi+fies
hu+mi+fy+ing
hu+mi+fied
hu+mili+ate
hu+mili+ates
hu+mili+at+ing
hu+mili+at+ed
hu+mili+at+ing+ly
hu+milia+tion
hu+milia+tions
hu+mil+ia+tor
hu+mil+ia+tors
hu+mil+ity
hu+mil+ities
Hum+ism
Hummel
humming+bird
humming+birds
hum+mock
hum+mocks
hum+mocky
hum+mus
hu+mor
U.S.
hu+mors
hu+mors
hu+mor+ing
hu+mored
hu+mor+al
hu+mor+esque
hu+mor+esques
hu+mor+ist
hu+mor+ists
hu+mor+less
hu+mor+ous
hu+mor+ous+ly
hu+mor+ous+
  ness
hu+mour
hu+mours
hu+mours
hu+mour+ing
hu+moured
hu+mour+less
hump
humps
humps
hump+ing
humped
hump+back
hump+backs

hump+backed
Humperdinck
humph
Humphrey
Humphries
hump+ty dump+
  ty
hump+ty dump+
  ties
humpy
humpies
humpi+er
humpi+est
hu+mus
Hun
Huns
Hu+nan
hunch
hunches
hunches
hunch+ing
hunched
hunch+back
hunch+backs
hunch+backed
hun+dred
hun+dreds or
hun+dred
hun+dredth
hun+dredths
hundred+weight
hundred+
  weights or
hundred+weight
hung
Hun+gar+ian
Hun+gar+ians
Hun+ga+ry
hun+ger
hun+gers
hun+gers
hun+ger+ing
hun+gered
Hung+nam
hun+gri+ly
hun+gri+ness
hun+gry
hun+gri+er
hun+gri+est
hunk
hunks
hunk+ers
hunky-dory
Hun+like
Hun+nish

hunt
hunts
hunts
hunt+ing
hunt+ed
hunt+away
hunt+aways
hunt+er
hunt+ers
hunter-killer
Hun+ting+don
place name
Huntingdon
surname
Hun+ting+don+
  shire
Hun+ting+ton
hunts+man
hunts+men
Huon
Hu+peh
Hu+pei
hur+dle
hur+dles
hur+dles
hur+dling
hur+dled
hur+dler
hur+dlers
hurdy-gurdy
hurdy-gurdies
hurl
hurls
hurls
hurl+ing
hurled
hur+ley
hur+leys
hurl+ing
hurly-burly
hurly-burlies
Hu+ron
Hu+rons or
Hu+ron
hur+rah
hur+rahs
hur+rah+ing
hur+rahed
hur+ri+cane
hur+ri+canes
hur+ried+ly
hur+ried+ness
hur+ry
hur+ries
hur+ry+ing

hur+ried
hurst
hursts
Hurst+mon+ceux
hurt
hurts
hurts
hurt+ing
hurt
hurt+ful
hurt+ful+ly
hurt+le
hurt+les
hurt+ling
hurt+led
Husain
hus+band
hus+bands
hus+bands
hus+band+ing
hus+band+ed
hus+band+er
hus+band+ers
husband+man
husband+men
hus+band+ry
hush
hushes
hushes
hush+ing
hushed
husha+by
husha+bies
hush-hush
husk
husks
husks
husk+ing
husked
huski+ly
huski+ness
husky
huskies
huski+er
huski+est
Huss
hus+sar
hus+sars
Hussein
Huss+ite
Huss+ites
Huss+it+ism
hus+sy
hus+sies
hus+tings

hus+tle
hus+tles
hus+tles
hus+tling
hus+tled
hus+tler
hus+tlers
Huston
hus+wife
hus+wives
hut
huts
huts
hut+ting
hut+ted
hutch
hutches
hut+ment
hut+ments
Hutton
Huxley
Hu Yaobang
Huygens
Huysmans
huz+zah
Hwan+ge
Hwang Hai
Hwang Ho
hwyl
hya+cinth
hya+cinths
hya+cin+thine
Hya+des
constellation
Hyades
nymphs
hy+aena
hy+aenas
hy+aenic
hya+line
hya+lite
hya+loid
hy+brid
hy+brids
hy+bridi+sa+tion
hy+bridi+sa+tions
hy+brid+ise
hy+brid+ises
hy+brid+is+ing
hy+brid+ised
hy+brid+ism
hy+brid+ity
hy+bridi+za+tion

hy+bridi+za+tions
hy+brid+ize
hy+brid+izes
hy+brid+iz+ing
hy+brid+ized
hy+brid+oma
hy+brid+omas
hy+da+tid
hy+da+tids
Hyde
Hy+dera+bad
hy+dra
hy+dras *or*
hy+drae
Hydra
monster
Hy+dra
constellation
hy+drac+id
hy+drac+ids
hy+dran+gea
hy+dran+geas
hy+drant
hy+drants
hy+drate
hy+drates
hy+drates
hy+drat+ing
hy+drat+ed
hy+dra+tion
hy+dra+tions
hy+dra+tor
hy+dra+tors
hy+drau+lic
hy+drau+li+cal+ly
hy+drau+lics
hy+dra+zine
hy+dric
hy+dride
hy+drides
hy+dril+la
hy+dril+las
hy+dro
hy+dros
hydro+car+bon
hydro+car+bons
hydro+cele
hydro+celes
hydro+cephal+ic
hydro+cepha+lous
hydro+cepha+lus
hydro+cepha+ly
hydro+chlo+ric

hydro+chlo+ride
hydro+chlo+rides
hydro+dy+nam+ics
hydro+elec+tric
hydro+elec+tric+ity
hydro+foil
hydro+foils
hydro+form+ing
hydro+gen
hydro+gen+ate
hydro+gen+ates
hydro+gen+at+ing
hydro+gen+at+ed
hydro+gena+tion
hydro+gena+tions
hydro+gen+ise
hydro+gen+ises
hydro+gen+is+ing
hydro+gen+ised
hydro+gen+ize
hydro+gen+izes
hydro+gen+iz+ing
hydro+gen+ized
hy+drog+enous
hy+drog+ra+pher
hy+drog+ra+phers
hydro+graph+ic
hy+drog+ra+phy
hy+droid
hy+droids
hydro+ki+net+ics
hydro+lase
hydro+lases
hydro+logi+cal
hy+drolo+gist
hy+drolo+gists
hy+drol+ogy
hydro+lyse
hydro+lyses
hydro+lys+ing
hydro+lysed
hy+droly+sis
hydro+lyte
hydro+lytes
hydro+lyt+ic
hydro+mel

hy+drom+eter
hy+drom+eters
hydro+met+ric
hydro+met+ri+cal
hydro+naut
hydro+nauts
hydro+path+ic
hy+dropa+thy
hydro+phile
hydro+philes
hydro+phil+ic
hydro+pho+bia
hydro+pho+bic
hydro+phone
hydro+phones
hydro+phyte
hydro+phytes
hydro+plane
hydro+planes
hydro+planes
hydro+plan+ing
hydro+planed
hydro+pon+ic
hydro+poni+cal+ly
hydro+pon+ics
hydro+pow+er
hydro+quin+ol
hydro+qui+none
hydro+sphere
hydro+stat+ic
hydro+stat+ics
hydro+thera+peu+tics
hydro+thera+py
hydro+ther+mal
hy+drot+ro+pism
hy+drous
hydro+vane
hydro+vanes
hy+drox+ide
hy+drox+ides
hy+droxy
hy+droxyl
hy+droxy+tryp+ta+mine
hydro+zoan
hydro+zoans
hy+ena
hy+enas
hy+enic
hy+giene
hy+gien+ic
hy+gieni+cal+ly
hy+gien+ics

hy+gien+ist
hy+gien+ists
hy+grom+eter
hy+grom+eters
hygro+met+ric
hygro+phyte
hygro+phytes
hygro+phyt+ic
hygro+scope
hygro+scopes
hygro+scop+ic
hygro+scopi+cal+
ly
hy+ing
hyla
hylas
hylo+morph+ism
hy+lo+zo+ism
hy+men
hy+mens
hy+men+al
hy+meneal
hy+meneals
hy+me+nop+ter+
an
hy+me+nop+ter+
ans *or*
hy+me+nop+
tera
hy+me+nop+ter+
on
hy+me+nop+ter+
ons
hy+men+op+ter+
ous
Hy+met+tian
Hy+met+tic
Hy+met+tus
hymn
hymns
hymns
hymn+ing
hymned
hym+nal
hym+nals
hym+nic
hym+no+dy
hym+nolo+gist
hym+nolo+gists
hym+nol+ogy
hy+oid
hy+os+cine
hy+os+cya+mine
hy+paethral
hy+pal+la+ge

Hypatia
hype
hypes
hypes
hyp+ing
hyped
hy+per
overexcited
hyper+acid+ity
hyper+ac+tive
hyper+ac+tiv+ity
hypera+cute
hyper+aemia
hyper+aes+the+
sia
hyper+aes+thet+
ic
hyper+ba+ton
hyper+bo+la
hyper+bo+las
or
hyper+bo+le
hyper+bo+le
hyper+bol+ic
hyper+boli+cal
hyper+boli+cal+ly
hyper+bo+lise
hyper+bo+lises
hyper+bo+lis+
ing
hyper+bo+lised
hyper+bo+lism
hyper+bo+lisms
hyper+bo+lize
hyper+bo+lizes
hyper+bo+liz+
ing
hyper+bo+lized
hyper+bo+loid
hyper+bo+loids
Hyper+bo+rean
Hyper+bo+reans
hyper+charge
hyper+cho+les+
ter+olaemia
hyper+cho+les+
ter+olemia
U.S.
hyper+civi+lised
hyper+civi+lized
hyper+clas+si+
cal
hyper+con+fi+
dence

hyper+con+form+
ity
hyper+con+
scious
hyper+conserva+
tive
hyper+cor+rect
hyper+criti+cal
hyper+criti+cal+ly
hyper+emia
hyper+emo+tion+
al
hyper+en+er+get+
ic
hyper+en+thu+si+
asm
hyper+es+the+
sia
U.S.
hyper+es+thet+ic
U.S.
hyper+ex+cite+
ment
hyper+func+tion+
al
hyper+gly+cae+
mia
hyper+gly+cae+
mic
hyper+gly+cemia
U.S.
hyper+gly+cemic
U.S.
hyper+gol+ic
hyper+icum
hyper+icums
hyper+in+fla+tion
hyper+in+tel+lec+
tual
hyper+in+tel+li+
gence
Hyperion
*mythical
character*
Hy+peri+on
satellite
hyper+mar+ket
hyper+mar+kets
hyper+metro+pia
hyper+met+ro+
py
hyper+nor+mal
hyper+on
hyper+ons
hyper+opia

hyper+op+ic
hyper+ortho+dox
hyper+physi+cal
hyper+py+rexia
hyper+ro+man+
tic
hyper+sen+si+
tive
hyper+sen+si+
tive+ness
hyper+sen+si+tiv+
ity
hyper+sen+ti+
men+tal
hyper+son+ic
hyper+son+ics
hyper+so+phis+ti+
cat+ed
hyper+space
hyper+sthene
hyper+tech+ni+
cal
hyper+ten+sion
hyper+ten+sive
hyper+text
hyper+texts
hyper+ther+mal
hyper+ther+mia
hyper+ther+my
hyper+thy+roid
hyper+thy+roids
hyper+thy+roid+
ism
hyper+ton+ic
hyper+tox+ic
hyper+tro+phy
hyper+tro+phies
hyper+tro+phies
hyper+tro+phy+
ing
hyper+tro+phied
hyper+ven+ti+la+
tion
hy+pethral
hy+pha
hy+phae
hy+phal
hy+phen
hy+phens
hy+phens
hy+phen+ing
hy+phened
hy+phen+ate
hy+phen+ates
hy+phen+at+ing

hy+phen+at+ed
hy+phena+tion
hy+phena+tions
hyp+noid
hyp+noi+dal
hyp+nolo+gist
hyp+nolo+gists
hyp+nol+ogy
hyp+no+pae+dia
hyp+no+pom+pic
hyp+no+sis
hyp+no+ses
hyp+no+thera+py
hyp+not+ic
hyp+not+ics
hyp+noti+cal+ly
hyp+no+ti+sa+
tion
hyp+no+ti+sa+
tions
hyp+no+tise
hyp+no+tises
hyp+no+tis+ing
hyp+no+tised
hyp+no+tis+er
hyp+no+tis+ers
hyp+no+tism
hyp+no+tisms
hyp+no+tist
hyp+no+tists
hyp+no+ti+za+
tion
hyp+no+ti+za+
tions
hyp+no+tize
hyp+no+tizes
hyp+no+tiz+ing
hyp+no+tized
hyp+no+tiz+er
hyp+no+tiz+ers
hypo
hypos
hypo+al+ler+gen+
ic
hypo+blast
hypo+blasts
hypo+caust
hypo+causts

hypo+cen+tre
hypo+cen+tres
hypo+chlor+ite
hypo+chlor+ites
hypo+chon+dria
hypo+chon+dri+
ac
hypo+chon+dri+
acs
hy+poco+rism
hy+poco+risms
hypo+co+ris+tic
hypo+cot+yl
hypo+cot+yls
hy+poc+ri+sy
hy+poc+ri+sies
hypo+crite
hypo+crites
hypo+criti+cal
hypo+criti+cal+ly
hypo+cy+cloid
hypo+cy+cloids
hypo+cy+cloi+dal
hypo+derm
hypo+der+mic
hypo+der+mics
hypo+der+mi+cal+
ly
hypo+der+mis
hypo+gas+trium
hypo+gas+tria
hypo+geal
hypo+gene
hypo+geous
hypo+geum
hypo+gea
hypo+nas+tic
hypo+nas+ty
hypo+phos+
phate
hypo+phos+
phates
hypo+phos+phite
hypo+phos+
phites
hypo+phys+eal
hypo+phys+ial
hy+pophy+sis

hy+pophy+ses
hypos+ta+sis
hypos+ta+ses
hypo+stat+ic
hypo+stati+cal
hypo+style
hypo+styles
hypo+sul+phite
hypo+ten+sion
hypo+ten+sive
hy+pot+enuse
hy+pot+enuses
hypo+tha+lam+ic
hypo+thala+mus
hypo+thala+mi
hy+poth+ec
hy+poth+ecs
hy+poth+ecate
hy+poth+ecates
hy+poth+ecat+
ing
hy+poth+ecat+
ed
hy+poth+eca+
tion
hy+poth+eca+
tions
hy+poth+eca+tor
hy+poth+eca+
tors
hypo+ther+mia
hy+poth+esis
hy+poth+eses
hy+poth+esise
hy+poth+esises
hy+poth+esis+
ing
hy+poth+esised
hy+poth+esis+er
hy+poth+esis+
ers
hy+poth+esist
hy+poth+esists
hy+poth+esize
hy+poth+esizes
hy+poth+esiz+
ing
hy+poth+esized

hy+poth+esiz+er
hy+poth+esiz+
ers
hypo+thet+ic
hypo+theti+cal
hypo+theti+cal+
ly
hypo+thy+roid
hypo+thy+roids
hypo+thy+roid+
ism
hypo+thy+roid+
isms
hypo+ton+ic
hy+poxia
hy+pox+ic
Hypsilantes
Hypsilantis
hyp+sog+ra+phy
hyp+som+eter
hyp+som+eters
hyp+som+etry
hy+rax
hy+raxes *or*
hy+races
Hyr+ca+nia
Hyr+ca+nian
hys+sop
hys+sops
hys+ter+ec+to+
my
hys+ter+ec+to+
mies
hys+te+re+sis
hys+ter+et+ic
hys+te+ria
hys+te+rias
hys+ter+ic
hys+ter+ics
hys+teri+cal
hys+teri+cal+ly
hys+ter+on prot+
er+on
hys+tri+co+
morph
hys+tri+co+
morphs
Hywel Dda

I

i
  i's
I
  I's *or*
  Is
iamb
  iambs
iambic
  iambics
iam+bus
  iam+bi *or*
  iam+buses
IATA
iat+ro+gen+ic
iat+ro+genic+ity
Iba+dan
Iba+gué
Ibarruri
Iberia
Iberian
  Iberians
ibe+ris
  ibe+rises
Ibert
ibex
  ibexes *or*
  ibices *or*
  ibex
ibis
  ibises *or*
  ibis
Ibi+za
Ibo
  Ibos *or*
  Ibo
Ibsen
ibu+prof+en
Icaria
Icar+ian
Icarus
ice
  ices
  ices
  ic+ing
  iced

ice+berg
ice+bergs
ice+blink
ice+blinks
ice+bound
ice+box
  ice+boxes
ice+breaker
ice+breakers
ice+cap
ice+caps
ice-cream
  adj.
ice cream
  noun
iced
ice+fall
  ice+falls
Içel
Ice+land
Ice+land+er
  Ice+land+ers
Ice+land+ic
ice-skate
ice-skates
ice-skating
ice-skated
ice skate
ice skates
ice-skater
ice-skaters
Ichang
I-ch'ang
I Ching
ich+neu+mon
ich+neu+mons
ich+no+graph+ic
ich+no+graphi+
  cal
ich+nog+ra+phy
ich+nog+ra+
  phies
ichor
ichors
ichor+ous

ich+thy+oid
ich+thy+oids
ich+thyoi+dal
ich+thyo+log+ic
ich+thyo+logi+cal
ich+thy+olo+gist
ich+thy+olo+
  gists
ich+thy+ol+ogy
ich+thyo+saur
ich+thyo+saurs
ich+thyo+saur+
  us
ich+thyo+saur+
  uses *or*
ich+thyo+sau+ri
ich+thyo+sis
ich+thy+ot+ic
ici+cle
ici+cles
ici+ly
ici+ness
ic+ing
ic+ings
icon
icons
Ico+nium
icono+clasm
icono+clast
icono+clasts
icono+clas+tic
ico+no+gra+pher
ico+no+gra+
  phers
icono+graph+ic
icono+graphi+cal
ico+no+gra+phy
ico+no+gra+
  phies
ico+nola+ter
ico+nola+ters
ico+nola+trous
ico+nola+try
icono+logi+cal
ico+nolo+gist

ico+nolo+gists
ico+nol+ogy
icono+scope
icono+scopes
icono+stas
icono+stases
ico+nos+ta+sis
ico+nos+ta+ses
ico+sa+he+dral
ico+sa+he+dron
ico+sa+he+
  drons *or*
ico+sa+he+dra
ic+tal
ic+tus
ic+tuses *or*
ic+tus
icy
  ici+er
  ici+est
id
ids
Ida
Ida+ho
ide
idea
ideas
ideal
ideals
ideali+sa+tion
ideali+sa+tions
ideal+ise
  ideal+ises
  ideal+is+ing
  ideal+ised
ideal+is+er
  ideal+is+ers
ideal+ism
ideal+ist
  ideal+ists
ideal+is+tic
ideal+is+ti+cal+ly
ideali+za+tion
ideali+za+tions
ideal+ize

ideal+izes
ideal+iz+ing
ideal+ized
ideal+iz+er
ideal+iz+ers
ideal+ly
ideal+ness
idée fixe
idées fixes
idem
iden+tic
iden+ti+cal
iden+ti+cal+ly
iden+ti+fi+able
iden+ti+fi+ca+
    tion
iden+ti+fi+ca+
    tions
iden+ti+fi+er
iden+ti+fi+ers
iden+ti+fy
iden+ti+fies
iden+ti+fy+ing
iden+ti+fied
Iden+ti+kit
Trademark
iden+tity
iden+tities
ideo+gram
ideo+grams
ideo+graph
ideo+graphs
id+eog+ra+phy
ideo+log+ic
ideo+logi+cal
ideo+logi+cal+ly
ideolo+gist
ideolo+gists
ideo+logue
ideo+logues
ideol+ogy
ideo+logies
ides
ides
id+io+cy
id+io+cies
id+io+lect
id+io+lects
idi+om
idi+oms
idio+mat+ic
idio+mati+cal+ly
idio+syn+cra+sy
idio+syn+cra+
    sies

idio+syn+crat+ic
idio+syn+crati+
    cal+ly
id+iot
id+iots
idi+ot+ic
idi+oti+cal+ly
idi+ot sa+vant
idi+ot sa+vants
    or
idi+ots sa+vant
idle
idles
idling
idled
idler
idlest
idle+ness
idler
idlers
idly
idol
idols
idola+ter
idola+ters
idola+tress
idola+tresses
idola+trous
idola+try
idola+tries
idoli+sa+tion
idol+ise
idol+ises
idol+is+ing
idol+ised
idol+is+er
idol+is+ers
idoli+za+tion
idol+ize
idol+izes
idol+iz+ing
idol+ized
idol+iz+er
idol+iz+ers
ido+lum
ido+lums
Idomeneus
id+yl
U.S.
id+yls
id+yll
id+ylls
idyl+lic
idyl+li+cal+ly
if

ifs
Ife
if+fy
if+fi+er
if+fi+est
Igbo
Igbo *or*
Igbos
Ig+dra+sil
ig+loo
ig+loos
iglu
iglus
Ignatius
Ignatius Loyola
ig+ne+ous
ig+nis fatuus
ig+nes fatui
ig+nit+abil+ity
ig+nit+able
ig+nite
ig+nites
ig+nit+ing
ig+nit+ed
ig+nit+er
ig+nit+ers
ig+nit+ibil+ity
ig+nit+ible
ig+ni+tion
ig+ni+tions
ig+ni+tron
ig+ni+trons
ig+no+bil+ity
ig+no+ble
ig+no+ble+ness
ig+no+bly
ig+no+mini+ous
ig+no+mini+ous+
    ly
ig+no+mini+ous+
    ness
ig+no+miny
ig+no+minies
ig+no+ra+mus
ig+no+ra+
    muses
ig+no+rance
ig+no+rances
ig+no+rant
ig+no+rant+ly
ig+nore
ig+nores
ig+nor+ing
ig+nored
ig+nor+er

ig+nor+ers
igua+na
igua+nas
igua+nian
igua+nians
iguano+don
iguano+dons
IJs+sel
Ika+ría
ikat
ikeba+na
Ikhnaton
ikon
ikons
il+eac
Ile-de-France
il+ei+tis
il+eos+to+my
il+eos+to+mies
Iles Co+mores
il+eum
il+eums
ilex
ilexes
Ili+am+na
Ili+gan
Ili+on
il+ium
il+ia
Il+ium
ilk
ilks
Il+kes+ton
Il+kley
ill
ills
worse
worst
I'll
ill-advised
ill-advised+ly
ill-affected
ill-assorted
il+la+tive
il+la+tive+ly
Il+la+war+ra
ill-bred
ill-breeding
ill-considered
ill-defined
ill-disposed
Ille-et-Vilaine
il+legal
il+legals
il+legal+ity

il+legal+ities
il+legal+ly
il+leg+ibil+ity
il+leg+ible
il+leg+ible+ness
il+leg+ibly
il+legiti+ma+cy
il+legiti+mate
il+legiti+mates
il+legiti+mate+ly
il+legiti+mate+
ness
ill-fated
ill-favoured
ill-favoured+ly
ill-favoured+ness
ill-founded
ill-gotten
ill hu+mour
ill-humoured
ill-humoured+ly
il+lib+er+al
il+lib+er+al+ity
il+lib+er+al+ly
Illich
il+lic+it
il+lic+it+ly
il+lic+it+ness
Illi+ma+ni
il+lim+it+abil+ity
il+lim+it+able
il+lim+it+able+
ness
Il+li+noian
Il+li+noians
Il+li+nois
Il+li+nois+ian
Il+li+nois+ians
il+lit+era+cy
il+lit+er+ate
il+lit+er+ates
il+lit+er+ate+ly
il+lit+er+ate+
ness
ill-judged
ill-mannered
ill-natured
ill-natured+ly
ill-natured+ness
ill+ness
ill+nesses
il+logi+cal
il+logi+cal+ity
il+logi+cal+ities
il+logi+cal+ly

ill-starred
ill tem+per
ill-tempered
ill-tempered+ly
ill-timed
ill-treat
ill-treats
ill-treating
ill-treated
il+lu+mi+nable
il+lu+mi+nance
il+lu+mi+nances
il+lu+mi+nant
il+lu+mi+nants
il+lu+mi+nate
il+lu+mi+nates
il+lu+mi+nates
il+lu+mi+nat+ing
il+lu+mi+nat+ed
il+lu+mi+na+ti
il+lu+mi+nat+ing
il+lu+mi+na+tion
il+lu+mi+na+
tions
il+lu+mi+na+tive
il+lu+mi+na+tor
il+lu+mi+na+
tors
il+lu+mine
il+lu+mines
il+lu+min+ing
il+lu+mined
ill-usage
ill-use
ill-uses
ill-using
ill-used
il+lu+sion
il+lu+sions
il+lu+sion+al
il+lu+sion+ary
il+lu+sioned
il+lu+sion+ism
il+lu+sion+ist
il+lu+sion+ists
il+lu+sion+is+tic
il+lu+sive
il+lu+so+ri+ly
il+lu+so+ri+ness
il+lu+so+ry
il+lus+trate
il+lus+trates
il+lus+trat+ing
il+lus+trat+ed
il+lus+tra+tion

il+lus+tra+tions
il+lus+tra+tion+al
il+lus+tra+tive
il+lus+tra+tor
il+lus+tra+tors
il+lus+tri+ous
il+lus+tri+ous+ly
il+lus+tri+ous+
ness
Il+lyria
Il+lyr+ian
Il+lyr+ians
Il+lyri+cum
Iloi+lo
I'm
im+age
im+ages
im+ages
im+ag+ing
im+aged
im+age+able
im+age+less
im+age+ry
im+age+ries
im+agi+nable
im+agi+nably
im+agi+nari+ly
im+agi+nary
im+agi+na+tion
im+agi+na+tions
im+agi+na+tive
im+agi+na+tive+
ly
im+agi+na+tive+
ness
im+ag+ine
im+ag+ines
im+ag+in+ing
im+ag+ined
im+ag+in+er
im+ag+in+ers
im+ag+ism
im+ag+ist
im+ag+ists
im+ag+is+tic
ima+go
ima+goes or
ima+gi+nes
imam
imams
imam+ate
imam+ates
imaum
imaums
im+bal+ance

im+bal+ances
im+becile
im+beciles
im+becile+ly
im+becil+ic
im+becil+ic+ally
im+becil+ity
im+becil+ities
im+bed
imbeds
im+bed+ding
im+bed+ded
im+bibe
im+bibes
im+bib+ing
im+bibed
im+bib+er
im+bib+ers
im+bri+cate
im+bri+cates
im+bri+cat+ing
im+bri+cat+ed
im+bri+cat+ed
im+bri+cate+ly
im+bri+ca+tion
im+bri+ca+tions
im+bro+glio
im+bro+glios
Im+bros
im+brue
im+brues
im+bru+ing
imbrued
im+brue+ment
im+bue
im+bues
im+bu+ing
im+bued
Imhotep
imi+tabil+ity
imi+table
imi+tate
imi+tates
imi+tat+ing
imi+tat+ed
imi+ta+tion
imi+ta+tions
imi+ta+tion+al
imi+ta+tive
imi+ta+tive+ly
imi+ta+tive+ness
imi+ta+tor
imi+ta+tors
im+macu+la+cy
im+macu+late

im+macu+late+ly
im+macu+late+
  ness
im+ma+nence
im+ma+nen+cy
im+ma+nent
im+ma+nent+ism
im+ma+nent+ly
Immanuel
im+ma+teri+al
im+ma+teri+al+
  ism
im+ma+teri+al+
  ist
im+ma+teri+al+
  ists
im+ma+teri+al+
  ity
im+ma+teri+al+ly
im+ma+ture
im+ma+ture+ly
im+ma+ture+
  ness
im+ma+tu+rity
im+meas+ur+abil+
  ity
im+meas+ur+
  able
im+meas+ur+
  able+ness
im+meas+ur+
  ably
im+medi+acy
im+medi+ate
im+medi+ate+ly
im+medi+ate+
  ness
im+memo+ri+al
im+memo+ri+al+
  ly
im+mense
im+mense+ly
im+mense+ness
im+men+si+ty
  im+men+si+ties
im+merse
  im+merses
im+mers+ing
im+mersed
im+mers+er
  im+mers+ers
im+mers+ible
im+mer+sion
  im+mer+sions
im+mi+grant

im+mi+grants
im+mi+grate
im+mi+grates
im+mi+grat+ing
im+mi+grat+ed
im+mi+gra+tion
im+mi+gra+
  tions
im+mi+gra+tor
im+mi+gra+tors
im+mi+gra+tory
im+mi+nent
im+mi+nent+ly
Im+ming+ham
im+mis+cibil+ity
im+mis+cible
im+mis+cibly
im+miti+gabil+ity
im+miti+gable
im+miti+gably
im+mo+bile
im+mo+bi+li+sa+
  tion
im+mo+bi+lise
im+mo+bi+lises
im+mo+bi+lis+
  ing
im+mo+bi+lised
im+mo+bi+lis+er
im+mo+bi+lis+
  ers
im+mo+bil+ity
im+mo+bi+li+za+
  tion
im+mo+bi+lize
im+mo+bi+lizes
im+mo+bi+liz+
  ing
im+mo+bi+lized
im+mo+bi+liz+er
im+mo+bi+liz+
  ers
im+mod+er+ate
im+mod+er+ate+
  ly
im+mod+er+ate+
  ness
im+mod+era+
  tion
im+mod+est
im+mod+est+ly
im+mod+es+ty
im+mo+late
im+mo+lates
im+mo+lating

im+mo+lat+ed
im+mo+la+tion
im+mo+la+tions
im+mo+la+tor
  im+mo+la+tors
im+mor+al
im+mo+ral+ity
  im+mo+ral+ities
im+mor+al+ly
im+mor+tal
im+mor+tals
im+mor+tali+sa+
  tion
im+mor+tal+ise
im+mor+tal+
  ises
im+mor+tal+is+
  ing
im+mor+tal+
  ised
im+mor+tal+is+er
im+mor+tal+is+
  ers
im+mor+tal+ity
im+mor+tali+za+
  tion
im+mor+tal+ize
im+mor+tal+izes
im+mor+tal+iz+
  ing
im+mor+tal+
  ized
im+mor+tal+iz+er
im+mor+tal+iz+
  ers
im+mor+tal+ly
im+mor+telle
im+mor+telles
im+mov+abil+ity
im+mov+able
im+mov+able+
  ness
im+mov+ably
im+move+abil+
  ity
im+move+able
im+move+able+
  ness
im+move+ably
im+mune
  im+munes
im+mun+isa+tion
im+mun+isa+
  tions
im+mun+ise

im+mun+ises
im+mun+is+ing
im+mun+ised
im+mun+is+er
  im+mun+is+ers
im+mun+ity
  im+mun+ities
im+mun+iza+tion
im+mun+iza+
  tions
im+mun+ize
  im+mun+izes
im+mun+iz+ing
im+mun+ized
im+mun+iz+er
  im+mun+iz+ers
im+mu+no+as+
  say
im+mu+no+as+
  says
im+mu+no+de+fi+
  cien+cy
im+mu+no+de+
  fi+cien+cies
im+mu+no+gen+
  ic
im+mu+no+geni+
  cal+ly
im+mu+no+globu+
  lin
im+mu+no+
  globu+lins
im+mu+no+log+
  ic
im+mu+no+logi+
  cal
im+mu+no+logi+
  cal+ly
im+mu+nolo+gist
im+mu+nolo+
  gists
im+mu+nol+ogy
im+mu+no+reac+
  tion
im+mu+no+reac+
  tions
im+mu+no+sup+
  pres+sant
im+mu+no+sup+
  pres+sants
im+mu+no+sup+
  pres+sion
im+mu+no+sup+
  pres+sive

im+mu+no+sup+
  pres+sives
im+mu+no+thera+
  peu+tic
im+mu+no+thera+
  py
im+mure
  im+mures
  im+mur+ing
  im+mured
im+mure+ment
im+mu+tabil+ity
im+mu+table
imp
  imps
  imps
  imp+ing
  imped
im+pact
  im+pacts
  im+pacts
  im+pact+ing
  im+pact+ed
im+pacted
im+pac+tion
im+pair
  im+pairs
  im+pair+ing
  im+paired
im+pair+able
im+pair+er
  im+pair+ers
im+pair+ment
im+pa+la
  im+pa+las or
  im+pa+la
im+pale
  im+pales
  im+pal+ing
  im+paled
im+pale+ment
  im+pale+ments
im+pal+er
im+pal+pabil+ity
im+pal+pable
im+pal+pably
im+pan+el
  im+pan+els
  im+pan+el+ling
  or
  im+pan+el+ing
  U.S.
  im+pan+el+led
  or
  im+pan+el+ed

U.S.
im+pan+el+ment
im+pan+el+
  ments
im+part
  im+parts
  im+part+ing
  im+part+ed
im+part+able
im+par+ta+tion
  im+par+ta+tions
im+par+tial
im+par+tial+ity
im+par+tial+ly
im+par+tial+ness
im+part+ibili+ty
im+part+ible
im+part+ibly
im+part+ment
  im+part+ments
im+pass+abil+ity
im+pass+able
  not able to be
  travelled through
im+pass+able+
  ness
im+pass+ably
im+passe
  im+passes
im+pass+ible
  not affected by
  pain or emotion
im+pass+ible+
  ness
im+pass+ibly
im+pas+sion
  im+pas+sions
  im+pas+sion+
  ing
  im+pas+sioned
  im+pas+sioned
  im+pas+sioned+
  ly
im+pas+sioned+
  ness
im+pas+sive
  im+pas+sive+ly
  im+pas+sive+
  ness
im+pas+siv+ity
im+pas+to
im+pa+tience
im+pa+ti+ens
  im+pa+ti+ens
im+pa+tient

im+pa+tient+ly
im+peach
  im+peaches
  im+peach+ing
  im+peached
im+peach+able
im+peach+ment
  im+peach+
  ments
im+pec+cabil+ity
im+pec+cable
im+pec+cably
im+pecu+ni+os+
  ity
im+pecu+ni+ous
im+pecu+ni+ous+
  ly
im+pecu+ni+ous+
  ness
im+ped+ance
  im+ped+ances
im+pede
  im+pedes
  im+ped+ing
  im+ped+ed
im+ped+er
  im+ped+ers
im+pedi+ment
  im+pedi+ments
  or
  im+pedi+men+
  ta
  Law
im+pedi+men+ta
im+pedi+men+tal
im+pedi+men+
  tary
im+pel
  im+pels
  im+pel+ling
  im+pelled
im+pel+lent
  im+pel+lents
im+pel+ler
  im+pel+lers
im+pend
  im+pends
  im+pend+ing
  im+pend+ed
im+pend+ence
  im+pend+ing
im+pen+etrabil+
  ity
im+pen+etrable

im+pen+etrable+
  ness
im+pen+etrably
im+peni+tence
im+peni+ten+cy
im+peni+tent
im+peni+tent+ly
im+peni+tent+
  ness
im+pera+tive
  im+pera+tives
im+pera+tive+ly
im+pera+tive+
  ness
im+pera+tor
  im+pera+tors
im+per+cep+tibil+
  ity
im+per+cep+tible
im+per+cep+tible+
  ness
im+per+cep+tibly
im+per+cep+tion
im+per+cep+tive
im+per+cep+tive+
  ly
im+per+cep+tive+
  ness
im+per+cipi+ent
im+per+fect
  im+per+fects
im+per+fec+tion
  im+per+fec+
  tions
im+per+fec+tive
  im+per+fec+
  tives
im+per+fec+tive+
  ly
im+per+fect+ly
im+per+fect+
  ness
im+per+fo+rate
im+per+fo+ra+
  tion
im+perial
  im+perials
im+peri+al+ism
  im+peri+al+isms
im+peri+al+ist
  im+peri+al+ists
im+peri+al+is+tic
im+peri+al+is+ti+
  cal+ly
im+peri+al+ly

im+peri+al+ness
im+per+il
  im+per+ils
  im+per+il+ling
  or
  im+per+il+ing
  U.S.
  im+per+illed or
  im+per+iled
  U.S.
im+per+il+ment
im+peri+ous
im+peri+ous+ly
im+peri+ous+
  ness
im+per+ish+abil+
  ity
im+per+ish+able
im+per+ish+able+
  ness
im+per+ish+ably
im+per+ma+
  nence
im+per+ma+nen+
  cy
im+per+ma+nent
im+per+ma+nent+
  ly
im+per+meabil+
  ity
im+per+meable
im+per+meable+
  ness
im+per+meably
im+per+mis+sibil+
  ity
im+per+mis+sible
im+per+son+al
im+per+son+ali+
  sa+tion
im+per+son+al+
  ise
  im+per+son+al+
  ises
  im+per+son+al+
  is+ing
  im+per+son+al+
  ised
im+per+son+al+
  ity
im+per+son+ali+
  za+tion
im+per+son+al+
  ize

im+per+son+al+
  izes
im+per+son+al+
  iz+ing
im+per+son+al+
  ized
im+per+son+al+
  ly
im+per+son+ate
im+per+son+
  ates
im+per+son+at+
  ing
im+per+son+at+
  ed
im+per+sona+
  tion
im+per+sona+
  tions
im+per+sona+tor
im+per+sona+
  tors
im+per+ti+nence
im+per+ti+
  nences
im+per+ti+nen+
  cy
im+per+ti+nen+
  cies
im+per+ti+nent
im+per+ti+nent+
  ly
im+per+turb+abil+
  ity
im+per+turb+able
im+per+turb+able+
  ness
im+per+turb+ably
im+per+vi+able
im+per+vi+ous
im+per+vi+ous+
  ly
im+per+vi+ous+
  ness
im+petigi+nous
im+peti+go
  im+peti+gos
  or
  im+peti+gi+nes
im+petu+os+ity
im+petu+ous
im+petu+ous+ly
im+petu+ous+
  ness
im+petus

im+petuses
Im+phal
impi
  impis or
  impies
im+pi+ety
  im+pi+eties
im+pinge
  im+pinges
  im+ping+ing
  im+pinged
im+pinge+ment
  im+pinge+
  ments
im+ping+er
  im+ping+ers
im+pi+ous
im+pi+ous+ly
im+pi+ous+ness
imp+ish
imp+ish+ly
imp+ish+ness
im+plac+abil+ity
im+plac+able
im+plac+ably
im+plant
  im+plants
  im+plant+ing
  im+plant+ed
im+plan+ta+tion
  im+plan+ta+
  tions
im+plau+sibil+ity
  im+plau+sibil+
  ities
im+plau+sible
im+plau+sible+
  ness
im+plau+sibly
im+ple+ment
  im+ple+ments
  im+ple+ments
  im+ple+ment+
  ing
  im+ple+ment+
  ed
im+ple+men+tal
im+ple+men+ta+
  tion
im+pli+cate
  im+pli+cates
  im+pli+cat+ing
  im+pli+cat+ed
im+pli+ca+tion
  im+pli+ca+tions

im+plica+tive
im+plica+tive+ly
im+plic+it
im+plic+it+ly
im+plic+it+ness
im+plied
im+plode
  im+plodes
  im+plod+ing
  im+plod+ed
im+plo+ra+tion
  im+plo+ra+tions
im+plore
  im+plores
  im+plor+ing
  im+plored
  im+plor+ing+ly
im+ply
  im+plies
  im+ply+ing
  im+plied
im+pol+der
  im+pol+ders
  im+pol+der+ing
  im+pol+dered
im+po+lite
im+po+lite+ly
im+po+lite+ness
  im+po+lite+
  nesses
im+poli+tic
im+poli+tic+ly
im+pon+der+abil+
  ity
im+pon+der+able
  im+pon+der+
  ables
  im+pon+der+able+
  ness
im+pon+der+ably
im+port
  im+ports
  im+ports
  im+port+ing
  im+port+ed
im+port+able
im+por+tance
im+por+tant
im+por+tant+ly
im+por+ta+tion
  im+por+ta+tions
im+port+er
  im+port+ers
im+por+tu+na+
  cy

im+por+tu+nate
im+por+tu+nate+
ly
im+por+tu+nate+
ness
im+por+tune
im+por+tunes
im+por+tun+ing
im+por+tuned
im+por+tune+ly
im+por+tun+er
im+por+tun+ers
im+por+tun+ity
im+pos+able
im+pose
im+poses
im+pos+ing
im+posed
im+pos+er
im+pos+ers
im+pos+ing
im+pos+ing+ly
im+pos+ing+ness
im+po+si+tion
im+po+si+tions
im+pos+sibil+ity
im+pos+sibil+
ities
im+pos+sible
im+pos+sible+
ness
im+pos+sibly
im+post
im+posts
im+posts
im+post+ing
im+post+ed
im+post+er
im+post+ers
im+pos+tor
im+pos+tors
im+pos+tor+ous
im+pos+trous
im+pos+ture
im+pos+tures
im+po+tence
im+po+ten+cy
im+po+tent
im+po+tent+ly
im+pound
im+pounds
im+pound+ing
im+pound+ed
im+pound+able
im+pound+age

im+pound+er
im+pound+ers
im+pound+ment
im+pov+er+ish
im+pov+er+
ishes
im+pov+er+ish+
ing
im+pov+er+
ished
im+pov+er+ish+
ment
im+prac+ti+cabil+
ity
im+prac+ti+cable
im+prac+ti+cable+
ness
im+prac+ti+cably
im+prac+ti+cal
im+prac+ti+cal+
ity
im+prac+ti+cal+
ly
im+pre+cate
im+pre+cates
im+pre+cat+ing
im+pre+cat+ed
im+pre+ca+tion
im+pre+ca+
tions
im+pre+ca+tory
im+pre+cise
im+pre+cise+ly
im+pre+cise+
ness
im+pre+ci+sion
im+preg+nabil+
ity
im+preg+nable
im+preg+na+bly
im+preg+na+
table
im+preg+nate
im+preg+nates
im+preg+nat+
ing
im+preg+nat+ed
im+preg+na+tion
im+preg+na+tor
im+preg+na+
tors
im+pre+sa+rio
im+pre+sa+rios
im+pre+scrip+
tibil+ity

im+pre+scrip+
tible
im+pre+scrip+
tibly
im+press
im+presses
im+presses
im+press+ing
im+pressed
im+press+er
im+press+ers
im+press+ible
im+pres+sion
im+pres+sions
im+pres+sion+
abil+ity
im+pres+sion+
able
im+pres+sion+
able+ness
im+pres+sion+al
im+pres+sion+al+
ly
im+pres+sion+
ism
im+pres+sion+ist
im+pres+sion+
ists
im+pres+sive
im+pres+sive+ly
im+pres+sive+
ness
im+prest
im+prests
im+pri+ma+tur
im+pri+ma+turs
im+print
im+prints
im+prints
im+print+ing
im+print+ed
im+print+ing
im+print+ings
im+pris+on
im+pris+ons
im+pris+on+ing
im+pris+oned
im+pris+on+ment
im+pris+on+
ments
im+prob+abil+ity
im+prob+abil+
ities
im+prob+able

im+prob+able+
ness
im+prob+ably
im+pro+bity
im+pro+bities
im+promp+tu
im+promp+tus
im+prop+er
im+prop+er+ly
im+prop+er+ness
im+pro+pri+ate
im+pro+pri+ates
im+pro+pri+at+
ing
im+pro+pri+at+
ed
im+pro+pria+tion
im+pro+pria+
tions
im+pro+pria+tor
im+pro+pria+
tors
im+pro+pri+ety
im+pro+pri+
eties
im+prov+abil+ity
im+prov+able
im+prov+able+
ness
im+prove
im+proves
im+prov+ing
im+proved
im+prove+ment
im+prove+
ments
im+prov+er
im+prov+ers
im+provi+dence
im+provi+dent
im+provi+dent+ly
im+provi+sa+tion
im+provi+sa+
tions
im+pro+vise
im+pro+vises
im+pro+vis+ing
im+pro+vised
im+pro+vis+er
im+pro+vis+ers
im+pru+dence
im+pru+dent
im+pru+dent+ly
im+pu+dence
im+pu+dences

im+pu+den+cy
im+pu+den+cies
im+pu+dent
im+pu+dent+ly
im+pu+dent+
ness
im+pugn
im+pugns
im+pugn+ing
im+pugned
im+pugn+able
im+pugn+er
im+pugn+ers
im+pugn+ment
im+pugn+ments
im+pulse
im+pulses
im+pul+sion
im+pul+sions
im+pul+sive
im+pul+sive+ly
im+pul+sive+
ness
im+pu+nity
im+pu+nities
im+pure
im+pur+er
im+pur+est
im+pure+ly
im+pure+ness
im+pu+rity
im+pu+rities
im+put+able
im+pu+ta+tion
im+pu+ta+tions
im+pu+ta+tive
im+pute
im+putes
im+put+ing
im+puted
im+put+er
in
in+abil+ity
in+abil+ities
in ab+sen+tia
in+ac+ces+sibil+
ity
in+ac+ces+sible
in+ac+ces+sible+
ness
in+ac+ces+sibly
in+ac+cu+ra+cy
in+ac+cu+ra+
cies
in+ac+cu+rate

in+ac+tion
in+ac+ti+vate
in+ac+ti+vates
in+ac+ti+vat+
ing
in+ac+ti+vat+ed
in+ac+ti+va+tion
in+ac+tive
in+ac+tive+ly
in+ac+tiv+ity
in+ad+equa+cy
in+ad+equa+
cies
in+ad+equate
in+ad+equate+ly
in+ad+mis+si+ble
in+ad+vert+ence
in+ad+vert+
ences
in+ad+vert+en+
cy
in+ad+vert+en+
cies
in+ad+vert+ent
in+ad+vert+ent+
ly
in+ad+vis+able
in+al+ien+abil+ity
in+al+ien+able
in+al+ien+able+
ness
in+al+ien+ably
in+al+ter+abil+ity
in+al+ter+able
in+al+ter+able+
ness
in+al+ter+ably
in+amo+ra+ta
in+amo+ra+tas
in+amo+ra+to
in+amo+ra+tos
in+ane
in+ane+ly
in+ani+mate
in+ani+mate+ly
in+ani+mate+
ness
ina+ni+tion
in+an+ity
in+an+ities
in+ap+pe+tence
in+ap+pli+cable
in+ap+po+site
in+ap+po+site+ly

in+ap+po+site+
ness
in+ap+pre+ciable
in+ap+pre+cia+
tive
in+ap+pro+pri+
ate
in+apt
in+ap+ti+tude
in+apt+ly
in+apt+ness
in+arch
in+arches
in+arch+ing
in+arched
in+ar+ticu+late
in+ar+tis+tic
in+at+ten+tive
in+audible
in+augu+ral
in+augu+rals
in+augu+rate
in+augu+rates
in+augu+rat+ing
in+augu+rat+ed
in+augu+ra+tion
in+augu+ra+
tions
in+augu+ra+tor
in+augu+ra+tors
in+augu+ra+to+
ry
in+aus+pi+cious
in-between
in+board
in+born
in+bred
in+breed
in+breeds
in+breed+ing
in+bred
in+breed+ing
in+breed+ings
in-built
in+cal+cu+labil+
ity
in+cal+cu+lable
in+cal+cu+lably
in+can+desce
in+can+desces
in+can+desc+
ing
in+can+desced
in+can+des+
cence

in+can+des+
cences
in+can+des+cent
in+can+des+cent+
ly
in+can+ta+tion
in+can+ta+tions
in+can+ta+tion+
al
in+ca+pable
in+ca+paci+tate
in+ca+paci+
tates
in+ca+paci+tat+
ing
in+ca+paci+tat+
ed
in+ca+pac+ity
in+ca+pac+ities
in-car
in+car+cer+ate
in+car+cer+ates
in+car+cer+at+
ing
in+car+cer+at+
ed
in+car+cera+tion
in+car+cera+
tions
in+car+cera+tor
in+car+cera+
tors
in+car+na+dine
in+car+na+dines
in+car+na+din+
ing
in+car+na+dined
in+car+nate
in+car+na+tion
in+car+na+tions
in+car+vil+lea
in+car+vil+leas
in+case
in+cases
in+cas+ing
in+cased
in+cau+tion
in+cau+tions
in+cau+tious
in+cau+tious+ly
in+cau+tious+
ness
in+cen+dia+rism
in+cen+di+ary
in+cen+di+aries

in+cense
in+censes
in+censes
in+cens+ing
in+censed
in+cense+ment
in+cen+so+ry
in+cen+so+ries
in+cen+tive
in+cen+tives
in+cept
in+cepts
in+cept+ing
in+cept+ed
in+cep+tion
in+cep+tions
in+cep+tive
in+cep+tives
in+cep+tive+ly
in+cep+tor
in+cep+tors
in+cer+ti+tude
in+cer+ti+tudes
in+ces+san+cy
in+ces+sant
in+ces+sant+ly
in+cest
in+cests
in+ces+tu+ous
in+ces+tu+ous+
  ly
in+ces+tu+ous+
  ness
inch
  inches
  inches
  inch+ing
  inched
in+cho+ate
  in+cho+ates
  in+cho+at+ing
  in+cho+at+ed
in+cho+ate+ly
in+cho+ate+ness
in+choa+tion
in+choa+tive
inch+worm
  inch+worms
in+ci+dence
  in+ci+dences
in+ci+dent
  in+ci+dents
in+ci+den+tal
  in+ci+den+tals
in+ci+den+tal+ly

in+ci+den+tal+
  ness
in+cin+er+ate
  in+cin+er+ates
  in+cin+er+at+
  ing
  in+cin+er+at+ed
in+cin+era+tion
  in+cin+era+tor
  in+cin+era+tors
in+cipi+ence
in+cipi+en+cy
in+cipi+ent
in+cipi+ent+ly
in+cise
  in+cises
  in+cis+ing
  in+cised
in+ci+sion
  in+ci+sions
in+ci+sive
  in+ci+sive+ly
  in+ci+sive+ness
in+ci+sor
  in+ci+sors
in+ci+ta+tion
in+cite
  in+cites
  in+cit+ing
  in+cit+ed
in+cite+ment
  in+cite+ments
in+cit+er
  in+cit+ers
in+cit+ing+ly
in+ci+vil+ity
  in+ci+vil+ities
in+clem+en+cy
in+clem+ent
in+clem+ent+ly
in+cli+na+tion
  in+cli+na+tions
in+cli+na+tion+al
in+cline
  in+clines
  in+clines
  in+clin+ing
  in+clined
  in+clined
in+clin+er
  in+clin+ers
in+cli+nom+eter
  in+cli+nom+
  eters
in+close

in+closes
in+clos+ing
in+closed
in+clos+ure
  in+clos+ures
in+clud+able
in+clude
  in+cludes
  in+clud+ing
  in+clud+ed
in+clud+ible
in+clu+sion
  in+clu+sions
in+clu+sive
  in+clu+sive+ly
  in+clu+sive+ness
in+cog+ni+ta
  in+cog+ni+tas
  in+cog+ni+to
  in+cog+ni+tos
in+cog+ni+zance
in+cog+ni+zant
in+co+her+ence
  in+co+her+
  ences
in+co+her+ency
  in+co+her+
  encies
in+co+her+ent
in+com+bus+
  tible
in+come
  in+comes
in+comer
  in+comers
in+com+ing
  in+com+ings
in+com+men+su+
  rabil+ity
in+com+men+su+
  rable
  in+com+men+
  su+rables
in+com+men+su+
  rably
in+com+men+su+
  rate
  in+com+men+su+
  rate+ly
  in+com+men+su+
  rate+ness
in+com+mode
  in+com+modes
  in+com+mod+
  ing

in+com+mod+
  ed
in+com+mo+di+
  ous
in+com+mo+di+
  ous+ly
in+com+mod+ity
  in+com+mod+
  ities
in+com+mu+ni+
  cable
  in+com+mu+ni+
  ca+do
  in+com+mu+ni+
  ca+tive
in+com+mut+
  able
in+com+pa+rabil+
  ity
in+com+pa+rable
  in+com+pa+rable+
  ness
  in+com+pa+rably
in+com+pat+ibil+
  ity
in+com+pat+ible
  in+com+pat+
  ibles
  in+com+pat+ible+
  ness
  in+com+pat+ibly
in+com+pe+
  tence
in+com+pe+ten+
  cy
in+com+pe+tent
  in+com+pe+
  tents
  in+com+pe+tent+
  ly
in+com+plete
in+com+pre+hen+
  sible
in+com+press+
  ible
in+con+ceiv+abil+
  ity
in+con+ceiv+able
  in+con+ceiv+able+
  ness
  in+con+ceiv+ably
in+con+clu+sive
in+con+gru+ent
in+con+gru+ity
  in+con+gru+ities

in+con+gru+ous
in+con+gru+ous+
ly
in+con+gru+ous+
ness
in+con+sequence
in+con+sequent
in+con+sequen+
tial
in+con+sequen+
ti+al+ity
in+con+sequen+
tial+ly
in+con+sequen+
tial+ness
in+con+sequent+
ly
in+con+sid+er+
able
in+con+sid+er+
able+ness
in+con+sid+er+
ably
in+con+sid+er+
ate
in+con+sid+er+
ate+ly
in+con+sid+er+
ate+ness
in+con+sid+era+
tion
in+con+sist+en+
cy
in+con+sist+en+
cies
in+con+sist+ent
in+con+sist+ent+
ly
in+con+sol+abil+
ity
in+con+sol+able
in+con+sol+able+
ness
in+con+sol+ably
in+con+so+nance
in+con+so+
nances
in+con+so+nant
in+con+spicu+
ous
in+con+spicu+
ous+ly
in+con+spicu+
ous+ness
in+con+stant

in+con+test+able
in+con+ti+nence
in+con+ti+nent
in+con+ti+nent+
ly
in+con+tro+vert+
ibil+ity
in+con+tro+vert+
ible
in+con+tro+vert+
ibly
in+con+ven+
ience
in+con+ven+
iences
in+con+ven+
iences
in+con+ven+
ienc+ing
in+con+ven+
ienced
in+con+ven+ient
in+con+vert+ible
in+co+ordi+na+
tion
in+cor+po+rate
in+cor+po+rates
in+cor+po+rat+
ing
in+cor+po+rat+
ed
in+cor+po+rat+
ed
in+cor+po+ra+
tion
in+cor+po+ra+
tions
in+cor+po+ra+
tive
in+cor+po+real
in+cor+po+real+
ity
in+cor+po+real+
ly
in+cor+po+reity
in+cor+rect
in+cor+rect+ly
in+cor+rect+ness
in+cor+ri+gibil+
ity
in+cor+ri+gible
in+cor+ri+gibles
in+cor+ri+gible+
ness
in+cor+ri+gibly

in+cor+rupt
in+cor+rupt+ibil+
ity
in+cor+rupt+ible
in+cor+rupt+ibly
in+cras+sate
in+cras+sa+tion
in+creas+able
in+crease
in+creases
in+creases
in+creas+ing
in+creased
in+creas+ed+ly
in+creas+er
in+creas+ers
in+creas+ing+ly
in+cred+ibil+ity
in+cred+ible
in+cred+ible+
ness
in+cred+ibly
in+cre+du+lity
in+credu+lous
in+credu+lous+ly
in+credu+lous+
ness
in+cre+ment
in+cre+ments
in+cre+men+tal
in+crimi+nate
in+crimi+nates
in+crimi+nat+ing
in+crimi+nat+ed
in+crimi+na+tion
in+crimi+na+tor
in+crimi+na+
tors
in+crimi+na+tory
in+crust
in+crusts
in+crust+ing
in+crust+ed
in+crust+ant
in+crust+ants
in+crus+ta+tion
in+crus+ta+
tions
in+cu+bate
in+cu+bates
in+cu+bat+ing
in+cu+bat+ed
in+cu+ba+tion
in+cu+ba+tions
in+cu+ba+tion+al

in+cu+ba+tive
in+cu+ba+tor
in+cu+ba+tors
in+cu+ba+tory
in+cu+bus
in+cu+bi or
in+cu+buses
in+cul+cate
in+cul+cates
in+cul+cat+ing
in+cul+cat+ed
in+cul+ca+tion
in+cul+ca+tions
in+cul+ca+tor
in+cul+ca+tors
in+cul+pate
in+cul+pates
in+cul+pat+ing
in+cul+pat+ed
in+cul+pa+tion
in+cul+pa+tions
in+cum+ben+cy
in+cum+ben+
cies
in+cum+bent
in+cum+bents
in+cu+nabu+la
in+cu+nabu+lar
in+cur
in+curs
in+cur+ring
in+curred
in+cur+abil+ity
in+cur+able
in+cur+ables
in+cur+able+ness
in+cur+ably
in+cu+ri+os+ity
in+cu+ri+ous
in+cu+ri+ous+ly
in+cur+rable
in+cur+sion
in+cur+sions
in+cur+sive
in+cus
in+cu+des
in+cuse
in+cuses
in+cuses
in+cus+ing
in+cused
in+da+ba
in+da+bas
in+debt+ed
in+debt+ed+ness

in+de+cen+cy
  in+de+cen+cies
in+de+cent
in+de+cent+ly
in+de+ci+pher+
  able
in+de+ci+sion
in+de+ci+sive
in+de+ci+sive+ly
in+de+ci+sive+
  ness
in+de+clin+able
in+deco+rous
in+de+co+rum
in+deed
in+de+fati+gabil+
  ity
in+de+fati+gable
in+de+fati+gably
in+de+fea+sibil+
  ity
in+de+fea+sible
in+de+fea+sibly
in+de+fen+sibil+
  ity
in+de+fen+sible
in+de+fen+sibly
in+de+fin+able
in+defi+nite
in+defi+nite+ly
in+defi+nite+ness
in+de+his+cence
in+de+his+cent
in+del+ibil+ity
in+del+ible
in+del+ible+ness
in+del+ibly
in+deli+ca+cy
  in+deli+ca+cies
in+deli+cate
in+deli+cate+ly
in+deli+cate+
  ness
in+dem+ni+fi+ca+
  tion
  in+dem+ni+fi+
    ca+tions
in+dem+ni+fi+er
in+dem+ni+fi+
  ers
in+dem+ni+fy
in+dem+ni+fies
in+dem+ni+fy+
  ing
in+dem+ni+fied

in+dem+nity
in+dem+nities
in+de+mon+
  strable
in+dene
in+dent
in+dents
in+dents
in+dent+ing
in+dent+ed
in+den+ta+tion
in+den+ta+tions
in+dent+er
in+dent+ers
in+den+tion
in+den+tions
in+dent+or
in+dent+ors
in+den+ture
in+den+tures
in+den+tures
in+den+tur+ing
in+den+tured
in+den+ture+ship
in+den+ture+
  ships
in+de+pend+
  ence
In+de+pend+
  ence
in+de+pend+en+
  cy
in+de+pend+en+
  cies
in+de+pend+ent
in+de+pend+
  ents
in+de+pen+dent+
  ly
in-depth
in+de+scrib+abil+
  ity
in+de+scrib+able
in+de+scrib+ably
in+de+struct+ible
in+de+ter+mi+
  nable
in+de+ter+mi+na+
  cy
in+de+ter+mi+
  nate
in+de+ter+mi+
  nate+ly
in+de+ter+mi+
  nate+ness

in+de+ter+min+
  ism
in+de+ter+min+
  ist
in+de+ter+min+
  ists
in+de+ter+min+is+
  tic
in+dex
  in+dexes *or*
  in+di+ces
in+dexes
in+dex+ing
in+dexed
in+dex+ation
in+dex+ations
in+dex+er
in+dex+ers
in+dex-linked
in+dex-link+ing
In+dia
India+man
India+men
In+dian
In+dians
In+di+ana
In+di+an+apo+lis
In+di+an+ian
In+di+an+ians
In+dic
in+di+cat+able
in+di+cate
  in+di+cates
in+di+cat+ing
in+di+cat+ed
in+di+ca+tion
in+di+ca+tions
in+dica+tive
in+dica+tives
in+dica+tive+ly
in+di+ca+tor
in+di+ca+tors
in+dica+tory
in+di+ces
in+di+cia
in+di+cial
in+dict
in+dicts
in+dict+ing
in+dict+ed
in+dict+able
in+dictee
in+dictees
in+dic+ter
in+dic+ters

in+dict+ment
  in+dict+ments
in+dic+tor
in+dic+tors
in+die
in+dies
In+dies
in+dif+fer+ence
in+dif+fer+ent
in+dif+fer+ent+
  ism
in+dif+fer+ent+
  ist
in+dif+fer+ent+
  ists
in+dif+fer+ent+ly
in+di+gence
in+dig+enous
in+dig+enous+ly
in+dig+enous+
  ness
in+di+gent
in+di+gents
in+di+gently
in+di+gest+ibil+
  ity
in+di+gest+ible
in+di+gest+ibly
in+di+ges+tion
in+dig+nant
in+dig+nant+ly
in+dig+na+tion
in+dig+nity
  in+dig+nities
in+di+go
  in+di+gos *or*
  in+di+goes
in+di+rect
in+di+rec+tion
in+di+rect+ly
in+di+rect+ness
in+dis+cern+ible
in+dis+creet
in+dis+creet+ly
in+dis+creet+
  ness
in+dis+crete
in+dis+cre+tion
  in+dis+cre+tions
in+dis+crimi+nate
in+dis+crimi+nate+
  ly
in+dis+crimi+nate+
  ness

in+dis+crimi+na+tion
in+dis+pen+sabil+ity
in+dis+pen+sable
in+dis+pen+sables
in+dis+pen+sable+ness
in+dis+pen+sably
in+dis+pose
in+dis+poses
in+dis+pos+ing
in+dis+posed
in+dis+po+si+tion
in+dis+po+si+tions
in+dis+put+able
in+dis+sol+uble
in+dis+sol+ubly
in+dis+tinct
in+dis+tinc+tive
in+dis+tinct+ly
in+dis+tinct+ness
in+dis+tin+guish+able
in+dite
in+dites
in+dit+ing
in+dit+ed
in+dite+ment
in+dite+ments
in+dit+er
in+dit+ers
in+dium
in+di+vid+ual
in+di+vid+uals
in+di+vidu+ali+sa+tion
in+di+vidu+al+ise
in+di+vidu+al+ises
in+di+vidu+al+is+ing
in+di+vidu+al+ised
in+di+vidu+al+is+er
in+di+vidu+al+is+ers
in+di+vidu+al+ism

in+di+vidu+al+isms
in+di+vidu+al+ist
in+di+vidu+al+ists
in+di+vidu+al+ity
in+di+vidu+al+ities
in+di+vidu+ali+za+tion
in+di+vidu+al+ize
in+di+vidu+al+izes
in+di+vidu+al+iz+ing
in+di+vidu+al+ized
in+di+vidu+al+iz+er
in+di+vidu+al+iz+ers
in+di+vid+ual+ly
in+di+vidu+ate
in+di+vidu+ates
in+di+vidu+at+ing
in+di+vidu+at+ed
in+di+vid+ua+tor
in+di+vid+ua+tors
in+di+vis+ibil+ity
in+di+vis+ible
in+di+vis+ibly
Indo+china
Indo-China
Indo+chinese
Indo-Chinese
Indo+chinese
Indo-Chinese
in+doc+tri+nate
in+doc+tri+nates
in+doc+tri+nat+ing
in+doc+tri+nat+ed
in+doc+tri+na+tion
in+doc+tri+na+tions
in+doc+tri+na+tor
in+doc+tri+na+tors

Indo-European
Indo-Europeans
Indo-Iranian
in+dol
in+dole
in+do+lence
in+do+lent
in+do+lent+ly
in+domi+tabil+ity
in+domi+table
in+domi+table+ness
in+domi+tably
In+do+nesia
In+do+nesian
In+do+nesians
in+door
in+doors
in+dorse
in+dorses
in+dors+ing
in+dorsed
Indra
in+draft
U.S.
in+drafts
in+draught
in+draughts
in+drawn
In+dre
Indre-et-Loire
in+dri
in+dris
in+dris
in+dris
in+du+bi+table
in+du+bi+tably
in+duce
in+duces
in+duc+ing
in+duced
in+duce+ment
in+duce+ments
in+duc+er
in+duc+ers
in+duc+ible
in+duct
in+ducts
in+duct+ing
in+duct+ed
in+duct+ance
in+duct+ances
in+duc+tile
in+duc+tion
in+duc+tions

in+duc+tion+al
in+duc+tive
in+duc+tive+ly
in+duc+tive+ness
in+duc+tor
in+duc+tors
in+due
in+dues
in+du+ing
in+dued
in+dulge
in+dulges
in+dulg+ing
in+dulged
in+dul+gence
in+dul+gences
in+dul+gent
in+dul+gent+ly
in+dulg+er
in+dulg+ers
in+dulg+ing+ly
in+du+na
in+du+nas
in+du+rate
in+du+rates
in+du+rat+ing
in+du+rat+ed
In+dus
in+du+sial
in+du+sium
in+du+sia
in+dus+trial
in+dus+tri+ali+sa+tion
in+dus+tri+al+ise
in+dus+tri+al+ises
in+dus+tri+al+is+ing
in+dus+tri+al+ised
in+dus+tri+al+ism
in+dus+tri+al+ist
in+dus+tri+al+ists
in+dus+tri+ali+za+tion
in+dus+tri+al+ize
in+dus+tri+al+izes
in+dus+tri+al+iz+ing
in+dus+tri+al+ized

in+dus+tri+al+ly
in+dus+tri+ous
in+dus+tri+ous+
  ly
in+dus+tri+ous+
  ness
in+dus+try
in+dus+tries
in+dwell
in+dwells
in+dwell+ing
in+dwelt
in+dwell+er
in+dwell+ers
in+ebri+ate
in+ebri+ates
in+ebri+ates
in+ebri+at+ing
in+ebri+at+ed
in+ebria+tion
in+ebria+tions
in+ebri+ety
in+ed+ibil+ity
in+ed+ible
in+ed+it+ed
in+edu+cabil+ity
in+edu+cable
in+ef+fabil+ity
in+ef+fable
in+ef+fable+ness
in+ef+fably
in+ef+face+able
in+ef+fec+tive
in+ef+fec+tive+ly
in+ef+fec+tive+
  ness
in+ef+fec+tual
in+ef+fec+tu+al+
  ity
in+ef+fec+tu+al+
  ly
in+ef+fi+ca+cious
in+ef+fi+ca+cious+
  ly
in+ef+fi+ca+cious+
  ness
in+ef+fi+ca+cy
in+ef+fi+cient
in+elas+tic
in+el+egant
in+eli+gible
in+eluc+tabil+ity
in+eluc+table
in+eluc+tably
in+ept

in+epti+tude
in+ept+ly
in+ept+ness
in+eq+uable
in+equal+ity
in+equal+ities
in+equi+table
in+equi+ty
in+equi+ties
in+eradi+cable
in+ert
in+er+tia
in+er+tial
in+ert+ly
in+ert+ness
in+es+cap+able
in+es+cap+ably
in+es+sen+tial
in+es+sen+tials
in+es+ti+mabil+
  ity
in+es+ti+mable
in+es+ti+mable+
  ness
in+es+ti+mably
in+evi+tabil+ity
in+evi+table
in+evi+table+
  ness
in+evi+tably
in+ex+act
in+ex+cus+able
in+ex+haust+ibil+
  ity
in+ex+haust+ible
in+ex+haust+ibly
in+exo+rabil+ity
in+exo+rable
in+exo+rably
in+ex+pe+di+ent
in+ex+pen+sive
in+ex+pe+ri+
  ence
in+ex+pert
in+ex+pi+able
in+ex+pi+able+
  ness
in+ex+pli+cable
in+ex+plic+it
in+ex+press+ible
in+ex+pres+sive
in ex+ten+so
in+ex+tin+guish+
  able
in ex+tre+mis

in+ex+tri+cabil+
  ity
in+ex+tri+cable
in+ex+tri+cable+
  ness
in+ex+tri+cably
in+fal+libil+ity
in+fal+lible
in+fal+libles
in+fal+lible+ness
in+fal+libly
in+fa+mous
in+fa+mous+ly
in+fa+mous+ness
in+fa+my
in+fa+mies
in+fan+cy
in+fan+cies
in+fant
in+fants
in+fan+ta
in+fan+tas
in+fan+te
in+fan+tes
in+fant+hood
in+fant+hoods
in+fan+ti+cid+al
in+fan+ti+cide
in+fan+ti+cides
in+fan+tile
in+fan+ti+lism
in+fan+ti+lisms
in+fan+til+ity
in+fan+til+ities
in+fan+try
in+fan+tries
in+fantry+man
in+fantry+men
in+farct
in+farcts
in+farct+ed
in+fatu+ate
in+fatu+ates
in+fatu+ates
in+fatu+at+ing
in+fatu+at+ed
in+fatu+at+ed
in+fat+ua+tion
in+fat+ua+tions
in+fea+sible
in+fect
in+fects
in+fect+ing
in+fect+ed
in+fec+ter

in+fec+ters
in+fec+tion
in+fec+tions
in+fec+tious
in+fec+tious+ly
in+fec+tious+
  ness
in+fec+tive
in+fec+tive+ly
in+fec+tive+ness
in+fec+tor
in+fec+tors
in+fe+lici+tous
in+fe+lic+ity
in+fe+lic+ities
in+fer
in+fers
in+fer+ring
in+ferred
in+fer+able
in+fer+ence
in+fer+ences
in+fer+en+tial
in+fer+en+tial+ly
in+fe+ri+or
in+fe+ri+ors
in+fe+ri+or+ity
in+fe+ri+or+ities
in+fe+ri+or+ly
in+fer+nal
in+fer+nal+ity
in+fer+nal+ly
in+fer+no
in+fer+nos
in+fer+rer
in+fer+rers
in+fer+tile
in+fer+til+ity
in+fest
in+fests
in+fest+ing
in+fest+ed
in+fes+ta+tion
in+fes+ta+tions
in+fest+er
in+fest+ers
in+feu+da+tion
in+feu+da+tions
in+fi+del
in+fi+dels
in+fi+del+ity
in+fi+del+ities
in+field
in+fields
in+fielder

in+fielders
in+fighter
in+fighters
in+fighting
in+fill
in+fills
in+fil+ling
in+fil+lings
in+fil+trate
in+fil+trates
in+fil+trates
in+fil+trat+ing
in+fil+trat+ed
in+fil+tra+tion
in+fil+tra+tions
in+fil+tra+tive
in+fil+tra+tor
in+fil+tra+tors
in+fi+nite
in+fi+nite+ly
in+fi+nite+ness
in+fini+tesi+mal
in+fini+tesi+
  mals
in+fini+tesi+mal+
  ly
in+fini+ti+val
in+fini+ti+val+ly
in+fini+tive
in+fini+tives
in+fini+tive+ly
in+fini+tude
in+fini+tudes
in+fin+ity
in+fin+ities
in+firm
in+fir+ma+ry
in+fir+ma+ries
in+fir+mity
in+fir+mities
in+firm+ly
in+firm+ness
in+fix
in+fixes
in+fixes
in+fix+ing
in+fixed
in+fixa+tion
in+fixa+tions
in+fix+ion
in+fix+ions
in fla+gran+te de+
  lic+to
in+flame
in+flames

in+flam+ing
in+flamed
in+flam+er
in+flam+ers
in+flam+mabil+ity
in+flam+mable
in+flam+mables
in+flam+mable+
  ness
in+flam+mably
in+flam+ma+tion
in+flam+ma+
  tions
in+flam+ma+to+ri+
  ly
in+flam+ma+tory
in+flat+able
in+flat+ables
in+flate
in+flates
in+flat+ing
in+flat+ed
in+flat+ed+ly
in+flat+ed+ness
in+flat+er
in+flat+ers
in+fla+tion
in+fla+tions
in+fla+tion+ary
in+fla+tion+ism
in+fla+tion+ist
in+fla+tion+ists
in+flat+or
in+flat+ors
in+flect
in+flects
in+flect+ing
in+flect+ed
in+flect+ed+ness
in+flec+tion
in+flec+tions
in+flec+tion+al
in+flec+tion+al+ly
in+flec+tion+less
in+flec+tive
in+flec+tor
in+flec+tors
in+flex+ible
in+flex+ion
in+flex+ions
in+flex+ion+al
in+flex+ion+al+ly
in+flex+ion+less
in+flict
in+flicts

in+flict+ing
in+flict+ed
in+flic+table
in+flic+ter
in+flic+ters
in+flic+tion
in+flic+tions
in+flic+tor
in+flic+tors
in-flight
in+flo+res+cence
in+flo+res+
  cences
in+flo+res+cent
in+flow
in+flows
in+flow+ing
in+flow+ings
in+flu+ence
in+flu+ences
in+flu+ences
in+flu+enc+ing
in+flu+enced
in+flu+ence+able
in+flu+enc+er
in+flu+enc+ers
in+flu+ent
in+flu+ents
in+flu+en+tial
in+flu+en+tial+ly
in+flu+en+za
in+flu+en+zas
in+flu+en+zal
in+flux
in+fluxes
info
in+fold
in+folds
in+fold+ing
in+fold+ed
in+form
in+forms
in+form+ing
in+formed
in+form+able
in+for+mal
in+for+mal+ity
in+for+mal+ities
in+for+mal+ly
in+form+ant
in+form+ants
in+for+ma+tion
in+for+ma+tions
in+for+ma+tion+
  al

in+forma+tive
in+for+ma+tive+
  ly
in+for+ma+tive+
  ness
in+forma+tory
in+formed
in+form+er
in+form+ers
info+tain+ment
in+fra
in+fract
in+fracts
in+fract+ing
in+fract+ed
in+frac+tion
in+frac+tions
in+frac+tor
in+frac+tors
in+fra dig
in+fran+gibil+ity
in+fran+gible
in+fran+gibly
infra+red
infra+son+ic
infra+sound
infra+struc+ture
infra+struc+
  tures
in+fre+quent
in+fringe
in+fringes
in+fring+ing
in+fringed
in+fringe+ment
in+fringe+ments
in+fring+er
in+fring+ers
in+fun+dibu+lar
in+furi+ate
in+furi+ates
in+furi+at+ing
in+furi+at+ed
in+furi+at+ing
in+furi+at+ing+ly
in+fuse
in+fuses
in+fus+ing
in+fused
in+fus+er
in+fus+ers
in+fu+sibil+ity
in+fu+sible
in+fu+sible+ness
in+fu+sion

in+ fu+ sions
in+ fu+ sive
in+ fu+ so+ rial
in+ fu+ so+ rial
in+ fu+ so+ rian
in+ fu+ so+ rians
in+ gath+ er
in+ gath+ ers
in+ gath+ er+ ing
in+ gath+ ered
in+ gemi+ nate
in+ gemi+ nates
in+ gemi+ nat+ ing
in+ gemi+ nat+ ed
in+ gen+ ious
in+ gen+ ious+ ly
in+ gen+ ious+ ness
in+ gé+ nue
in+ gé+ nues
in+ genu+ ity
in+ genu+ ities
in+ genu+ ous
in+ genu+ ous+ ly
in+ genu+ ous+ ness
in+ gest
in+ gests
in+ gest+ ing
in+ gest+ ed
in+ gest+ ible
in+ ges+ tion
in+ ges+ tive
in+ gle
in+ gles
ingle+ nook
ingle+ nooks
in+ glo+ ri+ ous
in+ go+ ing
in+ got
in+ gots
in+ graft
in+ grafts
in+ graft+ ing
in+ graft+ ed
in+ graf+ ta+ tion
in+ graf+ ta+ tions
in+ graft+ ment
in+ graft+ ments
in+ grain
in+ grains
in+ grains
in+ grain+ ing
in+ grained

in+ grained
in+ grain+ ed+ ly
in+ grain+ ed+ ness
in+ grate
in+ grates
in+ grate+ ly
in+ gra+ ti+ ate
in+ gra+ ti+ ates
in+ gra+ ti+ at+ ing
in+ gra+ ti+ at+ ed
in+ gra+ ti+ at+ ing
in+ gra+ ti+ at+ ing+ ly
in+ gra+ tia+ tion
in+ gra+ tia+ tions
in+ gra+ tia+ tory
in+ grati+ tude
in+ gre+ di+ ent
in+ gre+ di+ ents
in+ gress
in+ gresses
in+ gres+ sion
in+ gres+ sions
in-group
in-groups
in+ grow+ ing
in+ grown
in+ growth
in+ growths
in+ gui+ nal
in+ gulf
in+ gulfs
in+ gulf+ ing
in+ gulf+ ed
in+ gur+ gi+ tate
in+ gur+ gi+ tates
in+ gur+ gi+ tat+ ing
in+ gur+ gi+ tat+ ed
in+ gur+ gi+ ta+ tion
in+ hab+ it
in+ hab+ its
in+ hab+ it+ ing
in+ hab+ it+ ed
in+ hab+ it+ abil+ ity
in+ hab+ it+ able
in+ hab+ it+ ance
in+ hab+ it+ an+ cy
in+ hab+ it+ ant
in+ hab+ it+ ants
in+ habi+ ta+ tion
in+ hal+ ant

in+ hal+ ants
in+ ha+ la+ tion
in+ ha+ la+ tions
in+ hale
in+ hales
in+ hal+ ing
in+ haled
in+ hal+ er
in+ hal+ ers
In+ ham+ ba+ ne
in+ har+ mo+ ni+ ous
in+ here
in+ heres
in+ her+ ing
in+ hered
in+ her+ ent
in+ her+ ent+ ly
in+ her+ it
in+ her+ its
in+ her+ it+ ing
in+ her+ it+ ed
in+ her+ it+ abil+ ity
in+ her+ it+ able
in+ her+ it+ able+ ness
in+ her+ it+ ably
in+ her+ it+ ance
in+ her+ it+ ances
in+ her+ it+ ed
in+ heri+ tor
in+ heri+ tors
in+ heri+ tress
in+ heri+ tresses
in+ heri+ trix
in+ heri+ tri+ ces
or
in+ heri+ trixes
in+ hib+ it
in+ hib+ its
in+ hib+ it+ ing
in+ hib+ it+ ed
in+ hib+ it+ able
in+ hibi+ ter
in+ hibi+ ters
in+ hi+ bi+ tion
in+ hi+ bi+ tions
in+ hib+ it+ ive
in+ hibi+ tory
in+ hos+ pi+ table
in+ hos+ pi+ tal+ ity
in-house
in+ hu+ man
in+ hu+ mane+ ly
in+ hu+ man+ ity

in+ hu+ man+ ities
in+ hu+ man+ ly
in+ hu+ man+ ness
in+ hu+ ma+ tion
in+ hu+ ma+ tions
in+ hume
in+ humes
in+ hum+ ing
in+ hum+ ed
in+ hum+ er
in+ hum+ ers
in+ imi+ cal
in+ imi+ cal+ ity
in+ imi+ cal+ ly
in+ imi+ cal+ ness
in+ imi+ tabil+ ity
in+ imi+ table
in+ imi+ table+ ness
in+ imi+ tably
in+ iqui+ tous
in+ iqui+ tous+ ness
in+ iquity
in+ iquities
ini+ tial
ini+ tials
ini+ tials
ini+ tial+ ling or
ini+ tial+ ing
U.S.
ini+ tialled or
ini+ tialed
U.S.
ini+ tial+ er
ini+ tial+ ers
ini+ tiali+ sa+ tion
ini+ tiali+ sa+ tions
ini+ tial+ isc
ini+ tial+ ises
ini+ tial+ is+ ing
ini+ tial+ ised
ini+ tiali+ za+ tion
ini+ tiali+ za+ tions
ini+ tial+ ize
ini+ tial+ izes
ini+ tial+ iz+ ing
ini+ tial+ ized
ini+ tial+ ler
ini+ tial+ lers
ini+ tial+ ly
ini+ ti+ ate
ini+ ti+ ates
ini+ ti+ ates

ini+ti+at+ing
ini+ti+at+ed
ini+tia+tion
ini+tia+tions
ini+tia+tive
ini+tia+tives
ini+tia+tive+ly
ini+tia+tor
ini+tia+tors
ini+tia+to+ry
in+ject
in+jects
in+ject+ing
in+ject+ed
in+ject+able
in+jec+tion
in+jec+tions
in+jec+tive
in+jec+tor
in+jec+tors
in+ju+di+cious
in+junc+tion
in+junc+tions
in+junc+tive
in+junc+tive+ly
in+jur+able
in+jure
in+jures
in+jur+ing
in+jured
in+jured
in+jur+er
in+jur+ers
in+ju+ri+ous
in+ju+ri+ous+ly
in+ju+ri+ous+
ness
in+ju+ry
in+ju+ries
in+jus+tice
in+jus+tices
ink
inks
inks
ink+ing
inked
Inkatha
ink+blot
ink+blots
ink-cap
ink-caps
ink+er
ink+ers
ink+horn
ink+horns

inki+ness
ink+ling
ink+lings
ink+stand
ink+stands
ink+well
ink+wells
inky
inki+er
inki+est
in+laid
in+land
in+land+er
in+land+ers
in-law
in-laws
in+lay
in+lays
in+lays
in+lay+ing
in+laid
in+lay+er
in+lay+ers
in+let
in+lets
in+lets
in+let+ting
in+let
in+li+er
in+li+ers
in loco pa+ren+tis
in+ly
in+mate
in+mates
in me+mo+ri+am
in+most
inn
inns
in+nards
in+nate
in+nate+ly
in+nate+ness
in+ner
in+ners
in+ner+ly
inner+most
in+ner+ness
in+ner+vate
in+ner+vates
in+ner+vat+ing
in+ner+vat+ed
in+ner+va+tion
in+ner+va+tions
in+nings
In+nis+kil+ling

inn+keeper
inn+keepers
in+no+cence
in+no+cent
in+no+cents
in+no+cent+ly
in+no+cui+ty
in+nocu+ous
in+nocu+ous+ly
in+nocu+ous+
ness
in+nomi+nate
in+no+vate
in+no+vates
in+no+vat+ing
in+no+vat+ed
in+no+va+tion
in+no+va+tions
in+no+va+tion+al
in+no+va+tion+
ist
in+no+va+tion+
ists
in+no+va+tive
in+no+va+tor
in+no+va+tors
in+no+va+tory
Inns+bruck
in+nu+en+do
in+nu+en+dos
or
in+nu+en+does
In+nu+it
In+nu+it or
In+nu+its
in+nu+mer+abil+
ity
in+nu+mer+able
in+nu+mer+able+
ness
in+nu+mer+ably
in+nu+mera+cy
in+nu+mer+ate
in+nu+mer+ates
in+nu+mer+ous
in+ocu+late
in+ocu+lates
in+ocu+lat+ing
in+ocu+lat+ed
in+ocu+la+tion
in+ocu+la+tions
in+ocu+la+tive
in+ocu+la+tor
in+ocu+la+tors
in+of+fen+sive

in+of+fi+cious
in+op+er+abil+ity
in+op+er+able
in+op+er+able+
ness
in+op+er+ably
in+op+era+tive
in+op+por+tune
in+or+di+na+cy
in+or+di+nate
in+or+di+nate+ly
in+or+di+nate+
ness
in+or+gan+ic
in+or+gani+cal+ly
in+os+cu+late
in+os+cu+lates
in+os+cu+lat+
ing
in+os+cu+lat+
ed
in+os+cu+la+tion
in+os+cu+la+
tions
ino+si+tol
in+pa+tient
in+pa+tients
in per+pe+tuum
in+put
in+puts
in+puts
in+put+ting
in+put
in+quest
in+quests
in+qui+et
in+qui+et+ly
in+qui+etude
in+qui+line
in+qui+lines
in+qui+li+nous
in+quire
in+quires
in+quir+ing
in+quired
in+quir+er
in+quir+ers
in+quiry
in+quiries
in+qui+si+tion
in+qui+si+tions
In+qui+si+tion
in+qui+si+tion+al
in+qui+si+tion+
ist

in+qui+si+tion+
    ists
in+quisi+tive
in+quisi+tive+ly
in+quisi+tive+
    ness
in+quisi+tor
in+quisi+tors
in+quisi+to+rial
in+quisi+to+ri+al+
    ly
in+quisi+to+ri+al+
    ness
in+quor+ate
in+road
in+roads
in+rush
in+rushes
in+rushing
in+rushings
in+sa+lu+bri+ous
in+sane
in+sane+ly
in+sane+ness
in+sani+tary
in+san+ity
in+san+ities
in+sa+tiabil+ity
in+sa+tiable
in+sa+tiably
in+sa+ti+ate
in+sa+ti+ate+ly
in+sa+ti+ate+
    ness
in+scape
in+scapes
in+scrib+able
in+scrib+able+
    ness
in+scribe
in+scribes
in+scrib+ing
in+scribed
in+scrib+er
in+scrib+ers
in+scrip+tion
in+scrip+tions
in+scrip+tion+al
in+scrip+tive
in+scrip+tive+ly
in+scru+tabil+ity
in+scru+table
in+scru+table+
    ness
in+scru+tably

in+sect
in+sects
in+sec+tar+ium
in+sec+tar+iums
    or
in+sec+tar+ia
in+sec+tary
in+sec+taries
in+sec+ti+cid+al
in+sec+ti+cide
in+sec+ti+cides
in+sec+tile
in+sec+ti+vore
in+sec+ti+vores
in+sec+tivo+rous
insect-like
in+secure
in+secure+ly
in+secure+ness
in+secu+rity
in+secu+rities
in+sel+berg
in+sel+bergs
in+semi+nate
in+semi+nates
in+semi+nat+ing
in+semi+nat+ed
in+semi+na+tion
in+semi+na+
    tions
in+semi+na+tor
in+semi+na+
    tors
in+sen+sate
in+sen+sate+ly
in+sen+sate+
    ness
in+sen+sibil+ity
in+sen+sible
in+sen+sible+
    ness
in+sen+sibly
in+sen+si+tive
in+sen+ti+ence
in+sen+ti+ent
in+sepa+rable
in+sert
in+serts
in+sert+ing
in+sert+ed
in+sert+able
in+sert+er
in+sert+ers
in+ser+tion
in+ser+tions

in+ser+tion+al
in-service
in+ses+so+rial
in+set
in+sets
in+sets
in+set+ting
in+set
in+set+ter
in+set+ters
in+shal+lah
in+shore
in+side
in+sides
in+sid+er
in+sid+ers
in+sidi+ous
in+sidi+ous+ly
in+sidi+ous+ness
in+sight
in+sights
in+sight+ful
in+sig+nia
in+sig+nias or
in+sig+nia
in+sig+nifi+cance
in+sig+nifi+can+
    cy
in+sig+nifi+cant
in+sig+nifi+cant+
    ly
in+sin+cere
in+sin+cere+ly
in+sin+cer+ity
in+sin+cer+ities
in+sinu+ate
in+sinu+ates
in+sinu+at+ing
in+sinu+at+ed
in+sin+ua+tion
in+sin+ua+tions
in+sinua+tive
in+sinua+tor
in+sinua+tors
in+sinua+tory
in+sip+id
in+si+pid+ity
in+sip+id+ly
in+sist
in+sists
in+sist+ing
in+sist+ed
in+sist+ence
in+sist+en+cy
in+sist+ent

in+sist+ent+ly
in+sist+er
in+sist+ers
in+sist+ing+ly
in situ
in+so+bri+ety
in+so+bri+eties
in so far as
in+so+far as
in+so+la+tion
in+so+la+tions
in+sole
in+soles
in+so+lence
in+so+lent
in+so+lent+ly
in+sol+ubil+ity
in+sol+uble
in+sol+uble+ness
in+sol+ubly
in+solv+able
in+sol+ven+cy
in+sol+ven+cies
in+sol+vent
in+sol+vents
in+som+nia
in+som+nias
in+som+ni+ac
in+som+ni+acs
in+som+ni+ous
in+so+much
in+sou+ci+ance
in+sou+ci+ant
in+sou+ci+ant+ly
in+span
in+spans
in+span+ning
in+spanned
in+spect
in+spects
in+spect+ing
in+spect+ed
in+spect+able
in+spec+tion
in+spec+tions
in+spec+tive
in+spec+tor
in+spec+tors
in+spec+to+ral
in+spec+tor+ate
in+spec+tor+
    ates
in+spec+to+rial
in+spec+tor+ship

in+spec+tor+ships
in+spir+able
in+spi+ra+tion
in+spi+ra+tions
in+spira+tive
in+spira+tory
in+spire
in+spires
in+spir+ing
in+spired
in+spir+er
in+spir+ers
in+spir+ing+ly
in+spir+it
in+spir+its
in+spir+it+ing
in+spir+it+ed
in+spir+it+er
in+spir+it+ers
in+spir+it+ment
in+spir+it+ments
in+stabil+ity
in+stabil+ities
in+stal
in+stals
in+stal+ling
in+stalled
in+stall
in+stalls
in+stall+ing
in+stalled
in+stal+la+tion
in+stal+la+tions
in+stall+er
in+stall+ers
in+stall+ment
U.S.
in+stall+ments
in+stal+ment
in+stal+ments
in+stance
in+stances
in+stances
in+stanc+ing
in+stanced
in+stant
in+stants
in+stan+ta+neity
in+stan+ta+neous
in+stan+ta+neous+ly

in+stan+ta+neous+ness
in+stan+ter
in+stant+ly
in+star
in+stars
in+state
in+states
in+stat+ing
in+stat+ed
in+state+ment
in+state+ments
in+stead
in+step
in+steps
in+sti+gate
in+sti+gates
in+sti+gat+ing
in+sti+gat+ed
in+sti+ga+tion
in+sti+ga+tions
in+sti+ga+tive
in+sti+ga+tor
in+sti+ga+tors
in+stil
in+stils
in+stil+ling
in+stilled
in+still
U.S.
in+stills
in+still+ing
in+stilled
in+still+er
in+still+ers
in+still+ment
U.S.
in+stil+ment
in+stinct
in+stincts
in+stinc+tive
in+stinc+tive+ly
in+stinc+tual
in+stinc+tual+ly
in+sti+tute
in+sti+tutes
in+sti+tutes
in+sti+tut+ing
in+sti+tut+ed
in+sti+tut+er
in+sti+tut+ers
in+sti+tutes
in+sti+tu+tion
in+sti+tu+tions
in+sti+tu+tion+al

in+sti+tu+tion+ali+sa+tion
in+sti+tu+tion+al+ise
in+sti+tu+tion+al+ises
in+sti+tu+tion+al+is+ing
in+sti+tu+tion+al+ised
in+sti+tu+tion+al+ism
in+sti+tu+tion+ali+za+tion
in+sti+tu+tion+al+ize
in+sti+tu+tion+al+izes
in+sti+tu+tion+al+iz+ing
in+sti+tu+tion+al+ized
in+sti+tu+tion+al+ly
in+sti+tu+tion+ary
in+sti+tu+tor
in+sti+tu+tors
in-store
in+struct
in+structs
in+struct+ing
in+struct+ed
in+struct+ible
in+struc+tion
in+struc+tions
in+struc+tion+al
in+struc+tions
in+struc+tive
in+struc+tive+ly
in+struc+tive+ness
in+struc+tor
in+struc+tors
in+struc+tor+ship
in+struc+tor+ships
in+struc+tress
in+struc+tresses
in+stru+ment
in+stru+ments
in+stru+ments
in+stru+ment+ing

in+stru+ment+ed
in+stru+men+tal
in+stru+men+tals
in+stru+men+tal+ist
in+stru+men+tal+ists
in+stru+men+tal+ity
in+stru+men+tal+ities
in+stru+men+tal+ly
in+stru+men+ta+tion
in+stru+men+ta+tions
in+sub+or+di+nate
in+sub+or+di+nates
in+sub+or+di+nate+ly
in+sub+or+di+na+tion
in+sub+or+di+na+tions
in+sub+stan+tial
in+sub+stan+ti+al+ity
in+sub+stan+tial+ly
in+suf+fer+able
in+suf+fer+able+ness
in+suf+fer+ably
in+suf+fi+cien+cy
in+suf+fi+cien+cies
in+suf+fi+cient
in+suf+flate
in+suf+flates
in+suf+flat+ing
in+suf+flat+ed
in+suf+fla+tion
in+suf+fla+tions
in+suf+flat+or
in+suf+flat+ors
in+su+lar
in+su+lar+ism
in+su+lar+ity
in+su+lar+ly
in+su+late

in+su+lates
in+su+lat+ing
in+su+lat+ed
in+su+la+tion
in+su+la+tions
in+su+la+tor
in+su+la+tors
in+su+lin
in+sult
in+sults
in+sult+ing
in+sult+ed
in+sult+er
in+sult+ers
in+su+per+abil+
　ity
in+su+per+able
in+su+per+ably
in+sup+port+able
in+sup+port+able+
　ness
in+sup+port+ably
in+sur+abil+ity
in+sur+able
in+sur+ance
in+sur+ances
in+sure
in+sures
in+sur+ing
in+sured
in+sured
in+sur+er
in+sur+ers
in+sur+gence
in+sur+gences
in+sur+gen+cy
in+sur+gen+cies
in+sur+gent
in+sur+gents
in+sur+mount+
　able
in+sur+rec+tion
in+sur+rec+
　tions
in+sur+rec+tion+
　al
in+sur+rec+tion+
　ary
in+sur+rec+tion+
　aries
in+sur+rec+tion+
　ist
in+sur+rec+tion+
　ists
in+sus+cep+tible

in+tact
in+tact+ness
in+tag+li+at+ed
in+tag+lio
in+tag+lios or
　in+tag+li
in+take
in+takes
in+tan+gibil+ity
in+tan+gible
in+tan+gibles
in+tan+gibly
in+tar+sia
in+tar+sias
in+te+ger
in+te+gers
in+te+grabil+ity
in+te+grable
in+te+gral
in+te+grals
in+te+grali+ty
in+te+gral+ly
in+te+grand
in+te+grands
in+te+grant
in+te+grants
in+te+grate
in+te+grates
in+te+grat+ing
in+te+grat+ed
in+te+gra+tion
in+te+gra+tions
in+te+gra+tive
in+teg+rity
in+teg+rities
in+tegu+ment
in+tegu+ments
in+tegu+ment+al
in+tegu+men+
　tary
in+tel+lect
in+tel+lects
in+tel+lec+tion
in+tel+lec+tions
in+tel+lec+tive
in+tel+lec+tive+ly
in+tel+lec+tual
in+tel+lec+tuals
in+tel+lec+tu+al+
　ise
in+tel+lec+tu+al+
　ises
in+tel+lec+tu+al+
　is+ing

in+tel+lec+tu+al+
　ised
in+tel+lec+tu+al+
　ism
in+tel+lec+tu+al+
　ist
in+tel+lec+tu+al+
　ists
in+tel+lec+tu+al+
　is+tic
in+tel+lec+tu+al+
　ity
in+tel+lec+tu+al+
　ize
in+tel+lec+tu+al+
　izes
in+tel+lec+tu+al+
　iz+ing
in+tel+lec+tu+al+
　ized
in+tel+lec+tual+ly
in+tel+lec+tu+al+
　ness
in+tel+li+gence
in+tel+li+gences
in+tel+li+gent
in+tel+li+gen+tial
in+tel+li+gent+ly
in+tel+li+gent+sia
in+tel+li+gent+
　sias
in+tel+li+gibil+ity
in+tel+li+gi+ble
in+tel+li+gibly
in+tem+per+ance
in+tem+per+ate
in+tem+per+ate+
　ly
in+tem+per+ate+
　ness
in+tend
in+tends
in+tend+ing
in+tend+ed
in+tend+an+cy
in+tend+an+cies
in+tend+ant
in+tend+ants
in+tend+ed
in+tend+eds
in+tend+er
in+tend+ers
in+tense
in+tens+er
in+tens+est

in+tense+ly
in+tense+ness
in+ten+si+fi+ca+
　tion
in+ten+si+fi+ca+
　tions
in+ten+si+fi+er
in+ten+si+fi+ers
in+ten+si+fy
in+ten+si+fies
in+ten+si+fy+
　ing
in+ten+si+fied
in+ten+sion
in+ten+sions
in+ten+sion+al
in+ten+sity
in+ten+sities
in+ten+sive
in+ten+sives
in+ten+sive+ly
in+ten+sive+ness
in+tent
in+tents
in+ten+tion
in+ten+tions
in+ten+tion+al
in+ten+tion+al+
　ity
in+ten+tion+al+
　ities
in+ten+tion+al+ly
in+tent+ly
in+tent+ness
in+ter
in+ters
in+ter+ring
in+terred
inter+aca+dem+
　ic
inter+act
inter+acts
inter+act+ing
inter+act+ed
inter+ac+tion
inter+ac+tions
inter+ac+tive
in+ter alia
inter+al+lied
inter+atom+ic
inter+bank
inter+blend
inter+blends
inter+blend+ing
inter+blend+ed

inter+branch
inter+breed
  inter+breeds
  inter+breed+ing
  inter+bred
inter+ca+lary
inter+ca+late
  inter+ca+lates
  inter+ca+lat+ing
  inter+ca+lat+ed
inter+ca+la+tion
  inter+ca+la+
  tions
inter+caste
inter+cede
  inter+cedes
  inter+ced+ing
  inter+c+eded
inter+ced+er
  inter+ced+ers
inter+cel+lu+lar
inter+censal
inter+cept
  inter+cepts
  inter+cept+ing
  inter+cept+ed
inter+cept+er
  inter+cept+ers
inter+cep+tion
  inter+cep+tions
inter+cep+tive
inter+cep+tor
  inter+cep+tors
inter+ces+sion
  inter+ces+sions
inter+ces+sion+al
inter+ces+sor
  inter+ces+sors
inter+ces+so+ri+
al
inter+ces+sory
inter+change
  inter+changes
  inter+changes
  inter+chang+ing
  inter+changed
inter+change+abil+
ity
inter+change+
able
inter+change+
able+ness
inter+change+
ably
inter+city

inter-city
  inter-citys
inter+clasp
  inter+clasps
  inter+clasp+ing
  inter+clasp+ed
inter+class
inter+club
inter+col+legi+
ate
inter+co+lo+nial
inter+com
  inter+coms
inter+com+mu+ni+
cable
inter+com+mu+ni+
cate
  inter+com+mu+
ni+cates
  inter+com+mu+
ni+cat+ing
  inter+com+mu+
ni+cat+ed
inter+com+mu+ni+
ca+tion
inter+com+mu+
ni+ca+tions
inter+com+mu+ni+
ca+tive
inter+com+mun+
ion
inter+com+mu+
nity
inter+com+pa+ny
inter+con+nect
  inter+con+nects
  inter+con+nect+
ing
  inter+con+nect+
ed
inter+con+nec+
tion
  inter+con+nec+
tions
inter+con+so+
nan+tal
inter+con+ti+nen+
tal
inter+con+vert+
ible
inter+cos+tal
inter+coun+ty
inter+course
  inter+courses
inter+cru+ral

inter+cur+rence
  inter+cur+
  rences
inter+cur+rent
inter+de+nomi+
na+tion+al
inter+de+part+
ment+al
inter+de+part+
ment+al+ly
inter+de+pend
  inter+de+pends
  inter+de+pend+
ing
  inter+de+pend+
ed
inter+de+pend+
ence
inter+de+pend+
ent
inter+de+pend+
ent+ly
inter+dict
  inter+dicts
  inter+dicts
  inter+dict+ing
  inter+dict+ed
inter+dic+tion
  inter+dic+tions
inter+dic+tive
inter+dic+tive+ly
inter+dic+tor
  inter+dic+tors
inter+dic+tory
inter+digi+tal
inter+digi+tal+ly
inter+digi+tate
  inter+digi+tates
  inter+digi+tat+
ing
  inter+digi+tat+
ed
inter+dis+ci+pli+
nary
in+ter+est
  in+ter+ests
  in+ter+ests
  in+ter+est+ing
  in+ter+est+ed
  in+ter+est+ed
  in+ter+est+ed+ly
  in+ter+est+ed+
ness
  in+ter+est+ing
  in+ter+est+ing+ly

  in+ter+est+ing+
ness
inter+face
  inter+faces
  inter+faces
  inter+fac+ing
  inter+faced
inter+fa+cial
  inter+fa+cial+ly
inter+fac+ing
  inter+fac+ings
inter+fac+tion+al
inter+fere
  inter+feres
  inter+fer+ing
  inter+fered
inter+fer+ence
  inter+fer+ences
inter+feren+tial
inter+fer+ing
inter+fer+om+
eter
  inter+fer+om+
eters
inter+fero+met+
ric
inter+fero+met+ri+
cal+ly
inter+fer+om+
etry
inter+fer+on
  inter+fer+ons
inter+fi+bril+lar
inter+fi+brous
inter+flow
  inter+flows
  inter+flow+ing
  inter+flowed
inter+fold
  inter+folds
  inter+fold+ing
  inter+fold+ed
inter+fuse
  inter+fuses
  inter+fus+ing
  inter+fused
inter+fu+sion
  inter+fu+sions
inter+ga+lac+tic
inter+gla+cial
inter+gov+ern+
men+tal
inter+group
in+ter+im
inter+ion+ic

in+te+ri+or
in+te+ri+ors
in+te+ri+or+ise
in+te+ri+or+ises
in+te+ri+or+is+
ing
in+te+ri+or+ised
in+te+ri+or+ize
in+te+ri+or+izes
in+te+ri+or+iz+
ing
in+te+ri+or+ized
in+te+ri+or+ly
inter+ject
inter+jects
inter+ject+ing
inter+ject+ed
inter+jec+tions
inter+jec+tion+al
inter+jec+tion+al+
ly
inter+jec+tor
inter+jec+tors
inter+jec+tory
inter+knit
inter+knits
inter+knit+ting
inter+knit+ted
or
inter+knit
inter+lace
inter+laces
inter+lac+ing
inter+laced
In+ter+la+ken
inter+lard
inter+lards
inter+lard+ing
inter+lard+ed
inter+lay
inter+lays
inter+lay+ing
inter+laid
inter+leaf
inter+leaves
inter+leave
inter+leaves
inter+leav+ing
inter+leav+ed
in+ter+leu+kin
inter+library
inter+line
inter+lines
inter+lin+ing

inter+lined
inter+lin+eal
inter+lin+eal+ly
inter+lin+ear
inter+lin+ear+ly
inter+lin+eate
inter+lin+eates
inter+lin+eat+
ing
inter+lin+eat+ed
inter+line+ation
inter+lin+er
inter+lin+ers
inter+lin+ing
inter+lin+ings
inter+link
inter+links
inter+link+ing
inter+linked
inter+lobu+lar
inter+lock
inter+locks
inter+locks
inter+lock+ing
inter+locked
inter+locu+tor
inter+locu+tors
inter+locu+to+ri+
ly
inter+locu+tory
inter+locu+tress
inter+locu+
tresses
inter+locu+trice
inter+locu+tri+
ces
inter+locu+trix
inter+locu+tri+
ces or
inter+locu+trixes
inter+loper
inter+lopers
inter+lude
inter+ludes
inter+mar+riage
inter+mar+
riages
inter+mar+ry
inter+mar+ries
inter+mar+ry+
ing
inter+mar+ried
inter+media+cy
inter+medi+ary
inter+medi+aries

inter+medi+ate
inter+medi+ates
inter+medi+ates
inter+medi+at+
ing
inter+medi+at+
ed
inter+mediate-
acting
inter+medi+ate+
ly
inter+medi+ate+
ness
inter+media+tion
inter+media+tor
inter+media+
tors
in+ter+ment
in+ter+ments
inter+mesh
inter+meshes
inter+mesh+ing
inter+meshed
inter+metal+lic
inter+mez+zo
inter+mez+zos
or
inter+mez+zi
in+ter+mi+nable
in+ter+mi+nable+
ness
in+ter+mi+nably
inter+min+gle
inter+min+gles
inter+min+gling
inter+min+gled
inter+mis+sion
inter+mis+sions
in+ter+mis+sive
inter+mit
inter+mits
inter+mit+ting
inter+mit+ted
inter+mit+tence
inter+mit+ten+cy
inter+mit+tent
inter+mit+tent+ly
inter+mit+tor
inter+mit+tors
inter+mix
inter+mixes
inter+mix+ing
inter+mixed
inter+mix+able
inter+mix+ture

inter+mix+tures
inter+mus+cu+lar
in+tern
in+terns
in+terns
in+tern+ing
in+terned
in+ter+nal
in+ter+nals
in+ter+nali+sa+
tion
in+ter+nali+sa+
tions
in+ter+nal+ise
in+ter+nal+ises
in+ter+nal+is+
ing
in+ter+nal+ised
in+ter+nal+ity
in+ter+nali+za+
tion
in+ter+nali+za+
tions
in+ter+nal+ize
in+ter+nal+izes
in+ter+nal+iz+
ing
in+ter+nal+ized
in+ter+nal+ly
in+ter+nal+ness
inter+na+tion+al
inter+na+tion+
als
Inter+na+tion+al
Inter+na+tion+
als
inter+na+tion+ali+
sa+tion
inter+na+tion+al+
ise
inter+na+tion+al+
ises
inter+na+tion+al+
is+ing
inter+na+tion+al+
ised
inter+na+tion+al+
ism
inter+na+tion+al+
ist
inter+na+tion+al+
ists
inter+na+tion+al+
ity

inter+na+tion+ali+
za+tion
inter+na+tion+al+
ize
inter+na+tion+al+
izes
inter+na+tion+al+
iz+ing
inter+na+tion+al+
ized
inter+na+tion+al+
ly
in+terne
U.S., Canada
in+ternes
inter+necine
in+ternee
in+ternees
in+tern+ist
in+tern+ists
in+tern+ment
in+tern+ments
in+tern+ship
in+tern+ships
inter+nu+clear
inter+office
inter+os+seous
inter+pa+ri+etal
inter+pel+late
inter+pel+lates
inter+pel+lat+
ing
inter+pel+lat+ed
in+ter+pel+la+
tion
in+ter+pel+la+
tions
in+ter+pel+la+tor
in+ter+pel+la+
tors
inter+pen+etrable
inter+pen+etrant
inter+pen+etrate
inter+pen+
etrates
inter+pen+etrat+
ing
inter+pen+etrat+
ed
inter+pen+etra+
tion
inter+pen+etra+
tions
inter+pen+etra+
tive

inter+pen+etra+
tive+ly
inter+plait
inter+plaits
inter+plait+ing
inter+plait+ed
inter+plan+etary
inter+play
inter+plays
inter+plead+er
inter+plead+ers
Inter+pol
inter+po+lar
in+ter+po+late
in+ter+po+lates
in+ter+po+lat+
ing
in+ter+po+lat+
ed
in+ter+po+lat+er
in+ter+po+lat+
ers
in+ter+po+la+tive
in+ter+po+la+tor
in+ter+po+la+
tors
inter+pose
inter+poses
inter+pos+ing
inter+posed
inter+pos+er
inter+pos+ers
inter+po+si+tion
inter+po+si+
tions
in+ter+pret
in+ter+prets
in+ter+pret+ing
in+ter+pret+ed
in+ter+pret+abil+
ity
in+ter+pret+able
in+ter+pret+ably
in+ter+pre+ta+
tion
in+ter+pre+ta+
tions
in+ter+pre+ta+
tion+al
in+ter+pret+er
in+ter+pret+ers
inter+pret+er+
ship
inter+pret+er+
ships

in+ter+pre+tive
inter+pre+tress
inter+pre+
tresses
inter+pro+fes+
sion+al
inter+pro+vin+
cial
inter+ra+cial
inter+re+gion+al
inter+reg+nal
inter+reg+num
inter+reg+nums
or
inter+reg+na
inter+re+late
inter+re+lates
inter+re+lat+ing
inter+re+lat+ed
inter+re+la+tion
inter+re+la+
tions
inter+re+la+tion+
ship
inter+re+la+tion+
ships
inter+re+li+gious
in+ter+ro+gate
in+ter+ro+gates
in+ter+ro+gat+
ing
in+ter+ro+gat+
ed
in+ter+ro+ga+
tion
in+ter+ro+ga+
tions
in+ter+ro+ga+
tion+al
in+ter+roga+tive
in+ter+roga+
tives
in+ter+roga+tive+
ly
in+ter+ro+ga+tor
in+ter+ro+ga+
tors
in+ter+roga+tory
in+ter+roga+
tories
in+ter+rupt
in+ter+rupts
in+ter+rupt+ing
in+ter+rupt+ed
in+ter+rupt+ed

in+ter+rupt+er
in+ter+rupt+ers
in+ter+rupt+ible
in+ter+rup+tion
in+ter+rup+tions
in+ter+rup+tive
in+ter+rup+tive+
ly
in+ter+rup+tor
in+ter+rup+tors
inter+scho+las+
tic
inter+school
inter+sect
inter+sects
inter+sect+ing
inter+sect+ed
inter+sec+tion
inter+sec+tions
inter+sec+tion+al
inter+sep+tal
inter+sex
inter+sexes
inter+sex+ual
inter+sexu+al+ity
inter+sex+ual+ly
inter+so+ci+etal
inter+space
inter+spaces
inter+spaces
inter+spac+ing
inter+spaced
inter+spa+tial
inter+spa+tial+ly
inter+sperse
inter+sperses
inter+spers+ing
inter+spersed
inter+sper+sion
inter+sper+sions
inter+spi+nal
inter+state
inter+stel+lar
in+ter+stice
in+ter+stices
in+ter+sti+tial
in+ter+sti+tials
in+ter+sti+tial+ly
inter+ter+ri+to+
rial
inter+trib+al
inter+trib+al+ly
inter+tri+go
inter+tropi+cal
inter+twine

inter+twines
inter+twin+ing
inter+twined
inter+uni+ver+
sity
inter+urban
in+ter+val
in+ter+vals
inter+val+lic
inter+var+sity
inter+vene
inter+venes
inter+ven+ing
inter+vened
inter+ven+er
inter+ven+ers
inter+ven+or
inter+ven+ors
inter+ven+tion
inter+ven+tions
inter+ven+tion+
ist
inter+ven+tion+
ists
inter+ver+te+bral
inter+ver+tebral
inter+view
inter+views
inter+views
inter+view+ing
inter+viewed
inter+viewee
inter+viewees
inter+view+er
inter+view+ers
inter vi+vos
inter+volve
inter+volves
inter+volv+ing
inter+volved
inter+war
inter+weave
inter+weaves
inter+weav+ing
inter+wove or
inter+weaved
inter+wo+ven
or
inter+wove or
inter+weaved
inter+wind
inter+winds
inter+wind+ing
inter+wound
inter+wreathe

inter+wreathes
inter+wreath+
ing
inter+wreathed
inter+wrought
in+tes+ta+cy
in+tes+ta+cies
in+tes+tate
in+tes+tates
in+tes+ti+nal
in+tes+tine
in+tes+tines
inti
intis
in+ti+fa+da
in+ti+ma+cy
in+ti+ma+cies
in+ti+mate
in+ti+mates
in+ti+mate
in+ti+mates
in+ti+mat+ing
in+ti+mat+ed
in+ti+mate+ly
in+ti+mate+ness
in+ti+mat+er
in+ti+mat+ers
in+ti+ma+tion
in+ti+ma+tions
in+timi+date
in+timi+dates
in+timi+dat+ing
in+timi+dat+ed
in+timi+dat+ing
in+timi+da+tion
in+timi+da+tor
in+timi+da+tors
in+tinc+tion
in+tit+ule
in+tit+ules
in+tit+ul+ing
in+tit+uled
into
in+tol+er+able
in+tol+er+ance
in+tol+er+ant
in+to+nate
in+to+nates
in+to+nat+ing
in+to+nat+ed
in+to+na+tion
in+to+na+tions
in+to+na+tion+al
in+tone
in+tones

in+ton+ing
in+toned
in+ton+er
in+ton+ers
in toto
in+toxi+cable
in+toxi+cant
in+toxi+cants
in+toxi+cate
in+toxi+cates
in+toxi+cat+ing
in+toxi+cat+ed
in+toxi+cat+ing
in+toxi+cat+ing+
ly
in+toxi+ca+tion
in+toxi+ca+tions
in+trac+tabil+ity
in+trac+table
in+trac+table+
ness
in+trac+tably
intra+der+mal
intra+der+mal+ly
in+tra+dos
in+tra+dos or
in+tra+doses
intra+mu+ral
intra+mu+ral+ly
intra+mus+cu+lar
intra+mus+cu+lar+
ly
in+tran+si+gence
in+tran+si+gen+
cy
in+tran+si+gent
in+tran+si+
gents
in+tran+si+gent+
ly
in+tran+si+tive
in+tran+si+tive+
ly
in+tran+si+tive+
ness
in+tran+si+tiv+ity
intra+pre+neur
intra+pre+neurs
intra+uter+ine
intra+venous
intra+venous+ly
in-tray
in-trays
in+trench
in+trenches

in+trench+ing
in+trenched
in+trench+er
in+trench+ers
in+trench+ment
in+trep+id
in+tre+pid+ity
in+trep+id+ly
in+tri+ca+cy
in+tri+ca+cies
in+tri+cate
in+tri+cate+ly
in+tri+cate+ness
in+trigue
in+trigues
in+trigues
in+tri+guing
in+trigued
in+tri+guer
in+tri+guers
in+tri+guing+ly
in+trin+sic
in+trin+si+cal
in+trin+si+cal+ly
in+tro
in+tros
intro+duce
intro+duces
intro+duc+ing
intro+duced
intro+duc+er
intro+duc+ers
intro+duc+ible
intro+duc+tion
intro+duc+tions
intro+duc+tory
in+troit
in+troits
in+troi+tal
intro+mis+sible
intro+mis+sion
intro+mis+sions
intro+mit
intro+mits
intro+mit+ting
intro+mit+ted
intro+mit+tent
intro+spec+tion
intrc+spec+
tions
intro+spec+tive
intro+spec+tive+
ly
intro+ver+sion
intro+ver+sions

intro+ver+sive
intro+vert
 intro+verts
 intro+verts
 intro+vert+ing
 intro+vert+ed
intro+ver+tive
in+trude
 in+trudes
 in+trud+ing
 in+trud+ed
in+trud+er
 in+trud+ers
in+tru+sion
 in+tru+sions
 in+tru+sion al
in+tru+sive
in+tru+sive+ly
in+tru+sive+ness
in+trust
 in+trusts
 in+trust+ing
 in+trust+ed
in+tu+bate
 in+tu+bates
 in+tu+bat+ing
 in+tu+bat+ed
in+tu+ba+tion
 in+tu+ba+tions
in+tu+it
 in+tu+its
 in+tu+it+ing
 in+tu+it+ed
in+tu+it+able
in+tui+tion
 in+tui+tions
in+tui+tion+al
in+tui+tion+al+
 ism
in+tui+tion+al+ist
 in+tui+tion+al+
 ists
in+tui+tion+al+ly
in+tui+tion+ism
in+tui+tion+ist
 in+tui+tion+ists
in+tui+tive
in+tui+tive+ly
in+tui+tive+ness
in+tu+mesce
 in+tu+mesces
 in+tu+mesc+ing
 in+tu+mesced
in+tu+mes+
 cence

in+tu+mes+
 cences
in+tus+sus+cep+
 tion
in+tus+sus+cep+
 tions
Inu+it
 Inu+it *or*
 Inu+its
Inukti+tut
in+unc+tion
 in+unc+tions
in+un+dant
in+un+date
 in+un+dates
 in+un+dat+ing
 in+un+dat+ed
in+un+da+tion
 in+un+da+tions
in+un+da+tor
 in+un+da+tors
in+un+da+tory
in+ure
 in+ures
 in+ur+ing
 in+ured
in+ure+ment
 in+ure+ments
in ut+ero
in va+cuo
in+vad+able
in+vade
 in+vades
 in+vad+ing
 in+vad+ed
in+vad+er
 in+vad+ers
in+vagi+nable
in+vagi+nate
 in+vagi+nates
 in+vagi+nat+ing
 in+vagi+nat+ed
in+vagi+na+tion
 in+vagi+na+
 tions
in+va+lid
 in+va+lids
 in+va+lids
 in+va+lid+ing
 in+va+lid+ed
in+val+id
 not valid
in+vali+date
 in+vali+dates
 in+vali+dat+ing

 in+vali+dat+ed
in+vali+da+tion
 in+vali+da+tions
in+vali+da+tor
 in+vali+da+tors
in+va+lid+ity
in+val+id+ly
in+val+id+ness
in+valu+able
in+valu+able+
 ness
in+valu+ably
In+var
 Trademark
in+vari+abil+ity
in+vari+able
 in+vari+ables
in+vari+ably
in+vari+ance
in+vari+an+cy
in+vari+ant
 in+vari+ants
in+va+sion
 in+va+sions
in+va+sive
in+vec+tive
 in+vec+tives
in+vec+tive+ly
in+vec+tive+ness
in+veigh
 in+veighs
 in+veigh+ing
 in+veighed
in+veigh+er
 in+veigh+ers
in+vei+gle
 in+vei+gles
 in+vei+gling
 in+vei+gled
in+vei+gle+ment
in+vei+gler
 in+vei+glers
in+vent
 in+vents
 in+vent+ing
 in+vent+ed
in+vent+able
in+ven+tion
 in+ven+tions
in+ven+tive
in+ven+tive+ly
in+ven+tive+ness
in+ven+tor
 in+ven+tors

in+ven+to+ri+
 able
in+ven+to+ri+al
in+ven+to+ri+al+
 ly
in+ven+tory
 in+ven+tories
 in+ven+tories
 in+ven+tory+ing
 in+ven+toried
in+ven+tress
in+ve+rac+ity
 in+ve+rac+ities
In+ver+ary
In+ver+car+gill
In+ver+ness
Inverness-shire
in+verse
 in+verses
in+verse+ly
in+ver+sion
 in+ver+sions
in+ver+sive
in+vert
 in+verts
 in+verts
 in+vert+ing
 in+vert+ed
in+vert+ase
in+ver+tebrate
 in+ver+tebrates
in+vert+er
 in+vert+ers
in+vert+ibil+ity
in+vert+ible
in+ver+tor
 in+ver+tors
in+vest
 in+vests
 in+vest+ing
 in+vest+ed
in+vest+able
in+vest+ible
in+ves+ti+gate
 in+ves+ti+gates
 in+ves+ti+gat+
 ing
 in+ves+ti+gat+
 ed
in+ves+ti+ga+
 tion
 in+ves+ti+ga+
 tions
in+ves+ti+gative
in+ves+ti+ga+tor

in+ves+ti+ga+
  tors
in+ves+ti+ga+
  tory
in+ves+ti+tive
in+ves+ti+ture
in+ves+ti+tures
in+vest+ment
in+vest+ments
in+ves+tor
in+ves+tors
in+vet+era+cy
in+vet+er+ate
in+vet+er+ate+ly
in+vidi+ous
in+vidi+ous+ly
in+vidi+ous+ness
in+vigi+late
in+vigi+lates
in+vigi+lat+ing
in+vigi+lat+ed
in+vigi+la+tion
in+vigi+la+tions
in+vigi+la+tor
in+vigi+la+tors
in+vig+or+ate
in+vig+or+ates
in+vig+or+at+
  ing
in+vig+or+at+ed
in+vig+ora+tion
in+vig+ora+tive
in+vig+ora+tor
in+vig+ora+tors
in+vin+cibil+ity
in+vin+cible
in+vin+cible+
  ness
in+vin+cibly
in+vio+labil+ity
in+vio+lable
in+vio+lably
in+vio+la+cy
in+vio+late
in+vio+late+ly
in+vio+late+ness
in+vis+ibil+ity
in+vis+ible
in+vis+ibles
in+vis+ible+ness
in+vis+ibly
in+vi+ta+tion
in+vi+ta+tions
in+vite
  in+vites

in+vites
in+vit+ing
in+vit+ed
in+vit+er
  in+vit+ers
in+vit+ing
in+vit+ing+ness
in vi+tro
in vivo
in+vo+cable
in+vo+ca+tion
in+vo+ca+tions
in+vo+ca+tion+al
in+voca+tory
in+voice
in+voices
in+voices
in+voic+ing
in+voiced
in+voke
in+vokes
in+vok+ing
in+voked
in+vok+er
in+vok+ers
in+vo+lu+cral
in+vo+lu+crate
in+vo+lu+cre
in+vo+lu+cres
in+vo+lu+crum
in+vo+lu+crums
in+vol+un+tari+ly
in+vol+un+tari+
  ness
in+vol+un+tary
in+vo+lute
in+vo+lutes
in+vo+lutes
in+vo+lut+ing
in+vo+lut+ed
in+vo+lut+ed+ly
in+vo+lute+ly
in+vo+lu+tion
in+vo+lu+tion+al
in+volve
in+volves
in+volv+ing
in+volved
in+volve+ment
in+volve+ments
in+volv+er
in+volv+ers
in+vul+ner+abil+
  ity

in+vul+ner+able
in+vul+ner+able+
  ness
in+vul+ner+ably
in+ward
in+wards
in+ward+ly
in+ward+ness
in+wards
in+weave
in+weaves
in+weav+ing
in+wove or
in+weaved
in+wo+ven or
in+weaved
in+wrap
in+wraps
in+wrap+ping
in+wrapped
in+wrought
in+ya+la
in+ya+la or
in+ya+las
Io
iod+ic
iodide
iodides
iodine
iodi+sa+tion
iodi+sa+tions
iodise
iodises
iodis+ing
iodised
iodis+er
iodis+ers
iodi+za+tion
iodi+za+tions
iodize
iodizes
iodiz+ing
iodized
iodiz+er
iodiz+ers
iodo+form
iodop+sin
ion
ions
Io+na
Ionesco
Ionia
Ionian
Ionians
ion+ic

Ion+ic
Ion+ics
ion+is+able
ioni+sa+tion
ioni+sa+tions
ion+ise
ion+ises
ion+is+ing
ion+ised
ion+is+er
ion+is+ers
ionium
ion+iz+able
ioni+za+tion
ioni+za+tions
ion+ize
ion+izes
ion+iz+ing
ion+ized
ion+iz+er
ion+iz+ers
iono+sphere
iono+spher+ic
iota
iotas
IOU
IOUs
Iowa
Iowan
Iowans
ip+ecac
ip+ecacs
ip+ecacu+an+ha
ip+ecacu+an+
  has
Iphigenia
I-pin
ipo+moea
ipo+moeas
ippon
ippons
ipse dix+it
ipso fac+to
Ips+wich
Iqbal
Iqui+tos
ira+de
ira+des
Ira+kli+on
Iran
Ira+nian
Ira+nians
Iraq
Ira+qi
Ira+qis

iras+cibil+ity
iras+cible
iras+cible+ness
iras+cibly
irate
irate+ly
Ir+bil
ire
ire+ful
ire+ful+ness
Ire+land
place name
Ireland
surname
iren+ic
ireni+cal
ireni+cal+ly
Ireton
Iri+an Jaya
iri+da+ceous
iri+des+cence
  iri+des+cences
iri+des+cent
iri+des+cent+ly
irid+ium
iris
  irises *or*
  iri+des
Iris
Irish
Irish+man
  Irish+men
Irish+woman
  Irish+women
irit+ic
iri+tis
irk
  irks
  irk+ing
  irked
irk+some
irk+some+ly
irk+some+ness
Ir+kutsk
iron
  irons
  irons
  iron+ing
  ironed
iron+bark
  iron+barks
iron+bound
iron+clad
  iron+clads
iron+er

iron+ers
iron+ic
ironi+cal
ironi+cal+ly
ironi+cal+ness
iron+ing
  iron+ings
iron+like
iron+master
  iron+masters
iron+monger
  iron+mongers
iron+mongery
irons
Irons
Iron+side
ironsides
ironsides
iron+stone
  iron+stones
iron+ware
iron+wood
  iron+woods
iron+work
  iron+works
  iron+works
iro+ny
iro+nies
irony
of or like iron
Iro+quoi+an
Iro+quois
Iro+quois
ir+ra+di+ance
  ir+ra+di+ances
ir+ra+di+ate
  ir+ra+di+ates
  ir+ra+di+at+ing
  ir+ra+di+at+ed
ir+ra+dia+tion
  ir+ra+dia+tions
ir+ra+dia+tive
ir+ra+dia+tor
  ir+ra+dia+tors
ir+ra+tion+al
ir+ra+tion+al+ity
  ir+ra+tion+al+
    ities
ir+ra+tion+al+ly
Ir+ra+wad+dy
ir+re+claim+abil+
  ity
ir+re+claim+able
ir+re+claim+able+
  ness

ir+re+claim+ably
ir+rec+on+cil+
  abil+ity
ir+rec+on+cil+
  able
ir+rec+on+cil+
  ables
ir+rec+on+cil+
  able+ness
ir+rec+on+cil+
  ably
ir+re+cov+er+
  able
ir+re+cov+er+
  able+ness
ir+re+cov+er+
  ably
ir+re+cu+sable
ir+re+deem+abil+
  ity
ir+re+deem+able
ir+re+deem+able+
  ness
ir+re+deem+ably
ir+re+den+tism
  ir+re+den+tisms
ir+re+den+tist
  ir+re+den+tists
ir+re+duc+ibil+ity
ir+re+duc+ible
ir+re+duc+ibly
ir+ref+ra+gabil+
  ity
ir+ref+ra+gable
ir+ref+ra+gable+
  ness
ir+ref+ra+gably
ir+re+fran+gibil+
  ity
ir+re+fran+gible
ir+re+fran+gible+
  ness
ir+re+fran+gibly
ir+refu+tabil+ity
ir+refu+table
ir+refu+tably
ir+regu+lar
  ir+regu+lars
ir+regu+lar+ity
  ir+regu+lar+ities
ir+regu+lar+ly
ir+rel+evance
  ir+rel+evances
ir+rel+evan+cy
ir+rel+evan+cies

ir+rel+evant
ir+rel+evant+ly
ir+re+li+gion
ir+re+li+gion+ist
  ir+re+li+gion+
    ists
ir+re+li+gious
ir+re+li+gious+ly
ir+re+li+gious+
  ness
ir+re+medi+able
ir+re+medi+able+
  ness
ir+re+medi+ably
ir+re+mis+sibil+
  ity
ir+re+mis+sible
ir+re+mis+sible+
  ness
ir+re+mis+sibly
ir+re+mov+abil+
  ity
ir+re+mov+able
ir+re+mov+ably
ir+repa+rabil+ity
ir+repa+rable
ir+repa+rable+
  ness
ir+repa+rably
ir+re+place+able
ir+re+place+ably
ir+re+press+ibil+
  ity
ir+re+press+ible
ir+re+press+ible+
  ness
ir+re+press+ibly
ir+re+proach+abil+
  ity
ir+re+proach+
  able
ir+re+proach+
  able+ness
ir+re+proach+
  ably
ir+re+sist+ibil+ity
ir+re+sist+ible
ir+re+sist+ible+
  ness
ir+re+sist+ibly
ir+reso+lute
ir+reso+lute+ly
ir+reso+lute+
  ness
ir+reso+lu+tion

ir+reso+lu+tions
ir+re+spec+tive
ir+re+spec+tive+
ly
ir+re+spon+sibil+
ity
ir+re+spon+sible
ir+re+spon+sible+
ness
ir+re+spon+sibly
ir+re+spon+sive
ir+re+spon+sive+
ly
ir+re+spon+sive+
ness
ir+re+triev+abil+
ity
ir+re+triev+able
ir+re+triev+ably
ir+rev+er+ence
ir+rev+er+ences
ir+rev+er+ent
ir+rev+eren+tial
ir+rev+er+ent+ly
ir+re+vers+ibil+
ity
ir+re+vers+ible
ir+re+vers+ible+
ness
ir+re+vers+ibly
ir+revo+cabil+ity
ir+revo+cable
ir+revo+cable+
ness
ir+revo+cably
ir+ri+gable
ir+ri+gate
ir+ri+gates
ir+ri+gat+ing
ir+ri+gat+ed
ir+ri+ga+tion
ir+ri+ga+tions
ir+ri+ga+tive
ir+ri+ga+tor
ir+ri+ga+tors
ir+ri+tabil+ity
ir+ri+table
ir+ri+table+ness
ir+ri+tably
ir+ri+tan+cy
ir+ri+tant
ir+ri+tants
ir+ri+tate
ir+ri+tates
ir+ri+tat+ing

ir+ri+tat+ed
ir+ri+ta+tion
ir+ri+ta+tions
ir+ri+ta+tive
ir+ri+ta+tor
ir+ri+ta+tors
ir+rupt
ir+rupts
ir+rupt+ing
ir+rupt+ed
ir+rup+tion
ir+rup+tions
ir+rup+tive
Ir+tish
Ir+tysh
Ir+vine
Irving
is
Isaac
Isa+bel+la
colour
Isabella
name
isa+gog+ics
Isaiah
is+al+lo+bar
is+al+lo+bars
Isar
isa+tin
isa+tins
isa+tine
isa+tines
isa+tin+ic
Isau+ria
Isau+rian
Isau+rians
Iscariot
is+chae+mia
is+chae+mias
is+chaem+ic
is+che+mia
is+che+mias
is+chem+ic
Is+chia
is+chial
is+chium
is+chia
is+en+trop+ic
Isère
Iseult
Is+fa+han
Isherwood
Ishiguro
Ishmael
Ish+tar

isin+glass
Isis
Is+ken+de+run
Is+lam
Is+lama+bad
Is+lam+ic
Is+lami+sa+tion
Is+lam+ise
Is+lam+ises
Is+lam+is+ing
Is+lam+ised
Is+lami+za+tion
Is+lam+ize
Is+lam+izes
Is+lam+iz+ing
Is+lam+ized
is+land
is+lands
is+lands
is+land+ing
is+land+ed
is+land+er
is+land+ers
island-like
Is+lay
isle
isles
is+let
is+lets
Is+ling+ton
ism
isms
Is+mai+li
Is+mai+lis
Isma'ili
Isma'ilis
Is+mai+lia
Ismail Pasha
isn't
iso+bar
iso+bars
iso+bar+ic
iso+bar+ism
iso+cheim
iso+cheims
iso+chei+mal
iso+chi+mal
iso+chime
iso+chimes
isoch+ro+nal
isoch+ro+nal+ly
isoch+ro+nism
isoch+ro+nous
isoch+ro+nous+
ly

iso+cli+nal
iso+cli+nals
iso+cline
iso+clines
iso+clin+ic
iso+clin+ics
Isocrates
iso+dy+nam+ic
iso+geo+therm
iso+geo+therms
iso+geo+ther+
mal
iso+geo+ther+
mic
iso+gloss
iso+glosses
iso+glos+sal
iso+glot+tic
isogo+nal
isogo+nals
iso+gon+ic
iso+gon+ics
iso+hel
iso+hels
iso+hy+et
iso+hy+ets
iso+labil+ity
iso+lable
iso+late
iso+lates
iso+lates
iso+lat+ing
iso+lat+ed
iso+la+tion
iso+la+tion+ism
iso+la+tion+ist
iso+la+tion+ists
iso+la+tor
iso+la+tors
Isolde
iso+mer
iso+mers
iso+mer+ic
isom+er+ism
isom+er+isms
isom+er+ous
iso+met+ric
iso+met+rics
iso+met+ri+cal+
ly
iso+met+rics
iso+morph
iso+morphs
iso+mor+phic
iso+mor+phism

iso+mor+phous
iso+pleth
 iso+pleths
iso+pod
 iso+pods
isopo+dan
iso+prene
isos+celes
iso+seis+mal
 iso+seis+mals
isos+ta+sy
iso+stat+ic
isoth+er+al
iso+there
 iso+theres
iso+therm
 iso+therms
iso+ther+mal
 iso+ther+mals
iso+ther+mal+ly
iso+ton+ic
iso+to+nic+ity
iso+tope
 iso+topes
iso+top+ic
iso+topi+cal+ly
isoto+py
 isoto+pies
iso+trop+ic
iso+tropi+cal+ly
isot+ro+pous
isot+ro+py
I-spy
Is+ra+el
Is+rae+li
 Is+rae+lis or
 Is+rae+li
 Is+rael+ite
 Is+rael+ites
is+su+able
is+su+ance
 is+su+ances
is+sue
 is+sues
 is+sues
 is+su+ing

is+sued
is+su+er
 is+su+ers
Is+tan+bul
isth+mian
isth+moid
isth+mus
 isth+muses or
 isth+mi
is+tle
Is+tria
Is+trian
 Is+trians
it
 its
Ita+lia
Ital+ian
 Ital+ians
Ital+ian+ate
Ital+ian+esque
ital+ic
 ital+ics
Ital+ic
itali+ci+sa+tion
 itali+ci+sa+tions
itali+cise
 itali+cises
 itali+cis+ing
 itali+cised
itali+ci+za+tion
 itali+ci+za+tions
itali+cize
 itali+cizes
 itali+ciz+ing
 itali+cized
Ita+ly
itch
 itches
 itches
 itch+ing
 itched
itchi+ness
itchy
 itchi+er
 itchi+est
item

items
items
item+ing
itemed
itemi+sa+tion
 itemi+sa+tions
item+ise
 item+ises
 item+is+ing
 item+ised
item+is+er
 item+is+ers
itemi+za+tion
 itemi+za+tions
item+ize
 item+izes
 item+iz+ing
 item+ized
item+iz+er
 item+iz+ers
Ité+nez
it+er+ant
it+er+ate
 it+er+ates
 it+er+at+ing
 it+er+at+ed
it+era+tion
 it+era+tions
it+era+tive
Itha+ca
Itha+can
 Itha+cans
Ithunn
itin+era+cy
 itin+era+cies
itin+er+an+cy
 itin+er+an+cies
itin+er+ant
 itin+er+ants
itin+er+ant+ly
itin+er+ary
 itin+er+aries
itin+er+ate
 itin+er+ates
 itin+er+at+ing
 itin+er+at+ed

itin+era+tion
 itin+era+tions
it'll
Ito
its
belonging to it
it's
it is
it+self
itsy-bitsy
itty-bitty
Iulus
Iva+no+vo
I've
ivied
Ivi+za
ivo+ries
ivo+ry
 ivo+ries
Ivory
surname
Ivo+ry Coast
ivory-like
ivo+ry tow+er
 ivo+ry tow+ers
ivory-towered
ivo+ry+wood
 ivo+ry+woods
ivy
ivies
ivy-like
ixia
 ixias
Ixion
Ixio+nian
Ix+tac+ci+huatl
ix+tle
ix+tle
 ix+tles
izard
 izards
Izhevsk
Iz+mir
Iz+mit
Iz+nik
Iz+tac+ci+huatl

J

j
j's
J
  Js *or*
  J's
jab
  jabs
  jabs
jab+bing
jabbed
Jab+al+pur
jab+ber
  jab+bers
  jab+bers
jab+ber+ing
jab+bered
jab+ber+wocky
jab+ber+
  wockies
Jabir ibn Hayyan
jabi+ru
  jabi+rus
ja+bot
  ja+bots
ja+ça+na
  ja+ça+nas
jaca+ran+da
  jaca+ran+das
ja+cinth
  ja+cinths
jack
  jacks
  jacks
  jack+ing
  jacked
jack+al
  jack+als
jacka+napes
jacka+roo
  jacka+roos
jack+ass
  jack+asses
jack+boot
  jack+boots
  jack+boot+ed

jack+daw
  jack+daws
jack+eroo
  jack+eroos
jack+et
  jack+ets
  jack+ets
jack+et+ing
jack+et+ed
  jack+et+ed
Jack+ie
  Jack+ies
jack-in-office
  jacks-in-office
jack-in-the-box
  jack-in-the-
    boxes *or*
  jacks-in-the-box
jack+knife
  jack+knives
  jack+knifes
jack+knif+ing
jack+knifed
Jacklin
jack of all trades
  jacks of all
    trades
jack-o'-lantern
  jack-o'-lanterns
jack+pot
  jack+pots
Jack Russell
  Jack Russells
  jacks
jack+sie
  jack+sies
jack+snipe
  jack+snipe *or*
  jack+snipes
Jack+son
  place name
Jackson
  surname
Jack+son+ville
jack+straws

jack+sy
  jack+sies
Jack Tar
  Jack Tars
Jacky
  Jack+ies
Jacob
Jaco+bean
Jacobi
Jaco+bin
  Jaco+bins
Jaco+bin+ic
Jaco+bini+cal
Jaco+bin+ism
Jaco+bite
  Jaco+bites
Jaco+bit+ic
Jacobsen
jaco+net
  jaco+nets
Jac+quard
  Jac+quards
jac+ta+tion
  jac+ta+tions
jac+ti+ta+tion
  jac+ti+ta+tions
Ja+cuz+zi
  Trademark
  Ja+cuz+zis
jade
  jades
  jades
  jad+ing
  jad+ed
jad+ed
  jad+ed+ly
jad+ed+ness
jade+ite
  jade+ites
jad+ish
Ja+dot+ville
j'adoube
Jael
Jaén
Jaf+fa

Jaf+fas
Jaff+na
jag
  jags
  jags
jag+ging
jagged
jag+ged
jag+ged+ly
Jagger
jag+gy
  jag+gi+er
  jag+gi+est
jagu+ar
  jagu+ars
Jah+vism
Jah+vis+tic
Jah+wism
Jah+wis+tic
jai alai
jail
  jails
  jails
jail+ing
jailed
jail+bird
  jail+birds
jail+break
  jail+breaks
jail+er
  jail+ers
jail+or
  jail+ors
Jain
  Jains
Jai+na
  Jai+nas
Jain+ism
Jain+ist
  Jain+ists
Jai+pur
Ja+kar+ta
jake
Jal+an+dhar
jal+ap

jal+aps
Ja+la+pa
ja+lap+ic
Ja+lis+co
jal+op
jal+ops
ja+lop+py
ja+lop+pies
ja+lopy
ja+lopies
jalou+sie
jalou+sies
jam
jams
jams
jam+ming
jammed
Ja+mai+ca
Ja+mai+can
Ja+mai+cans
jamb
jambs
jambe
jambes
Jam+bi
jam+bo+ree
jam+bo+rees
James
Jameson
James+town
jam+mer
jam+mers
Jam+mu
jam+my
jam+mi+er
jam+mi+est
Jam+na+gar
jam-packed
Jam+shed+pur
Jamshid
Jamshyd
Janáček
Jan+dal
Trademark
Jan+dals
Janet
jan+gle
jan+gles
jan+gles
jan+gling
jan+gled
jan+gler
jan+glers
Ja+nicu+lum
Ja+ni+na

jan+is+sary
jan+is+saries
jani+tor
jani+tors
jani+to+ri+al
jani+zary
jani+zaries
Jan May+en
Jansen
Jan+sen+ism
Jan+sen+ist
Jan+sen+ists
Jan+sen+is+tic
jan+sky
jan+skys
Janu+ary
Janu+aries
Janus
Roman god
Ja+nus
moon of Saturn
ja+pan
ja+pans
ja+pans
ja+pan+ning
ja+panned
Ja+pan
Japa+nese
Japa+nese
jape
japes
japes
jap+ing
japed
jap+er
jap+ers
jap+ery
Japheth
ja+poni+ca
ja+poni+cas
Ja+pu+rá
Jaques-Dalcroze
jar
jars
jars
jar+ring
jarred
jar+di+nière
jar+di+nières
jar+gon
jar+gons
jarl
jarls
jarl+dom
jarl+doms

jar+rah
jar+rahs
Jarrett
jar+ring
jar+ring+ly
Jar+row
Jarry
Jaruzelski
jas+mine
jas+mines
Jason
jas+pé
jas+per
jas+pers
Jaspers
Jas+sy
jato
jatos
jaun+dice
jaun+dices
jaun+dices
jaun+dic+ing
jaun+diced
jaunt
jaunts
jaunts
jaunt+ing
jaunt+ed
jaun+ti+ly
jaun+ti+ness
jaun+ty
jaun+ti+er
jaun+ti+est
Jaurès
Java
Ja+van
Ja+vans
Java+nese
Java+nese
Ja+va+ri
Ja+va+ry
jave+lin
jave+lins
jaw
jaws
jaws
jaw+ing
jawed
Jawara
jaw+bone
jaw+bones
jaw+breaker
jaw+breakers
jaw+breaking
Jax+ar+tes

jay
jays
Jay
Ja+ya
Ja+ya+pu+ra
Jayawardene
Jay+cee
Jay+cees
jay+walk
jay+walks
jay+walk+ing
jay+walked
jay+walk+er
jay+walk+ers
jay+walk+ing
jazz
jazzes
jazz+ing
jazzed
jazzi+ly
jazzi+ness
jazzy
jazzi+er
jazzi+est
JCB
Trademark
JCBs
jeal+ous
jeal+ous+ly
jeal+ousy
jeal+ousies
jean
Jean
Jean de Meung
Jeanne d'Arc
jeans
Jeans
Jeb+el Musa
Jed+da
Jeep
Trademark
Jeeps
jee+pers
jee+pers cree+
 pers
jeer
jeers
jeers
jeer+ing
jeered
jeer+er
jeer+ers
jeer+ing
jeer+ings
jeer+ing+ly

Jefferson
surname
Jef+fer+son
place name
Jef+fer+so+nian
Jef+fer+so+
  nians
Jeffrey
Jeffreys
je+had
je+hads
Je+hol
Jehoshaphat
Je+ho+vah
Jehu
je+june
je+june+ly
je+june+ness
je+ju+num
je+ju+nums
Jekyll and Hyde
jell
  jells
  jel+ling
  jelled
jel+laba
jel+labas
jel+lab+ah
  jel+lab+ahs
Jellicoe
jel+lied
jel+li+fi+ca+tion
  jel+li+fi+ca+
    tions
jel+li+fy
jel+li+fies
jel+li+fy+ing
jel+li+fied
jel+ly
  jel+lies
  jel+lies
  jel+ly+ing
  jel+lied
jelly+fish
  jelly+fish *or*
  jelly+fishes
jelly-like
Je+mappes
jem+my
  jem+mies
  jem+mies
  jem+my+ing
  jem+mied
Jena
Jenghis Khan

Jenkins
Jenner
jen+net
  jen+nets
jen+ny
  jen+nies
Jensen
jeop+ard+ise
  jeop+ard+ises
  jeop+ard+is+ing
  jeop+ard+ised
jeop+ard+ize
  jeop+ard+izes
  jeop+ard+iz+ing
  jeop+ard+ized
jeop+ardy
Jephthah
je+quir+ity
  je+quir+ities
jer+bil
  jer+bils
jer+boa
  jer+boas
jer+emi+ad
  jer+emi+ads
Jeremiah
  Jeremiahs
jere+pi+go
  jere+pi+gos
Je+rez
Jeri+cho
jerk
  jerks
  jerks
  jerk+ing
  jerked
jerk+er
  jerk+ers
jerki+ly
jer+kin
  jer+kins
jerki+ness
jerky
  jerki+er
  jerki+est
jero+bo+am
  jero+bo+ams
Jeroboam
Jerome
jer+ry
  jer+ries
Jer+ry
  Jer+ries
jerry-build
  jerry-builds

jerry-building
jerry-built
jerry-builder
jerry-builders
jer+sey
  jer+seys
Jer+sey
Je+ru+sa+lem
Jespersen
jess
  jesses
jes+sa+mine
  jes+sa+mines
Jesse
jessed
Jes+sel+ton
jes+sie
  jes+sies
jest
  jests
  jests
jest+ing
jest+ed
jest+er
  jest+ers
Jesu
Jesu+it
  Jesu+its
Jesu+iti+cal
Jesus
jet
  jets
  jets
jet+ting
jet+ted
jeté
  jetés
Jethro
jet-propelled
jet+sam
jet-setter
  jet-setters
jet-setting
jet-ski
  jet-skis
jet-skiing
jet-skied *or*
jet-ski'd
jet ski
  jet skis
jet+ti+son
  jet+ti+sons
  jet+ti+son+ing
  jet+ti+soned
jet+ton

jet+tons
jet+ty
  jet+ties
jeu d'es+prit
jeux d'es+prit
Jevons
Jew
  Jews
  Jews
Jew+ing
Jewed
jew+el
  jew+els
  jew+els
jew+el+ling *or*
jew+el+ing
  U.S.
jew+elled *or*
jew+eled
  U.S.
jew+el+er
  U.S.
jew+el+ers
jewel+fish
  jewel+fish *or*
  jewel+fishes
jew+el+ler
  jew+el+lers
jew+el+lery
jew+el+ry
  U.S.
Jew+ess
  Jew+esses
jew+fish
  jew+fish *or*
  jew+fishes
Jew+ish
Jew+ish+ly
Jew+ish+ness
Jew+ry
  Jew+ries
jew's-ear
  jew's-ears
jew's-harp
  jew's-harps
Jezebel
  Jezebels
Jez+re+el
Jez+re+el+ite
  Jez+re+el+ites
Jhabvala
Jhan+si
Jhe+lum
Jiang Qing
Jiang+su

Jiang+xi
Jia+zhou
jib
 jibs
 jibs
 jib+bing
 jibbed
jib+ber
 jib+bers
jibe
 jibes
 jibes
 jib+ing
 jibed
Ji+bouti
Ji+bu+ti
Jid+da
jiff
 jiffs
jif+fy
 jif+fies
jig
 jigs
 jigs
 jig+ging
 jigged
jig+ger
 jig+gers
jig+gered
jigger+mast
 jigger+masts
jiggery-pokery
jig+gle
 jig+gles
 jig+gles
 jig+gling
 jig+gled
jig+gly
 jig+gli+er
 jig+gli+est
jig+saw
 jig+saws
ji+had
 ji+hads
Ji+lin
Ji+long
jilt
 jilts
 jilts
 jilt+ing
 jilt+ed
jim crow
 jim crows
jim-crowism
Jiménez

Jiménez de
 Cisneros
jim+jams
jim+my
 jim+mies
 jim+mies
jim+my+ing
jim+mied
Ji+nan
Jing+de+zhen
Jinghis Khan
jin+gle
 jin+gles
 jin+gles
 jin+gling
 jin+gled
jin+gly
 jin+gli+er
 jin+gli+est
jin+go
 jin+goes
 jin+go+ism
 jin+go+ist
 jin+go+ists
 jin+go+is+tic
Jin+ja
Jin+jiang
jink
 jinks
 jinks
 jink+ing
 jinked
jin+ker
 jin+kers
Jinnah
jin+nee
 jinn
jin+ni
 jinn
jin+rick+sha
 jin+rick+shas
 jin+rick+shaw
 jin+rick+shaws
 jin+riki+sha
 jin+riki+shas
jinx
 jinxes
 jinxes
 jinx+ing
 jinxed
Jin+zhou
jit+ter
 jit+ters
 jit+ters
 jit+ter+ing

jit+tered
jitter+bug
 jitter+bugs
 jitter+bugs
 jitter+bug+ging
 jitter+bugged
jit+teri+ness
jit+tery
jiu+jit+su
jiu+jut+su
jive
 jives
 jives
 jiv+ing
 jived
jiv+er
 jiv+ers
Joab
Joachim
Joan
Joan of Arc
job
 jobs
 jobs
 job+bing
 jobbed
Job
 Jobs
job+ber
 job+bers
job+bery
job+bing
Job+centre
 Job+centres
job+less
jobs+worth
 jobs+worths
Jocasta
Jochum
jock
 jocks
Jock
 Jocks
jock+ey
 jock+eys
 jock+eys
 jock+ey+ing
 jock+eyed
jock+strap
 jock+straps
jo+cose
jo+cose+ly
jo+cos+ity
 jo+cos+ities
jocu+lar

jocu+lar+ity
 jocu+lar+ities
jocu+lar+ly
joc+und
jo+cun+dity
 jo+cun+dities
joc+und+ly
Jodh+pur
Jodh+pu+ri
jodh+purs
Jodl
Joe Blake
 Joe Blakes
Joe Bloggs
Joel
Joe Pub+lic
joey
 joeys
Joffre
jog
 jogs
 jogs
 jog+ging
 jogged
jog+ger
 jog+gers
jog+ging
jog+gle
 jog+gles
 jog+gles
 jog+gling
 jog+gled
jog+gler
 jog+glers
Jog+ja+kar+ta
Jo+han+nes+
 burg
john
 johns
John
John Barley+corn
John Bull
 John Bulls
John Dory
 John Dories
John Hop
 John Hops
john+ny
 john+nies
John+ny Ca+nuck
 John+ny Ca+
 nucks
Johnny-come-
 lately

Johnny-come-
latelies *or*
Johnnies-come-
lately
John o'Groat's
Johns
Johnson
John+so+nian
John Thomas
John Thomases
Jo+hore
Jo+hore Bah+ru
joie de vi+vre
join
joins
joins
join+ing
joined
join+der
join+ders
join+er
join+ers
join+ery
joint
joints
joints
joint+ing
joint+ed
joint+ed
joint+ly
join+ture
join+tures
Joinville
joist
joists
jo+jo+ba
jo+jo+bas
joke
jokes
jokes
jok+ing
joked
jok+er
jok+ers
jok+ey
joki+er
joki+est
Jok+ja+kar+ta
joky
joki+er
joki+est
Joliot-Curie
jol+li+fi+ca+tion
jol+li+fi+ca+
tions

jol+li+fy
jol+li+fies
jol+li+fy+ing
jol+li+fied
jol+li+ness
jol+lity
jol+lities
jol+ly
jol+lies
jol+ly+ing
jol+lied
jol+li+er
jol+li+est
Jol+ly Rog+er
Jol+ly Rog+ers
Jolo
Jolson
jolt
jolts
jolts
jolt+ing
jolt+ed
Jonah
Jonahs
Jonas
Jonases
Jona+than
apple
Jona+thans
Jonathan
biblical character
Jones
Jongkind
jon+gleur
jon+gleurs
Jön+kö+ping
jon+quil
jon+quils
Jonson
Joplin
Jop+pa
Jordaens
Jor+dan
Jor+da+nian
Jor+da+nians
jo+rum
jo+rums
Jos
Joseph
Josephine
Josephus
josh
joshes
joshes
josh+ing

joshed
josh+er
josh+ers
Joshua
Josiah
joss
josses
jos+tle
jos+tles
jos+tles
jos+tling
jos+tled
jot
jots
jot+ting
jot+ted
jota
jotas
jot+ter
jot+ters
jot+ting
jot+tings
Jotun
Jotuns
Jo+tun+heim
Jotunn
Jotunns
Jo+tunn+heim
joule
joules
Joule
jounce
jounces
jounces
jounc+ing
jounced
jour+nal
jour+nals
jour+nal+ese
jour+nali+sa+tion
jour+nali+sa+
tions
jour+nal+ise
jour+nal+ises
jour+nal+is+ing
jour+nal+ised
jour+nal+ism
jour+nal+ist
jour+nal+ists
jour+nal+is+tic
jour+nal+is+ti+cal+
ly
jour+nali+za+tion
jour+nali+za+
tions

jour+nal+ize
jour+nal+izes
jour+nal+iz+ing
jour+nal+ized
jour+ney
jour+neys
jour+neys
jour+ney+ing
jour+neyed
jour+ney+er
jour+ney+ers
journey+man
journey+men
joust
jousts
jousts
joust+ing
joust+ed
joust+er
joust+ers
Jove
jo+vial
jo+vi+al+ity
jo+vi+al+ly
Jo+vian
of Jove or Jupiter
Jovian
Roman emperor
Jowett
jowl
jowls
jowled
joy
joys
joys
joy+ing
joyed
Joyce
Joyc+ean
Joyc+eans
joy+ful
joy+ful+ly
joy+ful+ness
joy+less
joy+less+ly
joy+less+ness
joy+ous
joy+ous+ly
joy+ride
joy+rides
joy-ride
joy-rides
joy-riding
joy-rode
joy-ridden

joy+rider
 joy+riders
joy+rid+ing
joy+stick
 joy+sticks
Juan Carlos
Juan de Fuca
Juantorena
Juá+rez
Mexican city
Juárez
Mexican
 statesman
Juba
Jubal
jub+bah
 jub+bahs
Jub+bul+pore
jube
church gallery
 jubes
jube
sweet
 jubes
ju+bi+lance
ju+bi+lant
ju+bi+lant+ly
ju+bi+late
 ju+bi+lates
 ju+bi+lat+ing
 ju+bi+lat+ed
ju+bi+la+tion
 ju+bi+la+tions
ju+bi+lee
 ju+bi+lees
Ju+daea
Ju+daean
 Ju+daeans
Judah
Ju+da+ic
Ju+dai+cal+ly
Ju+dai+sa+tion
 Ju+dai+sa+tions
Ju+da+ise
 Ju+da+ises
 Ju+da+is+ing
 Ju+da+ised
Ju+da+ism
Ju+da+is+tic
Ju+dai+za+tion
 Ju+dai+za+tions
Ju+da+ize
 Ju+da+izes
 Ju+da+iz+ing
 Ju+da+ized

Judas
Judases
Judas
 Maccabaeus
jud+der
jud+ders
jud+ders
jud+der+ing
jud+dered
Jude
Ju+dea
Ju+dean
 Ju+deans
judge
judges
judges
judg+ing
judged
judge ad+vo+
 cate
judge ad+vo+
 cates
judge+like
judge+ment
judge+ments
judge+men+tal
judg+er
judg+ers
judge+ship
judge+ships
judg+ment
judg+ments
Judg+ment
judg+men+tal
ju+di+ca+tory
 ju+di+ca+tories
ju+di+ca+ture
 ju+di+ca+tures
ju+di+cial
ju+di+cial+ly
ju+di+ci+ary
 ju+di+ci+aries
ju+di+cious
ju+di+cious+ly
ju+di+cious+ness
Judith
judo
ju+do+ist
 ju+do+ists
Judy
Judies
jug
jugs
jugs
jug+ging

jugged
ju+gate
jug+ger+naut
 jug+ger+nauts
jug+gins
jug+gle
jug+gles
jug+gles
jug+gling
jug+gled
jug+gler
jug+glers
Ju+go+slav
 Ju+go+slavs
Ju+go+sla+via
Ju+go+sla+vian
 Ju+go+sla+
 vians
jugu+lar
jugu+lars
Jugurtha
juice
juices
juice+less
juici+ly
juici+ness
juicy
juici+er
juici+est
Juiz de Fora
ju+jit+su
juju
jujus
ju+jube
 ju+jubes
ju+jut+su
juke+box
juke+boxes
juk+skei
ju+lep
 ju+leps
Julian
name
Jul+ian
adj.
Juliana
ju+li+enne
 ju+li+ennes
Julius
Jul+lun+dur
July
 Julies
jum+ble
 jum+bles
 jum+bles

jum+bling
jum+bled
jum+bly
jum+bo
 jum+bos
jum+buck
 jum+bucks
Jum+na
jump
jumps
jumps
jump+ing
jumped
jumped-up
jump+er
 jump+ers
jumpi+ly
jumpi+ness
jump-off
jump-offs
jump off
verb
jump-start
jump-starts
jump-starts
jump-starting
jump-started
jumpy
jumpi+er
jumpi+est
Junagadh
jun+co
jun+cos *or*
jun+coes
junc+tion
junc+tions
junc+ture
junc+tures
Jun+diaí
June
Junes
Ju+neau
Jung
Jung+frau
Jung+gar Pen+di
Jung+ian
jun+gle
jun+gles
jun+gly
jun+glier
jun+gliest
jun+ior
jun+iors
Jun+ior
ju+ni+per

ju+ni+pers
junk
 junks
 junks
 junk+ing
 junked
Jun+ker
 Jun+kers
Jun+ker+dom
Junkers
jun+ket
 jun+kets
 jun+kets
 jun+ket+ing
 jun+ket+ed
junkie
 junkies
junky
 junkies
Juno
jun+ta
 jun+tas
jun+to
 jun+tos
Jupiter
Roman god
Ju+pi+ter
planet
Jura

Ju+ras+sic
ju+rat
 ju+rats
ju+ridi+cal
ju+ridi+cal+ly
ju+ris+dic+tion
 ju+ris+dic+tions
ju+ris+dic+tion+
 al
ju+ris+pru+dence
ju+ris+pru+den+
 tial
ju+rist
 ju+rists
ju+ris+tic
ju+ris+ti+cal
ju+ror
 ju+rors
Ju+ruá
jury
 juries
jury+man
 jury+men
jury-rigged
jury+woman
 jury+women
just
jus+tice
 jus+tices

jus+tice+ship
jus+ti+ci+ar
 jus+ti+ci+ars
jus+ti+ci+ar+ship
jus+ti+ci+ary
 jus+ti+ci+aries
jus+ti+fi+abil+ity
jus+ti+fi+able
jus+ti+fi+ably
jus+ti+fi+ca+tion
 jus+ti+fi+ca+
 tions
jus+ti+fi+ca+tory
 jus+ti+fi+er
 jus+ti+fi+ers
jus+ti+fy
 jus+ti+fies
 jus+ti+fy+ing
 jus+ti+fied
Justin
just-in-time
jus+tle
 jus+tles
 jus+tling
 jus+tled
just+ly
just+ness
jut
 juts

juts
jut+ting
jut+ted
jute
jutes
Jut+land
Jut+land+er
 Jut+land+ers
jut+ting
Juvenal
ju+venes+cence
 ju+venes+
 cences
ju+venes+cent
ju+venile
 ju+veniles
ju+venile+ly
ju+venilia
jux+ta+pose
 jux+ta+poses
 jux+ta+pos+ing
 jux+ta+posed
jux+ta+po+si+
 tion
 jux+ta+po+si+
 tions
jux+ta+po+si+
 tion+al
Jyl+land

K

k
 k's
K
 Ks *or*
 K's
K2
Kaa+ba
ka+ba+la
 ka+ba+las
kab+ba+la
 kab+ba+las
ka+bu+ki
Ka+bul
 Ka+byle
 Ka+byles *or*
 Ka+byle
Kádár
kadi
 kadis
Ka+du+na
kaf+fir
Kaf+fir
 Kaf+firs *or*
 Kaf+fir
kaf+fir+boom
 kaf+fir+booms
kaf+fi+yeh
 kaf+fi+yehs
Kaf+fraria
Kaf+frar+ian
Kaf+ir
 Kaf+irs *or*
 Kaf+ir
Ka+fi+ri+stan
Kafka
Kafka+esque
kaf+tan
 kaf+tans
Ka+gera
Ka+go+shi+ma
kagoul
 kagouls
ka+ha+wai
 ka+ha+wais
Kahn

kai
kai+ak
 kai+aks
Kai+feng
kail
 kails
kail+yard
 kail+yards
kai+nite
Kair+ouan
Kair+wan
Kai+ser
 title
 Kai+sers
Kaiser
 surname
Kai+sers+lau+
 tern
kaka
 kakas
ka+ka+po
 ka+ka+pos
ka+kemo+no
 ka+kemo+nos
kala-azar
Ka+la+ha+ri
Kala+ma+zoo
kal+ash+ni+kov
 kal+ash+ni+
 kovs
Ka+lat
kale
 kales
ka+lei+do+scope
 ka+lei+do+
 scopes
ka+lei+do+scop+
 ic
kal+ends
Ka+leva+la
kale+yard
 kale+yards
Kal+gan
Kal+goor+lie
Kali

Kalidasa
Ka+li+man+tan
Ka+li+nin
 place name
Kalinin
 surname
Ka+li+nin+grad
Ka+lisz
Kal+mar
kal+mia
 kal+mias
Kal+muck
 Kal+mucks *or*
 Kal+muck
Kal+myk
 Kal+myks *or*
 Kal+myk
ka+long
 ka+longs
kal+pa
Ka+lu+ga
Kama
Kama+ku+ra
Ka+ma+su+tra
Kam+chat+ka
Kam+chat+kan
 Kam+chat+kans
kame
 kames
Kamensk-Uralski
Kamerlingh-
 Onnes
Ka+merun
Ka+met
ka+mi+ka+ze
 ka+mi+ka+zes
ka+mi+la+roi
Kam+pa+la
kam+pong
 kam+pongs
Kam+pu+chea
Kam+pu+chean
 Kam+pu+cheans
Ka+nak
 Ka+naks

Ka+naka
 Ka+nakas
Ka+nan+ga
Ka+na+ra
Ka+na+rese
 Ka+na+rese
Kana+za+wa
Kan+chen+jun+
 ga
Kan+chi+pu+ram
Kan+da+har
Kandinsky
Kan+dy
kan+ga
 kan+gas
kan+ga+roo
 kan+ga+roos
kangaroo-like
Kang+chen+jun+
 ga
Ka+Ngwa+ne
kan+ji
 kan+jis *or*
 kan+ji
Kano
Kan+pur
Kan+sas
Kan+su
Kant
Kant+ian
Kant+ian+ism
Kant+ism
KANU
Kao+hsiung
Kao-hsiung
Kao+lack
kao+lin
kao+lin+ic
kao+lin+ize
 kao+lin+izes
kao+lin+iz+ing
kao+lin+ized
kaon
 kaons
ka+pell+meis+ter

ka +pell +meis +
ter
Kap +fen +berg
Kapil Dev
ka +pok
kap +pa
kap +pas
ka +put
kara +bi +ner
kara +bi +ners
Ka +ra +chi
Ka +ra +fu +to
Ka +ra +gan +da
Karajan
Ka +ra +ko +ram
Ka +ra +ko +rum
kara +kul
kara +kuls
Karamanlis
kara +oke
kar +at
kar +ats
ka +ra +te
ka +ra +te +ka
ka +ra +te +kas
Kar +ba +la
Ka +relia
Ka +relian
Ka +relians
Ka +ri +ba
Ka +ri +ta +ne
Ka +ri +ta +nes
Karl-Marx-Stadt
Karloff
Kar +lo +vy Vary
Karls +kro +na
Karls +ruhe
kar +ma
kar +mic
Kar +nak
Kar +na +taka
Kärn +ten
Ka +roo
Ka +roos
ka +ross
ka +rosses
Karpov
kar +ri
kar +ris
Kar +roo
Kar +roos
karst
kart
karts

karyo
karyo +type
karyo +types
karyo +types
karyo +typ +ing
karyo +typed
karyo +typ +ic
karyo +typical
Ka +sai
kas +bah
kas +bahs
Kash +gar
Kashi
Kash +mir
Kash +miri
Kash +miris or
Kash +miri
Kash +mir +ian
Kash +mir +ians
kash +ruth
Kasparov
Kas +sa
Kas +sa +la
Kas +sel
Kastrop-Rauxel
kata
katas
kata +bat +ic
Ka +tan +ga
Ka +tar
Ka +thia +war
Kath +man +du
Kat +mai
Kat +man +du
Ka +to +wi +ce
Kat +rine
Kat +si +na
Kat +te +gat
ka +ty +did
ka +ty +dids
Katz
Ka +uai
Kauffmann
Kaufman
Kau +nas
Kaunda
kau +ri
kau +ris
kava
kavas
Ka +vál +la
Ka +wa +sa +ki
place name
Kawasaki
surname

Kay
kay +ak
kay +aks
kayo
kayos
kayos or
kayoes
kayo +ing
kayoed
Kay +seri
Ka +zak +stan
Ka +zan
place name
Kazan
surname
Ka +zan Ret +to
Kazantzakis
Kaz +bek
ka +zoo
ka +zoos
kea
keas
Kéa
Kean
Keaton
Keats
ke +bab
ke +babs
Keble
kecks
Kecs +ke +mét
Ked +ah
kedge
kedges
kedges
kedg +ing
kedged
ked +geree
ked +gerees
Ke +di +ri
Ked +ron
Ked +rons
Keegan
keek
keeks
keeks
keeked
keek +ing
keel
keels
keels
keel +ing
keeled
keel +age
keel +haul

keel +hauls
keel +haul +ing
keel +hauled
keel +son
keel +sons
Kee +lung
keen
keens
keens
keen +ing
keened
keen +er
keen +est
keen +er
keen +ers
keen +ly
keen +ness
keep
keeps
keeps
keep +ing
kept
keep +er
keep +ers
keep +ing
keep +net
keep +nets
keep +sake
keep +sakes
Kee +wa +tin
kef
kef +fi +yeh
kef +fi +yehs
Keflavík
keg
kegs
Keigh +ley
Kei +jo
Keitel
Kekkonen
keks
Kekulé von
Stradonitz
Ke +lan +tan
Keller
Kells
Kelly
ke +loid
ke +loids
kelp
kel +pie
kel +pies
Scots water
spirit,
sheepdog

kel+py
kel+pies
sheepdog
kel+son
kel+sons
kelt
kelts
Kelt
Kelts
kel+ter
kel+vin
kel+vins
Kelvin
Kemal Atatürk
Ke+mal+ism
Ke+ma+list
Ke+ma+lists
Ke+mero+vo
Kempe
Kempis
kempt
ken
kens
ken+ning
kenned
Ken+dal
Kendall
ken+do
Kendrew
Keneally
Ken+il+worth
Ké+ni+tra
Ken+ne+dy
place name
Kennedy
surname
ken+nel
ken+nels
ken+nels
ken+nel+ling
or
ken+nel+ing
U.S.
ken+nelled *or*
ken+neled
U.S.
Kennelly
ken+ning
ken+nings
ken+speckle
Kent
Kent+ish
Ken+tuck+ian
Ken+tuck+ians
Ken+tucky

Ken+ya
Ken+yan
Ken+yans
Kenyatta
Keos
Ke+phal+li+nía
kepi
kepis
Kepler
surname
Kep+ler
crater
kept
Kera+la
kera+tin
kera+tose
kerb
kerbs
Ker+be+la
kerb+ing
kerb+ings
kerb+stone
kerb+stones
Kerch
ker+chief
ker+chiefs
ker+chiefed
Kerenski
Kerensky
kerf
kerfs
ker+fuf+fle
ker+fuf+fles
Ker+gue+len
Kerk+ra+de
Kér+ky+ra
Ker+man
Ker+man+shah
ker+mes
ker+mis
kern
kerns
Kern
kerne
kernes
ker+nel
ker+nels
kernel-less
kero+sene
kero+sine
Kerouac
Kerr
Ker+ry
ker+sey
ker+sey+mere

Kesey
Kesselring
Kes+te+ven
kes+trel
kes+trels
Kes+wick
ketch
ket+ches
ketch+up
ketch+ups
ke+tone
ke+tones
ke+ton+ic
Ket+ter+ing
ket+tle
ket+tles
kettle+drum
kettle+drums
kettle+drummer
kettle+
  drummers
Kew
key
keys
keys
key+ing
keyed
key+board
key+boards
key+boards
key+board+ing
key+board+ed
key+board+er
key+board+ers
key+hole
key+holes
key+less
Keynes
Keynes+ian
Keynes+ian+ism
key+note
key+notes
key+notes
key+not+ing
key+not+ed
key+pad
key+pads
key-punch
key-punches
key-punching
key-punched
key punch
key punches
key+stone
key+stones

Kha+ba+rovsk
Khachaturian
khad+dar
kha+di
kha+ki
kha+kis
Khalid ibn Abdul
  Aziz
kha+lif
kha+lifs
Khal+ki+di+ki
Khal+kís
Khalsa
Khama
khan
khans
Khan
khan+ate
khan+ates
khan+ga
khan+gas
Kha+niá
Khar+kov
Khar+toum
Khar+tum
Khayyam
khe+di+val
khe+dive
khe+di+vial
Khe+lat
Kher+son
Khí+os
Khir+bet Qum+
  ran
Khmer
Khmers
Khmer+ian
Kho+dzhent
Kho+jent
Khomeini
Kho+tan
Khrushchev
Khufu
Khul+na
Khy+ber
ki+ang
ki+angs
Kiang+si
Kiang+su
Kiao+chow
kia ora
kib+ble
kib+bles
kib+bles
kib+bling

kib+bled
kib+butz
kib+but+zim
kibe
kibes
kib+lah
ki+bosh
ki+boshes
kick
kicks
kicks
kick+ing
kicked
kick+able
kick+back
kick+backs
kick back
verb
kick+down
kick+er
kick+ers
kick+off
kick+offs
kick off
verb
kick+shaw
kick+shaws
kick+shaws
kick+stand
kick+stands
kick-start
kick-starts
kick-starting
kick-started
kick-starter
kick-starters
kid
kids
kids
kid+ding
kid+ded
Kid
Kidd
kid+der
kid+ders
Kid+der+min+
ster
kid+die
kid+dies
kid+ding+ly
kid+dish+ness
kid+dy
kid+dies
kid+glove
adj.

kid glove
kid gloves
kid+like
kid+nap
kid+naps
kid+napped *or*
kid+naped
U.S.
kid+nap+ping *or*
kid+nap+ing
U.S.
kid+nap+per
kid+nap+pers
kid+ney
kid+neys
kid+ol+ogy
Ki+dron
kid+skin
kid+skins
kid+stakes
kief
kie+kie
kie+kies
Kiel
Kiel+ce
Kierkegaard
Kier+ke+gaard+
ian
kie+sel+guhr
Kiev
kif
Ki+ga+li
kike
kikes
Ki+klá+dhes
Ki+lauea
Kil+dare
kil+der+kin
kil+der+kins
ki+ley
ki+leys
ki+lim
ki+lims
Kili+man+ja+ro
Kil+ken+ny
kill
kills
kills
kill+ing
killed
Kil+lar+ney
kill+deer
kill+deers *or*
kill+deer
kill+er

kill+ers
kil+lick
kill+licks
kill+ing
Kil+lie+cran+kie
kil+li+fish
kil+li+fishes *or*
kil+li+fish
kill+ing
kill+ings
kill+joy
kill+joys
kil+lock
kil+locks
Kil+mar+nock
kiln
kilns
kilo
kilos
kilo+byte
kilo+bytes
kilo+calo+rie
kilo+calo+ries
kilo+cycle
kilo+cycles
kilo+gram
kilo+grams
kilo+gramme
kilo+grammes
kilo+hertz
kilo+meter
U.S.
kilo+meters
kilo+metre
kilo+metres
kilo+met+ric
kilo+ton
kilo+tons
kilo+volt
kilo+volts
kilo+watt
kilo+watts
kilowatt-hour
kilowatt-hours
kilt
kilts
kilts
kilt+ing
kilt+ed
kilt+ed
kil+ter
Ki+lung
Kilvert
Kim+ber+ley
kim+ber+lite
Kim Il Sung

ki+mo+no
ki+mo+nos
ki+mo+noed
kin
Kina+ba+lu
kin+aes+the+sia
kin+aes+thet+ic
Kin+car+dine+
shire
Kin+chin+jun+ga
kin+cob
kin+cobs
kind
kinds
kind+er
kind+est
kin+der+gar+ten
kin+der+gar+
tens
kind-hearted
kind-hearted+ly
kind-hearted+
ness
kin+dle
kin+dles
kin+dling
kin+dled
kin+dler
kin+dlers
kind+li+ness
kin+dling
kind+ly
kind+li+er
kind+li+est
kind+ness
kind+nesses
kin+dred
kine
kin+emat+ic
kin+emati+cal+ly
kin+emat+ics
kin+emato+graph
kin+emato+
graphs
ki+nesics
ki+nesis
kin+es+the+sia
U.S.
kin+es+thet+ic
U.S.
ki+net+ic
ki+neti+cal+ly
ki+net+ics
kin+folk

Chiefly U.S.,	kinky	Ki+ro+va+bad	kitsch
Canada	kinki+er	Ki+ro+vo+grad	kitschy
king	kinki+est	Kirsch	kit+ten
kings	Kinnock	Kirsch+was+ser	kit+tens
kings	kino	kir+tle	kit+ten+ish
king+ing	Kinross-shire	kir+tles	kit+ti+wake
kinged	Kinsey	Ki+ru+na	kit+ti+wakes
King	kins+folk	Kis+an+ga+ni	kit+ty
king+bird	Kin+sha+sa	Ki+shi+nev	kit+ties
king+birds	kin+ship	Kis+ma+yu	Kit+ty Hawk
king+bolt	kins+man	kis+met	Kit+we
king+bolts	kins+men	kiss	Kitz+bühel
king+cup	kins+woman	kisses	Kiu+shu
king+cups	kins+women	kisses	Kivu
king+dom	ki+osk	kiss+ing	Ki+wa+no
king+doms	ki+osks	kissed	*Trademark*
king+fish	Kio+to	kiss+able	Ki+wa+nos
king+fishes *or*	kip	kissa+gram	kiwi
king+fish	kips	kissa+grams	kiwis
king+fisher	kips	kiss-and-tell	Ki+zil Ir+mak
king+fishers	kip+ping	kiss+er	Kla+gen+furt
king+hood	kipped	kiss+ers	Klai+pe+da
king+hoods	Kipling	Kissinger	Klan
king+klip	kip+per	kist	Klan+ism
king+klips	kip+pers	kists	klax+on
king+let	kip+pers	Kist+na	klax+ons
king+lets	kip+per+ing	Ki+su+mu	Kléber
king+like	kip+pered	kit	Klee
king+li+ness	kip+skin	kits	Kleen+ex
king+ly	kip+skins	kits	Kleen+exes *or*
king+li+er	kir	kit+ting	Kleen+ex
king+li+est	Kirchhoff	kit+ted	Klein
king+maker	Kir+ghi+zia	Kitagawa	Kleist
king+makers	Kir+gi+zia	Kitaj	Klemperer
king-of-arms	Kiri+bati	Ki+ta+kyu+shu	klep+to+ma+nia
kings-of-arms	Ki+rin	kit+bag	klep+to+ma+ni+
king+pin	Ki+ri+ti+ma+ti	kit+bags	ac
king+pins	kirk	kitch+en	klep+to+ma+ni+
Kingsford-Smith	kirks	kitch+ens	acs
king+ship	Kirk	Kitch+ener	Kline
king+ships	Kirk+by	*place name*	klip+spring+er
king-size	*place name*	Kitchener	klip+spring+ers
king-sized	Kirkby	*surname*	Klon+dike
Kingsley	*surname*	kitch+en+ette	kloof
King's Lynn	Kirk+cal+dy	kitch+en+ettes	kloofs
King+ston	Kirk+cud+bright+	kitchen+ware	klys+tron
Kings+town	shire	kite	klys+trons
ki+nin	Kirk+patrick	kites	K-meson
ki+nins	Kir+kuk	kites	K-mesons
kink	Kirk+wall	kit+ing	knack
kinks	kir+mess	kit+ed	knacks
kin+ka+jou	Ki+rov	Kite mark	knack+er
kin+ka+jous	*place name*	Kite marks	knack+ers
kinki+ly	Kirov	kith	knack+ers
kinki+ness	*surname*	Kí+thi+ra	knack+er+ing

knack+ered
knack+er's yard
knack+er's
  yards
knack+ery
knack+eries
knag
  knags
knap
  knaps
  knap+ping
  knapped
knap+per
  knap+pers
knap+sack
  knap+sacks
knap+weed
  knap+weeds
knar
  knars
knave
  knaves
knav+ery
  knav+eries
knav+ish
knead
  kneads
  knead+ing
  knead+ed
  knead+er
  knead+ers
knee
  knees
  knees
  knee+ing
  kneed
knee+cap
  knee+caps
  knee+caps
  knee+cap+ping
  knee+capped
knee-deep
knee-high
knee+hole
  knee+holes
kneel
  kneels
  kneels
  kneel+ing
  knelt or
  kneeled
kneel+er
  kneel+ers
knees-up
  knees-ups

knell
  knells
  knells
  knell+ing
  knelled
  knelt
Knes+set
knew
knick+er+bock+
  ers
knick+ers
knick-knack
  knick-knacks
knife
  knives
  knifes
  knif+ing
  knifed
knife+like
knight
  knights
  knights
  knight+ing
  knight+ed
Knight
  knight+hood
  knight+hoods
  knight+li+ness
  knight+ly
Knight Tem+plar
  Knights Tem+
    plars or
  Knights Tem+
    plar
kni+pho+fia
  kni+pho+fias
knit
  knits
  knits
  knit+ting
  knit+ted
  knit+ter
  knit+ters
  knit+ting
  knit+wear
knives
knob
  knobs
  knobs
  knob+bing
  knobbed
knob+bly
  knob+bli+er
  knob+bli+est
knob+by

knob+bi+er
knob+bi+est
knob+ker+rie
  knob+ker+ries
knob+like
knob+stick
  knob+sticks
knock
  knocks
  knocks
  knock+ing
  knocked
  knock+about
    knock+abouts
    noun, adj.
  knock about
    verb
  knock-back
    knock-backs
  knock back
    verb
  knock+down
    noun, adj.
  knock down
    verb
  knock+er
    knock+ers
  knocking-shop
    knocking-shops
  knock-knee
    knock-knees
  knock-kneed
  knock-on
  knock+out
    knock+outs
  knock out
    verb
  knock-up
    knock-ups
  knock up
    verb
knoll
  knolls
Knos+sos
knot
  knots
  knots
  knot+ting
  knot+ted
  knot+grass
  knot+hole
    knot+holes
  knot+less
  knot+ted
  knot+ter

knot+ters
knot+ty
knot+ti+er
knot+ti+est
knout
  knouts
know
  knows
  know+ing
  knew
  known
know+able
know-all
  know-alls
know+er
  know+ers
know-how
know+ing
  know+ing+ly
  know+ing+ness
knowl+edg+able
knowl+edge
  knowl+edge+able
  knowl+edge+ably
known
Knox
Knox-Johnston
Knox+ville
knuck+le
  knuck+les
  knuck+les
  knuck+ling
  knuck+led
  knuckle-duster
    knuckle-dusters
  knuckle+head
    knuckle+heads
  knuckle+headed
knuck+ly
  knuck+lier
  knuck+liest
knur
  knurs
knurl
  knurls
  knurls
  knurl+ing
  knurled
knurr
  knurrs
Knut
k.o.
  k.o.'s
  k.o.'s
  k.o.'ing

k.o.'d
KO
KO's
KO's
KO'ing
KO'd
koa+la
koa+las
koan
koans
Ko+ba+rid
Kobe
Ko+blenz
kob+old
kob+olds
Koch
Ko+chi
ko+chia
ko+chias
Kodály
Ko+di+ak
koek+sis+ter
koek+sis+ters
koel
koels
Koestler
Kofu
Ko+hi+ma
kohl
Kohl
Köhler
kohl+ra+bi
kohl+ra+bies
koi+ne
Koi+ne
Ko+kand
ko+kanee
ko+kanees
Koko Nor
Kokoschka
Ko+ku+ra
kola
Kol+ding
Kol+ha+pur
ko+lin+sky
ko+lin+skies
kol+khoz
kol+khozes
Kol+mar
Kolmo+gorov
Köln
Kol Ni+dre
Kol Ni+dres
Ko+lom+na
Ko+ly+ma

Ko+ma+ti
ko+mat+ik
ko+mat+iks
Kom+mu+narsk
Kom+so+molsk
Ko+na+kri
Ko+na+kry
Kon+gur Shan
Kong Zi
Konia
Kö+nig+grätz
Kö+nigs+berg
Kó+nigs+hüt+te
Kon+stanz
Kon+ya
koo+doo
koo+doos
kook
kooks
kooka+bur+ra
kooka+bur+ras
kookie
kooki+er
kooki+est
kooky
kooki+er
kooki+est
Kooning
Koo+te+nai
Koo+te+nay
ko+peck
ko+pecks
Ko+peisk
Ko+peysk
kop+je
kop+jes
kop+pie
kop+pies
kora
koras
Ko+ran
Ko+ran+ic
Korbut
Kor+cë
Korchnoi
Korda
Kor+destan
Kor+do+fan
Ko+rea
Ko+rean
Ko+reans
korf+ball
Kó+rin+thos
kor+ma
kor+mas

Kor+sa+kof+fian
Kor+sa+kof+
fians
Kort+rijk
Korzybski
Kos
Kos+ci+us+ko
mountain
Kosciusko
surname
ko+sher
Kosovo-Metohi+
ja
Kossoff
Kossuth
Ko+stro+ma
Kosygin
Kota
Ko+ta+ba+ru
Kota Bha+ru
Ko+tah
Kota Kina+ba+lu
koto
kotos
ko+tu+ku
ko+tu+ku
kou+miss
kou+prey
kou+preys
Kov+no
Kov+rov
Ko+weit
kow+hai
kow+hais
Kow+loon
kow+tow
kow+tows
kow+tow+ing
kow+towed
Ko+zhi+kode
Kra
kraal
kraals
Krafft-Ebing
kraft
Kra+gu+je+vac
krait
kraits
Kra+ka+tau
Kra+ka+toa
Kra+kau
kra+ken
kra+kens
Kra+ków
Kra+ma+torsk

Kranj
krans
kranses
Kras+no+dar
Kras+no+yarsk
Krebs
Kre+feld
Kreisler
Kre+men+chug
krem+lin
krem+lins
Krem+lin
Krems
Kriemhild
Kriemhilde
krill
krill
Krim
krim+mer
Kriol
kris
krises
Krish+na
Krishnaism
Kris+tia+nia
Kris+tian+sand
Kristiansen
Kris+tian+stad
Krí+ti
Kri+voy Rog
kro+na
kro+nor
kró+na
kró+nur
kro+ne
kro+ner
Kro+nos
Kron+stadt
Kropotkin
Kruger
surname
Kru+ger
place name
Kru+ger+rand
Kru+ger+rands
Kru+gers+dorp
krumm+horn
krumm+horns
Krupp
Krym
kryp+ton
kry+tron
Kshat+ri+ya
Kua+la Lum+pur
Ku+ban

Kubelik
Kublai Khan
Kubrick
Kuch Bi+har
Ku+ching
ku+dos
kudu
kudus
Kuei+chou
Kuei-lin
Kuei-yang
Kuen+lun
ku+fi+yah
ku+fi+yahs
Kui+by+shev
Ku Klux Klan
Ku Klux Klan+ner
Ku Klux Klan+
ners
kuk+ri
kuk+ris
Kuku Nor
ku+lak
ku+laks
Ku+lun
Kum
Ku+ma+mo+to
ku+ma+ra
ku+ma+ras
Ku+masi
ku+mera
ku+meras
ku+mis
ku+mi+te

küm+mel
kum+quat
kum+quats
Kun
Kundera
Küng
kung fu
Kun+gur
Kun+lun
Kun+ming
K'un-ming
Kuo+pio
Ku+ra
kur+cha+to+vi+
um
Kurd
Kurds
Kur+destan
Kurd+ish
Kur+di+stan
Kure
Kur+gan
ku+ri
ku+ris
Kur+land
Kurosawa
Ku+ro+shio
kur+ra+jong
kur+ra+jongs
kur+saal
kur+saals
Kursk
kur+to+sis
kuru

Kush
Kus+ko+kwim
Ku+tai+si
Kutch
Kutuzov
Ku+wait
Ku+wai+ti
Ku+wai+tis
Kuy+by+shev
Kuz+bass
Kuznets
kvass
kwa+cha
kwa+chas
Kwa+ja+lein
Kwang+chow
Kwang+chow+an
Kwang+ju
Kwang+tung
Kwa+ra
kwashi+or+kor
Kwa+zu+lu
Kwei+chow
Kwei+lin
Kwei+sui
Kwei+yang
Kwen+lun
KWIC
KWOC
Ky
ky+ani+sa+tion
ky+an+ise
ky+an+ises
ky+an+is+ing

ky+an+ised
kya+nite
kya+nites
kya+nit+ic
ky+ani+za+tion
ky+an+ize
ky+an+izes
ky+an+iz+ing
ky+an+ized
Kyd
kyle
kyles
ky+lie
ky+lies
ky+loe
ky+loes
ky+mo+graph
ky+mo+graphs
ky+mo+graph+ic
Kym+ric
Kym+ry
Kynewulf
Kyong+song
Kyo+to
ky+pho+sis
ky+phot+ic
Kyprianou
Kyrie elei+son
Kyrie elei+sons
Ky+the+ra
kyu
kyus
Kyu+shu
Ky+zul Kum

L

l
l's
L
  Ls *or*
  L's
la
  Music
  las
la
laa+ger
laa+gers
laa+gers
laa+ger+ing
laa+gered
lab
labs
Laban
la+bel
  la+bels
  la+bels
  la+bel+ling *or*
  la+bel+ing
  U.S.
  la+belled *or*
  la+beled
  U.S.
la+bel+ler
  la+bel+lers
la+bia
la+bial
  la+bials
la+bial+ly
la+bi+ate
  la+bi+ates
Labiche
la+bile
la+bil+ity
la+bio+den+tal
  la+bio+den+tals
la+bium
  la+bia
la+bor
  U.S.
  la+bors
  la+bors

la+bor+ing
la+bored
la+bora+tory
  la+bora+tories
la+bored
  U.S.
la+bor+er
  U.S.
  la+bor+ers
la+bo+ri+ous
  la+bo+ri+ous+ly
  la+bo+ri+ous+
    ness
La+bor Par+ty
  Austral.
la+bour
la+bours
  la+bours
  la+bour+ing
  la+boured
  la+boured
  la+bour+er
  la+bour+ers
labour-intensive
La+bour+ite
  La+bour+ites
La+bour Par+ty
Lab+ra+dor
  Lab+ra+dors
la+bret
  la+brets
la+brum
  la+bra
La Bruyère
La+buan
la+bur+num
  la+bur+nums
laby+rinth
  laby+rinths
laby+rin+thine
lac
lac
  the number
    100 000
  lacs

Lacan
lac+co+lite
  lac+co+lites
lac+co+lith
  lac+co+liths
lace
  laces
  laces
  lac+ing
  laced
lace+bark
  lace+barks
Lac+edae+mon
Lac+edae+mo+
  nian
lac+er+ate
  lac+er+ates
  lac+er+at+ing
  lac+er+ated
lac+era+tion
  lac+era+tions
lace-up
  noun, adj.
  lace-ups
lace up
  verb
lace+wing
  lace+wings
lach+es
Lachesis
Lach+lan
lach+ry+mal
lach+ry+ma+tory
  lach+ry+ma+
    tories
lach+ry+mose
lach+ry+mose+ly
laci+ly
laci+ness
lac+ing
  lac+ings
la+cini+ate
  la+cini+at+ed
lack
  lacks

lack+ing
lacked
lacka+dai+si+cal
lacka+dai+si+cal+
  ly
lack+ey
  lack+eys
  lack+eys
  lack+ey+ing
  lack+eyed
lack+luster
  U.S.
lack+lustre
Laclos
La+co+nia
La+co+nian
  La+co+nians
la+con+ic
la+coni+cal+ly
lac+quer
  lac+quers
  lac+quers
  lac+quer+ing
  lac+quered
  lac+quer+er
  lac+quer+ers
lac+ri+mal
lac+ri+ma+tion
  lac+ri+ma+tions
lac+ri+ma+tory
la+crosse
lac+ry+mal
lac+ry+ma+tory
lac+tam
  lac+tams
lac+tate
  lac+tates
  lac+tates
  lac+tat+ing
  lac+tat+ed
lac+ta+tion
lac+teal
  lac+teals
lac+tes+cence
lac+tes+cent

lac+tic
lac+tif+er+ous
lac+tose
La Cum+bre
la+cu+na
  la+cu+nae *or*
la+cu+nas
la+cu+nar
la+cu+nary
la+cu+nose
la+cus+trine
lacy
  laci+er
  laci+est
lad
  lads
la+da+num
lad+der
  lad+ders
  lad+ders
  lad+der+ing
  lad+dered
lad+die
  lad+dies
lade
  lades
  lad+ing
  lad+ed
  lad+en *or*
  lad+ed
la-de-da
lad+en
la-di-da
ladies
lad+ing
Ladislas
la+dle
  la+dles
  la+dles
  la+dling
  la+dled
ladle+ful
  ladle+fuls
La+do+ga
lady
  ladies
Lady
  Ladies
lady+bird
  lady+birds
lady-in-waiting
  ladies-in-waiting
lady-killer
  lady-killers
lady+like

lady+love
  lady+loves
lady's fin+ger
  lady's fin+gers
Lady+ship
  Lady+ships
Lady+smith
lady's-slipper
  lady's-slippers
lady's-smock
  lady's-smocks
Laënnec
Laertes
lae+vo+ro+ta+
  tion
lae+vo+ro+ta+
  tions
lae+vo+ro+ta+
  tory
Lafayette
La Fayette
La Fontaine
Laforgue
lag
  lags
  lags
  lag+ging
  lagged
lag+an
la+ger
  la+gers
Lagerkvist
Lagerlof
lag+gard
  lag+gards
  lag+gard+ly
  lag+gard+ness
lag+ging
lago+morph
  lago+morphs
la+goon
  la+goons
La+gos
Lagrange
La+gran+gian
La Guai+ra
La Guardia
La Guay+ra
lah
  lahs
la+har
  la+hars
lah-di-dah
La+hore
Lah+ti

laic
  laics
lai+cal
lai+cal+ly
lai+ci+sa+tion
  lai+ci+sa+tions
lai+cise
  lai+cises
  lai+cis+ing
  lai+cised
lai+ci+za+tion
  lai+ci+za+tions
lai+cize
  lai+cizes
  lai+ciz+ing
  lai+cized
laid
laid-back
Lailat-ul-Qadr
  Lailat-ul-Qadrs
lain
Laine
Laing
Laing+ian
  Laing+ians
lair
  lairs
  lairs
  lair+ing
  laired
laird
  lairds
lais+ser faire
lais+sez faire
lais+sez pas+ser
la+ity
Laius
lake
  lakes
Lake+land
lakh
  lakhs
La Lí+nea
Lalique
Lal+lan
  Lal+lans
lal+la+tion
Lalo
lam
  lams
  lams
  lam+ming
  lammed
lama
  lamas

La+ma+ism
La+ma+ist
  La+ma+ists
La+ma+is+tic
La Man+cha
La Manche
Lamarck
La+marck+ian
  La+marck+ians
La+marck+ism
Lamartine
la+ma+sery
  la+ma+series
lamb
  lambs
  lambs
  lamb+ing
  lambed
Lamb
lam+ba+da
  lam+ba+das
Lam+ba+ré+né
lam+bast
  lam+basts
  lam+bast+ing
  lam+bast+ed
lam+baste
  lam+bastes
  lam+bast+ing
  lam+bast+ed
lamb+da
  lamb+das
lam+ben+cy
  lam+ben+cies
lam+bent
  lam+bent+ly
lam+bert
  lam+berts
Lambert
Lam+beth
lamb+ing
  lamb+ings
lamb+kin
  lamb+kins
lamb+like
lam+bre+quin
  lam+bre+quins
lamb+skin
  lamb+skins
lame
  lames
  lames
lam+ing
lamed
lam+er

lam+est
lamé
la+mel+la
la+mel+lae *or*
la+mel+las
la+mel+lar
lam+el+late
la+mel+li+branch
la+mel+li+
    branchs
la+mel+li+corn
la+mel+li+corns
lame+ly
lame+ness
la+ment
la+ments
la+ments
la+ment+ing
la+ment+ed
lam+en+table
lam+en+tably
la+men+ta+tion
la+men+ta+
    tions
la+ment+ed
la+ment+ed+ly
la+ment+er
la+ment+ers
la+ment+ing+ly
lami+na
lami+nae *or*
lami+nas
lami+nable
lami+nar
lami+nate
lami+nates
lami+nates
lami+nat+ing
lami+nat+ed
lami+nat+ed
lami+na+tion
lami+na+tions
lami+na+tor
lami+na+tors
lam+ing+ton
lam+ing+tons
lami+nose
Lam+mas
lam+mer+gei+er
lam+mer+gei+
    ers
lam+mer+gey+er
lam+mer+gey+
    ers
Lamont

lamp
lamps
lamp+black
Lam+pedu+sa
lamp+lighter
lamp+lighters
lam+poon
lam+poons
lam+poons
lam+poon+ing
lam+pooned
lam+poon+er
lam+poon+ers
lam+poon+ery
lam+poon+ist
lam+poon+ists
lamp+post
lamp+posts
lam+prey
lam+preys
La+nai
Lan+ark+shire
Lan+ca+shire
Lancaster
    surname
Lan+cas+ter
    place name
Lan+cas+trian
    Lan+cas+trians
lance
lances
lances
lanc+ing
lanced
lance+let
lance+lets
Lancelot
lan+ceo+late
lanc+er
lanc+ers
lan+cers
lan+cet
lan+cets
lance+wood
lance+woods
land
lands
lands
land+ing
land+ed
Land
    surname
Land
Länder
lan+dau

lan+daus
Landau
lan+dau+let
lan+dau+lets
land+ed
Landes
land+fall
land+falls
land+fill
land+form
land+forms
land+grave
land+graves
land-holder
land-holders
land-holding
land-holdings
land+ing
land+ings
land+lady
land+ladies
länd+ler
länd+lers
land+less
land+locked
land+lord
land+lords
land+lubber
land+lubbers
land+mark
land+marks
land+mass
land+masses
Landor
land+owner
land+owners
land+owner+ship
land+owner+
    ships
land+owning
Landowska
land+scape
land+scapes
land+scapes
land+scap+ing
land+scaped
land+scap+ist
land+scap+ists
Landseer
Land's End
Lands+hut
land+side
land+slide
land+slides
lands+man

lands+men
Landsteiner
land+ward
land+wards
lane
lanes
Lanfranc
lang
Lang
Lange
Langer
Langland
lang+lauf
lang+läuf+er
lang+läuf+ers
Langley
Langmuir
lan+gouste
lan+goustes
lan+gous+tine
lan+gous+tines
lang+syne
Langton
Langtry
lan+guage
lan+guages
langue
Langue+doc
langue d'oc
Languedoc-
    Roussill+lon
langue d'oïl
lan+guid
lan+guid+ly
lan+guid+ness
lan+guish
lan+guishes
lan+guish+ing
lan+guished
lan+guish+ing
lan+guish+ing+ly
lan+guish+ment
lan+guor
lan+guor+ous
lan+gur
lan+gurs
lan+iard
lan+iards
la+ni+ary
la+ni+aries
la+nif+er+ous
la+nig+er+ous
lank
lank+er
lank+est

Lankester
lanki+ly
lanki+ness
lank+ly
lank+ness
lanky
  lanki+er
  lanki+est
lan+ner
  lan+ners
lan+ner+et
  lan+ner+ets
lano+lin
lano+line
Lansbury
Lan+sing
lan+tern
  lan+terns
lantern-jawed
lan+tha+nide
  lan+tha+nides
lan+tha+num
lant+horn
  lant+horns
la+nu+go
  la+nu+gos
La+nus
lan+yard
  lan+yards
Lan+zhou
Laoag
Laocoon
La+odi+cea
la+odi+cean
  la+odi+ceans
Laoigh+is
Lao+is
Laomedon
Laos
Lao+tian
  Lao+tians
Lao-tzu
Lao Zi
lap
  laps
  laps
lap+ping
lapped
La Pal+ma
lapa+ro+scope
  lapa+ro+scopes
lapa+ros+co+py
lapa+ros+co+
  pies
lapa+rot+omy

lapa+rot+omies
La Paz
lap+dog
  lap+dogs
la+pel
  la+pels
la+pelled
lap+held
lapi+dary
lapi+daries
la+pil+lus
la+pil+li
lap+is lazu+li
Lap+ith
Lapi+thae or
  Lap+iths
lap-jointed
Laplace
Lap+land
Lap+land+er
  Lap+land+ers
La Pla+ta
Lapp
  Lapps
lap+per
  lap+pers
lap+pet
  lap+pets
Lapp+ish
laps+able
lapse
  lapses
  lapses
laps+ing
lapsed
laps+er
  laps+ers
laps+ible
lap+top
lap+wing
  lap+wings
lar+board
lar+cener
  lar+ceners
lar+cenist
  lar+cenists
lar+cenous
lar+ceny
lar+cenies
larch
  larches
lard
  lards
lard+ing

lard+ed
lar+der
  lar+ders
Lardner
lar+don
  lar+dons
lar+doon
  lar+doons
lardy
La+re+do
lares and pe+na+tes
large
  larg+er
  larg+est
large+ly
large+ness
large-scale
lar+gess
  lar+gesses
lar+gesse
  lar+gesses
lar+ghet+to
  lar+ghet+tos
larg+ish
lar+go
  lar+gos
lari+at
  lari+ats
La+ri+sa
La+ris+sa
lark
  larks
  larks
lark+ing
larked
Larkin
lark+ish
lark+spur
  lark+spurs
larky
  larki+er
  larki+est
larn
  larns
larn+ing
larned
La Rochefoucauld
La Ro+chelle
Larousse
lar+ri+gan
  lar+ri+gans
lar+ri+kin
  lar+ri+kins
lar+rup
  lar+rups

lar+rup+ping
lar+rupped
lar+rup+er
  lar+rup+ers
Lar+ry
lar+va
  lar+vae
lar+val
Larwood
la+ryn+gal
lar+yn+geal
lar+yn+git+ic
lar+yn+gi+tis
la+ryn+go+scope
la+ryn+go+
  scopes
lar+yn+gos+co+
  py
lar+yn+gos+co+
  pies
lar+yn+got+omy
lar+yn+got+
  omies
lar+ynx
la+ryn+ges or
  lar+ynxes
la+sa+gna
la+sa+gnas
la+sa+gne
  la+sa+gnes
La Salle
La Sca+la
las+car
  las+cars
Las+caux
las+civi+ous
las+civi+ous+ly
las+civi+ous+
  ness
Lasdun
lase
  lases
las+ing
lased
la+ser
  la+sers
lash
  lashes
  lashes
lash+ing
lashed
lash+er
  lash+ers
lash+ing
  lash+ings

Lashio
Lash+kar
lash-up
 lash-ups
Lasker
Laski
Las Pal+mas
La Spe+zia
lass
 lasses
Las+sa
Lassalle
las+sie
 las+sies
las+si+tude
las+so
 las+sos or
 las+soes
 las+sos
 las+so+ing
 las+soed
las+so+er
 las+so+ers
Lassus
last
 lasts
 lasts
 last+ing
 last+ed
last-ditch
last+er
 last+ers
last-gasp
last+ing
last+ing+ly
last+ing+ness
last+ly
Las Ve+gas
lat+ah
Lata+kia
latch
 latches
latch+key
 latch+keys
latch+string
 latch+strings
late
 lat+er
 lat+est
la+teen
late+ly
la+ten+cy
 la+ten+cies
La Tène
late+ness

la+tent
la+tent+ly
lat+er
lat+er+al
 lat+er+als
lat+er+al+ly
lat+er+ite
 lat+er+ites
lat+est
la+tex
 la+texes or
 lati+ces
lath
 laths
 laths
 lath+ing
 lathed
lathe
 lathes
 lathes
 lath+ing
 lathed
lath+er
 lath+ers
 lath+ers
 lath+er+ing
 lath+ered
lath+ery
la+thi
la+this
Latimer
Lat+in
 Lat+ins
La+ti+na
Lat+in+ate
Lat+ini+sa+tion
 Lat+ini+sa+tions
Lat+in+ise
 Lat+in+ises
 Lat+in+is+ing
 Lat+in+ised
 Lat+in+is+er
 Lat+in+is+ers
Lat+in+ism
 Lat+in+isms
Lat+in+ist
 Lat+in+ists
Lat+ini+za+tion
 Lat+ini+za+tions
Lat+in+ize
 Lat+in+izes
 Lat+in+iz+ing
 Lat+in+ized
Lat+in+iz+er
 Lat+in+iz+ers

lat+ish
lati+tude
 lati+tudes
lati+tu+di+nal
 lati+tu+di+nal+ly
lati+tu+di+nar+
 ian
 lati+tu+di+nar+
 ians
lati+tu+di+nari+
 an+ism
La+tium
Latour
La Tour
la+tria
la+trine
 la+trines
lat+ter
latter-day
lat+ter+ly
lat+tice
 lat+tices
 lat+tices
 lat+tic+ing
 lat+ticed
 lat+ticed
Lat+via
Lat+vian
 Lat+vians
laud
 lauds
 lauds
 laud+ing
 laud+ed
Laud
laud+abil+ity
laud+able
laud+able+ness
laud+ably
lau+da+num
lau+da+tion
lauda+tive
lauda+tory
Lauder
Laud+ian
 lauds
Laue
laugh
 laughs
 laughs
 laugh+ing
 laughed
laugh+able
laugh+able+ness
laugh+ably

laugh+er
 laugh+ers
laugh+ing
laugh+ing+ly
laugh+ter
Laughton
Laun+ces+ton
launch
 launches
 launches
 launch+ing
 launched
launch+er
 launch+ers
launch+ing
laun+der
 laun+ders
 laun+der+ing
 laun+dered
 laun+der+er
 laun+der+ers
Laun+der+ette
 Trademark
 Laun+der+ettes
laun+dress
 laun+dresses
laun+dry
 laun+dries
laundry+man
 laundry+men
laundry+woman
 laundry+women
Laura+sia
lau+reate
 lau+reates
lau+reate+ship
 lau+reate+ships
lau+rel
 lau+rels
 lau+rels
lau+rel+ling or
 lau+rel+ing
 U.S.
lau+relled or
 lau+reled
 U.S.
Laurel and Hardy
Lau+ren+tian
Laurier
lau+rus+ti+nus
 lau+rus+ti+
 nuses
Lau+sanne
Lautrec
lav

lavs
lava
la+va+bo
  la+va+boes *or*
  la+va+bos
lav+age
 lav+ages
La+val
place name
Laval
surname
lava+to+rial
lava+tory
 lava+tories
lave
laves
 lav+ing
laved
lav+en+der
la+ver
 la+vers
Laver
lav+ish
 lav+ishes
 lav+ish+ing
 lav+ished
 lav+ish+er
 lav+ish+ers
 lav+ish+ly
 lav+ish+ness
Lavoisier
law
 laws
Law
law-abiding
law+breaker
 law+breakers
 law+breaking
 law+breakings
Lawes
law+ful
law+ful+ly
law+ful+ness
law+giver
 law+givers
law+giving
lawks
law+less
law+less+ly
law+less+ness
Lawman
lawn
 lawns
lawny
Lawrence

law+ren+cium
Law+ren+tian
Lawson
law+suit
 law+suits
law+yer
 law+yers
lax
laxa+tive
 laxa+tives
lax+ity
lax+ly
lax+ness
Laxness
lay
 lays
 lays
 lay+ing
laid
lay+about
 lay+abouts
lay about
verb
Layamon
Layard
lay-by
 lay-bys
lay by
verb
lay+er
 lay+ers
 lay+ers
 lay+er+ing
 lay+ered
lay+er+ing
 lay+er+ings
lay+ette
 lay+ettes
lay+man
 lay+men
lay-off
 lay-offs
lay off
verb
lay+out
 lay+outs
lay out
verb
lay+woman
 lay+women
laz+ar
 laz+ars
laza+ret
laza+rets
laza+rette

laza+rettes
laza+ret+to
 laza+ret+tos
Lazarus
laze
lazes
lazes
laz+ing
lazed
la+zi+ly
la+zi+ness
La+zio
lazy
lazi+er
lazi+est
lazy+bones
L-dopa
lea
leas
leach
leaches
leaches
leach+ing
leached
Leach
leach+er
 leach+ers
Leacock
lead
 leads
 lead+ing
led
Leadbelly
lead+ed
lead+en
lead+en+ly
lead+en+ness
lead+er
 lead+ers
lead+er+less
lead+er+ship
lead-in
 lead-ins
lead+ing
lead-off
 lead-offs
lead off
verb
leaf
leaves
leafs
leaf+ing
leafed
leaf+age
leafi+ness

leaf+less
leaf+let
 leaf+lets
 leaf+lets
 leaf+let+ing
 leaf+let+ed
leaf+like
leaf+stalk
 leaf+stalks
leafy
leafi+er
 leafi+est
league
leagues
leagues
leagu+ing
leagued
leagu+er
 leagu+ers
Leah
leak
leaks
leaks
leak+ing
leaked
leak+age
 leak+ages
leak+er
 leak+ers
Leakey
leaki+ness
leaky
leaki+er
leaki+est
leal
leal+er
leal+est
leal+ly
le+al+ty
Leam+ing+ton
lean
leans
lean+ing
leaned *or*
leant
lean
 lean+er
 lean+est
Lean
lean-burn
Leander
lean+ing
 lean+ings
lean+ly
lean+ness

lean-to
  lean-tos
leap
  leaps
  leaps
  leap+ing
  leaped *or*
  leapt
  leap+er
  leap+ers
  leap+frog
  leap+frogs
  leap+frogs
  leap+frog+ging
  leap+frogged
Lear
learn
  learns
  learn+ing
  learned *or*
  learnt
learn+able
learn+ed
learn+ed+ly
learn+ed+ness
learn+er
  learn+ers
learn+ing
  learn+ings
leas+able
lease
  leases
  leases
  leas+ing
  leased
lease+back
  lease+backs
lease+hold
  lease+holds
  lease+holder
  lease+holders
leas+er
  leas+ers
leash
  leashes
  leashes
  leash+ing
  leashed
least
  least+ways
  least+wise
leath+er
  leath+ers
  leath+ers
  leath+er+ing

leath+ered
Leath+er+head
leath+eri+ness
leather+jacket
  leather+jackets
leath+ern
leather+neck
  leather+necks
leath+ery
leave
  to depart
  leaves
  leav+ing
  left
leave
  to grow leaves
  leaves
  leav+ing
  leaved
leaved
leav+en
  leav+ens
  leav+en+ing
  leav+ened
leav+en+ing
  leav+en+ings
Leav+en+worth
leav+er
  leav+ers
leaves
leave-taking
  leave-takings
  leav+ings
Leavis
Lea+vis+ite
  Lea+vis+ites
Leba+nese
Leba+non
Le+bens+raum
  Le+bens+raums
Leblanc
Lebrun
Le Carré
Lec+ce
lech
  leches
  leches
  lech+ing
  leched
Lech
lech+er
  lech+ers
lech+er+ous
  lech+er+ous+ly
lech+ery

lech+eries
leci+thin
  leci+thins
lecky
Lecky
Leconte de Lisle
Le Corbusier
Le Creu+sot
lec+tern
  lec+terns
lec+tion+ary
  lec+tion+aries
lec+tor
  lec+tors
lec+ture
  lec+tures
  lec+tures
  lec+tur+ing
  lec+tured
lec+tur+er
  lec+tur+ers
lec+ture+ship
  lec+ture+ships
led
Leda
Lederberg
le+der+ho+sen
ledge
  ledges
  ledged
ledg+er
  ledg+ers
  ledg+ers
  ledg+er+ing
  ledg+ered
ledgy
lee
  lees
Lee
leech
  leeches
  leeches
  leech+ing
  leeched
Leeds
leek
  leeks
Lee Kuan Yew
leer
  leers
  leers
  leer+ing
  leered
leeri+ness
leer+ing

leer+ing+ly
leery
  leeri+er
  leeri+est
lees
leet
  leets
Leeu+war+den
Leeuwenhoek
lee+ward
lee+way
Le Fanu
left
  lefts
left-hand
left-handed
  left-handed+ly
  left-handed+ness
left-hander
  left-handers
left+ism
left+ist
  left+ists
left-luggage
left+over
  left+overs
left+ward
  left+wards
left-wing
left-winger
  left-wingers
lefty
  lefties
leg
  legs
  legs
  leg+ging
  legged
lega+cy
  lega+cies
le+gal
  le+gal+ese
  le+gali+sa+tion
  le+gali+sa+tions
  le+gal+ise
  le+gal+ises
  le+gal+is+ing
  le+gal+ised
  le+gal+ism
  le+gal+ist
  le+gal+ists
  le+gal+is+tic
  le+gal+ity
  le+gal+ities
  le+gali+za+tion

le+gali+za+tions
le+gal+ize
le+gal+izes
le+gal+iz+ing
le+gal+ized
le+gal+ly
Le+gas+pi
leg+ate
leg+ates
lega+tee
lega+tees
leg+ate+ship
leg+ate+ships
le+ga+tion
le+ga+tions
le+ga+to
le+ga+tos
leg+end
leg+ends
leg+end+ary
Legendre
leg+er
Léger
leg+er+demain
leg+ged
leg+gi+ness
leg+gings
leg+gy
leg+gi+er
leg+gi+est
leg+horn
leg+horns
Leg+horn
leg+ibil+ity
leg+ible
leg+ibly
le+gion
le+gions
le+gion+ary
le+gion+aries
le+gion+naire
le+gion+naires
Le+gion+naire's
dis+ease
leg+is+late
leg+is+lates
leg+is+lat+ing
leg+is+lat+ed
leg+is+la+tion
leg+is+la+tive
leg+is+la+tive+ly
leg+is+la+tor
leg+is+la+tors
leg+is+la+ture
leg+is+la+tures

le+git
le+giti+ma+cy
le+giti+mate
le+giti+mates
le+giti+mat+ing
le+giti+mat+ed
le+giti+mate+ly
le+giti+ma+tion
le+giti+ma+ti+sa+
  tion
le+giti+ma+tise
le+giti+ma+tises
le+giti+ma+tis+
  ing
le+giti+ma+tised
le+giti+ma+ti+za+
  tion
le+giti+ma+tize
le+giti+ma+tizes
le+giti+ma+tiz+
  ing
le+giti+ma+tized
le+giti+mi+sa+
  tion
le+giti+mise
le+giti+mises
le+giti+mis+ing
le+giti+mised
le+giti+mism
le+giti+mist
le+giti+mists
le+giti+mi+za+
  tion
le+giti+mize
le+giti+mizes
le+giti+miz+ing
le+giti+mized
leg+less
Leg+ni+ca
leg-of-mutton
leg-o'-mutton
leg-pull
leg-pulls
leg+room
leg+uan
leg+uans
leg+ume
leg+umes
le+gu+mi+nous
leg+warmer
leg+warmers
leg+work
Lehár
Le Ha+vre
Lehmann

Lehmbruck
lei
leis
Leibnitz
Leib+nitz+ian
Leibniz
Leices+ter
Leices+ter+shire
Leichhardt
Lei+den
Leigh
Leighton
Lein+ster
Leip+zig
Lei+ria
leish+mania+sis
leish+ma+nio+sis
leis+ter
leis+ters
leis+ters
leis+ter+ing
leis+tered
lei+sure
lei+sured
lei+sure+li+ness
lei+sure+ly
Leith
leit+mo+tif
leit+mo+tifs
leit+mo+tiv
leit+mo+tivs
Lei+trim
Lei+zhou
lek
leks
lek+ker
Lely
Lemaître
Lé+man
Le Mans
lem+ma
lem+mas or
lem+ma+ta
lem+ming
lem+mings
lemming-like
Lem+nos
lem+on
lem+ons
lem+on+ade
lem+on+ades
lem+ony
le+mur
le+murs
lemu+roid

lemu+roids
Lena
lend
lends
lend+ing
lent
lend+er
lend+ers
lend+ing
Lendl
lend-lease
Lenglen
length
lengths
length+en
length+ens
length+en+ing
length+ened
length+en+er
length+en+ers
lengthi+ly
lengthi+ness
length+ways
length+wise
lengthy
lengthi+er
lengthi+est
le+ni+ence
le+ni+en+cy
le+ni+ent
le+ni+ent+ly
Lenin
Le+ni+na+bad
Le+ni+na+kan
Len+in+grad
Len+in+ism
Len+in+ist
Len+in+ists
leni+tive
leni+tives
len+ity
len+ities
Lennon
leno
lenos
Leno
lens
lenses
lent
Lent
len+ta+men+te
len+ten
len+ti+cel
len+ti+cels
len+ticu+lar

len+til
  len+tils
len+ti+vi+rus
  len+ti+vi+ruses
len+to
  len+tos
Lenya
Leo
Leo+ben
León
Leonard
Leo+nar+desque
Leonardo da Vinci
Leoncavallo
Leo+nid
  Leo+nids *or*
  Leo+nides
Leonidas
leo+nine
Leo+nine
leop+ard
  leop+ards
leop+ard+ess
Leopardi
Léo+pold+ville
leo+tard
  leo+tards
Le+pan+to
lep+er
  lep+ers
lepi+dop+ter+an
lepi+dop+ter+
  ans
  or
lepi+dop+tera
lepi+dop+ter+ist
lepi+dop+ter+
  ists
Lepidus
lep+re+chaun
  lep+re+chauns
lep+ro+sy
lep+rous
lep+to+dac+tyl+
  ous
lep+ton
  Greek currency
  lep+ta
lep+ton
  particle
  lep+tons
lep+to+spi+ro+
  sis
lep+to+spi+ro+
  ses

Lé+ri+da
Lermontov
Lerner
Ler+wick
Lesage
Le Sage
les+bian
  les+bians
les+bi+an+ism
Les+bos
Les Cayes
lese-majesty
le+sion
  le+sions
Le+so+tho
less
les+see
  les+sees
less+en
  less+ens
less+en+ing
less+ened
Lesseps
less+er
Less+er An+til+
  les
Lessing
les+son
  les+sons
les+sor
  les+sors
lest
Lés+vos
let
to permit or lease
  lets
  lets
  let+ting
  let
to hinder
  lets
  lets
  let+ting
  let+ted *or*
  let
Letch+worth
let+down
  let+downs
  let down
  verb
le+thal
le+thal+ity
  le+thal+ities
le+thal+ly

le+thar+gic
le+thar+gi+cal+ly
leth+ar+gy
  leth+ar+gies
Leth+bridge
Le+the
Le+thean
Leto
let-out
  let-outs
  let out
  verb
let's
let+ter
  let+ters
  let+ters
  let+ter+ing
  let+tered
let+tered
let+ter+er
  let+ter+ers
letter+head
  letter+heads
  let+ter+ing
letter-perfect
letter+press
Lett+ish
let+tuce
  let+tuces
let-up
  let-ups
  let up
  verb
Leucippus
leu+co+blast
  leu+co+blasts
leu+co+cyte
  leu+co+cytes
leu+co+cyt+ic
leu+co+ma
  leu+co+mas
leu+cot+omy
  leu+cot+omies
Leuc+tra
leu+kae+mia
leu+ke+mia
leu+ko+blast
  U.S.
  leu+ko+blasts
leu+ko+cyte
  U.S.
  leu+ko+cytes
leu+ko+cyt+ic
  U.S.
le+vant

Le+vant
le+vant+er
  le+vant+ers
Le+van+tine
  Le+van+tines
le+va+tor
  le+va+tors
levee
  levees
lev+el
  lev+els
  lev+els
lev+el+ling *or*
lev+el+ing
  U.S.
lev+elled *or*
lev+eled
  U.S.
lev+el+er
  U.S.
lev+el+ers
level-headed
level-headed+ly
lev+el+ler
  lev+el+lers
lev+el+ly
lev+el+ness
Le+ven
lev+er
  lev+ers
  lev+ers
  lev+er+ing
  lev+ered
lev+er+age
  lev+er+aged
lev+er+et
  lev+er+ets
Leverhulme
Le+ver+ku+sen
Leverrier
Levi
levi+able
le+via+than
  le+via+thans
levi+gate
  levi+gates
  levi+gat+ing
  levi+gat+ed
levi+ga+tion
Levis
  Trademark
Levi-Strauss
levi+tate
  levi+tates
  levi+tat+ing

levi+tat+ed
levi+ta+tion
levi+ta+tions
levi+ta+tor
levi+ta+tors
lev+ity
lev+ities
Lev+kas
levo+dopa
levy
levies
levies
levy+ing
levied
Lévy-Bruhl
lewd
lewd+er
lewd+est
lewd+ly
lewd+ness
Lew+es
lew+is
lew+ises
Lew+is
place name
Lewis
surname
Lewi+sham
lew+is+ite
lex+eme
lex+emes
lexi+cal
lexi+cal+ly
lexi+cog+ra+pher
lexi+cog+ra+
 phers
lexi+co+graph+ic
lexi+co+graphi+
 cal
lexi+cog+ra+phy
lexi+con
lexi+cons
lexi+gra+phy
Lex+ing+ton
lex+is
ley
Ley+den
place name
Leyden
surname
Ley+te
Lha+sa
lia+bil+ities
lia+bil+ity
lia+bil+ities

lia+ble
li+aise
li+aises
li+ais+ing
li+aised
liai+son
liai+sons
lia+na
lia+nas
li+ane
li+anes
Lian+yun+gang
Liao
Liao+dong
Liao+ning
Liao+tung
Liao+yang
liar
liars
Li+ard
Lias
Li+as+sic
lib
li+ba+tion
li+ba+tions
Libby
li+bel
li+bels
li+bels
li+bel+ling *or*
li+bel+ing
U.S.
li+belled *or*
li+beled
U.S.
li+bel+ist
li+bel+ists
U.S.
li+bel+ler
li+bel+lers
li+bel+lous
li+bel+ous
U.S.
lib+er+al
lib+er+als
Lib+er+al
Lib+er+als
lib+er+ali+sa+tion
lib+er+ali+sa+
 tions
lib+er+al+ise
lib+er+al+ises
lib+er+al+is+ing
lib+er+al+ised
lib+er+al+is+er

lib+er+al+is+ers
lib+er+al+ism
lib+er+al+ity
lib+er+al+ities
lib+er+ali+za+tion
lib+er+ali+za+
 tions
lib+er+al+ize
lib+er+al+izes
lib+er+al+iz+ing
lib+er+al+ized
lib+er+al+iz+er
lib+er+al+iz+ers
lib+er+al+ly
lib+er+al+ness
lib+er+ate
lib+er+ates
lib+er+at+ing
lib+er+at+ed
lib+er+at+ed
lib+era+tion
lib+era+tion+ist
lib+era+tion+ists
lib+era+tor
lib+era+tors
Li+be+rec
Li+beria
Li+berian
Li+berians
lib+er+tar+ian
lib+er+tar+ians
lib+er+tari+an+
 ism
lib+er+tin+age
lib+er+tine
lib+er+tines
lib+er+tin+ism
lib+er+ty
lib+er+ties
Lib+er+ty
Li+bia
li+bidi+nal
li+bidi+nal+ly
li+bidi+nous
li+bidi+nous+ly
li+bidi+nous+
 ness
li+bi+do
li+bi+dos
li+bra
li+brae
Li+bra
li+brar+ian
li+brar+ians
li+brar+ian+ship

li+brar+ian+
 ships
li+brary
li+braries
li+bra+tion
li+bra+tions
li+bret+tist
li+bret+tists
li+bret+to
li+bret+tos *or*
li+bret+ti
Li+breville
Lib+rium
Trademark
Libya
Liby+an
Liby+ans
lice
li+cence
li+cences
li+cens+able
li+cense
li+censes
li+cense
li+censes
li+cens+ing
li+censed
li+cen+see
li+cen+sees
li+cen+ser
li+cen+sers
li+cen+sor
li+cen+sors
li+cen+ti+ate
li+cen+ti+ates
li+cen+ti+ate+
 ship
li+cen+ti+ate+
 ships
li+cen+tious
li+cen+tious+ly
li+cen+tious+
 ness
lich
li+chee
li+chees
li+chen
li+chens
li+chened
li+chen+ous
Lich+field
Lichtenstein
lic+it
lic+it+ly
lic+it+ness

lick
 licks
 licks
 lick+ing
 licked
lick+er
 lick+ers
lick+er+ish
lickety-split
lick+ing
 lick+ings
lick+spittle
 lick+spittles
lico+rice
U.S.
lic+tor
 lic+tors
lid
 lids
lid+ded
Liddell Hart
Li+di+ce
lid+less
lido
 lidos
lie
to speak
* untruthfully*
 lies
 lies
 ly+ing
 lied
lie
to recline or be
* situated*
 lies
 ly+ing
 lay
 lain
Lie
Liebig
Liebknecht
Liech+ten+stein
lied
 lied+er
lie-down
noun
lie down
verb
lief
liege
 lieges
Li+ège
liege+man
 liege+men

lie-in
 lie-ins
lie in
verb
lien
li+erne
 li+ernes
Lies+tal
lieu
lieu+ten+an+cy
 lieu+ten+an+
  cies
lieu+ten+ant
 lieu+ten+ants
Lifar
life
 lives
life+blood
life+boat
 life+boats
life+guard
 life+guards
life+less
life+less+ly
life+less+ness
life+like
life+like+ness
life+line
 life+lines
life+long
lif+er
 lif+ers
life-saver
 life-savers
life-saving
life-size
life-sized
life+style
 life+styles
life-support
life+time
 life+times
Lif+fey
Lif+ford
LIFO
lift
 lifts
 lifts
 lift+ing
 lift+ed
 lift+er
 lift+ers
 lift+off
 lift+offs
 lift off

verb
liga+ment
 liga+ments
lig+and
 lig+ands
li+gate
 li+gates
 li+gat+ing
 li+gat+ed
li+ga+tion
 li+ga+tions
liga+ture
 liga+tures
 liga+tures
 liga+tur+ing
 liga+tured
li+ger
 li+gers
Ligeti
lig+ger
 lig+gers
lig+ging
light
to illuminate
 lights
 lights
 light+ing
 light+ed *or*
 lit
light
lacking weight
 light+er
 light+est
light+en
 light+ens
 light+en+ing
 light+ened
 light+en+ing
light+er
 light+ers
light+er+age
light-fingered
light-footed
light-footed+ly
light-headed
light-headed+ly
light-headed+
 ness
light-hearted
light-hearted+ly
light+house
 light+houses
light+ing
lighting-up
light+ish

light+less
light+ly
light+ness
light+ning
lights
light-sen+si+tive
light+ship
 light+ships
light+some
light+weight
 light+weights
lig+ne+ous
lig+nin
lig+nite
lig+nit+ic
lig+num vi+tae
lig+ro+in
Li+gu+ria
Li+gu+rian
 Li+gu+rians
lik+able
lik+able+ness
Li+ka+si
like
 likes
 likes
 lik+ing
 liked
like+able
like+able+ness
like+li+hood
like+li+ness
like+ly
 like+li+er
 like+li+est
like-minded
like-minded+ly
like-minded+ness
lik+en
 lik+ens
 lik+en+ing
 lik+ened
like+ness
 like+nesses
like+wise
lik+ing
li+lac
 li+lacs
Lilburne
lilia+ceous
Lilienthal
Lilith
Liliuokalani
Lille
Lillee

Lil+li+pu+tian
Lil+li+pu+tians
Lilo
Trademark
Lilos
Li+long+we
lilt
lilts
lilts
lilt+ing
lilt+ed
lily
lilies
lily-like
lily-livered
lily-white
lima
Lima
Li+mas+sol
limb
limbs
limbed
lim+ber
lim+bers
lim+bers
lim+ber+ing
lim+bered
lim+ber+ness
limb+less
lim+bo
lim+bos
Lim+burg
Lim+burg+er
lime
limes
limes
lim+ing
limed
lime+ade
lime+ades
lime+kiln
lime+kilns
lime+light
lim+er+ick
lim+er+icks
Lim+er+ick
lime+stone
lime+water
lim+ey
lim+eys
limi+ness
lim+it
lim+its
lim+its
lim+it+ing

lim+it+ed
lim+it+able
limi+tary
limi+ta+tion
limi+ta+tions
lim+it+ed
lim+it+ed+ly
lim+it+ed+ness
lim+it+ers
lim+it+less
lim+it+less+ly
lim+it+less+ness
limn
limns
limn+ing
limned
lim+ner
lim+ners
lim+no+logi+cal
lim+nolo+gist
lim+nolo+gists
lim+nol+ogy
Lím+nos
Li+moges
Li+mou+sin
lim+ou+sine
lim+ou+sines
limp
to walk with
uneven step
limps
limps
limp+ing
limped
limp
not firm
limp+er
limp+est
limp+er
limp+ers
lim+pet
lim+pets
lim+pid
lim+pid+ity
lim+pid+ly
lim+pid+ness
limp+ly
limp+ness
Lim+po+po
limp-wristed
limy
limi+er
limi+est
lin+able

Linacre
lin+age
Li+na+res
linch+pin
linch+pins
Lin+coln
place name
Lincoln
surname
Lin+coln+shire
linc+tus
linc+tuses
Lind
lin+dane
Lindbergh
Lindemann
lin+den
lin+dens
Lind+es+nes
Lin+dis+farne
Lindsay
Lind+sey
Lindwall
line
lines
lines
lin+ing
lined
line+able
lin+eage
lin+eages
line+age
lin+eal
lin+eal+ly
linea+ment
linea+ments
lin+ear
Lin+ear B
lin+ear+ity
lin+ear+ly
lin+ea+tion
lin+ea+tions
lined
line+man
line+men
lin+en
lin+ens
line-out
line-outs
lin+er
lin+ers
lines
lines+man
lines+men
line-up

line-ups
line up
verb
ling
ling *or*
lings
lin+ga
lin+gas
lin+gam
lin+gams
lin+ger
lin+gers
lin+ger+ing
lin+gered
lin+ger+er
lin+ger+ers
lin+gerie
lin+ger+ing
lin+ger+ing+ly
lin+go
lin+goes
lin+gua fran+ca
lin+gua fran+cas
or
lin+guae fran+
cae
Lin+gua Fran+ca
lin+gual
lin+guals
lin+gual+ly
lin+gui+form
lin+guist
lin+guists
lin+guis+tic
lin+guis+ti+cal+ly
lin+guis+tics
lini+ment
lini+ments
lin+ing
lin+ings
link
links
links
link+ing
linked
link+age
link+ages
link+man
link+men
Lin+kö+ping
links
Lin+lith+gow
linn
linns
Lin+naean

Linnaeus
Lin+nean
lin+net
lin+nets
Lin+nhe
lino
linos
li+no+cut
li+no+cuts
li+no+leum
Li+no+type
Trademark
Li+no+types
Lin Piao
lin+seed
linsey-woolsey
linsey-woolseys
lint
lin+tel
lin+tels
lint+er
lint+ers
linty
Linz
lion
lions
Lion
li+on+ess
li+on+esses
lion-hearted
li+oni+sa+tion
li+oni+sa+tions
li+on+ise
li+on+ises
li+on+is+ing
li+on+ised
li+on+is+er
li+on+is+ers
li+oni+za+tion
li+oni+za+tions
li+on+ize
li+on+izes
li+on+iz+ing
li+on+ized
li+on+iz+er
li+on+iz+ers
Lions
lip
lips
lips
lip+ping
lipped
li+pase
li+pases
Lipchitz

Li+petsk
li+pid
li+pids
li+pide
li+pides
Li+piz+zan+er
Li+piz+zan+ers
lip+less
lip+like
Li Po
li+pog+ra+phy
li+pog+ra+phies
lip+oid
lip+oids
lipo+pro+tein
lipo+pro+teins
lipo+suc+tion
lipo+suc+tions
Lip+pe
Lippi
Lip+pi+zan+er
Lip+pi+zan+ers
Lippmann
lip-read
lip-reads
lip-reading
lip-read
lip-reader
lip-readers
lip-reading
lip+stick
lip+sticks
lip-sync
lip-syncs
lip-syncing
lip-synced
lip-synch
lip-synchs
lip-synching
lip-synched
liq+ue+fa+cient
liq+ue+fa+cients
liq+ue+fac+tion
liq+ue+fac+tions
liq+ue+fi+able
liq+ue+fy
liq+ue+fies
liq+ue+fy+ing
liq+ue+fied
li+ques+cence
li+ques+cen+cy
li+ques+cent
li+queur
li+queurs
liq+uid

liq+uids
liq+uid+am+bar
liq+uid+am+bars
liq+ui+date
liq+ui+dates
liq+ui+dat+ing
liq+ui+dat+ed
liq+ui+da+tion
liq+ui+da+tions
liq+ui+da+tor
liq+ui+da+tors
liq+uid-crys+tal
liq+uid+ise
liq+uid+ises
liq+uid+is+ing
liq+uid+ised
liq+uid+is+er
liq+uid+is+ers
li+quid+ity
liq+uid+ize
liq+uid+izes
liq+uid+iz+ing
liq+uid+ized
liq+uid+iz+er
liq+uid+iz+ers
liq+uid+ly
liq+uor
liq+uors
liquo+rice
liquo+rish
lira
lire *or*
liras
lirio+den+dron
lirio+den+drons
or
lirio+den+dra
Lis+bon
Lis+burn
Li+sieux
lisle
lisp
lisps
lisps
lisp+ing
lisped
lisp+er
lisp+ers
lisp+ing
lisp+ings
lisp+ing+ly
lis+som
lis+some
lis+some+ly
lis+some+ness

lis+som+ly
lis+som+ness
list
lists
lists
list+ing
list+ed
list+able
list+ed
lis+ten
lis+tens
lis+ten+ing
lis+tened
lis+ten+er
lis+ten+ers
lis+ten+ing
lis+ter
lis+ters
Lister
lis+terio+sis
list+ing
list+ings
list+less
list+less+ly
list+less+ness
Liston
lists
Liszt
lit
lita+ny
lita+nies
li+tchi
li+tchis
li+ter
U.S.
li+ters
lit+era+cy
lit+er+al
lit+er+als
lit+er+al+ism
lit+er+al+ist
lit+er+al+is+tic
lit+er+al+is+tic
lit+er+al+ity
lit+er+al+ities
lit+er+al+ly
lit+er+al+ness
lit+er+ari+ly
lit+er+ari+ness
lit+er+ary
lit+er+ate
lit+er+ates
lit+er+ate+ly
lit+era+ti
lit+era+ture

lith+arge
lithe
lithe+ly
lithe+ness
lithia
lith+ic
lith+ium
li+tho
  li+thos
litho+graph
litho+graphs
litho+graphs
litho+graph+ing
litho+graphed
li+thog+ra+pher
  li+thog+ra+
  phers
litho+graph+ic
litho+graphi+cal+
  ly
li+thog+ra+phy
li+thol+ogy
  li+thol+ogies
litho+phyte
litho+phytes
litho+sphere
li+thoto+my
  li+thoto+mies
litho+trip+sy
Lithua+nia
Lithua+nian
  Lithua+nians
liti+gable
liti+gant
  liti+gants
liti+gate
liti+gates
liti+gat+ing
liti+gat+ed
liti+ga+tion
  liti+ga+tions
liti+ga+tor
  liti+ga+tors
li+ti+gious
li+ti+gious+ly
li+ti+gious+ness
lit+mus
li+to+tes
  li+to+tes
li+tre
  li+tres
lit+ter
  lit+ters
  lit+ter+ing
  lit+tered

lit+té+ra+teur
  lit+té+ra+teurs
litter+bug
  litter+bugs
lit+tle
Littlewood
lit+to+ral
  lit+to+rals
li+tur+gi+cal
li+tur+gi+cal+ly
lit+ur+gy
  lit+ur+gies
Liu Shao Qi
liv+abil+ity
liv+able
  liv+able+ness
live
  lives
  liv+ing
  lived
live+abil+ity
live+able
  live+able+ness
lived-in
live-in
  adj.
live in
  verb
live+li+hood
  live+li+hoods
live+li+ness
live+long
live+ly
  live+li+er
  live+li+est
liv+en
  liv+ens
  liv+en+ing
  liv+ened
liv+en+er
  liv+en+ers
liv+er
  liv+ers
liv+eried
liv+er+ish
  liv+er+ish+ness
Liv+er+pool
  place name
Liverpool
  surname
Liv+er+pud+lian
  Liv+er+pud+
  lians
liver+wort
  liver+worts

liver+wurst
  liver+wursts
liv+ery
  liv+eries
liv+ery
  adj.
livery+man
  livery+men
lives
live+stock
Livia Drusilla
liv+id
li+vid+ity
liv+id+ly
liv+id+ness
liv+ing
  liv+ings
Liv+ing+ston
Livingstone
Li+vo+nia
Li+vo+nian
  Li+vo+nians
Li+vor+no
Livy
liz+ard
  liz+ards
Liz+ard
Lju+blja+na
lla+ma
  lla+mas
Llan+daf
Llan+daff
Llan+dud+no
Llan+elli
Llan+elly
Llan+fair+pwll
Llan+fair+pwll+
  gwyn+gyll
Llan+go+llen
lla+no
  lla+nos
Lla+no Es+ta+ca+
  do
Llewellyn
Lloyd
Lloyd's
Llywelyn ap
  Gruffudd
lo
loach
  loaches
load
  loads
  loads
  load+ing

load+ed
load+ed
load+er
  load+ers
load+ing
  load+ings
loads
load+star
  load+stars
load+stone
  load+stones
loaf
  loaves
  loafs
loaf+ing
  loafed
loaf+er
  loaf+ers
loam
  loams
loams
loam+ing
  loamed
loami+ness
loamy
loan
  loans
  loans
loan+ing
  loaned
loanback
  loanbacks
loan back
  verb
Lo+an+da
loan+er
  loan+ers
loath
loathe
  loathes
loath+ing
  loathed
loath+er
  loath+ers
loath+ing
  loath+ings
loath+ly
loath+some
loath+some+ly
loath+some+ness
loaves
lob
  lobs
  lobs
  lob+bing

lobbed	lo+cali+za+tions	lo+co+mo+tive	loft+ed
Lobachevsky	lo+cal+ize	lo+co+mo+tives	lofti+ly
lo+bar	lo+cal+izes	lo+co+mo+tor	lofti+ness
lo+bate	lo+cal+iz+ing	lo+co+weed	lofty
lo+bate+ly	lo+cal+ized	Lo+crian	lofti+er
lob+by	lo+cal+ly	Lo+crians	lofti+est
lob+bies	lo+cal+ness	Lo+cris	log
lob+bies	Lo+car+no	locu+lar	logs
lob+by+ing	lo+cate	locu+lus	logs
lob+bied	lo+cates	locu+li	log+ging
lob+by+er	lo+cat+ing	lo+cum	logged
lob+by+ers	lo+cat+ed	lo+cums	lo+gan
lob+by+ism	lo+ca+ter	lo+cum te+nens	lo+gans
lob+by+ist	lo+ca+ters	lo+cum te+nen+	Lo+gan
lob+by+ists	lo+ca+tion	tes	logan+berry
lobe	lo+ca+tions	lo+cus	logan+berries
lobes	loca+tive	loci	loga+rithm
lo+bec+to+my	loca+tives	lo+cust	loga+rithms
lo+bec+to+mies	loch	lo+custs	loga+rith+mic
lo+belia	lochs	lo+cu+tion	log+book
lo+belias	lochia	lo+cu+tions	log+books
Lobengula	loch+ial	Lod	loge
Lo+bi+to	loci	lode	loges
lob+lol+ly	lock	lodes	log+ger
lob+lol+lies	locks	lo+den	log+gers
lo+bo+la	locks	lode+star	log+ger+head
lo+bo+lo	lock+ing	lode+stars	log+ger+heads
lo+boto+my	locked	lode+stone	log+gia
lo+boto+mies	lock+able	lode+stones	log+gias *or*
lob+scouse	Locke	lodge	log+gie
lob+ster	lock+er	lodges	log+ging
lob+sters	lock+ers	lodges	log+ic
lobu+lar	Lock+er+bie	lodg+ing	logi+cal
lobu+late	lock+et	lodged	logi+cal+ity
lob+ule	lock+ets	Lodge	logi+cal+ly
lob+ules	lock+jaw	lodge+ment	logi+cal+ness
lob+worm	lock+out	lodge+ments	lo+gi+cian
lob+worms	lock+outs	lodg+er	lo+gi+cians
lo+cal	lock out	lodg+ers	lo+gis+ti+cal
lo+cals	*verb*	lodg+ing	lo+gis+tics
lo+cale	lock+smith	lodg+ings	log+log
lo+cales	lock+smiths	lodg+ings	log+logs
lo+cal+is+able	lock+up	lodg+ment	logo
lo+cali+sa+tion	lock+ups	lodg+ments	logos
lo+cali+sa+tions	lock-up	Lodi	logo+gram
lo+cal+ise	*adj.*	lo+ess	logo+grams
lo+cal+ises	lock up	lo+ess+ial	log+or+rhea
lo+cal+is+ing	*verb*	Loewe	*U.S.*
lo+cal+ised	Lockyer	Loewi	log+or+rhoea
lo+cal+ism	loco	Lo+fo+ten and	log+os
lo+cal+isms	locos	Ves+ter+å+len	logo+type
lo+cal+ity	locos	loft	logo+types
lo+cal+ities	loco+ing	lofts	log+roll
lo+cal+iz+able	locoed	lofts	log+rolls
lo+cali+za+tion	lo+co+mo+tion	loft+ing	log+roll+ing

log+rolled
log+roll+er
log+roll+ers
log+roll+ing
log+roll+ings
log+wood
log+woods
Lohengrin
loin
 loins
loin+cloth
 loin+cloths
loins
Loire
Loire-Atlantique
Loi+ret
Loir-et-Cher
loi+ter
 loi+ters
 loi+ter+ing
 loi+tered
loi+ter+er
 loi+ter+ers
loi+ter+ing
 loi+ter+ings
Loki
loll
 lolls
 lolls
 loll+ing
 lolled
Lol+land
Lol+lard
 Lol+lards
Lol+lard+ism
loll+er
 loll+ers
loll+ing
lol+li+pop
 lol+li+pops
 lol+lop
 lol+lops
 lol+lop+ing
 lol+loped
lol+lo ros+so
 lol+lo ros+sos
lol+ly
 lol+lies
Lomax
Lom+bard
place name
 Lom+bards
Lombard
surname
Lom+bardy

Lom+bok
Lomé
Lo+mond
Lon+don
place name
London
surname
Lon+don+der+ry
Lon+don+er
 Lon+don+ers
Lon+dri+na
lone
lone+li+ness
 lone+ly
 lone+li+er
 lone+li+est
lone+ness
lon+er
 lon+ers
lone+some
 lone+some+ly
 lone+some+ness
long
 adj.
 long+er
 long+est
long
 verb
 longs
 long+ing
 longed
Long
long-acting
Long+ben+ton
long+boat
 long+boats
long+bow
 long+bows
long+cloth
long-dated
long-day
long-distance
long-drawn-out
Long Eaton
lon+geron
 lon+gerons
lon+gev+ity
long-faced
Longfellow
Long+ford
long+hand
long-headed
long-headed+ly
long-headed+
 ness

long+horn
 long+horns
Lon+gin+ean
long+ing
 long+ings
long+ing+ly
Longinus
long+ish
lon+gi+tude
 lon+gi+tudes
lon+gi+tu+di+nal
lon+gi+tu+di+nal+
 ly
long-lived
long-livedness
long-off
 long-offs
long-on
 long-ons
long-playing
long-range
longs
long+ship
 long+ships
long+shore
long+shore+man
 long+shore+
 men
long-sighted
long-sighted+
 ness
long-standing
long-suffer+ing
long-suffer+ing+
 ly
long-term
long+time
Lon+gueuil
lon+gueur
 lon+gueurs
Longus
long+ways
long-winded
long-winded+ly
long-winded+
 ness
long+wise
Long+year+byen
lo+nic+era
Lons-le-Saunier
loo
 loos
loo+fah
 loo+fahs
look

looks
looks
look+ing
looked
look+alike
 look+alikes
look+er
 look+ers
looker-on
 lookers-on
look-in
 noun
 look in
 verb
look+ing
look+out
 look+outs
 look out
 verb
look+over
 look+overs
 look over
 verb
look-see
 look-sees
loom
 looms
 looms
 loom+ing
 loomed
loon
 loons
looney
 looneys
looni+ness
loony
 loonies
looni+er
 looni+est
loop
 loops
 loops
 loop+ing
 looped
loop+er
 loop+ers
loop+hole
 loop+holes
 loop+holes
 loop+hol+ing
 loop+holed
loopy
 loopi+er
 loopi+est
Loos

loose	*place name*	losses	lounge
looses	Lorca	lost	lounges
loos+ing	*surname*	lot	lounges
loosed	lord	lots	loung+ing
loos+er	lords	lots	lounged
loos+est	Lord	lot+ting	loung+er
loose+box	Lords	lot+ted	loung+ers
loose+boxes	lord+less	Lot	loupe
loose-jointed	lord+like	Lot-et-Garonne	loupes
loose-jointed+	lord+li+ness	loth	lour
ness	lord+ly	Lo+thario	lours
loose-leaf	lord+li+er	Lo+tharios	lours
loose+ly	lord+li+est	Lo+thian	lour+ing
loos+en	lor+do+sis	Lo+thians	loured
loos+ens	lor+dot+ic	Lo+thring+en	Lourdes
loos+en+ing	Lords	lo+tion	Lou+ren+co
loos+ened	Lord's	lo+tions	Marques
loos+en+er	lords-and-ladies	lots	lourie
loos+en+ers	lord+ship	lot+tery	louries
loose+ness	lord+ships	lot+teries	lour+ing
loose+strife	Lord+ship	lot+to	louse
loot	Lord+ships	lo+tus	*insect*
loots	lore	lo+tuses	lice
loots	Lo+relei	lotus-eater	louses
loot+ing	Loren	lotus-eaters	lous+ing
loot+ed	Lorentz	loud	loused
loot+er	Lorenz	loud+er	louse
loot+ers	lor+gnette	loud+est	*unpleasant*
lop	lor+gnettes	loud+en	*person*
lops	Lo+rient	loud+ens	louses
lops	lori+keet	loud+en+ing	louse+wort
lop+ping	lori+keets	loud+ened	louse+worts
lopped	lo+ris	loud-hailer	lousi+ly
lope	lo+ris	loud-hailers	lousi+ness
lopes	lorn	loud+ish	lousy
lopes	Lorrain	loud+ly	lousi+er
lop+ing	Lor+raine	loud+mouth	lousi+est
loped	Lorris	loud+mouths	lout
lop-eared	lor+ry	loud+mouthed	louts
lop+per	lor+ries	loud+ness	Louth
lop+pers	lory	loud+speaker	lout+ish
lop+sided	lories	loud+speakers	Lou+vain
lop+sided+ly	los+able	lough	lou+ver
lop+sided+ness	Los Ala+mos	loughs	*U.S.*
lo+qua+cious	Los An+ge+les	Lough+bor+ough	lou+vers
lo+qua+cious+ly	lose	lou+is	lou+vered
lo+qua+cious+	loses	lou+is	*U.S.*
ness	los+ing	Louis	lou+vre
lo+quac+ity	lost	Lou+is+bourg	lou+vres
lo+quat	los+er	Lou+is+burg	Lou+vre
lo+quats	los+ers	lou+is d'or	lou+vred
lor	Losey	lou+is d'or	lov+abil+ity
lo+ran	los+ing	Loui+si+ana	lov+able
lo+rans	los+ings	Louis Philippe	lov+able+ness
Lor+ca	loss	Lou+is+ville	lov+ably

lov+age
love
  loves
  loves
  lov+ing
  loved
love+abil+ity
love+able
love+able+ness
love+ably
love+bird
  love+birds
love+bite
  love+bites
love-in-a-mist
Lovelace
love+less
love+less+ly
love+less+ness
love-lies-bleeding
love+li+ness
Lovell
love+lock
  love+locks
love+lorn
love+ly
  love+li+er
  love+li+est
love+making
lov+er
  lov+ers
love+sick
love+sick+ness
lovey-dovey
lov+ing
lov+ing+ly
lov+ing+ness
low
  lows
  lows
  low+ing
  lowed
  low+er
  low+est
Low
low+an
  low+ans
low+born
low+bred
low+brow
  low+brows
Low-Church
low-density
low-down
Löwe

Lowell
low+er
  low+ers
  low+er+ing
  low+ered
lower-case
  lower-cases
  lower-casing
  lower-cased
lower-class
low+er+ing
lower+most
low+est
Lowes+toft
low-key
low-keyed
low+land
  low+lands
Low+land
  low+land+er
  low+land+ers
Low+land+er
  Low+land+ers
  Low+lands
low+life
  low+lifes
low+li+ness
low-loader
  low-loaders
low+ly
  low+li+er
  low+li+est
low-minded
low-minded+ly
low-minded+ness
low+ness
low-pitched
low-pressure
low-profile
lowrie
  lowries
low-rise
  low-rises
lowry
  lowries
Lowry
low-spirit+ed
low-spirit+ed+
  ness
low-tech
low-tension
Low+veld
low-water
lox
loy+al

loy+al+ism
loy+al+ist
  loy+al+ists
Loy+al+ist
  Loy+al+ists
loy+al+ly
loy+al+ty
  loy+al+ties
Loyola
loz+enge
  loz+enges
loz+enged
loz+engy
Lo+zère
L-plate
  L-plates
Lua+la+ba
Lu+an+da
Lu+ang Pra+bang
luau
  luaus
lub+ber
  lub+bers
lub+ber+li+ness
lub+ber+ly
Lub+bock
Lü+beck
Lu+blin
lu+bra
  lu+bras
lub+ri+cant
  lub+ri+cants
lu+bri+cate
  lu+bri+cates
  lu+bri+cat+ing
  lu+bri+cat+ed
lu+bri+ca+tion
lu+bri+ca+tive
lu+bri+ca+tor
  lu+bri+ca+tors
lu+bri+cious
lu+bric+ity
lu+bri+cous
Lu+bum+ba+shi
Lucan
  surname
Lu+can
  of St. Luke
Lu+ca+nia
Lucas
Lucas van Leyden
Luc+ca
luce
  luces
lu+cent

lu+cent+ly
lu+cerne
Lu+cerne
Lucian
lu+cid
lu+cid+ity
lu+cid+ly
lu+cid+ness
lu+ci+fer
  lu+ci+fers
Lu+ci+fer
Lucilius
Lucina
luck
lucki+ly
lucki+ness
luck+less
luck+less+ly
luck+less+ness
Luck+now
lucky
  lucki+er
  lucki+est
lu+cra+tive
lu+cra+tive+ly
lu+cra+tive+ness
lu+cre
Lucretia
Lu+cretian
Lucretius
lu+cu+brate
  lu+cu+brates
  lu+cu+brat+ing
  lu+cu+brat+ed
lu+cu+bra+tion
  lu+cu+bra+tions
lu+cu+bra+tor
  lu+cu+bra+tors
Lu+cul+lan
Lu+cul+lean
Lu+cul+lian
Lucullus
Lucy
lud
  luds
Lü+da
Lud+dite
  Lud+dites
Ludendorff
Lü+den+scheid
Lü+der+itz
Lu+dhia+na
lu+di+crous
lu+di+crous+ly
lu+di+crous+ness

ludo
Lud+wigs+burg
Lud+wigs+ha+
 fen
luff
 luffs
 luffs
 luff+ing
 luffed
lug
 lugs
 lugs
 lug+ging
 lugged
Lu+gano
Lu+gansk
luge
 luges
 luges
 lug+ing
 luged
Lu+ger
Trademark
 Lu+gers
lug+gage
lug+ger
 lug+gers
lug+hole
 lug+holes
Lugo
lug+sail
 lug+sails
lu+gu+bri+ous
lu+gu+bri+ous+ly
lu+gu+bri+ous+
 ness
lug+worm
 lug+worms
Lukács
Luke
luke+warm
luke+warm+ly
luke+warm+ness
lull
 lulls
 lulls
 lull+ing
 lulled
lulla+by
 lulla+bies
 lulla+bies
 lulla+by+ing
 lulla+bied
Lully
lum+ba+go

lum+bar
lum+ber
 lum+bers
 lum+ber+ing
 lum+bered
 lum+ber+er
 lum+ber+ers
 lum+ber+ing
 lum+ber+ings
lumber+jack
 lumber+jacks
lumber+jacket
 lumber+jackets
lumber+yard
 lumber+yards
lu+men
 lu+mens or
 lu+mi+na
Lumière
lu+mi+nal
lu+mi+nance
lu+mi+nary
lu+mi+naries
lu+mi+nesce
lu+mi+nesces
lu+mi+nesc+ing
lu+mi+nesced
lu+mi+nes+cence
lu+mi+nes+cent
lu+mi+nos+ity
lu+mi+nos+ities
lu+mi+nous
lu+mi+nous+ly
lu+mi+nous+ness
lum+me
lum+mox
 lum+moxes
lum+my
lump
 lumps
 lumps
 lump+ing
 lumped
lum+pec+to+my
 lum+pec+to+
  mies
lump+en
lump+en+pro+le+
 tari+at
lump+fish
 lump+fish or
 lump+fishes
lumpi+ly
lumpi+ness
lump+ish

lump+ish+ly
lump+ish+ness
lumpy
 lumpi+er
 lumpi+est
Lumumba
Luna
lu+na+cy
 lu+na+cies
lu+nar
lu+nate
 lu+nat+ed
 lu+na+tic
 lu+na+tics
lunch
 lunches
 lunches
 lunch+ing
 lunched
lunch+eon
 lunch+eons
lunch+er
 lunch+ers
lunch+room
 lunch+rooms
Lund
Lundy
Lü+ne+burg
lu+nette
 lu+nettes
Lu+né+ville
lung
 lungs
lunge
 lunges
 lunges
 lung+ing
 lunged
lung+er
 lung+ers
lung+fish
 lung+fish or
 lung+fishes
lung+wort
 lung+worts
lu+nu+la
 lu+nu+lae
Luo+yang
Lu+per+ca+lia
 Lu+per+ca+lia
  or
 Lu+per+ca+lias
Lu+per+ca+lian
lu+pin
 lu+pins

lu+pine
lu+pines
U.S.
lu+pus
lu+pus vul+gar+is
lurch
 lurches
 lurches
 lurch+ing
 lurched
lurch+er
 lurch+ers
lure
 lures
 lures
 lur+ing
 lured
lur+er
 lur+ers
Lu+rex
Trademark
lu+rid
lu+rid+ly
lu+rid+ness
lurk
 lurks
 lurks
 lurk+ing
 lurked
lurk+er
 lurk+ers
lurk+ing
Lu+sa+ka
Lu+sa+tia
Lu+sa+tian
 Lu+sa+tians
lus+cious
lus+cious+ly
lus+cious+ness
lush
 lushes
 lushes
 lush+ing
 lushed
lush+ly
lush+ness
Lüshun
Lu+si+ta+nia
lust
 lusts
 lusts
 lust+ing
 lust+ed
lus+ter
U.S.

lus+ters
lus+ters
lus+ter+ing
lus+tered
lus+ter+less
U.S.
luster+ware
U.S.
lust+ful
lust+ful+ly
lust+ful+ness
lusti+ly
lusti+ness
lus+tral
lus+trate
lus+trates
lus+trat+ing
lus+trat+ed
lus+tra+tion
lus+tra+tions
lus+tre
lus+tres
lus+tres
lus+tring
lus+tred
lus+tre+less
lustre+ware
lus+trous
lus+trum
lus+trums *or*
lus+tra
lusty
lusti+er
lusti+est
lu+tan+ist
lu+tan+ists
lute
lutes
lutes
lut+ing
lut+ed
lu+tecium
lu+tein
lu+tein+iz+ing
lu+tenist
lu+tenists
lu+tetium
Luther
Lu+ther+an
Lu+ther+ans

Lu+ther+an+ism
Lu+ther+ism
Luthuli
lut+ist
lut+ists
Lu+ton
Lutuli
Lutyens
Lüt+zen
lux
lux
lux+ate
lux+ates
lux+at+ing
lux+at+ed
luxa+tion
luxa+tions
luxe
Lux+em+bourg
Luxemburg
Lux+or
luxu+ri+ance
luxu+ri+ances
luxu+ri+ant
luxu+ri+ant+ly
luxu+ri+ate
luxu+ri+ates
luxu+ri+at+ing
luxu+ri+at+ed
luxu+ria+tion
luxu+ri+ous
luxu+ri+ous+ly
luxu+ri+ous+ness
luxu+ry
luxu+ries
Lu+zon
Lvov
Lwów
ly+ase
ly+can+thrope
ly+can+thropes
ly+can+throp+ic
ly+can+thro+py
Lycaon
Lycao+nia
ly+cée
ly+cées
ly+ceum
ly+ceums
lych

ly+chee
ly+chees
lych+nis
Ly+cia
Ly+cian
Ly+cians
ly+co+po+dium
ly+co+po+
diums
Ly+cra
Trademark
Lycurgus
Lyd+da
lydd+ite
Lydgate
Lydia
Lyd+ian
Lyd+ians
lye
lyes
Lyell
ly+ing
lying-in
lyings-in
lyke-wake
lyke-wakes
Lyle
Lyly
Lyme
Lyme Re+gis
Lym+ing+ton
lymph
lym+phat+ic
lym+phat+ics
lym+pho+cyte
lym+pho+cytes
lym+pho+cyt+ic
lym+phoid
lym+pho+ma
lym+pho+ma+ta
or
lym+pho+mas
lynch
lynches
lynch+ing
lynched
Lynch
lynch+er
lynch+ers
lynch+et

lynch+ets
lynch+ing
lynch+ings
Lynn
lynx
lynxes *or*
lynx
lynx-eyed
lynx+like
Lyon
Lyon+nais
Ly+on+nesse
Ly+ons
place name
Lyons
surname
ly+rate
lyre
lyres
lyre+bird
lyre+birds
lyr+ic
lyr+ics
lyri+cal
lyri+cal+ly
lyri+cal+ness
lyri+cism
lyri+cisms
lyri+cist
lyri+cists
Lysander
lyse
lyses
lys+ing
lysed
Lysenko
ly+ser+gic
Lysias
Lysimachus
ly+sin
ly+sins
ly+sis
ly+ses
Ly+sol
Trademark
Lyth+am Saint
Anne's
lyt+ic
Lytton

M

m
ms
M
M's *or*
Ms
ma
mas
ma'am
ma'ams
Maa+ri+an+ha+
  mi+na
Maas
Maas+tricht
Mab
Mabuse
mac
macs
Mac
ma+ca+bre
mac+ad+am
maca+da+mia
maca+da+mias
mac+ad+ami+sa+
  tion
mac+ad+ami+sa+
  tions
mac+ad+am+ise
mac+ad+am+
  ises
mac+ad+am+is+
  ing
mac+ad+am+
  ised
mac+ad+am+is+
  er
mac+ad+am+is+
  ers
mac+ad+ami+za+
  tion
mac+ad+ami+za+
  tions
mac+ad+am+ize
mac+ad+am+
  izes

mac+ad+am+iz+
  ing
mac+ad+am+
  ized
mac+ad+am+iz+
  er
mac+ad+am+iz+
  ers
Ma+cao
Ma+ca+pá
ma+caque
ma+caques
maca+ro+ni
maca+ro+nis
  or
maca+ro+nies
maca+roon
maca+roons
Macarthur
MacArthur
Ma+cas+sar
Macáu
Macaulay
ma+caw
ma+caws
Macbeth
MacBride
mac+ca+ro+ni
mac+ca+ro+nis
  or
mac+ca+ro+nies
Mac+cles+field
Macdonald
MacDonald
mace
maces
mace+bearer
mace+bearers
ma+cedoine
ma+cedoines
Mac+edon
Mac+edo+nia
Mac+edo+nian
Mac+edo+nians
Ma+ceió

mac+er+ate
mac+er+ates
mac+er+at+ing
mac+er+at+ed
mac+era+tion
mac+era+tions
mac+era+tor
mac+era+tors
MacGuffin
MacGuffins
Mach
Machado
mach+air
mach+airs
Machel
ma+chete
ma+chetes
Machiavelli
Machia+vel+lian
Machia+vel+
  lians
Machia+vel+li+an+
  ism
ma+chico+late
ma+chico+lates
ma+chico+lat+
  ing
ma+chico+lat+
  ed
ma+chico+la+tion
ma+chico+la+
  tions
ma+chin+abil+ity
ma+chin+able
machi+nate
machi+nates
machi+nat+ing
machi+nat+ed
machi+na+tion
machi+na+tions
machi+na+tor
machi+na+tors
ma+chine
ma+chines
ma+chines

ma+chin+ing
ma+chined
ma+chine+able
machine-gun
machine-guns
machine-
  gunning
machine-gunned
ma+chine gun
ma+chine guns
ma+chin+ery
ma+chin+eries
machine-tooled
ma+chin+ist
ma+chin+ists
ma+chis+mo
macho
machos
Ma+chu Pic+chu
Ma+cí+as Ngue+
  ma
mac+in+tosh
mac+in+toshes
mack
macks
Mac+kay
Mackellar
Mac+ken+zie
  place name
Mackenzie
  surname
macke+rel
macke+rel *or*
macke+rels
Mackerras
Macki+nac
mack+in+tosh
mack+in+toshes
Mackintosh
Maclean
Macleod
Macmahon
Macmillan
MacMillan
MacNeice

Ma+con
U.S. town
Mâ+con
French town
Macpherson
Macquarie
surname
Mac+quarie
place name
mac+ra+mé
Macready
macro
macro+bi+ot+ic
macro+bi+ot+ics
macro+car+pa
macro+cephal+ic
macro+cephal+
  ous
macro+cepha+ly
macro+cli+mate
  macro+cli+
  mates
macro+cosm
  macro+cosms
macro+cos+mic
macro+cos+mi+
  cal+ly
macro+eco+nom+
  ic
macro+eco+nom+
  ics
macro+mol+
  ecule
  macro+mol+
  ecules
mac+ron
  mac+rons
macro+scop+ic
macro+scopi+cal+
  ly
macu+la
  macu+lae
macu+la lu+tea
  macu+lae lu+
  teae
macu+lar
macu+la+tion
  macu+la+tions
mac+ule
  mac+ules
mad
  mads
mad+ding
mad+ded
mad+der

mad+dest
Mada+gas+can
  Mada+gas+cans
Mada+gas+car
mad+am
  mad+ams *or*
  mes+dames
mad+ame
  mes+dames
mad+cap
  mad+caps
mad+den
  mad+dens
  mad+den+ing
  mad+dened
  mad+den+ing
  mad+den+ing+ly
mad+der
mad+ding
  mad+ding+ly
made
Ma+dei+ra
mad+eleine
  mad+eleines
mad+emoi+selle
  mes+de+moi+
  selles
made-up
mad+house
  mad+houses
Madh+ya Bha+rat
Madh+ya Pra+
  desh
Madi+son
place name
Madison
surname
mad+ly
mad+man
  mad+men
mad+ness
  mad+nesses
Ma+don+na
Virgin Mary
Madonna
singer
mad+ras
  mad+rases
Ma+dras
Ma+dre de Dios
mad+re+por+al
mad+re+pore
mad+re+pores
mad+re+po+rian
mad+re+por+ic

Ma+drid
mad+ri+gal
  mad+ri+gals
mad+ri+gal+
  esque
  mad+ri+gal+ian
  mad+ri+gal+ist
  mad+ri+gal+ists
Ma+du+ra
Ma+du+rai
Ma+du+rese
mad+woman
  mad+women
mae
Mae+an+der
Ma+eba+shi
Maecenas
mael+strom
  mael+stroms
Mael+strom
mae+nad
  mae+nads
mae+nad+ic
maes+to+so
  maes+to+sos
Maes+tricht
maes+tro
  maes+tri *or*
  maes+tros
Maeterlinck
Ma+ewo
Maf+eking
Ma+fia
Maf+ikeng
ma+fio+so
  ma+fio+sos *or*
  ma+fio+si
mag
  mags
ma+gainin
  ma+gainins
Ma+ga+lla+nes
maga+zine
  maga+zines
mag+da+len
  mag+da+lens
Mag+da+lena
mag+da+lene
  mag+da+lenes
Mag+da+lene
Mag+da+lenian
Mag+de+burg
Ma+gel+lan
place name
Magellan

surname
ma+gen+ta
Mag+gio+re
mag+got
  mag+gots
mag+goty
Ma+ghreb
Ma+ghre+bi
  Ma+ghre+bis
Ma+ghrib
Ma+ghri+bi
  Ma+ghri+bis
magi
ma+gian
mag+ic
  mag+ics
  mag+ics
mag+ick+ing
mag+icked
magi+cal
  magi+cal+ly
ma+gi+cian
  ma+gi+cians
ma+gilp
Ma+gi+not
mag+is+te+rial
mag+is+te+ri+al+
  ly
mag+is+tra+cy
  mag+is+tra+cies
mag+is+tral
mag+is+tral+ity
  mag+is+tral+
  ities
mag+is+trate
  mag+is+trates
mag+is+trate+
  ship
mag+is+tra+ture
  mag+is+tra+
  tures
Mag+le+mo+
  sean
Mag+le+mo+sian
mag+ma
  mag+mas *or*
  mag+ma+ta
mag+mat+ic
Mag+na Car+ta
Mag+na Char+ta
Mag+na Grae+cia
mag+na+nim+ity
  mag+na+nim+
  ities
mag+nani+mous

mag+nani+mous+
ly
mag+nate
mag+nates
mag+nate+ship
mag+ne+sia
mag+ne+sian
mag+ne+sic
mag+ne+sium
mag+net
mag+nets
mag+net+ic
mag+neti+cal+ly
mag+net+is+able
mag+neti+sa+
tion
mag+neti+sa+
tions
mag+net+ise
mag+net+ises
mag+net+is+ing
mag+net+ised
mag+net+is+er
mag+net+is+ers
mag+net+ism
mag+net+ite
mag+net+iz+able
mag+neti+za+
tion
mag+neti+za+
tions
mag+net+ize
mag+net+izes
mag+net+iz+ing
mag+net+ized
mag+net+iz+er
mag+net+iz+ers
mag+ne+to
mag+ne+tos
mag+ne+to+elec+
tric
mag+ne+to+elec+
tri+cal
mag+ne+to+elec+
tric+ity
mag+ne+tom+
eter
mag+ne+tom+
eters
mag+ne+tom+
etry
mag+ne+to+mo+
tive
mag+ne+to+
sphere

mag+ne+tron
mag+ne+trons
mag+ni+fi+able
Mag+nifi+cat
Mag+nifi+cats
mag+ni+fi+ca+
tion
mag+ni+fi+ca+
tions
mag+nifi+cence
mag+nifi+cent
mag+nifi+cent+ly
mag+nifi+co
mag+nifi+coes
mag+ni+fi+er
mag+ni+fi+ers
mag+ni+fy
mag+ni+fies
mag+ni+fy+ing
mag+ni+fied
mag+nilo+quence
mag+nilo+quent
mag+nilo+quent+
ly
Mag+ni+to+
gorsk
mag+ni+tude
mag+ni+tudes
mag+no+lia
mag+no+lias
mag+nox
mag+num
mag+nums
Magog
mag+pie
mag+pies
Magritte
mag+uey
mag+ueys
ma+gus
magi
Magus
Mag+yar
Mag+yars
Ma+gyar+or+
szág
Ma+ha+bha+ra+
ta
Ma+ha+bha+ra+
tam
Ma+ha+bha+ra+
tum
Ma+ha+jan+ga
Ma+hal+la el Ku+
bra

Ma+ha+na+di
ma+ha+ra+ja
ma+ha+ra+jas
ma+ha+ra+jah
ma+ha+ra+jahs
ma+ha+ra+nee
ma+ha+ra+nees
ma+ha+ra+ni
ma+ha+ra+nis
Ma+ha+rash+tra
ma+ha+ri+shi
ma+ha+ri+shis
ma+hat+ma
ma+hat+mas
Ma+ha+ya+na
Mah+di
Mah+dis
Mah+dism
Mah+dist
Mah+dists
Mahé
Mahfouz
Mahfuz
mah+jong
mah-jongg
Mahler
mahl+stick
mahl+sticks
ma+hoga+ny
ma+hoga+nies
Mahomet
ma+ho+nia
ma+ho+nias
Ma+hound
ma+hout
ma+houts
Mäh+ren
mah+seer
mah+seers
Maia
maid
maids
maid+en
maid+ens
maiden+hair
maid+en+head
maid+en+heads
Maid+en+head
maid+en+hood
maid+en+ish
maid+en+like
maid+en+li+ness
maid+en+ly
maid+servant
maid+servants

Maid+stone
Mai+du+gu+ri
mai+hem
Mai+kop
mail
mails
mails
mail+ing
mailed
mail+able
mail+bag
mail+bags
mail+box
mail+boxes
Mailer
Maillol
mail+lot
mail+lots
mail+man
mail+men
mail-order
adj.
mail or+der
noun
mail+sack
mail+sacks
mail+shot
mail+shots
maim
maims
maim+ing
maimed
mai mai
mai mais
Mai+moni+dean
Mai+moni+
deans
Maimonides
main
mains
Main
main+brace
main+braces
Maine
Maine-et-Loire
main+frame
main+frames
main+land
Main+land
main+land+er
main+land+ers
main+line
main+lines
main+lin+ing
main+lined

main-line
adj.
main line
noun
main+lin+er
main+lin+ers
main+ly
main+mast
main+masts
main+sail
main+sails
main+sheet
main+sheets
main+spring
main+springs
main+stay
main+stays
main+stream
main+street+ing
main+tain
main+tains
main+tain+ing
main+tained
main+tain+able
main+tain+er
main+te+nance
Maintenon
main+top
main+tops
main-topmast
main-topmasts
main+top+sail
main+top+sails
Mainz
ma+ioli+ca
mai+son+ette
mai+son+ettes
mai+son+nette
mai+son+nettes
Mait+land
place name
Maitland
surname
maî+tre d'hô+tel
maî+tres d'hô+
tel
maize
ma+jes+tic
ma+jes+ti+cal+ly
maj+es+ty
maj+es+ties
Maj+es+ty
Maj+es+ties
ma+joli+ca
ma+jor

ma+jors
ma+jors
ma+jor+ing
ma+jored
Major
Ma+jor+ca
major-domo
major-domos
ma+jor+ette
ma+jor+ettes
major-general+cy
major-general+
ship
ma+jor+ity
ma+jor+ities
ma+jor+ship
Ma+jun+ga
ma+jus+cu+lar
ma+jus+cule
ma+jus+cules
mak+able
Mak+ah
Mak+ahs
Ma+ka+lu
Ma+kas+ar
Ma+kas+sar
make
makes
mak+ing
made
make-believe
noun
make be+lieve
makes be+lieve
mak+ing be+
lieve
made be+lieve
Mak+edho+nia
make+over
make+overs
make over
verb
mak+er
mak+ers
Mak+er
make+shift
make+shifts
make-up
make-ups
make up
verb
make+weight
make+weights
Ma+ke+yev+ka

Ma+khach+ka+la
mak+ing
ma+kings
Mak+kah
mako
makos
Ma+kur+di
Mala+bar
Ma+la+bo
mal+ab+sorp+
tion
ma+lac+ca
ma+lac+cas
Ma+lac+ca
Malachi
mala+chite
mal+ad+just+ed
mal+ad+just+
ment
mal+ad+min+is+
ter
mal+ad+min+is+
ters
mal+ad+min+is+
ter+ing
mal+ad+min+is+
tered
mal+ad+min+is+
tra+tion
mala+droit
mala+droit+ly
mala+droit+ness
mala+dy
mala+dies
Má+la+ga
Mala+gasy
Mala+gasy *or*
Mala+gasies
ma+laise
Malamud
mala+mute
mala+mutes
Ma+lang
mala+prop+ism
mala+prop+isms
mal+ap+ro+pos
Mä+lar
ma+laria
ma+lar+ial
ma+lar+ian
ma+lari+ous
ma+lar+key
ma+lar+ky
Malatesta
Mala+thi+on

Trademark
Ma+la+tya
Ma+la+wi
Ma+lay
Ma+lays
Ma+laya
Mala+ya+laam
Mala+ya+lam
Ma+lay+an
Ma+lay+ans
Malayo-
Polynesian
Ma+lay+sia
Ma+lay+sian
Ma+lay+sians
Malcolm
mal+con+tent
mal+con+tents
mal de mer
Mal+dives
Mal+div+ian
Mal+don
male
males
Malé
ma+leate
ma+leates
Malebranche
mal+edic+tion
mal+edic+tions
mal+edic+tive
mal+edic+tory
mal+efac+tion
mal+efac+tor
mal+efac+tors
ma+lef+ic
ma+lefi+cent
mal+emute
mal+emutes
male+ness
Malenkov
Malevich
ma+levo+lence
ma+levo+lent
ma+levo+lent+ly
mal+fea+sance
mal+fea+sant
mal+fea+sants
mal+for+ma+tion
mal+for+ma+
tions
mal+formed
mal+func+tion
mal+func+tions
mal+func+tions

mal+func+tion+
  ing
mal+func+tioned
Malherbe
Mali
mal+ic
mal+ice
ma+li+cious
ma+li+cious+ly
ma+li+cious+
  ness
ma+lign
ma+ligns
ma+lign+ing
ma+ligned
ma+lig+nan+cy
ma+lig+nan+
  cies
ma+lig+nant
ma+lig+nant+ly
ma+lign+er
ma+lign+ers
ma+lig+nity
ma+lig+nities
ma+lign+ly
ma+lines
Ma+lines
ma+lin+ger
ma+lin+gers
ma+lin+ger+ing
ma+lin+gered
ma+lin+ger+er
ma+lin+ger+ers
Malinowski
mall
  malls
mal+lard
  mal+lard *or*
  mal+lards
Mallarmé
mal+le+abil+ity
mal+le+able
mal+le+ably
mal+lee
  mal+lees
mal+leo+lus
mal+leo+li
mal+let
  mal+lets
mal+le+us
mal+lei
Ma+llor+ca
mal+low
  mal+lows
malm

Mal+mé+dy
Malmö
malm+sey
mal+nu+tri+tion
mal+odor+ous
Malory
Malpighi
Mal+pigh+ian
mal+prac+tice
  mal+prac+tices
Malraux
malt
  malts
  malts
malt+ing
malt+ed
Mal+ta
malt+ed
Mal+tese
Mal+tese
Malthus
Mal+thu+sian
Mal+thu+sians
Mal+thu+si+an+
  ism
malt+ing
malt+ings
malt+ose
mal+treat
  mal+treats
  mal+treat+ing
  mal+treat+ed
mal+treat+er
  mal+treat+ers
mal+treat+ment
malt+ster
  malt+sters
malty
malti+er
malti+est
Ma+lu+ku
mal+va+ceous
Mal+vern
mal+ver+sa+tion
Mal+vi+nas
mam
  mams
mama
  mamas
Mama+luke
  Mama+lukes
mam+ba
  mam+bas
mam+bo
  mam+bos

mam+bos
mam+bo+ing
mam+boed
Mam+eluke
  Mam+elukes
Mamet
ma+mil+la
  ma+mil+lae
ma+mil+lary
mam+ma
  mother
  mam+mas
mam+ma
  milk-secreting
  organ
  mam+mae
mam+mal
  mam+mals
mam+ma+lian
  mam+ma+lians
mam+ma+ry
mam+mie
  mam+mies
mam+mil+la
  U.S.
  mam+mil+lae
mam+mil+lary
  U.S.
mam+mo+gram
  mam+mo+
    grams
mam+mog+ra+
  phy
mam+mon
Mam+mon
mam+mon+ish
mam+mon+ism
mam+mon+ist
  mam+mon+ists
mam+mon+ite
  mam+mon+ites
mam+moth
  mam+moths
mam+my
  mam+mies
Ma+mo+ré
man
  men
  mans
man+ning
manned
Man
mana
mana+cle
mana+cles

mana+cles
mana+cling
mana+cled
Ma+na+do
man+age
man+ages
man+ag+ing
man+aged
man+age+abil+ity
man+age+able
man+age+able+
  ness
man+age+ably
man+age+ment
man+age+
  ments
man+ag+er
man+ag+ers
man+ag+er+ess
man+ag+er+
  esses
mana+gerial
mana+geri+al+ly
man+ag+er+ship
man+ag+ing
Ma+na+gua
Ma+na+ma
ma+ña+na
Ma+náos
Ma+nas+sas
Manasseh
man-at-arms
men-at-arms
mana+tee
  mana+tees
Ma+naus
Manche
man+ches+ter
  man+ches+ters
Man+ches+ter
man+chi+neel
  man+chi+neels
Man+chou+kuo
Man+chu
  Man+chus *or*
  Man+chu
Man+chu+kuo
Man+chu+ria
Man+chu+rian
  Man+chu+rians
man+ci+ple
  man+ci+ples
Man+cu+nian
  Man+cu+nians
man+da+la

man+da+las
Man+da+lay
man+da+mus
man+da+muses
man+da+rin
man+da+rins
Man+da+rin
man+dar+in+ate
man+dar+in+
ates
man+da+tary
man+da+taries
man+date
man+dates
man+dates
man+dat+ing
man+dat+ed
man+da+tor
man+da+tors
man+da+to+ri+ly
man+da+tory
man+da+tories
Mandela
Mandelshtam
Mandelstam
Mandeville
man+di+ble
man+di+bles
man+dibu+lar
man+dibu+late
man+do+lin
man+do+lins
man+do+line
man+do+lines
man+do+lin+ist
man+do+lin+ists
man+drago+ra
man+drago+ras
man+drake
man+drakes
man+drel
man+drels
man+dril
man+drill
man+drills
mane
manes
maned
ma+nege
ma+neges
ma+nège
ma+nèges
ma+nes
Manes

Manet
ma+neu+ver
U.S.
ma+neu+vers
ma+neu+vers
ma+neu+ver+
ing
ma+neu+vered
ma+neu+ver+abil+
ity
U.S.
ma+neu+ver+
able
U.S.
ma+neu+ver+er
U.S.
ma+neu+ver+
ers
man+ful
man+ful+ly
man+ful+ness
man+ga+bey
man+ga+beys
Man+ga+lore
man+ga+nese
mange
man+gel+wur+zel
man+gel+wur+
zels
man+ger
man+gers
mange+tout
mange+touts
man+gey
man+gi+er
man+gi+est
man+gi+ly
man+gi+ness
man+gle
man+gles
man+gles
man+gling
man+gled
man+gled
man+gler
man+glers
man+go
man+goes *or*
man+gos
man+gold+wur+
zel
man+gold+wur+
zels
man+go+nel
man+go+nels

man+grove
man+groves
man+gy
man+gi+er
man+gi+est
man+handle
man+handles
man+handling
man+handled
Man+hat+tan
man+hole
man+holes
man+hood
man-hour
man-hours
man+hunt
man+hunts
Mani
ma+nia
ma+nias
ma+ni+ac
ma+ni+acs
ma+nia+cal
ma+nia+cal+ly
man+ic
man+ics
manic-depres+
sive
manic-depres+
sives
Mani+chaean
Mani+chaeans
Mani+chae+ism
Manichaeus
Mani+chean
Mani+cheans
Mani+chee
Mani+chees
Mani+che+ism
Manicheus
mani+cure
mani+cures
mani+cures
mani+cur+ing
mani+cured
mani+fest
mani+fests
mani+fests
mani+fest+ing
mani+fest+ed
mani+fest+able
mani+fes+ta+tion
mani+fes+ta+
tions
mani+fes+ta+tive

mani+fest+ly
mani+fes+to
mani+fes+toes
or
mani+fes+tos
mani+fold
mani+folds
mani+folds
mani+fold+ing
mani+fold+ed
mani+fold+ly
mani+fold+ness
mani+kin
mani+kins
Ma+nila
ma+nil+la
ma+nil+las
mani+oc
manio+ca
ma+nipu+labil+ity
ma+nipu+lable
ma+nipu+lat+able
ma+nipu+late
ma+nipu+lates
ma+nipu+lat+ing
ma+nipu+lat+ed
ma+nipu+la+tion
ma+nipu+la+
tions
ma+nipu+la+tive
ma+nipu+la+tor
ma+nipu+la+
tors
ma+nipu+la+tory
Ma+ni+pur
Ma+ni+sa
mani+to
mani+tos *or*
mani+to
Mani+to+ba
Mani+to+ban
Mani+to+bans
mani+tou
mani+tous *or*
mani+tou
mani+tu
mani+tus *or*
mani+tu
Mani+za+les
man+kind
Manley
man+like
man+li+ness
man+ly
man+li+er

man+li+est
man-made
Mann
man+na
Man+nar
manned
man+ne+quin
 man+ne+quins
man+ner
 man+ners
man+nered
Mannerheim
man+ner+ism
 man+ner+isms
man+ner+ist
 man+ner+ists
man+ner+is+tic
man+ner+is+ti+
 cal+ly
man+ner+less
man+ner+less+
 ness
man+ner+li+ness
man+ner+ly
man+ners
Mann+heim
place name
Mannheim
surname
man+ni+kin
 man+ni+kins
Manning
man+nish
man+nish+ly
man+nish+ness
ma+noeu+vrabil+
 ity
ma+noeu+vrable
ma+noeu+vre
 ma+noeu+vres
 ma+noeu+vres
 ma+noeu+vring
 ma+noeu+vred
 ma+noeu+vrer
 ma+noeu+vrers
man-of-war
men-of-war
Manolete
ma+nom+eter
 ma+nom+eters
mano+met+ric
mano+met+ri+cal
man+or
 man+ors
ma+no+rial

man+power
man+qué
Man+re+sa
man+sard
 man+sards
Mansart
manse
 manses
Mansell
man+servant
 men+servants
Mans+field
place name
Mansfield
surname
Mansholt
man+sion
 man+sions
man-sized
man+slaughter
Man+sû+ra
man+ta
man+tas
man+teau
 man+teaus *or*
 man+teaux
Mantegna
man+tel
 man+tels
man+tel+et
 man+tel+ets
mantel+piece
 mantel+pieces
man+tic
man+ti+cal+ly
man+til+la
 man+til+las
Man+ti+nea
Man+ti+neia
man+tis
 man+tises *or*
 man+tes
man+tis+sa
 man+tis+sas
man+tle
 man+tles
 man+tles
man+tling
man+tled
man+tlet
 man+tlets
Man+to+va
man+tra
 man+tras
man+tua

man+tuas
Man+tua
manu+al
 manu+als
manu+al+ly
manu+fac+tory
 manu+fac+
  tories
manu+fac+ture
 manu+fac+tures
 manu+fac+tures
 manu+fac+tur+
  ing
 manu+fac+tured
 manu+fac+tur+er
 manu+fac+tur+
  ers
 manu+fac+tur+
  ing
ma+nu+ka
 ma+nu+kas
Ma+nu+kau
manu+mis+sion
 manu+mis+
  sions
manu+mit
 manu+mits
 manu+mit+ting
 manu+mit+ted
ma+nure
 ma+nures
 ma+nures
 ma+nur+ing
 ma+nured
 ma+nur+er
 ma+nur+ers
ma+nus
 ma+nus
manu+script
 manu+scripts
Manutius
Manx
Manx+man
 Manx+men
Manx+wom+an
 Manx+wom+en
many
many-sided
many-sided+ness
man+za+nil+la
 man+za+nil+las
Manzoni
Mao+ism
Mao+ist
 Mao+ists

Mao+ri
 Mao+ris *or*
 Mao+ri
Maori+land
Mao Ze Dong
map
 maps
 maps
map+ping
mapped
Map
Mapes
ma+ple
 ma+ples
map+ping
 map+pings
Ma+pu+to
ma+quette
 ma+quettes
ma+quis
 ma+quis
mar
mars
mar+ring
marred
mara+bou
 mara+bous
mara+bout
 mara+bouts
ma+raca
 ma+racas
Mara+cai+bo
Mara+can+da
Ma+ra+cay
Maradona
ma+rae
 ma+raes
Ma+ra+jó
ma+ran+ta
 ma+ran+tas
Maraş
ma+ras+ca
 ma+ras+cas
mara+schi+no
 mara+schi+nos
ma+ras+mic
ma+ras+mus
Marat
mara+thon
 mara+thons
Mara+thon
ma+raud
 ma+rauds
 ma+raud+ing
 ma+raud+ed

ma+raud+er
ma+raud+ers
ma+raud+ing
mar+ble
mar+bles
mar+bles
mar+bling
mar+bled
mar+bled
mar+bles
mar+bling
Mar+burg
marc
marcs
Marc
mar+ca+site
mar+cato
Marceau
Marcellus
march
marches
marches
march+ing
marched
March
Marches
Marche
march+er
march+ers
Marches
march+ing
mar+chion+ess
mar+chion+
  esses
march+pane
Marciano
Marconi
Marco Polo
Marcos
Marcus Aurelius
  Antoninus
Marcuse
Mar del Pla+ta
Mar+di Gras
Marduk
mare
female horse
mares
mare
lunar plains
  ma+ria
Ma+ren+go
Marenzio
mare's-nest
  mare's-nests

mare's-tail
  mare's-tails
Margaret
mar+gar+ic
mar+ga+rine
  mar+ga+rines
Mar+ga+ri+ta
mar+gar+it+ic
Mar+gate
marge
marges
mar+gin
  mar+gins
  mar+gins
mar+gin+ing
mar+gined
mar+gin+al
mar+gin+als
mar+gi+na+lia
mar+gin+al+ity
mar+gin+al+ly
mar+gin+ate
mar+gin+ates
mar+gin+at+ing
mar+gin+at+ed
mar+gina+tion
mar+gra+vate
mar+gra+vates
mar+grave
mar+graves
mar+gra+vine
mar+gra+vines
mar+gue+rite
mar+gue+rites
ma+ria
mari+achi
mari+achis
Ma+ria+nao
Ma+ri+bor
Ma+rie Ga+lante
Ma+rie+hamn
Ma+ri+en+bad
mari+gold
mari+golds
ma+ri+hua+na
ma+ri+jua+na
ma+rim+ba
  ma+rim+bas
Marin
ma+ri+na
  ma+ri+nas
mari+nade
mari+nades
mari+nades
mari+nad+ing

mari+nad+ed
mari+nate
mari+nates
mari+nat+ing
mari+nat+ed
mari+na+tion
mari+na+tions
Ma+rin+du+que
ma+rine
  ma+rines
mari+ner
  mari+ners
Marinetti
Mari+ola+ter
  Mari+ola+ters
Mari+ola+trous
Mari+ola+try
mari+on+ette
  mari+on+ettes
Mar+ist
  Mar+ists
Maritain
mari+tal
mari+tal+ly
mari+time
Mari+tim+er
  Mari+tim+ers
Mari+times
Ma+rit+sa
Ma+riu+pol
Marius
Marivaux
mar+jo+ram
mark
  marks
  marks
mark+ing
marked
Mark
mark+down
  mark+downs
mark down
verb
marked
mark+ed+ly
mark+ed+ness
mark+er
  mark+ers
mar+ket
  mar+kets
  mar+kets
mar+ket+ing
mar+ket+ed
mar+ket+able
mar+ket+er

mar+ket+ers
mar+ket+ing
market+place
  market+places
Mark+ham
mar+khoor
  mar+khoors *or*
  mar+khoor
mar+khor
  mar+khors *or*
  mar+khor
Markiewicz
mark+ing
  mark+ings
mark+ka
  mark+kaa
Markova
marks+man
  marks+men
marks+man+ship
mark-up
  mark-ups
mark up
verb
marl
  marls
marl+ing
marled
Marl+bor+ough
place name
Marlborough
surname
Marley
mar+lin
  mar+lin *or*
  mar+lins
mar+line
  mar+lines
mar+line+spike
  mar+line+spikes
mar+lin+spike
  mar+lin+spikes
mar+lite
Marlowe
marl+stone
marly
mar+ma+lade
  mar+ma+lades
Mar+ma+ra
mar+mite
  mar+mites
Mar+mite
Trademark
Mar+mo+la+da
Mar+mo+ra

mar+mo+real
mar+mo+set
 mar+mo+sets
mar+mot
 mar+mots
Marne
Ma+roc
maro+cain
 maro+cains
ma+roon
 ma+roons
 ma+roons
ma+roon+ing
ma+rooned
Ma+ros
Marprelate
Marquand
marque
 marques
mar+quee
 mar+quees
mar+quess
 mar+quesses
mar+que+te+rie
 mar+que+te+
 ries
mar+que+try
 mar+que+tries
Marquette
Marquez
mar+quis
 mar+quises *or*
 mar+quis
Marquis
mar+quise
 mar+quises
mar+qui+sette
Mar+ra+kech
Mar+ra+kesh
mar+ram
mar+rer
 mar+rers
mar+ri
 mar+ris
mar+riage
 mar+riages
mar+riage+abil+
 ity
mar+riage+able
mar+ried
 mar+rieds
Marriner
mar+rons gla+
 cés
mar+row

mar+rows
marrow+bone
marrow+bones
marrow+fat
mar+rowy
mar+ry
mar+ries
mar+ry+ing
mar+ried
Marryat
Mars
Mar+sa+la
Marsalis
Mar+seil+laise
mar+seille
Mar+seille
mar+seilles
marsh
marshes
Marsh
mar+shal
 mar+shals
 mar+shals
mar+shal+ling
 U.S.
mar+shal+ing
mar+shalled
 U.S.
mar+shaled
mar+shal+cy
Marshall
 surname
Mar+shall
 place name
mar+shal+ling
mar+shal+ship
marshi+ness
marsh+mal+low
 sweet
 marsh+mal+
 lows
marsh mal+low
 plant
 marsh mal+lows
marshy
marshi+er
marshi+est
Marston
 surname
Mars+ton
 place name
mar+su+pial
 mar+su+pials
mar+su+pium
 mar+su+pia

mart
marts
Mar+ta+ban
mar+ta+gon
 mar+ta+gons
Martel
Mar+tel+lo
mar+ten
 mar+tens *or*
 mar+ten
Martens
Martha
mar+tial
Mar+tial
 of Mars
Martial
 surname
mar+tial+ism
mar+tial+ist
 mar+tial+ists
mar+tial+ly
Mar+tian
 Mar+tians
mar+tin
 mar+tins
Martin
Martin du Gard
mar+tin+et
 mar+tin+ets
mar+tin+gale
 mar+tin+gales
mar+ti+ni
 mar+ti+nis
Martini
 Trademark
Mar+ti+ni+can
 Mar+ti+ni+cans
Mar+ti+nique
mar+tin+mas
 Mar+tin+mases
Martinů
mar+tyr
 mar+tyrs
 mar+tyrs
mar+tyr+ing
mar+tyred
mar+tyr+dom
mar+tyri+sa+tion
 mar+tyri+sa+
 tions
mar+tyr+ise
 mar+tyr+ises
mar+tyr+is+ing
mar+tyr+ised
mar+tyri+za+tion

mar+tyri+za+
 tions
mar+tyr+ize
mar+tyr+izes
mar+tyr+iz+ing
mar+tyr+ized
mar+tyr+olo+gist
mar+tyr+olo+
 gists
mar+tyr+ol+ogy
mar+tyr+ol+
 ogies
mar+vel
mar+vels
mar+vel+ling
 or
mar+vel+ing
 U.S.
mar+velled *or*
mar+veled
 U.S.
Marvell
mar+vel+lous
mar+vel+lous+ly
mar+vel+lous+
 ness
marvel-of-Peru
marvels-of-Peru
mar+vel+ous
 U.S.
mar+vel+ous+ly
 U.S.
mar+vel+ous+
 ness
 U.S.
Marx
Marx+ian
Marx+ism
Marxism-
 Leninism
Marx+ist
 Marx+ists
Marxist-Leninist
Marxist-
 Leninists
Mary
 Maries
Mary+land
mar+zi+pan
Masaccio
Ma+sa+da
Ma+sai
 Ma+sais *or*
 Ma+sai
Ma+san

Masaryk
Mas+ba+te
Mascagni
mas+cara
mas+con
 mas+cons
mas+cot
 mas+cots
mas+cu+line
mas+cu+line+ly
mas+cu+lini+sa+
 tion
mas+cu+lin+ise
 mas+cu+lin+ises
 mas+cu+lin+is+
 ing
mas+cu+lin+
 ised
mas+cu+lin+ity
mas+cu+lini+za+
 tion
mas+cu+lin+ize
 mas+cu+lin+izes
 mas+cu+lin+iz+
 ing
 mas+cu+lin+ized
Masefield
ma+ser
ma+sers
Ma+se+ru
mash
 mashes
 mashes
 mash+ing
 mashed
Mash+ar+brum
mashed
mash+er
 mash+ers
Mash+er+brum
Mash+had
mashie
 mashies
mashy
 mashies
Masinissa
mask
 masks
 masks
 mask+ing
 masked
 masked
mask+er
 mask+ers
mas+ki+nonge

mas+ki+nonges
 or
mas+ki+nonge
maso+chism
maso+chist
 maso+chists
maso+chis+tic
maso+chis+ti+cal+
 ly
ma+son
ma+sons
ma+sons
ma+son+ing
ma+soned
Ma+son
Ma+sons
Mason-Dixon
ma+son+ic
ma+soni+cal+ly
Ma+son+ite
 Trademark
ma+son+ry
 ma+son+ries
Mas+qat
masque
 masques
mas+quer+ade
 mas+quer+ades
 mas+quer+ades
 mas+quer+ad+
 ing
 mas+quer+ad+
 ed
mas+quer+ad+er
 mas+quer+ad+
 ers
mass
 masses
 masses
 mass+ing
 massed
Mass
 Masses
Mas+sa
Mas+sa+chu+
 setts
mas+sa+cre
 mas+sa+cres
 mas+sa+cres
 mas+sa+cring
 mas+sa+cred
mas+sage
 mas+sages
 mas+sages
 mas+sag+ing

mas+saged
mas+sa+sau+ga
mas+sa+sau+
 gas
Massasoit
Mas+saua
Mas+sa+wa
mas+sé
 mas+sés
Masséna
Mas+se+net
masses
mas+seur
 mas+seurs
mas+seuse
 mas+seuses
Massey
mas+sif
 mas+sifs
Mas+sif Cen+tral
Massine
Massinger
Massinissa
mas+sive
mas+sive+ly
mas+sive+ness
mass-market
mass-produce
 mass-produces
 mass-produc+
 ing
 mass-produced
mass-produced
mass-produc+er
 mass-produc+
 ers
mast
 masts
 masts
mast+ing
mast+ed
mas+ta+ba
mas+ta+bas
mas+ta+bah
 mas+ta+bahs
mas+tec+to+my
 mas+tec+to+
 mies
mas+ter
 mas+ters
 mas+ters
mas+ter+ing
 mas+tered
Mas+ter
Mas+ters

master-at-arms
 masters-at-arms
mas+ter+ful
 mas+ter+ful+ly
 mas+ter+ful+
 ness
mas+ter+li+ness
mas+ter+ly
master+mind
 master+minds
 master+minds
 master+mind+
 ing
 master+mind+
 ed
master+piece
 master+pieces
master+stroke
 master+strokes
master+work
 master+works
mas+tery
 mas+teries
mast+head
 mast+heads
 mast+heads
 mast+head+ing
 mast+head+ed
mas+tic
 mas+tics
mas+ti+cate
 mas+ti+cates
 mas+ti+cat+ing
 mas+ti+cat+ed
mas+ti+ca+tion
 mas+ti+ca+tions
mas+ti+ca+tor
 mas+ti+ca+tors
 mas+ti+ca+tory
 mas+ti+ca+
 tories
mas+tiff
 mas+tiffs
mas+ti+tis
mas+to+don
 mas+to+dons
mas+toid
 mas+toids
mas+toid+itis
Mastroianni
mas+tur+bate
 mas+tur+bates
 mas+tur+bat+
 ing
 mas+tur+bat+ed

mas+tur+ba+tion
mas+tur+ba+tor
 mas+tur+ba+
  tors
mas+tur+ba+tory
Ma+su+ria
Ma+su+rian
 Ma+su+rians
mat
 mats
 mats
 mat+ting
 mat+ted
Mata+be+le+land
Ma+ta+di
mata+dor
 mata+dors
mata+gou+ri
 mata+gou+ris
Mata Hari
ma+tai
 ma+tais
Mata+mo+ros
Ma+tan+zas
Mata+pan
match
 matches
 matches
 match+ing
 matched
match+able
match+board
 match+boards
match+box
 match+boxes
match+ing
match+less
 match+less+ly
match+lock
 match+locks
match+maker
 match+makers
match+making
matchplay
adj.
match play
noun
match+stick
 match+sticks
match+wood
mate
 mates
 mates
 mat+ing
 mat+ed

maté
matés
mate+lot
 mate+lots
ma+ter
 ma+ters
ma+terial
 ma+terials
ma+teri+ali+sa+
 tion
 ma+teri+ali+sa+
 tions
ma+teri+al+ise
 ma+teri+al+ises
 ma+teri+al+is+
  ing
 ma+teri+al+ised
 ma+teri+al+is+er
 ma+teri+al+is+
  ers
ma+teri+al+ism
ma+teri+al+ist
 ma+teri+al+ists
ma+teri+al+is+tic
ma+teri+al+is+ti+
 cal+ly
ma+teri+al+ity
ma+teri+ali+za+
 tion
ma+teri+al+ize
 ma+teri+al+izes
 ma+teri+al+iz+
  ing
 ma+teri+al+ized
 ma+teri+al+iz+er
 ma+teri+al+iz+
  ers
ma+teri+al+ly
ma+teri+als
ma+teria medi+ca
ma+teri+el
ma+téri+el
ma+ter+nal
ma+ter+nal+ism
ma+ter+nal+is+
 tic
ma+ter+nal+ly
ma+ter+nity
mate+ship
matey
 maties
matey+ness
math
math+emat+ic
math+emati+cal

math+emati+cal+
 ly
math+ema+ti+
 cian
 math+ema+ti+
  cians
math+emat+ics
maths
Ma+thu+ra
Ma+til+da
 swag
Matilda
 name
mat+in
mat+in+al
mati+née
 mati+nées
mati+ness
mat+ins
Matisse
mat+lo
 mat+los
Mat+lock
mat+low
 mat+lows
Mato Gros+so
Mato Gros+so do
 Sul
Ma+to+pos
Ma+to+zi+nhos
mat+rass
 mat+rasses
ma+tri+arch
 ma+tri+archs
ma+tri+ar+chal
ma+tri+ar+chic
ma+tri+ar+chy
 ma+tri+ar+chies
ma+tric
 ma+trics
ma+tri+ces
mat+ri+cid+al
mat+ri+cide
 mat+ri+cides
ma+tricu+late
 ma+tricu+lates
 ma+tricu+lating
 ma+tricu+lated
ma+tricu+la+tion
 ma+tricu+la+
  tions
mat+ri+lin+eal
mat+ri+mo+nial
mat+ri+mo+ny
 mat+ri+mo+nies

ma+trix
 ma+tri+ces or
 ma+trixes
ma+tron
 ma+trons
ma+tron+al
ma+tron+hood
ma+tron+ly
ma+tron+ship
Ma+tsu
Ma+tsu+ya+ma
matt
 matts
 matt+ing
 matt+ed
mat+ta+more
 mat+ta+mores
matte
 mattes
 matt+ing
 matt+ed
 mat+ted
 mat+ter
 mat+ters
 mat+ters
 mat+ter+ing
 mat+tered
Mat+ter+horn
matter-of-course
adj.
mat+ter of course
noun
matter-of-fact
adj.
mat+ter of fact
noun
Matthew
Matthews
Matthias
Matthias I
 Corvinus
mat+tin
mat+ting
 mat+tings
 mat+tins
mat+tock
 mat+tocks
Mat+to Gros+so
mat+tress
 mat+tresses
matu+rate
 matu+rates
matu+rat+ing
matu+rat+ed
matu+ra+tion

matu+ra+tions
ma+tura+tive
ma+ture
ma+tures
ma+tur+ing
ma+tured
ma+ture+ly
ma+ture+ness
ma+tur+ity
ma+tur+ities
ma+tu+ti+nal
maty
maties
mati+er
mati+est
mat+za
mat+zas *or*
ma+tzoth
mat+zah
mat+zahs *or*
ma+tzoth
mat+zo
mat+zos *or*
ma+tzoth
mat+zoh
mat+zohs *or*
ma+tzoth
Mau+beuge
maud+lin
mau+ger
Maugham
mau+gre
Maui
maul
mauls
mauls
maul+ing
mauled
maul+er
maul+ers
Maul+main
maul+stick
maul+sticks
Mau+na Kea
Mau+na Loa
maun+der
maun+ders
maun+der+ing
maun+dered
maun+dy
maun+dies
Maun+dy
Maupassant
Maupertuis
Mau+re+ta+nia

Mau+re+ta+nian
Mau+re+ta+
  nians
Mauriac
Maurice
Mau+ri+ta+nia
Mau+ri+ta+nian
Mau+ri+ta+nians
Mau+ri+tian
Mau+ri+tians
Mau+ri+tius
Maurois
Maury
mau+so+leum
mau+so+leums
  or
mau+so+lea
mauve
mauves
ma+ven
ma+vens
mav+er+ick
mav+er+icks
ma+vin
ma+vins
ma+vis
ma+vises
maw
maws
mawk+ish
mawk+ish+ly
mawk+ish+ness
Mawson
maxi
max+il+la
max+il+lae
max+il+lary
max+im
max+ims
Maxim
maxi+ma
maxi+mal
maxi+mal+ly
Maximilian
maxi+min
maxi+mi+sa+tion
maxi+mi+sa+
  tions
max+im+ise
max+im+ises
max+im+is+ing
max+im+ised
maxi+mis+er
maxi+mis+ers
maxi+mi+za+tion

maxi+mi+za+
  tions
max+im+ize
max+im+izes
max+im+iz+ing
max+im+ized
maxi+miz+er
maxi+miz+ers
maxi+mum
maxi+mums *or*
maxi+ma
max+well
max+wells
Maxwell
may
mays
May
Mays
Maya
  Hindu goddess
Maya
  Indian tribe
  Maya *or*
  Mayas
Ma+ya+güez
Mayakovski
Mayakovsky
Ma+yan
  adj.
Ma+yan
  Ma+yans
may+be
May+day
  distress signal
May Day
  holiday
Ma+yence
Ma+yenne
Mayer
may+est
May+fair
may+flower
  may+flowers
May+flower
may+fly
  may+flies
may+hap
may+hem
Mayhew
May+ing
mayn't
Mayo
Ma+yon
may+on+naise
  may+on+naises

mayor
mayors
mayor+al
mayor+al+ty
  mayor+al+ties
mayor+ess
  mayor+esses
mayor+ship
Ma+yotte
may+pole
  may+poles
mayst
may+weed
  may+weeds
Mazarin
Ma+zat+lán
maze
mazes
mazes
maz+ing
mazed
maze+ment
ma+zour+ka
ma+zour+kas
Ma+zu
ma+zur+ka
ma+zur+kas
mazy
mazi+er
mazi+est
Mazzini
Mba+ba+ne
mba+qan+ga
mbi+ra
mbi+ras
Mbu+ji+ma+yi
McBride
McCarthy
McCar+thy+ism
McCar+thy+ist
  McCar+thy+ists
McCartney
McCormack
McCoy
McCullers
McDiarmid
McEnroe
McEwan
McGonagall
McKean
McKellen
McKenna
McKin+ley
  mountain
McKinley

surname
McLuhan
McMahon
McMillan
McQueen
me
mea cul+pa
mead
 meads
Mead
Meade
mead+ow
 mead+ows
meadow+sweet
 meadow+
  sweets
mead+owy
mea+ger
U.S.
mea+gre
mea+gre+ly
mea+gre+ness
meal
 meals
mealie
 mealies
meali+ness
meals-on-wheels
meal+worm
 meal+worms
mealy
 meali+er
 meali+est
mealy-mouthed
mean
 means
 means
 mean+ing
 meant
 mean+er
 mean+est
me+ander
 me+anders
 me+anders
 me+ander+ing
 me+andered
Me+ander
me+ander+ing
meanie
 meanies
mean+ing
 mean+ings
mean+ing+ful
mean+ing+ful+ly

mean+ing+ful+
 ness
mean+ing+less
mean+ing+less+
 ly
mean+ly
mean+ness
means
meant
mean+time
mean+while
meany
 meanies
Mearns
mea+sles
mea+sly
 mea+sli+er
 mea+sli+est
meas+ur+able
meas+ur+ably
meas+ure
 meas+ures
 meas+ures
 meas+ur+ing
 meas+ured
 meas+ured+ly
meas+ure+less
meas+ure+less+
 ly
meas+ure+ment
 meas+ure+
  ments
 meas+ures
meat
 meats
meat+ball
 meat+balls
Meath
meati+ly
meati+ness
meat+less
mea+tus
 mea+tuses *or*
 mea+tus
meaty
 meati+er
 meati+est
Mec+ca
Mec+ca+no
 Trademark
me+chan+ic
 me+chan+ics
me+chani+cal

me+chani+cal+
 ism
me+chani+cal+ly
me+chani+cal+
 ness
mecha+ni+cian
 mecha+ni+cians
me+chan+ics
mecha+ni+sa+
 tion
mecha+nise
 mecha+nises
 mecha+nis+ing
 mecha+nised
 mecha+nis+er
 mecha+nis+ers
mecha+nism
 mecha+nisms
mecha+nist
 mecha+nists
mecha+nis+tic
mecha+nis+ti+cal+
 ly
mecha+ni+za+
 tion
mecha+nize
 mecha+nizes
 mecha+niz+ing
 mecha+nized
 mecha+niz+er
 mecha+niz+ers
mecha+no+re+
 cep+tor
mecha+no+re+
 cep+tors
mecha+no+thera+
 py
Mech+elen
Mech+lin
Meck+len+burg
me+co+nium
meco+nop+sis
Med
mé+dail+lons
med+al
 med+als
med+al+ist
U.S.
 med+al+ists
me+dal+lion
 me+dal+lions
med+al+list
 med+al+lists
Me+dan
Medawar

med+dle
 med+dles
 med+dling
 med+dled
 med+dler
 med+dlers
med+dle+some
med+dle+some+
 ly
med+dle+some+
 ness
med+dling
Mede
 Medes
Medea
Me+del+lín
me+dia
plural of medium
me+dia
wall of blood
 vessel
 me+diae
Me+dia
me+di+aeval
me+di+aeval+ism
 me+di+aeval+
  isms
me+di+aeval+ist
 me+di+aeval+
  ists
me+dial
me+di+al+ly
me+dian
 me+dians
Me+dian
 Me+dians
me+di+an+ly
me+di+ant
 me+di+ants
me+di+as+ti+nal
me+di+as+ti+
 num
 me+di+as+ti+na
me+di+ate
 me+di+ates
 me+di+at+ing
 me+di+at+ed
me+di+ate+ly
me+di+a+tion
 me+dia+tions
me+dia+tor
 me+dia+tors
med+ic
 med+ics
medi+cable

medi+cal
medi+cals
medi+cal+ly
me+dica+ment
me+dica+ments
medi+cate
medi+cates
medi+cat+ing
medi+cat+ed
medi+ca+tion
medi+ca+tions
medi+ca+tive
Medi+cean
Medici
me+dici+nal
me+dici+nals
me+dici+nal+ly
medi+cine
medi+cines
med+ick
med+icks
medi+co
medi+cos
me+di+eval
me+di+eval+ism
me+di+eval+
  isms
me+di+eval+ist
me+di+eval+ists
Me+di+na
me+dio+cre
me+di+oc+rity
me+di+oc+rities
medi+tate
medi+tates
medi+tat+ing
medi+tat+ed
medi+ta+tion
medi+ta+tions
medi+ta+tive
medi+ta+tive+ly
medi+ta+tor
medi+ta+tors
Medi+ter+ra+
  nean
me+dium
me+dia *or*
me+diums
medium-dated
med+lar
med+lars
med+ley
med+leys
Mé+doc
me+dul+la

me+dul+las *or*
me+dul+lae
me+dul+la ob+
  lon+ga+ta
me+dul+la ob+
  lon+ga+tas *or*
me+dul+lae ob+
  lon+ga+tae
me+dul+lar
me+dul+lary
me+du+sa
me+du+sas *or*
me+du+sae
Medusa
Me+du+san
me+du+soid
me+du+soids
Med+way
meed
meeds
meek
meek+er
meek+est
meek+ly
meek+ness
meer+kat
meer+kats
meer+schaum
meer+schaums
Mee+rut
meet
meets
meets
meet+ing
met
meet+er
meet+ers
meet+ing
meet+ings
meet+ly
mega
mega+bit
mega+bits
mega+buck
mega+bucks
mega+cephal+ic
mega+cephal+
  ous
mega+cepha+ly
mega+cy+cle
mega+cy+cles
mega+death
mega+deaths
Megaera
mega+fau+na

mega+flop
mega+flops
mega+hertz
mega+hertz
mega+lith
mega+liths
mega+lith+ic
mega+lo+cepha+
  ly
mega+lo+ma+nia
mega+lo+ma+ni+
  ac
mega+lo+ma+ni+
  acs
mega+lo+ma+nia+
  cal
mega+lopo+lis
mega+lo+poli+
  tan
mega+lo+poli+
  tans
mega+lo+saur
mega+lo+saurs
mega+phone
mega+phones
mega+phon+ic
mega+pode
mega+podes
Mega+ra
mega+there
mega+theres
mega+ton
mega+tons
Meg+ger
Trademark
Meg+gers
Me+gha+la+ya
Me+gid+do
me+gilp
meg+ohm
meg+ohms
me+grim
me+grims
Mehemet Ali
Mei+ji
meio+sis
meio+ses
mei+ot+ic
mei+oti+cal+ly
Meir
Meis+sen
Meis+ter+sing+er
Meis+ter+sing+
  er *or*

Meis+ter+sing+
  ers
Meitner
Mé+ji+co
Mek+ka
Mek+nès
Me+kong
mela+leu+ca
mela+leu+cas
mela+mine
mel+an+cho+lia
mel+an+cho+li+
  ac
mel+an+cho+li+
  acs
mel+an+chol+ic
mel+an+chol+
  ics
mel+an+choly
mel+an+cholies
Melanchthon
Mela+nesia
Mela+nesian
Mela+nesians
me+lange
me+langes
mé+lange
mé+langes
mela+nin
mela+nism
mela+nis+tic
mela+no+ma
  mela+no+mas
  or
mela+no+ma+ta
mela+no+sis
mela+not+ic
Melba
Mel+bourne
place name
Melbourne
surname
Mel+bur+nian
Mel+bur+nians
Melchior
Melchizedek
meld
melds
melds
meld+ing
meld+ed
Meleager
me+lee
me+lees
mê+lée

mê +lées
Méliès
Melil +la
me +lio +rate
me +lio +rates
me +lio +rat +ing
me +lio +rat +ed
me +lio +ra +tion
me +lio +ra +tions
me +lio +ra +tive
me +lis +ma
me +lis +ma +ta
  or
me +lis +mas
Me +li +to +pol
Melk
mel +lif +er +ous
mel +lif +ic
mel +lif +lu +ence
mel +lif +lu +ent
mel +lif +lu +ous
mel +lif +lu +ous +ly
mel +lif +lu +ous +
  ness
mel +low
mel +lows
mel +low +ing
mel +lowed
mel +low +er
mel +low +est
mel +low +ness
me +lo +deon
me +lo +deons
me +lod +ic
me +lodi +cal +ly
me +lo +di +on
me +lo +di +ons
me +lo +dious
me +lo +di +ous +ly
me +lo +di +ous +
  ness
melo +dise
melo +dises
melo +dis +ing
melo +dised
melo +dis +er
melo +dis +ers
melo +dist
melo +dists
melo +dize
melo +dizes
melo +diz +ing
melo +dized
melo +diz +er
melo +diz +ers

melo +dra +ma
melo +dra +mas
melo +dra +mat +ic
melo +dra +mati +
  cal +ly
melo +drama +tist
melo +drama +
  tists
melo +dy
melo +dies
mel +on
mel +ons
Me +los
Melpomene
melt
melts
melts
melt +ing
melted
melted *or*
molt +en
melt +able
melt +down
melt +downs
melt +er
melt +ers
melt +ing +ly
Mel +ton Mow +
  bray
melt +water
Melville
  surname
Mel +ville
  place name
mem
mem +ber
  mem +bers
Mem +ber
  Mem +bers
mem +ber +less
mem +ber +ship
  mem +ber +ships
mem +brane
mem +branes
mem +brane +ous
mem +bra +nous
Me +mel
me +men +to
me +men +tos
  or
me +men +toes
me +men +to mori
me +men +to
  mori
Memlinc

Memling
Memnon
Mem +no +nian
memo
  memos
mem +oir
  mem +oirs
mem +oir +ist
  mem +oir +ists
mem +oirs
memo +ra +bilia
memo +rabil +ity
memo +rable
memo +rably
memo +ran +dum
memo +ran +
  dums *or*
memo +ran +da
me +mo +rial
  me +mo +rials
me +mo +rial +ise
me +mo +rial +
  ises
me +mo +rial +is +
  ing
me +mo +rial +
  ised
me +mo +ri +al +ize
me +mo +ri +al +
  izes
me +mo +ri +al +iz +
  ing
me +mo +ri +al +
  ized
me +mo +ri +al +ly
memo +rise
memo +rises
memo +ris +ing
memo +rised
memo +rize
memo +rizes
memo +riz +ing
memo +rized
memo +ry
memo +ries
Mem +phian
  Mem +phians
Mem +phis
Mem +phre +ma +
  gog
mem +sa +hib
  mem +sa +hibs
men
men +ace
  men +aces

men +aces
men +ac +ing
men +aced
men +ac +er
  men +ac +ers
men +ac +ing
men +ac +ing +ly
me +nad
me +nads
Me +na +do
mé +nage
mé +nages
mé +nage à trois
mé +nages à
  trois
me +nag +erie
me +nag +eries
Me +nam
Menander
Mencius
Mencken
mend
mends
mends
mend +ing
mend +ed
mend +able
men +da +cious
men +da +cious +ly
men +dac +ity
men +dac +ities
Mendel
Mendeleev
men +de +levium
Mendeleyev
Men +de +lian
Mendelssohn
mend +er
mend +ers
Men +deres
Mendès-France
men +di +can +cy
men +di +cant
men +di +cants
men +dic +ity
Men +dips
Men +do +za
  place name
Mendoza
  surname
me +neer
me +neers
Menelaus
Menes
men +folk

Mengelberg
Mengistu Haile
  Mariam
Meng-tze
Meng +zi
men +ha +den
  men +ha +den
men +hir
  men +hirs
me +nial
  me +nials
Meninga
me +nin +geal
me +nin +ges
men +in +git +ic
men +in +gi +tis
me +nin +go +coc +
  cus
  me +nin +go +coc +
  ci
men +inx
me +nis +coid
me +nis +cus
  me +nis +ci or
  me +nis +cuses
Men +non +ite
  Men +non +ites
Men +no +nit +ism
meno
Menon
  Menons
meno +pau +sal
meno +pause
me +no +rah
  me +no +rahs
Menorca
men +or +rha +gia
men +or +rhoea
Menotti
men +ses
  men +ses
Men +she +vik
  Men +she +viks
Men +she +vism
Men +she +vist
  Men +she +vists
men +strual
men +stru +ate
  men +stru +ates
  men +stru +at +
  ing
  men +stru +at +ed
  men +strua +tion
  men +strua +
  tions

men +struum
men +struums
  or
men +strua
men +sur +abil +ity
men +sur +able
men +su +ral
men +su +ra +tion
men +su +ra +tive
men +tal
men +tal +ism
men +tal +is +tic
men +tal +ity
  men +tal +ities
men +tal +ly
men +thol
men +tho +la +ted
men +tion
  men +tions
  men +tions
  men +tion +ing
  men +tioned
  men +tion +able
Men +ton
men +tor
  men +tors
Men +tor
men +tor +ing
menu
  menus
Menuhin
Menzies
meow
  meows
  meow +ing
  meowed
mepa +crine
me +peri +dine
Mephisto
Meph +is +to +
  phelean
Mephistopheles
Meph +is +to +
  phelian
me +phit +ic
me +phiti +cal
me +pro +ba +
  mate
Me +ra +no
Mer +ca
mer +can +tile
mer +can +til +ism
mer +can +til +ist
  mer +can +til +ists
mer +cap +tan

Mercator
mer +ce +nary
  mer +ce +naries
mer +cer
  mer +cers
mer +cer +ise
  mer +cer +ises
  mer +cer +is +ing
  mer +cer +ised
mer +cer +ize
  mer +cer +izes
  mer +cer +iz +ing
  mer +cer +ized
mer +cery
  mer +ceries
mer +chan +dise
  mer +chan +dises
  mer +chan +dis +
  ing
  mer +chan +dised
  mer +chan +dis +
  ing
mer +chant
  mer +chants
  mer +chants
  mer +chant +ing
  mer +chant +ed
Merchant
mer +chant +able
mer +chant +man
  mer +chant +men
Mer +cia
Mer +cian
  Mer +cians
mer +ci +ful
  mer +ci +ful +ly
  mer +ci +ful +ness
mer +ci +less
  mer +ci +less +ly
  mer +ci +less +
  ness
Merckx
Mercouri
mer +cu +rial
  mer +cu +rials
  mer +cu +ri +al +ity
  mer +cu +ri +al +ly
mer +cu +ric
Mer +cu +ro +
  chrome
  Trademark
mer +cu +rous
mer +cu +ry
  mer +cu +ries
Mercury

Roman god
Mer +cu +ry
  planet
mer +cy
  mer +cies
mere
  meres
  mer +est
mere
  Maori weapon
  meres
Meredith
mere +ly
mer +etri +cious
  mer +etri +cious +
  ly
  mer +etri +cious +
  ness
mer +gan +ser
  mer +gan +sers
  or
  mer +gan +ser
merge
  merges
  merg +ing
  merged
mer +gence
mer +ger
  mer +gers
Me +ric
Mé +ri +da
me +rid +ian
  me +rid +ians
me +ridio +nal
  me +ridio +nals
Mérimée
me +ringue
  me +ringues
me +ri +no
  me +ri +nos
Meri +on +eth +
  shire
me +ri +stem
  me +ri +stems
meri +stemat +ic
mer +it
  mer +its
  mer +its
  mer +it +ing
  mer +it +ed
  mer +it +ed
  mer +it +less
meri +toc +ra +cy
  meri +toc +ra +
  cies

meri+to+crat+ic
meri+to+ri+ous
meri+to+ri+ous+
 ly
meri+to+ri+ous+
 ness
mer+its
merl
 merls
merle
 merles
mer+lin
 mer+lins
Merlin
mer+maid
 mer+maids
mer+man
 mer+men
Meroë
Mero+vin+gian
 Mero+vin+gians
mer+ri+ly
mer+ri+ment
mer+ri+ness
mer+ry
 mer+ri+er
 mer+ri+est
merry-andrew
 merry-andrews
merry-go-round
 merry-go-rounds
merry+maker
 merry+makers
merry+making
merry+thought
 merry+thoughts
Merse
Mer+se+burg
Mer+sey
Mersey+side
Mer+sin
Mer+thyr Tyd+fil
 place name
Merton
 surname
me+sa
 me+sas
mé+sal+li+ance
 mé+sal+li+ances
Mesa Verde
mes+cal
 mes+cals
mes+ca+lin
mes+ca+line

mes+dames
mes+de+moi+
 selles
me+seems
mes+em+bry+an+
 themum
mes+em+bry+
 an+themums
mes+en+cepha+
 lon
mes+en+cepha+
 lons
mes+en+ter+ic
mes+en+teri+tis
mes+en+tery
mes+en+teries
mesh
meshes
meshes
mesh+ing
meshed
Meshach
Me+shed
me+sial
me+sic
mes+mer+ic
mes+meri+sa+
 tion
mes+mer+ise
mes+mer+ises
mes+mer+is+
 ing
mes+mer+ised
mes+mer+is+er
mes+mer+is+
 ers
mes+mer+ism
mes+mer+ist
mes+mer+ists
mes+meri+za+
 tion
mes+mer+ize
mes+mer+izes
mes+mer+iz+ing
mes+mer+ized
mes+mer+iz+er
mesne
meso+blast
meso+blasts
meso+blas+tic
meso+carp
meso+carps
meso+cephal+ic
meso+cephal+
 ics

meso+ceph+aly
meso+derm
meso+der+mal
meso+der+mic
Meso+lith+ic
Me+so+lon+ghi
Mesolóngion
meso+morph
meso+morphs
meso+mor+phic
meso+mor+
 phism
me+son
me+sons
me+son+ic
meso+phyte
meso+phytes
Meso+po+ta+mia
Meso+po+ta+
 mian
Meso+po+ta+
 mians
meso+sphere
Meso+zo+ic
mes+quit
mes+quits
mes+quite
mes+quites
mess
messes
messes
mess+ing
messed
mes+sage
mes+sages
mes+sages
mes+sag+ing
mes+saged
Messager
Messalina
Mes+sene
mes+sen+ger
mes+sen+gers
Mes+senia
Messerschmitt
Messiaen
Mes+si+ah
Mes+si+ahs
Mes+si+ah+ship
mes+si+an+ic
mes+sieurs
messi+ly
Mes+si+na
messi+ness
mess+mate

mess+mates
Messrs
messy
messi+er
messi+est
mes+ti+za
mes+ti+zo
mes+ti+zos *or*
mes+ti+zoes
mes+tra+nol
met
Meta
meta+bol+ic
meta+boli+cal+ly
me+tabo+lise
me+tabo+lises
me+tabo+lis+
 ing
me+tabo+lised
me+tabo+lism
me+tabo+lisms
me+tabo+lize
me+tabo+lizes
me+tabo+liz+ing
me+tabo+lized
meta+car+pal
meta+car+pals
meta+car+pus
meta+car+pi
meta+cen+ter
U.S.
meta+cen+ters
meta+cen+tre
meta+cen+tres
meta+cen+tric
met+age
met+ages
met+al
met+als
met+als
met+al+ling *or*
met+al+ing
U.S.
met+alled *or*
met+aled
U.S.
meta+lan+guage
meta+lan+
 guages
met+ali+za+tion
U.S.
met+ali+za+
 tions
met+al+ize
U.S.

met+al+izes
met+al+iz+ing
met+al+ized
met+alled
me+tal+lic
met+al+lif+er+
ous
met+al+li+sa+
tion
met+al+li+sa+
tions
met+al+lise
met+al+lises
met+al+lis+ing
met+al+lised
met+al+li+za+
tion
met+al+li+za+
tions
met+al+lize
met+al+lizes
met+al+liz+ing
met+al+lized
me+tal+lo+graph+
ic
met+al+log+ra+
phy
met+al+loid
met+al+loids
met+al+loi+dal
met+al+lur+gic
met+al+lur+gi+
cal
met+al+lur+gist
met+al+lur+
gists
met+al+lur+gy
metal+work
metal+worker
metal+workers
metal+working
me+tam+er+al
meta+mere
meta+meres
meta+mer+ic
me+tam+er+ism
meta+mict
meta+mic+ti+sa+
tion
meta+mic+ti+za+
tion
meta+mor+phic
meta+mor+phism
meta+mor+
phisms

meta+mor+phose
meta+mor+
phoses
meta+mor+phos+
ing
meta+mor+
phosed
meta+mor+pho+
sis
meta+mor+pho+
ses
meta+mor+phous
meta+phor
meta+phors
meta+phor+ic
meta+phori+cal
meta+phori+cal+
ly
meta+phrase
meta+phrases
meta+phrases
meta+phras+ing
meta+phrased
meta+phrast
meta+phrasts
meta+phras+tic
meta+phras+ti+
cal
meta+phras+ti+
cal+ly
meta+phys+ic
meta+phys+ics
meta+physi+cal
Meta+physi+cal
Meta+physi+
cals
meta+physi+cal+
ly
meta+phy+si+
cian
meta+phy+si+
cians
meta+physi+cist
meta+physi+
cists
meta+phys+ics
meta+psy+cho+
logi+cal
meta+psy+chol+
ogy
meta+sta+bil+ity
meta+sta+ble
me+tas+ta+sis
me+tas+ta+ses
me+tas+ta+sise

me+tas+ta+
sises
me+tas+ta+sis+
ing
me+tas+ta+
sised
me+tas+ta+size
me+tas+ta+
sizes
me+tas+ta+siz+
ing
me+tas+ta+
sized
meta+stat+ic
meta+stati+cal+
ly
meta+tar+sal
meta+tar+sals
meta+tar+sus
meta+tar+si
me+tath+esis
me+tath+eses
meta+thet+ic
meta+theti+cal
meta+zo+an
meta+zo+ans
meta+zo+ic
Metchnikoff
mete
metes
metes
met+ing
met+ed
me+tem+psy+
cho+sis
me+tem+psy+
cho+ses
me+tem+psy+
cho+sist
me+tem+psy+
cho+sists
me+teor
me+teors
me+teor+ic
me+teori+cal+ly
me+teor+ism
me+teor+ite
me+teor+ites
me+teor+it+ic
me+teor+oid
me+teor+oids
me+teor+oid+al
me+teoro+log+ic
me+teoro+logi+
cal

me+teoro+logi+
cal+ly
me+teor+olo+
gist
me+teor+olo+
gists
me+teor+ol+ogy
me+ter
U.S.
me+ters
me+ter
measuring device
me+ters
me+ters
me+ter+ing
me+tered
metha+don
metha+done
metham+pheta+
mine
metham+pheta+
mines
meth+anal
me+thane
metha+nol
me+thinks
metho
methos
meth+od
meth+ods
Meth+od
me+thod+ic
me+thodi+cal
me+thodi+cal+ly
meth+od+ise
meth+od+ises
meth+od+is+ing
meth+od+ised
meth+od+is+er
meth+od+is+ers
Meth+od+ism
Meth+od+ist
Meth+od+ists
Meth+od+is+ti+
cal
Meth+o+dius
meth+od+ize
meth+od+izes
meth+od+iz+ing
meth+od+ized
meth+od+iz+er
meth+od+iz+ers
meth+odo+logi+
cal

meth+ odo+ logi+
cal+ ly
meth+ od+ olo+
gist
meth+ od+ olo+
gists
meth+ od+ ol+ ogy
meth+ od+ ol+
ogies
me+ thought
meths
Me+ thu+ se+ lah
wine bottle
Me+ thu+ se+ lahs
Methuselah
person
me+ thyl
me+ thyls
meth+ yl+ ate
meth+ yl+ ates
meth+ yl+ at+ ing
meth+ yl+ at+ ed
meth+ yl+ ene
me+ thyl+ ic
me+ ticu+ lous
me+ ticu+ lous+ ly
me+ ticu+ lous+
ness
mé+ ti+ er
mé+ ti+ ers
Mé+ tis
Mé+ tis
Mé+ tisse
Mé+ tisses
me+ tol
meto+ nym+ ic
meto+ nymi+ cal
meto+ nymi+ cal+
ly
me+ tony+ my
me+ tony+ mies
met+ ope
met+ opes
me+ tre
me+ tres
metre-kilogram-
second
met+ ric
met+ ri+ cal
met+ ri+ cal+ ly
met+ ri+ cate
met+ ri+ cates
met+ ri+ cat+ ing
met+ ri+ cat+ ed
met+ ri+ ca+ tion

met+ ro
met+ ros
mét+ ro
mét+ ros
met+ ro+ nome
met+ ro+ nomes
met+ ro+ nom+ ic
met+ ro+ nym+ ic
met+ ro+ nym+
ics
me+ tropo+ lis
me+ tropo+ lises
met+ ro+ poli+ tan
met+ ro+ poli+
tans
met+ ro+ poli+ tan+
ism
me+ tror+ rha+ gia
Metternich
met+ tle
met+ tled
met+ tle+ some
Metz
Meung
Meurthe-et-
Moselle
Meuse
me+ vrou
me+ vrous
mew
mews
mews
mew+ ing
mewed
Me+ war
mewl
mewls
mewls
mewl+ ing
mewled
mews
Mexi+ cali
Mexi+ can
Mexi+ cans
Mexi+ co
Meyerbeer
Meyerhof
Meyerhold
mez+ cal
mez+ cals
mez+ ca+ line
Mé+ zières
me+ zu+ zah
me+ zu+ zahs *or*
me+ zu+ zoth

mez+ za+ nine
mez+ za+ nines
mez+ zo
mezzos
mezzo-soprano
mezzo-sopranos
mez+ zo+ tint
mez+ zo+ tints
mez+ zo+ tints
mez+ zo+ tint+
ing
mez+ zo+ tint+ ed
mho
mhos
mi
Mi+ ami
miaou
miaous
miaou+ ing
miaoued
miaow
miaows
miaow+ ing
miaowed
mi+ as+ ma
mi+ as+ ma+ ta
or
mi+ as+ mas
mi+ as+ mal
mi+ as+ mat+ ic
mi+ aul
mi+ auls
mi+ aul+ ing
mi+ auled
mica
micas
mi+ ca+ ceous
Micah
mice
mi+ cell
mi+ cells
mi+ cel+ la
mi+ cel+ las
mi+ celle
mi+ celles
Michael
Mich+ ael+ mas
Mich+ ael+
mases
Michelangelo
Michelet
Michelin
Michelozzo
Michelson
Michi+ gan

Michi+ gan+ der
Michi+ gan+ ders
Mi+ choa+ cán
Mick
Micks
mick+ ey
Mickey
Mickeys
Mickey Finn
Mickey Finns
Mickiewicz
mick+ le
micky
mi+ cro
mi+ cros
mi+ crobe
mi+ crobes
mi+ cro+ bial
mi+ cro+ bic
micro+ bio+ log+ ic
micro+ bio+ logi+
cal
micro+ bio+ logi+
cal+ ly
micro+ bi+ olo+
gist
micro+ bi+ olo+
gists
micro+ bi+ ol+ ogy
micro+ cephal+ ic
micro+ cepha+
lous
micro+ cepha+ ly
micro+ chemi+ cal
micro+ chem+ is+
try
micro+ chip
micro+ chips
micro+ cir+ cuit
micro+ cir+ cuits
micro+ cir+ cuit+ ry
micro+ cli+ mate
micro+ cli+ mates
micro+ cli+ mat+ ic
micro+ cli+ ma+ tol+
ogy
micro+ com+ put+
er
micro+ com+ put+
ers
micro+ cosm
micro+ cosms
micro+ cos+ mic
micro+ cos+ mi+
cal

micro+cos+mos
micro+dot
  micro+dots
micro+eco+
  nomic
micro+eco+nom+
  ics
micro+elec+tron+
  ics
micro+fiche
  micro+fiches
micro+film
  micro+films
  micro+films
  micro+film+ing
  micro+filmed
micro+grav+ity
micro+habi+tat
  micro+habi+tats
micro+light
  micro+lights
micro+lite
  micro+lites
micro+lith
  micro+liths
micro+lith+ic
mi+crom+eter
mi+crom+eters
micro+met+ric
micro+met+ri+cal
mi+crom+etry
micro+minia+turi+
  sa+tion
micro+minia+turi+
  za+tion
mi+cron
  mi+crons *or*
  mi+cra
Micro+nesia
Micro+nesian
  Micro+nesians
micro+or+gan+
  ism
  micro+or+gan+
  isms
micro+phone
  micro+phones
micro+phon+ic
micro+print
  micro+prints
micro+pro+ces+
  sor
  micro+pro+ces+
  sors
micro+scope

micro+scopes
micro+scop+ic
micro+scopi+cal
micro+scopi+cal+
  ly
mi+cros+co+pist
  mi+cros+co+
  pists
mi+cros+co+py
micro+sec+ond
  micro+sec+onds
micro+struc+ture
  micro+struc+
  tures
micro+sur+gery
micro+switch
  micro+switches
micro+tome
  micro+tomes
mi+croto+my
  mi+croto+mies
micro+wave
  micro+waves
  micro+waves
  micro+wav+ing
  micro+waved
mic+tu+rate
mic+tu+rates
mic+tu+rat+ing
mic+tu+rat+ed
mic+tu+ri+tion
mid
  mids
mid+air
Midas
mid-Atlantic
mid+brain
  mid+brains
mid+day
Mid+del+burg
mid+den
  mid+dens
mid+dle
  mid+dles
  mid+dles
  mid+dling
  mid+dled
middle-aged
middle+brow
  middle+brows
  middle+browed
middle-class
  adj.
mid+dle class
  mid+dle classes

middle+man
  middle+men
middle+most
middle-of-the-
  road
Mid+dles+brough
Mid+dle+sex
Mid+dle+ton
  place name
Middleton
  surname
middle+weight
  middle+weights
mid+dling
mid+dling+ly
mid+dy
  mid+dies
Mid+east
mid+field
Mid+gard
Mid+garth
midge
  midges
midg+et
  midg+ets
mid+gut
  mid+guts
mid+gy
midi
Midi
MIDI
Mid+ian
Midi+an+ite
  Midi+an+ites
Midi+an+it+ish
midi+nette
  midi+nettes
Midi-Pyrénées
mid+iron
  mid+irons
mid+land
  mid+lands
Mid+land+er
  Mid+land+ers
Mid+lands
mid+life
Mid+lo+thian
mid+most
mid+night
mid-off
  mid-offs
mid-on
  mid-ons
mid+point
  mid+points

mid+rib
  mid+ribs
mid+riff
  mid+riffs
mid+ship
  mid+ships
mid+ship+man
  mid+ship+men
  mid+ships
midst
mid+sum+mer
  mid+sum+mers
mid+term
  mid+terms
mid-Victorian
  mid-Victorians
mid+way
  mid+ways
Mid+way
mid+week
Mid+west
Mid+west+ern
Mid+west+ern+
  er
  Mid+west+ern+
  ers
mid-wicket
  mid-wickets
mid+wife
  mid+wives
mid+wife+ry
mid+win+ter
  mid+win+ters
mid+year
mien
  miens
Mie+res
Mies van der
  Rohe
miff
  miffs
  miffs
  miff+ing
  miffed
mif+fy
  mif+fi+er
  mif+fi+est
might
  mighti+ly
  mighti+ness
mighty
  mighti+er
  mighti+est
mi+gnon
mi+gnon+ette

mi+gnon+ettes
mi+gnonne
mi+graine
mi+graines
mi+grain+ous
mi+grant
mi+grants
mi+grate
mi+grates
mi+grat+ing
mi+grat+ed
mi+gra+tion
mi+gra+tions
mi+gra+tion+al
mi+gra+tor
mi+gra+tors
mi+gra+tory
mih+rab
mih+rabs
mi+ka+do
mi+ka+dos
mike
mikes
mikes
mik+ing
miked
Míko+nos
mil
mils
mi+la+di
mi+la+dies
mi+la+dy
mi+la+dies
mil+age
mil+ages
Mi+lan
Mil+an+ese
 Mil+an+ese
Mi+laz+zo
milch
mild
milds
mild+er
mild+est
mil+dew
mil+dews
mil+dews
mil+dew+ing
mil+dewed
mil+dewy
mild+ly
mild+ness
mile
miles
mile+age

mile+ages
mile+om+eter
mile+om+eters
mile+post
mile+posts
mil+er
mil+ers
Miles
Mi+lesian
Mi+lesians
mile+stone
mile+stones
Mi+letus
mil+foil
mil+foils
Mil+ford Ha+ven
Milhaud
mili+aria
mil+iary
mi+lieu
mi+lieus or
 mi+lieux
mili+tan+cy
mili+tant
mili+tants
mili+tant+ly
mili+tari+ly
mili+ta+ri+sa+
 tion
mili+ta+ri+sa+
 tions
mili+ta+rise
mili+ta+rises
mili+ta+ris+ing
mili+ta+rised
mili+ta+rism
mili+ta+rist
mili+ta+rists
mili+ta+ri+za+
 tion
mili+ta+ri+za+
 tions
mili+ta+rize
mili+ta+rizes
mili+ta+riz+ing
mili+ta+rized
mili+tary
mili+taries or
 mili+tary
mili+tate
mili+tates
mili+tat+ing
mili+tat+ed
mi+li+tia
mi+li+tias

mi+li+tia+man
mi+li+tia+men
milk
milks
milks
milk+ing
milked
milk-and-water
milk+er
milk+ers
milki+ly
milki+ness
milk+maid
milk+maids
milk+man
milk+men
milk+sop
milk+sops
milk+wort
milk+worts
milky
milki+er
milki+est
mill
mills
mills
mill+ing
milled
Mill
mill+able
Millais
Millay
mill+board
mill+dam
mill+dams
milled
mille+feuille
mille+feuilles
mille+fleurs
mil+le+nar+ian
 mil+le+nar+ians
mil+le+nari+an+
 ism
mil+le+nary
 mil+le+naries
mil+len+nial
mil+len+ni+al+ist
mil+len+ni+al+
 ists
mil+len+nium
mil+len+niums
 or
mil+len+nia
mil+le+ped
mil+le+peds

mil+le+pede
mil+le+pedes
mil+le+pore
mil+le+pores
mil+er
mil+lers
Miller
mil+lesi+mal
mil+let
mil+lets
Millet
mil+li+ard
mil+li+ards
mil+li+bar
mil+li+bars
Milligan
mil+li+gram
mil+li+grams
mil+li+gramme
mil+li+grammes
Millikan
mil+li+li+ter
U.S.
mil+li+li+ters
mil+li+li+tre
mil+li+li+tres
mil+li+meter
U.S.
mil+li+meters
mil+li+metre
mil+li+metres
mil+li+mi+cron
mil+li+mi+crons
mil+li+ner
mil+li+ners
mil+li+nery
mill+ing
mill+ings
mil+lion
mil+lions or
 mil+lion
mil+lion+aire
mil+lion+aires
mil+lion+air+ess
mil+lion+air+
 esses
mil+lionth
mil+lionths
mil+li+pede
mil+li+pedes
mil+li+sec+ond
mil+li+sec+onds
mill+pond
mill+ponds
mill+race

mill+races
mill+run
mill+runs
mill-run
adj.
Mills
mill+stone
mill+stones
mill+stream
mill+streams
mill+wheel
mill+wheels
mill+work
mill+wright
mill+wrights
Milne
mi+lom+eter
mi+lom+eters
mi+lord
mi+lords
Mí+los
milt
milts
milts
milt+ing
milt+ed
mil+ter
mil+ters
Miltiades
Milton
Mil+to+nian
Mil+ton+ic
Mil+wau+kee
Mil+wau+kee+an
Mil+wau+kee+
ans
mim
mime
mimes
mimes
mim+ing
mimed
Mimeo+graph
Trademark
Mimeo+graphs
Mimeo+graphs
Mimeo+graph+
ing
Mimeo+graphed
mim+er
mim+ers
mi+mesis
mi+met+ic
mi+meti+cal+ly
mim+ic

mim+ics
mim+ics
mim+ick+ing
mim+icked
mim+ick+er
mim+ick+ers
mim+ic+ry
mim+ic+ries
Mimir
mi+mo+sa
mi+mo+sas
mimu+lus
Min
mina
minae *or*
minas
Mina Has+san
Tani
mina+ret
mina+rets
mina+ret+ed
Mi+nas Ge+rais
mina+to+rial
mina+tory
mince
minces
minc+ing
minced
mince+meat
minc+er
minc+ers
Minch
minc+ing
minc+ing+ly
mind
minds
minds
mind+ing
mind+ed
Min+da+nao
mind-bending
mind-boggling
mind+ed
mind+er
mind+ers
mind+ful
mind+ful+ly
mind+ful+ness
mind+less
mind+less+ly
mind+less+ness
mind-numbing
mind-numbing+ly
Min+do+ro
mind-reader

mind-readers
mind-reading
mind-set
mind-sets
Mindszenty
mine
mines
mines
min+ing
mined
mine+field
mine+fields
mine+lay+er
mine+lay+ers
min+er
min+ers
min+er+al
min+er+als
min+er+ali+sa+
tion
min+er+al+ise
min+er+al+ises
min+er+al+is+
ing
min+er+al+ised
min+er+al+is+er
min+er+al+is+
ers
min+er+ali+za+
tion
min+er+al+ize
min+er+al+izes
min+er+al+iz+
ing
min+er+al+ized
min+er+al+iz+er
min+er+al+iz+
ers
min+er+al+og+ic
min+er+al+ogi+
cal
min+er+alo+gist
min+er+alo+
gists
min+er+al+ogy
Minerva
min+estro+ne
mine+sweeper
mine+sweepers
mine+sweeping
Ming
min+gle
min+gles
min+gling
min+gled

min+gler
min+glers
Mingus
min+gy
min+gi+er
min+gi+est
Mi+nho
mini
minis
minia+ture
minia+tures
minia+turi+sa+
tion
minia+turi+sa+
tions
minia+tur+ise
minia+tur+ises
minia+tur+is+ing
minia+tur+ised
minia+tur+ist
minia+tur+ists
minia+turi+za+
tion
minia+turi+za+
tions
minia+tur+ize
minia+tur+izes
minia+tur+iz+ing
minia+tur+ized
mini+bus
mini+buses
mini+cab
mini+cabs
mini+com+put+er
mini+com+put+
ers
min+im
min+ims
mini+mal
mini+mal+ism
mini+mal+ist
mini+mal+ists
mini+mal+ly
mini+max
mini+maxes
mini+mi+sa+tion
mini+mise
mini+mises
mini+mis+ing
mini+mised
mini+mis+er
mini+mis+ers
mini+mi+za+tion
mini+mize
mini+mizes

mini+miz+ing
mini+mized
mini+miz+er
mini+miz+ers
mini+mum
mini+mums *or*
mini+ma
min+ing
min+ion
min+ions
mini+pill
mini+pills
mini+se+ries
mini+se+ries
mini+skirt
mini+skirts
min+is+ter
min+is+ters
min+is+ters
min+is+ter+ing
min+is+tered
min+is+terial
min+is+teri+al+ly
min+is+trant
min+is+trants
mini+stra+tion
mini+stra+tions
min+is+tra+tive
min+is+try
min+is+tries
mini+ver
mink
mink *or*
minks
Minkowski
Min+ne+apo+lis
Minnelli
min+ne+ola
min+ne+olas
min+ne+sing+er
min+ne+sing+
ers
Min+ne+so+ta
Min+ne+so+tan
Min+ne+so+
tans
min+now
min+nows *or*
min+now
Mi+no+an
Mi+no+ans
mi+nor
mi+nors
mi+nors
mi+nor+ing

mi+nored
Mi+nor+ca
Mi+nor+can
Mi+nor+cans
mi+nor+ity
mi+nor+ities
Minos
Minotaur
Minsk
min+ster
min+sters
min+strel
min+strels
min+strel+sy
min+strel+sies
mint
mints
mints
mint+ing
mint+ed
mint+age
mint+ages
mint+er
mint+ers
Mintoff
minu+end
minu+ends
minu+et
minu+ets
mi+nus
mi+nuses
mi+nus+cu+lar
mi+nus+cule
mi+nus+cules
min+ute
min+utes
min+utes
min+ut+ing
min+ut+ed
mi+nute
very small
mi+nute+ly
Min+ute+man
Min+ute+men
mi+nute+ness
min+utes
mi+nu+tiae
minx
minxes
Min+ya
Mio+cene
mio+sis
mio+ses
mi+ot+ic
Mi+que+lon

Mir
Mirabeau
mira+cle
mira+cles
mi+racu+lous
mi+racu+lous+ly
mi+racu+lous+
ness
Mi+ra+flo+res
mi+rage
mi+rages
mire
mires
mires
mir+ing
mired
mire+poix
Miriam
mirk
mirki+ly
mirki+ness
mirky
Miró
mir+ror
mir+rors
mir+rors
mir+ror+ing
mir+rored
mirth
mirth+ful
mirth+ful+ness
mirth+less
mirth+less+ness
MIRV
MIRVs
mis+adapt
mis+adapts
mis+adapt+ing
mis+adapt+ed
mis+add
mis+adds
mis+add+ing
mis+add+ed
mis+add+ress
mis+add+resses
mis+add+ress+
ing
mis+add+ressed
mis+ad+min+is+
tra+tion
mis+ad+ven+ture
mis+ad+ven+
tures
misalign
mis+aligns

mis+align+ing
mis+aligned
mis+align+ment
mis+align+
ments
mis+al+li+ance
mis+al+li+ances
mis+an+thrope
mis+an+thropes
mis+an+throp+ic
mis+an+thropi+
cal
mis+an+thro+pist
mis+an+thro+
pists
mis+an+thro+py
mis+ap+pel+la+
tion
mis+ap+pel+la+
tions
mis+ap+pli+ca+
tion
mis+ap+pli+ca+
tions
mis+ap+ply
mis+ap+plies
mis+ap+ply+ing
mis+ap+plied
mis+ap+praise
mis+ap+praises
mis+ap+prais+
ing
mis+ap+praised
mis+ap+pre+
hend
mis+ap+pre+
hends
mis+ap+pre+
hend+ing
mis+ap+pre+
hend+ed
mis+ap+pre+hen+
sion
mis+ap+pre+
hen+sions
mis+ap+pre+hen+
sive
mis+ap+pre+hen+
sive+ness
mis+ap+pro+pri+
ate
mis+ap+pro+pri+
ates
mis+ap+pro+pri+
at+ing

mis+ap+pro+pri+
at+ed
mis+ap+pro+pria+
tion
mis+ap+pro+
pria+tions
mis+ar+range
mis+ar+ranges
mis+ar+rang+
ing
mis+ar+ranged
mis+ar+range+
ment
mis+ar+range+
ments
mis+as+so+ci+
ate
mis+as+so+ci+
ates
mis+as+so+ci+
at+ing
mis+as+so+ci+
at+ed
mis+as+so+cia+
tion
mis+as+so+cia+
tions
mis+be+come
mis+be+comes
mis+be+com+
ing
mis+be+came
mis+be+come
mis+be+got+ten
mis+be+have
mis+be+haves
mis+be+hav+ing
mis+be+haved
mis+be+hav+er
mis+be+hav+ers
mis+be+hav+iour
mis+be+lief
mis+be+liefs
mis+cal+cu+late
mis+cal+cu+
lates
mis+cal+cu+lat+
ing
mis+cal+cu+lat+
ed
mis+cal+cu+la+
tion
mis+cal+cu+la+
tions
mis+call

mis+calls
mis+call+ing
mis+called
mis+call+er
mis+call+ers
mis+car+riage
mis+car+riages
mis+car+ry
mis+car+ries
mis+car+ry+ing
mis+car+ried
mis+cast
mis+casts
mis+cast+ing
mis+cast
mis+cat+ego+
rise
mis+cat+ego+
rises
mis+cat+ego+
ris+ing
mis+cat+ego+
rised
mis+cat+ego+
rize
mis+cat+ego+
rizes
mis+cat+ego+riz+
ing
mis+cat+ego+
rized
mis+ce+gena+
tion
mis+cel+la+nea
mis+cel+la+
neous
mis+cel+la+
neous+ly
mis+cel+la+
neous+ness
mis+cel+la+nist
mis+cel+la+
nists
mis+cel+la+ny
mis+cel+la+nies
mis+chance
mis+char+ac+ter+
ise
mis+char+ac+
ter+ises
mis+char+ac+
ter+is+ing
mis+char+ac+
ter+ised

mis+char+ac+ter+
ize
mis+char+ac+
ter+izes
mis+char+ac+
ter+iz+ing
mis+char+ac+
ter+ized
mis+chief
mis+chiefs
mis+chie+vous
mis+chie+vous+
ly
mis+chie+vous+
ness
mis+choose
mis+chooses
mis+choos+ing
mis+chose
mis+chos+en
mis+cibil+ity
mis+cible
mis+clas+si+fy
mis+clas+si+fies
mis+clas+si+fy+
ing
mis+clas+si+
fied
mis+com+pu+ta+
tion
mis+com+pu+ta+
tions
mis+con+ceive
mis+con+ceives
mis+con+ceiv+
ing
mis+con+ceived
mis+con+ceiv+er
mis+con+ceiv+
ers
mis+con+cep+
tion
mis+con+cep+
tions
mis+con+duct
mis+con+ducts
mis+con+duct+
ing
mis+con+duct+
ed
mis+con+jec+
ture
mis+con+jec+
tures

mis+con+jec+
tur+ing
mis+con+jec+
tured
mis+con+struc+
tion
mis+con+struc+
tions
mis+con+strue
mis+con+strues
mis+con+stru+
ing
mis+con+strued
mis+copy
mis+copies
mis+copy+ing
mis+cop+ied
mis+count
mis+counts
mis+counts
mis+count+ing
mis+count+ed
mis+cre+ant
mis+cre+ants
mis+cue
mis+cues
mis+cues
mis+cu+ing
mis+cued
mis+date
mis+dates
mis+dat+ing
mis+dat+ed
mis+deal
mis+deals
mis+deals
mis+deal+ing
mis+dealt
mis+deal+er
mis+deal+ers
mis+deed
mis+deeds
mis+de+fine
mis+de+fines
mis+de+fin+ing
mis+de+fined
mis+de+mean
mis+de+means
mis+de+mean+
ing
mis+de+meaned
mis+de+mean+or
U.S.
mis+de+mean+
ors

mis+de+mean+
  our
mis+de+mean+
  ours
mis+di+ag+no+
  sis
mis+di+ag+no+
  ses
mis+di+rect
mis+di+rects
mis+di+rect+ing
mis+di+rect+ed
mis+di+rec+tion
mis+di+rec+
  tions
mis+doubt
mis+doubts
mis+doubt+ing
mis+doubt+ed
mis+edu+cate
mis+edu+cates
mis+edu+cat+
  ing
mis+edu+cat+
  ed
mis+edu+ca+tion
mise en scène
mis+em+ploy
mis+em+ploys
mis+em+ploy+
  ing
mis+em+ployed
Mi+seno
mi+ser
  mi+sers
mis+er+able
mis+er+able+
  ness
mis+er+ably
mi+sère
  mi+sères
Mis+erere
mis+eri+cord
  mis+eri+cords
mis+eri+corde
  mis+eri+cordes
mi+ser+li+ness
mi+ser+ly
mis+ery
  mis+eries
mis+es+ti+mate
mis+es+ti+
  mates
mis+es+ti+
  mates

mis+es+ti+mat+
  ing
mis+es+ti+mat+
  ed
mis+es+ti+ma+
  tion
mis+es+ti+ma+
  tions
mis+fea+sance
  mis+fea+sances
mis+file
mis+files
mis+fil+ing
mis+filed
mis+fire
mis+fires
mis+fires
mis+fir+ing
mis+fired
mis+fit
mis+fits
mis+fits
mis+fit+ting
mis+fit+ted
mis+for+tune
mis+for+tunes
mis+gauge
mis+gauges
mis+gaug+ing
mis+gauged
mis+give
mis+gives
mis+giv+ing
mis+gave
mis+giv+en
mis+giv+ing
mis+giv+ings
mis+gov+ern
mis+gov+erns
mis+gov+ern+
  ing
mis+gov+erned
mis+gov+ern+
  ment
mis+guide
mis+guides
mis+guid+ing
mis+guid+ed
mis+guid+ed
mis+guid+ed+ly
mis+han+dle
mis+han+dles
mis+han+dling
mis+han+dled
mis+hap

mis+haps
mis+hear
mis+hears
mis+hear+ing
mis+heard
Mishima
mis+hit
mis+hits
mis+hits
mis+hit+ting
mis+hit
mish+mash
  mish+mashes
Mish+na
  Mish+na+yoth
Mish+na+ic
Mish+nic
mis+iden+ti+fi+
  ca+tion
mis+iden+ti+fi+
  ca+tions
mis+iden+ti+fy
mis+iden+ti+fies
mis+iden+ti+fy+
  ing
mis+iden+ti+fied
mis+in+form
mis+in+forms
mis+in+form+
  ing
mis+in+formed
mis+in+for+ma+
  tion
mis+in+struct
mis+in+structs
mis+in+struct+
  ing
mis+in+struct+
  ed
mis+in+struc+
  tion
mis+in+struc+
  tions
mis+in+ter+pret
mis+in+ter+
  prets
mis+in+ter+pret+
  ing
mis+in+ter+pret+
  ed
mis+in+ter+pre+
  ta+tion
mis+in+ter+pre+
  ta+tions

mis+in+ter+pret+
  er
mis+in+ter+pret+
  ers
mis+judge
mis+judges
mis+judg+ing
mis+judged
mis+judge+ment
mis+judge+
  ments
mis+judg+er
mis+judg+ers
mis+judg+ment
mis+judg+ments
Mis+kolc
mis+la+bel
mis+la+bels
mis+la+bel+ling
mis+la+belled
mis+lay
mis+lays
mis+laying
mis+laid
mis+lead
mis+leads
mis+lead+ing
mis+led
mis+lead+er
mis+lead+ers
mis+lead+ing
mis+man+age
mis+man+ages
mis+man+ag+
  ing
mis+man+aged
mis+man+age+
  ment
mis+mar+riage
mis+mar+riages
mis+match
mis+matches
mis+matches
mis+match+ing
mis+matched
mis+meas+ure
mis+meas+ures
mis+meas+ur+
  ing
mis+meas+ured
mis+name
mis+names
mis+nam+ing
mis+named
mis+no+mer

mis+no+mers
misnumber
mis+num+bers
mis+num+ber+
  ing
mis+num+bered
miso
mi+soga+mist
mi+soga+mists
mi+soga+my
mi+sogy+nist
mi+sogy+nists
mi+sogy+nous
mi+sogy+ny
mis+per+cep+
  tion
mis+phrase
mis+phrases
mis+phras+ing
mis+phrased
mis+place
mis+places
mis+plac+ing
mis+placed
mis+placed
mis+place+ment
mis+play
mis+plays
mis+plays
mis+play+ing
mis+played
mis+prin+ci+pled
mis+print
mis+prints
mis+prints
mis+print+ing
mis+print+ed
mis+prise
mis+prises
mis+pris+ing
mis+prised
mis+pri+sion
mis+prize
mis+prizes
mis+priz+ing
mis+prized
mis+pro+nounce
mis+pro+
  nounces
mis+pro+nounc+
  ing
mis+pro+
  nounced
mis+pro+nun+cia+
  tion

mis+pro+nun+
  cia+tions
rnis+pro+por+
  tion
mis+pro+por+
  tions
mis+punc+tu+ate
mis+punc+tu+
  ates
mis+punc+tu+at+
  ing
mis+punc+tu+at+
  ed
mis+punc+tua+
  tion
mis+punc+tua+
  tions
mis+quo+ta+tion
mis+quo+ta+
  tions
mis+quote
mis+quotes
mis+quot+ing
mis+quot+ed
mis+read
mis+reads
mis+read+ing
mis+read
mis+rec+og+nise
mis+rec+og+
  nises
mis+rec+og+nis+
  ing
mis+rec+og+
  nised
mis+rec+og+nize
mis+rec+og+
  nizes
mis+rec+og+niz+
  ing
mis+rec+og+
  nized
mis+re+late
mis+re+lates
mis+re+lat+ing
mis+re+lat+ed
mis+re+la+tion
mis+re+la+tions
mis+re+mem+ber
mis+re+mem+
  bers
mis+re+mem+
  ber+ing
mis+re+mem+
  bered

mis+re+port
mis+re+ports
mis+re+port+ing
mis+re+port+ed
mis+rep+re+sent
mis+rep+re+
  sents
mis+rep+re+
  sent+ing
mis+rep+re+
  sent+ed
mis+rep+re+sen+
  ta+tion
mis+rep+re+sen+
  ta+tions
mis+rep+re+sen+
  ta+tive
mis+rhymed
mis+rule
mis+rules
mis+rul+ing
mis+ruled
miss
misses
misses
miss+ing
missed
Miss
Misses
mis+sal
mis+sals
mis+sel
mis+shape
mis+shapes
mis+shapes
mis+shap+ing
mis+shaped or
mis+shapen
mis+shap+en
mis+shap+en+
  ness
mis+sile
mis+siles
mis+sile+ry
mis+sil+ry
miss+ing
mis+sion
mis+sions
mis+sions
mis+sion+ing
mis+sioned
mis+sion+ary
mis+sion+aries
mis+sis
Mis+sis+sau+ga

Mis+sis+sip+pi
Mis+sis+sip+pian
Mis+sis+sip+
  pians
mis+sive
mis+sives
Mis+so+lon+ghi
Mis+souri
Mis+sou+rian
Mis+sou+rians
mis+spell
mis+spells
mis+spell+ing
mis+spelt or
mis+spelled
mis+spell+ing
mis+spell+ings
mis+spend
mis+spends
mis+spend+ing
mis+spent
mis+state
mis+states
mis+stat+ing
mis+stat+ed
mis+state+ment
mis+state+
  ments
mis+step
mis+steps
mis+sus
missy
missies
mist
mists
mists
mist+ing
mist+ed
mis+tak+able
mis+take
mis+takes
mis+takes
mis+tak+ing
mis+took
mis+tak+en
mis+tak+en
mis+tak+en+ly
mis+tak+en+ness
Mis+tas+si+ni
mis+teach
mis+teaches
mis+teach+ing
mis+taught
mis+ter
mis+ters

mis+ters
mis+ter+ing
mis+tered
Mis+ter
Mis+ters
mis+term
mis+terms
mis+term+ing
mis+termed
Mis+ti
mis+ti+gris
mis+ti+grises
misti+ly
mis+time
mis+times
mis+tim+ing
mis+timed
misti+ness
mis+ti+tle
mis+ti+tles
mis+ti+tling
mis+ti+tled
mis+tle+toe
mis+took
mis+tral
Mistral
mis+trans+late
mis+trans+lates
mis+trans+lat+
ing
mis+trans+lat+
ed
mis+treat
mis+treats
mis+treat+ing
mis+treat+ed
mis+treat+ment
mis+tress
mis+tresses
Mis+tress
Mis+tresses
mis+tri+al
mis+tri+als
mis+trust
mis+trusts
mis+trust+ing
mis+trust+ed
mis+trust+ful
mis+trust+ful+ly
mis+trust+ful+
ness
misty
misti+er
misti+est
mis+type

mis+types
mis+typ+ing
mis+typed
mis+under+stand
mis+under+
stands
mis+under+
stand+ing
mis+under+
stood
mis+under+stand+
ing
mis+under+
stand+ings
mis+under+stood
mis+us+age
mis+us+ages
mis+use
mis+uses
mis+uses
mis+us+ing
mis+used
mis+us+er
mis+us+ers
mis+value
mis+values
mis+valu+ing
mis+valued
Mitchell
Mitchum
mite
mites
mi+ter
U.S.
mi+ters
mi+ters
mi+ter+ing
mi+tered
Mith+gar+thr
Mith+ra
Mith+ra+ic
Mith+rai+cism
Mith+ra+ism
Mith+ra+ist
Mith+ra+ists
Mith+ras
mith+ri+dat+ic
mith+ri+da+tism
miti+gable
miti+gate
miti+gates
miti+gat+ing
miti+gat+ed
miti+ga+tion
miti+ga+tive

miti+ga+tor
miti+ga+tors
miti+ga+tory
Mi+ti+lí+ni
mi+to+chon+
drion
mi+to+chon+
dria
mi+to+sis
mi+tot+ic
mi+tral
mi+tre
mi+tres
mi+tres
mi+tring
mi+tred
mitt
mitts
mit+ten
mit+tens
Mitterrand
mit+ti+mus
mit+ti+muses
mix
mixes
mixes
mix+ing
mixed
mix+able
mixed
mix+ed+ness
mixed-up
mix+er
mix+ers
mix+ture
mix+tures
mix-up
mix-ups
miz+en
miz+ens
miz+en+mast
miz+en+masts
Mizoguchi
Mi+zo+ram
miz+zen
miz+zens
miz+zen+mast
miz+zen+masts
miz+zle
miz+zles
miz+zles
miz+zling
miz+zled
miz+zly
Mlle

Mlles
Mme
Mmes
mne+mon+ic
mne+mon+ics
mne+moni+cal+ly
mne+mon+ics
Mnemosyne
mo
mos
moa
moas
Moab
Mo+ab+ite
Mo+ab+ites
moan
moans
moans
moan+ing
moaned
moan+er
moan+ers
moan+ful
moan+ing
moat
moats
moats
moat+ing
moat+ed
mob
mobs
mobs
mob+bing
mobbed
mob+cap
mob+caps
mo+bile
mo+biles
Mo+bile
mo+bi+lis+able
mo+bi+li+sa+tion
mo+bi+li+sa+
tions
mo+bi+lise
mo+bi+lises
mo+bi+lis+ing
mo+bi+lised
mo+bil+ity
mo+bi+liz+able
mo+bi+li+za+tion
mo+bi+li+za+
tions
mo+bi+lize
mo+bi+lizes
mo+bi+liz+ing

mo+bi+lized
Möbius
mob+oc+ra+cy
mob+oc+ra+
cies
mob+ster
mob+sters
Mo+bu+tu
lake
Mobutu
surname
Mo+çam+bi+que
moc+ca+sin
moc+ca+sins
mo+cha
Mo+cha
mock
mocks
mocks
mock+ing
mocked
mock+er
mock+ers
mock+ers
mock+ery
mock+eries
mock-heroic
mock-heroics
mock+ing
mocking+bird
mocking+birds
mock+ing+ly
mock-up
mock-ups
mod
mods
mod+al
mo+dal+ity
mo+dal+ities
mo+dal+ly
mode
modes
mod+el
mod+els
mod+els
mod+el+ling or
mod+el+ing
U.S.
mod+elled or
mod+eled
U.S.
mod+el+er
U.S.
mod+el+ers
mod+el+ing

U.S.
mod+el+ler
mod+el+lers
mod+el+ling
mo+dem
mo+dems
Mo+dena
mod+er+ate
mod+er+ates
mod+er+ates
mod+er+at+ing
mod+er+at+ed
mod+era+tion
mod+era+tions
mod+era+to
mod+era+tor
mod+era+tors
mod+era+tor+
ship
mod+era+tor+
ships
mod+ern
mod+erns
mod+erni+sa+
tion
mod+erni+sa+
tions
mod+ern+ise
mod+ern+ises
mod+ern+is+ing
mod+ern+ised
mod+ern+is+er
mod+ern+is+ers
mod+ern+ism
mod+ern+ist
mod+ern+ists
mod+ern+is+tic
mod+ern+is+ti+
cal+ly
mo+der+nity
mo+der+nities
mod+erni+za+
tion
mod+erni+za+
tions
mod+ern+ize
mod+ern+izes
mod+ern+iz+ing
mod+ern+ized
mod+ern+iz+er
mod+ern+iz+ers
mod+ern+ness
mod+est
mod+est+ly
mod+es+ty

mod+es+ties
modi+cum
modi+cums
modi+fi+able
modi+fi+ca+tion
modi+fi+ca+
tions
modi+fi+ca+tive
modi+fi+ca+tory
modi+fi+er
modi+fi+ers
modi+fy
modi+fies
modi+fy+ing
modi+fied
Modigliani
mod+ish
mod+ish+ly
mod+ish+ness
mo+diste
mo+distes
Modred
modu+lar
modu+late
modu+lates
modu+lat+ing
modu+lat+ed
modu+la+tion
modu+la+tions
modu+la+tor
modu+la+tors
mod+ule
mod+ules
modu+lus
modu+li
mo+dus op+eran+
di
modi op+eran+
di
mo+dus vi+ven+
di
modi vi+ven+di
Moers
mog
mogs
Moga+discio
Moga+dishu
Moga+don
Trademark
Moga+dor
mog+gy
mog+gies
Mo+gi+lev
mo+gul
mo+guls

Mo+gul
Mo+guls
mo+hair
Mohammed
Mohammed
Ahmed
Mohammed Ali
Mo+ham+med+
an
Mo+ham+med+
ans
Mo+ham+med+
an+ism
Mo+ha+ve
Mo+hawk
Mo+hawks or
Mo+hawk
Mohenjo-Daro
mo+hi+can
mo+hi+cans
Mo+hi+lev
Moholy-Nagy
moi+dore
moi+dores
moi+ety
moi+eties
moil
moils
moil+ing
moiled
Moira
Moirai
moire
moi+ré
moi+rés
Moism
moist
mois+ten
mois+tens
mois+ten+ing
mois+tened
moist+ly
moist+ness
mois+ture
mois+tur+ise
mois+tur+ises
mois+tur+is+ing
mois+tur+ised
moist+ur+is+er
moist+ur+is+ers
mois+tur+ize
mois+tur+izes
mois+tur+iz+ing
mois+tur+ized
moist+ur+iz+er

moist+ur+iz+ers
Mo+ja+ve
moke
 mokes
Mo+kha
Mok+po
mo+lal
mo+lar
 mo+lars
mo+las+ses
mold
U.S.
 molds
 molds
 mold+ing
 mold+ed
Mol+dau
Mol+da+via
Mol+da+vian
 Mol+da+vians
mold+board
U.S.
 mold+boards
mold+er
U.S.
 mold+ers
 mold+ers
 mold+er+ing
 mold+ered
moldi+ness
U.S.
mold+ing
U.S.
 mold+ings
moldy
U.S.
 moldi+er
 moldi+est
mole
 moles
Mo+lech
mo+lecu+lar
mo+lecu+lar+ly
mol+ecule
 mol+ecules
mole+hill
 mole+hills
mole+skin
mo+lest
 mo+lests
 mo+lest+ing
 mo+lest+ed
mo+les+ta+tion
 mo+les+ta+
  tions

mo+lest+er
mo+lest+ers
Molière
Molina
Mo+li+se
moll
 molls
mol+li+fi+able
mol+li+fi+ca+tion
mol+li+fi+er
 mol+li+fi+ers
mol+li+fy
mol+li+fies
mol+li+fy+ing
mol+li+fied
mol+lusc
 mol+luscs
mol+lus+can
mol+lusk
 mol+lusks
U.S.
mol+lus+kan
U.S.
mol+ly
 mol+lies
molly+coddle
 molly+coddles
 molly+coddles
 molly+coddling
 molly+coddled
Molnár
Mo+loch
Mo+lo+kai
Mo+lo+po
Molo+tov
 place name
Molotov
 surname
molt
U.S.
 molts
 molts
 molt+ing
 molt+ed
mol+ten
Moltke
mol+to
Mo+luc+cas
moly
 molies
mo+lyb+de+nite
mo+lyb+de+num
mom
 moms
Mom+ba+sa

mo+ment
 mo+ments
mo+men+tari+ly
mo+men+tari+
  ness
mo+men+tary
mo+men+tous
mo+men+tous+ly
mo+men+tous+
  ness
mo+men+tum
mo+men+ta or
mo+men+tums
mom+ma
 mom+mas
Mommsen
Momus
 Momuses or
Momi
Mon
Mona+can
 Mona+cans
mon+acid
mon+acid+ic
Mona+co
Monaco-Ville
mon+ad
 mon+ads or
mona+des
mona+del+phous
mo+nad+ic
mo+nad+nock
 mo+nad+nocks
Mona+ghan
mo+nan+drous
mo+nan+dry
mon+arch
 mon+archs
mo+nar+chal
mo+nar+chi+al
mo+nar+chic
mo+nar+chi+cal
mon+ar+chism
mon+ar+chist
 mon+ar+chists
mon+ar+chis+tic
mon+ar+chy
 mon+ar+chies
mo+nar+da
 mo+nar+das
mon+as+te+rial
mon+as+tery
 mon+as+teries
mo+nas+tic
 mo+nas+tics

mo+nas+ti+cism
mon+atom+ic
mon+aural
mon+aural+ly
mona+zite
Mönchen-
  Gladbach
Monck
Monc+ton
Mon+day
 Mon+days
Mondrian
mo+necious
Monet
mon+etari+ly
mon+etar+ism
mon+etar+ist
 mon+etar+ists
mon+etary
mon+eti+sa+tion
mon+etise
 mon+etises
mon+etis+ing
mon+etised
mon+eti+za+tion
mon+etize
 mon+etizes
mon+etiz+ing
mon+etized
mon+ey
mon+eys or
 mon+ies
money+bags
money+changer
 money+
  changers
mon+eyed
money-grubber
 money-grubbers
money-grubbing
money+lender
 money+lenders
money+lending
money+maker
 money+makers
money+making
money-spinner
 money-spinners
mon+ger
 mon+gers
mon+ger+ing
mon+gol
 mon+gols
Mon+gol
 Mon+gols

Mon+go+lia
mon+go+lian
Mon+go+lian
Mon+go+lians
Mon+gol+ic
Mon+gol+ics
mon+go+lism
mon+gol+oid
mon+gol+oids
Mon+gol+oid
mon+goose
mon+gooses
mon+grel
mon+grels
mon+greli+sa+tion
mon+grel+ise
mon+grel+ises
mon+grel+is+ing
mon+grel+ised
mon+grel+ism
mon+greli+za+tion
mon+grel+ize
mon+grel+izes
mon+grel+iz+ing
mon+grel+ized
mon+grel+ly
mongst
mon+ick+er
mon+ick+ers
mon+ied
monies
moni+ker
moni+kers
mon+ism
mon+ist
mon+ists
mo+nis+tic
mo+ni+tion
mo+ni+tions
moni+tor
moni+tors
moni+tors
moni+tor+ing
moni+tored
moni+to+rial
moni+tor+ship
moni+tory
moni+tories
moni+tress
moni+tresses
monk
monks

Monk
mon+key
mon+keys
monk+fish
monk+fish *or*
monk+fishes
monk+ish
monks+hood
Mon+mouth
place name
Monmouth
surname
Mon+mouth+shire
Monnet
mono
monos
mono+ac+id
mono+ac+id+ic
mono+atom+ic
mono+ba+sic
mono+car+pic
mono+car+pous
mono+chro+ic
mono+chro+mat+ic
mono+chroma+tor
mono+chroma+tors
mono+chrome
mono+chromes
mono+chro+mic
mono+chrom+ist
mono+chrom+ists
mono+cle
mono+cles
mono+cled
mono+cli+nal
mono+cline
mono+clines
mono+clin+ic
mono+cli+nism
mono+cli+nous
mono+clo+nal
mono+coty+ledon
mono+coty+ledons
mono+coty+ledon+ous
mo+noc+ra+cy
mo+noc+ra+cies

mono+crat
mono+crats
mono+crat+ic
mo+nocu+lar
mo+nocu+lar+ly
mono+cul+ture
mono+cy+cle
mono+cy+cles
mono+cyte
mono+cytes
mo+nod+ic
mono+dist
mono+dists
mono+dy
mono+dies
mo+noecious
mono+fil
mono+fils
mono+fila+ment
mono+fila+ments
mo+noga+mist
mo+noga+mists
mo+noga+mous
mo+noga+my
mono+gen+esis
mo+nog+eny
mono+gram
mono+grams
mono+gram+matic
mono+graph
mono+graphs
mono+graphs
mono+graph+ing
mono+graphed
mo+nog+ra+pher
mo+nog+ra+phers
mono+graph+ic
mo+nog+ra+phist
mo+nog+ra+phists
mo+nogy+nous
mo+nogy+ny
mono+hull
mono+hulls
mono+lay+er
mono+lay+ers
mono+lin+gual
mono+lith
mono+liths
mono+lith+ic

mono+log+ic
mono+logi+cal
mono+log+ist
mono+log+ists
mono+logue
mono+logues
mono+ma+nia
mono+ma+ni+ac
mono+ma+ni+acs
mono+ma+nia+cal
mono+mark
mono+marks
mono+mer
mono+mers
mono+mer+ic
mono+me+tal+lic
mono+met+al+lism
mono+met+al+lisms
mono+met+al+list
mono+met+al+lists
mo+no+mial
mo+no+mials
mono+mor+phic
mono+mor+phous
Mo+non+ga+he+la
mono+nu+cleo+sis
mono+phon+ic
mon+oph+thong
mon+oph+thongs
Mo+nophy+site
Mo+nophy+sites
Mono+phy+sit+ic
mono+plane
mono+planes
mono+pole
mono+poles
mo+nopo+li+sa+tion
mo+nopo+li+sa+tions
mo+nopo+lise
mo+nopo+lises
mo+nopo+lis+ing

mo +nopo +lised
mo +nopo +lis +er
mo +nopo +lis +
  ers
mo +nopo +list
mo +nopo +lists
mo +nopo +lis +tic
mo +nopo +li +za +
  tion
mo +nopo +li +za +
  tions
mo +nopo +lize
mo +nopo +lizes
mo +nopo +liz +
  ing
mo +nopo +lized
mo +nopo +liz +er
mo +nopo +liz +
  ers
mo +nopo +ly
mo +nopo +lies
Mo +nopo +ly
Trademark
mono +rail
mono +rails
mono +sac +cha +
  ride
mono +sac +cha +
  rides
mono +ski
mono +skis
mono +skier
mono +skiers
mono +ski +ing
mono +so +dium
mono +sta +ble
mono +syl +lab +ic
mono +syl +labi +
  cal +ly
mono +syl +la +ble
mono +syl +la +
  bles
mono +theism
mono +theist
mono +theists
mono +theis +tic
mono +theis +ti +
  cal +ly
mono +tint
mono +tints
mono +tone
mono +tones
mo +noto +nous
mo +noto +nous +
  ly

mo +noto +nous +
  ness
mo +noto +ny
mo +noto +nies
mono +trema +
  tous
mono +treme
mono +tremes
mono +type
mono +types
Mono +type
Trademark
Mono +types
mono +typ +ic
mono +un +saturat +
  ed
mono +va +lence
mono +va +len +cy
mono +va +lent
mon +ox +ide
mon +ox +ides
Monroe
Mon +ro +via
Mons
Mon +sei +gneur
Messei +gneurs
mon +sieur
mes +sieurs
Mon +sig +nor
Mon +sig +nors
or
Mon +sig +nori
mon +soon
mon +soons
mon +soon +al
mons pu +bis
mon +tes pu +bis
Mons Ser +ra +tus
mon +ster
mon +sters
mon +stera
mon +steras
mon +strance
mon +strances
mon +stros +ity
mon +stros +ities
mon +strous
mon +strous +ly
mon +strous +
  ness
mons ven +er +is
mon +tes ven +er +
  is
mon +tage
mon +tages

Montagu
Montaigne
Montale
Mon +tana
place name
Montana
surname
Mon +tan +an
  Mon +tan +ans
mon +tane
Mon +tau +ban
Mont +bé +liard
Mont Blanc
mont +bre +tia
  mont +bre +tias
Montcalm
Mont Ce +nis
Mont Cer +vin
mon +te
  mon +tes
Mon +te Car +lo
Mon +te Cas +si +
  no
Mon +te Cor +no
Mon +te +go
Mon +te +ne +grin
  Mon +te +ne +
  grins
Mon +te +ne +gro
Mon +te +rey
Californian city
Mon +ter +rey
Mexican city
Montespan
Montesquieu
Montessori
Monteux
Monteverdi
Mon +te +vi +deo
Montezuma
Montfort
Montgolfier
Mont +gom +ery
place name
Montgomery
surname
Mont +gom +ery +
  shire
month
  months
Montherlant
month +ly
  month +lies
Mont +lu +çon
Mont +mar +tre

Mont +par +nasse
Mont +pel +ier
U.S.
Mont +pel +lier
France
Mon +treal
Mont +ré +al
Mon +treuil
Mon +treux
Montrose
Mont-Saint-
  Michel
Mont +ser +rat
monu +ment
monu +ments
Monu +ment
monu +men +tal
monu +men +tal +
  ly
Mon +za
moo
  moos
moo +ing
mooed
mooch
  mooches
mooch +ing
mooched
mooch +er
mooch +ers
mood
  moods
moodi +ly
moodi +ness
moody
moodi +er
moodi +est
Moody
Moog
Trademark
  Moogs
mooi
mooli
  moolis
mool +vi
  mool +vis
mool +vie
  mool +vies
Moom +ba
  Moom +bas
moon
  moons
moons
moon +ing
mooned

Moon	mop	mor+al+ize	Mo+relos
moon+beam	mops	mor+al+izes	more+over
moon+beams	mops	mor+al+iz+ing	more+pork
moon+calf	mop+ping	mor+al+ized	more+porks
moon+calves	mopped	mor+al+iz+er	mo+res
moon-faced	mope	mor+al+iz+ers	Mo+res+co
moon+less	mopes	mor+al+ly	Mo+res+cos
moon+light	mopes	Mor+ar	*or*
moon+lights	mop+ing	mo+rass	Mo+res+coes
moon+light+ing	moped	mo+rasses	Morgain le Fay
moon+light+ed	mo+ped	mora+to+rium	Mor+gan
moon+lighter	mo+peds	mora+to+ria *or*	Mor+gans
moon+lighters	mop+er	mora+to+riums	Morgan
moon+lit	mop+ers	Mo+ra+va	*surname*
moon+quake	mopes	Mo+ra+via	mor+ga+nat+ic
moon+quakes	mo+poke	Mo+ra+vian	mor+ga+nati+cal+
moon+scape	mo+pokes	Mo+ra+vians	ly
moon+scapes	mop+pet	Mo+ra+vi+an+	Morgan le Fay
moon+shine	mop+pets	ism	mor+gen
moon+shot	mop-up	mo+ray	mor+gens
moon+shots	mop-ups	mo+rays	morgue
moon+stone	mop up	Moray	morgues
moon+stones	*verb*	*surname*	mori+bund
moon+stricken	mopy	Mor+ay	mori+bun+dity
moon+struck	mo+quette	*place name*	mori+bund+ly
moony	mora	Mor+ay+shire	Mörike
mooni+er	morae *or*	mor+bid	Mo+ris+co
mooni+est	moras	mor+bid+ity	Mo+ris+cos *or*
moor	Mo+ra+da+bad	mor+bid+ities	Mo+ris+coes
moors	mo+rain+al	mor+bid+ly	mor+ish
moors	mo+raine	mor+bid+ness	Morisot
moor+ing	mo+raines	mor+bif+ic	Mor+ley
moored	mo+rain+ic	Mor+bi+han	*place name*
Moor	mor+al	mor+dan+cy	Morley
Moors	mor+als	mor+dant	*surname*
moor+age	mo+rale	mor+dants	Mor+mon
moor+ages	mor+ali+sa+tion	mor+dant+ly	Mor+mons
moor+cock	mor+ali+sa+	Mordecai	Mor+mon+ism
moor+cocks	tions	mor+dent	morn
Moore	mor+al+ise	mor+dents	morns
moor+hen	mor+al+ises	Mordred	mor+nay
moor+hens	mor+al+is+ing	more	Mornay
moor+ing	mor+al+ised	More	morn+ing
moor+ings	mor+al+is+er	Mo+rea	morn+ings
moor+ings	mor+al+is+ers	Moreau	morning-after
Moor+ish	mor+al+ist	More+cambe	morning-glory
moor+land	mor+al+ists	*place name*	morning-glories
moor+lands	mor+al+is+tic	Morecambe	morn+ings
moose	mor+al+is+ti+cal+	*surname*	Moro
moose	ly	more+ish	Moros *or*
moot	mo+ral+ity	mo+rel	Moro
moots	mo+ral+ities	mo+rels	Mo+roc+can
moots	mor+ali+za+tion	Mo+relia	Mo+roc+cans
moot+ing	mor+ali+za+	mo+rel+lo	mo+roc+co
moot+ed	tions	mo+rel+los	

Mo+roc+co
mor+on
mor+ons
Mo+ro+ni
mo+ron+ic
mo+roni+cal+ly
mo+ron+ism
mo+ron+ity
mo+rose
mo+rose+ly
mo+rose+ness
morph
morphs
Mor+phean
mor+pheme
mor+phemes
mor+phem+ic
mor+phemi+cal+
ly
Morpheus
mor+phia
mor+phine
mor+pho+gen+
esis
mor+pho+genet+
ic
mor+pho+log+ic
mor+pho+logi+
cal
mor+pho+logi+
cal+ly
mor+pholo+gist
mor+pholo+
gists
mor+phol+ogy
mor+phol+ogies
Morphy
mor+ris
Morris
Morrison
mor+ro
mor+ros
mor+row
mor+rows
Mors
Morse
mor+sel
mor+sels
mor+tal
mor+tals
mor+tal+ity
mor+tal+ities
mor+tal+ly
mor+tar
mor+tars

mor+tars
mor+tar+ing
mor+tared
mortar+board
mortar+boards
mort+gage
mort+gages
mort+gages
mort+gag+ing
mort+gaged
mort+gage+able
mort+ga+gee
mort+ga+gees
mort+gag+er
mort+gag+ers
mort+gag+or
mort+gag+ors
mor+tice
mor+tices
mor+tices
mor+tic+ing
mor+ticed
mor+ti+cian
mor+ti+cians
mor+ti+fi+ca+
tion
mor+ti+fi+ca+
tions
mor+ti+fi+er
mor+ti+fi+ers
mor+ti+fy
mor+ti+fies
mor+ti+fy+ing
mor+ti+fied
mor+ti+fy+ing
Mortimer
mor+tise
mor+tises
mor+tises
mor+tis+ing
mor+tised
mort+main
Morton
mor+tu+ary
mor+tu+aries
mor+wong
mor+wongs
mor+yah
mo+sa+ic
mo+sa+ics
Mo+sa+ic
mo+sai+cist
mo+sai+cists
mos+cha+tel
mos+cha+tels

Mos+cow
Moseley
Mo+selle
Moses
mo+sey
mo+seys
mo+sey+ing
mo+seyed
Moshesh
Moshoeshoe
Mos+kva
Mos+lem
Mos+lems or
Mos+lem
Mos+lem+ic
Mos+lem+ism
Mosley
mosque
mosques
mos+qui+to
mos+qui+toes
or
mos+qui+tos
moss
mosses
Moss
mos+sie
mos+sies
mossi+ness
moss+like
mos+so
moss+trooper
moss+troopers
mossy
mossi+er
mossi+est
most
Mo+staga+nem
most+ly
Mosul
mot
mots
MOT
MOTs
mote
mo+tel
mo+tels
mo+tet
mo+tets
moth
moths
moth+ball
moth+balls
moth+balls
moth+ball+ing

moth+balled
moth-eaten
moth+er
moth+ers
moth+ers
moth+er+ing
moth+ered
moth+er+hood
Moth+er+ing
mother-in-law
mothers-in-law
mother+land
mother+lands
moth+er+less
moth+er+li+ness
moth+er+ly
mother-of-pearl
moth+proof
moth+proofs
moth+proof+ing
moth+proofed
mothy
mothi+er
mothi+est
mo+tif
mo+tifs
mo+tile
mo+til+ity
mo+tion
mo+tions
mo+tions
mo+tion+ing
mo+tioned
mo+tion+less
mo+ti+vate
mo+ti+vates
mo+ti+vat+ing
mo+ti+vat+ed
mo+ti+va+tion
mo+ti+va+tions
mo+ti+va+tion+al
mo+tive
mo+tives
mo+tives
mo+tiv+ing
mo+tived
mo+tive+less
mot juste
mots justes
mot+ley
mot+leys
mo+to+cross
mo+tor
mo+tors
mo+tors

mo+tor+ing
mo+tored
motor+bicyc+le
motor+bicyc+les
motor+bike
motor+bikes
motor+boat
motor+boats
motor+bus
motor+buses
motor+cade
motor+cades
motor+car
motor+cars
motor+cycle
motor+cycles
motor+cycles
motor+cycling
motor+cycled
motor+cyclist
motor+cyclists
mo+tori+sa+tion
mo+tor+ise
mo+tor+ises
mo+tor+is+ing
mo+tor+ised
mo+tor+ist
mo+tor+ists
mo+tori+za+tion
mo+tor+ize
mo+tor+izes
mo+tor+iz+ing
mo+tor+ized
motor+man
motor+men
motor+way
motor+ways
Mo+town
Trademark
motte
mottes
mott+le
mott+les
mott+les
mott+ling
mott+led
mot+to
mot+toes *or*
mot+tos
moue
moues
mouf+flon
mouf+flons
mouil+lé

mou+jik
mou+jiks
mould
moulds
moulds
mould+ing
mould+ed
mould+able
mould+board
mould+boards
mould+er
mould+ers
mould+er+ing
mould+ered
mouldi+ness
mould+ing
mould+ings
mouldy
mouldi+er
mouldi+est
Moulin
Mou+lins
Moul+mein
moult
moults
moults
moult+ing
moult+ed
moult+er
moult+ers
mound
mounds
mounds
mound+ing
mound+ed
mound-builder
bird
mound-builders
Mound Build+er
prehistoric human
Mound Build+ers
mount
mounts
mounts
mount+ing
mount+ed
mount+able
moun+tain
moun+tains
moun+tain+eer
moun+tain+eers
moun+tain+eers
moun+tain+eer+
ing

moun+tain+
eered
moun+tain+eer+
ing
moun+tain+ous
Mountbatten
moun+tebank
moun+tebanks
moun+tebanks
moun+tebank+
ing
moun+tebanked
moun+tebank+
ery
mount+ed
mount+er
mount+ers
Mountie
Mounties
mount+ing
mount+ings
mounting-block
mounting-blocks
Mountjoy
Mounty
Mounties
mourn
mourns
mourn+ing
mourned
mourn+er
mourn+ers
mourn+ful
mourn+ful+ly
mourn+ful+ness
mourn+ing
mourn+ing+ly
mou+sa+ka
mou+sa+kas
mouse
mice
mouse+like
mous+er
mous+ers
mouse+trap
mouse+traps
mous+ey
mousi+er
mousi+est
mousi+ly
mousi+ness
mous+ing
mous+ings
mous+sa+ka
mous+sa+kas

mousse
mousses
mousse+line
Moussorgsky
mous+tache
mous+taches
mous+tached
Mous+terian
mousy
mousi+er
mousi+est
mouth
mouths
mouths
mouth+ing
mouthed
mouth+er
mouth+ers
mouth+ful
mouth+fuls
mouth+part
mouth+parts
mouth+piece
mouth+pieces
mouth+wash
mouth+washes
mouthy
mouthi+er
mouthi+est
mou+ton
mov+abil+ity
mov+able
mov+ables
mov+able+ness
mov+ably
move
moves
moves
mov+ing
moved
move+able
move+ables
move+ment
move+ments
mov+er
mov+ers
movie
movies
mov+ing
mov+ing+ly
mow
mows
mow+ing
mowed
mowed *or*

mown
mow+ er
mow+ ers
mown
Mo+ zam+ bique
Mozart
Mo+ zar+ tean
Mo+ zar+ tian
moz+ za+ rel+ la
Mr
  Messrs
Mrs
  Mrs *or*
  Mes+ dames
Ms
mu
  mus
Mubarak
much
much+ ness
mu+ ci+ lage
  mu+ ci+ lages
mu+ ci+ lagi+ nous
muck
  mucks
  muck+ ing
  mucked
muck+ er
  muck+ ers
muck+ er+ ish
muck+ le
muck+ rake
  muck+ rakes
  muck+ rak+ ing
  muck+ raked
muck+ rak+ er
  muck+ rak+ ers
muck+ rak+ ing
muck+ sweat
  muck+ sweats
mucky
  mucki+ er
  mucki+ est
mu+ cos+ ity
mu+ cous
mu+ cus
mud
  muds
  muds
  mud+ ding
  mud+ ded
mud+ di+ ly
mud+ di+ ness
mud+ dle
  mud+ dles

mud+ dles
mud+ dling
mud+ dled
mud+ dled
muddle+ headed
muddle+ headed+
  ness
mud+ dler
mud+ dlers
mud+ dling
mud+ dy
  mud+ dies
  mud+ dy+ ing
  mud+ died
  mud+ di+ er
  mud+ di+ est
mud+ fish
  mud+ fish *or*
  mud+ fishes
mud+ flow
  mud+ flows
mud+ guard
  mud+ guards
mud+ lark
  mud+ larks
mud+ pack
  mud+ packs
mud+ skipper
  mud+ skippers
mud+ slinger
  mud+ slingers
mud+ slinging
mud+ stone
mues+ li
mues+ lis
mu+ ez+ zin
  mu+ ez+ zins
muff
  muffs
  muffs
  muff+ ing
  muffed
muf+ fin
  muf+ fins
muf+ fle
  muf+ fles
  muf+ fles
  muf+ fling
  muf+ fled
muf+ fler
  muf+ flers
muf+ ti
  muf+ tis
Muf+ ti
  Muf+ tis

Mu+ fu+ li+ ra
mug
  mugs
  mugs
  mug+ ging
  mugged
Mugabe
mug+ ger
  mug+ gers
mug+ gi+ ness
mug+ gins
  mug+ gins
mug+ gy
  mug+ gi+ er
  mug+ gi+ est
Muhammad
Muhammad Ali
Mu+ ham+ mad+
  an
Mu+ ham+ mad+
  ans
Mu+ ham+ med+
  an
Mu+ ham+ med+
  ans
Mühl+ hau+ sen
Muir
mu+ ja+ hed+ din
mu+ ja+ he+ deen
Muk+ den
muk+ luk
  muk+ luks
mu+ lat+ to
  mu+ lat+ tos *or*
  mu+ lat+ toes
mul+ berry
  mul+ berries
mulch
  mulches
  mulch+ ing
  mulched
Mulciber
mulct
  mulcts
  mulcts
  mulct+ ing
  mulct+ ed
Muldoon
mule
  mules
mu+ leta
  mu+ letas
mu+ leteer
  mu+ leteers
mul+ ga

mul+ gas
Mul+ ha+ cén
Mül+ heim
Mül+ heim an der
  Ruhr
Mul+ house
mu+ li+ eb+ rity
mul+ ish
mul+ ish+ ly
mul+ ish+ ness
mull
  mulls
  mulls
  mull+ ing
  mulled
Mull
mul+ la
  mul+ las
mul+ lah
  mul+ lahs
mul+ lein
  mul+ leins
mul+ ler
  mul+ lers
Muller
Müller
mul+ let
  mul+ lets
mul+ li+ ga+ taw+
  ny
Mulliken
Mul+ lin+ gar
mul+ li+ on
  mul+ li+ ons
  mul+ li+ ons
  mul+ li+ on+ ing
  mul+ li+ oned
mul+ lock
  mul+ locks
mullo+ way
  mullo+ ways
Mulroney
Mul+ tan
mul+ tan+ gu+ lar
multi+ an+ gu+ lar
multi+ col+ oured
multi+ cul+ tur+ al
multi+ cul+ tur+ al+
  ism
multi+ fac+ et+ ed
multi+ fac+ to+ rial
multi+ fari+ ous
multi+ fari+ ous+ ly
mul+ ti+ fari+ ous+
  ness

multi+fo+li+ate
multi+form
multi+for+mity
multi+gym
multi+gyms
multi+hull
multi+hulls
multi+lat+er+al
multi+lat+er+al+
  ly
multi+lin+gual
multi+media
multi+mil+lion+
  aire
multi+mil+lion+
  aires
multi+na+tion+al
multi+na+tion+
  als
multi+pack
multi+packs
mul+tipa+rous
multi+par+tite
multi+par+ty
multi+ple
multi+ples
multiple-choice
multi+plex
multi+plexes
multi+plexes
multi+plex+ing
multi+plexed
multi+pli+able
multi+plic+able
multi+pli+cand
multi+pli+cands
multi+pli+ca+tion
multi+pli+ca+
  tions
multi+plic+ity
multi+plic+ities
multi+pli+er
multi+pli+ers
multi+ply
multi+plies
multi+ply+ing
multi+plied
multi+pro+ces+
  sor
multi+pro+ces+
  sors
multi+pur+pose
multi+racial
multi+skill+ing
multi+stage

multi+sto+rey
 multi+sto+reys
multi+task+ing
multi+track
multi+tude
multi+tudes
multi+tu+di+nous
multi+tu+di+nous+
  ly
multi+tu+di+nous+
  ness
multi-user
multi+va+len+cy
multi+va+lent
mum
mums
mums
mum+ming
mummed
Mumbai
mum+ble
mum+bles
mum+bles
mum+bling
mum+bled
mum+bler
mum+blers
mum+bling
mum+bling+ly
mum+bo
Mumford
mum+mer
mum+mers
Mum+mer+set
mum+mery
mum+meries
mum+mi+fi+ca+
  tion
mum+mi+fy
mum+mi+fies
mum+mi+fy+ing
mum+mi+fied
mum+my
mum+mies
mum+pish
mumps
mum+sy
mum+si+er
mum+si+est
munch
munches
munch+ing
munched
Munch
Mün+chen

München-
  Gladbach
mun+dane
mun+dane+ly
mun+dane+ness
Mu+nich
mu+nici+pal
mu+nici+pali+sa+
  tion
mu+nici+pali+sa+
  tions
mu+nici+pal+ise
mu+nici+pal+
  ises
mu+nici+pal+is+
  ing
mu+nici+pal+
  ised
mu+nici+pal+ity
mu+nici+pal+
  ities
mu+nici+pali+za+
  tion
mu+nici+pali+za+
  tions
mu+nici+pal+ize
mu+nici+pal+
  izes
mu+nici+pal+iz+
  ing
mu+nici+pal+
  ized
mu+nici+pal+ly
mu+nifi+cence
mu+nifi+cent
mu+nifi+cent+ly
mu+ni+ments
mu+ni+tion
mu+ni+tions
mu+ni+tion+ing
mu+ni+tioned
mu+ni+tions
Munro
Munros
Mun+ster
Mün+ster
munt+jac
munt+jacs
munt+jak
munt+jaks
Müntzer
muon
muons
muon+ic
mu+ral

mu+rals
mu+ral+ist
mu+ral+ists
Murasaki Shikibu
Murat
Murchison
Mur+cia
mur+der
mur+ders
mur+ders
mur+der+ing
mur+dered
mur+der+er
mur+der+ers
mur+der+ess
mur+der+esses
mur+der+ous
mur+der+ous+ly
mur+der+ous+
  ness
Murdoch
Mu+reş
mu+rex
mu+ri+ces
Murillo
murk
murki+ly
murki+ness
murky
murki+er
murki+est
Mur+mansk
mur+mur
mur+murs
mur+murs
mur+mur+ing
mur+mured
mur+mur+er
mur+mur+ers
mur+mur+ing
mur+mur+ings
mur+mur+ing+ly
mur+mur+ous
mur+phy
mur+phies
mur+rain
Mur+ray
river
Murray
surname
Mur+rum+bidgee
mur+ther
mur+thers
mur+thers
mur+ther+ing

mur+thered
mur+ther+er
mur+ther+ers
mus+ca+del
mus+ca+dels
mus+ca+dine
mus+ca+dines
mus+cae vo+li+
tan+tes
mus+cat
mus+cats
Mus+cat
mus+ca+tel
mus+ca+tels
mus+cle
mus+cles
mus+cles
mus+cling
mus+cled
muscle-bound
mus+cle+man
mus+cle+men
mus+cly
Mus+co+vite
Mus+co+vites
Mus+co+vy
mus+cu+lar
mus+cu+lar+ity
mus+cu+lar+ly
mus+cu+la+ture
mus+cu+la+
tures
muse
muses
muses
mus+ing
mused
Muse
Muses
mu+sette
mu+settes
mu+seum
mu+seums
Museveni
mush
mushes
mushes
mush+ing
mushed
mushi+ly
mushi+ness
mush+room
mush+rooms
mush+rooms
mush+room+ing

mush+roomed
mushy
mushi+er
mushi+est
mu+sic
mu+si+cal
mu+si+cals
mu+si+cal+ity
mu+si+cal+ly
musi+cas+sette
musi+cas+
settes
mu+si+cian
mu+si+cians
mu+si+cian+ly
mu+si+cian+ship
mu+si+co+logi+
cal
mu+si+colo+gist
mu+si+colo+
gists
mu+si+col+ogy
Musil
Musils
mu+sique con+
crète
musk
musks
mus+keg
mus+kegs
mus+kel+lunge
mus+kel+lunges
or
mus+kel+lunge
mus+ket
mus+kets
mus+ket+eer
mus+ket+eers
mus+ket+ry
mus+kie
mus+kies
Muskie
muski+ness
musk+melon
musk+melons
musk+rat
musk+rats or
musk+rat
musky
mus+kies
muski+er
muski+est
Mus+lim
Mus+lims or
Mus+lim

Mus+lim+ism
mus+lin
mus+lins
muso
musos
mus+quash
mus+quashes
muss
musses
musses
muss+ing
mussed
mus+sel
mus+sels
Musset
Mussolini
Mussorgsky
Mus+sul+man
Mus+sul+mans
mussy
must
musts
mus+tache
mus+taches
mus+tached
mus+ta+chio
mus+ta+chi+os
mus+ta+chi+oed
Mustafa Kemal
mus+tang
mus+tangs
mus+tard
mus+tards
mus+te+line
mus+ter
mus+ters
mus+ters
mus+ter+ing
mus+tered
musth
musti+ly
musti+ness
mus+ty
mus+ti+er
mus+ti+est
mu+tabil+ity
mu+table
mu+tably
mu+ta+gen
mu+ta+gens
mu+ta+gen+ic
mu+tant
mu+tants
Mu+ta+re
mu+tate

mu+tates
mu+tat+ing
mu+tat+ed
mu+ta+tion
mu+ta+tions
mu+ta+tion+al
mu+ta+tion+al+ly
mu+ta+tis mu+
tan+dis
mutch
mutches
mute
mutes
mutes
mut+ing
mut+ed
mute+ly
mute+ness
muti
mu+ti+late
mu+ti+lates
mu+ti+lat+ing
mu+ti+lat+ed
mu+ti+la+tion
mu+ti+la+tions
mu+ti+la+tive
mu+ti+la+tor
mu+ti+la+tors
mu+ti+neer
mu+ti+neers
mu+ti+nous
mu+ti+nous+ly
mu+ti+nous+
ness
mu+ti+ny
mu+ti+nies
mu+ti+nies
mu+ti+ny+ing
mu+ti+nied
mut+ism
Mutsuhito
mutt
mutts
mut+ter
mut+ters
mut+ters
mut+ter+ing
mut+tered
Mutter
mut+ter+ing
mut+ter+ings
mut+ton
mutton+chops
mutton+head
mutton+heads

mutton +headed
mut +tony
Mut +tra
mu +tu +al
mu +tu +al +ity
mu +tu +al +ly
mu +tu +el
  mu +tu +els
muu-muu
  muu-muus
Mu +zak
Trademark
mu +zhik
  mu +zhiks
Muzorewa
muz +zi +ly
muz +zi +ness
muz +zle
  muz +zles
  muz +zles
  muz +zling
  muz +zled
muzzle-loader
  muzzle-loaders
  muzzle-loading
muz +zler
  muz +zlers
muz +zy
  muz +zi +er
  muz +zi +est
Mwe +ru
my
my +al +gia
my +al +gic
mya +lism
my +all
  my +alls
Myanmar
my +celial
my +celium
  my +celia
My +cenae
My +cenaean
my +co +log +ic
my +co +logi +cal
my +colo +gist
  my +colo +gists
my +col +ogy

my +col +ogies
my +co +plas +ma
my +co +rhi +za
  my +co +rhi +zas
my +co +rhi +zal
my +cor +rhi +za
  my +cor +rhi +zae
my +cor +rhi +zal
my +co +sis
my +cot +ic
myco +tox +in
  myco +tox +ins
myco +tox +ol +
  ogy
myco +troph +ic
my +elin
my +eline
my +eli +tis
my +elo +ma
  my +elo +mas
    or
  my +elo +ma +ta
Myers
Myko +nos
My Lai
myna
  mynas
my +nah
  my +nahs
Myn +heer
  Myn +heers
myo +car +dial
myo +car +dium
  myo +car +dia
my +ol +ogy
  my +ol +ogies
my +ope
  my +opes
myo +pia
my +op +ic
my +opi +cal +ly
myo +sin
myo +sis
  myo +ses
my +ot +ic
myri +ad
  myri +ads

myria +pod
  myria +pods
Myr +mi +don
  Myr +mi +dons
    or
  Myr +mi +dones
my +roba +lan
  my +roba +lans
Myron
myrrh
myr +tle
  myr +tles
my +self
My +sia
My +sian
  My +sians
My +sore
mys +teri +ous
mys +teri +ous +ly
mys +teri +ous +
  ness
mys +tery
  mys +teries
mys +tic
  mys +tics
mys +ti +cal
mys +ti +cal +ly
mys +ti +cism
mys +ti +fi +ca +
  tion
  mys +ti +fi +ca +
    tions
mys +ti +fy
  mys +ti +fies
  mys +ti +fy +ing
  mys +ti +fied
  mys +ti +fy +ing
mys +tique
  mys +tiques
myth
  myths
myth +ic
mythi +cal
mythi +cal +ly
mythi +cise
  mythi +cises
mythi +cis +ing
mythi +cised

mythi +cist
  mythi +cists
mythi +cize
  mythi +cizes
mythi +ciz +ing
mythi +cized
mytho +logi +cal
my +tholo +gise
  my +tholo +gises
  my +tholo +gis +
    ing
  my +tholo +gised
my +tholo +gis +er
  my +tholo +gis +
    ers
my +tholo +gist
  my +tholo +gists
my +tholo +gize
  my +tholo +gizes
  my +tholo +giz +
    ing
  my +tholo +gized
my +tholo +giz +er
  my +tholo +giz +
    ers
my +thol +ogy
  my +thol +ogies
mytho +ma +nia
mytho +ma +ni +ac
  mytho +ma +ni +
    acs
mytho +poeia
mytho +poe +ic
my +thos
my +thoi
Myti +lene
myx +edema
myxo
myx +oedema
myxo +ma
  myxo +mas *or*
  myxo +ma +ta
  myxo +ma +to +sis
myx +oma +tous
myxo +my +cete
  myxo +my +
    cetes
myxo +vi +rus

N

n
n's
N
  N's or
  Ns
na
Na
NAAFI
Naafi
  Naafis
naan
naans
naar+tjie
  naar+tjies
nab
  nabs
  nab+bing
  nabbed
na+bla
  na+blas
Na+blus
na+bob
  na+bobs
Nabokov
Nabo+kov+ian
Naboth
na+celle
  na+celles
na+cre
na+cred
na+cre+ous
Nader
na+dir
  na+dirs
nae
nae+void
nae+vus
nae+vi
naff
naff+er
naff+est
nag
nags
nags
nag+ging

nagged
Na+ga+land
na+ga+na
Na+ga+no
Na+ga+sa+ki
nag+ger
nag+gers
Nagorno-
  Karabakh
Na+go+ya
Nag+pur
Nagy
Nagy+sze+ben
Nagy+vá+rad
Naha
Na+huatl
  Na+huatl or
  Na+hua+tls
Na+hum
nai+ad
  nai+ads or
  nai+ades
naïf
  naïfs
na+ïf+ly
nail
  nails
  nails
nail+ing
nailed
nail-biting
nail+brush
  nail+brushes
nail+er
  nail+ers
nail+file
  nail+files
nain+sook
  nain+sooks
Naipaul
nai+ra
  nai+ras
Nairn+shire
Nai+ro+bi
na+ive

na+ives
na+ïve
na+ïves
na+ive+ly
na+ïve+ly
na+ive+ness
na+ïve+ness
na+ive+té
na+ive+tés
na+ïve+té
na+ïve+tés
na+ive+ty
na+ive+ties
na+ked
na+ked+ly
na+ked+ness
Na+khi+che+van
Na+ku+ru
Nal+chik
NALGO
nam+able
Na+man+gan
Na+ma+qua+land
namby-pamby
namby-pambies
Nam Co
name
  names
  names
nam+ing
named
name+able
name-calling
name-dropper
  name-droppers
name-dropping
name+less
name+less+ness
name+ly
Na+men
name+plate
  name+plates
name+sake
  name+sakes
name+tape

name+tapes
Nam+hoi
Na+mibe
Na+mibia
Na+mib+ian
  Na+mib+ians
Namier
Nam Tso
Na+mur
nan
nans
nana
nanas
Nan+chang
Nan-ch'ang
Nan-ching
nan+cy
nan+cies
Nan+cy
NAND
Nan+da Devi
Nan+ga Par+bat
Nan+hai
Nan+jing
nan+keen
nan+keens
nan+kin
nan+kins
Nan+king
nan+na
nan+nas
Nan+ning
Nan-ning
nan+ny
nan+nies
nan+nies
nan+ny+ing
nan+nied
nan+ny+gai
nan+ny+gais
Nansen
Nan Shan
Nan+terre
Nantes
Nan+tong

Nan+tuck+et
Nan+tung
Naoise
Naomi
nap
  naps
  naps
  nap+ping
  napped
na+palm
  na+palms
  na+palms
  na+palm+ing
  na+palmed
nape
  napes
na+pery
  na+peries
Naphtali
naph+tha
  naph+thas
naph+tha+lene
naph+thal+ic
naph+thene
  naph+thenes
naph+thol
Na+pier
place name
Napier
surname
nap+kin
  nap+kins
Na+ples
na+po+le+on
  na+po+le+ons
Na+po+leon+ic
Na+po+li
nappe
  nappes
nap+py
  nap+pies
  nap+pi+er
  nap+pi+est
Nara
Narayan
Na+ra+yan+ganj
Nar+ba+da
Nar+bonne
narc
  narcs
nar+cism
nar+cis+sism
nar+cis+sist
  nar+cis+sists
nar+cis+sis+tic

nar+cis+sus
  nar+cis+suses
  or
  nar+cis+si
Narcissus
nar+co+analy+sis
  nar+co+analy+
    ses
nar+co+lep+sy
  nar+co+lep+sies
  nar+co+lep+tic
nar+co+sis
nar+cot+ic
  nar+cot+ics
nar+coti+cal+ly
nar+co+ti+sa+
    tion
nar+co+tise
  nar+co+tises
  nar+co+tis+ing
  nar+co+tised
nar+co+tism
nar+co+ti+za+
    tion
nar+co+tize
  nar+co+tizes
  nar+co+tiz+ing
  nar+co+tized
nard
  nards
nar+doo
  nar+doos
nar+es
nar+ghi+le
  nar+ghi+les
nar+gi+le
  nar+gi+les
nar+gi+leh
  nar+gi+lehs
nar+ial
nar+ine
nark
  narks
  narks
nark+ing
  narked
narky
  narki+er
  narki+est
Nar+ma+da
Nar+ra+gan+set
  Nar+ra+gan+set
  or
  Nar+ra+gan+
    sets

nar+rat+able
nar+rate
  nar+rates
  nar+rat+ing
  nar+rat+ed
nar+ra+tion
  nar+ra+tions
nar+ra+tive
  nar+ra+tives
nar+ra+tor
  nar+ra+tors
nar+row
  nar+rows
  nar+rows
  nar+row+ing
  nar+rowed
  nar+row+er
  nar+row+est
  nar+row+ly
narrow-minded
narrow-minded+
    ness
nar+row+ness
  nar+rows
nar+thex
  nar+thexes
Nar+va
Nar+vik
nar+wal
  nar+wals
nar+whal
  nar+whals
nar+whale
  nar+whales
nary
NASA
na+sal
  na+sals
na+sali+sa+tion
na+sal+ise
  na+sal+ises
  na+sal+is+ing
  na+sal+ised
na+sal+ity
  na+sal+ities
na+sali+za+tion
na+sal+ize
  na+sal+izes
  na+sal+iz+ing
  na+sal+ized
na+sal+ly
nas+cen+cy
nas+cen+cies
nas+cent
Nase+by

Nash
Nashe
Nash+ville
Na+sik
na+so+gas+tric
Nas+sau
Nasser
nas+tic
nas+ti+ly
nas+ti+ness
na+stur+tium
  na+stur+tiums
nas+ty
  nas+ties
  nas+ti+er
  nas+ti+est
na+tal
Na+tal
na+tant
na+ta+tion
  na+ta+tions
na+ta+to+rial
na+ta+tory
natch
na+tes
Nathan
Nathanael
nathe+less
nath+less
na+tion
  na+tions
na+tion+al
  na+tion+als
na+tion+ali+sa+
    tion
  na+tion+ali+sa+
    tions
na+tion+al+ise
  na+tion+al+ises
  na+tion+al+is+
    ing
  na+tion+al+ised
na+tion+al+ism
  na+tion+al+ist
  na+tion+al+ists
na+tion+al+is+tic
na+tion+al+ity
  na+tion+al+ities
na+tion+ali+za+
    tion
  na+tion+ali+za+
    tions
na+tion+al+ize
  na+tion+al+izes

na+tion+al+iz+
  ing
na+tion+al+ized
na+tion+al+ly
na+tion+hood
  na+tion+hoods
nation+wide
na+tive
  na+tives
native-born
na+tive+ly
na+tive+ness
  na+tive+nesses
na+tiv+ity
  na+tiv+ities
Na+tiv+ity
  Na+tiv+ities
Nato
NATO
na+tron
NATSOPA
nat+ter
  nat+ters
  nat+ters
nat+ter+ing
nat+tered
nat+ter+jack
  nat+ter+jacks
nat+ti+ly
nat+ti+ness
nat+ty
  nat+ti+er
  nat+ti+est
natu+ral
  natu+rals
natu+rali+sa+tion
natu+ral+ise
  natu+ral+ises
  natu+ral+is+ing
  natu+ral+ised
natu+ral+ism
natu+ral+ist
  natu+ral+ists
natu+ral+is+tic
natu+ral+is+ti+
  cal+ly
natu+rali+za+tion
natu+ral+ize
  natu+ral+izes
  natu+ral+iz+ing
  natu+ral+ized
natu+ral+ly
natu+ral+ness
na+ture
  na+tures

na+tur+ism
na+tur+ist
  na+tur+ists
na+turo+path
  na+turo+paths
na+turo+path+ic
na+tur+opa+thy
na+tur+opa+
  thies
nauch
nauches
Nau+cra+tis
naught
naughts
naugh+ti+ly
naugh+ti+ness
naugh+ty
  naugh+ti+er
  naugh+ti+est
nau+plius
  nau+plii
Nau+ru
Nau+ruan
  Nau+ruans
nau+sea
nau+seate
  nau+seates
  nau+seat+ing
  nau+seat+ed
  nau+seat+ing
nau+seous
  nau+seous+ly
  nau+seous+ness
Nausicaä
nautch
nautches
nau+ti+cal
  nau+ti+cal+ly
nau+ti+lus
  nau+ti+luses
    or
  nau+ti+li
Nava+ho
  Nava+ho *or*
  Nava+hos *or*
  Nava+hoes
Nava+jo
  Nava+jo *or*
  Nava+jos *or*
  Nava+joes
na+val
Nava+rat+ri
  Nava+rat+ris
nava+rin
  nava+rins

Nava+ri+no
Na+varre
nave
  naves
na+vel
  na+vels
navel+wort
  navel+worts
na+vicu+lar
  na+vicu+lars
navi+gabil+ity
navi+gable
navi+gably
navi+gate
  navi+gates
  navi+ga+ting
  navi+ga+ted
  navi+ga+tion
  navi+ga+tions
  navi+ga+tion+al
  navi+ga+tor
  navi+ga+tors
Náv+pak+tos
Navratilova
nav+vy
  nav+vies
navy
  navies
na+wab
  na+wabs
Nax+os
nay
  nays
Na+ya+rit
Naza+rene
  Naza+renes
Naza+reth
Naza+rite
  Naza+rites
Naze
Nazi
  Nazis
Na+zi+ism
Nazi+rite
  Nazi+rites
Na+zism
Ndja+me+na
N'dja+me+na
Ndo+la
Ne
Neagh
Ne+an+der+thal
Ne+an+der+
  thals
neap

neaps
Nea+poli+tan
  Nea+poli+tans
near
  nears
  nears
  near+ing
  neared
near+er
  near+est
near+by
Ne+arc+tic
near+ly
near+ness
near+side
  near+sides
near-sighted
near-sighted+ly
neat
  neat+er
  neat+est
neat
neat
  noun
neat+en
  neat+ens
  neat+en+ing
  neat+ened
neath
'neath
neat+ly
neat+ness
neat's-foot
neb
  nebs
Nebo
Ne+bras+ka
Ne+bras+kan
  Ne+bras+kans
Nebu+chad+nez+
  zar
  bottle
Nebuchadnezzar
  king
nebu+la
  nebu+lae *or*
  nebu+las
nebu+lar
nebu+los+ity
  nebu+los+ities
nebu+lous
  nebu+lous+ness
ne+ces+saries
nec+es+sari+ly
nec+es+sary

ne+ces+si+tar+
ian
ne+ces+si+tar+
ians
ne+ces+si+tari+
an+ism
ne+ces+si+tate
ne+ces+si+tates
ne+ces+si+tat+
ing
ne+ces+si+tat+
ed
ne+ces+si+tous
ne+ces+sity
ne+ces+sities
neck
necks
necks
neck+ing
necked
Neck+ar
neck+band
neck+bands
neck+cloth
neck+cloths
neck+er+chief
neck+er+chiefs
neck+ing
neck+lace
neck+laces
neck+line
neck+lines
neck+tie
neck+ties
neck+wear
nec+ro+bio+sis
ne+crola+try
ne+crola+tries
nec+ro+logi+cal
ne+crol+ogy
ne+crol+ogies
nec+ro+man+cer
nec+ro+man+
cers
nec+ro+man+cy
nec+ro+man+tic
nec+ro+phile
nec+ro+philes
nec+ro+philia
nec+ro+phil+ic
ne+cropo+lis
ne+cropo+lises
or
ne+cropo+leis
nec+rop+sy

nec+rop+sies
nec+ros+co+py
nec+ros+co+
pies
ne+cro+sis
ne+crot+ic
nec+tar
nec+tars
nec+tar+ine
nec+tar+ines
nec+tar+ous
nec+ta+ry
nec+ta+ries
ned+dy
ned+dies
Ne+der+land
nee
née
need
needs
needs
need+ing
need+ed
need+ful
need+ful+ness
nee+dle
nee+dles
nee+dles
nee+dling
nee+dled
needle+cord
needle+cords
needle+point
needle+points
need+less
need+less+ly
need+less+ness
needle+woman
needle+women
needle+work
needle+works
needs
needy
needi+er
needi+est
Néel
ne'er
ne'er-do-well
ne'er-do-wells
ne+fari+ous
ne+fari+ous+ly
ne+fari+ous+
ness
Nefertiti
ne+gate

ne+gates
ne+gat+ing
ne+gat+ed
ne+ga+ter
ne+ga+ters
ne+ga+tion
ne+ga+tions
nega+tive
nega+tives
nega+tives
nega+tiv+ing
nega+tived
nega+tive+ly
nega+tive+ness
nega+ti+vism
nega+tiv+ist
nega+tiv+ists
nega+tiv+ity
nega+tiv+ities
ne+ga+tor
ne+ga+tors
Neg+eb
Neg+ev
ne+glect
ne+glects
ne+glects
ne+glect+ing
ne+glect+ed
ne+glect+ful
neg+li+gee
neg+li+gees
neg+li+gée
neg+li+gées
neg+li+gence
neg+li+gences
neg+li+gent
neg+li+gent+ly
neg+li+gible
neg+li+gibly
ne+go+tiabil+ity
ne+go+tiabil+
ities
ne+go+tiable
ne+go+ti+ate
ne+go+ti+ates
ne+go+ti+at+ing
ne+go+ti+at+ed
ne+go+tia+tion
ne+go+tia+tions
ne+go+tia+tor
ne+go+tia+tors
Ne+gress
Ne+gresses
Ne+gril+lo
Ne+gril+los or

Ne+gril+loes
Neg+ri Sem+bi+
lan
Ne+gri+to
Ne+gri+tos or
Ne+gri+toes
ne+gri+tude
Ne+gro
Ne+groes
Ne+groid
Ne+groids
Ne+gro+ism
Neg+ro+pont
Ne+gros
ne+gus
ne+guses
Ne+he+mi+ah
Nehru
neigh
neighs
neighs
neigh+ing
neighed
neigh+bor
U.S.
neigh+bors
neigh+bors
neigh+bor+ing
neigh+bored
neigh+bor+hood
U.S.
neigh+bor+
hoods
neigh+bor+li+
ness
U.S.
neigh+bor+ly
U.S.
neigh+bour
neigh+bours
neigh+bours
neigh+bour+ing
neigh+boured
neigh+bour+hood
neigh+bour+
hoods
neigh+bour+li+
ness
neigh+bour+ly
Neill
Neis+se
nei+ther
Nejd
nek+ton
nel+ly

nel+lies
nel+son
nel+sons
Nel+son
place name
Nelson
surname
Ne+man
ne+mat+ic
nema+to+cyst
nema+to+cysts
nema+tode
nema+todes
Nem+bu+tal
Trademark
Ne+mea
Ne+mean
ne+mer+tean
ne+mer+teans
nem+er+tine
nem+er+tines
ne+mesia
ne+mesias
Nemesis
Nemeses
ne+mophi+la
neo+clas+sic
neo+clas+si+cal
neo+clas+si+
  cism
neo+co+lo+ni+al+
  ism
neo+co+lo+ni+al+
  ist
neo+co+lo+ni+
  al+ists
Neo-Darwin+ism
neo+dym+ium
neo+goth+ic
Neo+lith+ic
ne+olo+gise
ne+olo+gises
ne+olo+gis+ing
ne+olo+gised
ne+olo+gism
ne+olo+gisms
ne+olo+gist
ne+olo+gists
ne+olo+gize
ne+olo+gizes
ne+olo+giz+ing
ne+olo+gized
ne+ol+ogy
ne+ol+ogies
neo+my+cin

neon
neo+na+tal
neo+nate
neo+nates
neo+phyte
neo+phytes
neo+plasm
neo+plasms
Neo-Platonic
Neo-Platonism
neo+prene
neo+prenes
Neoptolemus
ne+ot+eny
neo+ter+ic
neo+ter+ics
Ne+pal
Nepa+lese
Ne+pali
Ne+pali *or*
Ne+palis
ne+pen+the
ne+pen+thes
nep+eta
nep+etas
neph+ew
neph+ews
ne+phol+ogy
ne+phrid+ium
ne+phrid+ia
neph+rite
neph+rites
ne+phrit+ic
ne+phri+tis
neph+rolo+gist
neph+rolo+gists
neph+rol+ogy
neph+ron
neph+rons
neph+ro+scope
neph+ro+
  scopes
neph+ro+sco+py
neph+ro+sco+
  pies
ne plus ul+tra
nepo+tism
nepo+tisms
nepo+tist
nepo+tists
Neptune
god
Nep+tune
planet
nep+tu+nium

nerd
nerds
Ne+reid
Ne+rei+des
Nereus
Neri
ne+rine
ne+rines
Nernst
Nero
nero+li
Ne+ru+da
Nerva
Nerval
ner+vate
ner+va+tion
ner+va+tions
ner+va+ture
ner+va+tures
nerve
nerves
nerves
nerv+ing
nerved
nerve+less
nerve+less+ly
nerve-racking
nerves
nerve-wracking
nerv+ine
nerv+ines
nerv+ous
nerv+ous+ly
nerv+ous+ness
ner+vure
ner+vures
nervy
nervi+er
nervi+est
nes+ci+ence
nes+ci+ent
ness
nesses
Ness
Nessus
nest
nests
nests
nest+ing
nest+ed
nes+tle
nes+tles
nes+tl+ing
nes+tled
nest+ling

nest+lings
Nestor
Nestorius
net
nets
nets
net+ting
net+ted
net
Ne+ta+ji
net+ball
net+balls
neth+er
Neth+er+land+er
Neth+er+land+
  ers
Neth+er+lands
nether+most
net+su+ke
net+su+kes
nett
net+ting
net+tle
net+tles
net+tles
net+tl+ing
net+tled
net+work
net+works
Neu+bran+den+
  burg
Neu+châ+tel
Neuilly-sur-Seine
neum
neums
Neumann
neume
neumes
Neu+mün+ster
neu+ral
neu+ral+gia
neu+ral+gic
neu+ral+ly
neu+ras+the+nia
neu+rit+ic
neu+ri+tis
neu+ro+chip
neu+ro+chips
neu+ro+com+put+
  er
neu+ro+com+
  put+ers
neu+ro+en+do+
  crine
neu+rog+lia

neu+rog+lias
neu+ro+lem+ma
neu+ro+lem+
  mas
neu+ro+logi+cal
neu+rol+ogy
neu+rol+ogies
neu+ro+mus+cu+
  lar
neu+ron
  neu+rons
neu+rone
  neu+rones
neu+ron+ic
neu+ro+path+ic
neu+ro+pathi+cal+
  ly
neu+ro+pa+thol+
  ogy
neu+ropa+thy
  neu+ropa+thies
neu+ro+physio+
  logi+cal
neu+ro+physi+ol+
  ogy
neu+rop+ter+an
neu+rop+ter+ous
neu+ro+sci+ence
neu+ro+sis
  neu+ro+ses
neu+ro+sur+gery
neu+ro+sur+gi+
  cal
neu+rot+ic
  neu+rot+ics
neu+roti+cal+ly
neu+roti+cism
  neu+roti+cisms
neu+roto+my
  neu+roto+mies
neu+ro+trans+
  mit+ter
neu+ro+trans+
  mit+ters
Neu+satz
Neuss
Neus+tria
Neus+trian
neu+ter
  neu+ters
  neu+ters
  neu+ter+ing
  neu+tered
neu+tral
  neu+trals

neu+trali+sa+tion
neu+tral+ise
  neu+tral+ises
  neu+tral+is+ing
  neu+tral+ised
  neu+tral+is+ers
neu+tral+ism
neu+tral+ist
  neu+tral+ists
neu+tral+ity
  neu+tral+ities
neu+trali+za+tion
neu+tral+ize
  neu+tral+izes
  neu+tral+iz+ing
  neu+tral+ized
  neu+tral+iz+er
  neu+tral+iz+ers
neu+tral+ly
neu+tret+to
  neu+tret+tos
neu+tri+no
  neu+tri+nos
neu+tron
  neu+trons
Neva
Ne+va+da
névé
  névés
nev+er
never+more
never-never
Ne+vers
never+the+less
Ne+vis
ne+void
U.S.
Nevski
ne+vus
U.S.
ne+vi
new
  new+er
  new+est
New+ark
new+born
New+bury
New+cas+tle
  place name
Newcastle
  surname
New+castle-
  under-Lyme
Newcomen

new+comer
  new+comers
new+el
  new+els
new+fan+gled
New+found+land
New+found+land+
  er
New+found+
  land+ers
New+gate
New+ham
New+ha+ven
  English port
New Ha+ven
  U.S. city
Ne Win
new+ish
Newlands
new+ly
newly+wed
  newly+weds
Newman
New+mar+ket
new+ness
New+port
New+ry
news
news+agent
  news+agents
news+cast
  news+casts
news+caster
  news+casters
news+dealer
  news+dealers
news+flash
  news+flashes
news+less
news+letter
  news+letters
news+monger
  news+mongers
news+paper
  news+papers
news+paper+
  man
news+paper+
  men
new+speak
news+print
news+read+er
  news+read+ers
news+reel
  news+reels

news+room
  news+rooms
news+stand
  news+stands
news+worthy
newsy
  newsi+er
  newsi+est
newt
  newts
new+ton
  new+tons
New+ton
  crater
Newton
  surname
New+to+nian
New+town
Newtown+abbey
New York+er
  New York+ers
New Zea+land
New Zea+land+er
New Zea+land+
  ers
Nexø
next
nex+us
  nex+us
Ney
Nez Per+cé
  Nez Per+cés *or*
  Nez Per+cé
ngaio
  ngaios
nga+ti
  nga+ti
Nha Trang
Ni
nia+cin
Ni+aga+ra
Nia+mey
Niarchos
nib
  nibs
  nibs
nib+bing
  nibbed
nib+ble
  nib+bles
  nib+bles
  nib+bling
  nib+bled
nib+bler
  nib+blers

Ni+belung	nick+name	Niepce	night+gowns
Ni+belungs *or*	nick+names	Nietzsche	night+hawk
Ni+belung+en	nick+names	Nie+tzschean	night+hawks
nib+lick	nick+nam+ing	Nie+tzscheans	nightie
nib+licks	nick+named	Nie+tzsche+ism	nighties
Ni+caea	Nico+bar	Niè+vre	night+in+gale
Ni+caean	Nicodemus	niff	night+in+gales
Nica+ra+gua	Nicol	niffs	Nightingale
Nica+ra+guan	Nicolai	niffs	night+jar
Nica+ra+guans	Nico+sia	niff+ing	night+jars
nice	ni+co+tia+na	niffed	night+life
nic+er	nico+tina+mide	niffy	night+lifes
nic+est	nico+tina+mides	niffi+er	night-light
Nice	nico+tine	niffi+est	night-lights
nice-looking	nico+tin+ic	Nifl+heim	night+long
nice+ly	nico+tin+ism	nif+ti+ly	night+ly
Ni+cene	nic+tate	nif+ti+ness	night+mare
nice+ness	nic+tates	nif+ty	night+mares
ni+cety	nic+tat+ing	nif+ti+er	night+mar+ish
ni+ceties	nic+tat+ed	nif+ti+est	nights
niche	nic+ta+tion	ni+gel+la	night+shade
niches	nic+ta+tions	Ni+ger	night+shirt
niches	Nic+the+roy	Ni+geria	night+shirts
nich+ing	nic+ti+tate	Ni+gerian	night+spot
niched	nic+ti+tates	Ni+gerians	night+spots
Nicholas	nic+ti+tat+ing	nig+gard	night-time
Nicholson	nic+ti+tat+ed	nig+gards	night-times
Ni+chrome	nic+ti+ta+tion	nig+gard+li+ness	night+wear
Trademark	nic+ti+ta+tions	nig+gard+ly	nighty
Nicias	Ni+da+ros	nig+ger	nighties
nic+ish	ni+dico+lous	nig+gers	ni+gres+cence
nick	nidi+fi+cate	nig+gle	ni+gres+cences
nicks	nidi+fi+cates	nig+gles	ni+gres+cent
nicks	nidi+fi+cat+ing	nig+gles	ni+hil+ism
nick+ing	nidi+fi+cated	nig+gling	ni+hil+ist
nicked	nidi+fi+ca+tion	nig+gled	ni+hil+ists
nick+el	nidi+fi+ca+tions	nig+gler	ni+hil+is+tic
nick+els	ni+difu+gous	nig+glers	ni+hil+ity
nick+els	nidi+fy	nig+gling	ni+hil ob+stat
nick+el+ling *or*	nidi+fies	nig+gly	Ni+hon
nick+el+ing	nidi+fy+ing	nig+gli+er	Nii+ga+ta
U.S.	nidi+fied	nig+gli+est	Nijinsky
nick+elled *or*	niece	nigh	Nij+megen
nick+eled	nieces	night	Ni+karia
U.S.	Nie+der+öster+	nights	Nike
nickel+odeon	reich	night+cap	Nik+kei
nickel+odeons	Nie+der+sach+	night+caps	Nik+ko
nick+er	sen	night+clothes	Ni+ko+lain+kau+
nick+ers	ni+el+lo	night+club	pun+ki
nick+ers	ni+el+li *or*	night+clubs	Ni+ko+la+yev
nick+er+ing	ni+el+los	night+dress	nil
nick+ered	Nielsen	night+dresses	Nile
Nicklaus	Nie+men	night+fall	nil+gai
nick-nack	Niemeyer	night+falls	nil+gai *or*
nick-nacks	Niemöller	night+gown	nil+gais

nil+ghau
nil+ghau *or*
nil+ghaus
Nil+gi+ris
Ni+lot+ic
Nilsson
nim+ble
nim+bler
nim+blest
nim+ble+ness
nim+bly
nim+bo+stra+tus
nim+bo+stra+ti
nim+bus
nim+bi *or*
nim+buses
Nîmes
Nimrod
Nim+rud
Nim+we+gen
nin+com+poop
nin+com+poops
nine
nines
nine+fold
nine+pins
nine+pins
nine+teen
nine+teens
nine+teenth
nine+teenths
nine+ti+eth
nine+ti+eths
nine+ty
nine+ties
Ni+neveh
Ni+nevite
Ni+nevites
Ning+bo
Ning+hsia
Ning+po
Ning+sia
Nin+ian
nin+ny
nin+nies
ninth
ninths
Ninus
Niobe
Nio+bean
nio+bium
nio+biums
nip
nips
nips

nip+ping
nipped
Nipi+gon
Nip+is+sing
nip+per
nip+pers
nip+pi+ly
nip+ple
nip+ples
nipple+wort
Nip+pon
Nip+pon+ese
Nip+pon+ese
Nip+pur
nip+py
nip+pi+er
nip+pi+est
Nirenberg
NIREX
nir+va+na
Nish
Ni+sha+pur
Ni+shi+no+mi+ya
nisi
Nissen
nit
nits
ni+ter
U.S.
Ni+terói
nit-picker
nit-pickers
nit-picking
ni+trate
ni+trates
ni+trates
ni+trat+ing
ni+trat+ed
ni+tra+tion
ni+tra+tions
ni+tre
ni+tric
ni+tride
ni+trides
ni+tri+fi+able
ni+tri+fi+ca+tion
ni+tri+fi+ca+
tions
ni+tri+fy
ni+tri+fies
ni+tri+fy+ing
ni+tri+fied
ni+trite
ni+trites

ni+tro
ni+tro+bac+te+
ria
ni+tro+ben+zene
ni+tro+ben+
zenes
ni+tro+cel+lu+
lose
ni+tro+gen
ni+trog+eni+sa+
tion
ni+trog+en+ise
ni+trog+en+ises
ni+trog+en+is+
ing
ni+trog+en+ised
ni+trog+eni+za+
tion
ni+trog+en+ize
ni+trog+en+izes
ni+trog+en+iz+
ing
ni+trog+en+ized
ni+trog+enous
ni+tro+glyc+er+in
ni+tro+glyc+er+
ine
ni+tro+methane
ni+trous
nit+ty
nit+ti+er
nit+ti+est
nitty-gritty
nit+wit
nit+wits
Niue
Niuean
Niueans
Niven
Ni+ver+nais
nix
nixes
nix+er
nix+ers
nixie
nixies
Nixon
Ni+zam
Ni+zams
Njord
Njorth
Nkomo
Nkrumah
no
noes *or*

nos
no'
No
No
no-account
no-accounts
Noah
nob
nobs
no-ball
no-balls
nob+ble
nob+bles
nob+bling
nob+bled
Nobel
no+belium
no+bilia+ry
no+bil+ity
no+bil+ities
no+ble
no+bles
no+bler
no+blest
noble+man
noble+men
no+ble+ness
noble+woman
noble+women
no+bly
no+body
no+bodies
nock
nocks
nock+ing
nocked
noc+tam+bu+la+
tion
noc+tam+bu+la+
tions
noc+tam+bu+
lism
noc+tam+bu+
lisms
noc+ti+lu+cent
noc+tu+id
noc+tu+ids
noc+tule
noc+tules
noc+tur+nal
noc+tur+nal+ity
noc+tur+nal+
ities
noc+tur+nal+ly

noc+turne
noc+turnes
nod
  nods
  nods
  nod+ding
  nod+ded
nod+al
nod+ding
nod+dle
nod+dles
nod+dles
nod+dling
nod+dled
nod+dy
nod+dies
node
  nodes
nodu+lar
nod+ule
  nod+ules
nodu+lose
nodu+lous
Noel
  Noels
Noël
  Noëls
no+et+ic
Nofretete
nog
  nogs
nogg
  noggs
nog+gin
  nog+gins
no-go
Noh
  Noh
noir
noise
  noises
  noises
  nois+ing
  noised
noise+less
noise+less+ly
noise+less+ness
noi+sette
  noi+settes
noisi+ly
noisi+ness
noi+some
noisy
  noisi+er
  noisi+est

Nolan
no+lens vo+lens
nol+le pros+equi
no+mad
  no+mads
no+mad+ic
no+mad+ism
no-man's-land
nom de guerre
  noms de guerre
nom de plume
  noms de plume
no+men+cla+ture
nomi+nal
  nomi+nals
nomi+nal+ism
nomi+nal+ist
  nomi+nal+ists
nomi+nal+ly
nomi+nate
  nomi+nates
  nomi+nat+ing
  nomi+nat+ed
nomi+na+tion
  nomi+na+tions
nomi+na+ti+val
nomi+na+tive
  nomi+na+tives
nomi+na+tor
  nomi+na+tors
nomi+nee
  nomi+nees
nomo+gram
  nomo+grams
nomo+graph
  nomo+graphs
non+aca+dem+ic
non+ac+cept+
  ance
non+ad+dic+tive
no+nage
no+na+genar+ian
  no+na+genar+
  ians
non+ag+gres+
  sion
nona+gon
  nona+gons
non+ago+nal
non+al+co+hol+
  ic
non+aligned
non+align+ment
  non+align+
  ments

non+ap+pear+
  ance
non+ap+pear+
  ances
non+at+tend+
  ance
non+at+tend+
  ances
non+at+trib+ut+
  able
non+ba+sic
non+bel+lig+er+
  ent
non+bio+logi+cal
non+break+able
non+car+bo+nat+
  ed
non-Catholic
  non-Catholics
nonce
  nonces
non+cer+ebral
non+cha+lance
non+cha+lant
non-Christian
  non-Christians
non+clas+sic
non+clas+si+cal
non+clas+si+fied
non+cleri+cal
non+clini+cal
non+col+legi+ate
non-com
  non-coms
non+com+bat+
  ant
non+com+bat+
  ants
non+com+bin+
  ing
non+com+mer+
  cial
non+com+mis+
  sioned
non+com+mit+tal
non+com+mu+ni+
  cant
non+com+mu+
  ni+cants
non+com+mu+ni+
  ca+tive
non+com+mu+
  nist
non+com+mu+
  nists

non+com+peti+
  tive
non+com+pli+
  ance
non com+pos
  men+tis
non+con+cili+
  atory
non+con+clu+
  sive
non+con+duc+
  tive
non+con+duc+
  tor
non+con+duc+
  tors
non+con+fi+den+
  tial
non+con+flict+
  ing
Non+con+form+
  ism
non+con+form+
  ist
non+con+form+
  ists
Non+con+form+
  ist
Non+con+form+
  ists
non+con+form+
  ity
non+con+form+
  ities
Non+con+form+
  ity
non+con+secu+
  tive
non+con+sent+
  ing
non+con+struc+
  tive
non+con+ta+
  gious
non+con+tribu+
  ting
non+con+tribu+
  tory
non+con+tro+ver+
  sial
non+con+ven+
  tion+al
non+con+vert+
  ible

non+co+op+era+tion
non+cor+robo+ra+tive
non+cor+rod+ing
non+crea+tive
non+crimi+nal
non+criti+cal
non+cul+ti+vat+ed
non+de+cidu+ous
non+de+liv+ery
non+de+liv+eries
non+demo+crat+ic
non+de+mon+strable
non+de+nomi+na+tion+al
non+de+part+men+tal
non+de+pend+ence
non+de+script
non+de+scripts
non+de+tach+able
non+deto+nat+ing
non+dis+ci+pli+nary
non+dis+crimi+nat+ing
non+di+vis+ible
non+doc+tri+nal
non+dog+mat+ic
non+domi+ciled
non+drink+er
non+drink+ers
non+drip
non+driv+er
non+driv+ers
none
non+earn+ing
non+eco+nom+ic
non+ef+fec+tive
non+elas+tic
non+en+tity
non+en+tities
non+equiva+lent
nones
nones
non+es+sen+tial

non+es+sen+tials
none+such
non+et
non+ets
none+the+less
non+ethi+cal
non-Euclid+ean
non+event
non+events
non+ex+change+able
non+ex+ist+ence
non+ex+ist+ent
non+ex+plo+sive
non+fac+tual
non+fa+tal
non+fat+ten+ing
non+fea+sance
non+fer+rous
non+fi+nite
non+flam+mable
non+flex+ible
non+flu+id
non+freez+ing
non+ful+fil+ment
non+func+tion+al
non+fu+sible
nong
nongs
non+gas+eous
non+gov+ern+men+tal
non+har+mon+ic
non+hu+man
no+nil+lion
no+nil+lions
non+in+fec+tious
non+in+flam+mable
non+in+flect+ed
non+in+her+it+able
non+in+tel+lec+tual
non+in+ter+sect+ing
non+inter+ven+tion
non+inter+ven+tions
non+in+toxi+cat+ing
non+iron
non+ir+ri+tant

non+ir+ri+tants
non+judg+men+tal
non+ju+ror
non+ju+rors
Non+ju+ror
Non+ju+rors
non+le+thal
non+lin+ear
non+lit+er+ary
non+logi+cal
non+lu+mi+nous
non+mag+net+ic
non+ma+lig+nant
non+mari+time
non+mem+ber
non+mem+bers
non+mem+ber+ship
non+met+al
non+met+als
non+met+al+lic
non+met+ric
non+mi+gra+tory
non+mili+tant
non+min+is+te+rial
non+mor+al
non-navigable
non-negoti+able
non-nuclear
non+ob+jec+tive
non+ob+serv+ance
non+oc+cur+rence
non+oc+cur+rences
no-nonsense
non+op+era+tion+al
non+op+era+tive
non+or+gan+ic
non+par+al+lel
non+pa+reil
non+pa+reils
non+pa+ren+tal
non+par+lia+men+tary
non+pa+ro+chial
non+par+tici+pat+ing
non+par+ti+san
non+par+ti+zan
non+par+ty

non+pay+ing
non+pay+ment
non+pay+ments
non+per+ma+nent
non+per+me+able
non+per+sis+tent
non+physi+cal
non+play+ing
non+plus
non+pluses
non+plusses
or
non+pluses
U.S.
non+plus+sing
or
non+plus+ing
U.S.
non+plussed
or
non+plused
U.S.
non+poi+son+ous
non+po+rous
non+prac+ti+sing
non+preda+tory
non+pre+scrip+tive
non+pro+fes+sion+al
non-profit-making
non+pro+lif+era+tion
non-pros
non-prosses
non-prosses
non-pros+sing
non-prossed
non pro+sequi+tur
non+ra+cial
non+radi+cal
non+ra+dio+ac+tive
non+read+er
non+read+ers
non+rec+og+ni+tion
non+re+cov+er+able
non+reg+is+tered

non+re+li+gious
non+re+new+
  able
non+rep+re+sen+
  ta+tion+al
non+rep+re+
  senta+tive
non+resi+dence
non+resi+den+cy
non+resi+dent
non+resi+dents
non+resi+den+
  tial
non+re+sis+tant
non+re+strict+ed
non+re+stric+tive
non+re+turn+able
non+rig+id
non+sched+uled
non+sci+en+tif+
  ic
non+sea+son+al
non+sec+ta+rian
non+secu+lar
non+seg+re+gat+
  ed
non+se+lec+tive
non+sense
non+sen+si+cal
non+sen+si+cal+
  ity
non+sen+si+cal+
  ly
non+sen+si+cal+
  ness
non se+qui+tur
non+sex+ist
non+sex+ual
non+skilled
non+slip
non+smok+er
  non+smok+ers
non+smok+ing
non+so+cial
non+sol+uble
non+speak+ing
non+spe+cial+ist
non+spe+cif+ic
non+spir+it+ual
non+stain+ing
non+stand+ard
non+start+er
  non+start+ers
non+sta+tis+ti+
  cal

non+stick
non+stop
non+struc+tur+al
non+sub+scrib+
  er
non+sub+scrib+
  ers
non+such
non+suit
non+suits
non+suits
non+suit+ing
non+suit+ed
non+sur+gi+cal
non+swim+mer
non+swim+
  mers
non+tax+able
non+teach+ing
non+tech+ni+cal
non+ter+ri+to+
  rial
non+tox+ic
non+trans+fer+
  able
non+tropi+cal
non trop+po
non-U
non+un+ion
  non+un+ions
non+ven+om+
  ous
non+ver+bal
non+vin+tage
non+vio+lent
non+vo+cal
non+vot+er
  non+vot+ers
non+vot+ing
noo+dle
noo+dles
nook
nooks
nookie
nookies
nooky
nookies
noon
noons
noon+day
noon+days
no-one
no one
noon+tide
noon+tides

noon+time
  noon+times
Noord+bra+bant
Noord+hol+land
noose
nooses
nooses
noos+ing
noosed
no-par
nor
NOR
nor+adrena+lin
nor+adrena+line
Nord
Nordenskjöld
  surname
Nor+den+skjöld
  sea
nor+dic
Nor+dic
Nord+kyn
Nord-Pas-de-
  Calais
Nordrhein-
  Westfalen
nor+epi+neph+
  rine
Nor+folk
Nor+ge
no+ria
  no+rias
Nori+cum
nork
  norks
norm
  norms
nor+mal
nor+mal+cy
  U.S.
  nor+mal+cies
nor+mali+sa+tion
nor+mal+ise
  nor+mal+ises
  nor+mal+is+ing
  nor+mal+ised
nor+mal+ity
  nor+mal+ities
nor+mali+za+tion
nor+mal+ize
  nor+mal+izes
  nor+mal+iz+ing
  nor+mal+ized
nor+mal+ly
Nor+man

Nor+mans
  people
Norman
  surname
Nor+man+dy
nor+ma+tive
Norn
  Norns
  goddess
Norn
  language
Norr+kö+ping
Norse
Norse+man
Norse+men
north
  norths
North
North+al+ler+ton
North+amp+ton
North+amp+ton+
  shire
north+bound
Northcliffe
north+east
North+east
north+easter
north+easter+ly
north+easter+
  lies
north+eastern
north+eastern+
  most
north+eastward
north+eastward+
  ly
north+er
north+ers
nor+ther+li+ness
nor+ther+ly
nor+ther+lies
north+ern
North+ern+er
North+ern+ers
north+ern+most
north+ing
north+ings
North+land
North+land+er
North+land+ers
North+man
North+men
north-northeast
north-northwest

North-Sea
adj.
North Sea
noun
North+um+ber+land
place name
Northumberland
surname
North+um+bria
North+um+brian
north+ward
north+wards
north+west
North+west
north+wester
north+westers
north+wester+ly
north+wester+lies
north+western+most
north+westward
north+westward+ly
North+wich
Nor+way
Nor+we+gian
Nor+we+gians
Nor+wich
nose
noses
noses
nos+ing
nosed
nose+bag
nose+bags
nose+band
nose+bands
nose+bleed
nose+bleeds
nose-dive
nose-dives
nose-diving
nose-dived
verb
nose dive
nose dives
noun
nose+gay
nose+gays
nose+less
nose+like
nose+piece
nose+pieces

nos+ey
nosi+er
nosi+est
nosh
noshes
noshes
nosh+ing
noshed
no-show
no-shows
nosh-up
nosh-ups
no-side
no-sides
nosi+ly
nosi+ness
noso+comi+al
noso+logi+cal
no+sol+ogy
nos+tal+gia
nos+tal+gic
nos+tal+gi+cal+ly
nos+toc
Nostradamus
nos+tril
nos+trils
nos+tro
nos+trum
nos+trums
nosy
nosi+er
nosi+est
not
NOT
nota bene
no+tabil+ity
no+tabil+ities
no+table
no+tables
no+tably
no+tar+ial
no+ta+rise
no+ta+rises
no+ta+ris+ing
no+ta+rised
no+ta+rize
no+ta+rizes
no+ta+riz+ing
no+ta+rized
no+ta+ry
no+ta+ries
no+ta+ry+ship
no+ta+tion
no+ta+tions
no+ta+tion+al

notch
notches
notches
notch+ing
notched
note
notes
notes
not+ing
not+ed
note+book
note+books
note+case
note+cases
not+ed
not+ed+ly
note+less
note+let
note+lets
note+paper
note+papers
note+worthi+ness
note+worthy
noth+ing
noth+ings
noth+ing+ness
no+tice
no+tices
no+tices
no+tic+ing
no+ticed
no+tice+able
no+tice+ably
no+ti+fi+able
no+ti+fi+ca+tion
no+ti+fi+ca+tions
no+ti+fi+er
no+ti+fi+ers
no+ti+fy
no+ti+fies
no+ti+fy+ing
no+ti+fied
no+tion
no+tions
no+tion+al
no+tion+al+ly
no+tions
no+to+chord
no+to+chords
no+to+ri+ety
no+to+ri+ous
no+to+ri+ous+ly
no+tor+nis

no+tor+nises
no-trump
no-trumps
no-trumper
no-trumps
Not+ting+ham
Not+ting+ham+shire
No+tus
not+with+stand+ing
Nouak+chott
nou+gat
nou+gats
nought
noughts
Nou+méa
noun
nouns
noun+al
nour+ish
nour+ishes
nour+ish+ing
nour+ished
nour+ish+er
nour+ish+ers
nour+ish+ing
nour+ish+ment
nous
nou+veau
nou+veau riche
nou+veaux riches
nou+veaux
Nouvelle-Calédonie
nou+velle cui+sine
nova
novae *or* novas
Nova Lis+boa
No+va+ra
Nova Sco+tia
No+va+ya Zem+lya
nov+el
nov+els
nov+el+ette
nov+el+ettes
nov+el+ist
nov+el+ists
nov+el+is+tic
no+vel+la

no+vel+las *or*
no+vel+le
Novello
nov+el+ty
nov+el+ties
No+vem+ber
No+vem+bers
no+vena
no+venae
Nov+go+rod
nov+ice
nov+ices
no+vi+ci+ate
no+vi+ci+ates
Novi Sad
no+vi+ti+ate
no+vi+ti+ates
No+vo+caine
Trademark
No+vo+kuz+
  netsk
No+vo+si+birsk
now
nowa+days
no+way
Now+el
Now+els
Now+ell
Now+ells
no+where
no+wise
nowt
Nox
nox+ious
nox+ious+ly
nox+ious+ness
Noy+on
noz+zle
 noz+zles
nth
n-type
nu
 nus
Nu
nu+ance
 nu+ances
nub
 nubs
nub+ble
 nub+bles
nub+bly
nub+by
Nu+bia
Nu+bian
 Nu+bians

nu+bile
nu+bil+ity
nu+cha
nu+chae
nu+chal
nu+clear
nu+clease
nu+cleases
nu+cleate
nu+cleates
nu+cleat+ing
nu+cleat+ed
nu+clei
nu+cleic
nu+cleo+lar
nu+cleo+lus
nu+cleo+li
nu+cleon
nu+cleons
nu+cleon+ic
nu+cleoni+cal+ly
nu+cleon+ics
nu+cleo+phil+ic
nu+cleo+side
nu+cleo+sides
nu+cleo+tide
nu+cleo+tides
nu+cleus
nu+clei *or*
nu+cleuses
nu+clide
nu+clides
nude
nudes
nude+ly
nudge
nudges
nudges
nudg+ing
nudged
nudg+er
nudg+ers
nu+di+branch
nu+di+branchs
nud+ism
nud+ist
nud+ists
nu+dity
nu+dities
Nuffield
nu+ga+tory
nug+get
nug+gets
nug+gety
nui+sance

nui+sances
Nu Jiang
Nu Jiangs
nuke
nukes
nukes
nuk+ing
nuked
Nu+ku'a+lo+fa
Nu+kus
null
nul+lah
nul+lahs
Null+ar+bor
nul+li+fi+ca+tion
nul+li+fy
nul+li+fies
nul+li+fy+ing
nul+li+fied
nul+lity
nul+lities
Nu+man+tia
Nu+man+tian
Nu+man+tians
numb
numbs
numb+ing
numbed
num+bat
num+bats
num+ber
num+bers
num+bers
num+ber+ing
num+bered
num+ber+less
number+plate
number+plates
numb+fish
numb+fish *or*
numb+fishes
num+bles
numb+ly
numb+ness
numb+skull
numb+skulls
nu+men
nu+mi+na
nu+mer+able
nu+mer+ably
nu+mera+cy
nu+mer+al
nu+mer+als
nu+mer+ate
nu+mer+ates

nu+mer+at+ing
nu+mer+at+ed
nu+mera+tion
nu+mera+tions
nu+mera+tive
nu+mera+tor
nu+mera+tors
nu+mer+ic
nu+meri+cal
nu+meri+cal+ly
nu+mero+logi+
  cal
nu+mer+ol+ogy
nu+mer+ol+
  ogies
nu+mer+ous
nu+mer+ous+ly
nu+mer+ous+
  ness
Nu+midia
Nu+mid+ian
Nu+mid+ians
nu+mi+nous
nu+mis+mat+ic
nu+mis+mati+cal+
  ly
nu+mis+mat+ics
num+mu+lite
num+mu+lites
num+skull
num+skulls
nun
nuns
Nunc Di+mit+tis
nun+cia+ture
nun+cia+tures
nun+cio
nun+cios
Nun+eaton
nun+hood
nun+hoods
nun+like
Nunn
nun+nery
nun+neries
NUPE
nup+tial
nup+tial+ly
nup+tials
nurd
nurds
nurd+ish
Nu+rem+berg
Nureyev
Nu+ri+stan

Nürn+berg
nurse
  nurses
  nurses
  nurs+ing
  nursed
nurse+ling
  nurse+lings
nurse+maid
  nurse+maids
nurse+ry
  nurse+ries
nursery+maid
  nursery+maids
nursery+man
  nursery+men
nurs+ing
nurs+ling
  nurs+lings
nur+ture
  nur+tures
  nur+tur+ing
  nur+tured
nur+tur+er
  nur+tur+ers
Nusa Teng+ga+ra
nut
  nuts
  nuts
  nut+ting
  nut+ted

nu+tant
nu+ta+tion
  nu+ta+tions
nut+brown
nut+case
  nut+cases
nut+cracker
  nut+crackers
nut+gall
  nut+galls
nut+hatch
  nut+hatches
nut+house
  nut+houses
nut+meg
  nut+megs
  nut+megs
  nut+meg+ging
  nut+megged
nu+tria
  nu+trias
nu+tri+ent
  nu+tri+ents
nu+tri+ment
  nu+tri+ments
  nu+tri+ment+al
nu+tri+tion
  nu+tri+tion+al
  nu+tri+tion+ist
  nu+tri+tion+ists
  nu+tri+tious

nu+tri+tious+ly
nu+tri+tious+
  ness
nu+tri+tive
  nu+tri+tives
nuts
nut+shell
  nut+shells
nut+ter
  nut+ters
nut+ti+ness
nut+ty
  nut+ti+er
  nut+ti+est
Nuuk
nux vomi+ca
  nux vomi+cas
nuz+zle
  nuz+zles
  nuz+zling
  nuz+zled
nya+la
  nya+la *or*
  nya+las
Ny+asa
Ny+asa+land
Ny+as+sa
nyc+ta+lo+pia
nyc+tit+ro+pism
nye
  nyes

Nye+man
Nye+re+re
Nyí+regy+há+za
Ny+kø+bing
ny+lon
  ny+lons
nymph
  nymphs
nym+pha
  nym+phae
nym+phal
nym+phean
nymph+et
  nymph+ets
nymph+like
nym+pho
  nym+phos
nym+pho+lep+sy
  nym+pho+lep+
   sies
nym+pho+lept
  nym+pho+lepts
nym+pho+lep+tic
nym+pho+ma+nia
nym+pho+ma+ni+ac
  nym+pho+ma+ni+acs
nys+tag+mus
  nys+tag+muses
Nyx

O

o
o's
o'
O
O's *or*
Os
oaf
oafs
oaf+ish
oaf+ish+ness
Oahu
oak
oaks
oak+en
Oak+ham
Oak+land
Oakley
Oaks
oakum
Oak+ville
oar
oars
oars
oar+ing
oared
oar+fish
oar+fish *or*
oar+fishes
oar+less
oar+like
oar+lock
oar+locks
oars+man
oars+men
oars+man+ship
oasis
oases
oast
oasts
oat
oats
oat+cake
oat+cakes
oat+en
Oates

oath
oaths
oat+meal
Oaxa+ca
Ob
Obadiah
Oban
ob+bli+ga+to
ob+bli+ga+tos
 or
ob+bli+ga+ti
ob+con+ic
ob+coni+cal
ob+cor+date
ob+du+ra+cy
ob+du+rate
ob+du+rate+ly
ob+du+rate+ness
obeah
obeahs
obedi+ence
obedi+ent
obedi+ent+ly
obei+sance
obei+sances
obei+sant
ob+elis+cal
ob+elisk
ob+elisks
ob+elis+koid
ob+elus
ob+eli
Ober+am+mer+
 gau
Ober+hau+sen
Ober+land
Oberon
 king of the fairies
Ober+on
 satellite of Uranus
Ober+öster+reich
obese
obese+ness
obesity
obey

obeys
obey+ing
obeyed
obey+er
obey+ers
ob+fus+cate
ob+fus+cates
ob+fus+cat+ing
ob+fus+cat+ed
ob+fus+ca+tion
ob+fus+ca+
 tions
ob+fus+ca+tory
obi
sash
obis *or*
obi
obi
witchcraft
obis
obit
obits
obi+ter dic+tum
obi+ter dic+ta
obi+tu+ar+ist
obi+tu+ar+ists
obi+tu+ary
obi+tu+aries
ob+ject
ob+jects
ob+jects
ob+ject+ing
ob+ject+ed
ob+jec+ti+fi+ca+
 tion
ob+jec+ti+fi+ca+
 tions
ob+jec+ti+fy
ob+jec+ti+fies
ob+jec+ti+fy+
 ing
ob+jec+ti+fied
ob+jec+tion
ob+jec+tions

ob+jec+tion+abil+
 ity
ob+jec+tion+able
ob+jec+tion+able+
 ness
ob+jec+tion+ably
ob+jec+tiv+al
ob+jec+tive
ob+jec+tives
ob+jec+tive+ly
ob+jec+tiv+ism
ob+jec+tiv+ist
ob+jec+tiv+ists
ob+jec+tiv+is+tic
ob+jec+tiv+ity
ob+jet d'art
ob+jets d'art
ob+jur+gate
ob+jur+gates
ob+jur+gat+ing
ob+jur+gat+ed
ob+jur+ga+tion
ob+jur+ga+tions
ob+jur+ga+tor
ob+jur+ga+tors
ob+jur+ga+tory
ob+late
ob+lates
ob+la+tion
ob+la+tions
ob+la+tion+al
ob+la+tory
ob+li+gable
ob+li+gate
ob+li+gates
ob+li+gat+ing
ob+li+gat+ed
ob+li+ga+tion
ob+li+ga+tions
ob+liga+tive
ob+li+ga+to
ob+li+ga+tos
 or
ob+li+ga+ti
ob+li+ga+tor

ob+li+ga+tors
ob+liga+to+ri+ly
ob+liga+tory
oblige
obliges
oblig+ing
obliged
ob+li+gee
ob+li+gees
oblig+er
oblig+ers
oblig+ing+ly
oblig+ing+ness
ob+li+gor
ob+li+gors
oblique
obliques
obliques
obliqu+ing
obliqued
oblique+ly
oblique+ness
obliqui+ty
obliqui+ties
oblit+erate
oblit+erates
oblit+erat+ing
oblit+erat+ed
oblit+era+tion
oblit+era+tions
oblit+era+tive
oblit+era+tor
oblit+era+tors
oblivi+on
oblivi+ons
oblivi+ous
ob+livi+ous+ly
ob+livi+ous+ness
ob+long
ob+longs
ob+lo+quy
ob+lo+quies
ob+nox+ious
ob+nox+ious+ly
ob+nox+ious+
ness
oboe
oboes
oboe d'amore
oboes d'amore
obo+ist
obo+ists
Obote
O'Brien
ob+scene

ob+scene+ly
ob+scen+ity
ob+scen+ities
ob+scur+ant
ob+scur+ants
ob+scu+rant+ism
ob+scu+rant+ist
ob+scu+rant+
ists
ob+scu+ra+tion
ob+scu+ra+
tions
ob+scure
ob+scures
ob+scur+ing
ob+scured
ob+scur+er
ob+scur+est
ob+scure+ly
ob+scure+ness
ob+scu+rity
ob+scu+rities
ob+se+quies
ob+se+qui+ous
ob+se+qui+ous+
ly
ob+se+qui+ous+
ness
ob+serv+able
ob+ser+vance
ob+ser+vances
ob+ser+vant
ob+ser+vant+ly
ob+ser+va+tion
ob+ser+va+
tions
ob+ser+va+tion+
al
ob+ser+va+tion+
al+ly
ob+ser+va+tory
ob+ser+va+
tories
ob+serve
ob+serves
ob+serv+ing
ob+served
ob+serv+er
ob+serv+ers
ob+sess
ob+sesses
ob+sess+ing
ob+sessed
ob+ses+sion
ob+ses+sions

ob+ses+sion+al
ob+ses+sion+al+
ly
ob+ses+sive
ob+ses+sive+ly
ob+ses+sive+
ness
ob+sid+ian
ob+so+lesce
ob+so+lesces
ob+so+lesc+ing
ob+so+lesced
ob+so+les+cence
ob+so+les+cent
ob+so+lete
ob+so+lete+ly
ob+so+lete+ness
ob+sta+cle
ob+sta+cles
ob+stet+ric
ob+stet+ri+cal
ob+stet+ri+cal+ly
ob+ste+tri+cian
ob+ste+tri+
cians
ob+stet+rics
ob+sti+na+cy
ob+sti+na+cies
ob+sti+nate
ob+sti+nate+ly
ob+strep+er+ous
ob+strep+er+ous+
ly
ob+strep+er+ous+
ness
ob+struct
ob+structs
ob+struct+ing
ob+struct+ed
ob+struc+tion
ob+struc+tions
ob+struc+tion+al
ob+struc+tion+
ism
ob+struc+tion+ist
ob+struc+tion+
ists
ob+struc+tive
ob+struc+tives
ob+struc+tive+ly
ob+struc+tive+
ness
ob+struc+tor
ob+struc+tors
ob+tain

ob+tains
ob+tain+ing
ob+tained
ob+tain+abil+ity
ob+tain+able
ob+tain+er
ob+tain+ers
ob+tain+ment
ob+trude
ob+trudes
ob+trud+ing
ob+trud+ed
ob+trud+er
ob+trud+ers
ob+tru+sion
ob+tru+sions
ob+tru+sive
ob+tru+sive+ly
ob+tru+sive+
ness
ob+tuse
ob+tuse+ly
ob+tuse+ness
ob+verse
ob+verses
ob+verse+ly
ob+ver+sion
ob+ver+sions
ob+vert
ob+verts
ob+vert+ing
ob+vert+ed
ob+vi+ate
ob+vi+ates
ob+vi+at+ing
ob+vi+at+ed
ob+via+tion
ob+via+tions
ob+vi+ous
ob+vi+ous+ly
ob+vi+ous+ness
oca+ri+na
oca+ri+nas
O'Casey
Occam
oc+ca+sion
oc+ca+sions
oc+ca+sions
oc+ca+sion+ing
oc+ca+sioned
oc+ca+sion+al
oc+ca+sion+al+ly
oc+ci+dent
Oc+ci+dent
oc+ci+den+tal

Oc+ci+den+tal
  Oc+ci+den+tals
oc+cipi+tal
  oc+cipi+tals
oc+ci+put
  oc+ci+puts *or*
  oc+cipi+ta
oc+clude
  oc+cludes
  oc+clud+ing
  oc+clud+ed
  oc+clud+ent
oc+clu+sion
  oc+clu+sions
  oc+clu+sive
oc+cult
  oc+cults
  oc+cult+ing
  oc+culted
oc+cul+ta+tion
  oc+cul+ta+tions
oc+cult+ism
oc+cult+ist
  oc+cult+ists
oc+cult+ness
oc+cu+pan+cy
  oc+cu+pan+cies
oc+cu+pant
  oc+cu+pants
oc+cu+pa+tion
  oc+cu+pa+tions
  oc+cu+pa+tion+
  al
oc+cu+pi+er
  oc+cu+pi+ers
oc+cu+py
  oc+cu+pies
  oc+cu+py+ing
  oc+cu+pied
oc+cur
  oc+curs
  oc+cur+ring
  oc+curred
  oc+cur+rence
  oc+cur+rences
oc+cur+rent
ocean
  oceans
ocean+ar+ium
  ocean+ar+iums
  or
  ocean+ar+ia
ocean-going
Oceania
Oce+an+ian

Oce+an+ians
ocean+ic
Ocea+nid
  Ocea+nids *or*
  Oceani+des
ocean+og+ra+
  pher
ocean+og+ra+
  phers
oceano+graph+ic
ocean+og+ra+
  phy
ocean+ol+ogy
Ocea+nus
ocel+lar
oc+el+late
oc+el+lat+ed
oc+el+la+tion
  oc+el+la+tions
ocel+lus
ocel+li
oc+elot
  oc+elots
och
oche
  oches
ocher
  ochers
  ochers
ocher+ing
  ochered
ocher+ous
och+loc+ra+cy
  och+loc+ra+cies
och+lo+crat
  och+lo+crats
  och+lo+crat+ic
och+one
ochre
  ochres
  ochres
ochring
  ochred
ochre+ous
ochrous
ochry
Ockeghem
ock+er
  ock+ers
Ockham
o'clock
O'Connell
octa
oc+tad
  oc+tads

oc+tad+ic
oc+ta+gon
  oc+ta+gons
oc+tago+nal
oc+ta+he+dron
  oc+ta+he+drons
  or
  oc+ta+he+dra
oc+tal
oc+tane
oc+tant
  oc+tants
oc+ta+roon
  oc+ta+roons
oc+ta+va+lent
oc+tave
  oc+taves
Octavian
oc+ta+vo
  oc+ta+vos
oc+ten+nial
oc+ten+ni+al+ly
oc+tet
  oc+tets
oc+til+lion
  oc+til+lions
  oc+til+lionth
Oc+to+ber
  Oc+to+bers
Oc+to+brist
  Oc+to+brists
oc+to+cen+te+
  nary
oc+to+cen+te+
  naries
oc+to+genar+ian
oc+to+genar+
  ians
oc+to+pus
  oc+to+puses
oc+to+roon
  oc+to+roons
oc+to+syl+lab+ic
oc+to+syl+la+ble
  oc+to+syl+la+
  bles
oc+troi
oc+trois
oc+tu+ple
  oc+tu+ples
  oc+tu+ples
oc+tu+pling
  oc+tu+pled
ocu+lar
  ocu+lars

ocu+lar+ist
  ocu+lar+ists
ocu+lar+ly
ocu+late
ocu+list
  ocu+lists
od
OD
  OD's
  OD's
  OD'ing
  OD'd
oda+lisk
  oda+lisks
oda+lisque
  oda+lisques
odd
  odds
odd+er
odd+est
odd+ball
  odd+balls
Odd+fellow
  Odd+fellows
odd+ity
  odd+ities
odd-jobber
  odd-jobbers
odd-jobman
odd-jobmen
odd+ly
odd+ment
  odd+ments
odd+ness
  odd+nesses
odds
odds-on
ode
  odes
Oden+se
odeon
  odeons
Oder
Odes+sa
odeum
  odea
odic
Odin
odi+ous
odi+ous+ness
odium
Odoacer
odom+eter
  odom+eters
odom+etry

odon+to+glos+
sum
odon+to+glos+
sums
odon+to+logi+cal
od+on+tolo+gist
od+on+tolo+
gists
od+on+tol+ogy
odor
odors
odor+if+er+ous
odor+if+er+ous+
ly
odor+if+er+ous+
ness
odori+phore
odori+phores
odor+less
odor+ous
odor+ous+ly
odor+ous+ness
odour
odours
odour+less
Odovacar
Odra
odyl
od+yle
Od+ys+sean
Odysseus
Od+ys+sey
Od+ys+seys
oede+ma
oede+ma+ta
oedema+tous
oedi+pal
oedi+pean
Oedipus
Oehlenschläger
oeno+logi+cal
oenolo+gist
oenolo+gists
oenol+ogy
Oenone
oeno+thera
oeno+theras
o'er
oer+sted
oer+steds
oesopha+geal
oesopha+gus
oesopha+gi
oes+tra+di+ol
oes+tral

oes+trin
oes+trins
oes+tro+gen
oes+tro+gens
oes+tro+gen+ic
oes+tro+geni+cal+
ly
oes+trous
oes+trus
oeuvre
oeuvres
of
off
Offa
of+fal
of+fals
Of+fa+ly
off+beat
off+beats
off-Broadway
off+cut
off+cuts
Of+fen+bach
place name
Offenbach
surname
of+fence
of+fences
of+fend
of+fends
of+fend+ing
of+fend+ed
of+fend+er
of+fend+ers
of+fense
of+fenses
of+fen+sive
of+fen+sives
of+fen+sive+ly
of+fen+sive+
ness
of+fer
of+fers
of+fers
of+fer+ing
of+fered
of+fer+ing
of+fer+ings
of+fer+tory
of+fer+tories
off+hand
off+handed+ly
off+handed+ness
of+fice
of+fices

of+fic+er
of+fic+ers
of+fic+ers
of+fic+er+ing
of+fic+ered
of+fi+cial
of+fi+cials
of+fi+cial+dom
of+fi+cial+ese
of+fi+cial+ly
of+fi+ci+ant
of+fi+ci+ants
of+fi+ci+ate
of+fi+ci+ates
of+fi+ci+at+ing
of+fi+ci+at+ed
of+fi+cia+tion
of+fi+cia+tions
of+fi+cia+tor
of+fi+cia+tors
of+fi+cious
of+fi+cious+ly
of+fi+cious+ness
of+fing
of+fings
of+fish
of+fish+ly
of+fish+ness
off-licence
off-licences
off-load
off-loads
off-load+ing
off-load+ed
off-peak
off-piste
off-putting
off-sales
off+set
off+sets
off+sets
off+set+ting
off+set
off+shoot
off+shoots
off+shore
off+side
off+sides
off+spring
off+springs
off+stage
off-the-wall
off-white
off-whites
oft

of+ten
Oga+den
ogam
Oga+sa+wa+ra
Gun+to
Og+bo+mo+sho
Ogden
ogee
ogees
og+ham
ogiv+al
ogive
ogives
ogle
ogles
ogles
ogling
ogled
ogler
oglers
Oglethorpe
Ogo+oué
Ogo+we
O grade
O grades
ogre
ogres
ogre+ish
ogress
Ogun
oh
O'Higgins
Ohio
Öhlenschläger
ohm
ohms
Ohm
ohm+age
ohm+ages
ohm+meter
ohm+meters
oho
oil
oils
oils
oil+ing
oiled
Oil
oil+can
oil+cans
oil+cloth
oil+cloths
oil+er
oil+ers
oil+field

oil+fields
oil+fired
oil+gas
oili+ly
oili+ness
oil-like
oil+man
oil+men
oil+skin
oil+skins
oil+stone
oil+stones
oily
oili+er
oili+est
oink
oint+ment
oint+ments
Oi+reach+tas
Oise
Oistrakh
Oita
Ojib+wa
Ojib+was *or*
Ojib+wa
o.k.
o.k.s
o.k.s
o.k.ing
o.k.ed
O.K.
O.K.s
O.K.s
O.K.ing
O.K.ed
OK
OKs
OKs
OKed
OKing
Oka+na+gan
oka+pi
oka+pis *or*
oka+pi
Oka+van+go
okay
okays
okays
okay+ing
okayed
Oka+ya+ma
Okee+cho+bee
O'Keeffe
Okefe+nokee
Okeghem

Okhotsk
Oki+na+wa
Ok+la+ho+ma
Okla+ho+man
Okla+ho+mans
Oko+van+go
okra
okras
Olaf
Öland
Olav
old
old+er
old+est
Old
Old Bai+ley
Oldcastle
old+en
Oldenbarneveldt
Ol+den+burg
place name
Oldenburg
surname
old-fashioned
old-fashioneds
Old+ham
oldie
oldies
old+ish
old-maidish
old+ness
old+ster
old+sters
old-time
old-timer
old-timers
Ol+du+vai
old-world
olé
olés
olea+ceous
oleagi+nous
olean+der
olean+ders
oleate
oleates
olein
oleo
oleo+mar+ga+rin
oleo+mar+ga+
rins
oleo+mar+ga+
rine
oleo+mar+ga+
rines

oleo+res+in
oleo+res+ins
oleo+res+in+ous
oleum
olea *or*
oleums
O lev+el
O lev+els
ol+fac+tion
ol+fac+tory
ol+fac+tories
oli+garch
oli+garchs
oli+gar+chic
oli+gar+chi+cal
oli+gar+chy
oli+gar+chies
Oli+go+cene
oli+go+chaete
oli+go+chaetes
oli+gopo+lis+tic
oli+gopo+ly
oli+gopo+lies
oli+go+sper+mia
oli+go+troph+ic
oli+got+ro+phy
oli+got+ro+
phies
Ólim+bos
olio
olios
Oliphant
oli+va+ceous
ol+ive
ol+ives
Oliver
Ol+ives
Olivier
oli+vine
oli+vines
olla
ollas
olla po+dri+da
Ol+mütz
ol+ogy
ol+ogies
Olo+mouc
olo+ro+so
olo+ro+sos
Ol+szt+yn
Olym+pia
Olym+pi+ad
Olym+pi+ads
Olym+pian
Olym+pians

Olym+pic
Olym+pics
Olym+pus
Olyn+thus
Omagh
Oma+ha
Oman
Oma+ni
Oma+nis
Omar
Omar Khayyám
oma+sum
oma+sa
Omay+yad
Omay+yads *or*
Omay+ya+des
om+ber
om+bre
om+buds+man
om+buds+men
Om+dur+man
omega
omegas
ome+let
U.S.
ome+lets
ome+lette
ome+lettes
omen
omens
omens
omen+ing
omened
omen+tum
omen+ta
omertà
omi+cron
omi+crons
omi+nous
omi+nous+ly
omi+nous+ness
omis+sible
omis+sion
omis+sions
omis+sive
omit
omits
omit+ting
omit+ted
omit+ter
omit+ters
Om+mi+ad
Om+mi+ads *or*
Om+mia+des
om+ni+bus

om+ni+buses
om+ni+com+pe+
  tence
om+ni+com+pe+
  tent
om+ni+di+rec+
  tion+al
om+ni+fari+ous
om+ni+fari+ous+
  ly
om+ni+fari+ous+
  ness
om+nif+ic
om+nifi+cence
om+nifi+cent
om+nipo+tence
om+nipo+tent
om+nipo+tents
om+nipo+tent+ly
om+ni+pres+
  ence
om+ni+pres+ent
om+nis+ci+ence
om+nis+ci+ent
om+nis+ci+ent+
  ly
omnium-gather+
  um
  omnium-gather+
  ums
om+ni+vore
om+ni+vores
om+niv+or+ous
om+niv+or+ous+
  ly
om+niv+or+ous+
  ness
Omphale
om+pha+los
  om+pha+li
Omsk
Omu+ta
on
On
ona+ger
  ona+gri *or*
  ona+gers
onan+ism
onan+ist
  onan+ists
onan+is+tic
Onassis
once
once-over
  once-overs

onc+er
onc+ers
onco+gene
onco+genes
on+co+gen+ic
on+coming
  on+comings
on+cost
  on+costs
on dit
  on dits
Ondo
one
  ones
one-armed
One+ga
one-horse
Onei+da
  Onei+das *or*
  Onei+da
O'Neill
one-liner
  one-liners
one-man
one+ness
one-night
one-off
  one-offs
one-parent
one-piece
  one-pieces
on+er+ous
on+er+ous+ly
on+er+ous+ness
one+self
one-sided
one-sidedly
one-sidedness
one-step
  one-steps
one-stop
one-time
one-to-one
one-track
one-up
one-upmanship
  one-upmanships
one-way
on+going
on+ion
  on+ions
onion+skin
  onion+skins
on+iony
Onit+sha

on-line
on+looker
  on+lookers
on+looking
only
ono+mas+tics
ono+mato+poeia
ono+mato+poe+
  ic
ono+mato+poei+
  cal+ly
ono+mato+po+et+
  ic
ono+mato+po+
  eti+cal+ly
On+on+da+ga
On+on+da+gas
  or
On+on+da+ga
on+rush
  on+rushes
on+set
  on+sets
on+shore
on+side
on+slaught
  on+slaughts
On+tarian
  On+tarians
On+tario
On+tarioan
  On+tarioans
onto
on+to+gen+esis
on+to+ge+net+ic
on+to+ge+neti+
  cal+ly
on+to+gen+ic
on+to+geni+cal+
  ly
on+tog+eny
on+to+logi+cal
on+to+logi+cal+
  ly
on+tol+ogy
  on+tol+ogies
onus
  onuses
on+ward
  on+wards
ony+chopho+ran
  ony+chopho+
  rans
onyx
oocyte

oocytes
oodles
ooga+mous
oog+amy
Ook+pik
Ook+piks
oolite
oolites
oo+lith
  ooliths
oolit+ic
oologi+cal
oolo+gist
  oolo+gists
ool+ogy
oolong
oomi+ac
oomi+acs
oomi+ak
  oomi+aks
oom+pah
oomph
oops
Oost+en+de
ooze
oozes
oozes
ooz+ing
oozed
oozi+ly
oozi+ness
oozy
oozi+er
oozi+est
opac+ity
opac+ities
opah
opahs
opal
opals
opa+lesce
opa+lesces
opa+lesc+ing
opa+lesced
opal+es+cence
opal+es+cent
opal+ine
opal+ines
opal-like
opaque
opaques
opaques
opaqu+ing
opaqued

opaque+ly
opaque+ness
ope
  opes
  op+ing
  oped
open
  opens
  opens
  open+ing
  opened
Open
open+able
open-and-shut
open+cast
open-ended
open+er
  open+ers
open-eyed
open-faced
open-handed
open-handed+ly
open-handed+
  ness
open-heart
open-hearted
open-hearted+
  ness
open-hearth
open+ing
  open+ings
open+ly
open-minded
open-minded+
  ness
open-mouthed
open+ness
open-plan
open-reel
open+work
op+era
  op+eras
op+era
op+er+abil+ity
op+er+able
op+er+ably
opé+ra bouffe
  opé+ras bouffes
opera buf+fa
  opera buf+fas
  or
  opere buffe
opé+ra co+mique
opé+ras co+
  miques

op+er+and
op+er+ands
op+er+ant
op+er+ants
opera se+ria
opera se+rias
  or
operas se+ria
  or
opere se+rie
op+er+ate
op+er+ates
op+er+at+ing
op+er+at+ed
op+er+at+ic
op+er+ati+cal+ly
op+er+at+ing
op+era+tion
op+era+tions
op+era+tion+al
op+era+tion+al+
  ism
op+era+tion+al+
  is+tic
op+era+tion+al+
  ly
op+era+tion+ism
op+era+tions
op+era+tive
  op+era+tives
op+era+tive+ly
op+era+tive+
  ness
op+era+tiv+ity
op+era+tor
op+era+tors
oper+cu+lar
oper+cu+lum
oper+cu+la *or*
oper+cu+lums
op+er+et+ta
op+er+et+tas
op+er+et+tist
op+er+et+tists
ophi+cleide
ophi+cleides
ophid+ian
ophid+ians
Ophir
oph+thal+mia
oph+thal+mic
oph+thal+mo+
  logi+cal
oph+thal+molo+
  gist

oph+thal+molo+
  gists
oph+thal+mol+
  ogy
oph+thal+mo+
  scope
oph+thal+mo+
  scopes
oph+thal+mo+
  scop+ic
opi+ate
opi+ates
opi+ates
opi+at+ing
opi+at+ed
opine
opines
opin+ing
opined
opin+ion
opin+ions
opin+ion+at+ed
opin+ion+at+ed+
  ly
opin+ion+at+ed+
  ness
opin+iona+tive
opin+iona+tive+ly
opin+iona+tive+
  ness
opioid
opioids
opium
Opor+to
opos+sum
  opos+sums *or*
  opos+sum
Oppenheimer
op+po+nen+cy
op+po+nent
  op+po+nents
op+por+tune
op+por+tune+ly
op+por+tune+
  ness
op+por+tun+ism
op+por+tun+ist
op+por+tun+ists
op+por+tun+is+
  tic
op+por+tu+nity
op+por+tu+
  nities
op+pos+abil+ity
op+pos+able

op+pos+ably
op+pose
  op+poses
  op+pos+ing
  op+posed
op+pos+er
op+pos+ers
op+po+site
op+po+sites
op+po+site+ly
op+po+site+ness
op+po+si+tion
op+po+si+tions
op+po+si+tion+al
op+po+si+tion+
  ist
op+po+si+tion+
  ists
op+po+si+tion+
  less
op+posi+tive
op+press
op+presses
op+press+ing
op+pressed
op+pres+sion
op+pres+sions
op+pres+sive
op+pres+sive+ly
op+pres+sive+
  ness
op+pres+sor
op+pres+sors
op+pro+bri+ous
op+pro+bri+ous+
  ly
op+pro+bri+ous+
  ness
op+pro+brium
op+pugn
  op+pugns
  op+pugn+ing
  op+pugned
op+pugn+er
op+pugn+ers
Ops
op+sin
op+son+ic
op+so+nin
opt
  opts
  opt+ing
  opt+ed
op+ta+tive
  op+ta+tives

op+tic
Trademark
op+tics
op+ti+cal
op+ti+cal+ly
op+ti+cian
op+ti+cians
op+tics
op+ti+mal
op+ti+mi+sa+tion
op+ti+mi+sa+tions
op+ti+mise
op+ti+mises
op+ti+mis+ing
op+ti+mised
op+ti+mism
op+ti+mists
op+ti+mis+tic
op+ti+mis+ti+cal+ly
op+ti+mi+za+tion
op+ti+mi+za+tions
op+ti+mize
op+ti+mizes
op+ti+miz+ing
op+ti+mized
op+ti+mum
op+ti+ma *or*
op+ti+mums
op+tion
op+tions
op+tions
op+tion+ing
op+tioned
op+tion+al
op+tion+al+ly
op+to+met+ric
op+tom+etrist
op+tom+etrists
op+tom+etry
op+to+phone
op+to+phones
opt-out
opt-outs
opt-out
verb
opu+lence
opu+lent
opu+lent+ly
opun+tia
opun+tias
opus

opuses *or*
op+era
Opus Dei
or
ora
or+ach
or+aches
or+ache
or+aches
ora+cle
ora+cles
Oracle
Trademark
oracu+lar
oracu+lar+ly
ora+cy
Ora+dea
oral
orals
oral+ly
Oran
orang
orangs
or+ange
or+anges
Or+ange
in place names
Orange
royal house
or+ange+ade
or+ange+ades
Orange+man
Orange+men
or+ang+ery
or+ang+eries
orange+wood
orang-outang
orang-outangs
orang-utan
orang-utans
orate
orates
orat+ing
orat+ed
ora+tion
ora+tions
ora+tor
ora+tors
ora+tori+cal
ora+tori+cal+ly
ora+to+rio
ora+to+rios
ora+tory
ora+tories
orb

orbs
orbs
orb+ing
orbed
or+bicu+lar
or+bicu+lar+ity
or+bicu+lar+ly
or+bicu+late
or+bicu+lat+ed
or+bit
or+bits
or+bits
or+bit+ing
or+bit+ed
or+bit+al
or+bit+als
or+bit+al+ly
orc
orcs
Or+cad+ian
Or+cad+ians
Orcagna
or+chard
or+chards
or+ches+tra
or+ches+tras
or+ches+tral
or+ches+tral+ly
or+ches+trate
or+ches+trates
or+ches+trat+ing
or+ches+trat+ed
or+ches+tra+tion
or+ches+tra+tions
or+ches+tra+tor
or+ches+tra+tors
or+chid
or+chids
or+chi+dec+to+my
or+chi+dec+to+mies
or+chil
or+chils
or+chis
or+chises
Or+cus
Orczy
Ord
or+dain
or+dains

or+dain+ing
or+dained
or+dain+er
or+dain+ers
or+dain+ment
or+dain+ments
or+deal
or+deals
or+der
or+ders
or+ders
or+der+ing
or+dered
or+der+er
or+der+ers
or+der+li+ness
or+der+ly
or+der+lies
or+di+nal
or+di+nals
or+di+nance
or+di+nances
or+di+nari+ly
or+di+nary
or+di+naries
or+di+nate
or+di+nates
or+di+na+tion
or+di+na+tions
ord+nance
Or+do+vi+cian
or+dure
Or+dzho+ni+ki+dze
ore
ores
öre
öre
oread
oreads
Örebro
orega+no
Or+egon
Orel
Oren+burg
Oren+se
Orestes
orfe
orfes
Orff
or+gan
or+gans
or+gan+die
or+gan+dies
or+gan+dy

or+gan+dies
or+ga+nelle
or+ga+nelles
organ-grinder
organ-grinders
or+gan+ic
or+gan+ics
or+gani+cal+ly
or+gani+sa+tion
or+gani+sa+
  tions
or+gani+sa+tion+
  al
or+gan+ise
or+gan+ises
or+gan+is+ing
or+gan+ised
or+gan+is+er
or+gan+is+ers
or+gan+ism
or+gan+isms
or+gan+is+mal
or+gan+is+mal+
  ly
or+gan+is+mic
or+gan+ist
or+gan+ists
or+gani+za+tion
or+gani+za+
  tions
or+gani+za+tion+
  al
or+gan+ize
or+gan+izes
or+gan+iz+ing
or+gan+ized
or+gan+iz+er
or+gan+iz+ers
or+gano+metal+
  lic
or+ga+non
or+ga+na *or*
or+ga+nons
or+gano+tin
or+ga+num
or+ga+na *or*
or+ga+nums
or+gan+za
or+gan+zas
or+gasm
or+gasms
or+gas+mic
or+gas+tic
or+geat
or+gi+as+tic

orgy
orgies
ori+bi
ori+bi *or*
ori+bis
ori+el
ori+els
ori+ent
ori+ents
ori+ents
ori+ent+ing
ori+ent+ed
Ori+ent
ori+en+tal
Ori+en+tal
Ori+en+tals
Ori+en+tal+ism
Ori+en+tal+isms
Ori+en+tal+ist
Ori+en+tal+ists
Ori+en+tal+is+tic
ori+en+tate
ori+en+tates
ori+en+tat+ing
ori+en+tat+ed
ori+en+ta+tion
ori+en+ta+tions
ori+en+ta+tion+al
ori+ent+eer
ori+ent+eers
ori+ent+eers
ori+ent+eer+ing
ori+ent+eered
ori+fice
ori+fices
ori+flamme
ori+ga+mi
ori+gan
ori+ga+num
Origen
ori+gin
ori+gins
origi+nal
origi+nals
origi+nal+ity
origi+nal+ities
origi+nal+ly
origi+nate
origi+nates
origi+nat+ing
origi+nat+ed
origi+na+tion
origi+na+tions
origi+na+tor
origi+na+tors

O-ring
O-rings
Ori+no+co
ori+ole
ori+oles
Orion
mythical giant
Ori+on
constellation
ori+son
ori+sons
Oris+sa
Ori+ya
Ori+ya
Ori+za+ba
Or+jo+ni+ki+dze
Ork+ney
Ork+ney+man
Ork+ney+men
Or+lan+do
Or+lé+ans
Orléans
surname
Or+lon
Trademark
or+lop
or+lops
Orly
Ormandy
or+mer
or+mers
or+mo+lu
Or+muz
or+na+ment
or+na+ments
or+na+ments
or+na+ment+ing
or+na+ment+ed
or+na+men+tal
or+na+men+tals
or+na+men+tal+
  ly
or+na+men+ta+
  tion
or+na+men+ta+
  tions
or+nate
or+nate+ly
or+nate+ness
Orne
or+neri+ness
or+nery
or+ni+tho+logi+
  cal

or+ni+tho+logi+
  cal+ly
or+ni+tholo+gist
or+ni+tholo+
  gists
or+ni+thol+ogy
or+ni+tho+rhyn+
  chus
or+ni+tho+rhyn+
  chuses
oro+gen+esis
oro+ge+net+ic
oro+gen+ic
orog+eny
Oron+tes
oro+tund
Orozco
or+phan
or+phans
or+phans
or+phan+ing
or+phaned
or+phan+age
or+phan+ages
Or+phean
Orpheus
Or+phic
Or+phi+cal+ly
or+pin
or+pins
or+pine
or+pines
Or+ping+ton
or+re+ry
or+re+ries
or+rice
or+ris
Orsini
Orsk
Ortega
Or+te+gal
Ortega y Gasset
or+thi+con
or+thi+cons
ortho+chro+mat+
  ic
ortho+chro+ma+
  tism
ortho+clase
ortho+don+tia
ortho+don+tic
ortho+don+tics
ortho+don+tist
ortho+don+tists
ortho+dox

Ortho+dox
ortho+doxy
ortho+doxies
ortho+ep+ic
ortho+epi+cal+ly
ortho+epy
ortho+gen+esis
ortho+ge+net+ic
ortho+geneti+cal+
ly
or+thogo+nal
or+thogo+nal+ly
or+thog+ra+pher
or+thog+ra+
phers
ortho+graph+ic
ortho+graphi+cal
ortho+graphi+cal+
ly
or+thog+ra+phist
or+thog+ra+
phists
or+thog+ra+phy
or+thog+ra+
phies
ortho+paedic
ortho+paedics
ortho+paedist
ortho+paedists
ortho+pedic
ortho+pedics
ortho+pedist
ortho+pedists
or+thop+ter+an
or+thop+ter+
ans
or+thop+ter+ous
or+thop+tic
or+thop+tics
or+thop+tist
or+thop+tists
ortho+rhom+bic
Ort+les
or+to+lan
or+to+lans
Orton
Oru+ro
Or+vie+to
Orwell
Or+wel+lian
Oryol
oryx
oryxes *or*
oryx
os

bone
ossa
os
mouth
ora
os
Osa+ka
Osborne
Os+car
award
Os+cars
Oscar
name
os+cil+late
os+cil+lates
os+cil+lat+ing
os+cil+lat+ed
os+cil+la+tion
os+cil+la+tions
os+cil+la+tor
os+cil+la+tors
os+cil+la+tory
os+cil+lo+gram
os+cil+lo+grams
os+cil+lo+graph
os+cil+lo+
graphs
os+cil+lo+graph+
ic
os+cil+log+ra+
phy
os+cil+lo+scope
os+cil+lo+
scopes
os+cine
os+ci+tance
os+ci+tances
os+ci+tan+cy
os+ci+tan+cies
os+ci+tant
os+cu+lar
os+cu+late
os+cu+lates
os+cu+lat+ing
os+cu+lat+ed
os+cu+la+tion
os+cu+la+tions
os+cu+la+tory
Osha+wa
Oshog+bo
osier
osiers
Osi+jek
Osi+rian
Osiris

Oslo
Osman
Os+man+li
Os+man+lis
os+mi+rid+ium
os+mium
os+mo+regu+la+
tion
os+mose
os+moses
os+mos+ing
os+mosed
os+mo+sis
os+mot+ic
os+moti+cal+ly
os+mund
os+munds
os+mun+da
os+mun+das
Os+na+brück
os+prey
os+preys
Ossa
os+sein
os+seous
os+seous+ly
Os+setia
Os+se+tian
Os+set+ic
Ossian
Os+si+an+ic
Ossietzky
os+si+fi+ca+tion
os+si+fi+er
os+si+fi+ers
os+si+fy
os+si+fies
os+si+fy+ing
os+si+fied
os+su+ary
os+su+aries
os+teal
os+teit+ic
os+tei+tis
Os+tend
os+ten+sibil+ity
os+ten+sible
os+ten+sibly
os+ten+sive
os+ten+sive+ly
os+ten+ta+tion
os+ten+ta+tions
os+ten+ta+tious
os+ten+ta+tious+
ly

os+teo+ar+thrit+
ic
os+teo+ar+thrit+
ics
os+teo+ar+thri+
tis
os+teo+logi+cal
os+teo+logi+cal+
ly
os+teolo+gist
os+teolo+gists
os+teol+ogy
os+teo+ma
os+teo+ma+ta
or
os+teo+mas
os+teo+ma+la+
cia
os+teo+ma+la+
cial
os+teo+ma+lac+
ic
os+teo+my+eli+
tis
os+teo+path
os+teo+paths
os+teo+path+ic
os+teo+pathi+cal+
ly
os+teopa+thy
os+teo+plas+ty
os+teo+plas+
ties
os+teo+po+ro+
sis
os+teo+po+rot+
ic
Öster+reich
Os+tia
os+ti+na+to
os+ti+na+tos
ost+ler
ost+lers
Ost+mark
Ost+marks
Ost+preus+sen
os+tra+cis+able
os+tra+cise
os+tra+cises
os+tra+cis+ing
os+tra+cised
os+tra+cis+er
os+tra+cis+ers
os+tra+cism
os+tra+cisms

os+tra+ciz+able
os+tra+cize
  os+tra+cizes
  os+tra+ciz+ing
  os+tra+cized
Os+tra+va
os+trich
  os+triches *or*
  os+trich
Ostwald
Oswald
Oś+wię+cim
Ota+go
otal+gia
oth+er
  oth+ers
other-directed
oth+er+ness
other+wise
other+worldli+
  ness
other+worldly
Othin
Oth+man
variant of
  Ottoman
Oth+mans
Othman
variant of
  Osman
otic
oti+ose
oti+ose+ness
oti+os+ity
oti+tis
oto+la+ryn+go+
  logi+cal
oto+lar+yn+golo+
  gist
  oto+lar+yn+golo+
  gists
oto+lar+yn+gol+
  ogy
oto+lith
  oto+liths
oto+lith+ic
oto+logi+cal
otolo+gist
  otolo+gists
otol+ogy
O'Toole
oto+rhino+lar+yn+
  gol+ogy
oto+scope
  oto+scopes

oto+scop+ic
Ot+ran+to
Ot+ta+wa
ot+ter
  ot+ters *or*
  ot+ter
Ot+ter+burn
Otto
ot+to+man
  ot+to+mans
Ot+to+man
  Ot+to+mans
Otway
ou
ous
Ouachi+ta
Oua+ga+dou+
  gou
oua+na+niche
  oua+na+niches
ou+baas
  ou+baases
Ouban+gui
oubli+ette
  oubli+ettes
ouch
Oudh
Oues+sant
ought
  oughts
Oui+ja
  Trademark
Ouj+da
Oulu
ouma
  oumas
ounce
  ounces
oupa
  oupas
our
  ours
our+self
our+selves
Ouse
ousel
  ousels
oust
  ousts
oust+ing
oust+ed
oust+er
  oust+ers
out
  outs

outs
out+ing
out+ed
out+act
  out+acts
  out+act+ing
  out+act+ed
out+age
  out+ages
out-and-out
out+back
out+bal+ance
  out+bal+ances
  out+bal+anc+ing
  out+bal+anced
out+bar+gain
  out+bar+gains
  out+bar+gain+
    ing
  out+bar+gained
out+bid
  out+bids
  out+bid+ding
  out+bid
  out+bid+den
    or
  out+bid
out+bluff
  out+bluffs
  out+bluff+ing
  out+bluffed
out+board
  out+boards
out+boast
  out+boasts
  out+boast+ing
  out+boast+ed
out+bound
out+box
  out+boxes
  out+box+ing
  outboxed
out+brave
  out+braves
  out+brav+ing
  out+braved
out+break
  out+breaks
out+build+ing
  out+build+ings
out+burst
  out+bursts
out+cast
  out+casts
out+caste

out+castes
out+castes
out+cast+ing
out+cast+ed
out+class
  out+classes
  out+class+ing
  out+classed
out+come
  out+comes
out+crop
  out+crops
  out+crops
  out+crop+ping
  out+cropped
out+cry
  out+cries
  out+cries
  out+cry+ing
  out+cried
out+dance
  out+dances
  out+danc+ing
  out+danced
out+dare
  out+dares
  out+dar+ing
  out+dared
out+dis+tance
  out+dis+tances
  out+dis+tanc+
    ing
  out+dis+tanced
out+do
  out+does
  out+do+ing
  out+did
  out+done
out+dodge
  out+dodges
  out+dodg+ing
  out+dodged
out+door
  out+doors
out+drink
  out+drinks
  out+drink+ing
  out+drank
  out+drunk
out+eat
  out+eats
  out+eat+ing
  out+ate
  out+eat+en
out+er

out+ers
outer+most
out+face
  out+faces
  out+fac+ing
  out+faced
out+fall
  out+falls
out+field
  out+fields
out+field+er
  out+field+ers
out+fight
  out+fights
  out+fight+ing
  out+fought
out+fit
  out+fits
  out+fits
  out+fit+ting
  out+fit+ted
  out+fit+ter
  out+fit+ters
out+flank
  out+flanks
  out+flank+ing
  out+flanked
out+flow
  out+flows
out+fly
  out+flies
  out+fly+ing
  out+flew
  out+flown
out+fox
  out+foxes
  out+fox+ing
  out+foxed
out+gen+er+al
  out+gen+er+als
  out+gen+er+al+
  ling *or*
  out+gen+er+al+
  ing
  U.S.
  out+gen+er+
  alled *or*
  out+gen+er+
  aled
  U.S.
out+go
  out+goes
  out+going
  out+went
  out+gone

out+going
out+goings
out+grow
  out+grows
  out+grow+ing
  out+grew
  out+grown
  out+growth
  out+growths
out+guess
  out+guesses
  out+guess+ing
  out+guessed
out+gun
  out+guns
  out+gun+ning
  out+gunned
out+hit
  out+hits
  out+hit+ting
  out+hit
out+house
  out+houses
out+ing
  out+ings
out+jockey
  out+jockeys
  out+jockey+ing
  out+jockeyed
out+jump
  out+jumps
  out+jump+ing
  out+jumped
out+land+ish
  out+land+ish+ly
  out+land+ish+
  ness
out+last
  out+lasts
  out+last+ing
  out+last+ed
out+laugh
  out+laughs
  out+laugh+ing
  out+laughed
out+law
  out+laws
  out+laws
  out+law+ing
  out+lawed
out+law+ry
  out+law+ries
out+lay
  out+lays
  out+lay+ing

out+laid
out+leap
  out+leaps
  out+leap+ing
  out+leapt *or*
  out+leaped
out+let
  out+lets
out+li+er
  out+li+ers
out+line
  out+lines
  out+lines
  out+lin+ing
  out+lined
out+live
  out+lives
  out+liv+ing
  out+lived
out+look
  out+looks
out+ly+ing
out+ma+neu+ver
  U.S.
  out+ma+neu+
  vers
  out+ma+neu+
  ver+ing
  out+ma+neu+
  vered
out+ma+noeu+
  vre
  out+ma+noeu+
  vres
  out+ma+noeu+
  vring
  out+ma+noeu+
  vred
out+match
  out+matches
  out+match+ing
  out+matched
out+mod+ed
  out+mod+ed+ly
  out+mod+ed+
  ness
out+most
out+num+ber
  out+num+bers
  out+num+ber+
  ing
  out+num+bered
out-of-door
out-of-doors
out-of-the-way

out+pace
  out+paces
  out+pac+ing
  out+paced
out+pa+tient
  out+pa+tients
out+per+form
  out+per+forms
  out+per+form+
  ing
  out+per+formed
out+place+ment
out+play
  out+plays
  out+play+ing
  out+played
out+point
  out+points
  out+point+ing
  out+point+ed
out+port
  out+ports
out+post
  out+posts
out+pour
  out+pours
  out+pours
  out+pour+ing
  out+poured
  out+pour+ing
  out+pour+ings
out+pro+duce
  out+pro+duces
  out+pro+duc+
  ing
  out+pro+duced
out+put
  out+puts
  out+puts
  out+put+ting
  out+put+ted *or*
  out+put
out+race
  out+races
  out+rac+ing
  out+raced
out+rage
  out+rages
  out+rages
  out+rag+ing
  out+raged
out+ra+geous
  out+ra+geous+ly
  out+ra+geous+
  ness

out+range
out+ranges
out+rang+ing
out+ranged
out+rank
out+ranks
out+rank+ing
out+ranked
outré
out+reach
out+reaches
out+reach+ing
out+reached
out+ride
out+rides
out+rid+ing
out+rode
out+rid+den
out+rid+er
out+rid+ers
out+rig+ger
out+rig+gers
out+right
out+ri+val
out+ri+vals
out+ri+val+ling
or
out+ri+val+ing
U.S.
out+ri+valled
or
out+ri+valed
U.S.
out+root
out+roots
out+root+ing
out+root+ed
out+run
out+runs
out+run+ning
out+ran
out+run
out+rush
out+rushes
out+sell
out+sells
out+sell+ing
out+sold
out+set
out+sets
out+shine
out+shines
out+shin+ing
out+shone
out+shoot

out+shoots
out+shoot+ing
out+shot
out+side
out+sides
out+sid+er
out+sid+ers
out+sing
out+sings
out+sing+ing
out+sang
out+sung
out+sit
out+sits
out+sit+ting
out+sat
out+size
out+sizes
out+skirts
out+smart
out+smarts
out+smart+ing
out+smart+ed
out+span
out+spans
out+spans
out+span+ning
out+spanned
out+speak
out+speaks
out+speak+ing
out+spoke
out+spo+ken
out+spo+ken
out+spread
out+spreads
out+spread+ing
out+spread
out+sprint
out+sprints
out+sprint+ing
out+sprint+ed
out+stand+ing
out+stand+ing+ly
out+stare
out+stares
out+star+ing
out+stared
out+sta+tion
out+sta+tions
out+stay
out+stays
out+stay+ing
out+stayed
out+step

out+steps
out+step+ping
out+stepped
out+stretch
out+stretches
out+stretch+ing
out+stretched
out+strip
out+strips
out+strip+ping
out+stripped
out+take
out+takes
out+talk
out+talks
out+talk+ing
out+talked
out+think
out+thinks
out+think+ing
out+thought
out+turn
out+turns
out+value
out+values
out+valu+ing
out+valued
out+vote
out+votes
out+vot+ing
out+vot+ed
out+walk
out+walks
out+walk+ing
out+walked
out+ward
out+ward+ly
out+ward+ness
out+wards
out+wear
out+wears
out+wear+ing
out+wore
out+worn
out+weigh
out+weighs
out+weigh+ing
out+weighed
out+wit
out+wits
out+wit+ting
out+wit+ted
out+with
out+work
out+works

out+works
out+work+ing
out+worked or
out+wrought
out+work+er
out+work+ers
ouzel
ouzels
ouzo
ova
ovum
oval
ovals
Oval
oval+ity
oval+ly
oval+ness
ovar+ian
ovari+ec+to+my
ovari+ec+to+
mies
ova+ry
ova+ries
ovate
ovate+ly
ova+tion
ova+tions
ova+tion+al
oven
ovens
ovens
oven+ing
ovened
oven+able
oven+bird
oven+birds
oven-like
oven-ready
oven+ware
over
overs
over+abun+
dance
over+ac+cen+tu+
ate
over+ac+cen+tu+
ates
over+ac+cen+tu+
at+ing
over+ac+cen+tu+
at+ed
over+act
over+acts
over+act+ing
over+act+ed

over+ac+tive
over+af+fect
over+af+fects
over+af+fect+ing
over+af+fect+ed
over+age
over+ag+gres+sive
over+all
over+alls
over+am+bi+tious
over+ana+lyse
over+ana+lyses
over+ana+lys+ing
over+ana+lysed
over+ani+ma+tion
over+anx+ious
over+ap+pre+cia+tive
over+ap+pre+hen+sive
over+arch
over+arches
over+arch+ing
over+arched
over+ar+gu+men+ta+tive
over+arm
over+as+sert
over+as+serts
over+as+sert+ing
over+as+sert+ed
over+as+ser+tive
over+as+ser+tive+ness
over+as+sess+ment
over+as+sess+ments
over+as+sured
over+at+ten+tive
over+at+ten+tive+ly
over+awe
over+awes
over+aw+ing
over+awed
over+bal+ance
over+bal+ances

over+bal+ances
over+bal+anc+ing
over+bal+anced
over+bear
over+bears
over+bear+ing
over+bore
over+borne
over+bear+ing
over+bear+ing+ly
over+bid
over+bids
over+bids
over+bid+ding
over+bid
over+bid+den
or
over+bid
over+board
over+bold
over+book
over+books
over+book+ing
over+booked
over+brave
over+build
over+builds
over+build+ing
over+built
over+bulky
over+bur+den
over+bur+dens
over+bur+dens
over+bur+den+ing
over+bur+dened
over+bur+den+some
over+busy
over+buy
over+buys
over+buy+ing
over+bought
over+ca+pac+ity
over+care+ful
over+cast
over+casts
over+casts
over+cast+ing
over+cast
over+cau+tious
over+cen+trali+sa+tion

over+cen+trali+sa+tions
over+cen+trali+za+tion
over+cen+trali+za+tions
over+ce+re+bral
over+charge
over+charges
over+charges
over+charg+ing
over+charged
over+civ+il
over+civi+lise
over+civi+lises
over+civi+lis+ing
over+civi+lised
over+civi+lize
over+civi+lizes
over+civi+liz+ing
over+civi+lized
over+cloud
over+clouds
over+cloud+ing
over+cloud+ed
over+coat
over+coats
over+come
over+comes
over+com+ing
over+came
over+come
over+com+mon
over+com+pen+sate
over+com+pen+sates
over+com+pen+sat+ing
over+com+pen+sat+ed
over+com+peti+tive
over+com+pla+cen+cy
over+com+plex
over+com+pli+cate
over+com+pli+cates
over+com+pli+cat+ing

over+com+pli+cat+ed
over+con+cern
over+con+fi+dent
over+con+sci+en+tious
over+con+serva+tive
over+con+sid+er+ate
over+con+sump+tion
over+cook
over+cooks
over+cook+ing
over+cooked
over+cor+rec+tion
over+cor+rec+tions
over+cost+ly
over+criti+cal
over+crop
over+crops
over+crop+ping
over+cropped
over+crowd
over+crowds
over+crowd+ing
over+crowd+ed
over+cul+ti+vate
over+cul+ti+vates
over+cul+ti+vat+ing
over+cul+ti+vat+ed
over+cu+ri+ous
over+deco+rate
over+deco+rates
over+deco+rat+ing
over+deco+rat+ed
over+de+fen+sive
over+def+er+en+tial
over+deli+cate
over+de+pend+ence
over+de+pend+ent

over+de+tailed
over+de+vel+op
over+de+vel+
 ops
over+de+vel+op+
 ing
over+de+vel+
 oped
over+dili+gent
over+di+lute
over+di+lutes
over+di+lut+ing
over+di+lut+ed
over+dis+tant
over+di+ver+si+
 fy
over+di+ver+si+
 fies
over+di+ver+si+
 fy+ing
over+di+ver+si+
 fied
over+do
over+does
over+do+ing
over+did
over+done
over+dos+age
over+dos+ages
over+dose
over+doses
over+doses
over+dos+ing
over+dosed
over+draft
over+drafts
over+dra+mat+ic
over+drama+tise
over+drama+
 tises
over+drama+tis+
 ing
over+drama+
 tised
over+drama+tize
over+drama+
 tizes
over+drama+tiz+
 ing
over+drama+
 tized
over+draw
over+draws
over+draw+ing
over+drew

over+drawn
over+dress
over+dresses
over+dresses
over+dress+ing
over+dressed
over+drink
over+drinks
over+drink+ing
over+drank
over+drunk
over+drive
over+drives
over+driv+ing
over+drove
over+driv+en
over+dub
over+dubs
over+dub+bing
over+dubbed
over+due
over+eager
over+eat
over+eats
over+eat+ing
over+ate
over+eat+en
over+edu+cate
over+edu+cates
over+edu+cat+
 ing
over+edu+cat+
 ed
over+ef+fu+sive
over+elabo+rate
over+elabo+
 rates
over+elabo+rat+
 ing
over+elabo+rat+
 ed
over+em+bel+
 lish
over+em+bel+
 lishes
over+em+bel+
 lish+ing
over+em+bel+
 lished
over+emo+tion+
 al
over+em+pha+
 sis
over+em+pha+
 ses

over+em+pha+
 sise
over+em+pha+
 sises
over+em+pha+
 sis+ing
over+em+pha+
 sised
over+em+pha+
 size
over+em+pha+
 sizes
over+em+pha+
 siz+ing
over+em+pha+
 sized
over+em+phat+ic
over+en+thu+si+
 asm
over+en+thu+si+
 as+tic
over+es+ti+mate
over+es+ti+
 mates
over+es+ti+
 mates
over+es+ti+mat+
 ing
over+es+ti+mat+
 ed
over+es+ti+ma+
 tion
over+es+ti+ma+
 tions
over+ex+act+ing
over+ex+cit+able
over+ex+cite
over+ex+cites
over+ex+cit+ing
over+ex+cit+ed
over+ex+er+cise
over+ex+er+
 cises
over+ex+er+cis+
 ing
over+ex+er+
 cised
over+ex+ert
over+ex+erts
over+ex+ert+ing
over+ex+ert+ed
over+ex+pand
over+ex+pands
over+ex+pand+
 ing

over+ex+pand+
 ed
over+ex+pan+
 sion
over+ex+pan+
 sions
over+ex+pen+di+
 ture
over+ex+plic+it
over+ex+pose
over+ex+poses
over+ex+pos+
 ing
over+ex+posed
over+ex+po+sure
over+ex+po+
 sures
over+ex+pres+
 sive
over+ex+tend
over+ex+tends
over+ex+tend+
 ing
over+ex+tend+
 ed
over+fa+mil+iar
over+fan+ci+ful
over+far
over+fas+tidi+
 ous
over+feed
over+feeds
over+feed+ing
over+fed
over+fill
over+fills
over+fill+ing
over+filled
over+fish
over+fishes
over+fish+ing
over+fished
over+flow
over+flows
over+flows
over+flow+ing
over+flowed
over+flown
over+fly
over+flies
over+fly+ing
over+flew
over+flown
over+fold
over+folds

over+fond
over+full
over+fund+ing
over+fur+nish
  over+fur+nishes
  over+fur+nish+ing
  over+fur+nished
over+gar+ment
over+gar+ments
over+gen+er+ali+sa+tion
over+gen+er+ali+sa+tions
over+gen+er+al+ise
  over+gen+er+al+ises
  over+gen+er+al+is+ing
  over+gen+er+al+ised
over+gen+er+ali+za+tion
over+gen+er+ali+za+tions
over+gen+er+al+ize
  over+gen+er+al+izes
  over+gen+er+al+iz+ing
  over+gen+er+al+ized
over+gen+er+ous
over+grow
  over+grows
  over+grow+ing
  over+grew
  over+grown
over+growth
over+hand
  over+hands
  over+hand+ing
  over+hand+ed
over+hang
  over+hangs
  over+hangs
  over+hang+ing
  over+hung
over+hasti+ly
over+hasty
over+haul
  over+hauls
  over+hauls

over+haul+ing
over+hauled
over+head
  over+heads
  over+heads
over+hear
  over+hears
  over+hear+ing
  over+heard
over+heat
  over+heats
  over+heat+ing
  over+heat+ed
over+hur+ried
over+ideal+ise
  over+ideal+ises
  over+ideal+is+ing
  over+ideal+ised
over+ideal+is+tic
over+ideal+ize
  over+ideal+izes
  over+ideal+iz+ing
  over+ideal+ized
Over+ijs+sel
over+im+agi+na+tive
over+im+press
  over+im+presses
  over+im+press+ing
  over+im+pressed
over+in+cline
  over+in+clines
  over+in+clin+ing
  over+in+clined
over+in+dulge
  over+in+dulges
  over+in+dulg+ing
  over+in+dulged
over+in+dul+gence
over+in+dus+tri+al+ise
  over+in+dus+tri+al+ises
  over+in+dus+tri+al+is+ing
  over+in+dus+tri+al+ised

over+in+dus+tri+al+ize
  over+in+dus+tri+al+izes
  over+in+dus+tri+al+iz+ing
  over+in+dus+tri+al+ized
over+in+flate
  over+in+flates
  over+in+flat+ing
  over+in+flat+ed
over+in+flu+ence
  over+in+flu+ences
  over+in+flu+enc+ing
  over+in+flu+enced
over+in+sist+ence
over+in+sure
  over+in+sures
  over+in+sur+ing
  over+in+sured
over+in+tel+lec+tual
over+in+tense
over+in+ter+est
over+in+vest
  over+in+vests
  over+in+vest+ing
  over+in+vest+ed
over+is+sue
  over+is+sues
  over+is+su+ing
  over+is+sued
over+joy
  over+joys
  over+joy+ing
  over+joyed
over+kill
over+la+den
over+land
  over+lands
  over+land+ing
  over+land+ed
  over+land+er
  over+land+ers
over+lap
  over+laps
  over+laps
  over+lap+ping

over+lapped
over+large
over+lav+ish
over+lay
  over+lays
  over+lays
  over+lay+ing
  over+laid
over+leaf
over+leap
  over+leaps
  over+leap+ing
  over+leaped *or* over+leapt
over+lie
  over+lies
  over+ly+ing
  over+lay
  over+lain
over+load
  over+loads
  over+loads
  over+load+ing
  over+load+ed
over+long
over+look
  over+looks
  over+look+ing
  over+looked
over+lord
  over+lords
  over+lord+ship
over+ly
over+mag+ni+fy
  over+mag+ni+fies
  over+mag+ni+fy+ing
  over+mag+ni+fied
over+man
  over+men
  over+mans
  over+man+ning
  over+manned
over+man+age
  over+man+ages
  over+man+ag+ing
  over+man+aged
over+many
over+master
  over+masters
  over+master+ing

over+mastered
over+match
over+matches
over+match+ing
over+matched
over+meas+ure
over+meas+ures
over+mod+est
over+modi+fy
over+modi+fies
over+modi+fy+ing
over+modi+fied
over+much
over+nice
over+night
over+op+ti+mism
over+op+ti+mis+tic
over+par+ticu+lar
over+pass
over+passes
over+passes
over+pass+ing
over+passed
or
over+past
over+pay
over+pays
over+pay+ing
over+paid
over+pes+si+mis+tic
over+play
over+plays
over+play+ing
over+played
over+popu+late
over+popu+lates
over+popu+lat+ing
over+popu+lat+ed
over+popu+la+tion
over+pow+er
over+pow+ers
over+pow+er+ing
over+pow+ered
over+pow+er+ful
over+praise
over+praises

over+prais+ing
over+praised
over+pre+cise
over+price
over+prices
over+pric+ing
over+priced
over+print
over+prints
over+prints
over+print+ing
over+print+ed
over+pro+duce
over+pro+duces
over+pro+duc+ing
over+pro+duced
over+pro+duc+tion
over+pro+tec+tive
over+proud
over+pub+li+cise
over+pub+li+cises
over+pub+li+cis+ing
over+pub+li+cised
over+pub+li+cize
over+pub+li+cizes
over+pub+li+ciz+ing
over+pub+li+cized
over+quali+fied
over+rate
over+rates
over+rat+ing
over+rat+ed
over+reach
over+reaches
over+reach+ing
over+reached
over+react
over+reacts
over+react+ing
over+react+ed
over+reac+tion
over+reac+tions
over+re+li+ance
over+re+strict
over+re+stricts

over+re+strict+ing
over+re+strict+ed
over+ride
over+rides
over+rides
over+rid+ing
over+rode
over+rid+den
over+rid+er
over+rid+ers
over+right+eous
over+ripe
over+ro+man+ti+cise
over+ro+man+ti+cises
over+ro+man+ti+cis+ing
over+ro+man+ti+cised
over+ro+man+ti+cize
over+ro+man+ti+cizes
over+ro+man+ti+ciz+ing
over+ro+man+ti+cized
over+rule
over+rules
over+rul+ing
over+ruled
over+run
over+runs
over+runs
over+run+ning
over+ran
over+run
over+scep+ti+cal
over+scru+pu+lous
over+seas
over+see
over+sees
over+see+ing
over+saw
over+seen
over+seer
over+seers
over+sell
over+sells
over+sell+ing
over+sold

over+sen+si+tive
over+set
over+sets
over+set+ting
over+set
over+se+vere
over+sew
over+sews
over+sew+ing
over+sewn or
over+sewed
over+sexed
over+shad+ow
over+shad+ows
over+shad+ow+ing
over+shad+owed
over+sharp
over+shoe
over+shoes
over+shoot
over+shoots
over+shoot+ing
over+shot
over+sight
over+sights
over+sim+pli+fy
over+sim+pli+fies
over+sim+pli+fy+ing
over+sim+pli+fied
over+size
over+sizes
over+skirt
over+skirts
over+sleep
over+sleeps
over+sleep+ing
over+slept
over+sleeve
over+sleeves
over+smart
over+so+lici+tous
over+so+phis+ti+cat+ed
over+spe+ciali+sa+tion
over+spe+ciali+sa+tions
over+spe+cial+ise

over+spe+cial+ises
over+spe+cial+is+ing
over+spe+cial+ised
over+spe+ciali+za+tion
over+spe+ciali+za+tions
over+spe+cial+ize
over+spe+cial+izes
over+spe+cial+iz+ing
over+spe+cial+ized
over+spend
over+spends
over+spends
over+spend+ing
over+spent
over+spill
over+spills
over+spills
over+spill+ing
over+spilt *or*
over+spilled
over+spread
over+spreads
over+spread+ing
over+spread
over+staff
over+staffs
over+staff+ing
over+staffed
over+state
over+states
over+stat+ing
over+stat+ed
over+state+ment
over+state+ments
over+stay
over+stays
over+stay+ing
over+stayed
over+steer
over+steers
over+steer+ing
over+steered
over+step
over+steps

over+step+ping
over+stepped
over+stimu+late
over+stimu+lates
over+stimu+lat+ing
over+stimu+lat+ed
over+stock
over+stocks
over+stock+ing
over+stocked
over+strain
over+strains
over+strain+ing
over+strained
over+stretch
over+stretches
over+stretch+ing
over+stretched
over+strict
over+strung
over+stuff
over+stuffs
over+stuff+ing
over+stuffed
over+sub+scribe
over+sub+scribes
over+sub+scrib+ing
over+sub+scribed
over+sub+tle
over+sup+ply
over+sup+plies
over+sup+ply+ing
over+sup+plied
over+sus+cep+tible
over+sus+pi+cious
over+sys+tem+at+ic
overt
over+take
over+takes
over+tak+ing
over+took
over+tak+en
over+tax
over+taxes

over+tax+ing
over+taxed
over+tech+ni+cal
over+throw
over+throws
over+throws
over+throw+ing
over+threw
over+thrown
over+thrust
over+thrusts
over+time
over+times
over+tim+ing
over+timed
over+tire
over+tires
over+tir+ing
over+tired
overt+ly
over+tone
over+tones
over+trade
over+trades
over+trad+ing
over+trad+ed
over+train
over+trains
over+train+ing
over+trained
over+trump
over+trumps
over+trump+ing
over+trumped
over+ture
over+tures
over+tures
over+tur+ing
over+tured
over+turn
over+turns
over+turns
over+turn+ing
over+turned
over+use
over+uses
over+us+ing
over+used
over+value
over+values
over+valu+ing
over+valued
over+view
over+vio+lent
over+wa+ter

over+wa+ters
over+wa+ter+ing
over+wa+tered
over+ween+ing
over+ween+ing+ness
over+weigh
over+weighs
over+weigh+ing
over+weighed
over+weight
over+weights
over+weight+ing
over+weight+ed
over+whelm
over+whelms
over+whelm+ing
over+whelmed
over+will+ing
over+wind
over+winds
over+wind+ing
over+wound
over+wise
over+work
over+works
over+work+ing
over+worked
over+write
over+writes
over+writ+ing
over+wrote
over+writ+ten
over+wrought
over+zeal+ous
Ovett
Ovid
Ovid+ian
ovi+du+cal
ovi+duct
ovi+ducts
ovi+duc+tal
Ovie+do
ovi+form
ovine
ovi+par+ity
ovipa+rous
ovipa+rous+ly
ovi+pos+it
ovi+pos+its
ovi+pos+it+ing
ovi+pos+it+ed

ovi+posi+tor
ovi+posi+tors
ovoid
ovoids
ovo+vi+vi+par+
ity
ovo+vi+vipa+
rous
ovu+lar
ovu+late
ovu+lates
ovu+lat+ing
ovu+lat+ed
ovu+la+tion
ovu+la+tions
ovule
ovules
ovum
ova
ow
owe
owes
ow+ing
owed
Owen
Owens
Ower+ri
ow+ing
owl
owls
owl+et
owl+ets
owl+ish
own
owns
own+ing
owned
own+er
own+ers
owner-occupier
owner-occupiers

own+er+ship
ox
oxen
oxa+lis
ox+blood
ox+bow
ox+bows
Ox+bridge
oxen
ox+eye
ox+eyes
ox-eyed
Ox+fam
Ox+ford
city
Oxford
person
Ox+ford+shire
oxi+dant
oxi+dants
oxi+date
oxi+dates
oxi+dat+ing
oxi+dat+ed
oxi+da+tion
oxi+da+tion+al
oxi+dation-
reduction
oxi+da+tive
ox+ide
ox+ides
oxi+di+sa+tion
oxi+dise
oxi+dises
oxi+dis+ing
oxi+dised
oxi+di+za+tion
oxi+dize
oxi+dizes
oxi+diz+ing
oxi+dized

ox+lip
ox+lips
Oxo+nian
Oxo+nians
ox+pecker
ox+peckers
ox+tail
ox+ter
ox+ters
ox+tongue
ox+tongues
Oxus
oxy+acety+lene
oxy+acid
oxy+acids
oxy+gen
oxy+gen+ate
oxy+gen+ates
oxy+gen+at+ing
oxy+gen+at+ed
oxy+gena+tion
oxy+gena+tions
oxy+gen+ic
oxy+gen+ise
oxy+gen+ises
oxy+gen+is+ing
oxy+gen+ised
oxy+gen+is+er
oxy+gen+is+ers
oxy+gen+ize
oxy+gen+izes
oxy+gen+iz+ing
oxy+gen+ized
oxy+gen+iz+er
oxy+gen+iz+ers
ox+yg+enous
oxy+hae+mo+glo+
bin
oxy+hy+dro+gen
oxy+mo+ron
oxy+mo+ra

oyer and ter+mi+
ner
oyes
oyez
Oyo
oys+ter
oys+ters
oys+ters
oys+ter+ing
oys+tered
oyster+catcher
oyster+catchers
Oz
Özal
Oza+lid
Trademark
Oza+lids
Ozark
ozo+cerite
ozo+kerite
ozone
ozone-friendly
ozon+ic
ozo+ni+sa+tion
ozo+ni+sa+tions
ozo+nise
ozo+nises
ozo+nis+ing
ozo+nised
ozo+nis+er
ozo+nis+ers
ozo+ni+za+tion
ozo+ni+za+tions
ozo+nize
ozo+nizes
ozo+niz+ing
ozo+nized
ozo+niz+er
ozo+niz+ers
ozo+no+sphere
ozo+nous

P

p
 p's
P
 P's *or*
Ps
pa
 pas
Pabst
pabu+lum
paca
 pacas
pace
 paces
 paces
 pac+ing
 paced
pace
pace+maker
 pace+makers
pac+er
 pac+ers
pace+setter
 pace+setters
pace+way
 pace+ways
pa+cha
 pa+chas
Pachelbel
pa+chi+si
Pa+chu+ca
pachy+derm
 pachy+derms
pachy+der+ma+
 tous
paci+fi+able
pa+cif+ic
Pa+cif+ic
pa+cifi+cal+ly
paci+fi+ca+tion
 paci+fi+ca+tions
paci+fi+er
 paci+fi+ers
paci+fism
paci+fist
 paci+fists

paci+fy
paci+fies
paci+fy+ing
paci+fied
Pacino
pack
packs
packs
pack+ing
packed
pack+able
pack+age
pack+ages
pack+ages
pack+ag+ing
pack+aged
pack+ag+er
pack+ag+ers
pack+ag+ing
pack+ag+ings
pack+er
pack+ers
pack+et
pack+ets
pack+ets
pack+et+ing
pack+et+ed
pack+horse
pack+horses
pack+ing
pack+ings
pack+saddle
pack+saddles
pack+thread
pact
pacts
pad
 pads
 pads
pad+ding
pad+ded
Pa+dang
pad+ding
pad+dle
 pad+dles

pad+dles
pad+dling
pad+dled
pad+dler
 pad+dlers
pad+dock
 pad+docks
pad+dy
 pad+dies
pad+emel+on
 pad+emel+ons
Pa+der+born
Paderewski
pad+lock
 pad+locks
 pad+locks
 pad+lock+ing
 pad+locked
Pa+do+va
pa+dre
 pa+dres
pad+saw
 pad+saws
Pad+ua
Pa+dus
paean
 paeans
paed+er+ast
 paed+er+asts
 paed+er+as+tic
 paed+er+as+ty
pae+di+at+ric
pae+dia+tri+cian
pae+dia+tri+
 cians
pae+di+at+rics
pae+do+mor+
 pho+sis
pae+do+phile
 pae+do+philes
pae+do+philia
pae+do+phili+ac
 pae+do+phili+
 acs
pa+el+la

pa+el+las
paeo+ny
 paeo+nies
Paes+tum
pa+gan
 pa+gans
Paganini
pa+gan+ise
 pa+gan+ises
 pa+gan+is+ing
 pa+gan+ised
pa+gan+ish
pa+gan+ism
pa+gan+ize
 pa+gan+izes
 pa+gan+iz+ing
 pa+gan+ized
page
 pages
 pages
 pag+ing
 paged
Page
pag+eant
 pag+eants
pag+eant+ry
 pag+eant+ries
page+boy
 page+boys
page-turner
 page-turners
pagi+nate
 pagi+nates
 pagi+nat+ing
 pagi+nat+ed
pagi+na+tion
 pagi+na+tions
Pagnol
pa+go+da
 pa+go+das
Pago Pago
Pa+hang
Pahlavi
 surname
Pah+la+vi

language
paid
paid-up
Paign+ton
pail
 pails
pail+lasse
 pail+lasses
pain
 pains
 pains
 pain+ing
 pained
Paine
pained
pain+ful
pain+ful+ly
pain+ful+ness
pain+killer
 pain+killers
pain+less
pains
pains+taking
pains+taking+ly
pains+taking+
 ness
paint
 paints
 paints
 paint+ing
 paint+ed
paint+box
 paint+boxes
paint+brush
 paint+brushes
paint+er
 paint+ers
paint+er+ly
paint+ing
 paint+ings
paint+work
pair
 pairs *or*
 pair
 pairs
 pair+ing
 paired
pais+ley
 pais+leys
Pais+ley
place name
Paisley
surname
pa+jam+as
U.S.

pa+keha
 pa+kehas
Paki
 Pakis
Pa+ki+stan
Pa+ki+stani
 Pa+ki+stanis
pa+ko+ra
 pa+ko+ras
pal
 pals
 pals
pal+ling
palled
pal+ace
 pal+aces
Palacio Valdés
pala+din
 pala+dins
palaeo+bota+nist
 palaeo+bota+
 nists
palaeo+bota+ny
Palaeo+cene
palaeo+cli+ma+
 tolo+gist
 palaeo+cli+ma+
 tolo+gists
palaeo+cli+ma+
 tol+ogy
palaeo+eco+logi+
 cal
palaeo+ecolo+
 gist
 palaeo+ecolo+
 gists
palaeo+ecol+ogy
palae+og+ra+
 pher
 palae+og+ra+
 phers
palaeo+graph+ic
palaeo+graphi+
 cal
palae+og+ra+phy
Palaeo+lith+ic
palaeo+mag+net+
 ism
palae+on+to+logi+
 cal
palae+on+tolo+
 gist
 palae+on+tolo+
 gists

palae+on+tol+
 ogy
Palaeo+zo+ic
pal+an+keen
 pal+an+keens
pal+an+quin
 pal+an+quins
pal+at+abil+ity
pal+at+able
pal+at+able+ness
pal+at+ably
pala+tal
 pala+tals
pala+tali+sa+tion
 pala+tali+sa+
 tions
pala+tal+ise
 pala+tal+ises
 pala+tal+is+ing
 pala+tal+ised
pala+tali+za+tion
 pala+tali+za+
 tions
pala+tal+ize
 pala+tal+izes
 pala+tal+iz+ing
 pala+tal+ized
pala+tal+ly
pal+ate
 pal+ates
pa+la+tial
pa+la+tial+ly
pa+lati+nate
 pa+lati+nates
Pa+lati+nate
 Pa+lati+nates
pala+tine
 pala+tines
Pala+tine
 Pala+tines
pa+la+ver
 pa+la+vers
Pa+la+wan
pale
 pales
 pal+ing
 paled
 pal+er
 pal+est
pale+face
 pale+faces
pale+ly
Pa+lem+bang
Pa+len+cia
pale+ness

Pa+len+que
Pa+ler+mo
Pal+es+tine
Pal+es+tin+ian
 Pal+es+tin+ians
Palestrina
pal+ette
 pal+ettes
Paley
pal+frey
 pal+freys
Pali
pali+mo+ny
pal+imp+sest
 pal+imp+sests
pal+in+drome
 pal+in+dromes
pal+in+drom+ic
pal+ing
 pal+ings
pali+sade
 pali+sades
pal+ish
pall
 palls
 palls
 pall+ing
 palled
Pal+la+dian
Pal+la+di+an+ism
Palladio
pal+la+dium
 pal+la+diums
Pallas
pall+bearer
 pall+bearers
pal+let
 pal+lets
pal+leti+sa+tion
pal+let+ise
 pal+let+ises
 pal+let+is+ing
 pal+let+ised
pal+leti+za+tion
pal+let+ize
 pal+let+izes
 pal+let+iz+ing
 pal+let+ized
pal+li+asse
 pal+li+asses
pal+li+ate
 pal+li+ates
 pal+li+at+ing
 pal+li+at+ed
pal+lia+tion

pal+lia+tions
pal+lia+tive
pal+lia+tives
pal+lia+tive+ly
pal+lid
pal+lid+ity
pal+lid+ly
pal+lid+ness
pall-mall
pall-malls
Pall Mall
pal+lor
pal+lors
pal+ly
pal+li+er
pal+li+est
palm
palms
palms
palm+ing
palmed
Pal+ma
place name
Palma
surname
pal+ma+ceous
pal+mar
pal+mate
pal+mat+ed
Palme
palm+er
palm+ers
Palmer
surname
Palm+er
place name
Palm+er+ston
place name
Palmerston
surname
pal+met+to
pal+met+tos
or
pal+met+toes
Pal+mi+ra
palm+ist
palm+ists
palm+is+try
palm-oil
palmy
palmi+er
palmi+est
pal+my+ra
pal+my+ras
Pal+my+ra

Palo Alto
Palo+mar
palo+mi+no
palo+mi+nos
Pa+los
palp
palps
pal+pabil+ity
pal+pable
pal+pably
pal+pate
pal+pates
pal+pat+ing
pal+pat+ed
pal+pa+tion
pal+pa+tions
pal+pe+bral
pal+pi+tant
pal+pi+tate
pal+pi+tates
pal+pi+tat+ing
pal+pi+tat+ed
pal+pi+ta+tion
pal+pi+ta+tions
pal+pus
pal+pi
pal+sied
pal+sy
pal+sies
pal+ter
pal+ters
pal+ter+ing
pal+tered
pal+tri+ly
pal+tri+ness
pal+try
pal+tri+er
pal+tri+est
pa+lu+dal
palu+dism
paly+no+logi+cal
paly+nolo+gist
paly+nolo+gists
paly+nol+ogy
Pa+mirs
pam+pas
pam+pean
pam+per
pam+pers
pam+per+ing
pam+pered
pam+per+er
pam+per+ers
pam+phlet
pam+phlets

pam+phlet+eer
pam+phlet+eers
pam+phlet+eers
pam+phlet+eer+
  ing
pam+phlet+
  eered
Pam+phylia
Pam+plo+na
pan
pans
pans
pan+ning
panned
Pan
pana+cea
pana+ceas
pana+cean
pa+nache
pa+naches
pa+na+da
Pa+na+ji
Pana+ma
Pana+ma+nian
Pana+ma+nians
Pan-Ameri+can
Pan-Ameri+can+
  ism
pana+tel+la
pana+tel+las
Pa+nay
pan+cake
pan+cakes
pan+cakes
pan+cak+ing
pan+caked
pan+chro+mat+ic
pan+chro+ma+
  tism
pan+cre+as
pan+cre+ases
pan+cre+at+ic
pan+crea+tin
pan+creo+zy+
  min
pan+da
pan+das
pan+da+nus
pan+da+nuses
Pandarus
Pan+dean
pan+dect
pan+dects
pan+dem+ic
pan+dem+ics

pan+de+mo+
  nium
pan+der
pan+ders
pan+ders
pan+der+ing
pan+dered
pan+dit
pan+dits
Pandora
Pandore
pane
panes
pané
pan+egyr+ic
pan+egyr+ics
pan+egyri+cal
pan+egyri+cal+ly
pan+egyr+ist
pan+egyr+ists
pan+el
pan+els
pan+els
pan+el+ling *or*
pan+el+ing
U.S.
pan+elled *or*
pan+eled
U.S.
pan+el+ing
U.S.
pan+el+ist
U.S.
pan+el+ists
pan+el+ling
pan+el+list
pan+el+lists
Pan-European
pang
pangs
pan+ga
pan+gas
Pan+gaea
Pan+gea
Pang-fou
pan+go+lin
pan+go+lins
Pan+go Pan+go
pan+han+dle
pan+han+dles
pan+han+dles
pan+han+dling
pan+han+dled
pan+han+dler
pan+han+dlers

Pan+hel+len+ic
pan+ic
 pan+ics
 pan+ics
 pan+ick+ing
 pan+icked
Pan+ic
pan+icky
pani+cle
 pani+cles
pani+cled
panic-stricken
panic-struck
pa+nicu+late
pan+jan+drum
 pan+jan+drums
Pan+jim
Pankhurst
Pan+mun+jom
pan+nage
pan+ni+er
 pan+ni+ers
pan+ni+kin
 pan+ni+kins
Pan+no+nia
pano+plied
pano+ply
 pano+plies
pan+op+tic
pano+ra+ma
 pano+ra+mas
pano+ram+ic
pano+rami+cal+ly
pan+pipes
pan+sy
 pan+sies
pant
 pants
 pants
 pant+ing
 pant+ed
pan+ta+lets
pan+ta+lettes
pan+ta+loon
 pan+ta+loons
 pan+ta+loons
pan+tech+ni+con
 pan+tech+ni+
 cons
Pan+tel+le+ria
pan+theism
pan+theist
 pan+theists
pan+theis+tic
pan+theis+ti+cal

pan+theis+ti+cal+
 ly
pan+the+on
 pan+the+ons
Pan+the+on
pan+ther
 pan+thers or
 pan+ther
panties
pan+ti+hose
pan+tile
 pan+tiles
pan+ti+soc+ra+
 cy
pan+ti+soc+ra+
 cies
pan+to
 pan+tos
pan+to+graph
 pan+to+graphs
pan+to+graph+ic
pan+to+mime
 pan+to+mimes
pan+to+mim+ic
pan+to+mim+ist
pan+to+mim+
 ists
pan+to+then+ic
pan+try
 pan+tries
pants
pan+ty+hose
Panufnik
pan+zer
 pan+zers
Paolozzi
Pao+ting
Pao-ting
Pao+tow
pap
 paps
papa
 father or pope
 papas
pa+pa
 soft clay
pa+pa+cy
 pa+pa+cies
Papadopoulos
pa+pa+in
pa+pal
pa+pal+ly
Papandreou
pa+pa+raz+zo
 pa+pa+raz+zi

pa+pa+vera+
 ceous
pa+pa+ver+ine
pa+paw
 pa+paws
pa+pa+ya
 pa+pa+yas
Pa+pe+ete
Papen
pa+per
 pa+pers
 pa+pers
pa+per+ing
pa+pered
paper+back
 paper+backs
paper+bark
 paper+barks
paper+boy
 paper+boys
paper+clip
 paper+clips
paper-cutter
 paper-cutters
pa+per+er
 pa+per+ers
paper+girl
 paper+girls
paper+hanger
 paper+hangers
paper+knife
 paper+knives
paper+weight
 paper+weights
paper+work
pa+pery
Pa+phi+an
Paph+la+go+nia
Pa+phos
 place name
Paphos
 mythical
 character
Paphus
papier-mâché
pa+pilio+na+
 ceous
pa+pil+la
 pa+pil+lae
pa+pil+lary
pa+pil+late
pap+il+lo+ma
 pap+il+lo+ma+
 ta or
pap+il+lo+mas

pap+il+lon
pap+il+lons
pap+il+lote
pap+il+lotes
pa+pist
 pa+pists
pa+pis+ti+cal
pa+pist+ry
pa+poose
 pa+pooses
pap+pose
pap+pous
pap+pus
 pap+pi
pap+ri+ka
Pa+pua
Pa+puan
 Pa+puans
papu+la
 papu+lae
papu+lar
pap+ule
 pap+ules
papy+rolo+gist
 papy+rolo+gists
papy+rol+ogy
pa+py+rus
 pa+py+ri or
 pa+py+ruses
par
para
 monetary unit
 paras or
 para
para
 soldier
 paras
Pará
pa+raba+sis
 pa+raba+ses
para+bio+sis
para+bi+ot+ic
para+ble
 para+bles
pa+rabo+la
 pa+rabo+las
para+bol+ic
para+boli+cal
para+boli+cal+ly
pa+rabo+loid
 pa+rabo+loids
pa+rabo+loi+dal
Paracelsus
pa+ra+ceta+mol

pa+ra+ceta+
mols
pa+rach+ro+nism
pa+rach+ro+
nisms
para+chute
para+chutes
para+chutes
para+chut+ing
para+chut+ed
para+chut+ist
para+chut+ists
Para+clete
pa+rade
pa+rades
pa+rades
pa+rad+ing
pa+rad+ed
pa+rad+er
pa+rad+ers
para+digm
para+digms
para+dig+mat+ic
para+di+sai+cal
para+dise
para+dises
para+disi+ac
para+di+sia+cal
para+dox
para+doxes
para+doxi+cal
para+doxi+cal+ly
par+af+fin
par+af+fins
para+glid+ing
para+gon
para+gons
para+graph
para+graphs
para+graphs
para+graph+ing
para+graphed
para+graphia
para+graph+ic
Para+guay
Para+guay+an
Para+guay+ans
para+hy+dro+
gen
Pa+raí+ba
para+keet
para+keets
par+al+de+hyde
para+leip+sis
para+leip+ses

para+lip+sis
para+lip+ses
par+al+lac+tic
par+al+lax
par+al+laxes
par+al+lel
par+al+lels
par+al+lels
par+al+lel+ing
par+al+leled
par+al+lel+epi+
ped
par+al+lel+epi+
peds
par+al+lel+epi+
pedon
par+al+lel+epi+
pedons
par+al+lel+ing
par+al+lel+ism
par+al+lelo+gram
par+al+lelo+
grams
pa+ralo+gism
pa+ralo+gisms
pa+ralo+gist
pa+ralo+gists
Para+lym+pi+an
Para+lym+pi+
ans
para+ly+sa+tion
para+ly+sa+
tions
para+lyse
para+lyses
para+lys+ing
para+lysed
pa+raly+sis
pa+raly+ses
para+lyt+ic
para+lyt+ics
para+ly+za+tion
U.S.
para+ly+za+
tions
para+lyze
U.S.
para+lyzes
para+lyz+ing
para+lyzed
para+mag+net+ic
para+mag+net+
ism
Para+mari+bo
para+mat+ta

para+mecium
para+mecia
para+med+ic
para+med+ics
para+medi+cal
para+medi+cals
pa+ram+eter
pa+ram+eters
para+met+ric
para+mili+tary
para+mount
para+mount+cy
para+mount+ly
par+amour
par+amours
Pa+ra+ná
pa+rang
pa+rangs
para+noia
para+noias
para+noi+ac
para+noi+acs
para+no+ic
para+no+ics
para+noid
para+noids
para+nor+mal
para+pente
para+pentes
para+pet
para+pets
par+aph
par+aphs
para+pher+na+lia
para+phrase
para+phrases
para+phrases
para+phras+ing
para+phrased
para+phras+tic
para+plegia
para+plegic
para+plegics
para+prax+is
para+praxes
para+psy+cholo+
gist
para+psy+
cholo+gists
para+psy+chol+
ogy
Para+quat
Trademark
paras+cend+ing
para+sele+ne

para+sele+nae
para+site
para+sites
para+sit+ic
para+siti+cal
para+siti+cal+ly
para+sit+ism
para+si+toid
para+si+toids
para+sit+olo+gist
para+sit+olo+
gists
para+sit+ol+ogy
para+ski+ing
para+sol
para+sols
para+sui+cide
para+sui+cides
para+sym+pa+
thet+ic
para+syn+the+
sis
para+syn+thet+ic
para+tac+tic
para+tax+is
para+thi+on
para+troops
para+vane
para+vanes
par avion
par+zo+an
para+zoa
par+boil
par+boils
par+boil+ing
par+boiled
par+buck+le
par+buck+les
par+buck+les
par+buck+ling
par+buck+led
Parcae
par+cel
par+cels
par+cels
par+cel+ling *or*
par+cel+ing
U.S.
par+celled *or*
par+celed
U.S.
parch
parches
parch+ing
parched

Par+chee+si
Trademark
parch+ment
parch+ments
pard
pards
par+don
par+dons
par+dons
par+don+ing
par+doned
par+don+able
par+don+ably
par+don+er
par+don+ers
Par+du+bi+ce
pare
pares
par+ing
pared
Paré
par+egor+ic
pa+rei+ra
pa+ren+chy+ma
par+en+chyma+
tous
par+ent
par+ents
par+ent+age
pa+ren+tal
par+en+ter+al
pa+ren+thesis
pa+ren+theses
pa+ren+thesise
pa+ren+thesises
pa+ren+thesis+
ing
pa+ren+thesised
pa+ren+thesize
pa+ren+thesizes
pa+ren+thesiz+
ing
pa+ren+thesized
par+en+thet+ic
par+en+the+ti+
cal
par+en+the+ti+
cal+ly
par+ent+hood
par+ent+ing
par+er
par+ers
par+er+gon
par+er+ga
pa+resis

pa+reses
pa+ret+ic
Pareto
par+fait
par+faits
par+get
par+gets
par+get+ing
par+get+ed
par+he+lia+cal
par+he+lic
par+he+li+on
par+he+lia
pa+ri+ah
pa+ri+ahs
Parian
Parians
Pa+ri+cu+tín
pa+ri+etal
pa+ri+etals
pari-mutuel
pari-mutuels *or*
paris-mutuels
par+ing
par+ings
pari pas+su
Par+is
place name
Paris
person's name
par+ish
par+ishes
pa+rish+ion+er
pa+rish+ion+ers
Pa+ris+ian
Pa+ris+ians
par+ity
par+ities
park
parks
parks
park+ing
parked
Park
par+ka
par+kas
Parker
Parkes
par+kin
par+kins
park+land
park+lands
parky
parki+er
parki+est

par+lance
par+lances
par+lan+do
par+ley
par+leys
par+leys
par+ley+ing
par+leyed
par+lia+ment
par+lia+ments
Par+lia+ment
Par+lia+ments
par+lia+men+tar+
ian
par+lia+men+tar+
ians
par+lia+men+ta+
ry
par+lor
U.S.
par+lors
par+lour
par+lours
par+lous
par+lous+ly
Par+ma
Parmenides
Par+me+san
Parmigianino
Par+na+hi+ba
Par+naí+ba
Par+nas+sian
Par+nas+sus
Parnell
Par+nel+lism
Par+nel+lite
Par+nel+lites
pa+ro+chial
pa+ro+chi+al+
ism
pa+ro+chi+al+ly
pa+rod+ic
pa+rodi+cal
paro+dist
paro+dists
paro+dy
paro+dies
paro+dies
paro+dy+ing
paro+died
pa+rol
pa+rols
pa+role
pa+roles
pa+roles

pa+rol+ing
pa+roled
pa+rolee
pa+rolees
paro+no+ma+sia
paro+no+ma+
sias
Pár+os
pa+rot+id
pa+rot+ids
paro+ti+tis
par+ox+ysm
par+ox+ysms
par+ox+ys+mal
par+quet
par+quets
par+quets
par+quet+ing
par+queted
par+quet+ry
parr
parrs *or*
parr
Parr
par+ra+keet
par+ra+keets
par+ra+mat+ta
par+ri+cid+al
par+ri+cide
par+ri+cides
par+rot
par+rots
par+rots
par+rot+ing
par+rot+ed
parrot-fashion
parrot+fish
parrot+fish *or*
parrot+fishes
par+ry
par+ries
par+ries
par+ry+ing
par+ried
Parry
parse
parses
pars+ing
parsed
par+sec
par+secs
Par+see
Par+sees
Par+see+ism
par+ser

par+sers
Par+si
Par+sis
Parsifal
par+si+mo+ni+
  ous
par+si+mo+ni+
  ous+ly
par+si+mo+ny
pars+ley
pars+leys
pars+nip
pars+nips
par+son
par+sons
par+son+age
par+son+ages
Parsons
part
parts
parts
part+ing
part+ed
par+take
par+takes
par+tak+ing
par+took
par+tak+en
par+tak+er
par+tak+ers
par+terre
par+terres
par+theno+gen+
  esis
par+theno+genet+
  ic
Par+the+non
Parthenopaeus
Parthenope
Par+thia
Par+thian
  Par+thians
par+tial
par+tials
par+tial+ity
  par+tial+ities
par+tial+ly
par+tial+ness
part+ible
par+tici+pant
  par+tici+pants
par+tici+pate
  par+tici+pates
par+tici+pat+ing
par+tici+pat+ed

par+tici+pa+tion
par+tici+pa+tor
  par+tici+pa+tors
  par+tici+pa+tory
par+ti+cipi+al
par+ti+cipi+al+ly
par+ti+ci+ple
  par+ti+ci+ples
par+ti+cle
  par+ti+cles
parti-coloured
par+ticu+lar
  par+ticu+lars
par+ticu+lari+sa+
    tion
par+ticu+lari+sa+
    tions
par+ticu+lar+ise
  par+ticu+lar+
    ises
par+ticu+lar+is+
    ing
par+ticu+lar+
    ised
par+ticu+lar+ism
par+ticu+lar+ist
  par+ticu+lar+
    ists
par+ticu+lar+ity
  par+ticu+lar+
    ities
par+ticu+lari+za+
    tion
par+ticu+lari+za+
    tions
par+ticu+lar+ize
  par+ticu+lar+
    izes
par+ticu+lar+iz+
    ing
par+ticu+lar+
    ized
par+ticu+lar+ly
par+ticu+late
  par+ticu+lates
part+ing
  part+ings
par+ti+san
  par+ti+sans
par+ti+san+ship
par+ti+ta
par+ti+te or
  par+ti+tas
par+tite
par+ti+tion

par+ti+tions
par+ti+tions
par+ti+tion+ing
par+ti+tioned
par+ti+tion+er
par+ti+tion+ers
par+ti+tion+ist
par+ti+tion+ists
par+ti+tive
  par+ti+tives
par+ti+tive+ly
par+ti+zan
  par+ti+zans
par+ti+zan+ship
part+ly
part+ner
part+ners
part+ners
part+ner+ing
part+nered
part+ner+ship
part+ner+ships
par+ton
  par+tons
Parton
par+took
par+tridge
  par+tridges or
  par+tridge
parts
part-time
part-timer
  part-timers
par+tu+ri+en+cy
par+tu+ri+ent
par+tu+ri+tion
par+ty
  par+ties
  par+ties
  par+ty+ing
  par+tied
par+venu
par+venus
par+venue
  par+venues
par+vo+vi+rus
  par+vo+vi+
    ruses
Parzival
pas
  pas
Pasa+dena
Pa+sar+ga+dae
Pa+say
pas+cal

pas+cals
Pascal
  surname
Pas+cal
  computer
  language
pas+chal
pas de basque
  pas de basque
Pas-de-Calais
pas de deux
  pas de deux
pash
  pashes
pa+sha
pa+shas
pashm
Pash+to
  Pash+to or
  Pash+tos
Pasionaria
Pasiphaë
Pasmore
paso do+ble
  paso do+bles
    or
  pasos do+bles
Pasolini
pasque+flow+er
  pasque+flow+
    ers
pas+quin+ade
  pas+quin+ades
pass
  passes
  passes
  pass+ing
  passed
pass+able
pass+able+ness
pass+ably
pas+sa+ca+glia
  pas+sa+ca+glias
pas+sage
  pas+sages
passage+way
  passage+ways
pass+book
  pass+books
Pass+chen+daele
pas+sé
pas+sen+ger
  pas+sen+gers
passe-partout
  passe-partouts

passe+pied
passe+pieds
passer-by
passers-by
pas+ser+ine
pas+ser+ines
pas+sim
pass+ing
pass+ings
pas+sion
pas+sions
Pas+sion
Pas+sions
pas+sion+al
pas+sion+ate
pas+sion+ate+ly
passion+flower
passion+flowers
pas+sion+less
pas+sive
pas+sives
pas+sive+ly
pas+sive+ness
pas+sivi+ty
pass+key
pass+keys
Pass+over
Pass+overs
pass+port
pass+ports
pass+word
pass+words
past
pasts
pas+ta
pas+tas
paste
pastes
pastes
past+ing
past+ed
paste+board
paste+boards
pas+tel
pas+tels
pas+tel+ist
pas+tel+ists
pas+tel+list
pas+tel+lists
pas+tern
pas+terns
Pasternak
paste-up
paste-ups
Pasteur

pas+teuri+sa+
 tion
pas+teur+ise
pas+teur+ises
pas+teur+is+ing
pas+teur+ised
pas+teur+is+er
pas+teur+is+ers
pas+teur+ism
pas+teuri+za+
 tion
pas+teur+ize
pas+teur+izes
pas+teur+iz+ing
pas+teur+ized
pas+teur+iz+er
pas+teur+iz+ers
pas+tic+cio
pas+tic+cios
pas+tiche
pas+tiches
pas+til
pas+tils
pas+tille
pas+tilles
pasti+ly
pas+time
pas+times
pasti+ness
Pas+to
pas+tor
pas+tors
pas+to+ral
pas+to+rals
pas+to+rale
pas+to+rales
pas+to+ral+ism
pas+tor+al+ist
pas+tor+al+ists
pas+to+ral+ly
pas+tor+ate
pas+tor+ates
pas+tor+ship
pas+tor+ships
pas+tra+mi
pas+try
pas+tries
pas+tur+age
pas+ture
pas+tures
pas+tures
pas+tur+ing
pas+tured
pasty
pasties

pasti+er
pasti+est
pat
pats
pats
pat+ting
pat+ted
pa+ta+gium
pa+ta+gia
Pata+go+nia
Pata+go+nian
patch
patches
patches
patch+ing
patched
patch+er
patch+ers
patchi+ly
patchi+ness
patchou+li
patchou+ly
patch+work
patchy
patchi+er
patchi+est
pate
pates
pâté
pâtés
pâté de foie gras
pâtés de foie
 gras
pa+tel+la
pa+tel+lae
pa+tel+lar
pat+en
pat+ens
pa+ten+cy
pa+tent
pa+tents
pa+tents
pa+tent+ing
pa+tent+ed
pa+tent+able
pa+tentee
pa+tentees
pa+tent+ly
pa+ten+tor
pa+ten+tors
pa+ter
pa+ters
Pater
pa+ter+fa+mili+
 as

pa+tres+fa+mili+
 as
pa+ter+nal
pa+ter+nal+ism
pa+ter+nal+ist
pa+ter+nal+ists
pa+ter+nal+is+tic
pa+ter+nal+is+ti+
 cal+ly
pa+ter+nal+ly
pa+ter+nity
pat+er+nos+ter
pat+er+nos+
 ters
Pat+er+nos+ter
Pat+er+nos+
 ters
Pat+er+son
place name
Paterson
surname
path
paths
Pa+than
Pa+thans
pa+thet+ic
pa+theti+cal+ly
path+finder
path+finders
path+less
patho+gen
patho+gens
patho+gen+esis
patho+genet+ic
patho+gen+ic
pa+thog+eny
patho+log+ic
patho+logi+cal
patho+logi+cal+ly
pa+tholo+gist
pa+tholo+gists
pa+thol+ogy
pa+thol+ogies
pa+thos
path+way
path+ways
Pa+tia+la
pa+tience
pa+tient
pa+tients
pa+tient+ly
pati+na
surface layer
pati+nas
pati+na

broad dish	pa+tron+ess	pau+low+nias	pawki+ness
pati+nae	pa+tron+esses	paunch	pawky
pa+tio	pat+ron+ise	paunches	pawki+er
pa+tios	pat+ron+ises	paunchi+ness	pawki+est
pa+tis+serie	pat+ron+is+ing	paunchy	pawl
pa+tis+series	pat+ron+ised	pau+per	pawls
Patmore	pat+ron+is+er	pau+pers	pawn
Pat+mos	pat+ron+is+ers	pau+per+ise	pawns
Pat+na	pat+ron+is+ing	pau+per+ises	pawns
pat+ois	pat+ron+is+ing+	pau+per+is+ing	pawn+ing
pat+ois	ly	pau+per+ised	pawned
Paton	pat+ron+ize	pau+per+ism	pawn+age
Pa+tras	pat+ron+izes	pau+per+ize	pawn+broker
pa+trial	pat+ron+iz+ing	pau+per+izes	pawn+brokers
pa+trials	pat+ron+ized	pau+per+iz+ing	pawn+broking
pa+tri+arch	pat+ron+iz+er	pau+per+ized	pawn+shop
pa+tri+archs	pat+ron+iz+ers	Pausanias	pawn+shops
pa+tri+ar+chal	pat+ron+iz+ing	pause	paw+paw
pa+tri+ar+chate	pat+ron+iz+ing+	pauses	paw+paws
pa+tri+ar+	ly	pauses	pax
chates	pat+ro+nym+ic	paus+ing	paxes
pa+tri+ar+chy	pat+ro+nym+ics	paused	Pax
pa+tri+ar+chies	pa+troon	pav	Paxes
pa+tri+cian	pa+troons	pavs	Paxton
pa+tri+cians	pat+sy	pa+van	pay
pat+ri+cid+al	pat+sies	pa+vans	*discharge a debt*
pat+ri+cide	pat+ten	pa+vane	pays
pat+ri+cides	pat+tens	pa+vanes	pay+ing
Patrick	pat+ter	Pavarotti	paid
pat+ri+lin+eal	pat+ters	pave	pay
pat+ri+mo+nial	pat+ters	paves	*Nautical*
pat+ri+mo+ny	pat+ter+ing	pav+ing	pays
pat+ri+mo+nies	pat+tered	paved	pay+ing
pa+tri+ot	pat+tern	pavé	payed
pa+tri+ots	pat+terns	pave+ment	pay+able
pat+ri+ot+ic	pat+terns	pave+ments	pay+back
pat+ri+oti+cal+ly	pat+tern+ing	pav+er	pay+backs
pat+ri+ot+ism	pat+terned	pav+ers	pay back
pa+tris+tic	Patti	Pavese	*verb*
pa+tris+ti+cal	Patton	Pa+via	pay+day
pa+tris+tics	pat+ty	pa+vil+ion	pay+days
Patroclus	pat+ties	pa+vil+ions	payee
pa+trol	patu	pav+ing	payees
pa+trols	patus	Pav+lo+dar	pay+er
pa+trols	patu+lous	Pavlov	pay+ers
pa+trol+ling	Pau	pav+lo+va	pay+load
pa+trolled	paua	pav+lo+vas	pay+loads
pa+trol+ler	pauas	Pavlova	pay+master
pa+trol+lers	pau+city	Pav+lo+vi+an	pay+masters
pa+trolo+gist	Paul	paw	pay+ment
pa+trolo+gists	Pauli	paws	pay+ments
pa+trol+ogy	Paul+ine	paws	pay+nim
pa+tron	Pauling	paw+ing	pay+nims
pa+trons	Paulinus	pawed	pay+off
pat+ron+age	pau+low+nia	pawki+ly	pay+offs

pay off
verb
pay+ola
  pay+olas
pay+out
  pay+outs
pay out
verb
pay+phone
  pay+phones
pay+roll
  pay+rolls
Pay+san+dú
Pays de la Loire
Paz
pea
  peas
Peabody
peace
peace+able
peace+able+ness
peace+ably
peace+ful
peace+ful+ly
peace+ful+ness
peace+keep+ing
peace+maker
  peace+makers
peace+making
peace+time
peach
  peaches
  peaches
  peach+ing
  peached
peachi+ness
peachy
  peachi+er
  peachi+est
pea+coat
  pea+coats
pea+cock
  pea+cocks
Peacock
pea+cock+ish
pea+fowl
  pea+fowls *or*
  pea+fowl
pea+hen
  pea+hens
peak
  peaks
  peaks
  peak+ing
  peaked

Peake
peaked
peak+ish
peaky
peal
  peals
  peals
  peal+ing
  pealed
pean
U.S.
  peans
pea+nut
  pea+nuts
  pea+nuts
pear
  pears
pearl
  pearls
pearli+ness
pearly
  pearlies
  pearli+er
  pearli+est
pear+main
  pear+mains
Pears
Pearse
Pearson
peart
peart+ly
Peary
peas+ant
  peas+ants
peas+ant+ry
peas+cod
  peas+cods
pease
  pease
pease+cod
  pease+cods
pea+shooter
  pea+shooters
pea+soup+er
  pea+soup+ers
peat
  peats
peaty
peb+ble
  peb+bles
  peb+bles
  peb+bling
  peb+bled
peb+bly
pe+can

pe+cans
pec+cable
pec+ca+dil+lo
  pec+ca+dil+los
  or
  pec+ca+dil+loes
pec+can+cy
pec+cant
pec+ca+ry
  pec+ca+ries *or*
  pec+ca+ry
Pe+cho+ra
peck
  pecks
  pecks
  peck+ing
  pecked
Peck
peck+er
  peck+ers
Peckinpah
peck+ish
Pe+cos
Pécs
pec+ten
  pec+tens *or*
  pec+ti+nes
pec+tic
pec+tin
  pec+tins
pec+to+ral
  pec+to+rals
  pec+to+ral+ly
pecu+late
  pecu+lates
  pecu+lat+ing
  pecu+lat+ed
pecu+la+tion
  pecu+la+tions
pecu+la+tor
  pecu+la+tors
pe+cu+liar
pe+cu+li+ar+ity
  pe+cu+li+ar+
  ities
pe+cu+liar+ly
pe+cu+ni+ari+ly
pe+cu+ni+ary
peda+gog
U.S.
  peda+gogs
peda+gog+ic
peda+gogi+cal
peda+gogi+cal+ly
peda+gogue

peda+gogues
peda+go+gy
ped+al
  ped+als
  ped+als
  ped+al+ling *or*
  ped+al+ing
  U.S.
  ped+alled *or*
  ped+aled
  U.S.
pe+dal
adj.
ped+ant
  ped+ants
pe+dan+tic
pe+dan+ti+cal+ly
ped+ant+ry
  ped+ant+ries
ped+ate
ped+dle
  ped+dles
  ped+dling
  ped+dled
ped+dler
  ped+dlers
ped+er+ast
  ped+er+asts
ped+er+as+tic
ped+er+as+ty
ped+es+tal
  ped+es+tals
pe+des+trian
  pe+des+trians
pe+des+tria+ni+
  sa+tion
pe+des+tri+an+
  ise
  pe+des+tri+an+
  ises
  pe+des+tri+an+
  is+ing
  pe+des+tri+an+
  ised
pe+des+tria+ni+
  za+tion
pe+des+tri+an+
  ize
  pe+des+tri+an+
  izes
  pe+des+tri+an+
  iz+ing
  pe+des+tri+an+
  ized
pe+di+at+ric

U.S.
pe+dia+tri+cian
U.S.
pe+dia+tri+cians
pe+di+at+rics
U.S.
pedi+cab
pedi+cabs
pedi+cel
pedi+cels
pedi+cel+late
pe+dicu+lo+sis
pe+dicu+lous
pedi+cure
pedi+cures
pedi+gree
pedi+grees
pedi+greed
pedi+ment
pedi+ments
pedi+ment+al
pedi+palp
pedi+palps
ped+lar
ped+lars
pe+dol+ogy
pe+dom+eter
pe+dom+eters
pe+do+phile
U.S.
pe+do+philes
pe+do+philia
U.S.
pe+dun+cle
pe+dun+cles
pe+dun+cu+lar
pe+dun+cu+late
pee
pees
pee+ing
peed
Pee+bles
Pee+bles+shire
peek
peeks
peeks
peek+ing
peeked
peeka+boo
peel
peels
peels
peel+ing
peeled
Peel

Peele
peel+er
peel+ers
peel+ing
peel+ings
Peel+ite
Peel+ites
peen
peens
Pee+ne+mün+de
peep
peeps
peeps
peep+ing
peeped
peep+er
peep+ers
peep+hole
peep+holes
Peep+ing Tom
peep+show
peep+shows
pee+pul
pee+puls
peer
peers
peers
peer+ing
peered
peer+age
peer+ages
peer+ess
peer+esses
peer+less
peeve
peeves
peeves
peev+ing
peeved
peeved
peev+ish
peev+ish+ly
peev+ish+ness
pee+wee
pee+wees
pee+wit
pee+wits
peg
pegs
pegs
peg+ging
pegged
Pega+sus
peg+board
peg+boards

peg+ma+tite
peg+ma+tites
peg-top
Pegu
Péguy
Pei
peign+oir
peign+oirs
Pei+pus
Pei+rae+us
Peirce
pejo+ra+tion
pe+jo+ra+tive
pe+jo+ra+tives
pe+jo+ra+tive+ly
pek+an
pek+ans
peke
pekes
Pe+kin+ese
Pe+kin+ese
Pe+king
Pe+king+ese
Pe+king+ese
pe+koe
pel+age
pel+ages
Pe+la+gian
Pe+la+gians
Pe+la+gi+an+ism
pe+lag+ic
Pelagius
pel+ar+go+nium
pel+ar+go+
  niums
Pelé
Pe+lée
Peleus
pelf
pel+ham
pel+hams
Pelham
Pelham Holles
Pelias
peli+can
peli+cans
Pe+li+on
pe+lisse
pe+lisses
Pel+la
pel+la+gra
pel+la+grous
pel+let
pel+lets
pel+lets

pel+let+ing
pel+let+ed
Pelletier
pel+li+tory
pel+li+tories
pell-mell
pel+lu+cid
pel+lu+cid+ity
pel+lu+cid+ly
pel+lu+cid+ness
pel+met
pel+mets
Pelo+pon+nese
Pelo+pon+ne+
  sian
Pelops
pe+lo+ta
Pe+lo+tas
pelt
pelts
pelts
pelt+ing
pelt+ed
pel+tate
pelt+ry
pelt+ries
pel+vic
pel+vi+metry
pel+vis
pel+vises *or*
pel+ves
Pem+ba
Pem+broke
Pem+broke+shire
pemi+can
pemi+cans
pem+mi+can
pem+mi+cans
pem+phi+gus
pen
pens
pens
pen+ning
penned *or*
pent
enclose
pe+nal
pe+nali+sa+tion
pe+nali+sa+
  tions
pe+nal+ise
pe+nal+ises
pe+nal+is+ing
pe+nal+ised
pe+nali+za+tion

pe+nali+za+ tions
pe+nal+ize
pe+nal+izes
pe+nal+iz+ing
pe+nal+ized
pen+al+ty
pen+al+ties
pen+ance
pen+ances
Pe+nang
pe+na+tes
pence
pen+chant
pen+chants
Pen+chi
pen+cil
pen+cils
pen+cils
pen+cil+ling or
pen+cil+ing
U.S.
pen+cilled or
pen+ciled
U.S.
pen+cil+er
U.S.
pen+cil+ers
pen+cil+ler
pen+cil+lers
pend
pends
pend+ing
pend+ed
pen+dant
pen+dants
pen+den+cy
pen+dent
pen+dents
pen+den+tive
pen+den+tives
Penderecki
pend+ing
pen+dragon
pen+dragons
pen+du+lous
pen+du+lous+ly
pen+du+lous+ ness
pen+du+lum
pen+du+lums
Penelope
pe+neplain
pe+neplains

pe+neplane
pe+neplanes
pen+etrabil+ity
pen+etrable
pen+etrant
pen+etrants
pen+etrate
pen+etrates
pen+etrat+ing
pen+etrat+ed
pen+etrat+ing
pen+etrat+ing+ly
pen+etra+tion
pen+etra+tions
pen+etra+tor
pen+etra+tors
Pe+neus
Peng+hu
P'eng-hu
Peng+pu
pen+guin
pen+guins
peni+cil+lin
peni+cil+lium
peni+cil+liums or
peni+cil+lia
pe+nile
pe+nil+li+on
pen+in+su+la
pen+in+su+las
Pen+in+su+la
pen+in+su+lar
pe+nis
pe+nises or
pe+nes
peni+tence
peni+tent
peni+tents
peni+ten+tial
peni+ten+tials
peni+ten+tial+ly
peni+ten+tia+ry
peni+ten+tia+ ries
peni+tent+ly
Pen+ki
pen+knife
pen+knives
pen+man
pen+men
pen+man+ship
Penn
pen+na
pen+nae

pen+nant
pen+nants
pen+nate
Penney
pen+ni
pen+nia or
pen+nis
pen+ni+less
pen+ni+less+ly
pen+ni+less+ ness
pen+nil+li+on
Pen+nines
pen+non
pen+nons
Penn+syl+va+nia
Penn+syl+va+ nian
Penn+syl+va+ nians
pen+ny
pen+nies or
pence
penny-dreadful
penny-dreadfuls
penny-farthing
penny-farthings
penny-pincher
penny-pinchers
penny-pinching
penny-royal
penny+royals
penny+weight
penny+weights
penny-wise
penny+wort
penny+worts
penny+worth
penny+worths
pe+no+logi+cal
pe+nolo+gist
pe+nolo+gists
pe+nol+ogy
pen+pusher
pen+pushers
pen+pushing
Pen+rith
Penrose
pen+sion
pen+sions
pen+sions
pen+sion+ing
pen+sioned
pen+sion+able
pen+sion+ary

pen+sion+er
pen+sion+ers
pen+sive
pen+sive+ly
pen+sive+ness
pen+ste+mon
U.S.
pen+ste+mons
pen+stock
pen+stocks
pent
pen+ta+cle
pen+ta+cles
pen+tad
pen+tads
pen+ta+dac+tyl
pen+ta+gon
pen+ta+gons
Pen+ta+gon
pen+tago+nal
pen+ta+gram
pen+ta+grams
pen+ta+he+dral
pen+ta+he+dron
pen+ta+he+ drons or
pen+ta+he+dra
pen+tam+er+ous
pen+tam+eter
pen+tam+eters
pen+tami+dine
pen+tane
pen+tan+gle
pen+tan+gles
pen+ta+no+ic
Pen+ta+teuch
Pen+ta+teuch+al
pen+tath+lon
pen+tath+lons
pen+ta+tom+ic
pen+ta+va+lent
pen+ta+zo+cine
Pen+tecost
Pen+tecosts
Pen+tecos+tal
Pen+tecos+tals
Pen+tecos+tal+ ist
Pen+tecos+tal+ ists
Pen+teli+kon
Penthesilea
Penthesileia
Pentheus
pent+house

pent+houses
pen+tode
pen+todes
pent+ste+mon
pent+ste+mons
pent-up
pen+ult
pen+ults
pe+nul+ti+mate
pe+nul+ti+
  mates
pe+num+bra
pe+num+brae
  or
pe+num+bras
pe+num+bral
pe+nu+ri+ous
pe+nu+ri+ous+ly
pe+nu+ri+ous+
  ness
penu+ry
Pen+za
Pen+zance
Penzias
peon
peons
pe+on+age
peo+ny
peo+nies
peo+ple
peo+ples
peo+ples
peo+pling
peo+pled
Peo+ria
pep
peps
pep+ping
pepped
pe+pero+mia
pe+pero+mias
pep+lum
pep+lums or
pep+la
pepo
pepos
pep+per
pep+pers
pep+pers
pep+per+ing
pep+pered
pepper-and-salt
pepper+corn
pepper+corns
pep+peri+ness

pepper+mint
pepper+mints
pep+pero+ni
pepper+tree
pepper+trees
pep+pery
pep+pi+ly
pep+pi+ness
pep+py
pep+pi+er
pep+pi+est
pep+sin
pep+tic
pep+tide
pep+tides
pep+tone
pep+tones
pep+ton+ic
Pepys
per
Pera
per+acid
per+acids
per+ad+ven+ture
Pe+raea
Pe+rak
per+am+bu+late
per+am+bu+
  lates
per+am+bu+lat+
  ing
per+am+bu+lat+
  ed
per+am+bu+la+
  tion
per+am+bu+la+
  tions
per+am+bu+la+
  tor
per+am+bu+la+
  tors
per+am+bu+la+
  tory
per an+num
per+cale
per capi+ta
per+ceiv+able
per+ceiv+ably
per+ceive
per+ceives
per+ceiv+ing
per+ceived
per+cent
per cent
per+cent+age

per+cent+ages
per+cen+tile
per+cen+tiles
per+cept
per+cepts
per+cep+tibil+ity
per+cep+tible
per+cep+tibly
per+cep+tion
per+cep+tions
per+cep+tion+al
per+cep+tive
per+cep+tive+ly
per+cep+tive+
  ness
per+cep+tiv+ity
per+cep+tual
Perceval
perch
perches
perches
perch+ing
perched
perch
  fish
perch or
  perches
per+chance
Per+cheron
Per+cherons
per+cipi+ence
per+cipi+ent
per+cipi+ents
per+cipi+ent+ly
Percival
per+co+lable
per+co+late
per+co+lates
per+co+lates
per+co+lat+ing
per+co+lat+ed
per+co+la+tion
per+co+la+tions
per+co+la+tor
per+co+la+tors
per con+tra
per+cuss
per+cusses
per+cuss+ing
per+cussed
per+cus+sion
per+cus+sions
per+cus+sion+ist
per+cus+sion+
  ists

per+cus+sive
per+cus+sive+ly
per+cus+sive+
  ness
per+cus+sor
per+cus+sors
per+cu+ta+neous
Percy
Per+di+do
per diem
per+di+tion
Per+du
per+dur+able
père
Pe+rea
per+egri+nate
per+egri+nates
per+egri+nat+
  ing
per+egri+nat+ed
per+egri+na+tion
per+egri+na+
  tions
per+egri+na+tor
per+egri+na+
  tors
per+egrine
Pe+rei+ra
Perelman
per+emp+to+ri+
  ly
per+emp+to+ri+
  ness
per+emp+tory
per+en+nial
per+en+nials
per+en+ni+al+ly
Peres
pe+re+stroi+ka
Pérez de Cuéllar
Pérez Galdós
per+fect
per+fects
per+fects
per+fect+ing
per+fect+ed
per+fect+ibil+ity
per+fect+ible
per+fec+tion
per+fec+tion+ism
per+fec+tion+ist
per+fec+tion+
  ists
per+fec+tive
per+fect+ly

per+fer+vid
per+fidi+ous
per+fidi+ous+ly
per+fidi+ous+
ness
per+fi+dy
per+fi+dies
per+fo+li+ate
per+fo+lia+tion
per+fo+rable
per+fo+rate
per+fo+rates
per+fo+rat+ing
per+fo+rat+ed
per+fo+rat+ed
per+fo+ra+tion
per+fo+ra+tions
per+fo+ra+tor
per+fo+ra+tors
per+force
per+form
per+forms
per+form+ing
per+formed
per+form+able
per+for+mance
per+for+mances
per+for+ma+tive
per+form+er
per+form+ers
per+fume
per+fumes
per+fumes
per+fum+ing
per+fumed
per+fum+er
per+fum+ers
per+fum+ery
per+fum+eries
per+func+to+ri+
ly
per+func+to+ri+
ness
per+func+tory
per+fuse
per+fuses
per+fus+ing
per+fused
per+fused
Per+ga+mum
per+go+la
per+go+las
Pergolesi
per+haps
peri

peris
peri+anth
peri+anths
peri+apt
peri+apts
peri+car+di+ac
peri+car+dial
peri+car+di+tis
peri+car+dium
peri+car+dia
peri+carp
peri+carps
peri+car+pial
peri+chon+drium
peri+chon+dria
peri+clase
Peri+clean
Pericles
peri+cli+nal
peri+cline
peri+clines
peri+cra+nium
peri+cra+nia
peri+dot
peri+gean
peri+gee
peri+gees
peri+gla+cial
Pé+ri+gueux
peri+he+lion
peri+he+lia
per+il
per+ils
peri+lous
peri+lous+ly
peri+lous+ness
peri+lune
peri+lunes
pe+rim+eter
pe+rim+eters
peri+met+ric
peri+na+tal
peri+neal
peri+neum
peri+nea
pe+ri+od
pe+ri+ods
pe+ri+od+ic
pe+ri+odi+cal
pe+ri+odi+cals
pe+ri+odi+cal+ly
pe+rio+dic+ity
perio+don+tal
perio+don+tics
peri+os+teal

peri+os+teum
peri+os+tea
peri+pa+tet+ic
peri+pa+tet+ics
Peri+pa+tet+ic
Peri+pa+tet+ics
peri+pa+teti+cal+
ly
peri+peteia
peri+peteias
pe+riph+er+al
pe+riph+er+al+ly
pe+riph+ery
pe+riph+eries
pe+riph+ra+sis
pe+riph+ra+ses
peri+phras+tic
peri+phras+ti+cal+
ly
peri+sarc
peri+sarcs
peri+scope
peri+scopes
peri+scop+ic
per+ish
per+ishes
per+ish+ing
per+ished
per+ish+abil+ity
per+ish+able
per+ish+ables
per+ish+able+
ness
per+ish+ing
per+ish+ing+ly
peri+sperm
pe+ris+so+dac+
tyl
pe+ris+so+dac+
tyls
peri+stal+sis
peri+stal+ses
peri+stal+tic
peri+stome
peri+stomes
peri+style
peri+styles
peri+to+neal
peri+to+neum
peri+to+nea or
peri+to+neums
peri+to+ni+tis
peri+wig
peri+wigs
peri+win+kle

peri+win+kles
per+jure
per+jures
per+jur+ing
per+jured
per+jur+er
per+jur+ers
per+juri+ous
per+jury
per+juries
perk
perks
perks
perk+ing
perked
perki+ly
perki+ness
perky
perki+er
perki+est
Per+lis
per+lite
Perlman
perm
perms
perms
perm+ing
permed
Perm
per+ma+frost
perm+al+loy
perm+al+loys
per+ma+nence
per+ma+nen+cy
per+ma+nen+
cies
per+ma+nent
per+ma+nent+ly
per+man+ga+
nate
per+me+abil+ity
per+me+able
per+me+ably
per+me+ance
per+me+ant
per+me+ate
per+me+ates
per+me+at+ing
per+me+at+ed
per+mea+tion
per+mea+tive
Per+mian
per+mis+sibil+ity
per+mis+sible

per+mis+sibly
per+mis+sion
  per+mis+sions
per+mis+sive
per+mis+sive+ly
per+mis+sive+
  ness
per+mit
  per+mits
  per+mits
per+mit+ting
per+mit+ted
per+mit+ter
  per+mit+ters
per+mit+tiv+ity
  per+mit+tiv+
    ities
per+mu+tate
  per+mu+tates
per+mu+tat+ing
per+mu+tat+ed
per+mu+ta+tion
  per+mu+ta+
    tions
per+mu+ta+tion+
  al
per+mute
  per+mutes
per+mut+ing
per+mut+ed
Per+nam+bu+co
per+ni+cious
per+ni+cious+ly
per+ni+cious+
  ness
per+nick+ety
Per+nik
Perón
pe+ro+neal
Peron+ist
  Peron+ists
pero+rate
  pero+rates
pero+rat+ing
pero+rat+ed
pero+ra+tion
  pero+ra+tions
per+ov+skite
per+ox+ide
  per+ox+ides
per+ox+id+ing
per+ox+id+ed
per+pen+dicu+lar

per+pen+dicu+
  lars
per+pen+dicu+lar+
  ity
per+pen+dicu+lar+
  ly
per+pe+trate
  per+pe+trates
per+pe+trat+ing
per+pe+trat+ed
per+pe+tra+tion
  per+pe+tra+
    tions
per+pe+tra+tor
  per+pe+tra+tors
per+pet+ual
per+pet+ual+ly
per+petu+ate
  per+petu+ates
per+petu+at+ing
per+petu+at+ed
per+petua+tion
per+pe+tu+ity
  per+pe+tu+ities
Per+pi+gnan
per+plex
  per+plexes
per+plex+ing
per+plexed
per+plex+ity
  per+plex+ities
per pro
per+qui+site
  per+qui+sites
Perrault
Perrier
  Trademark
  Perriers
Perrin
per+ron
  per+rons
per+ry
  per+ries
Perry
perse
Perse
per se
per+secute
  per+secutes
per+secut+ing
per+secut+ed
per+secu+tion
  per+secu+tions
per+secu+tive
per+secu+tor

per+secu+tors
Persephone
Per+sepo+lis
Perseus
  Greek hero
Per+seus
  constellation
per+sever+ance
per+sev+era+tion
  per+sev+era+
    tions
per+severe
  per+severes
per+sever+ing
per+severed
Pershing
Per+sia
Per+sian
  Per+sians
per+si+ennes
per+si+flage
per+sim+mon
Per+sis
per+sist
  per+sists
per+sist+ing
per+sist+ed
per+sis+tence
per+sis+ten+cy
per+sis+tent
per+sis+tent+ly
per+sist+er
  per+sist+ers
per+son
  per+sons
per+so+na
  per+so+nae
per+son+able
per+son+able+
  ness
per+son+ably
per+son+age
  per+son+ages
per+so+na gra+ta
  per+so+nae gra+
    tae
per+son+al
per+son+ali+sa+
  tion
per+son+ali+sa+
  tions
per+son+al+ise
  per+son+al+ises
  per+son+al+is+
    ing

per+son+al+ised
per+son+al+ity
  per+son+al+ities
per+son+ali+za+
  tion
  per+son+ali+za+
    tions
per+son+al+ize
  per+son+al+izes
  per+son+al+iz+
    ing
  per+son+al+ized
per+son+al+ly
per+so+na non
  gra+ta
per+so+nae non
  gra+tae
per+son+ate
  per+son+ates
per+son+at+ing
per+son+at+ed
per+son+ate
per+sona+tion
  per+sona+tions
per+sona+tive
per+sona+tor
  per+sona+tors
per+soni+fi+ca+
  tion
  per+soni+fi+ca+
    tions
per+soni+fi+er
  per+soni+fi+ers
per+soni+fy
  per+soni+fies
per+soni+fy+ing
per+soni+fied
per+son+nel
per+spec+tive
  per+spec+tives
per+spec+tive+ly
Per+spex
  Trademark
per+spi+ca+cious
per+spi+ca+cious+
  ly
per+spi+ca+cious+
  ness
per+spi+cac+ity
per+spi+cu+ity
per+spicu+ous
per+spicu+ous+ly
per+spicu+ous+
  ness
per+spi+ra+tion

per+spir+atory
per+spire
 per+spires
 per+spir+ing
per+spired
per+spir+ing+ly
per+suad+abil+
 ity
per+suad+able
per+suade
 per+suades
 per+suad+ing
per+suad+ed
per+suad+er
 per+suad+ers
per+sua+si+bil+
 ity
per+sua+sible
per+sua+sion
 per+sua+sions
per+sua+sive
per+sua+sive+ly
per+sua+sive+
 ness
pert
per+tain
 per+tains
 per+tain+ing
 per+tained
Perth
Perth+shire
per+ti+na+cious
per+ti+na+cious+
 ly
per+ti+na+cious+
 ness
per+ti+nac+ity
per+ti+nence
per+ti+nent
per+ti+nent+ly
pert+ly
pert+ness
per+turb
 per+turbs
 per+turb+ing
 per+turbed
per+turb+able
per+tur+ba+tion
per+turb+ing
per+tus+sal
per+tus+sis
Peru
Pe+ru+gia
Perugino
pe+ruke

pe+rukes
pe+rus+al
 pe+rus+als
pe+ruse
 pe+ruses
 pe+rus+ing
 pe+rused
pe+rus+er
 pe+rus+ers
Perutz
Pe+ru+vian
Pe+ru+vians
Peruzzi
perv
 pervs
per+vade
 per+vades
 per+vad+ing
 per+vad+ed
per+va+sion
 per+va+sions
per+va+sive
per+va+sive+ly
per+va+sive+
 ness
per+verse
per+verse+ly
per+verse+ness
per+ver+sion
 per+ver+sions
per+ver+sity
per+ver+sities
per+ver+sive
per+vert
 per+verts
 per+verts
 per+vert+ing
 per+vert+ed
per+vert+ed
per+vert+er
 per+vert+ers
per+ver+tible
per+vi+ous
per+vi+ous+ly
per+vi+ous+ness
pes
 pedes
Pes+ca+do+res
Pe+sca+ra
pe+seta
 pe+setas
Pesha+war
peski+ly
peski+ness
pesky

peski+er
peski+est
peso
 pesos
pes+sa+ry
 pes+sa+ries
pes+si+mism
pes+si+mist
 pes+si+mists
pes+si+mis+tic
pes+si+mis+ti+
 cal+ly
Pessoa
pest
 pests
Pestalozzi
pes+ter
 pes+ters
 pes+ter+ing
 pes+tered
pes+ti+cid+al
pes+ti+cides
pes+tif+er+ous
pes+ti+lence
 pes+ti+lences
pes+ti+lent
pes+ti+len+tial
pes+ti+len+tial+ly
pes+ti+lent+ly
pes+tle
 pes+tles
pes+to
pet
 pets
 pets
 pet+ting
 pet+ted
Pétain
pet+al
 pet+als
pet+al+ine
pet+alled
petal-like
pe+tard
 pe+tards
pe+tau+rist
 pe+tau+rists
pet+cock
 pet+cocks
pe+techia
 pe+techiae
pe+techial
pe+ter
 pe+ters

pe+ters
pe+ter+ing
pe+tered
Peter
Pe+ter+bor+ough
Pe+ter+lee
peter+man
peter+men
Pe+ters+burg
pe+ter+sham
 pe+ter+shams
Peterson
pethi+dine
petio+late
peti+ole
 peti+oles
pet+it
Petit
pe+tite
pet+it four
 pet+its fours
pe+ti+tion
 pe+ti+tions
 pe+ti+tions
pe+ti+tion+ing
pe+ti+tioned
pe+ti+tion+ary
pe+ti+tion+er
 pe+ti+tion+ers
pe+ti+tio prin+ci+
 pii
pet+it mal
 pet+it mals
Petöfi
Pet+ra
Petrarch
Pet+rar+chan
pet+rel
 pet+rels
Petrie
pet+ri+fac+tion
pet+ri+fi+ca+tion
pe+tri+fi+er
 pe+tri+fi+ers
pet+ri+fy
 pet+ri+fies
pet+ri+fy+ing
pet+ri+fied
pet+ro+chemi+
 cal
pet+ro+chemi+
 cals
pet+ro+chem+is+
 try
pet+ro+dol+lar

pet+ro+dol+lars
pet+ro+glyph
pet+ro+glyphs
Pet+ro+grad
pe+trog+ra+pher
pe+trog+ra+
phers
pet+ro+graph+ic
pet+ro+graphi+
cal
pe+trog+ra+phy
pet+rol
pet+ro+la+tum
petrol-bomb
petrol-bombs
petrol-bombing
petrol-bombed
pet+rol bomb
pet+rol bombs
pe+tro+leum
pet+ro+logi+cal
pe+trolo+gist
pe+trolo+gists
pe+trol+ogy
pe+trol+ogies
Petronius
Pet+ro+pav+
lovsk
Pe+tró+po+lis
pe+tro+sal
pet+rous
Pe+trovsk
Pet+ro+za+vodsk
Pet+sa+mo
pet+ter
pet+ters
pet+ti+coat
pet+ti+coats
pet+ti+fog
pet+ti+fogs
pet+ti+fog+ging
pet+ti+fogged
pet+ti+fog+ger
pet+ti+fog+gers
pet+ti+fog+gery
pet+ti+fog+ging
pet+ti+ly
pet+ti+ness
pet+tish
pet+tish+ly
pet+tish+ness
pet+ty
pet+ti+er
pet+ti+est
petu+lance

petu+lan+cy
petu+lant
petu+lant+ly
pe+tu+nia
pe+tu+nias
pe+tun+tse
Pevsner
pew
pews
pe+wit
pe+wits
pew+ter
pew+ter+er
pew+ter+ers
pe+yo+te
pfen+nig
pfen+nigs or
pfen+ni+ge
Pforz+heim
pha+celia
pha+celias
Phaea+cian
Phaea+cians
Phaedra
Phaedrus
Phae+thon
phae+ton
phae+tons
phage
phages
phago+cyte
phago+cytes
phago+cyt+ic
phago+cy+to+sis
phal+ange
pha+lan+ges
pha+lan+geal
pha+lan+ger
pha+lan+gers
phal+anx
phal+anxes or
pha+lan+ges
phala+rope
phala+ropes
phal+lic
phal+li+cism
phal+lism
phal+lus
phal+li or
phal+luses
phan+ero+gam
phan+ero+gams
phan+ero+gam+
ic

phan+er+oga+
mous
phan+tasm
phan+tasms
phan+tas+ma+go+
ria
phan+tas+ma+
go+rias
phan+tas+ma+go+
ric
phan+tas+ma+go+
ri+cal
phan+tas+ma+
gory
phan+tas+ma+
gories
phan+tas+mal
phan+tas+mic
phan+ta+sy
phan+ta+sies
phan+tom
phan+toms
Phar+aoh
Phar+aohs
Phar+aon+ic
Phari+sa+ic
Phari+sai+cal
Phari+sai+cal+ly
Phari+sa+ism
Phari+see
Phari+sees
Phari+see+ism
phar+ma+ceu+tic
phar+ma+ceu+ti+
cal
phar+ma+ceu+ti+
cal+ly
phar+ma+ceu+
tics
phar+ma+cist
phar+ma+cists
phar+ma+cog+no+
sist
phar+ma+cog+
no+sists
phar+ma+cog+no+
sy
phar+ma+co+logi+
cal
phar+ma+co+logi+
cal+ly
phar+ma+colo+
gist
phar+ma+colo+
gists

phar+ma+col+
ogy
phar+ma+co+
peia
U.S.
phar+ma+co+
peias
phar+ma+co+
poeia
phar+ma+co+
poeias
phar+ma+co+poe+
ial
phar+ma+cy
phar+ma+cies
Phar+sa+lus
pha+ryn+gal
phar+yn+geal
phar+yn+gi+tis
phar+ynx
pha+ryn+ges
or
phar+ynxes
phase
phases
phases
phas+ing
phased
phase-out
phase-outs
phase out
verb
pha+sic
phat+ic
pheas+ant
pheas+ants
Phebe
Pheidippides
phel+lem
phe+nac+etin
phe+nix
U.S.
phe+nixes
phe+no+bar+bi+
tal
phe+no+bar+bi+
tone
phe+no+cryst
phe+no+crysts
phe+nol
phe+nols
phe+nol+ic
phe+no+logi+cal
phe+nolo+gist
phe+nolo+gists

phe+nol+ogy
phenol+phthalein
phe+nom+ena
phe+nom+enal
phe+nom+enal+
ism
phe+nom+enal+
ist
phe+nom+enal+
ists
phe+nom+enal+
ly
phe+nom+eno+
logi+cal
phe+nom+enol+
ogy
phe+nom+enon
phe+nom+ena
or
phe+nom+
enons
phe+no+type
phe+no+types
phe+no+typ+ic
phe+no+typi+cal+
ly
phe+nyl
phenyl+alanine
phenyl+buta+
zone
phenyl+keton+
uria
phero+mone
phero+mones
phew
phi
phis
phial
phials
Phi Beta Kap+pa
Phid+ian
Phidias
Phidippides
Phila+del+phia
phila+del+phus
phila+del+
phuses
Phi+lae
phi+lan+der
phi+lan+ders
phi+lan+der+ing
phi+lan+dered
phi+lan+der+er
phi+lan+der+ers
phil+an+thrope

phil+an+thropes
phil+an+throp+ic
phil+an+thropi+
cal
phil+an+thropi+
cal+ly
phi+lan+thro+pist
phi+lan+thro+
pists
phi+lan+thro+py
phi+lan+thro+
pies
phila+tel+ic
phila+teli+cal+ly
phi+lat+elist
phi+lat+elists
phi+lat+ely
Philby
Philemon
phil+har+mon+ic
phil+har+mon+
ics
phil+hel+lene
phil+hel+lenes
phil+hel+lenic
phili+beg
phili+begs
Philip
Phil+ippe+ville
Phi+lip+pi
Phi+lip+pian
phi+lip+pic
phi+lip+pics
Phil+ip+pine
Phil+ip+pines
Phil+ip+popo+lis
Phi+lis+tia
Phi+lis+tian
Phil+is+tine
Phil+is+tines
Phil+is+tin+ism
Phillip
Phillips
phil+lu+men+ist
phil+lu+men+
ists
Philoctetes
philo+den+dron
philo+den+
drons *or*
philo+den+dra
phi+logy+nist
phi+logy+nists
phi+logy+ny
Philo Judaeus

philo+logi+cal
philo+logi+cal+ly
phi+lolo+gist
phi+lolo+gists
phi+lol+ogy
philo+mel
philo+mels
philo+mela
philo+melas
Philomela
philo+pro+geni+
tive
phi+loso+pher
phi+loso+phers
philo+soph+ic
philo+sophi+cal
philo+sophi+cal+
ly
phi+loso+phise
phi+loso+phises
phi+loso+phis+
ing
phi+loso+phised
phi+loso+phis+er
phi+loso+phis+
ers
phi+loso+phize
phi+loso+phizes
phi+loso+phiz+
ing
phi+loso+phized
phi+loso+phiz+er
phi+loso+phiz+
ers
phi+loso+phy
phi+loso+phies
phil+ter
U.S.
phil+ters
phil+tre
phil+tres
phi+mo+sis
phiz
phizes
Phiz
phle+bit+ic
phle+bi+tis
phle+boto+my
phle+boto+mies
Phleg+ethon
phlegm
phleg+mat+ic
phleg+mati+cal
phleg+mati+cal+
ly

phlegmy
phlo+em
phlo+gis+ton
phlox
phlox *or*
phloxes
phlyc+te+na
phlyc+te+nae
Phnom Penh
pho+bia
pho+bias
pho+bic
pho+bics
Pho+caea
Pho+cis
pho+co+melia
phoe+be
phoe+bes
Phoebe
goddess
Phoe+be
satellite
Phoebus
Phoe+ni+cia
Phoe+ni+cian
Phoe+ni+cians
phoe+nix
phoe+nixes
Phoe+nix
Phomvihane
phon
phons
pho+nate
pho+nates
pho+nat+ing
pho+nat+ed
pho+na+tion
phone
phones
phones
phon+ing
phoned
phone+card
phone+cards
phone-in
phone-ins
pho+neme
pho+nemes
pho+nemic
pho+nemi+cist
pho+nemi+cists
pho+nemics
pho+net+ic
pho+neti+cal+ly
pho+neti+cian

pho+neti+cians
pho+net+ics
pho+net+ist
pho+net+ists
pho+ney
pho+neys
pho+ni+er
pho+ni+est
pho+ney+ness
phon+ic
phoni+cal+ly
phon+ics
pho+ni+ness
U.S.
pho+no+gram
pho+no+grams
pho+no+gram+ic
pho+no+graph
pho+no+graphs
pho+no+graph+ic
pho+nog+ra+phy
pho+no+logi+cal
pho+no+logi+cal+ly
pho+nolo+gist
pho+nolo+gists
pho+nol+ogy
pho+nol+ogies
pho+non
pho+nons
pho+ny
U.S.
pho+nies
pho+ni+er
pho+ni+est
phoo+ey
phor+mium
phor+miums
phos+gene
phos+phate
phos+phates
phos+phat+ic
phos+pha+tide
phos+pha+tides
phos+pha+ti+dyl+
cho+line
phos+pha+ti+
dyl+cho+lines
phos+phene
phos+phenes
phos+phide
phos+phides
phos+phine
phos+phite
phos+phites

phos+pho+lip+id
phos+pho+lip+
ids
phos+phor
phos+phors
phos+pho+rate
phos+pho+rates
phos+pho+rat+
ing
phos+pho+rat+
ed
phos+pho+resce
phos+pho+
resces
phos+pho+resc+
ing
phos+pho+
resced
phos+pho+res+
cence
phos+pho+res+
cent
phos+phor+ic
phos+pho+rous
phos+pho+rus
phos+pho+
ruses
Phos+pho+rus
phot
phots
pho+tic
pho+to
pho+tos
photo+cell
photo+cells
photo+chemi+cal
photo+chem+is+
try
photo+chrom+ic
photo+com+po+
si+tion
photo+con+duc+
tive
photo+con+duc+
tiv+ity
photo+con+duc+
tor
photo+con+duc+
tors
photo+copi+er
photo+copi+ers
photo+copy
photo+copies
photo+copies
photo+copy+ing

photo+copied
photo+de+grad+
able
photo+elec+tric
photo+elec+tric+
ity
photo+elec+tron
photo+elec+
trons
photo+emis+sion
photo+emis+
sions
photo+en+grave
photo+en+
graves
photo+en+grav+
ing
photo+en+
graved
photo+en+grav+
ing
photo+en+grav+
ings
photo+flash
photo+flashes
photo+flood
photo+floods
photo+gen+ic
photo+geni+cal+
ly
photo+gram
photo+grams
photo+gram+
metry
photo+graph
photo+graphs
photo+graphs
photo+graph+
ing
photo+graphed
pho+tog+ra+pher
pho+tog+ra+
phers
photo+graph+ic
photo+graphi+cal+
ly
pho+tog+ra+phy
photo+gra+vure
photo+gra+
vures
photo+jour+nal+
ism
photo+jour+nal+
ist

photo+jour+nal+
ists
photo+ki+nesis
photo+li+thog+ra+
pher
photo+li+thog+
ra+phers
photo+li+thog+ra+
phy
photo+lu+mi+nes+
cence
pho+toly+sis
photo+lyt+ic
photo+mechani+
cal
photo+mechani+
cal+ly
pho+tom+eter
pho+tom+eters
pho+tom+etrist
pho+tom+etrists
pho+tom+etry
photo+micro+
graph
photo+micro+
graphs
photo+mi+crog+
ra+phy
photo+mon+tage
photo+mon+
tages
photo+multi+pli+
er
photo+multi+pli+
ers
pho+ton
pho+tons
photo+peri+od+
ic
photo+peri+od+
ism
photo+pho+bia
photo+pho+bic
photo+poly+mer
photo+poly+mers
photo+recep+tor
photo+recep+
tors
photo+sen+si+
tive
photo+sen+si+tiv+
ity
photo+set
photo+sets
photo+set+ting

photo+set
photo+set+ter
photo+set+ters
photo+sphere
photo+spher+ic
Photo+stat
Trademark
Photo+stats
Photo+stats
Photo+stat+ting
or
Photo+stat+ing
Photo+stat+ted
or
Photo+stat+ed
photo+stat+ic
photo+syn+the+
sis
photo+syn+the+
sise
photo+syn+the+
sises
photo+syn+the+
sis+ing
photo+syn+the+
sised
photo+syn+the+
size
photo+syn+the+
sizes
photo+syn+the+
siz+ing
photo+syn+the+
sized
photo+syn+thet+
ic
photo+syn+theti+
cal+ly
photo+tax+is
photo+trop+ic
photo+trop+ism
phras+al
phrase
phrases
phrases
phras+ing
phrased
phra+seo+gram
phra+seo+
grams
phra+seo+logi+
cal
phra+seol+ogy
phra+seol+ogies
phras+ing

phre+net+ic
phre+neti+cal+ly
phren+ic
phreno+logi+cal
phre+nolo+gist
phre+nolo+gists
phre+nol+ogy
phren+sy
phren+sies
Phrixus
Phrygia
Phryg+ian
Phryg+ians
Phryne
phthi+sis
phut
phuts
phy+co+my+cete
phy+co+my+
cetes
Phyfe
phy+la
phy+lac+tery
phy+lac+teries
phy+let+ic
phyllo
phyl+lode
phyl+lodes
phyl+lo+qui+
none
phyllo+tac+tic
phyl+lo+tax+is
phyl+lo+taxes
phyl+lo+taxy
phyl+lo+taxies
phyl+lox+era
phyl+lox+erae
or
phyl+lox+eras
phy+lo+gen+esis
phy+lo+gen+
eses
phy+lo+genet+ic
phy+lo+gen+ic
phy+log+eny
phy+log+enies
phy+lum
phy+la
phy+sa+lis
physi+cal
physi+cal+ly
physi+cals
phy+si+cian
phy+si+cians
physi+cist

physi+cists
phys+ics
physio
physios
physi+oc+ra+cy
physi+oc+ra+
cies
physio+crat
physio+crats
physi+og+nom+
ic
physi+og+nomi+
cal
physi+og+nomi+
cal+ly
physi+og+no+
mist
physi+og+no+
mists
physi+og+no+my
physi+og+no+
mies
physi+og+ra+
pher
physi+og+ra+
phers
physio+graph+ic
physio+graphi+
cal
physi+og+ra+phy
physio+logi+cal
physio+logi+cal+
ly
physi+olo+gist
physi+olo+gists
physi+ol+ogy
physio+thera+
pist
physio+thera+
pists
physio+thera+py
phy+sique
phy+siques
phyto+chrome
phyto+gen+esis
phy+tog+eny
phy+ton
phy+tons
phyto+pa+thol+
ogy
phyto+plank+ton
phyto+tox+in
phyto+tox+ins
pi
Greek letter

pis
pi
jumbled mixture
pies
pies
pi+ing
pied
Pia+cen+za
pi+acu+lar
Piaf
pi+affe
pi+affes
Piaget
pia+nism
pia+nis+si+mo
pia+nist
pia+nists
pia+nis+tic
pi+ano
pi+anos
pia+no
adj.
pi+ano+for+te
pi+ano+for+tes
Pia+no+la
Trademark
Pia+no+las
pi+as+ter
pi+as+ters
pi+as+tre
pi+as+tres
Piauí
Pia+ve
pi+az+za
pi+az+zas
pi+broch
pi+brochs
pic
pics *or*
pix
pica
picas
Picabia
pica+dor
pica+dors
Picard
Pic+ar+dy
pica+resque
pica+roon
pica+roons
Picasso
pica+yune
pica+yunes
Pic+ca+dil+ly
pic+ca+lil+li

pic+ca+nin
  pic+ca+nins
pic+ca+nin+ny
  pic+ca+nin+nies
Piccard
pic+co+lo
  pic+co+los
pick
  picks
  picks
  pick+ing
  picked
picka+back
  picka+backs
picka+nin+ny
U.S.
  picka+nin+nies
pick+ax
U.S.
  pick+axes
  pick+axes
  pick+ax+ing
  pick+axed
pick+axe
  pick+axes
  pick+axes
  pick+ax+ing
  pick+axed
pick+er
  pick+ers
pick+er+el
  pick+er+el or
  pick+er+els
Pickering
pick+et
  pick+ets
  pick+ets
  pick+et+ing
  pick+et+ed
pick+et+er
  pick+et+ers
Pickford
picki+ly
picki+ness
pick+ings
pick+le
  pick+les
  pick+les
  pick+ling
  pick+led
pick+led
pick+ler
  pick+lers
pick+lock
  pick+locks

pick-me-up
  pick-me-ups
pick+pocket
  pick+pockets
pick-up
  pick-ups
Pick+wick+ian
picky
  picki+er
  picki+est
pic+nic
  pic+nics
  pic+nics
  pic+nick+ing
  pic+nicked
  pic+nick+er
  pic+nick+ers
Pico de Aneto
Pico della
  Mirandola
Pico de Tei+de
pi+cot
  pi+cots
pico+tee
  pico+tees
Pict
  Picts
Pict+ish
pic+to+graph
  pic+to+graphs
  pic+to+graph+ic
  pic+tog+ra+phy
pic+to+rial
  pic+to+rials
  pic+to+ri+al+ly
pic+ture
  pic+tures
  pic+tures
  pic+tur+ing
  pic+tured
pic+tur+esque
pic+tur+esque+ly
pic+tur+esque+
  ness
pid+dle
  pid+dles
  pid+dling
  pid+dled
  pid+dler
  pid+dlers
  pid+dling
pid+dock
  pid+docks
pidg+in
  pidg+ins

pi-dog
  pi-dogs
pie
  pies
  pies
  pie+ing
  pied
pie+bald
  pie+balds
piece
  pieces
  pieces
  piec+ing
  pieced
pièce de ré+sis+
  tance
piece+meal
piece+work
pied
pied-à-terre
  pieds-à-terre
pied+mont
Pied+mont
pie-eyed
Pie+mon+te
pier
  piers
pierce
  pierces
  pierc+ing
  pierced
Pierce
  pierc+ing
  pierc+ing+ly
Pi+eria
Pi+eri+des
pi+eris
Piero della
  Francesca
Piero di Cosimo
Pierre
Pi+er+rot
  Pi+er+rots
pi+età
  pi+etàs
Pie+ter+mar+itz+
  burg
pi+etism
pi+etist
  pi+etists
pi+etis+tic
pi+etis+ti+cal
Pietro da Cortona
pi+ety
  pi+eties

pi+ezo+elec+tri+
  cal+ly
pi+ezo+elec+tric+
  ity
pif+fle
  pif+fles
pif+fling
pif+fled
pif+fling
pig
  pigs
  pigs
  pig+ging
  pigged
pi+geon
  pi+geons
pigeon+hole
  pigeon+holes
  pigeon+holes
  pigeon+hol+ing
  pigeon+holed
pigeon-toed
pig+face
pig+gery
  pig+geries
pig+gish
pig+gish+ly
pig+gish+ness
Piggott
pig+gy
  pig+gies
  pig+gi+er
  pig+gi+est
piggy+back
  piggy+backs
pig-headed
pig+let
  pig+lets
pig+meat
pig+ment
  pig+ments
pig+men+tary
pig+men+ta+tion
pig+my
  pig+mies
Pig+my
  Pig+mies
pig+nut
  pig+nuts
pig+pen
  pig+pens
pig-root
  pig-roots
  pig-rooting
  pig-rooted

pigs
Pigs
pig+skin
  pig+skins
pig+stick+er
  pig+stick+ers
pig+stick+ing
pig+sty
  pig+sties
pig+swill
pig+tail
  pig+tails
pika
  pikas
pi+kau
  pi+kaus
pike
  pikes
piked
pike+man
  pike+men
pike+perch
  pike+perch *or*
  pike+perches
pik+er
  pik+ers
pike+staff
  pike+staffs
pil+af
pil+aff
pi+las+ter
  pi+las+ters
pi+las+tered
Pilate
Pi+la+tus
pi+lau
pi+law
pil+chard
  pil+chards
Pil+co+ma+yo
pile
  piles
  piles
  pil+ing
  piled
pi+leate
pi+leat+ed
pile-driver
  pile-drivers
pi+leous
piles
pi+leum
  pi+lea
pile-up
  pile-ups

pile up
  verb
pi+leus
  pi+lei
pile+wort
  pile+worts
pil+fer
  pil+fers
  pil+fer+ing
  pil+fered
pil+fer+age
pil+fer+er
  pil+fer+ers
pil+grim
  pil+grims
pil+grim+age
  pil+grim+ages
Pil+grims
pi+lif+er+ous
pili+form
pil+ing
Pí+lion
pill
  pills
  pills
  pill+ing
  pilled
pil+lage
  pil+lages
  pil+lages
  pil+lag+ing
  pil+laged
pil+lag+er
  pil+lag+ers
pil+lar
  pil+lars
pillar-box
pill+box
  pill+boxes
pil+lion
  pil+lions
pil+li+winks
pil+lock
  pil+locks
pil+lo+ry
  pil+lo+ries
  pil+lo+ries
  pil+lo+ry+ing
  pil+lo+ried
pil+low
  pil+lows
  pil+lows
  pil+low+ing
  pil+lowed
pillow+case

pillow+cases
pillow+slip
  pillow+slips
Pí+los
pi+lose
pi+los+ity
pi+lot
  pi+lots
  pi+lots
  pi+lot+ing
  pi+loted
pi+lot+age
Pils
Pil+sen+er
Pils+ner
Pilsudski
pilu+lar
pil+ule
  pil+ules
pi+men+to
  pi+men+tos
pi+mien+to
  pi+mien+tos
pimp
  pimps
  pimps
  pimp+ing
  pimped
pim+per+nel
  pim+per+nels
pim+ple
  pim+ples
pim+pled
pim+pli+ness
pim+ply
pin
  pins
  pins
  pin+ning
  pinned
pi+na+ceous
pina+fore
  pina+fores
Pi+nar del Río
pi+nas+ter
  pi+nas+ters
pin+ball
pince-nez
  pince-nez
pin+cers
pinch
  pinches
  pinches
  pinch+ing
  pinched

pinch+beck
  pinch+becks
pinch+penny
  pinch+pennies
Pinckney
Pincus
pin+cushion
  pin+cushions
Pindar
Pin+dar+ic
Pin+dus
pine
  pines
  pines
  pin+ing
pined
pine+apple
  pine+apples
pi+nene
  pi+nenes
Pinero
Pines
pin+feather
  pin+feathers
pin+fold
  pin+folds
  pin+folds
  pin+fold+ing
  pin+fold+ed
ping
  pings
  pings
  ping+ing
pinged
ping+er
  ping+ers
Ping-Pong
  Trademark
pin+head
  pin+heads
pin+head+ed
pin+head+ed+
  ness
pin+hole
  pin+holes
pin+ion
  pin+ions
  pin+ions
  pin+ion+ing
  pin+ioned
Pi+niós
pink
  pinks
  pinks
  pink+ing

pinked
Pinkerton
pink+eye
pink-eye
pink-eyes
pinkie
pinkies
pink+ish
pink+ness
pinky
pinkies
pin+ria
pin+nae *or*
pin+nas
pin+nace
pin+naces
pin+na+cle
pin+na+cles
pin+na+cles
pin+na+cling
pin+na+cled
pin+nate
pin+nate+ly
pin+na+tion
pin+na+tions
pin+ni+ped
pin+ni+peds
pin+nu+lar
pin+nule
pin+nules
pin+ny
pin+nies
Pinochet
pi+noch+le
pi+noc+le
pin+point
pin+points
pin+points
pin+point+ing
pin+point+ed
pin+prick
pin+pricks
pin+pricks
pin+prick+ing
pin+pricked
Pinsk
pin+stripe
pin+stripes
pint
pints
pin+ta
tropical disease
pinta
pint of milk
pin+tail

pin+tails *or*
pin+tail
Pinter
pin+tle
pin+tles
pin+to
pin+tos
Pintoricchio
pint-size
pint-sized
Pinturicchio
pin-up
pin-ups
pin+wheel
pin+wheels
pin+worm
pin+worms
piny
pini+er
pini+est
Pin+yin
Pinzón
pion
pions
pio+neer
pio+neers
pio+neers
pio+neer+ing
pio+neered
pi+ous
pi+ous+ly
pi+ous+ness
pip
pips
pips
pip+ping
pipped
pi+pal
pi+pals
pipe
pipes
pipes
pip+ing
piped
pipe+clay
pipe+clays
pipe+clay+ing
pipe+clayed
pipe+fish
pipe+fish *or*
pipe+fishes
pipe+fitter
pipe+fitters
pipe+fitting
pipe+line

pipe+lines
pipe+lines
pipe+lin+ing
pipe+lined
pip+er
pip+ers
Piper
pi+peri+dine
pip+er+ine
pip+ero+nal
pi+pette
pi+pettes
pipi
pipi *or*
pipis
pip+ing
pipi+strelle
pipi+strelles
pip+it
pip+its
pip+kin
pip+kins
pip+pin
pip+pins
pip+sis+sewa
pip+sis+sewas
pip+squeak
pip+squeaks
pi+quan+cy
pi+quant
pi+quant+ly
pique
piques
piqu+ing
piqued
pi+qué
pi+quet
pi+ra+cy
pi+ra+cies
Pi+rae+us
pi+ra+gua
pi+ra+guas
Pirandello
Piranesi
pi+ra+nha
pi+ra+nhas
pi+rate
pi+rates
pi+rates
pi+rat+ing
pi+rat+ed
pi+rat+ic
pi+rati+cal
pi+rati+cal+ly
Pirithoüs

pi+rogue
pi+rogues
pirou+ette
pirou+ettes
pirou+ettes
pirou+et+ting
pirou+et+ted
Pisa
Pisanello
Pisano
pis+ca+to+rial
pis+ca+to+ri+al+ly
pis+ca+tory
Pi+sces
pis+ci+cul+tur+al
pis+ci+cul+ture
pis+ci+cul+tur+ist
pis+ci+cul+tur+ists
pis+ci+na
pis+ci+nae *or*
pis+ci+nas
pis+cine
pis+civo+rous
Pis+gah
pish
pishes
pish+ing
pished
Pish+pek
pisi+form
pisi+forms
Pisistratus
pis+mire
pis+mires
piss
pisses
pisses
piss+ing
pissed
Pissarro
pissed
piss-up
piss-ups
pis+ta+chio
pis+ta+chios
piste
pistes
pis+til
pis+tils
pis+til+late
Pis+toia
pis+tol

pis+tols
pis+tols
pis+tol+ling *or*
pis+tol+ing
U.S.
pis+tolled *or*
pis+toled
U.S.
pis+tole
pis+toles
pistol-whip
pistol-whips
pistol-whipping
pistol-whipped
pis+ton
pis+tons
pit
pits
pits
pit+ting
pit+ted
pita+pat
pita+pats
pita+pats
pita+pat+ting
pita+pat+ted
pitch
pitches
pitches
pitch+ing
pitched
pitch-black
pitch+blende
pitch-dark
pitch+er
pitch+ers
pitch+fork
pitch+forks
pitch+forks
pitch+fork+ing
pitch+forked
pitchi+ness
pitchy
pitchi+er
pitchi+est
pit+eous
pit+eous+ly
pit+eous+ness
pit+fall
pit+falls
pith
piths
piths
pith+ing
pithed

pit+head
pit+heads
pith+ecan+thro+
 pus
pith+ecan+thro+
 pi
pithi+ly
pithi+ness
pi+thos
pi+thoi
pithy
pithi+er
pithi+est
piti+able
piti+able+ness
piti+ably
piti+ful
piti+ful+ly
piti+ful+ness
piti+less
piti+less+ly
piti+less+ness
pit+man
 pit+men
Pitman
pi+ton
 pi+tons
pits
Pitt
pit+ta
pit+tance
pit+tances
pitter-patter
pitter-patters
pitter-patters
pitter-pattering
pitter-pattered
Pitts+burgh
pi+tui+tary
 pi+tui+taries
pity
pities
pities
pity+ing
pitied
pity+ing
pity+ing+ly
pity+ria+sis
più
piu+piu
piu+pius
Piu+ra
piv+ot
 piv+ots
piv+ots

piv+ot+ing
piv+ot+ed
piv+ot+al
pix
pix+el
 pix+els
pixie
pixies
pixi+lat+ed
pix+il+lat+ed
pixy
 pixies
Pizarro
pi+zazz
piz+za
piz+zas
piz+zazz
piz+ze+ria
piz+ze+rias
piz+zi+ca+to
piz+zle
piz+zles
plac+abil+ity
plac+able
plac+ard
 plac+ards
 plac+ards
plac+ard+ing
plac+ard+ed
pla+cate
pla+cates
pla+cat+ing
pla+cat+ed
pla+ca+tion
pla+ca+tions
placa+tory
place
places
places
plac+ing
placed
pla+cebo
pla+cebos *or*
pla+ceboes
place-kick
place-kicks
place-kicking
place-kicked
place kick
place kicks
place+ment
 place+ments
pla+cen+ta
pla+cen+tas *or*
pla+cen+tae

pla+cen+tal
plac+er
pla+cet
 pla+cets
plac+id
pla+cid+ity
plac+id+ly
plac+id+ness
plac+ing
plack+et
 plack+ets
plac+oid
pla+fond
pla+fonds
pla+gal
plage
 plages
pla+gia+rise
pla+gia+rises
pla+gia+ris+ing
pla+gia+rised
pla+gia+ris+er
pla+gia+ris+ers
pla+gia+rism
pla+gia+risms
pla+gia+rist
pla+gia+rists
pla+gia+ris+tic
pla+gia+rize
pla+gia+rizes
pla+gia+riz+ing
pla+gia+rized
pla+gia+riz+er
pla+gia+riz+ers
pla+gio+clase
pla+gio+clases
pla+gio+clas+tic
plague
plagues
plagues
plagu+ing
plagued
pla+guey
pla+gui+ly
pla+guy
plaice
plaice *or*
plaices
plaid
plaids
Plaid Cym+ru
plain
plains
plains
plain+ing

plained
plain+er
plain+est
plain+chant
plain+ly
plain+ness
plains+man
plains+men
plain+song
plain-spoken
plaint
plaints
plain+tiff
plain+tiffs
plain+tive
plain+tive+ly
plain+tive+ness
plait
plaits
plaits
plait+ing
plait+ed
plan
plans
plans
plan+ning
planned
pla+nar
pla+nar+ian
pla+nar+ians
planch+et
planch+ets
plan+chette
plan+chettes
Planck
plane
planes
planes
plan+ing
planed
plan+et
plan+ets
plan+etar+ium
plan+etar+iums
  or
plan+etaria
plan+etary
plan+et+oid
plan+et+oids
plan+etoi+dal
plan+gent
pla+nim+eter
pla+nim+eters
pla+nim+etry
plan+ish

plan+ishes
plan+ish+ing
plan+ished
plani+sphere
plani+spheres
plank
planks
planks
plank+ing
planked
plank+ing
plank+ton
plano-concave
plano-convex
plant
plants
plants
plant+ing
plant+ed
plant+able
Plantagenet
Plantagenets
plan+tain
plan+tains
plan+tar
plan+ta+tion
plan+ta+tions
plant+er
plant+ers
plan+ti+grade
plan+ti+grades
plaque
plaques
plash
plashes
plasm
plasms
plas+ma
plas+mat+ic
plas+mic
plas+mid
plas+mids
plas+mo+dial
plas+moly+sis
Plas+sey
plas+ter
plas+ters
plas+ters
plas+ter+ing
plas+tered
plaster+board
plas+tered
plas+ter+er
plas+ter+ers
plas+tic

plas+tics
plas+ti+cal+ly
Plas+ti+cine
Trademark
plas+ti+ci+sa+
  tion
plas+ti+cise
plas+ti+cises
plas+ti+cis+ing
plas+ti+cised
plas+ti+cis+er
plas+ti+cis+ers
plas+tic+ity
plas+ti+ci+za+
  tion
plas+ti+cize
plas+ti+cizes
plas+ti+ciz+ing
plas+ti+cized
plas+ti+ciz+er
plas+ti+ciz+ers
plas+tid
plas+tids
plas+tral
plas+tron
plas+trons
plat
plats
plats
plat+ting
plat+ted
Pla+ta
Pla+taea
plat+an
plat+ans
plat du jour
plats du jour
plate
plates
plates
plat+ing
plat+ed
Plate
plat+eau
plat+eaus *or*
plat+eaux
Plat+eau
plat+ed
plate+layer
plate+layers
plate+let
plate+lets
plat+en
plat+ens
plat+er

plat+ers
plat+form
plat+forms
Plath
plat+ing
plat+ings
plat+ini+rid+ium
plat+ini+rid+
  iums
plati+ni+sa+tion
plati+ni+sa+
  tions
plati+nise
plati+nises
plati+nis+ing
plati+nised
plati+ni+za+tion
plati+ni+za+
  tions
plati+nize
plati+nizes
plati+niz+ing
plati+nized
plati+num
platinum-blond
platinum-blonde
plati+tude
plati+tudes
plati+tu+di+nise
plati+tu+di+
  nises
plati+tu+di+nis+
  ing
plati+tu+di+
  nised
plati+tu+di+nize
plati+tu+di+
  nizes
plati+tu+di+niz+
  ing
plati+tu+di+
  nized
plati+tu+di+nous
Plato
philosopher
Pla+to
crater
Pla+ton+ic
Pla+toni+cal+ly
Pla+to+nism
Pla+ton+ist
Pla+ton+ists
pla+toon
pla+toons
Platt+deutsch

Platte
plat+te+land
plat+ter
 plat+ters
platy+hel+minth
platy+pus
 platy+puses
plat+yr+rhine
plat+yr+rhin+ian
plau+dit
 plau+dits
Plau+en
plau+sibil+ity
plau+sible
plau+sible+ness
plau+sibly
Plautus
play
 plays
 plays
 play+ing
 played
play+able
play-act
 play-acts
 play-acting
 play-acted
play-acting
play-actor
 play-actors
play+back
 play+backs
play back
verb
play+bill
 play+bills
play+boy
 play+boys
play+er
 play+ers
Player
play+fellow
 play+fellows
play+ful
play+ful+ly
play+goer
 play+goers
play+ground
 play+grounds
play+group
 play+groups
play+house
 play+houses
play+let
 play+lets

play+mate
 play+mates
play-off
 play-offs
play off
verb
play+pen
 play+pens
play+school
 play+schools
play+thing
 play+things
play+time
 play+times
play+wright
 play+wrights
pla+za
 pla+zas
plea
 pleas
plead
 pleads
plead+ing
plead+ed *or*
 plead *or*
 pled
 Scots, U.S.
plead+able
plead+er
 plead+ers
 plead+ings
pleas+ance
 pleas+ances
pleas+ant
pleas+ant+ly
pleas+ant+ry
 pleas+ant+ries
please
 pleases
pleas+ing
 pleased
pleased
pleas+ed+ly
Pleasence
pleas+ing
pleas+ing+ly
pleas+ur+able
pleas+ur+ably
pleas+ure
 pleas+ures
 pleas+ures
pleas+ur+ing
pleas+ured
pleat
 pleats

pleats
pleat+ing
pleat+ed
pleb
 plebs
ple+beian
 ple+beians
ple+beian+ism
ple+bis+ci+tary
plebi+scite
 plebi+scites
plec+tron
 plec+tra *or*
 plec+trons
plec+trum
 plec+tra *or*
 plec+trums
pled
Scots, U.S.
pledg+able
pledge
 pledges
 pledges
pledg+ing
 pledged
pledgee
 pledgees
pledg+er
 pledg+ers
pledg+et
 pledg+ets
pledg+or
 pledg+ors
plei+ad
 plei+ads
Pleiades
Greek myth
Pleia+des
constellation
Pleio+cene
Pleis+to+cene
ple+na+ri+ly
ple+na+ry
pleni+po+ten+ti+
 ary
 pleni+po+ten+ti+
 aries
pleni+tude
plen+teous
plen+teous+ly
plen+teous+ness
plen+ti+ful
plen+ti+ful+ly
plen+ti+ful+ness
plen+ty

plen+ties
Plen+ty
ple+num
 ple+nums *or*
 ple+na
pleo+chro+ic
ple+och+ro+ism
pleo+mor+phic
pleo+mor+phism
pleo+mor+phy
pleo+nasm
 pleo+nasms
pleo+nas+tic
ple+sio+saur
 ple+sio+saurs
ples+sor
 ples+sors
pletho+ra
ple+tho+ric
pleu+ra
 pleu+rae
pleu+ral
pleu+ri+sy
pleu+rit+ic
pleu+ro+pneu+
 mo+nia
Plev+en
Plev+na
Plexi+glas
Trademark
plex+or
 plex+ors
plex+us
 plex+uses *or*
 plex+us
pli+abil+ity
pli+able
pli+able+ness
pli+ably
pli+an+cy
pli+ant
pli+ant+ly
pli+cate
pli+cat+ed
pli+ca+tion
pli+ca+tions
plié
 pliés
pli+er
pli+ers
pli+ers
plight
 plights
 plights
plight+ing

plight+ed
plight+er
plight+ers
plim+sole
plim+soles
plim+soll
plim+solls
plinth
plinths
Pliny
Plio+cene
plis+sé
plod
plods
plod+ding
plod+ded
plod+der
plod+ders
plod+ding
plod+ding+ly
Plo+eş+ti
plonk
plonks
plonks
plonk+ing
plonked
plonk+er
plonk+ers
plop
plops
plops
plop+ping
plopped
plo+sion
plo+sions
plo+sive
plo+sives
plot
plots
plots
plot+ting
plot+ted
Plotinus
plot+ter
plot+ters
plough
ploughs
ploughs
plough+ing
ploughed
Plough
plough+er
plough+ers
plough+man
plough+men

plough+share
plough+shares
Plov+div
plov+er
plov+ers
plow
U.S.
plows
plows
plow+ing
plowed
plow+er
U.S.
plow+ers
plow+man
U.S.
plow+men
Plowright
plow+share
U.S.
plow+shares
ploy
ploys
pluck
plucks
plucks
pluck+ing
plucked
pluck+er
pluck+ers
plucki+ly
plucki+ness
plucky
plucki+er
plucki+est
plug
plugs
plugs
plug+ging
plugged
plug+ger
plug+gers
plug+hole
plug+holes
plug-ugly
plug-uglies
plum
plums
plum+age
plu+mate
plumb
plumbs
plumbs
plumb+ing
plumbed

plumb+able
plum+ba+go
plum+ba+gos
plumb+er
plumb+ers
plumb+ing
plum+bism
plume
plumes
plumes
plum+ing
plumed
plum+met
plum+mets
plum+mets
plum+met+ing
plum+met+ed
plum+my
plum+mi+er
plum+mi+est
plu+mose
plump
plumps
plumps
plump+ing
plumped
plump+er
plump+est
plump+ly
plump+ness
plu+mule
plu+mules
plumy
plumi+er
plumi+est
plun+der
plun+ders
plun+ders
plun+der+ing
plun+dered
plun+der+er
plun+der+ers
plunge
plunges
plunges
plung+ing
plunged
plung+er
plung+ers
plunk
plunks
plunks
plunk+ing
plunked
Plunket

Plunkett
plu+per+fect
plu+per+fects
plu+ral
plu+rals
plu+ral+ise
plu+ral+ises
plu+ral+is+ing
plu+ral+ised
plu+ral+ism
plu+ral+ist
plu+ral+ists
plu+ral+ist+ic
plu+ral+ity
plu+ral+ities
plu+ral+ize
plu+ral+izes
plu+ral+iz+ing
plu+ral+ized
plu+ral+ly
plus
pluses
plush
plush+ly
Plutarch
Pluto
Greek god
Plu+to
planet
plu+toc+ra+cy
plu+toc+ra+cies
plu+to+crat
plu+to+crats
plu+to+crat+ic
plu+to+crati+cal+
ly
plu+ton
plu+tons
Plu+to+nian
plu+ton+ic
plu+to+nium
Plutus
plu+vial
plu+vials
plu+vi+om+eter
plu+vi+om+
eters
plu+vio+met+ric
plu+vio+met+ri+
cal+ly
ply
plies
plies
ply+ing
plied

Plym+outh
ply+wood
pneu+mat+ic
 pneu+mat+ics
pneu+mati+cal+ly
pneu+mat+ics
pneu+ma+tol+
 ogy
pneu+mato+
 phore
pneu+mato+
 phores
pneu+mec+to+
 my
pneu+mec+to+
 mies
pneu+mo+coc+
 cus
pneu+mo+coc+
 ci
pneu+mo+co+nio+
 sis
pneu+mo+en+
 cepha+lo+gram
pneu+mo+en+
 cepha+lo+
 grams
pneu+mo+gas+
 tric
pneu+mo+nec+to+
 my
pneu+mo+nec+
 to+mies
pneu+mo+nia
pneu+mon+ic
pneu+mo+no+co+
 nio+sis
pneu+mo+tho+
 rax
Pnom Penh
po
 pos
Po
poach
 poaches
 poach+ing
 poached
 poach+er
 poach+ers
Pocahontas
po+chard
 po+chards *or*
 po+chard
pock
 pocks

pock+et
pock+ets
pock+ets
pock+et+ing
pock+et+ed
pocket+book
 pocket+books
pock+et+ful
pock+et+fuls
pocket+knife
 pocket+knives
pock+et+less
pock+mark
pock+marks
pock+marks
pock+mark+ing
pock+marked
pocky
poco
poco a poco
pod
 pods
 pods
pod+ding
pod+ded
po+dag+ra
pod+dy
pod+dies
podgi+ly
podgi+ness
Pod+go+ri+ca
Pod+go+rit+sa
podgy
podgi+er
podgi+est
po+dium
 po+diums *or*
 po+dia
Po+dolsk
podo+phyl+lin
podous
pod+sol
pod+zol
Poe
poem
poems
po+esy
po+esies
poet
poets
po+et+as+ter
 po+et+as+ters
po+et+ess
po+et+esses
po+et+ic

po+eti+cal
po+eti+cal+ly
po+eti+cise
po+eti+cises
po+eti+cis+ing
po+eti+cised
po+eti+cize
po+eti+cizes
po+eti+ciz+ing
po+eti+cized
po+et+ics
po+et+ise
po+et+ises
po+et+is+ing
po+et+ised
po+et+ize
po+et+izes
po+et+iz+ing
po+et+ized
poet lau+reate
 poets lau+reate
po+et+ry
po-faced
pog+rom
pog+roms
Po+hai
po+hu+tu+ka+wa
 po+hu+tu+ka+
 was
poi
pois
poign+ance
poign+an+cy
poign+ant
poign+ant+ly
poi+ki+lo+ther+
 mal
poi+ki+lo+ther+
 mic
poi+ki+lo+ther+
 my
Poincaré
poin+cia+na
 poin+cia+nas
poind
poinds
poind+ing
poind+ed
poin+set+tia
 poin+set+tias
point
points
points
point+ing
point+ed

point-blank
Point de Galle
pointe
 pointes
Pointe-à-Pitre
point+ed
point+ed+ly
Pointe-Noire
point+er
 point+ers
poin+til+lism
poin+til+list
 poin+til+lists
point+ing
point+less
point+less+ly
point-of-sale
points+man
 points+men
point-to-point
 point-to-points
poise
poises
poises
pois+ing
poised
poised
poi+son
poi+sons
poi+sons
poi+son+ing
poi+soned
poi+son+er
poi+son+ers
poi+son+ous
poi+son+ous+ly
poi+son+ous+
 ness
Poi+tiers
poi+tín
Poi+tou
Poitou-Charentes
poke
pokes
pokes
pok+ing
poked
poke+berry
 poke+berries
pok+er
 pok+ers
poker-faced
poke+root
poker+work
poke+weed

pok+ey	pole+axes	po+lite	pol+li+nates
poki+er	pole+axes	po+lite+ly	pol+li+nat+ing
poki+est	pole+ax+ing	po+lite+ness	pol+li+nat+ed
pokie	pole+axed	poli+tesse	pol+li+na+tion
pokies	pole+axe	Politian	pol+li+na+tor
poki+ly	pole+axes	poli+tic	pol+li+na+tors
poki+ness	pole+axes	po+liti+cal	pol+lin+ic
poky	pole+ax+ing	po+liti+cal+ly	pol+li+wog
poki+er	pole+axed	poli+ti+cian	pol+li+wogs
poki+est	pole+cat	poli+ti+cians	pol+lock
Pola	pole+cats *or*	po+liti+ci+sa+	pol+locks *or*
Po+land	pole+cat	tion	pol+lock
Polanski	po+lem+ic	po+liti+cise	Pollock
po+lar	po+lem+ics	po+liti+cises	poll+ster
Po+la+ri	po+lemi+cal	po+liti+cis+ing	poll+sters
po+lar+im+eter	po+lemi+cal+ly	po+liti+cised	pol+lu+tant
po+lar+im+eters	po+lemi+cist	po+liti+ci+za+	pol+lu+tants
po+lari+met+ric	po+lemi+cists	tion	pol+lute
Po+la+ris	po+lem+ics	po+liti+cize	pol+lutes
po+lari+sa+tion	pole+vault	po+liti+cizes	pol+lut+ing
po+lari+sa+tions	pole-vaults	po+liti+ciz+ing	pol+lut+ed
po+lari+scope	pole-vaulting	po+liti+cized	pol+lut+er
po+lari+scopes	pole-vaulted	poli+tick+ing	pol+lut+ers
po+lar+ise	pole vault	poli+tic+ly	pol+lu+tion
po+lar+ises	pole vaults	po+liti+co	pol+lu+tions
po+lar+is+ing	pole-vaulter	po+liti+cos	Pollux
po+lar+ised	pole-vaulters	poli+tics	Pollyanna
po+lar+is+er	po+ley	pol+ity	Pollyannas
po+lar+is+ers	po+lice	pol+ities	pol+ly+wog
po+lar+ity	po+lices	Polk	pol+ly+wogs
po+lar+ities	po+lic+ing	pol+ka	polo
po+lari+za+tion	po+liced	pol+kas	polos
po+lari+za+tions	police+man	pol+kas	Polo
po+lar+ize	police+men	pol+ka+ing	polo-naise
po+lar+izes	police+woman	pol+kaed	polo+naises
po+lar+iz+ing	police+women	poll	po+lo+nium
po+lar+ized	poli+cy	polls	po+lo+ny
po+lar+iz+er	poli+cies	polls	po+lo+nies
po+lar+iz+ers	policy+holder	poll+ing	Pol Pot
po+lar+og+ra+	policy+holders	polled	Pol+ska
phy	Polignac	pol+lack	Pol+ta+va
Po+lar+oid	po+lio	pol+lacks *or*	pol+ter+geist
Trademark	po+lio+my+eli+	pol+lack	pol+ter+geists
Po+lar+oids	tis	Pollack	pol+troon
pol+der	pol+ish	Pollaiuolo	pol+troons
pol+ders	pol+ishes	pol+lan	poly
pole	pol+ishes	pol+lans	polys
poles	pol+ish+ing	pol+lard	poly+am+ide
poles	pol+ished	pol+lards	poly+am+ides
pol+ing	Po+lish	pol+len	poly+an+drous
poled	pol+ished	Pollen	poly+an+dry
Pole	pol+ish+er	pol+lex	poly+an+thus
Poles	pol+ish+ers	pol+li+ces	poly+an+thuses
pole+ax	Pol+it+bu+ro	pol+li+cal	poly+atom+ic
U.S.	Pol+it+bu+ros	pol+li+nate	poly+ba+sic

Polybius
poly+car+boxy+
late
  poly+car+boxy+
lates
Polycarp
poly+car+pic
poly+car+pous
poly+car+py
poly+cen+trism
poly+chaete
  poly+chaetes
poly+chro+mat+
ic
poly+chro+ma+
tism
poly+chro+mic
poly+chro+mous
Polycleitus
Polycletus
poly+clin+ic
  poly+clin+ics
Polyclitus
poly+coty+ledon
  poly+coty+
ledons
poly+coty+ledon+
ous
Polycrates
poly+cy+clic
  poly+cy+clics
poly+cys+tic
poly+dac+tyl
  poly+dac+tyls
poly+dac+tyl+
ous
Polydeuces
poly+es+ter
  poly+es+ters
poly+eth+ene
  poly+eth+enes
poly+eth+yl+ene
  poly+eth+yl+
enes
po+lyga+mist
  po+lyga+mists
po+lyga+mous
  po+lyga+mous+
ly
po+lyga+my
poly+gene
  poly+genes
poly+gen+esis
poly+genet+ic
poly+glot

poly+glots
Polygnotus
poly+gon
  poly+gons
po+lygo+nal
po+lygo+nal+ly
po+lygo+num
po+lygo+nums
poly+graph
  poly+graphs
po+lygy+nous
po+lygy+ny
poly+he+dral
poly+he+dron
  poly+he+drons
or
poly+he+dra
Polyhymnia
poly+math
  poly+maths
po+lyma+thy
poly+mer
  poly+mers
poly+mer+ase
  poly+mer+ases
poly+mer+ic
po+lym+eri+sa+
tion
po+lym+eri+sa+
tions
poly+mer+ise
  poly+mer+ises
  poly+mer+is+
ing
  poly+mer+ised
po+lym+er+ism
po+lym+eri+za+
tion
po+lym+eri+za+
tions
poly+mer+ize
  poly+mer+izes
  poly+mer+iz+ing
  poly+mer+ized
po+lym+er+ous
poly+morph
  poly+morphs
poly+mor+phic
poly+mor+phism
poly+mor+phous
Poly+nesia
Poly+nesian
  Poly+nesians
poly+neu+ri+tis
Polynices

poly+no+mial
  poly+no+mials
poly+nu+cleo+
tide
poly+nu+cleo+
tides
po+lyn+ya
  po+lyn+yas
pol+yp
pol+yps
poly+pep+tide
  poly+pep+tides
poly+pet+al+ous
poly+pha+gia
po+lypha+gous
poly+phase
Polyphemus
poly+phone
  poly+phones
poly+phon+ic
poly+phoni+cal+
ly
po+lypho+nous
po+lypho+nous+
ly
po+lypho+ny
po+lypho+nies
poly+ploid
poly+ploi+dal
poly+ploi+dy
poly+pod
  poly+pods
poly+po+dy
  poly+po+dies
poly+poid
pol+yp+ous
poly+pro+pyl+
ene
poly+pro+pyl+
enes
poly+pus
poly+pi
poly+sac+cha+
ride
poly+sac+cha+
rides
poly+sac+cha+
rose
poly+sac+cha+
roses
poly+semous
poly+semy
poly+so+mic
poly+sty+rene
poly+syl+lab+ic

poly+syl+labi+cal+
ly
poly+syl+la+ble
  poly+syl+la+
bles
poly+syn+deton
poly+tech+nic
  poly+tech+nics
poly+tet+ra+fluo+
ro+ethy+lene
poly+theism
poly+theis+tic
poly+theis+ti+cal+
ly
poly+thene
  poly+thenes
poly+to+nal
poly+to+nal+ism
poly+to+nal+ity
poly+to+nal+ly
poly+un+satu+rat+
ed
poly+urethane
  poly+urethanes
poly+va+len+cy
poly+va+lent
poly+vi+nyl
Polyxena
poly+zoan
  poly+zoans
pom
  poms
pom+ace
po+ma+ceous
po+made
  po+mades
po+man+der
  po+man+ders
Pombal
pome
  pomes
pom+egran+ate
  pom+egran+
ates
pom+elo
  pom+elos
Pom+era+nia
Pom+era+nian
  Pom+era+nians
pom+fret
  pom+frets
pomfret-cake
  pomfret-cakes
pomi+cul+ture
pom+mel

pom+mels
pom+mels
pom+mel+ling
  or
pom+mel+ing
U.S.
pom+melled *or*
pom+meled
U.S.
Pom+mern
pom+my
pom+mies
pomo+logi+cal
pom+ol+ogy
Po+mo+na
Orkney Mainland
Pomona
goddess
Po+mo+rze
pomp
pomps
pom+pa+dour
pom+pa+dours
Pompadour
pom+pa+no
pom+pa+no *or*
pom+pa+nos
Pom+peii
Pom+pei+ian
Pom+pey
place name
Pompey
Roman general
Pompidou
pom+pom
pom+poms
pom-pom
pom-poms
pom+pon
pom+pons
pom+pos+ity
pom+pos+ities
pomp+ous
pomp+ous+ly
pomp+ous+ness
pon
ponce
ponces
ponces
ponc+ing
ponced
Pon+ce
Ponce de León
poncey
pon+cho

pon+chos
poncy
pond
ponds
pon+der
pon+ders
pon+der+ing
pon+dered
pon+der+able
pon+der+os+ity
pon+der+ous
pon+der+ous+ly
pon+der+ous+
  ness
Pon+di+cher+ry
pon+dok
pon+doks
Pon+do+land
pond+weed
pone
pones
pong
pongs
pongs
pong+ing
ponged
pon+ga
pon+gas
pon+gee
pon+gid
pon+gids
pon+go
pon+gos
pon+iard
pon+iards
pon+iards
pon+iard+ing
pon+iard+ed
pons Va+ro+lii
pon+tes Va+ro+
  lii
Pon+ta Del+ga+
  da
Pont+char+train
Pon+te+fract
Pon+te+ve+dra
Pontiac
Pon+tia+nak
Pon+tic
pon+ti+fex
pon+tifi+ces
pon+tiff
pon+tiffs
pon+tifi+cal
pon+tifi+cals

pon+tifi+cal+ly
pon+tifi+cals
pon+tifi+cate
pon+tifi+cates
pon+tifi+cat+ing
pon+tifi+cat+ed
Pontius Pilate
pon+toon
pon+toons
Pontoppidan
Pontormo
Pon+tus
Pon+tus Euxi+nus
Pon+ty+pool
Pon+ty+pridd
pony
ponies
pony+tail
pony+tails
pooch
pooches
poo+dle
poo+dles
poof
poofs
poof+ter
poof+ters
pooh
Pooh-Bah
Pooh-Bahs
pooh-pooh
pooh-poohs
pooh-poohing
pooh-poohed
pool
pools
pools
pool+ing
pooled
Poole
Pool Ma+lebo
pools
Poo+na
poop
poops
poops
poop+ing
pooped
pooper-scooper
pooper-
  scoopers
Poo+pó
poor
poor+er
poor+est

poor+house
poor+houses
poor+ly
poor+ness
poove
pooves
pop
pops
pops
pop+ping
popped
pop+corn
pope
popes
Pope
pope+dom
pope+doms
pop+ery
pop+eyed
pop+gun
pop+guns
pop+in+jay
pop+in+jays
pop+ish
pop+lar
pop+lars
pop+lin
pop+lit+eal
pop+mo+bil+ity
Po+po+ca+té+
  petl
Popov
pop+pa+dom
pop+pa+doms
pop+pa+dum
pop+pa+dums
pop+per
pop+pers
Popper
Pop+per+ian
Pop+per+ians
pop+pet
pop+pets
pop+ple
pop+ples
pop+pling
pop+pled
pop+py
pop+pies
poppy+cock
poppy+head
poppy+heads
pop+sy
pop+sies
popu+lace

popu+lar
popu+lars
popu+lari+sa+
tion
popu+lari+sa+
tions
popu+lar+ise
popu+lar+ises
popu+lar+is+ing
popu+lar+ised
popu+lar+is+er
popu+lar+is+ers
popu+lar+ity
popu+lari+za+
tion
popu+lari+za+
tions
popu+lar+ize
popu+lar+izes
popu+lar+iz+ing
popu+lar+ized
popu+lar+iz+er
popu+lar+iz+ers
popu+lar+ly
popu+late
popu+lates
popu+lat+ing
popu+lat+ed
popu+la+tion
popu+la+tions
Popu+lism
popu+list
popu+lists
Popu+list
Popu+lists
popu+lous
popu+lous+ly
popu+lous+ness
po+ran+gi
por+bea+gle
por+bea+gles
porce+lain
por+cel+la+
neous
porch
porches
por+cine
por+cu+pine
por+cu+pines
por+cu+pin+ish
por+cu+piny
pore
pores
pores
por+ing

pored
por+gy
por+gy or
por+gies
Pori
po+rif+er+an
po+rif+er+ans
Po+ri+rua
pork
pork+er
pork+ers
pork+pie
porky
porkies
porki+er
porki+est
porn
por+no
por+nog+ra+pher
por+nog+ra+
phers
por+no+graph+ic
por+no+graphi+
cal+ly
por+nog+ra+phy
poro+mer+ic
poro+mer+ics
po+ros+ity
po+ros+ities
po+rous
po+rous+ly
po+rous+ness
por+phy+ria
por+phy+rit+ic
por+phy+ry
por+phy+ries
Porphyry
por+poise
por+poise or
por+poises
por+ridge
por+rin+ger
por+rin+gers
Porsena
Porsenna
port
ports
ports
port+ing
port+ed
port+abil+ity
port+able
port+ables
port+ably
Por+ta+down

por+tage
por+tages
por+tag+ing
por+taged
Por+ta+ka+bin
Trademark
Por+ta+ka+bins
por+tal
por+tals
por+ta+men+to
por+ta+men+ti
por+ta+tive
Port-au-Prince
Port Blair
port+cul+lis
port+cul+lises
Porte
porte-cochere
porte-cocheres
por+tend
por+tends
por+tend+ing
por+tend+ed
por+tent
por+tents
por+ten+tous
por+ter
por+ters
Porter
por+ter+age
porter+house
porter+houses
port+fire
port+fires
port+fo+lio
port+fo+lios
Port-Gentil
Port Har+court
port+hole
port+holes
por+ti+co
por+ti+coes or
por+ti+cos
por+ti+ère
por+ti+ères
Por+ti+le de Fier
por+tion
por+tions
por+tions
por+tion+ing
por+tioned
por+tion+less
Port+land
port+li+ness
port+ly

port+li+er
port+li+est
port+man+teau
port+man+teaus
or
port+man+teaux
Port Mores+by
Pôr+to
Pôr+to Alegre
Por+to+bel+lo
Por+to Novo
Por+to Ri+can
Por+to Ri+cans
Por+to Rico
Pôr+to Ve+lho
por+trait
por+traits
por+trait+ist
por+trait+ists
por+trai+ture
por+trai+tures
por+tray
por+trays
por+tray+ing
por+trayed
por+tray+al
por+tray+als
por+tray+er
por+tray+ers
Port Said
Port-Salut
Ports+mouth
Por+tu+gal
Por+tu+guese
Por+tu+guese
por+tu+laca
por+tu+lacas
pose
poses
poses
pos+ing
posed
Poseidon
Po+sen
pos+er
pos+ers
po+seur
po+seurs
posh
posh+er
posh+est
pos+it
pos+its
pos+it+ing
pos+it+ed

po+si+tion
po+si+tions
po+si+tions
po+si+tion+ing
po+si+tioned
po+si+tion+al
posi+tive
posi+tives
posi+tive+ly
posi+tive+ness
posi+tiv+ism
posi+tiv+ist
posi+tiv+ists
posi+tron
posi+trons
posi+tro+nium
posi+tro+niums
po+sol+ogy
poss
pos+se
pos+ses
pos+se co+mi+ta+tus
pos+sess
pos+sesses
pos+sess+ing
pos+sessed
pos+sessed
pos+ses+sion
pos+ses+sions
pos+ses+sive
pos+ses+sives
pos+ses+sive+ly
pos+ses+sive+ness
pos+ses+sor
pos+ses+sors
pos+ses+so+ry
pos+set
pos+sibil+ity
pos+sibil+ities
pos+sible
pos+sibles
pos+sibly
pos+sum
pos+sums
post
posts
posts
post+ing
post+ed
post+age
post+al
post+al+ly
post+bag

post+bags
post+box
post+boxes
post+card
post+cards
post+clas+si+cal
post+code
post+codes
post+coit+al
post+con+so+nan+tal
post+con+va+les+cent
post-Darwinian
post+date
post+dates
post+dat+ing
post+dat+ed
post+de+vel+op+men+tal
post+di+ag+nos+tic
post+di+ges+tive
post+doc+tor+al
post+elec+tion
post+er
post+ers
poste res+tante
pos+teri+or
pos+teri+ors
pos+teri+or+ly
pos+ter+ity
pos+tern
pos+terns
post+femi+nist
post+femi+nists
post-Fordism
post-Fordist
post+free
post+gla+cial
post+gradu+ate
post+gradu+ates
post+haste
post+hu+mous
post+hu+mous+ly
post+hyp+not+ic
pos+tiche
pos+tiches
pos+til+ion
pos+til+ions
pos+til+lion
pos+til+lions

post+im+pres+sion+ism
post+im+pres+sion+ist
post+im+pres+sion+ists
post+ing
post+ings
post-Jurassic
post-Kantian
post-Keynesian
post+li+min+ium
post+li+minia
post+limi+ny
post+limi+nies
post+lude
post+ludes
post+man
post+men
post+mark
post+marks
post+marks
post+mark+ing
post+marked
post-Marxian
post+master
post+masters
post+meno+pau+sal
post+men+strual
post+me+rid+ian
post me+rid+iem
post+mil+len+ni+al+ism
post+mil+len+ni+al+ist
post+mil+len+ni+al+ists
post+mistress
post+mistresses
post+mod+ern+ism
post+mod+ern+ist
post+mod+ern+ists
post+mor+tem
post+mor+tems
post+na+sal
post+na+tal
post+nup+tial
post-obit
post-obits
post+op+era+tive

post-paid
post+pi+tui+tary
post+pone
post+pones
post+pon+ing
post+poned
post+pone+ment
post+pone+ments
post+posi+tive
post+posi+tives
post+pran+dial
post-Reforma+tion
post-Revolu+tion+ary
post+rider
post+riders
post+script
post+scripts
post-Socrat+ic
pos+tu+lant
pos+tu+lants
pos+tu+late
pos+tu+lates
pos+tu+lates
pos+tu+lat+ing
pos+tu+lat+ed
pos+tu+la+tion
pos+tu+la+tions
pos+tu+la+tor
pos+tu+la+tors
pos+tur+al
pos+ture
pos+tures
pos+tures
pos+tur+ing
pos+tured
pos+tur+er
pos+tur+ers
post-Victorian
post+war
post+woman
post+women
posy
posies
pot
pots
pots
pot+ting
pot+ted
po+tabil+ity
po+table
po+tae
po+taes

po+tage
po+tam+ic
pot+ash
po+tas+sic
po+tas+sium
po+ta+tion
 po+ta+tions
po+ta+to
 po+ta+toes
pot+bellied
pot+belly
 pot+bellies
pot+boiler
 pot+boilers
pot-bound
pot+boy
 pot+boys
potch
 potches
po+teen
Potemkin
po+tence
 po+tences
po+ten+cy
 po+ten+cies
po+tent
po+ten+tate
 po+ten+tates
po+ten+tial
 po+ten+tials
po+ten+ti+al+ity
 po+ten+ti+al+
  ities
po+ten+tial+ly
po+ten+ti+ate
 po+ten+ti+ates
 po+ten+ti+at+
  ing
 po+ten+ti+at+
  ed
po+ten+til+la
 po+ten+til+las
po+ten+ti+om+
 eter
 po+ten+ti+om+
  eters
po+ten+ti+om+
 etry
po+tent+ly
pot+ful
 pot+fuls
poth+er
 poth+ers
 poth+ers
 poth+er+ing

poth+ered
pot+herb
 pot+herbs
pot+hole
 pot+holes
pot+holer
 pot+holers
pot+holing
pot+hook
 pot+hooks
pot+house
 pot+houses
pot+hunter
 pot+hunters
po+tion
 po+tions
Potiphar
pot+latch
 pot+latches
pot+luck
pot+man
 pot+men
Po+to+mac
po+tom+eter
 po+tom+eters
poto+roo
 poto+roos
Po+to+sí
pot+pour+ri
 pot+pour+ris
Pots+dam
pot+shard
 pot+shards
pot+sherd
 pot+sherds
pot+tage
pot+ted
pot+ter
 pot+ters
 pot+ters
pot+ter+ing
pot+tered
Potter
pot+ter+er
 pot+ter+ers
Pot+teries
pot+tery
 pot+teries
pot+ti+ness
pot+tle
 pot+tles
pot+to
 pot+tos
pot+ty
 pot+ties

pot+ti+er
pot+ti+est
Potyomkin
pouch
 pouches
 pouches
 pouch+ing
 pouched
pouchy
pouf
 poufs
pouffe
 pouffes
pou+lard
 pou+lards
pou+larde
 pou+lardes
Poulenc
poult
 poults
poul+ter+er
 poul+ter+ers
poul+tice
 poul+tices
poul+try
poultry+man
 poultry+men
pounce
 pounces
 pounces
 pounc+ing
 pounced
pounc+er
 pounc+ers
pound
 pounds
 pounds
 pound+ing
 pound+ed
Pound
pound+age
pound+al
 pound+als
pound+er
 pound+ers
pour
 pours
 pour+ing
 poured
pour+boire
 pour+boires
pour+er
 pour+ers
pous+sin
 pous+sins

Poussin
pout
 pouts
 pouts
 pout+ing
 pout+ed
pout+er
 pout+ers
pout+ing+ly
pov+er+ty
poverty-stricken
pow
pow+an
 pow+ans
pow+der
 pow+ders
 pow+ders
 pow+der+ing
 pow+dered
pow+der+er
 pow+der+ers
pow+dery
Powell
pow+er
 pow+ers
 pow+ers
 pow+er+ing
 pow+ered
power+boat
 power+boats
 power+boating
power-dive
 power-dives
 power-diving
 power-dived
pow+er dive
 pow+er dives
pow+er+ful
pow+er+ful+ly
pow+er+ful+ness
power+house
 power+houses
pow+er+less
pow+er+less+ly
pow+er+less+
  ness
Powhatan
pow+wow
 pow+wows
 pow+wows
 pow+wow+ing
 pow+wowed
Pow+ys
 place name
Powys

surname	prag+ma+tism	prat+fall	preachi+fy+ing
pox	prag+ma+tist	prat+falls	preachi+fied
poxes	prag+ma+tists	prat+in+cole	preach+ment
Po+yang	Prague	prat+in+coles	preach+ments
Poz+nań	Pra+ha	Pra+to	preachy
Po+zsony	prai+rie	prat+tle	preachi+er
poz+zo+la+na	prai+ries	prat+tles	preachi+est
poz+zo+la+nas	praise	prat+tling	pre+ac+quaint
poz+zuo+la+na	praises	prat+tled	pre+ac+quaints
poz+zuo+la+nas	praises	prat+tler	pre+ac+quaint+
Poz+zuo+li	prais+ing	prat+tlers	ing
prac+ti+cabil+ity	praised	prau	pre+ac+quaint+
prac+ti+cable	praise+worthi+ly	praus	ed
prac+ti+cable+	praise+worthi+	prawn	pre+adapt
ness	ness	prawns	pre+adapts
prac+ti+cably	praise+worthy	prax+is	pre+adapt+ing
prac+ti+cal	Pra+krit	prax+ises *or*	pre+adapt+ed
prac+ti+cals	Pra+krits	praxes	pre+ad+dress
prac+ti+cal+ity	Pra+krit+ic	Praxiteles	pre+ad+dresses
prac+ti+cal+ities	pra+line	pray	pre+ad+dress+
prac+ti+cal+ly	pra+lines	prays	ing
prac+ti+cal+ness	prall+triller	pray+ing	pre+ad+dressed
prac+tice	prall+trillers	prayed	pre+ad+just
prac+tices	pram	prayer	pre+ad+justs
prac+tices	prams	*earnest petition*	pre+ad+just+ing
U.S.	prance	prayers	pre+ad+just+ed
prac+tic+ing	prances	pray+er	pre+ado+les+
U.S.	prances	*one who prays*	cent
prac+ticed	pranc+ing	pray+ers	pre+ado+les+
U.S.	pranced	prayer+ful	cents
prac+ticed	pranc+er	pre+ab+sorb	pre+ad+ver+tise
U.S.	pranc+ers	pre+ab+sorbs	pre+ad+ver+
prac+tise	pran+dial	pre+ab+sorb+	tises
prac+tises	prang	ing	pre+ad+ver+tis+
prac+tis+ing	prangs	pre+ab+sorbed	ing
prac+tised	prangs	pre+ac+cept	pre+ad+ver+
prac+tised	prang+ing	pre+ac+cepts	tised
prac+ti+tion+er	pranged	pre+ac+cept+	pre+am+ble
prac+ti+tion+ers	prank	ing	pre+am+bles
Pra+do	pranks	pre+ac+cept+ed	pre+am+pli+fi+er
prae+dial	pranks	pre+ac+cus+tom	pre+am+pli+fi+
prae+sid+ium	prank+ing	pre+ac+cus+	ers
prae+sid+iums	pranked	toms	pre+an+nounce
or	prank+ish	pre+ac+cus+	pre+an+nounces
prae+sidia	prank+ster	tom+ing	pre+an+nounc+
prae+tor	prank+sters	pre+ac+cus+	ing
prae+tors	prase	tomed	pre+an+
prae+to+rian	pra+seo+dym+	preach	nounced
prae+to+rians	ium	preaches	pre+ap+pear+
Praetorius	prate	preach+ing	ance
prae+tor+ship	prates	preached	pre+ap+pear+
prag+mat+ic	prat+ing	preach+er	ances
prag+mati+cal+	prat+ed	preach+ers	pre+ap+pli+ca+
ity	prat+er	preachi+fy	tion
prag+mati+cal+ly	prat+ers	preachi+fies	

pre+ap+pli+ca+
  tions
pre+ap+point
pre+ap+points
pre+ap+point+
  ing
pre+ap+point+
  ed
pre+arm
pre+arms
pre+arm+ing
pre+armed
pre+ar+range
pre+ar+ranges
pre+ar+rang+ing
pre+ar+ranged
pre+ar+ranged
pre+ar+range+
  ment
pre+ar+range+
  ments
pre+as+cer+tain
pre+as+cer+
  tains
pre+as+cer+tain+
  ing
pre+as+cer+
  tained
pre+as+sem+ble
pre+as+sem+
  bles
pre+as+sem+
  bling
pre+as+sem+
  bled
pre+as+sign
pre+as+signs
pre+as+sign+ing
pre+as+signed
pre+as+sump+
  tion
pre+as+sump+
  tions
pre+as+sur+ance
pre+as+sur+
  ances
preb+end
preb+ends
preb+ben+dal
preb+en+dary
preb+en+daries
pre+boil
pre+boils
pre+boil+ing
pre+boiled

pre-Byzantine
Pre+cam+brian
Pre-Cambrian
pre+can+cer+ous
pre+cari+ous
pre+cari+ous+ly
pre+cari+ous+
  ness
pre+cast
pre+cau+tion
pre+cau+tions
pre+cau+tion+ary
pre+cede
pre+cedes
pre+ced+ing
pre+ced+ed
prec+edence
prec+eden+cy
prec+edent
prec+edents
prec+edent+ed
prec+eden+tial
pre+ced+ing
pre-Celtic
pre+cen+sor
pre+cen+sors
pre+cen+sor+
  ing
pre+cen+sored
pre+cen+tor
pre+cen+tors
pre+cen+to+rial
pre+cen+tor+ship
pre+cept
pre+cepts
pre+cep+tive
pre+cep+tor
pre+cep+tors
pre+cep+to+ral
pre+cep+to+rial
pre+cep+tress
pre+cep+tresses
pre+ces+sion
pre+ces+sions
pre+ces+sion+al
pre+ces+sion+al+
  ly
pre+check
pre+checks
pre+check+ing
pre+checked
pre+chill
pre+chills
pre+chill+ing
pre+chilled

pre-Christian
pre-Christmas
pre+cinct
pre+cincts
pre+cincts
pre+ci+os+ity
  pre+ci+os+ities
pre+cious
pre+cious+ly
pre+cious+ness
preci+pice
preci+pices
preci+piced
pre+cipi+tabil+ity
pre+cipi+table
pre+cipi+tance
pre+cipi+tan+cy
pre+cipi+tant
  pre+cipi+tants
pre+cipi+tate
  pre+cipi+tates
  pre+cipi+tates
pre+cipi+tat+ing
pre+cipi+tat+ed
pre+cipi+tate+ly
pre+cipi+ta+tion
  pre+cipi+ta+
    tions
pre+cipi+ta+tor
  pre+cipi+ta+tors
pre+cipi+tous
pre+cipi+tous+ly
pre+cipi+tous+
  ness
pre+cis
  pre+cises
  pre+cis+ing
  pre+cised
pré+cis
pré+cis
  pré+cises
  pré+cis+ing
  pré+cised
pre+cise
pre+cise+ly
pre+cise+ness
pre+ci+sion
pre+ci+sion+ism
pre+ci+sion+ist
  pre+ci+sion+ists
pre+civi+li+sa+
  tion
pre+civi+li+za+
  tion

pre+clas+si+cal
pre+clude
pre+cludes
pre+clud+ing
pre+clud+ed
pre+clu+sion
pre+clu+sive
pre+co+cial
pre+co+cials
pre+co+cious
pre+co+cious+ly
pre+co+cious+
  ness
pre+coc+ity
pre+cog+ni+tion
pre+cog+ni+tive
pre+col+lege
pre+con+ceive
pre+con+ceives
pre+con+ceiv+
  ing
pre+con+ceived
pre+con+cep+
  tion
pre+con+cep+
  tions
pre+con+ces+
  sion
pre+con+ces+
  sions
pre+con+demn
pre+con+demns
pre+con+demn+
  ing
pre+con+
  demned
pre+con+di+tion
pre+con+di+
  tions
pre+con+di+
  tions
pre+con+di+tion+
  ing
pre+con+di+
  tioned
pre+co+ni+sa+
  tion
pre+co+nise
pre+co+nises
pre+co+nis+ing
pre+co+nised
pre+co+ni+za+
  tion
pre+co+nize
pre+co+nizes

pre+co+niz+ing
pre+co+nized
pre+con+struct
pre+con+structs
pre+con+struct+ing
pre+con+struct+ed
pre+con+sul+ta+tion
pre+con+sul+ta+tions
pre+con+trive
pre+con+trives
pre+con+triv+ing
pre+con+trived
pre+con+vic+tion
pre+con+vic+tions
pre+cook
pre+cooks
pre+cook+ing
pre+cooked
pre+cur+sive
pre+cur+sor
pre+cur+sors
pre+cur+sory
pre+da+ceous
pre+da+ceous+ness
pre+da+cious
pre+da+cious+ness
pre+dac+ity
pre-Darwin+ian
pre+date
pre+dates
pre+dat+ing
pre+dat+ed
pre+da+tion
pre+da+tions
preda+tor
preda+tors
preda+to+ri+ly
preda+to+ri+ness
preda+tory
pre+de+cease
pre+de+ceases
pre+de+ceas+ing
pre+de+ceased
pre+de+ces+sor
pre+de+ces+sors

pre+del+la
pre+del+le
pre+des+ig+nate
pre+des+ig+nates
pre+des+ig+nat+ing
pre+des+ig+nat+ed
pre+des+ti+nar+ian
pre+des+ti+nar+ians
pre+des+ti+nate
pre+des+ti+nates
pre+des+ti+nat+ing
pre+des+ti+nat+ed
pre+des+ti+na+tion
pre+des+tine
pre+des+tines
pre+des+tin+ing
pre+des+tined
pre+de+ter+mi+nable
pre+de+ter+mi+nate
pre+de+ter+mi+na+tion
pre+de+ter+mine
pre+de+ter+mines
pre+de+ter+min+ing
pre+de+ter+mined
pre+dial
predi+cabil+ity
predi+cable
predi+cables
pre+dica+ment
pre+dica+ments
predi+cant
predi+cants
predi+cate
predi+cates
predi+cates
predi+cat+ing
predi+cat+ed
predi+ca+tion
predi+ca+tions
pre+dica+tive

pre+dica+tive+ly
pre+dict
pre+dicts
pre+dict+ing
pre+dict+ed
pre+dict+abil+ity
pre+dict+able
pre+dict+ably
pre+dic+tion
pre+dic+tions
pre+dic+tive
pre+dic+tor
pre+dic+tors
pre+di+gest
pre+di+gests
pre+di+gest+ing
pre+di+gest+ed
pre+di+ges+tion
predi+kant
predi+kants
pre+di+lec+tion
pre+di+lec+tions
pre+dis+pos+al
pre+dis+pose
pre+dis+poses
pre+dis+pos+ing
pre+dis+posed
pre+dis+po+si+tion
pre+dis+po+si+tions
pre+dis+solve
pre+dis+solves
pre+dis+solv+ing
pre+dis+solved
pre+dis+tin+guish
pre+dis+tin+guishes
pre+dis+tin+guish+ing
pre+dis+tin+guished
pre+di+vide
pre+di+vides
pre+di+vid+ing
pre+di+vid+ed
pred+ni+so+lone
pred+ni+sone
pre+domi+nance
pre+domi+nant

pre+domi+nant+ly
pre+domi+nate
pre+domi+nates
pre+domi+nat+ing
pre+domi+nat+ed
pre+domi+nate+ly
pre+domi+na+tion
pre+doom
pre+dooms
pre+doom+ing
pre+doomed
pre+dy+nas+tic
pre-eclamp+sia
pre-elect
pre-elects
pre-electing
pre-elected
pre-election
pre-elections
pre-embryo
pre-embryos
pre-eminence
pre-eminent
pre-eminently
pre-empt
pre-empts
pre-empting
pre-empted
pre-emption
pre-emptions
pre-emptive
pre-emptor
pre-emptors
preen
preens
preen+ing
preened
preen+er
preen+ers
pre-engage
pre-engages
pre-engag+ing
pre-engaged
pre-engagement
pre-engagements
pre-enlistment
pre-enlistments
pre-establish
pre-establishes

pre-establish+
ing
pre-established
pre-estimate
pre-estimates
pre-estimat+ing
pre-estimated
pre-examine
pre-examines
pre-examin+ing
pre-examined
pre-exist
pre-exists
pre-exist+ing
pre-existed
pre-existence
pre-existences
pre-expose
pre-exposes
pre-expos+ing
pre-exposed
pre+fab
pre+fabs
pre+fab+ri+cate
pre+fab+ri+
cates
pre+fab+ri+cat+
ing
pre+fab+ri+cat+
ed
pre+fab+ri+ca+
tion
pre+fab+ri+ca+
tions
pref+ace
pref+aces
pref+aces
pref+ac+ing
pref+aced
pref+ac+er
pref+ac+ers
prefa+to+rial
prefa+tory
pre+fect
pre+fects
pre+fec+to+rial
pre+fec+ture
pre+fec+tures
pre+fer
pre+fers
pre+fer+ring
pre+ferred
pref+er+able
pref+er+ably
pref+er+ence

pref+er+ences
pref+er+en+tial
pref+er+en+tial+
ly
pre+fer+ment
pre+fer+ments
pre+figu+ra+tion
pre+figu+ra+
tions
pre+fig+ure
pre+fig+ures
pre+fig+ur+ing
pre+fig+ured
pre+fig+ure+
ment
pre+fig+ure+
ments
pre+fix
pre+fixes
pre+fixes
pre+fix+ing
pre+fixed
pre+fix+ion
pre+flight
pre+form
pre+forms
pre+form+ing
pre+formed
pre+for+ma+tion
pre+for+ma+
tions
pre+franked
pre+freeze
pre+freezes
pre+freez+ing
pre+froze
pre+fro+zen
pre+fron+tal
pre-German+ic
pre+gla+cial
preg+nable
preg+nan+cy
preg+nan+cies
preg+nant
preg+nant+ly
pre-Gothic
pre-Greek
pre+hard+en
pre+hard+ens
pre+hard+en+
ing
pre+hard+ened
pre+heat
pre+heats
pre+heat+ing

pre+heat+ed
pre+hen+sile
pre+hen+sil+ity
pre+hen+sion
pre+his+tor+ic
pre+his+tori+cal
pre+his+tori+cal+
ly
pre+his+to+ry
pre+his+to+ries
pre-Homeric
pre-ignition
pre+in+di+cate
pre+in+di+cates
pre+in+di+cat+
ing
pre+in+di+cat+
ed
pre+in+dus+trial
pre+in+form
pre+in+forms
pre+in+form+ing
pre+in+formed
pre+in+struct
pre+in+structs
pre+in+struct+
ing
pre+in+struct+
ed
pre+judge
pre+judges
pre+judg+ing
pre+judged
preju+dice
preju+dices
preju+dices
preju+dic+ing
preju+diced
preju+di+cial
preju+di+cial+ly
pre+kin+der+gar+
ten
prela+cy
prela+cies
pre+lap+sari+an
prel+ate
prel+ates
pre+lat+ic
pre+lati+cal
pre+limi+naries
pre+limi+nari+ly
pre+limi+nary
pre+limi+naries
pre+lims
pre+lo+cate

pre+lo+cates
pre+lo+cat+ing
pre+lo+cat+ed
prel+ude
prel+udes
prel+udes
prel+ud+ing
prel+ud+ed
pre+lu+dial
pre+mari+tal
pre-Marxian
prema+ture
prema+ture+ly
pre+medi+cal
pre+medi+ca+
tion
pre+medi+ca+
tions
pre+medi+tate
pre+medi+tates
pre+medi+tat+
ing
pre+medi+tat+
ed
pre+medi+ta+
tion
pre+medi+ta+tor
pre+medi+ta+
tors
pre+men+stru+al
prem+ier
prem+iers
premi+ere
premi+eres
premi+eres
premi+er+ing
premi+ered
prem+ier+ship
prem+ier+ships
pre+mil+lenar+ian
pre+mil+lenar+
ians
pre+mil+len+ni+al+
ism
pre+mil+len+ni+al+
ist
pre+mil+len+ni+
al+ists
Preminger
prem+ise
prem+ises
prem+ises
prem+is+ing
prem+ised
prem+ises

pre+mium
 pre+miums
pre+mix
 pre+mixes
 pre+mix+ing
 pre+mixed
pre+mo+lar
 pre+mo+lars
premo+ni+tion
 premo+ni+tions
pre+moni+tory
Pre+mon+stra+
 ten+sian
 Pre+mon+stra+
 ten+sians
pre+na+tal
 pre+na+tals
pre+nomi+nal
pren+tice
 pren+tices
pre+nup+tial
pre+oc+cu+pa+
 tion
 pre+oc+cu+pa+
 tions
pre+oc+cu+pied
pre+oc+cu+py
 pre+oc+cu+pies
 pre+oc+cu+py+
 ing
 pre+oc+cu+pied
pre+or+dain
 pre+or+dains
 pre+or+dain+ing
 pre+or+dained
prep
 preps
pre+pack
 pre+packs
 pre+pack+ing
 pre+packed
pre+pack+age
 pre+pack+ages
 pre+pack+ag+
 ing
 pre+pack+aged
pre+packed
pre+pala+tal
prepa+ra+tion
 prepa+ra+tions
pre+para+tive
 pre+para+tives
pre+para+tive+ly
pre+para+to+ri+
 ly

pre+para+tory
pre+pare
 pre+pares
 pre+par+ing
 pre+pared
 pre+par+ed+ness
 pre+par+er
 pre+par+ers
pre+pay
 pre+pays
 pre+pay+ing
 pre+paid
 pre+pay+able
pre+pense
pre+plan
 pre+plans
 pre+plan+ning
 pre+planned
pre+pon+der+
 ance
pre+pon+der+ant
 pre+pon+der+ant+
 ly
 pre+pon+der+ate
 pre+pon+der+
 ates
 pre+pon+der+at+
 ing
 pre+pon+der+at+
 ed
pre+pon+dera+
 tion
prepo+si+tion
 prepo+si+tions
 prepo+si+tion+al
 prepo+si+tion+al+
 ly
pre+pos+sess
 pre+pos+sesses
 pre+pos+sess+
 ing
 pre+pos+sessed
 pre+pos+sess+
 ing
 pre+pos+ses+
 sion
 pre+pos+ses+
 sions
pre+pos+ter+ous
 pre+pos+ter+ous+
 ly
 pre+pos+ter+ous+
 ness
pre+po+ten+cy
pre+po+tent

prep+py
 prep+pies
pre+pran+dial
pre+pu+bes+cent
 pre+pu+bes+
 cents
pre+pub+li+ca+
 tion
pre+puce
 pre+puces
pre+quel
 pre+quels
Pre-Raphael+ite
 Pre-Raphael+ites
 Pre-Raphael+it+
 ism
pre+re+cord
 pre+re+cords
 pre+re+cord+ing
 pre+re+cord+ed
pre-Reforma+tion
pre+reg+is+ter
 pre+reg+is+ters
 pre+reg+is+ter+
 ing
 pre+reg+is+
 tered
pre-Renais+sance
pre+requi+site
 pre+requi+sites
pre+re+tire+ment
pre+roga+tive
 pre+roga+tives
pre-Roman
pre-Romantic
pres+age
 pres+ages
 pres+ages
 pres+ag+ing
 pres+aged
pre+sage+ful
pre+sag+er
 pre+sag+ers
pre+sale
pres+byo+pia
pres+by+op+ic
pres+by+ter
 pres+by+ters
 pres+by+ter+ial
 pres+by+ter+ian
 pres+by+ter+
 ians
Pres+by+ter+ian
 Pres+by+ter+
 ians

pres+by+teri+an+
 ism
Pres+by+teri+an+
 ism
pres+by+tery
 pres+by+teries
pre+school
pre-school
pres+ci+ence
pres+ci+ent
pre+sci+en+ti+fic
Prescott
pre+scribe
 pre+scribes
 pre+scrib+ing
 pre+scribed
pre+scrib+er
 pre+scrib+ers
pre+script
 pre+scripts
pre+scrip+tion
 pre+scrip+tions
pre+scrip+tive
pre+scrip+tive+ly
pre+scrip+tive+
 ness
pre+se+lect
 pre+se+lects
 pre+se+lect+ing
 pre+se+lect+ed
pre+sell
 pre+sells
 pre+sell+ing
 pre+sold
pres+ence
 pres+ences
pres+ent
 in attendance
pre+sent
 to introduce
 pres+ents
 pre+sents
 pre+sent+ing
 pre+sent+ed
pre+sent+abil+ity
pre+sent+able
pre+sent+able+
 ness
pre+sent+ably
pres+en+ta+tion
 pres+en+ta+
 tions
pres+en+ta+tion+
 al

pres+en+ta+tion+
ism
pres+en+ta+tion+
ist
pres+en+ta+tion+
ists
pre+senta+tive
present-day
pre+sent+er
pre+sent+ers
pre+sen+tient
pre+sen+ti+ment
pre+sen+ti+
ments
pres+ent+ly
pre+sent+ment
pre+sent+ments
pres+ents
pre+serv+able
pres+er+va+tion
pres+er+va+
tions
pre+serva+tive
pre+serva+tives
pre+serve
pre+serves
pre+serves
pre+serv+ing
pre+served
pre+serv+er
pre+serv+ers
pre+set
pre+sets
pre+sets
pre+set+ting
pre+set
pre+shape
pre+shapes
pre+shap+ing
pre+shaped
pre+shrink
pre+shrinks
pre+shrink+ing
pre+shrank
pre+shrunk
pre+shrunk
pre+side
pre+sides
pre+sid+ing
pre+sid+ed
presi+den+cy
presi+den+cies
presi+dent
presi+dents
presi+den+tial

presi+den+tial+ly
presi+dent+ship
presi+dent+
ships
pre+sid+ium
pre+sid+iums
or
pre+sidia
Presley
pre+soak
pre+soaks
pre+soak+ing
pre+soaked
pre-Socrat+ic
press
presses
presses
press+ing
pressed
Press+burg
Pressburger
press-gang
press-gangs
press-ganging
press-ganged
press gang
press gangs
press+ing
press+ings
press+ing+ly
press+man
press+men
press+room
press+rooms
press-up
press-ups
pres+sure
pres+sures
pres+sures
pres+sur+ing
pres+sured
pressure-cook
pressure-cooks
pressure-
cooking
pressure-cooked
pres+suri+sa+
tion
pres+suri+sa+
tions
pres+sur+ise
pres+sur+ises
pres+sur+is+ing
pres+sur+ised

pres+suri+za+
tion
pres+suri+za+
tions
pres+sur+ize
pres+sur+izes
pres+sur+iz+ing
pres+sur+ized
press+work
Pres+tel
Trademark
Prester John
pres+ti+digi+ta+
tion
pres+ti+digi+ta+
tor
pres+ti+digi+ta+
tors
pres+tige
pres+tig+ious
pres+tis+si+mo
pres+tis+si+
mos
pres+to
pres+tos
Pres+ton
Pres+ton+pans
Prest+wich
Prest+wick
pre+sum+ably
pre+sume
pre+sumes
pre+sum+ing
pre+sumed
pre+sum+ed+ly
pre+sum+ing
pre+sump+tion
pre+sump+tions
pre+sump+tive
pre+sump+tive+
ly
pre+sump+tu+
ous
pre+sump+tu+
ous+ly
pre+sump+tu+
ous+ness
pre+sup+pose
pre+sup+poses
pre+sup+pos+
ing
pre+sup+posed
pre+sup+po+si+
tion

pre+sup+po+si+
tions
pre+sur+gi+cal
pre+tence
pre+tences
pre+tend
pre+tends
pre+tend+ing
pre+tend+ed
pre+tend+er
pre+tend+ers
pre+tense
U.S.
pre+tenses
pre+ten+sion
pre+ten+sions
pre+ten+tious
pre+ten+tious+ly
pre+ten+tious+
ness
pret+er+it
U.S.
pret+er+its
pret+er+ite
pret+er+ites
pre+term
pre+ter+mit
pre+ter+mits
pre+ter+mit+
ting
pre+ter+mit+ted
pre+ter+natu+ral
pre+ter+natu+ral+
ly
pre+test
pre+tests
pre+test+ing
pre+test+ed
pre+text
pre+texts
pre+tor
pre+tors
Pre+to+ria
Pretorius
pre+tor+ship
pret+ti+fi+ca+
tion
pret+ti+fi+er
pret+ti+fi+ers
pret+ti+fy
pret+ti+fies
pret+ti+fy+ing
pret+ti+fied
pret+ti+ly
pret+ti+ness

pret+ty
 pret+ties
 pret+ties
 pret+ty+ing
 pret+tied
 pret+ti+er
 pret+ti+est
pretty-pretty
pret+zel
 pret+zels
Preus+sen
pre+vail
 pre+vails
 pre+vail+ing
 pre+vailed
pre+vail+er
 pre+vail+ers
pre+vail+ing
pre+vail+ing+ly
preva+lence
preva+lent
preva+lent+ly
pre+vari+cate
 pre+vari+cates
 pre+vari+cat+ing
 pre+vari+cat+ed
pre+vari+ca+tion
 pre+vari+ca+tions
pre+vari+ca+tor
 pre+vari+ca+tors
pre+vent
 pre+vents
 pre+vent+ing
 pre+vent+ed
pre+vent+able
pre+vent+ably
pre+vent+ible
pre+vent+ibly
pre+ven+tion
 pre+ven+tions
pre+ven+tive
 pre+ven+tives
pre+ven+tive+ly
Prévert
pre+view
 pre+views
 pre+views
 pre+view+ing
 pre+viewed
Previn
pre+vi+ous
pre+vi+ous+ly

pre+vi+ous+ness
pre+vise
 pre+vises
 pre+vis+ing
 pre+vised
pre+vi+sion
 pre+vi+sions
Prévost d'Exiles
pre+war
pre+warm
 pre+warms
 pre+warm+ing
 pre+warmed
pre+wash
 pre+washes
 pre+washes
 pre+wash+ing
 pre+washed
prey
 preys
 preys
 prey+ing
 preyed
prey+er
 prey+ers
Priam
pria+pean
pri+ap+ic
pria+pism
Priapus
price
 prices
 prices
 pric+ing
 priced
price-fixing
price+less
price+less+ly
price+less+ness
pric+er
 pric+ers
price-sensitive
pricey
prici+er
prici+est
prick
 pricks
 pricks
 prick+ing
 pricked
prick+er
 prick+ers
prick+et
 prick+ets
prick+le

prick+les
prick+les
prick+ling
prick+led
prick+li+ness
prick+ly
 prick+li+er
 prick+li+est
pricy
prici+er
prici+est
pride
 prides
 prides
 prid+ing
 prid+ed
Pride
pride+ful
pride+ful+ly
prie-dieu
 prie-dieus or
 prie-dieux
pri+er
 pri+ers
priest
 priests
 priests
 priest+ing
 priest+ed
priest+craft
priest+ess
priest-hole
 priest-holes
priest+hood
Priestley
priest+like
priest+ly
 priest+li+er
 priest+li+est
prig
 prigs
prig+gery
prig+gish
prig+gish+ly
prig+gish+ness
Prigogine
prim
 prims
 prim+ming
 primmed
prim+mer
prim+mest
pri+ma+cy
 pri+ma+cies
pri+ma don+na

pri+ma don+nas
pri+mae+val
pri+mae+val+ly
pri+ma fa+cie
pri+mal
pri+ma+quine
pri+mari+ly
pri+ma+ry
 pri+ma+ries
pri+mate
 pri+mates
pri+ma+tial
prime
 primes
 primes
 prim+ing
 primed
prime+ness
pri+mer
 pri+mers
prime+time
prime+time
 adj.
prime time
 noun
pri+meval
pri+meval+ly
prim+ing
 prim+ings
primi+tive
 primi+tives
primi+tive+ly
primi+tive+ness
primi+tiv+ism
primi+tiv+ist
 primi+tiv+ists
prim+ly
prim+ness
pri+mo
 pri+mos or
 pri+mi
Primo de Rivera
pri+mo+geni+tary
pri+mo+geni+tor
 pri+mo+geni+tors
pri+mo+geni+ture
pri+mor+dial
pri+mor+di+al+ity
pri+mor+di+al+ly
primp
 primps
 primp+ing

primped
prim+rose
prim+roses
primu+la
primu+las
pri+mum mo+bi+
  le
Pri+mus
Trademark
  Pri+muses
prince
  princes
Prince
prince+dom
  prince+doms
prince+like
prince+ling
  prince+lings
prince+ly
  prince+li+er
  prince+li+est
prince's-feather
  prince's-feathers
prin+cess
  prin+cesses
Prince+ton
prin+ci+pal
  prin+ci+pals
  prin+ci+pal+ity
  prin+ci+pal+ities
  prin+ci+pal+ly
  prin+ci+pal+ship
  prin+ci+pal+
    ships
  prin+ci+pate
  prin+ci+pates
Prin+ci+pe
prin+ci+ple
  prin+ci+ples
  prin+ci+pled
prink
  prinks
  prink+ing
  prinked
print
  prints
  prints
  print+ing
  print+ed
print+able
print+er
  print+ers
  print+ing
  print+ings

print+maker
  print+makers
print-out
  print-outs
print out
  verb
pri+or
  pri+ors
Prior
pri+or+ate
  pri+or+ates
pri+or+ess
  pri+or+esses
pri+or+ity
  pri+or+ities
pri+ory
  pri+ories
Pri+pet
Priscian
prise
  prises
  prises
  pris+ing
  prised
prism
  prisms
pris+mat+ic
pris+mati+cal+ly
pris+on
  pris+ons
  pris+on+er
  pris+on+ers
pris+si+ly
pris+si+ness
pris+sy
  pris+si+er
  pris+si+est
pris+tine
Pritchett
prithee
pri+va+cy
pri+vate
  pri+vates
pri+va+teer
  pri+va+teers
  pri+va+teers
  pri+va+teer+ing
  pri+va+teered
pri+vate+ly
  pri+vates
pri+va+tion
  pri+va+tions
pri+vati+sa+tion
  pri+vati+sa+
    tions

pri+vat+ise
  pri+vat+ises
  pri+vat+is+ing
  pri+vat+ised
priva+tive
  priva+tive+ly
pri+vati+za+tion
  pri+vati+za+
    tions
pri+vat+ize
  pri+vat+izes
  pri+vat+iz+ing
  pri+vat+ized
priv+et
  priv+ets
privi+lege
  privi+leges
  privi+leges
  privi+leg+ing
  privi+leged
  privi+leged
privi+ly
priv+ity
  priv+ities
privy
  privies
  privi+er
  privi+est
Prix Gon+court
prize
  prizes
  prizes
  priz+ing
  prized
prize+fight
  prize+fights
  prize+fighter
  prize+fighters
  prize+fighting
pro
  pros
proa
  proas
pro+abo+li+tion
pro+ac+tive
pro-am
pro+amend+
  ment
pro-American
  pro-Americans
pro+an+nexa+
  tion
pro+ap+prov+al
pro+ar+bi+tra+
  tion

pro+auto+ma+
  tion
prob+abil+ity
  prob+abil+ities
prob+able
  prob+ables
  prob+ably
pro+band
  pro+bands
pro+bang
  pro+bangs
pro+bate
  pro+bates
  pro+bates
pro+bat+ing
  pro+bat+ed
pro+ba+tion
  pro+ba+tions
  pro+ba+tion+al
  pro+ba+tion+ary
  pro+ba+tion+er
  pro+ba+tion+ers
probe
  probes
  probes
  prob+ing
  probed
probe+able
prob+er
  prob+ers
pro+bib+li+cal
pro+bity
prob+lem
  prob+lems
prob+lem+at+ic
  prob+lem+ati+cal
  prob+lem+ati+cal+
    ly
pro bono pub+li+
  co
pro+bos+cid+ean
  pro+bos+cid+
    eans
pro+bos+cid+ian
  pro+bos+cid+
    ians
pro+bos+cis
  pro+bos+cises
  or
  pro+bos+ci+des
pro-British
pro+busi+ness
pro+caine
pro+capi+tal+ist
pro+cary+ote

pro+cary+otes
pro+ca+thedral
pro+ca+thedrals
pro+cedur+al
pro+cedur+al+ly
pro+cedure
pro+cedures
pro+ceed
pro+ceeds
pro+ceed+ing
pro+ceed+ed
pro+ceed+er
pro+ceed+ers
pro+ceed+ing
pro+ceed+ings
pro+ceeds
pro+cen+trali+sa+
tion
pro+cen+trali+za+
tion
pro+cess
pro+cesses
pro+cesses
pro+cess+ing
pro+cessed
pro+ces+sion
pro+ces+sions
pro+ces+sions
pro+ces+sion+
ing
pro+ces+sioned
pro+ces+sion+al
pro+ces+sion+
als
pro+ces+sor
pro+ces+sors
process-server
process-servers
procès-verbal
procès-verbaux
pro-choice
pro+chro+nism
pro+chro+nisms
pro+church
pro+claim
pro+claims
pro+claim+ing
pro+claimed
pro+claim+er
pro+claim+ers
proc+la+ma+tion
proc+la+ma+
tions
pro+clama+tory
pro+cleri+cal

pro+clit+ic
pro+clit+ics
pro+cliv+ity
pro+cliv+ities
Proclus
Procne
pro+con+scrip+
tion
pro+con+ser+va+
tion
pro+con+sul
pro+con+suls
pro+con+su+lar
Procopius
pro+cras+ti+nate
pro+cras+ti+
nates
pro+cras+ti+nat+
ing
pro+cras+ti+nat+
ed
pro+cras+ti+na+
tion
pro+cras+ti+na+
tions
pro+cras+ti+na+
tor
pro+cras+ti+na+
tors
pro+cre+ant
pro+cre+ate
pro+cre+ates
pro+cre+at+ing
pro+cre+at+ed
pro+crea+tion
pro+crea+tive
pro+crea+tor
pro+crea+tors
Pro+crus+tean
Procrustes
proc+tol+ogy
proc+tor
proc+tors
proc+to+rial
pro+cum+bent
pro+cur+able
procu+ra+cy
procu+ra+cies
pro+cur+al
pro+cur+als
procu+ra+tion
procu+ra+tions
procu+ra+tor
procu+ra+tors
procu+ra+to+rial

procu+ra+tor+
ship
procu+ra+tor+
ships
pro+cure
pro+cures
pro+cur+ing
pro+cured
pro+cure+ment
pro+cure+ments
pro+cur+er
pro+cur+ers
prod
prods
prods
prod+ding
prod+ded
prod+der
prod+ders
pro+demo+crat+
ic
prodi+gal
prodi+gals
prodi+gal+ity
prodi+gal+ly
pro+di+gious
pro+di+gious+ly
pro+di+gious+
ness
prodi+gy
prodi+gies
pro+dis+ar+ma+
ment
pro+dis+so+lu+
tion
pro+duce
pro+duces
pro+duc+ing
pro+duced
prod+uce
noun
pro+duc+er
pro+duc+ers
pro+duc+ibil+ity
pro+duc+ible
prod+uct
prod+ucts
pro+duc+tion
pro+duc+tions
pro+duc+tion+al
pro+duc+tive
pro+duc+tive+ly
pro+duc+tive+
ness
prod+uc+tiv+ity

pro+em
pro+ems
pro+emial
pro+en+force+
ment
pro+en+zyme
pro+en+zymes
pro-European
pro-Europeans
profa+na+tion
pro+fane
pro+fanes
pro+fan+ing
pro+faned
pro+fane+ly
pro+fane+ness
pro+fan+er
pro+fan+ers
pro+fan+ity
pro+fan+ities
pro+fas+cist
pro+fas+cists
pro+femi+nist
pro+femi+nists
pro+fess
pro+fesses
pro+fess+ing
pro+fessed
pro+fessed
pro+fess+ed+ly
pro+fes+sion
pro+fes+sions
pro+fes+sion+al
pro+fes+sion+
als
pro+fes+sion+al+
ism
pro+fes+sion+al+
ly
pro+fes+sor
pro+fes+sors
prof+es+so+rial
prof+es+sor+iate
prof+es+sor+
iates
pro+fes+sor+ship
pro+fes+sor+
ships
prof+fer
prof+fers
prof+fer+ing
prof+fered
pro+fi+cien+cy
pro+fi+cien+cies
pro+fi+cient

pro+fi+cients
pro+fi+cient+ly
pro+file
  pro+files
  pro+files
  pro+fil+ing
  pro+filed
pro+fil+er
  pro+fil+ers
pro+fil+ist
  pro+fil+ists
prof+it
  prof+its
  prof+its
  prof+it+ing
  prof+it+ed
prof+it+abil+ity
prof+it+able
prof+it+ably
profi+teer
  profi+teers
  profi+teers
  profi+teer+ing
  profi+teered
pro+fit+er+ole
  pro+fit+er+oles
prof+it+less
profit-sharing
prof+li+ga+cy
prof+li+gate
  prof+li+gates
prof+li+gate+ly
pro+for+eign
pro for+ma
pro+found
  pro+founds
pro+found+ly
Profumo
pro+fun+dity
  pro+fun+dities
pro+fuse
pro+fuse+ly
pro+fuse+ness
pro+geni+tive
pro+geni+tive+
  ness
pro+geni+tor
  pro+geni+tors
prog+eny
  prog+enies
pro+ges+ter+one
pro+ges+tin
  pro+ges+tins
pro+ges+to+gen

pro+ges+to+
  gens
prog+nath+ic
prog+na+thous
prog+no+sis
  prog+no+ses
prog+nos+tic
  prog+nos+tics
prog+nos+ti+
  cate
  prog+nos+ti+
  cates
  prog+nos+ti+cat+
  ing
  prog+nos+ti+cat+
  ed
prog+nos+ti+ca+
  tion
  prog+nos+ti+ca+
  tions
prog+nos+ti+ca+
  tive
prog+nos+ti+ca+
  tor
  prog+nos+ti+ca+
  tors
pro+gram
  pro+grams
  pro+grams
  pro+gram+ming
  pro+grammed
pro+gram+able
pro+gram+ma+
  ble
pro+gram+mat+
  ic
pro+gramme
  pro+grammes
  pro+grammes
  pro+gram+ming
  pro+grammed
pro+gram+mer
  pro+gram+mers
pro+gress
  pro+gresses
  pro+gress+ing
  pro+gressed
pro+gres+sion
  pro+gres+sions
pro+gres+sion+al
pro+gres+sive
  pro+gres+sives
pro+gres+sive+ly
pro+gres+sive+
  ness

pro+gres+siv+
  ism
pro+gres+siv+ist
pro+gres+siv+
  ists
pro+hib+it
  pro+hib+its
  pro+hib+it+ing
  pro+hib+it+ed
pro+hib+it+er
  pro+hib+it+ers
pro+hi+bi+tion
  pro+hi+bi+tions
Pro+hi+bi+tion
pro+hi+bi+tion+
  ary
pro+hi+bi+tion+
  ist
  pro+hi+bi+tion+
  ists
Pro+hi+bi+tion+
  ist
Pro+hi+bi+tion+
  ists
pro+hibi+tive
pro+hibi+tive+ly
pro+hibi+tive+
  ness
pro+hibi+tor
  pro+hibi+tors
pro+hibi+tory
pro+im+mi+
  gration
pro+in+dus+try
pro+in+te+gra+
  tion
pro+in+ter+ven+
  tion
pro+in+vest+
  ment
proj+ect
  proj+ects
pro+ject
  pro+jects
  pro+ject+ing
  pro+ject+ed
pro+jec+tile
  pro+jec+tiles
pro+jec+tion
  pro+jec+tions
pro+jec+tion+al
pro+jec+tion+ist
  pro+jec+tion+
  ists
pro+jec+tive

pro+jec+tor
  pro+jec+tors
pro+kary+ote
  pro+kary+otes
pro+kary+ot+ic
Prokofiev
Pro+kop+yevsk
pro+la+bour
pro+lac+tin
pro+lapse
  pro+lapses
  pro+lapses
  pro+laps+ing
  pro+lapsed
pro+late
pro+late+ly
prole
  proles
pro+legom+enal
pro+legom+enon
pro+legom+ena
pro+lep+sis
  pro+lep+ses
pro+lep+tic
pro+letar+ian
  pro+letar+ians
pro+letar+ian+
  ism
pro+letari+at
  pro+letari+ats
pro-life
pro-lifer
  pro-lifers
pro+lif+er+ate
  pro+lif+er+ates
  pro+lif+er+at+
  ing
  pro+lif+er+at+
  ed
pro+lif+era+tion
  pro+lif+era+
  tions
pro+lif+era+tive
pro+lif+ic
pro+lifi+ca+cy
pro+lifi+cal+ly
pro+lif+ic+ness
pro+lix
pro+lix+ity
pro+lix+ly
pro+locu+tor
  pro+locu+tors
pro+locu+tor+
  ship

pro+locu+tor+
 ships
pro+log
U.S.
 pro+logs
 pro+logs
 pro+log+ing
 pro+loged
Pro+log
pro+logue
 pro+logues
 pro+logues
 pro+logu+ing
 pro+logued
pro+long
 pro+longs
 pro+long+ing
 pro+longed
pro+lon+ga+tion
 pro+lon+ga+
  tions
pro+lu+sion
 pro+lu+sions
pro+lu+sory
prom
 proms
prom+enade
 prom+enades
 prom+enades
 prom+enad+ing
 prom+enad+ed
 prom+enad+er
 prom+enad+ers
pro+meth+azine
Pro+methean
Prometheus
pro+methium
pro+mili+tary
promi+nence
 promi+nences
promi+nent
promi+nent+ly
pro+mi+nor+ity
promis+cu+ity
 promis+cu+ities
pro+mis+cu+ous
pro+mis+cu+ous+
 ly
pro+mis+cu+ous+
 ness
prom+ise
 prom+ises
 prom+ises
 prom+is+ing
 prom+ised

promi+see
 promi+sees
prom+is+er
 prom+is+ers
prom+is+ing
prom+is+ing+ly
prom+is+sory
pro+mo
 pro+mos
pro+mod+ern
pro+mon+ar+
 chist
pro+mon+ar+
 chists
prom+on+tory
 prom+on+tories
pro+mote
 pro+motes
pro+mot+ing
pro+mot+ed
pro+mot+er
 pro+mot+ers
pro+mo+tion
 pro+mo+tions
pro+mo+tion+al
prompt
 prompts
 prompts
 prompt+ing
 prompt+ed
prompt+er
 prompt+ers
promp+ti+tude
prompt+ly
prompt+ness
prom+ul+gate
 prom+ul+gates
 prom+ul+gat+
  ing
 prom+ul+gat+ed
prom+ul+ga+tion
 prom+ul+ga+
  tions
prom+ul+ga+tor
 prom+ul+ga+
  tors
pro+nate
 pro+nates
 pro+nat+ing
 pro+nat+ed
pro+na+tion
pro+na+tion+al+
 ist
pro+na+tion+al+
 ists

pro+na+tor
 pro+na+tors
prone
prone+ly
prone+ness
prong
 prongs
 prongs
 prong+ing
pronged
pronged
prong+horn
 prong+horns
pro+nomi+nal
pro+nomi+nal+ly
pro+noun
 pro+nouns
pro+nounce
 pro+nounces
pro+nounc+ing
pro+nounced
pro+nounce+able
pro+nounced
pro+nounc+ed+ly
pro+nounce+
 ment
 pro+nounce+
  ments
pro+nounc+er
 pro+nounc+ers
pron+to
pro+nun+cia+tion
 pro+nun+cia+
  tions
proof
 proofs
 proofs
 proof+ing
 proofed
proof+read
 proof+reads
 proof+read+ing
 proof+read
proof+reader
 proof+readers
prop
 props
 props
prop+ping
propped
pro+pae+deu+tic
 pro+pae+deu+
  tics
propa+gan+da
 Propa+gan+da

Propa+gan+das
propa+gan+dise
 propa+gan+
  dises
 propa+gan+dis+
  ing
 propa+gan+
  dised
propa+gan+dism
propa+gan+dist
 propa+gan+
  dists
propa+gan+dize
 propa+gan+
  dizes
 propa+gan+diz+
  ing
 propa+gan+
  dized
propa+gate
 propa+gates
 propa+gat+ing
 propa+gat+ed
propa+ga+tion
 propa+ga+tions
 propa+ga+tion+al
 propa+ga+tive
 propa+ga+tor
 propa+ga+tors
pro+pane
pro pa+tria
pro+pel
 pro+pels
 pro+pel+ling
 pro+pelled
 pro+pel+lant
  pro+pel+lants
 pro+pel+lent
  pro+pel+lents
 pro+pel+ler
  pro+pel+lers
pro+pene
pro+pen+sity
 pro+pen+sities
prop+er
 prop+er+ly
 prop+er+ness
 prop+er+tied
 Propertius
 prop+er+ty
  prop+er+ties
proph+ecy
 proph+ecies
 proph+esi+able
 proph+esi+er

proph+esi+ers
proph+esy
  proph+esies
  proph+esy+ing
  proph+esied
proph+et
  proph+ets
Proph+et
proph+et+ess
  proph+et+esses
pro+phet+ic
pro+pheti+cal+ly
prophy+lac+tic
  prophy+lac+tics
prophy+lax+is
pro+pin+quity
pro+pi+ti+able
pro+pi+ti+ate
  pro+pi+ti+ates
  pro+pi+ti+at+ing
  pro+pi+ti+at+ed
pro+pi+tia+tion
  pro+pi+tia+tions
  pro+pi+tia+tor
  pro+pi+tia+tors
  pro+pi+tia+to+ry
pro+pi+tious
pro+pi+tious+ly
prop+jet
  prop+jets
prop+man
  prop+men
propo+lis
pro+po+nent
  pro+po+nents
Pro+pon+tis
pro+por+tion
  pro+por+tions
  pro+por+tions
  pro+por+tion+ing
  pro+por+tioned
pro+por+tion+able
pro+por+tion+ably
pro+por+tion+al
  pro+por+tion+als
pro+por+tion+al+ity
pro+por+tion+al+ly
pro+por+tion+ate

pro+por+tion+ates
pro+por+tion+at+ing
pro+por+tion+at+ed
pro+por+tion+ate+ly
pro+por+tion+ment
pro+pos+able
pro+po+sal
  pro+po+sals
pro+pose
  pro+poses
  pro+pos+ing
  pro+posed
pro+pos+er
  pro+pos+ers
pro+posi+ta
  pro+posi+tae
propo+si+tion
  propo+si+tions
  propo+si+tions
  propo+si+tion+ing
propo+si+tioned
propo+si+tion+al
pro+posi+tus
  pro+posi+ti
pro+pound
  pro+pounds
  pro+pound+ing
  pro+pound+ed
pro+pound+er
  pro+pound+ers
pro+prano+lol
pro+pri+etari+ly
pro+pri+etary
  pro+pri+etaries
pro+pri+etor
  pro+pri+etors
pro+pri+etorial
pro+pri+etress
  pro+pri+etresses
pro+pri+etrix
  pro+pri+etrixes
pro+pri+ety
  pro+pri+eties
pro+prio+cep+tive
pro+prio+cep+tor
pro+prio+cep+tors
prop+to+sis

prop+to+ses
pro+pul+sion
  pro+pul+sions
  pro+pul+sive
pro+pul+sory
pro+pyl
propy+laeum
  propy+laea
pro+pyl+ene
propy+lon
  propy+lons *or*
  propy+la
pro rata
pro+rat+able
pro+rate
  pro+rates
  pro+rat+ing
  pro+rat+ed
pro+ra+tion
  pro+ra+tions
pro+re+form
pro+res+to+ra+tion
pro+re+vi+sion
pro+revo+lu+tion+ary
pro+ro+ga+tion
  pro+ro+ga+tions
pro+rogue
  pro+rogues
  pro+rogu+ing
  pro+rogued
pro+sa+ic
pro+sai+cal+ly
pro+scenium
  pro+scenia *or*
  pro+sceniums
pro+sciut+to
pro+scribe
  pro+scribes
  pro+scrib+ing
  pro+scribed
pro+scrib+er
  pro+scrib+ers
pro+scrip+tion
  pro+scrip+tions
prose
  proses
pros+ecut+able
pros+ecute
  pros+ecutes
  pros+ecut+ing
  pros+ecut+ed
pros+ecu+tion

pros+ecu+tions
pros+ecu+tor
  pros+ecu+tors
prose+like
pros+elyte
  pros+elytes
  pros+elytes
pros+elyt+ing
pros+elyt+ed
pros+elyt+ic
pros+elyt+ise
  pros+elyt+ises
  pros+elyt+is+ing
pros+elyt+ised
pros+elyt+is+er
  pros+elyt+is+ers
pros+elyt+ism
pros+elyt+ize
  pros+elyt+izes
  pros+elyt+iz+ing
pros+elyt+ized
pros+elyt+iz+er
  pros+elyt+iz+ers
pros+en+cepha+lon
pros+en+cepha+la
pros+en+chy+ma
Pro+ser+pi+na
prosi+ly
pro+sim+ian
  pro+sim+ians
prosi+ness
pro+sit
pro+slav+ery
pro+sod+ic
proso+dist
  proso+dists
proso+dy
proso+po+peia
  proso+po+peias
proso+po+poeia
  proso+po+poeias
pros+pect
  pros+pects
pro+spect
  pro+spects
  pro+spect+ing
  pro+spect+ed
pro+spec+tive
pro+spec+tive+ly

pro+spec+tor
pro+spec+tors
pro+spec+tus
pro+spec+tuses
pros+per
pros+pers
pros+per+ing
pros+pered
pros+per+ity
pros+per+ous
pros+per+ous+ly
Prost
pros+ta+glan+din
pros+ta+glan+
dins
pros+tate
pros+tates
pros+the+sis
pros+the+ses
pros+thet+ic
pros+theti+cal+
ly
pros+thet+ics
pros+ti+tute
pros+ti+tutes
pros+ti+tutes
pros+ti+tut+ing
pros+ti+tut+ed
pros+ti+tu+tion
pros+ti+tu+tor
pros+ti+tu+tors
pros+trate
pros+trates
pros+trat+ing
pros+trat+ed
pros+tra+tion
pros+tra+tions
pro+style
pro+styles
prosy
prosi+er
prosi+est
pro+syn+di+cal+
ism
pro+tac+tin+ium
pro+tago+nism
pro+tago+nist
pro+tago+nists
Protagoras
prota+sis
prota+ses
pro+tea
pro+teas
pro+tean
pro+tease

pro+teases
pro+tect
pro+tects
pro+tect+ing
pro+tect+ed
pro+tect+ant
pro+tect+ants
pro+tec+tion
pro+tec+tion+
ism
pro+tec+tion+ist
pro+tec+tion+
ists
pro+tec+tive
pro+tec+tives
pro+tec+tive+ly
pro+tec+tive+
ness
pro+tec+tor
pro+tec+tors
Pro+tec+tor
pro+tec+tor+ate
pro+tec+tor+
ates
pro+tec+tress
pro+tect+tresses
pro+té+gé
pro+té+gés
pro+té+gée
pro+té+gées
pro+tein
pro+teins
pro+teina+ceous
pro+tein+ic
pro+tei+nous
pro tem+po+re
pro+teoly+sis
pro+teo+lyt+ic
pro+test
pro+tests
pro+tests
pro+test+ing
pro+test+ed
pro+test+ant
pro+test+ants
Prot+es+tant
Prot+es+tants
Prot+es+tant+
ism
pro+tes+ta+tion
pro+tes+ta+
tions
pro+test+er
pro+test+ers
pro+test+ing+ly

pro+tes+tor
pro+tes+tors
Proteus
pro+tha+la+mi+
on
pro+tha+la+mia
pro+tha+la+mium
pro+tha+la+mia
pro+thal+lium
pro+thal+lia
pro+thal+lus
pro+thal+li
proth+esis
pro+thet+ic
pro+theti+cal+ly
pro+throm+bin
pro+tist
pro+tists
pro+tium
proto+col
proto+cols
proto+hu+man
proto+hu+mans
Proto-Indo-
European
proto+mar+tyr
proto+mar+tyrs
pro+ton
pro+tons
proto+plasm
proto+plas+mic
proto+type
proto+types
proto+typ+ic
proto+zoan
proto+zoa or
proto+zoans
proto+zo+ic
proto+zo+on
proto+zoa
pro+tract
pro+tracts
pro+tract+ing
pro+tract+ed
pro+tract+ed+ly
pro+trac+tile
pro+trac+tion
pro+trac+tions
pro+trac+tor
pro+trac+tors
pro+trude
pro+trudes
pro+trud+ing
pro+trud+ed

pro+tru+sile
pro+tru+sion
pro+tru+sions
pro+tru+sive
pro+tu+ber+ance
pro+tu+ber+
ances
pro+tu+ber+an+
cy
pro+tu+ber+an+
cies
pro+tu+ber+ant
pro+tu+ber+ant+
ly
proud
proud+er
proud+est
Proudhon
proud+ly
proud+ness
pro+un+ion
pro+uni+ver+sity
Proust
prov+abil+ity
prov+able
prov+ably
prove
proves
prov+ing
proved
proved or
prov+en
prov+en
prov+enance
Pro+ven+çal
Pro+ven+çals
Pro+vence
prov+en+der
prov+erb
prov+erbs
pro+ver+bial
pro+ver+bi+al+ly
pro+vide
pro+vides
pro+vid+ing
pro+vid+ed
pro+vid+ed
provi+dence
Providence
God
Provi+dence
place name
provi+dent
provi+den+tial
provi+den+tial+ly

provi+dent+ly
pro+vid+er
 pro+vid+ers
pro+vid+ing
prov+ince
 prov+inces
Province+town
prov+ince+wide
pro+vin+cial
 pro+vin+cials
pro+vin+cial+ism
pro+vin+ci+al+ity
pro+vin+cial+ly
pro+virus
 pro+viruses
pro+vi+sion
 pro+vi+sions
 pro+vi+sions
 pro+vi+sion+ing
 pro+vi+sioned
pro+vi+sion+al
Pro+vi+sion+al
 Pro+vi+sion+als
pro+vi+sion+al+
 ly
pro+vi+sion+er
 pro+vi+sion+ers
pro+vi+so
 pro+vi+sos or
 pro+vi+soes
pro+vi+so+ri+ly
pro+vi+sory
Pro+vo
 Pro+vos
provo+ca+tion
provo+ca+tions
pro+voca+tive
pro+voca+tive+ly
pro+voke
 pro+vokes
 pro+vok+ing
 pro+voked
pro+vok+ing
pro+vok+ing+ly
prov+ost
 prov+osts
prow
 prows
pro+war
prow+ess
prowl
 prowls
 prowls
 prowl+ing
 prowled

prowl+er
 prowl+ers
proxi+mal
proxi+mal+ly
proxi+mate
proxi+mate+ly
prox+im+ity
 prox+im+ities
proxi+mo
proxy
 proxies
prude
 prudes
pru+dence
pru+dent
pru+den+tial
pru+den+tial+ly
Prudentius
pru+dent+ly
prud+ery
Prud'hon
prud+ish
prud+ish+ly
prui+nose
prun+able
prune
 prunes
 prunes
 prun+ing
 pruned
pru+nel+la
prun+er
 prun+ers
pru+ri+ence
pru+ri+ent
pru+ri+ent+ly
pru+ri+gi+nous
pru+ri+go
pru+rit+ic
pru+ri+tus
Prus+sia
Prus+sian
 Prus+sians
Prut
pry
 pries
 pries
 pry+ing
 pried
pry+er
 pry+ers
Prynne
Prze+myśl
psalm
 psalms

psalm+ic
psalm+ist
 psalm+ists
psalm+od+ic
psalmo+dist
 psalmo+dists
psalmo+dy
psalmo+dies
Psal+ter
 Psal+ters
psal+ter+ium
psal+teria
psal+tery
 psal+teries
psepho+logi+cal
psepho+logi+cal+
 ly
pse+pholo+gist
 pse+pholo+gists
pse+phol+ogy
pseud
 pseuds
Pseud+epig+ra+
 pha
Pseud+epi+graph+
 ic
Pseud+epi+
 graphi+cal
pseu+do
pseudo+an+tique
pseudo+ar+cha+
 ic
pseudoa+ris+to+
 crat+ic
pseudo+ar+tis+
 tic
pseudo-
 Bohemian
pseudo+carp
 pseudo+carps
pseudo+car+
 pous
pseudo+clas+sic
pseudo+clas+si+
 cal
pseudo+clas+si+
 cism
pseudo+cul+ti+
 vat+ed
pseudo+demo+
 crat+ic
pseudo-Elizabe+
 than
pseudo-Georgian
pseudo-Gothic

pseudo-Grecian
pseudo+his+tor+
 ic
pseudo+his+tori+
 cal
pseudo+lit+er+
 ary
pseudo+me+di+
 eval
pseudo+mod+ern
pseudo+morph
 pseudo+morphs
pseudo+mor+
 phic
pseudo+mor+
 phism
pseudo+mythi+
 cal
pseudo+nym
 pseudo+nyms
pseudo+nym+ity
pseu+dony+
 mous
pseudo-oriental
pseudo+philo+
 sophi+cal
pseudo+po+dium
pseudo+po+dia
pseudo+pro+fes+
 sion+al
pseudo+psycho+
 logi+cal
pseudo+schol+ar+
 ly
pseudo+sci+ence
 pseudo+sci+
 ences
pseudo+sci+en+
 tif+ic
pseudo+vec+tor
 pseudo+vec+
 tors
pseudo-Victorian
pshaw
psi
 psis
psilo+cy+bin
psit+ta+cine
psit+ta+co+sis
Pskov
pso+as
pso+ria+sis
pso+ri+at+ic
psst
psych

psychs
psych+ing
psyched
psyche
psyches
psych+ing
psyched
psy+che
psy+ches
Psyche
psychedel+ic
psychedeli+cal+ly
psy+chi+at+ric
psy+chi+at+ri+
cal
psy+chi+at+ri+
cal+ly
psy+chia+trist
psy+chia+trists
psy+chia+try
psy+chic
psy+chics
psy+chi+cal
psy+chi+cal+ly
psy+cho
psy+chos
psycho+ac+tive
psycho+ana+lyse
psycho+ana+
lyses
psycho+ana+lys+
ing
psycho+ana+
lysed
psycho+analy+
sis
psycho+ana+lyst
psycho+ana+
lysts
psycho+ana+lyt+
ic
psycho+ana+lyti+
cal
psycho+ana+lyti+
cal+ly
psycho+bio+logi+
cal
psycho+bi+olo+
gist
psycho+bi+olo+
gists
psycho+bi+ol+
ogy
psycho+chemi+
cal

psycho+chemi+
cals
psycho+dra+ma
psycho+dra+
mas
psycho+dy+nam+
ic
psycho+dy+nam+
ics
psycho+gen+ic
psycho+geni+cal+
ly
psycho+ki+nesis
psycho+lin+guist
psycho+lin+
guists
psycho+lin+guis+
tics
psycho+logi+cal
psycho+logi+cal+
ly
psy+cholo+gise
psy+cholo+
gises
psy+cholo+gis+
ing
psy+cholo+
gised
psy+cholo+gist
psy+cholo+gists
psy+cholo+gize
psy+cholo+
gizes
psy+cholo+giz+
ing
psy+cholo+
gized
psy+chol+ogy
psy+chol+ogies
psycho+met+ric
psycho+met+ri+
cal
psycho+met+ri+
cal+ly
psycho+met+rics
psy+chom+etry
psycho+mo+tor
psycho+neu+ro+
sis
psycho+neu+ro+
ses
psycho+path
psycho+paths
psycho+path+ic

psycho+pathi+cal+
ly
psycho+patho+
logi+cal
psycho+pa+thol+
ogy
psy+chopa+thy
psy+chopa+
thies
psycho+phar+ma+
col+ogy
psycho+physi+
cal
psycho+phys+ics
psycho+physio+
logi+cal
psycho+physi+ol+
ogy
psycho+sex+ual
psycho+sexu+al+
ly
psy+cho+sis
psy+cho+ses
psycho+so+cial
psycho+so+mat+
ic
psycho+sur+gery
psycho+sur+gi+
cal
psycho+thera+
peu+tic
psycho+thera+
peu+ti+cal+ly
psycho+thera+
pist
psycho+thera+
pists
psycho+thera+py
psy+chot+ic
psy+chot+ics
psy+choti+cal+ly
psy+choto+mi+
met+ic
psy+chrom+eter
psy+chrom+
eters
Ptah
ptar+mi+gan
ptar+mi+gans
or
ptar+mi+gan
pteri+do+logi+cal
pteri+dol+ogy
pteri+do+phyte
pteri+do+phytes

ptero+dac+tyl
ptero+dac+tyls
ptero+pod
ptero+pods
ptero+saur
ptero+saurs
Ptol+ema+ic
Ptolemy
pto+main
pto+mains
pto+maine
pto+maines
pto+sis
pto+ses
ptot+ic
ptya+lin
p-type
pub
pubs
pub+bing
pubbed
pub-crawl
pub-crawls
pub-crawls
pub-crawling
pub-crawled
pu+ber+tal
pu+ber+ty
pu+bes
pu+bes
pu+bes+cence
pu+bes+cent
pu+bic
pu+bis
pu+bes
pub+lic
pub+li+can
pub+li+cans
pub+li+ca+tion
pub+li+ca+tions
pub+li+cise
pub+li+cises
pub+li+cis+ing
pub+li+cised
pub+li+cist
pub+li+cists
pub+lic+ity
pub+li+cize
pub+li+cizes
pub+li+ciz+ing
pub+li+cized
pub+lic+ly
public-service
public-spirit+ed

pub+lish
  pub+lishes
  pub+lish+ing
  pub+lished
pub+lish+able
pub+lish+er
  pub+lish+ers
Puccini
puce
puck
  pucks
  pucks
  puck+ing
  pucked
pucka
puck+er
  puck+ers
  puck+ers
  puck+er+ing
  puck+ered
puck+ish
pud+ding
  pud+dings
pud+dingy
pud+dle
  pud+dles
  pud+dles
  pud+dling
  pud+dled
pud+dler
  pud+dlers
pud+dling
pud+dly
pu+den+cy
pu+den+dal
pu+den+dum
  pu+den+da
pudgi+ly
pudgi+ness
pudgy
  pudgi+er
  pudgi+est
pu+dic
Pud+sey
Pue+bla
pueb+lo
  pueb+los
Pueb+lo
  Pueb+lo *or*
  Pueb+los
pu+er+ile
pu+er+ile+ly
pu+er+il+ity
pu+er+per+al
Puer+to Ri+can

Puer+to Ri+cans
Puer+to Rico
puff
  puffs
  puffs
  puff+ing
  puffed
puff+ball
  puff+balls
puff+er
  puff+ers
puf+fin
  puf+fins
puff-puff
  puff-puffs
puffy
  puffi+er
  puffi+est
pug
  pugs
  pugs
  pug+ging
  pugged
puga+ree
  puga+rees
pug+ga+ree
  pug+ga+rees
pug+ging
pug+gish
pug+gree
  pug+grees
pu+gi+lism
pu+gi+list
  pu+gi+lists
pu+gi+lis+tic
pu+gi+lis+ti+cal+ly
Pugin
Pu+glia
pug+na+cious
pug+na+cious+ly
pug+nac+ity
pug-nosed
pug+ree
  pug+rees
puis+ne
pu+is+sance
pu+is+sant
pu+is+sant+ly
puke
  pukes
  puk+ing
  puked
pu+ke+ko
  pu+ke+kos

puk+ka
Pula
pul+chri+tude
pul+chri+tudi+
  nous
pule
  pules
pul+ing
  puled
pul+er
  pul+ers
Pulitzer
pull
  pulls
  pulls
  pull+ing
  pulled
pull+er
  pull+ers
pul+let
  pul+lets
pul+ley
  pul+leys
pull-in
  pull-ins
pull in
  verb
Pull+man
  Pull+mans
pull-out
  pull-outs
pull out
  verb
pull+over
  pull+overs
pul+lu+late
  pul+lu+lates
  pul+lu+lat+ing
  pul+lu+lat+ed
  pul+lu+la+tion
  pul+lu+la+tions
pull-up
  pull-ups
pull up
  verb
pul+mo+nary
pulp
  pulps
  pulps
  pulp+ing
  pulped
pul+pit
  pul+pits
pulp+wood
pulpy

pulpi+er
  pulpi+est
pul+que
  pul+ques
pul+sar
  pul+sars
pul+sate
  pul+sates
  pul+sat+ing
  pul+sat+ed
pul+sa+til+la
pul+sa+tion
  pul+sa+tions
pul+sa+tive
pul+sa+tor
  pul+sa+tors
pul+sa+tory
pulse
  pulses
  pulses
  puls+ing
  pulsed
pulse+jet
  pulse+jets
pulse+less
pul+sim+eter
  pul+sim+eters
pul+ver+is+able
pul+veri+sa+tion
pul+ver+ise
  pul+ver+ises
  pul+ver+is+ing
  pul+ver+ised
pul+ver+is+er
  pul+ver+is+ers
pul+ver+iz+able
pul+veri+za+tion
pul+ver+ize
  pul+ver+izes
  pul+ver+iz+ing
  pul+ver+ized
pul+ver+iz+er
  pul+ver+iz+ers
pul+veru+lent
puma
  pumas
pum+ice
  pum+ices
  pum+ices
  pum+ic+ing
  pum+iced
pu+mi+ceous
pum+mel
  pum+mels

pum+mel+ling
or
pum+mel+ing
U.S.
pum+melled *or*
pum+meled
U.S.
pump
  pumps
  pumps
  pump+ing
  pumped
pum+per+nick+el
pump+kin
  pump+kins
pun
  puns
  puns
  pun+ning
  punned
puna
  punas
Pu+na+ka
Pu+na+kha
punch
  punches
  punches
  punch+ing
  punched
Punch
punch+ball
  punch+balls
punch+bowl
  punch+bowls
punch-drunk
pun+cheon
  pun+cheons
punch+er
  punch+ers
punchi+ly
Pun+chi+nel+lo
  Pun+chi+nel+los
  or
  Pun+chi+nel+
  loes
punchi+ness
punch-up
  punch-ups
punchy
  punchi+er
  punchi+est
punc+tate
punc+ta+tion
  punc+ta+tions
punc+tilio

punc+tilios
punc+tili+ous
punc+tili+ous+ly
punc+tili+ous+
  ness
punc+tu+al
punc+tu+al+ity
punc+tu+al+ly
punc+tu+ate
  punc+tu+ates
  punc+tu+at+ing
  punc+tu+at+ed
punc+tua+tion
  punc+tua+tions
punc+ture
  punc+tures
  punc+tures
  punc+tur+ing
  punc+tured
pun+dit
  pun+dits
Pune
pun+ga
  pun+gas
pun+gen+cy
pun+gent
pun+gent+ly
Pu+nic
pu+ni+ness
pun+ish
  pun+ishes
  pun+ish+ing
  pun+ished
pun+ish+able
pun+ish+er
  pun+ish+ers
  pun+ish+ing
pun+ish+ment
  pun+ish+ments
pu+ni+tive
pu+ni+tive+ly
Pun+jab
Pun+ja+bi
  Pun+ja+bis
punk
  punks
pun+ka
  pun+kas
pun+kah
  pun+kahs
pun+net
  pun+nets
pun+ster
  pun+sters
punt

punts
punts
punt+ing
punt+ed
Pun+ta Arenas
punt+er
  punt+ers
puny
  puni+er
  puni+est
pup
  pups
  pups
  pup+ping
  pupped
pupa
  pupae *or*
  pupas
pu+pal
pu+pate
  pu+pates
  pu+pat+ing
  pu+pat+ed
pu+pa+tion
  pu+pa+tions
pu+pil
  pu+pils
pu+pil+age
U.S.
pu+pi+lary
pu+pil+lage
pu+pil+lary
pu+pipa+rous
pup+pet
  pup+pets
pup+pet+eer
  pup+pet+eers
pup+pet+ry
pup+py
  pup+pies
pup+py+hood
pup+py+ish
Pu+ra+na
pur+blind
Purcell
pur+chas+able
pur+chase
  pur+chases
  pur+chases
  pur+chas+ing
  pur+chased
  pur+chas+er
  pur+chas+ers
pur+dah
  pur+dahs

pure
  pur+er
  pur+est
pure+bred
  pure+breds
pu+rée
  pu+rées
  pu+rées
  pu+rée+ing
  pu+réed
pure+ly
pure+ness
pur+fle
  pur+fles
  pur+fles
  pur+fling
  pur+fled
pur+fling
  pur+flings
pur+ga+tion
pur+ga+tive
  pur+ga+tives
pur+ga+tive+ly
pur+ga+to+rial
pur+ga+tory
  pur+ga+tories
purge
  purges
  purges
  purg+ing
  purged
Puri
pu+ri+fi+ca+tion
  pu+ri+fi+ca+
  tions
pu+ri+fi+ca+tor
pu+ri+fi+ca+tors
pu+rifi+ca+tory
pu+ri+fi+er
  pu+ri+fi+ers
pu+ri+fy
  pu+ri+fies
  pu+ri+fy+ing
  pu+ri+fied
Pu+rim
  Pu+rims
pu+rin
pu+rine
pu+ri+ri
  pu+ri+ris
pur+ism
pur+ist
  pur+ists
pu+rist+ic
pu+ri+tan

pu+ri+tans
Pu+ri+tan
Pu+ri+tans
pu+ri+tani+cal
pu+ri+tani+cal+ly
pu+ri+tan+ism
Pu+ri+tan+ism
pu+rity
purl
 purls
 purls
 purl+ing
 purled
pur+ler
 pur+lers
pur+lieu
 pur+lieus
pur+lin
 pur+lins
pur+line
 pur+lines
pur+loin
 pur+loins
 pur+loin+ing
 pur+loined
pur+loin+er
 pur+loin+ers
pur+ple
 pur+ples
pur+ple+ness
pur+plish
pur+ply
pur+port
 pur+ports
 pur+port+ing
 pur+port+ed
pur+pose
 pur+poses
 pur+poses
 pur+pos+ing
 pur+posed
purpose-built
pur+pose+ful
pur+pose+ful+ly
pur+pose+ful+
 ness
pur+pose+less
pur+pose+ly
pur+pos+ive
pur+pos+ive+ly
pur+pos+ive+
 ness
pur+pu+ra
purr
 purrs

purrs
purr+ing
purred
purse
purses
purses
purs+ing
pursed
purs+er
purs+ers
purs+lane
purs+lanes
pur+su+ance
pur+su+ant
pur+su+ant+ly
pur+sue
pur+sues
pur+su+ing
pur+sued
pur+su+er
pur+su+ers
pur+suit
pur+suits
pur+sui+vant
pur+sui+vants
pu+ru+lence
pu+ru+lent
pu+ru+lent+ly
Pu+rús
pur+vey
pur+veys
pur+vey+ing
pur+veyed
pur+vey+ance
pur+vey+or
pur+vey+ors
pur+view
pur+views
pus
Pu+san
Pusey
push
 pushes
 pushes
 push+ing
 pushed
push-bike
push-bikes
push-button
adj.
push but+ton
 push but+tons
push+cart
 push+carts
push+chair

push+chairs
pushed
push+er
 push+ers
pushi+ly
pushi+ness
push+ing
push+ing+ly
Push+kin
 place name
Pushkin
 surname
push+over
 push+overs
push-pull
push-start
 push-starts
 push-starts
 push-starting
 push-started
Push+to
 Push+to *or*
 Push+tos
Push+tu
 Push+tu *or*
 Push+tus
push-up
 push-ups
pushy
 pushi+er
 pushi+est
pu+sil+la+nim+ity
pu+sil+lani+mous
pu+sil+lani+mous+
 ly
puss
 pusses
pussy
 pussies
pus+sy
pus+si+er
pus+si+est
pussy+foot
 pussy+foots
 pussy+foot+ing
 pussy+foot+ed
pus+tu+lant
pus+tu+lants
pus+tu+lar
pus+tu+late
pus+tu+lates
pus+tu+lat+ing
pus+tu+lat+ed
pus+tu+la+tion
pus+tule

pus+tules
put
 puts
 put+ting
 put
pu+ta+tive
pu+ta+tive+ly
put-down
 put-downs
put down
 verb
Putnam
put-put
 put-puts
 put-puts
 put-putting
 put-putted
pu+tre+fa+cient
pu+tre+fac+tion
pu+tre+fac+tive
pu+tre+fy
pu+tre+fies
pu+tre+fy+ing
pu+tre+fied
pu+tres+cence
pu+tres+cent
pu+trid
pu+trid+ity
pu+trid+ly
pu+trid+ness
putsch
 putsches
putt
 putts
 putts
 putt+ing
 putt+ed
put+tee
 put+tees
putt+er
 golf club
 putt+ers
putt+er
 U.S.
 putt+ers
 putt+er+ing
 putt+ered
put+ter
 person who puts
 put+ters
put+ter+er
 U.S.
 put+ter+ers
Puttnam
put+to

put+ti
put+ty
put+ties
put+ties
put+ty+ing
put+tied
Pu+tu+ma+yo
put-up
adj.
put up
verb
Puvis de
  Chavannes
Puy de Dôme
Puy de San+cy
Pu-yi
puz+zle
  puz+zles
  puz+zles
  puz+zling
  puz+zled
puz+zle+ment
puz+zler
  puz+zlers
  puz+zling
py+aemia
py+aemic
Pyd+na
pye-dog
  pye-dogs
py+elit+ic
py+eli+tis
py+emia
py+emic
pyg+maean
Pygmalion
pyg+mean
pyg+my
  pyg+mies
  Pyg+mies
pyin+ka+do

pyin+ka+dos
py+ja+mas
pyk+nic
py+lon
py+lons
py+lo+rus
py+lo+ri
Py+los
Pym
Pynchon
Pyong+yang
py+or+rhea
U.S.
py+or+rheal
U.S.
py+or+rhoea
py+or+rhoeal
py+or+rhoeic
py+ra+can+tha
py+ra+can+thas
pyra+mid
pyra+mids
pyra+mids
pyra+mid+ing
pyra+mid+ed
py+rami+dal
py+rami+dal+ly
pyra+midi+cal
pyra+midi+cal+ly
pyre
pyres
Pyr+enean
Pyr+enees
mountain range
Py+ré+nées
region
Py+rénées-
  Atlantiques
Py+rénées-
  Orientales
py+rethrin
py+rethrum

py+rethrums
py+ret+ic
Py+rex
Trademark
py+rexia
py+rex+ial
py+rex+ic
pyri+dine
pyri+dox+ine
py+rimi+dine
py+rite
py+ri+tes
  py+ri+tes *or*
  py+rites
py+rit+ic
pyro+elec+tric+
  ity
pyro+gal+lol
pyro+gen+ic
py+rog+enous
py+rog+ra+phy
  py+rog+ra+
    phies
pyro+lig+ne+ous
pyro+lig+nic
py+roly+sis
pyro+lyt+ic
pyro+ma+nia
pyro+ma+ni+ac
  pyro+ma+ni+
    acs
py+rom+eter
  py+rom+eters
pyro+met+ric
pyro+met+ri+cal
pyro+met+ri+cal+
  ly
py+rom+etry
py+rope
pyro+phor+ic
pyro+sis
pyro+stat

pyro+stats
pyro+stat+ic
pyro+tech+nic
pyro+tech+ni+cal
pyro+tech+nics
py+rox+ene
  py+rox+enes
py+roxy+lin
pyr+rhic
  pyr+rhics
Pyr+rhic
Pyrrho
Pyr+rho+nism
Pyr+rho+nist
  Pyr+rho+nists
Pyrrhus
Pythagoras
philosopher
Py+thago+ras
lunar crater
Py+thago+rean
  Py+thago+reans
Pytheas
Pythia
Pyth+ian
  Pyth+ians
Pythias
py+thon
  py+thons
Py+thon
py+thon+ess
  py+thon+esses
py+thon+ic
pyu+ria
P'yŏng-yang
pyx
  pyxes
pyx+id+ium
  pyx+idia
pyx+is
  pyxi+des

Q

q
q's
Q
Q's *or*
Qs
Qa+bis
Qaboos bin Said
Qaddafi
Qad+dish
Qad+dish+im
Qair+wan
QANTAS
QARANC
Qa+tar
Qa+ta+ri
Qa+ta+ris
qaw+wa+li
qaw+wa+lis
Qeshm
qi
Qing+dao
Qing+hai
Qi+qi+har
Qishm
Qom
Q-ship
Q-ships
qua
quack
quacks
quacks
quack+ing
quacked
quack+ery
quack+eries
quack+ish
quack+sal+ver
quack+sal+vers
quad
quads
Quad+ra+gesi+ma
Quad+ra+gesi+mal
quad+ran+gle

quad+ran+gles
quad+ran+gu+lar
quad+rant
quad+rants
quad+ran+tal
quad+ra+phon+ic
quad+ra+phon+ics
quad+rat
quad+rats
quad+rate
quad+rates
quad+rates
quad+rat+ing
quad+rat+ed
quad+rat+ic
quad+rat+ics
quad+ra+ture
quad+ra+tures
quad+rel+la
quad+rel+las
quad+ren+nial
quad+ren+nials
quad+ren+ni+al+ly
quad+ren+nium
quad+ren+niums *or*
quad+ren+nia
quad+ric
quad+rics
quad+ri+ceps
quad+ri+cepses *or*
quad+ri+ceps
quad+ri+fid
quad+ri+lat+er+al
quad+ri+lat+er+als
quad+rille
quad+rilles
quad+ril+lion
quad+ril+lions
quad+ril+lionth
quad+ri+no+mial

quad+ri+no+mials
quad+ri+plegia
quad+ri+plegic
quad+ri+va+lence
quad+ri+va+len+cy
quad+ri+va+lent
quad+riv+ium
quad+riv+ia
quad+roon
quad+roons
quad+ro+phon+ic
quad+ro+phon+ics
quad+ru+ma+nous
quad+ru+ped
quad+ru+peds
quad+ru+ped+al
quad+ru+ple
quad+ru+ples
quad+ru+ples
quad+ru+pling
quad+ru+pled
quad+ru+plet
quad+ru+plets
quad+ru+pli+cate
quad+ru+pli+cates
quad+ru+pli+cates
quad+ru+pli+cat+ing
quad+ru+pli+cat+ed
quad+ru+ply
quaes+tor
quaes+tors
quaes+to+ri+al
quaff
quaffs
quaff+ing
quaffed
quaff+er

quaff+ers
quag
quags
quag+ga
quag+gas *or*
quag+ga
quag+gy
quag+gi+er
quag+gi+est
quag+mire
quag+mires
qua+hog
qua+hogs
quaich
quaichs
Quai d'Orsay
quaigh
quaighs
quail
quails *or*
quail
quail
quails
quail+ing
quailed
quaint
quaint+er
quaint+est
quaint+ly
quaint+ness
quair
quairs
quake
quakes
quakes
quak+ing
quaked
Quak+er
Quak+ers
Quak+er+ess
Quak+er+ish
Quak+er+ism
quaki+ness
quaky
quaki+er

quaki+est
quali+fi+able
quali+fi+ca+tion
  quali+fi+ca+
   tions
quali+fied
quali+fi+er
  quali+fi+ers
quali+fy
  quali+fies
  quali+fy+ing
  quali+fied
quali+ta+tive
quali+ta+tive+ly
qual+ity
  qual+ities
qualm
  qualms
qualm+ish
quan+dang
  quan+dangs
quan+da+ry
  quan+da+ries
quan+dong
  quan+dongs
quango
  quangos
quant
  quants
  quants
  quant+ing
  quant+ed
Quant
quan+ta
quan+tic
  quan+tics
quan+ti+fi+able
quan+ti+fi+ca+
 tion
  quan+ti+fi+ca+
   tions
quan+ti+fi+er
  quan+ti+fi+ers
quan+ti+fy
  quan+ti+fies
  quan+ti+fy+ing
  quan+ti+fied
quan+ti+sa+tion
  quan+ti+sa+
   tions
quan+tise
  quan+tises
  quan+tis+ing
  quan+tised
quan+ti+ta+tive

quan+ti+ta+tive+
 ly
quan+ti+tive
quan+tity
  quan+tities
quan+ti+za+tion
  quan+ti+za+
   tions
quan+tize
  quan+tizes
  quan+tiz+ing
  quan+tized
quan+tong
  quan+tongs
quan+tum
  quan+ta
quan+tum me+
 ruit
qua+qua+ver+sal
quar+an+tine
  quar+an+tines
  quar+an+tines
  quar+an+tin+ing
  quar+an+tined
quark
  quarks
Quarles
quar+rel
  quar+rels
  quar+rels
  quar+relling *or*
  quar+rel+ing
  U.S.
  quar+relled *or*
  quar+reled
  U.S.
quar+rel+er
  U.S.
  quar+rel+ers
  quar+rel+ler
  quar+rel+lers
quar+rel+some
quar+rian
  quar+rians
quar+rion
  quar+rions
quar+ry
  quar+ries
  quar+ries
  quar+ry+ing
  quar+ried
quarry+man
  quarry+men
quart
  quarts

quar+tan
quarte
quar+ter
  quar+ters
  quar+ters
  quar+ter+ing
  quar+tered
  quarter+back
  quarter+backs
  quarter-bound
  quarter+deck
  quarter+decks
  quarter+final
  quarter+finals
  quarter-hour
  quarter-hours
  quar+ter+ing
  quar+ter+ings
  quarter+light
  quarter+lights
  quar+ter+ly
  quar+ter+lies
  quarter+master
  quarter+masters
  quarter-miler
  quarter-milers
  quar+tern
  quar+terns
  quar+ters
  quarter+staff
  quarter+staves
quar+tet
  quar+tets
  quar+tette
  quar+tettes
quar+tic
  quar+tics
quar+tile
  quar+tiles
quar+to
  quar+tos
quartz
  quartzes
  quartz+ite
  quartz+ites
qua+sar
  qua+sars
quash
  quashes
  quash+ing
  quashed
qua+si
Quasimodo
quas+sia
  quas+sias

qua+ter+cen+te+
 nary
qua+ter+cen+te+
 naries
qua+ter+cen+ten+
 nial
qua+ter+cen+
 ten+nials
qua+ter+nary
  qua+ter+naries
Qua+ter+nary
qua+ter+ni+on
  qua+ter+ni+ons
Quath+lam+ba
quat+rain
  quat+rains
Qua+tre Bras
quatre+foil
  quatre+foils
quat+tro+cen+to
qua+ver
  qua+vers
  qua+vers
  qua+ver+ing
  qua+vered
  qua+ver+ing+ly
quay
  quays
quay+age
  quay+ages
Quayle
quay+side
  quay+sides
quean
  queans
quea+si+ly
quea+si+ness
quea+sy
quea+si+er
quea+si+est
Que+bec
Que+bec+er
Que+bec+ers
Que+beck+er
Que+beck+ers
Qué+be+cois
Qué+be+cois
que+bra+cho
que+bra+chos
Quechua
Quechuas *or*
Quechua
Quech+uan
Quech+uans
queen

queens
queens
queen+ing
queened
Queen-Anne
queen+ly
queen+li+er
queen+li+est
Queens
Queens+ber+ry
Queens+land
Queens+land+er
Queens+land+ers
Queens+town
queer
queers
queers
queer+ing
queered
queer+er
queer+est
queer+ly
queer+ness
queer+nesses
quell
quells
quell+ing
quelled
quell+er
quell+ers
Quel+part
Que+moy
quench
quenches
quench+ing
quenched
quench+able
quench+er
quench+ers
Queneau
que+nelle
que+nelles
Quercia
Que+réta+ro
que+rist
que+rists
quern
querns
queru+lous
queru+lous+ly
queru+lous+ness
que+ry
que+ries
que+ries

que+ry+ing
que+ried
Quesnay
quest
quests
quests
quest+ing
quest+ed
quest+er
quest+ers
quest+ing+ly
ques+tion
ques+tions
ques+tions
ques+tion+ing
ques+tioned
ques+tion+able
ques+tion+able+ness
ques+tion+ably
ques+tion+er
ques+tion+ers
ques+tion+ing+ly
ques+tion+less
ques+tion+less+ly
ques+tion+naire
ques+tion+naires
ques+tor
ques+tors
Quet+ta
quet+zal
quet+zals or
quet+zales
Quet+zal+coa+tl
queue
queues
queues
queue+ing or
queu+ing
queued
queue-jump
queue-jumps
queue-jumping
queue-jumped
queue-jumper
queue-jumpers
Quezon y Molina
quib+ble
quib+bles
quib+bles
quib+bling
quib+bled
quib+bler

quib+blers
quib+bling
Qui+beron
quiche
quiches
quick
quicks
quick+er
quick+est
quick-change
quick+en
quick+ens
quick+en+ing
quick+ened
quick-freeze
quick-freezes
quick-freezing
quick-froze
quick-frozen
quickie
quickies
quick+lime
quick+ly
quick+ness
quick+sand
quick+sands
quick+set
quick+sets
quick+silver
quick+step
quick+steps
quick+steps
quick+step+ping
quick+stepped
quick-tempered
quick+thorn
quick+thorns
quick-witted
quick-witted+ly
quick-witted+ness
quid
tobacco
quids
quid
money
quid
quid+dity
quid+dities
quid+nunc
quid+nuncs
quid pro quo
quid pro quos
qui+es+cence
qui+es+cen+cy

qui+es+cent
qui+es+cent+ly
qui+et
qui+ets
qui+et+ing
qui+et+ed
qui+et+er
qui+et+est
qui+et+en
qui+et+ens
qui+et+en+ing
qui+et+ened
qui+et+ism
qui+et+ist
qui+et+ists
qui+et+ly
qui+et+ness
qui+etude
qui+etus
qui+etuses
quiff
quiffs
quill
quills
quills
quill+ing
quilled
Quil+mes
quilt
quilts
quilts
quilt+ing
quilt+ed
quilt+er
quilt+ers
quilt+ing
quilt+ings
Quim+per
quin
quins
qui+na+ry
quince
quinces
quin+cen+te+nary
quin+cen+te+naries
quin+cen+ten+nial
quin+cen+ten+nials
quin+cun+cial
quin+cunx
quin+cunxes
Quine

qui+nel+la
Qui Nhong
quini+dine
qui+nine
Quinn
quin+ol
quino+line
quino+lines
quin+qua+genar+
  ian
quin+qua+genar+
  ians
Quin+qua+gesi+
  ma
quin+que+cen+te+
  nary
quin+que+cen+
  te+naries
quin+quen+nial
quin+quen+nials
quin+quen+ni+al+
  ly
quin+quen+nium
quin+quen+nia
quin+que+reme
quin+que+remes
quin+que+va+
  lence
quin+que+va+len+
  cy
quin+que+va+
  lent
quin+sy
quint
quints
quin+tain
quin+tains
quin+tal
quin+tals
quin+tan
Quin+ta+na Roo
quinte
quin+tes+sence
quin+tes+sen+tial
quin+tet

quin+tets
quin+tette
quin+tettes
quin+til+lion
quin+til+lions
  or
quin+til+lion
quin+til+lionth
quin+tu+ple
quin+tu+ples
quin+tu+ples
quin+tu+pling
quin+tu+pled
quin+tu+plet
quin+tu+plets
quin+tu+pli+cate
quin+tu+pli+
  cates
quin+tu+pli+
  cates
quin+tu+pli+cat+
  ing
quin+tu+pli+cat+
  ed
quip
quips
quips
quip+ping
quipped
quip+ster
quip+sters
quire
quires
Quiri+nal
Quirinus
quirk
quirks
quirki+ness
quirki+nesses
quirky
quirki+er
quirki+est
quirt
quirts
quirts

quirt+ing
quirt+ed
quis+ling
quis+lings
quit
quits
quit+ting
quit+ted or
quit
  U.S.
quitch
quit+claim
quit+claims
quit+claims
quit+claim+ing
quit+claimed
quite
Qui+to
quit+rent
quit+rents
quits
quit+tance
quit+tances
quit+ter
quit+ters
quiv+er
quiv+ers
quiv+ers
quiv+er+ing
quiv+ered
quiv+ery
qui vive
Quixote
quix+ot+ic
quix+oti+cal+ly
quiz
quiz+zes
quiz+zes
quiz+zing
quizzed
quiz+zer
quiz+zers
quiz+zi+cal
quiz+zi+cal+ly
Qum

Qum+ran
Qun+gur
quod
quods
quod erat de+
  mon+stran+dum
quod+li+bet
quod+li+bets
quoin
quoins
quoit
quoits
quoits
quok+ka
quok+kas
quon+dam
quor+ate
Quorn
  Trademark
quor+um
quor+ums
quo+ta
quo+tas
quot+abil+ity
quot+able
quo+ta+tion
quo+ta+tions
quote
quotes
quotes
quot+ing
quot+ed
quoth
quotha
quo+tid+ian
quo+tid+ians
quo+tient
quo+tients
quo va+dis
quo war+ran+to
Qur'an
Qwa+qwa

R

r
r's
R
R's *or*
Rs
Ra
Ra+bat
Ra+baul
rab+bet
rab+bets
rab+bets
rab+bet+ing
rab+bet+ed
rab+bi
rab+bis
rab+bin+ate
rab+bin+ates
rab+bin+ic
Rab+bin+ic
rab+bini+cal
rab+bini+cal+ly
rab+bit
rab+bits *or*
rab+bit
rab+bits
rab+bit+ing
rab+bit+ed
rab+ble
rab+bles
rabble-rouser
rabble-rousers
rabble-rousing
Rabelais
Rab+elai+sian
Rab+elai+sians
Rab+elai+si+an+ism
Rabi
rab+ic
rab+id
ra+bid+ity
rab+id+ly
rab+id+ness
ra+bies
ra+bi+et+ic

rac+coon
rac+coons *or*
rac+coon
race
races
races
rac+ing
raced
Race
race+card
race+cards
race+course
race+courses
race+horse
race+horses
ra+ceme
ra+cemes
ra+cemic
rac+emism
rac+emose
rac+er
rac+ers
race+track
race+tracks
race+way
race+ways
Rachel
ra+chial
ra+chid+ial
ra+chis
ra+chises *or*
ra+chi+des
ra+chit+ic
ra+chi+tis
Rachmaninoff
Rachmaninov
Rach+man+ism
ra+cial
ra+cial+ism
ra+cial+isms
ra+cial+ist
ra+cial+ists
ra+cial+ly
raci+ly
Racine

raci+ness
rac+ism
rac+isms
rac+ist
rac+ists
rack
racks
racks
rack+ing
racked
rack-and-pinion
rack-and-pinions
rack+er
rack+ers
rack+et
rack+ets
rack+ets
rack+et+ing
rack+et+ed
rack+et+eer
rack+et+eers
rack+et+eers
rack+et+eer+ing
rack+et+eered
rack+et+eer+ing
rack+ety
Rackham
rack-rent
rack-rents
rack-rents
rack-renting
rack-rented
rack-renter
rack-renters
rac+on+teur
rac+on+teurs
ra+coon
ra+coons *or*
ra+coon
rac+quet
rac+quets
rac+quets
rac+quet+ing
rac+quet+ed
racy

raci+er
raci+est
rad
rads
rad+der
rad+dest
ra+dar
ra+dars
radar+scope
radar+scopes
Radcliffe
rad+dle
rad+dles
rad+dling
rad+dled
Radetzky
ra+dial
ra+dials
ra+di+al+ly
radial-ply
ra+dian
ra+dians
ra+di+ance
ra+di+ances
ra+di+an+cy
ra+di+an+cies
ra+di+ant
ra+di+ant+ly
ra+di+ata
ra+di+atas
ra+di+ate
ra+di+ates
ra+di+at+ing
ra+di+at+ed
ra+dia+tion
ra+dia+tions
ra+dia+tion+al
ra+dia+tive
ra+dia+tor
ra+dia+tors
radi+cal
radi+cals
radi+cal+ism
radi+cal+isms
radi+cal+is+tic

radi+cal+is+ti+cal+ly
radi+cal+ly
radi+cal+ness
radi+cand
 radi+cands
ra+dic+chio
 ra+dic+chios
radi+ces
radi+cle
 radi+cles
Radiguet
ra+dii
ra+dio
 ra+dios
 ra+dios
 ra+dio+ing
 ra+di+oed
radio+ac+tive
radio+ac+tive+ly
radio+ac+tiv+ity
radio+bio+logi+cal
radio+bio+logi+cal+ly
radio+bi+olo+gist
 radio+bi+olo+gists
radio+bi+ol+ogy
radio+car+bon
radio+chemi+cal
radio+chem+ist
 radio+chem+ists
radio+chem+is+try
radio-controlled
radio+el+ement
 radio+el+ements
radio+gram
 radio+grams
radio+graph
 radio+graphs
ra+di+og+ra+pher
 ra+di+og+ra+phers
radio+graph+ic
radio+graphi+cal+ly
ra+di+og+ra+phy
radio-immuno-assay
 radio-immuno-assays

radio+iso+tope
 radio+iso+topes
radio+iso+top+ic
radio+lar+ian
 radio+lar+ians
ra+di+olo+gist
 ra+di+olo+gists
ra+di+ol+ogy
ra+di+om+eter
 ra+di+om+eters
radio+met+ric
ra+di+om+etry
radio-opacity
radio-opaque
radio+pac+ity
radio+pag+er
 radio+pag+ers
radio+pag+ing
radio+paque
radio+scop+ic
radio+scopi+cal+ly
ra+di+os+co+py
radio+sonde
 radio+sondes
radio+tele+graph
 radio+tele+graphs
radio+tele+graphs
radio+tele+graph+ing
radio+tele+graphed
radio+tele+graph+ic
radio+teleg+ra+phy
radio+tele+phone
 radio+tele+phones
radio+tele+phon+ic
radio+telepho+ny
radio+tele+type
 radio+tele+types
radio+thera+pist
 radio+thera+pists
radio+thera+py
rad+ish
 rad+ishes
ra+dium
 ra+dius

ra+dii *or*
 ra+di+uses
ra+dix
 ra+di+ces *or*
 ra+dixes
Rad+nor
Ra+dom
ra+dome
 ra+domes
ra+don
radu+la
 radu+lae
radu+lar
Raeburn
Raf+fer+ty
raf+fia
 raf+fias
raff+ish
raff+ish+ly
raff+ish+ness
raf+fle
 raf+fles
 raf+fles
raf+fling
raf+fled
raf+fler
 raf+flers
Raffles
raf+fle+sia
 raf+fle+sias
Rafsanjani
raft
 rafts
 rafts
raft+ing
raft+ed
raft+er
 raft+ers
rag
 rags
 rags
rag+ging
 ragged
raga
 ragas
raga+muf+fin
 raga+muf+fins
rag-and-bone
rag+bag
 rag+bags
rag+bolt
 rag+bolts
rage
 rages
 rages

rag+ing
raged
rag+ged
rag+ged+ly
rag+ged+ness
rag+gedy
rag+gee
rag+gy
ragi
rag+lan
 rag+lans
Raglan
ra+gout
 ra+gouts
 ra+gouts
ra+gout+ing
ra+gouted
rag-rolling
rag+tag
rag+time
Ra+gu+sa
rag+weed
 rag+weeds
rag+worm
 rag+worms
rag+wort
 rag+worts
rah
rai
raid
 raids
 raids
raid+ing
raid+ed
raid+er
 raid+ers
rail
 rails
 rails
rail+ing
railed
rail+car
 rail+cars
rail+card
 rail+cards
rail+er
 rail+ers
rail+head
 rail+heads
rail+ing
 rail+ings
rail+lery
 rail+leries
rail+road
 rail+roads

rail +roads
rail +road +ing
rail +road +ed
rail +way
rail +ways
rai +ment
rain
rains
rains
rain +ing
rained
rain +bow
rain +bows
rain +coat
rain +coats
rain +fall
rain +falls
rain +for +est
rain +for +ests
Rai +ni +er
mountain
Rainier
prince
raini +ly
raini +ness
rain +less
rain +proof
rain +proofs
rain +proof +ing
rain +proofed
rain +storm
rain +storms
rain +water
rain +wear
rainy
raini +er
raini +est
Rais
rais +able
raise
raises
raises
rais +ing
raised
raise +able
rai +sin
rai +sins
rai +siny
rai +son d'être
rai +sons d'être
rai +ta
raj
raja
rajas
ra +jah

ra +jahs
Ra +ja +sthan
Raj +kot
Raj +poot
Raj +poots
Raj +put
Raj +puts
rake
rakes
rakes
rak +ing
raked
ra +kee
rake-off
rake-offs
rake off
verb
rak +er
rak +ers
raki
rak +ish
rak +ish +ly
rak +ish +ness
rale
rales
râle
râles
Ralegh
Ra +leigh
place name
Raleigh
surname
ral +len +tan +do
ral +li +er
ral +li +ers
ral +ly
ral +lies
ral +lies
ral +ly +ing
ral +lied
ral +ly +cross
ram
rams
rams
ram +ming
rammed
Ram
RAM
Rama +dan
Ramakrishna
Ra +mat Gan
Rambert
ram +ble
ram +bles
ram +bles

ram +bling
ram +bled
ram +bler
ram +blers
Ram +bo +esque
Ram +bo +ism
Ram +bouil +let
Ram +bouil +lets
ram +bunc +tious
ram +bunc +tious +
ness
ram +bu +tan
ram +bu +tans
Rameau
ram +ekin
ram +ekins
ram +equin
ram +equins
Rameses
rami +fi +ca +tion
rami +fi +ca +
tions
rami +fy
rami +fies
rami +fy +ing
rami +fied
Ra +mil +lies
ram +jet
ram +jets
ram +mer
ram +mers
ra +mose
ra +mose +ly
ra +mos +ity
ra +mous
ra +mous +ly
ramp
ramps
ramps
ramp +ing
ramped
ram +page
ram +pages
ram +pag +ing
ram +paged
ram +pa +geous
ram +pa +geous +
ly
ram +pag +er
ram +pag +ers
ram +pan +cy
ram +pant
ram +pant +ly
ram +part
ram +parts

ram +parts
ram +part +ing
ram +part +ed
ram +pi +on
ram +pi +ons
Ram +pur
ram +rod
ram +rods
Ramsay
Ramses
Ramsey
Rams +gate
ram +shack +le
ram +sons
ran
ranch
ranches
ranches
ranch +ing
ranched
ranch +er
ranch +ers
ranch +erie
ranch +eries
Ran +chi
ran +cid
ran +cid +ity
ran +cid +ness
ran +cor
U.S.
ran +cor +ous
ran +cor +ous +ly
ran +cour
rand
rands
Rand
Rand +ers
randi +ly
randi +ness
Randolph
ran +dom
ran +domi +sa +
tion
ran +domi +sa +
tions
ran +dom +ise
ran +dom +ises
ran +dom +is +ing
ran +dom +ised
ran +dom +is +ers
ran +dom +is +ers
ran +domi +za +
tion
ran +domi +za +
tions

ran+dom+ize
ran+dom+izes
ran+dom+iz+ing
ran+dom+ized
ran+dom+iz+er
ran+dom+iz+ers
ran+dom+ly
ran+dom+ness
randy
randies
randi+er
randi+est
ra+nee
ra+nees
rang
ran+ga+ti+ra
ran+ga+ti+ras
range
ranges
ranges
rang+ing
ranged
range+finder
range+finders
rang+er
rang+ers
Rang+er
Rang+ers
rangi+ly
rangi+ness
ran+gi+ora
ran+gi+oras
Ran+goon
rangy
rangi+er
rangi+est
rani
ranis
Ranjit Singh
rank
ranks
ranks
rank+ing
ranked
rank+er
rank+est
Rank
rank+er
rank+ers
rank+ing
rank+ings
ran+kle
ran+kles
ran+kling
ran+kled

rank+ly
rank+ness
ran+sack
ran+sacks
ran+sack+ing
ran+sacked
ran+sack+er
ran+sack+ers
ran+som
ran+soms
ran+soms
ran+som+ing
ran+somed
Ransom
Ransome
ran+som+er
ran+som+ers
rant
rants
rants
rant+ing
rant+ed
rant+er
rant+ers
rant+ing
rant+ings
rant+ing+ly
ra+nun+cu+la+
  ceous
ra+nun+cu+lus
ra+nun+cu+
  luses or
ra+nun+cu+li
rap
raps
raps
rap+ping
rapped
ra+pa+cious
ra+pa+cious+ly
ra+pa+cious+
  ness
ra+pac+ity
Rapacki
Ra+pal+lo
rape
rapes
rapes
rap+ing
raped
rape+seed
rape+seeds
Raphael
Rapha+el+esque
ra+phide

raphi+des
ra+phis
raphi+des
rap+id
rapid-fire
ra+pid+ity
rap+id+ly
rap+id+ness
rap+ids
ra+pi+er
ra+pi+ers
rap+ine
rap+ist
rap+ists
rap+pee
rap+pel
rap+pels
rap+pels
rap+pel+ling
rap+pelled
rap+port
rap+ports
rap+proche+
  ment
rap+proche+
  ments
rap+scal+lion
rap+scal+lions
rapt
rapt+ly
rap+tor
rap+tors
rap+to+rial
rap+ture
rap+tures
rap+tures
rap+tur+ing
rap+tured
rap+tur+ous
rara avis
ra+rae aves
rare
rar+er
rar+est
rare+bit
rare+bits
rare-earth
  adj.
rare earth
rare earths
rar+efac+tion
rar+efac+tions
rar+efac+tive
rar+efi+able
rar+efi+ca+tion

rar+efi+ca+tions
rar+efi+er
rar+efi+ers
rar+efy
rar+efies
rar+efy+ing
rar+efied
rare+ly
rare+ness
rar+ing
rar+ity
rar+ities
Ra+ro+ton+ga
ras+bo+ra
ras+bo+ras
ras+cal
ras+cals
ras+cal+ity
ras+cal+ities
ras+cal+ly
rase
rases
ras+ing
rased
ras+er
ras+ers
rash
rashes
rash+er
rash+ers
rash+ly
rash+ness
Rasht
Rask
Rasmussen
rasp
rasps
rasps
rasp+ing
rasped
rasp+berry
rasp+berries
rasp+er
rasp+ers
rasp+ish
Rasputin
Ras+ta
Ras+tas
Ras Tafari
Ras+ta+far+ian
Ras+ta+far+ians
ras+ter
ras+ters
rat
rats

rats
rat+ting
rat+ted
ra+ta
rat+tas
rat+abil+ity
rat+able
rat+ably
rata+fee
rata+fees
rata+fia
rata+fias
ra+tan
ra+tans
rata+tat
rata+tats
rata+tat-tat
rata+tat-tats
ra+ta+touille
rat+bag
rat+bags
rat-catcher
rat-catchers
ratch+et
ratch+ets
rate
rates
rates
rat+ing
rat+ed
rate+abil+ity
rate+able
rate+ably
rate-cap
rate-caps
rate-capping
rate-capped
ra+tel
ra+tels
rate+payer
rate+payers
Rathenau
ra+ther
rati+fi+able
rati+fi+ca+tion
rati+fi+ca+tions
rati+fi+er
rati+fi+ers
rati+fy
rati+fies
rati+fy+ing
rati+fied
rat+ing
rat+ings
ra+tio

ra+tios
ra+ti+oci+nate
ra+ti+oci+nates
ra+ti+oci+nat+
  ing
ra+ti+oci+nat+
  ed
ra+ti+oci+na+tion
ra+ti+oci+na+
  tions
ra+ti+oci+na+tive
ra+ti+oci+na+tor
ra+ti+oci+na+
  tors
ra+tion
ra+tions
ra+tions
ra+tion+ing
ra+tioned
ra+tion+al
ra+tion+als
ra+tion+ale
ra+tion+ales
ra+tion+ali+sa+
  tion
ra+tion+ali+sa+
  tions
ra+tion+al+ise
ra+tion+al+ises
ra+tion+al+is+
  ing
ra+tion+al+ised
ra+tion+al+is+er
ra+tion+al+is+
  ers
ra+tion+al+ism
ra+tion+al+ist
ra+tion+al+ists
ra+tion+al+is+tic
ra+tion+al+is+ti+
  cal+ly
ra+tion+al+ity
ra+tion+al+ities
ra+tion+ali+za+
  tion
ra+tion+ali+za+
  tions
ra+tion+al+ize
ra+tion+al+izes
ra+tion+al+iz+
  ing
ra+tion+al+ized
ra+tion+al+iz+er
ra+tion+al+iz+
  ers

ra+tion+al+ly
ra+tion+al+ness
rat+ite
rat+ites
rat+lin
rat+lins
rat+line
rat+lines
ra+toon
ra+toons
rats+bane
rat-tail
rat-tails
rat+tan
rat+tans
rat+ter
rat+ters
Rattigan
rat+ti+ly
rat+ti+ness
rat+tle
rat+tles
rat+tles
rat+tling
rat+tled
Rattle
rattle+brain
rattle+brains
rattle+head
rattle+heads
rattle+pate
rattle+pates
rat+tler
rat+tlers
rattle+snake
rattle+snakes
rattle+trap
rattle+traps
rat+tly
rat+toon
rat+toons
rat+ty
rat+ti+er
rat+ti+est
Ratushinskaya
rau+cous
rau+cous+ly
rau+cous+ness
raun+chi+ly
raun+chi+ness
raun+chy
raun+chi+er
raun+chi+est

Rauschenberg
rau+wol+fia
rau+wol+fias
rav+age
rav+ages
rav+ages
rav+ag+ing
rav+aged
rav+ag+er
rav+ag+ers
rave
raves
raves
rav+ing
raved
rav+el
rav+els
rav+els
rav+el+ling or
rav+el+ing
  U.S.
rav+elled or
rav+eled
  U.S.
Ravel
rav+el+ler
rav+el+lers
rav+el+ly
ra+ven
ra+vens
rav+en
rav+ens
rav+en+ing
rav+ened
rav+en+ing
rav+en+ing+ly
Ra+ven+na
rav+en+ous
rav+en+ous+ly
rav+en+ous+
  ness
rav+er
rav+ers
ra+vine
ra+vines
rav+ing
rav+ings
rav+ing+ly
ra+vio+li
rav+ish
rav+ishes
rav+ish+ing
rav+ished
rav+ish+er
rav+ish+ers

rav+ish+ing+ly
rav+ish+ment
rav+ish+ments
raw
Ra+wal+pin+di
raw+boned
raw+hide
raw+hides
ra+win+sonde
ra+win+sondes
raw+ish
Rawl+plug
Trademark
Rawl+plugs
raw+ly
raw+ness
Rawsthorne
ray
rays
rays
ray+ing
rayed
Ray
Rayleigh
ray+less
ray+let
ray+lets
ray+on
ray+ons
raze
razes
raz+ing
razed
raz+er
raz+ers
ra+zoo
ra+zoos
ra+zor
ra+zors
razor+back
razor+backs
razor+bill
razor+bills
razor-shell
razor-shells
razz
razzes
razzes
razz+ing
razzed
razzle-dazzle
razz+ma+tazz
re
res
Re

re+ab+sorb
re+ab+sorbs
re+ab+sorb+ing
re+ab+sorbed
re+ab+sorp+tion
re+ab+sorp+
  tions
re+ac+cept
re+ac+cepts
re+ac+cept+ing
re+ac+cept+ed
re+ac+cep+tance
re+ac+cep+
  tances
re+ac+claim
re+ac+claims
re+ac+claim+ing
re+ac+claimed
re+ac+cus+tom
re+ac+cus+
  toms
re+ac+cus+tom+
  ing
re+ac+cus+
  tomed
reach
reaches
reaches
reach+ing
reached
reach+able
reach+er
reach+ers
reach-me-down
reach-me-
  downs
re+ac+quaint
re+ac+quaints
re+ac+quaint+
  ing
re+ac+quaint+
  ed
re+ac+quaint+
  ance
re+ac+quaint+
  ances
re+ac+quire
re+ac+quires
re+ac+quir+ing
re+ac+quired
re+ac+qui+si+
  tion
re+ac+qui+si+
  tions
re+act

respond
re+acts
re+act+ing
re+act+ed
re-act
act again
re-acts
re-acting
re-acted
re+ac+tance
re+ac+tant
re+ac+tants
re+ac+tion
re+ac+tions
re+ac+tion+al
re+ac+tion+ary
re+ac+tion+
  aries
re+ac+tion+ism
re+ac+tion+ist
re+ac+tion+ists
re+ac+ti+vate
re+ac+ti+vates
re+ac+ti+vat+
  ing
re+ac+ti+vat+ed
re+ac+ti+va+tion
re+ac+ti+va+
  tions
re+ac+tive
re+ac+tive+ness
re+ac+tiv+ity
re+ac+tor
re+ac+tors
read
reads
read+ing
read
read+abil+ity
read+able
read+able+ness
read+ably
re+adapt
re+adapts
re+adapt+ing
re+adapt+ed
re+adap+ta+tion
re+adap+ta+
  tions
re+address
re+addresses
re+address+ing
re+addressed
Reade
read+er

read+ers
read+er+ship
read+er+ships
read+ily
readi+ness
read+ing
read+ings
Read+ing
re+adjourn
re+adjourns
re+adjourn+ing
re+adjourned
re+adjourn+ment
re+adjourn+
  ments
re+adjust
re+adjusts
re+adjust+ing
re+adjust+ed
re+admis+sion
re+admis+sions
re+admit
re+admits
re+admit+ting
re+admit+ted
re+adopt
re+adopts
re+adopt+ing
re+adopt+ed
read-out
read-outs
read out
verb
read-write
ready
readies
readi+er
readi+est
ready-made
ready-mades
ready-mix
ready-to-wear
ready-to-wears
re+affirm
re+affirms
re+affirm+ing
re+affirmed
re+affir+ma+tion
re+affir+ma+
  tions
re+affor+est
re+affor+ests
re+affor+est+
  ing
re+affor+est+ed

re+affor+esta+
  tion
Reagan
re+agent
  re+agents
real
real
  Spanish coin
  reals *or*
  rea+les
real
  Portuguese coin
  reis
re+al+gar
re+align
  re+aligns
  re+align+ing
  re+aligned
  re+align+ment
  re+align+ments
re+al+is+able
re+ali+sa+tion
  re+ali+sa+tions
re+al+ise
  re+al+ises
  re+al+is+ing
  re+al+ised
  re+al+is+er
  re+al+is+ers
re+al+ism
  re+al+isms
re+al+ist
  re+al+ists
re+al+is+tic
re+al+is+ti+cal+ly
re+al+ity
  re+al+ities
re+al+iz+able
re+ali+za+tion
  re+ali+za+tions
re+al+ize
  re+al+izes
  re+al+iz+ing
  re+al+ized
  re+al+iz+er
  re+al+iz+ers
re+allo+cate
  re+allo+cates
  re+allo+cat+ing
  re+allo+cat+ed
  re+allo+ca+tion
  re+allo+ca+tions
re+allot
  re+allots
  re+allot+ting

re+allot+ted
re+allot+ment
  re+allot+ments
re+al+ly
realm
  realms
real+ness
re+alter
  re+alters
  re+alter+ing
  re+altered
re+altera+tion
  re+altera+tions
real-time
re+al+tor
  re+al+tors
re+al+ty
ream
  reams
  reams
  ream+ing
  reamed
ream+er
  ream+ers
re+ana+lyse
  re+ana+lyses
  re+ana+lys+ing
  re+ana+lysed
re+analy+sis
  re+analy+ses
re+ani+mate
  re+ani+mates
  re+ani+mat+ing
  re+ani+mat+ed
  re+ani+ma+tion
  re+ani+ma+
    tions
reap
  reaps
  reap+ing
  reaped
reap+able
reap+er
  reap+ers
re+appear
  re+appears
  re+appear+ing
  re+appeared
re+appear+ance
  re+appear+
    ances
re+appli+ca+tion
  re+appli+ca+
    tions
re+apply

re+applies
  re+apply+ing
  re+applied
re+appoint
  re+appoints
  re+appoint+ing
  re+appoint+ed
  re+appoint+ment
  re+appoint+
    ments
re+appor+tion
  re+appor+tions
  re+appor+tion+
    ing
  re+appor+tioned
re+apprais+al
  re+apprais+als
re+appraise
  re+appraises
  re+apprais+ing
  re+appraised
rear
  rears
  rears
  rear+ing
  reared
Reardon
rear+er
  rear+ers
rear+guard
  rear+guards
re+argue
  re+argues
  re+argu+ing
  re+argued
re+arm
  re+arms
  re+arm+ing
  re+armed
re+arma+ment
  re+arma+ments
rear+most
re+arrange
  re+arranges
  re+arrang+ing
  re+arranged
re+arrange+ment
  re+arrange+
    ments
re+arrest
  re+arrests
  re+arrests
  re+arrest+ing
  re+arrest+ed
rear-view

rear+ward
rear+wards
rea+son
  rea+sons
  rea+sons
  rea+son+ing
  rea+soned
rea+son+able
rea+son+able+
  ness
rea+son+ably
rea+son+er
rea+son+ers
re+as+sem+ble
re+as+sem+bles
re+as+sem+
  bling
re+as+sem+
  bled
re+as+sem+bly
re+as+sem+
  blies
re+as+sert
  re+as+serts
  re+as+sert+ing
  re+as+sert+ed
re+as+ser+tion
  re+as+ser+tions
re+as+sess
  re+as+sesses
  re+as+sess+ing
  re+as+sessed
re+as+sess+
  ment
re+as+sess+
  ments
re+as+sign
  re+as+signs
  re+as+sign+ing
  re+as+signed
re+as+sign+ment
  re+as+sign+
    ments
re+as+sume
  re+as+sumes
  re+as+sum+ing
  re+as+sumed
re+as+sump+tion
  re+as+sump+
    tions
re+assur+ance
  re+assur+ances
re+assure
  re+assures
  re+assur+ing

re+assured
re+assur+er
re+assur+ers
re+assur+ing+ly
re+at+tach
re+at+taches
re+at+tach+ing
re+at+tached
re+at+tach+ment
re+at+tach+
ments
re+at+tempt
re+at+tempts
re+at+tempt+
ing
re+at+tempt+ed
Réaumur
reave
reaves
reav+ing
reaved *or*
reft
re+awak+en
re+awak+ens
re+awak+en+ing
re+awak+ened
re+bap+tise
re+bap+tises
re+bap+tis+ing
re+bap+tised
re+bap+tism
re+bap+tisms
re+bap+tize
re+bap+tizes
re+bap+tiz+ing
re+bap+tized
re+bat+able
re+bate
re+bates
re+bates
re+bat+ing
re+bat+ed
re+bate+able
re+bat+er
re+bat+ers
re+bec
re+becs
Rebecca
re+beck
re+becks
re+bel
re+bels
re+bels
re+bel+ling
re+belled

re+bel+lion
re+bel+lions
re+bel+lious
re+bel+lious+ly
re+bel+lious+
ness
re+bid
re+bids
re+bid+ding
re+bid
re+bind
re+binds
re+bind+ing
re+bound
re+birth
re+births
re+bore
re+bores
re+bor+ing
re+bored
re+born
re+bound
re+bounds
re+bound+ing
re+bound+ed
re+bo+zo
re+bo+zos
re+broad+cast
re+broad+casts
re+broad+cast+
ing
re+broad+cast
re+buff
re+buffs
re+buffs
re+buff+ing
re+buffed
re+build
re+builds
re+build+ing
re+built
re+buk+able
re+buke
re+bukes
re+bukes
re+buk+ing
re+buked
re+buk+er
re+buk+ers
re+bur+ial
re+bur+ials
re+bury
re+buries
re+bury+ing
re+buried

re+bus
re+buses
re+but+table
re+but+tal
re+but+tals
re+but+ter
re+but+ters
re+cal+ci+trance
re+cal+ci+trant
re+cal+ci+trants
re+cal+cu+late
re+cal+cu+lates
re+cal+cu+lat+
ing
re+cal+cu+lat+
ed
re+ca+les+cence
re+ca+les+cent
re+call
re+calls
re+calls
re+call+ing
re+called
re+call+able
re+cant
re+cants
re+cant+ing
re+cant+ed
re+can+ta+tion
re+can+ta+tions
re+cant+er
re+cant+ers
re+cap
re+caps
re+caps
re+cap+ping
re+capped
re+capi+tali+sa+
tion
re+capi+tali+sa+
tions
re+capi+tal+ise
re+capi+tal+ises
re+capi+tal+is+
ing
re+capi+tal+ised
re+capi+tali+za+
tion
re+capi+tali+za+
tions
re+capi+tal+ize
re+capi+tal+izes
re+capi+tal+iz+
ing
re+capi+tal+ized

re+ca+pitu+late
re+ca+pitu+
lates
re+ca+pitu+lat+
ing
re+ca+pitu+lat+
ed
re+ca+pitu+la+
tion
re+ca+pitu+la+
tions
re+ca+pitu+la+
tive
re+ca+pitu+la+
tory
re+cap+pable
re+cap+ture
re+cap+tures
re+cap+tures
re+cap+tur+ing
re+cap+tured
re+cast
re+casts
re+cast+ing
re+cast
rec+ce
rec+ces
rec+ces
rec+ce+ing
rec+ced *or*
rec+ceed
re+cede
re+cedes
re+ced+ing
re+ced+ed
re-cede
re-cedes
re-ceding
re-ceded
re+ceipt
re+ceipts
re+ceipts
re+ceipt+ing
re+ceipt+ed
re+ceiv+able
re+ceiv+ables
re+ceive
re+ceives
re+ceiv+ing
re+ceived
re+ceiv+er
re+ceiv+ers
re+ceiv+er+ship
re+cen+sion
re+cen+sions

re+cent
Re+cent
re+cent+ly
re+cent+ness
re+cep+ta+cle
 re+cep+ta+cles
re+cep+tion
 re+cep+tions
re+cep+tion+ist
 re+cep+tion+
  ists
re+cep+tive
re+cep+tive+ly
re+cep+tive+
  ness
re+cep+tiv+ity
re+cep+tor
 re+cep+tors
re+cess
 re+cesses
 re+cesses
 re+cess+ing
 re+cessed
re+ces+sion
 re+ces+sions
re+ces+sion+al
 re+ces+sion+als
re+ces+sive
 re+ces+sives
re+ces+sive+ly
re+ces+sive+
  ness
re+chal+lenge
 re+chal+lenges
 re+chal+leng+
  ing
 re+chal+lenged
re+charge
 re+charges
 re+charg+ing
 re+charged
re+charge+able
re+check
 re+checks
 re+checks
 re+check+ing
 re+checked
re+cher+ché
re+chris+ten
 re+chris+tens
 re+chris+ten+
  ing
 re+chris+tened
re+cidi+vism
re+cidi+vist

re+cidi+vists
re+cidi+vis+tic
re+cidi+vous
Re+ci+fe
reci+pe
 reci+pes
re+cipi+ence
re+cipi+ent
 re+cipi+ents
re+cip+ro+cal
 re+cip+ro+cals
re+cip+ro+cal+ity
re+cip+ro+cal+ly
re+cip+ro+cate
 re+cip+ro+cates
 re+cip+ro+cat+
  ing
 re+cip+ro+cat+
  ed
 re+cip+ro+ca+
  tion
 re+cip+ro+ca+
  tions
 re+cip+ro+ca+
  tive
 re+cip+ro+ca+tor
 re+cip+ro+ca+
  tors
 re+cip+ro+ca+
  tory
reci+proc+ity
 reci+proc+ities
re+cir+cu+late
 re+cir+cu+lates
 re+cir+cu+lat+
  ing
 re+cir+cu+lat+
  ed
re+ci+sion
 re+ci+sions
re+cit+able
re+cit+al
 re+cit+als
re+cit+al+ist
 re+cit+al+ists
reci+ta+tion
 reci+ta+tions
reci+ta+tive
 reci+ta+tives
re+cita+tive
 adj.
re+cite
 re+cites
 re+cit+ing
 re+cit+ed

re+cit+er
 re+cit+ers
reck
 recks
 reck+ing
 recked
reck+less
reck+less+ly
reck+less+ness
Reck+ling+hau+
  sen
reck+on
 reck+ons
 reck+on+ing
 reck+oned
reck+on+er
 reck+on+ers
 reck+on+ing
 reck+on+ings
re+claim
 re+claims
 re+claims
 re+claim+ing
 re+claimed
re+claim+able
re+claim+ant
 re+claim+ants
re+claim+er
 re+claim+ers
rec+la+ma+tion
 rec+la+ma+
  tions
ré+clame
re+clas+si+fi+ca+
  tion
 re+clas+si+fi+ca+
  tions
re+clas+si+fy
 re+clas+si+fies
 re+clas+si+fy+
  ing
 re+clas+si+fied
re+clin+able
rec+li+nate
rec+li+na+tion
 rec+li+na+tions
re+cline
 re+clines
 re+clin+ing
 re+clined
re+clin+er
 re+clin+ers
re+clothe
 re+clothes
 re+cloth+ing

re+clothed
re+cluse
 re+cluses
re+clu+sion
re+clu+sive
re+codi+fi+ca+
  tion
 re+codi+fi+ca+
  tions
re+codi+fy
 re+codi+fies
 re+codi+fy+ing
 re+codi+fied
rec+og+nis+abil+
  ity
rec+og+nis+able
rec+og+nis+ably
re+cog+ni+sance
 re+cog+ni+
  sances
re+cog+ni+sant
rec+og+nise
 rec+og+nises
 rec+og+nis+ing
 rec+og+nised
rec+og+nis+er
 rec+og+nis+ers
rec+og+ni+tion
 rec+og+ni+tions
re+cog+ni+tive
rec+og+niz+abil+
  ity
rec+og+niz+able
rec+og+niz+ably
re+cog+ni+zance
 re+cog+ni+
  zances
re+cog+ni+zant
rec+og+nize
 rec+og+nizes
 rec+og+niz+ing
 rec+og+nized
rec+og+niz+er
 rec+og+niz+ers
re+coil
 re+coils
 re+coil+ing
 re+coiled
re+coil+er
 re+coil+ers
rec+ol+lect
 rec+ol+lects
 rec+ol+lect+ing
 rec+ol+lect+ed
rec+ol+lec+tion

rec+ol+lec+tions
rec+ol+lec+tive
rec+ol+lec+tive+
  ly
re+colo+ni+sa+
  tion
re+colo+ni+sa+
  tions
re+colo+nise
re+colo+nises
re+colo+nis+ing
re+colo+nised
re+colo+ni+za+
  tion
re+colo+ni+za+
  tions
re+colo+nize
re+colo+nizes
re+colo+ni+zing
re+colo+nized
re+col+our
re+col+ours
re+col+our+ing
re+col+oured
re+com+bi+nant
re+com+bi+na+
  tion
re+com+bine
re+com+bines
re+com+bin+ing
re+com+bined
re+com+mence
re+com+
  mences
re+com+menc+
  ing
re+com+
  menced
re+com+mence+
  ment
re+com+mence+
  ments
rec+om+mend
rec+om+mends
rec+om+mend+
  ing
rec+om+mend+
  ed
rec+om+mend+
  able
rec+om+men+da+
  tion
rec+om+men+
  da+tions

rec+om+menda+
  tory
rec+om+mend+
  er
rec+om+mend+
  ers
re+com+mit
re+com+mits
re+com+mit+
  ting
re+com+mit+
  ted
re+com+mit+
  ment
re+com+mit+
  ments
rec+om+pense
rec+om+penses
rec+om+pens+
rec+om+pens+
  ing
rec+om+pensed
rec+om+pens+er
rec+om+pens+
  ers
re+com+pose
re+com+poses
re+com+pos+
  ing
re+com+posed
rec+on+cil+able
rec+on+cil+ably
rec+on+cile
rec+on+ciles
rec+on+cil+ing
rec+on+ciled
rec+on+cile+
  ment
rec+on+cile+
  ments
rec+on+cil+er
rec+on+cil+ers
rec+on+cilia+tion
rec+on+cilia+
  tions
rec+on+cilia+tory
re+con+dite
re+con+dite+ly
re+con+dite+
  ness
re+con+di+tion
re+con+di+tions
re+con+di+tion+
  ing

re+con+di+
  tioned
re+con+firm
re+con+firms
re+con+firm+ing
re+con+firmed
re+con+fir+ma+
  tion
re+con+fir+ma+
  tions
re+con+nais+
  sance
re+con+nais+
  sances
re+con+nect
re+con+nects
re+con+nect+
  ing
re+con+nect+ed
re+con+nec+tion
re+con+nec+
  tions
re+con+noi+ter
  U.S.
re+con+noi+ters
re+con+noi+ters
re+con+noi+ter+
  ing
re+con+noi+
  tered
rec+on+noi+ter+
  er
  U.S.
rec+on+noi+ter+
  ers
rec+on+noi+tre
rec+on+noi+tres
rec+on+noi+tres
rec+on+noi+
  tring
rec+on+noi+tred
rec+on+noi+trer
rec+on+noi+
  trers
re+con+quer
re+con+quers
re+con+quer+
  ing
re+con+quered
re+con+quest
re+con+quests
re+con+se+crate
re+con+se+
  crates

re+con+se+crat+
  ing
re+con+se+crat+
  ed
re+con+se+cra+
  tion
re+con+se+cra+
  tions
re+con+sid+er
re+con+sid+ers
re+con+sid+er+
  ing
re+con+sid+
  ered
re+con+sid+era+
  tion
re+con+sign
re+con+signs
re+con+sign+
  ing
re+con+signed
re+con+sign+
  ment
re+con+sign+
  ments
re+con+soli+date
re+con+soli+
  dates
re+con+soli+dat+
  ing
re+con+soli+dat+
  ed
re+con+soli+da+
  tion
re+con+soli+da+
  tions
re+con+stitu+ent
re+con+stitu+
  ents
re+con+sti+tute
re+con+sti+
  tutes
re+con+sti+tut+
  ing
re+con+sti+tut+
  ed
re+con+sti+tu+
  tion
re+con+struct
re+con+structs
re+con+struct+
  ing
re+con+struct+
  ed

re+con+struc+
tible
re+con+struc+
tion
re+con+struc+
tions
re+con+struc+
tive
re+con+struc+tor
re+con+struc+
tors
re+con+vene
re+con+venes
re+con+ven+ing
re+con+vened
re+con+ver+sion
re+con+ver+
sions
re+con+vert
re+con+verts
re+con+vert+ing
re+con+vert+ed
re+con+vey
re+con+veys
re+con+vey+ing
re+con+veyed
re+con+vict
re+con+victs
re+con+vict+ing
re+con+vict+ed
re+con+vic+tion
re+con+vic+
tions
rec+ord
rec+ords
rec+ords
rec+ord+ing
rec+ord+ed
re+cord+able
re+cord+er
re+cord+ers
re+cord+er+ship
re+cord+ing
re+cord+ings
re+count
narrate
re+counts
re+count+ing
re+count+ed
re-count
count again
re-counts
re-counts
re-counting
re-counted

re+count+al
re+count+als
re+coup
re+coups
re+coups
re+coup+ing
re+couped
re+coup+able
re+coup+ment
re+coup+ments
re+course
re+courses
re+cov+er
regain health
re+cov+ers
re+cov+er+ing
re+cov+ered
re-cover
cover again
re-covers
re-cover+ing
re-covered
re+cov+er+abil+
ity
re+cov+er+able
re+cov+er+er
re+cov+er+ers
re+cov+ery
re+cov+eries
rec+re+ance
rec+re+an+cy
rec+re+ant
rec+re+ants
rec+re+ate
amuse
rec+re+ates
rec+re+at+ing
rec+re+at+ed
re-create
create anew
re-creates
re-creating
re-created
rec+rea+tion
rec+rea+tions
re-creation
re-creations
rec+rea+tion+al
rec+rea+tive
rec+rea+tive+ly
rec+rea+tor
rec+rea+tors
re-creator
re-creators
re+crimi+nate

re+crimi+nates
re+crimi+nat+
ing
re+crimi+nat+ed
re+crimi+na+tion
re+crimi+na+
tions
re+crimi+na+tive
re+crimi+na+tor
re+crimi+na+
tors
re+crimi+na+tory
re+cross
re+crosses
re+cross+ing
re+crossed
re+cru+desce
re+cru+desces
re+cru+desc+
ing
re+cru+desced
re+cru+des+
cence
re+cru+des+
cences
re+cruit
re+cruits
re+cruits
re+cruit+ing
re+cruit+ed
re+cruit+able
re+cruit+er
re+cruit+ers
re+cruit+ment
re+cruit+ments
re+crys+tal+lise
re+crys+tal+
lises
re+crys+tal+lis+
ing
re+crys+tal+
lised
re+crys+tal+lize
re+crys+tal+
lizes
re+crys+tal+liz+
ing
re+crys+tal+
lized
rec+ta
rec+tal
rec+tal+ly
rec+tan+gle
rec+tan+gles
rec+tan+gu+lar

rec+tan+gu+lar+
ity
rec+tan+gu+lar+
ly
rec+ti
rec+ti+fi+able
rec+ti+fi+ca+tion
rec+ti+fi+ca+
tions
rec+ti+fi+er
rec+ti+fi+ers
rec+ti+fy
rec+ti+fies
rec+ti+fy+ing
rec+ti+fied
rec+ti+lin+eal
rec+ti+lin+eal+ly
rec+ti+lin+ear
rec+ti+lin+ear+ly
rec+ti+tude
rec+to
rec+tos
rec+to+cele
rec+to+celes
rec+tor
rec+tors
rec+tor+ate
rec+tor+ates
rec+tor+ial
rec+tor+ship
rec+tor+ships
rec+tory
rec+tories
rec+trix
rec+tri+ces
rec+tum
rec+tums *or*
rec+ta
rec+tus
rec+ti
re+cum+bence
re+cum+ben+cy
re+cum+bent
re+cum+bent+ly
re+cu+per+ate
re+cu+per+ates
re+cu+per+at+
ing
re+cu+per+at+
ed
re+cu+pera+tion
re+cu+pera+
tions
re+cu+pera+tive
re+cur

re+curs
re+cur+ring
re+curred
re+cur+rence
re+cur+rences
re+cur+rent
re+cur+rent+ly
re+cur+sion
re+cur+sions
re+cur+sive
re+curve
re+curves
re+curv+ing
re+curved
recu+sance
recu+san+cy
recu+sant
recu+sants
re+cy+clable
re+cy+cle
re+cy+cles
re+cy+cles
re+cy+cling
re+cy+cled
re+cy+cleable
red
reds
reds
red+ding
red+ded
red+der
red+dest
red
tidy
reds
red+ding
red *or*
red+ded
Red
Reds
re+dact
re+dacts
re+dact+ing
re+dact+ed
re+dac+tion
re+dac+tions
re+dac+tion+al
re+dac+tor
re+dac+tors
red+back
red+backs
red-blooded
red-blooded+
ness
red+breast

red+breasts
red+brick
red+cap
red+caps
red+coat
red+coats
red+cur+rant
red+cur+rants
redd
redds
redds
redd+ing
redd *or*
red+ded
red+den
red+dens
red+den+ing
red+dened
redd+er
redd+ers
Redding
red+dish
Red+ditch
red+dle
red+dles
red+dling
red+dled
re+deco+rate
re+deco+rates
re+deco+rat+ing
re+deco+rat+ed
re+deco+ra+tion
re+deco+ra+
tions
re+dedi+cate
re+dedi+cates
re+dedi+cat+ing
re+dedi+cat+ed
re+dedi+ca+tion
re+dedi+ca+
tions
re+deem
re+deems
re+deem+ing
re+deemed
re+deem+able
re+deem+er
re+deem+ers
Re+deem+er
re+de+fine
re+de+fines
re+de+fin+ing
re+de+fined
re+demp+tible
re+demp+tion

re+demp+tions
re+demp+tion+al
re+demp+tive
re+demp+tive+ly
re+demp+tory
re+deploy
re+deploys
re+deploy+ing
re+deployed
re+deploy+ment
re+deploy+
ments
re+describe
re+describes
re+describ+ing
re+described
re+design
re+designs
re+design+ing
re+designed
re+deter+mine
re+deter+mines
re+deter+min+
ing
re+deter+mined
re+devel+op
re+devel+ops
re+devel+op+
ing
re+devel+oped
re+devel+op+er
re+devel+op+
ers
re+devel+op+
ment
re+devel+op+
ments
red+eye
red+eyes
red-faced
red-faced+ly
red+fin
red+fins
red+fish
red+fish *or*
red+fishes
Redford
Redgrave
red-handed
red-handed+ly
red-handed+ness
red+head
red+heads
red-headed
red-hot

re+di+al
re+di+als
re+di+al+ling
re+di+alled
red+in+gote
red+in+gotes
red+in+te+grate
red+in+te+
grates
red+in+te+grat+
ing
red+in+te+grat+
ed
red+in+te+gra+
tion
red+in+te+gra+
tions
red+in+te+gra+
tive
re+di+rect
re+di+rects
re+di+rect+ing
re+di+rect+ed
re+di+rec+tion
re+di+rec+tions
re+dis+cov+er
re+dis+cov+ers
re+dis+cov+er+
ing
re+dis+cov+
ered
re+dis+cov+ery
re+dis+cov+
eries
re+dis+trib+ute
re+dis+trib+utes
re+dis+trib+ut+
ing
re+dis+trib+ut+
ed
re+dis+tri+bu+
tion
re+dis+tri+bu+
tions
re+di+vide
re+di+vides
re+di+vid+ing
re+di+vid+ed
re+di+vis+ion
re+di+vis+ions
red-lead
red-light
adj.
red light
red lights

red+line
red+lines
red+lin+ing
red+lined
Redmond
red+neck
red+necks
red+ness
redo
redos
redo+ing
redid
redone
redo+lence
redo+len+cy
redo+lent
redo+lent+ly
Redon
re+dou+ble
re+dou+bles
re+dou+bles
re+dou+bling
re+dou+bled
re+doubt
re+doubts
re+doubt+able
re+doubt+able+
ness
re+doubt+ably
re+dound
re+dounds
re+dound+ing
re+dound+ed
re+dox
red+poll
red+polls
re+draft
re+drafts
re+drafts
re+draft+ing
re+draft+ed
re+draw
re+draws
re+draw+ing
re+drew
re+drawn
re+dress
correct,
compensate
re+dresses
re+dress+ing
re+dressed
re-dress
dress again
re-dresses

re-dressing
re-dressed
re+dress+able
re+dress+er
re+dress+ers
re+dress+ible
re+dress+or
re+dress+ors
re+drill
re+drills
re+drill+ing
re+drilled
red+shank
red+shanks
red+skin
red+skins
red+start
red+starts
re+duce
re+duces
re+duc+ing
re+duced
re+duc+er
re+duc+ers
re+duc+ibil+ity
re+duc+ible
re+duc+ibly
re+duc+tase
re+duc+tases
re+duc+tio ad ab+
sur+dum
re+duc+tion
re+duc+tions
re+duc+tion+ism
re+duc+tion+
isms
re+duc+tion+ist
re+duc+tion+
ists
re+duc+tion+ist+
ic
re+duc+tive
re+dun+dan+cy
re+dun+dan+
cies
re+dun+dant
re+dun+dant+ly
re+du+pli+cate
re+du+pli+cates
re+du+pli+cat+
ing
re+du+pli+cat+
ed
re+du+pli+ca+
tion

re+du+pli+ca+
tions
re+du+pli+ca+
tive
red+wing
red+wings
red+wood
red+woods
re-echo
re-echoes
re-echoing
re-echoed
reed
reeds
reeds
reed+ing
reed+ed
reed+buck
reed+bucks *or*
reed+buck
reedi+ly
reedi+ness
reed+ing
reed+ings
re-edit
re-edits
re-editing
re-edited
reed+ling
reed+lings
reed+man
reed+men
reeds+man
reeds+men
re-educate
re-educates
re-educating
re-educated
re-education
re-educations
reedy
reedi+er
reedi+est
reef
reefs
reefs
reef+ing
reefed
reef+er
reef+ers
reek
reeks
reeks
reek+ing
reeked

reeky
reel
reels
reels
reel+ing
reeled
reel+able
re-elect
re-elects
re-electing
re-elected
re-election
re-elections
reel+er
reel+ers
reel-fed
re-eligible
reel-to-reel
re-emerge
re-emerges
re-emerging
re-emerged
re-emergence
re-emergences
re-emergent
re-emphasise
re-emphasises
re-emphasising
re-emphasised
re-emphasize
re-emphasizes
re-emphasizing
re-emphasized
re-employ
re-employs
re-employing
re-employed
re-employment
re-enact
re-enacts
re-enacting
re-enacted
re-enactment
re-enactments
re-enforce
re-enforces
re-enforcing
re-enforced
re-enforcement
re-enforcements
re-engage
re-engages
re-engaging
re-engaged
re-enter

re-enters
re-entering
re-entered
re-entrant
re-entrants
re-entry
re-entries
re-equip
re-equips
re-equipping
re-equipped
re-erect
re-erects
re-erecting
re-erected
re-establish
re-establishes
re-establishing
re-established
re-evaluate
re-evaluates
re-evaluating
re-evaluated
re-evaluation
re-evaluations
reeve
reeves
reeves
reev+ing
reeved *or*
rove
re-examine
re-examines
re-examin+ing
re-examined
re-exhibit
re-exhibits
re-exhibiting
re-exhibited
re-experience
re-experiences
re-experiencing
re-experienced
re-export
re-exports
re-exports
re-exporting
re-export+ed
re-exporta+tion
re-exporta+tions
re-exporter
re-exporters
ref
refs
re+fas+ten

re+fas+tens
re+fas+ten+ing
re+fas+tened
re+fec+tion
re+fec+tory
re+fec+tories
re+fer
re+fers
re+fer+ring
re+ferred
ref+er+able
ref+eree
ref+erees
ref+erees
ref+eree+ing
ref+ereed
ref+er+ence
ref+er+ences
ref+er+ences
ref+er+enc+ing
ref+er+enced
ref+er+en+dum
ref+er+en+dums
or
ref+er+en+da
ref+er+ent
ref+er+ents
ref+er+en+tial
re+fer+rable
re+fer+ral
re+fer+rals
re+ferred
re+fer+rer
re+fer+rers
re+fill
re+fills
re+fills
re+fill+ing
re+filled
re+fill+able
re+film
re+films
re+film+ing
re+filmed
re+fin+able
re+fine
re+fines
re+fin+ing
re+fined
re+fine+ment
re+fine+ments
re+fin+er
re+fin+ers
re+fin+ery
re+fin+eries

re+fin+ish
re+fin+ishes
re+fin+ish+ing
re+fin+ished
re+fit
re+fits
re+fits
re+fit+ting
re+fit+ted
re+fit+ment
re+fit+ments
re+flate
re+flates
re+flat+ing
re+flat+ed
re+fla+tion
re+fla+tions
re+flect
re+flects
re+flect+ing
re+flect+ed
re+flec+tance
re+flec+tion
re+flec+tions
re+flec+tion+al
re+flec+tive
re+flec+tive+ly
re+flec+tiv+ity
re+flec+tor
re+flec+tors
re+flet
re+flets
re+flex
re+flexes
re+flexes
re+flex+ing
re+flexed
re+flex+ibil+ity
re+flex+ible
re+flex+ion
re+flex+ions
re+flex+ion+al
re+flex+ive
re+flex+ives
re+flex+ive+ly
re+flex+ive+ness
re+flex+iv+ity
re+flex+olo+gist
re+flex+olo+
 gists
re+flex+ol+ogy
re+float
re+floats
re+float+ing
re+float+ed

re+flux
re+fluxes
re+fluxes
re+flux+ing
re+fluxed
re+fo+cus
re+fo+cuses *or*
re+fo+cusses
re+fo+cus+ing
 or
re+fo+cus+sing
re+fo+cused
 or
re+fo+cussed
re+fold
re+folds
re+fold+ing
re+fold+ed
re+for+est
re+for+ests
re+for+est+ing
re+for+est+ed
re+for+esta+tion
re+forge
re+forges
re+forg+ing
re+forged
re+form
improve
re+forms
re+forms
re+form+ing
re+formed
re-form
form anew
re-forms
re-forming
re-formed
re+form+able
ref+or+ma+tion
act of reform
ref+or+ma+
 tions
re-formation
new formation
re-formations
ref+or+ma+tion+
 al
re+forma+tive
re+forma+tory
re+forma+tories
re+form+er
re+form+ers
re+form+ism
re+form+isms

re+form+ist
re+form+ists
re+fract
re+fracts
re+fract+ing
re+fract+ed
re+fract+able
re+fract+ing
re+frac+tion
re+frac+tions
re+frac+tive
re+frac+tom+eter
re+frac+tom+eters
re+frac+to+met+ric
re+frac+tom+etry
re+frac+tor
re+frac+tors
re+frac+to+ri+ly
re+frac+to+ri+ness
re+frac+tory
re+frac+tories
re+frain
re+frains
re+frains
re+frain+ing
re+frained
re+frain+er
re+frain+ers
re+fran+gibil+ity
re+fran+gible
re+fran+gible+ness
re+freeze
re+freezes
re+freez+ing
re+froze
re+fro+zen
re+fresh
re+freshes
re+fresh+ing
re+freshed
re+fresh+er
re+fresh+ers
re+fresh+ment
re+fresh+ments
re+frig+er+ant
re+frig+er+ants
re+frig+er+ate
re+frig+er+ates
re+frig+er+at+ing

re+frig+er+at+ed
re+frig+era+tion
re+frig+era+tive
re+frig+era+tor
re+frig+era+tors
re+frig+era+tory
re+frig+era+tories
re+frin+gence
re+frin+gen+cy
re+frin+gent
reft
re+fu+el
re+fu+els
re+fu+el+ling
or
re+fu+el+ing
U.S.
re+fu+elled or
re+fu+eled
U.S.
ref+uge
ref+uges
refu+gee
refu+gees
refu+gee+ism
re+fu+gium
re+fu+gia
re+ful+gence
re+ful+gen+cy
re+ful+gent
re+ful+gent+ly
re+fund
reimburse
re+funds
re+funds
re+fund+ing
re+fund+ed
re-fund
discharge debt
re-funds
re-funding
re-funded
re+fund+able
re+fund+er
re+fund+ers
re+fur+bish
re+fur+bishes
re+fur+bish+ing
re+fur+bished
re+fur+bish+ment
re+fur+bish+ments

re+fur+nish
re+fur+nishes
re+fur+nish+ing
re+fur+nished
re+fus+able
re+fus+al
re+fus+als
re+fuse
reject
re+fuses
re+fus+ing
re+fused
ref+use
rubbish
re+fuse+nik
re+fuse+niks
re+fus+er
re+fus+ers
re+fus+nik
re+fus+niks
refu+table
refu+tably
refu+ta+tion
refu+ta+tions
re+fute
re+futes
re+fut+ing
re+fut+ed
re+fut+er
re+fut+ers
re+gain
re+gains
re+gain+ing
re+gained
re+gain+er
re+gain+ers
re+gal
re+gale
re+gales
re+gales
re+gal+ing
re+galed
re+gale+ment
re+gale+ments
re+ga+lia
re+gal+ity
re+gal+ities
re+gal+ly
re+gal+va+nise
re+gal+va+nises
re+gal+va+nis+ing
re+gal+va+nised
re+gal+va+nize
re+gal+va+nizes

re+gal+va+niz+ing
re+gal+va+nized
re+gard
re+gards
re+gards
re+gard+ing
re+gard+ed
re+gar+dant
re+gard+ful
re+gard+ful+ly
re+gard+less
re+gard+less+ly
re+gard+less+ness
re+gath+er
re+gath+ers
re+gath+er+ing
re+gath+ered
re+gat+ta
re+gat+tas
re+ge+la+tion
re+ge+la+tions
re+gen+cy
re+gen+cies
Re+gen+cy
re+gen+era+cy
re+gen+er+ate
re+gen+er+ates
re+gen+er+at+ing
re+gen+er+at+ed
re+gen+era+tion
re+gen+era+tions
re+gen+era+tive
re+gen+era+tive+ly
re+gen+era+tor
re+gen+era+tors
Re+gens+burg
re+gent
re+gents
re+gent+al
regent-bird
regent-birds
re+gent+ship
re+gent+ships
Reger
re+ger+mi+nate
re+ger+mi+nates

re+ger+mi+nat+ing
re+ger+mi+nat+ed
re+ger+mi+na+tion
re+ger+mi+na+tions
reg+gae
Reg+gio di Ca+la+bria
Reg+gio nell'Emilia
regi+cid+al
regi+cide
regi+cides
re+gild
re+gilds
re+gild+ing
re+gild+ed
re+gime
re+gimes
ré+gime
ré+gimes
regi+men
regi+mens
regi+ment
regi+ments
regi+ments
regi+ment+ing
regi+ment+ed
regi+men+tal
regi+men+tal+ly
regi+men+tals
Regin
Re+gi+na
Regiomontanus
re+gion
re+gions
re+gion+al
re+gion+al+ism
re+gion+al+isms
re+gion+al+ist
re+gion+al+ists
re+gion+al+ly
ré+gis+seur
ré+gis+seurs
reg+is+ter
reg+is+ters
reg+is+ters
reg+is+ter+ing
reg+is+tered
reg+is+trable
reg+is+trar
reg+is+trars

reg+is+trar+ship
reg+is+trar+ships
reg+is+tra+tion
reg+is+tra+tions
reg+is+try
reg+is+tries
re+glaze
re+glazes
re+glaz+ing
re+glazed
reg+let
reg+lets
reg+nal
reg+nan+cy
reg+nant
re+gorge
re+gorges
re+gorg+ing
re+gorged
re+grade
re+grades
re+grad+ing
re+grad+ed
re+gress
re+gresses
re+gress+ing
re+gressed
re+gres+sion
re+gres+sions
re+gres+sor
re+gres+sors
re+gret
re+grets
re+grets
re+gret+ting
re+gret+ted
re+gret+ful
re+gret+ful+ly
re+gret+ful+ness
re+gret+table
re+gret+tably
re+group
re+groups
re+group+ing
re+grouped
re+grow
re+grows
re+grow+ing
re+grew
re+grown
re+growth
re+growths
regu+lable

regu+lar
regu+lars
regu+lar+ise
regu+lar+ises
regu+lar+is+ing
regu+lar+ised
regu+lar+ity
regu+lar+ities
regu+lar+ize
regu+lar+izes
regu+lar+iz+ing
regu+lar+ized
regu+lar+ly
regu+late
regu+lates
regu+lat+ing
regu+lat+ed
regu+la+tion
regu+la+tions
regu+la+tive
regu+la+tive+ly
regu+la+tor
regu+la+tors
regu+la+tory
regu+lo
regu+lus
regu+luses or regu+li
Regulus
re+gur+gi+tant
re+gur+gi+tants
re+gur+gi+tate
re+gur+gi+tates
re+gur+gi+tat+ing
re+gur+gi+tat+ed
re+gur+gi+ta+tion
re+gur+gi+ta+tions
re+hab
re+habs
re+ha+bili+tate
re+ha+bili+tates
re+ha+bili+tat+ing
re+ha+bili+tat+ed
re+ha+bili+ta+tion
re+ha+bili+ta+tions
re+ha+bili+ta+tive

re+hang
re+hangs
re+hang+ing
re+hung
re+har+ness
re+har+nesses
re+har+ness+ing
re+har+nessed
re+hash
re+hashes
re+hashes
re+hash+ing
re+hashed
re+hear
re+hears
re+hear+ing
re+heard
re+hears+al
re+hears+als
re+hearse
re+hearses
re+hears+ing
re+hearsed
re+hears+er
re+hears+ers
re+heat
re+heats
re+heat+ing
re+heat+ed
re+heat+er
re+heat+ers
re+heel
re+heels
re+heel+ing
re+heeled
re+hire
re+hires
re+hir+ing
re+hired
re+ho+bo+am
re+ho+bo+ams
re+house
re+houses
re+hous+ing
re+housed
Reich
Reichs+mark
Reichs+marks
or
Reichs+mark
Reichs+tag
Reid
rei+fi+ca+tion
rei+fi+ca+tions

rei+fi+ca+tory
rei+fi+er
rei+fi+ers
rei+fy
rei+fies
rei+fy+ing
rei+fied
Rei+gate
reign
reigns
reigns
reign+ing
reigned
re+im+burs+able
re+im+burse
re+im+burses
re+im+burs+ing
re+im+bursed
re+im+burse+
  ment
re+im+burse+
  ments
re+im+burs+er
re+im+burs+ers
re+im+port
re+im+ports
re+im+ports
re+im+port+ing
re+im+port+ed
re+im+por+ta+
  tion
re+im+por+ta+
  tions
re+im+pose
re+im+poses
re+im+pos+ing
re+im+posed
re+im+pris+on
re+im+pris+ons
re+im+pris+on+
  ing
re+im+pris+
  oned
Reims
rein
reins
reins
rein+ing
reined
re+incar+nate
re+incar+nates
re+incar+nat+
  ing
re+incar+nat+ed
re+incar+na+tion

re+incar+na+
  tions
re+incar+na+tion+
  ist
re+incar+na+
  tion+ists
re+incor+po+rate
re+incor+po+
  rates
re+incor+po+rat+
  ing
re+incor+po+rat+
  ed
re+incor+po+ra+
  tion
re+incor+po+ra+
  tions
re+incur
re+incurs
re+incur+ring
re+incurred
rein+deer
rein+deer or
rein+deers
re+induce
re+induces
re+induc+ing
re+induced
re+induc+tion
re+induc+tions
re+infect
re+infects
re+infect+ing
re+infect+ed
re+infec+tion
re+infec+tions
re+inforce
re+inforces
re+inforc+ing
re+inforced
re+inforce+ment
re+inforce+
  ments
re+infuse
re+infuses
re+infus+ing
re+infused
re+infu+sion
re+infu+sions
Reinhardt
re+inocu+late
re+inocu+lates
re+inocu+lat+ing
re+inocu+lat+ed
re+inocu+la+tion

re+inocu+la+
  tions
re+insert
re+inserts
re+insert+ing
re+insert+ed
re+inser+tion
re+inser+tions
re+inspect
re+inspects
re+inspect+ing
re+inspect+ed
re+inspec+tion
re+inspec+tions
re+instate
re+instates
re+instat+ing
re+instat+ed
re+instate+ment
re+instate+
  ments
re+insta+tor
re+insta+tors
re+instruct
re+instructs
re+instruct+ing
re+instruct+ed
re+instruc+tion
re+instruc+tions
re+insur+ance
re+insure
re+insures
re+insur+ing
re+insured
re+insur+er
re+insur+ers
re+inte+grate
re+inte+grates
re+inte+grat+ing
re+inte+grat+ed
re+inte+gra+tion
re+inte+gra+
  tions
re+inter+pret
re+inter+prets
re+inter+pret+
  ing
re+inter+pret+
  ed
re+inter+pre+ta+
  tion
re+inter+pre+ta+
  tions
re+inter+ro+gate

re+inter+ro+
  gates
re+inter+ro+gat+
  ing
re+inter+ro+gat+
  ed
re+inter+ro+ga+
  tion
re+inter+ro+ga+
  tions
re+intro+duce
re+intro+duces
re+intro+duc+
  ing
re+intro+duced
re+intro+duc+
  tion
re+intro+duc+
  tions
re+invade
re+invades
re+invad+ing
re+invad+ed
re+inva+sion
re+inva+sions
re+invent
re+invents
re+invent+ing
re+invent+ed
re+inves+ti+gate
re+inves+ti+
  gates
re+inves+ti+gat+
  ing
re+inves+ti+gat+
  ed
re+inves+ti+ga+
  tion
re+inves+ti+ga+
  tions
re+it+er+ate
re+it+er+ates
re+it+er+at+ing
re+it+er+at+ed
re+it+era+tion
re+it+era+tions
re+it+era+tive
re+it+era+tive+ly
Reith
Rei+thean
reive
reives
reiv+ing
reived
reiv+er

reiv+ers
re+ject
re+jects
re+ject+ing
re+ject+ed
re+ject+er
re+ject+ers
re+jec+tion
re+jec+tions
re+jec+tive
re+jec+tor
re+jec+tors
re+jig
re+jigs
re+jig+ging
re+jigged
re+jig+ger
re+jig+gers
re+joice
re+joices
re+joic+ing
re+joiced
re+joic+er
re+joic+ers
re+join
re+joins
re+join+ing
re+joined
re+join+der
re+join+ders
re+judge
re+judges
re+judg+ing
re+judged
re+ju+venate
re+ju+venates
re+ju+venat+ing
re+ju+venat+ed
re+ju+vena+tion
re+ju+vena+
  tions
re+ju+vena+tor
re+ju+vena+tors
re+ju+venes+
  cence
re+ju+venes+
  cent
re+key
re+keys
re+key+ing
re+keyed
re+key+board
re+key+boards

re+key+board+
  ing
re+key+board+
  ed
re+kin+dle
re+kin+dles
re+kin+dling
re+kin+dled
re+la+bel
re+la+bels
re+la+bel+ling
  or
re+la+bel+ing
  U.S.
re+la+belled *or*
re+la+beled
  U.S.
re+lapse
re+lapses
re+lapses
re+laps+ing
re+lapsed
re+laps+er
re+laps+ers
re+lat+able
re+late
re+lates
re+lat+ing
re+lat+ed
re+lat+ed+ness
re+lat+er
re+lat+ers
re+la+tion
re+la+tions
re+la+tion+al
re+la+tion+ship
re+la+tion+ships
rela+tive
rela+tives
rela+tive+ly
rela+tive+ness
rela+tiv+ism
rela+tiv+ist
rela+tiv+ists
rela+tiv+is+tic
rela+tiv+ity
re+la+tor
re+la+tors
re+la+tum
re+la+ta
re+lax
re+laxes
re+lax+ing
re+laxed
re+lax+ant

re+lax+ants
re+laxa+tion
re+laxa+tions
re+lax+ed+ly
re+lax+er
re+lax+ers
re+lax+in
re+lax+ins
re+lay
pass message
re+lays
re+lays
re+lay+ing
re+layed
re-lay
lay anew
re-lays
re-laying
re-laid
re+learn
re+learns
re+learn+ing
re+learned
re+lease
re+leases
re+leases
re+leas+ing
re+leased
re+leas+er
re+leas+ers
rel+ega+table
rel+egate
rel+egates
rel+egat+ing
rel+egat+ed
rel+ega+tion
rel+ega+tions
re+lent
re+lents
re+lent+ing
re+lent+ed
re+lent+less
re+lent+less+ly
re+lent+less+
  ness
re+let
re+lets
re+let+ting
re+let
rel+evance
rel+evan+cy
rel+evant
rel+evant+ly
re+li+abil+ity
re+li+able

re+li+able+ness
re+li+ably
re+li+ance
re+li+ances
re+li+ant
re+li+ant+ly
rel+ic
rel+ics
rel+ict
rel+icts
re+lief
re+liefs
re+liev+able
re+lieve
re+lieves
re+liev+ing
re+lieved
re+liev+er
re+liev+ers
re+light
re+lights
re+light+ing
re+light+ed *or*
re+lit
re+li+gieuse
re+li+gieuses
re+li+gieux
re+li+gieux
re+li+gion
re+li+gions
re+li+gion+ism
reli+gion+ist
reli+gion+ists
re+ligi+ose
re+ligi+ose+ly
re+ligi+os+ity
re+li+gious
re+li+gious+ly
re+li+gious+ness
re+line
re+lines
re+lin+ing
re+lined
re+lin+quish
re+lin+quishes
re+lin+quish+ing
re+lin+quished
re+lin+quish+er
re+lin+quish+ers
re+lin+quish+
  ment
reli+quary
reli+quaries
re+liquiae
rel+ish

rel+ishes	re+marks	re+mem+	re+miss+ness
rel+ishes	re+mark+ing	brances	re+mit
rel+ish+ing	re+marked	re+mem+brancer	re+mits
rel+ished	re+mark+able	re+mem+	re+mits
rel+ish+able	re+mark+able+	brancers	re+mit+ting
re+liv+able	ness	re+mex	re+mit+ted
re+live	re+mark+ably	remi+ges	re+mit+table
re+lives	re+mark+er	re+mig+ial	re+mit+tal
re+liv+ing	re+mark+ers	re+mili+ta+ri+sa+	re+mit+tals
re+lived	re+marque	tion	re+mit+tal
re+load	re+marques	re+mili+ta+ri+sa+	re+mit+tals
re+loads	Remarque	tions	re+mit+tance
re+load+ing	re+mar+riage	re+mili+ta+rise	re+mit+tances
re+load+ed	re+mar+riages	re+mili+ta+rises	re+mit+tence
re+lo+cate	re+mar+ry	re+mili+ta+ris+	re+mit+tent
re+lo+cates	re+mar+ries	ing	re+mit+tent+ly
re+lo+cat+ing	re+mar+ry+ing	re+mili+ta+rised	re+mit+ter
re+lo+cat+ed	re+mar+ried	re+mili+ta+ri+za+	re+mit+ters
re+lo+ca+tion	re+mas+ter	tion	re+mix
re+lo+ca+tions	re+mas+ters	re+mili+ta+ri+za+	re+mixes
re+luc+tance	re+mas+ter+ing	tions	re+mixes
re+luc+tan+cy	re+mas+tered	re+mili+ta+rize	re+mix+ing
re+luc+tant	re+match	re+mili+ta+rizes	re+mixed
re+luc+tant+ly	re+matches	re+mili+ta+riz+	rem+nant
rel+uc+tiv+ity	Rembrandt	ing	rem+nants
rel+uc+tiv+ities	Rem+brandt+	re+mili+ta+rized	re+mod+el
rely	esque	re+mind	re+mod+els
relies	REME	re+minds	re+mod+el+ling
rely+ing	re+meas+ure	re+mind+ing	re+mod+elled
relied	re+meas+ures	re+mind+ed	re+modi+fi+ca+
REM	re+meas+ur+ing	re+mind+er	tion
re+main	re+meas+ured	re+mind+ers	re+modi+fi+ca+
re+mains	re+meas+ure+	re+mind+ful	tions
re+main+ing	ment	remi+nisce	re+modi+fy
re+mained	re+meas+ure+	remi+nisces	re+modi+fies
re+main+der	ments	remi+nisc+ing	re+modi+fy+ing
re+main+ders	re+medi+able	remi+nisced	re+modi+fied
re+main+ders	re+medi+ably	remi+nis+cence	re+mon+eti+sa+
re+main+der+	re+medial	remi+nis+	tion
ing	re+medi+al+ly	cences	re+mon+etise
re+main+dered	rem+edi+less	remi+nis+cent	re+mon+etises
re+mains	rem+edy	remi+nis+cent+ly	re+mon+etis+
re+make	rem+edies	re+mise	ing
re+makes	rem+edies	re+mises	re+mon+etised
re+makes	rem+edy+ing	re+mises	re+mon+eti+za+
re+mak+ing	rem+edied	re+mis+ing	tion
re+made	rem+mem+ber	re+mised	re+mon+etize
re+mand	re+mem+bers	re+miss	re+mon+etizes
re+mands	re+mem+ber+	re+mis+sibil+ity	re+mon+etiz+
re+mands	ing	re+mis+sible	ing
re+mand+ing	re+mem+bered	re+mis+sion	re+mon+etized
re+mand+ed	re+mem+ber+er	re+mis+sions	re+mon+strance
rema+nence	re+mem+ber+	re+mis+sive	re+mon+
re+mark	ers	re+mis+sive+ly	strances
re+marks	re+mem+brance	re+miss+ly	re+mon+strant

re+mon+strants
re+mon+strate
re+mon+strates
re+mon+strat+
    ing
re+mon+strat+
    ed
re+mon+stra+
    tion
re+mon+stra+
    tions
re+mon+stra+
    tive
re+mon+stra+tor
re+mon+stra+
    tors
re+mon+tant
re+mon+tants
remo+ra
remo+ras
re+morse
re+morse+ful
re+morse+ful+ly
re+morse+ful+
    ness
re+morse+less
re+mort+gage
re+mort+gages
re+mort+gag+
    ing
re+mort+gaged
re+mote
re+mot+er
re+mot+est
remote-controlled
re+mote+ly
re+mote+ness
remote-sensing
ré+mou+lade
re+mould
re+moulds
re+moulds
re+mould+ing
re+mould+ed
re+mount
re+mounts
re+mounts
re+mount+ing
re+mount+ed
re+mov+abil+ity
re+mov+able
re+mov+al
re+mov+als
re+mov+al+ist
re+mov+al+ists

re+move
re+moves
re+moves
re+mov+ing
re+moved
re+mov+er
re+mov+ers
Rem+scheid
re+mu+ner+able
re+mu+ner+ate
re+mu+ner+ates
re+mu+ner+at+
    ing
re+mu+ner+at+
    ed
re+mu+nera+tion
re+mu+nera+
    tions
re+mu+nera+tive
re+mu+nera+tive+
    ly
remu+nera+tor
remu+nera+tors
Remus
re+nais+sance
re+nais+sances
Re+nais+sance
re+nal
re+name
re+names
re+nam+ing
re+named
Renan
re+nas+cence
re+nas+cences
re+nas+cent
rend
rends
rend+ing
rent
Rendell
ren+der
ren+ders
ren+ders
ren+der+ing
ren+dered
ren+der+able
ren+der+er
ren+der+ers
ren+der+ing
ren+der+ings
ren+dez+vous
ren+dez+vous
ren+dez+vous

ren+dez+vous+
    ing
ren+dez+voused
rend+ible
ren+di+tion
ren+di+tions
ren+egade
ren+egades
re+nege
re+neges
re+neg+ing
re+neged
re+neg+er
re+neg+ers
re+nego+ti+able
re+nego+ti+ate
re+nego+ti+ates
re+nego+ti+at+
    ing
re+nego+ti+at+
    ed
re+nego+tia+tion
re+nego+tia+
    tions
re+negue
re+negues
re+negu+ing
re+negued
re+negu+er
re+negu+ers
re+new
re+news
re+new+ing
re+newed
re+new+able
re+new+al
re+new+als
re+new+er
re+new+ers
Ren+frew
Ren+frew+shire
Reni
reni+form
re+nin
Rennes
ren+net
ren+nin
Reno
Renoir
re+nomi+nate
re+nomi+nates
re+nomi+nat+
    ing
re+nomi+nat+ed
re+nomi+na+tion

re+nomi+na+
    tions
re+no+ti+fi+ca+
    tion
re+no+ti+fi+ca+
    tions
re+no+ti+fy
re+no+ti+fies
re+no+ti+fy+ing
re+no+ti+fied
re+nounce
re+nounces
re+nounces
re+nounc+ing
re+nounced
re+nounce+ment
re+nounce+
    ments
re+nounc+er
re+nounc+ers
reno+vate
reno+vates
reno+vat+ing
reno+vat+ed
reno+va+tion
reno+va+tions
reno+va+tive
reno+va+tor
reno+va+tors
re+nown
re+nowned
rent
rents
rents
rent+ing
rent+ed
rent+able
rent+al
rent+als
rent+er
rent+ers
rent-free
ren+tier
ren+tiers
rent-roll
rent-rolls
re+num+ber
re+num+bers
re+num+ber+ing
re+num+bered
re+nun+cia+tion
re+nun+cia+
    tions
re+nun+cia+tive
re+nun+cia+tory

re+oc+cu+pa+
 tion
re+oc+cu+pa+
 tions
re+oc+cu+py
re+oc+cu+pies
re+oc+cu+py+
 ing
re+oc+cu+pied
re+oc+cur
re+oc+curs
re+oc+cur+ring
re+oc+curred
re+oc+cur+rence
re+oc+cur+
 rences
re+open
re+opens
re+open+ing
re+opened
re+or+der
re+or+ders
re+or+der+ing
re+or+dered
re+or+gani+sa+
 tion
re+or+gani+sa+
 tions
re+or+gan+ise
re+or+gan+ises
re+or+gan+is+
 ing
re+or+gan+ised
re+or+gan+is+er
re+or+gan+is+
 ers
re+or+gani+za+
 tion
re+or+gani+za+
 tions
re+or+gan+ize
re+or+gan+izes
re+or+gan+iz+
 ing
re+or+gan+ized
re+or+gan+iz+er
re+or+gan+iz+
 ers
re+ori+ent
re+ori+ents
re+ori+ent+ing
re+ori+ent+ed
re+ori+en+ta+
 tion

re+ori+en+ta+
 tions
rep
reps
re+pack
re+packs
re+pack+ing
re+packed
re+pack+age
re+pack+ages
repack+ag+ing
repackaged
re+paint
re+paints
re+paint+ing
re+paint+ed
re+pair
re+pairs
re+pairs
re+pair+ing
re+paired
re+pair+able
re+pair+er
re+pair+ers
re+pair+man
re+pair+men
re+pand
re+pand+ly
re+pa+per
re+pa+pers
re+pa+per+ing
re+pa+pered
repa+rable
repa+rably
repa+ra+tion
repa+ra+tions
re+para+tive
re+para+tory
rep+ar+tee
rep+ar+tees
re+past
re+pasts
re+pat+ri+ate
re+pat+ri+ates
re+pat+ri+ates
re+pat+ri+at+
 ing
re+pat+ri+at+ed
re+pat+ria+tion
re+pat+ria+tions
re+pay
re+pays
re+pay+ing
re+paid
re+pay+able

re+pay+ment
re+pay+ments
re+peal
re+peals
re+peals
re+peal+ing
re+pealed
re+peal+able
re+peal+er
re+peal+ers
re+peat
re+peats
re+peats
re+peat+ing
re+peat+ed
re+peat+able
re+peat+ed+ly
re+peat+er
re+peat+ers
rep+echage
rep+echages
re+pel
re+pels
re+pel+ling
re+pelled
re+pel+lant
re+pel+lants
re+pel+lence
re+pel+len+cy
re+pel+lent
re+pel+lents
re+pel+lent+ly
re+pel+ler
re+pel+lers
re+pent
re+pents
re+pent+ing
re+pent+ed
re+pent+ance
re+pent+ances
re+pent+ant
re+pent+er
re+pent+ers
re+people
re+peoples
re+peopling
re+peopled
re+per+cus+sion
re+per+cus+
 sions
re+per+cus+sive
rep+er+toire
rep+er+toires
rep+er+to+rial
rep+er+tory

rep+er+tories
rep+etend
rep+etends
ré+pé+ti+teur
ré+pé+ti+teurs
rep+eti+tion
rep+eti+tions
rep+eti+tious
rep+eti+tious+ly
rep+eti+tious+
 ness
re+peti+tive
re+phrase
re+phrases
re+phras+ing
re+phrased
re+pine
re+pines
re+pin+ing
re+pined
re+place
re+places
re+plac+ing
re+placed
re+place+able
re+place+ment
re+place+ments
re+plac+er
re+plac+ers
re+plan
re+plans
re+plan+ning
re+planned
re+plant
re+plants
re+plant+ing
re+plant+ed
re+play
re+plays
re+plays
re+play+ing
re+played
re+plen+ish
re+plen+ishes
re+plen+ish+ing
re+plen+ished
re+plen+ish+er
re+plen+ish+ers
re+plen+ish+
 ment
re+plen+ish+
 ments
re+plete•
re+plete+ly
re+plete+ness

re+ple+tion
re+plevi+able
re+plev+in
re+plev+ins
re+plev+is+able
re+plevy
re+plevies
re+plevies
re+plevy+ing
re+plevied
rep+li+ca
rep+li+cas
rep+li+cate
rep+li+cates
rep+li+cat+ing
rep+li+cat+ed
rep+li+ca+tion
rep+li+ca+tions
rep+li+ca+tive
re+pli+er
re+pli+ers
re+ply
re+plies
re+plies
re+ply+ing
re+plied
re+point
re+points
re+point+ing
re+point+ed
re+popu+late
re+popu+lates
re+popu+lat+ing
re+popu+lat+ed
re+port
re+ports
re+ports
re+port+ing
re+port+ed
re+port+able
re+port+age
re+port+ages
re+port+ed
re+port+ed+ly
re+port+er
re+port+ers
re+pos+al
rest
re+pos+als
re+po+sal
placing
re+po+sals
re+pose
re+poses
re+poses

re+pos+ing
re+posed
re+pose+ful
re+pose+ful+ly
re+pos+er
re+pos+ers
re+po+si+tion
re+po+si+tions
re+po+si+tions
re+po+si+tion+
ing
re+po+si+tioned
re+posi+tory
re+posi+tories
re+pos+sess
re+pos+sesses
re+pos+sess+
ing
re+pos+sessed
re+pos+ses+sion
re+pos+ses+
sions
re+pos+ses+sor
re+pos+ses+
sors
re+pot
re+pots
re+pot+ting
re+pot+ted
re+pous+sé
re+pous+sés
repp
repped
rep+re+hend
rep+re+hends
rep+re+hend+
ing
rep+re+hend+ed
rep+re+hend+er
rep+re+hend+
ers
rep+re+hen+sibil+
ity
rep+re+hen+sible
rep+re+hen+sibly
rep+re+hen+sion
rep+re+hen+
sions
rep+re+sent
stand for
rep+re+sents
rep+re+sent+ing
rep+re+sent+ed
re-present
present again

re-presents
re-present+ing
re-present+ed
rep+re+sent+abil+
ity
rep+re+sent+able
rep+re+sen+ta+
tion
rep+re+sen+ta+
tions
re-presen+ta+
tion
re-presen+ta+
tions
rep+re+sen+ta+
tion+al
rep+re+sen+ta+
tion+al+ism
rep+re+sen+ta+
tion+al+is+tic
rep+re+sen+ta+
tion+ism
rep+re+sen+ta+
tion+ist
rep+re+sen+ta+
tion+ists
rep+re+senta+
tive
rep+re+senta+
tives
rep+re+senta+
tive+ly
rep+re+senta+
tive+ness
re+press
quell
re+presses
re+press+ing
re+pressed
re-press
press again
re-presses
re-pressing
re-pressed
re+press+er
re+press+ers
re+press+ible
re+pres+sion
re+pres+sions
re+pres+sive
re+press+or
re+press+ors
re+price
re+prices
re+pric+ing

re+priced
re+priev+able
re+prieve
re+prieves
re+prieves
re+priev+ing
re+prieved
re+priev+er
re+priev+ers
rep+ri+mand
rep+ri+mands
rep+ri+mands
rep+ri+mand+
ing
rep+ri+mand+ed
re+print
re+prints
re+prints
re+print+ing
re+print+ed
re+print+er
re+print+ers
re+pris+al
re+pris+als
re+prise
re+prises
re+prises
re+pris+ing
re+prised
re+pro
re+pros
re+proach
re+proaches
re+proaches
re+proach+ing
re+proached
re+proach+able
re+proach+er
re+proach+ers
re+proach+ful
re+proach+ful+ly
re+proach+ful+
ness
rep+ro+ba+cy
rep+ro+bate
rep+ro+bates
rep+ro+bates
rep+ro+bat+ing
rep+ro+bat+ed
rep+ro+bat+er
rep+ro+bat+ers
rep+ro+ba+tion
re+pro+cess
re+pro+cesses

re+pro+cess+
  ing
re+pro+cessed
re+pro+cess+ing
re+pro+duce
re+pro+duces
re+pro+duc+ing
re+pro+duced
re+pro+duc+er
re+pro+duc+ers
re+pro+duc+ible
re+pro+duc+ibly
re+pro+duc+tion
re+pro+duc+
  tions
re+pro+duc+tive
re+pro+duc+tive+
  ly
re+pro+duc+tive+
  ness
re+pro+gram+
  able
re+pro+gram+ma+
  ble
rep+ro+graph+ic
rep+ro+graphi+
  cal+ly
re+prog+ra+phy
re+proof
rebuke
  re+proofs
re-proof
renew
  re-proofs
  re-proofing
  re-proofed
re+prov+able
re+prove
  re+proves
  re+prov+ing
  re+proved
re+prov+er
  re+prov+ers
reprov+ing+ly
rep+tant
rep+tile
  rep+tiles
rep+til+ian
  rep+til+ians
Repton
re+pub+lic
  re+pub+lics
re+pub+li+can
  re+pub+li+cans
Re+pub+li+can

Re+pub+li+cans
re+pub+li+can+
  ism
re+pub+li+ca+
  tion
re+pub+li+ca+
  tions
re+pub+lish
  re+pub+lishes
  re+pub+lish+ing
  re+pub+lished
re+pu+di+able
re+pu+di+ate
  re+pu+di+ates
  re+pu+di+at+ing
  re+pu+di+at+ed
re+pu+dia+tion
  re+pu+dia+tions
re+pu+dia+tive
re+pu+dia+tor
  re+pu+dia+tors
re+pug+nance
re+pug+nant
  re+pug+nant+ly
re+pulse
  re+pulses
  re+pulses
  re+puls+ing
  re+pulsed
  re+puls+er
  re+puls+ers
re+pul+sion
  re+pul+sions
re+pul+sive
  re+pul+sive+ly
  re+pul+sive+ness
re+pur+chase
  re+pur+chases
  re+pur+chases
  re+pur+chas+
    ing
  re+pur+chased
re+puri+fy
  re+puri+fies
  re+puri+fy+ing
  re+puri+fied
repu+table
repu+tably
repu+ta+tion
  repu+ta+tions
re+pute
  re+putes
  re+put+ing
  re+put+ed
  re+put+ed+ly

re+quest
  re+quests
  re+quests
  re+quest+ing
  re+quest+ed
  re+quest+er
  re+quest+ers
Requi+em
  Requi+ems
requi+es+cat
  requi+es+cats
re+quire
  re+quires
  re+quir+ing
  re+quired
re+quire+ment
  re+quire+ments
re+quir+er
  re+quir+ers
requi+site
  requi+sites
requi+site+ly
requi+si+tion
  requi+si+tions
  requi+si+tions
  requi+si+tion+
    ing
  requi+si+tioned
requi+si+tion+ary
re+quit+able
re+quit+al
  re+quit+als
re+quite
  re+quites
  re+quit+ing
  re+quit+ed
re+quite+ment
  re+quite+ments
re+quit+er
  re+quit+ers
re+read
  re+reads
  re+read+ing
  re+read
re+rec+ord
  re+rec+ords
  re+rec+ord+ing
  re+rec+ord+ed
  re+rec+ord+ing
  re+rec+ord+ings
rere+dos
  rere+doses
re+roof
  re+roofs
  re+roof+ing

re+roofed
re+route
  re+routes
re+rout+ing
  re+rout+ed
re+run
  re+runs
  re+runs
  re+run+ning
  re+ran
res
  res
re+sal+able
re+sale
  re+sales
re+sale+able
re+sched+ule
  re+sched+ules
  re+sched+ul+ing
  re+sched+uled
re+scind
  re+scinds
  re+scind+ing
  re+scind+ed
  re+scind+able
  re+scind+er
  re+scind+ers
  re+scind+ment
  re+scind+ments
re+scis+sion
  re+scis+sions
re+script
  re+scripts
res+cue
  res+cues
  res+cues
  res+cu+ing
  res+cued
  res+cu+er
  res+cu+ers
re+seal
  re+seals
  re+seal+ing
  re+sealed
re+seal+able
re+search
  re+searches
  re+search+ing
  re+searched
  re+search+able
  re+search+er
  re+search+ers
re+seat
  re+seats
  re+seat+ing

re+seat+ed
re+sect
re+sects
re+sect+ing
re+sect+ed
re+sec+tion
re+sec+tions
re+sec+tion+al
re+sell
re+sells
re+sell+ing
re+sold
re+sem+blance
re+sem+blances
re+sem+blant
re+sem+ble
re+sem+bles
re+sem+bling
re+sem+bled
re+sem+bler
re+sem+blers
re+sent
re+sents
re+sent+ing
re+sent+ed
re+sent+ful
re+sent+ment
re+sent+ments
re+ser+pine
re+serv+able
res+er+va+tion
res+er+va+tions
re+serve
set aside
re+serves
re+serves
re+serv+ing
re+served
re-serve
serve again
re-serves
re-serving
re-served
re+serv+ed+ly
re+serv+ed+ness
reserve-grade
re+serv+er
re+serv+ers
re+serv+ist
re+serv+ists
res+er+voir
res+er+voirs
re+set
re+sets
re+sets

re+set+ting
re+set
re+set+ter
re+set+ters
re+set+tle
re+set+tles
re+set+tling
re+set+tled
re+set+tle+ment
re+set+tle+
ments
res ges+tae
re+shape
re+shapes
re+shap+ing
re+shaped
re+shuf+fle
re+shuf+fles
re+shuf+fles
re+shuf+fling
re+shuf+fled
re+side
re+sides
re+sid+ing
re+sid+ed
resi+dence
resi+dences
resi+den+cy
resi+den+cies
resi+dent
resi+dents
resi+den+tial
resi+den+tial+ly
resi+den+tiary
resi+den+tiaries
resi+dent+ship
resi+dent+ships
re+sid+er
re+sid+ers
re+sid+ual
re+sid+uals
re+sidu+al+ly
re+sidu+ary
resi+due
resi+dues
re+sid+uum
re+sidua
re+sign
give up
re+signs
re+sign+ing
re+signed
re-sign
sign again
re-signs

re-signing
re-signed
res+ig+na+tion
res+ig+na+tions
re+sign+ed+ly
re+sign+ed+ness
re+sign+er
re+sign+ers
re+sile
re+siles
re+sil+ing
re+siled
re+sile+ment
re+sili+ence
re+sili+en+cy
re+sili+ent
re+sili+ent+ly
res+in
res+ins
res+ins
res+in+ing
res+ined
res+in+ate
res+in+ates
res+in+at+ing
res+in+at+ed
res+in+ous
res+in+ous+ly
res+in+ous+ness
resi+pis+cence
resi+pis+cent
re+sist
re+sists
re+sists
re+sist+ing
re+sist+ed
re+sist+ance
re+sist+ances
Re+sist+ance
re+sist+ant
re+sist+ants
Re+sis+ten+cia
re+sist+er
re+sist+ers
re+sist+ibil+ity
re+sist+ible
re+sist+ibly
re+sis+tiv+ity
re+sist+less
re+sis+tor
re+sis+tors
re+sit
re+sits
re+sits
re+sit+ting

re+sat
re+site
re+sites
re+sit+ing
re+sited
res ju+di+ca+ta
Resnais
re+sole
re+soles
re+sol+ing
re+soled
re+sol+ubil+ity
re-solubil+ity
re+sol+uble
resolvable
re-soluble
dissolvable again
re+sol+uble+ness
re-soluble+ness
re-solubly
reso+lute
reso+lute+ly
reso+lute+ness
reso+lu+tion
reso+lu+tions
reso+lu+tion+er
reso+lu+tion+
ers
re+solv+abil+ity
re+solv+able
re+solv+able+
ness
re+solve
re+solves
re+solves
re+solv+ing
re+solved
re+solv+ed+ly
re+solv+ed+ness
re+sol+vent
re+sol+vents
re+solv+er
re+solv+ers
re+solv+ing
reso+nance
reso+nances
reso+nant
reso+nant+ly
reso+nate
reso+nates
reso+nat+ing
reso+nat+ed
reso+na+tion
reso+na+tions
reso+na+tor

reso+na+tors
re+sorb
 re+sorbs
 re+sorb+ing
 re+sorbed
re+sorb+ent
re+sor+cin+al
res+or+cin+ol
re+sorp+tion
 re+sorp+tions
re+sorp+tive
re+sort
have recourse
 re+sorts
 re+sorts
 re+sort+ing
 re+sort+ed
re-sort
sort again
 re-sorts
 re-sorting
 re-sorted
re+sort+er
 re+sort+ers
re+sound
reverberate
 re+sounds
 re+sound+ing
 re+sound+ed
re-sound
sound again
 re-sounds
 re-sounding
 re-sounded
re+sound+ing+ly
re+source
 re+sources
re+source+ful
re+source+ful+ly
re+source+ful+
 ness
re+source+less
re+spect
 re+spects
 re+spects
 re+spect+ing
 re+spect+ed
re+spect+abil+ity
re+spect+able
re+spect+ably
re+spect+er
 re+spect+ers
re+spect+ful
re+spect+ful+ly

re+spect+ful+
 ness
re+spec+tive
re+spec+tive+ly
Respighi
re+spir+abil+ity
res+pir+able
res+pi+ra+tion
res+pi+ra+tion+al
res+pi+ra+tor
 res+pi+ra+tors
res+pira+tory
re+spire
 re+spires
 re+spir+ing
 re+spired
res+pite
 res+pites
 res+pites
 res+pit+ing
 res+pit+ed
re+splend+ence
re+splend+en+cy
re+splend+ent
re+splend+ent+ly
re+spond
 re+sponds
 re+sponds
 re+spond+ing
 re+spond+ed
re+spond+ence
re+spond+ent
 re+spond+ents
re+spond+er
 re+spond+ers
re+sponse
 re+sponses
re+spons+er
 re+spons+ers
re+spon+sibil+ity
 re+spon+sibil+
 ities
re+spon+sible
re+spon+sible+
 ness
re+spon+sibly
re+spon+sive
re+spon+sive+ly
re+spon+sive+
 ness
re+spon+sor
 re+spon+sors
re+spon+so+ry

re+spon+so+
 ries
re+spray
 re+sprays
 re+sprays
 re+spray+ing
 re+sprayed
rest
 rests
 rests
 rest+ing
 rest+ed
re+start
 re+starts
 re+starts
 re+start+ing
 re+start+ed
re+state
 re+states
 re+stat+ing
 re+stat+ed
res+tau+rant
 res+tau+rants
 res+tau+ra+teur
 res+tau+ra+
 teurs
rest-cure
 rest-cures
rest+er
 rest+ers
rest+ful
rest+ful+ly
rest+ful+ness
rest+harrow
 rest+harrows
res+ti+tu+tion
 res+ti+tu+tions
res+ti+tu+tive
res+ti+tu+tory
res+tive
res+tive+ly
res+tive+ness
rest+less
rest+less+ly
rest+less+ness
re+stock
 re+stocks
 re+stock+ing
 re+stocked
re+stor+able
res+to+ra+tion
 res+to+ra+tions
re+stora+tive
 re+stora+tives
re+store

re+stores
re+stor+ing
re+stored
re+stor+er
 re+stor+ers
re+strain
 re+strains
 re+strain+ing
 re+strained
re+strain+able
re+strain+ed+ly
re+strain+er
 re+strain+ers
re+straint
 re+straints
re+strict
 re+stricts
re+strict+ing
re+strict+ed
re+strict+ed+ly
re+strict+ed+
 ness
re+stric+tion
 re+stric+tions
re+stric+tion+ist
 re+stric+tion+
 ists
re+stric+tive
re+stric+tive+ly
re+stric+tive+
 ness
re+string
 re+strings
 re+string+ing
 re+strung
re+struc+ture
 re+struc+tures
 re+struc+tur+ing
 re+struc+tured
re+style
 re+styles
 re+styl+ing
 re+styled
re+sub+mit
 re+sub+mits
 re+sub+mit+ting
 re+sub+mit+ted
re+sult
 re+sults
 re+sults
 re+sult+ing
 re+sult+ed
re+sult+ant
 re+sult+ants
re+sume

re+sumes
re+sum+ing
re+sumed
ré+su+mé
ré+su+més
re+sump+tion
re+sump+tions
re+sump+tive
re+sump+tive+ly
re+su+pi+nate
re+su+pi+na+tion
re+sup+ply
re+sup+plies
re+sup+ply+ing
re+sup+plied
re+sur+face
re+sur+faces
re+sur+fac+ing
re+sur+faced
re+surge
re+surges
re+surg+ing
re+surged
re+sur+gence
re+sur+gences
re+sur+gent
res+ur+rect
res+ur+rects
res+ur+rect+ing
res+ur+rect+ed
res+ur+rec+tion
res+ur+rec+tions
res+ur+rec+tion+al
res+ur+rec+tion+ism
res+ur+rec+tion+ist
res+ur+rec+tion+ists
re+sur+vey
re+sur+veys
re+sur+veys
re+sur+vey+ing
re+sur+veyed
re+sus+ci+tate
re+sus+ci+tates
re+sus+ci+tat+ing
re+sus+ci+tat+ed
re+sus+ci+ta+tion

re+sus+ci+ta+tions
re+sus+ci+ta+tive
re+sus+ci+ta+tor
re+sus+ci+ta+tors
ret
rets
ret+ting
ret+ted
re+ta+ble
re+ta+bles
re+tail
re+tails
re+tails
re+tail+ing
re+tailed
re+tail+er
re+tail+ers
re+tain
re+tains
re+tain+ing
re+tained
re+tain+able
re+tain+er
re+tain+ers
re+tain+ing
re+tain+ment
re+take
re+takes
re+takes
re+tak+ing
re+took
re+tak+en
re+tak+er
re+tak+ers
re+tali+ate
re+tali+ates
re+tali+at+ing
re+tali+at+ed
re+talia+tion
re+talia+tions
re+talia+tive
re+talia+tory
re+tard
re+tards
re+tard+ing
re+tard+ed
re+tard+ant
re+tard+ants
re+tar+da+tion
re+tar+da+tions
re+tarda+tive
re+tarda+tory

re+tard+er
re+tard+ers
re+tard+ment
re+tard+ments
retch
retches
retches
retch+ing
retched
rete
re+tia
re+tell
re+tells
re+tell+ing
re+told
re+ten+tion
re+ten+tions
re+ten+tive
re+ten+tive+ly
re+ten+tive+ness
re+tes+ti+fy
re+tes+ti+fies
re+tes+ti+fy+ing
re+tes+ti+fied
re+think
re+thinks
re+thinks
re+think+ing
re+thought
Reti
re+tial
re+ti+ar+ius
re+ti+arii
reti+cence
reti+cent
reti+cent+ly
reti+cle
reti+cles
reti+ticu+lar
re+ticu+late
re+ticu+lates
re+ticu+lat+ing
re+ticu+lat+ed
re+ticu+late+ly
re+ticu+la+tion
re+ticu+la+tions
reti+cules
reti+cules
re+ticu+lum
re+ticu+la
re+tie
re+ties
re+ty+ing
re+tied
re+ti+form

reti+na
reti+nas or
reti+nae
reti+nal
reti+nene
reti+ni+tis
reti+no+scop+ic
reti+no+scopi+cal+ly
reti+nos+co+pist
reti+nos+co+pists
reti+nos+co+py
reti+nos+co+pies
reti+nue
reti+nues
re+tir+al
re+tir+als
re+tire
re+tires
re+tir+ing
re+tired
re+tire+ment
re+tire+ments
re+tir+er
re+tir+ers
re+tir+ing+ly
re+ti+tle
re+ti+tles
re+ti+tling
re+ti+tled
re+tool
re+tools
re+tool+ing
re+tooled
re+tort
re+torts
re+torts
re+tort+ing
re+tort+ed
re+tort+er
re+tort+ers
re+touch
re+touches
re+touches
re+touch+ing
re+touched
re+touch+er
re+touch+ers
re+trace
*go back over
again*
re+traces
re+trac+ing

re+traced
re-trace
trace again
re-traces
re-tracing
re-traced
re+tract
re+tracts
re+tract+ing
re+tract+ed
re+tract+able
re+tract+ible
re+trac+tile
re+trac+til+ity
re+trac+tion
re+trac+tions
re+trac+tive
re+trac+tor
re+trac+tors
re+train
re+trains
re+train+ing
re+trained
re+trans+mis+
sion
re+trans+mis+
sions
re+trans+mit
re+trans+mits
re+trans+mit+
ting
re+trans+mit+
ted
re+tread
remould tyres
re+treads
re+treads
re+tread+ing
re+tread+ed
re-tread
tread again
re-treads
re-treading
re-trod
re-trodden *or*
re-trod
re+treat
re+treats
re+treats
re+treat+ing
re+treat+ed
re+trench
re+trenches
re+trench+ing
re+trenched

re+trench+ment
re+trench+
ments
re+tri+al
re+tri+als
ret+ri+bu+tion
ret+ri+bu+tions
re+tribu+tive
re+tribu+tive+ly
re+triev+able
re+triev+al
re+triev+als
re+trieve
re+trieves
re+trieves
re+triev+ing
re+trieved
re+triev+er
re+triev+ers
ret+ro
ret+ros
retro+act
retro+acts
retro+act+ing
retro+act+ed
retro+ac+tion
retro+ac+tions
retro+ac+tive
retro+ac+tive+ly
retro+ac+tiv+ity
retro+cede
retro+cedes
retro+ced+ing
retro+ced+ed
retro+ced+ence
retro+ced+ent
retro+ces+sion
retro+ces+sions
retro+ces+sive
retro+choir
retro+choirs
retro+fire
retro+fires
retro+fit
retro+fits
retro+fit+ting
retro+fit+ted
retro+flec+tion
retro+flec+tions
retro+flex
retro+flexed
retro+flex+ion
retro+flex+ions
retro+gra+da+
tion

retro+gra+da+
tions
retro+grade
retro+grades
retro+grad+ing
retro+grad+ed
retro+grade+ly
retro+gress
retro+gresses
retro+gress+ing
retro+gressed
retro+gres+sion
retro+gres+
sions
retro+gres+sive
retro+gres+sive+
ly
retro+rock+et
retro+rock+ets
re+trorse
retro+spect
retro+spec+tion
retro+spec+
tions
retro+spec+tive
retro+spec+
tives
retro+spec+tive+
ly
re+trous+sé
retro+ver+sion
retro+ver+sions
retro+vert+ed
Retro+vir
Trademark
retro+vi+rus
retro+vi+ruses
re+try
re+tries
re+try+ing
re+tried
ret+si+na
re+turf
re+turfs
re+turf+ing
re+turfed
re+turn
re+turns
re+turns
re+turn+ing
re+turned
re+turn+able
re+turn+er
re+turn+ers
re+turn+ing

re+tuse
re+type
re+types
re+typ+ing
re+typed
Reuben
re+uni+fi+ca+tion
re+uni+fi+ca+
tions
re+uni+fy
re+uni+fies
re+uni+fy+ing
re+uni+fied
re+union
re+unions
Réu+nion
re+unit+able
re+unite
re+unites
re+unit+ing
re+unit+ed
re+up+hol+ster
re+up+hol+sters
re+up+hol+ster+
ing
re+up+hol+
stered
Reus
re+us+able
re+use
re+uses
re+uses
re+us+ing
re+used
Reuter
Reut+ling+en
rev
revs
revs
rev+ving
revved
re+valu+ate
re+valu+ates
re+valu+at+ing
re+valu+at+ed
re+valua+tion
re+valua+tions
re+value
re+values
re+valu+ing
re+valued
re+vamp
re+vamps
re+vamps
re+vamp+ing

re+vamped
re+vanch+ism
re+vanch+ist
re+vanch+ists
re+var+nish
re+varn+ishes
re+var+nish+ing
re+var+nished
re+veal
re+veals
re+veals
re+veal+ing
re+vealed
re+veal+able
re+veal+er
re+veal+ers
re+veal+ing
re+veal+ing+ly
re+veil+le
re+veil+les
rev+el
rev+els
rev+els
rev+el+ling *or*
rev+el+ing
U.S.
rev+elled *or*
rev+eled
U.S.
rev+ela+tion
rev+ela+tions
Rev+ela+tion
rev+ela+tion+al
rev+ela+tion+ist
rev+ela+tion+ists
rev+el+ler
rev+el+lers
rev+el+ry
rev+el+ries
rev+enant
rev+enants
re+venge
re+venges
re+venges
re+veng+ing
re+venged
re+venge+ful
re+venge+ful+ly
re+venge+ful+ness
re+veng+er
re+veng+ers
re+veng+ing+ly
rev+enue

rev+enues
re+verb
re+verbs
re+ver+ber+ant+ly
re+ver+ber+ate
re+ver+ber+ates
re+ver+ber+at+ing
re+ver+ber+at+ed
re+ver+bera+tion
re+ver+bera+tions
re+ver+bera+tive
re+ver+bera+tor
re+ver+bera+tors
re+ver+bera+tory
re+vere
re+veres
re+ver+ing
re+vered
Revere
rev+er+ence
rev+er+ences
rev+er+ences
rev+er+enc+ing
rev+er+enced
Rev+er+ence
Rev+er+end
rev+er+ends
Rev+er+end
rev+er+ent
rev+er+en+tial
rev+er+en+tial+ly
rev+er+ent+ly
rev+erie
rev+eries
re+vers
re+vers
re+ver+sal
re+ver+sals
re+verse
re+verses
re+verses
re+vers+ing
re+versed
reverse-charge
re+verse+ly
re+vers+er
re+vers+ers
re+vers+ibil+ity
re+vers+ible
re+vers+ibles

re+vers+ibly
re+ver+sion
re+ver+sions
re+ver+sion+al
re+ver+sion+ary
re+vert
re+verts
re+vert+ing
re+vert+ed
re+vert+er
re+vert+ers
re+vert+ible
re+vet
re+vets
re+vet+ting
re+vet+ted
re+vet+ment
re+vet+ments
re+view
re+views
re+views
re+view+ing
re+viewed
re+view+er
re+view+ers
re+vile
re+viles
re+vil+ing
re+viled
re+vile+ment
re+vil+er
re+vil+ers
re+vis+al
re+vis+als
re+vise
re+vises
re+vises
re+vis+ing
re+vised
re+vis+er
re+vis+ers
re+vi+sion
re+vi+sions
re+vi+sion+ary
re+vi+sion+ism
re+vi+sion+ist
re+vi+sion+ists
re+vis+it
re+vis+its
re+vis+it+ing
re+vis+it+ed
re+vi+so+ry
re+vi+tal+ise
re+vi+tal+ises
re+vi+tal+is+ing

re+vi+tal+ised
re+vi+tal+ize
re+vi+tal+izes
re+vi+tal+iz+ing
re+vi+tal+ized
re+viv+abil+ity
re+viv+able
re+viv+al
re+viv+als
re+viv+al+ism
re+viv+al+isms
re+viv+al+ist
re+viv+al+ists
re+viv+al+is+tic
re+vive
re+vives
re+viv+ing
re+vived
re+viv+er
re+viv+ers
re+vivi+fi+ca+tion
re+vivi+fi+ca+tions
re+vivi+fy
re+vivi+fies
re+vivi+fy+ing
re+vivi+fied
revo+cabil+ity
revo+cable
revo+cably
revo+ca+tion
revo+ca+tions
revo+ca+tory
re+voice
re+voices
re+voic+ing
re+voiced
re+vok+abil+ity
re+vok+able
re+vok+ably
re+voke
re+vokes
re+vokes
re+vok+ing
re+voked
re+vok+er
re+vok+ers
re+volt
re+volts
re+volts
re+volt+ing
re+volt+ed
re+volt+ing+ly
revo+lute

revo+lu+tion
revo+lu+tions
revo+lu+tion+ary
revo+lu+tion+
 aries
Revo+lu+tion+ary
revo+lu+tion+ise
revo+lu+tion+
 ises
revo+lu+tion+is+
 ing
revo+lu+tion+
 ised
revo+lu+tion+is+
 er
revo+lu+tion+is+
 ers
revo+lu+tion+ist
revo+lu+tion+
 ists
revo+lu+tion+ize
revo+lu+tion+
 izes
revo+lu+tion+iz+
 ing
revo+lu+tion+
 ized
revo+lu+tion+iz+
 er
revo+lu+tion+iz+
 ers
re+volv+able
re+volve
re+volves
re+volv+ing
re+volved
re+volv+er
re+volv+ers
re+vue
re+vues
re+vul+sion
re+vul+sions
re+vul+sive
re+vul+sives
re+vul+sive+ly
re+ward
re+wards
re+wards
re+ward+ing
re+ward+ed
re+ward+less
re+wash
re+washes
re+wash+ing
re+washed

re+weigh
re+weighs
re+weigh+ing
re+weighed
re+weld
re+welds
re+weld+ing
re+weld+ed
re+wind
re+winds
re+winds
re+wind+ing
re+wound
re+wind+er
re+wind+ers
re+wir+able
re+wire
re+wires
re+wir+ing
re+wired
re+word
re+words
re+word+ing
re+word+ed
re+work
re+works
re+work+ing
re+worked
re+wrap
re+wraps
re+wrap+ping
re+wrapped
re+write
re+writes
re+writes
re+writ+ing
re+wrote
re+writ+ten
Rex
Rex+ine
Trademark
Reye
Rey+kja+vik
Reyn+ard
Reynaud
Reynolds
Rey+no+sa
re+zone
re+zones
re+zon+ing
re+zoned
rhab+do+man+
 cer
rhab+do+man+
 cers

rhab+do+man+cy
rhab+do+man+
 tist
rhab+do+man+
 tists
rha+chial
rha+chid+ial
rha+chis
rha+chises *or*
 rha+chi+des
Rhada+man+
 thine
Rhadamanthus
Rhadamanthys
Rhae+tia
rhap+sod+ic
rhap+so+dise
rhap+so+dises
rhap+so+dis+
 ing
rhap+so+dised
rhap+so+dist
rhap+so+dists
rhap+so+dize
rhap+so+dizes
rhap+so+diz+ing
rhap+so+dized
rhap+so+dy
rhap+so+dies
rhata+ny
rhata+nies
rhea
rheas
Rhea
Rhea Silvia
rhe+boks
rhe+boks *or*
 rhe+bok
Rhee
Rheims
Rhein
Rhein+land
Rheinland-Pfalz
Rhen+ish
rhe+nium
rheo+logi+cal
rhe+olo+gist
rhe+olo+gists
rhe+ol+ogy
rheo+stat
rheo+stats
rheo+stat+ic
rhe+sus
Rhesus
rheto+ric

rheto+rics
rhe+tori+cal
rhe+tori+cal+ly
rhe+tori+cian
rhe+tori+cians
rheum
rheums
rheu+mat+ic
rheu+mat+ics
rheu+mati+cal+ly
rheu+ma+tism
rheu+ma+tisms
rheu+ma+toid
rheu+ma+to+logi+
 cal
rheu+ma+tol+ogy
rheumy
rheumi+er
rheumi+est
Rheydt
rhi+nal
Rhine
Rhine+land
Rhineland-Palati+
 nate
rhine+stone
rhine+stones
rhi+ni+tic
rhi+ni+tis
rhi+no
rhi+nos *or*
 rhi+no
rhi+noc+er+os
rhi+noc+er+
 oses *or*
rhi+noc+er+os
rhi+no+cerot+ic
rhi+no+logi+cal
rhi+nolo+gist
rhi+nolo+gists
rhi+nol+ogy
rhi+no+plas+tic
rhi+no+plas+ty
rhi+no+plas+ties
rhi+nos+co+py
rhi+nos+co+pies
rhi+zo+car+pous
rhi+zoid
rhi+zoids
rhi+zoi+dal
rhi+zoma+tous
rhi+zome
rhi+zomes
rhi+zo+pod
rhi+zo+pods

rho
  rhos
rho+da+mine
  rho+da+mines
Rhode
Rhodes
Rho+desia
Rho+desian
  Rho+desians
Rho+dian
  Rho+dians
rho+dium
rho+do+chro+
  site
rho+do+den+
  dron
rho+do+den+
  drons
rhodo+lite
rhodo+nite
Rho+dope
rho+dop+sin
rhom+ben+cepha+
  lon
rhom+bic
rhom+bo+he+
  dral
rhom+bo+he+
  dron
  rhom+bo+he+
    drons *or*
rhom+bo+he+
  dra
rhom+boid
  rhom+boids
rhom+boi+dal
rhom+bus
  rhom+buses *or*
  rhom+bi
rhon+chus
  rhon+chi
Rhon+dda
Rhône
Rhône-Alpes
rhu+barb
  rhu+barbs
rhumb
  rhumbs
rhum+ba
  rhum+bas
rhyme
  rhymes
  rhymes
rhym+ing
rhymed

rhym+er
  rhym+ers
rhyme+ster
  rhyme+sters
rhym+ing
rhyo+lite
rhyo+lit+ic
Rhys
rhythm
  rhythms
rhyth+mic
rhyth+mi+cal
rhyth+mi+cal+ly
rhyth+mic+ity
ria
  rias
Ri+al+to
rib
  ribs
  ribs
rib+bing
ribbed
rib+ald
  rib+alds
rib+ald+ry
  rib+ald+ries
rib+and
  rib+ands
rib+band
  rib+bands
Ribbentrop
rib+bing
  rib+bings
Rib+ble
rib+bon
  rib+bons
  rib+bons
rib+bon+ing
rib+boned
ribbon+fish
  ribbon+fish *or*
  ribbon+fishes
ribbon+wood
  ribbon+woods
rib+cage
  rib+cages
Ribera
rib+less
ri+bo+fla+vin
ri+bo+fla+vine
ri+bo+nu+clease
  ri+bo+nu+
    cleases
ri+bose
ri+bo+so+mal

ri+bo+some
ri+bo+somes
rib-tickler
  rib-ticklers
rib-tickling
rib+wort
Ri+card+ian
  Ri+card+ians
Ricardo
Riccio
rice
  rices
  rices
ric+ing
riced
Rice
rich
rich+er
rich+est
Rich
Richard
Richards
Richardson
Richelieu
  surname
Rich+elieu
  river
riches
Richler
rich+ly
Rich+mond
rich+ness
Richter
Richthofen
rick
  ricks
  ricks
rick+ing
ricked
rick+eti+ness
rick+ets
rick+ett+sia
rick+ett+siae
  or
rick+ett+sias
rick+ett+sial
rick+ety
rick+rack
  rick+racks
rick+sha
  rick+shas
rick+shaw
  rick+shaws
rico+chet
  rico+chets

rico+chets
rico+chet+ing
  or
rico+chet+ting
rico+cheted *or*
rico+chet+ted
ri+cot+ta
ric+rac
  ric+racs
ric+tal
ric+tus
  ric+tus *or*
  ric+tuses
rid
  rids
rid+ding
  rid *or*
  rid+ded
rid+able
rid+dance
rid+den
rid+dle
  rid+dles
  rid+dles
rid+dling
  rid+dled
rid+dler
  rid+dlers
ride
  rides
  rides
rid+ing
rode
rid+den
ride+able
rid+er
  rid+ers
rid+er+less
ridge
  ridges
  ridges
ridg+ing
ridged
ridge+like
ridge+pole
  ridge+poles
ridge+way
  ridge+ways
ridgy
ridi+cule
  ridi+cules
  ridi+cules
ridi+cul+ing
ridi+culed
ri+dicu+lous

ri+dicu+lous+
  ness
rid+ing
  rid+ings
Ridley
Riefenstahl
Riemann
Rie+mann+ian
ries+ling
  ries+lings
rife
rife+ly
rife+ness
riff
  riffs
  riffs
  riff+ing
  riffed
rif+fle
  rif+fles
  rif+fles
  rif+fling
  rif+fled
riff+raff
ri+fle
  ri+fles
  ri+fles
  ri+fling
  ri+fled
rifle+bird
  rifle+birds
rifle+man
  rifle+men
ri+fler
  ri+flers
ri+fling
  ri+flings
rift
  rifts
  rifts
  rift+ing
  rift+ed
rig
  rigs
  rigs
  rig+ging
  rigged
Riga
riga+doon
riga+ma+role
  riga+ma+roles
rig+ger
  rig+gers
rig+ging
  rig+gings

right
  rights
  rights
  right+ing
  right+ed
right+able
right-angled
right+eous
right+eous+ly
right+eous+ness
right+er
  right+ers
right+ful
  right+ful+ly
right-hand
right-handed
right-handed+
  ness
right+ism
right+ist
  right+ists
right+ly
right-minded
right+ness
righto
right-thinking
right+ward
  right+wards
right-wing
adj.
right wing
noun
right-winger
  right-wingers
Rigi
rig+id
ri+gidi+fy
  ri+gidi+fies
  ri+gidi+fy+ing
  ri+gidi+fied
ri+gid+ity
rig+id+ly
rig+ma+role
  rig+ma+roles
ri+gor
  ri+gors
rig+or mor+tis
rig+or+ous
  rig+or+ous+ly
rig+our
  rig+ours
rig+out
  rig+outs
rig out
verb

Rig-Veda
Ri+je+ka
Rijks+mu+seum
Rijs+wijk
rile
  riles
ril+ing
riled
Riley
Rilke
rill
  rills
rim
  rims
  rims
rim+ming
rimmed
Rimbaud
rime
  rimes
  rimes
rim+ing
rimed
rim+er
  rim+ers
rime+ster
  rime+sters
rim-fire
Ri+mi+ni
ri+mose
Rimsky-Korsakov
rimu
  rimus
rimy
rimi+er
rimi+est
rind
  rinds
rinder+pest
ring
to encircle
  rings
  rings
ring+ing
ringed
ring
to toll
  rings
ring+ing
rang
rung
ring+bark
  ring+barks
  ring+bark+ing
  ring+barked

ring+bolt
  ring+bolts
ring+dove
  ring+doves
ringed
ring+er
  ring+ers
ring-fence
verb
  ring-fences
  ring-fencing
  ring-fenced
ring+hals
  ring+hals or
  ring+halses
ring-in
  ring-ins
ring in
verb
ring+ing
ring+leader
  ring+leaders
ring+let
  ring+lets
ring+let+ed
ring+master
  ring+masters
ring-necked
ring+side
  ring+sides
ring+tail
  ring+tails
ring+worm
  ring+worms
rink
  rinks
rinse
  rinses
  rinses
rins+ing
rinsed
rins+er
  rins+ers
Rio Bran+co
Río Bra+vo
Rio de Ja+nei+ro
Río de la Pla+ta
Río de Oro
Rio Grande
Rio Gran+de do
  Nor+te
Rio Gran+de do
  Sul
rioja
Río Muni

riot
  riots
  riots
  riot+ing
  riot+ed
ri+ot+er
  ri+ot+ers
ri+ot+ous
ri+ot+ous+ly
ri+ot+ous+ness
rip
  rips
  rips
  rip+ping
  ripped
ri+par+ian
  ri+par+ians
rip+cord
  rip+cords
ripe
  rip+er
  rip+est
ripe+ly
rip+en
  rip+ens
  rip+en+ing
  rip+ened
ripe+ness
ri+pieno
  ri+pieni *or*
  ri+pienos
rip-off
  rip-offs
rip off
verb
Rip+on
ri+poste
  ri+postes
  ri+postes
  ri+post+ing
  ri+post+ed
rip+per
  rip+pers
rip+ping+ly
rip+ple
  rip+ples
  rip+ples
  rip+pling
  rip+pled
rip+pler
  rip+plers
rip+ply
rip-roaring
rip+saw
  rip+saws

rip+snorter
  rip+snorters
  rip+snort+ing
rip+tide
  rip+tides
rise
  rises
  rises
  ris+ing
  rose
  ris+en
ris+er
  ris+ers
ris+ibil+ity
  ris+ibil+ities
ris+ible
  ris+ibly
ris+ing
  ris+ings
risk
  risks
  risks
  risk+ing
  risked
risk+er
  risk+ers
risk+ily
riski+ness
risky
  riski+er
  riski+est
ri+sot+to
  ri+sot+tos
ris+qué
ris+sole
  ris+soles
ri+sus sar+do+ni+
  cus
ri+tar+dan+do
rite
  rites
ri+tenu+to
ri+tor+nel+lo
  ri+tor+nel+los
    or
  ri+tor+nel+li
ritu+al
  ritu+als
ritu+al+ise
  ritu+al+ises
  ritu+al+is+ing
  ritu+al+ised
ritu+al+ism
ritu+al+ist
  ritu+al+ists

ritu+al+is+tic
ritu+al+is+ti+cal+
  ly
ritu+al+ize
  ritu+al+izes
  ritu+al+iz+ing
  ritu+al+ized
ritu+al+ly
ritzi+ly
ritzi+ness
ritzy
  ritzi+er
  ritzi+est
ri+val
  ri+vals
  ri+vals
  ri+val+ling *or*
  ri+val+ing
  U.S.
  ri+valled *or*
  ri+valed
  U.S.
ri+val+ry
  ri+val+ries
rive
  rives
  riv+ing
  rived
  rived *or*
  riv+en
riv+er
  riv+ers
Rivera
riv+er+ine
riv+er+less
Riv+ers
River+side
riv+et
  riv+ets
  riv+ets
  riv+et+ing
  riv+et+ed
riv+et+er
  riv+et+ers
  riv+et+ing
Rivi+era
ri+vi+ère
  ri+vi+ères
rivu+let
  rivu+lets
Ri+yadh
ri+yal
  ri+yals
Rizal
Rizzio

roach
  roaches
roach
fish
  roaches *or*
roach
road
  roads
road+block
  road+blocks
road-fund
road+holding
road+house
  road+houses
road+ie
  road+ies
road+less
road+roller
  road+rollers
road+stead
  road+steads
road+ster
  road+sters
road-test
  road-tests
  road-testing
  road-tested
road test
noun
road+way
  road+ways
road+work
road+worthi+
  ness
road+worthy
roam
  roams
  roams
  roam+ing
  roamed
roam+er
  roam+ers
roan
  roans
roar
  roars
  roars
  roar+ing
  roared
roar+er
  roar+ers
roar+ing+ly
roast
  roasts
  roasts

roast+ing
roast+ed
roast+er
roast+ers
roast+ing
roast+ings
rob
robs
rob+bing
robbed
Robbe-Grillet
Rob+ben
rob+ber
rob+bers
rob+bery
rob+beries
Robbia
Robbins
robe
robes
robes
rob+ing
robed
Roberts
Robeson
Robespierre
Robey
rob+in
rob+ins
ro+binia
ro+binias
Robinson
Robinson Crusoe
ro+bor+ant
ro+bor+ants
ro+bot
ro+bots
ro+bot+ic
ro+bot+ics
robot-like
Rob Roy
Rob+son
mountain
Robson
surname
ro+bust
ro+bus+tious
ro+bus+tious+ly
ro+bus+tious+
 ness
ro+bust+ly
ro+bust+ness
roc
rocs
Roca

ro+caille
roc+am+bole
Rocard
Roch+dale
Ro+chelle
roche mou+ton+
 née
roches mou+ton+
 nées
Roch+es+ter
place name
Rochester
surname
roch+et
roch+ets
rock
rocks
rocks
rock+ing
rocked
Rock
rocka+bil+ly
Rock+all
rock-bound
Rockefeller
rock+er
rock+ers
rock+ery
rock+eries
rock+et
rock+ets
rock+ets
rock+et+ing
rock+et+ed
rock+et+ry
rock+fish
rock+fish *or*
rock+fishes
Rock+ford
Rock+hamp+ton
Rockies
rocki+ly
rocki+ness
rock+ing
Rockingham
rock+ling
rock+lings *or*
rock+ling
rock'n'roll
rock'n'roller
rock'n'rollers
rock+rose
rock+roses
Rockwell
rocky

rocki+er
rocki+est
ro+co+co
rod
rods
Rodchenko
rode
ro+dent
ro+dents
rodent-like
ro+deo
ro+deos
Rodgers
Rodin
rod+like
Rodney
rodo+mon+tade
rodo+mon+
 tades
rodo+mon+tad+
 ing
rodo+mon+tad+
 ed
Rodrigo
roe
of fish
roes
roe
deer
roes *or*
roe
roe+buck
roe+bucks *or*
roe+buck
Roeg
roent+gen
roent+gens
Roentgen
Roe+se+la+re
Roethke
ro+ga+tion
ro+ga+tions
rog+er
Rogers
Roget
rogue
rogues
rogues
rogu+ing
rogued
ro+guery
ro+gueries
ro+guish
ro+guish+ly
roil

roils
roil+ing
roiled
rois+ter
rois+ters
rois+ter+ing
rois+tered
roist+er+er
roist+er+ers
roist+er+ous
roist+er+ous+ly
Roland
role
roles
rôle
rôles
role-playing
Rolf
Rolfe
roll
rolls
rolls
roll+ing
rolled
Rolland
roll+bar
roll+bars
roll+er
roll+ers
roll+er+ball
roll+er+balls
rol+ler der+by
rol+ler der+bies
roller-skate
verb
roller-skates
roller-skating
roller-skated
roll+er skate
roll+er skates
rol+lick
rol+licks
rol+licks
rol+lick+ing
rol+licked
rol+lick+ing
rol+lick+ings
roll+ing
Rollins
roll+mop
roll+mops
roll+neck
roll+necks
Rollo
roll-on

noun, adj.
roll-ons
roll on
verb
roll-on/roll-off
roll-out
 roll-outs
roll out
verb
roll-over
 roll-overs
roll over
verb
roll-up
 roll-ups
roll up
verb
roly-poly
 roly-polies
ROM
Roma
Ro+ma+gna
Ro+ma+ic
Romains
ro+man
 ro+mans
Ro+man
 Ro+mans
ro+man à clef
 ro+mans à clef
ro+mance
 ro+mances
 ro+mances
 ro+manc+ing
 ro+manced
Ro+mance
ro+man+cer
 ro+man+cers
Ro+man+esque
Roma+ni
 Roma+nis
Ro+ma+nia
Ro+ma+nian
 Ro+ma+nians
Ro+man+ic
Ro+mani+sa+tion
 Ro+mani+sa+
 tions
Ro+man+ise
 Ro+man+ises
 Ro+man+is+ing
 Ro+man+ised
Ro+man+ism
 Ro+man+ist
 Ro+man+ists

Ro+mani+za+tion
Ro+mani+za+
 tions
Ro+man+ize
Ro+man+izes
Ro+man+iz+ing
Ro+man+ized
Ro+ma+no
cheese
Romano
surname
Romanov
Ro+mansch
Ro+mansh
ro+man+tic
ro+man+tics
ro+man+ti+cal+ly
ro+man+ti+ci+sa+
 tion
ro+man+ti+ci+
 sa+tions
ro+man+ti+cise
ro+man+ti+
 cises
ro+man+ti+cis+
 ing
ro+man+ti+
 cised
ro+man+ti+cism
ro+man+ti+cist
ro+man+ti+cists
ro+man+ti+ci+za+
 tion
ro+man+ti+ci+
 za+tions
ro+man+ti+cize
ro+man+ti+cizes
ro+man+ti+ciz+
 ing
ro+man+ti+
 cized
Roma+ny
Roma+nies
ro+man+za
ro+man+zas
ro+maunt
 ro+maunts
Romberg
Rome
Romeo
 Romeos
Ro+mish
Rommel
Romney
surname

Rom+ney
marsh
romp
romps
romps
romp+ing
romped
Romulus
Ron+ces+valles
ron+da+vel
 ron+da+vels
ron+deau
ron+deaux
ron+del
ron+dels
ron+do
ron+dos
Ron+dô+nia
rone
 rones
rone+pipe
 rone+pipes
Ronsard
rönt+gen
rönt+gens
Röntgen
roo
 roos
rood
 roods
Roo+depoort-
 Marais+burg
roof
roofs
roofs
roof+ing
roofed
roof+er
roof+ers
roof+less
roof+tree
roof+trees
rooi+bos
rooi+kat
 rooi+kats
rook
rooks
rooks
rook+ing
rooked
rook+ery
rook+eries
rookie
rookies
room

rooms
rooms
room+ing
roomed
room+er
room+ers
room+ful
room+fuls
roomi+ly
roomi+ness
room+ing
room+mate
room+mates
roomy
roomi+er
roomi+est
Roosevelt
roost
roosts
roosts
roost+ing
roost+ed
Roost
roost+er
roost+ers
root
roots
roots
root+ing
root+ed
root-canal
root+er
root+ers
rooti+ness
root+ing
root+le
root+les
root+ling
root+led
root+less
root+let
root+lets
root+like
root+stock
root+stocks
rooty
rop+able
rope
ropes
ropes
rop+ing
roped
rope+able
rope+walk
rope+walks

ropey
 ropi+er
 ropi+est
ropi+ly
ropi+ness
ropy
 ropi+er
 ropi+est
Roque+fort
ro+quet
 ro+quets
 ro+quets
 ro+quet+ing
 ro+queted
Ro+rai+ma
ro-ro
ror+qual
 ror+quals
rort
 rorts
rorty
Rosa
ros+ace
 ros+aces
ro+sa+ceous
ro+sar+ian
 ro+sar+ians
Ro+sa+rio
ro+sar+ium
 ro+sar+iums or
 ro+saria
ro+sary
 ro+saries
Ros+cian
Roscius
Ros+com+mon
rose
 roses
rosé
 rosés
ro+seate
rose+bay
 rose+bays
Rosebery
rose+bud
 rose+buds
rose-coloured
rose-cut
rose+hip
 rose+hips
rose+like
ro+sel+la
 ro+sel+las
rose+mary
 rose+maries

Rosenberg
ro+seo+la
 ro+seo+las
ro+seo+lar
ro+sery
 ro+series
Ro+set+ta
 ro+sette
 ro+settes
rose-water
rose+wood
 rose+woods
Rosh Ha+sha+na
Rosh Ha+sha+
 nah
Ro+si+cru+cian
 Ro+si+cru+cians
rosi+ly
ros+in
 ros+ins
 ros+in+ing
 ros+ined
rosi+ness
ros+iny
Ros+kil+de
ROSPA
Ross
Rossellini
Rossetti
Rossini
Ros+si+ya
Rostand
ros+ter
 ros+ters
 ros+ters
 ros+ter+ing
 ros+tered
Ros+tock
Ros+tov
Rostov-on-Don
ros+tral
Rostropovich
ros+trum
 ros+trums or
 ros+tra
rosy
rosi+er
rosi+est
rot
 rots
rot+ting
rot+ted
rota
 rotas
Rota

rota+chute
 rota+chutes
rota+plane
 rota+planes
Ro+tar+ian
 Ro+tar+ians
ro+ta+ry
 ro+ta+ries
ro+tat+able
ro+tate
 ro+tates
ro+tat+ing
ro+tat+ed
ro+ta+tion
 ro+ta+tions
 ro+ta+tion+al
ro+ta+tive
ro+ta+tor
 ro+ta+tors
ro+ta+tory
rote
 rotes
ro+tenone
rot+gut
 rot+guts
Roth
Roth+er+ham
Rothermere
Rothe+say
Rothko
Rothschild
ro+ti+fer
 ro+ti+fers
ro+tif+er+al
ro+tif+er+ous
ro+tis+serie
 ro+tis+series
ro+to+gra+vure
ro+tor
 ro+tors
Ro+to+rua
Ro+to+va+tor
Trademark
 Ro+to+va+tors
rot+ten
rot+ten+ly
rot+ten+ness
rotten+stone
rot+ter
 rot+ters
Rott+ter+dam
Rott+wei+ler
 Rott+wei+lers
ro+tund
ro+tun+da

ro+tun+das
ro+tun+dity
ro+tund+ly
Rouault
Rou+baix
Roubiliac
Roubillac
rou+ble
 rou+bles
roué
 roués
Rou+en
rouge
 rouges
 rouges
roug+ing
rouged
rouge et noir
Rouget de Lisle
rough
 roughs
 roughs
rough+ing
roughed
rough+er
rough+est
rough+age
rough-and-ready
rough-and-tumble
rough-and-
 tumbles
rough+cast
 rough+casts
 rough+casts
rough+cast+ing
rough+cast
rough+cast+er
 rough+cast+ers
rough-cut
rough-cuts
rough-dry
rough-dries
rough-drying
rough-dried
rough+en
rough+ens
rough+en+ing
rough+ened
rough-hew
rough-hews
rough-hewing
rough-hewed
rough-hewed
 or
rough-hewn

rough +house
rough +ish
rough +ly
rough +neck
  rough +necks
rough +ness
rough +rider
  rough +riders
rough +shod
rou +lade
  rou +lades
Rou +lers
rou +lette
  rou +lettes
  rou +lettes
  rou +lett +ing
  rou +lett +ed
Rou +ma +nia
Rou +ma +nian
  Rou +ma +nians
Rou +me +lia
round
  rounds
  rounds
  round +ing
  round +ed
  round +er
  round +est
round +about
  round +abouts
roun +del
  roun +dels
roun +de +lay
  roun +de +lays
round +er
  round +ers
Round +head
  Round +heads
round +house
  round +houses
round +ish
round +ly
round +ness
round-shouldered
rounds +man
  rounds +men
round the clock
adv.
round-the-clock
adj.
round-trip
round +trip +ping
round +up
  round +ups
round up

verb
round +worm
  round +worms
roup
  roups
  roups
  roup +ing
  rouped
rouse
  rouses
  rous +ing
  roused
rouse +about
  rouse +abouts
rous +er
  rous +ers
rous +ing +ly
Rousseau
Rous +sil +lon
roust
  rousts
  roust +ing
  roust +ed
roust +about
  roust +abouts
rout
  routs
  routs
  rout +ing
  rout +ed
route
  routes
  routes
  route +ing
  rout +ed
route +march
  route +marches
rout +er
  rout +ers
rou +tine
  rou +tines
  rou +tine +ly
roux
rove
  roves
  roves
  rov +ing
  roved
rov +er
  rov +ers
Rov +er
  Rov +ers
rov +ing
row
  rows

rows
row +ing
rowed
ro +wan
  ro +wans
row +di +ly
row +di +ness
row +dy
  row +dies
  row +di +er
  row +di +est
  row +dy +ism
Rowe
row +el
  row +els
row +er
  row +ers
row +ing
Rowlandson
Rowley
row +lock
  row +locks
Rox +burgh +shire
roy +al
  royals
roy +al +ist
  roy +al +ists
roy +al +ly
roy +al +ty
  roy +al +ties
Royce
roz +zer
  roz +zers
Ruanda-Urundi
rub
  rubs
  rubs
  rub +bing
  rubbed
Rub al Kha +li
ru +ba +to
  ru +ba +tos
rub +ber
  rub +bers
rub +ber +ise
  rub +ber +ises
  rub +ber +is +ing
  rub +ber +ised
rub +ber +ize
  rub +ber +izes
  rub +ber +iz +ing
  rub +ber +ized
rubber +neck
  rubber +necks
  rubber +necks

  rubber +necking
  rubber +necked
rubber-stamp
verb
  rubber-stamps
  rubber-stamping
  rubber-stamped
  rub +ber stamp
  rub +ber stamps
rub +bery
rub +bing
  rub +bings
rub +bish
  rub +bishes
  rub +bish +ing
  rub +bished
rub +bishy
rub +ble
rub +bly
Rubbra
rub +down
  rub +downs
rub down
verb
rube
  rubes
ru +bel +la
ru +bel +lite
Rubens
ru +beo +la
Ru +bi +con
ru +bi +cund
ru +bi +cun +dity
ru +bid +ic
ru +bid +ium
ru +bigi +nous
Rubinstein
ru +ble
  ru +bles
ru +bric
  ru +brics
ru +bri +cal
ru +bri +cal +ly
ruby
  rubies
ruche
  ruches
ruch +ing
  ruch +ings
ruck
  rucks
  rucks
ruck +ing
rucked
ruck +sack

ruck+sacks
ruc+tion
  ruc+tions
ru+da+ceous
Ruda Slas+ka
rud+beckia
  rud+beckias
rudd
  rudds
Rudd
rud+der
  rud+ders
rud+der+less
rudder+post
  rudder+posts
rud+di+ly
rud+di+ness
rud+dle
  rud+dles
  rud+dling
  rud+dled
rud+dy
  rud+di+er
  rud+di+est
rude
  rud+er
  rud+est
rude+ly
rude+ness
ru+deral
  ru+derals
ru+di+ment
  ru+di+ments
ru+di+men+tal
ru+di+men+ta+ri+ly
ru+di+men+ta+ry
rud+ish
Rudolf
rue
  rues
  ru+ing
  rued
rue+ful
rue+ful+ly
rue+ful+ness
ruer
  ruers
ruff
  ruffs
ruffe
  ruffes
ruf+fian
  ruf+fians
ruf+fi+an+ism

ruf+fi+an+ly
ruf+fle
  ruf+fles
  ruf+fles
  ruf+fling
  ruf+fled
ruff+like
ru+fi+yaa
  ru+fi+yaas
ru+fous
rug
  rugs
ruga
  rugae
Rug+beian
  Rug+beians
rug+by
Rug+by
rug+ged
rug+ged+ly
rug+ged+ness
rug+ger
ru+gose
ru+gose+ly
ru+gos+ity
Ruhr
ruin
  ruins
  ruins
  ruin+ing
  ruined
ru+ina+tion
  ru+ina+tions
ru+in+ous
ru+in+ous+ly
ru+in+ous+ness
Ruisdael
rul+able
rule
  rules
  rules
  rul+ing
  ruled
rul+er
  rul+ers
Rules
rul+ing
  rul+ings
rum
rum
  rum+mer
  rum+mest
Ru+ma+nia
Ru+ma+nian
  Ru+ma+nians

rum+ba
rum+ble
  rum+bles
  rum+bles
  rum+bling
  rum+bled
rum+bler
  rum+blers
rum+bus+tious
rum+bus+tious+ly
rum+bus+tious+ness
Ru+melia
ru+men
  ru+mens *or*
  ru+mi+na
ru+mi+nant
  ru+mi+nants
ru+mi+nate
  ru+mi+nates
  ru+mi+nat+ing
  ru+mi+nat+ed
ru+mi+na+tion
  ru+mi+na+tions
ru+mi+na+tive
ru+mi+na+tive+ly
ru+mi+na+tor
  ru+mi+na+tors
rum+ly
rum+mage
  rum+mages
  rum+mages
  rum+mag+ing
  rum+maged
rum+mag+er
  rum+mag+ers
rum+mer
  rum+mers
rum+my
  rum+mies
rum+ness
ru+mor
U.S.
  ru+mors
  ru+mors
  ru+mor+ing
  ru+mored
ru+mour
  ru+mours
  ru+mours
  ru+mour+ing
  ru+moured
rump
  rumps

Rumpelstiltskin
rum+ple
  rum+ples
  rum+ples
  rum+pling
  rum+pled
rump+less
rum+ply
rum+pus
  rum+puses
run
  runs
  runs
  run+ning
  ran
  run
run+about
  run+abouts
run about
  verb
run-around
  noun
run around
  verb
run+away
  run+aways
run away
  verb
Run+corn
run+down
  run+downs
run-down
  adj.
run down
  verb
Rundstedt
rune
  runes
rung
  rungs
rung+less
ru+nic
run-in
  run-ins
run in
  verb
run+nel
  run+nels
run+ner
  run+ners
runner-up
  runners-up
run+ny
  run+ni+er
  run+ni+est

Run +ny +mede
run +off
  run +offs
run off
verb
run-of-the-mill
run-on
  run-ons
run on
verb
run-out
  run-outs
run out
verb
runt
  runts
run-through
  run-throughs
run through
verb
runti +ness
runt +ish
runty
run-up
  run-ups
run up
verb
run +way
  run +ways
Runyon
ru +pee
  ru +pees
Rupert
Ru +pert's Land
ru +pi +ah
  ru +pi +ah *or*
ru +pi +ahs
rup +tur +able
rup +ture
  rup +tures
rup +tures
rup +tur +ing
rup +tured
ru +ral
ru +rali +sa +tion
  ru +rali +sa +tions
ru +ral +ise

ru +ral +ises
ru +ral +is +ing
ru +ral +ised
ru +ral +ism
ru +ral +ist
  ru +ral +ists
ru +ral +ity
ru +rali +za +tion
  ru +rali +za +tions
ru +ral +ize
ru +ral +izes
ru +ral +iz +ing
ru +ral +ized
ru +ral +ly
Rurik
Ru +ri +ta +nia
Ru +ri +ta +nian
  Ru +ri +ta +nians
ruse
  ruses
Ruse
rush
  rushes
rushes
rush +ing
rushed
Rushdie
rush +er
  rush +ers
rush +like
Rush +more
rushy
rushi +er
rushi +est
rusk
  rusks
Rusk
Ruskin
Russ
Russell
rus +set
  rus +sets
rus +sety
Rus +sia
Rus +sian
  Rus +sians
Rus +siani +sa +
  tion

Rus +sian +ise
  Rus +sian +ises
Rus +sian +is +ing
Rus +sian +ised
Rus +siani +za +
  tion
Rus +sian +ize
  Rus +sian +izes
Rus +sian +iz +ing
Rus +sian +ized
rust
  rusts
rusts
rust +ing
rust +ed
rus +tic
  rus +tics
rus +ti +cal +ly
rus +ti +cate
  rus +ti +cates
rus +ti +cat +ing
rus +ti +cat +ed
rus +ti +cat +ing
rus +ti +ca +tion
  rus +ti +ca +tions
rus +ti +ca +tor
  rus +ti +ca +tors
rus +tic +ity
rusti +ly
rusti +ness
rus +tle
  rus +tles
rus +tles
rus +tling
rus +tled
rus +tler
  rus +tlers
rust +less
rust +proof
rusty
rusti +er
rusti +est
rut
  ruts
ruts
rut +ting

rut +ted
ru +ta +ba +ga
ru +ta +ba +gas
ru +ta +ceous
ruth
Ruth
Ru +the +nia
ru +the +nium
ruth +er +ford
  ruth +er +fords
Rutherford
ruth +er +for +dium
ruth +ful
ruth +ful +ly
ruth +ful +ness
ruth +less
ruth +less +ly
ruth +less +ness
ru +tile
Rut +land
rut +ti +ly
rut +ti +ness
rut +tish
rut +tish +ly
rut +tish +ness
rut +ty
  rut +ti +er
  rut +ti +est
Ru +wen +zo +ri
Ruyter
Rwan +da
Rya +zan
Ry +binsk
Ry +dal
Ryder
surname
Ry +der
golf cup
rye
  ryes
Rye
rye-grass
  rye-grasses
Ryle
Rys +wick
Ryu +kyu
Ryurik

S

s
s's
S
S's *or*
Ss
Saadi
Saar
Saar+brück+en
Saarinen
Saar+land
Saba
Sa+ba+dell
saba+dil+la
Sa+baean
 Sa+baeans
Sa+bah
Sabatier
Sabatini
sab+bat
 sab+bats
Sab+ba+tar+ian
 Sab+ba+tar+
  ians
Sab+ba+tari+an+
 ism
Sab+bath
 Sab+baths
sab+bati+cal
 sab+bati+cals
Sab+bati+cal
Sa+bean
 Sa+beans
sa+ber
U.S.
 sa+bers
 sa+bers
 sa+ber+ing
 sa+bered
sa+bin
 sa+bins
Sabin
Sab+ine
 Sab+ines
sab+kha
 sab+khas

sa+ble
sa+bles *or*
sa+ble
Sa+ble
sab+ot
 sab+ots
sabo+tage
 sabo+tages
sabo+tag+ing
 sabo+taged
sabo+teur
 sabo+teurs
sa+bra
 sa+bras
sa+bre
 sa+bres
 sa+bres
sa+bring
 sa+bred
sabre-rattling
sabre-toothed
sac
 sacs
sac+cate
sac+cha+ride
 sac+cha+rides
sac+cha+rim+
 eter
 sac+cha+rim+
  eters
sac+cha+rim+
 etry
 sac+cha+rim+
  etries
sac+cha+rin
 sac+cha+rins
sac+cha+rine
sac+cha+rose
sac+cule
 sac+cules
sac+cu+lus
 sac+cu+li
sac+er+do+tal
sac+er+do+tal+
 ism

sac+er+do+tal+ly
sa+chem
 sa+chems
sa+chet
 sa+chets
Sachs
Sach+sen
sack
 sacks
 sacks
sack+ing
 sacked
sack+but
 sack+buts
sack+cloth
sack+er
 sack+ers
sack+ing
sack+like
Sackville
Sackville-West
sac+like
sa+cral
sac+ra+ment
 sac+ra+ments
sac+ra+men+tal
 sac+ra+men+
  tals
sac+ra+men+tal+
 ism
sac+ra+men+tal+
 ity
Sac+ra+men+to
sa+crar+ium
sa+craria
sa+cred
sa+cred+ly
sa+cred+ness
sac+ri+fice
 sac+ri+fices
 sac+ri+fices
sac+ri+fic+ing
 sac+ri+ficed
sac+ri+fic+er
 sac+ri+fic+ers

sac+ri+fi+cial
sac+ri+fi+cial+ly
sac+ri+lege
sac+ri+legious
sac+ri+legious+ly
sac+ri+legist
 sac+ri+legists
sa+cring
sac+rist
 sac+rists
sac+ris+tan
 sac+ris+tans
sac+ris+ty
 sac+ris+ties
sa+cro+ili+ac
sac+ro+sanct
sac+ro+sanc+tity
sa+crum
sa+cra
sad
sad+der
sad+dest
Sadat
sad+den
sad+dens
sad+den+ing
sad+dened
sad+dhu
sad+dhus
sad+dle
sad+dles
sad+dles
sad+dling
sad+dled
saddle+back
saddle+backs
saddle-backed
saddle+bag
saddle+bags
saddle+bill
saddle+bills
saddle+bow
saddle+bows
saddle+cloth
saddle+cloths

saddle-like	Safi	sailed	saint+pau+lia
sad+dler	Sa+fid Rud	sail+able	saint+pau+lias
sad+dlers	saf+ra+nin	sail+board	Saint Pe+ters+
sad+dlery	saf+ra+nins	sail+boards	burg
sad+dleries	saf+ra+nine	sail+boarding	Saint-Pierre
saddle+tree	saf+ra+nines	sail+cloth	Saint-Quentin
saddle+trees	sag	sail+er	Saint-Saëns
Sad+du+cean	sags	sail+ers	Saint-Simon
Sad+du+cee	sags	sail+fish	Saint Vitus
Sad+du+cees	sag+ging	sail+fish or	Sai+pan
Sade	sagged	sail+fishes	Saïs
sa+dhu	saga	sail+ing	Sa+ite
sa+dhus	sagas	sail+less	saith
Sadi	sa+ga+cious	sail+or	saithe
sad+iron	sa+ga+cious+ly	sail+ors	saithes
sad+irons	sa+gac+ity	sail+plane	Sa+it+ic
sad+ism	saga+more	sail+planes	Sa+kai
sad+ist	saga+mores	sain+foin	sake
sad+ists	Sagan	saint	*benefit*
sa+dis+tic	sage	saints	sakes
sa+dis+ti+cal+ly	sages	saints	sake
sad+ly	sage+brush	saint+ing	*Japanese drink*
sad+ness	sage+ly	saint+ed	saké
sado+maso+	sage+ness	Saint-Brieuc	sa+ker
chism	sag+gar	Saint-Cloud	sa+kers
sado+maso+chis+	sag+gars	Saint-Denis	Sa+kha+lin
tic	sag+ger	Sainte-Beuve	Sakharov
Sa+do+wa	sag+gers	saint+ed	saki
sa+fa+ri	Sa+ghal+ien	Sainte Foy	sakis
sa+fa+ris	sag+it+tal	Saint Elmo	Saki
safe	Sag+it+tar+ian	Saint-Étienne	sal
safes	Sag+it+ta+rius	Saint-Exupéry	sals
saf+er	sag+it+tate	Saint Hel+ier	sa+laam
saf+est	sago	saint+hood	sa+laams
safe-breaker	sagos	Saint-John	sa+laams
safe-breakers	sa+gua+ro	Saint-Just	sa+laam+ing
safe-conduct	sa+gua+ros	Saint Kil+da	sa+laamed
safe-conducts	Sag+uenay	Saint Kitts-Nevis	sal+abil+ity
safe-deposit	Sa+gun+to	Saint-Laurent	*U.S.*
safe-deposits	Sa+ha+ra	Saint Leg+er	sal+able
safe+guard	Sa+har+an	saint+like	*U.S.*
safe+guards	sa+hib	saint+li+ly	sa+la+cious
safe+guards	sa+hibs	saint+li+ness	sa+la+cious+ly
safe+guard+ing	said	Saint-Lô	sa+la+cious+
safe+guard+ed	*adj., verb*	Saint-Louis	ness
safe+keeping	said	Saint Lu+cia	sa+lac+ity
safe+ly	*Muslim name*	saint+ly	sal+ad
safe+ness	saids	saint+li+er	sal+ads
safe+ty	Sai+da	saint+li+est	sa+lade
safe+ties	sai+ga	Saint-Maur-des-	Saladin
safety-deposit	Sai+gon	Fossés	Sa+la+do
safety-deposits	sail	Saint-Mihiel	Sala+man+ca
saf+fian	sails	Saint Mo+ritz	sala+man+der
saf+flow+er	sails	Saint-Nazaire	sala+man+ders
saf+fron	sail+ing	Saint-Ouen	Sa+lam+bria

sa+la+mi
  sa+la+mis
Sala+mis
sala+ried
sala+ry
  sala+ries
  sala+ries
  sala+ry+ing
  sala+ried
Salazar
sal+chow
  sal+chows
Sal+du+ba
sale
  sales
Sale
English town
Salé
French town
sale+abil+ity
sale+able
Sa+lem
Sa+ler+no
sale+room
  sale+rooms
sales+clerk
  sales+clerks
sales+man
  sales+men
  sales+man+ship
  sales+person
Sal+ford
Sa+lian
  Sa+lians
Sal+ic
sa+li+cin
sa+licy+late
  sa+licy+lates
sa+li+ence
sa+li+en+cy
sa+li+ent
  sa+li+ents
sa+li+en+tian
  sa+li+en+tians
sa+li+ent+ly
Salieri
sa+lina
  sa+linas
sa+line
Salinger
sa+lin+ity
sali+nom+eter
  sali+nom+eters
Salis+bury
sa+li+va

sali+vary
sali+vate
  sali+vates
  sali+vat+ing
  sali+vat+ed
sali+va+tion
Salk
sal+lee
  sal+lees
sal+low
  sal+lows
  sal+low+er
  sal+low+est
  sal+low+ish
  sal+low+ness
  sal+lowy
Sallust
sal+ly
sal+lies
sal+lies
sal+ly+ing
sal+lied
sal+ma+gun+di
  sal+ma+gun+dis
salm+on
  salm+ons *or*
  salm+on
sal+mo+nel+la
  sal+mo+nel+lae
sal+mo+noid
Salome
sa+lon
  sa+lons
Sa+lo+ni+ca
Sa+lo+ni+ka
sa+loon
  sa+loons
Sal+op
salo+pettes
Sal+opi+an
  Sal+opi+ans
sal+pi+glos+sis
sal+pin+gec+to+
  my
sal+pin+gec+to+
  mies
sal+pin+gi+tis
sal+pinx
sal+pin+ges
sal+sa
sal+sas
sal+si+fy
sal+si+fies
salt
salts

salts
salt+ing
salt+ed
SALT
Sal+ta
sal+ta+tion
  sal+ta+tions
sal+ta+to+rial
sal+ta+tory
salt+bush
  salt+bushes
salt+cellar
  salt+cellars
salt+ed
salt+tier
  salt+tiers
sal+ti+grade
Sal+til+lo
salti+ness
sal+tire
  salt+tires
salt+like
salt+ness
Sal+to
salt+pan
  salt+pans
salt+pe+ter
U.S.
salt+pe+tre
salts
sal+tus
  sal+tuses
salt+water
salt+works
salt+wort
  salt+worts
salty
salti+er
salti+est
sa+lu+bri+ous
sa+lu+bri+ous+ly
sa+lu+bri+ty
Sa+lu+ki
  Sa+lu+kis
salu+tari+ly
salu+tary
salu+ta+tion
  salu+ta+tions
sa+lu+ta+to+ri+ly
sa+lu+ta+tory
sa+lute
  sa+lutes
  sa+lutes
  sa+lut+ing
  sa+lut+ed

sa+lut+er
  sa+lut+ers
salv+able
Sal+va+dor
Sal+va+do+rian
  Sal+va+do+
  rians
sal+vage
  sal+vages
  sal+vages
  sal+vag+ing
  sal+vaged
sal+vage+able
sal+vag+er
  sal+vag+ers
sal+va+tion
  sal+va+tions
sal+va+tion+ist
  sal+va+tion+ists
salve
  salves
  salves
  salv+ing
  salved
sal+ver
  sal+vers
sal+via
  sal+vias
sal+vo
  sal+vos *or*
  sal+voes
Sal+vo
  Sal+vos
Sal+ween
Salz+burg
Salz+git+ter
Sam
SAM
Sa+mar
sa+ma+ra
  sa+ma+ras
Sa+ma+ra
Sa+ma+rang
Sa+maria
Sa+mari+tan
  Sa+mari+tans
sa+mar+ium
  sa+mar+iums
Sa+mar+kand
sam+ba
  sam+bas
sam+bas
  sam+ba+ing
  sam+baed
sam+bar

sam+bars *or*
sam+bar
Sam+bre
sam+bur
sam+burs *or*
sam+bur
same
same+ness
sam+foo
Sa+mian
Sa+mians
Sa+mian ware
Sa+mian wares
sami+sen
sami+sens
sam+ite
sa+miz+dat
Sam+mari+nese
Sam+ni+um
Sa+moa
Sa+mo+an
Sa+mo+ans
Sa+mos
sa+mo+sa
sa+mo+sas *or*
sa+mo+sa
Samo+thrace
samo+var
samo+vars
Samo+yed
Samo+yed *or*
Samo+yeds
samp
sam+pan
sam+pans
sam+phire
sam+ple
sam+ples
sam+ples
sam+pling
sam+pled
sam+pler
sam+plers
sam+pling
sam+plings
Samson
Sam+sun
Samuel
samu+rai
samu+rai
San
Sana
Sa+naa
San An+to+nian
San An+to+nio

sana+tive
sana+to+rium
sana+to+riums
or
sana+to+ria
San Ber+nar+di+
no
San Blas
San Cris+tó+bal
sanc+ti+fi+ca+
tion
sanc+ti+fied
sanc+ti+fi+er
sanc+ti+fi+ers
sanc+ti+fy
sanc+ti+fies
sanc+ti+fy+ing
sanc+ti+fied
sanc+ti+mo+ni+
ous
sanc+ti+mo+ni+
ous+ly
sanc+ti+mo+ni+
ous+ness
sanc+ti+mo+ny
sanc+tion
sanc+tions
sanc+tions
sanc+tion+ing
sanc+tioned
sanc+ti+tude
sanc+tity
sanc+tities
sanc+to+rum
sanc+tu+ary
sanc+tu+aries
sanc+tum
sanc+tums *or*
sanc+ta
Sanc+tus
sand
sands
sands
sand+ing
sand+ed
Sand
Sandage
San+da+kan
san+dal
san+dals
san+dalled
sandal+wood
san+da+rac
san+da+racs
san+da+rach

san+da+rachs
sand+bag
sand+bags
sand+bags
sand+bag+ging
sand+bagged
sand+bag+ger
sand+bag+gers
sand+bank
sand+banks
sand+blast
sand+blasts
sand+blasts
sand+blast+ing
sand+blast+ed
sand+blast+er
sand+blast+ers
sand-blind
sand-blindness
sand+box
sand+boxes
sand+boy
sand+boys
Sandburg
sand+er
sand+ers
sand+er+ling
sand+er+lings
Sanderson
sand+fly
sand+flies
sand+grouse
Sand+hurst
San Di+ego
sandi+ness
sand+like
sand+man
sand+men
sand+paper
sand+papers
sand+papers
sand+paper+ing
sand+papered
sand+piper
sand+pipers
sand+pit
sand+pits
San+dring+ham
Sandrocottus
sand+shoe
sand+shoes
sand+stone
sand+stones
sand+storm
sand+storms

sand+wich
sand+wiches
sand+wiches
sand+wich+ing
sand+wiched
sand+wort
sand+worts
sandy
sandi+er
sandi+est
sane
san+er
san+est
sane+ly
sane+ness
San Fer+nan+do
San+for+ise
Trademark
San+for+ises
San+for+is+ing
San+for+ised
San+for+ize
Trademark
San+for+izes
San+for+iz+ing
San+for+ized
San Fran+cis+can
San Fran+cis+
cans
San Fran+cis+co
sang
Sanger
sang-froid
san+go+ma
san+go+mas
San+graal
San+grail
San+greal
san+gria
san+grias
san+gui+nari+ly
san+gui+nari+
ness
san+gui+nary
san+guine
san+guines
san+guine+ly
san+guine+ness
san+guin+eous
san+guin+eous+
ness
San+hed+rin
sa+ni+es
San Il+de+fon+so
sani+tar+ian

sani+tar+ians
sani+tari+ness
sani+ta+rium
sani+ta+riums
or
sani+ta+ria
sani+tary
sani+ta+tion
sani+ti+sa+tion
sani+tise
sani+tises
sani+tis+ing
sani+tised
sani+ti+za+tion
sani+tize
sani+tizes
sani+tiz+ing
sani+tized
san+ity
San Jose
San Juan
sank
Sankey
Sankt Pöl+ten
San Luis Po+to+sí
San Mari+nese
San Ma+ri+no
San Martín
Sanmicheli
San Pe+dro Sula
San Remo
sans
San Sal+va+dor
sans-culotte
sans-culottes
San Se+bas+tián
san+ser+if
san+se+vieria
san+se+vierias
San+skrit
San+skrit+ic
San Ste+fa+no
San+ta
San+tas
San+ta Ana
Santa Ana
Santa Anna
San+ta Cata+li+na
San+ta Ca+ta+ri+na
San+ta Cla+ra
Santa Claus
San+ta Cruz
San+ta Fe

San+ta Ger+tru+dis
San+ta Isa+bel
San+ta Ma+ria
San+ta Mar+ta
San+ta Mau+ra
San+tan+der
San+ta+rém
San+ta Rosa de Co+pán
Santayana
San+tee
San+tia+go
San+tia+go de Com+po+ste+la
San+tia+go de Cuba
San+tia+go del Es+te+ro
San+to Do+min+go
san+toni+ca
san+to+nin
San+tos
São Fran+cis+co
São Mi+guel
Saône
Saône-et-Loire
São Pau+lo
Saor+stat Eir+eann
sap
saps
saps
sap+ping
sapped
sa+pan+wood
sa+pele
sap+id
sa+pid+ity
sa+pi+ence
sa+pi+ent
sa+pi+en+tial
sa+pi+ent+ly
sap+ling
sap+lings
sapo+dil+la
sapo+dil+las
sapo+na+ceous
sa+poni+fi+ca+tion
sa+poni+fy
sa+poni+fies
sa+poni+fy+ing
sa+poni+fied

sapo+nin
sapo+nins
sap+pan+wood
sap+per
sap+pers
Sapper
Sap+phic
Sap+phics
Sapphira
sap+phire
sap+phires
Sappho
Sap+po+ro
sap+py
sap+pi+er
sap+pi+est
sap+ro+gen+ic
sap+ro+gen+ous
sap+ro+phyte
sap+ro+phytes
sap+ro+phyt+ic
sap+ro+zo+ic
sap+sucker
sap+suckers
sap+wood
sara+band
sara+bands
sara+bande
sara+bandes
Sara+cen
Sara+cens
Sara+cen+ic
Sara+gos+sa
Sarah
Sa+ra+jevo
Sa+ransk
Sa+ra+tov
Sa+ra+wak
sar+casm
sar+cas+tic
sar+cas+ti+cal+ly
sarce+net
sar+co+carp
sar+co+carps
sar+co+ma
sar+co+ma+ta
or
sar+co+mas
sar+co+ma+to+sis
sar+co+ma+tous
sar+copha+gus
sar+copha+gi
or

sar+copha+guses
sar+co+plasm
sar+co+plas+mic
sar+cous
sard
Sardanapalus
sar+dar
sar+dars
Sar+de+gna
Sar+des
sar+dine
sar+dine *or*
sar+dines
Sar+dinia
Sar+din+ian
Sar+din+ians
Sar+dis
sar+di+us
sar+di+uses
sar+don+ic
sar+doni+cal+ly
sar+don+yx
Sardou
saree
sarees
Sar+gas+so
sar+gas+sum
sarge
Sargent
Sargeson
Sar+go+dha
sari
saris
Sark
Sar+ka
sark+ing
sark+ings
sar+ky
sar+ki+er
sar+ki+est
Sar+ma+tia
Sar+ma+tian
Sar+ma+tians
Sar+mat+ic
sar+men+tose
sar+men+tous
Sar+nen
Sar+nia
sar+nie
sar+nies
sa+rod
sa+rods
sa+rong
sa+rongs

sa+ros
sa+roses
Sa+ros
Sarpedon
Sarraute
Sarre
sar+ruso+phone
sar+ruso+
  phones
sar+sa+pa+ril+la
sar+sa+pa+ril+
  las
sar+sen
sar+sens
sarse+net
Sarthe
Sarto
sar+to+rial
sar+to+ri+al+ly
sar+to+rius
sar+to+rii
Sartre
Sar+um
Sa+sebo
sash
  sashes
  sashes
  sash+ing
  sashed
sash+ay
  sash+ays
  sash+ay+ing
  sash+ayed
sashi+mi
Sas+katch+ewan
Sas+katch+ewan+
  ian
  Sas+katch+
  ewan+ians
Sas+ka+toon
sas+quatch
sass
  sasses
  sass+ing
  sassed
sas+sa+by
sas+sa+bies
sas+sa+fras
sas+sa+frases
Sas+sa+ri
Sas+se+nach
Sas+se+nachs
sas+si+ly
sas+si+ness
Sassoon

sas+sy
sas+si+er
sas+si+est
sas+tra
sat
Satan
sa+tan+ic
sa+tani+cal+ly
Sa+tan+ism
Sa+tan+ist
  Sa+tan+ists
satch+el
satch+els
satch+elled
sate
  sates
  sat+ing
  sat+ed
sa+teen
sa+teens
sat+el+lite
  sat+el+lites
sa+ti+abil+ity
sa+ti+able
sa+ti+ably
sa+ti+ate
  sa+ti+ates
  sa+ti+at+ing
  sa+ti+at+ed
sa+tia+tion
Satie
sa+ti+ety
sat+in
  sat+ins
sati+net
sati+nette
satin+flower
satin+wood
sat+iny
sat+ire
  sat+ires
sa+tir+ic
sa+tiri+cal
sa+tiri+cal+ly
sati+ri+sa+tion
sati+rise
sati+ris+ing
sati+rised
sati+rist
sati+rists
sati+ri+za+tion
sati+rize
sati+rizes
sati+riz+ing

sati+rized
sat+is+fac+tion
sat+is+fac+tions
sat+is+fac+to+ri+
  ly
sat+is+fac+tory
sat+is+fi+able
sat+is+fice
sat+is+fices
sat+is+fic+ing
sat+is+ficed
sat+is+fic+er
sat+is+fic+ers
sat+is+fy
sat+is+fies
sat+is+fy+ing
sat+is+fied
sat+is+fy+ing
sat+is+fy+ing+ly
Sato Eisaku
sa+to+ri
sa+trap
sa+traps
sa+trapy
sa+trapies
sat+su+ma
sat+su+mas
Sa+tsu+ma
satu+rabil+ity
satu+rable
satu+rate
satu+rates
satu+rat+ing
satu+rat+ed
satu+rat+ed
satu+ra+tion
Sat+ur+day
Sat+ur+days
Saturn
Sat+ur+na+lia
  Sat+ur+na+lia
  or
  Sat+ur+na+lias
Sat+ur+na+lian
Sa+tur+nian
sat+ur+nine
sat+ur+nine+ly
sat+ya+gra+ha
sa+tyr
sa+tyrs
saty+ria+sis
sa+tyr+ic
sauce
sauces
sauces

sauc+ing
sauced
sauce+pan
sauce+pans
sau+cer
sau+cers
sau+cer+ful
sau+cer+fuls
sau+ci+ly
sau+ci+ness
saucy
sauci+er
sauci+est
Saud
Sau+di
  Sau+dis
sau+er+kraut
sau+ger
sau+gers
Saul
Sault Sainte Ma+
  rie
sau+na
sau+nas
Saunders
saun+ter
saun+ters
saun+ters
saun+ter+ing
saun+tered
saun+ter+er
saun+ter+ers
sau+rian
sau+rians
sau+ry
sau+ries
sau+sage
sau+sages
Saussure
Saus+sur+ean
sau+té
sau+tés
sau+tés
sau+té+ing *or*
sau+tée+ing
sau+téed
Sava
sav+able
sav+age
sav+ages
sav+ages
sav+ag+ing
sav+aged
Savage
surname

Sav+age	*U.S.*	saxes	scad *or*
place name	sa+vory	Saxe	scads
sav+age+ly	*U.S.*	saxe-blue	scads
sav+age+ness	sa+vories	*adj.*	Sca+fell
sav+age+ry	sa+vour	saxe blue	scaf+fold
sav+age+ries	sa+vours	*noun*	scaf+folds
Sa+vaii	sa+vours	Saxe-Coburg-	scaf+folds
sa+van+na	sa+vour+ing	Gotha	scaf+fold+ing
sa+van+nas	sa+voured	sax+horn	scaf+fold+ed
sa+van+nah	sa+vouri+ness	sax+horns	scaf+fold+er
sa+van+nahs	sa+vour+less	sax+ico+lous	scaf+fold+ers
Sa+van+nah	sa+voury	saxi+frage	scaf+fold+ing
sa+vant	sa+vouries	saxi+frages	scaf+fold+ings
sa+vants	sa+voy	Saxo	scal+able
sa+vante	sa+voys	Grammaticus	scal+able+ness
sa+vantes	Sa+voy	Sax+on	scal+ably
sa+vate	*place name*	Sax+ons	sca+lar
sa+vates	Savoy	Saxo+ny	sca+lars
save	*surname*	Saxony-Anhalt	scala+wag
saves	Sa+voy+ard	saxo+phone	scala+wags
saves	Sa+voy+ards	saxo+phones	scald
sav+ing	sav+vy	saxo+phon+ic	scalds
saved	sav+vies	sax+opho+nist	scalds
Save	sav+vy+ing	sax+opho+nists	scald+ing
save+able	sav+vied	say	scald+ed
sav+eloy	sav+vi+er	says	scald+er
sav+eloys	sav+vi+est	say+ing	scald+ers
sav+er	saw	said	scald+fish
sav+ers	saws	say+er	scald+fish *or*
Savery	saws	say+ers	scald+fishes
sav+in	saw+ing	Sayers	scale
sav+ine	sawed	say+ing	scales
sav+ing	sawn	say+ings	scales
savings	saw+bones	say-so	scal+ing
sav+ing+ly	saw+bones *or*	say-sos	scaled
sav+ings	saw+boneses	say+yid	scale+board
sav+ior	saw+dust	say+yids	scale+boards
U.S.	sawed-off	scab	sca+lene
sav+iors	saw+er	scabs	sca+lenus
Sav+ior	saw+ers	scabs	sca+leni
U.S.	saw+fish	scab+bing	scali+ness
sav+iour	saw+fish *or*	scabbed	scal+ing
sav+iours	saw+fishes	scab+bard	scal+lion
Sav+iour	saw+fly	scab+bards	scal+lions
Sa+voie	saw+flies	scab+bi+ly	scal+lop
savoir-faire	saw+horse	scab+bi+ness	scal+lops
Sa+vo+na	saw+horses	scab+by	scal+lops
Savonarola	saw+like	scab+bi+er	scal+lop+ing
sa+vor	saw+mill	scab+bi+est	scal+loped
U.S.	saw+mills	sca+bies	scal+lop+er
sa+vors	sawn	sca+bi+ous	scal+lop+ers
sa+vors	sawn-off	sca+bi+ouses	scal+lop+ing
sa+vor+ing	saw+yer	sca+brous	scal+ly
sa+vored	saw+yers	sca+brous+ly	scal+lies
sa+vori+ness	sax	scad	scal+ly+wag

scal+ly+wags
scalp
 scalps
 scalps
 scalp+ing
 scalped
scal+pel
 scal+pels
scalp+er
 scalp+ers
scaly
 scali+er
 scali+est
Sca+man+der
scamp
 scamps
 scamps
 scamp+ing
 scamped
scamp+er
 scamp+ers
 scamp+ers
 scamp+er+ing
 scamp+ered
scam+pi
scamp+ish
scan
 scans
 scans
 scan+ning
 scanned
scan+dal
 scan+dals
scan+dali+sa+
  tion
 scan+dal+ise
 scan+dal+ises
 scan+dal+is+ing
 scan+dal+ised
 scan+dali+za+
  tion
 scan+dal+ize
 scan+dal+izes
 scan+dal+iz+ing
 scan+dal+ized
scandal+monger
 scandal+
  mongers
scan+dal+ous
scan+dal+ous+ly
Scan+di+na+via
Scan+di+na+vian
 Scan+di+na+
  vians
scan+dium

scan+nable
scan+ner
scan+ners
scan+sion
 scan+sions
scant
 scants
 scant+ing
 scant+ed
scanti+ly
scanti+ness
scant+ling
 scant+lings
scant+ly
scanty
 scanti+er
 scanti+est
Scapa
scape
 scapes
 scapes
 scap+ing
 scaped
'scape
 'scapes
 'scap+ing
 'scaped
scape+goat
 scape+goats
scape+grace
 scape+graces
scaph+oid
scapu+la
 scapu+lae or
 scapu+las
scapu+lar
 scapu+lars
scar
 scars
 scars
 scar+ring
 scarred
scar+ab
 scar+abs
scara+bae+id
 scara+bae+ids
Scara+mouch
Scar+borough
scarce
 scarc+er
 scarc+est
scarce+ly
scarce+ness
scar+city
 scar+cities

scare
 scares
 scares
 scar+ing
 scared
scare+crow
 scare+crows
scare+monger
 scare+mongers
 scare+monger+
  ing
scar+er
 scar+ers
scarf
 scarfs or
 scarves
 scarfs
 scarf+ing
 scarfed
Scarfe
scarf+skin
 scarf+skins
Scargill
scari+fi+ca+tion
scari+fi+er
 scari+fi+ers
scari+fy
 scari+fies
 scari+fy+ing
 scari+fied
scar+la+ti+na
Scarlatti
scar+let
scarp
 scarps
 scarps
 scarp+ing
 scarped
scarp+er
 scarp+ers
 scarp+ers
 scarp+er+ing
 scarp+ered
Scarron
scarves
scary
 scari+er
 scari+est
scat
 scats
 scats
 scat+ting
 scat+ted
scathe
 scathes

scath+ing
scathed
scath+ing
scath+ing+ly
scato+logi+cal
sca+tol+ogy
scat+ter
 scat+ters
 scat+ters
 scat+ter+ing
 scat+tered
scatter+brain
 scatter+brains
scatter+brained
scat+ter+er
 scat+ter+ers
 scat+ter+ing
 scat+ter+ings
scat+ti+ly
scat+ti+ness
scat+ty
 scat+ti+er
 scat+ti+est
scaup
 scaups
scav+enge
 scav+enges
 scav+eng+ing
 scav+enged
scav+en+ger
 scav+en+gers
scav+en+gery
sce+na
 sce+ne
sce+nario
 sce+narios
scene
 scenes
scen+ery
 scen+eries
sce+nic
sce+ni+cal+ly
scent
 scents
 scents
 scent+ing
 scent+ed
scep+ter
 U.S.
 scep+ters
scep+tered
 U.S.
scep+tic
 scep+tics

Scep+tic
Scep+tics
scep+ti+cal
scep+ti+cism
Scep+ti+cism
scep+tre
scep+tres
scep+tred
Schaer+beek
Schaff+hau+sen
Schaumburg-
Lippe
sched+ule
sched+ules
sched+ules
sched+ul+ing
sched+uled
Scheel
Scheele
scheel+ite
Scheldt
Schelling
Schel+lin+gian
sche+ma
sche+ma+ta
sche+mat+ic
sche+mat+ics
sche+mati+cal+ly
sche+ma+ti+sa+
tion
sche+ma+tise
sche+ma+tises
sche+ma+tis+
ing
sche+ma+tised
sche+ma+tism
sche+ma+ti+za+
tion
sche+ma+tize
sche+ma+tizes
sche+ma+tiz+
ing
sche+ma+tized
scheme
schemes
schemes
schem+ing
schemed
schem+er
schem+ers
schem+ing
schem+ings
scher+zan+do

scher+zan+di
or
scher+zan+dos
scher+zo
scher+zi or
scher+zos
Schiaparelli
Schie+dam
Schiele
Schiller
schil+ling
schil+lings
schism
schisms
schis+mat+ic
schis+mat+ics
schis+mati+cal
schis+mati+cals
schis+mati+cal+
ly
schist
schists
schis+tose
schis+to+some
schis+to+somes
schis+to+so+mia+
sis
schi+zan+thus
schi+zan+thuses
schizo
schizos
schizo+carp
schizo+carps
schizo+car+pous
schiz+oid
schiz+oids
schizo+my+cete
schizo+my+
cetes
schizo+phre+nia
schizo+phre+
nias
schizo+phren+ic
schizo+phren+
ics
schizo+thy+mia
schizo+thy+mic
Schlegel
Schle+si+en
Schlesinger
Schles+wig
Schleswig-
Holstein
Schlick
Schlieffen

Schliemann
schlie+ren
schmaltz
schmaltzy
schmalz
Schmidt
Schnabel
schnap+per
schnap+pers
schnapps
schnaps
schnau+zer
schnau+zers
Schnittke
schnit+zel
schnit+zels
schnor+kle
schnor+kles
schnor+kles
schnor+kling
schnor+kled
schnoz+zle
schnoz+zles
Schoenberg
schol+ar
schol+ars
schol+ar+li+ness
schol+ar+ly
schol+ar+ship
schol+ar+ships
scho+las+tic
scho+las+ti+cal+
ly
scho+las+ti+cism
scho+li+ast
scho+li+asts
scho+li+as+tic
Schönberg
Schongauer
school
schools
schools
school+ing
schooled
school+boy
school+boys
school+fellow
school+fellows
school+girl
school+girls
school+house
school+houses
schoolie
schoolies
school+ing

school+ings
school+man
school+men
school+marm
school+marms
school+marm+ish
school+master
school+masters
school+mate
school+mates
school+mistress
school+
mistresses
Schools
school+teacher
school+teachers
school+teach+ing
schoon+er
schoon+ers
Schopenhauer
Scho+pen+hau+
er+ian
Scho+pen+hau+
er+ism
schot+tische
schot+tisches
Schreiner
Schrödinger
Schubert
Schumacher
Schuman
Schumann
schuss
schusses
schusses
schuss+ing
schussed
Schütz
schwa
schwas
Schwa+ben
Schwarzkopf
Schwarz+wald
Schwein+furt
Schweitzer
Schweiz
Schwe+rin
Schwitters
Schwyz
sci+at+ic
sci+ati+ca
sci+ence
sci+ences
sci+en+ter
sci+en+tial

sci+en+tif+ic
sci+en+tifi+cal+ly
sci+en+tism
sci+en+tist
sci+en+tists
sci+en+tis+tic
Sci+en+tolo+gist
Sci+en+tolo+gists
Sci+en+tol+ogy
Trademark
sci-fi
scili+cet
scil+la
scil+las
Scil+lies
Scil+lo+nian
Scil+ly
scimi+tar
scimi+tars
scin+tig+ra+phy
scin+til+la
scin+til+las
scin+til+lant
scin+til+late
scin+til+lates
scin+til+lat+ing
scin+til+lat+ed
scin+til+lat+ing
scin+til+la+tion
scin+til+la+tions
scio+lism
scio+list
scio+lists
scio+lis+tic
sci+on
sci+ons
Scipio
scir+rhoid
scir+rhus
scir+rhi *or*
scir+rhuses
scis+sion
scis+sor
scis+sors
scis+sor+ing
scis+sored
scis+sors
sciu+rine
scle+ra
scle+ren+chy+ma
scle+ri+tis
scle+ro+der+ma
scle+ro+der+mia
scle+ro+ma

scle+ro+ma+ta
or
scle+ro+mas
scle+ro+pro+tein
scle+ro+pro+
  teins
scle+ro+sis
scle+ro+ses
scle+rot+ic
scle+rot+ics
scle+rous
scoff
scoffs
scoffs
scoff+ing
scoffed
scoff+er
scoff+ers
scoff+ing
Scofield
scold
scolds
scolds
scold+ing
scold+ed
scold+er
scold+ers
scold+ing
scold+ings
sco+lio+sis
sco+li+ot+ic
scol+lop
scol+lops
scol+lops
scol+lop+ing
scol+loped
scom+broid
scom+broids
sconce
sconces
scone
scones
Scone
scoop
scoops
scoops
scoop+ing
scooped
scoop+er
scoop+ers
scoop+ful
scoop+fuls
scoot
scoots
scoots

scoot+ing
scoot+ed
scoot+er
scoot+ers
Scopas
scope
scopes
sco+pola+mine
Sco+pus
scor+bu+tic
scor+bu+ti+cal+
  ly
scorch
scorches
scorches
scorch+ing
scorched
scorch+er
scorch+ers
scorch+ing
score
scores
scores
scor+ing
scored
score+board
score+boards
score+card
score+cards
scor+er
scor+ers
sco+ria
sco+riae
sco+ri+fi+ca+tion
sco+ri+fi+er
sco+ri+fi+ers
sco+ri+fy
sco+ri+fies
sco+ri+fy+ing
sco+ri+fied
scor+ing
scorn
scorns
scorns
scorn+ing
scorned
scorn+er
scorn+ers
scorn+ful
scorn+ful+ly
Scor+pio
Scor+pios
scor+pi+on
scor+pi+ons

Scor+pi+on
Scorsese
Scot
Scots
scotch
scotches
scotches
scotch+ing
scotched
Scotch
Scotches
Scotch+man
Scotch+men
Scotch+woman
Scotch+women
sco+ter
sco+ters *or*
sco+ter
scot-free
Scot+land
sco+to+ma
sco+to+mas
or
sco+to+ma+ta
Scots
Scots+man
Scots+men
Scots+woman
Scots+women
Scott
Scot+ti+cism
Scot+tie
Scot+ties
Scot+tish
Scot+ty
Scot+ties
Scotus
scoun+drel
scoun+drels
scour
scours
scours
scour+ing
scoured
scour+er
scour+ers
scourge
scourges
scourges
scourg+ing
scourged
scour+ings
scouse
scouses
Scouse

Scouses	scram+blers	screech	scribed
scout	Scran+ton	screeches	Scribe
scouts	scrap	screeches	scrib+er
scouts	scraps	screech+ing	scrib+ers
scout+ing	scraps	screeched	scrim
scout+ed	scrap+ping	screech+er	scrims
Scout	scrapped	screech+ers	scrim+mage
Scouts	scrap+book	screechy	scrim+mages
scout+er	scrap+books	screed	scrim+mages
scout+ers	scrape	screeds	scrim+mag+ing
Scout+er	scrapes	screen	scrim+maged
Scout+ers	scrapes	screens	scrim+mag+er
Scout+ing	scrap+ing	screens	scrim+mag+ers
scow	scraped	screen+ing	scrimp
scows	scrap+er	screened	scrimps
scowl	scrap+ers	screen+able	scrimp+ing
scowls	scrap+er+board	screen+er	scrimped
scowls	scrap+er+	screen+ers	scrimpi+ness
scowl+ing	boards	screen+ing	scrimpy
scowled	scrap+heap	screen+ings	scrim+shank
scowl+er	scrap+heaps	screen+play	scrim+shanks
scowl+ers	scrap+pi+ly	screen+plays	scrim+shank+
scrab+ble	scrap+py	screen+writer	ing
scrab+bles	scrap+pi+er	screen+writers	scrim+shanked
scrab+bles	scrap+pi+est	screw	scrim+shaw
scrab+bling	scratch	screws	scrim+shaws
scrab+bled	scratches	screws	scrip
Scrab+ble	scratches	screw+ing	scrips
Trademark	scratch+ing	screwed	script
scrab+bler	scratched	screw+ball	scripts
scrab+blers	scratch+er	screw+balls	scripts
scrag	scratch+ers	screw+driver	script+ing
scrags	scratch+ing	screw+drivers	script+ed
scrags	scratch+ings	screwed	scrip+to+rium
scrag+ging	scratchy	screw+er	scrip+to+riums
scragged	scrawl	screw+ers	or
scrag+gi+ly	scrawls	screw-top	scrip+to+ria
scrag+gi+ness	scrawls	adj.	scrip+tur+al
scrag+gly	scrawl+ing	screw top	scrip+ture
scrag+gli+er	scrawled	screw tops	scrip+tures
scrag+gli+est	scrawly	screwy	Scrip+ture
scrag+gy	scrawni+ly	screwi+er	Scrip+tures
scrag+gi+er	scrawni+ness	screwi+est	script+writer
scrag+gi+est	scrawny	Scriabin	script+writers
scram	scrawni+er	scrib+al	script+writing
scrams	scrawni+est	scrib+ble	scrive+ner
scrams	scream	scrib+bles	scrive+ners
scram+ming	screams	scrib+bles	scrod
scrammed	screams	scrib+bling	scrods
scram+ble	scream+ing	scrib+bled	scrofu+la
scram+bles	screamed	scrib+bly	scrofu+lous
scram+bles	scream+er	scribe	scroll
scram+bling	scream+ers	scribes	scrolls
scram+bled	scree	scribes	scrolls
scram+bler	screes	scrib+ing	scroll+ing

scrolled
scroll+work
Scrooge
Scrooges
scrophu+laria+
  ceous
scro+tal
scro+tum
  scro+ta *or*
  scro+tums
scrounge
scrounges
scroung+ing
scrounged
scroung+er
scroung+ers
scrub
scrubs
scrubs
scrub+bing
scrubbed
scrub+ber
scrub+bers
scrub+by
scrub+bi+er
scrub+bi+est
scrub+land
scrub+lands
scruff
scruffs
scruffy
scruffi+er
scruffi+est
scrum
scrums
scrums
scrum+ming
scrummed
scrum+mage
scrum+mages
scrum+mages
scrum+mag+ing
scrum+maged
scrump
scrumps
scrump+ing
scrumped
scrump+tious
scrump+tious+ly
scrumpy
scrunch
scrunches
scrunches
scrunch+ing
scrunched

scru+ple
scru+ples
scru+ples
scru+pling
scru+pled
scru+pu+lous
scru+pu+lous+ly
scru+pu+lous+
  ness
scru+ti+neer
scru+ti+neers
scru+ti+nise
scru+ti+nises
scru+ti+nis+ing
scru+ti+nised
scru+ti+nis+er
scru+ti+nis+ers
scru+ti+nize
scru+ti+nizes
scru+ti+niz+ing
scru+ti+nized
scru+ti+niz+er
scru+ti+niz+ers
scru+ti+ny
scru+ti+nies
scry
scries
scry+ing
scried
scu+ba
scud
scuds
scuds
scud+ding
scud+ded
Scudamore
scuff
scuffs
scuffs
scuff+ing
scuffed
scuf+fle
scuf+fles
scuf+fles
scuf+fling
scuf+fled
scull
sculls
sculls
scull+ing
sculled
scull+er
scull+ers
scul+lery
scul+leries

Scullin
scul+lion
scul+lions
sculpt
sculpts
sculpt+ing
sculpt+ed
sculp+tor
sculp+tors
sculp+tress
sculp+tresses
sculp+tur+al
sculp+ture
sculp+tures
sculp+tures
sculp+tur+ing
sculp+tured
sculp+tur+esque
sculp+tur+esque+
  ly
scum
scums
scums
scum+ming
scummed
scum+bag
scum+bags
scum+ble
scum+bles
scum+bles
scum+bling
scum+bled
scum+my
scun+cheon
scun+cheons
scungy
scungi+er
scungi+est
scun+ner
scun+ners
scun+ners
scun+ner+ing
scun+nered
Scun+thorpe
scup
scups
scup+per
scup+pers
scup+pers
scup+per+ing
scup+pered
scurf
scurfy
scur+ril+ity
scur+ril+ous

scur+ri+lous+ly
scur+ry
scur+ries
scur+ries
scur+ry+ing
scur+ried
scur+vi+ly
scur+vi+ness
scur+vy
scur+vi+er
scur+vi+est
scut
scuts
scu+tage
scu+tages
Scu+ta+ri
scu+tate
scutch+eon
scutch+eons
scute
scutes
scu+tel+late
scu+tel+lum
scu+tel+la
scut+ter
scut+ters
scut+ters
scut+ter+ing
scut+tered
scut+tle
scut+tles
scut+tles
scut+tling
scut+tled
scuttle+butt
scuttle+butts
scu+tum
scu+ta
scuz+zy
scuz+zi+er
scuz+zi+est
Scylla
Scy+ros
scythe
scythes
scythes
scyth+ing
scythed
Scythia
Scyth+ian
Scyth+ians
sea
seas
sea+board
sea+boards

Seaborg
sea+borne
SEAC
sea+coast
sea+coasts
sea+cock
sea+cocks
sea+dog
light seen in fog
sea dog
old sailor
sea dogs
sea+farer
sea+farers
sea+faring
sea+food
sea+front
sea+fronts
sea-girt
sea+going
sea-green
adj.
sea green
noun
sea+gull
sea+gulls
sea+kale
seal
seals
seals
seal+ing
sealed
seal+able
seal+ant
seal+ants
sealed-beam
seal+er
seal+ers
seal-like
seal+skin
seal+skins
Sealy+ham
seam
seams
seams
seam+ing
seamed
sea+man
sea+men
seaman-like
sea+man+ly
sea+man+ship
Seami
seami+ness
seam+stress

seam+stresses
seamy
seami+er
seami+est
Sean+ad Éire+
ann
se+ance
se+ances
sé+ance
sé+ances
sea+plane
sea+planes
sea+port
sea+ports
sear
sears
sear+ing
seared
search
searches
searches
search+ing
searched
search+able
search+er
search+ers
search+ing
search+ing+ly
search+light
search+lights
Searle
sea+scape
sea+scapes
sea+shell
sea+shells
sea+shore
sea+shores
sea+sick
sea+sick+ness
sea+side
sea+son
sea+sons
sea+sons
sea+son+ing
sea+soned
sea+son+able
sea+son+able+
ness
sea+son+ably
sea+son+al
sea+son+al+ly
sea+soned
sea+son+er
sea+son+ers
sea+son+ing

sea+son+ings
seat
seats
seats
seat+ing
seat+ed
seat+ing
SEATO
Sea+ton
Se+at+tle
sea+ward
sea+way
sea+ways
sea+weed
sea+worthiness
sea+worthy
se+ba+ceous
Sebastian
Se+bas+to+pol
seb+or+rhea
U.S.
seb+or+rhoea
se+bum
sec
secs
se+cant
seca+teurs
se+cede
se+cedes
se+ced+ing
se+ceded
se+ced+er
se+ced+ers
se+ces+sion
se+ces+sions
se+ces+sion+ism
se+ces+sion+ist
se+ces+sion+
ists
sech
se+clude
se+cludes
se+clud+ing
se+clud+ed
se+clud+ed
se+clud+ed+ly
se+clud+ed+ness
se+clu+sion
sec+ond
give backing to
sec+onds
sec+onds
sec+ond+ing
sec+ond+ed
se+cond

transfer
se+conds
se+cond+ing
se+cond+ed
sec+ond+ari+ly
sec+ond+ari+
ness
sec+ond+ary
sec+ond+aries
second-best
adj.
second-class
adj.
sec+ond class
noun
second-degree
se+conde
sec+ond+er
sec+ond+ers
second-genera+
tion
adj.
sec+ond gen+era+
tion
noun
second-hand
sec+ond+ly
se+cond+ment
second-rate
second-sighted
second-string
adj.
sec+ond string
noun
se+cre+cy
se+cre+cies
se+cret
se+crets
sec+re+taire
sec+re+taires
sec+re+tar+ial
sec+re+tari+at
sec+re+tari+ats
sec+re+tary
sec+re+taries
sec+retary-
general
sec+re+taries-
general
sec+re+tary+ship
se+crete
se+cretes
se+cret+ing
se+cret+ed
se+cre+tion

se+cre+tions
se+cre+tive
se+cre+tive+ly
se+cre+tive+ness
se+cret+ly
se+cre+tor
se+cre+tors
se+cre+tory
sect
sects
sec+tar+ian
sec+tar+ians
sec+tari+an+ism
sec+tary
sec+taries
sec+tion
sec+tions
sec+tions
sec+tion+ing
sec+tioned
sec+tion+al
sec+tion+al+ise
sec+tion+al+ises
sec+tion+al+is+ing
sec+tion+al+ised
sec+tion+al+ism
sec+tion+al+ist
sec+tion+al+ists
sec+tion+al+ize
sec+tion+al+izes
sec+tion+al+iz+ing
sec+tion+al+ized
sec+tion+al+ly
sec+tor
sec+tors
sec+tor+al
sec+to+rial
secu+lar
secu+lars
secu+lari+sa+tion
secu+lar+ise
secu+lar+ises
secu+lar+is+ing
secu+lar+ised
secu+lar+ism
secu+lar+ist
secu+lar+ists
secu+lar+ity
secu+lar+ities

secu+lari+za+tion
secu+lar+ize
secu+lar+izes
secu+lar+iz+ing
secu+lar+ized
secu+lar+ly
se+cund
Se+cun+dera+bad
se+cur+able
se+cure
se+cures
se+cur+ing
se+cured
se+cure+ly
se+cure+ment
se+cur+er
se+cur+ers
se+cu+riti+sa+tion
se+cu+riti+za+tion
se+cu+rity
se+cu+rities
se+dan
se+dans
Se+dan
se+date
se+dates
se+dat+ing
se+dat+ed
se+date+ly
se+date+ness
se+da+tion
se+da+tions
seda+tive
seda+tives
Seddon
sed+en+tari+ly
sed+en+tari+ness
sed+en+tary
Se+der
Se+ders
sedge
sedges
Sedge+moor
Sedgwick
sedgy
se+di+lia
sedi+ment
sedi+ments
sedi+men+tari+ly
sedi+men+tary

sedi+men+ta+tion
se+di+tion
se+di+tions
se+di+tion+ary
se+di+tious
se+duce
se+duces
se+duc+ing
se+duced
se+duc+er
se+duc+ers
se+duc+ible
se+duc+tion
se+duc+tions
se+duc+tive
se+duc+tive+ly
se+duc+tive+ness
se+duc+tress
se+duc+tresses
se+du+lity
sedu+lous
sedu+lous+ly
sedu+lous+ness
se+dum
se+dums
see
sees
sees
see+ing
saw
seen
seed
seeds
seeds
seed+ing
seed+ed
seed+bed
seed+beds
seed+cake
seed+cakes
seed+er
seed+ers
seedi+ly
seedi+ness
seed+less
seed+ling
seed+lings
seedy
seedi+er
seedi+est
Seeger
see+ing
seek

seeks
seek+ing
sought
seek+er
seek+ers
See+land
seem
seems
seem+ing
seemed
seem+ing
seem+ing+ly
seem+ly
seem+li+er
seem+li+est
seen
seep
seeps
seeps
seep+ing
seeped
seep+age
seep+ages
seer
seers
seer+sucker
see+saw
see+saws
see+saws
see+saw+ing
see+sawed
seethe
seethes
seeth+ing
seethed
seeth+ing
seeth+ing+ly
see-through
adj.
see through
verb
Seferis
seg+ment
seg+ments
seg+ments
seg+ment+ing
seg+ment+ed
seg+men+tal
seg+men+tary
seg+men+ta+tion
seg+men+ta+tions
Se+go+via
place name
Segovia

surname
Segrè
seg+re+gate
 seg+re+gates
 seg+re+gat+ing
 seg+re+gat+ed
seg+re+ga+tion
 seg+re+ga+tion+
 al
 seg+re+ga+tion+
 ist
 seg+re+ga+tion+
 ists
seg+re+ga+tive
seg+re+ga+tor
 seg+re+ga+tors
segue
 segues
 segues
 segue+ing
 segued
se+gui+dil+la
 se+gui+dil+las
seiche
 seiches
Seid+litz
seif
sei+gneur
 sei+gneurs
sei+gneu+rial
sei+gneury
 sei+gneuries
sei+gnior
 sei+gniors
sei+gnio+rial
sei+gniory
 sei+gniories
seine
 seines
 seines
 sein+ing
 seined
Seine
Seine-et-Marne
Seine-Maritime
Seine-Saint-Denis
seis+able
seise
 seises
 seis+ing
 seised
seis+er
 seis+ers
sei+sin
 sei+sins

seism
seis+mic
seis+mo+graph
 seis+mo+graphs
seis+mog+ra+
 pher
 seis+mog+ra+
 phers
seis+mo+graph+
 ic
seis+mo+log+ic
seis+mo+logi+cal
seis+mo+logi+cal+
 ly
seis+molo+gist
 seis+molo+gists
seis+mol+ogy
seiz+able
seize
 seizes
 seiz+ing
 seized
sei+zin
U.S.
 sei+zins
sei+zure
 sei+zures
Sek+on+di
se+la+chian
Se+lan+gor
Selby
sel+dom
se+lect
 se+lects
 se+lect+ing
 se+lect+ed
se+lec+tion
 se+lec+tions
se+lec+tive
 se+lec+tive+ly
 se+lec+tiv+ity
se+lect+ness
se+lec+tor
 se+lec+tors
Selene
sel+enite
se+lenium
se+lenog+ra+
 pher
se+leno+graph+
 ic
se+lenog+ra+phy
Seles
Se+leu+cia
self

selves
self-abasement
self-abhor+rence
self-abnega+tion
self-absorbed
self-absorp+tion
self-abuse
self-accusa+tion
self-acting
self-addressed
self-adhesive
self-adjust+ing
self-advance+
 ment
self-advertise+
 ment
self-aggran+dize+
 ment
self-aggran+diz+
 ing
self-analy+sis
self-appoint+ed
self-assert+ing
self-assertion
self-assertive
self-assess+ment
self-assurance
self-assured
self-aware
self-cater+ing
self-censor+ship
self-centred
self-centred+ness
self-certi+fi+ca+
 tion
 self-certi+fi+ca+
 tions
self-cleaning
self-closing
self-coloured
self-command
self-conceit
self-condem+na+
 tion
self-confessed
self-confidence
self-confident
self-confident+ly
self-congratu+la+
 tion
self-conscious
self-conscious+ly
self-conscious+
 ness

self-consis+ten+
 cy
self-consis+tent
self-contained
self-contain+ed+
 ness
self-contra+dic+
 tory
self-control
self-controlled
self-correct+ing
self-criticism
self-deceit
self-deception
self-deceptive
self-defeat+ing
self-defence
self-defensive
self-degrada+tion
self-delusion
self-denial
 self-denials
 self-denying
self-depend+ent
self-destruct
 self-destructs
 self-destruct+
 ing
 self-destruct+ed
self-destruction
self-determi+na+
 tion
self-determined
self-determin+ing
self-develop+
 ment
self-discipline
self-disciplined
self-doubt
 self-doubts
self-drive
self-educat+ed
self-efface+ment
self-effacing
self-elect+ed
self-employed
self-employ+
 ment
self-esteem
self-evidence
self-evident
self-evident+ly
self-examina+tion
self-existent
self-expand+ing

self-explana+tory
self-expres+sion
self-express+ive
self-fertili+za+tion
self-financed
self-financ+ing
self-focus+ing
self-fulfill+ing
self-fulfil+ment
self-generat+ing
self-governed
self-govern+ing
self-govern+ment
self-hate
self+heal
 self+heals
self-help
self-hypnosis
self-hypnotism
self-image
 self-images
self-import+ance
self-import+ant
self-import+ant+
 ly
self-imposed
self-improve+
 ment
self-induced
self-induction
 self-inductions
self-indulgence
self-indulgent
self-inflict+ed
self-interest
self-interest+ed
self+ish
self+ish+ly
self+ish+ness
self-judgment
self-justifi+ca+
 tion
self-knowledge
self+less
self+less+ly
self+less+ness
self-loading
self-locking
self-love
self-made
self-mockery
self-motivat+ed
self-mutila+tion
self-operat+ing

self-opinion+at+
 ed
self-paro+dy
self-perpetuat+
 ing
self-pity
self-pitying
self-pitying+ly
self-pollinat+ed
self-pollina+tion
self-portrait
 self-portraits
self-possessed
self-posses+sion
self-powered
self-praise
self-prepared
self-preser+va+
 tion
self-proclaimed
self-produced
self-professed
self-promo+tion
self-pronounc+
 ing
self-propa+gat+
 ing
self-propelled
self-propel+ling
self-propul+sion
self-protec+tion
self-punish+ment
self-raising
self-realiza+tion
self-regard
self-regula+tory
self-reliance
self-reliant
self-renuncia+tion
self-reproach
self-reproach+ful
self-respect
self-respect+ing
self-restraint
self-restrict+ed
self-reveal+ing
self-righteous
self-righteous+ly
self-righteous+
 ness
self-righting
self-rule
self-sacrifice
self-sacrific+ing
self+same

self-satisfac+tion
self-satisfied
self-sealing
self-seeker
 self-seekers
self-seeking
self-service
self-serving
self-sown
self-starter
 self-starters
self-styled
self-sufficien+cy
self-sufficient
self-sufficient+ly
self-suffic+ing
self-support+ing
self-taught
self-tender
 self-tenders
self-trained
self-will
self-willed
self-winding
self-worship
Sel+juk
 Sel+juks
Selkirk
 surname
Sel+kirk
 place name
Sel+kirk+shire
sell
 sells
 sell+ing
 sold
sell+able
Sel+la+field
sell-by
sell+er
 sell+ers
Sellers
Sel+lo+tape
 Trademark
 Sel+lo+tapes
 Sel+lo+tap+ing
 Sel+lo+taped
sell+out
 noun
sell out
 verb
sel+syn
 sel+syns
Selt+zer
sel+va

sel+vas
sel+vage
sel+vages
sel+vaged
sel+vedge
sel+vedges
selves
Sem
se+man+tic
se+man+ti+cal+ly
se+man+ti+cist
se+man+ti+cists
se+man+tics
sema+phore
sema+phores
sema+phores
sema+phor+ing
sema+phored
sema+phor+ic
Se+ma+rang
se+ma+siol+ogy
se+mat+ic
sem+blance
sem+blances
Semele
sem+eme
sem+emes
se+men
Se+me+roe
Se+me+ru
se+mes+ter
se+mes+ters
semi
semis
semi+ag+ri+cul+
 tur+al
semi+an+nual
semi+an+nu+al+
 ly
semi+aquat+ic
semi+ar+id
semi+auto+mat+
 ic
semi+auto+mat+
 ics
semi+auto+mati+
 cal+ly
semi+autono+
 mous
semi+breve
semi+breves
semi+cir+cle
semi+cir+cles
semi+cir+cu+lar
semi+civi+lised

semi+civi+lized
semi+clas+si+cal
semi+co+lon
  semi+co+lons
semi+con+duc+
  tor
  semi+con+duc+
  tors
semi+con+scious
semi+con+scious+
  ly
semi+con+scious+
  ness
semi+dark+ness
semi+de+tached
semi+di+rect
semi+di+vine
semi+docu+men+
  tary
  semi+docu+men+
  taries
semi+dome
  semi+domes
semi+dry
semi+el+lip+ti+
  cal
semi+fic+tion+al
semi+fi+nal
  semi+fi+nals
  semi+fi+nal+ist
  semi+fi+nal+ists
semi+flu+id
  semi+flu+ids
semi+hard
semi-independ+
  ent
semi-industrial
semi-invalid
  semi-invalids
semi+leg+end+
  ary
semi+lit+er+ate
semi+lu+nar
semi+mythi+cal
semi+nal
  semi+nal+ly
semi+nar
  semi+nars
semi+nar+ial
semi+nar+ian
  semi+nar+ians
semi+nary
  semi+naries
semi+nif+er+ous
semi+nude

semi+of+fi+cial
se+mi+ot+ic
se+mi+ot+ics
Se+mi+pa+la+
  tinsk
semi+para+sit+ic
semi+perma+
  nent
semi+per+meabil+
  ity
semi+per+
  meable
semi+plas+tic
semi+po+liti+cal
semi+po+rous
semi+precious
semi+pri+vate
semi+pro+fes+
  sion+al
semi+pro+fes+
  sion+als
semi+pro+fes+
  sion+al+ly
semi+pub+lic
semi+qua+ver
  semi+qua+vers
Se+mira+mis
semi+re+tired
semi+re+tire+
  ment
  semi+re+tire+
  ments
semi+rig+id
semi+ru+ral
semi+se+ri+ous
semi+skilled
semi+sol+id
semi+sol+us
  semi+sol+uses
semi+sweet
Se+mite
  Se+mites
Se+mit+ic
semi+tone
  semi+tones
semi+ton+ic
semi+trail+er
  semi+trail+ers
semi+trained
semi+trans+lu+
  cent
semi+trans+par+
  ent
semi+tropi+cal
semi+trop+ics

semi+truth+ful
semi+ur+ban
semi+vow+el
  semi+vow+els
semi+year+ly
Semmelweis
semo+li+na
Sem+pach
sem+per+vi+vum
  sem+per+vi+
  vums
sem+pi+ter+nal
sem+pi+ter+nal+
  ly
sem+pli+ce
sem+pre
semp+stress
  semp+stresses
Sem+tex
  Trademark
sen
sen+ate
  sen+ates
Sen+ate
  Sen+ates
sena+tor
  sena+tors
sena+to+rial
send
  sends
send+ing
  sent
send+able
Sen+dai
send+er
  send+ers
send+off
  send+offs
send off
  verb
send-up
  send-ups
send up
  verb
Sen+eca
  tribe
  Sen+ecas *or*
  Sen+eca
Seneca
  name
Sen+egal
Sen+ega+lese
  Sen+ega+lese
Sen+egam+bia
se+nes+cence

se+nes+cent
sen+eschal
  sen+eschals
Senghor
se+nile
se+nil+ity
sen+ior
  sen+iors
Sen+ior
sen+ior+ity
  sen+ior+ities
Sen+lac
sen+na
  sen+nas
Senna
Sennacherib
Sen+nar
sen+night
  sen+nights
se'nnight
  se'nnights
se+ñor
  se+ñors *or*
  se+ñores
se+ño+ra
  se+ño+ras
se+ño+ri+ta
  se+ño+ri+tas
sen+sa+tion
  sen+sa+tions
sen+sa+tion+al
sen+sa+tion+al+
  ise
sen+sa+tion+al+
  ises
sen+sa+tion+al+
  is+ing
sen+sa+tion+al+
  ised
sen+sa+tion+al+
  ism
sen+sa+tion+al+
  ist
sen+sa+tion+al+
  ists
sen+sa+tion+al+
  is+tic
sen+sa+tion+al+
  ize
sen+sa+tion+al+
  izes
sen+sa+tion+al+
  iz+ing
sen+sa+tion+al+
  ized

sen+sa+tion+al+
  ly
sense
  senses
  senses
  sens+ing
  sensed
sense+less
sense+less+ly
sense+less+ness
sen+sibil+ity
  sen+sibil+ities
sen+sible
sen+sible+ness
sen+sibly
sen+si+ti+sa+
  tion
  sen+si+ti+sa+
    tions
sen+si+tise
  sen+si+tises
  sen+si+tis+ing
  sen+si+tised
  sen+si+tis+er
  sen+si+tis+ers
sen+si+tive
sen+si+tive+ly
sen+si+tiv+ity
  sen+si+tiv+ities
sen+si+ti+za+tion
  sen+si+ti+za+
    tions
sen+si+tize
  sen+si+tizes
  sen+si+tiz+ing
  sen+si+tized
  sen+si+tiz+er
  sen+si+tiz+ers
sen+si+tom+eter
  sen+si+tom+
    eters
sen+so+mo+tor
sen+sor
  sen+sors
sen+so+ri+mo+
  tor
sen+so+rium
  sen+so+riums
    or
  sen+so+ria
sen+so+ry
sen+sual
sen+su+al+ism
sen+su+al+ist
  sen+su+al+ists

sen+su+al+ity
  sen+su+al+ities
sen+su+al+ly
sen+su+ous
sen+su+ous+ly
sen+su+ous+
  ness
sent
sen+tence
  sen+tences
  sen+tences
  sen+tenc+ing
  sen+tenced
sen+ten+tial
sen+ten+tious
sen+ten+tious+ly
sen+ten+tious+
  ness
sen+tience
sen+ti+ent
  sen+ti+ents
sen+ti+ment
  sen+ti+ments
sen+ti+ment+al
sen+ti+men+tali+
  sa+tion
sen+ti+men+tal+
  ise
  sen+ti+men+tal+
    ises
  sen+ti+men+tal+
    is+ing
  sen+ti+men+tal+
    ised
sen+ti+men+tal+
  ism
sen+ti+men+tal+
  ist
  sen+ti+men+tal+
    ists
sen+ti+men+tal+
  ity
  sen+ti+men+tal+
    ities
sen+ti+men+tali+
  za+tion
sen+ti+men+tal+
  ize
  sen+ti+men+tal+
    izes
  sen+ti+men+tal+
    iz+ing
  sen+ti+men+tal+
    ized

sen+ti+men+tal+
  ly
sen+ti+nel
  sen+ti+nels
  sen+ti+nels
  sen+ti+nel+ling
    or
  sen+ti+nel+ing
  U.S.
  sen+ti+nelled
    or
  sen+ti+neled
  U.S.
sen+try
  sen+tries
sen+za
Seoul
sep+al
  sep+als
sep+al+ous
sepa+rabil+ity
sepa+rable
sepa+rable+ness
sepa+rably
sepa+rate
  sepa+rates
  sepa+rat+ing
  sepa+rat+ed
sepa+rate+ly
sepa+rate+ness
  sepa+rates
sepa+ra+tion
  sepa+ra+tions
sepa+ra+tism
sepa+ra+tist
  sepa+ra+tists
sepa+ra+tive
sepa+ra+tor
  sepa+ra+tors
Se+phar+di
  Se+phar+dim
  Se+phar+dic
se+pia
  se+pias
se+poy
  se+poys
sep+pu+ku
sep+sis
sept
  septs
sep+ta
sep+tal
Sep+tem+ber
  Sep+tem+bers
sep+te+nary

sep+te+naries
sep+ten+nial
sep+tet
  sep+tets
sep+tic
  sep+tics
sep+ti+cae+mia
  sep+ti+cae+mic
sep+ti+cal+ly
sep+ti+cemia
  U.S.
sep+tic+ity
sep+til+lion
  sep+til+lions
    or
  sep+til+lion
sep+til+lionth
  sep+til+lionths
sep+time
sep+tua+genar+
  ian
  sep+tua+genar+
    ians
Sep+tua+gesi+
  ma
  Sep+tua+gesi+
    mas
Sep+tua+gint
sep+tum
  sep+ta
sep+tu+ple
  sep+tu+ples
  sep+tu+pling
  sep+tu+pled
sep+tu+pli+cate
  sep+tu+pli+
    cates
sep+ul+cher
  U.S.
  sep+ul+chers
  sep+ul+chers
  sep+ul+cher+ing
  sep+ul+chered
se+pul+chral
se+pul+chral+ly
sep+ul+chre
  sep+ul+chres
  sep+ul+chres
  sep+ul+chring
  sep+ul+chred
sep+ul+ture
  sep+ul+tures
se+quel
  se+quels
  se+quela
se+quela

se+quelae
se+quence
se+quences
se+quenc+ing
se+quent
se+quents
se+quen+tial
se+quen+ti+al+ity
se+quen+tial+ly
se+quent+ly
se+ques+ter
se+ques+ters
se+ques+ter+ing
se+ques+tered
se+ques+tral
se+ques+trate
se+ques+trates
se+ques+trat+ing
se+ques+trat+ed
se+ques+tra+tion
se+ques+tra+tions
se+ques+tra+tor
se+ques+tra+tors
se+ques+trum
se+ques+tra
se+quin
se+quins
se+quined
se+quoia
se+quoias
sé+rac
sé+racs
se+ra+glio
se+ra+glios
se+rail
se+rails
Se+ra+jevo
Se+ram
se+ra+pe
se+ra+pes
ser+aph
ser+aphs *or*
ser+aphim
se+raph+ic
Sera+pis
Serb
Serbs
Ser+bia
Ser+bian

Ser+bians
Serbo-Croat
Serbo-Croa+tian
Sercq
sere
seres
seres
ser+ing
sered
Ser+em+ban
ser+enade
ser+enades
ser+enades
ser+enad+ing
ser+enad+ed
ser+enad+er
ser+enad+ers
ser+en+dip+ity
se+rene
se+rene+ly
se+ren+ity
se+ren+ities
serf
serfs
serf+dom
serf+hood
serge
ser+geant
ser+geants
se+rial
se+rials
se+riali+sa+tion
se+riali+sa+tions
se+rial+ise
se+rial+ises
se+rial+is+ing
se+rial+ised
se+rial+ism
se+riali+za+tion
se+riali+za+tions
se+rial+ize
se+rial+izes
se+rial+iz+ing
se+rial+ized
se+rial+ly
se+ri+ate
se+ria+tim
se+ri+ceous
seri+cul+tur+al
seri+cul+ture
seri+cul+tur+ist
seri+cul+tur+ists
se+ries

se+ries
series-wound
ser+if
ser+ifs
seri+graph
seri+graphs
se+rig+ra+phy
ser+in
ser+ins
se+rin+ga
se+rin+gas
Se+rin+ga+pa+tam
se+rio+com+ic
se+rio+comi+cal+ly
se+ri+ous
se+ri+ous+ly
se+ri+ous+ness
ser+jeant
ser+jeants
ser+mon
ser+mons
ser+mon+ise
ser+mon+ises
ser+mon+is+ing
ser+mon+ised
ser+mon+is+er
ser+mon+is+ers
ser+mon+ize
ser+mon+izes
ser+mon+iz+ing
ser+mon+ized
ser+mon+iz+er
ser+mon+iz+ers
sero+con+ver+sion
sero+con+vert
sero+con+verts
sero+con+vert+ing
sero+con+vert+ed
se+ro+log+ic
se+ro+logi+cal
se+rol+ogy
sero+posi+tive
se+ros+ity
sero+tine
sero+to+nin
se+rous
ser+ow
ser+ows
ser+pent
ser+pents

ser+pen+tine
ser+pen+tines
ser+pi+go
ser+pi+gos
SERPS
Serps
ser+rate
ser+rates
ser+rat+ing
ser+rat+ed
ser+rat+ed
ser+ra+tion
ser+ra+tions
ser+ried
ser+ri+form
ser+ru+late
ser+ru+la+tion
ser+ru+la+tions
Sertorius
se+rum
se+rums *or*
se+ra
serv+able
ser+val
ser+vals *or*
ser+val
serv+ant
serv+ants
serve
serves
serves
serv+ing
served
serve+able
serv+er
serv+ers
Servetus
Ser+via
Ser+vian
Ser+vians
ser+vice
ser+vices
ser+vices
ser+vic+ing
ser+viced
ser+vice+abil+ity
ser+vice+able
ser+vice+ably
ser+vice+man
ser+vice+men
ser+vices
ser+vice+woman
ser+vice+women
ser+vi+ette

ser+vi+ettes
ser+vile
ser+vil+ity
serv+ing
serv+ings
ser+vi+tor
ser+vi+tors
ser+vi+tude
ser+vo
ser+vos
ser+vo+mecha+
  nism
ser+vo+mecha+
  nisms
ser+vo+mo+tor
ser+vo+mo+
  tors
sesa+me
sesa+moid
ses+qui+cen+ten+
  nial
ses+qui+cen+
  ten+nials
ses+qui+cen+ten+
  ni+al+ly
ses+sile
ses+sil+ity
ses+sion
  ses+sions
ses+sion+al
Sessions
ses+terce
  ses+terces
ses+ter+tius
  ses+ter+tiuses
ses+tet
  ses+tets
ses+ti+na
  ses+ti+nas
Ses+tos
set
  sets
  sets
  set+ting
  set
seta
  setae
se+ta+ceous
set-aside
  set-asides
set aside
verb
set+back
  set+backs
  set back

verb
Seth
setif+er+ous
se+tig+er+ous
set-in
adj.
set in
verb
set+line
  set+lines
set+off
  set+offs
set-off
Printing fault
  set-offs
set off
verb
Seton
Seto Nai+kai
se+tose
set+screw
  set+screws
sett
  setts
set+tee
  set+tees
set+ter
  set+ters
set+ting
  set+tings
set+tle
  set+tles
  set+tles
set+tling
  set+tled
set+tle+able
set+tle+ment
  set+tle+ments
set+tler
  set+tlers
set+tlings
set-to
  set-tos
set to
verb
Se+tú+bal
set+up
  set+ups
set-up
adj.
set up
verb
Seurat
Se+van
Se+vas+to+pol

sev+en
  sev+ens
sev+en+fold
  sev+ens
sev+en+teen
  sev+en+teens
sev+en+teenth
  sev+en+teenths
sev+enth
  sev+enths
Seventh-Day
sev+en+ti+eth
  sev+en+ti+eths
sev+en+ty
  sev+en+ties
sev+er
  sev+ers
sev+er+ing
  sev+ered
sev+er+able
sev+er+al
  sev+er+al+ly
  sev+er+al+ty
  sev+er+al+ties
sev+er+ance
  sev+er+ances
se+vere
  se+vere+ly
  se+ver+ity
  se+ver+ities
Sev+ern
Se+ver+na+ya
  Zem+lya
Severus
Se+veso
Sévigné
Se+ville
Sèvres
sew
  sews
  sew+ing
  sewed
  sewn
sew+age
Seward
Sewell
sew+er
  sew+ers
  sew+ers
  sew+er+ing
  sew+ered
sew+er+age
  sew+ing
  sewn
sex

sexes
  sexes
  sex+ing
  sexed
sexa+genar+ian
sexa+genar+
  ians
Sexa+gesi+ma
Sexa+gesi+mas
sexa+gesi+mal
sexa+gesi+mals
sex+cen+te+nary
sex+cen+te+
  narys
sexed
sexi+ly
sexi+ness
sex+ism
sex+ist
  sex+ists
sex+less
sex+linked
sexo+logi+cal
sex+olo+gist
  sex+olo+gists
sex+ol+ogy
sex+par+tite
sext
sex+tan
sex+tant
  sex+tants
sex+tet
  sex+tets
sex+tette
  sex+tettes
sex+til+lion
  sex+til+lions
  or
sex+til+lion
sex+ton
  sex+tons
sex+tu+ple
  sex+tu+ples
sex+tup+let
  sex+tup+lets
sex+ual
sexu+al+ity
  sexu+al+ities
sex+ual+ly
sexy
sexi+er
  sexi+est
Sey+chelles
Sey+han
Seymour

Sfax
Sfor+za
sfor+zan+do
sfor+zan+dos
sfor+za+to
sfor+za+tos
sgraf+fi+to
sgraf+fi+ti
sh
Shaan+xi
Sha+ba
shab+bi+ly
shab+bi+ness
shab+by
shab+bi+er
shab+bi+est
Sha+bu+oth
Sha+bu+oths
Sha+che
shack
shacks
shacks
shack+ing
shacked
shack+le
shack+les
shack+les
shack+ling
shack+led
shack+ler
shack+lers
Shackleton
shad
shad or
shads
Shadbolt
shad+dock
shad+docks
shade
shades
shades
shad+ing
shad+ed
shade+less
shades
shadi+ly
shadi+ness
shad+ing
shad+ings
sha+doof
sha+doofs
shad+ow
shad+ows
shad+ows
shad+ow+ing

shad+owed
shadow-box
shadow-boxes
shadow-boxing
shadow-boxed
shadow-boxing
shad+ow+er
shad+ow+ers
shad+ow+graph
shad+ow+
  graphs
shad+owi+ness
shad+owy
Shadrach
shady
shadi+er
shadi+est
SHAEF
Shaffer
shaft
shafts
shafts
shaft+ing
shaft+ed
Shaftesbury
shag
shags
shags
shag+ging
shagged
shag+gi+ly
shag+gi+ness
shag+gy
shag+gi+er
shag+gi+est
sha+green
shah
shahs
shah+dom
shah+doms
Shah Jahan
Shah+ja+han+pur
Shaka
shak+able
shake
shakes
shak+ing
shook
shak+en
shake+able
shake+down
shake+downs
shake down
verb
shak+er

shak+ers
Shak+ers
Shakespeare
Shake+spear+
  ean
Shake+spear+
  eans
Shake+spear+ian
Shake+spear+
  ians
shake-up
shake-ups
shake up
verb
Shakh+ty
shaki+ly
shaki+ness
shako
shakos or
shakoes
shaky
shaki+er
shaki+est
shale
shales
shall
shal+lop
shal+lops
shal+lot
shal+lots
shal+low
shal+lows
shal+low+er
shal+low+est
shal+low+ly
shal+low+ness
sha+lom alei+
  chem
shalt
shaly
sham
shams
shams
sham+ming
shammed
sham+able
sham+an
sham+ans
sham+an+ism
sham+an+ist
sham+an+ists
Sha+mash
shama+teur
  shama+teurs
sham+ble

sham+bles
sham+bles
sham+bling
sham+bled
sham+bles
sham+bo+lic
shame
shames
shames
sham+ing
shamed
shame+able
shame+faced
shame+fac+ed+ly
shame+ful
shame+ful+ly
shame+ful+ness
shame+less
shame+less+ly
shame+less+
  ness
Shamir
sham+my
sham+mies
Sha+mo
sham+poo
sham+poos
sham+poos
sham+poo+ing
sham+pooed
sham+rock
sham+rocks
sha+mus
sha+muses
Shan+dong
shan+dy
shan+dies
Shang
shang+hai
shang+hais
shang+hais
shang+hai+ing
shang+haied
Shang+hai
Shangri-la
shank
shanks
shanks
shank+ing
shanked
Shankar
Shankara
Shankaracharya
Shankly
shanks

Shan+non
place name
Shannon
surname
shan+ny
 shan+nies
Shan+si
shan't
Shan+tou
Shan+tow
shan+tung
Shan+tung
shan+ty
 shan+ties
shanty+town
 shanty+towns
Shan+xi
shap+able
shape
 shapes
 shapes
shap+ing
shaped
shape+able
shaped
shape+less
shape+less+ness
shape+li+ness
shape+ly
 shape+li+er
 shape+li+est
shap+er
 shap+ers
shape+up
 shape+ups
shape up
verb
shar+able
shard
 shards
share
 shares
 shares
shar+ing
shared
share+crop
share+crops
share+crop+
 ping
share+cropped
share+crop+per
share+crop+
 pers
share+holder
 share+holders

share-milker
 share-milkers
shar+er
 shar+ers
share+ware
Sha+ri
sha+ria
sha+rif
 ash+raf
shark
 sharks
shark+like
shark+skin
Sha+ron
sharp
 sharps
sharp+er
sharp+est
Sharp
sharp+en
sharp+ens
sharp+en+ing
sharp+ened
sharp+en+er
sharp+en+ers
sharp+er
sharp+ers
Sharpe+ville
sharp+ish
sharp+ly
sharp+ness
sharp-set
sharp+shooter
sharp+shooters
sharp+shooting
sharp-tongued
sharp-witted
sharp-witted+ly
sharp-witted+
 ness
shas+ter
shas+tra
Shatt-al-Arab
shat+ter
shat+ters
shat+ter+ing
shat+tered
shat+ter+ing+ly
shatter+proof
shav+able
shave
 shaves
shav+ing
shaved
shav+en

shave+able
shave+ling
 shave+lings
shav+en
shav+er
 shav+ers
Sha+vian
 Sha+vians
shav+ing
 shav+ings
Sha+vu+ot
 Sha+vu+ots
Shaw
shawl
 shawls
shawm
 shawms
shay
 shays
Shcheg+lovsk
Shcher+ba+kov
she
shea
 sheas
shead+ing
 shead+ings
sheaf
sheaves
shear
 shears
shear+ing
sheared *or*
shore
Archaic,
 Austral., N.Z.
sheared *or*
 shorn
shear+er
 shear+ers
shear+legs
shear+ling
 shear+lings
shears
shear+water
 shear+waters
sheat+fish
 sheat+fish *or*
 sheat+fishes
sheath
 sheaths
sheathe
 sheathes
sheath+ing
sheathed
sheath+ing

sheath+ings
sheave
 sheaves
 sheaves
sheav+ing
sheaved
sheaves
She+ba
place name
Sheba
surname
she+bang
 she+bangs
she+bean
 she+beans
she+been
 she+beens
She+chem
shed
 sheds
 sheds
shed+ding
shed
she'd
shed+able
shed+dable
shed+der
 shed+ders
sheen
 sheens
sheeny
 sheenies
sheep
 sheep
sheep+cote
 sheep+cotes
sheep-dip
 sheep-dips
sheep+dog
 sheep+dogs
sheep+fold
 sheep+folds
sheep+ish
sheep+ish+ly
sheep+ish+ness
sheep+like
sheepo
 sheepos
sheep+shank
 sheep+shanks
sheep+skin
 sheep+skins
sheep+walk
 sheep+walks
sheer

sheers
sheers
sheer+ing
sheered
sheer+er
sheer+est
sheer+legs
sheer+ly
sheer+ness
Sheer+ness
sheet
sheets
sheets
sheet+ing
sheet+ed
sheet+ing
Shef+field
sheik
sheiks
sheik+dom
sheik+doms
sheikh
sheikhs
sheikh+dom
sheikh+doms
shei+la
shei+las
shek+el
shek+els
Shel+burne
shel+drake
shel+drakes *or*
shel+drake
shel+duck
shel+ducks *or*
shel+duck
shelf
shelves
shelf+like
shell
shells
shells
shell+ing
shelled
she'll
shel+lac
shel+lacs
shel+lacs
shel+lack+ing
shel+lacked
shell+back
shell+backs
Shelley
shell+fire
shell+fish

shell+fish *or*
shell+fishes
shell-less
shell-like
shell+proof
shell-shocked
shelly
Shel+ta
shel+ter
shel+ters
shel+ters
shel+ter+ing
shel+tered
shel+tered
shel+ter+er
shel+ter+ers
shel+tie
shel+ties
shel+ty
shel+ties
shelve
shelves
shelv+ing
shelved
shelv+er
shelv+ers
shelves
shelv+ing
Shem
she+nani+gan
she+nani+gans
Shen+si
Shen+yang
she-oak
she-oaks
She+ol
Shepard
shep+herd
shep+herds
shep+herds
shep+herd+ing
shep+herd+ed
shepherd's-purse
Shep+pey
Sheraton
sher+bet
sher+bets
Sher+borne
Sher+brooke
sherd
sherds
she+reef
ash+raf
she+ria
Sheridan

she+rif
ash+raf
sher+iff
sher+iffs
sher+iff+dom
sher+iff+doms
Sherman
Sher+pa
Sher+pas *or*
Sher+pa
Sherrington
sher+ry
sher+ries
sher+wa+ni
sher+wa+nis
Sherwood
surname
Sher+wood
place name
she's
Shet+land
Shevardnadze
shew
shews
shew+ing
shewed
shewn *or*
shewed
shew+bread
Shi+a
Shi+as
Shi+ah
Shi+ahs
shi+at+su
shib+bo+leth
shib+bo+leths
shick+ered
shied
shiel
shiels
shield
shields
shields
shield+ing
shield+ed
shiel+ing
shiel+ings
shi+er
shi+er
shi+ers
shi+est
shift
shifts
shifts
shift+ing

shift+ed
shift+er
shift+ers
shifti+ly
shifti+ness
shift+less
shift+less+ness
shifty
shifti+er
shifti+est
shi+gel+la
shi+gel+las
Shih+chia+
  chuang
Shih+kia+chwang
Shi+ism
Shi+isms
Shi+ite
Shi+ites
Shi+it+ic
Shi+jia+zhuang
Shi+ko+ku
shil+la+la
shil+la+las
shil+lelagh
shil+lelaghs
shil+ling
shil+lings
Shil+long
shilly+shalli+er
shilly+shalli+ers
shilly+shally
shilly+shallies
shilly+shallies
shilly+shally+ing
shilly+shallied
Shi+loh
shi+ly
shim
shims
shims
shim+ming
shimmed
shim+mer
shim+mers
shim+mers
shim+mer+ing
shim+mered
shim+mery
shim+my
shim+mies
shim+mies
shim+my+ing
shim+mied
Shi+mo+no+seki

shin	ship+pable	shit+ting	shod
shins	ship+per	shit+ted *or*	shoe+black
shins	ship+pers	shit	shoe+blacks
shin+ning	ship+ping	Shit+tim	shoe+horn
shinned	ship+shape	shit+ty	shoe+horns
Shi+nar	ship+worm	shit+ti+er	shoe+lace
shin+bone	ship+worms	shit+ti+est	shoe+laces
shin+bones	ship+wreck	shiv	shoe+maker
shin+dig	ship+wrecks	shivs	shoe+makers
shin+digs	ship+wrecks	Shiva	Shoemaker
shin+dy	ship+wreck+ing	shiva+ree	shoe+making
shin+dies	ship+wrecked	shiva+rees	sho+er
shine	ship+wright	shiv+er	sho+ers
shines	ship+wrights	shiv+ers	shoe+shine
shin+ing	ship+yard	shiv+ers	shoe+string
shone	ship+yards	shiv+er+ing	shoe+strings
shin+er	shi+ra+lee	shiv+ered	shoe+tree
shin+ers	shi+ra+lees	shiv+er+er	shoe+trees
shin+gle	Shi+raz	shiv+er+ers	sho+far
shin+gles	shire	shiv+er+ing	sho+fars *or*
shin+gles	shires	shiv+ery	sho+froth
shin+gling	Shi+ré	Shi+zuo+ka	sho+gun
shin+gled	shirk	Shko+dër	sho+guns
shin+gler	shirks	Shoa	sho+gun+ate
shin+glers	shirks	shoal	sho+gun+ates
shin+gly	shirk+ing	shoals	Sho+la+pur
shini+ness	shirked	shoals	Sholokhov
Shin+to	shirr	shoal+ing	shone
Shin+to+ism	shirrs	shoaled	shoo
Shin+to+ist	shirrs	shock	shoos
Shin+to+ists	shirr+ing	shocks	shoo+ing
shin+ty	shirred	shocks	shooed
shin+ties	shirr+ing	shock+ing	shoo-in
shiny	shirr+ings	shocked	shoo-ins
shini+er	shirt	shock+abil+ity	shook
shini+est	shirts	shock+able	shooks
ship	shirti+ly	shock+er	shoon
ships	shirt+ing	shock+ers	shoot
ships	shirt+ings	shock+headed	shoots
ship+ping	shirt+sleeve	shock-horror	shoots
shipped	shirt+sleeves	shock+ing	shoot+ing
ship+board	shirt-tail	shock+ing+ly	shot
ship+builder	shirt-tails	Shockley	shoot+er
ship+builders	shirt+waist	shock+proof	shoot+ers
ship+building	*U.S.*	shod	shoot+ing
ship+load	shirt+waists	shod+di+ly	shop
ship+loads	shirt+waister	shod+di+ness	shops
ship+master	shirt+waisters	shod+dy	shops
ship+masters	shirty	shod+dies	shop+ping
ship+mate	shirti+er	shod+di+er	shopped
ship+mates	shirti+est	shod+di+est	shop-floor
ship+ment	shish	shoe	*adj.*
ship+ments	shit	shoes	shop floor
ship+owner	shits	shoes	*noun*
ship+owners	shits	shoe+ing	sho+phar

sho+phars *or*
sho+phroth
shop+keeper
shop+keepers
shop+keeping
shop+lifter
shop+lifters
shop+lifting
shop+per
shop+pers
shop+ping
shop+soiled
shop+talk
shop+walker
shop+walkers
shor+an
shor+ans
shore
shores
shores
shor+ing
shored
shore+less
shore+line
shore+lines
shore+ward
shorn
short
short+er
short+est
short-acting
short+age
short+ages
short+bread
short+breads
short+cake
short+cakes
short-change
short-changes
short-changing
short-changed
short-circuit
short-circuits
short-circuit+ing
short-circuit+ed
short cir+cuit
short cir+cuits
short+coming
short+comings
short-cut
short-cuts
short-cutting
short-cut
short cut
short cuts

short-dated
short-day
short+en
short+ens
short+en+ing
short+ened
short+en+ing
short+fall
short+falls
short+hand
short-handed
short+horn
short+horns
shortie
shorties
short-list
short-lists
short-listing
short-listed
short list
noun
short-lived
short+ly
short+ness
short-order
adj.
short-range
shorts
short-sighted
short-sighted+ly
short-sighted+
ness
short-spoken
short-tempered
short-term
short-termism
short-time
short-waisted
short-wave
adj.
short wave
noun
short-winded
shorty
shorties
Shostakovich
shot
shots
shot+gun
shot+guns
shot-putter
shot-putters
shot+ten
should
shoul+der

shoul+ders
shoul+ders
shoul+der+ing
shoul+dered
should+est
shouldn't
shouldst
shout
shouts
shouts
shout+ing
shout+ed
shout+er
shout+ers
shove
shoves
shoves
shov+ing
shoved
shove-halfpen+ny
shov+el
shov+els
shov+els
shov+el+ling
or
shov+el+ing
U.S.
shov+elled *or*
shov+eled
U.S.
shov+el+er
U.S.
shov+el+ers
shovel+head
shovel+heads
shov+el+ler
shov+el+lers
shov+er
shov+ers
show
shows
shows
show+ing
showed
shown *or*
showed
show+boat
show+boats
show+bread
show+case
show+cases
show+cases
show+cas+ing
show+cased
show+down

show+downs
show+er
show+ers
show+ers
show+er+ing
show+ered
show+ery
show+girl
show+girls
showi+ly
showi+ness
show+ing
show+ings
show-jumper
show-jumpers
show+jumping
show+man
show+men
show+man+ship
show+man+
ships
shown
show-off
show-offs
show off
verb
show+piece
show+pieces
show+place
show+places
show+room
show+rooms
showy
showi+er
showi+est
shrank
shrap+nel
shred
shreds
shreds
shred+ding
shred+ded *or*
shred
shred+der
shred+ders
Shreve+port
shrew
shrews
shrewd
shrewd+er
shrewd+est
shrewd+ly
shrewd+ness
shrew+ish
Shrews+bury

shriek
 shrieks
 shrieks
 shriek+ing
 shrieked
shriek+er
 shriek+ers
shrie+val
 shriev+al+ty
 shriev+al+ties
shrift
shrike
 shrikes
shrill
 shrills
 shrill+ing
 shrilled
 shrill+er
 shrill+est
 shrill+ness
 shril+ly
shrimp
 shrimps
 shrimps
 shrimp+ing
 shrimped
shrimp+er
 shrimp+ers
shrine
 shrines
 shrines
 shrin+ing
 shrined
shrine+like
shrink
 shrinks
 shrinks
 shrink+ing
 shrank or
 shrunk
 shrunk or
 shrunk+en
shrink+able
shrink+age
 shrink+ages
shrink+er
 shrink+ers
shrink+ing
shrink-wrap
 shrink-wraps
 shrink-wrapping
 shrink-wrapped
shrive
 shrives
 shriv+ing

shrove or
 shrived
 shriv+en or
 shrived
shriv+el
 shriv+els
 shriv+el+ling
  or
 shriv+el+ing
  U.S.
 shriv+elled or
 shriv+eled
  U.S.
shriv+er
 shriv+ers
Shrop+shire
shroud
 shrouds
 shrouds
 shroud+ing
 shroud+ed
 shroud+less
shrove
Shrove+tide
 Shrove+tides
shrub
 shrubs
shrub+bery
 shrub+beries
 shrub+bi+ness
shrub+by
 shrub+bi+er
 shrub+bi+est
shrub+like
shrug
 shrugs
 shrugs
 shrug+ging
 shrugged
shrunk
 shrunk+en
shtoom
shuck
 shucks
 shucks
 shuck+ing
 shucked
 shuck+er
 shuck+ers
 shucks
shud+der
 shud+ders
 shud+ders
 shud+der+ing
 shud+dered

shud+der+ing
shud+der+ing+ly
shud+dery
shuf+fle
 shuf+fles
 shuf+fles
 shuf+fling
 shuf+fled
shuffle+board
 shuffle+boards
shuf+fler
 shuf+flers
shuf+ti
 shuf+ties
shuf+ty
 shuf+ties
Shu+fu
shun
 shuns
 shun+ning
 shunned
shunt
 shunts
 shunts
 shunt+ing
 shunt+ed
shunt-wound
shush
 shushes
 shush+ing
 shushed
Shu+shan
shut
 shuts
 shuts
 shut+ting
 shut
shut+down
 shut+downs
shut down
 verb
Shute
shut+eye
shut-in
 shut-ins
shut-off
 shut-offs
shut+out
 shut+outs
shut out
 verb
shut+ter
 shut+ters
 shut+ters
 shut+ter+ing

shut+tered
shut+ter+ing
 shut+ter+ings
shut+tle
 shut+tles
 shut+tles
 shut+tling
 shut+tled
shuttle+cock
 shuttle+cocks
shwa
 shwas
shy
 shies
 shies
 shy+ing
 shied
 shy+er or
 shi+er
 shy+est or
 shi+est
shy+er
 shy+ers
Shy+lock
 Shy+locks
shy+ly
shy+ness
shy+ster
 shy+sters
si
 sis
Si
sial
si+al+ic
Si+al+kot
Siam
sia+mang
 sia+mangs
Sia+mese
 Sia+mese
Sian
Siang
Siang+tan
sib
 sibs
Sibelius
Si+beria
Si+berian
 Si+berians
sibi+lance
sibi+lan+cy
sibi+lant
 sibi+lants
sibi+lant+ly
sibi+late

sibi+lates
sibi+lat+ing
sibi+lat+ed
sibi+la+tion
sibi+la+tions
Si+biu
sib+ling
sib+lings
sib+yl
sib+yls
sib+yl+line
sic
sics
sick+ing
sicked
Sica
sic+ca+tive
sic+ca+tives
Si+chuan
Si+ci+lia
Si+cil+ian
Si+cil+ians
si+cil+iano
si+cil+ianos
Sici+ly
sick
sicks
sick+ing
sicked
sick+er
sick+est
sick+bay
sick+bays
sick+en
sick+ens
sick+en+ing
sick+ened
sick+en+er
sick+en+ers
sick+en+ing
sick+en+ing+ly
Sickert
sickie
sickies
sick+ish
sick+le
sick+les
sickle+bill
sickle+bills
sickle-cell
sick+li+ness
sick+ly
sick+li+er
sick+li+est
sick+ness

sick+nesses
sic tran+sit glo+
ria mun+di
Sicy+on
si+dal+cea
si+dal+ceas
Siddhartha
Siddons
side
sides
sides
sid+ing
sid+ed
side+band
side+bands
side+board
side+boards
side+boards
side+burns
side+car
side+cars
side+kick
side+kicks
side+light
side+lights
side+line
side+lines
side+lines
side+lin+ing
side+lined
side+lines
side+long
si+dereal
si+dereal+ly
si+der+ite
si+dero+lite
si+dero+lites
si+der+osis
si+dero+stat
si+dero+stats
side-saddle
side-saddles
side+show
side+shows
side+slip
side+slips
side+slips
side+slip+ping
side+slipped
sides+man
sides+men
side-splitting
side+step
side+steps
side+step+ping

side+stepped
side step
noun
side+step+per
side+step+pers
side+stroke
side+strokes
side+swipe
side+swipes
side+swipes
side+swip+ing
side+swiped
side+swip+er
side+swip+ers
side+track
side+tracks
side+tracks
side+track+ing
side+tracked
side-valve
side+walk
side+walks
side+wall
side+walls
side+ward
side+wards
side+ways
side+winder
side+winders
Sidi-bel-Abbès
sid+ing
sid+ings
si+dle
si+dles
si+dling
si+dled
Sidmouth
Sidney
Si+don
Si+do+nian
Sid+ra
Siegbahn
siege
sieges
Sieg+en
Siegfried
sie+mens
SI unit
sie+mens
Siemens
surname
Si+ena
Sienkiewicz
si+en+na
si+er+ra

si+er+ras
Si+er+ra Leo+ne
Si+er+ra Le+on+
ean
Si+er+ra Le+on+
eans
Si+er+ra Ma+dre
Si+er+ra Mo+
rena
si+er+ran
si+es+ta
si+es+tas
sieve
sieves
sieves
siev+ing
sieved
sieve+like
Sieyès
sift
sifts
sift+ing
sift+ed
sift+er
sift+ers
sift+ings
sigh
sighs
sighs
sigh+ing
sighed
sigh+er
sigh+ers
sight
sights
sights
sight+ing
sight+ed
sight+able
sight+ed
sight+less
sight+less+ly
sight+less+ness
sight+li+ness
sight+ly
sight+li+er
sight+li+est
sight-read
sight-reads
sight-reading
sight-read
sight-reader
sight-readers
sight-reading
sight+screen

sight+screens	sign+er	Sikorsky	silk+worm
sight+see	sign+ers	si+lage	silk+worms
sight+sees	sig+net	sild	silky
sight+see+ing	sig+nets	silds	silki+er
sight+saw	sig+nifi+cance	si+lence	silki+est
sight+seen	sig+nifi+cances	si+lences	sill
sight+see+ing	sig+nifi+cant	si+lences	sills
sight+seer	sig+nifi+cant+ly	si+lenc+ing	sil+la+bub
sight+seers	sig+ni+fi+ca+tion	si+lenced	sil+la+bubs
Sigismund	sig+ni+fi+ca+	si+lenc+er	Sillanpää
sig+la	tions	si+lenc+ers	sil+li+ness
sig+las	sig+nifi+ca+tive	si+lene	Sillitoe
sig+ma	sig+ni+fi+er	si+lenes	sil+ly
sig+mas	sig+ni+fi+ers	si+lent	sil+lies
sig+moid	sig+ni+fy	si+lent+ly	sil+li+er
sig+moids	sig+ni+fies	si+lent+ness	sil+li+est
Sigmund	sig+ni+fy+ing	Silenus	silo
sign	sig+ni+fied	Si+lesia	silos
signs	si+gnior	Si+lesian	Si+lo+am
signs	si+gniors *or*	Si+lesians	Silone
sign+ing	si+gniori	si+lex	silt
signed	si+gnor	sil+hou+ette	silts
sign+able	si+gnors *or*	sil+hou+ettes	silts
Signac	si+gnori	sil+hou+ettes	silt+ing
sig+nal	si+gno+ra	sil+hou+ett+ing	silt+ed
sig+nals	si+gno+ras *or*	sil+hou+ett+ed	sil+ta+tion
sig+nals	si+gno+re	sili+ca	silty
sig+nal+ling *or*	si+gno+re	sili+cate	Si+lu+rian
sig+nal+ing	si+gno+ri	sili+cates	si+lu+rid
U.S.	Signorelli	si+li+ceous	si+lu+rids
sig+nalled *or*	Signoret	si+lic+ic	sil+va
sig+naled	si+gnori+na	si+lici+fi+ca+tion	sil+vas *or*
U.S.	si+gnori+nas	si+lici+fy	sil+vae
sig+nal+er	*or*	si+lici+fies	sil+van
U.S.	si+gnori+ne	si+lici+fy+ing	sil+vans
sig+nal+ers	si+gnory	si+lici+fied	Silvanus
sig+nal+ise	si+gnories	si+li+cious	sil+ver
sig+nal+ises	sign+post	sili+con	sil+vers
sig+nal+is+ing	sign+posts	sili+cone	sil+vers
sig+nal+ised	sign+posts	sili+cones	sil+ver+ing
sig+nal+ize	sign+post+ing	sili+co+sis	sil+vered
sig+nal+izes	sign+post+ed	si+li+qua	silver-eye
sig+nal+iz+ing	Sigurd	si+li+quae *or*	silver-eyes
sig+nal+ized	Sihanouk	si+li+quas	silver+fish
sig+nal+ler	sika	si+lique	silver+fish *or*
sig+nal+lers	sikas	si+liques	silver+fishes
sig+nal+ly	Si+kang	sili+quose	silver-gilt
signal+man	Sikh	sili+quous	sil+veri+ness
signal+men	Sikhs	silk	sil+ver+ing
sig+na+tory	Sikh+ism	silks	silver-plate
sig+na+tories	Si Kiang	silk-cotton	silver-plates
sig+na+ture	Si+king	silk+en	silver-plating
sig+na+tures	Sik+kim	silki+er	silver-plated
sign+board	Sik+ki+mese	silki+ness	sil+ver plate
sign+boards	Sikorski	silk+like	*noun*

silver+side
silver+smith
silver+smiths
silver+smithing
silver+ware
silver+weed
silver+weeds
sil+very
sil+vi+cul+tur+al
sil+vi+cul+ture
sil+vi+cul+tur+ist
sil+vi+cul+tur+
  ists
sima
Sim+birsk
Simenon
Simeon
Simeon Stylites
Sim+fero+pol
sim+ian
  sim+ians
simi+lar
simi+lar+ity
  simi+lar+ities
simi+lar+ly
simi+le
  simi+les
si+mili+tude
  si+mili+tudes
Sim+la
sim+mer
  sim+mers
  sim+mers
  sim+mer+ing
  sim+mered
sim+nel
Simon
Simonides
simon-pure
si+mo+ny
si+moom
  si+mooms
si+moon
  si+moons
sim+pa+ti+co
sim+per
  sim+pers
  sim+pers
  sim+per+ing
  sim+pered
  sim+per+ing
  sim+per+ing+ly
sim+ple
  sim+ples
  sim+pler

sim+plest
simple-hearted
simple-minded
simple-minded+ly
simple-minded+
  ness
sim+ple+ton
  sim+ple+tons
sim+plic+ity
  sim+plic+ities
sim+pli+fi+ca+
  tion
  sim+pli+fi+ca+
    tions
sim+pli+fy
  sim+pli+fies
  sim+pli+fy+ing
  sim+pli+fied
sim+plism
sim+plis+tic
sim+plis+ti+cal+
  ly
Sim+plon
simp+ly
Simpson
surname
Simp+son
place name
simu+la+crum
  simu+la+cra
simu+late
  simu+lates
  simu+lat+ing
  simu+lat+ed
  simu+lated
simu+la+tion
  simu+la+tions
simu+la+tive
simu+la+tor
  simu+la+tors
sim+ul+cast
  sim+ul+casts
  sim+ul+casts
  sim+ul+cast+ing
  sim+ul+cast+ed
sim+ul+ta+neity
sim+ul+ta+neous
sim+ul+ta+neous+
  ly
sim+ul+ta+neous+
  ness
sin
  sins
  sins
  sin+ning

sinned
Si+nai
Si+na+ic
Si+na+it+ic
Si+na+loa
sin+an+thro+pus
  sin+an+thro+
    puses
Sinatra
since
sin+cere
sin+cere+ly
sin+cere+ness
sin+cer+ity
sin+cipi+tal
sin+ci+put
  sin+ci+puts *or*
  sin+cipi+ta
Sinclair
Sind
sine
  sines
sine
prep.
si+necure
  si+necures
si+necur+ism
si+necur+ist
  si+necur+ists
sine die
sine qua non
sin+ew
  sin+ews
sin+ewi+ness
sin+ew+less
sin+ewy
sin+fo+nia
  sin+fo+nie
sin+fo+niet+ta
  sin+fo+niet+tas
sin+ful
sin+ful+ly
sin+ful+ness
sing
  sings
  sing+ing
  sang
  sung
sing+able
Sin+ga+pore
Sin+ga+po+rean
  Sin+ga+po+
    reans
singe
  singes

singes
singe+ing
singed
sing+er
sing+ers
Singer
Singh
Sin+gha+lese
Sin+ha+leses
  or
Sin+gha+lese
sing+ing
sin+gle
sin+gles
sin+gles
sin+gling
sin+gled
single-acting
single-breasted
single-decker
single-deckers
single-end
single-ends
single-foot
single-foots
single-footing
single-footed
single-handed
single-handed+ly
single-handed+
  ness
single-lens
single-minded
single-minded+ly
single-minded+
  ness
sin+gle+ness
sin+gles
single-sex
single+stick
  single+sticks
sin+glet
  sin+glets
sin+gle+ton
  sin+gle+tons
single-track
single+tree
  single+trees
sin+gly
sing+song
  sing+songs
sin+gu+lar
  sin+gu+lars
sin+gu+lari+sa+
  tion

sin+gu+lar+ise
sin+gu+lar+ises
sin+gu+lar+is+ing
sin+gu+lar+ised
sin+gu+lar+ity
sin+gu+lar+ities
sin+gu+lari+za+tion
sin+gu+lar+ize
sin+gu+lar+izes
sin+gu+lar+iz+ing
sin+gu+lar+ized
sin+gu+lar+ly
sin+gul+tus
sin+gul+tuses
sinh
Sin+ha+lese
  Sin+ha+leses
  or
  Sin+ha+lese
Si+ning
sin+is+ter
sin+is+ter+ly
sin+is+ter+ness
sin+is+tral
sin+is+tral+ly
sin+is+tror+sal
sin+is+trorse
Si+nit+ic
sink
  sinks
  sink+ing
  sank *or*
  sunk
  sunk *or*
  sunk+en
sink+able
sink+er
  sink+ers
sink+hole
  sink+holes
sink+ing
sin+less
sin+less+ly
sin+less+ness
sin+ner
  sin+ners
Sinn Féin
Si+no+logi+cal
Si+nolo+gist
  Si+nolo+gists
Si+no+logue
  Si+no+logues

Si+nol+ogy
Sino-Tibetan
sin+se+mil+la
sin+ter
  sin+ters
  sin+ters
  sin+ter+ing
  sin+tered
Sint Maar+ten
Sin+tra
sinu+ate
sinu+ate+ly
sinu+os+ity
sinu+os+ities
sinu+ous
sinu+ous+ly
si+nus
si+nuses
si+nusi+tis
si+nus+oid
  si+nus+oids
si+nusoi+dal
Sion
Siouan
Sioux
Sioux
sip
sips
sips
sip+ping
sipped
si+phon
si+phons
si+phons
si+phon+ing
si+phoned
si+phon+al
si+phon+ic
si+pho+no+phore
si+pho+no+phores
Si+ple
sip+per
sip+pers
sip+pet
sip+pets
sir
sirs
Sir
Si+ra+cu+sa
Siraj-ud-daula
sir+dar
  sir+dars
sire
sires

sires
sir+ing
sired
si+ren
  si+rens
si+renian
  si+renians
Si+ret
Sir+ius
sir+loin
  sir+loins
si+roc+co
  si+roc+cos
si+ro+nise
  si+ro+nises
si+ro+nis+ing
  si+ro+nised
si+ro+nize
  si+ro+nizes
si+ro+niz+ing
  si+ro+nized
si+ro+set
sir+rah
sir+ree
sir+up
  sir+ups
sis
  sises
si+sal
  si+sals
Sisera
sis+kin
  sis+kins
Sisley
sis+sy
  sis+sies
sis+ter
  sis+ters
sis+ter+hood
  sis+ter+hoods
sister-in-law
  sisters-in-law
sis+ter+li+ness
sis+ter+ly
Sis+tine
sis+trum
sis+tra
Sisy+phean
Sisyphus
sit
  sits
  sit+ting
  sat
si+tar
  si+tars

si+tar+ist
  si+tar+ists
sit+com
  sit+coms
sit-down
  noun, adj.
  sit-downs
sit down
  verb
site
  sites
  sites
sit+ing
sit+ed
sith
sit-in
  sit-ins
sit+ka
Sit+ka
sit+kam+er
  sit+kam+ers
Si+tsang
sit+ter
  sit+ters
Sitter
sit+ting
  sit+tings
situ+ate
  situ+ates
  situ+at+ing
  situ+at+ed
situa+tion
  situa+tions
situa+tion+al
sit-up
  sit-ups
sit up
  verb
Sitwell
sitz
Siva
Si+va+ism
Si+vas
six
  sixes
Six
six+er
  six+ers
six+fold
six+mo
  six+mos
six+pence
  six+pences
six-shooter
  six-shooters

sixte	skate+board	*U.S.*	skiff
six+teen	skate+boards	sker+rick	skiffs
six+teens	skate+boards	sker+ricks	skif+fle
six+teen+mo	skate+board+	sker+ry	ski+ing
six+teen+mos	ing	sker+ries	ski+jor+er
six+teenth	skate+board+ed	sketch	ski+jor+ers
six+teenths	skate+board+er	sketches	ski+jor+ing
sixth	skate+board+	sketches	ski-jump
sixths	ers	sketch+ing	ski-jumps
sixth-form	skate+board+ing	sketched	ski-jumping
sixth-former	skat+er	sketch+book	ski-jumped
sixth-formers	skat+ers	sketch+books	ski jump
six+ti+eth	Skaw	sketch+er	*noun*
six+ti+eths	skean-dhu	sketch+ers	Skik+da
six+ty	skean-dhus	sketchi+ly	skil+ful
six+ties	ske+dad+dle	sketchi+ness	skil+ful+ly
sixty-fourmo	ske+dad+dles	sketchy	skill
sixty-fourmos	ske+dad+dles	sketchi+er	skills
sixty-nine	ske+dad+dling	sketchi+est	skilled
sixty-nines	ske+dad+dled	skew	skil+less
siz+able	skeet	skews	skil+let
siz+ably	skein	skews	skil+lets
size	skeins	skew+ing	skill+ful
sizes	skel+etal	skewed	*U.S.*
sizes	skel+eton	skew+back	skill+ful+ly
siz+ing	skel+etons	skew+backs	*U.S.*
sized	skel+eton+ise	skew+bald	skill-less
size+able	skel+eton+ises	skew+balds	skil+ly
size+ably	skel+eton+is+	skew+er	skil+lies
sized	ing	skew+ers	skim
siz+er	skel+eton+ised	skew+ers	skims
siz+ers	skel+eton+ize	skew+er+ing	skims
siz+zle	skel+eton+izes	skew+ered	skim+ming
siz+zles	skel+eton+iz+	skew+ness	skimmed
siz+zles	ing	skew+whiff	skim+mer
siz+zling	skel+eton+ized	ski	skim+mers
siz+zled	skeleton-like	skis *or*	skim+mia
siz+zler	Skel+mers+dale	ski	skim+mias
siz+zlers	Skelton	skis	skimp
siz+zling	Skelton+ic	ski+ing	skimps
sjam+bok	skep	skied *or*	skimp+ing
sjam+boks	skeps	ski'd	skimped
ska	skep+tic	ski+bob	skimpi+ly
Ska+gen	*U.S.*	ski+bobs	skimpi+ness
Skag+er+rak	skep+tics	ski+bob+ber	skimpy
skald	Skep+tic	ski+bob+bers	skimpi+er
skalds	*U.S.*	skid	skimpi+est
skald+ic	Skep+tics	skids	skin
Skara Brae	skep+ti+cal	skids	skins
skat	*U.S.*	skid+ding	skins
skate	skep+ti+cal+ly	skid+ded	skin+ning
skates	*U.S.*	skied	skinned
skates	skep+ti+cism	Ski+en	skin-deep
skat+ing	*U.S.*	ski+er	skin-diver
skat+ed	Skep+ti+cism	ski+ers	skin-divers

skin+flint
skin+flints
skin+ful
skin+fuls
skin+head
skin+heads
skink
skinks
skin+less
skin+like
skinned
Skinner
skin+ny
skin+ni+er
skin+ni+est
skint
skin+tight
skip
skips
skips
skip+ping
skipped
skip+jack
skip+jack *or*
skip+jacks
ski+plane
ski+planes
skip+per
skip+pers
skip+pers
skip+per+ing
skip+pered
skip+ping
skipping-rope
skipping-ropes
Skip+ton
skirl
skirls
skirls
skirl+ing
skirled
skir+mish
skir+mishes
skir+mishes
skir+mish+ing
skir+mished
skir+mish+er
skir+mish+ers
Skí+ros
skirt
skirts
skirts
skirt+ing
skirt+ed
skirt+ed

skirt+ing
skirt+ings
skirt+ings
skit
skits
skite
skites
skites
skit+ing
skit+ed
skit+ter
skit+ters
skit+ter+ing
skit+tered
skit+tish
skit+tish+ly
skit+tish+ness
skit+tle
skit+tles
skive
skives
skiv+ing
skived
skiv+er
skiv+ers
skiv+vy
skiv+vies
skiv+vies
skiv+vy+ing
skiv+vied
skoal
skol
Skop+je
Skryabin
skua
skuas
skul+dug+gery
skulk
skulks
skulks
skulk+ing
skulked
skulk+er
skulk+ers
skull
skulls
skull+cap
skull+caps
skull+dug+gery
U.S.
skunk
skunk *or*
skunks
sky
skies

skies
sky+ing
skied
sky-blue
adj.
sky+dive
sky+dives
sky+div+ing
sky+dived *or*
sky+dove
U.S.
sky+dived
sky+div+er
sky+div+ers
sky+div+ing
Skye
sky-high
sky+jack
sky+jacks
sky+jack+ing
sky+jacked
sky+lark
sky+larks
sky+larks
sky+lark+ing
sky+larked
sky+light
sky+lights
sky+line
sky+rocket
sky+rockets
sky+rockets
sky+rocket+ing
sky+rocket+ed
Sky+ros
sky+sail
sky+sails
sky+scraper
sky+scrapers
sky+ward
sky+writer
sky+writers
sky+writing
slab
slabs
slabs
slab+bing
slabbed
slab+ber
slab+bers
slab+ber+ing
slab+bered
slack
slacks
slacks

slack+ing
slacked
slack+er
slack+est
slack+en
slack+ens
slack+en+ing
slack+ened
slack+er
slack+ers
slack+ly
slack+ness
slacks
slag
slags
slags
slag+ging
slagged
slag+ging
slag+gings
slag+gy
slain
slak+able
slake
slakes
slak+ing
slaked
slake+able
sla+lom
sla+loms
slam
slams
slams
slam+ming
slammed
slam+mer
slam+mers
slan+der
slan+ders
slan+ders
slan+der+ing
slan+dered
slan+der+er
slan+der+ers
slan+der+ous
slang
slangs
slangs
slang+ing
slanged
slangi+ly
slangi+ness
slangy
slant
slants

slants	slaughter+	sleds	sleeve
slant+ing	houses	sled+ing	sleeves
slant+ed	slaugh+ter+ous	sled+ed	sleeves
slant+ing	Slav	sledge	sleev+ing
slant+ways	Slavs	sledges	sleeved
slant+wise	slave	sledges	sleeve+less
slap	slaves	sledg+ing	sleeve+like
slaps	slaves	sledged	sleev+ing
slaps	slav+ing	sledge+hammer	sleigh
slap+ping	slaved	sledge+	sleighs
slapped	slave-driver	hammers	sleighs
slap+dash	slave-drivers	sledg+er	sleigh+ing
slap+happy	slave+holder	sledg+ers	sleighed
slap+happier	slave+holders	sleek	sleight
slap+happiest	slave+holding	sleeks	slen+der
slap+stick	slav+er	sleek+ing	slen+der+ise
slap+sticks	slav+ers	sleeked	slen+der+ises
slap-up	slav+ers	sleek+er	slen+der+is+ing
slash	slav+er+ing	sleek+est	slen+der+ised
slashes	slav+ered	sleek+ly	slen+der+ize
slashes	slav+er+er	sleek+ness	slen+der+izes
slash+ing	slav+er+ers	sleeky	slen+der+iz+ing
slashed	slav+ery	sleep	slen+der+ized
slash+er	slave-trader	sleeps	slen+der+ly
slash+ers	slave-traders	sleeps	slen+der+ness
slash+ing	slave-trading	sleep+ing	slept
Śląsk	slav+ey	slept	Sles+vig
slat	slav+eys	sleep+er	sleuth
slats	Slav+ic	sleep+ers	sleuths
slate	Slav+ics	sleepi+ly	sleuths
slates	slav+ish	sleepi+ness	sleuth+ing
slates	slav+ish+ly	sleep+ing	sleuthed
slat+ing	Slav+kov	sleep+less	sleuth+hound
slat+ed	Sla+vo+nia	sleep+less+ly	sleuth+hounds
slat+er	Sla+vo+nian	sleep+less+ness	slew
slat+ers	Sla+vo+nians	sleep-out	slews
slath+er	Sla+von+ic	sleep-outs	slews
slath+ers	Sla+von+ics	sleep out	slew+ing
slat+ing	slaw	*verb*	slewed
slat+ings	slay	sleep+walk	Slezs+ko
slat+tern	slays	sleep+walks	slice
slat+terns	slay+ing	sleep+walk+ing	slices
slat+tern+li+ness	slew	sleep+walked	slices
slat+tern+ly	slain	sleep+walk+er	slic+ing
slaty	slay+er	sleep+walk+ers	sliced
slati+er	slay+ers	sleep+walk+ing	slice+able
slati+est	sleaze	sleepy	slic+er
slaugh+ter	slea+zi+ly	sleepi+er	slic+ers
slaugh+ters	slea+zi+ness	sleepi+est	slick
slaugh+ters	slea+zy	sleet	slicks
slaugh+ter+ing	slea+zi+er	sleets	slicks
slaugh+tered	slea+zi+est	sleets	slick+ing
slaugh+ter+er	sled	sleet+ing	slicked
slaugh+ter+ers	*U.S.*	sleet+ed	slick+er
slaughter+house	sleds	sleety	slick+est

slick+er
slick+ers
slick+ly
slick+ness
slid+able
slid+den
slide
 slides
 slid+ing
 slid
 slid *or*
 slid+den
slid+er
slid+ers
slid+ing
sli+er
sli+est
slight
 slights
 slights
 slight+ing
 slight+ed
 slight+er
 slight+est
slight+ing+ly
slight+ly
slight+ness
Sli+go
sli+ly
slim
 slim+mer
 slim+mest
Slim
slime
 slimes
 slimes
 slim+ing
 slimed
slim+line
slim+mer
slim+mers
slim+ming
slim+ness
slimy
 slimi+er
 slimi+est
sling
 slings
 slings
 sling+ing
 slung
sling+back
sling+backs
sling+er
sling+ers

sling+shot
 sling+shots
slink
 slinks
 slink+ing
 slunk
slinki+ly
slinki+ness
slinky
 slinki+er
 slinki+est
slip
 slips
 slips
 slip+ping
 slipped
slip+case
 slip+cases
slip+cover
 slip+covers
slipe
 slipes
slip+knot
 slip+knots
slip+less
slip-on
 slip-ons
slip+over
 slip+overs
slip+page
 slip+pages
slip+per
 slip+pers
 slip+pered
 slip+peri+ness
slipper+wort
slip+pery
slip+pi+ness
slip+py
slip+pi+er
slip+pi+est
slip+shod
slip+stream
 slip+streams
slip-up
 slip-ups
slip up
 verb
slip+ware
slip+way
slip+ways
slit
 slits
slit+ting
slit

slith+er
 slith+ers
 slith+ers
 slith+er+ing
 slith+ered
 slith+ery
slit+ter
 slit+ters
sliv+er
 sliv+ers
 sliv+ers
 sliv+er+ing
 sliv+ered
Sloan
Sloane
 Sloanes
slob
 slobs
slob+ber
 slob+bers
 slob+ber+ing
 slob+bered
 slob+ber+er
 slob+ber+ers
slob+bery
sloe
 sloes
sloe-eyed
slog
 slogs
 slogs
 slog+ging
 slogged
slo+gan
 slo+gans
slog+ger
 slog+gers
slo-mo
 slo-mos
sloop
 sloops
sloot
 sloots
slop
 slops
 slops
 slop+ping
 slopped
slope
 slopes
 slopes
 slop+ing
 sloped
slop+er
 slop+ers

slop+ing
slop+pi+ly
slop+pi+ness
slop+py
 slop+pi+er
 slop+pi+est
slosh
 sloshes
 sloshes
 slosh+ing
 sloshed
sloshy
slot
 slots
 slots
slot+ting
slot+ted
sloth
 sloths
sloth+ful
sloth+ful+ly
sloth+ful+ness
slot+ter
 slot+ters
slouch
 slouches
 slouches
 slouch+ing
 slouched
 slouch+ing
slough
 sloughs
 sloughs
 slough+ing
 sloughed
Slough
sloughy
Slo+vak
 Slo+vaks
Slo+vakia
Slo+vak+ian
 Slo+vak+ians
slov+en
 slov+ens
Slo+vene
 Slo+venes
Slo+venia
Slo+venian
 Slo+venians
slov+en+li+ness
slov+en+ly
slow
 slows
 slow+ing

slowed
slow+er
slow+est
slow+coach
slow+coaches
slow+ly
slow-mo
slow-mos
slow-motion
adj.
slow mo+tion
noun
slow+ness
slow+worm
slow+worms
slub
slubs
slubs
slub+bing
slubbed
sludge
sludges
sludgy
slue
slues
slues
slue+ing
slued
slug
slugs
slugs
slug+ging
slugged
slug+gard
slug+gards
slug+gard+ly
slug+gish
slug+gish+ly
slug+gish+ness
sluice
sluices
sluices
sluic+ing
sluiced
sluice+gate
sluice+gates
sluice+like
slum
slums
slums
slum+ming
slummed
slum+ber
slum+bers
slum+bers

slum+ber+ing
slum+bered
slum+ber+er
slum+ber+ers
slum+ber+ous
slum+ber+ous+ly
slum+ber+ous+
ness
slum+my
slump
slumps
slumps
slump+ing
slumped
slung
slunk
slur
slurs
slurs
slur+ring
slurred
slurp
slurps
slurps
slurp+ing
slurped
slur+ry
slur+ries
slush
slushes
slushes
slush+ing
slushed
slushi+ness
slushy
slushi+er
slushi+est
slut
sluts
Sluter
slut+tish
slut+tish+ness
sly
sly+er *or*
sli+er
sly+est *or*
sli+est
sly+ly
sly+ness
slype
slypes
smack
smacks
smacks
smack+ing

smacked
smack+er
smack+ers
small
smalls
small+er
small+est
small+holder
small+holders
small+holding
small+holdings
small+ish
small-minded
small-minded+ly
small-minded+
ness
small+ness
small+pox
small-scale
small-time
small-timer
small-timers
smalt
smarm
smarms
smarm+ing
smarmed
smarmi+ly
smarmi+ness
smarmy
smarmi+er
smarmi+est
smart
smarts
smarts
smart+ing
smart+ed
smart+er
smart+est
Smart
smart-aleck
adj.
smart al+eck
noun
smart-alecky
smart+en
smart+ens
smart+en+ing
smart+ened
smart+ly
smart+ness
smarts
smash
smashes
smashes

smash+ing
smashed
smash+able
smash-and-grab
smashed
smash+er
smash+ers
smash+ing
smash-up
smash-ups
smash up
verb
smat+ter
smat+ters
smat+ters
smat+ter+ing
smat+tered
smat+ter+er
smat+ter+ers
smat+ter+ing
smat+ter+ings
smear
smears
smears
smear+ing
smeared
smeari+ly
smeari+ness
smeary
smec+tic
smeg+ma
smell
smells
smells
smell+ing
smelt *or*
smelled
smell+er
smell+ers
smelli+ness
smell+ing
smelly
smelli+er
smelli+est
smelt
smelt *or*
smelts
smelts
smelt+ing
smelt+ed
smel+ter
smel+ters
Smetana
smew
smews

smid+gen	smogs	smooth+ing	smuts
smid+gens	smog+gy	smoothed	smuts
smid+gin	smok+able	smooth+er	smut+ting
smid+gins	smoke	smooth+est	smut+ted
smi+lax	smokes	smooth+bore	smutch
smile	smokes	smooth+bores	smutches
smiles	smok+ing	smooth+bored	smutches
smiles	smoked	smooth+en	smutch+ing
smil+ing	Smoke	smooth+ens	smutched
smiled	smoke+able	smooth+en+ing	smutchy
smil+er	smoke-dried	smooth+ened	Smuts
smil+ers	smoke+ho	smooth+er	smut+ti+ly
Smiles	smoke+hos	smooth+ers	smut+ti+ness
smil+ing	smoke+house	smoothie	smut+ty
smil+ing+ly	smoke+houses	smoothies	smut+ti+er
smirch	smoke+less	smooth+ly	smut+ti+est
smirches	smok+er	smooth+ness	Smyr+na
smirches	smok+ers	smooth-spoken	snack
smirch+ing	smoke+stack	smooth-tongued	snacks
smirched	smoke+stacks	smoothy	snacks
smirk	smoki+ly	smoothies	snack+ing
smirks	smoki+ness	smor+gas+bord	snacked
smirks	smok+ing	smote	snaf+fle
smirk+ing	smo+ko	smoth+er	snaf+fles
smirked	smo+kos	smoth+ers	snaf+fles
smirk+er	smoky	smoth+ers	snaf+fling
smirk+ers	smoki+er	smoth+er+ing	snaf+fled
smirk+ing	smoki+est	smoth+ered	sna+fu
smirk+ing+ly	Smoky	smoth+ery	sna+fues
smite	smol+der	smoul+der	sna+fu+ing
smites	*U.S.*	smoul+ders	sna+fued
smit+ing	smol+ders	smoul+ders	snag
smote	smol+ders	smoul+der+ing	snags
smit+ten *or*	smol+ders	smoul+dered	snags
smit	smol+der+ing	smudge	snag+ging
smit+er	smol+dered	smudges	snagged
smit+ers	Smo+lensk	smudges	snaggle+tooth
smith	Smollett	smudg+ing	snaggle+teeth
smiths	smolt	smudged	snag+gy
Smith	smolts	smudgi+ly	snail
smith+er+eens	smooch	smudgi+ness	snails
smith+ery	smooches	smudgy	snail-like
smith+eries	smooches	smug	snake
Smithson	smooch+ing	smug+ger	snakes
smithy	smooched	smug+gest	snake+bird
smithies	smoodge	smug+gle	snake+birds
smit+ten	smoodges	smug+gles	snake+bite
smock	smoodg+ing	smug+gling	snake+bites
smocks	smoodged	smug+gled	snake+like
smocks	smooge	smug+gler	snake+root
smock+ing	smooges	smug+glers	snake+roots
smocked	smoog+ing	smug+gling	snake+skin
smock+ing	smooged	smug+ly	snake+skins
smock+like	smooth	smug+ness	snaki+ly
smog	smooths	smut	snaki+ness
	smooths		

snaky
 snaki+er
 snaki+est
snap
 snaps
 snaps
 snap+ping
 snapped
 snap+dragon
 snap+dragons
snap+less
snap+per
 snap+per *or*
 snap+pers
snap+pi+ly
snap+pi+ness
snap+ping
snap+py
 snap+pi+er
 snap+pi+est
snap+shot
 snap+shots
snare
 snares
 snares
 snar+ing
 snared
snar+er
 snar+ers
snarl
 snarls
 snarls
 snarl+ing
 snarled
snarl+er
 snarl+ers
snarl+ing
snarl-up
 snarl-ups
snarly
snatch
 snatches
 snatches
 snatch+ing
 snatched
snatch+er
 snatch+ers
snatchi+ly
snatchy
 snatchi+er
 snatchi+est
snaz+zi+ly
snaz+zi+ness
snaz+zy
 snaz+zi+er

snaz+zi+est
sneak
 sneaks
 sneaks
 sneak+ing
 sneaked
 sneak+ers
 sneaki+ly
 sneaki+ness
 sneak+ing
 sneak+ing+ly
sneaky
 sneaki+er
 sneaki+est
sneer
 sneers
 sneers
 sneer+ing
 sneered
 sneer+er
 sneer+ers
 sneer+ing
sneeze
 sneezes
 sneezes
 sneez+ing
 sneezed
 sneez+er
 sneez+ers
sneeze+wood
 sneeze+woods
 sneeze+wort
 sneeze+worts
sneezy
snick
 snicks
 snicks
 snick+ing
 snicked
 snick+er
 snick+ers
 snick+ers
 snick+er+ing
 snick+ered
snide
 snid+er
 snid+est
 snide+ly
 snide+ness
sniff
 sniffs
 sniffs
 sniff+ing
 sniffed
 sniff+er

sniff+ers
sniffi+ly
sniffi+ness
sniff+ing
snif+fle
 snif+fles
 snif+fles
 snif+fling
 snif+fled
snif+fler
 snif+flers
 snif+fles
snif+fly
snif+fy
 snif+fi+er
 snif+fi+est
snif+ter
 snif+ters
snig
 snigs
snig+ging
 snigged
snig+ger
 snig+gers
 snig+gers
 snig+ger+ing
 snig+gered
snig+ging
snip
 snips
 snips
snip+ping
 snipped
snipe
 snipe *or*
 snipes
 snipes
 snip+ing
 sniped
snipe+fish
 snipe+fish *or*
 snipe+fishes
snip+er
 snip+ers
snip+pet
 snip+pets
snip+peti+ness
snip+pety
 snips
snitch
 snitches
 snitches
 snitch+ing
 snitched
 snitchy

snitchi+er
snitchi+est
sniv+el
 sniv+els
 sniv+els
sniv+el+ling *or*
sniv+el+ing
 U.S.
sniv+elled *or*
sniv+eled
 U.S.
sniv+el+ler
 sniv+el+lers
 sniv+el+ling
snob
 snobs
snob+bery
snob+bish
snob+bish+ly
SNOBOL
Sno-Cat
 Trademark
 Sno-Cats
snoek
 snoeks
snog
 snogs
 snogs
snog+ging
 snogged
snood
 snoods
snook
 snook *or*
 snooks
snook+er
 snook+ers
 snook+ers
 snook+er+ing
 snook+ered
snoop
 snoops
 snoops
 snoop+ing
 snooped
snoop+er
 snoop+ers
snooper+scope
 snooper+scopes
snoopy
snoot
 snoots
snooti+ly
snooti+ness
snooty

snooti+er
snooti+est
snooze
  snoozes
  snoozes
  snooz+ing
  snoozed
snooz+er
  snooz+ers
snoozy
snore
  snores
  snores
  snor+ing
  snored
snor+er
  snor+ers
snor+kel
  snor+kels
  snor+kels
  snor+kel+ling
    or
  snor+kel+ing
  U.S.
  snor+kelled *or*
  snor+keled
  U.S.
Snorri Sturluson
snort
  snorts
  snorts
  snort+ing
  snort+ed
snort+er
  snort+ers
snort+ing
snort+ing+ly
snot
  snots
snot+ti+ly
snot+ti+ness
snot+ty
  snot+ti+er
  snot+ti+est
snout
  snouts
snout+ed
snout+less
snout+like
snow
  snows
  snows
  snow+ing
  snowed
Snow

snow+ball
snow+balls
snow+balls
snow+ball+ing
snow+balled
snow+berry
snow+berries
snow-blind
snow+blower
snow+blowers
snow+board
snow+boards
snow+board+ing
snow+bound
snow+cap
snow+caps
snow+capped
Snow+don
  mountain
Snowdon
  surname
Snow+donia
snow+drift
snow+drifts
snow+drop
snow+drops
snow+fall
snow+falls
snow+field
snow+fields
snow+flake
snow+flakes
snowi+ly
snowi+ness
snow-in-summer
snow+less
snow+like
snow+man
snow+men
snow+mobile
snow+mobiles
snow+plough
snow+ploughs
snow+shoe
snow+shoes
snow+sho+er
snow+sho+ers
snow+storm
snow+storms
snow-white
snowy
snowi+er
snowi+est
snub
  snubs

snubs
snub+bing
snubbed
snub+ber
  snub+bers
snub-nosed
snuff
  snuffs
  snuffs
  snuff+ing
  snuffed
snuff+box
  snuff+boxes
snuff-dipping
snuff+er
  snuff+ers
snuffi+ness
snuf+fle
  snuf+fles
  snuf+fles
  snuf+fling
  snuf+fled
  snuf+fles
snuf+fly
snuffy
snuffi+er
snuffi+est
snug
  snugs
  snugs
  snug+ging
  snugged
snug+ger
snug+gest
snug+gery
  snug+geries
snug+gle
  snug+gles
  snug+gles
  snug+gling
  snug+gled
snug+ly
snug+ness
so
  sos
soak
  soaks
  soaks
  soak+ing
  soaked
soak+away
  soak+aways
soak+er
  soak+ers

  soak+ing
  soak+ings
so-and-so
  so-and-sos
Soane
soap
  soaps
  soaps
  soap+ing
  soaped
soap+berry
  soap+berries
soap+box
  soap+boxes
soapi+ly
soapi+ness
soap+less
soap+like
soap+stone
soap+suds
soap+sudsy
soap+wort
  soap+worts
soapy
  soapi+er
  soapi+est
soar
  soars
  soar+ing
  soared
soar+er
  soar+ers
Soares
sob
  sobs
  sobs
  sob+bing
  sobbed
so+ber
  so+bers
  so+ber+ing
  so+bered
so+ber+er
so+ber+est
so+ber+ing
so+ber+ly
Sobers
so+bri+ety
so+bri+quet
  so+bri+quets
soca
soc+age
so-called
soc+cer
So+che

So-ch'e
So+chi
so+cia+bil+ity
so+cia+ble
so+cia+bly
so+cial
 so+cials
so+cial+ise
 so+cial+ises
 so+cial+is+ing
 so+cial+ised
so+cial+ism
so+cial+ist
 so+cial+ists
so+cial+is+tic
so+cial+ite
 so+cial+ites
so+ci+al+ity
 so+ci+al+ities
so+cial+ize
 so+cial+izes
 so+cial+iz+ing
 so+cial+ized
so+cial+ly
so+ci+etal
so+ci+etal+ly
so+ci+ety
 so+ci+eties
so+cio+biolo+gy
so+cio+eco+nom+
 ic
so+cio+eco+
 nomi+cal+ly
so+cio+lin+guist
 so+cio+lin+
 guists
so+cio+lin+guis+
 tics
so+cio+logi+cal
so+ci+olo+gist
 so+ci+olo+gists
so+ci+ol+ogy
so+cio+met+ric
so+ci+om+etrist
 so+ci+om+
 etrists
so+ci+om+etry
so+cio+path
 so+cio+paths
so+cio+path+ic
so+ci+opa+thy
so+cio+po+liti+
 cal
sock
 socks

socks
sock+ing
socked
sock+et
 sock+ets
 sock+ets
 sock+et+ing
 sock+et+ed
sock+eye
 sock+eyes
so+cle
 so+cles
So+co+tra
Socrates
So+crat+ic
So+crati+cal+ly
So+crati+cism
 So+crati+cisms
Soc+ra+tist
 Soc+ra+tists
sod
 sods
 sods
sod+ding
sod+ded
soda
 sodas
so+dal+ity
 so+dal+ities
so+da+mide
sod+den
sod+dens
sod+den+ing
sod+dened
sod+den+ness
sod+ding
Soddy
so+dium
Sod+om
Sod+oms
sodo+mite
 sodo+mites
sodo+my
Soekarno
Soem+ba
Soem+ba+wa
Soe+ra+ba+ja
so+ever
sofa
 sofas
sof+fit
 sof+fits
So+fia
soft
 softs

soft+er
soft+est
sof+ta
 sof+tas
soft+ball
 soft+balls
soft-boiled
soft-core
soft-cover
sof+ten
 sof+tens
sof+ten+ing
sof+tened
sof+ten+er
 sof+ten+ers
sof+ten+ing
soft-headed
soft-headed+
 ness
soft+hearted
soft+hearted+ly
soft+hearted+
 ness
softie
 softies
soft+ly
soft+ness
soft-pedal
 soft-pedals
 soft-pedalling
  or
 soft-pedaling
  U.S.
 soft-pedalled
  or
 soft-pedaled
  U.S.
softs
soft-soap
 soft-soaps
 soft-soaping
 soft-soaped
soft soap
 noun
soft-spoken
soft+ware
soft+wood
 soft+woods
softy
 softies
SOGAT
Sog+dian
 Sog+dians
Sog+dia+na
sog+gi+ly

sog+gi+ness
sog+gy
sog+gi+er
sog+gi+est
soh
 sohs
Soho
soi-disant
soi+gné
soi+gnée
soil
 soils
 soils
soil+ing
soiled
soi+ree
 soi+rees
Sois+sons
soixante-neuf
so+journ
 so+journs
 so+journs
so+journ+ing
so+journed
so+journ+er
 so+journ+ers
soke
 sokes
So+ko+to
So+ko+tra
sol
 sols
Sol
sola
sol+ace
 sol+aces
 sol+aces
sol+ac+ing
sol+aced
sol+ac+er
 sol+ac+ers
so+lan
 so+lans
sola+na+ceous
so+la+num
 so+la+nums
so+lar
so+lar+ium
 so+laria *or*
 so+lar+iums
so+la+tium
so+la+tia
sold
sol+der
 sol+ders

sol+ders
sol+der+ing
sol+dered
sol+der+able
sol+der+er
sol+der+ers
sol+der+ing
sol+dier
sol+diers
sol+diers
sol+dier+ing
sol+diered
sol+dier+ly
sol+diery
sol+dieries
sole
shoe underside
soles
sole
fish
sole *or*
soles
sol+ecism
sol+ecisms
sol+ecist
sol+ecists
sol+ecis+tic
sol+ecis+ti+cal+
ly
sole+ly
sol+emn
sol+em+ness
so+lem+ni+fi+ca+
tion
so+lem+ni+fy
so+lem+ni+fies
so+lem+ni+fy+
ing
so+lem+ni+fied
sol+em+ni+sa+
tion
sol+em+nise
sol+em+nises
sol+em+nis+ing
sol+em+nised
sol+em+nis+er
sol+em+nis+ers
so+lem+nity
so+lem+nities
sol+em+ni+za+
tion
sol+em+nize
sol+em+nizes
sol+em+niz+ing
sol+em+nized

sol+em+niz+er
sol+em+niz+ers
sol+emn+ly
sol+emn+ness
sole+ness
so+leno+don
so+leno+dons
so+lenoid
so+lenoids
so+lenoi+dal
So+lent
So+leure
sol-fa
sol-fas
sol-fas
sol-faing
sol-faed
sol+fa+ta+ra
sol+fa+ta+ras
sol+fège
sol+fèges
sol+feg+gio
sol+feg+gi *or*
sol+feg+gios
soli
so+lic+it
so+lic+its
so+lic+it+ing
so+lic+it+ed
so+lici+ta+tion
so+lici+ta+tions
so+lici+tor
so+lici+tors
so+lici+tor+ship
so+lici+tous
so+lici+tous+
ness
so+lici+tude
sol+id
sol+ids
soli+da+go
soli+da+gos
soli+dar+ity
soli+dar+ities
so+lidi+fi+ca+
tion
so+lidi+fi+er
so+lidi+fi+ers
so+lidi+fy
so+lidi+fies
so+lidi+fy+ing
so+lidi+fied
so+lid+ity
sol+id+ly
sol+id+ness

solid-state
soli+dus
soli+di
soli+fluc+tion
soli+flux+ion
So+li+hull
so+lilo+quise
so+lilo+quises
so+lilo+quis+ing
so+lilo+quised
so+lilo+quis+er
so+lilo+quis+ers
so+lilo+quist
so+lilo+quists
so+lilo+quize
so+lilo+quizes
so+lilo+quiz+ing
so+lilo+quized
so+lilo+quiz+er
so+lilo+quiz+ers
so+lilo+quy
so+lilo+quies
Soliman
So+ling+en
sol+ip+sism
sol+ip+sist
sol+ip+sists
sol+ip+sis+tic
soli+taire
soli+taires
soli+tari+ly
soli+tari+ness
soli+tary
soli+taries
soli+tude
soli+tudes
soli+tu+di+nous
sol+mi+sa+tion
sol+mi+za+tion
solo
solos *or*
soli
solos
solo+ing
soloed
so+lo+ist
so+lo+ists
Solomon
surname
Solo+mon
place name
Solo+mo+nian
Solo+mon+ic
Solon
So+lo+nian

So+lon+ic
So+lo+thurn
sol+stice
sol+stices
sol+sti+tial
Solti
sol+ubil+ity
sol+ubil+ities
sol+uble
sol+ubly
so+lus
so+lute
so+lutes
so+lu+tion
so+lu+tions
So+lu+trean
solv+able
solva+tion
Solvay
solve
solves
solv+ing
solved
sol+ven+cy
sol+vent
sol+vents
Sol+way
Solyman
Solzhenitsyn
soma
biology
so+ma+ta *or*
somas
soma
drink
somas
So+ma+li
So+ma+lis *or*
So+ma+li
So+ma+lian
So+ma+lians
So+ma+li+land
so+mat+ic
so+mati+cal+ly
so+ma+to+gen+
ic
so+ma+to+type
so+ma+to+
types
som+ber
U.S.
som+ber+ly
U.S.
som+ber+ness
U.S.

som+bre
som+bre+ly
som+bre+ness
som+brero
som+breros
som+brous
some
some+body
some+bodies
some+day
some+how
some+one
some+place
som+er+sault
som+er+saults
som+er+saults
som+er+sault+ing
som+er+sault+ed
Som+er+set
place name
Somerset
surname
some+thing
some+time
some+times
some+way
some+what
some+where
Somme
som+melier
som+meliers
som+nam+bu+lance
som+nam+bu+lant
som+nam+bu+lants
som+nam+bu+late
som+nam+bu+lates
som+nam+bu+lat+ing
som+nam+bu+lat+ed
som+nam+bu+la+tion
som+nam+bu+la+tor
som+nam+bu+la+tors
som+nam+bu+lism

som+nam+bu+list
som+nam+bu+lists
som+nif+er+ous
som+nif+ic
som+no+lence
som+no+len+cy
som+no+lent
som+no+lent+ly
Somnus
son
sons
Son
so+nance
so+nant
so+nants
so+nar
so+nars
so+na+ta
so+na+tas
son+dage
son+dages
sonde
sondes
Sondheim
sone
sones
son et lu+mi+ère
song
songs
Song
song+bird
song+birds
Song Coi
Song+hua
Song Koi
son+go+lo+lo
son+go+lo+los
song+ster
song+sters
song+stress
song+writer
song+writers
son+ic
son+ics
son-in-law
sons-in-law
son+less
son+net
son+nets
son+nets
son+net+ing
son+net+ed
son+net+eer

son+net+eers
son+ny
son+nies
so+no+buoy
so+no+buoys
So+no+ra
son+or+ant
son+or+ants
so+nor+ity
so+nor+ities
so+no+rous
so+no+rous+ly
so+no+rous+ness
son+sie
son+si+er
son+si+est
son+sy
son+si+er
son+si+est
Sontag
Soo+chow
sook
sooks
sool
sools
sool+ing
sooled
soon
Soong
soot
soots
soot+ing
soot+ed
sooth
sooths
soothe
soothes
sooth+ing
soothed
sooth+er
sooth+ers
sooth+ing
sooth+ing+ly
sooth+say+er
sooth+say+ers
sooti+ly
sooti+ness
sooty
sooti+er
sooti+est
sop
sops
sops
sop+ping

sopped
Soper
So+phi
So+phies
Sophia
soph+ism
soph+isms
soph+ist
soph+ists
so+phis+tic
so+phis+ti+cal
so+phis+ti+cal+ly
so+phis+ti+cate
so+phis+ti+cates
so+phis+ti+cates
so+phis+ti+cat+ing
so+phis+ti+cat+ed
so+phis+ti+cat+ed
so+phis+ti+ca+tion
so+phis+ti+ca+tions
so+phis+ti+ca+tor
so+phis+ti+ca+tors
soph+ist+ry
soph+ist+ries
Sopho+clean
Sophocles
sopho+more
sopho+mores
So+phy
So+phies
sopo+rif+ic
sopo+rif+ics
sop+pi+ly
sop+pi+ness
sop+ping
sop+py
sop+pi+er
sop+pi+est
so+pra+ni+no
so+pra+ni+nos
so+pra+no
so+pra+nos *or*
so+pra+ni
Sopwith
So+ra+ta
sorb

sorbs
sor+befa+cient
sor+befa+cients
sor+bet
sor+bets
sorb+ic
sor+bi+tol
sor+bo
Sor+bonne
sor+cer+er
sor+cer+ers
sor+cer+ess
sor+cer+esses
sor+cery
sor+ceries
sor+did
sor+did+ly
sor+did+ness
sor+di+no
sor+di+ni
sore
sores
sore+head
sore+heads
sore+ly
sore+ness
sor+ghum
sor+ghums
So+ro+ca+ba
so+ror+ity
so+ror+ities
sorp+tion
sor+rel
sor+rels
Sor+ren+to
sor+ri+ly
sor+ri+ness
sor+row
sor+rows
sor+rows
sor+row+ing
sor+rowed
sor+row+ful
sor+row+ful+ly
sor+row+ful+
  ness
sor+ry
sor+ri+er
sor+ri+est
sort
sorts
sorts
sort+ing
sort+ed
sort+able

sort+er
sort+ers
sor+tie
sor+ties
sor+ties
sor+tie+ing
sor+tied
sor+ti+lege
sor+ti+leges
SOS
SOSs
so+sa+tie
so+sa+ties
Sos+no+wiec
so-so
sos+te+nu+to
sot
sots
so+te+ri+ol+ogy
Soto
sot+tish
sot+to voce
sou
sous
sou+brette
sou+brettes
sou+bri+quet
sou+bri+quets
Sou+dan
souf+fle
souf+fles
souf+flé
souf+flés
souf+fléed
Sou+frière
sough
soughs
soughs
sough+ing
soughed
sought
souk
souks
sou+kous
soul
souls
soul-destroy+ing
soul+ful
soul+ful+ly
soul+ful+ness
soul+less
soul+less+ness
soul-searching
sound
sounds

sounds
sound+ing
sound+ed
sound+er
sound+est
Sound
sound+able
sound+box
sound+boxes
sound+er
sound+ers
sound+ing
sound+ings
sound+less
sound+less+ness
sound+ly
sound+ness
sound+post
sound+posts
sound+proof
sound+proofs
sound+proof+
  ing
sound+proofed
sound+track
sound+tracks
Souness
soup
soups
soup+çon
soup+çons
Souphanouvong
soupy
soupi+er
soupi+est
sour
sours
sours
sour+ing
soured
Sour
source
sources
sources
sourc+ing
sourced
sour+dough
sour+doughs
sour+ish
sour+ly
sour+ness
sour+puss
sour+pusses
Sousa
sou+sa+phone

sou+sa+phones
sou+sa+phon+ist
sou+sa+phon+
  ists
souse
souses
souses
sous+ing
soused
sous+lik
sous+liks
Sousse
sou+tane
sou+tanes
sou+ter+rain
sou+ter+rains
south
South
south+bound
Southcott
South+down
South+downs
south+east
South+east
south+easter
south+easters
south+easter+ly
south+easter+
  lies
south+eastern
south+eastern+
  most
south+eastward
south+
  eastwards
Southend-on-Sea
south+er
south+ers
south+er+ii+ness
south+er+ly
south+er+lies
south+ern
South+ern
South+ern+er
South+ern+ers
south+ern+most
Southey
south+ing
south+ings
south+paw
south+paws
South+port
south-southeast
south-southwest
south+ward

south+wards
South+wark
Southwell
south+west
South+west
south+wester
south+westers
south+wester+ly
south+wester+
lies
south+western+
most
south+westward
Soutine
sou+venir
sou+venirs
sou'+west+er
sou'+west+ers
sov+er+eign
sov+er+eigns
sov+er+eign+ly
sov+er+eign+ty
sov+er+eign+
ties
So+vetsk
so+vi+et
so+vi+ets
So+vi+et
so+vi+eti+sa+
tion
so+vi+et+ise
so+vi+et+ises
so+vi+et+is+ing
so+vi+et+ised
so+vi+et+ism
so+vi+et+isms
so+vi+eti+za+
tion
so+vi+et+ize
so+vi+et+izes
so+vi+et+iz+ing
so+vi+et+ized
So+vi+ets
sow
sows
sows
sow+ing
sowed
sown *or*
sowed
sow+er
sow+ers
So+we+to
sown
soy

soya
soy+bean
U.S.
soy+beans
Soyinka
soz+zled
spa
spas
Spaak
space
spaces
spaces
spac+ing
spaced
space-age
adj.
space age
noun
space-bar
space-bars
space+craft
space+crafts
spaced
Space In+va+
ders
Trademark
space+man
space+men
space+port
space+ports
spac+er
spac+ers
space+ship
space+ships
space+suit
space+suits
space-time
space+walk
space+walks
space+walks
space+walk+ing
space+walked
space+woman
space+women
spacey
spaci+er
spaci+est
spa+cial
spac+ing
spac+ings
spa+cious
spa+cious+ly
spa+cious+ness
spade
spades

spades
spad+ing
spad+ed
spad+er
spad+ers
spade+work
spa+dix
spa+di+ces
spa+ghet+ti
spa+hee
spa+hees
spa+hi
spa+his
Spain
spake
Spa+la+to
Spal+ding
Spam
Trademark
span
spans
spans
span+ning
spanned
span+drel
span+drels
span+dril
span+drils
span+gle
span+gles
span+gles
span+gling
span+gled
span+gly
Span+iard
Span+iards
span+iel
span+iels
Span+ish
Spanish-
American
Spanish-
Americans
spank
spanks
spanks
spank+ing
spanked
spank+er
spank+ers
spank+ing
spank+ings
span+ner
span+ners
span+spek

span+speks
spar
spars
spars
spar+ring
sparred
spa+rax+is
spare
spares
spares
spar+ing
spared
spare+ly
spare+ness
spare-part
spar+er
spar+ers
spare+rib
spare+ribs
spar+ing
spar+ing+ly
spar+ing+ness
spark
sparks
sparks
spark+ing
sparked
Spark
spark+ing
spark+ish
spar+kle
spar+kles
spar+kles
spar+kling
spar+kled
spar+kler
spar+klers
spar+kling
sparks
sparky
sparki+er
sparki+est
spar+ring
spar+row
spar+rows
sparrow+grass
sparrow+hawk
sparrow+hawks
sparse
spars+er
spars+est
sparse+ly
sparse+ness
spar+sity
Spar+ta

Spartacus
Spar+tan
 Spar+tans
spasm
 spasms
spas+mod+ic
spas+modi+cal
spas+modi+cal+
 ly
Spassky
spas+tic
 spas+tics
spas+ti+cal+ly
spat
 spats
 spats
 spat+ting
 spat+ted
spatch+cock
 spatch+cocks
 spatch+cocks
 spatch+cock+
  ing
 spatch+cocked
spate
 spates
spa+tha+ceous
spathe
 spathes
spath+ic
spath+ose
spa+tial
spa+ti+al+ity
spa+tial+ly
spa+tio+tem+por+
 al
spa+tio+tem+po+
 ral+ly
spat+ter
 spat+ters
 spat+ters
 spat+ter+ing
 spat+tered
spatter+dash
 spatter+dashes
spatu+la
 spatu+las
spatu+lar
spatu+late
spav+in
spav+ined
spawn
 spawns
 spawns
 spawn+ing

spawned
spawn+er
spawn+ers
spay
 spays
 spay+ing
 spayed
speak
 speaks
 speak+ing
 spoke
 spo+ken
speak+able
speak+easy
 speak+easies
speak+er
 speak+ers
Speak+er
 Speak+ers
speak+er+ship
speak+ing
spear
 spears
 spears
 spear+ing
 speared
spear+head
 spear+heads
 spear+heads
 spear+head+ing
 spear+head+ed
spear+man
 spear+men
spear+mint
spec
 specs
spe+cial
 spe+cials
 spe+cials
 spe+cial+ling
 spe+cialled
spe+ciali+sa+tion
spe+ciali+sa+
 tions
spe+cial+ise
 spe+cial+ises
 spe+cial+is+ing
 spe+cial+ised
spe+cial+ism
spe+cial+ist
 spe+cial+ists
spe+ci+al+ity
spe+ci+al+ities
spe+ciali+za+tion

spe+ciali+za+
 tions
spe+cial+ize
 spe+cial+izes
 spe+cial+iz+ing
 spe+cial+ized
spe+cial+ly
spe+cial+ness
spe+cial+ty
 spe+cial+ties
spe+cia+tion
spe+cie
spe+cies
spe+cies
spe+cies
speci+fi+able
spe+cif+ic
 spe+cif+ics
spe+cifi+cal+ly
speci+fi+ca+tion
speci+fi+ca+
 tions
speci+fi+ca+tive
speci+fic+ity
speci+fy
 speci+fies
 speci+fy+ing
 speci+fied
speci+men
 speci+mens
spe+ci+os+ity
 spe+ci+os+ities
spe+cious
spe+cious+ly
spe+cious+ness
speck
 specks
 specks
 speck+ing
 specked
speck+le
 speck+les
 speck+les
 speck+ling
 speck+led
 speck+led
specs
spec+ta+cle
 spec+ta+cles
 spec+ta+cled
 spec+ta+cles
spec+tacu+lar
 spec+tacu+lars
 spec+tacu+lar+ly
spec+tate

spec+tates
spec+tat+ing
spec+tat+ed
spec+ta+tor
 spec+ta+tors
spec+ter
 U.S.
 spec+ters
Spector
spec+tra
spec+tral
spec+tral+ity
spec+tral+ly
spec+tre
 spec+tres
spec+tro+graph
 spec+tro+
  graphs
spec+tro+graph+
 ic
spec+tro+graphi+
 cal+ly
spec+trog+ra+
 phy
spec+tro+he+lio+
 graph
 spec+tro+he+lio+
  graphs
spec+tro+he+lio+
 graph+ic
spec+trom+eter
 spec+trom+
  eters
spec+tro+met+
 ric
spec+trom+etry
spec+tro+pho+
 tom+eter
 spec+tro+pho+
  tom+eters
spec+tro+photo+
 met+ric
spec+tro+pho+
 tom+etry
spec+tro+scope
 spec+tro+
  scopes
spec+tro+scop+
 ic
spec+tro+scopi+
 cal
spec+tros+co+
 pist
 spec+tros+co+
  pists

spec+tros+co+py
spec+trum
spec+tra
specu+lar
specu+late
specu+lates
specu+lat+ing
specu+lat+ed
specu+la+tion
specu+la+tions
specu+la+tive
specu+la+tor
specu+la+tors
specu+lum
specu+la *or*
specu+lums
sped
speech
speeches
speechi+fi+er
speechi+fi+ers
speechi+fy
speechi+fies
speechi+fy+ing
speechi+fied
speech+less
speech+less+ly
speech+less+
ness
speed
speeds
speeds
speed+ing
sped *or*
speed+ed
speed+ball
speed+balls
speed+boat
speed+boats
speed+er
speed+ers
speedi+ly
speedi+ness
speedo
speedos
speed+om+eter
speed+om+
eters
speed-up
speed-ups
speed up
verb
speed+way
speed+ways
speed+well

speed+wells
speedy
speedi+er
speedi+est
spek
spe+laeo+logi+
cal
spe+laeolo+gist
spe+laeolo+
gists
spe+laeol+ogy
spe+leo+logi+cal
spe+leolo+gist
spe+leolo+gists
spe+leol+ogy
spell
spells
spells
spell+ing
spelt *or*
spelled
spell+able
spell+bind
spell+binds
spell+bind+ing
spell+bound
spell+bind+er
spell+bind+ers
spell+bound
spell+er
spell+ers
spel+li+can
spel+li+cans
spell+ing
spell+ings
spelt
spel+ter
spe+lunk+er
spe+lunk+ers
spe+lunk+ing
Spence
spen+cer
spen+cers
Spencer
surname
Spen+cer
place name
spend
spends
spend+ing
spent
spend+able
spend+er
spend+ers
Spender

spend+thrift
spend+thrifts
Spengler
Spenser
Spen+serian
Spen+serians
spent
sperm
sperms
sper+ma+ceti
sper+mat+ic
sper+mati+cal+ly
sper+ma+tid
sper+ma+tids
sper+mato+cyte
sper+mato+
cytes
sper+mato+gen+
esis
sper+ma+to+
genet+ic
sper+mato+go+
nium
sper+mato+go+
nia
sper+ma+to+
phyte
sper+ma+to+
phytes
sper+ma+to+
phyt+ic
sper+ma+to+zo+
al
sper+ma+to+zo+
an
sper+ma+to+zo+
ic
sper+ma+to+zo+
on
sper+ma+to+
zoa
sper+mic
sper+mi+ci+dal
sper+mi+cide
sper+mi+cides
sper+mo+phyte
sper+mo+
phytes
sper+mous
spew
spews
spew+ing
spewed
spew+er
spew+ers

Spey
Spey+er
sphag+nous
sphag+num
sphai+ree
sphal+er+ite
sphene
sphe+noid
sphe+noids
spher+al
sphere
spheres
spheres
spher+ing
sphered
spher+ic
spheri+cal
spheri+cal+ly
spheri+cal+ness
sphe+roid
sphe+roids
sphe+roi+dal
sphe+roi+dic+ity
sphe+rom+eter
sphe+rom+eters
spheru+lar
spher+ule
spher+ules
spheru+lite
spheru+lit+ic
sphinc+ter
sphinc+ters
sphinc+ter+al
sphinx
sphinxes *or*
sphin+ges
Sphinx
sphra+gis+tic
sphra+gis+tics
sphyg+mo+graph
sphyg+mo+
graphs
sphyg+mo+graph+
ic
sphyg+mog+ra+
phy
sphyg+mo+ma+
nom+eter
spic-and-span
spi+cate
spic+ca+to
spice
spices
spices
spic+ing

spiced
Spice
spice+bush
spici+ly
spici+ness
spick-and-span
spicu+late
spic+ule
  spic+ules
spicy
  spici+er
  spici+est
spi+der
  spi+ders
spider+man
  spider+men
spider+wort
spi+dery
spiel
  spiels
  spiels
  spiel+ing
  spieled
Spielberg
spi+er
  spi+ers
spiffi+ly
spif+fing
spif+fy
  spif+fi+er
  spif+fi+est
spig+ot
  spig+ots
spike
  spikes
  spikes
  spik+ing
  spiked
spike+let
  spike+lets
spike+nard
spiky
  spiki+er
  spiki+est
spile
  spiles
  spiles
  spil+ing
  spiled
  spili+kin
  spili+kins
spill
  spills
  spills
  spill+ing

spilt *or*
spilled
spill+age
  spill+ages
Spillane
spill+er
  spill+ers
spil+li+kin
  spil+li+kins
  spil+li+kins
spill+over
  spill+overs
spill over
  verb
spill+way
  spill+ways
spilt
spin
  spins
  spins
  spin+ning
  spun
spi+na bi+fi+da
spin+ach
spi+nal
  spi+nal+ly
spin+dle
  spin+dles
  spin+dles
  spin+dling
  spin+dled
spindle+legs
spindle+shanks
spin+dly
  spin+dli+er
  spin+dli+est
spin+drift
spin-dry
  spin-dries
  spin-drying
  spin-dried
spin-dryer
  spin-dryers
spine
  spines
spine-chiller
  spine-chillers
spine-chilling
spined
spi+nel
spine+less
spine+less+ly
spine+less+ness
spin+et
  spin+ets

spini+fex
spini+ness
spin+na+ker
  spin+na+kers
spin+ner
  spin+ners
spin+ner+et
  spin+ner+ets
spin+ney
  spin+neys
spin+ning
spin-off
  spin-offs
spi+nose
spin+out
  noun
spin out
  verb
Spinoza
spin+ster
  spin+sters
spin+ster+hood
spin+ster+ish
spiny
  spini+er
  spini+est
spiny-finned
spira+cle
  spira+cles
spi+racu+lar
spi+racu+late
spi+raea
spi+ral
  spi+rals
  spi+rals
  spi+ral+ling *or*
  spi+ral+ing
  U.S.
  spi+ralled *or*
  spi+raled
  U.S.
spi+ral+ly
spi+rant
  spi+rants
spire
  spires
  spires
spir+ing
  spired
spi+rea
  U.S.
Spires
spi+ril+lum
  spi+ril+la
spir+it

spir+its
spir+its
spir+it+ing
spir+it+ed
Spir+it
spir+it+ed
spir+it+ed+ly
spir+it+ed+ness
spir+it+ism
spir+it+ist
  spir+it+ists
spir+it+is+tic
spir+it+less
spiri+tous
spir+itu+al
  spir+itu+als
spir+itu+ali+sa+
  tion
spir+itu+al+ise
  spir+itu+al+ises
spir+itu+al+is+
  ing
  spir+itu+al+ised
spir+itu+al+is+er
spir+itu+al+is+
  ers
spir+itu+al+ism
spir+itu+al+ity
spir+itu+al+ities
spir+itu+ali+za+
  tion
spir+itu+al+ize
  spir+itu+al+izes
spir+itu+al+iz+
  ing
  spir+itu+al+ized
spir+itu+al+iz+er
spir+itu+al+iz+
  ers
spir+itu+al+ly
spir+itu+el
spir+itu+os+ity
spir+itu+ous
spir+itu+ous+
  ness
spi+ro+chaete
  spi+ro+chaetes
spi+ro+chete
  U.S.
  spi+ro+chetes
spi+ro+graph
  spi+ro+graphs
spi+ro+graph+ic
spi+ro+gy+ra
spirt

spirts
spiry
spit
  spits
  spits
  spit+ting
  spat *or*
  spit
spite
  spites
  spites
  spit+ing
  spit+ed
spite+ful
  spit+fire
  spit+fires
Spit+head
Spits+ber+gen
spit+ter
  spit+ters
spit+ting
spit+tle
spit+toon
  spit+toons
spitz
  spitzes
Spitz
spiv
  spivs
spiv+vy
splake
  splakes
splanch+nic
splash
  splashes
  splashes
  splash+ing
  splashed
splash+down
  splash+downs
splash down
verb
splashy
  splashi+er
  splashi+est
splat
  splats
splat+ter
  splat+ters
  splat+ters
  splat+ter+ing
  splat+tered
splay
  splays
  splays

splay+ing
splayed
splay+foot
  splay+feet
  splay+footed
spleen
  spleens
spleen+ish
spleen+wort
spleeny
splen+dent
splen+did
splen+did+ly
splen+did+ness
splen+dif+er+ous
splen+dor
U.S.
splen+dors
splen+dour
  splen+dours
sple+net+ic
  sple+net+ics
sple+neti+cal+ly
sple+nial
splen+ic
sple+nius
sple+nii
sple+no+mega+
  ly
splice
  splices
  splices
  splic+ing
  spliced
splic+er
  splic+ers
spline
  splines
  splines
  splin+ing
  splined
splint
  splints
  splints
  splint+ing
  splint+ed
splin+ter
  splin+ters
  splin+ters
  splin+ter+ing
  splin+tered
splin+tery
split
  splits
  splits

split+ting
split
Split
split-level
  splits
split-screen
split-second
adj.
split sec+ond
noun
split+ter
  split+ters
  split+ting
split-up
  split-ups
split up
verb
splodge
  splodges
  splodges
  splodg+ing
  splodged
splodgy
splotch
  splotches
splotchy
splurge
  splurges
  splurges
  splurg+ing
  splurged
splut+ter
  splut+ters
  splut+ters
  splut+ter+ing
  splut+tered
  splut+ter+er
  splut+ter+ers
Spock
spode
spoil
  spoils
  spoils
  spoil+ing
  spoilt *or*
  spoiled
spoil+age
  spoil+ages
spoil+er
  spoil+ers
  spoils
spoil+sport
  spoil+sports
spoilt
Spo+kane

spoke
spokes
spokes
spok+ing
spoked
spoke+shave
  spoke+shaves
spokes+man
  spokes+men
spokes+person
  spokes+persons
  or
  spokes+peo+ple
spokes+woman
  spokes+women
spo+lia+tion
spo+lia+tory
spon+da+ic
spon+dee
  spon+dees
spon+dy+li+tis
sponge
  sponges
  sponges
  spong+ing
  sponged
spong+er
  spong+ers
spon+gi+form
spon+gy
spon+gi+er
  spon+gi+est
spon+sion
  spon+sions
spon+son
  spon+sons
spon+sor
  spon+sors
  spon+sors
  spon+sor+ing
  spon+sored
  spon+sored
spon+so+rial
spon+sor+ship
  spon+sor+ships
spon+ta+neity
  spon+ta+neities
spon+ta+neous
spon+ta+neous+
  ly
spon+ta+neous+
  ness
spoof
  spoofs

spoofs
spoof+ing
spoofed
spoof+er
spoof+ers
spook
spooks
spooks
spook+ing
spooked
spooky
spooki+er
spooki+est
spool
spools
spools
spool+ing
spooled
spoon
spoons
spoons
spoon+ing
spooned
spoon+bill
spoon+bills
spoon+drift
spoon+er+ism
spoon+er+isms
spoon+ey
spoonies
spooni+er
spooni+est
spoon-feed
spoon-feeds
spoon-feeding
spoon-fed
spoon+ful
spoon+fuls
spoony
spoonies
spooni+er
spooni+est
spoor
spoors
spoors
spoor+ing
spoored
Spora+des
spo+rad+ic
spo+radi+cal+ly
spo+ran+gial
spo+ran+gium
spo+ran+gia
spore
spores

spores
spor+ing
spored
spo+ro+gen+esis
spo+ro+rog+enous
spo+ro+go+nium
spo+ro+go+nia
spo+ro+phyl
spo+ro+phyls
spo+ro+phyll
spo+ro+phylls
spo+ro+phyte
spo+ro+phytes
spo+ro+phyt+ic
spo+ro+zo+an
spo+ro+zo+ans
spor+ran
spor+rans
sport
sports
sports
sport+ing
sport+ed
sport+er
sport+ers
sport+ful+ly
sport+ful+ness
sporti+ly
sporti+ness
sport+ing
sport+ing+ly
spor+tive
spor+tive+ly
spor+tive+ness
sports
sports+cast
sports+casts
sports+caster
sports+casters
sports+man
sports+men
sportsman-like
sports+man+ly
sports+man+ship
sports+wear
sports+wears
sports+woman
sports+women
sporty
sporti+er
sporti+est
spor+ule
spor+ules
spot
spots

spots
spot+ting
spot+ted
spot-check
spot-checks
spot-checking
spot-checked
spot check
noun
spot+less
spot+less+ly
spot+less+ness
spot+light
spot+lights
spot+lights
spot+light+ing
spot+lit *or*
spot+light+ed
spot-on
spot+ted
spot+ter
spot+ters
spot+tie
spot+ties
spot+ti+ly
spot+ti+ness
spot+ty
spot+ti+er
spot+ti+est
spot-weld
spot-welds
spot-welds
spot-welding
spot-welded
spot-welder
spot-welders
spous+al
spous+als
spous+al+ly
spouse
spouses
spouses
spous+ing
spoused
spout
spouts
spouts
spout+ing
spout+ed
spout+er
spout+ers
spout+ing
sprag
sprags
sprain

sprains
sprains
sprain+ing
sprained
sprang
sprat
sprats
sprawl
sprawls
sprawls
sprawl+ing
sprawled
sprawly
spray
sprays
sprays
spray+ing
sprayed
spray+er
spray+ers
spread
spreads
spreads
spread+ing
spread
spread+able
spread-eagle
spread-eagles
spread-eagling
spread-eagled
spread+er
spread+ers
spread+sheet
spread+sheets
sprech+ge+sang
spree
sprees
sprig
sprigs
sprigs
sprig+ging
sprigged
sprig+ger
sprig+gers
sprig+gy
spright+li+ness
spright+ly
spright+li+er
spright+li+est
spring
springs
springs
spring+ing
sprang *or*
sprung

sprung	sprint+ers	spumed	squab+bling
spring+board	sprit	spu+mous	squab+bled
spring+boards	sprits	spumy	squab+bler
spring+bok	sprite	spun	squab+blers
spring+bok *or*	sprites	spunk	squab+by
spring+boks	sprit+sail	spunks	squad
Spring+bok	sprit+sails	spunki+ly	squads
Spring+boks	spritz+er	spunky	squad+die
spring-clean	spritz+ers	spunki+er	squad+dies
spring-cleans	sprock+et	spunki+est	squad+dy
spring-cleans	sprock+ets	spur	squad+dies
spring-cleaning	sprout	spurs	squad+ron
spring-cleaned	sprouts	spurs	squad+rons
spring-cleaning	sprouts	spur+ring	squa+lene
springe	sprout+ing	spurred	squal+id
springes	sprout+ed	spurge	squa+lid+ity
springes	spruce	spurges	squal+id+ly
spring+ing	spruces	spu+ri+ous	squal+id+ness
springed	sprucer	spu+ri+ous+ly	squall
spring+er	sprucest	spu+ri+ous+ness	squalls
spring+ers	spruce+ly	spurn	squalls
Spring+field	spruce+ness	spurns	squall+ing
spring+haas	sprue	spurns	squalled
spring+haas *or*	sprues	spurn+ing	squall+er
spring+ha+se	spru+ik	spurned	squall+ers
springi+ly	spru+iks	spurn+er	squal+ly
springi+ness	spru+ik+ing	spurn+ers	squal+or
spring+ing	spru+iked	spurt	squa+ma
spring+ings	spru+ik+er	spurts	squa+mae
spring+less	spru+ik+ers	spurts	squa+mate
spring+like	spruit	spurt+ing	squa+ma+tion
Springs	spruits	spurt+ed	squa+ma+tions
Springsteen	sprung	Sput+nik	squa+mose
spring+tail	spry	sput+ter	squa+mous
spring+tails	spry+er *or*	sput+ters	squan+der
spring+tide	spri+er	sput+ters	squan+ders
spring+time	spry+est *or*	sput+ter+ing	squan+der+ing
springy	spri+est	sput+tered	squan+dered
springi+er	spry+ly	sput+ter+er	squan+der+er
springi+est	spry+ness	sput+ter+ers	squan+der+ers
sprin+kle	spud	spu+tum	square
sprin+kles	spuds	spu+ta	squares
sprin+kles	spuds	spy	squares
sprin+kling	spud+ding	spies	squar+ing
sprin+kled	spud+ded	spies	squared
sprin+kler	Spud	spy+ing	square-bashing
sprin+klers	spue	spied	square-dance
sprin+kling	spues	spy+glass	square-dances
sprin+klings	spu+ing	spy+glasses	square-dancing
sprint	spued	squab	square-danced
sprints	spu+er	squabs *or*	square dance
sprints	spu+ers	squab	*noun*
sprint+ing	spume	squab+ble	square-dancer
sprint+ed	spumes	squab+bles	square-dancers
sprint+er	spum+ing	squab+bles	square+ly

square+ness
squar+er
squar+ers
square-rigged
squar+rose
squash
squashes
squashes
squash+ing
squashed
squash+er
squash+ers
squashi+ly
squashi+ness
squashy
squashi+er
squashi+est
squat
squats
squats
squat+ting
squat+ted
squat+ly
squat+ness
squat+ter
squat+ters
squat+toc+ra+cy
squat+toc+ra+
cies
squaw
squaws
squawk
squawks
squawks
squawk+ing
squawked
squawk+er
squawk+ers
squeak
squeaks
squeaks
squeak+ing
squeaked
squeaki+ly
squeaki+ness
squeaky
squeaki+er
squeaki+est
squeaky-clean
squeal
squeals
squeals
squeal+ing
squealed
squeal+er

squeal+ers
squeam+ish
squeam+ish+ly
squeam+ish+
ness
squee+gee
squee+gees
squee+gees
squee+gee+ing
squee+geed
squeez+able
squeeze
squeezes
squeezes
squeez+ing
squeezed
squeez+er
squeez+ers
squelch
squelches
squelches
squelch+ing
squelched
squelch+er
squelch+ers
squelchy
squib
squibs
squibs
squib+bing
squibbed
squid
squid or
squids
squif+fy
squif+fi+er
squif+fi+est
squig+gle
squig+gles
squig+gles
squig+gling
squig+gled
squig+gler
squig+glers
squig+gly
squil+gee
squil+gees
squill
squills
squinch
squinches
squint
squints
squints
squint+ing

squint+ed
squint+er
squint+ers
squinty
squir+ar+chal
squir+ar+chi+cal
squir+ar+chy
squir+ar+chies
squire
squires
squires
squir+ing
squired
squire+ar+chal
squire+ar+chi+cal
squire+ar+chy
squire+ar+chies
squi+reen
squi+reens
squire+ling
squire+lings
squirm
squirms
squirms
squirm+ing
squirmed
squirm+er
squirm+ers
squirmy
squir+rel
squir+rels or
squir+rel
squir+rels
squir+rel+ling
or
squir+rel+ing
U.S.
squir+relled or
squir+reled
U.S.
squirrel-cage
squirt
squirts
squirts
squirt+ing
squirt+ed
squirt+er
squirt+ers
squirt+ing
squish
squishes
squishes
squish+ing
squished
squishy

squit
squits
squiz
squizzes
Sr+bi+ja
Sri Lan+ka
Sri+na+gar
stab
stabs
stabs
stab+bing
stabbed
Sta+bat Ma+ter
stab+ber
stab+bers
sta+bile
sta+biles
sta+bi+li+sa+tion
sta+bi+li+sa+
tions
sta+bi+lise
sta+bi+lises
sta+bi+lis+ing
sta+bi+lised
sta+bi+li+ser
sta+bi+li+sers
sta+bil+ity
sta+bil+ities
sta+bi+li+za+tion
sta+bi+li+za+
tions
sta+bi+lize
sta+bi+lizes
sta+bi+liz+ing
sta+bi+lized
sta+bi+li+zer
sta+bi+li+zers
sta+ble
sta+bles
sta+bles
sta+bling
sta+bled
stable+boy
stable+boys
stable+man
stable+men
sta+ble+ness
sta+bling
sta+blings
stab+lish
stab+lishes
stab+lish+ing
stab+lished
sta+bly
Sta+broek

stac+ca+to
sta+chys
stack
  stacks
  stacks
  stack+ing
  stacked
stack+able
stacked
stack+er
  stack+ers
stad+hold+er
  stad+hold+ers
sta+dia
  sta+dias
sta+dium
  sta+diums *or*
  sta+dia
stadt+hold+er
  stadt+hold+ers
Staël
staff
  staffs *or*
  staves
  staffs
  staff+ing
  staffed
Staf+fa
Staf+ford
place name
Stafford
surname
Staf+ford+shire
stag
  stags
  stags
  stag+ging
  stagged
stage
  stages
  stages
  stag+ing
  staged
stage+coach
  stage+coaches
stage+craft
stage+hand
  stage+hands
stage-manage
  stage-manages
  stage-manag+
    ing
  stage-managed
stag+er
  stag+ers

stage-struck
stag+ey
U.S.
  stag+i+er
  stag+i+est
stag+fla+tion
stag+ger
  stag+gers
  stag+gers
  stag+ger+ing
  stag+gered
  stag+ger+er
  stag+ger+ers
  stag+ger+ing
  stag+ger+ing+ly
  stag+gers
stagi+ly
stagi+ness
stag+ing
  stag+ings
Sta+gi+ra
stag+nan+cy
stag+nant
stag+nate
  stag+nates
  stag+nat+ing
  stag+nat+ed
stag+na+tion
stagy
stagi+er
stagi+est
staid
staid+ly
staid+ness
stain
  stains
  stains
  stain+ing
  stained
stain+abil+ity
stain+able
  stained
stain+er
  stain+ers
Stainer
Staines
stain+less
stain+less+ly
stair
  stairs
stair+case
  stair+cases
  stairs
stair+way

stair+ways
stair+well
  stair+wells
stake
  stakes
  stakes
  stak+ing
  staked
stake+out
  stake+outs
stake out
verb
Sta+kha+nov+
  ism
Sta+kha+nov+ite
  Sta+kha+nov+
  ites
sta+lac+ti+form
stal+ac+tite
  stal+ac+tites
stal+ac+tit+ic
stal+ac+titi+cal
sta+lag
  sta+lags
stal+ag+mite
  stal+ag+mites
stal+ag+mit+ic
stal+ag+miti+cal
stale
  stales
stal+ing
  staled
stal+er
stal+est
stale+mate
  stale+mates
  stale+mates
  stale+mat+ing
  stale+mat+ed
stale+ness
Sta+lin
place name
Stalin
surname
Sta+li+na+bad
Sta+lin+grad
Sta+lin+ism
Sta+lin+ist
  Sta+lin+ists
Sta+li+no+grod
Sta+linsk
stalk
  stalks
  stalks
  stalk+ing

stalked
stalk-and-slash
stalked
stalk+er
  stalk+ers
stalki+ly
stalki+ness
stalking-horse
  stalking-horses
stalk+like
stalky
stalki+er
stalki+est
stall
  stalls
  stalls
  stall+ing
  stalled
stall-feed
  stall-feeds
  stall-feed+ing
  stall-fed
stall+holder
  stall+holders
stal+lion
  stal+lions
stal+wart
  stal+warts
stal+wart+ly
stal+wart+ness
Stam+boul
Stam+bul
sta+men
  sta+mens *or*
  stami+na
Stam+ford
stami+na
stami+nate
stami+nif+er+ous
stam+mer
  stam+mers
  stam+mers
  stam+mer+ing
  stam+mered
  stam+mer+er
  stam+mer+ers
  stam+mer+ing
  stam+mer+ings
stamp
  stamps
  stamps
  stamp+ing
  stamped
stam+pede
  stam+pedes

stam+pedes
stam+ped+ing
stam+ped+ed
stam+ped+er
stam+ped+ers
stamp+er
stamp+ers
stamp+ing
stance
stances
stanch
stanches
stanch+ing
stanched
stanch+able
stanch+er
stanch+ers
stan+chion
stan+chions
stan+chions
stan+chion+ing
stan+chioned
stand
stands
stands
stand+ing
stood
stand+ard
stand+ards
standard-bearer
standard-
  bearers
standard-gauge
adj.
stand+ard gauge
noun
stand+ardi+sa+
  tion
stand+ardi+sa+
  tions
stand+ard+ise
stand+ard+ises
stand+ard+is+
  ing
stand+ard+ised
stand+ard+is+er
stand+ard+is+
  ers
stand+ardi+za+
  tion
stand+ardi+za+
  tions
stand+ard+ize
stand+ard+izes

stand+ard+iz+
  ing
stand+ard+ized
stand+ard+iz+er
stand+ard+iz+
  ers
stand-by
stand-bys
stand by
verb
stand+er
stand+ers
stand-in
stand-ins
stand in
verb
stand+ing
stand+ings
Standish
stand+off
stand+offs
stand-off
adj.
stand off
verb
stand+offish
stand+offish+
  ness
stand+out
stand+outs
stand out
verb
stand+over
noun, adj.
stand over
verb
stand+pipe
stand+pipes
stand+point
stand+points
stand+still
stand+stills
stand-up
adj.
stand up
verb
Stanford
stan+hope
stan+hopes
Stanislaus
Stanislavski
Stanislavsky
stank
stanks
stank+ing

stanked
Stan+ley
place name
Stanley
surname
Stan+ley+ville
Stan+na+ries
stan+na+ry
stan+na+ries
stan+nic
stan+nite
stan+nous
Stans
stan+za
stan+zas
stan+zaed
stan+za+ic
sta+pelia
sta+pelias
sta+pes
sta+pes *or*
sta+pedes
staphy+lo+coc+
  cal
staphy+lo+coc+
  cus
staphy+lo+coc+
  ci
staphy+lo+plas+
  tic
staphy+lo+plas+
  ty
sta+ple
sta+ples
sta+ples
sta+pling
sta+pled
sta+pler
sta+plers
star
stars
stars
star+ring
starred
Star
Sta+ra Za+go+ra
star+board
star+boards
star+board+ing
star+board+ed
starch
starches
starches
starch+ing
starched

starch+er
starch+ers
starchi+ly
starchi+ness
starch-reduced
starchy
starchi+er
starchi+est
star-crossed
star+dom
star+dust
stare
stares
stares
star+ing
stared
star+er
star+ers
star+fish
star+fish *or*
star+fishes
star+gaze
star+gazes
star+gaz+ing
star+gazed
star+gaz+er
star+gaz+ers
star+gaz+ing
stark
stark+er
stark+est
Stark
stark+ly
stark-naked
stark+ness
star+less
star+let
star+lets
star+light
star+like
star+ling
star+lings
star-of-Bethlehem
stars-of-
  Bethlehem
Starr
star+ri+ness
star+ry
star+ri+er
star+ri+est
starry-eyed
star-spangled
star-studded
start
starts

starts	state+li+er	statu+esque+	stead+fast
start+ing	state+li+est	ness	stead+fast+ly
start+ed	state+ment	statu+ette	stead+fast+ness
start+er	state+ments	statu+ettes	steadi+ly
start+ers	state-of-the-art	stat+ure	steadi+ness
start+ing	*adj.*	stat+ures	stead+ing
star+tle	state of the art	sta+tus	stead+ings
star+tles	*noun*	sta+tuses	steady
star+tling	state+room	sta+tus quo	steadies
star+tled	state+rooms	stat+ute	stead+ies
star+tler	States	stat+utes	steady+ing
star+tlers	state+side	statu+to+ri+ly	steadied
star+tling	states+man	statu+tory	steadi+er
start-up	states+men	Stauffenberg	steadi+est
adj.	statesman-like	staunch	steady-state
start up	states+man+ly	staunches	*adj.*
verb	states+man+ship	staunch+ing	steady state
star+va+tion	states+woman	staunched	*noun*
starve	states+women	staunch+er	steak
starves	stat+ic	staunch+est	steaks
starv+ing	stati+cal+ly	staunch+able	steak+house
starved	stat+ice	staunch+er	steak+houses
starve+ling	stat+ics	staunch+ers	steal
starve+lings	sta+tion	staunch+ly	steals
Star Wars	sta+tions	staunch+ness	steal+ing
star+wort	sta+tions	Sta+vang+er	stole
star+worts	sta+tion+ing	stave	sto+len
stash	sta+tioned	staves	steal+er
stashes	sta+tion+ary	staves	steal+ers
stashes	sta+tion+er	stav+ing	stealth
stash+ing	sta+tion+ers	staved *or*	Stealth
stashed	sta+tion+ery	stove	stealthy
sta+sis	station+master	staves	stealthi+er
sta+sies	station+masters	staves+acre	stealthi+est
stat+able	stat+ism	staves+acres	steam
state	stat+ist	Stav+ro+pol	steams
states	stat+ists	stay	steams
states	sta+tis+tic	stays	steam+ing
stat+ing	sta+tis+tics	stays	steamed
stat+ed	sta+tis+ti+cal	stay+ing	steam+boat
state+able	sta+tis+ti+cal+ly	stayed	steam+boats
state+craft	stat+is+ti+cian	stay-at-home	steam-boiler
state+hood	stat+is+ti+cians	stay-at-homes	steam-boilers
State+house	sta+tis+tics	stay+er	steam-engine
U.S. seat of state	Statius	stay+ers	steam-engines
legislature	sta+tor	stay+ing	steam+er
State+houses	sta+tors	stays	steam+ers
state house	stato+scope	stay+sail	steami+ness
N.Z. council	stato+scopes	stay+sails	steam+ing
house	statu+ary	stead	steam+roller
state houses	statue	steads	steam+rollers
state+less	statues	steads	steam+rollers
state+less+ness	statu+esque	stead+ing	steam+roller+
state+li+ness	statu+esque+ly	stead+ed	ing
state+ly		Stead	steam+rollered

steam+ship
steam+ships
steam-shovel
steam-shovels
steamy
steami+er
steami+est
ste+ap+sin
ste+aric
stea+rin
stea+rine
stea+tite
stea+tit+ic
stea+toly+sis
stea+to+py+ga
stea+to+py+gia
stea+to+pyg+ic
stea+to+py+gous
Ste+bark
sted+fast
sted+fast+ly
sted+fast+ness
steed
steeds
steel
steels
steels
steel+ing
steeled
Steel
Steele
steel+head
steel+heads or
steel+head
steeli+ness
steel+worker
steel+workers
steel+works
steely
steel+yard
steel+yards
Steen
steen+bok
steen+boks or
steen+bok
steep
steeps
steeps
steep+ing
steeped
steep+er
steep+est
steep+en
steep+ens
steep+en+ing

steep+ened
steep+er
steep+ers
stee+ple
stee+ples
steeple+chase
steeple+chases
steeple+chases
steeple+chas+ing
steeple+chased
steeple+chas+er
steeple+chas+ers
steeple+chas+ing
stee+pled
steeple+jack
steeple+jacks
steep+ly
steep+ness
steer
steers
steers
steer+ing
steered
steer+able
steer+age
steer+age+way
steer+er
steer+ers
steer+ing
steers+man
steers+men
Stefansson
Steffens
stego+saur
stego+saurs
stego+saur+us
stego+saur+uses
Stei+er
Stei+er+mark
stein
steins
Stein
Steinbeck
stein+bok
stein+boks or
stein+bok
Steiner
Steinitz
Steinway
ste+lar
ste+le
ste+lae or

ste+les
stel+lar
stel+late
stel+lat+ed
stel+late+ly
stel+lu+lar
stel+lu+lar+ly
stem
stems
stems
stem+ming
stemmed
stem+like
stem+ma
stem+mas
stemmed
Sten
stench
stenches
sten+cil
sten+cils
sten+cils
sten+cil+ling
or
sten+cil+ing
U.S.
sten+cilled or
sten+ciled
U.S.
Stendhal
steno
steno+graph
steno+graphs
steno+graphs
steno+graph+ing
steno+graphed
ste+nog+ra+pher
ste+nog+ra+phers
steno+graph+ic
ste+nog+ra+phy
ste+no+sis
ste+no+ses
ste+not+ic
Steno+type
Trademark
Steno+types
steno+typ+ist
steno+typ+ists
steno+typy
Sten+tor
sten+to+rian
step
steps

steps
step+ping
stepped
step+brother
step+brothers
step+child
step+children
step+daughter
step+daughters
step-down
step-downs
step down
verb
step+father
step+fathers
stepha+no+tis
Stephen
Stephenson
step-in
noun, adj.
step-ins
step in
verb
step+ladder
step+ladders
step+like
step+mother
step+mothers
step-parent
step-parents
step-parenting
steppe
steppes
step+per
step+pers
Steppes
step+ping
step+sister
step+sisters
step+son
step+sons
step-up
noun, adj.
step-ups
step up
verb
ste+ra+dian
ste+ra+dians
ster+co+ra+ceous
stere
steres
ste+reo
ste+reos

ste+reo+chem+is+
try
ste+reo+graph
ste+reo+graphs
ste+reo+iso+mer
ste+reo+iso+
mers
ste+reo+isom+er+
ism
ste+reo+phon+ic
ste+reo+phoni+
cal+ly
ste+reoph+ony
ste+reo+scope
ste+reo+scopes
ste+reo+scop+ic
ste+reos+co+py
ste+reo+spe+cif+
ic
ste+reo+type
ste+reo+types
ste+reo+types
ste+reo+typ+ing
ste+reo+typed
ste+reo+typed
ste+reo+typ+er
ste+reo+typ+ist
ste+reo+typ+
ists
ste+reo+typy
ste+reo+vi+sion
ste+ric
ste+ri+cal
ster+ile
ster+ile+ly
steri+li+sa+tion
steri+li+sa+tions
steri+lise
steri+lises
steri+lis+ing
steri+lised
steri+lis+er
steri+lis+ers
ste+ril+ity
steri+li+za+tion
steri+li+za+tions
steri+lize
steri+lizes
steri+liz+ing
steri+lized
steri+liz+er
steri+liz+ers
ster+ling
Ster+li+ta+mak
stern

sterns
stern+er
stern+est
Stern
ster+nal
Sternberg
Sterne
stern+fore+most
stern+ly
stern+most
stern+ness
stern+post
stern+posts
ster+num
ster+na *or*
ster+nums
ster+nu+ta+tion
ster+nu+ta+
tions
ster+nu+ta+tor
ster+nu+ta+tors
ster+nu+ta+tory
stern+ward
stern+wards
stern+way
stern-wheeler
stern-wheelers
ster+oid
ster+oids
ste+roi+dal
ster+ol
ster+ols
ster+to+rous
ster+to+rous+ly
ster+to+rous+
ness
stet
stets
stets
stet+ting
stet+ted
stetho+scope
stetho+scopes
stetho+scop+ic
ste+thos+co+py
stet+son
stet+sons
Stet+tin
ste+vedore
ste+vedores
ste+vedores
ste+vedor+ing
ste+vedored
Ste+ven+age
Stevenson

stew
stews
stews
stew+ing
stewed
stew+ard
stew+ards
stew+ards
stew+ard+ing
stew+ard+ed
stew+ard+ess
stew+ard+esses
stew+ard+ship
Stewart
surname
Stew+art
place name
stewed
Steyr
sthen+ic
Stheno
stib+ine
stib+nite
stick
sticks
sticks
stick+ing
stuck *or*
sticked
support a plant
stick+er
stick+ers
sticki+ly
sticki+ness
stick+ing
stick-in-the-mud
stick-in-the-
muds
stick+le
stick+les
stick+ling
stick+led
stickle+back
stickle+backs
stick+ler
stick+lers
stick-up
stick-ups
sticky
stickies
sticky+ing
stickied
sticki+er
sticki+est
sticky+beak

sticky+beaks
sticky+beaks
sticky+beak+ing
sticky+beaked
Stieglitz
stiff
stiffs
stiffs
stiff+ing
stiffed
stiff+er
stiff+est
stiff+en
stiff+ens
stiff+en+ing
stiff+ened
stiff+en+er
stiff+en+ers
stiff+ish
stiff+ly
stiff-necked
stiff+ness
sti+fle
sti+fles
sti+fling
sti+fled
stig+ma
stig+mas *or*
stig+ma+ta
stig+mat+ic
stig+mat+ics
stig+ma+ti+sa+
tion
stig+ma+ti+sa+
tions
stig+ma+tise
stig+ma+tises
stig+ma+tis+ing
stig+ma+tised
stig+ma+tis+er
stig+ma+tis+ers
stig+ma+tism
stig+ma+ti+za+
tion
stig+ma+ti+za+
tions
stig+ma+tize
stig+ma+tizes
stig+ma+tiz+ing
stig+ma+tized
stig+ma+tiz+er
stig+ma+tiz+ers
stil+bene
stil+bes+trol
U.S.

stil+boes+trol	sting+er	stip+pling	stoats
stile	sting+ers	stip+pled	sto+chas+tic
stiles	stin+gi+ly	stip+pler	stock
sti+let+to	stin+gi+ness	stip+plers	stocks
sti+let+tos	sting+ing	stipu+lar	stocks
Stilicho	sting+ray	stipu+late	stock+ing
still	sting+rays	stipu+lates	stocked
stills	stin+gy	stipu+lat+ing	stock+ade
stills	*mean*	stipu+lat+ed	stock+ades
still+ing	stin+gi+er	stipu+la+tion	stock+ades
stilled	stin+gi+est	stipu+la+tions	stock+ad+ing
still+er	stingy	stipu+la+tor	stock+ad+ed
still+est	*stinging*	stipu+la+tors	stock+breeder
stil+lage	stingi+er	stip+ule	stock+breeders
stil+lages	stingi+est	stip+ules	stock+breeding
still+birth	stink	stir	stock+broker
still+births	stinks	stirs	stock+brokers
still+born	stinks	stirs	stock+bro+ker+
still-life	stink+ing	stir+ring	age
adj.	stank *or*	stirred	stock+broking
still life	stunk	stir-fry	stock+er
still lifes	stunk	stir-fries	stock+ers
still+ness	stink+er	stir-frying	stock+fish
stil+ly	stink+ers	stir-fried	stock+fish *or*
stilt	stink+horn	stirk	stock+fishes
stilts	stink+horns	stirks	Stockhausen
stilts	stink+ing	Stir+ling	stock+holder
stilt+ing	stink+ing+ly	*place name*	stock+holders
stilt+ed	stink+ing+ness	Stirling	stock+holding
stilt+ed	stinko	*surname*	Stock+holm
stilt+ed+ly	stink+weed	Stir+ling+shire	stock+horse
stilt+ed+ness	stink+wood	stirps	stock+horses
Stil+ton	stint	stir+pes	stocki+ly
Stil+tons	stints	stir+rer	stocki+ness
Stilwell	stints	stir+rers	stocki+net
stimu+lant	stint+ing	stir+ring	stocki+nets
stimu+lants	stint+ed	stir+ring+ly	stock+ing
stimu+late	stint+er	stir+rup	stock+ings
stimu+lates	stint+ers	stir+rups	stock+inged
stimu+lat+ing	stipe	stitch	stock+ist
stimu+lat+ed	stipes	stitches	stock+ists
stimu+lat+ing	sti+pel	stitches	stock+jobber
stimu+la+tion	sti+pels	stitch+ing	stock+jobbers
stimu+la+tions	sti+pel+late	stitched	stock+jobbery
stimu+la+tive	sti+pend	stitch+er	stock+jobbing
stimu+la+tives	sti+pends	stitch+ers	stock+man
stimu+la+tor	sti+pen+di+ary	stitch+wort	stock+men
stimu+la+tors	sti+pen+di+aries	stitch+worts	stock+pile
stimu+lus	sti+pes	sti+ver	stock+piles
stimu+li	stipi+tes	sti+vers	stock+piles
sting	sti+pi+form	St John	stock+pil+ing
stings	stipi+ti+form	stoa	stock+piled
stings	stip+ple	stoae *or*	stock+pil+er
sting+ing	stip+ples	stoas	stock+pil+ers
stung	stip+ples	stoat	Stock+port

stock+pot
stock+pots
stock+room
stock+rooms
stock+route
stock+routes
stocks
stock-still
stock+taking
Stock+ton
place name
Stockton
surname
Stockton-on-
  Tees
stocky
stocki+er
stocki+est
stock+yard
stock+yards
stodge
stodges
stodgi+ly
stodgi+ness
stodgy
stodgi+er
stodgi+est
sto+ic
sto+ics
Sto+ic
Sto+ics
stoi+cal
stoi+cal+ly
stoi+chei+om+
  etry
stoi+chio+met+
  ric
stoi+chi+om+etry
stoi+cism
stoke
stokes
stok+ing
stoked
stoke+hold
stoke+holds
stoke+hole
stoke+holes
Stoke-on-Trent
stok+er
stok+ers
Stoker
Stokowski
STOL
STOLs
stole

stoles
stol+en
stol+id
sto+lid+ity
stol+id+ly
stol+id+ness
sto+lon
sto+lons
sto+lonif+er+ous
Stolypin
sto+ma
sto+ma+ta
stom+ach
stom+achs
stom+achs
stom+ach+ing
stom+ached
stomach+ache
stomach+aches
stom+ach+er
stom+ach+ers
sto+mach+ic
sto+mach+ics
sto+machi+cal
sto+ma+ta
sto+ma+tit+ic
sto+ma+ti+tis
sto+ma+to+log+
  ical
sto+ma+tol+ogy
stomp
stomps
stomps
stomp+ing
stomped
stomp+er
stomp+ers
stone
stones
stones
ston+ing
stoned
Stone-Age
adj.
Stone Age
noun
stone-blind
stone+chat
stone+chats
stone-cold
stone+crop
stone+crops
stone+cutter
stone+cutters
stone+cutting

stoned
stone-deaf
stone+fish
stone+fish *or*
stone+fishes
stone+fly
stone+flies
Stone+henge
stone+mason
stone+masons
stone+mason+ry
ston+er
ston+ers
Stones
stone+wall
stone+walls
stone+wall+ing
stone+walled
stone+wall+er
stone+wall+ers
stone+ware
stone+washed
stone+work
stone+worker
stone+workers
stoney
stoni+er
stoni+est
stoni+ly
stoni+ness
stonk+ered
stony
stoni+er
stoni+est
stony-broke
stony-hearted
stony-
  heartedness
stood
stooge
stooges
stooges
stoog+ing
stooged
stook
stooks
stooks
stook+ing
stooked
stook+er
stook+ers
stool
stools
stools
stool+ing

stooled
stoop
stoops
stoops
stoop+ing
stooped
stoop+ing
stop
stops
stops
stop+ping
stopped
stop+bank
stop+banks
stop+cock
stop+cocks
stope
stopes
stopes
stop+ing
stoped
Stopes
stop+gap
stop+gaps
stop-go
stop+light
stop+lights
stop-loss
stop+off
stop+offs
stop off
verb
stop+over
stop+overs
stop over
verb
stop+pable
stop+page
stop+pages
Stoppard
stopped
stop+per
stop+pers
stop+pers
stop+per+ing
stop+pered
stop+ping
stop+pings
stop+watch
stop+watches
stor+able
stor+age
sto+rax
store
stores

stores
stor+ing
stored
store+house
store+houses
store+keeper
store+keepers
store+keeping
store+room
store+rooms
stores
sto+rey
sto+reys
Storey
sto+reyed
sto+ried
stork
storks
storks+bill
storks+bills
storm
storms
storms
storm+ing
stormed
storm+bound
storm-cock
storm-cocks
stormi+ly
stormi+ness
Stor+mont
stormy
stormi+er
stormi+est
Stor+no+way
Stor+thing
Stor+ting
sto+ry
sto+ries
sto+ries
sto+ry+ing
sto+ried
story+board
story+boards
story+book
story+books
story+teller
story+tellers
story+telling
stoup
stoups
Stour+bridge
stoush
stoushes
stoushes

stoush+ing
stoushed
stout
stouts
stout+er
stout+est
Stout
stout+hearted
stout+hearted+ly
stout+hearted+
  ness
stout+ly
stout+ness
stove
stoves
stoves
stov+ing
stoved
stove+pipe
stove+pipes
stow
stows
stow+ing
stowed
stow+age
stow+ages
stow+away
stow+aways
stow away
  verb
Stowe
stra+bis+mal
stra+bis+mic
stra+bis+mi+cal
stra+bis+mus
Strabo
Strachey
Strad
Strads
strad+dle
strad+dles
strad+dles
strad+dling
strad+dled
strad+dler
strad+dlers
Stradivari
Stradi+var+ius
Stradi+var+
  iuses
strafe
strafes
strafes
straf+ing
strafed

straf+er
straf+ers
Strafford
strag+gle
strag+gles
strag+gling
strag+gled
strag+gler
strag+glers
strag+gly
straight
straights
straight+er
straight+est
straight+away
straight+aways
straight+edge
straight+edges
straight+en
straight+ens
straight+en+ing
straight+ened
straight+en+er
straight+en+ers
straight-faced
straight+forward
straight+forward+
  ly
straight+forward+
  ness
straight+jacket
straight+jackets
straight-laced
straight+ly
straight+ness
straight-out
straight+way
strain
strains
strains
strain+ing
strained
strained
strain+er
strain+ers
strait
straits
strait+en
strait+ens
strait+en+ing
strait+ened
strait+jacket
strait+jackets
strait+jackets
strait+jacket+ing

strait+jacket+ed
strait-laced
strait+ly
strait+ness
strake
strakes
Stral+sund
stra+mo+nium
stra+mo+niums
strand
strands
strands
strand+ing
strand+ed
Strand
strange
strang+er
strang+est
strange+ly
strange+ness
stran+ger
stran+gers
stran+gle
stran+gles
stran+gling
stran+gled
strangle+hold
strangle+holds
stran+gler
stran+glers
stran+gles
stran+gu+late
stran+gu+lates
stran+gu+lat+
  ing
stran+gu+lat+ed
stran+gu+la+tion
stran+gu+ry
Stran+raer
strap
straps
straps
strap+ping
strapped
strap+hanger
strap+hangers
strap+hanging
strap+ping
Stras+bourg
stra+ta
strata+gem
strata+gems
stra+tal
stra+tegic
stra+tegi+cal

stra+tegi+cal+ly
stra+tegics
strat+egist
strat+egists
strat+egy
strat+egies
Stratford-on-
  Avon
Stratford-upon-
  Avon
strath
straths
Strath+clyde
strath+spey
strath+speys
stra+ticu+late
stra+ticu+la+tion
strati+fi+ca+tion
strati+fi+ca+
  tions
strati+fy
strati+fies
strati+fy+ing
strati+fied
strati+graph+ic
strati+graphi+cal
stra+tig+ra+phy
stra+tig+ra+
  phies
strato+cu+mu+
  lus
strato+cu+mu+li
strato+pause
strato+sphere
strato+spher+ic
strato+spheri+cal
stra+tum
stra+ta *or*
stra+tums
stra+tus
stra+ti
Straus
Strauss
Stravinsky
straw
straws
straw+berry
straw+berries
straw+board
straw+flower
straw+flowers
strawy
stray
strays
strays

stray+ing
strayed
stray+er
stray+ers
strays
streak
streaks
streaks
streak+ing
streaked
streaked
streak+er
streak+ers
streaki+ness
streak+like
streaky
streaki+er
streaki+est
stream
streams
streams
stream+ing
streamed
stream+er
stream+ers
stream+let
stream+lets
stream+line
stream+lines
stream+lines
stream+lin+ing
stream+lined
stream+lined
stream-of-
  conscious+ness
  adj.
stream of con+
  scious+ness
  noun
streamy
streami+er
streami+est
Streep
street
streets
street+car
street+cars
street-credible
street+walker
street+walkers
street+walking
street+wise
Streicher
Streisand
stre+lit+zia

stre+lit+zias
strength
strengths
strength+en
strength+ens
strength+en+ing
strength+ened
strength+en+er
strength+en+ers
strenu+ous
strenu+ous+ly
strenu+ous+ness
strep
streps
stre+pi+to+so
strep+to+car+
  pus
strep+to+car+
  puses
strep+to+coc+cal
strep+to+coc+cic
strep+to+coc+
  cus
strep+to+coc+ci
strep+to+my+cin
strep+to+thri+cin
stress
stresses
stresses
stress+ing
stressed
stress+ful
stretch
stretches
stretches
stretch+ing
stretched
stretch+abil+ity
stretch+able
stretch+er
stretch+ers
stretch+ers
stretch+er+ing
stretch+ered
stretcher-bearer
stretcher-
  bearers
stretchi+ness
stretch+marks
stretchy
stretchi+er
stretchi+est
Stret+ford
stret+to
stret+tos *or*

stret+ti
strew
strews
strew+ing
strewed
strewn *or*
strewed
strew+er
strew+ers
strewth
stria
striae
stri+ate
stri+ates
stri+at+ing
stri+at+ed
stria+tion
stria+tions
strick+en
strick+en+ly
strict
strict+er
strict+est
strict+ly
strict+ness
stric+ture
stric+tures
stric+tured
stride
strides
strides
strid+ing
strode
strid+den
stri+dence
stri+den+cy
stri+dent
stri+dent+ly
strid+er
strid+ers
stri+dor
stri+dors
stridu+lant
stridu+late
stridu+lates
stridu+lat+ing
stridu+lat+ed
stridu+la+tion
stridu+la+tor
stridu+la+tors
stridu+lous
stridu+lous+ness
strife
strig+il

strig+ils
stri+gose
strike
  strikes
  strikes
strik+ing
  struck
strike+bound
strike+breaker
  strike+breakers
strike+breaking
strike-off
noun
strike off
verb
strik+er
  strik+ers
strik+ing
strik+ing+ly
strik+ing+ness
Stri+mon
Strindberg
Strine
string
  strings
  strings
string+ing
  strung
string+board
  string+boards
stringed
strin+gen+cy
strin+gen+do
strin+gent
strin+gent+ly
string+er
  string+ers
string+halt
stringi+ly
stringi+ness
string+like
string+piece
  string+pieces
stringy
  stringi+er
  stringi+est
stringy-bark
  stringy-barks
strip
  strips
  strips
strip+ping
  stripped
stripe
  stripes

stripes
strip+ing
striped
striped
strip+ling
  strip+lings
strip+per
  strip+pers
strip-search
  strip-searches
  strip-searches
  strip-searching
  strip-searched
  strip-searching
strip+tease
  strip+teaser
  strip+teasers
stripy
  stripi+er
  stripi+est
strive
  strives
  striv+ing
  strove
  striv+en
  striv+er
  striv+ers
strobe
  strobes
stro+bile
  stro+biles
  stro+bi+lus
  stro+bi+luses
  or
  stro+bi+li
stro+bo+scope
  stro+bo+scopes
  stro+bo+scop+ic
  stro+bo+scopi+
  cal
  stro+bo+scopi+
  cal+ly
strode
Stroessner
stroga+noff
Stroheim
stroke
  strokes
  strokes
  strok+ing
  stroked
stroke+play
adj.
stroke play
noun

stroll
  strolls
  strolls
stroll+ing
  strolled
stroll+er
  stroll+ers
stro+ma
  stro+ma+ta
stro+mat+ic
  stro+ma+tous
Strom+bo+li
Strom+bo+lian
strong
  strong+er
  strong+est
strong-arm
  strong-arms
  strong-arming
  strong-armed
strong+box
  strong+boxes
strong+hold
  strong+holds
strong+ly
strong-minded
  strong-minded+ly
  strong-minded+
  ness
strong+ness
strong+point
  strong+points
strong+room
  strong+rooms
strong-willed
stron+tium
strop
  strops
  strops
strop+ping
  stropped
stro+phan+thin
  stro+phan+thus
stro+phe
  stro+phes
stroph+ic
strop+pi+ly
strop+pi+ness
strop+py
  strop+pi+er
  strop+pi+est
strove
strow
  strows
  strow+ing

strowed
strown *or*
  strowed
struck
struc+tur+al
  struc+tur+al+ism
  struc+tur+al+ist
  ists
struc+ture
  struc+tures
  struc+tures
struc+tur+ing
  struc+tured
  struc+tured
stru+del
  stru+dels
strug+gle
  strug+gles
  strug+gles
  strug+gling
  strug+gled
  strug+gling
strum
  strums
strum+ming
  strummed
stru+ma
  stru+mae
Stru+ma
strum+mer
  strum+mers
stru+mose
  stru+mous
strum+pet
  strum+pets
strung
strut
  struts
  struts
strut+ting
  strut+ted
stru+thi+ous
strut+ter
  strut+ters
strut+ting
  strut+ting+ly
strych+nine
Stry+mon
Stuart
stub
  stubs
  stubs
stub+bing

stubbed
stub+bi+ly
stub+bi+ness
stub+ble
stub+bled
stubble-jumper
stubble-jumpers
stub+born
stub+born+ly
stub+born+ness
Stubbs
stub+by
stub+bies
stub+bi+er
stub+bi+est
stuc+co
stuc+coes *or*
stuc+cos
stuc+coes *or*
stuc+cos
stuc+co+ing
stuc+coed
stuck
stuck-up
stuck-upness
stud
studs
studs
stud+ding
stud+ded
stud+book
stud+books
stud+ding
studding+sail
studding+sails
stu+dent
stu+dents
stud+horse
stud+horses
stud+ied
stud+ied+ly
stud+ied+ness
stu+dio
stu+dios
stu+di+ous
stu+di+ous+ly
stu+di+ous+ness
study
studies
stud+ies
study+ing
stud+ied
stuff
stuffs
stuff+ing

stuffed
stuffed
stuff+er
stuff+ers
stuffi+ly
stuffi+ness
stuff+ing
stuff+ings
stuffy
stuffi+er
stuffi+est
stul+ti+fi+ca+tion
stul+ti+fi+er
stul+ti+fi+ers
stul+ti+fy
stul+ti+fies
stul+ti+fy+ing
stul+ti+fied
stum
stum's
stum+ming
stummed
stum+ble
stum+bles
stum+bles
stum+bling
stum+bled
stum+bler
stum+blers
stum+bling
stum+bling+ly
stu+mer
stu+mers
stump
stumps
stumps
stump+ing
stumped
stump+er
stump+ers
stumpi+ness
stumpy
stumpi+er
stumpi+est
stun
stuns
stun+ning
stunned
stung
stunk
stun+ner
stun+ners
stun+ning
stun+ning+ly
stun+sail

stun+sails
stuns'l
stuns'ls
stunt
stunts
stunts
stunt+ing
stunt+ed
stunt+ed
stunt+ed+ness
stu+pa
stu+pas
stupe
stupes
stu+pefa+ci+ent
stu+pefa+ci+
ents
stu+pefac+tion
stu+pefy
stu+pefies
stu+pefy+ing
stu+pefied
stu+pefy+ing
stu+pen+dous
stu+pen+dous+ly
stu+pen+dous+
ness
stu+pid
stu+pids
stu+pid+er
stu+pid+est
stu+pid+ity
stu+pid+ities
stu+pid+ness
stu+por
stu+pors
stu+por+ous
stur+di+ly
stur+di+ness
stur+dy
stur+di+er
stur+di+est
stur+geon
stur+geons
Sturt
stut+ter
stut+ters
stut+ters
stut+ter+ing
stut+tered
stut+ter+er
stut+ter+ers
stut+ter+ing
stut+ter+ing+ly
Stutt+gart

Stuyvesant
sty
sties
sties
sty+ing
stied
stye
styes
Styg+ian
sty+lar
style
styles
styles
styl+ing
styled
style+book
style+books
styl+er
styl+ers
sty+let
sty+lets
styl+ing
styli+sa+tion
styli+sa+tions
styl+ise
styl+ises
styl+is+ing
styl+ised
styl+ish
styl+ish+ly
styl+ish+ness
styl+ist
styl+ists
sty+lis+tic
sty+lis+ti+cal+ly
sty+lite
sty+lites
sty+lit+ic
styli+za+tion
styli+za+tions
styl+ize
styl+izes
styl+iz+ing
styl+ized
sty+lo+bate
sty+lo+bates
sty+lo+graph
sty+lo+graphs
sty+loid
sty+lops
sty+lo+pes
sty+lus
sty+li *or*
sty+luses
sty+mie

sty+mies
sty+mies
sty+mie+ing
sty+mied
sty+my
sty+mies
sty+mies
sty+my+ing
sty+mied
styp+tic
styp+tics
sty+rene
Styria
Styx
su+abil+ity
su+able
Sua+kin
Suárez
sua+sion
sua+sive
suave
suav+er
suav+est
suave+ly
suave+ness
suav+ity
sub
 subs
 subs
 sub+bing
 subbed
sub+ab+do+min+
 al
sub+acid
sub+acid+ity
sub+acid+ness
sub+acute
su+ba+dar
 su+ba+dars
sub+agent
 sub+agents
su+bah+dar
 su+bah+dars
sub+al+pine
sub+al+tern
 sub+al+terns
sub+al+ter+na+
 tion
sub+ant+arc+tic
sub+aqua
sub+aquat+ic
sub+aque+ous
sub+arc+tic
sub+ar+ti+cle
 sub+ar+ti+cles

sub+atom+ic
sub+av+er+age
sub+ax+il+la+ry
sub+base+ment
 sub+base+
  ments
sub+branch
sub+branches
sub+cat+ego+ry
 sub+cat+ego+
  ries
sub+cell
 sub+cells
sub+chap+ter
 sub+chap+ters
sub+chief
 sub+chiefs
sub+class
 sub+classes
sub+clas+si+fi+
  ca+tion
 sub+clas+si+fi+
  ca+tions
sub+clas+si+fy
 sub+clas+si+fies
 sub+clas+si+fy+
  ing
 sub+clas+si+
  fied
sub+clause
 sub+clauses
sub+cla+vian
sub+clini+cal
sub+clini+cal+ly
sub+com+mand+
  er
 sub+com+mand+
  ers
sub+com+mis+
  sion
 sub+com+mis+
  sions
 sub+com+mis+
  sion+er
 sub+com+mis+
  sion+ers
sub+com+mit+
  tee
 sub+com+mit+
  tees
sub+con+scious
sub+con+scious+
  ly
sub+con+scious+
  ness

sub+con+ti+nent
sub+con+ti+
  nents
sub+con+ti+nen+
  tal
sub+con+tract
 sub+con+tracts
 sub+con+tracts
 sub+con+tract+
  ing
 sub+con+tract+
  ed
 sub+con+trac+
  tor
 sub+con+trac+
  tors
sub+con+tra+ry
 sub+con+tra+
  ries
sub+cra+nial
sub+criti+cal
sub+cul+tur+al
sub+cul+ture
 sub+cul+tures
sub+cu+ta+
  neous
 sub+cu+ta+
  neous+ly
sub+dea+con
 sub+dea+cons
 sub+dea+con+
  ate
sub+de+pot
 sub+de+pots
sub+dis+trict
 sub+dis+tricts
sub+di+vide
 sub+di+vides
 sub+di+vid+ing
 sub+di+vid+ed
sub+di+vi+sion
 sub+di+vi+sions
sub+domi+nant
 sub+domi+nants
sub+du+able
sub+du+al
sub+due
 sub+dues
 sub+du+ing
 sub+dued
sub+dued
 sub+du+ral
sub+edit
 sub+edits
 sub+edit+ing

sub+edit+ed
sub+edi+tor
 sub+edi+tors
sub+en+try
 sub+en+tries
sub+equa+to+rial
su+bereous
su+ber+ic
su+ber+ose
sub+fami+ly
 sub+fami+lies
sub+file
 sub+files
sub+floor
 sub+floors
sub+fore+man
 sub+fore+men
sub+freez+ing
sub+func+tion
 sub+func+tions
sub+fusc
sub+ge+ner+ic
sub+ge+nus
  or
 sub+ge+nuses
sub+group
 sub+groups
sub+head
 sub+heads
sub+head+ing
 sub+head+ings
sub+hu+man
sub+in+dex
 sub+in+dices
  or
 sub+in+dexes
subi+tise
 subi+tises
 subi+tis+ing
 subi+tised
subi+tize
 subi+tizes
 subi+tiz+ing
 subi+tized
su+bi+to
sub+ja+cen+cy
sub+ja+cent
sub+ja+cent+ly
sub+ject
 sub+jects
 sub+jects
 sub+ject+ing
 sub+ject+ed
 sub+ject+able

sub+jec+tion
sub+jec+tions
sub+jec+tive
sub+jec+tives
sub+jec+tive+ly
sub+jec+tive+
  ness
sub+jec+tiv+ism
sub+jec+tiv+ist
sub+jec+tiv+ists
sub+jec+tiv+ity
sub+join
sub+joins
sub+join+ing
sub+joined
sub+join+der
sub+join+ders
sub ju+di+ce
sub+ju+gable
sub+ju+gate
sub+ju+gates
sub+ju+gat+ing
sub+ju+gat+ed
sub+ju+ga+tion
sub+ju+ga+tor
sub+ju+ga+tors
sub+junc+tive
sub+junc+tives
sub+junc+tive+ly
sub+lease
sub+leases
sub+leases
sub+leas+ing
sub+leased
sub+les+see
sub+les+sees
sub+les+sor
sub+les+sors
sub+let
sub+lets
sub+let+ting
sub+let
sub+lieu+ten+an+
  cy
sub+lieu+ten+ant
sub+lieu+ten+
  ants
sub+li+mate
sub+li+mates
sub+li+mates
sub+li+mat+ing
sub+li+mat+ed
sub+li+ma+tion
sub+lime
sub+limes

sub+lim+ing
sub+limed
sub+lime+ly
sub+limi+nal
sub+limi+nal+ly
sub+lim+ity
sub+lin+gual
sub+lu+nary
sub-machine-gun
sub-machine-
  guns
sub+mar+gin+al
sub+mar+gin+al+
  ly
sub+ma+rine
sub+ma+rines
sub+ma+rin+er
sub+ma+rin+ers
sub+me+di+ant
sub+me+di+
  ants
sub+merge
sub+merges
sub+merg+ing
sub+merged
sub+merg+ence
sub+merg+
  ences
sub+merg+ibil+
  ity
sub+merg+ible
sub+merg+ibles
sub+merse
sub+merses
sub+mers+ing
sub+mersed
sub+mers+ibil+ity
sub+mers+ible
sub+mers+ibles
sub+mer+sion
sub+mer+sions
sub+micro+scop+
  ic
sub+minia+ture
sub+mis+sible
sub+mis+sion
sub+mis+sions
sub+mis+sive
sub+mis+sive+ly
sub+mis+sive+
  ness
sub+mit
sub+mits
sub+mit+ting
sub+mit+ted

sub+mit+table
sub+mit+tal
sub+mit+tals
sub+mit+ter
sub+mit+ters
sub+mo+lecu+lar
sub+mul+ti+ple
sub+mul+ti+ples
sub+nor+mal
sub+nor+mals
sub+nor+mal+ity
sub+nu+clear
sub+of+fice
sub+of+fices
sub+or+bi+tal
sub+or+der
sub+or+ders
sub+or+di+nal
sub+or+di+nate
sub+or+di+
  nates
sub+or+di+
  nates
sub+or+di+nat+
  ing
sub+or+di+nat+
  ed
sub+or+di+nate+
  ly
sub+or+di+nat+
  ing
sub+or+di+na+
  tion
sub+or+di+na+
  tive
sub+orn
sub+orns
sub+orn+ing
sub+orned
sub+or+na+tion
sub+or+na+
  tions
sub+or+na+tive
sub+orn+er
sub+orn+ers
Su+bo+ti+ca
sub+ox+ide
sub+ox+ides
sub+para+graph
sub+para+
  graphs
sub+phy+lum
sub+phy+la
sub+plot
sub+plots

sub+poe+na
sub+poe+nas
sub+poe+nas
sub+poe+na+
  ing
sub+poe+naed
sub+re+gion
sub+re+gions
sub+ro+gate
sub+ro+gates
sub+ro+gat+ing
sub+ro+gat+ed
sub+ro+ga+tion
sub+ro+ga+
  tions
sub rosa
sub+rou+tine
sub+rou+tines
sub+satu+ra+tion
sub+satu+ra+
  tions
sub+scapu+lar
sub+scapu+lars
sub+scribe
sub+scribes
sub+scrib+ing
sub+scribed
sub+scrib+er
sub+scrib+ers
sub+script
sub+scripts
sub+scrip+tion
sub+scrip+tions
sub+scrip+tive
sub+sec+tion
sub+sec+tions
sub+se+quence
sub+se+
  quences
sub+se+quent
sub+se+quent+ly
sub+se+quent+
  ness
sub+se+ries
sub+se+ries
sub+serve
sub+serves
sub+serv+ing
sub+served
sub+ser+vi+ence
sub+ser+vi+en+
  cy
sub+ser+vi+ent
sub+ser+vi+ent+
  ly

sub+set
sub+sets
sub+shrub
sub+shrubs
sub+side
sub+sides
sub+sid+ing
sub+sid+ed
sub+sid+ence
sub+sid+ences
sub+sid+er
sub+sid+ers
sub+sidi+ari+ly
sub+sidi+ari+
ness
sub+sidi+ary
sub+sidi+aries
sub+si+di+sa+
tion
sub+si+di+sa+
tions
sub+si+dise
sub+si+dises
sub+si+dis+ing
sub+si+dised
sub+si+dis+er
sub+si+dis+ers
sub+si+di+za+
tion
sub+si+di+za+
tions
sub+si+dize
sub+si+dizes
sub+si+diz+ing
sub+si+dized
sub+si+diz+er
sub+si+diz+ers
sub+si+dy
sub+si+dies
sub+sist
sub+sists
sub+sist+ing
sub+sist+ed
sub+sist+ence
sub+sist+ent
sub+soil
sub+soils
sub+soils
sub+soil+ing
sub+soiled
sub+son+ic
sub+spe+cies
sub+spe+cies
sub+stance
sub+stances

sub+stand+ard
sub+stan+tial
sub+stan+tials
sub+stan+tial+
ism
sub+stan+tial+ist
sub+stan+tial+
ists
sub+stan+ti+al+
ity
sub+stan+tial+ly
sub+stan+tial+
ness
sub+stan+ti+ate
sub+stan+ti+
ates
sub+stan+ti+at+
ing
sub+stan+ti+at+
ed
sub+stan+tia+
tion
sub+stan+tia+
tions
sub+stan+ti+val
sub+stan+ti+val+
ly
sub+stan+tive
sub+stan+tives
sub+stan+tive+ly
sub+sta+tion
sub+sta+tions
sub+stitu+ent
sub+stitu+ents
sub+sti+tut+able
sub+sti+tute
sub+sti+tutes
sub+sti+tutes
sub+sti+tut+ing
sub+sti+tut+ed
sub+sti+tu+tion
sub+sti+tu+
tions
sub+sti+tu+tive
sub+stra+tal
sub+strate
sub+strates
sub+stra+tive
sub+stra+tum
sub+stra+ta
sub+struc+tur+al
sub+struc+ture
sub+struc+tures
sub+sum+able
sub+sume

sub+sumes
sub+sum+ing
sub+sumed
sub+sump+tion
sub+sump+tions
sub+sur+face
sub+sys+tem
sub+sys+tems
sub+tem+per+
ate
sub+ten+an+cy
sub+ten+an+
cies
sub+ten+ant
sub+ten+ants
sub+tend
sub+tends
sub+tend+ing
sub+tend+ed
sub+ter+fuge
sub+ter+fuges
sub+termi+nal
sub+ter+ra+nean
sub+ter+ra+nean+
ly
sub+ter+ra+
neous+ly
sub+tile
sub+til+er
sub+til+est
sub+tile+ly
sub+tile+ness
sub+tili+sa+tion
sub+til+ise
sub+til+ises
sub+til+is+ing
sub+til+ised
sub+til+ity
sub+tili+za+tion
sub+til+ize
sub+til+izes
sub+til+iz+ing
sub+til+ized
sub+til+ty
sub+til+ties
sub+ti+tle
sub+ti+tles
sub+ti+tles
sub+ti+tling
sub+ti+tled
sub+tle
sub+tler
sub+tlest
sub+tle+ness
sub+tle+ty

sub+tle+ties
sub+tly
sub+ton+ic
sub+ton+ics
sub+to+tal
sub+to+tals
sub+to+tals
sub+to+tal+ling
or
sub+to+tal+ing
U.S.
sub+to+talled
or
sub+to+taled
U.S.
sub+tract
sub+tracts
sub+tract+ing
sub+tract+ed
sub+tract+er
sub+tract+ers
sub+trac+tion
sub+trac+tions
sub+trac+tive
sub+tra+hend
sub+tra+hends
sub+tropi+cal
sub+trop+ics
su+bu+late
sub+urb
sub+urbs
sub+ur+ban
sub+ur+ban+ise
sub+ur+ban+
ises
sub+ur+ban+is+
ing
sub+ur+ban+
ised
sub+ur+ban+ite
sub+ur+ban+
ites
sub+ur+ban+ize
sub+ur+ban+
izes
sub+ur+ban+iz+
ing
sub+ur+ban+
ized
sub+ur+bia
sub+va+ri+ety
sub+va+ri+eties
sub+ven+tion
sub+ven+tions
sub+ver+sion

sub+ver+sions
sub+ver+sive
sub+ver+sives
sub+ver+sive+ly
sub+ver+sive+
    ness
sub+vert
sub+verts
sub+vert+ing
sub+vert+ed
sub+vert+er
sub+vert+ers
sub+way
sub+ways
sub+zero
suc+ce+da+
    neous
suc+ce+da+neum
suc+ce+da+nea
suc+ceed
suc+ceeds
suc+ceed+ing
suc+ceed+ed
suc+ceed+er
suc+ceed+ers
suc+ceed+ing+ly
suc+cess
suc+cesses
suc+cess+ful
suc+cess+ful+ly
suc+cess+ful+
    ness
suc+ces+sion
suc+ces+sions
suc+ces+sion+al
suc+ces+sive
suc+ces+sive+ly
suc+ces+sive+
    ness
suc+ces+sor
suc+ces+sors
suc+cinct
suc+cinct+ly
suc+cinct+ness
suc+cor
U.S.
suc+cors
suc+cors
suc+cor+ing
suc+cored
suc+co+tash
Suc+coth
Suc+coths
suc+cour
suc+cours

suc+cours
suc+cour+ing
suc+coured
suc+cu+bus
suc+cu+bi
suc+cu+lence
suc+cu+len+cy
suc+cu+lent
suc+cu+lents
suc+cu+lent+ly
suc+cumb
suc+cumbs
suc+cumb+ing
suc+cumbed
suc+cur+sal
suc+cur+sals
such
such+like
Su-chou
Sü+chow
suck
sucks
sucks
suck+ing
sucked
suck+er
suck+ers
suck+ers
suck+er+ing
suck+ered
suck+le
suck+les
suck+ling
suck+led
suck+ler
suck+lers
suck+ling
suck+lings
Suckling
sucks
su+crase
su+cre
su+cres
Su+cre
place name
Sucre
surname
su+crose
suc+tion
suc+to+rial
Su+dan
Su+da+nese
su+dar+ium
su+daria
su+da+to+rium

su+da+to+ria
su+da+tory
su+da+tories
Sud+bury
sudd
sud+den
sud+dens
sud+den+ly
sud+den+ness
Su+deten+land
Su+detes
su+dor
su+dor+al
su+dor+if+er+
    ous
su+dor+if+er+
    ous+ness
su+dor+if+ic
su+dor+if+ics
suds
sudsy
sue
sues
su+ing
sued
Sue
suede
suer
suers
suet
Suetonius
su+ety
Suez
suf+fer
suf+fers
suf+fer+ing
suf+fered
suf+fer+able
suf+fer+ance
suf+fer+er
suf+fer+ers
suf+fer+ing
suf+fer+ings
suf+fice
suf+fices
suf+fic+ing
suf+ficed
suf+fi+cien+cy
suf+fi+cien+cies
suf+fi+cient
suf+fi+cient+ly
suf+fix
suf+fixes
suf+fixes
suf+fix+ing

suf+fixed
suf+fo+cate
suf+fo+cates
suf+fo+cat+ing
suf+fo+cat+ed
suf+fo+cat+ing
suf+fo+ca+tion
Suf+folk
suf+fra+gan
suf+fra+gans
suf+fra+gan+ship
suf+frage
suf+frages
suf+fra+gette
suf+fra+gettes
suf+frag+ism
suf+fra+gist
suf+fra+gists
suf+fru+ti+cose
suf+fuse
suf+fuses
suf+fus+ing
suf+fused
suf+fu+sion
suf+fu+sions
suf+fu+sive
Sufi
Sufis
Su+fic
Su+fism
Sufu
sug
sugs
sug+ging
sugged
sug+ar
sug+ars
sug+ars
sug+ar+ing
sug+ared
sugar-coat
sugar-coats
sugar-coating
sugar-coated
sug+ared
sug+ari+ness
sug+ar+ing
sugar+plum
sugar+plums
sug+ary
sug+gest
sug+gests
sug+gest+ing
sug+gest+ed
sug+gest+er

sug+gest+ers
sug+gest+ibil+ity
sug+gest+ible
sug+ges+tion
sug+ges+tions
sug+ges+tive
sug+ges+tive+ly
sug+ges+tive+
ness
sug+ging
Suharto
sui+cid+al
sui+cid+al+ly
sui+cide
sui+cides
sui gen+eris
su+int
Suisse
suit
suits
suits
suit+ing
suit+ed
suit+abil+ity
suit+able
suit+able+ness
suit+ably
suit+case
suit+cases
suite
suites
suit+ing
suit+or
suit+ors
Sui+yüan
Su+kar+na+pu+
ra
Sukarno
Su+khu+mi
su+ki+ya+ki
Suk+koth
Suk+koths
Su+la+we+si
sul+cate
sul+cus
sul+ci
sul+fur
U.S.
sul+fu+ric
U.S.
sulk
sulks
sulks
sulk+ing
sulked

sulki+ly
sulki+ness
sulky
sulkies
sulki+er
sulki+est
Sulla
sul+lage
sul+len
sul+lens
sul+len+ly
sul+len+ness
Sullivan
Sul+lom Voe
sul+ly
sul+lies
sul+ly+ing
sul+lied
Sully-Prudhomme
sul+pha
sul+pha+dia+zine
sul+pha+nila+
mide
sul+phate
sul+phates
sul+phates
sul+phat+ing
sul+phat+ed
sul+pha+tion
sul+phide
sul+phides
sul+phite
sul+phites
sul+phit+ic
sul+phona+mide
sul+phona+
mides
sul+phone
sul+phones
sul+phon+ic
sul+phon+me+
thane
sul+phur
sul+phur+ate
sul+phur+ates
sul+phur+at+ing
sul+phur+at+ed
sulphur-bottom
sulphur-bottoms
sul+phu+reous
sul+phu+ric
sul+phu+rise
sul+phu+rises
sul+phu+ris+ing

sul+phu+rised
sul+phu+ri+za+
tion
sul+phu+rize
sul+phu+rizes
sul+phu+riz+ing
sul+phu+rized
sul+phur+ous
sul+phur+ous+ly
sul+phur+ous+
ness
sul+tan
sul+tans
sul+tana
sul+tanas
sul+tan+ate
sul+tan+ates
sul+tri+ly
sul+tri+ness
sul+try
sul+tri+er
sul+tri+est
sum
sums
sums
sum+ming
summed
su+mac
U.S.
su+macs
su+mach
su+machs
Su+ma+tra
Su+ma+tran
Su+ma+trans
Sum+ba
Sum+ba+wa
Su+mer
Su+me+rian
Su+me+rians
sum+ma cum lau+
de
sum+mari+ly
sum+ma+ri+sa+
tion
sum+ma+rise
sum+ma+rises
sum+ma+ris+ing
sum+ma+rised
sum+ma+ris+er
sum+ma+ris+
ers
sum+ma+rist
sum+ma+rists

sum+ma+ri+za+
tion
sum+ma+rize
sum+ma+rizes
sum+ma+riz+ing
sum+ma+riz+er
sum+ma+riz+ers
sum+mary
sum+maries
sum+ma+tion
sum+ma+tions
sum+ma+tion+al
sum+ma+tive
sum+mer
sum+mers
sum+mers
sum+mer+ing
sum+mered
summer+house
summer+houses
sum+mer+ly
sum+mer+sault
sum+mer+saults
sum+mer+saults
sum+mer+sault+
ing
sum+mer+sault+
ed
summer+time
summer season
sum+mer time
*daylight-saving
time*
summer+weight
sum+mery
summing-up
summings-up
sum+mit
sum+mits
sum+mon
sum+mons
sum+mon+ing
sum+moned
sum+mons
sum+monses
sum+monses
sum+mons+ing
sum+monsed
sum+mum bo+
num
sumo
sump
sumps
sump+ter

sump+ters
sump+tua+ry
sump+tu+ous
sump+tu+ous+ly
sump+tu+ous+
　ness
Sum+ter
Sumy
sun
　suns
　suns
sun+ning
sunned
sun+baked
sun+bathe
　sun+bathes
　sun+bath+ing
sun+bathed
sun+bather
　sun+bathers
sun+beam
　sun+beams
Sun+belt
sun+bird
　sun+birds
sun+bonnet
　sun+bonnets
sun+burn
sun+burned
sun+burnt
sun+burst
　sun+bursts
Sunbury-on-
　Thames
sun-cured
sun+dae
　sun+daes
Sun+day
　Sun+days
Sunday-school
adj.
Sun+day school
　Sun+day schools
sun+der
　sun+ders
　sun+der+ing
　sun+dered
Sun+der+land
sun+dew
　sun+dews
sun+dial
　sun+dials
sun+dog
　sun+dogs
sun+down

sun+downs
sun+downer
　sun+downers
sun+dress
　sun+dresses
sun-dried
sun+dry
　sun+dries
Sunds+vall
sun+fast
sun+fish
　sun+fish or
　sun+fishes
sun+flower
　sun+flowers
sung
Sung
Sun+ga+ri
Sung+kiang
sun+glass
　sun+glasses
　sun+glasses
sun-god
　sun-gods
sunk
sunk+en
sun+less
　sun+less+ly
sun+light
sun+lit
Sun+na
Sun+ni
sun+ni+ly
sun+ni+ness
Sun+nite
　Sun+nites
sun+ny
sun+ni+er
sun+ni+est
sun+rise
　sun+rises
sun+roof
　sun+roofs
sun+set
　sun+sets
sun+shade
　sun+shades
sun+shine
　sun+shines
sun+shiny
sun+spot
　sun+spots
sun+stroke
sun+suit

sun+suits
sun+tan
sun+tans
sun+tanned
sun+trap
　sun+traps
sun+ward
Suo+mi
sup
　sups
　sups
sup+ping
supped
su+per
　su+pers
Su+per
super+abil+ity
super+able
super+able+ness
super+ably
super+abound
　super+abounds
super+abound+
　ing
super+abound+
　ed
super+an+nu+ate
super+an+nu+
　ates
super+an+nu+at+
　ing
super+an+nu+at+
　ed
super+an+nu+at+
　ed
super+an+nua+
　tion
super+an+nua+
　tions
su+perb
su+perb+ly
su+perb+ness
super+cal+en+
　der
super+cal+en+
　ders
super+cal+en+
　ders
super+cal+en+
　der+ing
super+cal+en+
　dered
super+cal+en+
　dered
super+car+go

super+car+goes
super+charge
super+charges
super+charg+ing
super+charged
super+char+ger
super+char+
　gers
super+cili+ary
super+cili+ous
super+cili+ous+ly
super+cili+ous+
　ness
super+class
super+classes
super+co+lum+
　nar
super+col+um+
　nia+tion
super+con+duct+
　ing
super+con+duc+
　tion
super+con+duc+
　tive
super+con+duc+
　tiv+ity
super+con+duc+
　tor
super+con+duc+
　tors
super+con+fi+
　dent
super+con+ti+
　nent
super+con+ti+
　nents
super+cool
super+cools
super+cool+ing
super+cooled
super+criti+cal
super+cyni+cal
super+dose
　super+doses
super-duper
super+ef+fec+
　tive
super+ef+fi+cient
super+ego
　super+egos
super+el+eva+
　tion
　super+el+eva+
　tions

super+ emi+ nence
super+ emi+ nent
super+ emi+ nent+ ly
super+ ero+ ga+ tion
super+ eroga+ tory
super+ fami+ ly
super+ fami+ lies
super+ fe+ cun+ da+ tion
super+ fe+ ta+ tion
super+ fi+ cial
super+ fi+ ci+ al+ ity
super+ fi+ cial+ ly
super+ fi+ cies
super+ fi+ cies
super+ fine
super+ fine+ ness
super+ fix
super+ fixes
super+ fluid
super+ fluids
super+ flu+ id+ ity
super+ flu+ ity
super+ flu+ ities
super+ flu+ ous
super+ flu+ ous+ ly
super+ flu+ ous+ ness
super+ gi+ ant
super+ gi+ ants
super+ glue
super+ grass
super+ grasses
super+ grav+ ity
super+ heat
super+ heats
super+ heat+ ing
super+ heat+ ed
super+ heat+ er
super+ heat+ ers
super+ heavy
super+ het
super+ hets
super+ hu+ man
super+ hu+ man+ ly
super+ im+ pose
super+ im+ poses
super+ im+ pos+ ing

super+ im+ posed
super+ im+ po+ si+ tion
super+ in+ duce
super+ in+ duces
super+ in+ duc+ ing
super+ in+ duced
super+ in+ duc+ tion
super+ in+ tel+ lec+ tual
super+ in+ tel+ li+ gent
super+ in+ tend
super+ in+ tends
super+ in+ tend+ ing
super+ in+ tend+ ed
super+ in+ tend+ ence
super+ in+ tend+ en+ cy
super+ in+ tend+ en+ cies
super+ in+ ten+ dent
super+ in+ ten+ dents
su+ peri+ or
su+ peri+ ors
Su+ peri+ or
su+ peri+ or+ ess
su+ peri+ or+ ity
super+ la+ tive
super+ la+ tives
super+ la+ tive+ ly
super+ la+ tive+ ness
super+ lun+ ar
super+ lun+ ary
super+ luxu+ ri+ ous
super+ man
super+ men
super+ mar+ ket
super+ mar+ kets
super+ mem+ brane
super+ mem+ branes
super+ mun+ dane
super+ nal

super+ nal+ ly
super+ na+ tant
super+ na+ ta+ tion
super+ na+ ta+ tions
super+ natu+ ral
super+ natu+ ral+ ism
super+ natu+ ral+ ist
super+ natu+ ral+ ists
super+ natu+ ral+ is+ tic
super+ natu+ ral+ ly
super+ natu+ ral+ ness
super+ nor+ mal
super+ nor+ mal+ ity
super+ nor+ mal+ ly
super+ no+ va
super+ no+ vae
or
super+ no+ vas
super+ nu+ mer+ ary
super+ nu+ mer+ aries
super+ or+ der
super+ or+ ders
super+ or+ di+ nate
super+ or+ di+ nates
super+ phos+ phate
super+ poly+ mer
super+ poly+ mers
super+ pose
super+ poses
super+ pos+ ing
super+ posed
super+ po+ si+ tion
super+ pow+ er
super+ pow+ ers
super+ pow+ ered
super+ pure
super+ re+ fine
super+ re+ fines
super+ re+ fin+ ing
super+ re+ fined

super+ rich
super+ satu+ rat+ ed
super+ satu+ ra+ tion
super+ scribe
super+ scribes
super+ scrib+ ing
super+ scribed
super+ script
super+ scripts
super+ scrip+ tion
super+ scrip+ tions
super+ sede
super+ sedes
super+ sed+ ing
super+ sed+ ed
super+ sed+ ence
super+ se+ dure
super+ sen+ si+ tive
super+ ses+ sion
super+ sex
super+ sexes
super+ son+ ic
super+ soni+ cal+ ly
super+ son+ ics
super+ star
super+ stars
super+ sti+ tion
super+ sti+ tions
super+ sti+ tious
super+ sti+ tious+ ly
super+ sti+ tious+ ness
super+ store
super+ stores
super+ stra+ tum
super+ stra+ ta
or
super+ stra+ tums
super+ string
super+ struc+ tur+ al
super+ struc+ ture
super+ struc+ tures
super+ suf+ fi+ cien+ cy
super+ sym+ me+ try

super+tank+er
super+tank+ers
super+tax
super+taxes
super+ton+ic
super+ton+ics
super+vene
super+venes
super+ven+ing
super+vened
super+veni+ence
su+per+veni+ent
super+ven+tion
super+vise
super+vises
super+vis+ing
super+vised
super+vi+sion
super+vi+sor
super+vi+sors
super+vi+sor+ship
super+vi+sory
su+pi+nate
su+pi+nates
su+pi+nat+ing
su+pi+nat+ed
su+pi+na+tion
su+pine
su+pines
su+pine+ly
su+pine+ness
sup+per
sup+pers
sup+per+less
sup+plant
sup+plants
sup+plant+ing
sup+plant+ed
sup+plant+er
sup+plant+ers
sup+ple
sup+ples
sup+pling
sup+pled
supple+jack
supple+jacks
sup+ple+ly
sup+plement
sup+plements
sup+plements
sup+plement+ing
sup+plement+ed

sup+ple+men+ta+ri+ly
sup+plemen+ta+ry
sup+plemen+ta+ries
sup+plemen+ta+tion
sup+plemen+ta+tions
sup+ple+ness
sup+pli+able
sup+pli+ant
sup+pli+ants
sup+pli+ant+ly
sup+pli+cant
sup+pli+cants
sup+pli+cate
sup+pli+cates
sup+pli+cat+ing
sup+pli+cat+ed
sup+pli+ca+tion
sup+pli+ca+tions
sup+pli+ca+tory
sup+pli+er
sup+pli+ers
sup+ply
sup+plies
sup+plies
sup+ply+ing
sup+plied
sup+port
sup+ports
sup+ports
sup+port+ing
sup+port+ed
sup+port+able
sup+port+er
sup+port+ers
sup+port+ing
sup+port+ive
sup+pos+able
sup+pose
sup+poses
sup+pos+ing
sup+posed
sup+posed
sup+pos+ed+ly
sup+pos+er
sup+pos+ers
sup+po+si+tion
sup+po+si+tions

sup+po+si+tion+al
sup+po+si+tion+al+ly
sup+po+si+tious
sup+po+si+tious+ly
sup+po+si+tious+ness
sup+posi+ti+tious
sup+posi+ti+tious+ly
sup+posi+ti+tious+ness
sup+posi+tive
sup+posi+tives
sup+posi+tive+ly
sup+posi+tory
sup+posi+tories
sup+press
sup+presses
sup+press+ing
sup+pressed
sup+press+er
sup+press+ers
sup+press+ible
sup+pres+sion
sup+pres+sions
sup+pres+sive
sup+pres+sor
sup+pres+sors
sup+pu+rate
sup+pu+rates
sup+pu+rat+ing
sup+pu+rat+ed
sup+pu+ra+tion
sup+pu+ra+tive
supra+limi+nal
supra+limi+nal+ly
supra+mo+lecu+lar
supra+na+tion+al
supra+na+tion+al+ism
supra+or+bit+al
supra+renal
su+prema+cist
su+prema+cists
su+prema+cy
su+prema+tism
su+preme
Su+preme
su+prême
su+preme+ly

su+pre+mo
su+pre+mos
Su+qu+tra
Sur
sura
suras
Su+ra+ba+ja
Su+ra+ba+ya
su+rah
Su+ra+kar+ta
su+ral
Su+rat
sur+base
sur+bases
sur+cease
sur+ceases
sur+ceas+ing
sur+ceased
sur+charge
sur+charges
sur+charges
sur+charg+ing
sur+charged
sur+cin+gle
sur+cin+gles
sur+coat
sur+coats
sur+cu+lose
surd
surds
sure
sur+er
sur+est
sure-fire
sure-footed
sure-footed+ly
sure-footed+ness
sure+ly
sure+ness
sure+ty
sure+ties
sure+ty+ship
surf
surfs
surfs
surf+ing
surfed
sur+face
sur+faces
sur+faces
sur+fac+ing
sur+faced
surface-active
sur+fac+er
sur+fac+ers

surface-to-air
sur+fac+tant
sur+fac+tants
surf+board
surf+boards
surf+boat
surf+boats
surf+caster
surf+casters
surf+casting
sur+feit
sur+feits
sur+feits
surf+feit+ing
surf+feit+ed
surf+er
surf+ers
surfie
surfies
surf+ing
surf-rider
surf-riders
surfy
surge
surges
surges
surg+ing
surged
sur+geon
sur+geons
surgeon+fish
surgeon+fish
   or
surgeon+fishes
surg+er
surg+ers
sur+gery
sur+geries
sur+gi+cal
sur+gi+cal+ly
Su+ri+ba+chi
su+ri+cate
su+ri+cates
Su+ri+nam
sur+li+ly
sur+li+ness
sur+ly
sur+li+er
sur+li+est
sur+mise
sur+mises
sur+mises
sur+mis+ing
sur+mised
sur+mount

sur+mounts
sur+mount+ing
sur+mount+ed
sur+mount+able
sur+name
sur+names
sur+names
sur+nam+ing
sur+named
sur+nam+er
sur+nam+ers
sur+pass
sur+passes
sur+pass+ing
sur+passed
sur+pass+able
sur+pas+sing
sur+pass+ing+ly
sur+plice
sur+plices
sur+plus
sur+pluses
sur+pris+al
sur+prise
sur+prises
sur+prises
sur+pris+ing
sur+prised
sur+pris+ed+ly
sur+pris+ing
sur+pris+ing+ly
sur+ra
sur+re+al
sur+re+al+ism
sur+re+al+ist
sur+re+al+ists
sur+re+al+is+tic
sur+re+but+tal
sur+re+but+tals
sur+re+but+ter
sur+re+but+ters
sur+re+join+der
sur+re+join+
   ders
sur+ren+der
sur+ren+ders
sur+ren+ders
sur+ren+der+ing
sur+ren+dered
sur+rep+ti+tious
sur+rep+ti+tious+
   ly
sur+rep+ti+tious+
   ness

sur+rey
sur+reys
Sur+rey
place name
Surrey
surname
sur+ro+ga+cy
sur+ro+gate
sur+ro+gates
sur+ro+gates
sur+ro+gat+ing
sur+ro+gat+ed
sur+ro+gate+ship
sur+ro+ga+tion
sur+ro+ga+tions
sur+round
sur+rounds
sur+rounds
sur+round+ing
sur+round+ed
sur+round+ing
sur+round+ings
sur+sum cor+da
sur+tax
sur+taxes
sur+taxes
sur+tax+ing
sur+taxed
Surtees
sur+ti+tles
sur+tout
sur+touts
sur+veil+lance
sur+veil+lant
sur+veil+lants
sur+vey
sur+veys
sur+veys
sur+vey+ing
sur+veyed
sur+vey+ing
sur+vey+or
sur+vey+ors
sur+vey+or+ship
sur+viv+al
sur+viv+als
sur+viv+al+ism
sur+viv+al+ist
sur+viv+al+ists
sur+vive
sur+vives
sur+viv+ing
sur+vived
sur+vi+vor
sur+vi+vors

sus
susses
sus+sing
sussed
Susa
Su+sah
Susanna
sus+cep+tance
sus+cep+tibil+ity
sus+cep+tibil+
   ities
sus+cep+tible
sus+cep+tibly
su+shi
sus+lik
sus+liks
sus+pect
sus+pects
sus+pects
sus+pect+ing
sus+pect+ed
sus+pend
sus+pends
sus+pend+ing
sus+pend+ed
sus+pend+er
sus+pend+ers
sus+pend+ibil+ity
sus+pend+ible
sus+pense
sus+pense+ful
sus+pens+ible
sus+pen+sion
sus+pen+sions
sus+pen+sive
sus+pen+sive+ly
sus+pen+sive+
   ness
sus+pen+sory
sus+pen+sories
sus+pi+cion
sus+pi+cions
sus+pi+cion+al
sus+pi+cious
sus+pi+cious+ly
sus+pi+cious+
   ness
Sus+que+han+na
suss
susses
suss+ing
sussed
Sus+sex
sus+tain

sus+tains	swab	swal+low+er	swa+raj+ist
sus+tain+ing	swabs	swal+low+ers	swa+raj+ists
sus+tained	swabs	swallow+tail	sward
sus+tain+able	swab+bing	swallow+tails	swards
sus+tained	swabbed	swallow-tailed	swards
sus+tain+ed+ly	swab+ber	swam	sward+ing
sus+tain+er	swab+bers	swa+mi	sward+ed
sus+tain+ers	Swa+bia	swa+mies or	swarf
sus+tain+ing	Swa+bian	swa+mis	swarm
sus+tain+ment	Swa+bians	swamp	swarms
sus+te+nance	swad+die	swamps	swarms
sus+ten+ta+tion	swad+dies	swamps	swarm+ing
su+sur+rate	swad+dle	swamp+ing	swarmed
su+sur+rates	swad+dles	swamped	swart
su+sur+rat+ing	swad+dling	swamp+land	swarth
su+sur+rat+ed	swad+dled	swamp+lands	swarthi+ly
su+sur+ra+tion	swad+dling	swampy	swarthi+ness
Sutcliffe	swad+dy	swampi+er	swarthy
Suth+er+land	swad+dies	swampi+est	swarthi+er
place name	swag	swan	swarthi+est
Sutherland	swags	swans	swash
surname	swags	swans	swashes
Sut+lej	swag+ging	swan+ning	swashes
sut+ler	swagged	swanned	swash+ing
sut+lers	swage	Swan	swashed
su+tra	swages	Swa+nee	swash+buck+ler
su+tras	swages	swank	swash+buck+
sut+tee	swag+ing	swanks	lers
sut+tees	swaged	swanks	swash+buck+ling
sut+tee+ism	swag+er	swank+ing	swas+ti+ka
Sut+ton	swag+ers	swanked	swas+ti+kas
Sutton-in-	swag+ger	swanki+ly	swat
Ashfield	swag+gers	swanki+ness	swats
su+tur+al	swag+gers	swanky	swats
su+ture	swag+ger+ing	swanki+er	swat+ting
su+tures	swag+gered	swanki+est	swat+ted
su+tures	swag+ger+er	swan+like	Swat
su+tur+ing	swag+ger+ers	swan+nery	swatch
su+tured	swag+ger+ing+ly	swan+neries	swatches
Suva	swag+gie	swan's-down	swath
Suvorov	swag+gies	Swan+sea	swaths
Su+wan+nee	swag+man	swan-upping	swathe
su+ze+rain	swag+men	swap	swathes
su+ze+rains	Swa+hi+li	swaps	swathes
su+ze+rain+ty	Swa+hi+lis or	swaps	swath+ing
su+ze+rain+ties	Swa+hi+li	swap+ping	swathed
Su+zhou	Swa+hi+lian	swapped	Swa+tow
Sval+bard	swain	SWAPO	swat+ter
svelte	swains	Swapo	swat+ters
Sven+ga+li	swal+low	swap+per	sway
Sven+ga+lis	swal+lows	swap+pers	sways
Sverd+lovsk	swal+lows	swap+tion	sways
Sve+ri+ge	swal+low+ing	swap+tions	sway+ing
Svevo	swal+lowed	swa+raj	swayed
Sviz+ze+ra	swal+low+able	swa+raj+ism	sway-back

sway-backed
Swa+zi+land
swear
 swears
 swear+ing
 swore
 sworn
swear+er
swear+ers
swear+word
 swear+words
sweat
 sweats
 sweats
 sweat+ing
 sweat+ed
sweat+band
 sweat+bands
sweat+ed
sweat+er
 sweat+ers
sweati+ly
sweati+ness
sweat+ing
 sweats
sweat+shirt
 sweat+shirts
sweat+shop
 sweat+shops
sweaty
 sweati+er
 sweati+est
swede
 swedes
Swede
 Swedes
Swe+den
Swedenborg
Swe+dish
Sweelinck
sweep
 sweeps
 sweeps
 sweep+ing
 swept
sweep+er
 sweep+ers
sweep+ing
sweep+ing+ly
sweep+ing+ness
sweep-saw
 sweep-saws
sweep+stake
 sweep+stakes
 sweep+stakes

U.S.
sweepy
sweet
 sweets
 sweet+er
 sweet+est
Sweet
sweet-and-sour
sweet+bread
 sweet+breads
sweet+brier
 sweet+briers
sweet+en
 sweet+ens
 sweet+en+ing
 sweet+ened
sweet+en+er
 sweet+en+ers
 sweet+en+ing
 sweet+en+ings
sweet+heart
 sweet+hearts
sweetie
 sweeties
sweet+ing
 sweet+ings
sweet+ish
sweet+ly
sweet+meat
 sweet+meats
sweet+ness
sweet+sop
 sweet+sops
sweet-talk
 sweet-talks
 sweet-talking
 sweet-talked
sweet talk
 noun
swell
 swells
 swells
 swell+ing
 swelled
 swol+len *or*
 swelled
 swell+ing
 swell+ings
swel+ter
 swel+ters
 swel+ters
 swel+ter+ing
 swel+tered
 swel+ter+ing
 swel+ter+ing+ly

swept
swept+back
swept+wing
swerv+able
swerve
 swerves
 swerves
 swerv+ing
 swerved
swerv+er
 swerv+ers
Sweyn
swift
 swifts
 swift+er
 swift+est
Swift
swift+let
 swift+lets
swift+ly
swift+ness
swig
 swigs
 swigs
 swig+ging
 swigged
swig+ger
 swig+gers
swill
 swills
 swills
 swill+ing
 swilled
swill+er
 swill+ers
swim
 swims
 swim+ming
 swam
 swum
swim+mable
swim+mer
 swim+mers
 swim+mer+et
 swim+mer+ets
swim+ming
swim+ming+ly
swim+suit
 swim+suits
Swinburne
swin+dle
 swin+dles
 swin+dles
 swin+dling
 swin+dled

swin+dler
 swin+dlers
Swin+don
swine
 swines
 people
 swine
 pigs
swine+herd
 swine+herds
swing
 swings
 swings
 swing+ing
 swung
swing+boat
 swing+boats
swinge
 swinges
 swinge+ing *or*
 swing+ing
 swinged
 swinge+ing
swing+er
 swing+ers
swing+ing
swing+ing+ly
swin+gle
 swin+gles
 swin+gles
 swin+gling
 swin+gled
swingle+tree
 swingle+trees
swing-wing
 swing-wings
swingy
 swingi+er
 swingi+est
swin+ish
 swin+ish+ly
 swin+ish+ness
swipe
 swipes
 swipes
 swip+ing
 swiped
swirl
 swirls
 swirls
 swirl+ing
 swirled
swirl+ing
swirly
swish

swishes
swishes
swish+ing
swished
swishy
Swiss
switch
  switches
  switches
  switch+ing
  switched
switch+back
  switch+backs
switch+blade
  switch+blades
switch+board
  switch+boards
switch+er
  switch+ers
switch+gear
  switch+gears
switch+man
  switch+men
swith+er
  swith+ers
  swith+ers
  swith+er+ing
  swith+ered
Swithin
Swithun
Switz+er
  Switz+ers
Swit+zer+land
swiv+el
  swiv+els
  swiv+els
  swiv+el+ling *or*
  swiv+el+ing
  U.S.
  swiv+elled *or*
  swiv+eled
  U.S.
swiz
  swizes
swizz
  swizzes
swiz+zle
  swiz+zles
  swiz+zles
  swiz+zling
  swiz+zled
swob
  swobs
  swobs
  swob+bing

swobbed
swol+len
swol+len+ness
swoon
  swoons
  swoons
  swoon+ing
  swooned
  swoon+ing
swoop
  swoops
  swoops
  swoop+ing
  swooped
swoosh
  swooshes
  swooshes
  swoosh+ing
  swooshed
swop
  swops
  swops
  swop+ping
  swopped
sword
  swords
sword+bearer
  sword+bearers
sword+fish
  sword+fish *or*
  sword+fishes
sword+play
swords+man
  swords+men
  swords+man+
  ship
sword+stick
  sword+sticks
sword+tail
  sword+tails
swore
sworn
swot
  swots
  swots
  swot+ting
  swot+ted
swounds
'swounds
swum
swung
swy
Syba+ris
syba+rite
  syba+rites

Syba+rite
  Syba+rites
syba+rit+ic
Syba+rit+ic
syba+riti+cal+ly
syba+rit+ism
syca+more
  syca+mores
sy+co+nium
sy+co+nia
syco+phan+cy
  syco+phan+cies
syco+phant
  syco+phants
syco+phan+tic
syco+phan+ti+cal+
  ly
sy+co+sis
Syd+ney
  place name
Sydney
  surname
Sy+ene
sy+enite
sy+enit+ic
Syk+tyv+kar
syl+la+bary
  syl+la+baries
syl+la+bi
syl+lab+ic
  syl+lab+ics
syl+labi+cal+ly
syl+labi+cate
  syl+labi+cates
  syl+labi+cat+ing
  syl+labi+cat+ed
syl+labi+ca+tion
  syl+labi+ca+
  tions
syl+labi+fi+ca+
  tion
  syl+labi+fi+ca+
  tions
syl+labi+fy
  syl+labi+fies
  syl+labi+fy+ing
  syl+labi+fied
syl+la+ble
  syl+la+bles
  syl+la+bles
  syl+la+bling
  syl+la+bled
syl+la+bub
  syl+la+bubs
syl+la+bus

syl+la+buses
  or
syl+la+bi
syl+lep+sis
  syl+lep+ses
syl+lep+tic
syl+lep+ti+cal+ly
syl+lo+gise
  syl+lo+gises
  syl+lo+gis+ing
  syl+lo+gised
syl+lo+gism
  syl+lo+gisms
syl+lo+gis+tic
syl+lo+gize
  syl+lo+gizes
  syl+lo+giz+ing
  syl+lo+gized
sylph
  sylphs
  sylph+like
syl+va
  syl+vas *or*
  syl+vae
syl+van
  syl+vans
syl+van+ite
Sylvanus
syl+vi+cul+ture
sym+bi+ont
  sym+bi+onts
sym+bi+on+tic
sym+bi+on+ti+
  cal+ly
sym+bio+sis
sym+bi+ot+ic
sym+bol
  sym+bols
  sym+bols
  sym+bol+ling
  or
  sym+bol+ing
  U.S.
  sym+bolled *or*
  sym+boled
  U.S.
sym+bol+ic
sym+boli+cal
sym+boli+cal+ly
sym+boli+sa+
  tion
  sym+boli+sa+
  tions
sym+bol+ise
  sym+bol+ises

sym+bol+is+ing
sym+bol+ised
sym+bol+ism
sym+bol+isms
sym+bol+ist
sym+bol+ists
sym+bol+is+tic
sym+bol+is+ti+cal+ly
sym+boli+za+tion
sym+boli+za+tions
sym+bol+ize
sym+bol+izes
sym+bol+iz+ing
sym+bol+ized
sym+met+ri+cal
sym+me+try
sym+me+tries
Symonds
Symons
sym+pa+thec+to+my
sym+pa+thec+to+mies
sym+pa+thet+ic
sym+pa+theti+cal+ly
sym+pa+thise
sym+pa+thises
sym+pa+this+ing
sym+pa+thised
sym+pa+this+er
sym+pa+this+ers
sym+pa+thize
sym+pa+thizes
sym+pa+thiz+ing
sym+pa+thized
sym+pa+thiz+er
sym+pa+thiz+ers
sym+pa+tho+lyt+ic
sym+pa+tho+lyt+ics
sym+pa+tho+mi+met+ic
sym+pa+tho+mi+met+ics
sym+pa+thy
sym+pa+thies
sym+phon+ic

sym+pho+ny
sym+pho+nies
sym+phys+eal
sym+phys+ial
sym+phy+sis
sym+phy+ses
sym+po+dial
sym+po+di+al+ly
sym+po+dium
sym+po+dia
sym+po+sium
sym+po+siums
or
sym+po+sia
symp+tom
symp+toms
symp+to+mat+ic
symp+to+mati+cal+ly
symp+toma+tol+ogy
syn+aer+esis
syn+aes+the+sia
syn+aes+thet+ic
syna+gog+al
syna+gogi+cal
syna+gogue
syna+gogues
syn+apse
syn+apses
syn+ap+sis
syn+ap+ses
syn+ap+tic
syn+ap+ti+cal+ly
syn+ar+thro+dial
syn+ar+thro+sis
syn+ar+thro+ses
sync
syncs
sync+ing
synced
syn+carp
syn+carps
syn+car+pous
synch
synchs
synch+ing
synched
syn+chro
syn+chros
syn+chro+cy+clo+tron
syn+chro+mesh

syn+chro+meshes
syn+chron+ic
syn+chroni+cal+ly
syn+chro+nic+ity
syn+chro+ni+sa+tion
syn+chro+ni+sa+tions
syn+chro+nise
syn+chro+nises
syn+chro+nis+ing
syn+chro+nised
syn+chro+nis+er
syn+chro+nis+ers
syn+chro+nism
syn+chro+nisms
syn+chro+nis+tic
syn+chro+nis+ti+cal+ly
syn+chro+ni+za+tion
syn+chro+ni+za+tions
syn+chro+nize
syn+chro+nizes
syn+chro+niz+ing
syn+chro+nized
syn+chro+niz+er
syn+chro+niz+ers
syn+chro+nous
syn+chro+nous+ly
syn+chro+nous+ness
syn+chro+tron
syn+chro+trons
syn+cli+nal
syn+cline
syn+clines
Syn+com
syn+co+pal
syn+co+pate
syn+co+pates
syn+co+pat+ing
syn+co+pat+ed
syn+co+pa+tion
syn+co+pa+tions

syn+co+pa+tor
syn+co+pa+tors
syn+co+pe
syn+co+pes
syn+cop+ic
syn+cret+ic
syn+cre+ti+sa+tion
syn+cre+tise
syn+cre+tises
syn+cre+tis+ing
syn+cre+tised
syn+cre+tism
syn+cre+tisms
syn+cre+tist
syn+cre+tists
syn+cre+tis+tic
syn+cre+ti+za+tion
syn+cre+tize
syn+cre+tizes
syn+cre+tiz+ing
syn+cre+tized
syn+dac+tyl
syn+dac+tyls
syn+dac+tyl+ism
syn+de+sis
syn+des+mo+sis
syn+des+mo+ses
syn+des+mot+ic
syn+det+ic
syn+deti+cal+ly
syn+dic
syn+dics
syn+di+cal
syn+di+cal+ism
syn+di+cal+ist
syn+di+cal+is+tic
syn+di+cate
syn+di+cates
syn+di+cates
syn+di+cat+ing
syn+di+cat+ed
syn+di+cat+ed
syn+di+ca+tion
syn+di+ca+tions
syn+drome
syn+dromes
syn+drom+ic
syne
syn+ec+do+che
syn+ec+do+ches
syn+ec+doch+ic

syn+ec+dochi+
cal
syn+ecious
syn+eco+log+ic
syn+eco+logi+cal
syn+eco+logi+cal+
ly
syn+ecol+ogy
syn+er+esis
syn+er+get+ic
syn+er+gic
syn+er+gism
syn+er+gisms
syn+er+gist
syn+er+gists
syn+er+gy
syn+er+gies
syn+esis
syn+es+the+sia
U.S.
syn+es+thet+ic
U.S.
syn+gam+ic
syn+ga+mous
syn+ga+my
Synge
syn+gen+esis
syn+od
syn+ods
syn+od+al
syn+od+ic
syn+oecious
syno+nym
syno+nyms
syno+nym+ic
syno+nymi+cal
syno+nym+ity
syn+ony+mous
syn+ony+mous+
ly
syn+ony+mous+
ness
syn+ony+my
syn+ony+mies
syn+op+sis
syn+op+ses
syn+op+sise
syn+op+sises
syn+op+sis+ing
svn+op+sised
syn+op+size
syn+op+sizes
syn+op+siz+ing

syn+op+sized
syn+op+tic
syn+op+tics
syn+op+ti+cal+ly
syn+op+tist
syn+op+tists
syno+via
syno+vial
syno+vit+ic
syno+vi+tis
syn+roc
syn+tac+tic
syn+tac+ti+cal
syn+tac+ti+cal+ly
syn+tac+tics
syn+tagm
syn+tagms
syn+tag+ma
syn+tag+ma+ta
syn+tag+mat+ic
syn+tax
syn+taxes
synth
synths
syn+the+sis
syn+the+ses
syn+the+si+sa+
tion
syn+the+sise
syn+the+sises
syn+the+sis+ing
syn+the+sised
syn+the+sist
syn+the+sists
syn+the+si+za+
tion
syn+the+size
syn+the+sizes
syn+the+siz+ing
syn+the+sized
syn+the+siz+er
syn+the+siz+ers
syn+thet+ic
syn+thet+ics
syn+theti+cal
syn+theti+cal+ly
syn+the+ti+sa+
tion
syn+the+tise
syn+the+tises
syn+the+tis+ing
syn+the+tised
syn+the+ti+za+
tion

syn+the+tize
syn+the+tizes
syn+the+tiz+ing
syn+the+tized
syphi+lis
syphi+lit+ic
syphi+loid
sy+phon
sy+phons
sy+phons
sy+phon+ing
sy+phoned
Sy+ra+cuse
Syr Dar+ya
Syria
Syri+ac
Syr+ian
Syr+ians
sy+rin+ga
sy+rin+gas
sy+ringe
sy+ringes
sy+ringes
sy+ring+ing
sy+ringed
sy+rin+geal
sy+rin+go+my+
elia
sy+rin+go+my+el+
ic
syr+inx
syr+in+ges or
syr+inxes
Syr+inx
syr+up
syr+ups
syr+upy
sys+sar+co+sis
sys+sar+co+ses
sys+sar+cot+ic
sys+tal+tic
sys+tem
sys+tems
sys+tem+at+ic
sys+tem+ati+cal+
ly
sys+tem+at+ics
sys+tema+ti+sa+
tion
sys+tema+ti+sa+
tions
sys+tema+tise

sys+tema+tises
sys+tema+tis+
ing
sys+tema+tised
sys+tema+tis+er
sys+tema+tis+
ers
sys+tema+tism
sys+tema+tisms
sys+tema+tist
sys+tema+tists
sys+tema+ti+za+
tion
sys+tema+ti+za+
tions
sys+tema+tize
sys+tema+tizes
sys+tema+tiz+
ing
sys+tema+tized
sys+tema+tiz+er
sys+tema+tiz+
ers
sys+tem+ic
sys+tem+ics
sys+temi+cal+ly
sys+tem+ise
sys+tem+ises
sys+tem+is+ing
sys+tem+ised
sys+tem+is+er
sys+tem+is+ers
sys+tem+ize
sys+tem+izes
sys+tem+iz+ing
sys+tem+ized
sys+tem+iz+er
sys+tem+iz+ers
sys+tems
sys+to+le
sys+tol+ic
Syz+ran
syzy+gal
syzy+geti+cal+ly
sy+zyg+ial
syzy+gy
syzy+gies
Szcze+cin
Sze+chwan
Sze+ged
Szell
Szom+bat+hely
Szymanowski

T

t
t's
't
T
T's *or*
Ts
ta
Taal
tab
tabs
tabs
tab+bing
tabbed
tab+ard
tab+ards
taba+ret
Ta+bas+co
Trademark
tab+by
tab+bies
tab+er+nac+le
tab+er+nac+les
tab+er+nacu+lar
ta+bes
ta+bes
ta+bes+cence
ta+bes+cent
ta+bes dor+sa+
lis
ta+bet+ic
'tab+la
tab+las
tab+la+ture
tab+la+tures
ta+ble
ta+bles
ta+bles
ta+bling
ta+bled
Ta+ble
tab+leau
tab+leaux *or*
tab+leaus
ta+bleau vi+vant

ta+bleaux vi+
vants
table+cloth
table+cloths
ta+ble d'hôte
ta+bles d'hôte
table+land
table+lands
table+spoon
table+spoons
tab+let
tab+lets
table-turning
table+ware
tab+loid
tab+loids
ta+boo
ta+boos
ta+boos
ta+boo+ing
ta+booed
ta+bor
ta+bors
Ta+bor
tabo+ret
tabo+rets
ta+bour
ta+bours
tabou+ret
tabou+rets
Ta+briz
tabu
tabus
tabus
tabu+ing
tabued
tabu+lable
tabu+lar
tabu+la rasa
tabu+lae ra+sae
tabu+lar+ly
tabu+late
tabu+lates
tabu+lat+ing
tabu+lat+ed

tabu+la+tion
tabu+la+tions
tabu+la+tor
tabu+la+tors
taca+ma+hac
taca+ma+hacs
ta+cet
ta+cets
ta+cet+ing
ta+cet+ed
tach+eom+eter
tach+eom+eters
tach+eom+etry
ta+chisme
ta+chis+to+
scope
ta+chis+to+
scopes
ta+chis+to+scop+
ic
tacho+graph
tacho+graphs
ta+chom+eter
ta+chom+eters
ta+chom+etry
tachy+car+dia
ta+chyg+ra+phy
ta+chym+eter
ta+chym+eters
tachy+on
tachy+ons
tachy+phy+lax+is
tac+it
tac+it+ly
taci+turn
taci+tur+nity
taci+turn+ly
Tacitus
tack
tacks
tacks
tack+ing
tacked
tack+er
tack+ers

tackies
tacki+ly
tacki+ness
tack+le
tack+les
tack+les
tack+ling
tack+led
tack+ler
tack+lers
tacky
tacki+er
tacki+est
tac+ma+hack
tac+ma+hacks
Tacna-Arica
tac+node
tac+nodes
Ta+co+ma
tact
tact+ful
tact+ful+ness
tac+tic
tac+tics
tac+ti+cal
tac+ti+cal+ly
tac+ti+cian
tac+ti+cians
tac+tics
tac+tile
tac+til+ity
tact+less
tact+less+ness
Tad+mor
tad+pole
tad+poles
Ta+dzhik
Ta+dzhik
tae+di+um vi+tae
Tae+gu
Tae+jon
tae kwon do
tael
taels
ta'en

tae+nia
 tae+niae
tae+nia+sis
taf+fe+ta
 taf+fe+tas
taf+fia
taff+rail
 taff+rails
Taf+fy
 Taf+fies
tafia
Ta+fi+la+let
Ta+fi+lelt
Taft
tag
 tags
 tags
tag+ging
tagged
Ta+ga+log
 Ta+ga+logs *or*
 Ta+ga+log
Ta+gan+rog
ta+get+es
ta+glia+tel+le
Tagore
Ta+gus
Ta+hi+ti
Ta+hi+tian
Ta+hoe
tahr
 tahrs
tah+sil
 tah+sils
Tai
 Tais *or*
 Tai
taia+ha
 taia+has
t'ai chi
t'ai chi ch'uan
Tai+chung
T'ai-chung
tai+ga
tai+hoa
tail
 tails
 tails
tail+ing
tailed
tail+back
 tail+backs
tail+board
 tail+boards
tail+gate

board at rear of lorry
tail+gates
 tail+gates
tail+gat+ing
tail+gat+ed
tail gate
 gate of lock
 tail gates
tail+ing
 tail+ings
tail+lamp
 tail+lamps
tail+less
tail+light
 tail+lights
tai+lor
tai+lors
tai+lors
tai+lor+ing
tai+lored
tailor+bird
 tailor+birds
tailor-made
 tailor-mades
tailor's-tack
 tailor's-tacks
tail+piece
 tail+pieces
tail+pipe
 tail+pipes
tail+plane
 tail+planes
tail+race
 tail+races
tails
tail+skid
 tail+skids
tail+spin
 tail+spins
tail+stock
 tail+stocks
tail+wind
 tail+winds
Tai+nan
T'ai-nan
Tai+na+ron
Tai+no
 Tai+nos *or*
 Tai+no
taint
 taints
 taints
taint+ing
taint+ed

taint+less
tai+pan
 tai+pans
Tai+pei
T'ai-pei
Tai+sho
Tai+wan
Tai+wan+ese
Tai+yuan
T'ai-y'uan
taj
 tajes
Taj Ma+hal
Tajo
tak+able
ta+ka+he
 ta+ka+hes
Taka+mat+su
Ta+kao
take
 takes
 takes
 tak+ing
 took
 tak+en
take+able
take+away
 take+aways
take away
 verb
take-down
 adj.
take down
 verb
 tak+en
take+off
 take+offs
take off
 verb
take+out
 take+outs
take out
 verb
take+over
 take+overs
take over
 verb
tak+er
 tak+ers
take-up
 noun
take up
 verb
tak+in
 tak+ins

tak+ing
 tak+ings
tak+ing+ly
tak+ing+ness
Ta+ko+ra+di
tala+poin
 tala+poins
ta+laria
Ta+la+vera de la
 Rei+na
Talbot
talc
 talcs
 talcs
talck+ing *or*
 talc+ing
talcked *or*
 talced
Tal+ca
Tal+ca+hua+no
talc+ose
tal+cous
tal+cum
tale
 tales
tal+ent
 tal+ents
tal+ent+ed
ta+les
 ta+les+man
 ta+les+men
Taliesin
tali+grade
tali+on
tali+pes
tali+pot
tal+is+man
 tal+is+mans
tal+is+man+ic
talk
 talks
 talks
 talk+ing
 talked
talka+tive
talka+tive+ly
talka+tive+ness
talk+back
 noun
talk back
 verb
talk+er
 talk+ers
talkie
 talkies

talking-to	ta+luses	Tam+il	Tan+ga
talking-tos	tal+weg	Ta+mil Nadu	Tan+gan+yi+ka
tall	tal+wegs	Tam+mer+fors	Tan+gan+yi+kan
tall+er	tam	tam+my	Tan+gan+yi+
tall+est	tams	tam+mies	kans
tal+lage	tam+able	tam-o'-shanter	Tange
tal+lages	ta+ma+le	tam-o'-shanters	tan+gen+cy
Tal+la+has+see	ta+ma+les	tamp	tan+gen+cies
tall+boy	ta+man+dua	tamps	tan+gent
tall+boys	ta+man+duas	tamp+ing	tan+gents
Talleyrand-	tama+rack	tamped	tan+gen+tial
Périgord	tama+racks	Tam+pa	tan+gen+ti+al+ity
Tal+lin	ta+ma+ri	tam+per	tan+gen+tial+ly
Tal+linn	ta+ma+ril+lo	tam+pers	tan+ge+rine
Tallis	ta+ma+ril+los	tam+pers	tan+ge+rines
tal+lith	tama+rin	tam+per+ing	Tan+ge+rine
tal+lai+sim	tama+rins	tam+pered	Tan+ge+rines
tal+lithes	tama+rind	Tam+pe+re	tangi
tal+li+toth	tama+rinds	tam+per+er	tangis
tall+ness	tama+risk	tam+per+ers	tan+gibil+ity
tal+low	tama+risks	Tam+pi+co	tan+gible
tal+lows	Ta+ma+tave	tam+pi+on	tan+gible+ness
tal+low+ing	Ta+mau+li+pas	tam+pi+ons	tan+gibly
tal+lowed	Tambo	tam+pon	Tan+gier
tal+lowy	Tam+bo+ra	tam+pons	tan+gle
tal+ly	tam+bour	tam+pons	tan+gles
tal+lies	tam+bours	tam+pon+ing	tan+gles
tal+lies	tam+bours	tam+poned	tan+gling
tal+ly+ing	tam+bour+ing	tam+pon+age	tan+gled
tal+lied	tam+boured	tam-tam	tan+gly
tally-ho	tam+boura	tam-tams	tan+go
tally-hos	tam+bouras	Tam+worth	tan+gos
tally-hos	tam+bou+rin	tan	tan+goes
tally-hoing	tam+bou+rins	tans	tan+go+ing
tally-hoed or	tam+bou+rine	tans	tan+goed
tally-ho'd	tam+bou+rines	tan+ning	tan+gram
tally+man	tam+bou+rin+ist	tanned	tan+grams
tally+men	tam+bou+rin+	tan+ner	Tang+shan
tally+woman	ists	tan+nest	Tanguy
tally+women	Tam+bov	Tana	tangy
Tal+mud	Tamburlaine	tana+ger	tangi+er
Tal+mud+ic	tame	tana+gers	tangi+est
Tal+mudi+cal	tames	Tana+gra	tanh
Tal+mud+ism	tam+ing	Tana+na	Ta+nis
Tal+mud+ist	tamed	Ta+na+na+rive	Tan+jore
Tal+mud+ists	tam+er	tan+bark	Tan+jung+pri+ok
tal+on	tam+est	Tancred	tank
tal+ons	tame+able	tan+dem	tanks
ta+loned	tame+ly	tan+dems	tanks
Talos	tame+ness	Tan+djung+pri+	tank+ing
ta+lus	tam+er	ok	tanked
anklebone	tam+ers	tan+doori	tan+ka
ta+li	Tamerlane	tang	tan+kas or
ta+lus	Tam+il	tangs	tan+ka
rock pile	Tam+ils or	Tang	tank+age

tank+ard	Tan+trist	tap+holes	tar+di+ly
tank+ards	Tan+trists	tap+house	tar+di+ness
tank+er	tan+trum	tap+house	tar+dy
tank+ers	tan+trums	tap+houses	tar+di+er
tan+nable	Tan+za+nia	tapio+ca	tar+di+est
Tan+nen+berg	Tan+za+nian	ta+pir	tare
tan+ner	Tan+za+nians	ta+pirs *or*	tares
tan+ners	Tao	ta+pir	tares
tan+nery	Taoi+seach	tap+is	tar+ing
tan+neries	Tao+ism	tap+is	tared
Tannhäuser	Tao+ist	tap+per	Ta+ren+tum
tan+nic	Tao+ists	tap+pers	targe
tan+nin	Tao+is+tic	tap+pet	targes
tan+nins	ta+on+ga	tap+pets	tar+get
tan+nish	ta+on+gas	tap+room	tar+gets
Tan+noy	tap	tap+rooms	tar+gets
Trademark	taps	tap+root	tar+get+ing
Tan+noys	taps	tap+roots	tar+get+ed
Tans	tap+ping	taps	tar+iff
tan+sy	tapped	tap+ster	tar+iffs
tan+sies	tapa	tap+sters	tar+iffs
Tan+ta	Ta+pa+jós	tar	tar+iff+ing
tan+ta+li+sa+tion	tap-dance	tars	tar+iffed
tan+ta+li+sa+	tap-dances	tars	Ta+rim
tions	tap-dancing	tar+ring	Tarkington
tan+ta+lise	tap-danced	tarred	Tarkovsky
tan+ta+lises	tap dance	Tara	tar+la+tan
tan+ta+lis+ing	tap dances	Ta+ra+bu+lus el	Tar+mac
tan+ta+lised	tap-dancer	Gharb	*Trademark*
tan+ta+lis+ing	tap-dancers	Ta+ra+bu+lus	Tar+macs
tan+ta+lis+ing+ly	tap-dancing	esh Sham	Tar+mack+ing
tan+ta+lite	tape	ta+ra+did+dle	Tar+macked
tan+ta+li+za+tion	tapes	ta+ra+did+dles	tarn
tan+ta+li+za+	tapes	ta+ra+ki+hi	tarns
tions	tap+ing	ta+ra+ki+his	Tarn
tan+ta+lize	taped	ta+ra+ma+sa+la+	tar+na+tion
tan+ta+lizes	tape+like	ta	Tarn-et-Garonne
tan+ta+liz+ing	tap+er	ta+ran+tass	tar+nish
tan+ta+lized	*person who tapes*	ta+ran+tasses	tar+nishes
tan+ta+liz+ing	tap+ers	tar+an+tel+la	tar+nishes
tan+ta+liz+ing+ly	tap+per	tar+an+tel+las	tar+nish+ing
tan+ta+lum	*become narrower*	tar+ant+ism	tar+nished
tan+ta+lus	ta+pers	Ta+ran+to	tar+nish+able
tan+ta+luses	ta+pers	ta+ran+tu+la	Tar+no+pol
Tantalus	ta+per+ing	ta+ran+tu+las	Tar+nów
tan+ta+mount	ta+pered	*or*	taro
tan+ta+ra	ta+per+er	ta+ran+tu+lae	taros
tan+ta+ras	ta+per+ers	Ta+ra+wa	ta+rot
tan+tivy	ta+per+ing	ta+raxa+cum	ta+rots
tan+tivies	tap+es+tried	ta+raxa+cums	tar+pan
tant mieux	tap+es+try	Tarbes	tar+pans
tan+to	tap+es+tries	tar+boosh	tar+pau+lin
tant pis	tape+worm	tar+booshes	tar+pau+lins
Tan+tric	tape+worms	Tar+de+noi+sian	Tarpeia
Tan+trism	tap+hole	tar+di+grade	tar+pon
		tar+di+grades	

tar+pons *or*
tar+pon
Tarquin
tar+ra+did+dle
tar+ra+did+dles
tar+ra+gon
Tar+ra+go+na
Tar+ra+sa
tar+ri+er
tar+ri+ers
tar+ri+ness
tar+ry
tar+ries
tar+ry+ing
tar+ried
tar+sal
tar+sals
tar+seal
tar+seals
Tar+shish
tar+sia
tar+sias
tar+si+er
tar+si+ers
tar+sus
tar+si
Tar+sus
tart
tarts
tar+tan
tar+tans
tar+taned
tar+tar
tar+tars
Tar+tar
Tar+tars
Tar+tar+ean
Tar+tar+ian
tar+tar+ic
Tar+tar+ic
Tar+ta+rus
Tar+ta+ry
tart+let
tart+lets
tart+ly
tart+ness
tar+trate
tar+trates
tar+trat+ed
tar+tra+zine
Tar+tu
tarty
tarti+er
tarti+est
tar+whine

tar+whines
Tar+zan
Tar+zans
Tash+kent
ta+sim+eter
ta+sim+eters
tasi+met+ric
ta+sim+etry
task
tasks
tasks
task+ing
tasked
task+master
task+masters
task+mistress
task+mistresses
task+work
Tasman
Tas+man
Tas+ma+nia
Tas+ma+nian
Tas+ma+nians
tass
tasses
Tass
tas+sel
tas+sels
tas+sels
tas+sel+ling *or*
tas+sel+ing
tas+selled *or*
tas+seled
U.S.
tas+sie
tas+sies
Tas+sie
Tas+sies
Tasso
Tas+sy
Tas+sies
tast+able
taste
tastes
tastes
tast+ing
tast+ed
taste+ful
taste+ful+ly
taste+ful+ness
taste+less
taste+less+ly
taste+less+ness
tast+er

tast+ers
tasti+ly
tasti+ness
tasty
tasti+er
tasti+est
tat
tats
tat+ting
tat+ted
ta-ta
Ta+tar
Ta+tars
Ta+tar+ic
Ta+ta+ry
Tate
ta+ter
ta+ters
Tati
tatou+ay
tatou+ays
tat+ter
tat+ters
tat+ters
tat+ter+ing
tat+tered
tat+ter+de+mal+
ion
tat+ter+de+mal+
ions
tat+ter+sall
Tat+ter+sall's
tat+ti+ly
tat+ti+ness
tat+ting
tat+tle
tat+tles
tat+tles
tat+tling
tat+tled
tat+tler
tat+tlers
tattle+tale
tattle+tales
tat+too
tat+toos
tat+toos
tat+too+ing
tat+tooed
tat+too+er
tat+too+ers
tat+too+ist
tat+too+ists
tat+ty
tat+ti+er

tat+ti+est
Tatum
tau
taus
taught
taunt
taunts
taunts
taunt+ing
taunt+ed
taunt+ing
Taun+ton
taupe
Tau+po
Tau+ranga
tau+rine
tau+roma+chy
Tau+rus
Tau+ruses
taut
taut+en
taut+ens
taut+en+ing
taut+ened
taut+ly
taut+ness
tau+tog
tau+togs
tau+to+logi+cal
tau+tol+ogy
tau+tol+ogies
tau+to+mer
tau+to+mers
tau+to+mer+ic
tau+tom+er+ism
tau+to+nym
tau+to+nyms
tau+to+nym+ic
tau+tony+mous
tau+tony+my
Tavener
tav+ern
tav+erns
ta+ver+na
ta+ver+nas
Taverner
taw
taws
taws
taw+ing
tawed
tawa
tawas
taw+dri+ly
taw+dri+ness

taw+dry
 taw+dri+er
 taw+dri+est
taw+er
 taw+ers
taw+ni+ness
taw+ny
taws
 tawses
tawse
 tawses
tax
 taxes
 taxes
 tax+ing
 taxed
tax+able
taxa+tion
 taxa+tions
taxa+tion+al
tax-deduct+ible
tax+eme
 tax+emes
tax+emic
tax+er
 tax+ers
taxi
 taxis *or*
 taxies
 taxis *or*
 taxies
 taxi+ing *or*
 taxy+ing
 taxied
taxi+der+mal
taxi+der+mic
taxi+der+mist
 taxi+der+mists
taxi+der+my
taxi+meter
 taxi+meters
tax+ing
tax+ing+ly
tax+is
taxi+way
 taxi+ways
tax+on
 taxa
taxo+nom+ic
taxo+nomi+cal
taxo+nomi+cal+
 ly
tax+ono+mist
 tax+ono+mists
tax+ono+my

tax+payer
 tax+payers
Tay
Taylor
Tay-Sachs
Tay+side
taz+za
 taz+zas
T-bar
 T-bars
Tbi+li+si
T-bone
T-cell
 T-cells
Tchad
Tchaikovsky
te
 tes
tea
 teas
tea+cake
 tea+cakes
teach
 teaches
 teach+ing
 taught
teach+able
teach+er
 teach+ers
teach-in
 teach-ins
teach+ing
 teach+ings
tea+cup
 tea+cups
tea+house
 tea+houses
teak
teal
 teals *or*
 teal
team
 teams
 teams
 team+ing
 teamed
tea-maker
 tea-makers
team-mate
 team-mates
team+ster
 team+sters
team+work

tea+pot
 tea+pots
tea+poy
 tea+poys
tear
 tears
 tears
 tear+ing
 tore
 torn
tear+able
tear+away
 tear+aways
tear away
 verb
tear+er
 tear+ers
tear+ful
 tear+ful+ly
 tear+ful+ness
 tear+ing
tear-jerker
 tear-jerkers
tear+less
tea+room
 tea+rooms
tears
tease
 teases
 teases
 teas+ing
 teased
tea+sel
 tea+sels
 tea+sels
 tea+sel+ling *or*
 tea+sel+ing
 U.S.
 tea+selled *or*
 tea+seled
 U.S.
tea+sel+ler
 tea+sel+lers
teas+er
 teas+ers
tea+shop
 tea+shops
teas+ing
 teas+ing+ly
tea+spoon
 tea+spoons
teat
 teats
tea+zel
 tea+zels

tea+zels
tea+zel+ling *or*
tea+zel+ing
U.S.
tea+zelled *or*
tea+zeled
U.S.
tea+zle
 tea+zles
 tea+zles
 tea+zling
 tea+zled
tech
 techs
techi+ly
techi+ness
tech+ne+tium
tech+nic
 tech+nics
tech+ni+cal
tech+ni+cal+ity
 tech+ni+cal+
 ities
tech+ni+cal+ly
tech+ni+cal+ness
tech+ni+cian
 tech+ni+cians
Tech+ni+col+or
 Trademark
tech+nics
tech+nique
 tech+niques
tech+noc+ra+cy
 tech+noc+ra+
 cies
tech+no+crat
 tech+no+crats
tech+no+crat+ic
tech+no+logi+cal
tech+nolo+gist
 tech+nolo+gists
tech+nol+ogy
 tech+nol+ogies
techy
techi+er
techi+est
tec+ton+ic
tec+ton+ics
tec+tri+cial
tec+trix
tec+tri+ces
Tecumseh
ted
 teds
 teds

ted+ding
ted+ded
ted+der
ted+ders
Tedder
ted+dy
ted+dies
Te De+um
  Te De+ums
te+di+ous
te+di+ous+ness
te+dium
tee
  tees
  tees
  tee+ing
  teed
tee-hee
tee-hees
tee-hees
tee-heeing
tee-heed
teem
  teems
  teem+ing
  teemed
teen
teen+age
  teen+ager
  teen+agers
  teens
teensy-weensy
tee+ny
  tee+ni+er
  tee+ni+est
teeny+bopper
teeny+boppers
tee+pee
  tee+pees
Tees
tee shirt
  tee shirts
Tees+side
tee+ter
  tee+ters
  tee+ters
  tee+ter+ing
  tee+tered
teeth
teethe
  teethes
  teeth+ing
  teethed
teeth+ing
tee+to+tal

tee+to+tal+ism
tee+to+tal+ler
  tee+to+tal+lers
tee+to+tum
  tee+to+tums
teff
Tef+lon
  Trademark
teg
  tegs
teg+men
  teg+mi+na
  teg+mi+nal
Te+gu+ci+gal+pa
tegu+ment
  tegu+ments
te-hee
  te-hees
  te-hees
  te-heeing
  te-heed
Te+he+ran
Teh+ran
Te+huan+tepec
Tei+de
te igi+tur
Teilhard de
  Chardin
Tejo
Te Kanawa
tek+tite
  tek+tites
tel+aes+the+sia
tel+aes+thet+ic
tela+mon
  tela+mones *or*
  tela+mons
Telamon
Tela+nai+pu+ra
tel+an+gi+ec+ta+
  sia
tel+an+gi+ec+ta+
  ses
tel+an+gi+ec+ta+
  sis
tel+an+gi+ec+ta+
  ses
tel+an+gi+ec+tat+
  ic
Tel Aviv
tele+cast
  tele+casts
  tele+casts
  tele+cast+ing
  tele+cast *or*

tele+cast+ed
tele+cast+er
  tele+cast+ers
tele+com
tele+com+mu+ni+
  ca+tions
tele+com+mut+
  er
  tele+com+mut+
  ers
  tele+com+mut+
  ing
tele+coms
tel+edu
  tel+edus
tele+gen+ic
tele+geni+cal+ly
tel+eg+no+sis
tel+egon+ic
te+lego+nous
Telegonus
te+lego+ny
  te+lego+nies
tele+gram
  tele+grams
tele+graph
  tele+graphs
  tele+graphs
  tele+graph+ing
  tele+graphed
te+leg+ra+pher
tele+graph+ic
te+leg+ra+phist
  te+leg+ra+
  phists
te+leg+ra+phy
Tel+egu
  Tel+egus *or*
  Tel+egu
tele+ki+ne+sis
tele+ki+net+ic
Te+lema+chus
Telemann
tel+emark
  tel+emarks
tele+mar+ket+ing
Tele+mes+sage
  Trademark
  Tele+mes+
  sages
te+lem+eter
  te+lem+eters
  te+lem+eters
  te+lem+eter+ing
  te+lem+etered

tele+met+ric
te+lem+etry
tel+en+cephal+ic
tel+en+cepha+
  lon
  tel+en+cepha+
  lons
teleo+logi+cal
tele+olo+gist
  tele+olo+gists
tele+ol+ogy
  tele+ol+ogies
tel+eost
  tel+eosts
tele+path+ic
te+lepa+thise
  te+lepa+thises
  te+lepa+this+ing
  te+lepa+thised
te+lepa+thist
  te+lepa+thists
te+lepa+thize
  te+lepa+thizes
  te+lepa+thiz+ing
  te+lepa+thized
te+lepa+thy
tele+phone
  tele+phones
  tele+phones
  tele+phon+ing
  tele+phoned
tele+phon+er
  tele+phon+ers
tele+phon+ic
te+lepho+nist
  te+lepho+nists
te+lepho+ny
tele+photo
tele+pho+tog+ra+
  phy
tele+print+er
  tele+print+ers
Tele+prompt+er
  Trademark
  Tele+prompt+
  ers
Tele+ran
  Trademark
  Tele+rans
tele+sales
tele+scope
  tele+scopes
  tele+scopes
  tele+scop+ing
  tele+scoped

tele+scop+ic
tele+scopi+cal+ly
te+les+co+py
tele+spec+tro+
　scope
tele+spec+tro+
　scopes
tele+ste+reo+
　scope
tele+ste+reo+
　scopes
tel+es+the+sia
U.S.
tel+es+thet+ic
U.S.
te+les+tich
te+les+tichs
Tele+text
Trademark
tele+thon
　tele+thons
Tele+type
Trademark
　Tele+types
　Tele+types
　Tele+typ+ing
　Tele+typed
tele+type+writ+
　er
U.S.
　tele+type+writ+
　ers
tele+van+gelist
tele+van+gelists
tele+vise
　tele+vises
　tele+vis+ing
　tele+vised
tele+vi+sion
　tele+vi+sions
tele+vis+ual
tele+work+ing
tel+ex
　tel+exes
　tel+exes
　tel+ex+ing
　tel+exed
Tel+ford
place name
Telford
surname
Teli+don
Trademark
tell
　tells

tells
tell+ing
told
Tell
tell+able
Tell el Amar+na
tell+er
tell+ers
Teller
tell+ing
tell+ing+ly
tell+tale
tell+tales
tel+lu+rian
tel+lu+rians
tel+lu+ric
tel+lu+ri+on
tel+lu+ri+ons
tel+lu+rium
tel+lu+rom+eter
tel+lu+rom+
　eters
Tellus
tel+ly
tel+lies
Te+loek+be+
　toeng
tel+pher+age
tel+son
tel+sons
Telu+gu
Telu+gus *or*
Telu+gu
Te+luk+be+tung
Tema
Tém+bi
tem+blor
tem+blors *or*
tem+blores
tem+er+ari+ous
te+mer+ity
Tem+es+vár
temp
temps
temps
temp+ing
temped
Tem+pe
tem+per
tem+pers
tem+pers
tem+per+ing
tem+pered
tem+pera
tem+peras

tem+per+able
tem+pera+ment
tem+pera+
　ments
tem+pera+men+
　tal
tem+pera+men+
　tal+ly
tem+per+ance
tem+per+ate
tem+per+ate+ly
tem+per+ate+
　ness
tem+pera+ture
tem+pera+tures
tem+pered
tem+per+er
tem+per+ers
tem+pest
tem+pests
tem+pes+tu+ous
tem+pes+tu+ous+
　ly
tem+pes+tu+ous+
　ness
tem+pi
Tem+plar
Tem+plars
tem+plate
tem+plates
tem+ple
tem+ples
Temple
tem+plet
tem+plets
tem+po
tem+pos *or*
tem+pi
tem+po+ral
tem+po+ral+ity
tem+po+ral+
　ities
tem+po+ral+ly
tem+po+rari+ly
tem+po+rari+
　ness
tem+po+rary
tem+po+raries
tem+po+ri+sa+
　tion
tem+po+rise
tem+po+rises
tem+po+ris+ing
tem+po+rised
tem+po+ris+er

tem+po+ris+ers
tem+po+ri+za+
　tion
tem+po+rize
tem+po+rizes
tem+po+riz+ing
tem+po+rized
tem+po+riz+er
tem+po+riz+ers
tempt
tempts
tempt+ing
tempt+ed
tempt+able
temp+ta+tion
temp+ta+tions
tempt+er
tempt+ers
tempt+ing
tempt+ing+ly
tempt+ress
tempt+resses
Te+mu+co
ten
tens
ten+abil+ity
ten+able
ten+able+ness
ten+ably
ten+ace
ten+aces
te+na+cious
te+na+cious+ly
te+na+cious+
　ness
te+nac+ity
te+nacu+lum
te+nacu+la
ten+an+cy
ten+an+cies
ten+ant
ten+ants
ten+ants
ten+ant+ing
ten+ant+ed
ten+ant+able
ten+ant+less
ten+ant+ry
ten+ant+ries
tench
tenches
tend
tends
tend+ing

tend+ed
ten+den+cious
ten+den+cious+ly
ten+den+cious+ness
ten+den+cy
ten+den+cies
ten+den+tious
ten+den+tious+ly
ten+den+tious+ness
ten+der
ten+ders
ten+ders
ten+der+ing
ten+dered
ten+der+er
ten+der+est
ten+der+er
ten+der+ers
tender+foot
tender+foots
or
tender+feet
tender+hearted
ten+deri+sa+tion
ten+der+ise
ten+der+ises
ten+der+is+ing
ten+der+ised
ten+der+is+er
ten+der+is+ers
ten+deri+za+tion
ten+der+ize
ten+der+izes
ten+der+iz+ing
ten+der+ized
ten+der+iz+er
ten+der+iz+ers
tender+loin
tender+loins
ten+der+ly
ten+der+ness
ten+don
ten+dons
ten+dril
ten+drils
te+neb+ri+ous
ten+ebrism
ten+ebrist
ten+ebrists
ten+ebrous
Ten+edos
ten+ement

ten+ements
ten+emen+tal
Ten+erife
te+nes+mic
te+nes+mus
ten+et
ten+ets
ten+fold
ten-gallon
Ten+gri Khan
Ten+gri Nor
te+nia
te+niae
te+nia+sis
U.S.
Teniers
ten+ner
ten+ners
Ten+nes+sean
Ten+nes+seans
Ten+nes+see
Tenniel
ten+nis
Tennyson
Ten+ny+so+nian
Ten+ny+so+nians
Teno
Te+noch+ti+tlan
ten+on
ten+ons
ten+ons
ten+on+ing
ten+oned
ten+on+er
ten+on+ers
ten+or
ten+ors
te+nor+rha+phy
te+nor+rha+phies
teno+syno+vi+tis
te+noto+mist
te+noto+mists
te+noto+my
te+noto+mies
ten+pin
ten+rec
ten+recs
tense
tenses
tenses
tens+ing
tensed
tens+er

tens+est
tense+less
tense+ly
tense+ness
ten+sile
ten+sile+ness
ten+sil+ity
ten+sim+eter
ten+sim+eters
ten+si+om+eter
ten+si+om+eters
ten+sion
ten+sions
ten+sion+al
ten+sion+less
ten+sor
ten+sors
ten+so+rial
tent
tents
tents
tent+ing
tent+ed
ten+ta+cle
ten+ta+cles
ten+ta+cled
ten+tacu+lar
tent+age
tent+ages
ten+ta+tion
ten+ta+tive
ten+ta+tive+ly
ten+ta+tive+ness
tent+ed
tent+er
ten+ters
ten+ters
ten+ter+ing
ten+tered
tenter+hook
tenter+hooks
tenth
tenths
tenu+is
tenu+es
tenu+ity
tenu+ous
tenu+ous+ly
tenu+ous+ness
ten+ure
ten+ures
tenu+rial
te+nu+to
Tenzing Norgay

teo+cal+li
teo+cal+lis
te+pee
te+pees
teph+ra
Te+pic
tep+id
te+pid+ity
tep+id+ly
te+pid+ness
te+qui+la
te+qui+las
Te+rai
Te+rais
tera+ki+hi
tera+ki+his
tera+tism
tera+tisms
tera+to+gen
tera+to+gens
tera+to+gen+ic
tera+toid
tera+tolo+gist
tera+tolo+gists
tera+tol+ogy
tera+tol+ogies
tera+to+ma
tera+to+ma+ta
or
tera+to+mas
ter+bic
ter+bium
Terborch
Ter Borch
terce
Ter+cei+ra
ter+cel
ter+cels
ter+cen+te+nary
ter+cen+te+naries
ter+cen+ten+nial
ter+cen+ten+nials
ter+cet
ter+cets
ter+ebene
ter+ebinth
ter+ebinths
ter+ebin+thine
te+re+do
te+re+dos *or*
te+re+di+nes
Terence
Teresa

Tereshkova
Te+re+si+na
te+rete
ter+gal
ter+gi+ver+sate
ter+gi+ver+
  sates
ter+gi+ver+sat+
  ing
ter+gi+ver+sat+
  ed
ter+gi+ver+sa+
  tion
ter+gi+ver+sa+
  tions
ter+gi+ver+sa+
  tor
ter+gi+ver+sa+
  tors
ter+gum
  ter+ga
term
  terms
  terms
term+ing
termed
ter+ma+gant
ter+ma+gants
ter+mer
  ter+mers
ter+mi+nabil+ity
ter+mi+nable
ter+mi+nable+
  ness
ter+mi+nably
ter+mi+nal
ter+mi+nals
ter+mi+nal+ly
ter+mi+nate
  ter+mi+nates
ter+mi+nat+ing
ter+mi+nat+ed
ter+mi+na+tion
  ter+mi+na+tions
ter+mi+na+tive
ter+mi+na+tor
  ter+mi+na+tors
ter+mi+no+logi+
  cal
ter+mi+nolo+gist
ter+mi+nolo+
  gists
ter+mi+nol+ogy
ter+mi+nol+
  ogies

ter+mi+nus
ter+mi+ni or
ter+mi+nuses
Terminus
ter+mi+nus ad
  quem
ter+mi+nus a quo
ter+mi+tar+ium
  ter+mi+tar+ia
ter+mite
  ter+mites
ter+mit+ic
term+less
term+ly
ter+mor
  ter+mors
terms
tern
  terns
ter+na+ry
ter+nate
ter+nate+ly
terne
Ter+ni
Ter+no+pol
tero+tech+nol+
  ogy
ter+pene
  ter+penes
ter+pin+eol
Terpsichore
Terp+si+cho+real
Terp+si+cho+
  rean
  Terp+si+cho+
    reans
ter+ra
ter+ra alba
ter+race
  ter+races
  ter+races
ter+rac+ing
ter+raced
  ter+rac+ing
  ter+rac+ings
terra-cotta
  adj.
ter+ra cot+ta
  noun
ter+ra fir+ma
ter+rain
  ter+rains
ter+ra in+cog+ni+
  ta

ter+ras in+cog+
  ni+tas
Ter+ra+my+cin
  Trademark
ter+ra+pin
  ter+ra+pins
ter+rar+ium
  ter+rar+iums
  or
  ter+raria
ter+ra si+gil+la+
  ta
ter+raz+zo
  ter+raz+zos
Terre Adélie
ter+rene
  ter+renes
terre+plein
  terre+pleins
ter+res+trial
  ter+res+trials
ter+res+tri+al+ly
ter+ret
  ter+rets
terre-verte
ter+ri+ble
ter+ri+ble+ness
ter+ri+bly
ter+rico+lous
ter+ri+er
  ter+ri+ers
ter+rif+ic
ter+rifi+cal+ly
ter+ri+fy
  ter+ri+fies
  ter+ri+fy+ing
  ter+ri+fied
ter+ri+fy+ing
ter+ri+fy+ing+ly
ter+rig+enous
ter+rine
  ter+rines
ter+ri+to+rial
Ter+ri+to+rial
  Ter+ri+to+rials
ter+ri+to+ri+al+
  ity
  ter+ri+to+ri+al+
    ities
ter+ri+to+ri+al+ly
ter+ri+tory˙
  ter+ri+tories
ter+ror
  ter+rors
ter+ror+ful

ter+rori+sa+tion
ter+ror+ise
  ter+ror+ises
ter+ror+is+ing
ter+ror+ised
ter+ror+is+er
  ter+ror+is+ers
ter+ror+ism
ter+ror+ist
  ter+ror+ists
ter+rori+za+tion
ter+ror+ize
  ter+ror+izes
ter+ror+iz+ing
ter+ror+ized
ter+ror+iz+er
  ter+ror+iz+ers
ter+ror+less
terror-stricken
terror-struck
ter+ry
  ter+ries
Terry
terse
  ters+er
  ters+est
terse+ly
terse+ness
ter+tial
ter+tian
  ter+tians
ter+tiary
  ter+tiaries
Ter+tiary
Tertullian
Te+ruel
ter+va+len+cy
ter+va+lent
Tery+lene
  Trademark
ter+za rima
  ter+ze rime
tes+la
  SI unit
tes+las
tesla
  coil
Tesla
tes+sel+late
  tes+sel+lates
  tes+sel+lat+ing
  tes+sel+lat+ed
tes+sera
  tes+serae
tes+ser+al

Tes+sin
tes+si+tu+ra
test
  tests
  tests
  test+ing
  test+ed
tes+ta
  tes+tae
test+able
tes+ta+ceous
tes+ta+cy
  tes+ta+cies
tes+ta+ment
  tes+ta+ments
Tes+ta+ment
  Tes+ta+ments
tes+ta+men+tal
tes+ta+men+tary
tes+tate
  tes+tates
tes+ta+tor
  tes+ta+tors
tes+ta+trix
  tes+ta+trixes
test-bed
  test-beds
test-drive
  test-drives
  test-driving
  test-drove
  test-driven
test+er
  test+ers
tes+tes
tes+ti+cle
  tes+ti+cles
tes+ticu+lar
tes+ticu+late
tes+ti+fi+ca+tion
  tes+ti+fi+ca+
    tions
tes+ti+fi+er
  tes+ti+fi+ers
tes+ti+fy
  tes+ti+fies
  tes+ti+fy+ing
  tes+ti+fied
tes+ti+ly
tes+ti+mo+nial
  tes+ti+mo+nials
tes+ti+mo+ny
  tes+ti+mo+nies
tes+ti+ness
test+ing

tes+tis
  tes+tes
tes+tos+ter+one
test-tube
  adj.
test tube
  test tubes
tes+tu+di+nal
tes+tu+do
  tes+tu+di+nes
tes+ty
  tes+ti+er
  tes+ti+est
teta+nal
teta+noid
teta+nus
teta+ny
tetchi+ly
tetchi+ness
tetchy
  tetchi+er
  tetchi+est
tête-à-tête
  tête-à-têtes or
  tête-à-tête
tête-bêche
teth+er
  teth+ers
  teth+ers
  teth+er+ing
  teth+ered
Tethys
  Greek goddess
Te+thys
  sea, satellite
tet+ra
tetra+ba+sic
tetra+ba+sic+ity
tetra+chlo+ro+
  me+thane
tetra+chord
  tetra+chords
tetra+chor+dal
tetra+cy+clic
tetra+cy+cline
tet+rad
  tet+rads
tetra+ethyl
tetra+fluo+ro+eth+
  ene
tetra+gon
  tetra+gons
te+trago+nal
te+trago+nal+ly

Tetra+gram+ma+
  ton
tetra+he+dral
tetra+he+dron
  tetra+he+drons
  or
  tetra+he+dra
te+tral+ogy
  te+tral+ogies
te+tram+er+ous
te+tram+eter
  te+tram+eters
tetra+plegia
tetra+plegic
tetra+ploid
  tetra+ploids
tetra+pod
  tetra+pods
te+trap+ter+ous
te+trarch
  te+trarchs
te+trarch+ate
  te+trarch+ates
te+trar+chic
te+trar+chy
  te+trar+chies
tetra+stich
  tetra+stichs
tetras+ti+chal
tetra+stich+ic
tetra+va+len+cy
tetra+va+lent
Tetrazzini
tet+rode
  tet+rodes
te+trox+ide
  te+trox+ides
tet+ryl
Te+tuán
Tetzel
Teucer
Teu+crian
  Teu+crians
Teu+to+bur+ger
  Wald
Teu+ton
  Teu+tons
Teu+ton+ic
Te+vere
Tewkes+bury
Tex+an
  Tex+ans
Tex+as
Tex-Mex
text

texts
text+book
  text+books
  text+book+ish
tex+tile
  tex+tiles
tex+tu+al
  tex+tu+al+ism
  tex+tu+al+ist
  tex+tu+al+ists
  tex+tu+al+ly
tex+tur+al
  tex+tur+al+ly
tex+ture
  tex+tures
  tex+tures
tex+tur+ing
tex+tured
Tey+de
Tezel
TGAT
Thabana-Ntlenya+
  na
Thackeray
Thaddeus
Tha+den+tso+
  nya+ne
Thadeus
Thai
  Thais or
  Thai
Thai+land
Thaïs
tha+lam+ic
thala+mus
thala+mi
tha+las+saemia
tha+las+semia
  U.S.
tha+las+sic
tha+ler
  tha+ler or
  tha+lers
Thales
Thalia
tha+lido+mide
thal+lium
thal+loid
thal+lo+phyte
  thal+lo+phytes
thal+lo+phyt+ic
thal+lus
thal+li or
  thal+luses
thal+weg

thal+wegs
Thames
than
than+age
thana+tolo+gy
thana+top+sis
thana+top+ses
Thanatos
Thana+tot+ic
thane
thanes
Than+et
Than+ja+vur
thank
thanks
thank+ing
thanked
thank+ful
thank+ful+ly
thank+ful+ness
thank+less
thank+less+ly
thank+less+ness
thanks
thanks+giving
thanks+givings
Thanks+giving
Thap+sus
thar
thars
Thá+sos
that
thatch
thatches
thatches
thatch+ing
thatched
thatch+er
thatch+ers
Thatcher
Thatch+er+ism
Thatch+er+ite
Thatch+er+ites
thau+ma+tol+ogy
thau+ma+trope
thau+ma+tropes
thau+ma+tropi+
cal
thau+ma+turge
thau+ma+turges
thau+ma+tur+gic
thau+ma+tur+gy
thaw
thaws
thaws

thaw+ing
thawed
the
the+an+throp+ic
the+an+thro+
pism
the+ar+chy
the+ar+chies
thea+ter
U.S.
thea+ters
thea+tre
thea+tres
theatre-in-the-
round
theatres-in-the-
round
the+at+ri+cal
the+at+ri+cal+ity
the+at+ri+cal+ly
the+at+ri+cal+
ness
the+at+ri+cals
the+at+rics
The+ba+ic
The+ba+id
the+ba+ine
The+ban
The+bans
Thebes
the+ca
the+cae
the+cate
the+co+dont
the+co+donts
thé dan+sant
thés dan+sant
thee
theft
thefts
thegn
thegns
Theiler
the+ine
their
theirs
the+ism
the+ist
the+ists
the+is+tic
the+is+ti+cal
them
the+mat+ic
theme
themes

themes
them+ing
themed
Themis
Themistocles
them+selves
then
the+nar
the+nars
thence
thence+forward
thence+forwards
theo+bro+mine
theo+cen+tric
the+oc+ra+cy
the+oc+ra+cies
the+oc+ra+sy
the+oc+ra+sies
theo+crat
theo+crats
theo+crat+ic
The+oc+ri+tan
The+oc+ri+tans
The+oc+ri+tean
The+oc+ri+
teans
Theocritus
Theoderic
the+odi+cean
the+odi+cy
the+odi+cies
the+odo+lite
the+odo+lites
the+odo+lit+ic
Theodora
Theodorakis
Theodoric
theo+gon+ic
the+ogo+nist
the+ogo+nists
the+ogo+ny
the+ogo+nies
theo+lo+gian
theo+lo+gians
theo+logi+cal
theo+logi+cal+ly
the+olo+gi+sa+
tion
the+olo+gise
the+olo+gises
the+olo+gis+ing
the+olo+gised
the+olo+gis+er
the+olo+gis+ers
the+olo+gist

the+olo+gists
the+olo+gi+za+
tion
the+olo+gize
the+olo+gizes
the+olo+giz+ing
the+olo+gized
the+olo+giz+er
the+olo+giz+ers
the+ol+ogy
the+ol+ogies
the+oma+chy
the+oma+chies
theo+man+cy
theo+ma+nia
theo+ma+ni+ac
theo+ma+ni+acs
theo+phan+ic
the+opha+ny
the+opha+nies
Theophrastus
theo+phyl+line
theo+rem
theo+rems
theo+remat+ic
theo+rem+ic
theo+ret+ic
theo+reti+cal
theo+reti+cal+ly
theo+reti+cian
theo+reti+cians
theo+ret+ics
theo+ri+sa+tion
theo+ri+sa+
tions
theo+rise
theo+rises
theo+ris+ing
theo+rised
theo+ris+er
theo+ris+ers
theo+rist
theo+rists
theo+ri+za+tion
theo+ri+za+
tions
theo+rize
theo+rizes
theo+riz+ing
theo+rized
theo+riz+er
theo+riz+ers
theo+ry
theo+ries
theo+soph+ic

theo+sophi+cal
the+oso+phist
  the+oso+phists
the+oso+phy
  the+oso+phies
Thera
thera+peu+tic
thera+peu+ti+cal+
  ly
thera+peu+tics
thera+pist
  thera+pists
thera+py
  thera+pies
Thera+va+da
there
there+about
  U.S.
there+abouts
there+after
there+at
there+by
there+for
there+fore
there+from
there+in
there+into
there+of
there+on
Theresa
Thérèse de
  Lisieux
there+to
there+to+fore
there+under
there+upon
there+with
there+with+al
The+re+zi+na
the+ri+an+throp+
  ic
the+ri+an+thro+
  pism
the+rio+mor+
  phic
therm
  therms
ther+mae
ther+mal
  ther+mals
ther+mali+sa+
  tion
ther+mal+ise
  ther+mal+ises
  ther+mal+is+ing

ther+mal+ised
ther+mali+za+
  tion
ther+mal+ize
  ther+mal+izes
  ther+mal+iz+ing
  ther+mal+ized
ther+mal+ly
ther+mi+on
  ther+mi+ons
ther+mi+on+ic
ther+mi+on+ics
ther+mis+tor
  ther+mis+tors
Ther+mit
  Trademark
Ther+mite
ther+mo+baro+
  graph
  ther+mo+baro+
    graphs
ther+mo+ba+rom+
  eter
  ther+mo+ba+
    rom+eters
ther+mo+chemi+
  cal
ther+mo+chem+
  ist
  ther+mo+chem+
    ists
ther+mo+chem+
  is+try
ther+mo+cline
  ther+mo+clines
ther+mo+cou+ple
  ther+mo+cou+
    ples
ther+mo+dy+
  nam+ic
ther+mo+dy+
  nami+cal
ther+mo+dy+
  nam+ics
ther+mo+elec+
  tric
ther+mo+elec+tri+
  cal
ther+mo+elec+
  tric+ity
ther+mo+elec+
  tron
  ther+mo+elec+
    trons

ther+mo+gen+
  esis
ther+mo+gram
  ther+mo+grams
ther+mo+graph
  ther+mo+graphs
ther+mo+graph+
  ic
ther+mog+ra+
  phy
ther+mo+junc+
  tion
  ther+mo+junc+
    tions
ther+mo+la+bile
ther+mo+lu+mi+
  nes+cence
ther+moly+sis
ther+mo+lyt+ic
ther+mo+mag+
  net+ic
ther+mom+eter
  ther+mom+
    eters
ther+mom+etry
ther+mo+nu+
  clear
ther+mo+phil
  ther+mo+phils
ther+mo+phile
  ther+mo+philes
ther+mo+phil+ic
ther+mo+pile
  ther+mo+piles
ther+mo+plas+tic
  ther+mo+plas+
    tics
Ther+mopy+lae
Ther+mos
  Trademark
Ther+moses
ther+mo+set+
  ting
ther+mo+si+phon
  ther+mo+si+
    phons
ther+mo+sphere
ther+mo+sta+ble
ther+mo+stat
  ther+mo+stats
ther+mo+stat+ic
ther+mo+stati+
  cal+ly
ther+mo+stat+ics
ther+mo+tax+ic

ther+mo+tax+is
ther+mo+trop+ic
ther+mo+tro+
  pism
the+roid
Theroux
Thersites
the+sau+rus
  the+sau+ri *or*
  the+sau+ruses
these
The+sean
Theseus
Thesiger
the+sis
  the+ses
Thes+pian
  Thes+pians
Thespis
Thes+sa+li+an
  Thes+sa+li+ans
Thes+sa+lo+nian
  Thes+sa+lo+
    nians
Thes+sa+lo+ní+ki
Thes+sa+ly
the+ta
  the+tas
Thetis
the+ur+gic
the+ur+gi+cal
the+ur+gist
  the+ur+gists
the+ur+gy
  the+ur+gies
thew
  thews
thew+less
thewy
they
they'd
they'll
they're
they've
thia+min
thia+mine
thia+zine
thia+zole
thick
  thick+er
  thick+est
thick+en
  thick+ens
  thick+en+ing
  thick+ened

thick+en+er
thick+en+ers
thick+en+ing
thick+en+ings
thick+et
thick+ets
thick+head
thick+heads
thick+headed
thickie
thickies
thick+ish
thick-knee
thick-knees
thick+ly
thick+ness
thick+set
thick+sets
thick-skinned
thick-skulled
thick-witted
thick-witted+ly
thick-witted+
ness
thicky
thickies
thief
thieves
Thiers
thieve
thieves
thiev+ing
thieved
thiev+ery
thiev+ing
thiev+ish
thigh
thighs
thigh+bone
thigh+bones
thim+ble
thim+bles
thim+ble+ful
thim+ble+fuls
thimble+rig
thimble+rigs
thimble+rigger
thimble+riggers
Thim+bu
Thim+phu
thin
thins
thin+ning
thinned
thin+ner

thin+nest
thine
thin-film
thing
things
thinga+ma+bob
thinga+ma+
bobs
thing-in-itself
things-in-
themselves
thingu+ma+bob
thingu+ma+
bobs
think
thinks
thinks
think+ing
thought
think+able
think+er
think+ers
think+ing
think-tank
think-tanks
thin+ly
thin+ner
thin+ners
thin+ness
thin-skinned
thiol
thiols
thio+nin
thio+nine
thio+phen
thio+phene
thio+sul+phate
thio+sul+phates
thio+ura+cil
thio+urea
third
thirds
third-class
adj.
third class
noun
third-degree
adj.
third de+gree
noun
third+ly
third-rate
Thirl+mere
thirst
thirsts

thirsts
thirst+ing
thirst+ed
thirsti+ly
thirsti+ness
thirsty
thirsti+er
thirsti+est
thir+teen
thir+teens
thir+teenth
thir+teenths
thir+ti+eth
thir+ti+eths
thir+ty
thir+ties
thirty-twomo
thirty-twomos
this
Thisbe
this+tle
this+tles
thistle+down
this+tly
thith+er
thither+to
thither+ward
thixo+trope
thixo+tropes
thixo+trop+ic
thix+ot+ro+py
tho
tho'
thole
tholes
tholes
thol+ing
tholed
thole+pin
thole+pins
tho+los
tho+loi
Thomas
Tho+mism
Thompson
Trademark
Thomson
thon
Thon+bu+ri
thong
thongs
Thor
tho+rac+ic
tho+ra+co+plas+
ty

tho+ra+co+plas+
ties
thor+ax
thor+axes *or*
tho+ra+ces
Thorburn
Thoreau
tho+ric
tho+rium
thorn
thorns
Thorn
thorn+bill
thorn+bills
Thorndike
Thorne
thorni+ly
thorni+ness
thorn+less
thorny
thorni+er
thorni+est
tho+ron
thor+ough
thorough+bred
thorough+breds
Thorough+bred
Thorough+breds
thorough+fare
thorough+fares
thorough+going
thor+ough+ly
thor+ough+ness
thorough+paced
thorp
thorps
thorpe
thorpes
Thorpe
Thors+havn
Thorvaldsen
Thorwaldsen
those
Thoth
thou
thous *or*
thou
though
thought
thoughts
thought+ful
thought+ful+ly
thought+ful+ness
thought+less
thought+less+ly

thought+less+
ness
thought-out
thou+sand
thou+sands
thou+sandth
thou+sandths
Thrace
Thra+cian
Thra+cians
thrall
thralls
thralls
thrall+ing
thralled
thrash
thrashes
thrashes
thrash+ing
thrashed
thrash+er
thrash+ers
thrash+ing
thrash+ings
thra+soni+cal
thra+soni+cal+ly
thrawn
thread
threads
threads
thread+ing
thread+ed
thread+bare
thread+er
thread+ers
threadi+ness
thread+like
thread+worm
thread+worms
thready
threadi+er
threadi+est
threat
threats
threat+en
threat+ens
threat+en+ing
threat+ened
threat+en+ing
threat+en+ing+ly
three
threes
three-card
three-colour
three-D

3-D
three-decker
three-deckers
three-dimen+sion+
al
three+fold
three-legged
three-phase
three-ply
three-point
three-quarter
three-quarters
three-ring
three+score
three+some
three+somes
threm+ma+tol+
ogy
thre+node
thre+nodes
thre+nod+ic
threno+dist
threno+dists
threno+dy
threno+dies
thresh
threshes
threshes
thresh+ing
threshed
thresh+er
thresh+ers
thresh+ing
thresh+old
thresh+olds
threw
thrice
thrift
thrifts
thrifti+ly
thrifti+ness
thrift+less
thrift+less+ly
thrifty
thrifti+er
thrifti+est
thrill
thrills
thrills
thrill+ing
thrilled
thrill+er
thrill+ers
thrill+ing
thrips

thrips
thrive
thrives
thriv+ing
thrived *or*
throve
thrived *or*
thriv+en
thro
thro'
throat
throats
throati+ly
throaty
throati+er
throati+est
throb
throbs
throbs
throb+bing
throbbed
throes
throm+bin
throm+bo+cyte
throm+bo+cytes
throm+bo+cyt+ic
throm+bo+em+
bo+lism
throm+bose
throm+boses
throm+bos+ing
throm+bosed
throm+bo+sis
throm+bo+ses
throm+bot+ic
throm+bus
throm+bi
throne
thrones
thrones
thron+ing
throned
throng
throngs
throngs
throng+ing
thronged
thros+tle
thros+tles
throt+tle
throt+tles
throt+tling
throt+tled
throt+tler

throt+tlers
through
through+out
through+put
through+way
through+ways
throve
throw
throws
throws
throw+ing
threw
thrown
throw+away
throw+aways
throw away
verb
throw+back
throw+backs
throw back
verb
throw+er
throw+ers
throw-in
throw-ins
throw in
verb
thrown
thru
U.S.
thrum
thrums
thrums
thrum+ming
thrummed
thrush
thrushes
thrust
thrusts
thrusts
thrust+ing
thrust
thrust+er
thrust+ers
Thu+cydi+dean
Thucydides
thud
thuds
thuds
thud+ding
thud+ded
thug
thugs
thug+gery
thug+gish

thu+ja
 thu+jas
Thu+le
thu+lium
thumb
 thumbs
 thumbs
 thumb+ing
 thumbed
thumb-index
 thumb-indexes
 thumb-indexing
 thumb-indexed
thumb in+dex
 thumb in+dexes
thumb+nail
 thumb+nails
thumb+nut
 thumb+nuts
thumb+screw
 thumb+screws
thumb+tack
 thumb+tacks
Thum+mim
thump
 thumps
 thumps
 thump+ing
 thumped
thump+er
 thump+ers
thump+ing
Thun
thun+ber+gia
 thun+ber+gias
thun+der
 thun+ders
 thun+ders
 thun+der+ing
 thun+dered
thunder+bolt
 thunder+bolts
thunder+clap
 thunder+claps
thunder+cloud
 thunder+clouds
thun+der+er
 thun+der+ers
thunder+head
 thunder+heads
thun+der+ing
thun+der+ous
thunder+storm
 thunder+storms
thunder+stricken

thunder+struck
thun+dery
Thurber
Thur+gau
thu+ri+ble
 thu+ri+bles
Thu+rin+gia
Thu+rin+gian
 Thu+rin+gians
Thurs+day
 Thurs+days
thus
thu+ya
 thu+yas
thwack
 thwacks
 thwacks
 thwack+ing
 thwacked
thwart
 thwarts
 thwarts
 thwart+ing
 thwart+ed
thy
Thy+es+tean
Thyestes
Thy+es+tian
thy+la+cine
 thy+la+cines
thyme
thy+mine
thy+mol
thy+mus
 thy+muses or
 thy+mi
thymy
thy+ra+tron
 thy+ra+trons
thy+ris+tor
 thy+ris+tors
thy+roid
 thy+roids
thy+ro+tro+phin
thy+ro+tro+pin
thy+rox+in
thy+rox+ine
thyrse
 thyrses
thyr+sus
 thyr+si
thy+self
ti
 tis
Tia Jua+na

Tian+jin
Tian Shan
ti+ara
 ti+aras
 ti+araed
Ti+ber
Ti+be+ri+tas
Tiberius
Ti+bes+ti
Ti+bet
Ti+bet+an
 Ti+bet+ans
tibia
 tibiae or
 tibias
tib+ial
Tibullus
Ti+bur
tic
 tics
tic dou+lou+reux
tichy
 tichi+er
 tichi+est
Ti+ci+no
tick
 ticks
 ticks
 tick+ing
 ticked
tick-bird
 tick-birds
tick+er
 tick+ers
tick+et
 tick+ets
 tick+et+ing
 tick+et+ed
ticket-of-leave
 adj.
tick+et of leave
 tick+ets of leave
tick+ing
tick+le
 tick+les
 tick+les
 tick+ling
 tick+led
tick+ler
 tick+lers
tick+lish
 tick+lish+ly
 tick+lish+ness
tick+tack

tick+tacks
tick+tock
 tick+tocks
 tick+tocks
 tick+tock+ing
 tick+tocked
Ti+con+dero+ga
tid+al
tid+al+ly
tid+bit
 U.S.
tid+bits
tid+dler
 tid+dlers
tid+dly
 tid+dli+er
 tid+dli+est
tiddly+winks
tide
 tides
 tides
 tid+ing
 tid+ed
tide+land
 tide+lands
tide+less
tide+mark
 tide+marks
tide-rip
 tide-rips
tide+waiter
 tide+waiters
tide+water
 tide+waters
tide+way
 tide+ways
tidi+ly
tidi+ness
tid+ings
tidy
 tidies
 tidies
 tidy+ing
 tidied
 tidi+er
 tidi+est
tie
 ties
 ties
 ty+ing
 tied
tie-and-dye
 tied
tie-dyed
tie-in

tie-ins
tie in
verb
T'ien-ching
Tien Shan
Tien+tsin
tie+pin
tie+pins
Tiepolo
tier
row
tiers
tiers
tier+ing
tiered
tier
person who ties
tiers
tierce
tier+cel
tier+cels
Tier+ra del Fue+
go
tie-up
tie-ups
tie up
verb
tiff
tiffs
tiffs
tiff+ing
tiffed
tif+fa+ny
Tiffany
tif+fin
Tif+lis
tig
tigs
tigs
tig+ging
tigged
ti+ger
ti+gers
Tiger
tiger+eye
ti+ger+ish
tiger's-eye
tight
tight+er
tight+est
tight+en
tight+ens
tight+en+ing
tight+ened
tight+fisted

tight+knit
tight-lipped
tight+ly
tight+ness
tight+rope
tight+ropes
tights
tig+lon
tig+lons
ti+gon
ti+gons
Ti+gré
ti+gress
ti+gresses
ti+grid+ia
Ti+gris
ti+grish
Ti+hua
Ti+hwa
Ti+jua+na
tike
tikes
tiki
tikis
tik+ka
til+ak
til+ak *or*
til+aks
Til+burg
til+bury
til+buries
Til+bury
til+de
til+des
Tilden
tile
tiles
tiles
til+ing
tiled
til+er
til+ers
til+ing
till
tills
tills
till+ing
tilled
till+able
till+age
till+er
till+ers
till+ers
till+er+ing
till+ered

till+er+less
Till Eulenspiegel
Tilley
Tillich
Til+sit
tilt
tilts
tilts
tilt+ing
tilt+ed
tilt+er
tilt+ers
tilth
tilt+yard
tilt+yards
Tima+ru
tim+bal
tim+bals
tim+bale
tim+bales
tim+ber
tim+bers
tim+bers
tim+ber+ing
tim+bered
tim+ber+ing
timber+yard
timber+yards
tim+bre
tim+bres
tim+brel
tim+brels
Tim+buk+tu
time
times
times
tim+ing
timed
time-honoured
time+keeper
time+keepers
time+keeping
time-lag
time-lags
time-lapse
time+less
time+less+ly
time+less+ness
time+ly
time+li+er
time+li+est
time-out
time-outs
time+piece

time+pieces
tim+er
tim+ers
Times
time+saver
time+savers
time+saving
time+scale
time+scales
time-served
time+server
time+servers
time+table
time+tables
time+tables
time+tabling
time+tabled
time+worn
tim+id
ti+mid+ity
tim+id+ly
tim+ing
Ti+mi+şoa+ra
ti+moc+ra+cy
ti+moc+ra+cies
Ti+mor
tim+or+ous
tim+or+ous+ly
tim+or+ous+ness
Timoshenko
timo+thy
Timothy
Timour
tim+pa+ni
tim+pa+nist
tim+pa+nists
Timur
tin
tins
tins
tin+ning
tinned
tina+mou
tina+mous
Tinbergen
tinc+to+rial
tinc+ture
tinc+tures
tinc+tures
tinc+tur+ing
tinc+tured
Tindal
Tindale
tin+der
tinder+box

tinder+boxes
tin+dery
tine
  tines
tinea
tin+eal
tined
tin+foil
ting
  tings
  tings
  ting+ing
  tinged
Ting
ting-a-ling
  ting-a-lings
tinge
  tinges
  tinges
  tinge+ing *or*
  ting+ing
  tinged
tin+gle
  tin+gles
  tin+gles
  tin+gling
  tin+gled
tin+gler
  tin+glers
tin+gling
tin+gly
ti+ni+ly
ti+ni+ness
tink+er
  tink+ers
  tink+ers
  tink+er+ing
  tink+ered
tink+er+er
  tink+er+ers
tin+kle
  tin+kles
  tin+kles
  tin+kling
  tin+kled
tinned
tin+ni+ly
tin+ni+ness
tin+ni+tus
tin+ny
  tin+nies
  tin+ni+er
  tin+ni+est
tin-opener

tin-openers
Tin Pan Al+ley
tin-plate
  tin-plates
  tin-plating
  tin-plated
  tin plate
    noun
tin+pot
tin+sel
  tin+sels
  tin+sels
  tin+sel+ling *or*
  tin+sel+ing
    U.S.
  tin+selled *or*
  tin+seled
    U.S.
Tin+sel+town
tin+smith
  tin+smiths
tin+stone
tint
  tints
  tints
  tint+ing
  tint+ed
tint+er
  tint+ers
tin+tin+nabu+la+
  tion
tin+tin+nabu+la+
  tions
Tintoretto
tin+ware
tin+works
tiny
  tini+er
  tini+est
tip
  tips
  tips
  tip+ping
  tipped
tip+less
tip-off
  tip-offs
  tip off
    verb
tip+per
  tip+pers
Tip+per+ary
tip+pet
  tip+pets
Tippett

tip+ple
  tip+ples
  tip+ples
  tip+pling
  tip+pled
tip+pler
  tip+plers
tip+si+ly
tip+si+ness
tip+staff
  tip+staffs
tip+ster
  tip+sters
tip+sy
  tip+si+er
  tip+si+est
tip+toe
  tip+toes
  tip+toe+ing
  tip+toed
tip+top
tip-up
ti+rade
  ti+rades
Ti+ran
Ti+ra+na
Ti+ra+në
tire
  make tired
  tires
  tir+ing
  tired
tire
  U.S.
  tires
  tired
Ti+ree
tire+less
tire+less+ly
tire+less+ness
Tiresias
tire+some
tire+some+ly
tire+some+ness
tire+woman
  tire+women
Tîr+gu Mu+reş
Ti+rich Mir
tir+ing
tiro
  tiros
Ti+rol
Ti+ro+lean
  Ti+ro+leans
Tiro+lese

Tirpitz
Tiru+chi+ra+pal+
  li
Ti+ru+nel+veli
'tis
Ti+sa
ti+sane
  ti+sanes
Tish+ri
  Tish+ris
Tisiphone
Tissot
tis+sue
  tis+sues
  tis+sues
  tis+su+ing
  tis+sued
Ti+sza
tit
  tits
ti+tan
  ti+tans
Ti+tan
  Ti+tans
Ti+tan+esque
Ti+tan+ess
  Ti+tan+esses
Titania
ti+tan+ic
ti+ta+nium
tit+bit
  tit+bits
titchy
  titchi+er
  titchi+est
ti+ter
  U.S.
  ti+ters
tit+fer
  tit+fers
tith+able
tithe
  tithes
  tithes
  tith+ing
  tithed
Tithonus
titi
  titis
Titian
  painter
Ti+tian
  colour
Ti+ti+ca+ca
tit+il+late

tit+il+lates
tit+il+lat+ing
tit+il+lat+ed
titi+vate
titi+vates
titi+vat+ing
titi+vat+ed
titi+va+tion
titi+va+tions
tit+lark
tit+larks
ti+tle
ti+tles
ti+tles
ti+tling
ti+tled
title+holder
title+holders
tit+mouse
tit+mice
Tito
Ti+to+grad
ti+trat+able
ti+trate
ti+trates
ti+trat+ing
ti+trat+ed
ti+tra+tion
ti+tra+tions
ti+tre
ti+tres
tit+ter
tit+ters
tit+ters
tit+ter+ing
tit+tered
tit+ter+er
tit+ter+ers
tit+ti+vate
tit+ti+vates
tit+ti+vat+ing
tit+ti+vat+ed
tit+tle
tit+tles
tittle-tattle
tittle-tattles
tittle-tattling
tittle-tattled
tittle-tattler
tittle-tattlers
tit+tup
tit+tups
tit+tups
tit+tup+ping *or*
tit+up+ing

U.S.
tit+tupped *or*
tit+tuped
U.S.
titu+ba+tion
titu+lar
titu+lars
Titus
Tiu
Tivo+li
tiz+zy
tiz+zies
Tji+re+bon
T-junction
T-junctions
Tlax+ca+la
Tlem+cen
tme+sis
T-number
T-numbers
to
toad
toads
toad+fish
toad+fish *or*
toad+fishes
toad+flax
toad+flaxes
toad-in-the-hole
toad+ish
toad+stone
toad+stool
toad+stools
toady
toadies
toadies
toady+ing
toad+ied
toady+ish
toady+ism
Toa+ma+si+na
to-and-fro
adj.
to and fro
adv.
toast
toasts
toasts
toast+ing
toast+ed
toast+er
toast+ers
toastie
toasties
toast+master

toast+masters
toast+mistress
toast+
  mistresses
toasty
toasties
to+bac+co
to+bac+cos *or*
to+bac+coes
to+bac+co+nist
to+bac+co+
  nists
To+ba+go
To+ba+go+nian
To+ba+go+
  nians
to+bog+gan
to+bog+gans
to+bog+gans
to+bog+gan+ing
to+bog+ganed
to+bog+gan+er
to+bog+gan+
  ers
to+bog+gan+ist
to+bog+gan+
  ists
To+bol
To+bolsk
To+bruk
toby
tobies
To+can+tins
toc+ca+ta
toc+ca+tas
Toc H
To+char+ian
To+char+ians
to+coph+er+ol
Tocqueville
toc+sin
toc+sins
tod
to+day
Todd
tod+dle
tod+dles
tod+dles
tod+dling
tod+dled
tod+dler
tod+dlers
tod+dy

tod+dies
to-do
to-dos
toe
toes
toes
toe+ing
toed
toe+cap
toe+caps
toed
toe+hold
toe+holds
toe-in
toe-ins
toe+nail
toe+nails
toe+nails
toe+nailing
toe+nailed
toe+rag
toe+rags
toey
toff
toffs
tof+fee
tof+fees
toffee-apple
toffee-apples
toffee-nosed
tof+fy
tof+fies
toft
tofts
tofu
tog
togs
togs
tog+ging
togged
toga
togas
togaed
to+geth+er
to+geth+er+ness
tog+gery
tog+gle
tog+gles
tog+gles
tog+gling
tog+gled
Tog+li+at+ti
Togo
To+go+land
To+go+land+er

To+go+land+ers
To+go+lese
togs
to+he+roa
to+he+roas
to+hunga
to+hungas
toil
 toils
 toils
 toil+ing
 toiled
toile
 toiles
toil+er
 toil+ers
toi+let
 toi+lets
toi+let+ry
 toi+let+ries
toi+lette
 toi+lettes
toil+ful
toil+some
toil+some+ly
toil+some+ness
toi+toi
 toi+tois
Tojo
to+ka+mak
 to+ka+maks
To+kay
 To+kays
to+ken
 to+kens
 to+kens
 to+ken+ing
 to+kened
to+ken+ism
To+khar+ian
 To+khar+ians
toko+loshe
 toko+loshes
Tokugawa
 Iyeyasu
To+kyo
tol+booth
 tol+booths
tol+bu+ta+mide
told
tole
To+ledo
tol+er+abil+ity
tol+er+able
tol+er+ably

tol+er+ance
tol+er+ances
tol+er+ant
tol+er+ant+ly
tol+er+ate
tol+er+ates
tol+er+at+ing
tol+er+at+ed
tol+era+tion
tol+era+tion+ist
tol+era+tion+
 ists
To+le+tum
To+li+ma
Tolkien
toll
 tolls
 tolls
 toll+ing
 tolled
toll+booth
 toll+booths
toll+gate
 toll+gates
toll+house
 toll+houses
tol+lie
 tol+lies
Tolstoy
Tol+tec
 Tol+tecs or
 Tol+tec
tolu
To+lu+ca
tolu+ene
to+lui+dine
tom
 toms
toma+hawk
 toma+hawks
to+ma+to
 to+ma+toes
tomb
 tombs
tom+bac
Tombaugh
tom+bo+la
Tom+bouc+tou
tom+boy
 tom+boys
tom+boy+ish
tom+boy+ish+ly
tomb+stone
 tomb+stones
Tom Collins

Tom Collinses
Tom, Dick, and
 Harry
Tom, Dick, or
 Harry
tome
 tomes
to+men+tose
to+men+tum
 to+men+ta
tom+fool
 tom+fools
tom+fool+ery
tom+fool+eries
tom+fool+ish+
 ness
tom+my
 tom+mies
Tom+my gun
 Tom+my guns
tommy+rot
to+mog+ra+phy
to+mor+row
 to+mor+rows
tom+pi+on
 tom+pi+ons
Tomsk
tom+tit
 tom+tits
tom-tom
 tom-toms
ton
 tons
to+nal
to+nal+ity
 to+nal+ities
to+nal+ly
Ton+bridge
ton+do
 ton+di
tone
 tones
 tones
 ton+ing
 toned
tone-deaf
tone+less
tone+less+ly
to+neme
 to+nemes
to+nemic
ton+er
 ton+ers
tong
 tongs

ton+ga
ton+gas
Tonga
Tong+king
tongs
tongue
 tongues
 tongues
 tongu+ing
 tongued
 tongued
tongue-lash
 tongue-lashes
 tongue-lashing
 tongue-lashed
 tongue-lashing
 tongue-lashings
tongue+less
tongue+like
tongue-tie
 tongue-tied
 tongu+ing
ton+ic
 ton+ics
toni+cal+ly
to+nic+ity
 to+nic+ities
to+night
Ton+kin
Ton+le Sap
ton+nage
 ton+nages
tonne
 tonnes
ton+neau
 ton+neaus or
 ton+neaux
to+nom+eter
 to+nom+eters
tono+met+ric
ton+sil
 ton+sils
ton+sil+lar
ton+sil+lec+to+
 my
ton+sil+lec+to+
 mies
ton+sil+lit+ic
ton+sil+li+tis
ton+so+rial
ton+sure
 ton+sures
 ton+sures
 ton+sur+ing
 ton+sured

ton+sured
ton+tine
ton+tines
ton-up
ton-ups
to+nus
too
took
tool
tools
tool+er
tool+ers
tool+ing
tool-maker
tool-makers
tool-making
tool+room
tool+rooms
toot
toots
toots
toot+ing
toot+ed
toot+er
toot+ers
tooth
teeth
tooths
tooth+ing
toothed
tooth+ache
tooth+aches
tooth+brush
tooth+brushes
toothed
toothi+ly
toothi+ness
tooth+less
tooth+like
tooth+paste
tooth+pastes
tooth+pick
tooth+picks
tooth+some
tooth+wort
tooth+worts
toothy
toothi+er
toothi+est
too+tle
too+tles
too+tles
too+tling
too+tled
too+tler

too+tlers
Too+woom+ba
top
tops
tops
top+ping
topped
to+paz
to+pazes
top+coat
top+coats
top-dress
top-dresses
top-dressing
top-dressed
tope
topes
topes
top+ing
toped
to+pee
to+pees
To+pe+ka
top+er
top+ers
top-flight
top+gal+lant
top+gal+lants
top-hat
adj.
top hat
top hats
top-heavy
To+phet
To+pheth
to+phus
to+phi
topi
topis
to+pia+rist
to+pia+rists
to+pi+ary
to+pi+aries
top+ic
top+ics
topi+cal
topi+cal+ity
topi+cal+ly
top+knot
top+knots
top+less
top-level
top+loftiness
top+lofty
top+mast

top+masts
top+most
top+notch
top+notch+er
top+notch+ers
to+pog+ra+pher
to+pog+ra+
    phers
topo+graph+ic
topo+graphi+cal
to+pog+ra+phy
to+pog+ra+
    phies
topo+log+ic
topo+logi+cal
topo+logi+cal+ly
to+polo+gist
to+polo+gists
to+pol+ogy
to+pol+ogies
Topolski
top+per
top+pers
top+ping
top+pings
top+ple
top+ples
top+pling
top+pled
tops
top+sail
top+sails
top-secret
top+side
top+sides
top+soil
top+spin
topsy-turvy
top-up
top-ups
top up
verb
toque
toques
tor
tors
To+rah
Tor+bay
torc
torcs
torch
torches
torch+bearer
torch+bearers
tor+chère

tor+chères
tor+chier
tor+chiers
tor+chiere
tor+chieres
tore
torea+dor
torea+dors
to+re+ro
to+re+ros
tor+ic
to+rii
to+rii
To+ri+no
tor+ment
tor+ments
tor+ments
tor+ment+ing
tor+ment+ed
tor+ment+ed
tor+men+til
tor+men+tils
tor+ment+ing
tor+men+tor
tor+men+tors
torn
tor+nad+ic
tor+na+do
tor+na+does
    or
tor+na+dos
to+roid
to+roids
to+roi+dal
To+ron+to
To+ron+to+nian
To+ron+to+
    nians
tor+pe+do
tor+pe+does
tor+pe+does
tor+pe+do+ing
tor+pe+doed
torpedo-like
tor+pid
tor+pid+ity
tor+pid+ly
tor+por
tor+quate
Tor+quay
torque
torques
Torquemada
tor+ques
tor+queses

torr
  torr
Tor+rance
Tor+re del Gre+
  co
tor+re+fac+tion
tor+re+fy
  tor+re+fies
  tor+re+fy+ing
  tor+re+fied
Tor+rens
tor+rent
  tor+rents
  tor+ren+tial
Tor+re+ón
Torricelli
tor+rid
tor+rid+ity
tor+rid+ly
tor+rid+ness
tor+sion
tor+sion+al
tor+sion+al+ly
torsk
  torsks *or*
  torsk
tor+so
  tor+sos *or*
  tor+si
tort
  torts
torte
  tortes
Tortelier
tor+ti+col+lis
tor+til+la
  tor+til+las
tor+toise
  tor+toises
tortoise+shell
Tor+to+la
tor+tri+cid
  tor+tri+cids
Tor+tu+ga
tor+tu+os+ity
  tor+tu+os+ities
tor+tu+ous
tor+tu+ous+ly
tor+tu+ous+ness
tor+ture
  tor+tures
  tor+tures
  tor+tur+ing
  tor+tured
tor+tur+er

tor+tur+ers
tor+tur+ous
tor+tur+ous+ly
To+rún
to+rus
to+ri
Tory
  Tories
To+ry+ish
To+ry+ism
Tos+ca+na
Toscanini
tosh
toss
  tosses
  tosses
  toss+ing
  tossed
toss+er
  toss+ers
toss-up
  toss-ups
toss up
  verb
tot
  tots
  tots
  tot+ting
  tot+ted
to+tal
  to+tals
  to+tals
  to+tal+ling *or*
  to+tal+ing
  U.S.
  to+talled *or*
  to+taled
  U.S.
to+tali+sa+tor
to+tali+sa+tors
to+tal+is+er
to+tal+is+ers
to+tali+tar+ian
to+tali+tari+an+
  ism
to+tal+ity
  to+tal+ities
to+tali+za+tor
to+tali+za+tors
to+tal+iz+er
to+tal+iz+ers
to+tal+ly
to+ta+quine
to+ta+ra
  to+ta+ras

tote
  totes
  totes
  tot+ing
  tot+ed
to+tem
  to+tems
to+tem+ic
to+tem+ism
tot+er
  tot+ers
toth+er
t'oth+er
to+ti+pal+mate
tot+ter
  tot+ters
  tot+ters
  tot+ter+ing
  tot+tered
tot+ter+er
  tot+ter+ers
tot+tery
tot+ting
tou+can
  tou+cans
touch
  touches
  touches
  touch+ing
  touched
touch+able
touch-and-go
touch+down
  touch+downs
touch down
  verb
tou+ché
  touched
touch+er
  touch+ers
touch+hole
  touch+holes
touchi+ly
touchi+ness
touch+ing
touch+ing+ly
touch+line
  touch+lines
touch+mark
  touch+marks
touch-me-not
  touch-me-nots
touch+paper
touch+stone
  touch+stones

touch-type
  touch-types
  touch-typing
  touch-typed
touch-typist
  touch-typists
touch-up
  touch-ups
touch up
  verb
touch+wood
touchy
touchi+er
touchi+est
tough
  toughs
  toughs
  tough+ing
  toughed
tough+er
tough+est
tough+en
  tough+ens
  tough+en+ing
  tough+ened
tough+ly
tough-minded
tough-minded+
  ness
tough+ness
Toul
Tou+lon
Tou+louse
Toulouse-Lautrec
tou+pee
  tou+pees
tour
  tours
  tours
  tour+ing
  toured
tou+ra+co
  tou+ra+cos
Tou+raine
Tou+rane
Tour+coing
tour de force
  tours de force
Touré
tour+er
  tour+ers
tour+ism
tour+ist
  tour+ists
tour+is+tic

tour+isty	tow+els	*U.S.*	tra+cheate
tour+ma+line	tow+els	tox+ic	tra+che+itis
Tour+nai	tow+el+ling *or*	toxi+cal+ly	tra+che+oto+my
tour+na+ment	tow+el+ing	toxi+cant	tra+che+oto+
tour+na+ments	*U.S.*	toxi+cants	mies
tour+nedos	tow+elled *or*	tox+ic+ity	tra+cho+ma
tour+nedos	tow+eled	toxi+ic+ities	tra+choma+tous
Tourneur	*U.S.*	toxi+co+log+ic	tra+chyte
tour+ney	tow+el+ling	toxi+co+logi+cal	trac+ing
tour+neys	tow+er	toxi+colo+gist	trac+ings
tour+neys	tow+ers	toxi+colo+gists	track
tour+ney+ing	tow+ers	toxi+col+ogy	tracks
tour+neyed	tow+er+ing	tox+in	tracks
tour+ni+quet	tow+ered	tox+ins	track+ing
tour+ni+quets	tow+er+ing	toxin-antitox+in	tracked
Tours	tow+head	toxo+ca+ria+sis	track+er
tou+sle	tow+heads	tox+oid	track+ers
tou+sles	tow+headed	tox+oids	track+ing
tou+sles	tow+hee	tox+ophi+lite	track+laying
tou+sling	tow+hees	tox+ophi+lites	tracks
tou+sled	tow+line	tox+ophi+ly	track+suit
Toussaint	tow+lines	toxo+plas+mic	track+suits
L'Ouverture	town	toxo+plas+mo+	tract
tout	towns	sis	tracts
touts	townee	toy	trac+tabil+ity
touts	townees	toys	trac+table
tout+ing	Townes	toys	trac+table+ness
tout+ed	townie	toy+ing	trac+tably
tout à fait	townies	toyed	Trac+tar+ian
tout de suite	town+ish	To+ya+ma	Trac+tar+ians
tout+er	town+land	Toynbee	Trac+tari+an+ism
tout+ers	town+lands	tra+beate	trac+tate
tout le monde	town+scape	tra+beat+ed	trac+tates
to+va+rich	town+scapes	tra+becu+la	trac+tion
to+va+riches	towns+folk	tra+becu+lae	trac+tion+al
to+va+risch	Townshend	tra+becu+lar	trac+tive
to+va+risches	town+ship	tra+becu+late	trac+tor
to+va+rish	town+ships	Trab+zon	trac+tors
to+va+rishes	towns+man	trace	Tracy
tow	towns+men	traces	trad
tows	towns+people	traces	trad+able
tows	Towns+ville	trac+ing	trade
tow+ing	towns+woman	traced	trades
towed	towns+women	trace+abil+ity	trades
tow+able	towny	trace+able	trad+ing
tow+age	townies	trace+able+ness	trad+ed
tow+ages	tow+path	trace+ably	trade+able
to+ward	tow+paths	trac+er	trade-in
to+wards	tow+rope	trac+ers	trade-ins
tow+bar	tow+ropes	trac+eried	trade in
tow+bars	tox+aemia	trac+ery	*verb*
tow+boat	tox+aemic	trac+eries	trade+mark
tow+boats	tox+emia	tra+chea	trade+marks
tow-coloured	*U.S.*	tra+cheae	trade+marks
tow+el	tox+emic	tra+cheal	trade+mark+ing

trade+ marked
trade-off
trade-offs
trad+ er
trad+ ers
trad+ es+ can+ tia
trad+ es+ can+ tias
trades+ folk
trades+ man
trades+ men
trades+ people
trades+ woman
trades+ women
trad+ ing
tra+ di+ tion
tra+ di+ tions
tra+ di+ tion+ al
tra+ di+ tion+ al+ ism
tra+ di+ tion+ al+ ist
tra+ di+ tion+ al+ ists
tra+ di+ tion+ al+ is+ tic
tra+ di+ tion+ al+ ly
tra+ di+ tion+ less
tra+ duce
tra+ duces
tra+ duc+ ing
tra+ duced
tra+ duce+ ment
tra+ duce+ ments
tra+ duc+ er
tra+ duc+ ers
Tra+ fal+ gar
traf+ fic
traf+ fics
traf+ fick+ ing
traf+ ficked
traf+ fi+ ca+ tor
traf+ fi+ ca+ tors
traf+ fick+ er
traf+ fick+ ers
traga+ canth
traga+ canths
tra+ gedian
tra+ gedians
tra+ gedi+ enne
tra+ gedi+ ennes
trag+ edy
trag+ edies
tragi+ ic
tragi+ cal
tragi+ cal+ ly

tragi+ com+ edy
tragi+ com+ edies
tragi+ com+ ic
trago+ pan
trago+ pans
tra+ gus
tra+ gi
Traherne
trail
trails
trails
trail+ ing
trailed
trail+ blazer
trail+ blazers
trail+ blazing
trail+ er
trail+ ers
train
trains
trains
train+ ing
trained
train+ able
train+ band
train+ bands
train+ bearer
train+ bearers
trainee
trainees
train+ er
train+ ers
train+ ing
traipse
traipses
traipses
traips+ ing
traipsed
trait
traits
trai+ tor
trai+ tors
trai+ tor+ ous
trai+ tress
trai+ tresses
Trajan
tra+ jec+ tory
tra+ jec+ tories
Tra+ lee
tram
trams
tram+ less
tram+ line
tram+ lines

tram+ mel
tram+ mels
tram+ mels
tram+ mel+ ling
or
tram+ mel+ ing
U.S.
tram+ melled or
tram+ meled
U.S.
tra+ mon+ tane
tra+ mon+ tanes
tramp
tramps
tramps
tramp+ ing
tramped
tramp+ er
tramp+ ers
tramp+ ing
tramp+ ish
tram+ ple
tram+ ples
tram+ ples
tram+ pling
tram+ pled
tram+ pler
tram+ plers
tram+ po+ line
tram+ po+ lines
tram+ po+ lines
tram+ po+ lin+ ing
tram+ po+ lined
tram+ po+ lin+ er
tram+ po+ lin+ ers
trance
trances
trances
tranc+ ing
tranced
trance+ like
tranche
tranches
tran+ nie
tran+ nies
tran+ ny
tran+ nies
tran+ quil
tran+ quil+ ity
U.S.
tran+ qui+ li+ za+ tion
U.S.
tran+ quil+ ize
U.S.

tran+ quil+ izes
tran+ quil+ iz+ ing
tran+ quil+ ized
tran+ quil+ iz+ er
U.S.
tran+ quil+ iz+ ers
tran+ quil+ li+ sa+ tion
tran+ quil+ lise
tran+ quil+ lises
tran+ quil+ lis+ ing
tran+ quil+ lised
tran+ quil+ lis+ er
tran+ quil+ lis+ ers
tran+ quil+ lity
tran+ quil+ li+ za+ tion
tran+ quil+ lize
tran+ quil+ lizes
tran+ quil+ liz+ ing
tran+ quil+ lized
tran+ quil+ liz+ er
tran+ quil+ liz+ ers
tran+ quil+ ly
trans+ act
trans+ acts
trans+ act+ ing
trans+ act+ ed
trans+ ac+ ti+ nide
trans+ ac+ ti+ nides
trans+ ac+ tion
trans+ ac+ tions
trans+ ac+ tion+ al
trans+ ac+ tor
trans+ ac+ tors
trans+ al+ pine
trans+ ami+ nase
trans+ ami+ nases
trans+ at+ lan+ tic
Trans+ cau+ ca+ sia
Trans+ cau+ ca+ sian
Trans+ cau+ ca+ sians
trans+ ceiv+ er
trans+ ceiv+ ers
trans+ cend
trans+ cends
trans+ cend+ ing
trans+ cend+ ed
tran+ scend+ ence

tran+scend+en+cy
trans+cend+ent
trans+cend+ents
tran+scen+den+tal
tran+scen+den+tal+ism
tran+scen+den+tal+ist
tran+scen+den+tal+ists
tran+scen+den+tal+ly
tran+scend+ent+ly
trans+con+ti+nen+tal
trans+con+ti+nen+tal+ly
tran+scrib+able
tran+scribe
tran+scribes
tran+scrib+ing
tran+scribed
tran+scrib+er
tran+scrib+ers
tran+script
tran+scripts
tran+scrip+tase
tran+scrip+tion
tran+scrip+tions
tran+scrip+tion+al
tran+scrip+tive
trans+duc+er
trans+duc+ers
tran+sect
tran+sects
tran+sect+ing
tran+sect+ed
tran+sec+tion
tran+sec+tions
tran+sept
tran+septs
tran+sep+tal
trans+fer
trans+fers
trans+fers
trans+fer+ring
trans+ferred
trans+fer+able
trans+feree
trans+ferees

trans+fer+ence
trans+fer+rable
trans+fer+rin
trans+fer+rins
trans+figu+ra+tion
trans+figu+ra+tions
Trans+figu+ra+tion
Trans+figu+ra+tions
trans+fig+ure
trans+fig+ures
trans+fig+ur+ing
trans+fig+ured
trans+fig+ure+ment
trans+fig+ure+ments
trans+fix
trans+fixes
trans+fix+ing
trans+fixed or
trans+fixt
trans+fix+ion
trans+form
trans+forms
trans+forms
trans+form+ing
trans+formed
trans+form+able
trans+for+ma+tion
trans+for+ma+tions
trans+for+ma+tion+al
trans+forma+tive
trans+form+er
trans+form+ers
trans+fus+able
trans+fuse
trans+fuses
trans+fus+ing
trans+fused
trans+fus+er
trans+fus+ers
trans+fus+ible
trans+fu+sion
trans+fu+sions
trans+fu+sive
trans+gen+ic
trans+gress
trans+gresses

trans+gress+ing
trans+gressed
trans+gres+sion
trans+gres+sions
trans+gres+sive
trans+gres+sor
trans+gres+sors
tran+ship
tran+ships
tran+ship+ping
tran+shipped
tran+ship+ment
tran+ship+ments
trans+hu+mance
trans+hu+mant
tran+si+ence
tran+si+ent
tran+si+ents
tran+si+ent+ly
tran+sis+tor
tran+sis+tors
tran+sis+tor+ise
tran+sis+tor+ises
tran+sis+tor+is+ing
tran+sis+tor+ised
tran+sis+tor+ize
tran+sis+tor+izes
tran+sis+tor+iz+ing
tran+sis+tor+ized
trans+it
trans+its
trans+its
trans+it+ing
trans+it+ed
tran+si+tion
tran+si+tions
tran+si+tion+al
tran+si+tion+al+ly
tran+si+tive
tran+si+tive+ly
tran+si+tive+ness
tran+si+tiv+ity
tran+si+to+ri+ness
tran+si+tory

Trans-Jordan
Trans-Jordanian
Trans-Jordanians
Trans+kei
Trans+kei+an
Trans+kei+ans
trans+lat+able
trans+late
trans+lates
trans+lat+ing
trans+lat+ed
trans+la+tion
trans+la+tions
trans+la+tion+al
trans+la+tor
trans+la+tors
trans+lit+er+ate
trans+lit+er+ates
trans+lit+er+at+ing
trans+lit+er+at+ed
trans+lit+era+tion
trans+lit+era+tions
trans+lit+era+tor
trans+lit+era+tors
trans+lo+ca+tion
trans+lo+ca+tions
trans+lu+cence
trans+lu+cen+cy
trans+lu+cent
trans+lu+cent+ly
trans+lu+nar
trans+lu+nary
trans+mi+grate
trans+mi+grates
trans+mi+grat+ing
trans+mi+grat+ed
trans+mi+gra+tion
trans+mi+gra+tions
trans+mi+gra+tory
trans+mis+sible
trans+mis+sion
trans+mis+sions
trans+mis+sive

trans+mis+siv+
  ity
trans+mis+siv+
  ities
trans+mit
trans+mits
trans+mit+ting
trans+mit+ted
trans+mit+table
trans+mit+tal
trans+mit+tance
trans+mit+ter
trans+mit+ters
trans+mog+ri+fi+
  ca+tion
trans+mog+ri+fi+
  ca+tions
trans+mog+ri+fy
trans+mog+ri+
  fies
trans+mog+ri+
  fy+ing
trans+mog+ri+
  fied
trans+mon+tane
trans+mon+
  tanes
trans+mut+abil+
  ity
trans+mut+able
trans+mu+ta+
  tion
trans+mu+ta+
  tions
trans+mu+ta+
  tion+al
trans+mu+ta+tive
trans+mute
trans+mutes
trans+mut+ing
trans+mut+ed
trans+na+tion+al
trans+ocean+ic
tran+som
tran+soms
tran+somed
tran+son+ic
trans+par+en+cy
trans+par+en+
  cies
trans+par+ent
trans+par+ent+ly
trans+par+ent+
  ness
tran+spi+ra+tion

tran+spira+tory
tran+spire
tran+spires
tran+spir+ing
tran+spired
trans+plant
trans+plants
trans+plants
trans+plant+ing
trans+plant+ed
trans+plant+able
trans+plan+ta+
  tion
trans+plan+ta+
  tions
tran+spond+er
tran+spond+ers
trans+port
trans+ports
trans+port+ing
trans+port+ed
trans+port+able
trans+por+ta+
  tion
trans+por+ta+
  tions
trans+port+er
trans+port+ers
trans+pos+able
trans+pos+al
trans+pos+als
trans+pose
trans+poses
trans+pos+ing
trans+posed
trans+pos+er
trans+pos+ers
trans+po+si+tion
trans+po+si+
  tions
trans+pos+on
trans+pos+ons
trans+put+er
trans+put+ers
trans+sex+ual
trans+sex+uals
trans+ship
trans+ships
trans+ship+ping
trans+shipped
trans+ship+ment
trans+ship+
  ments
tran+sub+stan+
  tia+tion

tran+sub+stan+
  tia+tions
tran+sub+stan+
  tia+tion+al+ist
tran+sub+stan+
  tia+tion+al+ists
tran+su+da+tion
tran+su+da+
  tions
tran+sude
tran+sudes
tran+sud+ing
tran+sud+ed
transu+ra+nian
transu+ran+ic
transu+ra+nium
Trans+vaal
Trans+vaal+er
Trans+vaal+ers
Trans+vaal+ian
trans+ver+sal
trans+ver+sals
trans+ver+sal+ly
trans+verse
trans+verses
trans+verse+ly
trans+ves+tism
trans+ves+tite
trans+ves+tites
trans+ves+ti+
  tism
Tran+syl+va+nia
Tran+syl+va+
  nian
Tran+syl+va+
  nians
trap
traps
traps
trap+ping
trapped
Tra+pa+ni
Tra+pa+nis
trap-door
adj.
trap door
trap doors
trapes
trapeses
trapeses
trapes+ing
trapesed
tra+peze
tra+pezes
tra+pezial

tra+pezium
tra+peziums *or*
  tra+pezia
tra+pezius
  tra+peziuses
trap+ezoid
trap+ezoids
trap+like
trap+per
trap+pers
trap+pings
Trap+pist
Trap+pists
trap+rock
traps
trap+shooter
trap+shooters
trap+shooting
trash
trashes
trash+ing
trashed
trashi+ly
trashi+ness
trashy
trashi+er
trashi+est
Tra+si+mene
trass
trat+to+ria
trat+to+rias
trau+ma
trau+ma+ta *or*
  trau+mas
trau+mat+ic
trau+mati+cal+ly
trau+ma+ti+sa+
  tion
trau+ma+tise
trau+ma+tises
trau+ma+tis+ing
trau+ma+tised
trau+ma+ti+za+
  tion
trau+ma+tize
trau+ma+tizes
trau+ma+tiz+ing
trau+ma+tized
trav+ail
trav+ails
trav+ails
trav+ail+ing
trav+ailed
Trav+an+core
trav+el

trav+els	treach+er+ous+	Trebi+zond	trem+bly
trav+els	ness	tre+ble	tre+men+dous
trav+el+ling *or*	treach+ery	tre+bles	tre+men+dous+ly
trav+el+ing	treach+eries	tre+bles	tre+men+dous+
U.S.	trea+cle	tre+bling	ness
trav+elled *or*	trea+cly	tre+bled	tremo+lo
trav+eled	tread	tre+bly	tremo+los
U.S.	treads	trebu+chet	trem+or
trav+eled	treads	trebu+chets	trem+ors
U.S.	tread+ing	tre+buck+et	trem+ors
trav+elled	trod	tre+buck+ets	trem+or+ing
trav+el+ler	trod+den *or*	tre+cen+tist	trem+ored
trav+el+lers	trod	tre+cen+tists	trem+or+ous
trav+el+ler's	tread+er	tre+cen+to	tremu+lous
trav+el+ling	tread+ers	tree	tremu+lous+ly
travelling-wave	trea+dle	trees	tremu+lous+ness
adj.	trea+dles	trees	tre+nail
trav+el+ling wave	trea+dles	tree+ing	tre+nails
trav+el+ling	trea+dling	treed	trench
waves	trea+dled	Tree	trenches
trav+elog	tread+mill	tree+hopper	trenches
U.S.	tread+mills	tree+hoppers	trench+ing
trav+elogs	trea+son	tree+less	trenched
trav+elogue	trea+son+able	tree+less+ness	trench+an+cy
trav+elogues	trea+son+ably	tree+like	trench+ant
Traven	trea+son+ous	tre+en	trench+ant+ly
Travers	treas+ure	tree+nail	Trenchard
tra+vers+al	treas+ures	tree+nails	trench+er
tra+vers+als	treas+ures	treen+ware	trench+ers
trav+erse	treas+ur+ing	tref	trencher+man
trav+erses	treas+ured	tre+foil	trencher+men
trav+erses	treas+ur+er	tre+foils	trend
trav+ers+ing	treas+ur+ers	tre+foiled	trends
trav+ersed	Treas+ur+er	trek	trends
tra+vers+er	Treas+ur+ers	treks	trend+ing
tra+vers+ers	treas+ur+er+ship	treks	trend+ed
trav+er+tine	treasure-trove	trek+king	trendi+ly
trav+es+ty	treasure-troves	trekked	trendi+ness
trav+es+ties	treas+ury	trel+lis	trend+setter
trav+es+ties	treas+uries	trel+lises	trend+setters
trav+es+ty+ing	Treas+ury	trel+lises	trend+setting
trav+es+tied	treat	trel+lis+ing	trendy
tra+vois	treats	trel+lised	trendies
tra+vois	treats	trellis+work	trendi+er
trawl	treat+ing	trema+tode	trendi+est
trawls	treat+ed	trema+todes	Treng+ga+nu
trawls	treat+able	trem+ble	Trent
trawl+ing	treat+er	trem+bles	trente et qua+
trawled	treat+ers	trem+bles	rante
trawl+er	trea+tise	trem+bling	Tren+to
trawl+ers	trea+tises	trem+bled	Tren+ton
tray	treat+ment	trem+bler	tre+pan
trays	treat+ments	trem+blers	tre+pans
treach+er+ous	trea+ty	trem+bles	tre+pans
treach+er+ous+ly	trea+ties	trem+bling	tre+pan+ning

tre+panned	tri+an+gu+lat+	tri+cen+ten+	tri+clin+ia
trepa+na+tion	ing	nials	tri+col+or
trepa+na+tions	tri+an+gu+lat+	tri+ceps	U.S.
tre+pang	ed	tri+cepses or	tri+col+ors
tre+pangs	tri+an+gu+late+ly	tri+ceps	tri+col+our
trephi+na+tion	tri+an+gu+la+tion	tri+chia+sis	tri+col+ours
trephi+na+tions	tri+an+gu+la+	tri+chi+na	tri+col+oured
tre+phine	tions	tri+chi+nae	tri+corn
tre+phines	Tri+as+sic	Trichi+nopo+ly	tri+corns
tre+phines	tri+ath+lon	trichi+no+sis	tri+cot
tre+phin+ing	tri+ath+lons	trichi+nous	tri+cus+pid
tre+phined	tri+atom+ic	tri+chlo+ride	tri+cus+pids
trepi+da+tion	trib+ade	tri+chlo+rides	tri+cy+cle
tres+pass	trib+ades	tri+cholo+gist	tri+cy+cles
tres+passes	trib+ad+ism	tri+cholo+gists	tri+cy+clist
tres+passes	trib+al	tri+chol+ogy	tri+cy+clists
tres+pass+ing	trib+al+ism	tricho+mo+nia+	tri+dent
tres+passed	trib+al+ist	sis	tri+dents
tres+pass+er	trib+al+ists	tri+chop+ter+an	Tri+dent
tres+pass+ers	trib+al+is+tic	tri+chop+ter+	Tri+dents
tress	tri+ba+sic	ans	tri+den+tal
tresses	tribe	tri+cho+sis	tri+den+tate
tresses	tribes	tricho+tom+ic	Tri+den+tine
tress+ing	tribes+man	tri+choto+mous	Tri+den+tines
tressed	tribes+men	tri+choto+my	Tri+den+tum
tressy	tri+bo+elec+tric+	tri+choto+mies	tri+ecious
tres+tle	ity	tri+chro+ism	tried
tres+tles	tri+bol+ogy	tri+chro+mat+ic	tri+ella
trestle+work	tri+bo+lu+mi+nes+	tri+chro+ma+	tri+ellas
tre+val+ly	cence	tism	tri+en+nial
tre+val+lies	tri+bo+lu+mi+nes+	tri+chro+mic	tri+en+nials
Trevelyan	cent	trick	tri+en+ni+al+ly
Trèves	tri+brach	tricks	tri+en+nium
Trevino	tri+brachs	tricks	tri+en+niums
Tre+vi+so	tri+bro+mo+etha+	trick+ing	or
Trevithick	nol	tricked	tri+en+nia
trews	tribu+la+tion	trick+ery	Tri+ent
trey	tribu+la+tions	tricki+ly	tri+er
treys	tri+bu+nal	tricki+ness	tri+ers
tri+able	tri+bu+nals	trick+le	Trier
tri+ac+id	tribu+nate	trick+les	Tri+este
tri+ad	trib+une	trick+les	tri+fa+cial
tri+ads	trib+unes	trick+ling	tri+fec+ta
Tri+ad	trib+une+ship	trick+led	tri+fid
Tri+ads	tribu+tari+ly	trick+si+ness	tri+fle
tri+ad+ic	tribu+tary	trick+ster	tri+fles
tri+ad+ism	tribu+taries	trick+sters	tri+fles
tri+age	trib+ute	trick+sy	tri+fling
tri+al	trib+utes	trick+si+er	tri+fled
tri+als	trice	trick+si+est	tri+fler
tri+an+gle	trices	tricky	tri+flers
tri+an+gles	tri+cen+ten+ary	tricki+er	tri+fling
tri+an+gu+lar	tri+cen+ten+	tricki+est	tri+fling+ly
tri+an+gu+late	aries	tri+clin+ic	tri+fo+cal
tri+an+gu+lates	tri+cen+ten+nial	tri+clin+ium	tri+fo+cals

tri+fo+rium
 tri+fo+ria
tri+fur+cate
tri+fur+cat+ed
trig
 trigs
 trig+ging
 trigged
tri+gemi+nal
trig+ger
 trig+gers
 trig+gers
 trig+ger+ing
 trig+gered
trigger+fish
 trigger+fish *or*
 trigger+fishes
trigger-happy
trig+ly
tri+glyc+er+ide
 tri+glyc+er+ides
tri+glyph
 tri+glyphs
trig+ness
trigo+nal
trigo+no+met+ric
trigo+no+met+ri+
 cal
trigo+nom+etry
tri+graph
 tri+graphs
tri+he+dral
 tri+he+drals
tri+he+dron
 tri+he+drons
 or
 tri+he+dra
trike
 trikes
tri+lat+er+al
tril+by
 tril+bies
tri+lin+gual
tri+lin+gual+ism
tri+lith
 tri+liths
tri+lith+ic
tri+lith+on
 tri+lith+ons
trill
 trills
 trills
 trill+ing
 trilled
tril+lion

tril+lions
 tril+lionth
 tril+lionths
tril+lium
 tril+liums
tri+lo+bate
tri+lo+bite
 tri+lo+bites
 tri+lo+bit+ic
tril+ogy
 tril+ogies
trim
 trims
 trims
 trim+ming
 trimmed
trim+mer
trim+mest
Trim
tri+ma+ran
 tri+ma+rans
tri+mer
 tri+mers
trim+er+ous
trim+mes+ter
 tri+mes+ters
 tri+mes+tral
 tri+mes+tri+al
trim+eter
 trim+eters
tri+metha+di+one
trim+ly
trim+mer
 trim+mers
trim+ming
 trim+mings
trim+ness
tri+mo+lecu+lar
tri+month+ly
tri+mor+phism
Tri+na+cria
Tri+na+crian
tri+nal
tri+na+ry
Trin+co+ma+lee
trine
 trines
Trini+dad
Trini+dad+ian
 Trini+dad+ians
 Trini+tar+ian
 Trini+tar+ians
Trini+tari+an+ism
tri+ni+tro+glyc+
 er+in

tri+ni+tro+tolu+
 ene
tri+ni+tro+tolu+ol
trini+ty
 trini+ties
Trini+ty
trin+ket
 trin+kets
tri+no+mial
 tri+no+mials
trio
 trios
tri+ode
 tri+odes
tri+oecious
trio+lein
trio+let
 trio+lets
tri+ox+ide
 tri+ox+ides
trip
 trips
 trips
trip+ping
 tripped
tri+par+tite
 tri+par+tite+ly
tripe
trip+hammer
 trip+hammers
tri+phibi+ous
triph+thong
 triph+thongs
triph+thong+al
tri+pin+nate
tri+plane
 tri+planes
tri+ple
 tri+ples
 tri+ples
 tri+pling
 tri+pled
tri+plet
 tri+plets
Tri+plex
Trademark
trip+li+cate
 trip+li+cates
 trip+li+cates
 trip+li+cat+ing
 trip+li+cat+ed
 trip+li+ca+tion
 trip+li+ca+tions
trip+loid
 trip+loids

tri+ply
tri+pod
 tri+pods
tripo+dal
tripo+li
Tripo+li
Tripo+li+ta+nia
Tripo+li+ta+nian
 Tripo+li+ta+
 nians
tri+pos
 tri+poses
trip+per
trip+pers
trip+tane
Triptolemus
trip+tych
 trip+tychs
trip+tyque
 trip+tyques
Tripu+ra
trip+wire
 trip+wires
tri+reme
 tri+remes
tri+sect
 tri+sects
tri+sect+ing
tri+sect+ed
tri+sec+tion
 tri+sec+tions
tri+shaw
 tri+shaws
tris+keli+on
 tri+skelia
Trismegistus
tris+mus
Tristan
Tris+tan da Cu+
 nha
triste
Tristram
tri+syl+lab+ic
tri+syl+la+ble
 tri+syl+la+bles
trite
 trit+er
 trit+est
trite+ly
trite+ness
tri+the+ism
tri+the+ist
 tri+the+ists
triti+cum
trit+ium

tri+ton	tro+chal	troop	trot+ters
tri+tons	tro+chan+ter	troops	trou+ba+dour
Triton	tro+chan+ters	troops	trou+ba+dours
tri+tone	troche	troop+ing	trou+ble
tri+tones	troches	trooped	trou+bles
tritu+rate	tro+chee	troop+er	trou+bles
tritu+rates	tro+chees	troop+ers	trou+bling
tritu+rates	troch+lea	troop+ship	trou+bled
tritu+rat+ing	troch+leae	troop+ships	trouble+maker
tritu+rat+ed	tro+choid	tro+paeo+lum	trouble+makers
tritu+ra+tion	tro+choids	tro+paeo+lums	trouble+making
tritu+ra+tions	trod	or	trou+bler
tri+umph	trod+den	tro+paeo+la	trou+blers
tri+umphs	trode	trope	trouble+shooter
tri+umphs	trog+lo+dyte	tropes	trouble+
tri+umph+ing	trog+lo+dytes	troph+ic	shooters
tri+umphed	trog+lo+dyt+ic	tropho+blast	trouble+shooting
tri+um+phal	tro+gon	tropho+blasts	trou+ble+some
tri+um+phant	tro+gons	tropho+zo+ite	trou+ble+some+
tri+um+phant+ly	troi+ka	tropho+zo+ites	ness
tri+um+vir	troi+kas	tro+phy	trou+blous
tri+um+virs or	Troilus	tro+phies	trou+blous+ly
tri+um+vi+ri	Trois Ri+vières	trop+ic	trough
tri+um+vi+ral	Tro+jan	trop+ics	troughs
tri+um+vi+rate	Tro+jans	tropi+cal	trounce
tri+um+vi+rates	troll	tropi+cal+ity	trounces
tri+une	trolls	tropi+cal+ly	trounc+ing
tri+unity	trolls	tropic+bird	trounced
tri+va+len+cy	troll+ing	tropic+birds	troupe
tri+va+lent	trolled	tro+pism	troupes
Tri+van+drum	troll+er	tro+pis+mat+ic	troupes
triv+et	troll+ers	tropo+pause	troup+ing
triv+ets	trol+ley	tropo+sphere	trouped
trivia	trol+leys	tropo+spher+ic	troup+er
triv+ial	trolley+bus	trop+po	troup+ers
trivi+ali+sa+tion	trolley+buses	Tros+sachs	trou+ser
trivi+al+ise	trol+lius	trot	trou+sers
trivi+al+ises	trol+liuses	trots	trous+seau
trivi+al+is+ing	trol+lop	trots	trous+seaux or
trivi+al+ised	trol+lops	trot+ting	trous+seaus
trivi+al+ity	Trollope	trot+ted	trout
trivi+al+ities	trom+bone	Trot	trout or
trivi+ali+za+tion	trom+bones	Trots	trouts
trivi+al+ize	trom+bon+ist	troth	trou+vère
trivi+al+izes	trom+bon+ists	troths	trou+vères
trivi+al+iz+ing	trom+mel	trot+line	trove
trivi+al+ized	trom+mels	trot+lines	troves
trivi+al+ly	trompe	Trotski	trow
trivi+al+ness	trompes	Trotsky	trows
trivium	trompe l'oeil	Trot+sky+ism	trow+ing
trivia	trompe l'oeils	Trot+sky+ist	trowed
Tro+as	tron	Trot+sky+ists	Trow+bridge
tro+car	tronc	Trot+sky+ite	trow+el
tro+cars	troncs	Trot+sky+ites	trow+els
tro+cha+ic	Trond+heim	trot+ter	trow+els

trow+el+ling
or
trow+el+ing
U.S.
trow+elled *or*
trow+eled
U.S.
troy
Troy
Troyes
Trst
tru+an+cy
tru+an+cies
tru+ant
tru+ants
tru+ants
tru+ant+ing
tru+ant+ed
truce
truces
truck
trucks
trucks
truck+ing
trucked
truck+er
truck+ers
truckie
truckies
truck+ing
truck+le
truck+les
truck+ling
truck+led
truck+ler
truck+lers
trucu+lence
trucu+len+cy
trucu+lent
trucu+lent+ly
Trudeau
trudge
trudges
trudges
trudg+ing
trudged
trudg+en
trudg+er
trudg+ers
true
trues
tru+ing
trued
tru+er
tru+est

true-blue
adj.
true blue
true blues
true-life
true+love
true+loves
Trueman
true+ness
Truffaut
truf+fle
truf+fles
trug
trugs
tru+go
tru+ism
tru+isms
tru+is+tic
Trujillo
trull
trulls
tru+ly
Truman
tru+meau
tru+meaux
trump
trumps
trumps
trump+ing
trumped
trump+ery
trump+eries
trum+pet
trum+pets
trum+pets
trum+pet+ing
trum+pet+ed
trum+pet+er
trum+pet+ers
trumps
trun+cate
trun+cates
trun+cat+ing
trun+cat+ed
trun+cat+ed
trun+ca+tion
trun+ca+tions
trun+cheon
trun+cheons
trun+dle
trun+dles
trun+dles
trun+dling
trun+dled
trun+dler

trun+dlers
trunk
trunks
trunk+fish
trunk+fish *or*
trunk+fishes
trunk+ing
trunks
trun+nion
trun+nions
Tru+ro
truss
trusses
trusses
truss+ing
trussed
trust
trusts
trusts
trust+ing
trust+ed
trust+able
trus+tee
trus+tees
trus+tee+ship
trus+tee+ships
trust+er
trust+ers
trust+ful
trust+ful+ly
trusti+ly
trusti+ness
trust+ing
trust+worthi+ly
trust+worthi+
  ness
trust+worthy
trusty
trusties
trusti+er
trusti+est
truth
truths
truth+ful
truth+ful+ly
truth+ful+ness
truth-function
truth-functions
truth+less
truth-value
truth-values
try
tries
tries
try+ing

tried
try+ing
try+ing+ly
try-on
try-ons
try on
verb
try+out
try+outs
try out
verb
trypa+no+some
trypa+no+
  somes
trypa+no+so+mia+
  sis
tryp+sin
tryp+tic
tryp+to+phan
try+sail
try+sails
tryst
trysts
Tsa+na
tsar
tsars
tsar+dom
tsar+doms
tsar+evitch
tsar+evitches
tsa+rev+na
tsa+rev+nas
tsa+ri+na
tsa+ri+nas
tsar+ism
tsar+ist
tsar+ists
tsa+rit+sa
tsa+rit+sas
Tsa+ri+tsyn
Tse+li+no+grad
tset+se
T-shirt
T-shirts
Tshombe
Tsi+nan
Tsing+hai
Tsing+tao
Tsing+yuan
tso+tsi
tso+tsis
T-square
T-squares
T-stop
T-stops

tsu+na+mi
 tsu+na+mis *or*
 tsu+na+mi
Tsu+shi+ma
Tswa+na
 Tswa+na *or*
 Tswa+nas
tua+ta+ra
 tua+ta+ras
tub
 tubs
 tubs
 tub+bing
 tubbed
tuba
 tubas *or*
 tubae
tu+bal
Tubal-cain
tub+bable
tub+ber
 tub+bers
tub+bi+ness
tub+by
 tub+bi+er
 tub+bi+est
tube
 tubes
 tubes
 tub+ing
 tubed
tube+less
tu+ber
 tu+bers
tu+ber+cle
 tu+ber+cles
tu+ber+cu+lar
 tu+ber+cu+lars
tu+ber+cu+late
tu+ber+cu+la+
 tion
tu+ber+cu+lin
tuberculin-tested
tu+ber+cu+lo+sis
tu+ber+cu+lous
tu+ber+ose
 tu+ber+oses
tu+ber+ous
tu+bi+fex
 tu+bi+fex *or*
 tu+bi+fexes
tub+ing
Tü+bing+en
Tubman
tub-thumper

tub-thumpers
tub-thumping
tubu+lar
tu+bule
 tu+bules
tuck
 tucks
 tucks
 tuck+ing
 tucked
Tuck
tuck+er
 tuck+ers
 tuck+ers
 tuck+er+ing
 tuck+ered
tucker-bag
 tucker-bags
tucker+box
 tucker+boxes
tuck+et
 tuck+ets
tuck-in
 tuck-ins
 tuck in
 verb
Tuc+son
Tu+cu+mán
Tu+dor
 Tu+dors
Tues+day
 Tues+days
tufa
tu+fa+ceous
tuff
tuffa+ceous
tuf+fet
 tuf+fets
tuft
 tufts
 tufts
 tuft+ing
 tuft+ed
tufty
Tu Fu
tug
 tugs
 tugs
 tug+ging
 tugged
Tu+ge+la
tug+ger
 tug+gers
tui

tuis
tui+tion
tui+tion+al
Tula
tu+la+rae+mia
tu+la+raemic
tu+la+remia
 U.S.
tu+la+remic
 U.S.
tu+lip
 tu+lips
tulip+wood
Tull
Tullamore
tulle
Tully
Tul+sa
tum+ble
 tum+bles
 tum+bles
 tum+bling
 tum+bled
tumble+down
tum+bler
 tum+blers
tumble+weed
 tumble+weeds
tum+brel
 tum+brels
tum+bril
 tum+brils
tu+mefa+cient
tu+mefac+tion
 tu+mefac+tions
tu+mefy
 tu+mefies
 tu+mefy+ing
 tu+mefied
tu+mes+cence
tu+mes+cent
tu+mid
tu+mid+ity
tu+mid+ly
tu+mid+ness
tum+my
 tum+mies
tu+mor
 U.S.
 tu+mors
tu+mor+ous
tu+mour
 tu+mours
tu+mult
 tu+mults

tu+mul+tu+ous
tu+mul+tu+ous+
 ly
tu+mul+tu+ous+
 ness
tu+mu+lus
 tu+mu+li
tun
 tuns
 tuns
 tun+ning
 tunned
tuna
 tuna *or*
 tunas
tun+able
Tun+bridge
tun+dra
tune
 tunes
 tunes
 tun+ing
 tuned
tune+able
tune+ful
tune+ful+ly
tune+ful+ness
tune+less
tune+less+ly
tune+less+ness
tun+er
 tun+ers
tune-up
 tune-ups
 tune up
 verb
tung+sten
Tung+ting
Tung-t'ing
Tun+gus+ic
Tun+gus+ka
tu+nic
 tu+nics
tu+ni+cate
 tu+ni+cates
 tu+ni+cat+ed
tun+ing
Tu+nis
Tu+ni+sia
Tu+ni+sian
 Tu+ni+sians
tun+nage
 tun+nages
tun+nel
 tun+nels

tun+nels	tur+bi+nates	Turk	*verb*
tun+nel+ling *or*	tur+bi+nat+ed	Turks	turn+out
tun+nel+ing	tur+bi+na+tion	Tur+ka+na	turn+outs
U.S.	tur+bine	Tur+ke+stan	turn out
tun+nelled *or*	tur+bines	Tur+ke+sta+ni	*verb*
tun+neled	tur+bit	Tur+ke+sta+nis	turn+over
U.S.	tur+bits	tur+key	turn+overs
tun+nel+er	tur+bo+charg+er	tur+keys *or*	turn over
U.S.	tur+bo+charg+	tur+key	*verb*
tun+nel+ers	ers	Tur+key	turn+pike
tun+nel+ler	tur+bo+fan	Tur+ki	turn+pikes
tun+nel+lers	tur+bo+fans	Tur+kic	turn+round
tun+ny	tur+bo+gen+era+	Turk+ish	turn+rounds
tun+nies *or*	tor	Tur+ki+stan	turn+spit
tun+ny	tur+bo+gen+era+	Turks	turn+spits
tup	tors	Turk's-head	turn+stile
tups	tur+bo+jet	Turk's-heads	turn+stiles
tups	tur+bo+jets	Tur+ku	turn+stone
tup+ping	tur+bo+prop	tur+mer+ic	turn+stones
tupped	tur+bo+props	tur+moil	turn+table
Tu+pa+ma+ro	tur+bo+super+	turn	turn+tables
Tu+pa+ma+ros	charg+er	turns	turn-up
tu+pelo	tur+bo+super+	turns	turn-ups
tu+pelos	charg+ers	turn+ing	turn up
Tupi	tur+bot	turned	*verb*
Tupis *or*	tur+bot *or*	turn+about	tur+pen+tine
Tupi	tur+bots	turn+abouts	tur+peth
Tu+pian	tur+bu+lence	turn+around	tur+peths
tu+pik	tur+bu+lent	turn+arounds	Turpin
tu+piks	tur+bu+lent+ly	turn+buckle	tur+pi+tude
Tupolev	turd	turn+buckles	turps
tup+pence	turds	turn+coat	tur+quoise
tup+pences	tu+reen	turn+coats	tur+ret
tup+pen+ny	tu+reens	turn+cock	tur+rets
Tu+pun+ga+to	turf	turn+cocks	tur+ret+ed
tuque	turfs *or*	turn+down	tur+tle
tuques	turves	*adj.*	tur+tles
tu+ra+co	turfs	turn down	turtle+back
tu+ra+cos	turf+ing	*verb*	turtle+backs
Tu+ra+nian	turfed	turn+er	turtle-dove
Tu+ra+nians	turf+man	turn+ers	turtle-doves
tur+ban	turf+men	Turner	turtle+neck
tur+bans	Turgenev	turn+ing	turtle+necks
tur+baned	tur+ges+cence	turn+ings	turves
tur+ba+ry	tur+ges+cent	tur+nip	Tus+can
tur+ba+ries	tur+gid	tur+nips	Tus+cans
tur+bel+lar+ian	tur+gid+ity	turn+key	Tus+ca+ny
tur+bel+lar+ians	tur+gid+ly	turn+keys	tusche
tur+bid	tur+gid+ness	turn-off	Tus+cu+lan
tur+bid+ity	tur+gor	turn-offs	Tus+cu+lum
tur+bid+ly	Tu+rin	turn off	tush
tur+bid+ness	Turing	*verb*	tusk
tur+bi+nal	turi+on	turn-on	tusks
tur+bi+nals	turi+ons	turn-ons	tusks
tur+bi+nate	Turishcheva	turn on	tusk+ing

tusked	Tu+va+lu+ans	twelve+mo	twinges
tusked	tux+edo	twelve+mos	twinges
tusk+er	tux+edos	twelve+month	twing+ing
tusk+ers	Tux+tla Gu+tiér+	twelve+months	twinged
tus+sah	rez	twelve-tone	twink
tus+sahs	tu+yère	twen+ti+eth	twinks
Tussaud	tu+yères	twen+ti+eths	twin+kle
tus+ser	Tver	twen+ty	twin+kles
tus+sers	twad+dle	twen+ties	twin+kles
tus+sis	twad+dles	twenty-twenty	twin+kling
tus+sises	twad+dling	'twere	twin+kled
tus+sive	twad+dled	twerp	twin+kler
tus+sle	twad+dler	twerps	twin+klers
tus+sles	twad+dlers	twi+bil	twin+kling
tus+sles	twain	twi+bils	twin+klings
tus+sling	Twain	twi+bill	twin+ning
tus+sled	twang	twi+bills	Twins
tus+sock	twangs	twice	twin-screw
tus+socks	twangs	Twick+en+ham	twin+set
tus+socky	twang+ing	twid+dle	twin-sets
tus+sore	twanged	twid+dles	twin-tub
tus+sores	twangy	twid+dles	twin-tubs
tut	'twas	twid+dling	twirl
Tutankhamen	twat	twid+dled	twirls
Tutankhamun	twats	twid+dler	twirls
tu+telage	tway+blade	twid+dlers	twirl+ing
tu+telar	tway+blades	twig	twirled
tu+telars	tweak	twigs	twirl+er
tu+telary	tweaks	twigs	twirl+ers
tu+telaries	tweaks	twig+ging	twirp
tu+tor	tweak+ing	twigged	twirps
tu+tors	tweaked	twig+gy	twist
tu+tors	twee	twig+gi+er	twists
tu+tor+ing	tweed	twig+gi+est	twists
tu+tored	tweeds	twi+light	twist+ing
tu+tor+age	Tweed	twi+lit	twist+ed
tu+to+rial	Tweed+dale	twill	twist+er
tu+to+rials	Tweedsmuir	twills	twist+ers
tu+tor+ship	tweedy	twills	twit
tut+san	tweedi+er	twill+ing	twits
tut+ti	tweedi+est	twilled	twits
tutti-frutti	'tween	'twill	twit+ting
tutti-fruttis	tweet	twin	twit+ted
tut-tut	tweets	twins	twitch
tut-tuts	tweet+ing	twins	twitches
tut-tuts	tweet+ed	twin+ning	twitches
tut-tutting	tweet+er	twinned	twitch+ing
tut-tutted	tweet+ers	twine	twitched
tut+ty	twee+zers	twines	twitch+er
tutu	twelfth	twines	twitch+ers
tutus	twelfths	twin+ing	twite
Tutu	twelve	twined	twites
Tu+tui+la	twelves	twin+er	twit+ter
Tu+va+lu	twelve-inch	twin+ers	twit+ters
Tu+va+lu+an	twelve-inches	twinge	twit+ters

twit+ter+ing
twit+tered
twit+ter+er
twit+ter+ers
twit+tery
twixt
twixt
two
twos
two-by-four
two-by-fours
two-dimen+sion+al
two-edged
two-faced
two+fold
two-handed
two-pack
two+pence
two+pences
two+pen+ny
two-phase
two-piece
two-pieces
two-ply
two-plies
two-sided
two+some
two+somes
two-step
two-steps
two-stroke
two-time
two-times
two-timing
two-timed
two-timer
two-timers
two-tone
twould
two-up
two-way
twy+er
twy+ers
Tyan-Shan
Ty+burn
Tyche
tych+ism
ty+coon
ty+coons
tyke

tykes
Tyler
ty+lo+pod
ty+lo+pods
Tylor
tym+bal
tym+bals
tym+pan
tym+pans
tym+pa+ni
tym+pan+ic
tym+pa+nist
tym+pa+nists
tym+pa+ni+tes
tym+pa+nit+ic
tym+pa+ni+tis
tym+pa+num
tym+pa+nums
or
tym+pa+na
Tyndale
Tyndall
Tyndareus
Tyne
Tyne+mouth
Tyne+side
Tyn+wald
typ+al
type
types
typ+ing
typed
type+cast
type+casts
type+cast+ing
type+cast
type+face
type+faces
type+script
type+scripts
type+set
type+sets
type+set+ting
type+set
type+set+ter
type+set+ters
type+write
type+writes
type+writ+ing
type+wrote

type+writ+ten
type+writ+er
type+writ+ers
type+writ+ing
typh+lit+ic
typh+li+tis
Ty+phoe+an
Typhoeus
ty+phoid
Typhon
ty+phon+ic
ty+phoon
ty+phoons
ty+phous
ty+phus
typi+cal
typi+cal+ity
typi+cal+ly
typi+cal+ness
typi+fi+ca+tion
typi+fi+ca+tions
typi+fy
typi+fies
typi+fy+ing
typi+fied
typ+ist
typ+ists
typo
typos
ty+pog+ra+pher
ty+pog+ra+phers
ty+po+graph+ic
ty+po+graphi+cal
ty+po+graphi+cal+ly
ty+pog+ra+phy
ty+po+logi+cal
ty+polo+gist
ty+polo+gists
ty+pol+ogy
ty+pol+ogies
Tyr
ty+ran+nic
ty+ran+ni+cal
ty+ran+ni+cal+ly
ty+ran+ni+cide
ty+ran+ni+cides
tyr+an+nise
tyr+an+nises
tyr+an+nis+ing

tyr+an+nised
tyr+an+nis+er
tyr+an+nis+ers
tyr+an+nize
tyr+an+nizes
tyr+an+niz+ing
tyr+an+nized
tyr+an+niz+er
tyr+an+niz+ers
ty+ran+no+saur
ty+ran+no+saurs
ty+ran+no+saur+us
ty+ran+no+saur+uses
tyr+an+nous
tyr+an+ny
tyr+an+nies
ty+rant
ty+rants
tyre
tyres
Tyre
Tyr+ian
Tyr+ians
tyro
tyros
Ty+rol
Ty+ro+lean
Ty+ro+leans
Tyro+lese
Ty+rone
ty+ro+sine
ty+ro+thri+cin
Tyrr
Tyson
Tyu+men
tzar
tzars
Tzara
tzat+zi+ki
Tze+kung
tzet+ze
Tzi+gane
Tzi+ganes
Tzu-kung
Tzu-po

U

u
u's
U
U's *or*
Us
UB40
UB40s
Uban+gi
Ubangi-Shari
U-bend
U-bends
ub+er+ri+ma fi+
des
ubi+ety
ubiqui+tar+ian
ubiqui+tar+ians
ubiqui+tar+ianism
ubiqui+tous
ubiqui+tous+ly
ubiquity
U-boat
U-boats
Uca+ya+li
UCCA
Uccello
Udai+pur
udal
ud+der
ud+ders
Udi+ne
Ud+murt
udom+eter
udom+eters
UEFA
Uele
Ufa
Uf+fi+zi
ufol+ogist
ufol+ogists
ufol+ogy
Ugan+da
Ugan+dan
Ugan+dans
Uga+rit+ic
ugh

Ugli
Trademark
Uglis *or*
Uglies
ug+li+fi+ca+tion
ug+li+fy
ug+li+fies
ug+li+fy+ing
ug+li+fied
ug+li+ly
ug+li+ness
ugly
ug+li+er
ug+li+est
Ugrian
Ugrians
Ugric
uh-huh
uh+lan
uh+lans
Uhland
uhu+ru
Uin+ta
uit+land+er
uit+land+ers
Uji+ji
Uj+jain
Ujung Pan+dang
ukase
ukases
uke+lele
uke+leles
Ukrain+ian
Ukrain+ians
uku+lele
uku+leles
Ulan Ba+tor
Ulanova
Ulan-Ude
Ulbricht
ul+cer
ul+cers
ul+cer+ate
ul+cer+ates
ul+cer+at+ing

ul+cer+at+ed
ul+cera+tion
ul+cera+tions
ul+cera+tive
ul+cer+ous
ul+cer+ous+ly
ulema
ulemas
ul+lage
ul+lages
Ulls+wa+ter
Ulm
ulna
ulnae *or*
ulnas
ul+nar
ulot+ri+chous
ul+ster
ul+sters
Ul+ster
Ul+ster+man
Ul+ster+men
Ul+ster+wo+man
Ul+ster+wo+
men
ul+te+ri+or
ul+te+ri+or+ly
ul+ti+ma
ul+ti+mas
ul+ti+mate
ul+ti+mates
ul+ti+mate+ly
ul+ti+mate+ness
ul+ti+ma+tum
ul+ti+ma+tums
or
ul+ti+ma+ta
ul+ti+mo
ultimo+geniture
ul+tra
ul+tras
ultra+cen+tri+
fuge
ultra+cen+tri+
fuges

ultra+con+ser+va+
tive
ultra+con+ser+
va+tives
ultra-distance
ultra+fiche
ultra+fiches
ultra+high
ultra+ism
ultra+isms
ultra+ist
ultra+ists
ultra+ma+rine
ultra+ma+rines
ultra+micro+
scope
ultra+micro+
scopes
ultra+micro+scop+
ic
ultra+mod+ern
ultra+mod+ern+
ism
ultra+mod+ern+
ist
ultra+mod+ern+
ists
ultra+mod+ern+is+
tic
ultra+mon+tane
ultra+mon+
tanes
ultra+mun+dane
ultra+na+tion+al
ultra+na+tion+al+
ism
ultra+na+tion+al+
isms
ultra+na+tion+al+
ist
ultra+na+tion+al+
ists
ultra+short
ultra+son+ic
ultra+soni+cal+ly

ultra+son+ics
ultra+sound
ultra+struc+ture
ultra+struc+
tures
ultra+vio+let
ul+tra vi+res
ultra+vi+rus
ultra+vi+ruses
ulu+lant
ulu+late
ulu+lates
ulu+lat+ing
ulu+lat+ed
ulu+la+tion
ulu+la+tions
Ul+ya+novsk
Ulysses
Umar
Umay+yad
Umay+yads or
Umay+yades
um+bel
um+bels
um+bel+lar
um+bel+late
um+bel+lif+er
um+bel+lif+ers
um+bel+lif+er+
ous
um+bel+lule
um+bel+lules
um+ber
um+bers
um+bili+cal
um+bili+cate
um+bili+ca+tion
um+bili+ca+
tions
um+bili+cus
um+bili+ci
um+ble
um+bles
umbo
um+bo+nes or
umbos
um+bo+nal
um+bo+nate
um+bon+ic
um+bra
um+brae or
um+bras
um+brage
um+brages
um+bra+geous

um+bral
um+brel+la
um+brel+las
um+brella-like
Um+bria
Um+brian
Um+brians
umi+ak
umi+aks
um+laut
um+lauts
um+pire
um+pires
um+pires
um+pir+ing
um+pired
ump+teen
ump+teenth
Um+ta+li
Um+ta+ta
un
'un
un+abashed
un+abat+ed
un+ab+bre+vi+at+
ed
un+able
un+abridged
un+aca+dem+ic
un+ac+cen+ted
un+ac+cen+tu+at+
ed
un+ac+cep+table
un+ac+cli+ma+
tised
un+ac+cli+ma+
tized
un+ac+com+mo+
dat+ing
un+ac+com+pa+
nied
un+ac+com+
plished
un+ac+count+abil+
ity
un+ac+count+
able
un+ac+count+
ably
un+ac+count+ed
un+ac+counted-
for
un+ac+cred+it+
ed

un+ac+cus+
tomed
un+ac+cus+
tomed+ness
un+ac+knowl+
edged
una cor+da
un+ac+quaint+ed
un+act+ed
un+ac+tion+able
un+adapt+able
un+adapt+ed
un+ad+dressed
un+adopt+ed
un+adorned
un+adul+ter+at+
ed
un+ad+van+ta+
geous
un+ad+ven+tur+
ous
un+ad+ver+tised
un+ad+vis+able
un+ad+vised
un+ad+vis+ed+ly
un+ad+vis+ed+
ness
un+af+fect+ed
un+af+fect+ed+ly
un+af+fect+ed+
ness
un+af+fili+at+ed
un+afraid
un+aid+ed
un+alarmed
Una+las+ka
un+al+ien+able
un+aligned
un+al+layed
un+al+le+vi+at+
ed
un+al+lied
un+al+low+able
un+al+loyed
un+al+ter+able
un+al+tered
un+am+bigu+ous
un+am+bi+tious
un-Ameri+can
un-Ameri+can+
ism
un-Ameri+can+
isms
un+ami+able
un+am+pli+fied

Unamuno
un+amused
una+nim+ity
unani+mous
unani+mous+ly
un+an+nounced
un+an+swer+
able
un+an+swered
un+an+tici+pat+
ed
un+apolo+get+ic
un+ap+par+ent
un+ap+peal+able
un+ap+peal+ing
un+ap+pe+tis+
ing
un+ap+pe+tiz+
ing
un+ap+plied
un+ap+point+ed
un+ap+por+
tioned
un+ap+pre+ci+at+
ed
un+ap+pre+cia+
tive
un+ap+proach+
able
un+ap+proach+
able+ness
un+ap+proach+
ably
un+ap+pro+pri+
at+ed
un+ap+proved
un+apt
un+apt+ly
un+apt+ness
un+ar+gu+able
un+ar+gu+ably
un+arm
un+arms
un+arm+ing
un+armed
un+armed
un+ar+ticu+lat+
ed
un+ar+tis+tic
un+ashamed
un+asked
un+as+pi+rat+ed
un+aspir+ing
un+as+sail+able

un+as+sail+able+
ness
un+as+sail+ably
un+as+ser+tive
un+as+simi+lat+
ed
un+as+sist+ed
un+as+sort+ed
un+as+sumed
un+as+sum+ing
un+as+sum+ing+
ly
un+as+sum+ing+
ness
un+atoned
un+at+tached
un+at+tain+able
un+at+tained
un+at+tempt+ed
un+at+tend+ed
un+at+trac+tive
un+aus+pi+cious
un+authen+tic
un+author+ised
un+author+ized
un+avail+able
un+avail+ing
un+avail+ing+ly
un+avoid+abil+ity
un+avoid+able
un+avoid+able+
ness
un+avoid+ably
un+aware
un+aware+ness
un+awares
un+backed
un+bal+ance
un+bal+ances
un+bal+anc+ing
un+bal+anced
un+bal+anced
un+bap+tised
un+bap+tized
un+bar
un+bars
un+bar+ring
un+barred
un+bear+able
un+bear+ably
un+beat+able
un+beat+en
un+be+com+ing
un+be+com+ing+
ly

un+be+com+ing+
ness
un+be+fit+ting
un+be+got+ten
un+be+hold+en
un+be+known
un+be+lief
un+be+liev+abil+
ity
un+be+liev+able
un+be+liev+ably
un+be+liev+er
un+be+liev+ers
un+be+liev+ing
un+be+liev+ing+
ly
un+belt
un+belts
un+belt+ing
un+belt+ed
un+bend
un+bends
un+bend+ing
un+bent
un+bend+ing
un+bend+ing+ly
un+bend+ing+
ness
un+bi+ased
un+bid+den
un+bind
un+binds
un+bind+ing
un+bound
un+bleached
un+blem+ished
un+blessed
un+bless+ed+
ness
un+blink+ing
un+block
un+blocks
un+block+ing
un+blocked
un+blush+ing
un+blush+ing+ly
un+bolt
un+bolts
un+bolt+ing
un+bolt+ed
un+born
un+bos+om
un+bos+oms
un+bos+om+ing
un+bos+omed

un+bound+ed
un+bound+ed+ly
un+bound+ed+
ness
un+bowed
un+brace
un+braces
un+brac+ing
un+braced
un+break+able
un+bri+dle
un+bri+dles
un+bri+dling
un+bri+dled
un+bri+dled+ly
un+bri+dled+
ness
un+bro+ken
un+bro+ken+ly
un+bro+ken+
ness
un+bruised
un+buck+le
un+buck+les
un+buck+ling
un+buck+led
un+built
un+bun+dling
un+bun+dlings
un+bur+den
un+bur+dens
un+bur+den+ing
un+bur+dened
un+bur+ied
un+but+ton
un+but+tons
un+but+ton+ing
un+but+toned
un+caged
uncalled-for
un+can+ni+ly
un+can+ni+ness
un+can+ny
un+can+ni+er
un+can+ni+est
un+cap
un+caps
un+cap+ping
un+capped
uncared-for
un+cashed
un+caught
un+ceas+ing
un+cen+sored

un+cen+sured
un+cer+emo+ni+
ous
un+cer+emo+ni+
ous+ly
un+cer+emo+ni+
ous+ness
un+cer+tain
un+cer+tain+ly
un+cer+tain+ty
un+cer+tain+
ties
un+chain
un+chains
un+chain+ing
un+chained
un+chal+lenge+
able
un+chal+lenged
un+change+able
un+changed
un+chang+ing
un+chap+er+
oned
un+char+ac+ter+
is+tic
un+charged
un+chari+table
un+chart+ed
un+char+tered
un+chaste
un+checked
un+chiv+al+rous
un+cho+sen
un+chris+tian
un+chris+tian+ly
un+church
un+churches
un+church+ing
un+churched
un+cial
un+cials
un+ci+al+ly
un+ci+nate
un+cir+cum+
cised
un+cir+cum+ci+
sion
un+civ+il
un+civi+lised
un+civi+lis+ed+
ness
un+ci+vil+ity
un+civi+lized

un+civi+liz+ed+
  ness
un+civ+il+ly
un+clad
un+claimed
un+clasp
  un+clasps
  un+clasp+ing
  un+clasped
un+clas+si+fied
un+cle
  un+cles
un+clean
un+cleaned
un+clean+li+ness
un+clean+ly
un+clean+ness
un+clear
Un+cle Sam
Un+cle Tom
  Un+cle Toms
Un+cle Tom+ism
un+clog
  un+clogs
  un+clog+ging
  un+clogged
un+close
  un+closes
  un+clos+ing
  un+closed
un+clothe
  un+clothes
  un+cloth+ing
  un+clothed or
    un+clad
un+cloud+ed
un+clut+tered
un+coil
  un+coils
  un+coil+ing
  un+coiled
un+col+lect+ed
un+col+oured
un+combed
un+com+fort+
  able
un+com+fort+
  able+ness
un+com+fort+
  ably
un+com+mer+
  cial
un+com+mit+ted
un+com+mon
un+com+mon+ly

un+com+mon+
  ness
un+com+mu+ni+
  ca+tive
un+com+mu+ni+
  ca+tive+ly
un+com+mu+ni+
  ca+tive+ness
un+com+pan+ion+
  able
un+com+pen+sat+
  ed
un+com+peti+
  tive
un+com+plain+
  ing
un+com+plet+ed
un+com+pli+cat+
  ed
un+com+pli+men+
  ta+ry
un+com+pound+
  ed
un+com+pre+
  hend+ing
un+com+pro+mis+
  ing
un+com+pro+mis+
  ing+ly
un+con+cealed
un+con+cern
un+con+cerned
un+con+cern+ed+
  ly
un+con+clud+ed
un+con+demned
un+con+di+tion+
  al
un+con+di+tion+
  al+ly
un+con+di+
  tioned
un+con+di+
  tioned+ness
un+con+du+cive
un+con+fi+dent
un+con+fined
un+con+firmed
un+con+form+
  abil+ity
un+con+form+
  able
un+con+form+
  able+ness

un+con+form+
  ably
un+con+form+ity
un+con+form+
  ities
un+con+gen+ial
un+con+nect+ed
un+con+quered
un+con+scion+
  able
un+con+scion+
  ably
un+con+scious
un+con+scious+
  ly
un+con+se+crat+
  ed
un+con+sent+ing
un+con+sid+ered
un+con+sti+tu+
  tion+al
un+con+sti+tu+
  tion+al+ity
un+con+strained
un+con+strict+ed
un+con+sum+
  mat+ed
un+con+tami+nat+
  ed
un+con+test+ed
un+con+trol+
  lable
un+con+trolled
un+contro+ver+
  sial
un+con+ven+tion+
  al
un+con+ven+tion+
  al+ity
un+con+ven+tion+
  al+ly
un+con+vert+ed
un+con+vinced
un+con+vinc+ing
un+cooked
un+cool
un+co+opera+
  tive
un+co+ordi+nat+
  ed
un+cork
  un+corks
  un+cork+ing
  un+corked

un+cor+robo+rat+
  ed
un+cor+rupt+ed
un+count+able
un+count+ed
un+cou+ple
  un+cou+ples
  un+cou+pling
  un+cou+pled
un+couth
un+couth+ly
un+couth+ness
un+cov+enant+
  ed
un+cov+er
  un+cov+ers
  un+cov+er+ing
  un+cov+ered
un+crea+tive
un+criti+cal
un+crowd+ed
un+crowned
unc+tion
  unc+tions
unc+tion+less
unc+tu+os+ity
unc+tu+ous
unc+tu+ous+ly
unc+tu+ous+
  ness
un+cul+ti+vat+ed
un+cul+tured
un+curbed
un+cured
un+curl
  un+curls
  un+curl+ing
  un+curled
un+cut
un+dam+aged
un+damped
un+dat+ed
un+daunt+ed
un+daunt+ed+ly
un+daunt+ed+
  ness
un+deca+gon
  un+deca+gons
un+de+ceiv+able
un+de+ceive
  un+de+ceives
  un+de+ceiv+ing
  un+de+ceived
un+de+ceiv+er
  un+de+ceiv+ers

un+de+cid+ed
un+de+cid+ed+ly
un+de+cid+ed+
  ness
un+de+clared
un+de+deco+rat+ed
un+de+feat+ed
un+de+fend+ed
un+de+filed
un+de+fin+able
un+de+fined
un+de+mand+ing
un+demo+crat+ic
un+de+mon+stra+
  tive
un+de+ni+able
un+de+ni+able+
  ness
un+de+ni+ably
un+de+nied
un+de+pend+
  able
un+der
under+achieve
  under+achieves
  under+achiev+
    ing
  under+achieved
  under+achieve+
    ment
  under+achiev+er
  under+achiev+
    ers
under+act
  under+acts
  under+act+ing
  under+act+ed
under+age
under+arm
under+belly
  under+bellies
under+bid
  under+bids
  under+bid+ding
  under+bid
  under+bid+der
  under+bid+ders
under+body
  under+bodies
under+bred
under+breeding
under+buy
  under+buys
  under+buy+ing
  under+bought

under+capi+tal+
  ise
under+capi+tal+
  ises
under+capi+tal+
  is+ing
under+capi+tal+
  ised
under+capi+tal+
  ize
under+capi+tal+
  izes
under+capi+tal+
  iz+ing
under+capi+tal+
  ized
under+carriage
under+carriages
under+charge
  under+charges
  under+charg+
    ing
  under+charged
under+clad
under+class
  under+classes
under+clothed
under+clothes
under+coat
  under+coats
  under+coats
  under+coat+ing
  under+coat+ed
under+cook
  under+cooks
  under+cook+ing
  under+cooked
under+cov+er
under+croft
  under+crofts
under+cur+rent
  under+cur+rents
under+cut
  under+cuts
  under+cuts
  under+cut+ting
  under+cut
under+de+vel+op
  under+de+vel+
    ops
  under+de+vel+
    op+ing
  under+de+vel+
    oped

under+de+vel+
  oped
under+do
  under+does
  under+do+ing
  under+did
  under+done
under+dog
  under+dogs
under+done
under+dressed
under+eat
  under+eats
  under+eat+ing
  under+ate
  under+eat+en
under+edu+cat+
  ed
under+em+
  ployed
under+es+ti+
  mate
  under+es+ti+
    mates
  under+es+ti+
    mates
  under+es+ti+
    mat+ing
  under+es+ti+
    mat+ed
under+es+ti+ma+
  tion
  under+es+ti+ma+
    tions
under+ex+pose
  under+ex+poses
  under+ex+pos+
    ing
  under+ex+
    posed
under+ex+po+
  sure
  under+ex+po+
    sures
under+feed
  under+feeds
  under+feed+ing
  under+fed
under+felt
  under+felts
under+floor
under+foot
under+fund+ed
under+fur
  under+furs

under+gar+ment
  under+gar+
    ments
under+gird
  under+girds
  under+gird+ing
  under+gird+ed
    or
  under+girt
under+glaze
  under+glazes
under+go
  under+goes
  under+go+ing
  under+went
  under+gone
  under+go+er
  under+go+ers
under+gradu+ate
  under+gradu+
    ates
under+ground
  under+grounds
under+grown
under+growth
  under+growths
under+hand
  under+hand+ed
under+hung
under+in+sured
under+lay
  under+lays
  under+lays
  under+lay+ing
  under+laid
  under+lay+er
  under+lay+ers
under+lie
  under+lies
  under+ly+ing
  under+lay
  under+lain
  under+li+er
  under+li+ers
under+line
  under+lines
  under+lines
  under+lin+ing
  under+lined
  under+lin+en
  under+lin+ens
under+ling
  under+lings
under+men+
  tioned

under+mine
under+mines
under+min+ing
under+mined
under+min+er
under+min+ers
under+most
under+named
under+neath
under+nour+ish
under+nour+ishes
under+nour+ish+ing
under+nour+ished
under+nour+ish+ment
under+paid
under+pants
under+part
under+parts
under+pass
under+passes
under+pay
under+pays
under+pay+ing
under+paid
under+pay+ment
under+pay+ments
under+peo+pled
under+pin
under+pins
under+pin+ning
under+pinned
under+pin+ning
under+pin+nings
under+play
under+plays
under+play+ing
under+played
under+popu+lat+ed
under+price
under+prices
under+pric+ing
under+priced
under+privi+leged
under+pro+duce
under+pro+duces
under+pro+duc+ing

under+pro+duced
under+pro+duc+tion
under+proof
under+quote
under+quotes
under+quot+ing
under+quot+ed
under+rate
under+rates
under+rat+ing
under+rat+ed
under+ri+pened
under+score
under+scores
under+scores
under+scor+ing
under+scored
under+sea
under+seal
under+seals
under+seals
under+seal+ing
under+sealed
under+sec+re+tary
under+sec+re+taries
under+sell
under+sells
under+sell+ing
under+sold
under+sell+er
under+sell+ers
under+sexed
under+shirt
under+shirts
under+shoot
under+shoots
under+shoot+ing
under+shot
under+shorts
under+side
under+sides
under+signed
under+sized
under+skirt
under+skirts
under+slung
under+spend
under+spends
under+spend+ing

under+spent
under+staffed
under+stand
under+stands
under+stand+ing
under+stood
under+stand+able
under+stand+ably
under+stand+ing
under+stand+ings
under+stand+ing+ly
under+state
under+states
under+stat+ing
under+stat+ed
under+state+ment
under+state+ments
under+steer
under+steers
under+steer+ing
under+steered
under+study
under+studies
under+studies
under+study+ing
under+stud+ied
under+sup+ply
under+sup+plies
under+sup+ply+ing
under+sup+plied
under+sur+face
under+sur+faces
under+take
under+takes
under+tak+ing
under+took
under+tak+en
under+tak+er
under+tak+ers
under+tak+ing
under+tak+ings
under+things
under+thrust
under+thrusts
under+tone
under+tones

under+tow
under+tows
under+trained
under+trick
under+tricks
under+valu+ation
under+valu+ations
under+value
under+val+ues
under+valu+ing
under+val+ued
under+valu+er
under+valu+ers
under+vest
under+vests
under+wa+ter
under+wear
under+weight
under+whelm
under+whelms
under+whelm+ing
under+whelmed
under+wing
under+wings
under+wood
under+world
under+worlds
under+write
under+writes
under+writ+ing
under+wrote
under+writ+ten
under+writ+er
under+writ+ers
un+de+served
un+de+serv+ing
un+de+sign+ing
un+de+sir+abil+ity
un+de+sir+able
un+de+sir+ables
un+de+sir+able+ness
un+de+sir+ably
un+de+sired
un+de+tect+ed
un+de+ter+mined
un+de+terred
un+de+vel+oped
un+di+ag+nosed
un+dies
un+dif+fer+en+ti+at+ed

un+di+gest+ed
un+dig+ni+fied
un+di+lut+ed
un+di+min+ished
un+dimmed
un+dine
un+dines
un+dip+lo+matic
un+di+rect+ed
un+dis+cern+ing
un+dis+ci+plined
un+dis+closed
un+dis+cov+ered
un+dis+crimi+nat+ing
un+dis+mayed
un+dis+posed
un+dis+put+ed
un+dis+tin+guish+able
un+dis+tin+guished
un+dis+trib+ut+ed
un+dis+turbed
un+di+vid+ed
undo
un+does
un+do+ing
un+did
un+done
un+docu+ment+ed
un+do+ing
un+do+ings
un+doubt+able
un+doubt+ed
un+doubt+ed+ly
un+drained
un+dreamed
un+dreamt
un+dress
un+dresses
un+dress+ing
un+dressed
un+drink+able
Undset
un+due
un+du+lance
un+du+lant
un+du+late
un+du+lates
un+du+lat+ing
un+du+lat+ed
un+du+la+tion

un+du+la+tions
un+du+la+tor
un+du+la+tors
un+du+la+tory
un+du+ly
un+du+ti+ful
un+dyed
un+dy+ing
un+dy+ing+ly
un+earned
un+earth
un+earths
un+earth+ing
un+earthed
un+earth+li+ness
un+earth+ly
un+ease
un+easi+ly
un+easi+ness
un+easy
un+easi+er
un+easi+est
un+eat+able
un+eat+en
un+eco+nom+ic
un+eco+nomi+cal
un+edi+fy+ing
un+edit+ed
un+edu+cable
un+edu+cat+ed
un+elect+able
un+eman+ci+pat+ed
un+em+bar+rassed
un+em+bel+lished
un+emo+tion+al
un+em+ploy+abil+ity
un+em+ploya+ble
un+em+ployed
un+em+ploy+ment
un+en+cum+bered
un+end+ing
un+en+dowed
un+en+dur+able
un+en+gaged
un+en+joy+able
un+en+light+ened

un+en+ter+pris+ing
un+en+thu+si+as+tic
un+en+vi+able
un+equal
un+equaled
U.S.
un+equalled
un+equipped
un+equivo+cal
un+equivo+cal+ly
un+equivo+cal+ness
un+err+ing
un+err+ing+ly
un+err+ing+ness
un+es+cap+able
UNESCO
un+escort+ed
un+es+sen+tial
un+ethi+cal
un+even
un+even+ly
un+even+ness
un+event+ful
un+event+ful+ly
un+event+ful+ness
un+ex+ag+ger+at+ed
un+ex+am+pled
un+ex+cep+tion+able
un+ex+cep+tion+ably
un+ex+cep+tion+al
un+ex+cep+tion+al+ly
un+ex+cit+ed
un+ex+cused
un+ex+pec+ted
un+ex+pect+ed+ly
un+ex+pect+ed+ness
un+ex+pe+ri+enced
un+ex+pired
un+ex+plain+able
un+ex+plained
un+ex+ploit+ed
un+ex+plored
un+ex+pressed

un+ex+pur+gat+ed
un+ex+tin+guished
un+fad+ing
un+fail+ing
un+fail+ing+ly
un+fail+ing+ness
un+fair
un+fair+ly
un+fair+ness
un+faith+ful
un+faith+ful+ly
un+faith+ful+ness
un+fa+mil+iar
un+fa+mili+ar+ity
un+fa+mil+iar+ly
un+fash+ion+able
un+fas+ten
un+fas+tens
un+fas+ten+ing
un+fas+tened
un+fa+thered
un+fath+om+able
un+fath+om+able+ness
un+fath+om+ably
un+fath+om+ed
un+fa+vor+able
U.S.
un+fa+vor+ably
U.S.
un+fa+vour+able
un+fa+vour+ably
un+fa+voured
un+fazed
un+fed
un+fed+er+at+ed
un+feel+ing
un+feel+ing+ly
un+feel+ing+ness
un+feigned
un+fer+ment+ed
un+fer+ti+lised
un+fer+ti+lized
un+fet+ter
un+fet+ters
un+fet+ter+ing
un+fet+tered
un+fin+ished
un+fit
un+fits
un+fit+ting
un+fit+ted
un+fit+ly

un+fit+ness
un+fit+ting
un+fix
 un+fixes
 un+fix+ing
 un+fixed
un+flag+ging
un+flap+pabil+ity
un+flap+pable
un+flap+pably
un+flat+ter+ing
un+fledged
un+flinch+ing
un+flinch+ing+ly
un+fold
 un+folds
 un+fold+ing
 un+fold+ed
 un+fold+er
 un+fold+ers
un+for+bear+ing
un+force+able
un+forced
un+fore+see+
 able
un+fore+seen
un+fore+told
un+for+get+table
un+for+giv+able
un+for+giv+en
un+for+giv+ing
un+for+got+ten
un+formed
un+for+mu+lat+
 ed
un+for+sak+en
un+forth+com+
 ing
un+for+ti+fied
un+for+tu+nate
 un+for+tu+nates
un+for+tu+nate+
 ly
un+found
un+found+ed
un+found+ed+ly
un+found+ed+
 ness
un+framed
un+franked
un+freeze
 un+freezes
 un+freez+ing
 un+froze
 un+fro+zen

un+fre+quent+ed
un+friend+ed
un+friend+li+ness
un+friend+ly
un+friend+li+er
un+friend+li+est
un+frock
 un+frocks
 un+frock+ing
 un+frocked
un+fruit+ful
un+ful+filled
un+fund+ed
un+fun+ny
un+furl
 un+furls
 un+furl+ing
 un+furled
un+fur+nished
un+gain+li+ness
un+gain+ly
 un+gain+li+er
 un+gain+li+est
Ungaretti
Un+ga+va
un+gen+er+ous
un+gen+tle+man+
 ly
un+glazed
un+god+li+ness
un+god+ly
 un+god+li+er
 un+god+li+est
un+gov+ern+able
un+gov+ern+able+
 ness
un+gov+ern+ably
un+gra+cious
un+grad+ed
un+gram+mati+
 cal
un+grate+ful
un+ground+ed
un+grudg+ing
un+gual
un+guard+ed
un+guard+ed+ly
un+guard+ed+
 ness
un+guent
 un+guents
un+guicu+late
 un+guicu+lates
un+guid+ed
un+guis

un+gues
un+gu+late
 un+gu+lates
un+ham+pered
un+hand
 un+hands
 un+hand+ing
 un+hand+ed
un+handy
un+hap+pi+ly
un+hap+pi+ness
un+hap+py
 un+hap+pi+er
 un+hap+pi+est
un+hard+ened
un+harmed
un+harm+ful
un+har+mo+ni+
 ous
un+har+ness
 un+har+nesses
 un+har+ness+
 ing
 un+har+nessed
un+har+rowed
un+har+vest+ed
un+hatched
un+healed
un+healthi+ly
un+healthi+ness
un+healthy
 un+healthi+er
 un+healthi+est
un+heard
unheard-of
un+heat+ed
un+heed+ed
un+heed+ful
un+heed+ing
un+helped
un+help+ful
un+her+ald+ed
un+he+ro+ic
un+hesi+tat+ing
un+hewn
un+hin+dered
un+hinge
 un+hinges
 un+hing+ing
 un+hinged
un+hitch
 un+hitches
 un+hitch+ing
 un+hitched
un+ho+li+ness

un+ho+ly
 un+ho+li+er
 un+ho+li+est
un+hon+oured
un+hook
 un+hooks
 un+hook+ing
 un+hooked
unhoped-for
un+horse
 un+horses
 un+hors+ing
 un+horsed
un+housed
un+hou+seled
un+hu+man
un+hur+ried
un+hurt
un+hy+gien+ic
un+hy+phen+at+
 ed
uni
 unis
Uni+at
 Uni+ats
Uni+ate
 Uni+ates
Uni+at+ism
uni+ax+ial
uni+cam+er+al
uni+cam+er+al+
 ism
uni+cam+er+al+
 ist
uni+cam+er+al+
 ists
uni+cam+er+al+ly
UNICEF
uni+cel+lu+lar
uni+cel+lu+lar+ity
uni+corn
 uni+corns
uni+cy+cle
 uni+cy+cles
uni+cy+clist
 uni+cy+clists
un+iden+ti+fi+
 able
un+iden+ti+fied
un+idio+mat+ic
uni+di+rec+tion+
 al
UNIDO
uni+fi+able
uni+fi+ca+tion

uni+fi+ca+tions
Uni+fi+ca+tion
uni+fied
uni+fi+er
uni+fi+ers
uni+form
uni+forms
uni+forms
uni+form+ing
uni+formed
uni+formi+tar+ian
uni+formi+tar+ians
uni+formi+tari+an+ism
uni+form+ity
uni+form+ities
uni+form+ly
uni+form+ness
uni+fy
uni+fies
uni+fy+ing
uni+fied
uni+lat+er+al
Uni+lat+er+al
uni+lat+er+al+ism
uni+lat+er+al+ly
un+il+lu+mi+nat+ed
un+il+lu+mi+nat+ing
un+il+lus+trat+ed
un+im+agi+nable
un+im+agi+nably
un+im+agi+na+tive
un+im+agi+na+tive+ly
un+im+ag+ined
Uni+mak
un+im+paired
un+im+pas+sioned
un+im+peach+able
un+im+peach+ably
un+im+ped+ed
un+im+por+tant
un+im+pos+ing
un+im+pressed
un+im+pres+sion+able
un+im+proved

un+in+closed
un+in+cor+po+ra+ted
un+in+cum+bered
un+in+fect+ed
un+in+flu+en+tial
un+in+forma+tive
un+in+formed
un+in+hab+it+able
un+in+hab+it+ed
un+in+hib+it+ed
un+ini+ti+at+ed
un+in+jured
un+in+spired
un+in+spir+ing
un+in+struct+ed
un+in+struc+tive
un+in+sured
un+in+tel+li+gent
un+in+tel+li+gible
un+in+tend+ed
un+in+tend+ed+ly
un+in+ten+tion+al
un+in+ten+tion+al+ly
un+in+ter+est+ed
un+in+ter+est+ed+ly
un+in+ter+est+ed+ness
un+in+ter+est+ing
un+in+ter+rupt+ed
un+in+vent+ive
un+in+vest+ed
un+in+ves+ti+gat+ed
un+in+vit+ed
un+in+vit+ing
un+in+voked
un+in+volved
un+ion
un+ions
Un+ion
Un+ions
un+ioni+sa+tion
un+ioni+sa+tions
un+ion+ise

un+ion+ises
un+ion+is+ing
un+ion+ised
un+ion+ism
Un+ion+ism
un+ion+ist
un+ion+ists
Un+ion+ist
Un+ion+ists
un+ioni+za+tion
un+ioni+za+tions
un+ion+ize
un+ion+izes
un+ion+iz+ing
un+ion+ized
uni+po+lar
uni+po+lar+ity
unique
unique+ly
unique+ness
un+ironed
uni+sex
uni+sexu+al
uni+sexu+al+ity
uni+sexual+ly
uni+son
uniso+nal
uniso+nant
uniso+nous
unit
units
uni+tar+ian
uni+tar+ians
Uni+tar+ian
Uni+tar+ians
Uni+tari+an+ism
uni+tary
Unitas
unite
unites
unites
unit+ing
unit+ed
unit+ed
Unit+ed
unit+ed+ly
unit+ed+ness
uniti+sa+tion
uniti+sa+tions
unit+ise
unit+ises
unit+is+ing
unit+ised
uni+tive

uniti+za+tion
uniti+za+tions
unit+ize
unit+izes
unit+iz+ing
unit+ized
unity
unities
uni+va+len+cy
uni+va+lent
uni+valve
uni+valves
uni+ver+sal
uni+ver+sals
uni+ver+sali+sa+tion
uni+ver+sali+sa+tions
uni+ver+sal+ise
uni+ver+sal+ises
uni+ver+sal+is+ing
uni+ver+sal+ised
uni+ver+sal+ism
uni+ver+sal+isms
Uni+ver+sal+ism
Uni+ver+sal+ist
Uni+ver+sal+ists
uni+ver+sal+ity
uni+ver+sali+za+tion
uni+ver+sali+za+tions
uni+ver+sal+ize
uni+ver+sal+izes
uni+ver+sal+iz+ing
uni+ver+sal+ized
uni+ver+sal+ly
uni+verse
uni+verses
uni+ver+sity
uni+ver+sities
UNIX
Trademark
un+joined
un+just
un+jus+ti+fi+able
un+jus+ti+fi+ably
un+jus+ti+fied
un+just+ly

un+just+ness
un+kempt
un+kempt+ly
un+kempt+ness
un+kept
un+kind
un+kind+er
un+kind+est
un+kind+ly
un+kind+ness
un+kissed
un+knit
un+knits
un+knit+ting
un+knit+ted
un+know+able
un+know+ing
un+know+ing+ly
un+known
un+knowns
Un+known
un+known+ness
un+la+belled
un+lace
un+laces
un+lac+ing
un+laced
un+lade
un+lades
un+lad+ing
un+lad+ed
un+la+den
un+lady+like
un+laid
un+la+ment+ed
un+latch
un+latches
un+latch+ing
un+latched
un+law+ful
un+lay
un+lays
un+lay+ing
un+laid
un+lead+ed
un+learn
un+learns
un+learn+ing
un+learnt or
un+learned
un+learn+ed
un+learn+ed+ly
un+leash
un+leashes
un+leash+ing

un+leashed
un+leav+ened
un+less
un+let+tered
un+lib+er+at+ed
un+li+censed
un+light+ed
un+lik+able
un+like
un+like+li+hood
un+like+li+ness
un+like+ly
un+like+li+er
un+like+li+est
un+like+ness
un+lim+ber
un+lim+bers
un+lim+ber+ing
un+lim+bered
un+lim+it+ed
un+lim+it+ed+ly
un+lim+it+ed+
  ness
un+lined
un+list+ed
Un+list+ed
un+lit
un+load
un+loads
un+load+ing
un+load+ed
un+load+er
un+load+ers
un+lock
un+locks
un+lock+ing
un+locked
un+lock+able
un+locked
unlooked-for
un+loose
un+looses
un+loos+ing
un+loosed
un+loos+en
un+loos+ens
un+loos+en+ing
un+loos+ened
un+lov+able
un+loved
un+love+li+ness
un+love+ly
un+lov+ing
un+lucki+ly
un+lucki+ness

un+lucky
un+lucki+er
un+lucki+est
un+mag+ni+fied
un+make
un+makes
un+mak+ing
un+made
un+man
un+mans
un+man+ning
un+manned
un+man+age+
  able
un+man+li+ness
un+man+ly
un+manned
un+man+nered
un+man+ner+li+
  ness
un+man+ner+ly
un+marked
un+mar+ket+able
un+mar+ried
un+mask
un+masks
un+mask+ing
un+masked
un+mask+er
un+mask+ers
un+matched
un+ma+tured
un+mean+ing
un+mean+ing+ly
un+mean+ing+
  ness
un+meant
un+meas+ured
un+meet
un+meet+ly
un+meet+ness
un+me+lo+di+
  ous
un+melt+ed
un+memor+able
un+men+tion+
  able
un+men+tion+
  able+ness
un+men+tion+
  ables
un+men+tion+
  ably
un+men+tioned

un+mer+chant+
  able
un+mer+ci+ful
un+mer+ci+ful+ly
un+mer+ci+ful+
  ness
un+mer+it+ed
un+me+thodi+cal
un+met+ri+cal
un+mind+ful
un+mind+ful+ly
un+mind+ful+
  ness
un+miss+able
un+mis+tak+able
un+mis+tak+ably
un+mis+take+
  able
un+mis+tak+en
un+miti+gat+ed
un+miti+gat+ed+
  ly
un+mixed
un+modi+fied
un+moor
un+moors
un+moor+ing
un+moored
un+mor+al
un+mo+ral+ity
un+mor+al+ly
un+mo+ti+vat+
  ed
un+mount+ed
un+mourned
un+mov+able
un+moved
un+mur+mur+ing
un+mu+si+cal
un+muz+zle
un+muz+zles
un+muz+zling
un+muz+zled
un+mys+ti+fied
un+nam+able
un+named
un+natu+ral
un+natu+ral+ly
un+natu+ral+
  ness
un+navi+gable
un+navi+gat+ed
un+nec+es+sari+
  ly

un+nec+es+sari+
ness
un+nec+es+sary
un+need+ed
un+ne+go+ti+
able
un+neigh+bour+
ly
un+nerve
  un+nerves
  un+nerv+ing
  un+nerved
un+no+ticed
un+num+bered
un+ob+jec+tion+
able
un+ob+lig+ing
un+ob+served
un+ob+struct+ed
un+ob+tain+able
un+ob+tained
un+ob+tru+sive
un+oc+cu+pied
un+of+fend+ed
un+of+fend+ing
un+of+fen+sive
un+of+fi+cial
un+of+fi+cial+ly
un+of+fi+cious
un+opened
un+op+posed
un+or+dained
un+or+gan+ised
un+or+gan+ized
un+origi+nal
un+ortho+dox
un+os+ten+ta+
tious
un+os+ten+ta+
tious+ly
un+pack
  un+packs
  un+pack+ing
  un+packed
  un+pack+er
    un+pack+ers
un+paged
un+paid
un+paired
un+pal+at+able
un+par+al+leled
un+par+don+able
un+par+lia+men+
tari+ly

un+par+lia+men+
tari+ness
un+par+lia+men+
ta+ry
un+pas+teur+
ised
un+pas+teur+
ized
un+pat+ent+ed
un+pat+ri+ot+ic
un+peg
  un+pegs
  un+peg+ging
  un+pegged
un+peo+ple
  un+peo+ples
  un+peo+pling
  un+peo+pled
un+per+ceived
un+per+cep+tive
un+per+fect+ed
un+per+fo+rat+
ed
un+per+formed
un+per+son
  un+per+sons
un+per+suad+ed
un+per+turb+able
un+per+turbed
un+philo+sophi+
cal
un+pick
  un+picks
  un+pick+ing
  un+picked
un+pin
  un+pins
  un+pin+ning
  un+pinned
un+pit+ied
un+pity+ing
un+placed
un+planned
un+play+able
un+pleas+ant
un+pleas+ant+ly
un+pleas+ant+
ness
  un+pleas+ant+
  nesses
un+pleas+ing
un+ploughed
un+plug
  un+plugs
  un+plug+ging

un+plugged
un+plumbed
un+point+ed
un+po+lar+ised
un+po+lar+ized
un+pol+ished
un+poli+tic
un+polled
un+pol+lut+ed
un+popu+lar
un+popu+lar+ity
un+popu+lar+ly
un+popu+lat+ed
un+posed
un+prac+ti+cable
un+prac+ti+cal
un+prac+ti+cal+
ity
un+prac+ti+cal+
ly
un+prac+ticed
U.S.
un+prac+tised
un+prec+edent+
ed
un+prec+edent+
ed+ly
un+pre+dict+abil+
ity
un+pre+dict+able
un+pre+dict+able+
ness
un+pre+dict+ed
un+preju+diced
un+preju+diced+
ly
un+pre+medi+tat+
ed
un+pre+pared
un+pre+pos+
sess+ing
un+pre+scribed
un+pre+sent+
able
un+pressed
un+pre+sump+tu+
ous
un+pre+tend+ing
un+pre+ten+tious
un+priced
un+prin+ci+pled
un+prin+ci+pled+
ness
un+print+able

un+print+able+
ness
un+print+ably
un+pro+claimed
un+pro+duc+tive
un+pro+fessed
un+pro+fes+sion+
al
un+pro+fes+sion+
al+ly
un+prof+it+able
un+pro+hib+it+
ed
un+prom+is+ing
un+prompt+ed
un+pro+nounce+
able
un+pro+nounced
un+pro+pi+tious
un+pro+tect+ed
un+pro+test+ing
un+proved
un+prov+en
un+pro+vid+ed
un+pro+voked
un+pub+lished
un+pun+ished
un+put+down+
able
un+quali+fi+able
un+quali+fied
un+quenched
un+ques+tion+
abil+ity
un+ques+tion+
able
un+ques+tion+
ably
un+ques+tioned
un+ques+tion+
ing
un+qui+et
un+qui+et+ly
un+qui+et+ness
un+quot+able
un+quote
  un+quotes
  un+quot+ing
  un+quot+ed
un+rav+el
  un+rav+els
  un+rav+el+ling
  or
  un+rav+el+ing
  U.S.

un+rav+elled
or
un+rav+eled
U.S.
un+read
un+read+abil+ity
un+read+able
un+readi+ly
un+readi+ness
un+ready
un+real
un+re+al+ised
un+re+al+is+tic
un+re+al+ity
un+re+al+ities
un+re+al+ized
un+re+al+ly
un+rea+son
un+rea+sons
un+rea+son+able
un+rea+son+able+
ness
un+rea+son+ably
un+rea+soned
un+rea+son+ing+
ly
un+re+cep+tive
un+rec+og+nis+
able
un+rec+og+nised
un+rec+og+niz+
able
un+rec+og+nized
un+rec+om+
mend+ed
un+rec+om+
pensed
un+rec+on+ciled
un+re+con+
struct+ed
un+re+cord+ed
un+re+deemed
un+reel
un+reels
un+reel+ing
un+reeled
un+re+fined
un+re+flect+ed
un+re+flect+ing
un+re+freshed
un+re+gen+era+
cy
un+re+gen+er+
ate

un+re+gen+er+
ates
un+re+gen+er+
ate+ly
un+reg+is+tered
un+regu+lat+ed
un+re+hearsed
un+re+lat+ed
un+re+lent+ing
un+re+lent+ing+
ly
un+re+lent+ing+
ness
un+re+li+able
un+re+li+gious
un+re+li+gious+ly
un+re+mark+able
un+re+mem+
bered
un+re+mit+ting
un+re+mit+ting+
ly
un+re+mit+ting+
ness
un+re+morse+ful
un+re+mu+nera+
tive
un+re+newed
un+re+nowned
un+re+pealed
un+re+peat+able
un+re+pent+ant
un+rep+re+senta+
tive
un+rep+re+sent+
ed
un+re+proved
un+re+quest+ed
un+re+quit+ed
un+re+served
un+re+serv+ed+
ly
un+re+serv+ed+
ness
un+re+sist+ing
un+re+solved
un+re+spon+sive
un+rest
un+rest+ed
un+re+strained
un+re+strict+ed
un+re+vealed
un+re+veal+ing
un+re+vised

un+re+ward+ed
un+re+ward+ing
un+rid+den
un+rid+dle
un+rid+dles
un+rid+dling
un+rid+dled
un+rid+dler
un+rid+dlers
un+rig
un+rigs
un+rig+ging
un+rigged
un+right+eous
un+right+eous+ly
un+right+eous+
ness
un+rip
un+rips
un+rip+ping
un+ripped
un+ripe
un+rip+ened
un+ripe+ness
un+ri+valled
un+roll
un+rolls
un+roll+ing
un+rolled
un+ro+man+tic
un+round+ed
un+ruf+fled
un+ruf+fled+ness
un+ruled
un+ru+li+ness
un+ru+ly
un+ru+li+er
un+ru+li+est
UNRWA
un+sad+dle
un+sad+dles
un+sad+dling
un+sad+dled
un+sad+dling
un+safe
un+said
un+sala+ried
un+sale+able
un+salt+ed
un+sanc+tioned
un+sani+tary
un+sat+is+fac+
tory
un+sat+is+fied
un+sat+is+fy+ing

un+satu+rat+ed
un+satu+ra+tion
un+satu+ra+
tions
un+saved
un+sa+vori+ly
U.S.
un+sa+vori+ness
U.S.
un+sa+vory
U.S.
un+sa+vouri+ly
un+sa+vouri+
ness
un+sa+voury
un+say
un+says
un+say+ing
un+said
un+say+able
un+scarred
un+scathed
un+scent+ed
un+sched+uled
un+schol+ar+ly
un+schooled
un+sci+en+tif+ic
un+scram+ble
un+scram+bles
un+scram+bling
un+scram+bled
un+scram+bler
un+scram+blers
un+scratched
un+screened
un+screw
un+screws
un+screw+ing
un+screwed
un+script+ed
un+scru+pu+lous
un+scru+pu+lous+
ly
un+scru+pu+lous+
ness
un+seal
un+seals
un+seal+ing
un+sealed
un+seam
un+seams
un+seam+ing
un+seamed
un+sea+son+able

un+sea+son+able+
  ness
un+sea+son+ably
un+sea+soned
un+seat
 un+seats
un+seat+ing
un+seat+ed
un+sea+wor+thy
un+se+clud+ed
un+secured
un+seed+ed
un+see+ing
un+seem+li+ness
un+seem+ly
un+seen
 un+seens
un+seg+re+gat+
  ed
un+se+lect+ed
un+se+lec+tive
un+self+con+
  scious
un+self+ish
un+self+ish+ly
un+self+ish+ness
un+sen+ti+men+
  tal
un+set
un+set+tle
 un+set+tles
 un+set+tling
 un+set+tled
un+set+tled+
  ness
un+set+tle+ment
un+sex
 un+sexes
 un+sex+ing
 un+sexed
un+shak+able
un+shak+en
un+shap+en
un+shared
un+shaved
un+shav+en
un+sheathe
 un+sheathes
 un+sheath+ing
 un+sheathed
un+shed
un+shield+ed
un+ship
 un+ships

un+ship+ping
un+shipped
un+shock+able
un+shod
un+shrink+able
un+sight+ed
un+sight+ed+ly
un+sight+li+ness
un+sight+ly
un+signed
un+sink+able
un+sized
un+skil+ful
un+skil+ful+ly
un+skil+ful+ness
un+skilled
un+skill+ful
U.S.
un+skill+ful+ly
U.S.
un+skill+ful+ness
U.S.
un+sling
 un+slings
 un+sling+ing
 un+slung
un+smil+ing
un+snap
 un+snaps
 un+snap+ping
 un+snapped
un+snarl
 un+snarls
 un+snarl+ing
 un+snarled
un+so+ciabil+ity
un+so+ciable
un+so+ciable+
  ness
un+so+cial
un+sold
un+so+lic+it+ed
un+solved
un+so+phis+ti+
  cat+ed
un+so+phis+ti+
  cat+ed+ly
un+so+phis+ti+
  cat+ed+ness
un+so+phis+ti+
  ca+tion
un+sort+ed
un+sought
un+sound
un+sound+ly

un+sound+ness
un+sown
un+spar+ing
un+spar+ing+ly
un+spar+ing+
  ness
un+speak+able
un+speak+able+
  ness
un+speak+ably
un+spe+cial+ised
un+spe+cial+ized
un+speci+fied
un+spec+tacu+
  lar
un+spoiled
un+spo+ken
un+sport+ing
un+spot+ted
un+sta+ble
un+sta+ble+ness
un+sta+bly
un+stained
un+stat+ed
un+statesman-
  like
un+steadi+ly
un+steadi+ness
un+steady
un+step
 un+steps
 un+step+ping
 un+stepped
un+stick
 un+sticks
 un+stick+ing
 un+stuck
un+stint+ed
un+stop
 un+stops
 un+stop+ping
 un+stopped
un+stop+pable
un+stop+pably
un+stopped
un+strained
un+strap
 un+straps
 un+strap+ping
 un+strapped
un+stri+at+ed
un+string
 un+strings
 un+string+ing
 un+strung

un+striped
un+struc+tured
un+strung
un+stuck
un+stud+ied
un+sub+dued
un+sub+stan+tial
un+sub+stan+ti+
  al+ity
un+sub+stan+tial+
  ly
un+sub+stan+ti+
  at+ed
un+sub+tle
un+suc+cess+ful
un+suit+able
un+suit+ed
un+sul+lied
un+sung
un+su+per+vised
un+sup+port+
  able
un+sup+port+ed
un+sure
un+sur+mount+
  able
un+sur+pass+
  able
un+sur+passed
un+sus+cep+tible
un+sus+pect+ed
un+sus+pect+ed+
  ly
un+sus+pect+ed+
  ness
un+sus+pect+ing
un+sus+tained
un+sweet+ened
un+swerv+ing
un+sym+pa+thet+
  ic
un+sys+tem+at+
  ic
un+taint+ed
un+tal+ent+ed
un+tamed
un+tan+gle
 un+tan+gles
 un+tan+gling
 un+tan+gled
un+tapped
un+tast+ed
un+taught
un+taxed
un+teach+able

un+ten+abil+ity
un+ten+able
un+ten+able+
   ness
un+ten+ably
un+tend+ed
Un+ter den Lin+
   den
Un+ter+wal+den
un+test+ed
un+teth+ered
un+thanked
un+thank+ful
un+think+able
un+think+ably
un+think+ing+ly
un+think+ing+
   ness
un+thought+ful
unthought-of
un+thread
un+threads
un+thread+ing
un+thread+ed
un+throne
un+thrones
un+thron+ing
un+throned
un+ti+di+ly
un+ti+di+ness
un+ti+dy
un+ti+dies
un+ti+dy+ing
un+ti+died
un+ti+di+er
un+ti+di+est
un+tie
un+ties
un+ty+ing
un+tied
un+til
un+time+li+ness
un+time+ly
un+tinged
un+tir+ing
un+tit+led
unto
un+to+geth+er
un+told
un+touch+abil+
   ity
un+touch+able
un+touch+ables
un+touched
un+to+ward

un+to+ward+ly
un+to+ward+
   ness
un+trained
un+tram+melled
un+trans+fer+
   able
un+trav+eled
U.S.
un+trav+elled
un+treat+ed
un+tried
un+trod+den
un+trou+bled
un+true
un+tru+ly
un+truss
un+trusses
un+truss+ing
un+trussed
un+trust+wor+
   thy
un+truth
un+truths
un+truth+ful
un+truth+ful+ly
un+truth+ful+
   ness
un+tuck
un+tucks
un+tuck+ing
un+tucked
un+tu+tored
un+twine
un+twines
un+twin+ing
un+twined
un+twist
un+twists
un+twist+ing
un+twist+ed
un+us+able
un+used
un+usual
un+usu+al+ly
un+ut+ter+able
un+ut+ter+able+
   ness
un+ut+ter+ably
un+ut+tered
un+val+ued
un+van+quished
un+var+ied
un+var+nished
un+vary+ing

un+veil
un+veils
un+veil+ing
un+veiled
un+veil+ing
un+veil+ings
un+veri+fi+able
un+veri+fied
un+versed
un+vi+able
un+voice
un+voices
un+voic+ing
un+voiced
un+waged
un+want+ed
un+wari+ly
un+wari+ness
un+warmed
un+warned
un+war+rant+
   able
un+war+rant+
   able+ness
un+war+rant+
   ably
un+war+rant+ed
un+wary
un+washed
un+watched
un+wa+ver+ing
un+wea+ried
un+wea+ried+ly
un+wea+ried+
   ness
un+wea+ry
un+wea+ry+ing
un+wed
un+wed+ded
un+weighed
un+wel+come
un+well
un+wept
un+whole+some
un+whole+some+
   ness
un+wieldi+ly
un+wieldi+ness
un+wieldy
un+willed
un+will+ing
un+will+ing+ly
un+will+ing+ness
un+wind
un+winds

un+wind+ing
un+wound
un+wind+able
un+wink+ing
un+wise
un+wise+ly
un+wise+ness
un+wish
un+wishes
un+wish+ing
un+wished
unwished-for
un+with+ered
un+wit+nessed
un+wit+ting
un+wit+ting+ly
un+wit+ting+
   ness
un+wont+ed
un+wont+ed+ly
un+work+able
un+work+man+
   like
un+world+li+ness
un+world+ly
un+worn
un+wor+ried
un+worthi+ly
un+worthi+ness
un+wor+thy
un+wound+ed
un+wrap
un+wraps
un+wrap+ping
un+wrapped
un+writ+ten
un+yield+ing
un+yoke
un+yokes
un+yok+ing
un+yoked
un+zip
un+zips
un+zip+ping
un+zipped
up
ups
ups
up+ping
upped
up-anchor
up-anchors
up-anchor+ing
up-anchored
up-and-coming

up-and-down
up-and-over
up-and-under
 up-and-unders
Upani+shad
 Upani+shads
upas
 upases
up+beat
 up+beats
up+braid
 up+braids
 up+braid+ing
 up+braid+ed
up+braid+er
 up+braid+ers
up+braid+ing
 up+braid+ings
up+bring+ing
 up+bring+ings
up+cast
 up+casts
 up+casts
 up+cast+ing
 up+cast
up+country
up+date
 up+dates
 up+dat+ing
 up+dat+ed
 up+date+able
up+dat+er
 up+dat+ers
Updike
up+draught
 up+draughts
up+end
 up+ends
 up+end+ing
 up+end+ed
up+front
up+grade
 up+grades
 up+grad+ing
 up+grad+ed
up+grad+er
 up+grad+ers
up+heav+al
 up+heav+als
up+heave
 up+heaves
 up+heav+ing
 up+heaved or
 up+hove
up+hill

up+hills
up+hold
 up+holds
 up+hold+ing
 up+held
up+hold+er
 up+hold+ers
up+hol+ster
 up+hol+sters
 up+hol+ster+ing
 up+hol+stered
up+hol+ster+er
 up+hol+ster+ers
 up+hol+stery
 up+hol+steries
up+keep
up+land
 up+lands
up+lift
 up+lifts
 up+lifts
 up+lift+ing
 up+lift+ed
 up+lift+er
 up+lift+ers
 up+light+er
 up+light+ers
up-market
up+most
Upolu
upon
up+per
 up+pers
Up+per
upper+cut
 upper+cuts
 upper+cuts
 upper+cut+ting
 upper+cut
upper+most
up+pish
 up+pish+ly
 up+pish+ness
up+pi+ty
Upp+sa+la
up+raise
 up+raises
 up+rais+ing
 up+raised
 up+rais+er
 up+rais+ers
up+rear
 up+rears
 up+rear+ing
 up+reared

up+right
 up+rights
 up+right+ly
 up+right+ness
up+rise
 up+rises
 up+rises
 up+ris+ing
 up+rose
 up+ris+en
up+ris+er
 up+ris+ers
 up+ris+ing
 up+ris+ings
up+roar
 up+roars
 up+roari+ous
 up+roari+ous+ly
 up+roari+ous+
  ness
up+root
 up+roots
 up+root+ing
 up+root+ed
 up+root+er
 up+root+ers
up+rush
 up+rushes
up+sa+dai+sy
Up+sa+la
up+scale
up+set
 up+sets
 up+sets
 up+set+ting
 up+set
 up+set+ter
 up+set+ters
 up+set+ting+ly
up+shot
 up+shots
up+side
 up+sides
upside-down
 up+sides
up+si+lon
 up+si+lons
up+stage
 up+stages
 up+stag+ing
 up+staged
up+stairs
up+stand+ing
up+start
 up+starts

up+state
 up+states
 up+stat+er
 up+stat+ers
up+stream
up+stretched
up+stroke
 up+strokes
up+surge
 up+surges
 up+surges
 up+surg+ing
 up+surged
up+sweep
 up+sweeps
 up+sweeps
 up+sweep+ing
 up+swept
up+swing
 up+swings
upsy-daisy
up+take
 up+takes
up+throw
 up+throws
up+thrust
 up+thrusts
up+tight
up+time
up-to-date
up-to-dateness
up+town
up+town+er
 up+town+ers
up+turn
 up+turns
 up+turns
 up+turn+ing
 up+turned
up+ward
 up+ward+ly
 up+ward+ness
 up+wards
up+wind
Ur
ura+cil
urae+mia
urae+mic
urae+us
 urae+uses
Ural
Ural-Altaic
Ura+lian
Ural+ic
Urals

ura+naly+sis
ura+naly+ses
ura+nide
ura+nides
uran+ism
ura+nium
ura+nog+ra+pher
ura+nog+ra+
   phers
ura+no+graph+ic
ura+nog+ra+phy
Uranus
Greek god
Ura+nus
planet
urate
urates
urat+ic
ur+ban
ur+bane
ur+bane+ly
ur+bane+ness
ur+bani+sa+tion
ur+bani+sa+
   tions
ur+ban+ise
ur+ban+ises
ur+ban+is+ing
ur+ban+ised
ur+ban+ism
ur+ban+ite
ur+ban+ites
ur+ban+ity
ur+ban+ities
ur+bani+za+tion
ur+bani+za+
   tions
ur+ban+ize
ur+ban+izes
ur+ban+iz+ing
ur+ban+ized
urbi et orbi
ur+ceo+late
ur+chin
ur+chins
Urdu
urea
urea-
   formaldehyde
ureal
ureic
ureide
ureides
ure+mia
ure+mic

ureter
ureters
ureter+al
urethan
urethane
urethra
urethrae *or*
urethras
urethral
urethrit+ic
urethri+tis
urethro+scope
urethro+scopes
urethro+scop+ic
urethros+co+py
uret+ic
Urey
Urfa
Urga
urge
urges
urges
urg+ing
urged
ur+gen+cy
ur+gen+cies
ur+gent
ur+gent+ly
Uri
Uriah
uric
uri+dine
uri+nal
uri+nals
uri+naly+sis
uri+naly+ses
uri+nary
uri+naries
uri+nate
uri+nates
uri+nat+ing
uri+nat+ed
uri+na+tion
uri+na+tions
uri+na+tive
urine
uri+no+geni+tal
Ur+mia
Urm+ston
urn
urns
urn+field
urn+fields
urn+like
uro+geni+tal

uro+lith
uro+liths
uro+lith+ic
uro+log+ic
urolo+gist
urolo+gists
urol+ogy
uro+pyg+ial
uro+pyg+ium
uro+pyg+iums
uro+scop+ic
uros+co+pist
uros+co+pists
uros+co+py
Ursa
ur+sine
Ur+spra+che
Ur+spra+chen
Ursula
Ur+su+line
Ur+su+lines
Ur+text
Ur+texts
ur+ti+ca+ceous
ur+ti+caria
ur+ti+ca+tion
ur+ti+ca+tions
Urua+pan
Uru+guay
Uru+guay+an
Uru+guay+ans
Urum+chi
Urum+qi
Urun+di
urus
uruses
uru+shi+ol
us
us+abil+ity
us+able
us+age
us+ages
us+ance
us+ances
USDAW
use
uses
uses
us+ing
used
use+abil+ity
use+able
used
use+ful
use+ful+ly

use+ful+ness
use+less
use+less+ly
use+less+ness
user
users
user-friendly
Ush+ant
Ush+as
ush+er
ush+ers
ush+ers
ush+er+ing
ush+ered
Usher
ush+er+ette
ush+er+ettes
Usk
Üs+küb
Üs+kü+dar
Usnach
Usnech
Us+pal+la+ta
us+que+baugh
us+que+baughs
Ussher
Us+su+ri
Ústí nad La+bem
Ustinov
Ust-Kameno+
   gorsk
Ust Urt
Ust+yurt
usu+al
usu+als
usu+al+ly
usu+al+ness
usu+fruct
usu+fruc+tu+ary
usu+fruc+tu+
   aries
Usum+bu+ra
usu+rer
usu+rers
usu+ri+ous
usurp
usurps
usurp+ing
usurped
usur+pa+tion
usur+pa+tions
usurp+er
usurp+ers
usu+ry
usu+ries

ut
Utah
ute
 utes
uten+sil
 uten+sils
u+ter+ine
uter+us
 uteri
Ut+gard
Utgard-Loki
Uther Pendragon
Uti+ca
uti+lis+able
uti+li+sa+tion
 uti+li+sa+tions
uti+lise
 uti+lises
 uti+lis+ing
 uti+lised
utili+tar+ian
 utili+tar+ians

utili+tari+an+ism
util+ity
 util+ities
uti+liz+able
uti+li+za+tion
 uti+li+za+tions
uti+lize
 uti+lizes
 uti+liz+ing
 uti+lized
uti+liz+er
 uti+liz+ers
ut+most
Uto+pia
 Uto+pias
Uto+pian
 Uto+pians
Uto+pi+an+ism
Utrecht
utri+cle
 utri+cles
utricu+lar

utricu+li+tis
Utrillo
Ut+tar Pra+desh
ut+ter
 ut+ters
ut+ter+ing
 ut+tered
ut+ter+able
ut+ter+able+ness
ut+ter+ance
 ut+ter+ances
ut+ter+er
 ut+ter+ers
ut+ter+ly
utter+most
U-turn
 U-turns
uva+rov+ite
 uva+rov+ites
uvea
 uveas
uveal

uvu+la
uvu+las or
uvu+lae
uvu+lar
 uvu+lars
Ux+bridge
Ux+mal
uxo+rial
uxo+ri+al+ly
uxo+ri+cid+al
uxo+ri+cide
 uxo+ri+cides
uxo+ri+ous
uxo+ri+ous+ly
uxo+ri+ous+ness
Uz+bek
Uz+beks or
Uz+bek
Uz+beki+stan

V

v
v's
V
V's *or*
Vs
Vaal
Vaasa
vac
vacs
va+can+cy
va+can+cies
va+cant
va+cant+ly
va+cat+able
va+cate
va+cates
va+cat+ing
va+cat+ed
va+ca+tion
va+ca+tions
va+ca+tions
va+ca+tion+ing
va+ca+tioned
va+ca+tion+er
va+ca+tion+ers
va+ca+tion+ist
va+ca+tion+ists
vac+ci+nal
vac+ci+nate
vac+ci+nates
vac+ci+nat+ing
vac+ci+nat+ed
vac+ci+na+tion
vac+ci+na+tions
vac+ci+na+tor
vac+ci+na+tors
vac+cine
vac+cines
vac+cinia
vache+rin
vache+rins
vac+il+late
vac+il+lates
vac+il+lat+ing
vac+il+lat+ed

vac+il+la+tion
vac+il+la+tions
vac+il+la+tor
vac+il+la+tors
vacua
va+cu+ity
va+cu+ities
vacuo+lar
vacu+ole
vacu+oles
vacu+ous
vacu+ous+ly
vacuum
vacuums *or*
vacua
vacuums
vacuum+ing
vacuumed
vacuum-packed
vade me+cum
vade me+cums
Va+do+da+ra
va+dose
Va+duz
vaga+bond
vaga+bonds
vaga+bond+age
va+gal
va+gary
va+garies
va+gi+na
va+gi+nas *or*
va+gi+nae
vagi+nal
vagi+nate
vagi+nec+tomy
vagi+nec+
tomies
vagi+nis+mus
vagi+ni+tis
va+goto+my
va+goto+mies
va+go+to+nia
va+go+to+nias
va+gran+cy

va+grant
va+grants
va+grant+ly
vague
vaguer
vaguest
vague+ly
vague+ness
va+gus
va+gi
vail
vails
vails
vail+ing
vailed
vain
vain+er
vain+est
vain+glo+ri+ous
vain+glo+ry
vain+glo+ries
vain+ly
vain+ness
vair
Vais+ya
Va+lais
val+ance
val+ances
val+anced
Val-de-Marne
Val+di+via
Val-d'Oise
vale
vales
val+edic+tion
val+edic+tions
val+edic+tory
val+edic+tories
va+lence
va+lences
Va+lence
Va+len+cia
Va+len+ci+ennes
va+len+cy
va+len+cies

Valens
val+en+tine
val+en+tines
Valentine
Valentino
va+lerian
va+lerians
Valerian
va+ler+ic
Valéry
val+et
val+ets
va+leta
va+letas
va+let de cham+
bre
va+lets de cham+
bre
Va+let+ta
val+etu+di+nar+
ian
val+etu+di+nar+
ians
val+etu+di+nari+
an+ism
val+etu+di+nary
val+etu+di+
naries
val+gus
Val+hall
Val+hal+la
val+iant
val+iant+ly
val+id
vali+date
vali+dates
vali+dat+ing
vali+dated
vali+da+tion
vali+da+tions
va+lid+ity
val+id+ly
va+line
va+lines
va+lise

va +lises
Va +lium
Trademark
Va +liums
Val +kyr
Val +kyrs
Val +kyr +ian
Val +kyrie
Val +kyries
Va +lla +do +lid
val +la +tion
val +la +tions
val +lecu +la
val +lecu +lae
Val +le d'Ao +sta
Val +let +ta
val +ley
val +leys
Val +lom +bro +sa
val +lum
Va +lois
place name
Valois
family name
Va +lo +na
va +lo +nia
val +or
U.S.
val +ori +sa +tion
val +ori +sa +tions
val +or +ise
val +or +ises
val +or +is +ing
val +or +ised
val +ori +za +tion
val +ori +za +tions
val +or +ize
val +or +izes
val +or +iz +ing
val +or +ized
val +or +ous
val +our
Val +pa +raí +so
valse
valses
valu +able
valu +ables
valu +ably
valu +ate
valu +ates
valu +at +ing
valu +at +ed
valua +tion
valua +tions
valua +tion +al

valua +tor
valua +tors
value
values
values
valu +ing
valued
value-added
val +ued
value +less
valu +er
valu +ers
Valu +er Gen +er +al
Valu +er Gen +er +als
valu +ta
valu +tas
val +vate
valve
valves
valve +less
valve +like
val +vu +lar
val +vu +li +tis
va +moose
va +mooses
va +moos +ing
va +moosed
vamp
vamps
vamps
vamp +ing
vamped
vam +pire
vam +pires
vam +pir +ic
vam +pir +ism
van
vans
Van
va +na +dium
Van Allen
Vanbrugh
Van Buren
Van +cou +ver
place name
Vancouver
surname
van +dal
van +dals
Van +dal
Van +dals
Van +dal +ic
van +dal +ise

van +dal +ises
van +dal +is +ing
van +dal +ised
van +dal +ism
van +dal +is +tic
van +dal +ize
van +dal +izes
van +dal +iz +ing
van +dal +ized
Van de Graaf
Van +de +mo +nian
Van +de +mo +nians
Vanderbilt
Van der Post
van der Waals
van der Weyden
Van Diemen
Van Dyck
surname
Vandyke
surname
Van +dyke
adj.
vane
vanes
vaned
Vä +nern
van Eyck
Van Gogh
van +guard
van +guards
va +nil +la
va +nil +lic
van +il +lin
Va +nir
van +ish
van +ishes
van +ish +ing
van +ished
van +ish +er
van +ish +ers
van +ity
van +ities
van +quish
van +quishes
van +quish +ing
van +quished
van +quish +able
van +quish +er
van +quish +ers
van +tage
van +tages
van't Hoff
Va +nua Levu

Va +nu +atu
van +ward
vap +id
va +pid +ity
va +pid +ities
vap +id +ly
va +por
U.S.
va +pors
va +por +er
U.S.
va +por +ers
va +por +es +cence
va +por +es +cent
va +po +ret +to
va +po +ret +tos
or
va +po +ret +ti
va +por +if +ic
va +por +im +eter
va +por +im +eters
va +pori +sa +tion
va +por +ise
va +por +ises
va +por +is +ing
va +por +ised
va +por +is +er
va +por +is +ers
va +por +ish
U.S.
va +pori +za +tion
va +por +ize
va +por +izes
va +por +iz +ing
va +por +ized
va +por +iz +er
va +por +iz +ers
vapor-like
U.S.
va +por +os +ity
va +por +os +ities
vap +or +ous
va +por +ous +ly
va +pory
U.S.
va +pour
va +pours
va +pour +er
va +pour +ers
va +pour +ish
vapour-like
va +poury
Var

va+rac+tor
va+rac+tors
Varah
Va+ra+na+si
Var+dar
Vard+ha+ma+na
var+ec
Va+rese
place name
Varèse
surname
Vargas
Vargas Llosa
vari+abil+ity
vari+able
vari+ables
variable-
geometry
vari+able+ness
variable-sweep
vari+ably
vari+ance
vari+ances
vari+ant
vari+ants
vari+ate
vari+ates
vari+ation
vari+ations
vari+ation+al
vari+cel+la
vari+ces
vari+col+ored
U.S.
vari+col+oured
vari+cose
vari+co+sis
vari+cos+ity
vari+cos+ities
vari+coto+my
vari+coto+mies
var+ied
var+ied+ly
varie+gate
varie+gates
varie+gat+ing
varie+gat+ed
varie+gat+ed
varie+ga+tion
varie+ga+tions
va+ri+etal
va+ri+etals
va+ri+etal+ly
va+ri+ety
va+ri+eties

vari+form
vari+form+ly
va+rio+la
va+rio+lar
vari+ole
vari+oles
vari+olite
vari+olites
vario+lit+ic
vari+om+eter
vari+om+eters
vario+rum
vario+rums
vari+ous
vari+ous+ly
vari+ous+ness
var+is+tor
var+is+tors
Vari+typ+er
Trademark
Vari+typ+ers
var+ix
var+ices
var+let
var+lets
var+let+ry
var+mint
var+mints
var+na
var+nas
Var+na
var+nish
var+nishes
var+nishes
var+nish+ing
var+nished
var+nish+er
var+nish+ers
Varro
var+sity
var+sities
Varu+na
var+us
varve
varves
vary
varies
vary+ing
varied
vary÷ing
vas
vasa
Vasari
vas+cu+lar
vas+cu+lar+ity

vas+cu+lar+ly
vas de+fe+rens
vasa de+fe+ren+
tia
vase
vases
vas+ec+to+my
vas+ec+to+mies
Vas+eline
Trademark
Vashti
vaso+ac+tive
vaso+con+stric+
tor
vaso+con+stric+
tors
vaso+di+la+tor
vaso+di+la+tors
vaso+in+hibi+tor
vaso+in+hibi+
tors
vaso+mo+tor
vaso+pres+sin
vaso+pres+sins
vaso+pres+sor
vaso+pres+sors
vas+sal
vas+sals
vas+sal+age
vast
vast+er
vast+est
vast+ly
vast+ness
vasty
vasti+er
vasti+est
vat
vats
vats
vat+ting
vat+ted
vat-dyed
vat+ic
Vati+can
Vät+tern
Vau+cluse
Vaud
vau+de+ville
vau+de+villes
vau+de+vil+lian
vau+de+vil+lians
Vau+dois
Vaughan
vault

vaults
vaults
vault+ing
vault+ed
vault+er
vault+ers
vault+ing
vaunt
vaunts
vaunts
vaunt+ing
vaunt+ed
vaunt+er
vaunt+ers
Vaux+hall
vava+sor
vava+sors
vava+sour
vava+sours
V-Day
V-Days
veal
veal+er
veal+ers
vec+tor
vec+tors
vec+tors
vec+tor+ing
vec+tored
vec+to+rial
Veda
Vedas
ve+da+lia
ve+da+lias
Ve+dan+ta
Ve+dan+tic
Ve+dan+tist
Ve+dan+tists
ve+dette
ve+dettes
Ve+dic
veer
veers
veers
veer+ing
veered
veg
vegges
veg+ging
vegged
Vega
ve+gan
ve+gans
veg+eburg+er
veg+eburg+ers

Veg+emite
Trademark
veg+eta+ble
veg+eta+bles
veg+etal
veg+etar+ian
veg+etar+ians
veg+etari+an+
ism
veg+etate
veg+etates
veg+etat+ing
veg+etat+ed
veg+eta+tion
veg+eta+tion+al
veg+eta+tive
veg+eta+tive+ly
veg+gie
veg+gies
ve+he+mence
ve+he+ment
ve+he+ment+ly
ve+hi+cle
ve+hi+cles
ve+hicu+lar
Veii
veil
veils
veils
veil+ing
veiled
veiled
veil+ed+ly
veil+er
veil+ers
veil+ing
veil-like
vein
veins
veins
vein+ing
veined
vein+ing
vein+less
vein+let
vein+lets
vein+like
veiny
ve+la+men
ve+lami+na
ve+lar
Velásquez
Velázquez
Vel+cro
Trademark

veld
veld+skoen
veld+skoens
veldt
ve+leta
ve+letas
veli+ger
veli+gers
Vel+lore
vel+lum
ve+lo+ce
ve+loci+pede
ve+loci+pedes
ve+loci+ped+ist
ve+loci+ped+
ists
ve+loc+ity
ve+loc+ities
ve+lo+drome
ve+lo+dromes
ve+lour
ve+lours
ve+lou+té
ve+lou+tés
Vel+sen
ve+lum
ve+la
ve+lure
ve+lures
ve+lu+ti+nous
vel+vet
vel+vets
vel+vet+een
vel+vet+eens
velvet-like
vel+vety
vena
venae
vena cava
venae cavae
ve+nal
ve+nal+ity
ve+nal+ly
ve+na+tion
ve+na+tion+al
vend
vends
vend+ing
vend+ed
Ven+da
ven+dace
ven+daces *or*
ven+dace
ven+dee
ven+dees

Ven+dée
vend+er
vend+ers
ven+det+ta
ven+det+tas
ven+det+tist
ven+det+tists
vend+ibil+ity
vend+ible
vend+ibles
Vendôme
ven+dor
ven+dors
ve+neer
ve+neers
ve+neers
ve+neer+ing
ve+neered
ve+neer+er
ve+neer+ers
ve+neer+ing
ven+epunc+ture
ven+epunc+
tures
ven+er+abil+ity
ven+er+able
ven+er+able+
ness
ven+er+ably
ven+er+ate
ven+er+ates
ven+er+at+ing
ven+er+at+ed
ven+era+tion
ven+era+tor
ven+era+tors
ve+nereal
ve+nere+olo+gist
ve+nere+olo+
gists
ve+nere+ol+ogy
ven+ery
ven+esec+tion
ven+esec+tions
Ve+netia
Ve+netian
Ve+netians
Ve+neto
Ve+nezia
Ve+nezia Giu+lia
Ve+nezia Tri+den+
ti+na
Ven+ezue+la
Ven+ezue+lan
Ven+ezue+lans

venge+ance
venge+ful
venge+ful+ly
ve+nial
ve+ni+al+ity
ve+ni+al+ly
Ven+ice
ven+in
ven+ins
veni+punc+ture
veni+punc+tures
veni+son
Ve+ni+te
Venizelos
Ven+lo
Ven+loo
ven+om
ven+oms
ven+om+ous
ven+om+ous+ly
ven+om+ous+
ness
ve+nose
ve+nos+ity
ve+nous
vent
vents
vents
vent+ing
vent+ed
vent+er
vent+ers
ven+ti+lable
ven+ti+late
ven+ti+lates
ven+ti+lat+ing
ven+ti+lat+ed
ven+ti+la+tion
ven+ti+la+tions
ven+ti+la+tor
ven+ti+la+tors
ven+tral
ven+tral+ly
ven+tri+cle
ven+tri+cles
ven+tri+cose
ven+tricu+lar
ven+tricu+lus
ven+tricu+li
ven+tri+lo+quial
ven+tri+lo+qui+al+
ly
ven+trilo+quise
ven+trilo+quises

ven+trilo+quis+
ing
ven+trilo+quised
ven+trilo+quism
ven+trilo+quist
ven+trilo+quists
ven+trilo+quize
ven+trilo+quizes
ven+trilo+quiz+
ing
ven+trilo+quized
ven+trilo+quy
Ventris
ven+ture
ven+tures
ven+tures
ven+tur+ing
ven+tured
ven+tur+er
ven+tur+ers
Ven+tur+er
Ven+tur+ers
ven+ture+some
Venturi
ven+tu+rous
venue
venues
ven+ule
ven+ules
Venus
goddess
Ve+nus
planet
Ve+nus+berg
Venus fly+trap
Venus fly+traps
Ve+nu+sian
Ve+nu+sians
Venus's-flytrap
Venus's-flytraps
ve+ra+cious
ve+ra+cious+ly
ve+ra+cious+
ness
ve+rac+ity
Vera+cruz
ve+ran+da
ve+ran+das
ve+ran+dah
ve+ran+dahs
vera+trin
vera+trine
verb
verbs
ver+bal

ver+bali+sa+tion
ver+bali+sa+
tions
ver+bal+ise
ver+bal+ises
ver+bal+is+ing
ver+bal+ised
ver+bal+ism
ver+bal+ist
ver+bal+ists
ver+bali+za+tion
ver+bali+za+
tions
ver+bal+ize
ver+bal+izes
ver+bal+iz+ing
ver+bal+ized
ver+bal+ly
ver+bas+cum
ver+bas+cums
ver+ba+tim
ver+be+na
ver+be+nas
ver+bi+age
ver+bose
ver+bose+ly
ver+bos+ity
ver+bo+ten
Ver+cel+li
Vercingetorix
ver+dan+cy
ver+dant
verd an+tique
ver+dant+ly
Verde
Verdi
ver+dict
ver+dicts
ver+di+gris
Ver+dun
ver+dure
ver+dured
Ve+ree+ni+ging
verge
verges
verges
verg+ing
verged
ver+ger
ver+gers
Vergil
Ver+gil+ian
ver+glas
ver+glases
ve+ridi+cal

ve+ridi+cal+ity
ve+ridi+cal+ly
veri+est
veri+fi+able
veri+fi+ably
veri+fi+ca+tion
veri+fi+ca+tory
veri+fi+er
veri+fi+ers
veri+fy
veri+fies
veri+fy+ing
veri+fied
veri+ly
veri+simi+lar
veri+si+mili+tude
veri+si+mili+
tudes
ver+ism
ve+ris+mo
ver+ist
ver+ists
ver+ist+ic
veri+table
veri+table+ness
veri+tably
ver+ity
ver+juice
Verkhne-Udinsk
ver+kramp+te
ver+kramp+tes
Verlaine
ver+lig+te
ver+lig+tes
Vermeer
ver+meil
ver+mi+cel+li
ver+mi+cid+al
ver+mi+cide
ver+mi+cides
ver+micu+lar
ver+micu+late
ver+micu+la+tion
ver+micu+lite
ver+micu+lites
ver+mi+form
ver+mi+fu+gal
ver+mi+fuge
ver+mi+fug+es
ver+mil+ion
ver+mil+ions
ver+min
ver+mi+nous
ver+mis
ver+mes

Ver+mont
Ver+mont+er
Ver+mont+ers
ver+mouth
ver+mouths
ver+nacu+lar
ver+nacu+lars
ver+nacu+lar+ly
ver+nal
ver+nali+sa+tion
ver+nal+ise
ver+nal+ises
ver+nal+is+ing
ver+nal+ised
ver+nali+za+tion
ver+nal+ize
ver+nal+izes
ver+nal+iz+ing
ver+nal+ized
ver+nal+ly
ver+na+tion
Verne
ver+ni+er
ver+ni+ers
ver+nis+sage
ver+nis+sages
Ver+no+le+ninsk
Ver+ny
Ve+ro+na
Vero+nal
Trademark
Vero+nese
(person) from
Verona
Vero+nese
Veronese
surname
ve+roni+ca
ve+roni+cas
Verrazano
Verrazzano
Verrocchio
ver+ru+ca
ver+ru+cas *or*
ver+ru+cae
ver+ru+cose
ver+ru+cos+ity
ver+ru+cous
Ver+sailles
ver+sant
ver+sants
ver+sa+tile
ver+sa+tile+ly
ver+sa+til+ity
ver+sa+til+ities

verse
 verses
 verses
 vers+ing
 versed
 versed
ver+si+cle
 ver+si+cles
ver+si+col+or
U.S.
ver+si+col+our
ver+si+fi+ca+tion
ver+si+fi+er
 ver+si+fi+ers
ver+si+fy
 ver+si+fies
 ver+si+fy+ing
 ver+si+fied
ver+sion
 ver+sions
ver+sion+al
vers li+bre
ver+so
 ver+sos
verst
 versts
ver+sus
ver+te+bra
 ver+te+brae or
 ver+te+bras
ver+te+bral
 ver+te+bral+ly
ver+te+brate
 ver+te+brates
ver+te+bra+tion
ver+tex
 ver+texes or
 ver+ti+ces
ver+ti+cal
 ver+ti+cals
ver+ti+cal+ity
 ver+ti+cal+ly
ver+ti+ces
ver+ti+cil
 ver+ti+cils
ver+tic+il+late
ver+tigi+nous
ver+tigi+nous+ly
ver+ti+go
ver+tu
Vertumnus
Veru+la+mium
ver+vain
 ver+vains
verve

ver+vet
 ver+vets
Verwoerd
very
Very
Vesalius
vesi+ca
 vesi+cae
vesi+cal
vesi+cant
 vesi+cants
vesi+cate
 vesi+cates
 vesi+cat+ing
 vesi+cat+ed
 vesi+ca+tion
vesi+ca+tory
 vesi+ca+tories
vesi+cle
 vesi+cles
ve+sicu+lar
ve+sicu+late
 ve+sicu+lates
 ve+sicu+lat+ing
 ve+sicu+lat+ed
Vespasian
ves+per
 ves+pers
 ves+per+tine
ves+pi+ary
 ves+pi+aries
ves+pid
 ves+pids
ves+pine
Vespucci
ves+sel
 ves+sels
vest
 vests
 vests
 vest+ing
 vest+ed
ves+ta
 ves+tas
Vesta
ves+tal
 ves+tals
vest+ed
ves+ti+ary
 ves+ti+aries
 ves+ti+bule
 ves+ti+bules
ves+tige
 ves+tiges
ves+tig+ial

vest+ment
 vest+ments
 vest+ment+al
vest-pocket
ves+tral
ves+try
 ves+tries
vestry+man
 vestry+men
ves+tur+al
ves+ture
 ves+tures
Ve+su+vi+us
vet
 vets
 vets
vet+ting
vet+ted
vetch
 vetches
vetch+ling
 vetch+lings
vet+er+an
 vet+er+ans
vet+eri+nary
veto
 vetoes
 vetoes
ve+to+ing
 ve+toed
ve+to+er
 ve+to+ers
vex
 vexes
vex+ing
 vexed
vexa+tion
vexa+tious
 vexa+tious+ly
 vexed
vex+ed+ly
vex+er
 vex+ers
vex+il+late
vex+il+lolo+gist
 vex+il+lolo+
   gists
vex+il+lol+ogy
vex+il+lum
 vex+il+la
via
vi+abil+ity
vi+able
Via Dolo+ro+sa
via+duct

via+ducts
vial
 vials
via me+dia
vi+and
 vi+ands
Via+reg+gio
vi+ati+cum
 vi+ati+cums or
 vi+ati+ca
vibes
Vi+borg
vi+bracu+lum
 vi+bracu+la
vi+bran+cy
vi+brant
 vi+brant+ly
vi+bra+phone
 vi+bra+phones
vi+bra+phon+ist
 vi+bra+phon+
   ists
vi+brate
 vi+brates
 vi+brat+ing
 vi+brat+ed
vi+bra+tile
vi+bra+tion
 vi+bra+tions
 vi+bra+tion+al
vi+bra+tions
vi+bra+to
 vi+bra+tos
vi+bra+tor
 vi+bra+tors
vi+bra+tory
vi+bris+sa
 vi+bris+sae
vi+bris+sal
vi+bur+num
 vi+bur+nums
vic+ar
 vic+ars
vic+ar+age
 vic+ar+ages
vi+car+ial
vi+cari+ate
 vi+cari+ates
vi+cari+ous
 vi+cari+ous+ly
 vi+cari+ous+ness
vi+car+ly
vice
 vices
 vices

vicing
viced
vice-chairman
vice-chairmen
vice-chairman+
ship
vice-chairman+
ships
vice-chancel+lor+
ship
vice-chancel+lor+
ships
vice+ge+ren+cy
vice+ge+ren+
cies
vice+ge+rent
vice+ge+rents
vi+cen+nial
Vi+cen+za
vice-presiden+cy
vice-presiden+
cies
vice+re+gal
vice+re+gal+ly
vice+reine
vice+reines
vice+roy
vice+roys
vice+roy+al+ty
vice+roy+al+ties
vice+roy+ship
vice+roy+ships
vice ver+sa
vi+chy
Vi+chy
vi+chy+ssoise
vici+nage
vici+nages
vici+nal
vi+cin+ity
vi+cin+ities
vi+cious
vi+cious+ly
vi+cious+ness
vi+cis+si+tude
vi+cis+si+tudes
vi+cis+si+tu+di+
nous
Vicks+burg
Vicky
Vico
vic+tim
vic+tims
vic+timi+sa+tion
vic+tim+ise

vic+tim+ises
vic+tim+is+ing
vic+tim+ised
vic+tim+is+er
vic+tim+is+ers
vic+timi+za+tion
vic+tim+ize
vic+tim+izes
vic+tim+iz+ing
vic+tim+ized
vic+tim+iz+er
vic+tim+iz+ers
vic+tor
vic+tors
Victor
vic+to+ria
vic+to+rias
Vic+to+ria
place name
Victoria
person
Vic+to+rian
Vic+to+rians
Vic+to+ri+ana
Vic+to+ri+an+
ism
vic+to+ri+ous
vic+to+ri+ous+ly
vic+to+ry
vic+to+ries
Victory
vict+ual
vict+uals
vict+ual+ling *or*
vict+ual+ing
U.S.
vict+ualled *or*
vict+ualed
U.S.
vict+ual+ler
vict+ual+lers
victual-less
vict+uals
vi+cu+na
vi+cu+nas
vi+cu+ña
vi+cu+ñas
vid
vids
Vidal
vide
vi+deli+cet
video
videos
videos

video+ing
videoed
video+phone
video+phones
Video+tex
Trademark
video+text
vidi+con
vidi+cons
vie
vies
vy+ing
vied
Vi+en+na
Vienne
Vi+en+nese
Vi+en+nese
Vien+ti+ane
vier
viers
Vier+wald+stät+
ter+see
Vi+et+nam
Viet Nam
Vi+et+nam+ese
vieux jeu
view
views
views
view+ing
viewed
view+able
View+data
Trademark
view+er
view+ers
view+finder
view+finders
view+ing
view+ings
view+less
view+point
view+points
Vigée-Lebrun
vi+gesi+mal
vi+gia
vi+gias
vig+il
vig+ils
vigi+lance
vigi+lant
vigi+lan+te
vigi+lan+tes
vigi+lan+tism
vigi+lant+ly

vigne+ron
vigne+rons
vi+gnette
vi+gnettes
vi+gnettes
vi+gnet+ting
vi+gnet+ted
vi+gnet+tist
vi+gnet+tists
Vignola
Vigny
Vigo
vig+or
U.S.
vig+oro
vig+or+ous
vig+or+ous+ly
vig+our
Vii+pu+ri
Vi+jaya+wa+da
Vi+king
Vi+kings
vile
vil+er
vil+est
vile+ly
vile+ness
vili+fi+ca+tion
vili+fi+ca+tions
vili+fi+er
vili+fi+ers
vili+fy
vili+fies
vili+fy+ing
vili+fied
vili+pend
vili+pends
vili+pend+ing
vili+pend+ed
vili+pend+er
vili+pend+ers
vil+la
vil+las
Villa
Vil+lach
vil+lage
vil+lages
vil+lag+er
vil+lag+ers
Vil+la+her+mo+
sa
vil+lain
vil+lains
vil+lain+ess
vil+lain+ous

vil+lain+ous+ly
vil+lain+ous+ness
vil+lainy
 vil+lainies
Villa-Lobos
vil+la+nelle
 vil+la+nelles
vil+lein
 vil+leins
vil+lein+age
Villeneuve
Ville+ur+banne
Villiers
vil+li+form
Villon
vil+los+ity
vil+lous
vil+lus
 vil+li
Vil+ni+us
Vil+ny+us
vim
Vimi+nal
vi+min+eous
vina
 vinas
vi+na+ceous
vinai+grette
Vin+cennes
Vincent de Paul
vin+cibil+ity
vin+cible
vin+cris+tine
vin+cu+lum
 vin+cu+la
vin de pays
 vins de pays
Vin+dhya Pra+
 desh
vin+di+cabil+ity
vin+di+cable
vin+di+cate
 vin+di+cates
 vin+di+cat+ing
 vin+di+cat+ed
vin+di+ca+tion
vin+di+ca+tor
 vin+di+ca+tors
vin+di+ca+tory
vin+dic+tive
vin+dic+tive+ly
vin+dic+tive+
 ness
vin du pays
 vins du pays

vine
vines
Vine
vine+dresser
vine+dressers
vin+egar
vin+egars
vin+egar+ish
vin+egary
Vine+land
vin+ery
vin+eries
vine+yard
vine+yards
vingt-et-un
vin+ho ver+de
vini+cul+tur+al
vini+cul+ture
vini+cul+tur+ist
 vini+cul+tur+ists
vi+nif+er+ous
Vin+land
Vin+ni+tsa
vino
 vinos
vin or+di+naire
 vins or+di+
 naires
vi+nos+ity
vi+nous
vin+tage
 vin+tages
 vin+tag+er
 vin+tag+ers
vint+ner
vint+ners
viny
vi+nyl
 vi+nyls
viol
 viols
vio+la
 vio+las
vio+lable
vio+la da gam+ba
 vio+las da gam+
 ba
vio+la d'amo+re
 vio+las d'amo+
 re
vio+late
 vio+lates
 vio+lat+ing
 vio+lat+ed
vio+la+ter

vio+la+ters
vio+la+tion
 vio+la+tions
vio+la+tor
 vio+la+tors
vio+lence
vio+lent
vio+lent+ly
vio+let
 vio+lets
vio+lin
 vio+lins
vio+lin+ist
 vio+lin+ists
vi+ol+ist
 vi+ol+ists
Viollet-le-Duc
vio+lon+cel+list
 vio+lon+cel+
 lists
vio+lon+cel+lo
 vio+lon+cel+los
vi+per
vi+pers
vi+per+ish
vi+per+ous
vi+ra+go
 vi+ra+goes or
 vi+ra+gos
virago-like
vi+ral
Virchow
vir+elay
 vir+elays
Viren
vireo
 vireos
vi+res+cence
 vi+res+cences
vi+res+cent
vir+gate
 vir+gates
Virgil
Vir+gil+ian
vir+gin
 vir+gins
Vir+gin
vir+gin+al
 vir+gin+als
 vir+gin+al+ist
 vir+gin+al+ists
 vir+gin+al+ly
Vir+ginia
Vir+gin+ian
 Vir+gin+ians

vir+gin+ity
vir+gin+ium
virgin's-bower
 virgin's-bowers
Vir+go
 Vir+gos
vir+go in+tac+ta
vir+gule
 vir+gules
viri+des+cence
viri+des+cent
vi+rid+ian
 vi+rid+ians
vi+rid+ity
vir+ile
viri+lism
vi+ril+ity
vi+ro+logi+cal
vi+rol+ogy
 vi+rol+ogies
vir+tu
vir+tual
vir+tu+al+ity
 vir+tu+al+ities
 vir+tu+al+ly
vir+tue
 vir+tues
vir+tu+os+ic
vir+tu+os+ity
vir+tuo+so
 vir+tuo+sos or
 vir+tuo+si
vir+tu+ous
vir+tu+ous+ly
viru+lence
viru+len+cy
viru+lent
viru+lent+ly
vi+rus
 vi+ruses
vis
 vir+es
visa
 visas
vis+age
 vis+ages
Vi+sa+kha+pat+
 nam
vis-à-vis
 vis-à-vis
Vis+by
vis+ca+cha
 vis+ca+chas
vis+cera
vis+cer+al

vis+cer+al+ly
vis+cid
vis+cid+ity
Visconti
vis+cose
vis+cos+ity
vis+count
  vis+counts
vis+count+cy
  vis+count+cies
vis+count+ess
  vis+count+
  esses
vis+cous
vis+cous+ly
vis+cus
vis+cera
vise
U.S.
  vises
  vises
vis+ing
vised
Vi+seu
Vi+sha+kha+pat+
  nam
Vishinsky
Vishnu
Vish+nu+ism
vis+ibil+ity
  vis+ibil+ities
vis+ible
vis+ibly
vi+sion
vi+sions
vi+sion+ary
vi+sion+aries
vis+it
  vis+its
  vis+its
  vis+it+ing
  vis+it+ed
  vis+it+able
visi+tant
  visi+tants
vis+ita+tion
  vis+ita+tions
Vis+ita+tion
visi+tor
  visi+tors
Vis+lin+sky Za+
  liv
vi+sor
vi+sors
vis+ta

vis+tas
vis+taed
Vis+tu+la
vis+ual
  vis+uals
visu+ali+sa+tion
  visu+ali+sa+
  tions
visu+al+ise
  visu+al+ises
  visu+al+is+ing
  visu+al+ised
visu+ali+za+tion
  visu+ali+za+
  tions
visu+al+ize
  visu+al+izes
  visu+al+iz+ing
  visu+al+ized
visu+al+ly
vi+tal
  vi+tals
vi+tali+sa+tion
vi+tal+ise
  vi+tal+ises
  vi+tal+is+ing
  vi+tal+ised
vi+tal+ism
vi+tal+ist
  vi+tal+ists
  vi+tal+is+tic
vi+tal+ity
vi+tali+za+tion
vi+tal+ize
  vi+tal+izes
  vi+tal+iz+ing
  vi+tal+ized
vi+tal+ly
vita+min
  vita+mins
vita+min+ic
Vi+tebsk
vi+tel+lin
  vi+tel+lins
vi+tel+lus
  vi+tel+luses or
  vi+tel+li
vi+ti+ate
  vi+ti+ates
  vi+ti+at+ing
  vi+ti+at+ed
vi+tia+tion
  vi+tia+tions
vi+tia+tor
  vi+tia+tors

viti+cul+ture
viti+cul+tur+ist
  viti+cul+tur+ists
Viti Levu
Vi+to+ria
  Spanish city
Vi+tó+ria
  Brazilian port
vit+re+ous
vit+re+ous+ly
vi+tres+cence
  vi+tres+cences
vi+tres+cent
vit+ri+fi+able
vit+ri+fi+ca+tion
vit+ri+fy
  vit+ri+fies
  vit+ri+fy+ing
  vit+ri+fied
vit+rine
  vit+rines
vit+ri+ol
  vit+ri+ols
vit+ri+ol+ic
vit+ri+oli+sa+tion
vit+ri+ol+ise
  vit+ri+ol+ises
  vit+ri+ol+is+ing
  vit+ri+ol+ised
vit+ri+oli+za+tion
vit+ri+ol+ize
  vit+ri+ol+izes
  vit+ri+ol+iz+ing
  vit+ri+ol+ized
Vi+tru+vian
Vitruvius Pollio
vit+tle
  vit+tles
vi+tu+per+ate
  vi+tu+per+ates
  vi+tu+per+at+
  ing
  vi+tu+per+at+ed
vi+tu+pera+tion
  vi+tu+pera+
  tions
vi+tu+pera+tor
  vi+tu+pera+tors
viva
  vivas
  vivas
viva+ing
vivaed
vi+va+ce
vi+va+cious

vi+va+cious+ly
vi+va+cious+
  ness
vi+va+cious+
  nesses
vi+vac+ity
vi+vac+ities
Vivaldi
vi+var+ium
  vi+var+iums or
  vi+varia
viva voce
vive
Vivian
viv+id
viv+id+ly
viv+id+ness
vivi+fi+ca+tion
  vivi+fi+ca+tions
vivi+fy
  vivi+fies
  vivi+fy+ing
  vivi+fied
vi+vip+ar+ity
vi+vip+ar+ous
  vi+vipa+rous+ly
vivi+sect
  vivi+sects
  vivi+sect+ing
  vivi+sect+ed
vivi+sec+tion
  vivi+sec+tions
  vivi+sec+tion+al
  vivi+sec+tion+ist
  vivi+sec+tion+
  ists
vivi+sec+tor
  vivi+sec+tors
vivo
vix+en
  vix+ens
vix+en+ish
vix+en+ly
Vi+yel+la
  Trademark
Vi+za+ga+pa+
  tam
viz+ard
  viz+ards
  viz+ard+ed
vi+zier
  vi+ziers
vi+zier+ate
  vi+zier+ates
vi+zier+ial

vi+zier+ship
vi+zier+ships
vi+zor
vi+zors
vizs+la
vizs+las
Vlaar+ding+en
Vla+di+kav+kaz
Vla+di+mir
place name
Vladimir
personal name
Vla+di+vos+tok
Vlaminck
vlei
vleis
Vlis+sing+en
Vlo+në
Vlo+rë
Vl+ta+va
V-neck
adj.
V neck
V necks
V-necked
adj.
vo+cab
vo+cabs
vo+cable
vo+cables
vo+cably
vo+cabu+lary
vo+cabu+laries
vo+cal
vo+cals
vo+cal cords
vo+cal+ic
vo+cali+sa+tion
vo+cali+sa+
tions
vo+cal+ise
vo+cal+ises
vo+cal+ise
vo+cal+ises
vo+cal+is+ing
vo+cal+ised
vo+cal+is+er
vo+cal+is+ers
vo+cal+ism
vo+cal+isms
vo+cal+ist
vo+cal+ists
vo+cal+ity
vo+cal+ities
vo+cali+za+tion

vo+cali+za+
tions
vo+cal+ize
vo+cal+izes
vo+cal+iz+ing
vo+cal+ized
vo+cal+iz+er
vo+cal+iz+ers
vo+cal+ly
vo+ca+tion
vo+ca+tions
vo+ca+tion+al
voca+tive
voca+tives
vo+ces
vo+cif+er+ate
vo+cif+er+ates
vo+cif+er+at+
ing
vo+cif+er+at+ed
vo+cif+era+tion
vo+cif+era+
tions
vo+cif+er+ous
vo+cif+er+ous+ly
vo+cif+er+ous+
ness
vo+cod+er
vo+cod+ers
vod+ka
vod+kas
voe
voes
voet+sek
voets+toets
voets+toots
Vogel
Vogelweide
vogue
vogue+ing
voguish
voice
voices
voices
voic+ing
voiced
voiced
voice+less
voice+less+ly
voice-over
voice-overs
voice+print
voice+prints
voic+er
voic+ers

void
voids
voids
void+ing
void+ed
void+able
void+ance
void+ances
void+er
void+ers
voile
voiles
Voio+tia
Voi+vo+di+na
Voj+vo+di+na
vo+lant
vo+lar
vola+tile
vola+tiles
vola+tile+ness
vo+lati+lise
vo+lati+lises
vo+lati+lis+ing
vo+lati+lised
vola+til+ity
vo+lati+liz+able
vo+lati+liza+tion
vo+lati+lize
vo+lati+lizes
vo+lati+liz+ing
vo+lati+lized
vol-au-vent
vol-au-vents
vol+can+ic
vol+cani+cal+ly
vol+can+ic+ity
vol+can+ism
vol+ca+no
vol+ca+noes
or
vol+ca+nos
vol+cano+logi+
cal
vol+can+ol+ogy
vole
voles
Vol+ga
Vol+go+grad
voli+tant
vo+li+tion
vo+li+tions
vo+li+tion+al
voli+tive
vol+ley
vol+leys

vol+leys
vol+ley+ing
vol+leyed
volley+ball
volley+balls
vol+ley+er
vol+ley+ers
Vo+log+da
Vó+los
Volsung
volt
volts
vol+ta
vol+te
Vol+ta
in place names
Volta
surname
volt+age
volt+ages
vol+ta+ic
Voltaire
Vol+tair+ean
Vol+tair+eans
Vol+tair+ian
Vol+tair+ians
volt+am+eter
volt+am+eters
vol+ta+met+ric
volt+am+meter
volt+am+meters
volt-ampere
volt-amperes
Vol+ta Re+don+
da
volte
voltes
volte-face
volte-face
volt+me+ter
volt+me+ters
Vol+tur+no
vol+ubil+ity
vol+uble
vol+uble+ness
vol+ubly
vol+ume
vol+umes
volu+met+ric
volu+met+ri+cal+
ly
vo+lu+mi+nos+
ity
vo+lu+mi+nous

vo+lu+mi+nous+
ly
Völund
vol+un+tar+ily
vol+un+ta+rism
vol+un+ta+rist
vol+un+ta+rists
vol+un+tary
vol+un+taries
vol+un+tary+ism
vol+un+tary+ist
vol+un+tary+
ists
vol+un+teer
vol+un+teers
vol+un+teers
vol+un+teer+ing
vol+un+teered
vo+lup+tu+ary
vo+lup+tu+aries
vo+lup+tu+ous
vo+lup+tu+ous+
ly
vo+lup+tu+ous+
ness
vol+ute
vol+utes
vo+lut+ed
vo+lu+tion
vo+lu+tions
vo+mer
vo+mers
vom+it
vom+its
vom+it+ing
vom+it+ed
vom+it+er
vom+it+ers
vomi+tory
vomi+tories
von Braun
von Euler
von Laue
Vonnegut
von Rundstedt
von Stroheim
voo+doo
voo+doos
voo+doos
voo+doo+ing
voo+dooed
voo+doo+ist
voo+doo+ists
voor+kam+er

voor+kam+ers
Voor+trek+ker
Voor+trek+kers
vo+ra+cious
vo+ra+cious+
ness
vo+rac+ity
Vor+arl+berg
Vo+ro+nezh
Vo+ro+shi+lov+
grad
Vo+ro+shi+lovsk
Vorster
vor+tex
vor+texes *or*
vor+ti+ces
vor+ti+cal
vor+ti+cel+la
vor+ti+cel+lae
vor+ti+cism
vor+ti+cist
vor+ti+cists
Vortumnus
Vosges
vos+tro ac+count
vos+tro ac+
counts
vot+able
vo+tar+ess
vo+ta+rist
vo+ta+rists
vo+ta+ry
vo+ta+ries
vote
votes
votes
vot+ing
vot+ed
vot+er
vot+ers
vo+tive
vouch
vouches
vouch+ing
vouched
vouch+er
vouch+ers
vouch+safe
vouch+safes
vouch+saf+ing
vouch+safed
vous+soir
vous+soirs
vow

vows
vows
vow+ing
vowed
vow+el
vow+els
vow+eli+sa+tion
vow+eli+za+tion
vow+el+ise
vow+el+ises
vow+el+is+ing
vow+el+ised
vow+eli+za+tion
vow+el+ize
vow+el+izes
vow+el+iz+ing
vow+el+ized
vowel-like
vow+er
vow+ers
vox
vo+ces
vox pop
vox po+pu+li
voy+age
voy+ages
voy+ages
voy+ag+ing
voy+aged
voy+ag+er
voy+ag+ers
vo+ya+geur
vo+ya+geurs
vo+yeur
vo+yeurs
vo+yeur+ism
vo+yeur+is+tic
V-sign
V-signs
VTOL
Vuel+ta Aba+jo
vug
vugs
vug+gy
Vuillard
Vulcan
god
Vul+can
planet
vul+ca+nian
Vul+ca+nian
vul+cani+sa+tion
vul+can+ise
vul+can+ises

vul+can+is+ing
vul+can+ised
vul+can+ism
vul+can+ite
vul+cani+za+tion
vul+can+ize
vul+can+izes
vul+can+iz+ing
vul+can+ized
vul+cano+logi+
cal
vul+can+ol+ogy
vul+gar
vul+gar+ian
vul+gar+ians
vul+gari+sa+tion
vul+gar+ise
vul+gar+ises
vul+gar+is+ing
vul+gar+ised
vul+gar+ism
vul+gar+isms
vul+gar+ity
vul+gar+ities
vul+gari+za+tion
vul+gar+ize
vul+gar+izes
vul+gar+iz+ing
vul+gar+ized
vul+gar+ly
vul+gate
vul+gates
Vul+gate
vul+ner+abil+ity
vul+ner+abil+
ities
vul+ner+able
vul+ner+ably
vul+ner+ary
vul+ner+aries
vul+pine
vul+ture
vul+tures
vul+tur+ine
vul+tur+ous
vul+va
vul+vae *or*
vul+vas
vul+var
vul+vi+tis
Vyat+ka
Vy+borg
vy+ing
Vyshinsky

W

w
w's
W
W's *or*
Ws
WAAC
WAACs
Waadt
WAAF
WAAFs
Waal
Wa+bash
wab+ble
wab+bles
wab+bles
wab+bling
wab+bled
Wace
wacke
wackes
wacki+ly
wacki+ness
wacky
wacki+er
wacki+est
wad
wads
wads
wad+ding
wad+ded
wad+able
Wa+dai
Wad+den+zee
wad+ding
wad+dle
wad+dles
wad+dles
wad+dling
wad+dled
wad+dler
wad+dlers
wad+dling
wad+dy
wad+dies
wad+dies

wad+dy+ing
wad+died
wade
wades
wades
wad+ing
wad+ed
Wade
wade+able
wad+er
wad+ers
wad+ers
wadi
wadies
Wadi Hal+fa
Wad Me+da+ni
wady
wadies
wa+fer
wa+fers
wa+fers
wa+fer+ing
wa+fered
wa+fery
waf+fle
waf+fles
waf+fles
waf+fling
waf+fled
waf+fling
waf+flings
waft
wafts
wafts
waft+ing
waft+ed
wag
wags
wags
wag+ging
wagged
wage
wages
wages
wag+ing

waged
wage+less
wa+ger
wa+gers
wa+gers
wa+ger+ing
wa+gered
wa+ger+er
wa+ger+ers
wag+ga
wag+gas
Wag+ga Wag+ga
wag+gish
wag+gle
wag+gles
wag+gles
wag+gling
wag+gled
wag+gly
wag+gon
wag+gons
wag+gon+er
wag+gon+ers
wag+gon+ette
wag+gon+ettes
wag+gon+less
waggon+load
waggon+loads
Wagner
Wag+ne+rian
Wag+ne+rians
Wag+ner+ite
Wag+ner+ites
Wagner-Jauregg
wag+on
wag+ons
wag+on+er
wag+on+ers
wag+on+ette
wag+on+ettes
wag+on+less
wagon-lit
wagons-lits
wagon+load
wagon+loads

Wa+gram
wag+tail
wag+tails
Wa+ha+bi
Wa+ha+bis
Wa+ha+bism
Wah+ha+bi
Wah+ha+bis
Wah+ha+bism
wa+hi+ne
wa+hi+nes
wa+hoo
wa+hoos
wah-wah
wah-wahs
waif
waifs
waif+like
Wai+ka+re+mo+ana
Wai+ka+to
Wai+ki+ki
wail
wails
wails
wail+ing
wailed
wail+er
wail+ers
wain
wains
wain+scot
wain+scots
wain+scots
wain+scot+ing
wain+scot+ed
wain+scot+ing
wain+scot+ting
wain+wright
wain+wrights
waist
waists
waist+band
waist+bands
waist+coat

waist+coats
waist+coated
waist+less
waist+line
waist+lines
wait
waits
waits
wait+ing
wait+ed
wait-a-bit
wait-a-bits
Waite
wait+er
wait+ers
wait+ing
wait+ress
wait+resses
wait+resses
wait+ress+ing
wait+ressed
waive
waives
waiv+ing
waived
waiv+er
waiv+ers
Wajda
Wa+ka+ya+ma
wake
wakes
wakes
wak+ing
woke
woken
Wake+field
wake+ful
wake+ful+ly
wake+ful+ness
wak+en
wak+ens
wak+en+ing
wak+ened
wak+er
wak+ers
wake-robin
wake-robins
wake-up
Waksman
Wa+la+chia
Wa+la+chian
Wa+la+chians
Wal+brzych
Wal+che+ren

Walcott
Wal+den+burg
Wal+den+ses
Wal+den+sian
Wal+den+sians
Waldheim
wal+do
wal+dos *or*
wal+does
Wal+dorf
wald+ster+ben
wale
wales
wales
wal+ing
waled
Wales
Walesa
Wal+hall
Wal+hal+la
walk
walks
walks
walk+ing
walked
walk+able
walk+about
walk+abouts
walk+er
walk+ers
walkie-talkie
walkie-talkies
walk-in
walk+ing
Walk+man
Trademark
walk+out
walk+outs
walk out
verb
walk+over
walk+overs
walk over
verb
walk-through
walk-throughs
walk through
verb
walk+way
walk+ways
Wal+kyrie
Wal+kyries
walky-talky
walky-talkies
wall

walls
walls
wall+ing
walled
Wall
wal+la
wal+las
wal+la+by
wal+la+bies *or*
wal+la+by
Wal+la+by
Wal+la+bies
Wallace
Wal+la+chia
wal+lah
wal+lahs
wal+la+roo
wal+la+roos *or*
wal+la+roo
Wal+la+sey
wall+board
walled
Wallenberg
Wallenstein
Waller
wal+let
wal+lets
wall+eye
wall+eyes *or*
wall+eye
wall+eyed
wall+flower
wall+flowers
Wal+lis
place name
Wallis
surname
wall-less
Wal+loon
Wal+loons
wal+lop
wal+lops
wal+lops
wal+lop+ing
wal+loped
wal+lop+er
wal+lop+ers
wal+lop+ing
wal+lop+ings
wal+low
wal+lows
wal+lows
wal+low+ing
wal+lowed
wal+low+er

wal+low+ers
wall+paper
wall+papers
wall+papers
wall+papering
wall+papered
wall+poster
wall+posters
Walls+end
wall-to-wall
wal+ly
wal+lies
wal+nut
wal+nuts
Walpole
wal+rus
wal+ruses *or*
wal+rus
Wal+sall
Wal+sing+ham
place name
Walsingham
surname
Walter
Walton
waltz
waltzes
waltzes
waltz+ing
waltzed
waltz+er
waltz+ers
Wal+vis Bay
wam+pum
wan
wan+ner
wan+nest
Wan+chü+an
Wan-ch'uan
wand
wands
wan+der
wan+ders
wan+ders
wan+der+ing
wan+dered
wan+der+er
wan+der+ers
wan+der+ing
wan+der+ings
wan+der+lust
wan+deroo
wan+deroos
wan+doo
wan+doos

Wands+worth
wane
wanes
wanes
wan+ing
waned
wan+ey
Wan+ga+nui
wan+gle
wan+gles
wan+gles
wan+gling
wan+gled
wan+gler
wan+glers
Wan+hsien
Wan-Hsien
wank
wanks
wanks
wank+ing
wanked
wan+kel
wank+er
wank+ers
Wan+kie
wan+ly
wanna+be
wanna+bes
wanna+bee
wanna+bees
Wanne-Eickel
wan+ness
want
wants
wants
want+ing
want+ed
want+er
want+ers
want+ing
wan+ton
wan+tons
wan+tons
wan+ton+ing
wan+toned
wan+ton+ly
wan+ton+ness
Wan+xian
wany
wap+en+take
wap+en+takes
wapi+ti
wapi+tis
war

wars
wars
war+ring
warred
Wa+ran+gal
wa+ra+tah
wa+ra+tahs
Warbeck
war+ble
war+bles
war+bles
war+bling
war+bled
war+bler
war+blers
Warburg
ward
wards
wards
ward+ing
ward+ed
Ward
war+den
war+dens
war+der
war+ders
ward+less
war+dress
war+dresses
ward+robe
ward+robes
ward+room
ward+rooms
ward+ship
ward+ships
ware
wares
war+ing
war+ed
ware+house
ware+houses
ware+houses
ware+hous+ing
ware+housed
ware+house+
man
ware+house+
men
ware+hous+ing
ware+hous+ings
wares
war+fare
war+fa+rin
war+head
war+heads

Warhol
war+horse
war+horses
wari+ly
wari+ness
War+ley
war+like
war+lock
war+locks
Warlock
war+lord
war+lords
Warl+piri
warm
warms
warm+ing
warmed
warm+er
warm+est
warm-blooded
warm-blooded+
ness
warm-down
warm-downs
warm+er
warm+ers
warm-hearted
warm-hearted+ly
warm-hearted+
ness
warm+ing
warm+ish
warm+ly
warm+ness
war+monger
war+mongers
war+monger+ing
warmth
warm-up
warm-ups
warm up
verb
warn
warns
warn+ing
warned
warn+er
warn+ers
warn+ing
warn+ings
warn+ing+ly
warp
warps
warps
warp+ing

warped
warp+age
war+path
war+paths
warped
warp+er
warp+ers
war+plane
war+planes
war+rant
war+rants
war+rants
war+rant+ing
war+rant+ed
war+rant+abil+ity
war+rant+able
war+rant+ably
war+ran+tee
war+ran+tees
war+rant+er
war+rant+ers
war+ran+tor
war+ran+tors
war+ran+ty
war+ran+ties
war+ren
war+rens
War+ren
war+rig+al
war+rig+als
War+ring+ton
war+ri+or
war+ri+ors
War+saw
war+ship
war+ships
wart
warts
War+ta
Wart+burg
wart+hog
wart+hogs
war+time
warty
War+wick
place
Warwick
person
War+wick+shire
wary
wari+er
wari+est
was
wash
washes

washes	wasn't	watch+dog	water+fowl
wash+ing	wasp	watch+dogs	water+fowls
washed	wasps	watch+er	water+front
Wash	Wasp	watch+ers	water+fronts
wash+abil+ity	Wasps	watch+ful	Water+gate
wash+able	WASP	watch+ful+ly	Waterhouse
wash-and-wear	WASPs	watch+ful+ness	wa+ter+ing
wash+basin	waspi+ly	watch-glass	wa+ter+less
wash+basins	waspi+ness	watch-glasses	water+logged
wash+board	wasp+ish	watch+maker	Wa+ter+loo
wash+boards	wasp+ish+ly	watch+makers	water+man
wash+cloth	wasp+like	watch+making	water+men
wash+cloths	wasp-waisted	watch+man	water+man+ship
wash+day	waspy	watch+men	water+mark
wash+days	was+sail	watch+strap	water+marks
washed-out	was+sails	watch+straps	water+marks
washed-up	was+sails	watch+tower	water+mark+ing
wash+er	was+sail+ing	watch+towers	water+marked
wash+ers	was+sailed	watch+word	water+melon
washer+man	was+sail+er	watch+words	water+melons
washer+men	was+sail+ers	wa+ter	water+proof
washer+woman	Wassermann	wa+ters	water+proofs
washer+women	wast	wa+ters	water+proofs
wash+ery	Wast	wa+ter+ing	water+proof+
wash+eries	wast+age	wa+tered	ing
wash-hand	waste	water+borne	water+proofed
washi+ness	wastes	water+buck	water-repellent
wash+ing	wastes	water+bucks	water-resistant
wash+ings	wast+ing	water+color	Waters
Wash+ing+ton	wast+ed	*U.S.*	water+shed
place name	wast+ed	water+colors	water+sheds
Washington	waste+ful	water+color+ist	water+side
surname	waste+ful+ly	*U.S.*	water+sider
Wash+ing+to+	waste+ful+ness	water+color+	water+siders
nian	waste+land	ists	water-ski
Wash+ing+to+	waste+lands	water+colour	water-skis
nians	waste+paper	water+colours	water-skis
washing-up	wast+er	water+colour+ist	water-skiing
wash+out	wast+ers	water+colour+	water-skied *or*
wash+outs	wast+ing	ists	water-ski'd
wash out	wast+ing+ly	water-cool	water-skier
verb	wast+rel	water-cools	water-skiers
wash+room	wast+rels	water-cool+ing	water-skiing
wash+rooms	wat	water-cooled	water+spout
wash+stand	wats	water-cooled	water+spouts
wash+stands	wa+tap	water+course	water+tight
wash+tub	wa+taps	water+courses	water+way
wash+tubs	watch	water+craft	water+ways
wash+up	watches	water+cress	water+weed
noun	watches	watered-down	water+weeds
wash up	watch+ing	wa+ter+er	water+works
verb	watched	wa+ter+ers	water+worn
washy	watch+able	water+fall	wa+tery
washi+er	watch+case	water+falls	Wat+ford
washi+est	watch+cases	Wa+ter+ford	Watson

Watson-Watt	wavi+ly	way-out	weap+on+less
watt	wavi+ness	way+side	wea+pon+ry
watts	wavy	way+sides	wear
Watt	wavi+er	way+ward	wears
watt+age	wavi+est	way+ward+ly	wear+ing
watt+ages	wawl	way+ward+ness	wore
Watteau	wawls	way+worn	worn
Wat+ten+scheid	wawl+ing	Wa+ziri+stan	Wear
watt-hour	wawled	we	wear+abil+ity
watt-hours	wax	weak	wear+able
wat+tle	waxes	weak+er	wear+er
wat+tles	waxes	weak+est	wear+ers
wat+tles	wax+ing	weak+en	wea+ri+less
wat+tling	waxed	weak+ens	wea+ri+ly
wat+tled	wax+berry	weak+en+ing	wea+ri+ness
watt+meter	wax+berries	weak+ened	wear+ing
watt+meters	wax+bill	weak+en+er	wear+ing+ly
Watts	wax+bills	weak+en+ers	wea+ri+some
Waugh	wax+en	weak+ish	wea+ri+some+ly
waul	wax+er	weak-kneed	wea+ry
wauls	wax+ers	weak-kneedly	wea+ries
waul+ing	wax+eye	weak+ling	wea+ry+ing
wauled	wax+eyes	weak+lings	wea+ried
wave	waxi+ly	weak+ly	wea+ri+er
waves	waxi+ness	weak+li+er	wea+ri+est
waves	wax+plant	weak+li+est	wea+ry+ing
wav+ing	wax+plants	weak-minded	wea+ry+ing+ly
waved	wax+wing	weak-minded+ly	wea+sand
wave+band	wax+wings	weak-minded+	wea+sands
wave+bands	wax+work	ness	wea+sel
wave+form	wax+works	weak+ness	wea+sel or
wave+forms	waxy	weak+nesses	wea+sels
wave+front	waxi+er	weal	wea+sels
wave+fronts	waxi+est	weals	wea+sel+ling or
wave+guide	way	weald	wea+sel+ing
wave+guides	ways	wealds	U.S.
wave+length	way+bill	Weald	wea+selled or
wave+lengths	way+bills	wealth	wea+seled
wave+less	way+farer	wealthi+ly	U.S.
wave+let	way+farers	wealthi+ness	wea+sel+ly
wave+lets	way+faring	wealthy	weath+er
wave+like	way+farings	wealthi+er	weath+ers
Wavell	Way+land	wealthi+est	weath+er+ing
wa+ver	way+lay	wean	weath+ered
wa+vers	way+lays	weans	weather-beaten
wa+vers	way+lay+ing	weans	weather+board
wa+ver+ing	way+laid	wean+ing	weather+boards
wa+vered	way+lay+er	weaned	weather+
wa+ver+er	way+lay+ers	wean+er	boarding
wa+ver+ers	way+leave	wean+ers	weather-bound
wa+ver+ing	way+leaves	wean+ling	weather+cock
wa+ver+ing+ly	way+mark	wean+lings	weather+cocks
wa+vey	way+marks	weap+on	weath+ered
wa+veys	way+marked	weap+ons	weath+er+er
	Wayne	weap+oned	weath+er+ers

weather+glass
weather+
  glasses
weath+er+ing
weath+er+li+
  ness
weath+er+ly
weather+man
weather+men
weather+proof
weather+proofs
weather+proof+
  ing
weather+
  proofed
weather-wise
weather+worn
weave
  weaves
  weaves
weav+ing
wove *or*
weaved
wo+ven *or*
weaved
weav+er
  weav+ers
weaver+bird
  weaver+birds
web
  webs
  webs
web+bing
webbed
Webb
webbed
web+bing
  web+bings
web+by
  web+bi+er
  web+bi+est
we+ber
  we+bers
Weber
Webern
web+foot
  web+feet
web-footed
web+less
Webster
web-toed
web+wheel
  web+wheels
wed
  weds

wed+ding
wed+ded *or*
  wed
we'd
wed+ded
wed+ding
  wed+dings
Wedekind
wedge
  wedges
  wedges
wedg+ing
  wedged
wedge+like
wedge-tailed
Wedg+wood
  Trademark
wedgy
  wedgi+er
  wedgi+est
wed+lock
Wednes+day
wee
  weer
  weest
wee
  wees
  wees
wee+ing
weed
weed
  weeds
  weeds
weed+ing
weed+ed
weed+er
  weed+ers
weed+killer
  weed+killers
weed+less
  weeds
weedy
  weedi+er
  weedi+est
week
  weeks
week+day
  week+days
week+end
  week+ends
  week+ends
week+end+ing
week+end+ed
  week+ends
week+ly

week+lies
week+night
  week+nights
Weelkes
ween
  weens
ween+ing
  weened
wee+ny
  wee+ni+er
  wee+ni+est
weeny-bopper
  weeny-boppers
weep
  weeps
weep+ing
  wept
weep+er
  weep+ers
weepi+ly
weepi+ness
weep+ing
weep+ing+ly
weepy
  weepies
  weepi+er
  weepi+est
wee+ver
  wee+vers
wee+vil
  wee+vils
wee+vily
wee-wee
  wee-wees
  wee-wees
  wee-weeing
  wee-weed
weft
Wegener
Weichsel
wei+ge+la
  wei+ge+las
weigh
  weighs
weigh+ing
  weighed
weigh+able
weigh+bridge
  weigh+bridges
weigh+er
  weigh+ers
weigh-in
  weigh-ins
weigh in
  verb

weight
  weights
  weights
weight+ing
weight+ed
weight+ed
weight+er
  weight+ers
weighti+ly
weighti+ness
weight+ing
  weight+ings
weight+less
weight+less+
  ness
weight+lifter
  weight+lifters
weight+lifting
weighty
  weighti+er
  weighti+est
Wei+hai
  Wei-hai
Weil
Weill
Weil's dis+ease
Wei+mar
Wei+mar+an+er
  Wei+mar+an+
  ers
Weinberg
weir
  weirs
weird
  weirds
weird+er
  weird+est
weir+die
  weir+dies
weird+ly
weird+ness
weir+do
  weir+dos
Weis+mann+ism
Weisshorn
Weissmuller
Weizmann
weka
  wekas
welch
  welches
welch+ing
  welched
Welch
welch+er

welch+ers
wel+come
  wel+comes
  wel+comes
  wel+com+ing
wel+comed
wel+come+ly
wel+com+er
  wel+com+ers
weld
  welds
  welds
  weld+ing
  weld+ed
Weld
weld+abil+ity
weld+able
weld+er
  weld+ers
Weldon
wel+dor
  wel+dors
wel+fare
wel+kin
Wel+kom
well
  bet+ter
  best
well
  wells
  wells
  well+ing
  welled
we'll
well-accept+ed
well-accustomed
well-acknowledged
well-acquaint+ed
well-acted
well-adapted
well-adjust+ed
well-adminis+tered
well-advertised
well-advised
well-affect+ed
well-aimed
well-aired
well-applied
well-appoint+ed
well-argued
well-armed
well-arranged
well-assort+ed

well-assured
well-attend+ed
well-attest+ed
well-authenti+cat+ed
well-aware
well+away
well-balanced
well-behaved
well+being
well-beloved
  well-beloveds
well-blessed
well-bred
well-built
well-calculat+ed
well-chosen
well-clothed
well-compensat+ed
well-concealed
well-conditioned
well-conduct+ed
well-confirmed
well-connect+ed
well-considered
well-construct+ed
well-content+ed
well-controlled
well-cooked
well-covered
well-cultivat+ed
well-defend+ed
well-defined
well-demonstrat+ed
well-described
well-deserved
well-developed
well-devised
well-digest+ed
well-disciplined
well-disposed
well-document+ed
well-done
well-dressed
well-earned
well-educat+ed
well-employed
well-endowed
well-equipped
Welles
Wellesley

well-established
well-esteemed
well-favoured
well-fed
well-financed
well-finished
well-fitted
well-formed
well-fortified
well-fought
well-found
well-founded
well-furnished
well-governed
well-groomed
well-grounded
well-guarded
well-handled
well+head
  well+heads
well-heeled
well-hidden
well-housed
wel+lies
well-illustrat+ed
well-inclined
well-informed
Wel+ling+bor+ough
Wel+ling+ton
place
Wellington
person
wel+ling+ton+ia
  wel+ling+ton+ias
wel+ling+tons
well-intentioned
well-judged
well-justified
well-kept
well-knit
well-known
well-liked
well-loved
well-made
well-managed
well-mannered
well-marked
well-matched
well-meaning
well-merited
well-mixed
well-motivat+ed
well-nigh

well-noted
well-off
well-oiled
well-ordered
well-organised
well-organized
well-paid
well-phrased
well-placed
well-planned
well-played
well-pleased
well-practised
well-prepared
well-preserved
well-proportioned
well-protect+ed
well-provid+ed
well-qualified
well-read
well-reasoned
well-received
well-recommend+ed
well-regard+ed
well-regulat+ed
well-rehearsed
well-remembered
well-represent+ed
well-respect+ed
well-reviewed
well-ripened
well-rounded
Wells
well-satisfied
well-schooled
well-seasoned
well-secured
well-shaped
well-situat+ed
well-spent
well-spoken
well+spring
  well+springs
well-stacked
well-stocked
well-suited
well-supplied
well-support+ed
well-taught
well-tempered
well-thought-of
well-thumbed
well-timed

well-to-do
well-trained
well-travelled
well-treated
well-tried
well-trodden
well-turned
well-understood
well-upholstered
well-used
well-wisher
 well-wishers
well-wishing
well-woman
 well-women
well-worn
well-written
well-wrought
Wels
welsh
 welshes
welsh+ing
welshed
Welsh
welsh+er
 welsh+ers
Welsh+man
 Welsh+men
Welsh+woman
 Welsh+women
welt
 welts
 welts
welt+ing
welt+ed
wel+ter
wel+ters
wel+ters
wel+ter+ing
wel+tered
wel+ter+weight
wel+ter+
 weights
Wel+wyn
Wem+bley
wen
 wens
Wenceslas
Wenceslaus
wench
 wenches
 wenches
wench+ing
wenched
wench+er

wench+ers
Wen-chou
Wen+chow
wend
 wends
wend+ing
wend+ed
Wend
 Wends
Wen+dy
wens+ley+dale
 wens+ley+dales
went
wen+tle+trap
 wen+tle+traps
Wentworth
Wen+zhou
wept
were
we're
were+gild
 were+gilds
weren't
were+wolf
 were+wolves
wer+geld
 wer+gelds
wer+gild
 wer+gilds
Werner
wert
We+ser
We+ser+mün+de
Wesker
wes+kit
Wesley
Wes+ley+an
 Wes+ley+ans
Wes+ley+an+ism
Wes+sex
west
West
west+bound
west+er+ing
West+er+lies
west+er+li+ness
west+er+ly
 west+er+lies
west+ern
West+ern
 West+erns
west+ern+er
west+ern+ers
west+erni+sa+
 tion

west+ern+ise
west+ern+ises
west+ern+is+
 ing
west+ern+ised
west+erni+za+
 tion
west+ern+ize
west+ern+izes
west+ern+iz+ing
west+ern+ized
west+ern+most
West+fa+len
west+ing
 west+ings
West+meath
West+min+ster
West+mor+land
west-northwest
Weston-super-
 Mare
West+pha+lia
West+pha+lian
 West+pha+lians
west-southwest
west+ward
west+ward+ly
wet
 wets
 wets
wet+ting
wet or
wet+ted
wet+ter
wet+test
weth+er
 weth+ers
wet+land
 wet+lands
wet+ly
wet+ness
wet-nurse
 wet-nurses
wet-nursing
wet-nursed
wet nurse
 wet nurses
wet+table
wet+ter
 wet+ters
Wet+ter+horn
wet+ting
wet+tish
we've
Wex+ford

Wey+mouth
whack
 whacks
 whacks
whack+ing
whacked
whack+er
 whack+ers
whack+ing
whacky
whacki+er
whacki+est
whale
 whales or
 whale
 whales
whal+ing
whaled
whale+boat
 whale+boats
whale+bone
 whale+bones
whal+er
 whal+ers
whal+ing
wham
 whams
 whams
wham+ming
whammed
wha+nau
 wha+naus
whang
 whangs
 whangs
whang+ing
whanged
Whanga+rei
whangee
 whangees
whare
 whares
whare+puni
 whare+punis
wharf
 wharves or
 wharfs
 wharfs
wharf+ing
wharfed
wharf+age
 wharf+ages
wharfie
 wharfies
wharf+in+ger

wharf+in+gers
Wharton
wharve
  wharves
what
what+ev+er
what+not
  what+nots
whats+her+name
whats+his+name
whats+it
  whats+its
whats+its+name
what+so+ev+er
whaup
  whaups
wheal
  wheals
wheat
  wheats
wheat+ear
  wheat+ears
wheat+en
wheat+meal
Wheatstone
whee
whee+dle
  whee+dles
  whee+dling
  whee+dled
whee+dler
  whee+dlers
whee+dling
whee+dling+ly
wheel
  wheels
  wheels
  wheel+ing
  wheeled
wheel+barrow
  wheel+barrows
wheel+base
  wheel+bases
wheel+chair
  wheel+chairs
wheeled
wheel+er
  wheel+ers
Wheeler
wheeler-dealer
  wheeler-dealers
wheel+house
  wheel+houses
wheelie
  wheelies

wheels
wheel+wright
  wheel+wrights
wheeze
  wheezes
  wheezes
  wheez+ing
  wheezed
  wheez+er
  wheez+ers
  wheezi+ly
  wheezi+ness
  wheezy
  wheezi+er
  wheezi+est
whelk
  whelks
  whelky
whelm
  whelms
  whelm+ing
  whelmed
whelp
  whelps
  whelps
  whelp+ing
  whelped
when
  whens
when+as
whence
whence+so+ever
when+ever
when+so+ever
whenua
where
  wheres
where+abouts
where+as
where+at
where+by
where+fore
  where+fores
where+from
where+in
where+of
where+on
where+so+ever
where+to
where+upon
wher+ever
where+with
where+with+al
wher+ry
  wher+ries

wherry+man
wherry+men
whet
  whets
  whets
whet+ting
whet+ted
wheth+er
whet+stone
  whet+stones
whet+ter
  whet+ters
whew
whey
whey+face
  whey+faces
whey+faced
which
which+ever
which+so+ever
whick+er
  whick+ers
  whick+er+ing
  whick+ered
whid+ah
  whid+ahs
whiff
  whiffs
  whiffs
whiff+ing
  whiffed
whif+fle
  whif+fles
  whif+fling
  whif+fled
whif+fle+tree
  whif+fle+trees
Whig
  Whigs
Whig+gery
Whig+gish
Whig+gism
while
  whiles
  whiled
  whil+ing
  whiles
whi+lom
whilst
whim
  whims
whim+brel
  whim+brels
whim+per
  whim+pers

whim+pers
whim+per+ing
whim+pered
whim+per+er
  whim+per+ers
whim+per+ing
  whim+per+ings
whim+per+ing+ly
whim+sey
  whim+seys
whim+si+er
whim+si+est
whim+si+cal
whim+si+cal+ity
whim+si+cal+
  ities
whim+si+cal+ly
whim+sy
  whim+sies
whim+si+er
whim+si+est
whin
whin+chat
  whin+chats
whine
  whines
  whines
whin+ing
  whined
whin+er
  whin+ers
whinge
  whinges
  whinges
whinge+ing
  whinged
whinge+ing
  whinge+ings
whin+ing
whin+ing+ly
whin+ny
  whin+nies
  whin+nies
whin+ny+ing
  whin+nied
whin+stone
whiny
whini+er
whini+est
whip
  whips
  whips
whip+ping
  whipped
whip+cord

whip+cords
whip+lash
whip+lashes
whip+like
whip+pers
whipper-in
whippers-in
whip+per+snap+
    per
whip+per+snap+
    pers
whip+pet
whip+pets
whip+ping
whip+pings
whip+ple+tree
whip+ple+trees
whip+poor+will
whip+poor+wills
whip-round
whip-rounds
whip round
verb
whips
whip+saw
whip+saws
whip+saws
whip+saw+ing
whip+sawed
whip+sawed
    or
whip+sawn
whip+stitch
whip+stitches
whip+stock
whip+stocks
whir
whirs
whirs
whir+ring
whirred
whirl
whirls
whirls
whirl+ing
whirled
whirl+er
whirl+ers
whirli+gig
whirli+gigs
whirl+ing
whirl+ing+ly
whirl+pool
whirl+pools

whirl+wind
whirl+winds
whirly+bird
whirly+birds
whirr
whirrs
whirrs
whirr+ing
whirred
whish
whishes
whisht
whisk
whisks
whisks
whisk+ing
whisked
whisk+er
whisk+ers
whisk+ered
whisk+ery
whis+key
whis+keys
whis+ky
whis+kies
whis+per
whis+pers
whis+pers
whis+per+ing
whis+pered
whis+per+er
whis+per+ers
whis+per+ing
whist
whis+tle
whis+tles
whis+tles
whis+tling
whis+tled
whistle-blower
whistle-blowers
whis+tler
whis+tlers
Whistler
whistle-stop
adj.
whis+tle stop
whis+tle stops
whit
Whit
Whits
Whitaker
Whitbread
Whit+by

white
whites
whites
whit+ing
whit+ed
whit+er
whit+est
White
Whites
white+bait
white+bait
white+beam
white+beams
white+cap
white+caps
white-collar
whit+ed
white+damp
white-eye
white-eyes
Whitefield
white+fish
species
white+fish or
white+fishes
white fish
edible marine fish
in general
white+fly
white+flies
White+hall
Whitehead
White+horse
white-hot
white-knuckle
Whitelaw
white-livered
white+ly
whit+en
whit+ens
whit+en+ing
whit+ened
whit+en+er
whit+en+ers
white+ness
whit+en+ing
white+out
noun
white out
verb
whites
white-slaver
white-slavers
white+thorn
white+thorns

white+throat
white+throats
white+wall
white+walls
white+wash
white+washes
white+washes
white+wash+ing
white+washed
white+wash+er
white+wash+ers
white+wood
white+woods
whit+ey
whit+eys
whith+er
whither+so+ever
whit+ing
whit+ings
whit+ish
Whitlam
Whit+ley
whit+low
whit+lows
Whitman
Whit+ney
mountain
Whitney
surname
Whit+sun
Whit+suns
Whit+sun+day
Scots
Whit+sun+days
Whit+sun+tide
Whit+sun+tides
Whittier
Whittington
whit+tle
whit+tles
whit+tling
whit+tled
Whittle
whity
whities
whiz
whiz+zes
whiz+zes
whiz+zing
whizzed
whiz-bang
whiz-bangs
whizz
whizzes
whizzes

whizz+ing	whooshes	wick+et	wield+ers
whizzed	whoosh+ing	wick+ets	wieldy
whizz-bang	whooshed	wicket+keeper	wieldi+er
whizz-bangs	whop	wicket+keepers	wieldi+est
who	whops	wicki+up	Wien
Who	whops	wicki+ups	wie+ner
WHO	whop+ping	Wickliffe	wie+ners
whoa	whopped	Wick+low	Wiener
who-does-what	whop+per	wicky+up	Wie+ner Neu+
who+dun+it	whop+pers	wicky+ups	stadt
who+dun+its	whop+ping	Wiclif	Wie+ner schnit+
who+dun+nit	whore	wid+der+shins	zel
who+dun+nits	whores	wide	Wie+ner schnit+
who+ever	whores	wides	zels
whole	whor+ing	wid+er	wiener+wurst
wholes	whored	wid+est	wiener+wursts
whole+food	whore+dom	wide-angle	Wies+ba+den
whole+foods	whore+house	wide-awake	Wiesel
whole+hearted	whore+houses	wide-awakes	Wiesenthal
whole+hearted+	whore+monger	wide-body	wife
ly	whore+mongers	wide-eyed	wives
whole+meal	whore+mongery	wide+ly	wife+hood
whole+ness	whore+son	wid+en	wife+ly
whole+sale	whore+sons	wid+ens	wig
whole+sales	whor+ish	wid+en+ing	wigs
whole+sal+ing	whorl	wid+ened	wigs
whole+saled	whorls	wid+en+er	wig+ging
whole+sal+er	whorled	wid+en+ers	wigged
whole+sal+ers	whortle+berry	wide+ness	Wig+an
whole+some	whortle+berries	wide-open	wig+eon
whole+some+ly	who's	wide+spread	wig+eons
whole+some+	whose	widg+eon	wigged
ness	who+so	widg+eons	wig+ging
whole-tone	who+so+ever	widg+et	wig+gings
adj.	why	widg+ets	wig+gle
whole tone	whys	wid+ish	wig+gles
whole tones	Why+al+la	Wid+nes	wig+gles
whole-wheat	whyd+ah	wid+ow	wig+gling
who'll	whyd+ahs	wid+ows	wig+gled
whol+ly	wic+ca	wid+ows	wig+gler
whom	Wic+ca	wid+ow+ing	wig+glers
whom+ever	Wichi+ta	wid+owed	wig+gly
whoop	wick	wid+ow+er	wig+gli+er
whoops	wicks	wid+ow+ers	wig+gli+est
whoops	Wick	wid+ow+hood	wight
whoop+ing	wick+ed	wid+ow's	wights
whooped	wick+ed+er	width	Wight
whoo+pee	wick+ed+est	widths	wig+less
whoo+pees	wick+ed+ly	Wieland	Wigner
whoop+er	wick+ed+ness	wield	Wig+town+shire
whoop+ers	wick+ed+	wields	wig+wag
whoop+ing	nesses	wield+ing	wig+wags
whoops	wick+er	wield+ed	wig+wags
whoosh	wick+ers	wield+able	wig+wag+ging
whooshes	wicker+work	wield+er	wig+wagged

wig+wag+ger
wig+wag+gers
wig+wam
wig+wams
wiki+up
wiki+ups
Wilberforce
wil+co
wild
wilds
wild+er
wild+est
wild+cat
wild+cats *or*
wild+cat
wild+cats
wild+cat+ting
wild+cat+ted
wild+cat+ter
wild+cat+ters
wild+cat+ting
Wilde
wil+de+beest
wil+de+beests
or
wil+de+beest
wil+der
wil+ders
wil+der+ing
wil+dered
Wilder
wil+der+ness
wil+der+nesses
Wil+der+ness
wild-eyed
wild+fire
wild+fowl
wild+fowls
wild+fowl+er
wild+fowl+ers
wild+fowl+ing
wild-goose
wild+ing
wild+ings
wild+ish
wild+life
wild+ly
wild+ness
wild+wood
wild+woods
wile
wiles
wiles
wil+ing
wiled

wil+ful
wil+ful+ly
wil+ful+ness
Wil+helms+ha+
  ven
Wil+helm+stras+
  se
wili+ness
wili+nesses
Wilkes
Wilkins
will
wills
wills
will+ing
willed
willed
Wil+lem+stad
will+er
will+ers
wil+let
wil+lets
will+ful
U.S.
will+ful+ly
U.S.
will+ful+ness
U.S.
William
Williams
Wil+liams+burg
Williamson
wil+lie
wil+lies
wil+lies
will+ing
will+ing+ly
will+ing+ness
Willis
wil+li+waw
wil+li+waws
will-o'-the-wisp
will-o'-the-wisps
wil+low
wil+lows
wil+low+herb
wil+low+herbs
wil+lowy
will+power
Wills
wil+ly
wil+lies
willy-nilly
willy-willy
willy-willies

Wil+ming+ton
Wil+no
Wilson
Trademark
wilt
wilts
wilts
wilt+ing
wilt+ed
Wil+ton
Wil+tons
Wilt+shire
wily
wili+er
wili+est
wim+ble
wim+bles
wim+bles
wim+bling
wim+bled
Wim+ble+don
wimp
wimps
wimps
wimp+ing
wimped
WIMP
wimp+ish
wim+ple
wim+ples
wim+ples
wim+pling
wim+pled
wimpy
wimpi+er
wimpi+est
Wimpy
Trademark
Wimpies
win
wins
wins
win+ning
won
wince
winces
winces
winc+ing
winced
winc+er
winc+ers
win+cey+ette
winch
winches
winches
winch+ing

winched
Win+ches+ter
Trademark
Winckelmann
wind
current of air
  winds
  winds
  wind+ing
  wind+ed
wind
coil or twist
  winds
  winds
  wind+ing
  wound
wind
blow bugle etc.
  winds
  wind+ing
  wind+ed *or*
  wound
wind+able
wind+age
wind+ages
wind+bag
wind+bags
wind+blown
wind-borne
wind-bound
wind+break
wind+breaks
wind+burn
wind+cheater
wind+cheaters
wind-chill
wind+ed
wind+er
wind+ers
Win+der+mere
wind+fall
wind+falls
wind+flower
wind+flowers
Wind+hoek
wind+hover
wind+hovers
windi+ly
windi+ness
wind+ing
wind+ings
wind+ing+ly
winding-up
wind+jam+mer
wind+jam+mers

wind+lass
wind+lasses
wind+lasses
wind+lass+ing
wind+lassed
wind+less
win+dle+straw
win+dle+straws
wind+mill
wind+mills
wind+mills
wind+mill+ing
wind+milled
win+dow
win+dows
win+dows
win+dow+ing
win+dowed
window-dresser
window-dressers
window-dressing
window+pane
window+panes
window-shop
window-shops
window-shopping
window-shopped
window-shopper
window-shoppers
window-shopping
window+sill
window+sills
wind+pipe
wind+pipes
wind+row
wind+rows
Wind+scale
wind+screen
wind+screens
wind+shield
wind+shields
wind+sock
wind+socks
Wind+sor
place name
Windsor
surname
wind+storm
wind+storms
wind+sucker

wind+suckers
wind-sucking
wind+surfing
wind+swept
wind-up
wind-ups
wind up
verb
wind+ward
Wind+ward
windy
windi+er
windi+est
wine
wines
wines
win+ing
wined
wine+bibber
wine+bibbers
wine+bibbing
wine+glass
wine+glasses
wine+less
wine+press
wine+presses
win+ery
win+eries
wine+skin
wine+skins
wing
wings
wings
wing+ing
winged
Wingate
wing-case
wing-cases
wing+ding
wing+dings
winged
wing+er
wing+ers
wing+less
wing+like
wing+man
wing+men
wing+span
wing+spans
wing+spread
wing+spreads
wink
winks
winks
wink+ing

winked
wink+er
wink+ers
win+kle
win+kles
win+kles
win+kling
win+kled
winkle-pickers
win+nable
Win+ne+ba+go
Win+ne+ba+
  gos *or*
Win+ne+ba+go
win+ner
win+ners
win+ning
win+nings
win+ning+ly
win+ning+ness
Win+ni+peg
Win+ni+peg+ger
Win+ni+peg+
  gers
Win+ni+pego+sis
win+now
win+nows
win+nows
win+now+ing
win+nowed
win+now+er
win+now+ers
wino
winos
win+some
win+some+ly
Winston-Salem
win+ter
win+ters
win+ters
win+ter+ing
win+tered
win+ter+er
win+ter+ers
winter+green
win+teri+sa+tion
win+teri+sa+
  tions
win+ter+ise
win+ter+ises
win+ter+is+ing
win+ter+ised
win+teri+za+tion
win+teri+za+
  tions

win+ter+ize
win+ter+izes
win+ter+iz+ing
win+ter+ized
win+ter+less
Win+ter+thur
winter+time
winter+times
winter+weight
win+tery
win+tri+er
win+tri+est
win+tri+ly
win+tri+ness
win+try
win+tri+er
win+tri+est
winy
wini+er
wini+est
wipe
wipes
wipes
wip+ing
wiped
wipe+out
wipe+outs
wipe out
verb
wip+er
wip+ers
wire
wires
wires
wir+ing
wired
wire+draw
wire+draws
wire+draw+ing
wire+drew
wire+drawn
wire-gauge
wire-gauges
wire-guided
wire-haired
wire+less
wire+lesses
wire+lesses
wire+less+ing
wire+lessed
wire+like
wire+puller
wire+pullers
wire+pulling
wire+pullings

wire+tap
wire+taps
wire+tapping
wire+tapped
wire+tapper
wire+tappers
wire+work
wire+works
wire+works
wire+works
wire+worm
wire+worms
wiri+ly
wiri+ness
wir+ing
Wir+ral
wiry
wiri+er
wiri+est
wis
wisses
wis+sing
wist
Wisbech
Wis+con+sin
Wis+con+sin+ite
Wis+con+sin+ites
Wisden
wis+dom
wis+doms
wise
wises
wis+ing
wised
wis+er
wis+est
wisea+cre
wisea+cres
wise+crack
wise+cracks
wise+cracks
wise+crack+ing
wise+cracked
wise+crack+er
wise+crack+ers
wise+ly
Wiseman
wise+ness
wi+sent
wi+sents
wish
wishes
wishes
wish+ing

wished
wish+bone
wish+bones
wish+er
wish+ers
wish+ful
wish+ful+ly
wish+ful+ness
wishy-washy
Wis+la+ny Za+
lew
Wis+mar
wisp
wisps
wisp+like
wispy
wispi+er
wispi+est
wist
wis+te+ria
wis+te+rias
wist+ful
wist+ful+ly
wist+ful+ness
wit
wits
wit+ting
wot
wist
wit+an
wit+ans
witch
witches
witches
witch+ing
witched
witch+craft
witch-elm
witch-elms
witch+ery
witch+eries
witches'-broom
witches'-
brooms
witch+et+ty
witch+et+ties
witch+ety
witch+eties
witch-hunt
witch-hunts
witch-hunting
witch+ing
witch+ing+ly
witch+like
wit+ena+gemot

wit+ena+
gemots
with
with+al
with+draw
with+draws
with+draw+ing
with+drew
with+drawn
with+draw+al
with+draw+als
with+draw+er
with+draw+ers
with+draw+ing
with+drawn
withe
withes
withes
with+ing
withed
with+er
with+ers
with+er+ing
with+ered
with+er+er
with+er+ers
with+er+ing+ly
with+ers
with+er+shins
with+hold
with+holds
with+hold+ing
with+held
with+hold+er
with+hold+ers
with+in
with+out
with+stand
with+stands
with+stand+ing
with+stood
with+stand+er
with+stand+ers
withy
withies
wit+less
wit+less+ly
wit+less+ness
wit+ling
wit+lings
wit+ness
wit+nesses
wit+nesses
wit+ness+ing
wit+nessed

wit+ness+er
wit+ness+ers
wits
Witt
Wit+ten+berg
wit+ter
wit+ters
wit+ter+ing
wit+tered
Wittgenstein
Witt+gen+steini+
an
wit+ti+cism
wit+ti+cisms
wit+ti+ly
wit+ti+ness
wit+ting
wit+ting+ly
wit+ty
wit+ti+er
wit+ti+est
Wit+wa+ters+
rand
wive
wives
wiv+ing
wived
wi+vern
wi+verns
wives
wiz
wiz+zes
wiz+ard
wiz+ards
wiz+ard+ly
wiz+ard+ry
wiz+en
wiz+ens
wiz+en+ing
wiz+ened
wiz+ened
woad
wob+be+gong
wob+be+gongs
wob+ble
wob+bles
wob+bles
wob+bling
wob+bled
wob+bler
wob+blers
wob+bli+ness
wob+bly
wob+blies
wob+bli+er

wob+bli+est
Wodan
Wodehouse
Woden
wodge
  wodges
woe
  woes
woe+be+gone
woe+ful
woe+ful+ly
woe+ful+ness
wog
  wogs
wog+gle
  wog+gles
Wöhler
wok
  woks
woke
wok+en
Wo+king
wold
Wolds
wolf
  wolves
  wolfs
  wolf+ing
  wolfed
Wolf
Wolfe
wolf+fish
  wolf+fish or
  wolf+fishes
wolf+hound
  wolf+hounds
wolf+ish
Wolfit
wolf+like
wolf+ram
wolf+ram+ite
Wolfram von
  Eschenbach
wolfs+bane
wolf's-bane
Wolfs+burg
wolf-whistle
  wolf-whistles
  wolf-whistling
  wolf-whistled
  wolf whis+tle
  wolf whis+tles
Wol+lon+gong
Wollstonecraft
Wol+of

Wol+of or
Wol+ofs
Wolsey
Wol+ver+hamp+
  ton
wol+ver+ine
wol+ver+ines
wolves
wom+an
wom+en
wom+ans
wom+an+ing
wom+aned
wom+an+hood
wom+an+ise
wom+an+ises
wom+an+is+ing
wom+an+ised
wom+an+is+er
wom+an+is+ers
wom+an+ish
wom+an+ish+ly
wom+an+ish+
  ness
wom+an+ize
wom+an+izes
wom+an+iz+ing
wom+an+ized
wom+an+iz+er
wom+an+iz+ers
wom+an+kind
wom+an+less
woman-like
wom+an+ly
womb
  wombs
wom+bat
  wom+bats
wombed
womb+like
wom+en
wom+en+folk
Wom+en's
wom+era
  wom+eras
won
won+der
  won+ders
  won+ders
  won+der+ing
  won+dered
Wonder
won+der+er
won+der+ers
won+der+ful

won+der+ful+ly
wonder+land
  wonder+lands
won+der+ment
  won+der+ments
wonder+work
  wonder+works
wonder-worker
  wonder-workers
wonder-working
  wonder-
    workings
won+drous
won+drous+ly
won+drous+ness
won+ky
  won+ki+er
  won+ki+est
wont
  wonts
  wont+ing
  wont+ed
won't
wont+ed
woo
  woos
  woo+ing
  wooed
wood
  woods
  woods
  wood+ing
  wood+ed
Wood
wood+bine
wood+carver
  wood+carvers
wood+carving
  wood+carvings
wood+chuck
  wood+chucks
wood+cock
  wood+cocks
wood+craft
wood+cut
  wood+cuts
wood+cutter
  wood+cutters
  wood+cutting
wood+ed
wood+en
wooden+head
  wooden+heads
wooden+headed

wooden+headed+
  ness
wood+en+ly
wood+grouse
  wood+grouse
    or
  wood+grouses
woodi+ness
wood+land
  wood+lands
wood+lander
  wood+landers
wood+lark
  wood+larks
wood+louse
  wood+lice
wood+man
  wood+men
wood+note
  wood+notes
wood+pecker
  wood+peckers
wood+pile
  wood+piles
wood+ruff
  wood+ruffs
  woods
Woods
wood+screw
  wood+screws
wood+shed
  wood+sheds
woods+man
  woods+men
Wood+stock
Woodward
wood+wind
wood+work
wood+worker
  wood+workers
wood+working
wood+worm
  wood+worms
woody
woodi+er
woodi+est
wood+yard
  wood+yards
woo+er
  woo+ers
woof
  woofs
  woofs
  woof+ing
  woofed

woof+er
woof+ers
woo+ing
Wookey Hole
wool
wools
wool+en
U.S.
wool+ens
Woolf
wool+fell
wool+fells
wool+gather+ing
wool+grower
wool+growers
wool+growing
woolled
wool+len
wool+lens
Woolley
wool-like
wool+li+ly
wool+li+ness
wool+ly
wool+li+er
wool+li+est
woolly-butt
woolly-butts
woolly-minded
wool+pack
wool+packs
wool+sack
wool+sacks
wool+shed
wool+sheds
Woolworth
wooly
U.S.
wooli+er
wooli+est
woom+era
woom+eras
Woom+era
Woop Woop
woosh
wooshes
wooshes
woosh+ing
wooshed
Wootton
woozi+ly
woozi+ness
woozy
woozi+er
woozi+est

wop
wops
Worces+ter
Worces+ter+
  shire
word
words
words
word+ing
word+ed
Word
word+age
word-blind
word+book
word+books
word+break
word+breaks
wordi+ly
wordi+ness
word+ing
word+less
word+less+ly
word-perfect
word+play
words
Wordsworth
Words+worth+
  ian
Words+worth+
  ians
wordy
wordi+er
wordi+est
wore
work
works
works
work+ing
worked
work+abil+ity
work+able
work+able+ness
worka+day
worka+hol+ic
worka+hol+ics
work+bag
work+bags
work+bench
work+benches
work+book
work+books
work+day
work+days
worked
work+er

work+ers
worker-priest
worker-priests
work+fare
work+force
work+forces
work-harden
work-hardens
work-harden+
  ing
work-hardened
work+horse
work+horses
work+house
work+houses
work-in
work-ins
work in
verb
work+ing
work+ings
working-class
adj.
work+ing class
noun
work-in-progress
work+less
work+load
work+loads
work+man
work+men
work+man+like
work+man+ly
work+man+ship
work+mate
work+mates
work-out
work-outs
work out
verb
work+people
work+room
work+rooms
works
work+shop
work+shops
work+shy
Work+sop
work-study
work+table
work+tables
work+top
work+tops
work-to-rule
work-to-rules

work+week
work+weeks
world
worlds
world-beater
world-beaters
world-class
world+li+ness
world+ling
world+lings
world+ly
world+li+er
world+li+est
world-shaking
world-weariness
world-weary
world+wide
worm
worms
worms
worm+ing
wormed
WORM
worm+cast
worm+casts
worm-eaten
worm+er
worm+ers
worm+hole
worm+holes
worm+holed
wormi+ness
worm+like
worms
Worms
worm+wood
wormy
wormi+er
wormi+est
worn
worn+ness
worn-out
wor+ried
wor+ried+ly
wor+ri+ment
wor+ri+ments
wor+ri+some
wor+ri+some+ly
wor+rit
wor+rits
wor+rit+ing
wor+rit+ed
wor+ry
wor+ries
wor+ries

wor+ry+ing	wouldst	Wrath	wretch+ed+ness
wor+ried	wound	wrath+ful	Wrex+ham
wor+ry+guts	wounds	wrath+ful+ly	wrick
wor+ry+guts	wounds	wrath+ful+ness	wricks
wor+ry+ing	wound+ing	wreak	wrick+ing
wor+ry+ing+ly	wound+ed	wreaks	wricked
worse	wound+ed	wreak+ing	wri+er
wors+en	wound+ing	wreaked	wri+est
wors+ens	wound+ing+ly	wreak+er	wrig+gle
wors+en+ing	wound+wort	wreak+ers	wrig+gles
wors+ened	wound+worts	wreath	wrig+gles
wor+ship	wove	wreaths	wrig+gling
wor+ships	wo+ven	wreathe	wrig+gled
wor+ship+ping	wow	wreathes	wrig+gler
or	wows	wreath+ing	wrig+glers
wor+ship+ing	wows	wreathed	wrig+gly
U.S.	wow+ing	wreath+like	wright
wor+shipped	wowed	wreck	wrights
or	wow+ser	wrecks	Wright
wor+shiped	wow+sers	wrecks	wring
U.S.	wrack	wreck+ing	wrings
Wor+ship	wracks	wrecked	wrings
Wor+ships	wraith	wrecked	wring+ing
wor+ship+ful	wraiths	wreck+er	wrung
wor+ship+ful+ly	wraith+like	wreck+ers	wring+er
wor+ship+ful+	Wran	wreck+ing	wring+ers
ness	Wrans	Wre+kin	wrin+kle
wor+ship+per	Wran+gell	wren	wrin+kles
wor+ship+pers	wran+gle	wrens	wrin+kles
Wors+ley	wran+gles	Wren	wrin+kling
worst	wran+gles	Wrens	wrin+kled
worsts	wran+gling	wrench	wrin+klies
worst+ing	wran+gled	wrenches	wrin+kly
worst+ed	wran+gler	wrenches	wrin+kli+er
wor+sted	wran+glers	wrench+ing	wrin+kli+est
wor+steds	wrap	wrenched	wrist
wort	wraps	wrest	wrists
worts	wraps	wrests	wrist+band
worth	wrap+ping	wrests	wrist+bands
wor+thi+ly	wrapped	wrest+ing	wrist+let
wor+thi+ness	wrap+around	wrested	wrist+lets
Wor+thing	wrap+arounds	wrest+er	wrist+watch
worth+less	wrap+over	wrest+ers	wrist+watches
worth+less+ly	wrap+overs	wres+tle	wristy
worth+less+ness	wrapped	wres+tles	wristi+er
worth+while	wrap+per	wres+tles	wristi+est
wor+thy	wrap+pers	wres+tled	writ
wor+thies	wrap+ping	wres+tler	writs
wor+thi+er	wrap+pings	wres+tlers	writ+able
wor+thi+est	wrap+round	wres+tling	write
wot	wrap+rounds	wretch	writes
Wotan	wrasse	wretches	writ+ing
would	wrasses	wretch+ed	wrote
would-be	wrath	wretch+ed+ly	writ+ten
wouldn't	wraths	wretch+ed	write-down

write-downs
write down
verb
write-off
write-offs
write off
verb
writ+er
writ+ers
writ+er's
write-up
write-ups
write up
verb
writhe
writhes
writhes
writh+ing
writhed
writh+er
writh+ers
writ+ing
writ+ings
writ+ten
wrong
wrongs
wrongs
wrong+ing
wronged

wrong+doer
wrong+doers
wrong+doing
wrong+doings
wrong+er
wrong+ers
wrong-foot
wrong-foots
wrong-footing
wrong-footed
wrong+ful
wrong+ful+ly
wrong+ful+ness
wrong-headed
wrong-headed+ly
wrong-headed+
ness
wrong+ly
wrong+ness
wrote
wroth
wrought
wrought-up
wrung
wry
wries
wry+ing
wried
wri+er *or*

wry+er
wri+est *or*
wry+est
wry+bill
wry+bills
wry+er
wry+est
wry+ly
wry+neck
wry+necks
wry+ness
Wu+chang
Wu-ch'ang
Wu+han
Wu-hsi
Wu+hsien
Wuhu
Wulfila
Wu-lu-mu-ch'i
wun+der+kind
wun+der+kinds
or
wun+der+kind+
er
Wup+per+tal
wurst
wursts
Würt+tem+berg
Würz+burg

Wu+sih
wuth+er+ing
Wu+tsin
Wu+xi
Wyatt
wych-elm
wych-elms
Wycherley
wych-hazel
wych-hazels
Wyclif
Wycliffe
Wycliff+ism
Wyc+lif+fite
Wyc+lif+fites
Wyc+lif+ism
Wyc+lif+ite
Wyc+lif+ites
Wye
Wykeham
wynd
wynds
Wyndham
Wyo+ming
WYSIWYG
wy+vern
wy+verns

XYZ

x
x's
X
X's
Xs
xan+the+in
xan+thene
Xan+thian
xan+thic
xan+thine
xan+thines
Xanthippe
xan+thoch+ro+
ism
xan+tho+ma
xan+tho+phyl
xan+tho+phyls
xan+tho+phyll
xan+tho+phylls
xan+tho+phyll+
ous
xan+thous
Xan+thus
Xantippe
Xavier
x-axis
x-axes
X-chromosome
X-chromosomes
Xe
xe+bec
xe+becs
Xenakis
Xenocrates
Xeno+crat+ic
xe+noga+mous
xe+noga+my
xe+noga+mies
xe+no+ge+neic
xeno+glos+sia
xeno+lith
xeno+liths
xeno+lith+ic
xen+on
Xenophanes

xeno+phile
xeno+philes
xeno+phobe
xeno+phobes
xeno+pho+bia
xeno+pho+bic
Xenophon
Xe+res
xe+ric
xe+ri+cal+ly
xe+ro+der+ma
xe+ro+der+mat+
ic
xe+ro+der+mat+
ous
xe+ro+der+mia
xe+rog+ra+pher
xe+rog+ra+
phers
xe+ro+graph+ic
xe+ro+graphi+cal+
ly
xe+rog+ra+phy
xe+ro+phile
xe+ro+philes
xe+rophi+lous
xe+rophi+ly
xe+roph+thal+
mia
xe+roph+thal+
mic
xe+ro+phyte
xe+ro+phytes
xe+ro+phyt+ic
xe+ro+phyti+cal+
ly
xe+ro+phyt+ism
Xer+ox
Trademark
Xer+oxes
Xer+oxes
Xer+ox+ing
Xer+oxed
Xerxes
Xho+sa

Xho+sa *or*
Xho+sas
Xho+san
xi
xis
Xi
Xia Gui
Xiang
Xiang+tan
Ximenes
Ximenez
Xin+gú
Xi+ning
Xin+jiang Uygur
xiphi+ster+num
xiphi+ster+na
xiph+oid
xiph+oids
Xmas
Xmases
Xo+chi+mil+co
x-ray
x-rays
x-rays
x-raying
x-rayed
X-ray
X-rays
X-rays
X-raying
X-rayed
Xuan-tong
Xuthus
Xu+zhou
xy+lem
xy+lene
xy+lenes
xy+lo+carp
xy+lo+carps
xy+lo+car+pous
xy+lo+graph
xy+lo+graphs
xy+lo+graphs
xy+lo+graph+
ing

xy+lo+graphed
xy+log+ra+phy
xy+lopha+gous
xy+lo+phone
xy+lo+phones
xy+lo+phon+ic
xy+lopho+nist
xy+lopho+nists
xy+lose
xys+ter
xys+ters
y
y's
Y
Y's *or*
Ys
yab+bie
yab+bies
yab+bies
yab+by+ing
yab+bied
yab+by
yab+bies
yab+bies
yab+by+ing
yab+bied
yacht
yachts
yachts
yacht+ing
yacht+ed
yacht+ie
yacht+ies
yacht+ing
yachts+man
yachts+men
yachts+man+ship
yachts+woman
yachts+women
yack
yacks
yack+ing
yacked
yack+er
yackety-yak

yaf+fle
yaf+fles
Yafo
yah
Ya+ha+ta
ya+hoo
ya+hoos
ya+hoo+ism
Yah+veh
Yah+vism
Yah+vist
Yah+vis+tic
Yah+weh
Yah+wism
Yah+wist
Yah+wis+tic
yak
yaks
yaks
yak+king
yakked
yak+ka
yak+ker
Ya+kutsk
Yale
Trademark
Yal+ta
Yalu
yam
yams
Yamagata
Yamasaki
yam+mer
yam+mers
yam+mer+ing
yam+mered
yam+mer+er
yam+mer+ers
Ya+mous+souk+
  ro
Yan+an
Yang
Yan+gon
Yang+tze
Ya+ni+na
yank
yanks
yanks
yank+ing
yanked
Yank
Yanks
Yan+kee
Yan+kees
Yan+tai

Ya+oun+de
yap
yaps
yaps
yap+ping
yapped
Yap
ya+pok
ya+poks
yap+per
yap+pers
yap+py
Ya+pu+rá
Ya+qui
yar+bor+ough
yar+bor+oughs
yard
yards
Yard
yard+age
yard+arm
yard+arms
Yar+die
Yar+dies
yard+stick
yard+sticks
Yar+kand
Yar+mouth
yar+mul+ke
yar+mul+kes
yarn
yarns
yarns
yarn+ing
yarned
yarn-dyed
Ya+ro+slavl
yar+ran
yar+rans
yar+row
yar+rows
yash+mac
yash+macs
yash+mak
yash+maks
yata+ghan
yata+ghans
Ya+un+de
yaup
yaups
yaups
yaup+ing
yauped
yaup+er
yaup+ers

Ya+va+rí
yaw
yaws
yaws
yaw+ing
yawed
Ya+wa+ta
yawl
yawls
yawn
yawns
yawns
yawn+ing
yawned
yawn+er
yawn+ers
yawn+ing
yawn+ing+ly
yawp
yawps
yawps
yawp+ing
yawped
yawp+er
yawp+ers
yaws
y-axis
y-axes
Yazd
Yb
Y-chromosome
Y-chromosomes
yclept
ye
yea
yeah
yean
yeans
yean+ing
yeaned
yean+ling
yean+lings
year
years
year+book
year+books
year+ling
year+lings
year+long
year+ly
yearn
yearns
yearn+ing
yearned
yearn+er

yearn+ers
yearn+ing
yearn+ings
yearn+ing+ly
year-round
yeast
yeasts
yeast+ing
yeast+ed
yeasti+ly
yeasti+ness
yeast+less
yeast+like
yeasty
yeasti+er
yeasti+est
Yeats
yegg
yeggs
Yeisk
Ye+ka+te+rin+
  burg
Ye+ka+te+ri+no+
  dar
Ye+ka+te+ri+no+
  slav
Ye+li+sa+vet+
  grad
Ye+li+sa+vet+pol
Yelizaveta
  Petrovna
yell
yells
yells
yel+ling
yelled
yell+er
yell+ers
yel+low
yel+lows
yel+lows
yel+low+ing
yel+lowed
yel+low+er
yel+low+est
yellow-bellied
yellow-belly
coward
  yellow-bellies
yel+low bel+ly
fish
  yel+low bel+lies
yellow+hammer

yellow+
  hammers
yel+low+ish
Yellow+knife
yel+low+ly
yel+low+ness
yel+lows
Yellow+stone
yellow+wood
  yellow+woods
yel+lowy
yelp
  yelps
  yelps
  yelp+ing
  yelped
  yelp+er
  yelp+ers
Yelt+sin
Yem+en
Yem+eni
  Yem+enis
yen
currency
  yen
yen
longing
  yens
  yens
  yen+ning
  yenned
Yen+an
Ye+ni+sei
Ye+ni+sey
Yen+tai
Yen-t'ai
yeo+man
  yeo+men
yeo+man+ly
yeo+man+ry
yep
yer+ba
  yer+bas
Ye+re+van
Yerwa-Maidugu+
  ri
yes
  yeses
ye+shi+va
  ye+shi+vahs
  or
  ye+shi+voth
Ye+şil Ir+mak
Ye+şil+köy
yes+ter

yes+ter+day
  yes+ter+days
yes+ter+year
  yes+ter+years
yes+treen
yet
yeti
  yetis
Yevtushenko
yew
  yews
Yeysk
Yezd
Y-fronts
Trademark
Yg+dra+sil
Ygerne
Ygg+dra+sil
Yi+bin
Yichang
yid
  yids
Yid+dish
Yid+dish+er
  Yid+dish+ers
yield
  yields
  yields
  yield+ing
  yield+ed
  yield+able
  yield+er
  yield+ers
  yield+ing
Yin
Yin+chuan
Yin-ch'uan
Yin+chwan
Ying+kou
Ying+kow
yip+pee
  yips
ylang-ylang
  ylang-ylangs
ylem
Ymer
Ymir
yo
yob
  yobs
yob+bery
  yob+beries
yob+bish
yob+bo
  yob+bos

yo+del
yo+dels
yo+dels
yo+del+ling *or*
yo+del+ing
U.S.
yo+delled *or*
yo+deled
U.S.
yo+del+ler
  yo+del+lers
yoga
  yogas
yogh
  yoghs
yo+ghourt
  yo+ghourts
yo+ghurt
  yo+ghurts
yogi
  yo+gis *or*
  yo+gin
yo+gic
yo+gurt
  yo+gurts
Yog+ya+kar+ta
yo-heave-ho
yo+him+bine
yo-ho-ho
yoicks
yoke
  yokes *or*
  yoke
  yokes
yok+ing
yoked
yo+kel
  yo+kels
Yo+ko+ha+ma
Yo+ko+su+ka
Yola
yolk
  yolks
yolky
Yom Kip+pur
  Yom Kip+purs
yomp
  yomps
  yomp+ing
  yomped
yon
yond
yon+der
yoni
Yon+kers

yonks
Yonne
yoo-hoo
YOP
yore
york
  yorks
york+ing
yorked
York
york+er
  york+ers
york+ie
  york+ies
York+ist
  York+ists
York+shire
York+town
Yo+ru+ba
  Yo+ru+bas *or*
  Yo+ru+ba
Yo+ru+ban
Yoshihito
Yoshkar-Ola
you
you'd
you'll
young
  young+er
  young+est
Young
young+ish
young+ling
  young+lings
young+ster
  young+sters
Youngs+town
youn+ker
  youn+kers
your
you're
yours
your+self
  your+selves
youth
  youths
youth+ful
youth+ful+ly
youth+ful+ness
you've
yowl
  yowls
  yowls
  yowl+ing
  yowled

yowl+er
yowl+ers
yo-yo
yo-yos
yo-yos
yo-yoing
yo-yoed
Ypres
Ypsilanti
Yser
Yseult
Ys+sel
yt+ter+bia
yt+ter+bium
yt+tria
yt+trium
yuan
yuan
Yüan
Yu+ca+tán
yuc+ca
yuc+cas
yuck
yucky
yucki+er
yucki+est
Yüen
Yu+go+slav
Yu+go+slavs
Yu+go+sla+via
Yu+go+sla+vian
Yu+go+sla+
vians
yuk
Yukawa
yuk+ky
yuk+ki+er
yuk+ki+est
Yu+kon
Yu+kon+er
Yu+kon+ers
yu+lan
yu+lans
yule
yules
yum+my
yum+mi+er
yum+mi+est
Yün+nan
yup+pie
yup+pies
yup+pie+dom
yup+pi+fi+ca+
tion
yup+pi+fy

yup+pi+fies
yup+pi+fy+ing
yup+pi+fied
yup+py
yup+pies
Yur+ev
yurt
yurts
Yu+zov+ka
z
z's
Z
Z's *or*
Zs
Zaan+dam
Zaan+stad
za+ba+glio+ne
za+ba+glio+nes
Za+brze
Za+ca+te+cas
Zachariah
Zacharias
Zachary
Za+cyn+thus
zaf+fer
zaf+fre
Zaga+zig
Za+greb
Zagreus
zai+bat+su
Za+ïre
Za+ïr+ese
Za+ïr+ian
Za+ïr+ians
Zá+kin+thos
za+kous+ki
za+kus+ki
Zama
Zam+be+se
Zam+be+zi
Zam+be+zian
Zam+bia
Zam+bian
Zam+bians
Zam+bo+an+ga
zam+buck
zam+bucks
Zamenhof
Za+mo+ra
Zamyatin
za+ni+ly
za+ni+ness
Zan+te
ZANU
zany

zanies
zani+er
zani+est
Zan+zi+bar
Zan+zi+ba+ri
Zan+zi+ba+ris
zap
zaps
zaps
zap+ping
zapped
Zapata
za+pa+tea+do
za+pa+tea+dos
Za+po+rozh+ye
Zappa
zap+py
zap+pi+er
zap+pi+est
ZAPU
Zaqa+ziq
Za+ra+go+za
Zarathustra
Zara+thus+trian
Zara+thus+
trians
Zara+thus+tric
Zara+thus+trics
za+reba
za+rebas
za+ree+ba
za+ree+bas
zarf
zarfs
Za+ria
Zar+qa
zar+zue+la
zar+zue+las
z-axis
z-axes
Zea
zeal
Zea+land
zeal+ot
zeal+ots
Zeal+ot
Zeal+ots
zeal+ot+ry
zeal+ous
zeal+ous+ly
zeal+ous+ness
Zeami
ze+bec
ze+becs
ze+beck

ze+becks
Zebedee
zeb+ra
mammal
zeb+ras *or*
zeb+ra
Zebra
bond
Zebras
zebra+wood
zebra+woods
ze+brine
ze+broid
zebu
zebus
Zebulun
Zechariah
zed
zeds
Zedekiah
zedo+ary
zedo+aries
zee
zees
Zee+brug+ge
Zee+land
Zee+land+er
Zee+land+ers
Zeffirelli
zein
zeins
Zeist
Zeit+geist
Zeit+geists
Zen
ze+na+na
ze+na+nas
Zend
Zends
Zend-Avesta
Zend+ic
Zen+ic
Zen+ist
Zen+ists
zen+ith
zen+iths
zen+ith+al
Zenobia
zeo+lite
zeo+lites
zeo+lit+ic
Zephaniah
zeph+yr
zeph+yrs
Zephyrus

zep+pe+lin
zep+pe+lins
Zeppelin
Zer+matt
zero
 zeros *or*
 zeroes
 zeroes
 ze+ro+ing
 ze+roed
zero-rated
zeroth
zest
 zests
 zests
zest+ing
zest+ed
zest+ful
zest+ful+ly
zest+ful+ness
zesty
zeta
 zetas
ZETA
 ZETAs
Zet+land
zeug+ma
 zeug+mas
zeug+mat+ic
Zeus
Zeuxis
Zhang+jia+kou
Zhang+zhou
Zhao Ziyang
Zhda+nov
Zhe+jiang
Zheng+zhou
Zhi+to+mir
Zhivkov
zho
 zhos *or*
 zho
Zhou En Lai
Zhukov
Zia ul Haq
zib+el+ine
 zib+el+ines
zib+et
 zib+ets
Zi+bo
zi+dov+udine
Ziegfeld
ziff
 ziffs
zig+gu+rat

zig+gu+rats
Zi+gong
zig+zag
zig+zags
zig+zags
zig+zag+ging
zig+zagged
zilch
zil+lion
zil+lions *or*
zil+lion
Zilpah
Zim+ba+bwe
Zim+ba+bwean
Zim+ba+bweans
Zim+mer
Trademark
Zim+mers
zinc
zinc+ic
zinc+ite
zinc+ites
zincky
zin+co+graph
zin+co+graphs
zin+cog+ra+pher
zin+cog+ra+
 phers
zin+cog+ra+phy
zincy
zing
zings
zings
zing+ing
zinged
zingy
zingi+er
zingi+est
zin+jan+thro+pus
zinky
zin+nia
zin+nias
Zinoviev
Zi+nov+ievsk
Zion
Zi+on+ism
Zi+on+ist
Zi+on+ists
Zi+on+is+tic
zip
zips
zips
zip+ping
zipped
Zipangu

zip+per
zip+pers
zip+py
zip+pi+er
zip+pi+est
zirc+al+loy
zirc+al+loys
zir+con
zir+cons
zir+con+ic
zir+co+nium
Ziska
zit
 zits
zith+er
zith+ers
zith+er+ist
zith+er+ists
Zla+to+ust
zlo+ty
zlo+tys *or*
zlo+ty
zo
 zos *or*
 zo
Zoan
zo+di+ac
zo+di+acs
zo+dia+cal
Zoffany
zo+ic
Zola
Zoll+ver+ein
Zom+ba
zom+bi
zom+bis
zom+bie
zom+bies
zon+al
zo+nat+ed
zo+na+tion
zo+na+tions
zone
zones
zones
zon+ing
zoned
zone+time
zone+times
zon+ing
zon+ings
zonked
zoo
zoos

zoo+geog+ra+
 pher
zoo+geog+ra+
 phers
zoo+geo+graph+
 ic
zoo+geo+graphi+
 cal+ly
zoo+geog+ra+
 phy
zo+og+ra+pher
zo+og+ra+phers
zoo+graph+ic
zoo+graphi+cal
zo+og+ra+phy
zo+oid
zo+oids
zo+oid+al
zo+ola+trous
zo+ola+try
zoo+logi+cal
zo+olo+gist
zo+olo+gists
zo+ol+ogy
zo+ol+ogies
zoom
zooms
zooms
zoom+ing
zoomed
zoo+mor+phic
zoo+mor+phism
zoo+phile
zoo+philes
zo+ophi+lism
zoo+pho+bia
zo+opho+bous
zoo+phyte
zoo+phytes
zoo+phyt+ic
zoo+phyti+cal
zoo+plank+ton
zoo+plank+tons
zoo+spore
zoo+spores
zoo+spor+ic
zo+os+por+ous
zo+os+ter+ol
zo+os+ter+ols
zoot
zoo+tech+nics
zoo+tom+ic
zoo+tomi+cal
zoo+tomi+cal+ly
zo+oto+mist

zo+oto+mists
zo+oto+my
zoo+tox+in
  zoo+tox+ins
zo+ril
  zo+rils
zo+rille
  zo+rilles
Zoroaster
Zo+ro+as+trian
  Zo+ro+as+trians
Zo+ro+as+tri+an+
  ism
Zo+ro+as+trism
Zorrilla y Moral
zos+ter
Zou+ave
  Zou+aves
Zoug
zouk
zounds
Zsigmondy
zuc+chet+to

zuc+chet+tos
zuc+chi+ni
zuc+chi+ni *or*
  zuc+chi+nis
Zug
Zug+spit+ze
zug+zwang
zug+zwangs
zug+zwangs
zug+zwang+ing
zug+zwanged
Zui+der Zee
Zuid+hol+land
Zu Jiang
Zukerman
Zulu
  Zulus *or*
  Zulu
Zu+lu+land
Zun+garia
Zurbarán
Zü+rich
Zuy+der Zee

Zweig
Zwickau
zwie+back
  zwie+backs
Zwingli
Zwing+lian
  Zwing+lians
zwit+teri+on
  zwit+teri+ons
Zwol+le
Zworykin
zyga+pophy+sis
  zyga+pophy+
  ses
zy+go+dac+tyl
  zy+go+dac+tyls
  zy+go+dac+tyl+
  ous
zy+go+ma
  zy+go+ma+ta
zy+go+mat+ic
zy+go+mor+phic
zy+go+mor+
  phous

zy+go+phyte
  zy+go+phytes
zy+go+spore
zy+go+spores
zy+go+spor+ic
zy+gote
  zy+gotes
zy+got+ic
zy+goti+cal+ly
zy+mase
zy+mo+gen
  zy+mo+gens
zy+mo+log+ic
zy+mo+logi+cal
zy+molo+gist
  zy+molo+gists
zy+mol+ogy
zy+moly+sis
zy+mo+sis
  zy+mo+ses
zy+mot+ic
zy+mur+gy

COLLINS
ELECTRONIC
REFERENCE

For details of Collins machine-readable
electronic dictionary of spelling and
hyphenation, and other electronic reference
products, please apply to:

COLLINS Dictionaries: Dept. RDH
PO Box, Glasgow G4 ONB